84

Editor-in-Chief
Asa S. Knowles

Chancellor, Northeastern University

THE
INTERNATIONAL
ENCYCLOPEDIA
OF HIGHER
EDUCATION

Volume 2

A

Jossey-Bass Publishers

San Francisco • Washington • London • 1978

THE INTERNATIONAL ENCYCLOPEDIA OF HIGHER EDUCATION
Volume 2
Asa S. Knowles, Editor-in-Chief

Copyright © 1977 by: Jossey-Bass, Inc., Publishers
433 California Street
San Francisco, California 94104
&
Jossey-Bass Limited
28 Banner Street
London EC1Y 8QE

Library of Congress Cataloging in Publication Data

Main entry under title:

The international encyclopedia of higher education.

Includes index.
1. Education, Higher—Dictionaries.   I. Knowles,
Asa Smallidge, 1909–
LB15.157   378′.003   77-73647
ISBN 0-87589-323-6 (set)
ISBN 0-87589-325-2 (v. 2)

Manufactured in the United States of America
Composition by Chapman's Phototypesetting
Printing by Hamilton Printing Company
Binding by Payne Edition Bindery

COVER DESIGN BY WILLI BAUM

FIRST EDITION
First printing: December 1977
Second printing: November 1978

Code 7724

THE
INTERNATIONAL
ENCYCLOPEDIA
OF HIGHER
EDUCATION

ACADEMIC ASSOCIATION OF THE UNIVERSITY OF SINGAPORE
(Kesatuan akademis Universiti Singapura)

The *Kesatuan akademis Universiti Singapura* (Academic Association of the University of Singapore) was set up in 1965 to promote the ideal of an autonomous national university; increase recruitment of local personnel to the staff of the university; secure effective organization of the teaching staff, the library administrative staff, and student health physicians; and promote the social, educational, and academic welfare of the members.

Full membership is open to all local nationals (including Malaysians), although expatriate staff members may participate as associate members. Membership dues are minimal. The association's programs and priorities are determined by an executive committee, which is elected on an annual basis.

Originally the association lobbied for measures to ensure better opportunities for brilliant local nationals to prepare for academic careers. Since this task has been accomplished, the focus of the association is now on promoting the social and intellectual pursuits of the university members. The association has hosted a number of seminars on themes pertaining to contemporary social and educational issues affecting the academic community. It has also collaborated with staff organizations of other institutions of higher learning in sponsoring seminars and workshops.

The association publishes *Kesatuan Bulletin. Suara universiti,* and proceedings of conferences/seminars.

University of Singapore
Bukit Timah Road
Singapore 10

C. M. SEAH

ACADEMIC COMMUNITY
See Agriculture in Higher Education: Agricultural Research, Extension Services, and Field Stations; Public Service Role of Higher Education; Town-Gown Relations; Towns, University; Urban University.

ACADEMIC COUNCILS
See Governance and Control of Higher Education.

ACADEMIC DRESS AND INSIGNIA

In many countries universities and other institutions providing higher education prescribe or permit the wearing of certain types of academic dress or insignia by selected groups within the institution. There are, however, several countries in which neither academic dress nor insignia is used, and a number of countries for which information on academic dress is not available. Thus, this study is selective, focusing on the most characteristic forms and customs in academic dress in a representative group of countries. Further, the constant changes in higher education are paralleled by changes in academic dress. Thus, only the principal features of the systems that were in use in 1975 will be considered.

In this study "academic dress" means any garment or article made principally of natural or synthetic fibers, while "academic insignia" means any article made principally of metal, the garment or article in each case being used to indicate an office in, or a degree or other qualification awarded by, a university or similar institution or body. Academic insignia also includes such items as coats of arms or badges of office, and any type of mace or staff of office used in universities and other institutions of higher education. "Faculty" means a department of learning, such as law, medicine, or engineering. "Degree" means the academic rank marking a certain level of proficiency in a particular field of learning—for example, Bachelor of Science, Master of Arts, Doctor of Laws, architect, civil engineer.

Regulations and customs governing academic dress and insignia vary from one country or group of countries to another. Differences arise from varying historical, political, ideological, and religious traditions, as well as from geographical and climatic conditions. However, in most countries, academic dress may be worn by the titular and/or executive heads of universities and other institutions of higher education—chancellors, vice-chancellors, presidents, rectors, or directors; senior administrative officers; deans of faculties and members of the teaching staff; recipients of degrees, diplomas, or other qualifications. Students in some instances also wear academic dress or insignia.

The Oxford-Cambridge System of Academic Dress

The first system of academic dress to be considered is that currently in use in England, Scotland, Northern Ireland, Australia, Bangladesh, Botswana, the Republic of Ireland, Ghana, Guyana, Hong Kong, Kenya, Lesotho, Malawi, Malaysia, Malta, New Zealand, Nigeria, Pakistan, Papua New Guinea, Sierra Leone, the Republic of South Africa, the University of the South Pacific (in Suva, Fiji), Swaziland, Tanzania, Uganda, and Zambia. The unifying feature of the academic dress in all these places is that it is based on that of the ancient English universities of Oxford and Cambridge, and consists of a gown, a hat, and possibly a hood.

Gowns. The Oxford and Cambridge bachelors' and masters' gowns (Figures 1 to 4) are predominantly the gowns for bachelor's and master's degrees in the universities in the above places, though the sleeves are sometimes modified to give individuality or for greater comfort in tropical areas. Chinese features have been incorporated into gowns of the Chinese University of Hong Kong. The University of Ghana trims its gowns with distinctive types of locally manufactured *kente* cloth. Bachelors' and masters' gowns have traditionally been made of black material, but recently colors such as blue, gray, light brown, and maroon have been introduced.

At Oxford, Cambridge, and a limited number of other universities, there are distinctive gowns for all or certain bachelor's and master's degrees, but the general custom is for a university to prescribe one style of bachelor's gown and one style of master's gown. Doctors customarily have a "full-dress" gown for ceremonial occasions, the scarlet (bright red of varying shades) doctoral gowns of Oxford and Cambridge being overwhelmingly the prototypes for gowns for doctors other than Doctors of Philosophy. (Figures 5 and 6 show the Oxford and Cambridge doctoral

Figure 2. Oxford M.A.

Figure 1. Oxford B.A.

Figure 3. Cambridge B.A.

Figure 5. Oxford doctorate full dress.

Figure 4. Cambridge M.A.

Figure 6. Cambridge doctorate full dress.

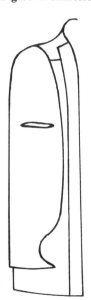

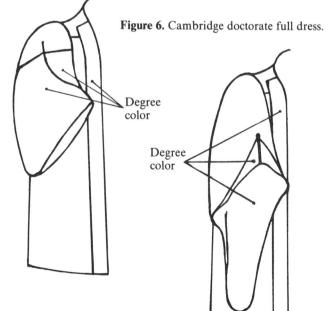

Degree color

Degree color

gowns.) Often the Oxford gown has facings down each side in front and on the sleeves, and the Cambridge gown has facings down each side in front and sleeve linings, of a color distinctive either of the degree or of the university. Colors other than scarlet are also being used for doctoral full-dress gowns, including blue, darker shades of red, purple, gold, and black.

In the places listed above, the degree of Doctor of Philosophy is commonly considered to be junior in status to other doctorates. Thus, the gown for the Doctor of Philosophy may be either identical to that for other doctorates but with distinctively colored facings, of a different basic color from other doctorates but with the same colored facings, or of an entirely distinctive design. It may also follow the Cambridge custom of being the master's gown with some additional trimming. Frequently, doctors also have an "undress" gown for nonceremonial use—usually the master's gown with some additional trimming.

Hoods. The hood, apparently used by all persons in medieval times as a head covering, is the second item of academic dress based on the Oxford-Cambridge tradition. It has currently become the symbol of some measure of higher education, not necessarily a degree in the strict sense of the word. It is worn over the gown, hanging down the back and kept in place by a neckband passing under the chin. Each university has its own scheme of hoods, the varying colors, trimmings, and shapes of which indicate, ideally as simply as possible, the wearer's qualification and the awarding institution. The principal shapes that the hood takes are shown in Figures 7 to 12, but the proportions of the various parts of the hood often differ from one university to another. There is no uniformity in the colors used to indicate faculties or departments of learning or in the method of indicating the level of the qualification. Thus, the same colors indicate different faculties, and there may well be doubt concerning the exact color sensation a name is intended to suggest. However, several universities and

other institutions have recently defined their colors by reference to the named and numbered color samples in the British Colour Council's *Dictionary of Colour Standards.*

The simplest hood is of one color only, but such hoods are rare even when trimmed in some way (for example, with white fur). Two-colored hoods are common, the hood being basically of one color trimmed with a second. Examples of such trimming are an inside facing (Figure 10), a complete lining (Figure 9), an edging on the outside (Figure 7), or a binding (Figure 11). A lining may be turned over on to the outside, as shown in Figure 8, to form a narrow edging. The proliferation of degrees and qualifications, as well as the increasing number of awarding institutions, has led to increasing combinations of such trimmings and the development of multicolored hoods. Some of the schemes used to indicate degrees and other qualifications are tabulated in Table 1, but these are not the only schemes in use, and some schemes are without any regularity. If a school uses the scheme indicated for the bachelor's degree, that school will then follow the variations noted for the master's and doctoral degrees.

Within the various hood schemes, cords and/or bands and other forms of trimming are often added to differentiate degrees and universities. Obviously, it becomes increasingly difficult as new institutions and degrees are established to devise uncomplicated, dignified, and distinctive hoods, which explains the search for colors other than black or scarlet as the basic colors of hoods. In some few schemes, the same hood represents more than one degree at the same level; sometimes the same hood is used at different degree levels, the precise degree being indicated by differing gowns. In a few rare instances "shot" materials, which combine two or more colors, or watered materials are used. Commonly the Oxford simple or burgon shapes are used for bachelor's and master's degrees, and either the Oxford doctorate

Figure 7. Oxford simple shape.

Figure 8. Oxford burgon shape.

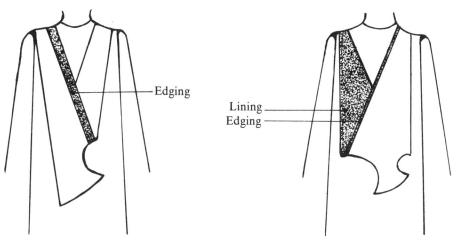

Figure 9. Oxford doctorate shape.

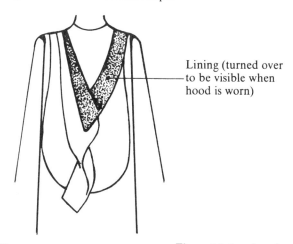

Figure 10. Cambridge shape.

Figure 11. London shape.

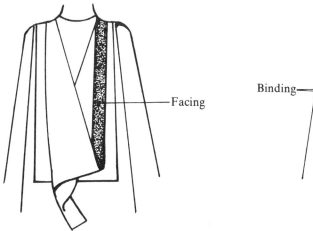

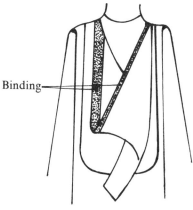

TABLE 1. HOOD SCHEMES

Bachelor	Master	Doctor
Degree color trimmed with white fur	Black lined with degree color	Scarlet lined with degree color
Degree color bound with white fur	Black lined with degree color	Degree color lined with white silk or ermine fur
Black or other color faced, bound, or edged with degree color	Black or other color lined, or lined and edged, with degree color	Scarlet or other color lined, or lined and edged, with degree color
Black lined with degree color, bound with white fur or silk	Black lined, or lined and edged, with degree color	Scarlet lined, or lined and edged, with degree color
Black lined with degree color, faced with white fur	Black lined with degree color	Degree color
Black or other color lined with degree color	Black or other color lined, or lined and edged, with degree color	Scarlet or other color lined, or lined and edged, with degree color
Black edged with degree color	Degree color edged with black	Degree color edged with black and lined with white
Gray lined with degree color	Gray lined and edged with degree color	Gray
Green faced with white fur and edged with degree color	Green lined with degree color	Red lined with degree color
Black faced with a university color and bound with degree color	Black lined with a university color and bound with degree color	Scarlet lined with a university color and bound with degree color
Blue faced half with university color and half with degree color	Blue lined with university color and faced with degree color	Scarlet lined with university color and faced with degree color
Green lined and edged with degree color	Green lined with white and bound with degree color	Green lined and edged with degree color; shape different from bachelor
Dove gray bound with degree color	Dove gray lined with degree color	Scarlet lined with dove gray and bound with degree color

or the Cambridge shape for doctoral degrees. Sometimes the change of shape occurs at master's level; if the bachelor's hood is lined with the degree color, change of shape or of the basic color is the simplest method of indicating the higher degree. The hood for the Doctor of Philosophy may follow any one of the four practices outlined above for the gown for this degree.

Since diversity is the principal feature of hoods used by universities following the Oxford-Cambridge tradition, there must inevitably be duplication of hoods. However, differences of shape or other nuances may enable apparently similar hoods to be distinguished from each other.

Hats. Hats follow three major designs. Bachelors and masters customarily wear a black cloth mortarboard (Figure 13), the tassel of which is usually black but may be of another color. Women sometimes wear a soft square black cloth cap (Figure 14). Colors other than black are sometimes used for the hat, usually to match the gown. When not wearing their full-dress gowns, doctors usually wear the same hat as mas-

Figure 12. Aberdeen shape.

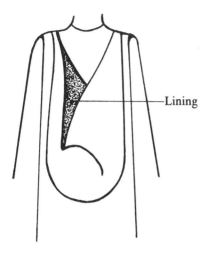

Lining

Figure 13. Mortarboard.

Figure 14. Women's soft cap.

Figure 15. Doctoral velvet bonnet.

Gold cord

Gold tassel

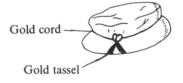

Figure 16. American bachelor.

Figure 17. American master.

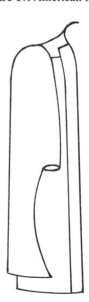

ters. With the full-dress gown, doctors customarily wear a round black velvet bonnet, which, if it follows the Cambridge style, is trimmed between crown and brim with gold cord and tassels (Figure 15). The Oxford bonnet is similarly trimmed with black ribbon. The four ancient Scottish universities use a square soft-crowned black velvet hat, which has been adopted by certain other universities, while yet others prescribe a black velvet mortarboard with black or colored tassel. For Doctors of Philosophy, frequently only a hat indicative of the junior status of this degree is prescribed.

Student academic dress. Students, if required to wear academic dress, generally wear a black gown of either the Oxford scholar or the Cambridge or London undergraduate pattern, together with a black cloth mortarboard, or sometimes for women, a soft black cap. In the four ancient Scottish universities, students wear a red gown, and the use of colors other than black for undergraduate gowns is not unknown.

Academic dress for administrative officers. It is virtually universal practice for chancellors, pro-chancellors, and vice-chancellors to wear specially designed gowns of office, which, if they follow Oxford-Cambridge tradition, are of some rich material trimmed with varying amounts of gold or silver lace and ornaments. These gowns may incorporate the colors of the university and/or locally significant floral or other symbols in their design. The customary hat worn with these gowns is a black velvet mortarboard with gold or silver lace trimming and tassel. Special gowns and hats may be prescribed for senior administrative officers and deans of faculties. These special gowns are worn only on ceremonial occasions; when no special official gowns are prescribed, officers and members of the teaching staff of universities wear the dress appropriate to their academic qualifications. The use of gowns, hoods, and hats on other than ceremonial occasions appears, in general, to be declining.

Variations on the Oxford-Cambridge Tradition

The tradition of academic dress founded at Oxford and Cambridge forms the basis for such dress in many other countries. In such former British colonies as Canada and India, for example, academic dress is basically in the Oxford-Cambridge model with modifications drawn from United States practice and from Indian dress, respectively.

Academic dress in Canada. In Canada, for historical and geographical reasons, academic dress has developed along four lines. First, some institutions follow the Oxford-Cambridge system outlined above. In others, aspects of the United States academic dress system are incorporated into the Oxford-Cambridge system. In some instances the United States system has been adopted, with or without modification. Finally, certain French-language universities use a costume that emphasizes the wearer's university office and that makes use of quite distinctive styles of garments. In many English-language universities, the dress for a Doctor of Philosophy is designed to emphasize the important place of this degree in Canadian higher education, while the dress for the other doctorates—often only awarded as honorary degrees—follows the normal Oxford-Cambridge tradition except in the case of Doctors of Medicine. This latter degree is awarded after a period of undergraduate study, and its dress is frequently indicative of its junior status. When the same degree may be awarded as both an honorary and an earned degree, Canadian practice often distinguishes between the two by some difference in dress.

Academic dress in India. In India the older universities prescribe for their officers and graduates academic dress following, perhaps somewhat loosely, the Oxford-Cambridge tradition, frequently with some type of Indian headgear optionally replacing the mortarboard. Certain newer universities have followed the precedent set by the older ones, but some have chosen to indicate degrees by some type of trimming on a gown only, by some type of scarf worn with a gown, or by a scarf or hood worn simply with prescribed outdoor clothing. Institutions predominantly concerned with Sanskrit or Indian culture and learning use distinctively trimmed gowns or Indian-style garments and headdresses to indicate their officers and their degrees. Some institutions have dispensed completely with academic dress in any form or have retained it only for their officers.

Academic dress in Sri Lanka. In Sri Lanka academic dress is currently under revision, but the hood has never been used because it is derived from an ecclesiastical tradition foreign to the country. In its place, some form of garland or scarf has been used, together with a modified Oxford-type gown. One of the most interesting features of academic dress in Sri Lanka has been the use, in the two Buddhist universities, of a fan of varying size, design, and colors to indicate certain offices and degrees. The fan is used because the Buddhist monk *(bhikku)* customarily carries a palm-leaf fan; this has been adapted to provide regalia for a modern university whose teaching is oriented toward Buddhist culture and philosophy.

Academic Dress in the United States

In the United States the system of academic dress originated at the end of the nineteenth century, when interest arose in the adoption of such dress. It seemed desirable to create a uniform system that all institutions might follow rather than to have each develop its own scheme of academic dress. At a conference of interested institutions held at Columbia University on May 16, 1895, a system of academic dress was formulated that could be adopted by all institutions of higher education. This original system has been reviewed by committees appointed in 1932 and 1959 by the American Council on Education; although

certain modifications have been made, the current system is substantially the same as that originally formulated.

Gowns. The system provides, first, for three types of gowns, each made of suitable black material (Figures 16, 17, and 18). The derivation from Oxford gowns is clearly apparent. The bachelor's gown has always been worn closed in front; and, when no hood is worn, women may optionally wear a white collar. Prior to 1960 the master's gown was the same as the gown shown in Figure 2, but since 1960 the shape of the sleeve has been modified as shown in Figure 17, and the gown may be worn open or closed in front, as may the doctoral gown. The doctoral gown is faced down each front and around the neck with velvet, and three horizontal velvet bars trim each sleeve. The velvet may be black or the color distinctive of the discipline in which the degree is awarded.

Hoods. The system also provides for each degree a hood made of the same black material as the gown. Bachelor's and master's hoods follow the Oxford simple shape shown in Figure 7 and are thirty-six and forty-two inches long, respectively. Doctor's hoods are of the special shape shown in Figure 19 and are forty-eight inches long. Hoods are bound with velvet or velveteen of the discipline color, one-half inch wide inside and two, three, and five inches wide outside for bachelor's, master's and doctoral degrees, respectively. For six-year specialist degrees, institutions may use forty-five-inch-long hoods with four inches of velvet on the outside.

The colors currently used to indicate the various disciplines are as follows: agriculture—maize; arts, humanities, letters—white; commerce, accountancy, business—drab or sapphire blue; dentistry—lilac; economics—copper; education—light blue; engineering—orange; fine arts and architecture—brown; forestry—russet; journalism—crimson; law—purple; library science—lemon; medicine—green; music—pink; nursing—apricot; oratory (speech)—silver gray; pharmacy—olive green; philosophy—dark blue; physical education—sage green; public administration, including foreign service—peacock blue; public health—salmon pink; science—golden yellow; social work—citron; theology—scarlet; veterinary science—gray.

Sapphire blue as an alternative to drab is too easily confused with the other blues to be recommended, as are the additional colors sometimes used by robe makers for new disciplines. The range of colors that can be distinguished clearly from each other is virtually exhausted, and new interdisciplinary areas will have to use the color of the discipline most nearly indicative of the new field of learning.

Prior to 1960 the exact title of the degree determined the color of the velvet on the hood, and thus a Master of Arts in teaching required white. Since 1960 the rule has been that the color representing the major field of work is to be used, and thus a Master of Science in engineering requires orange rather than golden yellow. Hoods are lined with the official color or colors of the institution awarding the degree. If there is only one color, this lines all of the inside. Two colors can be combined by placing one, two, or more V-shaped chevrons of one color across a field of another, and the chevron may be placed point upward to form an inverted V-shape. Rather than a chevron, a horizontal bar or bars may be used, or one color may be placed in the upper half or in the left-hand side of the hood and the other in the bottom half or the right-hand side. More than two colors can be shown by having chevrons or bars of different colors, by separating two colors by a chevron of a third, or by dividing the chevron or bar into two or more adjoining colors. A limited number of unique arrangements of colors is also found.

The idea of distinguishing institutions by a colored hood lining is certainly the weakest aspect of this system because many institutions use identical colors and arrangements or use colors virtually indistinguishable from each other. It should also be noted that many institutions have dispensed entirely with the bachelor's hood, and some also with the master's hood, at ceremonies at which degrees are conferred. There is, of course, nothing to prevent a graduate from purchasing the hood indicative of his degree and wearing it on appropriate occasions subsequent to the graduation ceremony.

Hats. The recommended hat is the black mortarboard of material to match the gown for bachelors and masters or, for doctors only, of velvet. The tassel may be either black or the color appropriate to the discipline in which the degree is awarded. The doctoral hat may have a gold tassel. Soft square-topped black hats are permissible for women, and some institutions prescribe a soft black velvet hat for doctors.

Variations on the 1895 system. The most interesting and certainly the most significant current development in academic dress in the United States is the deliberate policy of many of the most influential institutions to break away from the rigid uniformity of the system used since 1895. Harvard University has never entirely conformed to the 1895 system of academic dress. Standard gowns and hats have been used, but the hood is a modification of the simple shape shown in Figure 7 and made of black silk lined with crimson. The discipline of the wearer's degree is indicated by a colored "crow's-foot" (a design of twisted braid) on the front of the gown, which now for doctors may be of crimson trimmed with black velvet. Yale University has allowed its masters and doctors the option of wearing Yale blue rather than black gowns. A small number of institutions have always used individual schemes of hoods.

The new developments in United States academic dress are of significant magnitude and follow three definite lines. First, all graduates wear standard pattern but distinctively colored or trimmed gowns, together with standard hoods and hats. Second, in addition to distinctive gowns, specially designed hoods and probably a

Figure 18. American doctor.

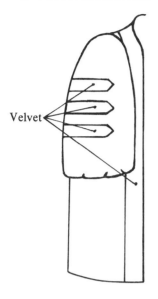

Velvet

Figure 19. Doctoral hood with a chevron across the lining (Doctor of Philosophy).

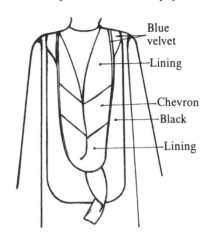

Blue velvet

Lining

Chevron

Black

Lining

Figure 20. Part of a Swedish rector's chain of office.

Figure 21. Enlarged representation of Swedish Doctor of Medicine hat badge and ring.

special doctoral hat are prescribed. Finally, while bachelors and masters wear standard dress, all doctors or honorary doctors wear distinctive gowns and hats and possibly a special hood.

Academic dress for presidents of institutions. The 1895 system never provided distinctive dress for presidents of institutions, but it noted that occasionally the chief executive officer of an institution might have some distinctive dress or insignia. This has long been the practice at Harvard and Yale Universities; at the latter the president also has a chain of office. The practice of having special dress for the president of an institution is increasing. It is also customary for members of the governing bodies of institutions to wear doctoral gowns (trimmed with black velvet), together with either the hood proper to the wearer's degree or with a hood of special design prescribed by the institution. Increasingly, it is the practice to prescribe distinctive academic dress for members of governing bodies.

Academic Dress in Europe

In Europe in many instances the academic dress currently in use is the latest development in a chain of tradition reaching back to medieval times. It tends to differ from the Oxford-Cambridge and United States systems in that the emphasis is on the office or function of the wearer in a particular institution rather than on the possession of a particular academic qualification. Within this generalization the systems of academic dress and insignia in use tend to be related to national entities.

Academic dress in Scandinavia. In the Scandinavian countries of Denmark, Finland, Iceland, Norway, and Sweden, rectors (executive heads) of universities and similar institutions wear a chain of office that passes over each shoulder and around the wearer's neck and customarily has a medallion of some form in the front. In Norway such a chain may be worn with or without a distinctive gown; in Finland it is usually worn with a distinctive sleeveless cape; and in Denmark, Iceland, and Swe-

den it is worn with full evening dress, including a tailcoat and white bow tie.

In all these countries doctors wear a distinctive ring, and in Sweden and Finland this custom is extended also to certain holders of master's degrees and other professional qualifications. A most interesting custom in Finland and Sweden is the wearing by doctors of a hat with a high stiff crown and pleated sides, which has a small badge on the front indicating the wearer's degree and awarding institution. This hat, worn with the rectorial chain of office and, in Finland the rectorial cape, is made of black silk (except for the hat for Finnish Doctors of Law, which is of red silk). Doctors wear this hat on all ceremonial occasions, together with full evening dress; in Sweden the collar of the tailcoat may have a prescribed design embroidered in black silk. Figures 20 and 21 show, respectively, part of a Swedish rector's chain of office and an enlarged representation of a doctoral hat badge and ring.

Academic dress in the Netherlands, Belgium, France, and the Federal Republic of Germany. In the Netherlands and Belgium academic dress consists basically of a black gown with varying types of black braid and/or velvet trimming, to which the nonstate institutions often add colors distinctive of the faculty in which the wearer teaches. In the Netherlands rectors wear a chain of office, and various types of capes—usually of some shade of red—are prescribed for doctors or perhaps only for honorary doctors. In Belgium the rector's office is indicated in the state universities and institutions by an ermine scarf worn over the right shoulder and in the nonstate universities by a distinctive gown and hat or device. Honorary doctors are invested with a special type of scarf, of distinctive colors, worn over the left shoulder. This scarf is trimmed in various ways, back and front, with white fur.

In France it was the custom for the rector and members of the academic staff of universities to wear a colorful and elaborate academic dress, but the use of such costume appears almost to have fallen away. The same situation prevails in the Federal Republic of Germany, where the use of academic dress has been completely abandoned, and the once universally worn rectorial and professorial gowns have disappeared from the field of higher education.

Academic dress in Spain. In Spain there is a uniform system of academic dress, which consists of a black gown, faced in front with black velvet or satin and having narrow wrist-length sleeves edged in some instances with white lace, worn over a colored satin foundation. An elbow-length cape is worn with this gown, that of rectors being of black velvet and in other instances of the color distinctive of the wearer's faculty— for example, red for law, gold yellow for medicine, sky blue for letters, dark blue for science, and orange for economic sciences. An octagonal black hat with a large tuft in the center of the flat crown is worn with this gown and cape. The tuft is of the same color as the cape, and for rectors and doctors the sides of the hat are covered with loose threads also of the same color as the cape. Rectors, deans of faculties, and doctors also wear an academic medal suspended from a cord round the neck. The same type of costume is worn in the technical universities and privately controlled institutions.

Academic dress in Central European countries. As is to be expected in a country where local cantonal influence is strong, universities in Switzerland have differences of principle concerning the use of academic dress. Usage varies from, on the one hand, no academic dress or insignia being used, to the other extreme, in which the rector and all the members of the teaching staff wear gowns and hats. Between these extremes, usage varies from that in which only the rector wears academic dress to its being worn by the rector, the deans of the faculties, and certain members of the academic staff. In all instances, however, such gowns and hats as are worn are black with the addition of either trimming of a single color or trimming in the color distinctive

of the wearer's faculty. Rectors wear a chain of office, and in one instance special insignia is prescribed for the deans.

In Austria academic dress consists basically of a black gown and hat, the gown being trimmed either with a single color for all those persons in an institution who wear such dress or with a color distinctive of the rectorial office and, for deans and others, with the color distinctive of their faculty. Rectors and deans of faculties wear a chain of office. In the Austrian system the wearing of academic dress is often confined to the rector, deans of faculties, elected members of the university senate, and professors acting as promoters at the ceremony when the doctorate is awarded.

In Czechoslovakia it is customary for the rectors to wear a gown of red of varying shades, the remaining academic dress being basically black with some type of trimming, which may be black or a color. Rectors and deans of faculties wear a chain of office.

In Poland the use of academic costume is virtually universal in universities and similar institutions, and it assumes a quite distinctive form of a gown, cape reaching to the elbow or wrist, and a square hat. Rectors generally wear a red gown and an ermine fur cape, red hat and gloves, and a special rectorial ring. A special staff of office is carried before the rector by a person specially appointed to this duty. Deans of faculties and professors generally wear a black gown with a cape and a black square hat and black gloves. The cape and gown are trimmed in various ways with the color distinctive of the wearer's faculty, and rectors and deans of faculties wear a chain of office with their academic dress. Some of these chains are of considerable age, while others are new and functional in their design.

In Italy it generally remains the custom for rectors, deans of faculties, and professors to wear fairly elaborate academic dress that varies from one university to another. Frequently the rector's costume is embellished with ermine fur, and deans of faculties often wear sashes of a color indicating their faculty transversely across the body. Scarves, cords, tassels, and sleeve linings of the color of the wearer's faculty are commonly added to the basic gown, which is usually black although other colors are sometimes used.

Academic Dress in the Middle East and Africa

Little information relating to the Middle East and Africa is available, in part because these countries have no tradition of distinctive dress for members of universities. There are thus three possibilities open to universities in these countries: to adopt, possibly with some modifications, the type of dress used in Western European universities; to adopt, again perhaps with modifications, as has been done in the Sudan, some local garment; or not to use any academic dress at all.

The first course has been adopted by the state universities in Turkey, the universities in Iran, the University of Kuwait, and at least one university in Saudi Arabia. In each case a black gown with some form of trimming is used. In the state universities in Turkey, the gown is trimmed with the color distinctive of the wearer's faculty, and a scarf and black hat have been added. The scarf is worn over the left shoulder and trimmed with the same color as the gown and with gold motifs. Rectors of these universities wear a white gown, scarf, and hat. One privately controlled university in Turkey uses only a special type of scarf worn over ordinary clothes and passing over both shoulders to hang down at the back and the front.

In Iran it is customary to place the university's insignia on the colored facing down each front of a black gown and to join the insignia by a gold cord ending in gold tassels. The status of the wearer is commonly indicated by adding to the colored front facings perpendicular gold braid edgings, varying from four for the chancellor or rector to one for professors, while those of lower grades have the facing

of the color alone. Recipients of degrees customarily wear a plain black gown.

The University of Kuwait uses a black gown trimmed with blue and yellow, the status of the wearer being indicated by three, two, or one infinity marks on the sleeves. The status of the wearer of the gown in the University of Riyadh, in Saudi Arabia, is indicated by between one and four horizontal colored bars on each sleeve or by a plain untrimmed sleeve.

It is interesting to note that while in France the custom of wearing academic dress is declining, certain universities in African countries, now independent but formerly under French administration, use the French type of academic dress. One university in Lebanon also uses the French type of academic dress, while another university and certain colleges in that country use the United States system. The Bar-Ilan University in Israel uses a cape and beret for its graduates; in the other universities and institutions of university level in Israel no academic dress is used.

Academic Dress in the Far East

In the Far East there is also no tradition of academic dress. In the universities and colleges of the Republic of the Philippines, the system of academic dress most commonly used is that of the United States, though in some few instances the Spanish system of academic dress is used for holders of master's and doctoral degrees. The United States system is used almost universally, so far as information can be obtained, in the universities and colleges of the Republic of Korea. There appear to be, however, certain significant modifications in the colors that designate the various departments of learning. Bachelors do not usually wear a hood nor, on some occasions, do masters, but it is general custom for doctors to wear the hood. In one institution in the Republic of Korea, academic dress is based on the costume worn in Korea during the Yi dynasty (1392 to 1910).

In the Republic of China there are varying usages in academic dress, but the standard practice is for bachelors to wear a plain black gown with wrist-length sleeves. Some institutions add a black collar coming to a point on the chest; a band of color on the collar indicates the degree. Masters customarily wear a gown of the pattern shown in Figure 2, to which may be added a hood of varying design. Frequently, however, the hood is the same as that worn by masters in the United States. The doctoral dress customarily follows that of the United States system, but there is one instance of a purple gown for doctors with a unique hood.

In Thailand, the only other country in the Far East from which it has been possible to obtain information, there is no uniform procedure relating to academic dress. At Chulalongkorn University an entirely unique type of dress is prescribed. It consists of a white lawn gown with front facings, a border round the bottom, sleeve facings, and velvet bands around the elbow trimmed with gold braid. The velvet is black for bachelors and masters and red for doctors, the degree being indicated by the width and color of a narrow band in the center of the velvet. The university insignia is placed on each front facing near the top of the gown.

Thammasat University uses a black gown with a scarf over the left shoulder. The scarf is the color of the degree and similar to that formerly in general use in France. It is trimmed, back and front, with horizontal bands of knitted white wool—three bands for doctors, two for masters, and one band for bachelors.

Kasetsart University and Mahidol University use black gowns, the design generally following that used in the United States, but with several significant modifications. Thus, at Kasetsart University, bachelors do not wear a hood, but the yoke of the gown is trimmed with cord of the color distinctive of the degree and ending in two tassels on the chest in front. Masters wear a gown of the pattern shown in Figure 2, and an Oxford simple shape hood of black lined with green and bound with the

degree color. Doctors wear a black gown with front facings and three horizontal bars on each sleeve of blue velvet; their hood is black lined with green with two chevrons. The hood is bound with velvet of the color of the department in which the degree is awarded.

At Mahidol University all gowns have wrist-length sleeves and are faced down each front with the degree color, the doctoral gown also having three horizontal bars of this color on each sleeve. The width of the front facing varies with the degree, being widest for doctors and narrowest for bachelors. All hoods are of the shape shown in Figure 19 and are of black lined with blue and edged with varying widths of the degree color.

Academic Dress in Central and South America

Central and South America are two further areas about which it is difficult to be precise. It is known that in some universities in Central America the Spanish system of academic costume is worn; in others no academic dress is used; and in yet others the United States system, with or without significant modification, is used.

In the two universities of the Republic of Panama, the general custom is for the rector and professors to wear a black gown with colored trimming and around the neck a ribbon, of the color of the wearer's faculty, from which is suspended a medal. Graduates wear an untrimmed black gown and a medal suspended from a ribbon of the color of the faculty in which the degree is awarded.

In Venezuela it is the general custom for the rector, deans of faculties, and members of the teaching staff to wear black gowns with or without faculty-colored facings. It is customary for deans and professors to wear the medal that all graduates of the Venezuelan universities receive when their degree is awarded. This medal is suspended from a ribbon of the color distinctive of the faculty in which the degree is awarded. The rector of each university wears a special gold medal suspended from a ribbon of the Venezuelan national colors of red, yellow, and blue.

In Brazil academic dress appears to be generally in use and to a certain extent reflects the style formerly used in Portugal. Because of lack of information it is impossible to be more specific. In Peru, the only other South American country about which information is available, the general custom is for a medal to be worn from a ribbon round the wearer's neck, and with ordinary clothes rather than with any form of gown, though in some instances a gown alone or gown and some type of cape or hood is used. In the state universities the suspending ribbon for rectors is of equal parts of red, white, and red—the national colors— and the medal is of gold. The medal worn by members of the academic staff is of gold for doctors and of silver for bachelors and is suspended from a ribbon of the color distinctive of the faculty in which the wearer's degree has been awarded. In the private universities the same custom of wearing a medal prevails, but the colors of the ribbon appear to vary from one institution to another.

In concluding this survey of academic dress it should be emphasized that, in several of the countries following the Oxford-Cambridge tradition and in the United States, the use of academic dress is not confined to institutions of higher education as such. There appears to be a growing tendency for professional associations in various fields to adopt some form of academic dress—perhaps a gown and hat alone, or gown, hat, and hood—for those who hold certain qualifications. Despite some indications to the contrary, it would appear that on the whole there is still a widespread usage of academic dress and, in some instances, of insignia together with or rather than academic dress alone.

Academic Insignia

Academic insignia, discussed above to some extent, is insignia used to indicate offices in, or degrees awarded by, universities and similar institutions. In addition to this type, however, insignia is also used to identify the university or institution in various ways. Into this category fall such insignia as coats of arms, devices of various kinds, and seals. Coats of arms are shields and similar devices that follow the Western European heraldic tradition and are devised in terms of certain specific rules relating to heraldry. In certain instances, these coats of arms have been granted by the heraldic authority having jurisdiction over the country in which the university or institution is situated. In other instances, coats of arms have simply been devised and adopted, in which case they do not always adhere to the rules of heraldry.

Insignia may also take the form of some device symbolic of the university's philosophy or of the local culture of the country. The adoption of a device based on local culture or other similar basis is often preferable to forcing local ideas into the constraints of a tradition that is often entirely foreign.

The coat of arms or symbol of the university or institution is often reproduced on its seal. A reproduction of the seal— many of which in Western European universities are of great antiquity—may be used to identify the university or institution on its letterheads, certificates, and publications. The seal is also customarily impressed on the certificates awarded to recipients of the university's degrees and qualifications. In some form, it may also be used on flags and banners, as may the other types of insignia mentioned above. A selection of examples of university devices is shown in Figure 22.

Mention has already been made of chains of office worn by holders of certain offices in universities and similar institutions. Such chains of office may be of plain links with a medallion suspended from the lowest point in front. The medallion bears some device characteristic of the university or institution, such as its coat of arms, seal, or a representation of its founder or other notable person connected with its history.

Figure 22. University insignia. (1) University of Oxford: England; (2) University of Cambridge: England; (3) University of Dundee: Scotland; (4) Fu Jen Catholic University: Republic of China; (5) University of Calicut: India; (6) Massey University: New Zealand; (7) University College, Cork: Republic of Ireland; (8) University of Oslo: Norway; (9) University of Victoria, Toronto, Ontario: Canada; (10) Chulalongkorn University: Thailand; (11) Jean Bédel Bokassa University: Central African Republic; (12) University of Isfahan: Iran.

Alternatively, chains of office may consist of ornamental links or plaques, or both, with various types of embellishment thereon and a medallion as described above. It is not uncommon to find incorporated into the chain of office the coat of arms or symbol of the town or city in which the university or institution is located. When the chain is that of the dean of a faculty, devices symbolic of the faculty over which the dean presides are frequently included, either on the chain itself or on the medallion.

An interesting usage of academic insignia occurs in the Soviet Union, where no form of academic dress or insignia of the type outlined above is used. Graduates of universities and institutes of higher education wear in the lapel a badge distinctive of the institution that has awarded their degree. These badges differ for each university or institution.

A final type of insignia is the mace, staff, or scepter that is carried before the titular or executive head of the university or institution on ceremonial occasions. These are found most often, but not exclusively, in Western Europe. Many of the older universities have several such items of insignia dating often from medieval times. They are frequently of intricate design and of great beauty, reflecting the craftsmanship of the age in which they were fabricated. However, this does not mean that the more modern items of this kind, although perhaps simpler and more functional in design, are less beautiful or less appropriate indicators of the importance of the person before whom they are carried. As symbols of a particular office, they add a measure of dignity to the pageantry of the occasions on which they are used.

Bibliography

Rogers, F. R. S., Franklyn, C. A. H., Shaw, G. W., and Boyd, A. H. (Eds.) *The Degrees and Hoods of the World's Universities and Colleges.* Lewes, England: W. E. Baxter, 1970.
Shaw, G. W. *Academical Dress of British Universities.* Cambridge, England: W. Heffer, 1966.
Sheard, K. *Academic Heraldry in America.* Marquette: Northern Michigan University, 1962.
Smith, H. H., and Sheard, K. *Academic Dress and Insignia of the World.* Cape Town, South Africa: A. A. Balkema, 1970.

HUGH H. SMITH

See also: Academic Dress, History of.

ACADEMIC DRESS, HISTORY OF

Academic dress was adopted by most European universities founded during the Middle Ages and the Renaissance. Universities in Italy, Portugal, France, the German-speaking states, the Netherlands, Belgium, and Switzerland prescribed some form of academic dress, generally having its source in ecclesiastical dress. However, it was at the University of Oxford that the symbolic system of academic dress had its origin and its major development. Teaching began at Oxford as early as 1117, when a group of scholars gathered around St. Frideswide, the mother church of Christ Church Cathedral at Cardinal College (now known as Christ Church). The theologian Robert Pollen arrived to lecture at Oxford in 1133, and gradually a university came into being. The secondary source of academic dress, Cambridge University, began as a teaching center in approximately 1209 but was not recognized as a *studium generale* (customary medieval designation of a community organized for learning and instruction) until the bull of Pope John XXII in 1318. (Oxford was recognized as a *studium generale* in approximately 1163.)

Originally, all members of a university were clerics; that is, they were either in holy orders or in minor orders, or at least were tonsured as belonging to the lower grade of the clericature. Accordingly, they were subject to clerical discipline and, in particular, were required to wear clerical dress. Academic dress is thus ecclesiastical in origin, with the exception of that of the faculties of law and medicine, which, in the sixteenth century, adopted some lay details in their bonnets and their undress (nonceremonial) gowns.

Throughout the Middle Ages academic dress developed and evolved at both Oxford and Cambridge. Its evolution may be divided approximately into three periods: from the beginning to about the close of the fifteenth century, from about 1500 to about 1636 (date of the Laudian Statutes), and from 1636 to the present.

At first, dress in the universities was very simple, and undergraduates and bachelors were under very strict and definite discipline; masters and doctors enjoyed much greater freedom. Gradually, faculties arose and titles of degrees came into being, such as bachelor's and master's degrees in grammar and arts and bachelor's and doctoral degrees in theology and canon law. Degrees in physic (medicine) came much later, and later still (about 1500) came those of bachelor and doctor in music.

The earliest dress for undergraduates and bachelors consisted of a black habit, the habit of the Benedictines, or of other religious orders. With this was worn a black hood, lined with cheap white rabbit fur; under the habit all wore the plain black cassock *(sub-tunica)*. A distinctly academic or official garment was at first confined to masters. This garment was not the modern gown or *toga,* but the *cappa* or cope, with a border and a hood lined with miniver. The use of expensive fur, such as ermine or miniver, was forbidden to bachelors.

As faculties evolved, colors were adopted that distinguished their members. Grammar, arts, and theology continued to wear black; the law faculty adopted blue. Thus, bachelors in arts wore black hoods lined with cheap white fur, masters wore black hoods lined with ermine or miniver, bachelors in theology wore black cloth hoods lined with black, or used their master's hoods, while doctors in theology adopted scarlet cloth hoods lined with black. Doctors probably began to line their hoods with silk toward the end of the fourteenth century. The *Books of the Chancellor and the Proctors* of 1426 permitted masters to line their hoods with silk between Easter and All Saints Day, while an Oxford statute of May 24, 1432, stated that silk linings were to be restricted to masters and to those of

high rank, noble birth, or great elevation or wealth. Students and bachelors were prohibited from wearing miniver, pure white, pure gray, cotton, tartary cloth, or silk *(sericus)*.

In announcing to Paris University his exaltation to the Chair of St. Peter, Pope Benedict XII (1334–1342) granted the use of scarlet robes *(capuchons rouges)* to doctors in theology and canon law. Doctors at Oxford began to wear scarlet robes about the middle of the fourteenth century. Some wore purple robes, and in the time of the Edwards (fourteenth century) doctors adopted some shade of red for their *cappae* (copes), while masters and the higher bachelors retained their black ones.

An important Oxford statute of March 5, 1490, addressed nongraduate scholars and bachelors; all bachelors were ordered to wear their hoods fully lined with fur. (Debasement of hoods had already begun, as robe makers merely partly lined or edged them.) The statute proclaimed, "Whereas certain bachelors have been seen walking abroad careless of the safety of their souls, in fancy boots, with their scanty hoods insufficiently lined with fur [they] are hereby given fourteen days in which to have their scanty hoods fully lined with fur." Penalties were imposed for noncompliance.

By the middle of the fifteenth century the main robes had come into use and were well established (Figures 1, 2, and 3).

The most valuable record of academic dress in Oxford at that period is the Chaundler Manuscript in the Bodleian Library at Oxford. The probable date of the manuscript is 1463. A picture in the manuscript shows the warden of New College, Oxford, surrounded by members of the college. The carefully drawn details of the picture have made possible an understanding of the academic dress of the time. By its evidence, doctors wore the cassock *(sub-tunica),* over it the habit, chimere, or tabard *(cappa clausa)* with a single central slit for doctors in theology and two side slits for other doctors. Over the habit was a hood (or, if a high church dignitary, an almuce with furred edges and small tails); on the head was a small round skullcap *(pileus)*.

Bachelors in the superior faculties (other than bachelors in theology) wore the cassock, habit, and hood, but no cap, as did masters. Bachelors in divinity were usually masters; they wore no cap but wore the black habit. Bachelors in arts wore the cassock, the gown or habit of their order (not the *cappa clausa*), a black hood lined with cheap white fur, and no cap.

During the second half of the fifteenth century degrees in medicine were instituted. The faculty of medicine adopted the dress of the faculty of law, so the bachelor in physic wore a blue hood lined with white fur (and does so still at Oxford). Doctors in physic wore scarlet hoods, which should have been lined with blue (as were the lawyers), but they and the doctors in canon law seem to have had them lined with crimson silk.

Academic Dress after the Reformation

Inevitably, after the Reformation, academic dress became more secular, with the cassocks and the habits of the religious orders no longer being worn. Bachelors in arts wore instead black gowns with wide open winglike sleeves, with no habit or cap, although they retained their old hoods. Masters and bachelors in theology adopted black gowns, open in front, with Tudor half sleeves, and a large appendage behind the elbow that extended gradually until it reached the hem of the gown *(toga talaris)*. Bachelors in the superior faculties (other than Bachelors in Theology) and doctors in civil law, medicine, and music wore black cloth gowns with long closed sleeves (half sleeves to the elbow) with square-ended pendants to the hem of the gown. Their hoods remained the same. In full dress, doctors wore gowns of scarlet cloth with wide bell-shaped sleeves, civic or secular, and nonecclesiastical.

The only pre-Reformation item of academic dress retained was the *cappa clausa* (worn over the cassock). This had been the earliest official dress of masters and thus was academic rather than ecclesiastical in

Figure 1. A "Doctor in Physic," second half fourteenth century.

Figure 2. A Doctor of Law.

Figure 3. A Doctor in Medicine, 'temp:' Henry VII, 1485–1509.

From H. Norris, *Costume and Fashion*, vol. II, 1927, pp. 258, 95, and 74, reproduced in Charles A. H. Franklyn, *Academical Dress from the Middle Ages to the Present Day Including Lambeth Degrees*, Lewes, England: W. E. Baxter, 1970. By permission.

origin. Henry VIII, in "An Act for the Reformation of Excess in Apparel" (1533), expressly permitted its use by bachelors and doctors in divinity, doctors in canon or civil law, and doctors in the newer sciences. All were allowed to wear the "sleveless cote" in scarlet, violet, or murrey (mulberry). Doctors at Oxford also retained (and still retain) their scarlet habits as a convocation dress, worn over the gown, with the hood worn over the habit. At Cambridge this handsome and dignified academic robe was discontinued, except for the vice-chancellor when presenting for degrees, but any doctor is still entitled to have one made.

Sometime between 1550 and 1600 doctors in music adopted full-dress festal robes of cream figured damask silk with bell-shaped sleeves of rich salmon pink or cerise silk. They wore hoods of the same pattern as those of the other doctors; the hoods were made of cream figured damask silk, fully lined with salmon pink silk. This remains the ceremonial robe of doctors in music and is regarded as the most beautiful robe in the world.

Anthony Wood (1892) states that the large open bell-shaped sleeves were introduced into both Oxford and Cambridge from Geneva by the Puritan element. They were then enforced by law as one of the results of the Hampton Court Conference of 1604, which ordered that the sleeves of gowns and robes were to be "straight and wide at the wrist."

In 1636 the Laudian Statutes (or the Caroline Code) were put through under the chancellor of the University of Oxford by William Laud, lord archbishop of Canterbury. The statutes laid down very strict regulations concerning the dress of heads, fellows, and scholars of colleges, and the observance of moderation in dress by men. Academic dress suited to each degree and faculty was enacted, all graduates were ordered to wear gown *(toga)* and scarf *(epomidas)* adapted to their degree and faculty, and square or round caps, particularly at sermons, ordinary lectures, and public disputations.

During the civil war scarlet robes were looked on with disfavor by the Puritans. However, when Thomas, the third Lord Fairfax, and Oliver Cromwell visited Oxford in 1649, they wore scarlet robes when created Doctors of Civil Law.

Academic Dress after the Restoration

After the Restoration in 1660, Paul Hoode, vice-chancellor of the University of Oxford, issued a proclamation recalling the statutes of the university (evidently those relating to academic dress in the Laudian Statutes) and ordering every graduate to appear in his "formalities" and undergraduates to wear caps and gowns. In 1666 John Fell, then vice-chancellor of Oxford, introduced a motion "to restore formalities and habits much neglected in the late interval." Thus, academic dress was restored to pre–civil war usage.

Two sets of plates of the academic dress of Oxford and Cambridge in 1674 and 1675, now in the Bodleian Library at Oxford, show exactly what robes were then worn by the members of these two universities. The plates, by George Edwards (1674) and David Loggan (1675), reveal that all gowns were full length to the ankles (including the commoners') and that all hoods for all degrees were of the very full pattern, consisting of a large shoulder cape, hood proper (cowl), and liripipe (tail). All the Oxford and Cambridge hoods seem to have been the same for the corresponding degrees; no hoods are shown in what is called the simple shape. Academic dress continued much the same to about 1770 (a year of new statutes), when robe makers seem to have reduced the hoods of all bachelors (except bachelors in theology) and masters to a simpler shape by removing the cape.

Academic Caps

In the early Middle Ages the wearing of a cap was the exclusive privilege of doctors, and this cap was one of the four doctoral insignia (the cap, the kiss, the ring, and the book). Even archbishops and bishops were forbidden to wear the cap unless they were doctors; the cap was the simple black skullcap or *pileus* still worn in the Roman Catholic church. However, by 1350, or before, all theologians (religious orders excepted), canon lawyers, and doctors in civil law were forced to wear caps.

After 1564 caps came under several statutes and decrees. In 1564 the square cap was ordered for heads of houses, colleges, and halls at Oxford; graduate fellows were not allowed to go about in public and outside college walls unless wearing caps, which had to be square. Caps were allowed to graduates at Cambridge in 1575. In 1576 all those bound by decree to wear caps were ordered to wear square caps.

By Oxford statute, bachelors were allowed in 1580 to wear a square cap "humbly and submissively in the Schools." In 1601 the square cap (*pileus quadratus*) was again ordered for all fellows (of all degrees) and scholars. Sons of nobles and gentlemen and fellow-commoners were to wear the round cap (*pileus rotundus*). In 1620 the wearing of square caps by masters, in congregation or convocation, was again enforced, penalties being instituted for noncompliance. In 1636 the Laudian Statutes also prescribed caps.

The earliest cap was the *calotte* or skullcap worn by canons and church dignitaries in the twelfth and thirteenth centuries, followed by the round skullcap of doctors, between 1300 and 1500. The square cap was devised about 1490 by sewing together four pieces of cloth, forming four horns and four seams, or ridges, from which developed the biretta. In the Tudor age, the square cap in velvet with a soft top, no tuft or tassel, grew into a beautiful cap with an ear flap around the back of the head (known as the Thomas Cranmer cap). Beautiful round Tudor caps came into use by doctors in the secular faculties, and in Stuart times round caps in velvet and in silk were authorized for all graduates except those in arts and theology (who were restricted to square caps) and for noblemen and gentlemen-commoners.

Bibliography

Franklyn, C. A. H. *Academical Dress from the Middle Ages to the Present Day Including Lambeth Degrees.* Lewes, England: W. E. Baxter, 1970.

Gibson, S. (Ed.) *Statuta Antiqua Universitatis Oxoniensis.* Oxford, England: Clarendon Press, 1931.

Hargreaves-Maudsley, W. H. *A History of Academical Dress in Europe.* Oxford, England: Clarendon Press, 1963.

Rashdall, W. H. *The Universities of Europe in the Middle Ages.* (F. M. Powicke and A. B. Emden, Eds.) Oxford, England: Clarendon Press, 1936. (Published originally 1895.)

Rogers, F. R. S. "The Origin and Development of Academic Costume." Unpublished master's thesis, University of Bristol, 1962.

Rogers, F. R. S., Franklyn, C. A. H., Shaw, G. W., and Boyd, A. H. (Eds.) *The Degrees and Hoods of the World's Universities and Colleges.* Lewes, England: W. E. Baxter, 1972.

Shaw, G. W. *Academical Dress of British Universities.* Cambridge, England: W. Heffer, 1966.

Wood, A. *The Life and Times of Anthony Wood M.A., Antiquary of Oxford, 1632–1695.* Oxford, England: Oxford Historical Society, 1892.

CHARLES A. H. FRANKLYN

See also: Academic Dress and Insignia.

ACADEMIC DUE PROCESS
See Due Process and Grievance Procedures.

ACADEMIC FREEDOM

Academic freedom is the freedom of the teacher within his or her field of study. It is a safeguard that allows researchers and teachers in institutions of higher learning to pursue their work without the inhibition, prohibition, or direction of political, ecclesiastical, or other administrative authorities, regardless of their personal philosophies, behavior, or life-style. It is a liberty granted to these individuals to assure them the opportunity for examination and challenge of doctrines, dogma, and received opinions in the interest of advancing knowledge for the benefit of all society. For the individual it entails, as Arthur O. Lovejoy pointed out, the freedom "to investigate and discuss the problems of his science and to express his conclusion, whether through publication or in the instruction of students, without interference" ("Academic Freedom," 1930, p. 384). For scholars academic freedom is a precondition of teaching or advancing knowledge not only on philosophical grounds but on the basis of efficiency of inquiry (Polanyi, 1947).

From a legal point of view, there is no definition of academic freedom, but one commentator suggests a useful definition as "that freedom of members of the academic community, assembled in colleges and universities, which underlies the effective performance of their functions of teaching, learning, practice of the arts and research. The right to academic freedom is recognized in order to enable faculty members and students to carry on their roles" (Fuchs, 1967).

Difficulties arise in terms of describing the boundaries of academic freedom: at what point does the shield of academic freedom cease to assure teachers and researchers that their actions may be carried on with impunity? This is a concern that has been examined carefully by the American Association of University Professors (AAUP), a United States organization long active in the advocacy and protection of academic freedom. In its 1940 *Statement of Principles on Academic Freedom,* the AAUP states, in part, "The teacher is entitled to freedom in the classroom in discussing his subject, but he should be careful not to introduce into his teaching controversial matter which has no relation to his subject" (quoted in Joughin, 1967, pp. 35f). The real question, however, is how to distinguish between the teacher as teacher and the citizen who also happens to be a teacher. The AAUP states, "The college or university teacher is a citizen, a member of a learned profession and an officer of an educational institution. When he speaks or writes as a citizen, he should be free from institutional censorship or discipline, but his special position in the community

imposes special obligations; as a man of learning and as an educational officer, he should remember that the public may judge his profession and his institution by his utterances. Hence he should at all times be accurate, should exercise appropriate restraint, should show respect for the opinion of others and should make every effort to indicate that he is not an institutional spokesman" (quoted in Joughin, 1967, p. 36).

This is a statement subscribed to by most United States institutions of higher learning, and it has served as a model for consideration in other countries. Difficulties still exist, however, in attempting to determine precisely the parameters of academic freedom in the ambiguous nature of "appropriate restraint." One explication of the concept suggests that restraint applied to *manner* of expression is acceptable, but any restraint on the *matter* of expression would be an infringement of academic freedom. Thus, an attempt to discipline an individual for failure to observe standards of academic responsibility would be subject to the following interpretation in terms of academic freedom: "A violation [of academic responsibility] may consist of serious intemperateness of expression, intentional falsehood, incitement of misconduct, or conceivably, some other impropriety of circumstances. It may not lie, however, in the error of unpopularity, even though gross, of the ideas contained in an utterance" (R. F. Fuchs, quoted in Taylor, 1963, p. 42). Thus, academic freedom is committed to the protection of the circulation, exploration, and advancement of ideas but not of any excessive mode of advocating them.

This is an aspect of academic freedom as an institutional freedom. It is also a professional freedom, a functional freedom: "Here, indeed, lies its full significance. An educator has various other tasks to do, subsidiary to his primary function. . . . But the reason he belongs to the guild of educations, the reason he has a place in an institution of higher learning, is that he is first and foremost engaged in the pursuit and communication of knowledge. This function is a community service. . . . The service of the educator is not a service to his students alone or to his institution or to his profession. It is a service to his country. A service to civilization, a service to mankind. The fulfillment of this incalculable service depends on the healthful maintenance of the freedom of the scholar" (MacIver, 1955).

A few examples may suffice to indicate the long intellectual history of academic freedom. In the thirteenth century Godfrey of Fontaines, a member of the University of Paris faculty of theology, asserted that "to bind men to an opinion on questions on which there may be a diversity of views without danger to faith would impede the pursuit of truth" (Hofstadter and Metzger, 1955, p. 31). Tommaso Campanella's "The Defense of Galileo" in 1623 enunciated "the first rational argument to be published in support of the freedom of scientific investigation" (Sutton, 1953, p. 311). John Milton, in *Areopagitica*, and John Stuart Mill, in *On Liberty* both argued for an environment in which truth or received opinion could be challenged.

The emergence of academic freedom as a formal doctrine took place in Germany in the nineteenth century, largely as a result of Wilhelm von Humboldt's administration of the University of Berlin. There he developed the concept of academic self-government and the concept that became known in Western European universities as *Lehrfreiheit,* freedom of teaching. (Concommitantly he developed *Lernfreiheit,* the freedom of the student to choose his own curriculum.) *Lehrfreiheit* had two main aspects: "It meant, in the first place, that a professor or lecturer was free to teach according to his convictions, unhampered by political or other restrictions. In the second place, it implied that he was free to choose his subjects, on which to lecture, without reference to a prescribed syllabus" (Samuel and Thomas, 1949, p. 115).

During the nineteenth century *Lehrfrei-* *heit* suffered abuses from within, as some professors "used their freedom to preach a tendenciously nationalist philosophy that stood in glaring contrast to the objectivity that *Lehrfreiheit* was intended to secure." Threats came from without as well. In 1899 a law (the *Lex Arons*) was enacted in Germany, which stated that "the deliberate promotion of Social Democratic purposes is incompatible with a teaching post in a royal university" (Samuel and Thomas, 1949, p. 117). Theology professors were expected to be Christian, and hostility to the state was unacceptable in those teaching political science (Paulsen, 1906).

In its transmission to other countries of Western Europe, the concept of *Lehrfreiheit* became greatly broadened, particularly in the United States and the United Kingdom. By the turn of the century, John Dewey (1902) could feel that academic freedom was secure and unthreatened in the United States.

In post–1918 Germany, *Lehrfreiheit* was assured by Article 142 of the Weimar constitution, but it was still subjected to frequent abuse. With the ascent of Hitler to the chancellorship, *Lehrfreiheit* was replaced by *Kämpfende Wissenschaft*—a militant scholarship—and academic freedom disappeared from German universities until after World War II (Samuel and Thomas, 1949, pp. 127–134).

The influence of German concepts of academic freedom on United States institutions was strong in the latter half of the nineteenth century. "If one were to single out the chief German contribution to the American conception of academic freedom, it would be the assumption that academic freedom, like academic searching, defined the true university" (Hofstadter and Metzger, 1955). In this case, Presidents Charles W. Eliot of Harvard, William Rainey Harper of the University of Chicago, Julius H. Seelye of Amherst, and Daniel Coit Gilman of Johns Hopkins supported and advanced this concept. In turn, the leaders in the battles for academic freedom in United States universities in the early years of the twentieth century were scholars who had studied in Germany.

In the United Kingdom the German ideals have been carried forward to a point where academic freedom "would be infringed if any authority, either inside or outside the university, were to forbid a university officer to take a certain line in his teaching or in his published work; and it would be a scandalous infringement if he were to be dismissed from his office for refusing to comply" (Ashby, 1966, p. 292). Indeed, Chorley (1963) considered that academic freedom is enjoyed as fully in English universities as anywhere else in the world.

Similarly, in France "the liberty of the professor to determine how he teaches and to express his views gave him an academic freedom seldom equaled anywhere" (Burn, 1971, p. 34).

Japanese universities were established using nineteenth-century German universities as models, but Western concepts of academic freedom did not emerge until after World War II, when the classroom practice of indoctrinating a single set of values was abandoned in exchange for "a complete freedom of expression and teaching. . . . The freedom to teach and to learn are practiced with few restrictions" (Burn, 1976, p. 265).

Because academic freedom depends upon a willing and irrevocable ceding of authority, it is a concept alien to universities in countries governed by totalitarian or authoritarian regimes. Because its existence implies and encourages dissent, academic freedom is unacceptable to such governments. This is not to say that a university without autonomy cannot ensure its members academic freedom. For example, the Prussian constitution of 1850 provided that "Science and the teaching of it are free" ("Academic Freedom," 1930, p. 387). Academic freedom, however, is not generally compatible with authoritarian regimes; it no longer is allowed in Cuba, for example (Salazar, 1976).

In some developing nations that have modeled their universities on Western European institutions, academic freedom may be considered an irrelevant curiosity in that it cannot be related to immediate fulfillment of national purpose. As Eni Njoku (1959), a scholar who became vice-chancellor of the University of Lagos, commented, "Although the principle of academic freedom is accepted, it is important to realize that it has still to justify itself in the Nigerian context. It is not easy to argue that academic freedom is necessary in order to train the professional manpower required by the Nigerian society. . . . The scholar has not yet fully arrived in Nigeria and the advantages to be gained by giving him freedom are not yet obvious . . . [academic freedom] is merely one of the embellishments attached in its country of origin to an imported product."

Despite the exotic nature of the philosophy of academic freedom in developing countries, Ashby (1966, p. 320) feels that there have been no infringements of academic freedom, in the narrowest sense of the idea, in universities in African Commonwealth countries. In a broader understanding of the phrase—the freedom to hold political opinions unacceptable to the government—there have been infringements, conspicuously by the white governments of Rhodesia and South Africa.

The concept of academic freedom in the developing nations is changing in response to the special circumstances of universities in those countries. Emerging nations consider universities as the best hope for eradicating poverty, ignorance, and disease. Concentration on these important but comparatively short-term goals has meant a closer relationship to governments and to parties with an immediate political stake in these issues; this in turn has meant impatience and disenchantment with traditional roles and attributes of the university. In 1972 the forty-two countries represented by the Association of African Universities stated: "The emerging university of the 1970's in Africa must, therefore, shed its foreign forms and cloak; it must not just pursue knowledge for its own sake, but for the sake of and the amelioration of the conditions of the life and work of the ordinary man and woman. . . . Even in the pursuit of its traditional functions of promotion and dissemination of knowledge, as well as research, the university must place emphasis on that which is immediately relevant and useful" (Yesufu, 1973). To the extent that the teacher must subordinate his own intellectual interests to the priorities of the state, academic freedom might be considered to be eroded.

In governments relatively new to positions of world power and influence, there is a simple and direct relationship between manpower needs and educational resources. Accordingly, traditional academic freedom is completely alien to the educational context of such countries as the People's Republic of China. Research problems for solution are determined by the government, and educational means are directed toward this end. Academicians do participate, however, in the definition of problems, particularly in the natural sciences. The understanding of and commitment to the political and social system by both teachers and students, as a precondition of their participation in higher education, eliminates any possibility of the existence of academic freedom as it developed in the West (Ballantine, 1975).

In the Arab countries of the Middle East, academic freedom was essentially an import from the West as a part of the total concept of a university. Freedom of inquiry, embodied in academic freedom, found, at best, an uneasy accommodation within the essentially authoritarian tradition of the Arab world. Although it has not been disavowed as an ideal, academic freedom in the Western sense has not yet emerged in practice (Matthews and Akrian, 1948).

In India planning for higher education came under the influence of English models, which had a salutary effect on concepts of academic freedom and the role of the faculty member. As early as 1919 the Cal-

cutta University Commission was urging that "A body of university teachers of this character, well selected, holding their post by a secure tenure, and therefore independent, would form an element in the shaping of public thought in India the value of which it is impossible to overestimate" (cited in Ashby, 1966).

In the United States the concept of academic freedom, as developed in the Federal Republic of Germany, was broadened. Rudolph (1962, p. 413) has pointed out that "the German conception applied only to life within the academic walls and did not address itself to the privileges of the professor once he chose to go beyond the university. . . . the American academician was able to break down the distinction between inner freedom and outer restraint which characterizes the German definition."

Academic freedom more broadly defined was more easily infringed. A series of cases in the 1890s and early 1900s at the University of Wisconsin (Curti and Carstenson, 1949, pp. 508ff.), Marietta College (Beach, 1935, p. 227), Indiana University (Woodburn, 1940, pp. 414ff.), Brown University (Bronson, 1914, pp. 461ff.), and Stanford University (Elliott, 1937, pp. 362ff.) tested the limits of academic freedom and made the subject a matter of continually current interest to the teaching profession. This interest was of sufficient breadth and depth to lead, in 1915, to the establishment of the American Association of University Professors. The journal of this association over the years charts the course, case by case, of attempts to infringe on academic freedom and of resistance to those attempts. The association has published the definitive United States handbook on academic freedom.

The threats against which academic freedom has had to be on guard are primarily political, whether national, local, or intramural. The disappearance of academic freedom under such manifestly repressive regimes as those of Nazi Germany and Fascist Italy was complete, as there was no recourse (Minio-Paluello, 1946). Apparent attempts at restricting academic freedom in the United States, however, have resulted—especially in the post–World War II years—in recourse to the courts, thereby providing continuing commentaries on the essence and the limits of academic freedom. Thus, in 1957 the United States Supreme Court noted an emerging aspect of academic freedom—its extension to students: "The essentiality of freedom in the community of American universities is almost self-evident . . . Teachers and students must always remain free to inquire, to study and to evaluate, to gain new maturity and understanding: otherwise our civilization will stagnate and die" (354 U.S. 234, 250 [1957]). To these words of Chief Justice Earl Warren, Justice Felix Frankfurter added, "For society's good— if understanding be an essential need of society—inquiries into these problems, speculation about them, stimulation in others of reflection upon them, must be left as unfettered as possible" (354 U.S. 234, 262 [1957]).

The tendency of the courts has been to broaden further the definition of academic freedom. One commentator has suggested that academic freedom is now an attribute of the *university;* "the faculty and students must have complete and unqualified freedom to inquire and investigate, to interpret data, and to arrive at and announce conclusions in and out of the classroom, without the fear or reality of sanctions or controls of any kind, whether direct or indirect, whether pecuniary or related to status, or advancement, whether from within or from without the institutions. This is a societal interest which is independent of, although not superior to, the right of the individual scholar as a citizen to the exercise of freedom of inquiry and expression" (DeBardeleben, 1969).

Despite the increased acceptance of the principles of academic freedom within the educational community, new threats of infringement appear with each change in educational emphasis. In the student crisis years of the 1960s, a Canadian scholar stated that "the major threat to academic freedom in recent years has not been autocratic government or university bureaucrats or reactionary board members, but groups of students, small in number but highly visible because of their actions. These groups want to censor what is taught at the university and to choose who may teach on the basis of their own radical ideological commitments" (Hanly, 1955). Similarly, the economic constraints of the 1970s brought "wholesale encroachments upon academic freedom" (Bowen, 1973, p. 2), with sweeping demands for accountability, imposition of rigid budget systems, and increased regulation for economic reasons of such matters as tenure and teaching loads (Bowen, 1973, p. 2). Inflation, by reducing the purchasing power of universities, with consequent limitation of educational programs, has also threatened academic freedom (Wallace, 1974).

Among nonacademics, there is occasionally opposition to the exercise of academic freedom. Often this opposition derives from a larger antiintellectualism. Such opponents conceive of academic freedom as "the right to teach what employers do not want taught, without such teaching affecting in any manner the teacher's salary, tenure, promotion or assignment. Such objections usually "lack all the specific and objective qualifications which can in some degree be measured" (Zoll, 1952, p. 11).

In many countries during the 1960s and 1970s, increased costs of higher education and, in some cases, increased reliance by universities on government funds, led to a reexamination of government expenditures for educational purposes. In turn, this emphasis on costs raised the question of whether external control of university funds is a threat to autonomy and, consequently, a threat to academic freedom. In the United Kingdom the issues of institutional autonomy and academic freedom were raised clearly as the traditional role of the University Grants Committee as a buffer between the universities and the government changed to that of an agency making strategic decisions on the allocations of resources to universities, according to social priorities and national needs. The committee itself described the consequences of this changed role: "The dilemma is clear. On the one hand if each university does that which is right in its own eyes, with no regard for the totality of university provision or for national needs, there is a clear danger that anarchy and licence, under the universally respected name of academic freedom, will result. On the other hand, if the committee becomes too *dirigiste,* too tidy-minded and too much concerned with overall planning, there is an equally clear danger that the free growth of academic institutions will be stunted by excessive control" (quoted in Halsey and Trow, 1971, p. 88).

Clearly, there is a dilution of institutional autonomy, but "the question of individual right to free doctrinal expression is nowhere in question" (Halsey and Trow, 1971, p. 92).

In 1974 the University Grants Committee reported: "We can confirm after five years further experience the comment of our predecessors that no minister or official 'has shown the slightest inclination to reduce the independence of the committee or of the universities.'" The *dirigiste* role of the committee, however, had actually increased to a point where the committee was "more and more determining what shall be taught and studied in our universities and at which university a particular branch of learning shall be pursued." By 1976 university autonomy had been eroded to a point which led Lord Crowther-Hunt to comment that "the universities are now subordinate to, and dependent on, the UGC and whatever the fine intentions of the UGC, there is no doubt that it will still further erode the so-called autonomy of the universities over the next five years." He charged that *dirigism* had changed the committee from a buffer between the universities and the government to an agency of the government: "For just as the universities have become more and more controlled by the UGC, so the UGC has allowed itself to become more and more subordinate to the government." It was not alleged, however, that the erosion of autonomy had resulted in the abridgement of academic freedom.*

In differentiating between an appropriate government influence on the universities and an inappropriate influence on academic freedom, Eric Ashby suggests that "government influence on the movement of universities must be confined to over all social policy (such as the proportion of the age group to receive post-secondary education)" (quoted in Halsey and Trow, 1971, p. 87). On the other hand, he contends, "it would be crazy for the layman to tell the professor how to teach" (p. 96).

Dressel (1972, p. 12) makes a sharp distinction between university autonomy and academic freedom: "The imposition of role definitions and some operational controls on universities will not seriously interfere with their autonomy . . . such controls have little to do with academic freedom." Consideration of institutional purpose as well as institutional autonomy raises similar concerns. Morison (1970, p. 634) has proposed that "the academic community will have to recognize that academic freedom, like most other freedoms, has its limits. In the last analysis, agreement on what limits are can only be reached by some sort of political process. As a contribution to that process, we might begin by drawing a sharp distinction between the right of the university to determine the broad general directions of its research program and the right to tell individual investigators at a particular point in time what they can do and cannot do."

Bibliography

"Academic Freedom." In E. R. A. Seligman (Ed.), *Encyclopedia of Social Science.* Vol. 1., pp. 384–387. New York: Macmillan, 1930.

*Quoted material in this paragraph is from "The UGC and the Universities" (1976).

Ashby, E. *Universities: British, Indian, African.* Cambridge, Massachusetts: Harvard University Press, 1966.

Ballantine, D. S. *International Support for Emerging Universities.* Washington, D.C.: American Council on Education, 1975.

Beach, A. G. *A Pioneer College: The Story of Marietta.* Marietta, Ohio: Marietta College, 1935.

Bowen, H. R. "Academic Freedom and the Financing of Higher Education." Paper presented at meeting of American Council on Education, Washington, D.C., October 1973.

Bronson, W. C. *The History of Brown University, 1764–1914.* Providence, Rhode Island: Brown University, 1914.

Burn, B. A. *Higher Education in Nine Countries.* New York: McGraw-Hill, 1971.

Chorley, R. S. T. "Academic Freedom in the United Kingdom." *Law and Contemporary Problems,* 1963, *28,* 647–671.

Curti, M., and Carstenson, V. *The University of Wisconsin: A History. 1848–1925.* Madison: University of Wisconsin Press, 1949.

DeBardeleben, A. "The University's External Constituency." In W. P. Metzger, S. H. Kadish, A. DeBardeleben, and E. J. Bloustein, *Dimensions of Academic Freedom.* Urbana: University of Illinois Press, 1969.

Dewey, J. "Academic Freedom." *Educational Review,* January 1902, *23,* 1–14.

Dressel, P. L. *Return to Responsibility.* San Francisco: Jossey-Bass, 1972.

Elliott, O. E. *Stanford University: The First Twenty-Five Years.* Stanford, California: Stanford University Press, 1937.

Fuchs, R. F. "Academic Freedom, Its Basic Philosophy, Function and History." In L. Joughin (Ed.), *Academic Freedom and Tenure.* Madison: University of Wisconsin Press, 1967. Appendix E, pp. 242–263.

Halsey, A. H., and Trow, M. A. *The British Academics.* Cambridge, Massachusetts: Harvard University Press, 1971.

Hanly, C. "Problems of Academic Freedom in Canada." In P. Seabury (Ed.), *Universities in the Western World.* New York: Free Press, 1955.

Hofstadter, R., and Metzger, W. P. *The Development of Academic Freedom in the United States.* New York: Columbia University Press, 1955.

Joughin, L. (Ed.) *Academic Freedom and Tenure.* Madison: University of Wisconsin Press, 1967.

MacIver, R. M. *Academic Freedom in Our Time.* New York: Columbia University Press, 1955.

Matthews, R. D., and Akrian, M. *Education in the Arab Countries of the Near East.* Washington, D.C.: American Council on Education, 1948.

Minio-Paluello, L. *Education in Fascist Italy.* London: Oxford University Press, 1946.

Morison, R. S. "Some Aspects of Policy-Making in the American University." *Daedalus,* Summer 1970, pp. 609–644.

Njoku, E. "The Relationship Between University and Society in Nigeria." *The Scholar and Society,* 1959, *13,* 82–86.

Paulsen, F. *The German Universities and University Study.* (Translated by F. Thilly and W. W. Elwong.) New York: Scribner's, 1906.

Polanyi, M. *The Foundations of Academic Freedom.* Occasional Pamphlet No. 6. London: Society for Freedom in Service, 1947.

Rudolph, R. *The American College and University.* New York: Knopf, 1962.

Salazar, J. "No Academic Freedom in Cuba." *Boston Herald,* June 27, 1976.

Samuel, R. H., and Thomas, R. H. *Education and Society in Modern Germany.* London: Routledge and Kegan Paul, 1949.

Sutton, R. B. "The Phrase *Libertas Philosophandi.*" *Journal of the History of Ideas,* April 1953, *14,* 310–316.

Taylor, W. "Academic Freedom and Tenure: The University of Illinois." *AAUP Bulletin,* March 1963, *49*(1), 25–43.

"The UGC and the Universities." *Times* (London) *Higher Education Supplement,* May 28, 1976, p. 15.

Wallace, W. "Inflation Is 'Main Threat' to Academic Freedom." *Times* (London) *Higher Education Supplement,* December 13, 1974, p. 7.

Woodburn, J. A. *History of Indiana University.* Bloomington: Indiana University Bookstore, 1940.

Yesufu, T. M. (Ed.) *Creating the African University: Emerging Issues of the 1970s.* Ibadan, Nigeria: Oxford University Press, 1973.

Zoll, A. A. In *Can We Afford Academic Freedom?* Harvard Law School Forum. Boston: Beacon Press, 1952.

FRANK A. TREDINNICK, JR.

See also: Due Process and Grievance Procedures; Political Persecution of Academics.

ACADEMIC PERSONNEL ADMINISTRATION

See Academic Freedom; Academic Tenure; Affirmative Action; Due Process and Grievance Procedures; Political Persecution of Academics; Recruitment, Appointment, Promotion, and Termination of Academic Personnel; Remuneration: Faculty, Staff, and Chief Executive Officers; Workloads of Academic Personnel.

ACADEMIC PLANNING SECTION
(Directie Rectoraat—Academische Planning), Belgium

The Academic Planning Section was set up at the University of Antwerp, in Belgium, at the university's founding in October 1971. The section promotes the improvement of university teaching through research in higher education. On a national level, the section studies the cooperation of Dutch-speaking universities in Belgium, especially with respect to educational planning, research management, and organizational structure. Other research topics, which focus primarily on the problems of the University of Antwerp, include higher education administration, especially academic policies, and curricula and instruction. In addition to research activities, the section designs curricula and provides a documentation service.

The section is funded by the government. Its staff includes two research professionals, eight administrative personnel, and two secretaries.

Universiteit Antwerpen
Universiteitsplein 1
2610 Wilrijk
Antwerp, Belgium

ACADEMIC POLICIES

See Academic Freedom; Academic Tenure; Access to Higher Education; Affirmative Action; Calendars, Academic; Credit, Assessment of Learning for Postsecondary Education; Curriculum and Instruction; Degrees, Diplomas, and Certificates; Due Process and Grievance Procedures; Educational Resources: Learning Resources Centers; Exchange, International; Financial Aid; General Administration, Organization for; Governance and Control of Higher Education: Governance and Administration; Independent Study; Interdisciplinarity; Interinstitutional Cooperation; Languages of Instruction; Participatory Democracy; Recruitment, Appointment, Promotion, and Termination of Academic Personnel; Women and Higher Education; Workloads of Academic Personnel.

ACADEMIC STANDARDS AND ACCREDITATION: INTERNATIONAL

The regulation and maintenance of academic standards have long been a major concern of higher learning the world over. The first "keepers of the standards" were religious scholars or other learned men, such as the *shaykhs* (Islamic scholars) who taught in the mosques and *madrassas* (centers of advanced learning) in the Islamic world; the Buddhist monks, Brahmin teachers, and Hindu *gurus* of the East; and the monastic scholars of the Catholic church in medieval Europe. Learning was organized around these famous teachers or groups of teachers at established academies or centers of religious study. Students who successfully completed their studies often were granted a license to teach—the *ijazah* in the Islamic world and the *licencia docendi* in medieval Europe. This licensing of teachers was an embryonic attempt to control academic standards, the assumption being that by controlling those empowered to transmit knowledge, the quality of the knowledge being imparted would be maintained.

A second early form of "quality control"—the utilization of entrance examinations as a form of selecting those qualified to pursue higher learning—may be traced as far back as the sixth-century Buddhist center of learning at Nalanda, India. Over the centuries, the use of various types of entrance examinations has become a universal practice and in many instances constitutes a nation's first attempt to establish uniform academic standards.

In Great Britain the external examination developed by Oxford and Cambridge and later adapted by the University of London emerged as a third form of control. Under the Oxford-Cambridge system, external examiners from one institution reviewed the performances of students of another institution. Under the University of London plan, students in distant nations of the British Commonwealth enrolled in local colleges and universities but sat for examinations administered by the only degree-granting authority in the land, the University of London.

As in the Middle East and Europe, where higher learning prospered under the auspices of Islamic and Catholic religious centers, many of the early institutions of higher learning in the United States developed under the auspices of the Protestant church. Some institutions, such as Oxford and Cambridge Universities and later institutions patterned after the Oxford-Cambridge model, were self-governing from their very beginning. But as the structures of higher education became more solidified and colleges and universities became increasingly dependent on public funding, the reins of higher education governance began to pass from religious authorities to the authority of the state. In the wake of these changes, there evolved a variety of procedures, both formal and informal, for the regulation of academic standards.

The first pattern is that in which the authority to establish academic standards is vested in the institutions themselves under the overall direction of national or state ministries or agents empowered by the governments to act in their behalf.

The second pattern is that of standardization through examinations—entrance examinations, as originated at Nalanda; state examinations for degrees and licensing, as practiced by the medieval guilds; and external examinations in the tradition of Oxford, Cambridge, and the University of London.

The third principal pattern is that of accreditation by external agents, including voluntary accreditation, a system which, although developed in (and once unique to) the United States, has been adopted in other nations. Accreditation in the American sense of external, independent organizations that invite institutions into membership on the basis of on-site inspections of courses, programs, admissions standards, degree requirements, and adequacy of facilities and academic services has no parallel in the higher education systems of most nations. The principal exceptions are

Japan and the Philippines, where United States influence was extensive following World War II. There exist in many nations, however, independent external agents authorized to supervise the educational quality of programs and degrees.

Institutional Autonomy and the Role of the Ministries

There are many procedures used by governments to establish and maintain educational standards. In some countries, national Ministries of Education have direct responsibility for the approval of new curricula and the approval of course syllabi within those curricula. In most countries, however, the ministries exercise only indirect control, by virtue of their responsibility to oversee the implementation of laws governing the establishment of new institutions, their structure and divisions (as in Colombia, Japan, and Hungary); university reform; admissions procedures, including limitations on enrollment; student/teacher ratios; the appointment and promotion of faculty and administrative staff (as in the Federal Republic of Germany); and the appropriation of finances, including allocations for such ancillary functions as university research and library development. Even private institutions in such countries as Italy and Japan must comply with most of the laws governing state institutions if their degrees are to be "legally recognized."

In many nations, especially socialist nations, higher education falls under the jurisdiction of more than one ministry. Universities, for example, may be under the jurisdiction of the Ministry of Education, while the courses and curricula of agricultural schools are under the supervision of the Ministry of Agriculture, medical schools under the Ministry of Health, schools of technology under the Ministry of Science or the Ministry of Technology, and military colleges under the Ministry of Defense.

Still another variation is found in the Federal Republic of Germany, where the power to regulate standards is vested in the several states, the chief function of the national Ministry of Education being the formulation of broad policies designed to bring higher learning into line with national goals and objectives.

The implementation of government policy in most educational systems, however, rests with the university councils and academic senates of the individual institutions, the membership of which is comprised of university faculty and the chief administrative officers.

Monitoring Academic Standards Through Examinations

The concept of the examination is as old as that of learning itself. It is perhaps for this reason that one finds greater uniformity in examination practices than virtually any other aspect of higher learning. The use of an admissions examination or series of examinations is a common practice in higher education the world over. To this may be added the practice of requiring students to pass a secondary school examination, frequently called the school-leaving examination, as a preliminary step toward university admission. In many nations statewide maturation and entrance examinations are supplemented by the entrance examination of the individual institutions to which the students apply.

Once enrolled, students in most countries outside the United States are left to their own scholastic devices until they decide that they are ready to sit for final examinations. In some instances, such as the external degree program of the University of London or the correspondence study of the British Open University, the examination is the only form of quality evaluation in use. Both the University of London and the Open University guarantee the quality of their programs through the use of standardized tests.

In *The British Academics,* Halsey and Trow (1971, p. 38) make the point that "British universities have a strong centrifugal tendency evident in the comparable standard of their degrees which has been maintained hitherto by a voluntary system of external examining involving the interchange of staff between universities for examining purposes, by the role played by London in the development of the provincial colleges and by the more diffuse influence of Oxford and Cambridge."

Under the external examination system, tests administered and marked by the staff of one institution are passed on to external examiners on the staff of another institution, who then review the marks, propose changes when necessary, and confer with the staff of the examining institution as to the final assessment of the examinations. Examinations are held, for the most part, at the end of the student's first year and again at the conclusion of his studies.

A somewhat different procedure has been followed by the University of London, which for years fostered the development of many colleges in the Commonwealth that lacked degree-granting authority. Students attended local institutions but obtained University of London degrees after the successful completion of London's external examinations.

The use of the external examination has given rise to a variety of administrative agents, such as the West African Examinations council, serving the member countries of the Gambia, Ghana, Liberia, Nigeria, and Sierra Leone. The Universities of Cambridge and London also maintain membership on the council, which conducts examinations on behalf of the examining boards of the University of London, the Royal Society of Arts, the City and Guilds of London Institute, and the Educational Testing Service in Princeton, New Jersey. The council also conducts such national examinations as the entrance and final examinations for teacher training colleges in member countries.

The University of London continues to offer its degrees through affiliated colleges in the Commonwealth, but the London pattern has been modified by some countries to form an internal system of affiliated colleges that functions under the supervision of a nearby university. In Australia, for example, teachers colleges in some states have been affiliated with local universities in an effort to upgrade the standards of the nonuniversity segment of tertiary education. In the state of Victoria, degrees and diplomas of several local single-purpose colleges must be approved by the Victoria Institute of Colleges, established in 1965 for "the development and improvement of institutions offering tertiary education in Victoria, other than in universities" (Australian Commission on Advanced Education, 1972, p. 107).

In Canada some provincial institutions hold their degree-granting power in abeyance in deference to their affiliations with major universities. In addition, most notably in the province of Alberta, two-year colleges are so closely bound to local senior institutions that faculty appointments and curriculum and entrance requirements are, by statutory provision, controlled by the senior university.

The pattern of affiliated colleges also exists in Pakistan, where colleges and other institutions affiliated with universities are regularly inspected by the Affiliation Committee of the individual university academic councils in order to evaluate the educational standards of the junior institutions and to recommend improvements for granting further affiliation.

Validation of Degrees and Standards by External Agents

The establishment and preservation of standards in some nations is the province of independent but government-endorsed bodies. These include the Council for National Academic Awards (CNAA) in Great Britain, the Australian Council on Awards in Advanced Education, the University Grants Commission in India, and the *Instituto colombiano para del fomento de la educación superior* (Colombian Institute for the Promotion of Higher Education) in Colombia. In Mexico the National Association of Universities and Institutes of Higher Education assists the secretariat of education in the establishment and main-

tenance of academic standards.

Council for National Academic Awards. The CNAA was founded by royal charter and given the authority to award degrees and other academic distinctions to graduates of the polytechnics and further education institutions that do not themselves have degree-granting powers. The council's degrees are comparable in standard to those of universities although sometimes more pragmatic in their orientation. In some professions the CNAA degree is sufficient to exempt degree recipients from examinations required by individual professions. Courses are validated and bachelor's, master's, and doctoral degrees awarded in a wide variety of fields ranging from the sciences and engineering to business, social studies, education, and the arts and humanities.

The council's procedures for the validation of degrees is similar to those employed by the universities, where internal boards and committees review the academic content of and facilities and funding for new programs. The CNAA makes use of on-site visitations by panels of academics from universities and polytechnics that review course proposals in light of stated aims, projected syllabi, internal methods of evaluation, adequacy of facilities, and availability of funding.

Many observers have suggested that the CNAA ought to shift its emphasis away from the validation of degree programs toward the accreditation of the institution as a whole. The ultimate end result of such a move would be that of "accredited" colleges seeking degree-granting powers of their own in lieu of CNAA degrees awarded in the colleges' behalf. The next question then becomes at what point the universities might be brought into a national system of accreditation. But this move would seem to be some distance in the future (Tolley, 1974, p. 16).

Australian Council on Awards in Advanced Education. The CNAA's effort to establish consistency in academic degrees has its parallel in the work of the Australian Council on Awards in Advanced Education, established in 1971 as a nonstatutory body by agreement of the six state ministers and the Commonwealth minister for education and science. Unlike the CNAA, however, the Australian council does not award degrees but seeks instead to promote consistency on the nomenclature used for awards in advanced education and to assist in the development of meaningful relationships between courses and their associated awards (Australian Commission on Advanced Education, 1972, p. 120).

Colombian Institute for the Promotion of Higher Education. The *Instituto colombiano para el fomento de la educación superior* (ICFES), an outgrowth of the Colombian Association of Universities, was officially sanctioned by extraordinary decree in 1968. Authorized by the Ministry of Education to serve as the controlling authority for all public and private higher education, the ICFES approves the establishment of all new universities and evaluates new programs within existing universities. The accreditation of a new program is dependent on ICFES approval after a series of ICFES staff on-site visitations to the institution concerned. When the program's first graduates have completed their studies, the program is reevaluated to determine how well it has fulfilled its objectives. ICFES is more than a "keeper of the standards," however; it also finances university research in education and organizes commissions to study university administrative structures and curricular reform.

University grants committees: India. In nations following the British system of education, university grants committees, independent and sometimes statutory agencies, function as buffers between ministries and colleges and universities.

The first such committee was established in Great Britain in 1919 for the purpose of advising the government on the financial needs of the universities. Since that time, grants committees with greatly augmented responsibilities have been established in several nations. Such committees do not profess to be agents for academic standards, but their influence is considerable by virtue of their power to determine financial appropriations. Their on-site visitations for the purpose of studying financial needs pursuant to academic programs, staff, and library and research facilities have the effect of monitoring existing educational quality in addition to determining the level of financing needed to maintain, if not to improve, that quality. This is particularly true in India, where the University Grants Commission (UGC) is a statutory agency with strong links to the Ministry of Education and regulatory powers enabling it to exercise considerable influence over academic standards.

In 1975 the Indian UGC announced a series of guidelines designed to regulate the expansion and quality of Indian higher education institutions, the growth of which many observers felt had gotten out of hand. These guidelines set forth new minimum qualifications for academic staff, new guidelines for the initiation of graduate studies, and new requirements for the establishment of new institutions and new programs (Abraham, 1975, p. 8).

In spite of the existence of the UGC, or perhaps because of its unsatisfactory control of standards, India also has experimented with the concept of voluntary accreditation in certain of its key professions.

Voluntary accreditation, or peer group evaluation for the purpose of maintaining and improving educational standards, originated in the United States and spread to other nations, largely through American influence. The precedent for such activity lies in the work of the medieval guilds, which sought to protect the standards of their profession by prescribing the methods by which an apprentice could become a master of his trade. The direct descendants of the guilds are the professional societies that currently function in many countries in the interests of academic quality within a given field. The United States has the greatest number of professional accrediting agencies, but such societies exist elsewhere as well. The Indian Medical Council, for example, establishes and regulates the standards for medical education, the Bar Council regulates standards for legal education, and the Chartered Accountants Act sets standards for the accounting profession. Technical education is under the supervision of the All India Council for Technical Education. The interesting aspect of India's professional accreditation is the fact that each of the above-mentioned bodies was established by act of parliament or ministerial resolution rather than by the voluntary organization of practitioners in the field.

The Indian Medical Council, first established by parliamentary act in 1933, was given the power by a new act of parliament in 1956 to establish medical qualifications; to requisition information on courses of study and examinations; to appoint visitors and inspectors to publicly report on the conduct of examinations and the adequacy of staff, equipment, and other facilities; to recommend to the central government the withdrawal of recognition previously granted; and to define minimum standards for medical education as well as postgraduate medical education for the guidance of the universities.

The Bar Council, established by the Advocates Act of 1961, is empowered to recognize and to continually inspect those universities whose law degrees constitute satisfactory preparation for the role of advocate and to prescribe the standards of legal education to which said universities must adhere in order to maintain Bar Council recognition. The Chartered Accountants Act of 1949 set forth similar regulations for the profession of accountancy.

The All India Council for Technical Education was established by a 1945 resolution of the Ministry of Education rather than by parliamentary act, but its function is similar to the other agencies by virtue of its responsibility to continuously survey existing facilities and to make proper proposals for the development of technical education.

Institutional accreditation—the public recognition of educational quality in all segments of a college's or university's course offerings—has been most extensively developed outside the United States in Japan and in the Philippines, where United States influence since World War II has been extensive.

Japanese University Accrediting Association. In 1947 forty-six national, public, and private universities founded the Japanese University Accrediting Association to measure and to evaluate an institution "in terms of its stated objectives, the purposes it seeks to serve, and its entirety as an institution of higher learning" (Japanese University Accrediting Association, 1967, p. 211). At that time, standards were set forth by the association regarding the faculties of an institution; student quotas; admissions qualifications; courses of instruction and units of academic credit; degree requirements; the nature of an institution's facilities; and standards for the assets, maintenance, and administration of a university.

In 1949 the association established criteria for the accreditation of graduate school standards, briefly specifying degree requirements for the master's and doctoral degrees and further specifying that an institution must have the necessary facilities and teaching staff to carry out programs of graduate study (Japanese University Accrediting Association, 1967, p. 216).

In 1959 the association was reorganized to form a foundation, and its purposes and qualifications for membership were more carefully defined. The purposes of the foundation were "to make surveys and studies on universities at home and abroad for the qualitative evaluation of the universities in this country and simultaneously to contribute to international cooperation in university education" (Japanese University Accrediting Association, 1967, p. 217). At this time, two types of membership were established: supporting membership was accorded full member institutions having one or more accredited faculties, and associate membership was granted to those institutions whose faculties were not as yet accredited. In the spring of 1976, the association had 83 supporting member institutions and 159 associate members. Within these institutions there were 224 registered (or accredited) faculties and 197 nonregistered faculties.

The activities of the foundation include surveys and studies of foreign and domestic materials on colleges and universities; the institution, revision, and application of accreditation standards for the upgrading of colleges and universities; the dispensation of aid and advice relative to the improvement of education; the conduct of seminars and conferences relative to academic standards; and the international exchange of information and publication of materials on university education.

Philippine Accrediting Association of Schools, Colleges and Universities. Exploratory accreditation efforts began early in the 1950s in the Philippines through the efforts of the Association of Christian Schools (ACS), the Catholic Educational Association of the Philippines (CEAP), and the Philippine Association of Colleges and Universities (PACU). It was not until 1957, however, that the Philippine Accrediting Association of Schools, Colleges and Universities (PAASCU) was founded, and it was some ten years later before PAASCU was officially recognized by the Philippine Department of Education as the first national accrediting association.

Although originally established primarily through the efforts of the CEAP, PAASCU membership includes public, private sectarian (but non-Catholic), and private nonsectarian institutions as well. Its membership is still proportionately small, however, in a country having more than six hundred colleges and universities.

PAASCU activities follow much the same pattern as those of the Japanese Accrediting Association and of United States regional accrediting associations. These include assisting institutions in self-evaluation and in developing standards and criteria for assessing the implementation of those stan-

dards in the areas of liberal arts, agriculture, engineering, commerce, and teacher education.

"The major problems that confront the PAASCU," according to past president Paul Hebert, "deal with the qualitative expansion of its membership, the official involvement and membership of state-supported institutions, the granting of greater autonomy to member schools by the government, the growth of its influence without succumbing to political pressure and interference, and the financial viability for carrying out its rapidly expanding service function" (Hebert, 1970, p. 7).

In a 1974 report on the future of accreditation in the Philippines, the issue appeared in broader perspective, with two models being proposed for consideration: the United States system of accreditation and the university grants committee approach. Proponents of the grants committee feel that institutional accreditation must be preceded by standardization of degree programs, more readily attained under the financial impetus of national quinquennial grants for program development. Proponents of voluntary accreditation as pioneered by PAASCU argue that government-controlled accreditation will stress minimum standards geared to national government planning at the expense of academic excellence and institutional autonomy (National Board of Education, 1974).

The resolution of academic standards lies at the very heart of the tradition of higher learning. Just as a variety of higher education systems and structures has evolved over the centuries, a similar diversity for quality control within those systems and structures has been developed in the nations of the world. One cannot presume to say that one method of evaluation is better than another. One can only seek to ascertain whether specific methods of control or accreditation satisfactorily serve the systems in which they operate. Accreditation systems, like the institutions they accredit, should seek to evaluate their performance in light of their own stated objectives. To the extent that they are able to do so, they will have satisfactorily served the cause of quality in learning.

Bibliography

Abraham, A. S. "UGC Initiates Campaign To Raise Standards." *Times* (London) *Higher Education Supplement,* August 29, 1975, p. 8.

Australian Commission on Advanced Education. *Third Report on Advanced Education.* Canberra: Australian Government Publishing Service, 1972.

Haggerty, W. J. *Higher and Professional Education in India.* Washington, D.C.: U.S. Government Printing Office, 1969.

Halsey, A. H., and Trow, M. A. *The British Academics.* Cambridge, Massachusetts: Harvard University Press, 1971.

Hebert, P. "Accreditation—Its Role." Paper presented at Seminar on Higher Education, Presidential Commission to Survey Philippine Education, Taol Vista Lodge, June 13–14, 1970.

Japanese University Accreditation Association. *Japanese Universities and Colleges.* Tokyo: Japanese University Accreditation Association, 1967.

MacArthur, B. "A Day with the CNAA—'Guardian of Academic Standards'." *Times* (London) *Higher Education Supplement,* June 6, 1975, p. 8.

National Board of Education. *Final Report of the Committee on Higher Education.* Manila, Philippines: National Board of Education, April 18, 1974.

Philippine Accrediting Association of Schools, Colleges and Universities. *Manual of Accrediting for Colleges and Universities.* Manila: Philippine Accrediting Association of Schools, Colleges and Universities, 1969.

Taylor, W. "Approaches Differ but Standards Are the Same." *Times* (London) *Higher Education Supplement,* May 30, 1975, p. 3.

Tolley, G. "Accreditation for All." *Times* (London) *Higher Education Supplement,* June 21, 1974, p. 16.

ASA S. KNOWLES

JOY WINKIE VIOLA

ACADEMIC STANDARDS AND ACCREDITATION: UNITED STATES

The programs presented by postsecondary educational institutions in the United States would be more uniform if all the states maintained similar educational policies or if the federal government played a dominant role in regulating educational practices. Since neither the states nor the federal government exercises control over all postsecondary education, the institutions themselves have developed their own internal systems of evaluation and external evaluation systems called accreditation. In general, accreditation systems operate through private regional and national educational and professional associations, which have adopted criteria for the quality of educational programs and have developed procedures for evaluating the extent to which institutions or programs have attained that level of quality.

Definitions

"Accreditation" is the process through which a legally responsible agency or association grants public recognition to a school, institute, college, university, or specialized program of study that meets certain established qualifications and educational standards. Accreditation is determined through initial and periodic evaluations. The purpose of the accreditation process is to provide an acceptable professional evaluation of the quality of educational institutions, or programs, and to encourage consistent improvement in such programs.

"Adverse accrediting action" normally is defined as the denial or the withdrawal of accreditation or preaccreditation status. "Institutional accreditation" signifies that the institution as a whole is achieving its educational objectives while meeting or exceeding the agreed-to minimum quantitative and qualitative standards. "Professional accreditation," or "program accreditation," denotes the review and approval of the quality of professional programs in terms of predetermined standards by professional associations or an organization of professional associations having a common interest and acting on behalf of all members of the group in accrediting matters; for example, the Engineers' Council for Professional Development.

"Representatives of the public" are laymen in the sense that they are not currently educators in, or members of, the profession for which the students are being prepared, nor are they in any way directly related to the institutions or programs being evaluated.

The Accreditation Process

To evaluate the quality of institutions and programs, all recognized accrediting organizations and associations follow the procedure listed below:

1. The accrediting agency or association, in collaboration with institutions and programs, publicly establishes the standards by which it judges the quality of the institution or program. These standards usually deal with the academic achievement of students, the competence of the faculty, the effectiveness of administrative techniques, the appropriateness of the curriculum, the quality of the library and other educational resources, the adequacy of physical facilities, the stability of financial support, and the fair and equitable treatment of students.

2. The institution clearly states its objectives and goals and the means to achieve them. It will be this statement against which the institution's achievements will be evaluated. The Council on Postsecondary Accreditation (later described) clearly states that accreditation is intended to encourage the diversity of American postsecondary education and allow institutions to achieve their particular objectives and goals.

3. The administration of the institution or program is required to submit a written analysis of how well that institution or program conforms to the standards. This analysis is an important part of the procedure and is usually exhaustive in nature.

4. The accrediting agency carefully studies the submitted analysis and then sends visiting committees to examine the institution or program in light of the analysis. The size of the committee is proportional to the size of the institution. In certain specialized situations a team may contain as few as two members; for a large univer-

sity the committee could number in excess of twenty-five. The visiting committee, in turn, writes its own reports based on its observations of the program or institution.

5. These reports are transmitted, usually with recommendations, with a copy to the head of the institution or program being accredited, to a decision-making body within the accrediting agency, composed of educators, practitioners of specific professions (in the case of professional or program accrediting), representatives of the general public, and sometimes students. On favorable action of the decision-making body, the institution or program is added to the accrediting agency's listing. In the event that the visiting committee's recommendations are unfavorable, the program or institution head has the right to appeal the committee's findings.

6. All accrediting requires reevaluation at specified intervals, which may vary between two and ten years. In this way the accreditation process tends to foster continuous program and institutional self-evaluation and self-improvement.

Scope of Accreditation

It is important to recognize that the lists of accredited institutions indicate only those institutions that meet the accreditation standards; they in no way indicate a ranking of institutions by the degree to which they surpass these standards. Accrediting agencies do not rank accredited institutions. They expect that every accredited college will adequately accomplish its own stated purposes and that these purposes are appropriate for the institution. They recognize that American colleges and universities differ in the types of students they admit and in the range of programs they offer. Thus, it should not be assumed that the graduates of every accredited college will have acquired the same knowledge or be competent in exactly the same skills. Although the graduation requirements of accredited colleges and universities in the United States are not identical, it can be assumed that the degrees awarded by all accredited institutions are based on at least a common minimum level of quality. For this reason, accreditation can justifiably be used as a general indication of good academic training.

Voluntary accreditation in the United States is the closest equivalent to the systems of external examinations and government supervision of universities employed by some other nations. It differs, however, in that it is a self-regulating mechanism; that is, the institutions or programs voluntarily initiate, promulgate, and adhere to basic minimum criteria. The accrediting organizations operate with little power and exercise only the positive sanction of publicizing those institutions and programs that have been examined by their peers and found to meet the criteria or the negative sanction of withholding public announcement of accreditation.

The lists of accredited institutions and programs are widely used in the United States. Many students refer to them when deciding which institution to attend; school officials use them in advising students about postsecondary education; and university officials rely on them to some extent in granting recognition for study completed at other institutions. For many professions, state licensing boards limit eligibility for the license to practice to graduates of accredited programs. The United States Civil Service Commission requires that candidates for certain positions must be graduates of accredited institutions.

Accreditation can be a helpful guide to students and educational officials in other countries, particularly for determining the overall quality of an institution. In general, nonaccredited institutions are deficient in one or more features normally considered necessary for adequate education. These features may include library materials, laboratory equipment, competent faculty, or adequate financial standing. Many good institutions, however, may not have all their professional offerings accredited. The casual observer should not base an educational choice solely on whether a particular program of study is accredited if that course is offered at an institution that has been evaluated and accredited as a whole.

Examples of Accrediting Procedures

Consider a new college that has been established in the state of Pennsylvania and has received legal authority from the state to grant academic degrees. If it wishes to be accredited by the appropriate regional association of schools and colleges, of which there are six in the United States, it applies for membership as a "candidate" for accreditation by the Middle States Association of Colleges and Schools, which serves Pennsylvania. The institution must normally remain a candidate until it has graduated (or is in the year in which it will graduate) its first class. After its faculty and staff have prepared a thorough report on institutional objectives and operations, the college is visited by a small group of faculty and administrators, specifically designated for this purpose, from other institutions that are members of the association. The team may spend several days at the candidate institution, meeting with its officials, observing classes, and evaluating its facilities and programs. Following this visit, the team writes an evaluation report, containing suggestions about possible improvements in the curriculum and faculty. This information is considered by the Commission on Higher Education of the association, and if the college is found to meet the standards for membership, it is permitted to join the association, thereby becoming a candidate for accreditation in the association.

A second institution, a liberal arts college in Illinois, for example, has been a member of the North Central Association of Colleges and Schools for ten years and is due for reevaluation. Its president reports to the association all major changes that have occurred in the college during the decade, and the institution is visited by a group of administrators and faculty from other institutions belonging to the association. As a result of their visit, the group makes several recommendations concerning areas of concern, perhaps in the freshman curricula or in admission and the student housing policies, or in the area of financial resources. The association votes to continue the college's membership with the requirement that a report be made within two years to demonstrate progress in eliminating the stated shortcomings.

A third institution, for instance, a state university elsewhere in the country, has been subject to interference in its operations by certain officials of the state government. Following a visit to the institution and an investigation of the situation, its regional association may place the institution on probation, with the requirement that the university's board of trustees be permitted to govern the university without external interference if its membership in the association and its accreditation are to be preserved.

As a fourth example, a proprietary school has been advertising guaranteed job placement following training. The investigating team ascertains that a substantial portion of the graduates are unable to find employment and requests the school to cease such advertising. If the school refuses to comply, the accrediting agency, affording due process to the school, including show cause and appeal, will drop the school from its list of accredited schools.

Costs of Accreditation

The costs of accreditation are met by the institutions themselves, except in a few professional fields where the individual members of the organization contribute support for accreditation through their membership dues. The costs of accreditation, both for individual programs and institutional accreditation, increased during the 1970s. This increase was caused by inflationary economic conditions in the United States and by increased numbers of specialized educational programs. Even so, because accreditation makes extensive use of volunteer, nonpaid evaluators and deci-

sion-making bodies, the nongovernmental process is considerably less expensive than the costs of a similar process administrered by a national government.

The Role of the Council on Postsecondary Accreditation

In 1975 the Council on Postsecondary Accreditation (COPA) was formed by the merger of the National Commission on Accrediting (the nongovernmental authorizing body for professional programatic accrediting agencies) and the Federation of Regional Accrediting Commissions of Higher Education (the grouping of the regional accrediting agencies). To this merger were joined four independent agencies which accredit special-purpose institutions. Among COPA's functions is the recognition and regular review of all recognized accrediting agencies to assure the integrity and consistency of their policies and procedures.

The Role of the Federal Government

Since 1952, when the United States Congress enacted the first of many pieces of legislation tying federal funding to accredited schools, the Commissioner of Education has pubished an annual list of "recognized" accrediting agencies. Initially, this list consisted of those agencies already recognized by the academic community as acceptable. By 1968, when more agencies had come into being and federal funding for various programs had greatly increased, the process of recognition became more formal and agencies were required to meet certain published criteria and to be reviewed at least every four years. For purposes of determining eligibility of colleges and universities for United States government assistance under certain legislation, the United States Commissioner of Education is required to publish a list of nationally recognized accrediting agencies and associations determined to be reliable authorities as to the quality of training offered by educational institutions and programs. Most collegiate institutions thus attain eligibility for federal funds by way of accreditation or preaccreditation. In some legislation provision is made for special qualifying steps that may be taken as alternatives to the normal accreditation process.

If an institution is accredited by an agency recommended for approval by the National Advisory Committee on Accreditation and Institutional Eligibility and is placed on the commissioner's list of recognized agencies, that institution and students attending it become eligible for various federal subsidies.

In requesting national recognition by the United States Commissioner of Education for federal funding eligibility or by the Council on Postsecondary Accreditation for quality determination, an accrediting agency or association must show the geographical scope of its operations as well as the type and levels of institutions or programs to be covered; the nature of its administrative staff; the use of qualified persons to serve as evaluators; fiscal solvency as evidenced by an external audit of its resources; and the procedures and standards for granting, denying, reaffirming, revoking, and reinstating accreditation. Each agency must also demonstrate its responsibility to the interests of students; the general public; the academic, professional, or occupational fields involved; and the institutions or programs under review. Finally, each agency also must prove its autonomy and reliability by showing freedom from conflict of interest and general acceptance of its policies and practices by those whom it seeks to judge. Detailed statements on the methods and procedures to be followed by accrediting bodies in seeking official recognition are published by the United States Office of Education and by the Council on Postsecondary Accreditation.

Recognized Accrediting Agencies and Associations

The following list combines the postsecondary accrediting bodies recognized on January 1, 1977, by both the United

States Commissioner of Education and the Council on Postsecondary Accreditation.

INSTITUTIONAL—REGIONAL

New England Association of Schools and Colleges
(Connecticut, Maine, Massachusetts, New Hampshire, Rhode Island, Vermont)
Richard J. Bradley, Executive Director
131 Middlesex Turnpike
Burlington, Massachusetts 01803

Commission on Independent Schools
Ralph O. West, Director of Evaluation

Commission on Institutions of Higher Education
William J. MacLeod, Director of Evaluation

Commission on Vocational, Technical, Career Institutions
Daniel S. Maloney, Director of Evaluation

Western Association of Schools and Colleges
(California, Hawaii, territory of Guam and such other areas in the Pacific Trust Territories as may apply to it)

Accrediting Commission for Community and Junior Colleges, WASC
Harry D. Wiser, Executive Director
P.O. Box 4065
Modesto, California 95352

Accrediting Commission for Schools, WASC
Lyle Siverson, Executive Director
1499 Bayshore Highway
Burlingame, California 94010

Accrediting Commission for Senior Colleges and Universities, WASC
Kay J. Andersen, Executive Director
% Mills College, Box 9990
Oakland, California 94613

Northwest Association of Schools and Colleges
(Alaska, Idaho, Montana, Nevada, Oregon, Utah, Washington)

Commission on Colleges, NASC
James F. Bemis, Executive Director
3700-B University Way N.E.
Seattle, Washington 98105

Southern Association of Colleges and Schools
(Alabama, Florida, Georgia, Kentucky, Louisiana, Mississippi, North Carolina, South Carolina, Tennessee, Texas, Virginia)

Commission on Colleges, SACS
Gordon W. Sweet, Executive Secretary
795 Peachtree Street NE
Atlanta, Georgia 30308

Commission on Occupational Education Institutions, SACS

Bob E. Childers, Executive Secretary
795 Peachtree Street NE
Atlanta, Georgia 30308

*Middle States Association of Colleges and
Secondary Schools*
(Canal Zone, Delaware, District of Columbia,
Maryland, New Jersey, New York,
Pennsylvania, Puerto Rico, Virgin Islands)

Commission on Higher Education, MSACSS
Robert Kirkwood, Executive Secretary
3624 Market Street
Philadelphia, Pennsylvania 19104

North Central Association of Colleges and Schools
(Arizona, Arkansas, Colorado, Illinois,
Indiana, Iowa, Kansas, Michigan, Minnesota,
Missouri, Nebraska, New Mexico, North
Dakota, Ohio, Oklahoma, South Dakota,
West Virginia, Wisconsin, Wyoming)

Commission on Institutions of Higher
   Education, NCACS
Thurston E. Manning, Director
P.O. Box 2276
Boulder, Colorado 80302

Commission on Schools, NCACS
P.O. Box 2276
Boulder, Colorado 80302

INSTITUTIONAL—NATIONAL
AND SPECIALIZED

Architecture:
National Architectural Accrediting Board,
   Inc.
Hugo G. Blasdel, Executive Director
1735 New York Avenue NW
Washington, D.C. 20006

Art:
National Association of Schools of Art
Roger Gilmore, Director
Commission on Accreditation and
   Membership, NASA
School of the Art Institute of Chicago
Michigan Avenue at Adams Street
Chicago, Illinois 60603

Bible college education:
American Association of Bible Colleges
John Mostert, Executive Director
Box 543
Wheaton, Illinois 60187

Blind and visually handicapped education:
National Accreditation Council for Agencies
   Serving the Blind and Visually
   Handicapped
Richard W. Bleecker, Executive Director
79 Madison Avenue
New York, New York 10016

Blood bank technology:
Council on Medical Education, American
   Medical Association, in cooperation with
   the Committee on Education, American
   Association of Blood Banks
Ralph C. Kuhli, Secretary
Committee on Allied Health and
   Accreditation
535 North Dearborn Street
Chicago, Illinois 60610

Business:
American Assembly of Collegiate Schools of
   Business
William K. Laidlaw, Jr., Managing Director
760 Office Parkway, Suite 50
St. Louis, Missouri 63141

Association of Independent Colleges and
   Schools
Dana R. Hart, Executive Secretary
Accrediting Commission, AICS
1730 M Street NW
Washington, D.C. 20036

Chiropractic:
Council on Chiropractic Education
Orval L. Hidde, Chairman
Commission on Accreditation, CCE
1434 East Main Street
Watertown, Wisconsin 53094

Clinical pastoral education:
Association for Clinical Pastoral Education,
   Inc.
Charles E. Hall, Jr., Executive Director
Interchurch Center, Suite 450
475 Riverside Drive
New York, New York, 10027

Construction education:
American Council for Construction
   Education
Eugene Thorson, Executive Secretary
1140 NW63, Glenbrook Centre
Suite 511
Oklahoma City, Oklahoma 73116

Cosmetology:
Cosmetology Accrediting Commission
James R. Dunne, Executive Director
1707 L Street NW, Suite 440
Washington, D.C. 20036

Cytotechnology:
Council on Medical Education, American
   Medical Association, in cooperation with
   the Cytotechnology Programs Review
   Committee, American Society of Cytology
Ralph C. Kuhli, Secretary
Committee on Allied Health and
   Accreditation
535 North Dearborn Street
Chicago, Illinois 60610

Dental and dental auxiliary programs:
American Dental Association
Thomas J. Ginley, Secretary
Commission on Accreditation of Dental and
　Dental Auxiliary Programs, ADA
211 East Chicago Avenue
Chicago, Illinois 60611

Dietetics:
American Dietetic Association
Gloria Archer, Coordinator
Program Evaluation, ADA
430 North Michigan Avenue
Chicago, Illinois 60611

Engineering:
Engineers' Council for Professional
　Development
David R. Reyes-Guerra, Executive Director
345 East 47th Street
New York, New York 10017

Forestry:
Society of American Foresters
Orlo Jackson, Director of Professional
　Programs, SAF
5400 Grosvenor Lane
Washington, D.C. 20014

Funeral service education:
American Board of Funeral Service
　Education
William H. Ford, Administrator
201 Columbia Street
Fairmont, West Virginia 26554

Histologic technology:
Council on Medical Education, American
　Medical Association, in cooperation with
　the National Accrediting Agency for
　Clinical Laboratory Sciences, sponsored by
　the American Society for Medical
　Technology and the American Society of
　Clinical Pathologists
Ralph C. Kuhli, Secretary
Committee on Allied Health and
　Accreditation
535 North Dearborn Street
Chicago, Illinois 60610

Home study education:
National Home Study Council
William A. Fowler, Executive Secretary
Accrediting Commission, NHSC
1601 18th Street NW
Washington, D.C. 20009

Hospital administration:
Accrediting Commission on Education for
　Health Services Administration
Gary L. Filerman, Executive Secretary
One Dupont Circle NW, Suite 420
Washington, D.C. 20036

Industrial technology:
National Association for Industrial
　Technology
Gene Strandberg, Executive Director
P.O. Box 627
Charleston, Illinois 61920

Interior design education:
Foundation for Interior Design Education
　Research
John Mead, Administrator
730 Fifth Avenue
New York, New York 10019

Journalism:
American Council on Education for
　Journalism
Baskett Mosse, Executive Secretary
Accrediting Committee, ACEJ
563 Essex Court
Deerfield, Illinois 60015

Laboratory assistant education:
Council on Medical Education, American
　Medical Association, in cooperation with
　the National Accrediting Agency for
　Clinical Laboratory Sciences, sponsored by
　the American Society for Medical
　Technology and the American Society of
　Clinical Pathologists
Ralph C. Kuhli, Secretary
Committee on Allied Health and
　Accreditation
535 North Dearborn Street
Chicago, Illinois 60610

Landscape architecture:
American Society of Landscape Architects
Samuel Miller, Director
Education and Research, ASLA
1750 Old Meadow Road
McLean, Virginia 22101

Law:
American Bar Association
Frederick R. Franklin, Staff Director
Section of Legal Education and Admissions
　to the Bar
1155 East 60th Street
Chicago, Illinois 60637

Librarianship:
American Library Association
Elinor Yungmeyer, Accreditation Officer
Committee on Accreditation, ALA
50 East Huron Street
Chicago, Illinois 60611

Medical assistant education:
Accrediting Bureau of Medical Laboratory
　Schools
Hugh A. Woosley, Administrator
Oak Manor Offices, 29089 US-20 West
Elkhart, Indiana 46514

Council on Medical Education, American
Medical Association, in cooperation with
the Curriculum Review Board, American
Association of Medical Assistants
Ralph C. Kuhli, Secretary
Committee on Allied Health and
Accreditation
535 North Dearborn Street
Chicago, Illinois 60610

Medical laboratory technician education:
Accrediting Bureau of Medical Laboratory
Schools
Hugh A. Woosley, Administrator
Oak Manor Offices, 29089 US-20 West
Elkhart, Indiana 46514

Council on Medical Education, American
Medical Association, in cooperation with
the National Accrediting Agency for
Clinical Laboratory Sciences, sponsored by
the American Society for Medical
Technology and the American Society of
Clinical Pathologists
Ralph C. Kuhli, Secretary
Committee on Allied Health and
Accreditation
535 North Dearborn Street
Chicago, Illinois 60610

Medical record education:
Council on Medical Education, American
Medical Association, in cooperation with
the Education and Registration
Committee, American Medical Record
Association
Ralph C. Kuhli, Secretary
Committee on Allied Health and
Accreditation
535 North Dearborn Street
Chicago, Illinois 60610

Medical technology:
Council on Medical Education, American
Medical Association, in cooperation with
the National Accrediting Agency for
Clinical Laboratory Sciences, sponsored by
the American Society for Medical
Technology and the American Society of
Clinical Pathologists
Ralph C. Kuhli, Secretary
Committee on Allied Health and
Accreditation
535 North Dearborn Street
Chicago, Illinois 60610

Medicine:
Liaison Committee on Medical Education,
representing the Council on Medical
Education, American Medical Association,
and the Executive Council, Association of
American Medical Colleges

even-numbered years:
Richard L. Egan, Secretary
Council on Medical Education, AMA
535 North Dearborn Street
Chicago, Illinois 60610
odd-numbered years:
John A. D. Cooper, President
Association of American Medical Colleges
One Dupont Circle NW, Suite 200
Washington, D.C. 20036

Music:
National Association of Schools of Music
Samuel Hope, Executive Director
11250 Roger Bacon Drive, No. 5
Reston, Virginia 22090

Nuclear medicine technology:
Council on Medical Education, American
Medical Association, in cooperation with
the Joint Review Committee on
Educational Programs in Nuclear Medicine
Technology, sponsored by the American
College of Radiology, American Society of
Clinical Pathologists, American Society
for Medical Technology, American Society
of Radiologic Technologists, and the
Society of Nuclear Medicine
Ralph C. Kuhli, Secretary
Committee on Allied Health and
Accreditation
535 North Dearborn Street
Chicago, Illinois 60610

Nursing:
American Association of Nurse Anesthetists
Edward L. Kaleita, Executive Staff Secretary
Council on Accreditation, AANA
111 East Wacker Drive, Suite 929
Chicago, Illinois 60601

National Association for Practical Nurse
Education and Service, Inc.
Lucille L. Etheridge, Executive Director
122 East 42nd Street
New York, New York 10017

National League for Nursing, Inc.
Margaret E. Walsh, General Director and
Secretary
10 Columbus Circle
New York, New York 10019

Occupational therapy:
Council on Medical Education, American
Medical Association, in cooperation with
the Accreditation Committee, American
Occupational Therapy Association
Ralph C. Kuhli, Secretary
Committee on Allied Health and
Accreditation
535 North Dearborn Street
Chicago, Illinois 60610

Occupational, trade, and technical education:
National Association of Trade and Technical
Schools
William A. Goddard, Secretary
Accrediting Commission, NATTS
2021 L Street NW
Washington, D.C. 20036

Optometry:
American Optometric Association
William M. Chapman, Executive Secretary
Council on Optometric Education, AOA
7000 Chippewa Street
St. Louis, Missouri 63119

Osteopathic medicine:
American Osteopathic Association
Philip Pumerantz, Director
Office of Osteopathic Education, AOA
212 East Ohio Street
Chicago, Illinois 60611

Pharmacy:
American Council on Pharmaceutical
Education
Daniel A. Nona, Executive Director
One East Wacker Drive
Chicago, Illinois 60601

Physical therapy:*
Council on Medical Education, American
Medical Association, in cooperation with
the Committee on Accreditation in
Education, American Physical Therapy
Association
Ralph C. Kuhli, Secretary
Committee on Allied Health and
Accreditation
535 North Dearborn Street
Chicago, Illinois 60610

*This arrangement was dissolved December
31, 1976. No new arrangement has been
recognized.

Physician's assistant education:
Council on Medical Education, American
Medical Association, in cooperation with
the Joint Review Committee on
Educational Programs for Physician's
Assistants, sponsored by the American
Academy of Family Physicians, American
Academy of Pediatrics, American Academy
of Physician's Assistants, American
College of Physicians, American College
of Surgeons, and the American Society of
Internal Medicine
Ralph C. Kuhli, Secretary
Committee on Allied Health and
Accreditation
535 North Dearborn Street
Chicago, Illinois 60610

Podiatry:
American Podiatry Association
John L. Bennett, Director
Council on Podiatry Education, APA
20 Chevy Chase Circle NW
Washington, D.C. 20015

Psychology:
American Psychological Association
Carolyn J. Suber, Associate Educational
Affairs Officer
1200 17th Street NW
Washington, D.C. 20036

Public health:
Council on Education for Public Health
Janet A. Strauss, Executive Director
1015 18th Street NW
Washington, D.C. 20036

Rabbinical and Talmudic education:
Association of Advanced Rabbinical and
Talmudic Schools
Abraham J. Tannenbaum, Executive
Director
Accreditation Commission, AARTS
175 Fifth Avenue, Room 711
New York, New York 10010

Radiologic technology:
Council on Medical Education, American
Medical Association, in cooperation with
the Joint Review Committee on Education
in Radiologic Technology, sponsored by
the American Society of Radiologic
Technologists and the American College
of Radiology
Ralph C. Kuhli, Secretary
Committee on Allied Health and
Accreditation
535 North Dearborn Street
Chicago, Illinois 60610

Rehabilitation counseling:
Council of Rehabilitation Counseling
Brockman Schumacher, President
Rehabilitation Institute
Southern Illinois University
1001 South Elizabeth
Carbondale, Illinois 62901

Respiratory therapy:
Council on Medical Education, American
Medical Association, in cooperation with
the Joint Review Committee for
Respiratory Therapy Education,
sponsored by the American Association for
Respiratory Therapy Education, American
College of Chest Physicians, American
Society of Anesthesiologists, and the
American Thoracic Society
Ralph C. Kuhli, Secretary

Committee on Allied Health and
  Accreditation
535 North Dearborn Street
Chicago, Illinois 60610

Social work:
Council on Social Work Education
Alfred Stamm, Director
Division of Standards and Accreditation,
  CSWE
345 East 46th Street
New York, New York 10017

Speech pathology and audiology:
American Speech and Hearing Association
Noel D. Matkin, Chairman
Education and Training Board, ASHA
9030 Old Georgetown Road
Washington, D.C. 20014

Teacher education:
National Council for Accreditation of
  Teacher Education
Rolf W. Larson, Director
1750 Pennsylvania Avenue NW
Washington, D.C. 20006

Theology:
Association of Theological Schools in the
  United States and Canada
Jesse H. Ziegler, Executive Director
P.O. Box 396
Vandalia, Ohio 45377

Veterinary medicine:
American Veterinary Medical Association
R. Leland West, Assistant Director
Scientific Activities, AVMA
930 North Meacham Road
Schaumburg, Illinois 60196

Other:
New York State Board of Regents
Ewald Nyquist, Commissioner of Education
State Education Department
The University of the State of New York
Albany, New York 12224

Bibliography

Blauch, L. E. (Ed.) *Accreditation in Higher Edu-
    cation.* Washington, D.C.: U.S. Government
    Printing Office, 1959.
Burns, N. "Accreditation." In *Encyclopedia of
    Educational Research.* New York: Macmillan,
    1960.
Deferrari, R. J. *Self-Evaluation and Accreditation
    in Higher Education.* Washington, D.C.:
    Catholic University of America Press, 1959.
Division of Eligibility and Agency Evaluation.
    *Criteria and Procedures for Listing by the U.S.
    Commissioner of Education and Current List.*
    Washington, D.C.: Bureau of Postsecondary

Education, Office of Education, U.S. De-
    partment of Health, Education and Wel-
    fare, 1976.
Dressel, P. L. *The New Colleges: Towards an
    Appraisal.* Iowa City, Iowa: American Col-
    lege Testing Program, 1971.
Fisk, Roberts and Duryea, E. D. *Academic Collec-
    tive Bargaining and Regional Accreditation.*
    Washington, D.C.: Council on Postsecon-
    dary Accreditation, 1977.
Geiger, L. G. *Voluntary Accreditation: A History
    of the North Central Association.* Evanston,
    Illinois: North Central Association of Col-
    leges and Schools, 1970.
Heilbron, L. H. *Confidentiality and Accreditation.*
    Washington, D.C.: Council on Postsecon-
    dary Accreditation, 1976.
Kaplan, W. A. *Respective Roles of Federal Govern-
    ment, State Governments, and Private Accredit-
    ing Agencies in the Governance of Postsecondary
    Education.* Washington, D.C.: Council on
    Postsecondary Accreditation, 1976.
Miller, J. W. *Organizational Structure of Non-
    Governmental Postsecondary Accreditation: Re-
    lationship to Uses of Accreditation.* Washington,
    D.C.: National Commission on Accrediting,
    1973.
Nevins, J. F. *A Study of the Organization and the
    Operation of Voluntary Accrediting Agencies.*
    Washington, D.C.: Catholic University of
    America Press, 1959.
Orlans, H. *Private Accreditation and Public Eligi-
    bility.* Lexington, Massachusetts: Heath,
    1975.
Puffer, C. E. (Ed.) *Regional Accreditation of
    Institutions of Higher Education.* Washington,
    D.C.: Federation of Regional Accrediting
    Commissions of Higher Education, 1970.
Selden, W. K. *Accreditation and the Public Interest.*
    Washington, D.C.: Council on Postsecon-
    dary Accreditation, 1976.
Selden, W. K. *Accreditation: A Struggle over Stan-
    dards in Higher Education.* New York: Harper
    & Row, 1960.
Zook, G. F., and Haggerty, M. E. *The Evaluation
    of Higher Institutions.* Chicago: University of
    Chicago Press, 1936.

JAMES M. PHILLIPS

EUGENE I. VAN ANTWERP

ACADEMIC TENURE

Academic tenure, a term in common use in
Australia, Canada, the United Kingdom,
and the United States, has been defined as
"an arrangement under which faculty appointments in an institution of higher edu-

cation are continued until retirement for age or physical disability, subject to dismissal for adequate cause or unavoidable termination on account of financial exigency or change of institutional program" (American Association of University Professors and Association of American Colleges, 1973, p. 256). Other terms for security of employment used in the bibliography entries cited below include lifetime appointment, appointment not subject to review, becoming established, confirmation in employment, titularization, permanent and pensionable employment, confirmation on permanent establishment, and continuing appointment.

These terms—and the term *academic tenure* itself—are not simply alternative names for a single set of employee provisions. Rather, each one refers to the "job security" aspect of employment situations that may vary considerably among institutions within each nation. An adequate review of variations in tenure provisions requires as well an examination of institutional provisions for the classification, appointment, promotion, retirement, and dismissal of faculty members. These provisions, in turn, generally reflect both the national or cultural attitudes toward higher education and teachers and the mechanisms that the sponsoring society historically has used to administer its educational and other public service enterprises.

Tenure will be considered here as job security in relation to faculty personnel policies. Tenure as a protection of "academic freedom" will not be considered, except indirectly, although it may be an issue of equal or sometimes greater importance. Briefly, a sound academic personnel system will ensure that faculty members will be able to teach and carry out research subject only to high standards of professional competence and that they shall be free from political or other inappropriate interference in their teaching and research. Although such interference may take many forms other than loss of a job, academic tenure ensures that tenured faculty members cannot be dismissed from their positions without due process and without the use of appropriate academic criteria.

Faculty Personnel Systems

Most faculty personnel systems are designed to employ two large classes of persons: those who hope for a career in college teaching in the employing institution or in the educational system of which it is a part, and those who are assumed to be only temporary or part-time employees. Among the second group are persons fully employed elsewhere and those in student status who have not yet completed the necessary academic requirements for admission to the first formal step in a teaching career. Tenure is ordinarily not available to members of the second group. The following provisions, therefore, apply to the first group, the career teachers.

Qualifications for initial selection of members of the career group ordinarily include, as a minimum, a basic academic degree such as a master's degree, a doctorate, or a professional degree in the United States, or the passing of a competitive national examination such as the *agrégation* in France. Selection among qualified candidates may be made on additional bases, such as interviews, research writings, recommendations of former colleagues, and public lectures. A final formal decision to appoint may be made by an academic department or faculty, by a senior university administrator, by a minister of education, by a combination of these, or—in some cases—by the crown.

In many educational systems, the initial appointment is for a fixed term and leads to the possibilities of termination, of reappointment for another fixed term, or, at the end of the fixed-term appointment, of permanent appointment. This period of impermanent, fixed-term appointments is the probationary period and may range from one year (in Indonesia, for example) to five years or more. (The maximum in the United States is usually seven years.)

Movement from a probationary appointment to a tenured one may be virtually automatic in the absence of demonstrable incompetence, but more often it is based on some consideration of probationary performance. In personnel systems in which the number of tenured positions is not limited by law or quotas, a favorable recommendation of a professional group ("peer review") based on the candidate's performance in teaching, research, and other duties and on an estimate of future potential for professional growth is often the only requirement. This procedure is essentially noncompetitive among the candidates. Where tenured vacancies are limited, "peer review" will include a recommendation by the reviewing body of the best qualified among the candidates, thus introducing an important element of competition. Ordinarily, opportunities for achieving tenure are open only to those already employed in the institution. However, in some countries (such as France) tenured vacancies are open to all formally qualified candidates, both internal and external, on the basis of competitive examinations and occasionally other provisions, such as the achievement of a position on a promotion list following the examinations. In theory no preference is given to local candidates.

In many systems the initial award of tenure does not necessarily carry a promotion in rank. Even when promotion accompanies tenure, later advancement to the highest rank is not ensured. Like the initial award of tenure, subsequent promotions may come nearly automatically on the basis of seniority alone. More often promotions are the result of a peer review of performance in teaching, research, or other duties, or of a move by a teacher to a vacancy at higher rank in another institution. In some European and European-based systems, vacancies in the higher ranks are limited. Promotion in these systems requires, first, completion of a prescribed course of work or of an examination that entitles the candidate's name to be placed on a promotion list, and then selection from that list for a particular vacancy. Often the highest position in a discipline or faculty (the chair, the professorship, or the Latin American equivalent, the *cátedra*) is filled in this way. To remain in the lower rank held at the award of tenure is usually disadvantageous, despite the security of employment, since there are limitations on salary even when automatic salary increases can be expected.

A full tenure system provides for employment (but not promotion) until a specified retirement age or, rarely, for life, as in the Federal Republic of Germany. Retirement, usually with a pension, may be optional at any age after a specified number of years of service (for example, after thirty years in Mexico) and mandatory at a maximum age. In some systems, retirement age is related to rank. At the University of Indonesia, for example, retirement for the junior ranks is mandatory at age fifty-six, for the middle ranks and professors at age sixty-five, with the possibility of extension for professors until age seventy-five. Pension benefits vary considerably among nations.

Termination of the employment of tenured faculty members before retirement occurs as the result of resignation, death, or incapacitating illness, or may be brought about by action of the institution under one of two conditions: dismissal for cause or termination because of a change in the program of the institution. There is much variation in the procedures required to terminate for cause, although in civil service systems and in many autonomous systems minimum procedures ("due process") require that adequate cause be defined narrowly to include only matters of professional incompetence or of gross misconduct affecting the faculty member's work; that the institution prefer written charges and bear the burden of proving them; that there be an impartial hearing with all parties having the right to summon and cross-examine witnesses; and that there be granted the right of appeal from an adverse decision. In the case of termination resulting from a change in the institution's program (either because of a shift in student enrollments or because of financial exigency), a tenured faculty member may be found "redundant" (in Great Britain, for example) and be released, usually with the payment of compensation related to salary. Sometimes the faculty member is also granted "layoff rights," guaranteeing that the teacher so terminated has prior claim to his position if it is reinstated within two or three years.

The legal strength of tenure lies in the procedures required of the institution wishing to release a faculty member. Faculty personnel systems, from a worldwide viewpoint, may be divided into three categories on this criterion: those in which there is no legally binding system guaranteeing continued employment (for example, in the Soviet Union, Brazil, and Bermuda); those in which the system calls only for the payment of money should a decision to release a tenured faculty member be taken (for example, Monash and Sydney Universities in Australia in 1972); those in which some formal due process is called for either in civil service regulations or in the autonomous institution's contracts with its faculty members. It should be noted, however, that even systems without legally binding dismissal procedures may in fact operate so as to ensure the continued employment of faculty members in the absence of incompetence or misconduct. In Japan, for example, the social pattern that has been called "the life service system" appears to ensure continued employment for all employees, industrial as well as governmental and educational.

The attitude a culture takes toward higher education and toward teachers will determine in part the kind of personnel system it chooses for its institutions of higher education. Benjamin (1965, p. 59) observes that "when a culture regards a higher education institution chiefly as an instrument for the preservation and transmission of well-defined fields of knowledge

to a new generation, it is understandable that the doctrine of life ownership of a *cátedra* should be accepted." The traditional personnel systems in Japan and many Latin American countries reflect this attitude. Each field of study is headed by a professor on a permanent appointment. Additional faculty members qualified for advancement may serve in the field, and may even achieve a measure of job security through either law or custom, but they may also wait in junior ranks for a vacancy that never occurs in their professional lifetimes.

Benjamin goes on to note that "when the university is thought to be primarily the highest teaching, research, and service instrument of a dynamic society, the system of the *cátedra* falls into disrepute." Two different systems may replace it. "When individual intellectual achievement, often against strong competition, is considered a mark of great social distinction, it is inevitable that individual performance in a competitive examination should be the prime measure of a professor." This alternative is illustrated in the traditional personnel system in the Federal Republic of Germany, which was undergoing reform in 1975. Finally, "where cooperative research, cooperative administration, and cooperative learning are looked upon as marks of modern efficiency, a professorial candidate's record of experience in such enterprises is much more heavily weighted." This attitude is reflected in the personnel systems common to modern Canadian, Australian, British, and United States faculty personnel policies.

However, cultural attitudes alone do not determine the nature of faculty personnel systems. Such systems are also affected by the mechanisms that each society has used historically for administering service organizations. In some countries, government-funded agencies may be branches of the civil service, with employees of such agencies falling under the general provisions of civil service employment, including competitive examinations, promotion lists, and termination and dismissal regulations.

Where there is a majority of colleges and universities under civil service, private or independent colleges may pattern their personnel practices on the civil service, even though not legally required to do so. A second administrative pattern is found in the establishment of publicly financed institutions under autonomous governing boards. The governing boards are responsible for setting and administering the personnel policies of their institution or group of institutions. Thus, while faculty members may formally be employees of the state, the provisions for their employment are designed specifically for the conduct of education rather than being bound to regulations designed for other governmental employment situations. The third administrative pattern arises out of private enterprise, whereby the relations between an institution and its employees are matters of individual contract, with no formal relation to governmental employment requirements. However, even in these institutions (whether individually owned or established under a board of directors), which have considerable legal freedom to establish personnel policies, there is a tendency to reflect the prevailing social and administrative patterns.

Even in countries where all three administrative arrangements exist side by side, it is possible to identify characteristic national patterns that most institutions follow. Thus, in Canada, the United States, and Great Britain, and increasingly in Australia, the characteristic pattern is that of autonomous institutions administering their own regulations, even when some institutions are government funded. In France, the Federal Republic of Germany, Austria, some Latin American countries, and other nations whose systems derive from these, the dominant mode is that of the civil service, with national competitive examinations, a fairly strict hierarchy of ranks, and special privileges accruing to those in the highest ranks. In countries with an extensive private higher education system, like the United States, Japan, and the Philippines,

part of the system may follow the model of an autonomous board of directors (as in the "nonprofit" institutions in the United States), while the rest follow the pattern of individual ownership and administration. The latter pattern occurs in proprietary institutions, where there is likely to be no formal provision for tenure, but where many faculty members may teach for a lifetime.

Current Issues

There have been many changes in higher education internationally in the 1970s, and each change has raised difficult questions about the kind of personnel system that is suitable for the present and future. The most important issues relating to tenure are those of providing for rapid growth, accommodating cessation of growth, anticipating the rise of collective bargaining, maintaining both autonomy and social accountability, meeting new civil rights requirements, and surviving political change.

Many nations with higher education systems originally designed for elite student clienteles have massively expanded their scope, while other countries with no colleges or universities have entered the higher education field. In both cases, the first problem has been finding enough people to serve as faculty members. Characteristically, when personnel systems that were designed for a stable student body and that emphasize a limited academic program (preparation for national examinations, or the encouragement of research, or the teaching of special vocational skills) wish to expand, they must seek a much wider range of faculty talent at a time when fewer qualified candidates are available. In the developing nations the shortage has often been met by importing foreign professors, usually on temporary appointments. Also, in developing nations tenure has frequently been awarded to native-born and only marginally prepared faculty members, a practice that has proven to be unsatisfactory for the long run.

In countries with well-developed systems, two patterns have been followed. In the United States and Canada, and to some extent in Australia, many new faculty members were appointed in a time of rapid growth, given tenure, and promoted on the basis of general criteria rather than by competition for limited vacancies in the higher ranks. Even when all these appointees were fully qualified, the effect on the balance among ranks has been considerable. For example, in 1974–75 in the United States, professors comprised 27.2 percent of the teaching staff, and 95 percent of these professors held tenure. The corresponding figures for the other ranks were: associate professors, 27.2 percent, 81 percent tenured; assistant professors, 33.5 percent, 29 percent tenured; instructors, 10.8 percent, 11 percent tenured. In all ranks combined, 60 percent of the faculty members held tenure *(AAUP Bulletin,* 1975, pp. 136, 139). In Canada the situation in 1974–75 was similar. For example, in a list of the numbers of faculty members by rank in twenty-three universities, McMaster University reported a faculty of 500, of which 189 were professors, 156 associate professors, and 155 assistant professors *(Canadian Association of University Teachers Bulletin,* 1975, p. 31). In contrast, in the humanities in France, Gaussen (1973, pp. 373–374) reported a distribution of ranks as follows: professors, 7.5 percent; senior lecturers and readers *(maîtres de conférences),* 19.5 percent; lecturers *(maîtres-assistants),* 29 percent; and assistant lecturers, 44 percent. Assistant lecturers are limited to five-year terms in universities. If they are not promoted to one of the rigidly controlled vacancies at the end of this period, they may claim positions in the secondary school system, where their status under civil service gives them tenure. The possibilities for eventual promotion to professor are extremely limited.

The differences in personnel systems between the United States and Canada, on the one hand, and France, on the other, may shortly be reduced, because all three countries are experiencing a rapid decline in the rate of enrollment increase even though enrollments may not have actually stopped rising. Under the policies in the United States and Canada, large numbers of faculty members have been tenured and promoted to higher ranks without regard to "vacancies"; in France large numbers have been given tenure, but because of the civil service's limitation on numbers in the top ranks, most of these are in junior grades with little hope of promotion. In the United States college and university administrations have considered setting limits on the numbers of professorships, associate professorships, or tenured positions generally, and a few institutions have done so. In response, faculty organizations are raising serious challenges to the establishment of quotas, on the grounds that the institutions are changing contractual obligations.

A reduction in the rate of growth has sometimes reflected an actual decline in enrollments, or at least a shift of student interest away from some fields of study. These changes have begun to force consideration of "retrenchment measures" and "redundancy" and to initiate discussion on selection methods for the release of faculty. Although tradition says that nontenured faculty will be released before tenured, in actual cases the situation is not quite as simple as it appears (Furniss, "Retrenchment," 1974).

The decline in the job market and the threat of layoffs have helped to stimulate new activity in faculty groups, such as the Canadian Association of University Teachers, the National Union of Teachers (United Kingdom), the Federation of Australian University Staff Associations, and the American Association of University Professors. These groups wish to prescribe procedures to protect the positions of their members, and they have contributed to the growth of faculty unionization. In mid 1975 there were 266 unionized faculty groups on 431 American campuses (Kelley, 1975).

Increasingly, too, the move from elite to mass education has raised questions about the quality of education offered to a much more diverse student group, and in turn about whether a system that provides tenure does not also encourage mediocrity and the perpetuation of irrelevant standards for faculty performance. It cannot be said with any certainty that one employment system is better than another, but the civil service systems appear to be under special attack. The French system has been criticized for providing little opportunity for the initial appointment or the later advancement of teachers whose talents do not run to the research requirements traditional in gaining promotion. Thus, say the critics, French education will be forever run by those with ideas too elite, too narrow, or too antiquated for the responsibilities of a mass education system.

Similarly, the system in India grew out of the British Indian Educational Service, which was subordinate to the Indian Civil Service in the nineteenth and early twentieth centuries. The Indian system fostered the development of British and Indian college teachers who "came to expect little more than the bureaucratic mete of promotions, increments and pensions, and to retain them, generally developed cautious attitudes towards public issues as well" (Gilbert, 1972, p. 411). The legacy of this is noted by Gilbert (1972): "Under the difficult circumstances of independent India, of greatly expanded numbers, poorer secondary school preparation, linguistic difficulties and an aggravated tradition of student disorder, the better side of this inheritance, that of devoted teaching, still struggles to survive, while the poorer side, a depressed and hopeless state of mind, has waxed and prospered." In a recent report on faculty status in eleven European countries, the Council for Cultural Co-operation of the Council of Europe asserts, "Teachers ought not to be in the same category as civil servants" (Council of Europe, 1973b, p. 17).

Even when faculty members are not civil servants, however, the institutions they serve are not exempt from national laws protecting all citizens' rights or from special laws that may be established with respect to employment. In the United States in the 1960s and 1970s, new laws and new applications of existing laws to university employment have increasingly affected the institutions' autonomy in employment practices, especially regarding discriminatory practices involving race, sex, national origin, age, and religion. One of the more difficult questions relating to tenure is whether, in a time of retrenchment, it is legally permissible to terminate nontenured before tenured faculty when the result is to dismiss more women or minority members than white males. Finally, academic tenure has not always ensured security for tenured faculty members in times of political change, especially when the ruling powers may view the institutions as sources of strong political opposition (Socolow, 1973).

The experience of many countries in the quarter century since 1950 indicates that no faculty employment system is equally suited to periods of stability, periods of rapid growth, and periods of restabilization or decline. Even systems without tenure provisions, while they may provide opportunity for retrenchment without precipitating legal action, nevertheless may not prove attractive to the best qualified teachers. Therefore, those institutions whose aim is to provide high quality of education will be at a disadvantage. During the late 1970s and early 1980s, systems will need to be developed to accommodate sharply reduced demand after a period of rapid growth. The resulting changes may suggest the outlines of one or more systems better suited to fluctuations in demand, changes in social needs, and alterations of familiar administrative structures.

The most accurate information available about details of tenure in a particular institution must be sought from the institution itself. Even with this information, however, a reader from another culture will have

difficulty with the academic and legal terms
as well as with the unwritten assumptions
that lie behind the regulations.

Few comprehensive surveys of actual
tenure regulations country by country
have been made, although some collections
of college and university tenure documents
exist in the offices of the Canadian Association of University Teachers and the American Association of University Professors.
For American institutions that have faculty
collective bargaining, a collection of contracts is being made at the Academic Collective Bargaining Information Service
(1818 R Street NW, Washington, D.C.
20009). Texts of these contracts have been
deposited in the Educational Resources
Information Center Clearinghouse on
Higher Education (ERIC/HE), One Dupont Circle, Washington, D.C. 20036.
Regulations affecting civil service systems
of faculty employment country by country
may be obtained from the ministries of
education of these countries.

Bibliography

Altbach, P. G., and Kelly, D. H. *Higher Educa-
tion in Developing Nations: A Selected Bibli-
ography, 1969–1974.* New York: Praeger,
1974.
American Association of University Professors.
Policy Documents and Reports. Washington,
D.C.: American Association of University
Professors, 1977.
American Association of University Professors.
Bulletin, 1975, *61*(2), 136, 139.
American Association of University Professors
and Association of American Colleges. *Fac-
ulty Tenure: A Report and Recommendations by
the Commission on Academic Tenure in Higher
Education.* San Francisco: Jossey-Bass, 1973.
Benjamin, H. R. W. *Higher Education in the
American Republics.* New York: McGraw-Hill,
1965.
Blackburn, R. T. *Tenure: Aspects of Job Security
on the Changing Campus.* Atlanta, Georgia:
Southern Regional Education Board, 1972.
Burn, B. B., Altbach, P. G., Kerr, C., and
Perkins, J. A. *Higher Education in Nine Coun-
tries.* New York: McGraw-Hill, 1971.
Canadian Association of University Teachers,
Bulletin, March 1975, *23*(5), 31.
Canadian Association of University Teachers/

Association canadienne des professeurs
d'université. *C.A.U.T. Handbook.* (2nd ed.)
Ottawa, Ontario: Canadian Association of
University Teachers, 1973.
Carr, R. K., and Van Eyck, D. K. *Collective Bar-
gaining Comes to the Campus.* Washington,
D.C.: American Council on Education, 1973.
Council of Europe/Conseil de l'Europe. *Mobility
of University Staff.* Strasbourg, France: Coun-
cil of Europe, 1973a.
Council of Europe/Conseil de l'Europe. *Access
to University Careers in the Member States of
the Council for Cultural Co-operation.* Stras-
bourg, France: Council of Europe, 1973b.
Finken, M. W., Goldstein, R. A., and Osborne,
W. B. *A Primer on Collective Bargaining for
College and University Faculty.* Washington,
D.C.: American Association of University
Professors, 1975.
Furniss, W. T. *Steady-State Staffing in Tenure-
Granting Institutions and Related Papers.*
Washington, D.C.: American Council on
Education, 1973.
Furniss, W. T. "Steady-State Staffing: Issues
for 1974." *Educational Record*, 1974, *55*(2),
87–95.
Furniss, W. T. "Retrenchment, Layoff, and
Termination." *Educational Record*, 1974,
55(3), 159–170.
Furniss, W. T. *Grievance Procedures: A Working
Paper.* Washington, D.C.: American Council
on Education, 1975.
Furniss, W. T., and El-Khawas, E. H. *Faculty
Tenure and Contract Systems: 1972 and 1974.*
Washington, D.C.: American Council on
Education, 1974.
Gaussen, F. "The Human Cost of French Uni-
versity Expansion." *Minerva*, 1973, *11*(3),
372–386.
Gilbert, I. A. "The Indian Academic Profes-
sion: The Origins of a Tradition of Subordi-
nation." *Minerva*, 1972, *10*(3), 384–411.
Halsey, A. H., and Trow, M. A. *The British
Academics.* Cambridge, Massachusetts: Harvard University Press, 1971.
Harris, R. S. *A Bibliography of Higher Education
in Canada, Supplement 1971.* Toronto, Ontario: University of Toronto Press, 1971.
Kelley, E. P., Jr. *Special Report #12 Update,
July 1975.* Washington, D.C.: Academic Collective Bargaining Information Service,
1975.
Morris, A. "Flexibility and the Tenured Academic." *Higher Education Review*, 1974, *6*(2),
3–25.
National Union of Teachers. *Colleges' Reorganization: Safeguarding Tenure and Status.* London: National Union of Teachers, 1974.

"The Reform of Japanese Higher Education."
    Minerva, 1973, *11*(3), 387–414.
"Salaries of Full-Time Teaching Staff at Cana-
    dian Universities 1974–75." *Bulletin*, Ottawa:
    Canadian Association of University Teach-
    ers, March 1975, *23*(5), 30–31.
Shils, E. "The Academic Profession in India."
    Minerva, 1969, *7*(2), 345–372.
Socolow, D. J. "The Argentine Professorate:
    Occupational Insecurity and Political Inter-
    ference." *Cooperative Education Review*, Oc-
    tober 1973, *17*, 375–388.

W. TODD FURNISS

See also: Academic Freedom; Due Process and
Grievance Procedures; Legal Status of Faculty
Unionization in the United States; Political
Persecution of Academics.

ACADEMIC YEAR ABROAD PROGRAMS

See Exchange, International: Study Abroad.

ACADEMIES

Election to a modern academy—an association of learned persons organized for
the advancement of research and the development of scientific and humanistic knowledge—represents in most countries the
highest formal recognition of intellectual
achievement that a society can bestow. One
of the world's most sophisticated intellectual institutions, the academy is by its nature very selective; yet by tradition the
scope of its interests is nothing short of
universal.

Development of Academies

The academy has undergone many
changes in the course of its history. The
first was founded in the fourth century
B.C., when Plato gathered around him a
group of scholars to discuss philosophy in
an olive grove north of Athens. The place
was known as *academia,* and the name attached itself to Plato's school and to similar
schools founded later by his followers.
Thus, in ancient Greece the term referred
to a particular learning institution. However, in denoting a group of scholars in-

volved in a dialog to develop ideas that they
felt were essential to their culture, Plato's
original academy was the true spiritual
progenitor of its modern counterparts.

This original academy was not abolished
until A.D. 529, when Emperor Justinian I
(527–565), who was suspicious of its pagan
origins, ordered it closed. In the meanwhile, however, the term had gained currency outside of Greece, where it was used
to denote any association formed to preserve and advance higher learning. Thus,
in the third century B.C., the Museum, a
society for the cultivation of science and
letters, founded by Ptolemy I in Alexandria, was considered an academy. The
concept of the academy could also be fitted
to the needs of cultures with sharply different religious world views. Muslims, for
example, opened academies for higher Islamic studies from Samarkand to Córdoba.
In eighth-century France, Charlemagne
sponsored the creation of an academy
where learned men might come together
to discuss and promote the precepts of
Christianity, and Alfred the Great opened a
similar institution in ninth-century Anglo-
Saxon England. All these institutions undertook teaching, and the use of the term
academy to designate a school persists today.
In the United States, for example, specialized institutions of higher education—especially those devoted to fine arts or military study—are called academies, as are
some general, private secondary schools.

As the term *university* came to be more
widely used for teaching institutions, the
term *academy* became disassociated from
teaching and began to signify merely a
society devoted to the advancement of a
particular branch of knowledge. In 1270
such a society, dedicated to speculative
thought, was founded in Florence; and in
1323 troubadours, meeting together for
the promotion of poetic arts, called themselves the *Académie des jeux floraux* (Academy of Floral Games). By the end of the
fourteenth century, such academic associations, mostly devoted to poetry, were
common throughout France and Italy.

The revival of humanistic learning during the Renaissance added still another dimension to the concept of the academy. In 1438–39 a group of Greek and Western scholars summoned a council at Florence. From this meeting grew the *Accademia Platonica,* which derived its name from Plato's fourth-century school and which sought to promote knowledge of ancient Greek literature and Platonic philosophy. During the same period the *Accademia Pontaniana* opened in Naples for the advancement of literary style; it was followed by the *Accademia Romana* or *Pomponiana* for the study of ancient Roman works and the *Accademia Aldina* in Venice in 1494. This latter society marked a transition from concern with only the classical world by including among its aims the printing and editing of Italian as well as classical works. Many other academic societies began to appear—particularly in Italy—for the advancement of literature and the humanities; and while in their informality and lack of structured projects they differ dramatically from the modern academy, in their basic aim of promulgating humanistic study they can claim an important place in its development.

It was not until the sixteenth and seventeenth centuries, however, that three important events defined the structure and function of today's academies. First, in 1582 the *Accademia della Crusca* was founded in Florence with the aim of examining and purifying the Italian language. The societies that had existed until then were largely discussion groups that were formed under the patronage of a wealthy individual and often collapsed at the individual's death. Many of their members were noteworthy in intellectual history, but as the societies themselves had few sustained projects or regular policy of publication, they left, in general, little of permanent scholarly accomplishment. Not satisfied simply with the study and encouragement of learning, the members of the new *accademia* collaborated to compose the world's first major dictionary, *Vocabolario degli Accademici della Crusca,* published in Venice in 1612. This academy, which became incorporated with two others, survives to this day. Thus, by the early seventeenth century, the concept of sustained scholarly effort, which characterizes the function of the modern academy, had been established.

The second major step in the evolution of the modern academy was the founding of the first science academy in 1560, when the *Academia Secretorum Naturae* opened in Naples. Until that time learned societies had been devoted largely to the study of classics and language. The *Academia Secretorum Naturae* was followed in 1575 by the *Academia de ciencias matemáticas,* a Spanish organization also devoted to the advancement of scientific knowledge. Both of these associations were short-lived, but in 1603 the *Accademia dei Lincei,* which counted Galileo among its first members, was established in Rome. This academy was the progenitor of the modern *Accademia nazionale dei Lincei* (Rome) and the *Pontificia Academia Scientiarum* (Vatican City). The concept of a science academy spread quickly throughout Europe. In Germany the *Societas Ereunitica* was opened in Rostock in 1622, and the *Academia Naturae Curiosorum* began in Schweinfurt in 1652. In 1662 the present Royal Society was incorporated in London, and by 1666 the French *Académie des sciences* was functioning in the Louvre.

The third major event, which influenced the structure more than the intellectual function of the academy, occurred in 1634, when Cardinal Richelieu gave his protection to an informal literary society in Paris. This group became a state institution, the *Académie française,* on the granting of a royal charter and letters patent on January 29, 1635, and continues its original aim of developing and protecting the French language as part of the *Institut de France.* Whether Richelieu's motive was to create a brain trust for the king or an institution that would aid in the political overthrow of the feudal lords is of less importance in retrospect than that he set a precedent for the academy as a national institution.

Both the Royal Society and the *Académie des sciences* were founded as national societies. Their fame and accomplishments motivated other nations to create their own nationally authorized academies. Thus, in 1711 the *Societät der Scienzien* in Berlin was incorporated as the *Königlich preussische Societät der Wissenschaften* by Frederick III of Prussia; the *Real academia española* was founded in 1713 in Spain for the protection of the Spanish language; the Imperial Academy of Science (now the *Akademiia nauk SSSR:* Academy of Sciences of the USSR) was opened in 1724; and the small Swedish academy founded by Linnaeus in 1739 became, two years later, the *Kungliga svenska vetenskapsakademien* (Royal Swedish Academy of Sciences). Even the emerging United States felt it necessary to have an official learned society; before its revolution was completed, the American Academy of Arts and Sciences, founded by Benjamin Franklin in 1743, was established by a congressional act of 1779. By the mid twentieth century almost every developed nation has its own nationally sponsored academy.

Thus, by the end of the eighteenth century the day of the informal princely society had passed and the modern academy had been born.

The Modern Academy

In 1975 the *Conseil international de la philosophie et des sciences humaines* (International Council of Philosophy and Humanistic Studies), under the auspices of UNESCO, cited over seventy national academies among its members. This is by no means a complete list of such learned associations throughout the world, since besides national academies—recognized by government statute and responsible to national intellectual concerns—private academies still exist, and it is difficult to determine their exact numbers. One of the most notable of the private academies is the *Académie Goncourt* in France. Endowed by Edmond de Goncourt in 1896, it awards annual literary prizes of considerable prestige and provides a small annuity to its ten members.

Structure and financing. Most academies are currently divided into classes; that is, they have assumed under one structure the different functions of scientific and humanistic study pursued by separate institutions in the sixteenth, seventeenth, and eighteenth centuries. The *Institut de France,* for example, comprises the *Académie française,* the *Académie des inscriptions et belles-lettres,* the *Académie des sciences,* the *Académie des beaux-arts,* and the *Académie des sciences morales et politiques.* Classes may be further subdivided into sections covering specific fields. In Great Britain science and humanities are still the province of separate institutions: the Royal Society represents the United Kingdom in the sciences, while the British Academy represents it in historical, philosophical, and philological studies. The latter academy is divided into fourteen subsections: ancient history; medieval history; Biblical, theological, and religious studies; Oriental and African studies; classical literature and philosophy; medieval and modern literature and philology; philosophy; jurisprudence; economics and economic history; archeology; the history of art; social and political studies; modern history 1500–1800; and modern history from 1800. Each branch, class, or section is staffed by scholars prominent in the field.

In the mid 1970s academies are no longer informal gatherings but associations carefully regulated by constitutions and clearly defined statutes. In some countries, particularly in the Soviet Union and countries of Eastern Europe, national academies have an official status and are considered as government agencies. In the Western nations national academies are recognized by their governments but generally retain an autonomous self-regulating structure. Normally each is directed by a president, who may be appointed by the government or elected by the membership, and a vice-president, usually from another section.

There is generally a permanent secretary and an executive committee or board. Each section comes under the control of a chairman, who is assisted by an administrative staff and committees.

Although many academies are directly subsidized by the government, others operate under grants, private contributions, and special endowment funds. Many receive funds from several sources. In the United States, for example, the American Academy of Arts and Sciences receives contributions from the government, private foundations, interested individuals, and endowment funds. Special projects may receive special funding. For example, the Israel Academy of Sciences and Humanities is represented on the board of governors of the United States–Israel Binational Foundation, which finances projects of concern to both countries.

Membership. In general, members are either ordinary (natives of the country) or corresponding (natives of another country, whose participation is usually honorary). Some academies have as few as six ordinary members (Australian Academy of the Humanities; Ghana Academy of Arts and Sciences); others have as many as 2000 *(Koninklijk Nederlands aardrijkskundig genootschap:* Royal Dutch Geographical Society, Amsterdam) or 2300 (American Academy of Arts and Sciences). Nonetheless, selection is highly competitive, with new members generally being elected or nominated by secret ballot. Limitations are usually placed on the size of the group, and selection is a singular honor. One of the most prestigious academies, the *Académie française,* for example, accepts a new candidate only when one of its forty seats has been made vacant by death. Tenure is for life, although in some institutions, such as the British Academy, fellows become senior fellows at the age of seventy-two and as such are not included in the membership total.

Functions. As the academies have become more formal in structure and selective in membership, their functions have become at once broader and more specific. In general, their work consists of fostering and promoting work in science and humanities; advising the government on research and scientific projects of national importance; representing their countries' scientific and humanistic scholarly community at international meetings and conferences; organizing symposia, congresses, and cultural exchanges; and publishing works that contribute to the advancement of science and the humanities. For this latter purpose most academies maintain their own publishing houses. Many also award prizes. Probably the best known are the Nobel prizes in literature awarded annually by the Swedish Academy *(Svenska akademien)* and the Nobel prizes in chemistry and physics awarded each fall by the Royal Swedish Academy of Sciences *(Kungliga svenska vetenskapsakademien).*

The major projects of most academies are essentially national. Many of those devoted to the humanities have, in the tradition established by the *Accademia della Crusca,* concentrated a large part of their efforts on purifying and preserving the national language. The *Académie française* and the *Svenska akademien* are only two of the many involved in such work. Priority is also given to projects of a regional character. Thus, the science section of the Israel Academy of Sciences and Humanities is conducting a study on the Pleistocene stratum of the Central River Jordan Valley, revealed by excavations at Ubeidiya, while the humanities section devotes special attention to research on the Bible and the Talmud.

International Cooperation

By the mid twentieth century almost all academies had developed international affiliations. Before World War I the International Association of Academies, which included among its members institutions devoted to humanistic and to scientific study, was the chief agency for international cooperation and coordination. As areas of study grew more specialized, however, it became more practical to found separate organizations for academies and classes of academies according to their special interest.

In 1919 two organizations came into being—the International Union of Academies (IUA) and the International Research Council (IRC). Their aim was to coordinate and facilitate the exchange of information and views on an international level between members of academies that were concerned with humanities on the one hand and mathematics and natural science on the other. The IUA effects its aims through appropriate collective projects in the fields of philology; archeology; history; and moral, political, and social sciences. Its projects range from the preparation of a dictionary of medieval Latin to a concordance and indices of Muslim traditions. The IRC, renamed the International Council of Scientific Unions in 1931, acts as a coordinating administrative body for international unions in scientific fields; establishes committees to coordinate planning of scientific activities on an international basis, such as the Scientific Committee on the Problems of the Environment and the Committee on the Teaching of Science; organizes commissions to promote studies of particular scientific fields, such as geodynamics and radiometeorology; and encourages the foundation of permanent services, such as the Federation of Astronomical and Geophysical Services for the worldwide collection of astronomical and geophysical information.

After World War II, UNESCO assumed responsibility for further developing organizations to promote international cooperation and in 1949 sponsored the creation of the International Council of Philosophy and Humanistic Studies, with the stated aim of encouraging respect for cultural autonomy by the comparative study of civilizations, contributing to international understanding through a better knowledge of men, and developing international co-

operation in philosophy and humanistic studies. As a coordinating body for international unions that are devoted to humanistic study, it counts among its members the IUA as well as such specialized commissions and committees as the International Committee of Historical Sciences, the International Commission of Folk Art and Folklore, and the International Union of Orientalists. Altogether its membership represents over eighty-six countries.

Another representative organization established under the sponsorship of UNESCO, the Royal Academy of Sciences, and the American Academy of Arts and Sciences is the International Foundation for Sciences, founded in May 1972. Its membership includes academies and other representative scientific bodies from sixteen different countries. Its expressed aim is to promote natural, social, and behavioral scientific and technological research in developing countries and to encourage young scientists from these countries who are involved in such work.

In addition to these four general organizations, more specialized associations of academies exist for particular branches of humanistic study and for pure and applied sciences. The need for such bodies was underscored at the 1974 meeting of the IUA in a call for "intensification of international collaboration between academies" *(Compte rendu de la quarante-huitième session annuelle du comité,* 1974, p. 15).

Problems and Trends

Academies have come a long way from Plato's meetings of scholars in the olive grove north of Athens, but today many face a crisis of identity and role. Since World War II their structure and role in relation to the intellectual world have changed, as the president's report at the 48th annual session of the IUA noted *(Compte rendu de la quarante-huitième session annuelle du comité,* 1974). Before the war, the role of academies as the highest research authority was clearly defined. Since the war, Eastern

European academies have become affiliated with institutes and centers of research and consequently have a large source of funds and researchers available to them. Their role in scientific work has become considerably more important than in Western Europe, where academies have retained their traditional structure apart from national research organizations and from new university-sponsored research institutes staffed and directed by professors. As a consequence, the role of Western national academies in the scientific life of their nations has not expanded and in some cases has proportionally decreased. This problem has been particularly severe for those academies devoted to the human sciences. The rise of interest in technology and the positive sciences has served to overshadow and lessen interest in the historical and philological work traditionally associated with these academies. Stress on the social and behavioral sciences has come at the expense of moral and political sciences.

In light of these problems, an effort is being made by Western academies to create research centers under their direction and to broaden the scope of their activities to projects that have international importance. Academies, which in the past have focused on problems of national concern and which have operated independently, are being encouraged to take on work that has global implications and to operate in collaboration with extranational academies. It has been suggested, for example, that the IUA create a section that will be entirely devoted to developing such collaboration *(Compte rendu de la quarante-huitième session annuelle du comité,* 1974, pp. 12–16). On the premise that research should not be conducted entirely outside of academies that have the benefit of a long scientific tradition and a selective, dispassionate membership, the president of the IUA foresees their future role as promoting a cordial detente between researchers devoted to scientific work in the country that is the country of all, "the country of truth."

Bibliography

"The Academies in Seventeenth Century Spanish Literature." *Publications of the Modern Language Association,* June 1960, pp. 367–376.

Accademie e istituti di cultura: Statuti e regolamenti. Rome: Fratelli Palombi, 1939.

Compte rendu de la quarante-huitième session annuelle du comité, Bruxelles, du 16 au 22 juin 1974. Brussels: International Union of Academies, 1974.

Compte rendu de la quarante-neuvième session annuelle du comité, Munich, du 15 au 21 juin 1975. Brussels: International Union of Academies, 1975.

Directory of Selected Research Institutions in Eastern Europe. New York: Columbia University Press, 1967.

Directory of Selected Research Institutions in Mainland China. Washington, D.C.: National Science Foundation, 1970.

Directory of Selected Scientific Institutions in the USSR. Columbus, Ohio: Battelle Memorial Institute, 1963.

Herter, H. *Platon Akademie.* Bonn, Federal Republic of Germany: Verlag Bonner Universitäts-Buchdruckerei Gebr. Scheur, 1952.

Kiger, J. C. *American Learned Societies.* Washington, D.C.: Public Affairs Press, 1963.

Trois siècles de l'Académie française. Paris: Académie française, 1935.

ANTOINETTE FREDERICK

ACADEMY FOR EDUCATIONAL DEVELOPMENT, United States

The Academy for Educational Development is a nonprofit, tax-exempt planning organization in the United States that assists universities, colleges, schools, government agencies, and other organizations in developing future educational plans and improving operations and programs. Originally organized in 1961 to conduct research on long-range planning and budgeting in higher education, the academy has expanded its research activities to include studies of all areas of educational operations—goals, finances, curriculum, administration and organization, instructional arrangements, faculty quality, student services, and physical facilities—on all educational levels. In 1969 the academy established a communication institute to study the relationship between mass communications and education and in 1970 created a management division to conduct research on the management of colleges and universities.

In addition to research activities, the academy designs and administers new programs for educational institutions, social agencies, and governments in the United States and abroad. Fostering educational and cultural activities that transcend national boundaries, the academy maintains a data bank on international programs at colleges and universities in the United States. The institute's management division sponsors management training programs and operates an information center on college management.

Governed by a board of directors, the academy is funded by contractual research services and by grants for special projects. The academy's staff includes more than sixty-five full-time members. Panels of advisers—national and international figures in education, government, business, foundations, letters, and communications— regularly provide counsel on questions of policy and planning for major academy programs. In addition, the academy augments its staff by enlisting outside experts with special experience and knowledge for specific projects.

The academy publishes occasional papers by recognized experts on critical issues and innovations in education, as well as reports growing out of academy projects and intended primarily, but often not exclusively, for the client. Most of these publications are available free of charge from the publications department of the academy's New York office. Research reports on studies of university management conducted by the management division are available free of charge from the academy's Washington, D.C., office.

680 Fifth Avenue
New York, New York 10019 USA
1414 22nd Street NW
Washington, D.C. 20037 USA

ACCESS OF MINORITIES: BLACKS IN THE UNITED STATES

Black people constitute the largest of the racial and ethnic minorities of the American population; according to the 1974 census estimate, 11 percent of all Americans were black (24,000,000 out of a total population of 211,000,000). Blacks have also been the most ill treated of the minorities. They have suffered the indignities of chattel slavery, legal and customary segregation, and economic and social discrimination. Despite tremendous adversity, however, they have managed to progress significantly toward achieving a full and equal participation in American society. The greatest tragedy of the United States is that the goal of full equality for blacks remains unrealized and that problems of race still beset the American community. Perhaps nowhere are the tragedies and triumphs of the black experience better illustrated than in the field of American higher education.

In 1974, 814,000 black students were enrolled in American higher education, on both a full- and part-time basis (full-time enrollment was approximately 600,000). But blacks continued to be underrepresented as students: only about 18 percent aged eighteen to twenty-four years were enrolled in colleges and universities as opposed to 25 percent of whites of comparable age. The further one ascends the educational ladder, the fewer blacks one finds. A high attrition rate exists among blacks because many have been ill prepared for a degree course. In addition, more blacks than whites tend to enroll in two-year colleges and technical schools. Despite general underrepresentation, however, the percentage of blacks in colleges and universities has risen sharply in recent years, increasing 55.5 percent from 1970 to 1974, compared with 15.1 percent for white enrollment during the same period. Thus, despite problems, the participation of blacks in contemporary higher education is much greater than in the past (Bureau of the Census, 1975, pp. 92–94; Pifer, 1973, pp. 29–30).

History of Blacks in American Higher Education

As early as 1619, black Africans were imported into the American colonies to serve as slaves. Though at one time black slavery was practiced in every colony, shortly after national independence (1776) the northern states abolished the institution and freed their slaves. Slavery continued to flourish, however, in the southern states because of the labor required for the southern plantation economies. In 1860, on the eve of the American Civil War, which resulted in the abolition of slavery, there were about four million black slaves and slightly under a half million free blacks in the United States.

The ethos of slavery did much to condition the character of education for blacks in pre–Civil War America. The southern states passed legislation that prohibited the provision of even the most elementary kinds of schooling for slaves because education was thought to make slaves unruly and even rebellious. Higher education was, of course, out of the question for slaves. In the northern states, some education was provided for free blacks, usually on a segregated basis, and a few blacks were able to achieve a higher education. Three or four went to European universities, some matriculated at one of the few northern colleges that would accept blacks, and still others went to colleges that were set up specifically to educate blacks. According to the best estimate, only twenty-eight blacks received degrees from American institutions of higher education prior to 1860 (Bowles and DeCosta, 1971, p. 12).

The first black college graduates in the United States were John Brown Russworm and Edward Jones, who in 1826 received their degrees from, respectively, Bowdoin College in Brunswick, Maine, and Amherst College in Amherst, Massachusetts. Many of the early graduates of northern colleges were sponsored by the American Colonization Society, whose aim was to resettle freed slaves in Liberia and to provide that country with an educated elite. Because of their abolitionist leanings, other colleges—notably Oberlin College in Oberlin, Ohio, and Berea College in Berea, Kentucky—made a regular practice of admitting black students. On the eve of the Civil War, certain church groups established colleges specifically for the education of blacks: the Institute for Colored Youth, founded in 1837 in Pennsylvania by the Quakers and later to become Cheyney State College; the Ashmun Institute, founded in 1854 in Pennsylvania by the Presbyterians and later to become Lincoln University; and Wilberforce University, founded in 1856 in Ohio by the Methodist Episcopal Church. Though prior to the Civil War none of these institutions offered more than a secondary school course, they are remembered today as the first of the Negro colleges (Bowles and DeCosta, 1971, pp. 11–26).

Development of the Negro college. The years immediately following the end of the Civil War (1865) witnessed the founding of several other institutions of higher education designed specifically for blacks. Established initially by northern church groups, these colleges were located in the South in order to educate the vast population of black slaves freed by the Emancipation Proclamation (1863). Among the more famous institutions established in this period were Atlanta University, Atlanta, Georgia, founded in 1865 by the American Baptist Mission Society; Walton College, Nashville, Tennessee, founded in 1865 by the Methodist Episcopal Church and later to become the Meharry Medical College; Fisk University, Nashville, Tennessee, founded in 1866 by the American Missionary Association; and Howard University, Washington, D.C., founded by Congregationalists in 1867 and aided throughout its history by the United States federal government. A further expansion of Negro colleges occurred following the passage of the Morrill-McComas Act of 1890. Under the terms of this act, states were allowed to establish "separate but equal" publicly supported land-grant colleges designed for blacks. Seventeen black colleges and universities were set up under the terms of the act. An additional seventeen black institutions that had been established before passage of the act were subsequently supported under its provisions. Since the Civil War, a slowly increasing number of blacks has managed to attend predominantly white colleges and universities. Nonetheless, until the middle of the twentieth century the vast majority of all black graduates has come from the Negro colleges.

It is difficult to count the total number of Negro colleges that have been established in the United States. Some have long since passed out of existence, some have merged with other institutions, many have changed their names, and a few, which began as predominantly black institutions, have since become predominantly white. In 1975 there were 105 Negro colleges and universities, which, for the most part, had their origins in the segregated educational system of the post–Civil War American South. Most began by offering an elementary and secondary school curriculum and later added collegiate departments. In 1900 the number of black graduates was fairly small (about 2500), and the number of blacks then enrolled in collegiate programs was only about 700 to 800 (Drake, 1971, pp. 838–839). By 1910 Negro college enrollments had climbed to about 3500; by 1920, to 7000; by 1930, to 22,000; by 1940, to 45,000; and by 1950 (on the eve of the abolition of legalized segregation), to 90,000. During the time of legal segregation, over half of the graduates of the Negro colleges went into school teaching. A smaller percentage entered the ministry, some went into business, and a few went into such professions as medicine, law, and dentistry. The few who completed doctoral degrees in academic subjects (most of whom studied in northern graduate schools) invariably returned to the Negro colleges for teaching positions (Bond, 1972).

The onus of segregation and discrimi-

nation weighed heavily upon the Negro colleges and universities, whose control was for many years strictly in the hands of whites. In the case of publicly supported institutions, southern state legislatures determined the finances, and the legislatures were never as generous in the support of black schools as they were of white schools. Private institutions were for many years financially controlled by church groups and private philanthropies, which were dominated by northern whites (McPherson, 1970). Notable among these private groups were the Peabody Education Fund, the John F. Slater Fund, the Phelps-Stokes Fund, and the General Education Board, which was founded by John D. Rockefeller, Sr.

Many of the decisions made by whites with regard to black higher education were, at their worst, the products of a cynical neglect and, at their best, of a well-meaning paternalism. Perhaps the most important policy decision affecting the development of Negro colleges and universities displayed a measure of both attitudes. Negro institutions were urged to eschew the traditional, liberal arts approach to higher education and instead to emphasize such practical—some would say menial—subjects as blacksmithing, farming, and cooking. Some who made this suggestion wished to keep the black man "in his place"; others sincerely believed that meaningful black progress ought to be gradual. The institutions that stressed this practical approach to higher education were the Hampton Institute (founded in Virginia in 1868 by Samuel Chapman Armstrong) and the Tuskegee Institute (founded in Alabama in 1881 by Booker T. Washington, a former pupil of Armstrong's at Hampton). For many years, such institutions received the most financial assistance, despite the vigorous protests of men like W. E. B. Du Bois, who championed the academic curriculum. Some would argue that the decision to emphasize the practical as opposed to the academic did much to retard the development of Negro colleges as true institutions of higher education. Eventually the academics triumphed, and even Hampton and Tuskegee now offer a highly academic curriculum (Bullock, 1967, pp. 60–146).

The Negro college today. Of the 105 Negro colleges existing today, 85 are four-year institutions, which grant the bachelor's degree, and 20 are two-year junior colleges, which award the associate's diploma. Twenty-three of the four-year institutions offer graduate courses that can lead to the Master of Arts degree; Howard and Atlanta Universities have graduate departments that offer the Ph.D. Meharry Medical College and Howard University have medical schools; and four other black institutions have law schools. Of the four-year institutions, fifty are privately supported and the remaining thirty-five are publicly financed. All, except for Wilberforce University and Central State University in Ohio and Lincoln University and Cheyney State College in Pennsylvania, are located either in the South or in the border states of Kentucky, Missouri, Oklahoma, and West Virginia.

The Negro colleges can look back with pride upon a history of tremendous achievement, made despite the adversities of segregation. Virtually alone for almost a century, these colleges provided the means for blacks to attain a higher education. As late as 1947, 80 to 90 percent of all blacks with degrees had obtained their degrees at Negro colleges and universities. In 1975 almost all black dentists, 80 percent of all black doctors, 75 percent of all black military officers, and 60 percent of all blacks serving in high-level civil service positions were graduates of those predominantly black institutions. Moreover, the school system for blacks set up in the legally segregated American South was staffed primarily by the graduates of the Negro colleges (Pifer, 1973, p. 32).

Despite their achievements, however, Negro colleges are beset with problems. For example, the standards of education offered at the Negro colleges and universities have been questioned. It was once assumed that black institutions were merely comical caricatures of white colleges. Though they

are less smug in their phraseology, some modern critics continue to argue that the academic standards and educational ambiance of the typical Negro college are inferior to those of the typical white college (Jencks and Riesman, 1967). Recent surveys of Negro colleges, however, suggest that the range of quality among black schools is comparable to that found among all American colleges and universities (McGrath, 1965; Bowles and DeCosta, 1971, pp. 258–259). Despite the evidence presented by such reports, the old erroneous stereotype of the inferiority of the typical Negro college persists in many quarters.

Another problem for the Negro colleges is finances. Negro colleges have traditionally served an economically deprived clientele. Thus, unlike their richer white counterparts, they cannot rely heavily upon tuition fees, alumni gifts, and endowment income. Instead, they must seek financial assistance from government, private philanthropy, and public contribution. Thus, the supply of money for Negro colleges is greatly affected by the overall state of the economy, by political machinations, and, above all, by the priorities of public and private contributors. Consider the course of one relatively new development—the involvement of the federal government in the support of Negro colleges. Prior to 1960, Negro colleges and universities, save Howard University, received little federal support. As a result of the massive social programs of the administration of President Lyndon Johnson during the 1960s, the federal government, through the Department of Health, Education and Welfare, embarked on a vigorous program of aid for Negro colleges. By 1970 federal appropriations for Negro colleges were $125,000,000 annually (Pifer, 1973, p. 34). Because of the change in the political and economic climate, however, appropriations for Negro colleges dropped significantly during the 1970s.

Consider also foundational, or philanthropic, aid. Though it is difficult to arrive at accurate totals, a fair guess is that philanthropic aid to Negro colleges amounted to only $1,000,000 annually in the early 1960s but increased sharply to $23,000,000 in 1966. It leveled off during the late 1960s and early 1970s to approximately $19,000,000 (Pifer, 1973, pp. 34–35). Because of the worsened state of the economy during the middle 1970s, the amount of philanthropic support dropped. The extent of that drop, although difficult to estimate, has been mitigated partially by an ambitious Ford Foundation scheme, initiated in 1972, to assist in black higher education over a five-year period: $50,000,000 is earmarked for a black fellowship program and $50,000,000 for the improvement of certain outstanding black colleges. Even with the Ford assistance, however, some institutions were hard hit by the mid 1970s' recession: in the summer of 1975, Fisk University, a Ford recipient, had to lay off 11 percent of its full-time faculty and reduce the salaries of its remaining teachers by 20 percent. Moreover, it is doubtful that the Ford Foundation, whose portfolio was especially hard hit by the economic recession, will continue to give as much support to black colleges and universities when the present program expires.

To coordinate fund-raising activities and to better become the masters of their own financial fate, a number of Negro colleges joined together in 1944 to form the United Negro College Fund. The fund solicits money from business corporations and private individuals and divides its revenues among member institutions on a formula basis. It raises money only for student aid and for general operating expenses; its funds cannot be used for capital expenditures. In 1975 the fund included forty-one member institutions and reported that it had raised (in 1974) almost $13,000,000 (United Negro College Fund, 1975).

Perhaps the greatest problem facing the Negro colleges today is their need to reevaluate their role in higher education. Some people have argued that the Negro colleges, which were creations of the age

of legal segregation, have outlived their purpose now that blacks are legally entitled to attend almost any college or university of their choice. Moreover, as an ironic outcome of recent court decisions and legislation aimed at barring discrimination in student admissions and faculty hiring, many Negro colleges may lose their predominantly black character. Already a few formerly all-black colleges have become predominantly white.

There are strong reasons, however, for preserving the Negro colleges, reasons that are economic, pedagogical, political, and cultural. Blacks are still economically more deprived than whites, and the costs of a college education, especially at a private, predominantly white school, are out of the question for many blacks. Though they have recently felt obliged to raise tuition, Negro colleges, even private ones, still generally cost less than do other institutions. Moreover, the Negro institutions are located primarily in areas that have high concentrations of black population, allowing a number of students to save the costs of having to live away from home.

Pedagogically, the Negro colleges have traditionally provided an educational experience that brings out the best in many black students. Many black high school graduates are ill prepared to do college-level work. Negro colleges generally have recognized this fact and have developed special programs to provide black youth with the skills needed for academic success. Moreover, many black students, especially those with origins in the rural South and urban ghettos, would be handicapped if they had to pursue their education on predominantly white campuses. Many who have known only a black environment all their lives need the more comfortable social situation of a black college if they are to learn well.

The Negro college also serves as an avenue of political power. The colleges continue to provide talented blacks with leadership opportunities in higher education which are unavailable to them elsewhere. There are more black deans and department heads in the Negro colleges than there are in predominantly white institutions; and, even though every Negro college presently has a black president, in 1975 only one predominantly white school (Michigan State University) had a black president. Further, the Negro colleges have served to make their students politically aware. Some suggest that in forming a predominantly black student body, the colleges create a "critical mass" of people who can discover that they share similar concerns and who can learn from each other how best to contend with their problems. It was no accident that the sit-ins of the civil rights movement of the 1960s were largely conducted by Negro college students (Bullock, 1967, pp. 194–277). Blacks also look to the Negro colleges as "their" institutions; the colleges are important bases of black power and pride. The importance blacks attach to their colleges can be seen in the establishment during the 1960s of a number of new black colleges, such as Nairobi College in East Palo Alto, California. Such schools represent a new effort by blacks to control their own educational destiny.

This leads to a final reason for the continuance of the Negro college: to a large extent they embody the particular cultural spirit of the Afro-American. They have pioneered in the development of teaching and research about the black experience in America. Predominantly black institutions like Atlanta University, Howard University, and Fisk University serve as important repositories for documents relating to black history and as important centers for black-related research. In this way, Negro colleges make a rich contribution to the overall diversity of American higher education.

Desegregation of Predominantly White Colleges and Universities

Until recently, the enrollment of black students in predominantly white institutions has been more the exception than

the rule. As late as 1938, 97 percent of all black students in American higher education attended the historically Negro colleges. By 1954, however, 40 percent of all blacks in colleges and universities were attending predominantly white institutions, and, by the end of the 1960s, the proportion of blacks enrolled in predominantly white schools grew to more than half. This trend has continued and is caused primarily by two factors: the migration of southern blacks to the North and West and the concerted attack upon the legal bases of segregation (Pifer, 1973, pp. 37–38).

From 1790 to 1910, 90 percent of all black people lived in the southern region of the United States. With the mechanization of southern agriculture and the lure of better employment possibilities outside the South, black people, about the time of World War I, began to migrate northward and, to a lesser extent, westward. As blacks migrated from the South, they began increasingly to attend the predominantly white colleges and universities of the North and West, universities that traditionally were not subject to the restrictions of legal segregation.

Legal segregation of the races was a characteristic practice of the southern and border states. In 1896 the Supreme Court of the United States, in *Plessy* v. *Ferguson,* gave sanction to the practice. The court said that segregation did not deny the equal protection of the law, provided that the states which chose to practice segregation provided facilities for each race which were equal in kind and quality. Thus was born the doctrine of "separate but equal." Soon after the *Plessy* decision, however, certain groups were formed to forward the cause of black civil rights, most notably the National Association for the Advancement of Colored People (NAACP), which was founded in 1909. The legal arm of the association, the Legal Defense Fund, almost single-handedly overturned the system of legal segregation through its arguments in an important series of cases. The most influential of those cases focused on the desegregation of institutions of higher education.

At first, the Legal Defense Fund challenged the principle of "equal" in the legal phrase "separate but equal." In a series of cases in the 1930s and early 1940s, the Legal Defense Fund argued that it was improper for a state to provide certain types of university programs at publicly supported institutions for whites while not providing comparable programs within the state for blacks. Faced with the expense of instituting "separate but equal" facilities, a few states chose or were legally compelled to admit blacks to their previously all-white state universities. The first such instance came with the *Murray* decision of 1935, which resulted in Donald Murray's admission to the law school of the University of Maryland. Other states, however, complied with court rulings by setting up allegedly comparable facilities for blacks. Thus, Lincoln University, a black school in Missouri, gained a school of journalism; and Kentucky State University, a black land-grant institution, acquired a college of engineering.

In 1945 the NAACP changed its strategy by attacking the principle of "separate" in the familiar phrase. As a result of a court decision of 1946, the state of Texas set up a "separate but equal" law school at Texas Southern University (a black institution). The plaintiff in that case argued that the new institution was not comparable with the established law school at the University of Texas and continued to sue for admission there. The Supreme Court, in *Sweatt* v. *Painter*, agreed, saying that the faculty, facilities, and reputation of the University of Texas law school were vastly superior to those of Texas Southern. Hence, Sweatt would be denied equal protection of the law if he were not admitted to the University of Texas. In *McLaurin* v. *Oklahoma Board of Regents* (1950), the Supreme Court further ruled that blacks admitted to a predominantly white college or university could not be segregated within the institution. McLaurin, admitted to the University of Oklahoma, had been forced to attend class

out of the sight of his fellow students; to eat in the school cafeteria at a time when other students would not be there; and to study in the library only at a specially assigned table. The Court decided that McLaurin was receiving an inferior education because he was prohibited from profiting from intellectual exchange with his fellow students.

By 1954 legal action had resulted in a considerable erosion of absolute segregation in higher education. By that date, blacks were enrolled in at least twenty-two of the previously all-white public colleges and universities of the South. Only the state universities of Florida, Alabama, Georgia, Mississippi, and South Carolina remained totally segregated. Though the number of blacks on any one previously all-white campus was quite small, the principle of their right to attendance was gradually established. More importantly, that principle served to make the total rejection of legal segregation all the more inevitable. In 1954 the Supreme Court of the United States, in *Brown* v. *Board of Education*, reversed the *Plessy* decision of 1896 and held that separate facilities are by their very nature inferior. It ordered that legal segregation cease immediately in all public institutions. During the next decade, blacks exercised their new rights by enrolling in the few remaining publicly supported universities that were still all white. To take such action called for great personal courage on the part of black students and required the occasional use of federal marshals and troops. As a result, in 1975 blacks were enrolled in every American public college and university.

The *Brown* decision gave blacks the right to enroll in public institutions only, however. Blacks could still be barred from private colleges and universities because the federal government then had no power to influence the policies of privately controlled and funded institutions. That situation changed dramatically, however, with the passage of the Civil Rights Act of 1964, which, among its provisions, empowered the government to withdraw federal funds from any college or university that did not demonstrate a commitment toward eliminating discrimination in its hiring policies and in its student admissions. Since almost every college and university in the United States, private as well as public, is dependent upon government grants for research, capital expenditures, and financial assistance for students, the act barred discrimination in virtually all private as well as public institutions of higher education.

Blacks in Predominantly White Colleges and Universities

The actions of the federal government since 1964 have demonstrated that it is serious in its intent to integrate American colleges and universities in all areas: the student body, the administration, and the faculty. In 1968 the government established the federal Office of Civil Rights and charged it with the responsibility, among other things, of collecting statistics to document the extent of compliance with civil rights legislation. The office surveys American higher education every two years, and it has insisted, from time to time, that institutions be more diligent in their recruitment of blacks and other minorities or else suffer the loss of federal funds. In the most far-reaching case to date, the federal district court of Washington, D.C., ordered in 1970 that federal funds be terminated in ten states (nine of them southern) because they had not demonstrated sufficient commitment to integration.

But the extent of integration required by law in any given institution is still unclear. Surely the number of blacks in colleges and universities ought to be more than a token few. At the same time, should every institution—let alone every academic department—be penalized if its student body and staff contain blacks in a proportion lower than the proportion of blacks in the total population? Few blacks, for example, may wish to become foresters; ought a school of forestry with few black

professors and students be penalized? The question is presently moot.

The speed of integration is another question. Institutions must not be permitted to move so slowly as to postpone almost indefinitely an equitable participation of blacks. In the mid 1970s, however, insufficient numbers of well-trained blacks were available to integrate effectively most academic departments. Thus far, the federal government has recognized this difficulty and has deemed legally compliant those institutions that—though they may have relatively few black students and staff members—have pledged to take "affirmative action" to rectify the situation.

In attempting to integrate quickly, many colleges and universities have indulged in questionable practices. Some prestigious institutions bent on integrating their staffs have "raided" the historically Negro colleges for professors. Although the practice has increased the number of black scholars on predominantly white campuses, it has also had a negative effect upon the academic programs of many black colleges. Some predominantly white institutions have also created lower admissions standards for blacks and made scholarship assistance more available for black students than for whites. Some people have charged that, under the pretext of providing blacks with an equal educational opportunity, blacks are actually being shown favoritism over whites. Others have countered that, because blacks have been so discriminated against in the past, they must be given more opportunity, at least for the time being, if they are to achieve eventual parity with whites.

In the 1970s there was an attempt, in the *deFunis* case, to resolve the legal issues involved in such admissions practices. A student named deFunis applied to the law school of the University of Washington. His test score on the law school admissions test was below that required for white admissions but above that for black admissions; because he was white, deFunis was rejected. He then sued for admission in the courts, arguing that he had been the subject of "reverse discrimination," which resulted in his being denied equal protection of the law. The Supreme Court, however, declared the case moot in 1974 because, by that time, deFunis had been accepted into the law school. The fundamental issues raised by the case are still unresolved.

Whatever the unresolved legal and moral issues, blacks are now being actively recruited by most colleges and universities, and special programs have been instituted to facilitate their growing participation in American higher education. For example, in the early 1970s the federal government instituted a program of financial assistance (the Basic Opportunity Grants) for students who are economically poor, which is the situation of most blacks. Some state governments, universities, and colleges have also instituted special programs of financial aid for blacks and other minorities. As we have noted, the Ford Foundation has embarked on an ambitious program of fellowship assistance for students. In addition, many colleges and universities have instituted special remedial courses that aim to upgrade the academic skills of entering students who are black or of other minority affiliation. Perhaps the most ambitious remedial course is included in the "open admissions" program of the City University of New York. Begun in 1970, the open admissions program grants college admission to any applicant from the New York City school system, no matter how poor the student's previous educational background. Poorly prepared students are provided with remedial work until they are ready to commence the regular collegiate program (Healy, 1972). All such programs of financial aid and academic support are expensive, however, and their future in economically uncertain times is in question.

The presence of blacks in predominantly white colleges and universities has resulted in considerable change in academic programs. Most notably, it has occasioned the development of courses that focus on the black experience in America. In 1975 approximately two hundred institutions had entire departments, institutes, or programs in "Black Studies." Some have charged that the course content of black studies programs is academically inferior and, moreover, that its very presence in the curriculum encourages a resegregation of blacks once they have arrived at predominantly white colleges, because most black studies majors tend to be black. Further, some critics have said that a major in black studies does not lead to promising avenues of employment as does, say, an academic major in economics or sciences—fields in which blacks are underrepresented (Pifer, 1973, p. 43). Although such criticism of black studies programs may have a good deal of validity, colleges and universities still ought to investigate more seriously academic areas that bear upon the Afro-American experience. Perhaps the solution lies in a better integration of black-related studies into the traditional disciplinary offerings (Robinson, Foster, and Ogilvie, 1969).

The large-scale participation of blacks in American higher education is an extremely recent phenomenon. Throughout most of American history, blacks were denied equal access to colleges and universities, a situation that changed only within the past few decades. Although the problems of full integration are far from resolved, remarkable progress has been made. It remains to be seen whether the commitment to eradicating the vestiges of racial discrimination will continue until the final goal of full and equal opportunity for blacks in higher education is achieved.

Bibliography

Bond, H. M. *Black American Scholars: A Study of Their Beginnings.* Detroit: Balame Publishing, 1972.

Bowles, F., and DeCosta, F. *Between Two Worlds: A Profile of Negro Higher Education.* A Carnegie Commission on Higher Education report. New York: McGraw-Hill, 1971.

Bullock, H. A. *A History of Negro Education in the South from 1619 to the Present.* Cambridge, Massachusetts: Harvard University Press, 1967.

Bureau of the Census, United States Department of Commerce. *The Social and Economic Status of the Black Population in the United States, 1974.* Current Population Reports, Special Studies Series P-23, No. 54. Washington, D.C.: U.S. Government Printing Office, 1975.

Drake, St. C. "The Black University in the American Social Order." *Daedalus,* Summer 1971, *100,* 838–839.

Healy, T. "The City University of New York." In W. R. Niblett and R. F. Butts (Eds.), *Universities Facing the Future: An International Perspective.* San Francisco: Jossey-Bass, 1972.

Jencks, C., and Riesman, D. "The American Negro College." *Harvard Educational Review,* Winter 1967, *37,* 3–60.

McGrath, E. J. *The Predominantly Negro Colleges and Universities in Transition.* New York: Teachers College Press, Columbia University, 1965.

McPherson, J. M. "White Liberals and Black Power in Negro Education, 1865–1915." *American Historical Review,* June 1970, *75,* 1357–1379.

Pifer, A. *The Higher Education of Blacks in the United States.* New York: Carnegie Corporation of New York, 1973.

Robinson, A. L., Foster, C. C., and Ogilvie, D. H. (Eds.) *Black Studies in the University: A Symposium.* New Haven, Connecticut: Yale University Press, 1969.

United Negro College Fund. *Facts Booklet.* New York: United Negro College Fund, 1975.

CHARLES H. LYONS

ACCESS OF MINORITIES: SOVIET UNION, PEOPLE'S REPUBLIC OF CHINA, AND ISLAMIC NATIONS

Contemporary social scientists generally describe a minority as a group of people that has been differentiated by others in a society on the bases of language, race, religion, nationality, and sometimes occupation when it is manifested in caste form. Generally, due to one or more of these factors, a minority group is discriminated against from without and is self-segregating from within. In some societies, a minority, such as the Bantu people of South Africa or the black people of Rhodesia, numerically constitutes the majority of the population. Essential to a definition of minority is the power relationship between the majority and the minority. A minority, according to Wirth (1945, p. 347), is "a group of people who, because of their physical and cultural characteristics, are singled out from the others in the society in which they live for differential and unequal treatment, and who therefore regard themselves as objects of collective discrimination. The existence of a minority in a society implies the existence of a corresponding dominant group with higher social status and greater privileges. Minority status carries with it the exclusion from full participation in the life of the society."

Since education and especially higher education is generally perceived as a means to enhance one's social, political, and economic status, competition for it is acute in most societies. Thus minorities have faced problems in their admission to and passage through higher education institutions, and they have posed problems for the governance of these institutions and the contents of their curricula. In turn, educational decisions regarding minorities generally fall into two broad categories—economic and political—both of which are anchored to the question of "Who shall be educated?" Economically, given the scarcity of resources, the decision makers, who generally represent the dominant group, have been able to recruit a far greater proportion of members of their own groups into educational institutions than are represented by their proportion in the population of the country. Politically, they have generally been less reluctant to provide primary and secondary education for minorities to develop and to acculturate the minority to the majority's norms, values, and ways of life. Acculturation and political socialization of minorities often take place purportedly to strengthen national unity, patriotism, and security.

Minorities have generally perceived these majority decisions as inequitable and biased. They have often asked for proportionate representation in the enrollments and governance of higher education institutions and in the determination of curricula contents. Their success in achieving these goals often has depended on the dominant group's perception of the minority and of the nature of a good society and of education as well as the minority group's self-perception.

Socialist Attitudes Toward the Education of Minorities

In some societies, such as the Soviet Union and the People's Republic of China, the ideological bases of socialism have played a major role in the development of education for minority citizens. The development of a socialist society, or the good society, according to Soviet and Chinese ideology, is dependent on the development of all human resources, regardless of ethnicity. Lenin's statements that socialism does not take place in an illiterate society and that an illiterate person is outside politics have played key roles in the allocation of resources to education and in the education of minorities. A much more elaborate discussion of the rationale for resource allocation in socialist societies has been advanced by Engels (1962, pp. 400–409). His view that it is necessary to improve the standard of living of the backward peoples to the level enjoyed by the most advanced ones has been influential in shaping Soviet and Chinese educational and economic decision making. By taxing richer regions in each of these countries more heavily and investing the proceeds in less developed areas, the development of the human and physical capital of minorities in both of these societies has been speeded up (Hu, 1970; Shorish, 1975).

For the decision makers of China and the Soviet Union, education also constitutes one of the most important vehicles of behavioral and political change in the hands of the state. Thus educational and other socialist institutions have been theoretically designed to develop the socialist man—an omnicompetent person, internationalist, humanitarian, and a good communist. The development of such a person is not dependent on his or her ethnicity. Similarly, the socialist culture is to be composed from the best parts of the cultures of all the peoples of the country, and only those aspects of the culture are promulgated that are in harmony with the ideals of socialism—in other words, the proletarian culture.

There are also economic arguments in favor of investment in the human capital of people in the socialist countries. Strumilin (1968) calculated the rates of return to investment in formal education to be consistently higher than that of investment in alternative areas such as physical capital and on-the-job training. There are still other factors involved in the education of national minorities. Factors such as cooptation of minorities into the social system, by means of political socialization, for example, to diminish dissent, have been documented by scholars of the socialist affairs.

The Soviet Union

The demand for higher education is a derived demand. Those who obtain an elementary education want secondary education, and those achieving secondary education seek still more advanced or specialized education. Because of this factor combined with the economic and political ideologies of socialism and the rewards deriving from education, over the past half century the educational development of Soviet minorities has been very impressive, both in terms of years of education attained and of numbers of people attaining them. Prior to 1917, for example, in Soviet Central Asia (an area settled by the Uzbeks, Tadzhiks, Turkmens, Kirgiz, and Karakalpaks) no higher education institution existed, and no more than 5 percent of the population were literate. By 1970 the area had 100 percent literacy; one out of every four persons was attending school; and more than 360 persons per 10,000 population had acquired higher education. In this and other cases the Soviets have been able to substantially reduce the educational differential that previously existed among various nationalities of the Soviet Union (Silver, 1974; Shorish, 1973).

In 1970 the Soviet Union still had about 105 different nationalities speaking about as many languages (Lewis, 1972, pp. 25–43), with the Russians constituting about 53 percent of the population. Although by 1976 it is quite possible that the national minorities constituted a distinct majority of the population, the Russian language has been selected to act as the *lingua franca* of the country, and close to 76 percent of the population communicate in Russian, either as their mother tongue or as a second language. The pressure to learn Russian is high and a substantial amount of resources is invested in the development of Russian as the language of the Soviet Union. Even though minorities need not know Russian to get a higher education in most disciplines, since minority tongues are used at all levels of formal education, students without a knowledge of Russian remain tied to their place of birth with little chance of social and political mobility (Shorish, 1976). Moreover, the nationalism of the minorities, often a reaction to the Soviet nationalities policy, has created conflicts with the nationalism of the Russians; such conflict may not be conducive to the development of the socialist man and a monolithic proletarian culture (Bennigsen and Lemercier-Quelquejay, 1967; Conquest, 1967). Many minorities who have acquired higher education are often unable to occupy roles congruent with their level of expectations, whereas Russians and other Slavs are far overrepresented in the higher echelons of the central government and the Communist party.

The People's Republic of China

The People's Republic of China, like the Soviet Union, is a multinational and multilingual state. In addition to the Han people, it contains fifty-four different national minorities divided into ethnolinguistic groups of Sino-Tibetan, Indo-European, Austro-Asiatic, and Altaic. The population of these minorities has not been calculated exactly, but it has been estimated to be between 5 and 6 percent of the total population, or about fifty to sixty million people. Ten of the minorities have a population of a million or more, and the rest range from a few hundred to several hundred thousand.

In comparison with the minorities in the Soviet Union, the proportion of minorities in the People's Republic of China is thus small, but they occupy more than 50 percent of the country's land area. The largest groups occupy the five autonomous borderland regions of Sinkiang-Uyghur, Inner Mongolia, Kwangsi Chuang, Ningsia Hui, and Tibet. Only in Tibet is the indigenous population in the majority. In the other four regions, the titular nationalities have become distinct minorities due to the immigration of the Han people, particularly since the Cultural Revolution in 1966, when hundreds of thousands of educated young men and women from the congested areas of the eastern coast homesteaded in the more sparsely populated areas of the country. The primary task of these young Han immigrants has been to bring the revolution to the national minorities who, according to some Chinese, are still tied to outmoded and reactionary traditions and cultures. This immigration may contribute significantly to the economic development of the minority regions in the years to come, but the reaction of the minorities to the Han people has often been less than enthusiastic, and in certain cases has resulted in their ouster.

As in the Soviet Union, all minorities in the People's Republic of China have been declared to be equal with the Han majority before the law. Article 4 of the 1975 constitution states that "the People's Republic of China is a unitary multinational state. The areas where regional national authority is exercised are all inalienable parts of the People's Republic of China. All the nationalities are equal. Binationality chauvinism and local nationality chauvinism must be opposed. All nationalities have the freedom to use their own spoken and written languages."

Participation of minorities in higher education in the People's Republic of China follows the same economic ideology and political rationale as in the Soviet Union. The aim of education in China is to promote not only production but also the development of the new Chinese socialist man. The underlying ideology as outlined by Lenin and articulated by Mao Tse-tung is to include progressive and popular aspects of every past culture of the peoples of China. Yet as in the Soviet Union, the process of deciding what is "reactionary" and "progressive" has created confusion at almost all levels of Chinese society and has been compounded at the local level among minorities.

The Chinese have also followed Stalin's dictum that the "culture of Soviet People be proletarian and socialist in content and national in form" in striving to standardize the content of the Han and minority cultures. Theoretically, the role of education in this process has been to facilitate the realization of the socialist culture, but since the Cultural Revolution, the Chinese have aimed to place education in "harmony" with the economic needs of the local environment by making curricula functional in preparing students for solving local economic problems. For example, the Kazakh and Yughur children in Sinkiang province in the northwest are trained to understand problems in animal husbandry, desert agriculture, cotton growing, irrigation, and erosion, whereas those in the Pearl River Delta receive special education in the growing of rice and tropical agriculture. Neither of these student groups can apply this knowledge effectively when they are removed from their native areas. It would seem that this provincialism in education would hinder movements of population, not only between rural and urban areas in the same province but also between provinces, and

that it would also hinder development of Chinese socialist culture, which includes standardization of selected aspects of Han Chinese culture (such as language) and rapprochement between the many cultures of this multinational country.

The ideological imperatives that have led to the immigration of young Hans into the hinterlands and the economic and political imperatives that have led to the vocational, localized curricula are also unmasking contradictory policies and creating potentially conflicting situations among national minorities.

Unfortunately, we do not know the exact number of Han immigrants in the areas traditionally dominated by the minorities or the number of minority students enrolled in higher education. Until quite recently, few institutions of higher education were in the minority regions of China, and most minority students were trained in so-called Institutes of Nationalities situated in Han-dominated areas like Peking and Wuhan. Since the Cultural Revolution, several higher learning institutes have been built in titular minority areas, although their number and the number of students enrolled in them are also not known. Several generalizations can be made, however. Since 1966, the minority as well as students from the Han nationality, after graduating from the higher education establishments of China, have, in general, no more than twelve years of formal education. Of these, nine years are devoted to the elementary and middle schools. After graduation from middle schools, all students spend at least two years of "practical works" on a farm or in a factory. In general, university training is presently no more than three years. Selection of students for the higher education establishments is based upon recommendations by coworkers. Often commitment to the ideals of Chinese socialism, rather than competency in a particular area, is sufficient reason for admission to the universities. The curriculum in higher education is also practically oriented, as at all levels of Chinese formal education. Pure research is pursued in many of the country's professional institutes.

The Islamic Nations and Minority Access to Education

As in most other educational systems, ideology plays a major role in education in Muslim countries of the Near and the Middle East, where "The Islamic faith is the base of all educational philosophies and theories" and where almost all the constitutions of these countries state that education should inculcate the essentials of the Islamic faith in children (Jaradat, 1975, pp. 66–68).

In Islam, ethnicity based on race, language, or nationality is of little importance in determining the status of minorities. Only religion is critical. Theoretically, the only criterion for induction into all levels of Islamic education, society, and the state is adherence to the faith. Thus, only a Muslim can receive all the benefits offered by the social system, and full participation in the affairs of the state is the domain of devout Muslims. Therefore, in a declared Islamic state, non-Muslims often feel isolated, self-segregated, and insecure (Smith, 1957, p. 80). It is probably true that

Nowhere in the Muslim world (except perhaps in Indonesia?) do Muslims feel that a non-Muslim member of their nation is "one of us." And nowhere do the minorities feel accepted. Indeed in many instances there is very serious trepidation. A great many Muslims are genuinely unaware of the insecurity and apprehension of their non-Muslim minorities. Many do not see the problem: it simply does not occur to them that non-Muslims would expect to be included in the group along with them. Others content themselves, though they do not content the minorities, by a serene assurance that Islam treats minorities well (Smith, 1957, p. 80).

To protect the rights, customs, traditions, and religions of those citizens who are non-Muslims and yet are citizens of an Islamic nation, the institution of *millet* came into existence during the Ottoman Empire. *Millet* referred to a community of non-Muslims, mostly Jews and Christians. According to Hodgson, "The Greek Ortho-

dox Armenians, Jacobite (Syrian) and Coptic Christians, and the Jewish communities . . . were given great authority over their own; but heretics in their midst were left to the mercies of the established bishops that they rejected, who were granted both ecclesiastical and civil judical authority over them" (1974, *3*, 125). In leaving the task of social and political integration of non-Muslims to these religious institutions, the Ottomans condemned them "to exclusion from effective incorporation in the Ottoman structure of society; and it was for this reason, and not from deliberate anti-Christian policy, that the *millet* system proved fatal to it in the end" (Gibb and Bowen, 1957, *1*, 74).

Even though a non-Muslim is by definition outside the faith and therefore a minority, he can acquire any form and level of education in schools established by the government and those provided by his own faith. But his education will not provide all the options that similar education provides a Muslim, such as participating in government. Only those with proper ideological commitments—that is, those belonging to Mohammed's *Ummah*, the Islamic community—can participate in decisions concerning the affairs of the state and the faith. In many ways, therefore, the Muslims' attitudes toward minorities are similar to those of other dominant groups with different ideologies and doctrines regarding other ethnic, linguistic, or national minorities.

Bibliography

Allworth, E. (Ed.) *Soviet Nationality Problems.* New York: Columbia University Press, 1971.

Allworth, E. (Ed.) *The Nationality Question in Soviet Central Asia.* New York: Praeger, 1973.

Bacon, E. *Central Asians Under Russian Rule: A Study in Culture Change.* Ithaca, New York: Cornell University Press, 1966.

Bennigsen, A., and Lemercier-Quelquejay, C. *Islam in the Soviet Union.* New York: Praeger, 1967.

Bilinsky, Y. "Education of the Non-Russian Peoples in the USSR, 1917–1967: An Essay." *Slavic Review,* September 1968, *27*(3).

Connor, W. "Ethnology and the Peace of South Asia." *World Politics,* 1969, *22*(1), 51–86.

Conquest, R. (Ed.) *Soviet Nationalities Policy in Practice.* New York: Praeger, 1967.

Dryer, J. "China's Minority Nationalities in the Cultural Revolution." *The China Quarterly,* 1969(35), 96–109.

Engels, F. *Anti-Duhring.* (3rd English ed.) Moscow: Foreign Languages Publishing House, 1962.

Gibb, H. A. R., and Bowen, H. *Islamic Society and the West: A Study of the Impact of Western Civilization on Muslim Culture in the Near East.* Vol. 1. New York: Oxford University Press, 1957.

Goldhagen, E. (Ed.) *Ethnic Minorities in the Soviet Union.* New York: Praeger, 1968.

Hodgson, M. G. S. *The Venture of Islam.* Vol. 1: *The Classical Age of Islam;* Vol. 2: *The Expansion of Islam in the Middle Periods;* Vol. 3: *The Gunpowder Empires and Modern Times.* Chicago: University of Chicago Press, 1974.

Hu, C. T. *The Education of National Minorities in Communist China.* Washington, D.C.: Institute of International Education, Office of Education, United States Department of Health, Education and Welfare, 1970.

Jaradat, I. "Islam and Education for Development." In *From Muslim to Islamic.* Proceedings of the Fourth Annual Convention of the Association of Muslim Social Scientists. Indianapolis, Indiana: Association of Muslim Social Scientists, 1975.

Katz, Z., Rogers, R., and Harned, F. (Eds.) *Handbook of Major Soviet Nationalities.* New York: Free Press, 1975.

Kunstadter, P. *Southeast Asian Tribes, Minorities and Nations.* Princeton, New Jersey: Princeton University Press, 1967.

Lewis, E. G. *Multilingualism in the Soviet Union.* The Hague: Mouton, 1972.

Lo, J. P. "Five Years of the Sinkiang-Uyghur Autonomous Region, 1955–1960." *The China Quarterly,* October–November 1961, pp. 92–105.

Medlin, W. K., Cave, W. M., and Carpenter, F. *Education and Development in Central Asia: A Case Study of Social Change in Uzbekistan.* Leiden, Netherlands: E. J. Brill, 1971.

Moseley, G. *The Party and the National Question in China.* Cambridge, Massachusetts: MIT Press, 1966.

Moseley, G. "China's Fresh Approach to the National Minority Question." *The China Quarterly,* 1969, No. 24, pp. 15–27. October–December 1965.

Schlesinger, R. (Ed.) *The Nationalities Problem and Soviet Administration.* London: Routledge and Kegan Paul, 1956.

Schwarz, H. G. "Communist Language Policies for China's Ethnic Minorities: The First Decade." *The China Quarterly,* October–December 1962, pp. 170–182.

Shorish, M. M. "Who Shall Be Educated: Selection and Integration in Soviet Central Asia." In E. Allworth (Ed.), *The Nationality Question in Soviet Central Asia.* New York: Praeger, 1973.

Shorish, M. M. "Soviet Developmental Strategies in Central Asia." *Canadian Slavonic Papers,* Summer-Fall 1975, *17*(2, 3).

Shorish, M. M. "The Pedagogical, Linguistic and Logistical Problems of Teaching Russian to the Local Central Asians." *Slavic Review,* September 1976, pp. 443–462.

Silver, B. "Levels of Sociocultural Development Among Soviet Nationalities: A Partial Test of the Equalization Hypothesis." *The American Political Science Review,* 1974, *68*(4), 1618–1637.

Smith, W. C. *Islam in Modern History.* Princeton, New Jersey: Princeton University Press, 1957.

Strumilin, S. G. "The Economic Significance of National Education." In *Readings in the Economics of Education.* Paris: UNESCO, 1968, pp. 413–450.

Tuzmukhamedov, R. A. *How the National Question Was Solved in Soviet Central Asia (A Reply to Falsifiers).* (D. Fidlon, Trans.) Moscow: Progress Publishers, 1973.

Vaidyanath, R. *The Formation of the Soviet Central Asian Republics: A Study in Soviet Nationalities Policy, 1917–1936.* New Delhi: People's Publishing House, 1967.

Wirth, L. "The Problem of Minority Groups." In R. Linton (Ed.), *The Science of Man in the World Crisis.* New York: Columbia University Press, 1945.

M. MOBIN SHORISH

ACCESS OF MINORITIES: SPANISH-SPEAKING PEOPLES

Spanish-speaking Americans of diverse heritage constitute nearly 6 percent of the total population of the United States. This group is uniformly persistent in retaining the use of the Spanish language. In a country where higher education is almost totally oriented to the English language, this characteristic has had a distinct impact upon their access to advanced education.

Population Characteristics

Spanish-speaking Americans are estimated to total over nine million by the

Bureau of the Census (1973) and twelve million by the Cabinet Committee on Opportunities for Spanish Speaking People (1972). Many experts consider the higher figure to be the more accurate of the two. Since both figures were determined by surveys conducted in 1970 and 1971, and since birthrates and immigration rates for Spanish-speaking people are higher than for other groups, the current total may be taken to be considerably higher than either estimate (Bureau of the Census, 1971). The number of Spanish-speaking people in the United States places it in fifth position among the Spanish-speaking nations of the world, being exceeded only by Mexico, Spain, Argentina, and Colombia.

Spanish-speaking Americans come from three dominant backgrounds: Mexico, Puerto Rico, and Cuba. Mexican Americans (Chicanos) form the largest single component of Spanish-speaking people in the United States. The 1970 census reported more than five million Chicanos living in the Southwest. This group has been increasing rapidly. During the 1960s over 400,000 persons of Mexican birth were admitted to the United States. Furthermore, birthrates for Mexican-American women are significantly higher than for other groups.

Puerto Ricans constitute the second largest group. Figures, which do not include those living in Puerto Rico (a self-governing commonwealth of the United States), place the total at nearly two million. Between 1960 and 1970 the number of Puerto Ricans living in the United States rose by 55 percent. This group has tended to concentrate in the large cities of the East and Middle West, where, even under the best of circumstances, the relatively stable educational systems of these cities would have difficulty coping with a rapid influx of students who speak a different language.

Cubans are the third largest Spanish-speaking group, totaling 570,000. Of these, 250,000 immigrated since 1965 directly from Cuba for political and other reasons. The majority live in Florida.

Persons from other Spanish-speaking backgrounds total over two million. This figure does not include a large number of illegal aliens from Mexico and from Central and South America. Estimates of these aliens range between two and five million, and approximately a half million are deported each year (Bureau of the Census, 1973).

Educational Backgrounds and Needs

Among Spanish-speaking persons between twenty-five and thirty-five years of age, the median number of years of education completed in 1970 was 11.7, compared with 12.6 for Americans of English-speaking backgrounds and 12.2 for blacks. The level for those thirty-five years and older was 8.5, compared with the national average of 12.0. An estimated 100,000 Spanish-speaking students were enrolled in higher education as undergraduates in 1976.

The proportion of college graduates among those aged twenty-five years and older varies sharply with Spanish-speaking subgroups. A comparison sheds considerable light on the need for increased higher education for those of Puerto Rican and Mexican heritage. The percent of adults with a college degree ranges from a high of 12.7 percent for Cubans to a low of 1.6 percent for Mexican Americans. Spanish-speaking people of Central or South American origin report that 11.2 percent of all adults have college degrees, whereas only 2.4 percent of Americans of Puerto Rican background have earned degrees. Since the national average for all persons in the United States is 11.2 percent, it is evident that Spanish-speaking Americans of Mexican and Puerto Rican origin are well below the norm, and other subgroups are above average (Cabinet Committee on Opportunities for Spanish Speaking People, 1973).

The number of Spanish-speaking students enrolled in colleges and universities in the United States is estimated to be between 105,000 and 160,000. The low figure is that cited by the Office for Civil Rights and, if accurate, reflects a 1 percent enrollment, which is considerably less than the

6 percent Spanish-speaking population (United States Department of Health, Education and Welfare, 1974).

The United States Commission for Civil Rights points out that school districts in the Southwest have difficulty in keeping Spanish-speaking students enrolled. Such students made up 17.2 percent of elementary and secondary enrollments in this area in 1970 but, in the same year, made up only 5.6 percent of the college undergraduate enrollments in the same area. Also, the secondary schools of the region seem to have an exceptionally high dropout rate, although the role played by the migrant workers in this rate is not clear (United States Department of Health, Education and Welfare, 1974).

A study conducted by the College Entrance Examination Board reviewed the factors that tend to affect access to higher education by Spanish-speaking high school graduates (College Entrance Examination Board, 1972). This study indicated that one major impediment is financial in nature. A lack of active recruitment by some institutions appeared to also be an impediment.

The attitude of the United States government during the 1960s and the 1970s has been to encourage minority groups to seek recognition and preservation of their distinctive cultural status. The growing number of Spanish-speaking Americans suggests that the United States might become a multicultural country somewhat in the manner of the English-French cultures of Canada. But quite clearly, bilingual education and financial assistance are needed by Spanish-speaking Americans in metropolitan areas and the Southwest. The fact that the Spanish-speaking minority most in need of educational assistance are concentrated in the Southwest and in certain West and East Coast cities makes planning for this need somewhat easier. Already, government-supported programs aimed at improving bilingual schools and staff in these areas are well under way, and financial assistance for minority students is becoming more available.

One further important avenue by which educational opportunities for minorities may be expedited is the development of facilities specifically designed for a given minority group. This approach has been applied most successfully in the case of the American Indian. A similar institution, designed for Mexican-Americans, is the *Colegio Jacinto Trevino*, in Mercedes, Texas. A major goal of this institution is to train teachers to work in bilingual schools. The ultimate value of such institutions could be significant, and the progress achieved by the *Colegia Jacinto Trevino* deserves careful consideration.

Bibliography

Burma, J. (Ed.) *Mexican Americans in the United States.* San Francisco: Canfield Press, 1970.

Bureau of the Census. *Bureau of the Census Report P-20, No. 224.* Washington, D.C.: U.S. Government Printing Office, 1971.

Bureau of the Census. *1970 Census of the Population.* Washington, D.C.: U.S. Government Printing Office, 1973.

Cabinet Committee on Opportunities for Spanish Speaking People. *Annual Report for 1971.* Washington, D.C.: U.S. Government Printing Office, 1972.

Cabinet Committee on Opportunities for Spanish Speaking People. *Spanish-Surnamed American College Graduates, 1971–1972.* Washington, D.C.: U.S. Government Printing Office, 1973.

College Entrance Examination Board. *Admission of Minority Students to Midwestern Colleges.* Princeton, New Jersey: CEEB, 1970.

College Entrance Examination Board. *A Chance to Go to College: A Directory of 800 Colleges That Have Special Help for Students from Minorities and Low-Income Families.* Princeton, New Jersey: CEEB, 1971.

College Entrance Examination Board. "Access to College for Mexican Americans in the Southwest." In *Higher Education Surveys Report, Report No. 6.* Princeton, New Jersey: CEEB, 1972.

Grebler, L., Moore, J. W., and Guzman, R. C. *The Mexican American People: The Nation's Second Largest Minority.* New York: Free Press, 1970.

Moore, J. W., and Cuéllar, A. *Mexican Americans.* Englewood Cliffs, New Jersey: Prentice-Hall, 1970.

Rolle, A. F. *The Immigrant Upraised.* Norman: University of Oklahoma Press, 1968.

Steiner, S. *La Raza: The Mexican Americans.* New York: Harper & Row, 1970.

United States Department of Health, Education and Welfare, Office for Civil Rights. *Racial and Ethnic Enrollment Data from Institutions of Higher Education, Fall 1972.* Washington, D.C.: Department of Health, Education and Welfare, 1974.

Watkins, B. T. "Graduate Schools: Unfair to Chicanos?" *Chronicle of Higher Education,* December 16, 1974, p. 1.

PEPE BARRÓN

ACCESS OF MINORITIES: THE NORTH AMERICAN INDIAN

It should be clearly understood that the term *North American Indian* includes all Indian tribes in the United States, Canada, and Mexico. It also includes Eskimos and the native inhabitants of the Aleutian Islands known as Aleuts.

Indian Higher Education in the United States

Approximately eighty treaties between the United States and various Indian tribes and bands mention that education would be provided the Indians in exchange for ceded lands. Congress has recognized these treaties and has made an effort to carry out their provisions, which include scholarships to enable Indians to continue their education in colleges and universities.

In the years following the signing of these treaties, the federal government offered educational loans to Indians desiring to attend college. The loans, however, required both cosigners and collateral, neither of which most Indians could provide, and therefore only a few Indians were able to take advantage of them. Some treaty provisions included the offering of scholarships, but Bureau of Indian Affairs records indicate that as few as seventy-one Indians were attending college or vocational schools under bureau scholarships in 1934.

After World War II, Indian students began to attend college in greater numbers.

Indian veterans seeking to enroll had a choice of Veterans Administration funding or aid from a newly initiated Bureau of Indian Affairs grant program. The number of those choosing bureau funding grew from 178 in the program's first year, 1949, to 400 in 1959 and to 3189 in 1969. This grant program has become the major item in the bureau's higher education budget, which amounted to over thirty-five million dollars for fiscal year 1977 and served over 17,000 Indian youths in 1976.

Recent efforts have permitted Indian students to use these bureau funds to attend private or sectarian colleges as well as public institutions and to receive funding from more than one federal program simultaneously. By exercising their rights as dual citizens (citizens of the United States and members of Indian tribes), Indian students may receive regular funding through federal programs open to all students as well as the Bureau of Indian Affairs, provided the total amount does not result in "overawarding," as established by the appropriate college or university federal aid office. As a result, Indian students may now attend their choice of colleges and enroll in their choice of major fields of study with a large portion of their college financial needs provided through federal grants. The bureau's portion of the student's financial aid varies with individual financial need, and it ranges from $200 to over $7500 for advanced degree students with families. The bureau grant to students for 1975–76 averaged about $2000.

Native American students under Bureau of Indian Affairs sponsorship attend over five hundred different American institutions, but the majority attend approximately fifty institutions, most of which are situated in Oklahoma, Arizona, New Mexico, California, Montana, North Dakota, South Dakota, Minnesota, Alaska, and Oregon. In general, the students choose institutions with strong academic offerings in the field of their major; but the existence of an active Indian student center and a native American studies program, as well as attractive financial aid packages, has influenced their greater enrollment at particular institutions.

Although a few students earn the Associate in Arts degree each year, most native Americans earn bachelor's and advanced degrees. About 1600 will earn undergraduate degrees in the academic year 1975–76, and about 40 are expected to gain a doctoral or other advanced degree.

In early years, most Indian students selected training in education, business, and nursing, largely because of their associations with professionals in these fields. However, in recent years their choices have expanded beyond those directly related to reservation needs and now include fields like law, medicine, health, social welfare, conservation, ecology, and environmental sciences. Under the Indian Preference Act, Indians have preference in hiring and promotions within the Bureau of Indian Affairs and in the Indian Health Service (a branch of the United States Public Health Service), two of the largest organizations working with Indian people, and Indian college and university graduates now occupy a large number of key positions in these organizations. This gives them a distinct advantage in assuming leadership positions and in furthering Indian involvement in shaping vital programs for their people.

During the initial phases of higher education programs for native Americans, Indian students found little recognition of Indian cultural contributions or lifestyles in college and university curricula. In many cases, American history was presented in a manner derogatory to the Indian peoples and embarrassing to native American students. Although attempts to correct the teaching and writing about culture and history have been under way for many years, only since 1970 have these new attitudes become visible in institutions of higher learning. Over two hundred American institutions now offer some recognition of Indian culture, often through courses in Indian languages, history, phi-

losophy, arts, crafts, foods, and family patterns. Such changes have given Indian people a new pride in their culture and an increased motivation to attend institutions of higher learning.

Other factors have also influenced the increased educational pursuits of native Americans. Speaking English as a first language has enabled Indian students to speed up the learning process, and it has stimulated better attendance at schools of all levels. Indian leaders and parents take more interest in the educational processes of their children; and, perhaps most important, the self-motivation of the Indian peoples has grown in recent years as they have demanded a more relevant role in American society. The general public is becoming more aware and appreciative of the cultural and practical contributions of Indians, not only as craftsmen, artists, entertainers, athletes, and political figures but also as professionals who have made unique contributions in education, engineering, science, architecture, and other specialties.

Certain Indian tribes are now operating their own colleges on their own reservations. Ten such colleges have requested federal funding to support their efforts; if they are successful, it is estimated that as many as fifty Indian communities may soon request similar aid to found their own colleges. Typical of the autonomous colleges sought by Indian communities is the Navajo Community College, located in northeastern Arizona on the largest Indian reservation in the United States. Initiated by the Navajo Tribal Council and founded in 1969 by funds from the United States Office of Economic Opportunity, businesses, foundations, and the tribe, it is now largely supported by the Bureau of Indian Affairs. It is the first Indian college to be located on the reservation and serves a population of more than 140,000 Navajos. It offers a conventional three-track program: (1) college-level transfer courses, such as English, mathematics, history, and biology; (2) vocational and technical courses in nursing, auto mechanics, commercial art, secretarial work, and welding; and (3) part-time, off-campus courses for adults in such subjects as basic English, beginning mathematics, driver education, livestock management, community agriculture, home economics, and child care.

In addition to fulfilling a critical need for Indian community leadership and development, graduates of colleges such as Navajo Community College are helping to raise the educational achievements of Indian people in general. Reservation development programs, furthermore, ensure that many of these graduates will have immediate job opportunities at home.

Indian Higher Education in Canada

Canadian Indians live primarily on reserves in much the same manner as do Indian tribes in the United States. Federal schools on the reserves provide free education through grade 13. Completion of grade 13 is necessary for entry to higher education. Despite the presence of these schools, more than 51 percent of Indian youths fail to complete grade 13, as compared with 17 percent among non-Indians. The number of Indians living on reserves who complete programs of higher education has been extremely low. Through 1975, for example, only twelve Indians had graduated from such programs in the history of the province of Alberta. Of the 20,000 students registered at the University of Alberta in 1976, fewer than .1 percent were native Indian. The practice of sending Indian students from remote reservations to the cities to complete their education has been responsible for the low number of Indian university graduates. Indian students find the transition too extreme and do not remain.

Project Morning Star is an experimental program aimed at providing a transition from high school education on the reserves to city life on the university campus. Organized by an Indian education council in a joint venture with the University of Al-

berta, it marks a first step in Indian educational autonomy and freedom from federal control and bears several implications for the future direction of higher education for reserve Indians ("Degree Experiment Brings Indian Autonomy Nearer," 1976).

Under Project Morning Star, lecturers are sent from the university to teach university courses at an Indian high school located one hundred miles from the main campus of the university and within easy reach of five Indian reservations. Although these courses take place in intensive six-week units rather than over the usual length of a term, their content, for the most part, is identical with the curriculum being followed on the university campus. After completing two of the four years necessary to obtain a B.Ed. degree on the local campus, students can teach in any school of the province's educational system for up to five years before needing to complete the remaining two years required for the degree. They also have the option, however, to enroll directly at Edmonton for the remaining two years.

Perhaps the most important change brought about by Project Morning Star has been the inclusion of native Indian studies as a part of its program. As well as attending lectures from visiting professors, the students spend time with elders and medicine men in order to learn the traditional approaches to Indian life and philosophy.

The progress of this first experiment in independent native education is being followed with great care by the Department of Indian Affairs and Northern Development, which is very sensitive to native initiative and concerned about its own control over federal funds. The university must be careful, therefore, to maintain the level of the reservation program at a standard equal to that at Edmonton. Also watching the program closely is the National Indian Brotherhood, which represents the views of Indian band councils from all over Canada and which advocates the need for a separate school system for treaty

Indians, free from the control of the federal department.

Bibliography

Billington, R. A. *America's Frontier Heritage.* New York: Holt, Rinehart and Winston, 1966.

Bureau of Indian Affairs. *The California Indian.* Washington, D.C.: U.S. Government Printing Office, 1968.

Cook, S. F. *The Conflict Between the California Indian and White Civilization.* Berkeley: University of California Press, 1943.

Dale, E. E. *The Indians of the Southwest.* Norman: University of Oklahoma Press, 1949.

"Degree Experiment Brings Indian Autonomy Nearer." *Times* (London) *Higher Education Supplement,* January 2, 1976.

Ellison, W. H. "The Federal Indian Policy in California." *Mississippi Valley Historical Review,* 1922, *9,* 37–67.

Indian Chiefs of Alberta. *Citizens Plus.* Edmonton: Indian Association of Alberta, 1970.

McLuhan, T. C. (Ed.) *Touch the Earth.* New York: Pocket Books, 1972.

Morris, A. *The Treaties of Canada with the Indians.* Toronto, Ontario: Coles, 1971.

LEROY FALLING

ACCESS OF WOMEN STUDENTS TO HIGHER EDUCATION

See Women and Higher Education: Access of Women Students to Higher Education.

ACCESS TO HIGHER EDUCATION

The term *access* became topical in discussions of educational policy in the 1960s (Bowles, 1963; UNESCO, 1968), the use of this term marking a profound change in attitudes regarding the right to educational opportunity after World War II. On an international plane, the new attitude was embodied in Article 26 of the Universal Declaration of Human Rights adopted by the General Assembly of the United Nations on December 10, 1948, which stated not only that "every person has the right to education" but also that "technical and professional education shall be made generally available and higher education shall be equally accessible to all on the basis of merit" (United Nations, 1948).

Changes in Conceptions of Higher Education Access

During the three decades since the United Nations statement was adopted, conceptions as to what comprises higher education have been greatly enlarged, particularly in highly developed countries. Although there is far from a consensus on this expanded meaning of higher education, a general move toward extending the range of higher-level institutions and programs is in progress. Once identified largely with admission to universities and university-level institutions, the phrase *access to higher education* now most frequently refers to entrance to any form of postsecondary or postcompulsory education (Organisation for Economic Co-operation and Development, 1974). At the same time, distinctions are maintained among selection criteria for such sectors of higher education as the universities, technical institutions, teachers colleges, and other specialized professional schools.

Paralleling the expanded conception of the scope of higher education, and in many respects contributing to that changed conception, has been a new outlook regarding the grounds for entry to higher education. Particularly in the developed countries, what was long viewed as an "elite" stage of education, to which entry was a privilege of family or of talent, has gradually shifted toward what some authors refer to as a "mass" stage, seen as a right for all who meet at least minimal requirements (Trow, 1974). The transition from elite to mass access is difficult to mark precisely, since it typically involves a convergence of changes in both secondary education and in higher-level education. When the percentage of youth admitted to higher-level institutions is less than 10 percent, selection is often assumed to be restricted to an elite group, supposedly of above average academic ability. When the percentage enrolled increases to 15 to 20 percent or more of youth, students of a broader range of abilities are expected to be able to take advantage of at least some form of postsecondary study, a perspective on both the criteria for selection and the nature of higher education that is referred to as mass education. A still more open policy, in which educational opportunity of some form is available to all who wish it, is referred to as "universal" education.

Discussions of the availability of educational opportunity have thus usually been couched in terms of the percentage of youth of student age who enroll in some form of higher education, with particular concern for the opportunities offered for groups that have traditionally been poorly represented, including youths from working-class and peasant families; females; and members of minority language, racial, and religious groups. Discrimination with respect to opportunity for these groups, particularly in programs of greatest demand and highest prestige is widespread and is a major access issue, as is the rate of success of such students after admission. In three decades the problem of higher education access has thus been steadily reformulated from an initial focus on admission to highly selective university programs to the availability of a diversity of forms of educational experience and the opportunities for successful completion of these experiences for students of much more varied background and interest than the traditional university student.

The consequences of the changed perspective on access can be observed most dramatically in the increasing proportion of youths enrolled in higher-level studies throughout the world. The numbers of students enrolled in educational programs beyond the secondary level (tertiary level institutions, in UNESCO terms) has increased from about 6,700,000 in 1950 to some 35,000,000 in the mid 1970s. This fivefold increase is far in excess of the growth in the size of the youth population over the same period, estimated for the 20- to 24-year age group as increasing from

219,300,000 in 1950 to 352,100,000 in 1975. It thus represents a significant increase in the enrollment rate of students as a percentage of the population aged 20–24 for countries throughout the world (Bowles, 1963, p. 97; UNESCO, 1974, p. 299).

As of 1970, the UNESCO statistics graphed in Figure 1 indicated that in the countries in the developed world generally, and especially in Northern America, Europe and the USSR, and Oceania, the possibilities for enrollment in postsecondary studies were no longer limited to the so-called elite group. Enrollment rates had more than doubled since 1960, moving from about 12 to 24 percent on an overall basis. On the other hand, opportunities for postsecondary education in the developing countries continued to be very limited as of 1970, with students representing less than 5 percent of the 20- to 24-year age population. Nevertheless, the access rates had also doubled in this group of countries between 1960 and 1970, with especially high levels of growth reported for the Arab states and for Latin America (UNESCO, 1974). (Significant omissions from the UNESCO statistics are enrollment data for the People's Republic of China, the Democratic People's Republic of Korea, and the Socialist Republic of Vietnam. The People's Republic of China, under the new policy of higher education access in effect since the Cultural Revolution, should be watched with close attention because it is the country with the largest population in the world and is a unique case of a very abrupt shift in policies governing educational priorities. As of 1975 available reports emphasize changes in selection procedures, particularly in their basis in social and political qualities deemed to contribute to the development of the People's Republic rather than the traditional aim—to select an intellectual elite—and speculations of the impact of these policies on the traditional university role of scholarship and scientific research.)

The general trend toward expansion in higher education access has thus occurred

Figure 1. Students as percentage of the population aged 20–24 (1960–1970). *Source:* UNESCO Statistical Yearbook 1974, © UNESCO 1975. Reprinted by permission of UNESCO.

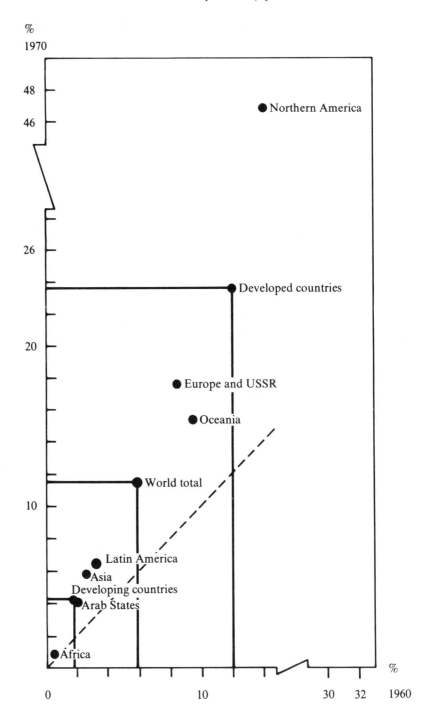

in countries of diverse levels of development, but the actual possibilities of access vary so markedly that they are best understood by examining the distinctive educational practices of systems at different levels of access.

Comparison of Systems Varying in Access Level

The specific character of practices governing access to higher education at differing levels of access is suggested by the contrasting features of representative systems that vary in their higher education enrollment rates as follows: (1) *elite access systems* (highly selective, enrolling fewer than 10 percent of the age cohort); (2) *systems in transition to mass access* (selective, enrolling from 10 to 20 percent of age cohort); (3) *mass access systems* (enrolling more than 20 percent of the age cohort); (4) *systems in transition toward universal access* (at which enrollment rates of 35 to 40 percent of age cohort would be typical).

Within each of these categories, systems vary, but they tend to be generally similar with respect to their economic resources and the existence of certain educational practices that tend to liberalize higher education access—notably, postponement of the age when selection for higher education is critical, availability of a range of institutions and programs, and financial support for students.

Elite systems of access. The highly selective systems of higher education are now most typical of countries in which the level of economic development is comparatively low and the level of educational development is also low, as evidenced by limited availability of primary school education and by illiteracy rates. Opportunity for education at primary and secondary levels is, in fact, a major determinant of who will receive higher education in these countries. Secondary school programs and examination procedures are similar to those of pre–World War II Europe, on which they were modeled. Financial support is often available for university students, but the costs

of preparatory studies are frequently prohibitive. Thus, the ability to enroll in preparatory studies is a major selective hurdle in these systems.

Expansion of higher education in these elite systems has been contained, in part because the limited opportunities for preparatory education restrict the number of candidates. This situation is changing, and the political pressure for university growth is often strong. Where fiscal restraints have been removed, as in the Arab states, enrollment has expanded greatly and, with new university development, is expected to continue to grow. A significant aspect of this enrollment increase is the much greater participation of women in higher education in the Arab states.

Although change is occurring in the practices governing higher education access in certain developing countries, and may indeed be imminent in others, the critical changes that mark transition to mass access systems have not occurred. Higher education offerings are still largely limited to university programs that emphasize professional studies such as law, and there is a marked avoidance of technical-mathematical fields and of practical fieldwork.

Systems in transition to mass access. In contrast to the elite systems, the systems of the Western European countries have now largely moved toward much broader access. Because the change from a traditional elite-oriented access process to one of mass character requires a fundamental reorientation in educational philosophy, this transition phase has provoked extended discussion. Numerous governmental commissions and extragovernmental study groups, such as the Parliamentary Committee under Lord Robbins in the United Kingdom (Committee on Higher Education, 1963) and the Education Committee (U68) in Sweden, have been organized. On the international level, such commissions have included those of the European Ministers of Education (Faure and others, 1968), the Organisation for

Figure 2. Selection process for elite, mass, and universal access.

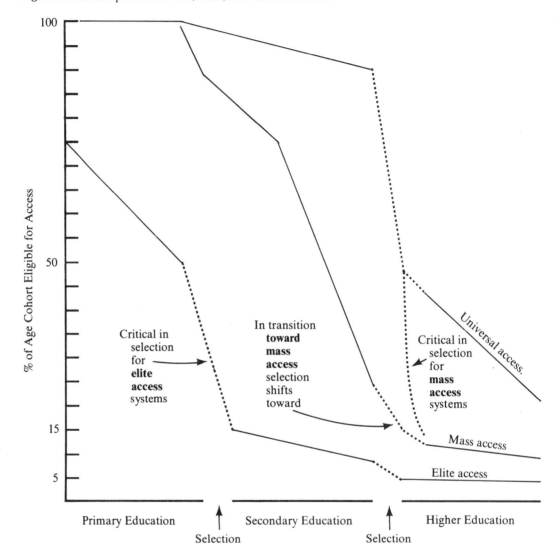

Economic Co-operation and Development (OECD, 1974), and the European Cultural Foundation (Sauvy and others, 1973). These organizations analyze and evaluate alternative lines of development and prepare recommendations for necessary legislation. (The Council of Europe News Letter provides a continuing report on these developments.) A dominant feature of these discussions is the conflict between those who argue for expanded opportunity and press for changes that relax the rigid selection process and those who fear the conse-

quences for the continued quality of education. The arguments for restriction build on diverse grounds, including the fear of creating an educated body of unemployed and the concern that any expansion of higher education will necessarily weaken it (the famous "more means worse" argument of Kingsley Amis). (See Janne, 1968, for an outline of these arguments.) An underlying belief in the argument for restriction is that there is only a limited pool of talent suitable for higher studies.

In retrospect, it would seem that the

expanded demand for higher education following from the measures taken to reform and expand secondary education opportunities after World War II in Western Europe was not anticipated. The changes, designed to reduce the selectivity of secondary education, especially for the first cycle of studies, greatly expanded the pool of potential candidates for higher education. In countries such as France, where passing the school-leaving examination is the basis for university matriculation, demand has been far in excess of capacity. Hugely swollen classes and serious delays in completion of programs have occurred. A much slower expansion of secondary education delayed such developments in the Federal Republic of Germany, but in this country, too, the number of students who now qualify for university admission greatly exceeds program capacity. A much resented practice of limiting numbers through restricting admission to certain classes, or by adding special admission tests, has been introduced in an attempt to control the numbers in the most popular programs such as medicine and psychology, while more fundamental reforms in admission practices are under consideration.

Discussions and recommendations in the OECD countries, with Sweden perhaps in the vanguard, now point toward a general reform or restructuring of postsecondary education aimed not only at expanding the alternatives but also at extending the paths of entry so as to provide greater opportunity for working adults. At the same time, the aim is to protect the selective character of university programs. The solution proposed to the seeming conflict between expanded numbers with a right to higher education and the need to maintain programs of high quality is thus a policy of program diversification. However, educational traditions and supporting political forces frequently limit the possibility of attracting students to new alternatives.

Mass access systems. The number of countries in which over 20 percent of youth are now eligible to enroll in some form of post-secondary study is still quite limited but includes Canada and Japan, as well as most parts of the United States. The systems of the Soviet Union and the socialist countries of Eastern Europe, where the common school plan of ten years' compulsory education has been implemented, also provide high levels of access. A key characteristic of the countries that now provide advanced education to a large fraction of their youth is the prior availability of secondary schooling to all and the existence of a diversity of postsecondary options.

There are two distinct prototypes for systems of this type: the United States system, as it has developed over the last century, and the post-Revolution system in the Soviet Union. In both systems, selection is by examination for preferred programs but provisions for transfer, for later entry, and for part-time study provide great flexibility. Although the general level of opportunity for enrollment in these countries is thus comparatively high, there are notable variations within each country, from state to state in the United States (Carnegie Foundation, 1976) and by region elsewhere. Also, despite significant advances in access for minority groups and for women, these groups still suffer from inequities of opportunity, particularly with respect to preferred programs. Provisions for student support also represent a critical problem that has been a dominant element in recent federal higher education policy in the United States. The forms for such support and the formulas for its distribution are foci around which a major share of national educational policy is being worked out. Appropriations have, however, regularly lagged behind perceived need.

Student support in the Soviet Union is quite different insofar as all students who are admitted to higher education receive state support as long as they make satisfactory progress. Because manpower needs are the prime concern in determining the enrollment of a given program, the number of students admitted is planned in terms of national objectives rather than student demand. There is strong competition for preferred places, especially in prestige programs, such as those in the science and technical fields at Moscow State University. Many more students enroll in nonuniversity programs in technical and pedagogical institutes. The majority of students in the USSR are enrolled in part-time and correspondence study, and were it not for these programs and the inclusion of part-time enrollment in the national statistics, the rate of access for the Soviet system would be less than 15 percent (Revenko, 1973). These programs, which encourage students to gain experience as workers, also represent a continuing effort to enroll working-class people in higher education. Despite these efforts, class discrimination in the Soviet Union is far from eliminated in higher education (Sauvy and others, 1973).

Systems in transition toward universal access. The stage of universal opportunity of access, in which, as one exponent puts it, "we are no longer prepared to tell anyone that he should not try to go" (Birenbaum, 1971), is as yet open to consideration in only the most affluent of countries, notably the United States. It is important to distinguish the goal of universal opportunity for access from universal attendance. Universal access means elimination of financial barriers to attendance and provision of necessary places: "We define universal access as a condition where (1) all college age persons are financially able to attend college if they otherwise wish to do so and (2) there are places for them" (Carnegie Foundation, 1975, p. 118).

The universal access target is now approached in a few western states of the United States, where high school graduation qualifies for admission to at least some form of higher education and alternative forms are widely available. Self-selection on the part of the students, reflected in the decision to apply, may be as significant as institutional decision to admit in determining who gains access. Good information

about alternatives can be critical. Financial support based on student need is stated as a condition of universal access (Carnegie Foundation, 1975) but is not now fully available.

The conditions necessary for universal access will thus be costly but are not beyond the capacity to pay in the United States, according to the most recent Carnegie Foundation studies (1975, 1976). A private sector of higher education and a range of public institutions are viewed as essential for providing universal access opportunities without diminishing the strength of the institutions needed for the advancement of knowledge and the critical evaluation of society (Carnegie Commission, 1973; Trow, 1975).

Outlook on Higher Education Access in the Mid 1970s

Although enrollments have continued to increase in higher education institutions in the 1970s, the main wave of expansion now appears to be over. Particularly in the developed countries, the rate of growth in the size of student bodies is declining, and actual enrollments are expected to fall off during the coming decade. Decrease of the youth population after the postwar "baby boom" is one major factor in these projections, accompanied by a generally more sober outlook on the future expansion of higher education. Some of the factors underlying this outlook may be temporary, but they include certain long-standing problems of educational access.

1. *Equalization of opportunity.* Evidence of differential selectivity by social class and by racial, sex, or language group is still widespread and is used to challenge the legitimacy of selection procedures. Expansion and improvement of lower-level education are critical steps in relieving this problem. In the meantime special recruitment procedures and supportive education programs are providing short-range solutions in some countries.

2. *Unemployed graduates.* Fears that large numbers of highly educated people will

be unemployed worry educational policy-makers. These fears have recently been reinforced in countries such as the United States, where the job market shrank while graduates from a period of major expansion increased. The problem has been partly one of mismatch between the fields of specialty in which students were prepared and those the market sought. However, a more basic question is whether any country can afford to educate more people than it can employ in high-level occupations. Some argue that employment should not be a major concern; intrinsic values of studies should receive more weight.

3. *Threats to scholarly excellence and the continuance of a high level of culture.* These two concerns, although separable, predominate among intellectuals, including some faculty, who fear the erosion of teaching conditions that they view as essential through the pressures of expanded enrollment. These concerns have been reinforced by evidence of declining student academic performance. Many people who support the liberalization of educational access have mixed feelings about its effect on educational and cultural standards. Advocates of educational reform have usually been products of selective systems, who have demonstrated their own merit by successfully passing the hurdles of such systems. Others, who may well have opposed liberalization to begin with, believe that only a minority of youth—perhaps 10 to 15 percent—have the ability to pursue higher education and that they should be screened early for thorough university preparation.

4. *Competition for limited public resources.* Expanded higher education, particularly in times of inflation, is a costly venture. Arguments for education's investment value, both for the state and for the individual, may still be valid but are now somewhat weakened.

Some new issues have now been added to the discussion of higher education expansion, notably in those systems in which educational opportunity is now most accessible.

1. *The value of higher education to the student.* There is growing skepticism about the rewards of higher education, especially in terms of added income.

2. *Differential support for expensive programs.* Support for research universities may be in jeopardy by a tendency toward the leveling of the resources allocated to the various sectors in expanded higher education systems.

3. *Timing of higher education.* The legitimacy of higher education geared primarily to full-time students in the 18–21 age group is increasingly questioned. Some proposals argue for more flexible lifetime possibilities with public support.

The extensive literature on higher education access issues now available from national and international bodies, both governmental and extragovernmental, provides evidence of the keen interest in these issues and of the types of arguments which underlie their continuing political import. (See, for example, Carnegie Commission on Higher Education, 1973; Carnegie Foundation for the Advancement of Teaching, 1975, 1976; Education Project of the European Cultural Foundation, 1973; Organisation for Economic Cooperation and Development (OECD), 1974, 1975; and UNESCO, 1972.)

Bibliography

Birenbaum, W. M. "Who Should Go to College?" In P. R. Rever (Ed.), *Open Admissions and Equal Access.* ACT Monograph 4. Iowa City, Iowa: American College Testing Program, 1971.

Bowles, F. *Report of the International Study of University Admissions.* Vol. 1: *Access to Higher Education.* Paris: UNESCO, 1963.

Carnegie Commission on Higher Education. *The Purposes and the Performance of Higher Education in the United States.* New York: McGraw-Hill, 1973.

Carnegie Foundation for the Advancement of Teaching. *More Than Survival: Prospects for Higher Education in a Period of Uncertainty.* San Francisco: Jossey-Bass, 1975.

Carnegie Foundation for the Advancement of Teaching. *The States and Higher Education.* San Francisco: Jossey-Bass, 1976.

Committee on Higher Education. *Report of the*

Committee Appointed by the Prime Minister Under the Chairmanship of Lord Robbins, 1961–1963. London: H. M. Stationery Office, 1963.

Council of Europe, Documentation Center for Education in Europe. *News Letter* (quarterly).

Faure, E., and others. *Learning to Be: The World of Education Today and Tomorrow.* Paris: UNESCO, 1972.

Janne, H. "Access to Higher Education from the Point of View of the Social, Economic and Cultural Origins of Students." In *Access to Higher Education in Europe: Comparative Background Documents and Report of the Conference.* Paris: UNESCO, 1968, pp. 39–87.

Organisation for Economic Co-operation and Development. *Policies for Higher Education: General Report.* Paris: OECD, 1974.

Organisation for Economic Co-operation and Development. *Education, Inequality and Life Chances.* (2 vols.) Paris: OECD, 1975.

Revenko, T. *L'enseignement supérieur en Union soviétique.* Paris: OECD, 1973.

Sauvy, A., with Girard, A., Jacquard, A., and Lagmeau-Markiewicz, J. *Access to Education: New Possibilities.* (English Ed.) Vol. 3. The Hague: Nijhoff, 1973.

Trow, M. "Problems in the Transition from Elite to Mass Higher Education." In *Policies for Higher Education: General Report.* Paris: OECD, 1974, pp. 51–101.

Trow, M. "The Public and Private Lives of Higher Education." *Daedalus,* Winter 1975, 2, 113–127.

UNESCO. *Access to Higher Education in Europe: Comparative Background Documents and Report of the Conference.* Paris: UNESCO, 1968.

UNESCO. *Statistical Yearbook, 1974.* Paris: UNESCO, 1975.

United Nations. *Universal Declaration of Human Rights.* New York: United Nations, 1948.

MARY CORCORAN

See also: Access of Minorities; Women and Higher Education: Access of Women Students to Higher Education.

ACCESS TO HIGHER EDUCATION (Higher Education Report), Multinational

Access to Higher Education: International Study of University Admissions (Paris: UNESCO and International Association of Universities, 1963) is a two-volume study prepared by UNESCO and the International Association of Universities (IAU), under the chairmanship of F. Bowles, with a grant from the Carnegie Corporation of New York. The study examines university admissions internationally and presents data on the specific admission policies of twelve countries. The following findings and recommendations are reported.

The expansion of primary and secondary education after World War II, with little concern for the potential effect on higher education, led to excessive demands for higher education in many countries. As a consequence, universities were forced to implement more restrictive admission policies. Better methods are needed to discharge admission responsibilities—among them, a shift in the selection process, from competitive examination to orientation and guidance. To accomplish this shift, the investigators recommend a maximum of two entrance examinations, an advisory role for secondary schools in final selections, and a single admission fee to be paid at the end of the process. They also recommend restrictions in opportunities for repeated attempts at admission, alternative institutions and programs for those who fail to be admitted to disciplines of their first choice, sufficient financial assistance to superior students pursuing fields of study regarded as national priority, and professional admission guidance and counseling staffs at the universities.

ACCOUNTABILITY

During the 1970s institutions of higher education increasingly have faced charges, by the public and by government bodies alike, that they have failed to discharge responsibly the mandate of accountability. The demand for greater accountability also has been heard within institutions themselves, with regard to the management of internal affairs and the reform of institutional governance. In view of the traditional meaning of the concept of accountability, the current use of the term to sustain an indictment of the objectives or performance of colleges and universities is surprising, and deserving of comment. The currently fashionable use of the term is less than a decade old, as evidenced by the fact that there is no reference to accountability as a major discussion theme in the *Education Index* prior to 1970 (Mortimer, 1972, p. 47).

The principle of accountability, however, is scarcely a contemporary social invention. On the contrary, it is a social device which has long been inherent in the functioning of associations or organizations of any type—whether educational, economic, religious, social, legal, or political. In its basic sense, "to be accountable" simply means "to be answerable legally or morally for the discharge of some duty, trust, or debt." If answerability on the part of officeholders, as bearers of some social or institutional trust, has characteristically been a feature of the functioning of social institutions and if accountability is not a new concept or invention, some explanation is needed as to why the clamor for "greater accountability" has only recently reached such a crescendo. Several reasons come to mind.

Educational institutions are by no means alone in facing the charge of failure to respond to the mandate of accountability. Since the mid-1960s there has occurred a marked erosion of confidence in traditional authorities and in the functioning of a wide array of social, political, and economic institutions. Older forms of value consensus have dissolved, and adversarial and litigious relationships have become more prevalent, as the legitimacy of institutions and of their leaders increasingly has been challenged. Conflicts of various kinds have escalated to the point where traditional mechanisms for conflict resolution are no longer able to mute or to contain disputes within acceptable bounds. The unreasonably high expectations of the 1960s, as to what could be achieved by educational and other major national institutions, have not been realized. In addition, by virtue of their greatly expanded claims on the public purse, colleges and universities have lost the "low profile" which they formerly enjoyed. All of these trends have generated a deep malaise; and the cry of accountability is in large part an expression of this malaise, a voicing of disenchantment with the performance and potentialities of existing institutional forms.

The demand for accountability also has gained impetus through pressures for greater participation in decision making, whether by workers in industrial firms, citizens in governmental affairs, or students and academic staff in the governance of educational institutions. In significant measure this trend toward "participatory democracy" also has been directed toward the imposing of more stringent limitations on the discretionary powers of officeholders, or of devising what are deemed to be more effective sanctions forcing such individuals to fulfill their particular obligations. To some degree the cry for accountability functions as "an instrument of persuasion" (Bowen, 1973), sometimes almost as a club, to ensure compliance with popular social or governmental aims. Hence, as Etzioni (1975) has remarked, its contemporary use is highly "symbolic." Sociologically, the call for accountability often functions as a hortatory political slogan or as a "cue word" to mobilize followers in some cause. Its use has thus become strongly emotive, a mode of employment of the term rendered easier by the fact that in current polemic its cognitive content is frequently minimal.

No dispassionate observer of the educational scene would wish to claim that institutions of higher education are not in need of reform or that they should be exempt from all criticism. Undiscriminating attack on these institutions, however, or unreasonable expectations as to their capacity within existing resources to discharge the formidable tasks being laid upon them, may well destroy fragile institutional forms and values. Yet, in the name of accountability, colleges and universities are being summoned not only to discharge their traditional functions but to assume even greater responsibilities. They are exhorted, for instance, to achieve higher productivity, to attain greater efficiency, to get on with the job of measuring educational outcomes, to be more relevant, to develop new forms of continuing education, to be more open and accessible (especially to disadvantaged minorities), to strive for flexibility and abandon rigidity, and to accomplish all these goals while at the same time implementing more and more participatory systems of management and governance. The weight of all these demands may be so heavy as to subject colleges and universities to a stress beyond their capacity to repair. In consequence, efforts must be made to separate legitimate demands from those which are illegitimate and unreasonable. In this regard, the first requirement is to clarify the meaning and function of accountability and to specify the "transactional frame" (Sibley, 1974a) within which accountability must exist if it is to function properly.

Conditions of Accountability

There are four conditions essential to the existence of genuine accountability. First of all, accountability is a triadic relation. In its simplest form, accountability prevails when person X, holding an office within a formally defined structure, is held responsible to a second officeholder, Y, for the discharge of some trust or set of duties, Z. (X and Y may of course be corporate bodies, not individual persons.) For example, if one considers the relationship between the dean of a university faculty and the president of his institution, one might say "The dean is accountable to the president," meaning that he is obliged to give an accounting of and to justify to the president what he has done or failed to do. Should the dean (X) refuse to give such an accounting, or should the president (Y) find his account in some respect deficient, the president is empowered to inflict upon the dean some appropriate sanction or penalty or to request a higher authority, such as the governing body of the institution in question,

to do so. In his turn, of course, the president is accountable to his governing board; and the board itself, in a public institution, is accountable to the government or to one of its agencies, such as a university grants commission or a statewide coordinating or governing board.

Second, the accountability relationship is asymmetrical in that in a given context X may be accountable to Y but Y may not be accountable to X. This is not to say that Y does not have responsibilities toward X; in fact, he may have some responsibilities which are absolutely essential to the proper functioning of accountability. "To be accountable," however, is not coterminous or identical in meaning with "to be responsible."

Third, X (the bearer of accountability, the executor of some stipulated trust) must in the discharge of that trust be allowed a measure of autonomy appropriate to the nature of his task. In many current discussions of accountability, this point is ignored or completely overlooked. Yet no point is more fundamental. Every association or organization, if it is to survive at all, must be ready to deal promptly with sudden contingencies and to respond to challenges which will require the exercise of responsible judgment on the part of those entrusted with the management of its affairs. General objectives or policies may be set by the organization at large, but these general objectives must be interpreted and put into action. It is impossible to specify fully in advance explicit rules governing the conduct of an officeholder in every conceivable circumstance. If such instructions were in fact possible, there would be no need for anyone to assume the responsibility carried, for instance, by deans and university presidents: a clerk in principle (and ultimately a machine) could do the job. The role of an officeholder such as a dean or president is not slavishly to follow a detailed set of blueprints but to create—to interpret through his decisions certain broad objectives, largely normative in nature, which are not themselves fully interpreted or capable of being interpreted prior to his activity. In short, the concept of accountability entails the existence of a field for judgment and autonomous decision making on the part of X—the bearer of accountability. This does not mean that everything can be left to X's judgment, but if X is not allowed to make independent judgments and decisions, he is not acting as a person under trust. When, in the spirit of participatory decision making, X is held accountable and yet allowed no initiative or independence of action, but is instead continuously subjected to the outcomes of referenda or to collective approval of everything he proposes, the result is an inherently contradictory if not impossible state of affairs. Only an autonomous decision maker can be held accountable.

A fourth condition essential to the existence of accountability is that X must have at his command adequate means and resources to execute his trust. Such means and resources usually include adequate personnel support and material resources as well as the management or governance structures necessary to make his decisions operative. If sufficient means to discharge a task are not available, its execution cannot be morally or rationally expected. And yet, where such a situation exists, as unfortunately it often does, the call for sanctions is clearly unjustified and is destructive of the relationships inherent in the very nature of accountability.

Many current discussions of accountability fasten too exclusively on the responsibilities of X toward Y, to the neglect of those which fall upon Y, the person or body who exacts accountability. The responsibilities of Y toward X are correlative with those of X to Y. In fact, there is between X and Y a kind of implicit *contract of accountability.* When Y confers his trust upon X, and says to X: "I shall hold you accountable," Y's words contextually entail a set of promises or pledges toward X. Not only is Y pledging a sphere of autonomy to X and assuring X that he will have the means

and resources adequate to the discharge of his trust; Y also is pledging some degree of confidence in X and indicating that a conscientious attempt on the part of X to discharge his duties will be accepted as a defense, at least in part, against the imposition of some sanctions upon X—should such ever be necessary. In sum, while the relationship of accountability is itself asymmetrical, or one-way, from X to Y, the relationships of responsibility are two-way, or symmetrical. Under the pathological conditions now characterizing much of contemporary institutional life, whether in education, in politics, or in society as a whole, this correlativity of responsibility is too frequently ignored—with consequences that may seriously impair or violate the basic transactional frame of accountability (Sibley, 1974a).

Failure and Defeat of Accountability

Before one can rightly charge that some agent occupying a position of trust has failed to be accountable, it is necessary to make a distinction between the failure and the defeat of accountability. Within the context of accountability, there is a structure of relationships designed to achieve a certain set of objectives. If these objectives are not attained, the cause will lie in either or both of two circumstances. If the attainment of an objective is within the power of X and Y conjointly, but through some defect they do not properly exercise that power, the result is what may be called a failure of accountability. Because of human failings, responsibilities which could have been discharged were not discharged. When, however, a given objective is not attained as a result of forces totally beyond the power of the agents concerned, the result may be termed a defeat of accountability.

It is at this point that much of the current rhetoric about accountability goes astray. Institutions of higher learning are nowadays beset by an array of difficulties so formidable that they find it virtually impossible to meet the demands placed upon them. Within this context, many may have been defeated, yet not have failed in their quest to remain accountable. Where such is the case, cries for "more accountability," though psychologically explicable, may be nonetheless unreasonable. Authority may be so eroded, power so dispersed, adversarial relationships so entrenched, resources so inadequate that the task cannot be fulfilled. The clamor for greater accountability is then thoroughly unjustified and utterly lacking in the dimensions of moral and rational criticism. Far from preserving accountability, attacks of such a punitive and political kind destroy the transactional frame within which accountability must function.

Within the sphere of higher education, certain key forces operate to defeat accountability. Institutions of higher learning in the Western world are diverse in scale, resources, organizational complexity, tradition, and outlook; but certain circumstances appear to be universal. In many contemporary institutions, for instance, efficient governance is impeded by problems arising from the sheer size or scale of the institution. Whether in the physical, biological, or social realm, scientists since the days of Aristotle have noted that it is impossible to disregard the changes which inevitably ensue in the functioning of a physical instrument, a biological organism, or a social institution when scale is radically altered. Size and function are interrelated. The growth of an organization may be functional up to a certain size; beyond that range, it becomes positively dysfunctional. As Gallant and Prothero (1972) have shown, various dysfunctions have attended the increase in scale of educational institutions. Dysfunctional size renders mythical the old notion of a "community of scholars." Large size eliminates, at one level after another, the possibility of the interactions needed to maintain a community. "Dead-end specialization," which often accompanies large-scale university enterprises, produces an isolation which makes "craft idiocy" the norm. As institutions grow, administrative complexity in-

creases disproportionately to the mere arithmetical increase in numbers. Large bureaucracies struggle in vain to "inform" and to "communicate." Anonymity and impersonality, loss of community, and bureaucratic complexity all conspire to diminish the possibility of fruitful human interaction. Specialization and differentiation act as centrifugal forces, destroying or loosening the shared sense of values which, when the institution was of a more manageable scale and complexity, held it together in a genuine form of community and made its governance a viable undertaking.

In large, complex "multiversities" and in smaller institutions as well, accountability can be defeated by modes of governance that are antithetical to the institution's proper functioning. Whatever may be said about the merits of the trend toward full "participatory democracy," its application poses serious difficulties (Hart, 1972). In its most extreme form, the demand for participation can severely paralyze the decision-making process. Rigidity and inflexibility are maximized at a time when flexibility and initiative, in the face of the challenges confronting educational institutions, are more imperative than ever before. Moreover, the growing tendency to rely upon departmental committees, academic senates, or boards of trustees, not to set policies but to make specific operational decisions, carries with it a direct threat to accountability, in that the imposition of *sanctions* (a necessary element in the very definition of accountability) is rendered impossible. Sanctions can be meaningfully imposed only upon *individuals,* not upon collectivities.

Participation in decision making has not only become more widely based; it also has become more "fluid" in nature. The constant change in composition of committees—coupled with the growing practice of term appointments (often of very short duration) for departmental chairmen, deans, and presidents—creates a fluidity of participation and an instability in decision making that renders it difficult if not impossible to locate "the author" of a given decision or action. In such circumstances, the search for some X to be "held accountable" is usually a fruitless mission or a punitive expedition in search of a scapegoat. When power is dispersed everywhere, it is, in effect, nowhere.

The consequence of these developments is that in the university of today "no one can say who decides what, and no one even knows who gets to decide who decides what" (Dressel and Faricy, 1972, p. 4). The involvement of so many individuals and groups in decision making, with the consequent destruction of accountability, is likely to push educational institutions toward a political or collective bargaining model of the university, the ultimate end of which may well be further diminution of autonomy and hence of the very possibility of true accountability (Dressel and Faricy, 1972).

Still other factors conspire to defeat accountability. In institutions of higher learning and elsewhere, the traditional loci of decision making are shifting. Since the 1960s the powers of university presidents and boards of trustees have become severely attenuated (Glenny, 1971). Reluctance to admit this fact blurs distinctions which accountability requires. Decision making is increasingly layered, with a proliferation of levels. Moreover, many decisions now tend to be made by anonymous persons or bodies, hidden away within the complex structures of governmental bodies or their agencies. The very anonymity of such functionaries, who in effect may make many important decisions simply by the manner in which they filter information passing through their hands, makes accountability totally inoperative. Genuine communication between governments and educational institutions is undermined if not rendered impossible by this developing complexity and thickening of layers of control.

Finally, our colleges and universities are becoming severely hampered by the disappearance of reserve resources or "slack" in the system. No system of any kind can function without adequate reserves of power to meet the stresses which unforeseen and dramatic changes can induce. The effects of financial retrenchment in support of higher education, together with the ravages of inflation, have increased the "net energy load" on the system—the differential between the demands placed upon it and the energy actually available— to the point where outright system failure is threatened or actually being experienced.

If the call to accountability is to function in a positive manner, a number of far-reaching issues must be addressed. First, efforts must be made to ensure that the requisite conditions of accountability are maintained or, where necessary, reinstated. Second, economic conditions are such that institutions of higher education will have to respond to the demand for more efficient models of management and governance. Inefficiency and lack of genuine accountability at this level are an open invitation to those who would tamper with institutional autonomy. Finally, institutions will need to reappraise their role and mission, as well as their types and levels of programs, in keeping with probable levels of funding. To accomplish this, educators and administrators alike will need to cultivate on the part of political authorities a better understanding of the idiosyncrasies inherent in the unique nature of higher education. Indeed, it is at the interface between colleges and universities on the one hand and government or its agencies on the other that many of the factors defeating accountability are rooted. More efficient and effective relationships at this point are therefore mandatory. Retreat to the ivory tower is no longer a live option. Colleges and universities must surrender much of their erstwhile independence from state control; and yet, in the long run, the interests of both government and higher education are best served if they can reach a mutual accommodation, in which educational institutions are assured a reasonable degree of autonomy and adequate levels of resources in return for a viable level of accountability. If the contemporary debate over accountability can be directed to the better perception of such basic realities, it will have been a constructive episode in the history and development of higher education.

Bibliography

Allison, G. T. *Essence of Decision.* Boston: Little, Brown, 1971.

Austin, J. L. "Performative Utterances." In J. O. Urmson and G. L. Warnock (Eds.), *J. L. Austin: Philosophical Papers.* Oxford, England: Clarendon Press, 1970.

Balderston, F. E. *Managing Today's University.* San Francisco: Jossey-Bass, 1974.

Bennis, W. *The Leaning Ivory Tower.* San Francisco: Jossey-Bass, 1973.

Bowen, H. R. "Holding Colleges Accountable." *Chronicle of Higher Education,* April 23, 1973, 7, 28.

Bowen, H. R. (Ed.) *New Directions for Institutional Research: Evaluating Institutions for Accountability,* no. 1. San Francisco: Jossey-Bass, 1974.

Dressel, P. L., and Faricy, W. H. *Return to Responsibility.* San Francisco: Jossey-Bass, 1972.

Etzioni, A. "Alternative Conceptions of Accountability: The Example of Health Administration." *Public Administration Review,* May–June 1975, 35, 279–286.

Gallant, J. A., and Prothero, J. W. "Weight-Watching at the University: The Consequences of Growth." *Science,* January 28, 1972, 175, 381–388.

Glenny, L. A. "The Anonymous Leaders of Higher Institutions." In *Institutional Research and Institutional Policy.* Proceedings of the 11th Annual Forum of the Association for Institutional Research, Denver, Colorado, 1971. Tallahassee, Florida: Association for Institutional Research, 1971.

Hart, D. K. "Theories of Government Related to Decentralization and Citizen Participation." Special issue of *Public Administration Review,* October 1972, 32, 603–621.

Mortimer, K. P. *Accountability in Higher Education.* ERIC Clearinghouse on Higher Education. Washington, D.C.: American Association for Higher Education, 1972.

Nisbet, R. *The Degradation of the Academic Dogma.* New York: Basic Books, 1971.

Parsons, T., and Platt, G. M. *The American University.* Cambridge, Massachusetts: Harvard University Press, 1973.

Perkins, J. A. (Ed.) *The University as Organiza-* *tion.* A Report for the Carnegie Commission on Higher Education. New York: McGraw-Hill, 1973.

Sibley, W. M. "The Transactional Frame of Accountability." In H. R. Bowen (Ed.), *Evaluating Institutions for Accountability.* San Francisco: Jossey-Bass, 1974a.

Sibley, W. M. "Institutional Accountability—Concept, Dogma, and Reality." *Stoa,* 1974b, 4(2), 67–77.

Thompson, J. D. *Organizations in Action.* New York: McGraw-Hill, 1967.

Ulam, A. *The Fall of the American University.* LaSalle, Illinois: Library Press, 1973.

Vickers, G. "The Management of Conflict." *Futures,* June 1972, 4(2), 126–144.

Wildavsky, A. "The Self-Evaluating Organization." *Public Administration Review,* September–October 1972, 32(5), 509–520.

W. M. SIBLEY

See also: Autonomy; Governance and Control of Higher Education; Participatory Democracy.

ACCOUNTANCY (Field of Study)

Accounting has often been called "the language of business," both private and public, because it encompasses any data relating to measurement of enterprise or social goals. Furthermore, accounting is involved with many aspects of internal control of resources, especially in the 1970s, when assets are becoming scarce. Although accounting uses were narrowly defined for centuries, the computer has greatly expanded the parameters of the discipline. In fact, the name *accounting* may be changed to *information system.*

Even though changes are taking place rapidly in the nature and role of accounting, the orthodox divisions of the field still are (1) financial accounting, which deals with reporting enterprise income and the status of financial well-being; (2) cost or managerial accounting, which deals with the various aspects of product and service costs; and (3) governmental accounting, which deals with governmental financial data at all levels. Accountants are usually classified as (1) professional public accountants, who serve a range of clients; (2) private accountants, who serve individual enterprises; and (3) governmental accountants, who have responsibilities for taxes, budgeting, and public reporting. Recently, however, because the rapid growth in world trade, investment, transportation, and development programs since the 1950s has increased the need for international accounting, a new classification has been proposed: (1) domestic accounting and (2) international accounting.

Accounting is related to several other disciplines, particularly statistics, operations research, decision theory, and computer science. The behavioral sciences also can be regarded as allied fields because many data influence behavior, especially in decision making. Another related field, human resource accounting, aids personnel managers because it computes the educational levels, skill development, and practical experience of employees, as well as training costs and employee turnover.

Accounting has become an international discipline. Standardization between countries is now being sought because intelligent investment decisions require it. Another trend in the field, the area of accounting and economic development policy, concerns the relationship between "good accounting" and a rising standard of living of the peoples of the world.

Some aspects of the practice of accounting can be traced back to the Greeks, Romans, and Egyptians, but professional practice in its currently accepted form in the Western world is just over one century old. For a major portion of this time, persons who wished to enter the practice have had some preparatory work plus some form of internship or apprenticeship with able practitioners. Recently, however, university education for the profession has become widely available.

In the United States, university education for professional accounting started in the 1870s, but it was only after World War II that a sizable number of institutions offered suitable curricula. In the mid 1970s there were more than 600 such institutions,

graduating about 40,000 candidates per year. A majority of these earned the bachelor's degree, but advanced degrees are becoming more prevalent. Nearly all of the accounting programs in universities are affiliated with the university's school of business. Many junior colleges and technical institutes also offer a substantial number of accounting courses, which lead either to more advanced work in the universities or to careers as assistants in the offices of accountants.

In Europe university education for accounting has developed substantially since the 1950s. In the United Kingdom, for example, much of the instruction is in the polytechnics, but several of the newer city universities now have organized curricula. On the continent much of the university education for accounting involves a wider curriculum base than in the United States. In the Federal Republic of Germany the number of top practitioners is quite limited compared with the population, and these individuals have many years of educational background. In France several of the newer universities are stressing accounting. In the Netherlands, where accounting has had a long and honorable history, the curriculum stresses business economics but includes only a modest amount of technical education in accounting. A similar curricular emphasis exists in Scandinavia. In Italy the practice of accounting is divided into tax work and auditing. Most of the Italian professional accountants studied liberal arts in the major universities and received their practical education on the job.

In Africa the North African countries have begun some university work in accounting. In Middle Africa, Nigeria has the most business schools, and these include accounting curricula. Newer countries of Middle Africa—for example, Tanzania, Zambia, Ghana, and Kenya—are beginning organized curricula in accounting. South Africa has had accounting curricula in the universities for many decades, and in the 1970s nearly one dozen universities and colleges in South Africa offered programs.

In the Middle East, only a few of the countries have organized curricula in accounting, but the number is growing rapidly. In Egypt accountancy majors in the universities also take a certain proportion of general and liberal education courses. Israel has several business schools which give moderate attention to accounting subjects. Saudi Arabia is also establishing business schools that offer courses in management accounting. In Iraq and Iran accounting is being taught at a limited number of universities. In Pakistan Canadians have helped develop the accounting instruction in at least two universities, but much of the instruction is done by institutes in private schools. India has numerous commerce schools which give accounting instruction as a major part of the curriculum. Several universities also stress accounting as part of their business economics programs. In Thailand the two major universities have accounting departments in their business schools. Faculty members in these departments are educated both in Thailand and abroad. In addition, several large private business schools emphasize accounting subjects.

In Malaysia and Singapore the business schools are usually associated with universities and have grown very rapidly since the 1950s; in addition, some private colleges with superior reputations, like Stamford College in Singapore, offer courses in accounting. Indonesia is beginning to offer management instruction (which pays modest attention to accounting subjects) in more than one university.

Since the 1950s Australia has become one of the leading countries in accounting instruction, with programs in more than a score of institutions. In New Zealand accounting is offered in each of the four major universities and in some of the regional colleges.

The Philippines has, in proportion to its population, more business schools which stress accounting subjects than most other countries. Each of the major universities

also has a strong emphasis on accounting.

After World War II, Japan began to stress accounting instruction in many of its numerous universities, especially in the larger cities. In the mid 1970s young people have many opportunities for studying accounting, but the selection process is quite strict. The profession of accounting is well organized in Japan, and educational levels of Japanese accountants are quite high. Many of the Japanese accounting professors have studied in other countries, and they are well aware of developments in North America and Europe. Accounting instruction in the commerce schools of the universities and colleges is superior in quality and quantity.

After the Republic of Korea won its independence, more than a dozen universities were established or reestablished in the major cities. In Seoul and Pusan accounting instruction is available at each of the significant universities. As in Japan, Thailand, and Australia, many of the faculty members have studied abroad. The literature of accounting, written in Korean, is substantial, and the profession has made much progress in attaining public and legislative recognition. Competition for places at the universities, however, continues to be very keen.

Canada has about forty business schools, most of them associated with universities in several provinces. In nearly all of these schools, accounting is offered as a separate discipline; and there is much interchange with the United States in faculty and text materials. The professional accounting organizations have also made special efforts to encourage their members to continue their education and to prepare themselves for more responsible posts.

In the countries to the south of the United States, Mexico has been in the forefront in accounting education. All of the large cities now have universities with accounting enrollments. Large amounts of materials from the United States have been translated into Spanish and are used by students and practicing accountants. The profession of accounting is also well organized in Mexico, and the standards of practice are constantly improving.

In Central America accounting is not well recognized in the relatively few universities and there are only limited enrollments in the available programs. Consequently, many of the prospective accounting practitioners study in the United States or in Mexico. A graduate business school with a limited amount of accounting instruction was established in Central America in the 1970s.

In South America, Colombia has a few modest programs in accounting instruction, with moderately sizable enrollments, but these are not proportionate to the population. The graduate business school in Medellín earned a superior reputation in the 1965–1975 decade. Accounting instruction has been offered in a few institutions in Peru on a modest basis, and the graduate business school in Lima also gives moderate attention to accounting. Argentina has had extensive curricula in commerce subjects for many decades. Enrollments in one or two of the major universities have been very large, even by standards of other countries. There is ample text material prepared by staff members in the country, along with translations from English, German, and other European languages. Under various aid programs Brazil has established a few well-recognized business schools, even at the graduate level. In each of these schools, accounting has received varying degrees of attention. The practice of accounting is regulated by the federal government of Brazil, as in many other Latin American countries, and the organizations of professional accountants offer continuing education opportunities for the members. Venezuela has recently begun to stress management and business educational opportunities for university students. With its tremendous resources, Venezuela may be in the forefront in accounting education in the very near future.

University education for accounting, as this brief survey shows, is both dynamic and in a state of flux. Many problems, however, remain to be solved: the role of university training versus practical experience in the attainment of educational and technical proficiency; the proper balance between accounting education, education for a broad business understanding, and education for general cultural and social understanding; the emphasis on theory versus the emphasis on practice in accountancy training; and, finally, the proper balance between international and national accounting matters.

PAUL GARNER

Levels and Programs of Study

Programs in accountancy generally require as a prerequisite a secondary education, though applicants with relevant work experience and aptitude may be admitted with lower educational qualifications. For entry to programs sponsored by professional accounting associations, such as those of chartered accounts and registered industrial accountants, greater emphasis may be placed on experience than academic qualifications. The following awards are given: certificate or diploma, bachelor's degree (B.B.A., B.Com., B.Sc.), master's degree (M.B.A.), the doctorate (Ph.D.), or their equivalents.

Programs leading to an award not equivalent to a first university degree consist primarily of study and practice in accountancy. These programs are concerned mainly with the practical aspects of keeping accounts and preparing financial and other statements; relatively little time is spent on accountancy theory or the general principles of record keeping. The programs, generally full time for more than one year, are usually given in a college of technology, community college, business college, or similar institution. Principal course content usually includes general accountancy; preparation of financial statement and other operational statements required for business management; maintenance of inventory records and records of purchases, sales, and costs; valuation of assets; preparation of a corporation income tax return; and preparation of statistical returns. Some programs of this kind may include the study of relevant commercial law, tax law, business correspondence, office machine operation, and computer operation.

Programs leading to a first university degree consist primarily of instruction and group discussion dealing with the principles and practices of business management, with specialization in accountancy. Some emphasis is given to management practice, but the stress is on cost accounting, auditing, and public accounting. A background is usually provided in other functional areas of business, such as statistics, production, law, marketing, and personnel relations. Programs leading to a qualification such as that of chartered accountant or certified public accountant are included at this level. Principal course content usually includes specialized business administration subjects, such as general accountancy, commercial law, taxation, corporation finance, inventory control, accounting records and systems, financial statement analysis, funds flow statements, budgeting and governmental systems, product costing, standard costs, and return on investment and capital acquisitions. Usual background courses are economic theory, money and banking, industrial relations, statistics, and courses in the humanities, political science, public administration, and the sciences.

Programs that lead to a postgraduate university degree consist primarily of study; seminar or group discussion; and research dealing with the principles and practices of business administration, with emphasis on accountancy. Background study in other areas of business administration is usually included. An important part of the Ph.D. programs is original research work involving the preparation and defense of a dissertation or thesis. Principal course content and areas of research usually include general accounting, analysis of financial statements, flow of funds analysis, taxation, auditing of financial records, and applica-

tion of electronic computers to accounting procedures. In addition, many programs include some study of other business administration subjects, such as commercial law, corporation finance, and purchasing policy. Usual background studies include economic theory, money and banking, international trade, statistics, mathematics, and behavioral sciences.

[This section was based on UNESCO's *International Standard Classification of Education (ISCED): Three Stage Classification System, 1974* (Paris: UNESCO, 1974), with revisions by Paul Garner.]

Major National and International Organizations

INTERNATIONAL

Association of International Accountants
P.O. Box 38
Link House
Billericay, Essex, England

Confederation of Asian and Pacific
    Accountants (CAPA)
6th Floor, Woodward House
99 The Terrace
P.O. 10046
Wellington, New Zealand

Council for International Progress in
    Management (CIPM)
135 West 50th Street
New York, New York 10020 USA

European Union of Public Accountants
Union européenne des experts comptables
    économiques et financiers (UEC)
139 rue Faubourg Saint-Honoré
75008 Paris, France

Financial Executives Institute (FEI)
633 Third Avenue
New York, New York 10017 USA

Foundation for the Advancement of
    International Business Administration
64 Ferndale Drive
Hastings-on-Hudson, New York 10706 USA

Inter-American Accounting Conference
P.O. Box 2165
San Juan, Puerto Rico 00903

International Accounting Standards
    Committee
3 Street, Helen's Place
London EC3A 6DN, England

International Association of Students in
Business and Economics
Association internationale des étudiants en
sciences économiques et commerciales
(AIESEC)
45 avenue Legrand
B1050 Brussels, Belgium

International Centre for Advanced Technical
and Vocational Training
140 Corso Unità d'Italia
10127 Turin, Italy

International Committee for Scientific
Management
Comité international de l'organisation
scientifique
1 rue de Varembé
1211 Geneva 20, Switzerland

International Co-ordination Committee for
the Accountancy Profession
Cecilienallee 36
D-4 Düsseldorf 30, Federal Republic of
Germany

International Council of Practitioners of the
International Plan of Accounts
Conseil international des practiciens du plan
comptable international (CIPCI)
21 rue Ernest Havaux
1040 Brussels, Belgium

International Finance Corporation (IFC)
Société financière internationale (SFI)
1818 H Street NW
Washington, D.C. 20433 USA

Society for International Development (SID)
1346 Connecticut Avenue NW
Washington, D.C. 20036 USA
(European Office: 49 rue de la Glacière,
75013 Paris, France.)

NATIONAL

Argentina:
Federación argentina de colegios
graduados en ciencias económicas
Viamonte 1592
Buenos Aires

Australia:
Institute of Chartered Accountants in
Australia
333 George Street
P.O. Box 3921
Sydney, New South Wales 2000

Belgium:
Société royale chambre belge des
comptables
2 Galerie de la Reine
Brussels 1000

Brazil:
Instituto dos auditóres independêntes
do Brasil
Rua Antonio de Godoi
88-16 Andar
São Paulo 01034

Canada:
Canadian Institute of Chartered
Accountants
250 Bloor Street East
Toronto, Ontario M4W 1G5

Chile:
Sociedad nacional de contadores
Casilla 3863
Santiago

Federal Republic of Germany:
Institut der Wirtschaftsprüfer in
Deutschland, e.V.
Cecilienallee 36
D-4 Düsseldorf 30

France:
Conseil supérieur de l'ordre des experts
comptables et des comptables agréés
109 boulevard Malesherbes
Paris 8e

India:
Institute of Chartered Accountants
of India
P.O. Box 268
Indraprastha Marg
New Delhi 11001

Ireland:
Institute of Chartered Accountants in
Ireland
7 Fitzwilliam Place
Dublin 2

Italy:
Federazione nazionale dei collegi dei
ragionieri
Piazza Scuole Pie
7-9 Bis.
16123 Genoa

Japan:
Japanese Institute of Certified Public
Accountants
Kabuki Building
4-12-15
Ginza, Chuo-ku, Tokyo

Netherlands:
Nederlands instituut van
registeraccountants
Mensinge 2, Postbus 7984
Europa Boulevard
Amsterdam 1011

Switzerland:
> Chambre suisse des sociétés fiduciaires
> et des experts-comptables
> Limmatquai 120
> 80001 Zurich

United Kingdom:
> Institute of Chartered Accountants in
> England and Wales
> Chartered Accountants' Hall
> Moorgate Place
> London EC2R 6EQ, England

United States:
> American Accounting Association
> 653 S. Orange Avenue
> Sarasota, Florida 33577
> > Includes a Committee on International
> > Accounting.

> American Institute of Certified Public
> Accountants
> 1211 Avenue of the Americas
> New York, New York 10036

> National Association of Accountants
> (NAA)
> 919 Third Avenue
> New York, New York 10022

Additional associations are listed in: "A World Directory of Accountancy Bodies." *The Accountant's Diary and Yearbook 1975.* London: Gee, annual.

Principal Information Sources

GENERAL

Guides to the literature sources of accounting include the following:

Current Accounting Literature 1973: A Supplement to Current Accounting Literature 1971 Listing Books, Pamphlets and Periodicals of Current Interest Added to Seven Accounting Libraries in the British Isles During 1973. London: Mansell, 1974. The 1971 volume, plus supplements for 1972 and 1973, mainly includes books held by the Library of the Institute of Chartered Accountants in England and Wales.

Demarest, R. R. *Accounting Information Sources.* Detroit: Gale Research, 1970.

Mueller, G. G. *A Bibliography of International Accounting.* (Rev. ed.) Seattle: Graduate School of Business Administration, University of Washington, 1968. Copies available from the author.

Aspects of education for accountancy are found in:

Edwards, J. D. (Ed.) *Accounting Education Problems and Prospects.* Sarasota, Florida: American Accounting Association, 1974.

"Foreign Educational Credential Evaluation by IQAC." New York: American Institute of Certified Public Accountants, International Qualifications Appraisal Committee, 1973. Memorandum sent June 1, 1973, to state or other jurisdictional boards of accountancy.

Osman, A. C. "Cybernetics Paradigm for Research and Development in Accountancy Education and Training." Paper presented at International Conference on Education for International Public Accountancy, London, December 1972.

Roy, R. H., and MacNeil, J. H. *Horizons for a Profession: The Common Body of Knowledge for Certified Public Accountants.* New York: American Institute of Certified Public Accountants, 1967.

Williams, D. Z. *Accounting Education: A Statistical Survey, 1972–73.* New York: American Institute of Certified Public Accountants, 1974.

Comparative accounting information is found in the following:

Accounting Principles and Reporting Practices: A Survey in 38 Countries. New York: Price Waterhouse, 1973.

American Accounting Association, Committee on International Accounting. "Report." *Accounting Review,* 1973, *48,* 121–167, supplement.

American Accounting Association, Committee on International Accounting. "Report." *Accounting Review,* 1974, *49,* 251–269, supplement.

Berg, K. B., and others. *Readings in International Accounting.* Boston: Houghton Mifflin, 1969. A collection of articles on various aspects of international accounting.

Garner, P. *Development of International Accounting Standards and Conventions: Past Accomplishments and Future Potentials and Strategies.* University, Alabama: Center for Business and Economic Research, University of Alabama, 1973.

International Accounting Standards Committee. *Commentary on the Statements of International Accounting Standards.* New York: American Institute of Certified Public Accountants, 1974.

Mueller, G. G. *Studies in Accounting.* Seattle: Graduate School of Business Administration, University of Washington, 1962–. Presentations of the essentials of accounting and auditing in various countries are found in this series.

Mueller, G. G. *International Accounting.* New York: Macmillan, 1967. A detailed textbook presentation of problems in international accounting.

Professional Accounting in 30 Countries. (Rev. ed.)

New York: American Institute of Certified Public Accountants, 1975. Gives data on accounting principles, auditing standards, reporting practices, and professional requirements in various countries.

CURRENT BIBLIOGRAPHIES

Bibliographies, indexes, and abstracts specifically directed to accounting subjects are:

Accountants' Digest. Syracuse, New York: Germain, 1935–.
Accountants' Index. New York: American Institute of Certified Public Accountants, 1923–.
Accounting and Data Processing Abstracts. Wembley, England: Anbar, 1970–.
CCH Accounting Articles. Chicago: Commerce Clearing House, 1965–.
Topical Index. New York: National Association of Accountants, 1946–.

General indexing and abstracting services in which subjects of interest to accountants can be found are:

Business Periodicals Index. New York: Wilson, 1958–.
Management Index. Ottawa, Ontario: Keith Business Library, 1963–.
Public Affairs Information Service Bulletin. New York: Public Affairs Information Service, 1915–.

PERIODICALS

Among the important journals in the field of accounting are the following: *Abacus* (Nigeria), *Accountancy* (England and Wales), *Accountancy* (Ireland), *Accountant* (UK), *Accountant* (Netherlands), *Accountants' Digest* (US), *Accountants' Journal* (New Zealand), *Accountants' Journal* (Philippines), *Accountants' Magazine* (UK), *Accounting Review* (US), *Bilanz- und Buchhaltungs-Praxis* (FRG), *Bukhhalterski uchiot* (USSR), *Canadian Chartered Accountant, Chartered Accountant* (India), *Chartered Accountant in Australia, CPA Journal* (US), *Finanzas y contabilidad* (Mexico), *International Accountant* (UK), *International Journal of Accounting Education and Research* (US), *Journal of Accountancy* (US), *Journal of Accounting Research* (US), *Journal U.E.C.* (FRG), *Management Accounting* (UK), *Management Accounting* (US), *National Public Accountant* (US), *Practical Accountant* (US), *Revision og regnskabsvaesen* (Denmark), *Revue française de comptabilité, Roeh haheshbon* (Israel), *Der schweizer Treuhander, South African Chartered Accountant, Wirtschaftsprüfung* (FRG).

For more complete listings of accounting journals see:

Accountants' Index. New York: American Institute of Certified Public Accountants, 1923–.

Current Accounting Literature 1971. London: Institute of Chartered Accountants in England and Wales, 1971–. With supplements.
Ulrich's International Periodicals Directory. New York: Bowker, biennial.

ENCYCLOPEDIAS, DICTIONARIES, HANDBOOKS

Accountants' Encyclopedia. Englewood Cliffs, New Jersey: Prentice-Hall, 1962.
Accountants' International Study Group. *Comparative Glossary of Accounting Terms in Canada, the United Kingdom and the United States: A Selection of Terms with Different Meanings in Three Nations.* New York: American Institute of Certified Public Accountants, 1975.
Davidson, S. (Ed.) *Handbook of Modern Accounting.* New York: McGraw-Hill, 1970.
Dickey, R. I., and others (Eds.) *Accountants' Cost Handbook.* (2nd ed.) New York: Ronald Press, 1960.
Dictionary of Accounting and Business Terms: Diccionario de terminos contables y comerciales. New York: Arthur Andersen, 1962. An excellent Spanish-English/English-Spanish listing of accounting terms.
Kohler, E. L. *Dictionary for Accountants.* (5th ed.) Englewood Cliffs, New Jersey: Prentice-Hall, 1975.
Lasser, J. K. *Standard Handbook for Accountants.* New York: McGraw-Hill, 1956.
Lexique UEC. (2nd ed.) Düsseldorf, Federal Republic of Germany: IdW Verlag GmbH, 1975. Defines terms dealing with taxation, banking, stock exchange dealings, costing, and electronic data processing in Danish, Dutch, English, French, German, Italian, Portuguese, and Spanish. (Sold in Great Britain by Gee and Co., London.)
Williams, R. I., and Doris, L. (Eds.) *Encyclopedia of Accounting Systems.* Englewood Cliffs, New Jersey: Prentice-Hall, 1957.
Wixon, R., Kell, W. G., and Bedford, N. M. (Eds.) *Accountants' Handbook.* (5th ed.) New York: Ronald Press, 1970.

DIRECTORIES

For guides to colleges and universities offering courses in accounting consult the following:

American Universities and Colleges. Washington, D.C.: American Council on Education, quadrennially.
Commonwealth Universities Yearbook. London: Association of Commonwealth Universities, annual.
International Handbook of Universities. Paris: International Association of Universities, triennially.
Patterson's American Education. Mount Prospect, Illinois: Educational Directories, annual.

The following centers specialize in international accounting:

Center for International Accounting
University of Lancaster
Bailrigg, Lancaster, England

Center for International Accounting
University of Washington
Seattle, Washington 98195 USA

Center for International Education and
   Research in Accounting
College of Commerce and Business
   Administration
University of Illinois
Urbana, Illinois 61801 USA

A listing of national accounting institutes in most nations of the world can be found in:

The Accountant's Diary and Yearbook 1975. London: Gee, annual.

ACCOUNTING AND FINANCIAL REPORTING

See Financial Affairs: Accounting and Financial Reporting.

ACCREDITATION

See Academic Standards and Accreditation: International; Academic Standards and Accreditation: United States.

ACCREDITATION, REGIONAL

See Academic Standards and Accreditation: United States.

ACCREDITATION, REGULATIONS OF THE UNITED STATES GOVERNMENT

See Academic Standards and Accreditation: United States.

ACTION, United States

In July 1971 ACTION was established as an independent United States agency to streamline existing federal volunteer programs, develop ways to make the most effective use of volunteers, and provide opportunities for all Americans to serve their communities through volunteer work. The new agency grouped seven volunteer organizations, each with its own legislative mandate and guidelines: Peace Corps, Volunteers in Service to America, National Student Volunteer Program, Retired Senior Volunteer Program, Foster Grandparent Program, Service Corps of Retired Executives, and Active Corps of Executives. Through ACTION, these programs maintain their own identity and purpose while cooperating to provide strong overall support to community efforts.

The Peace Corps was founded in 1961 to help developing countries meet their needs for trained manpower; promote better understanding of Americans among the people being served; and encourage better understanding of other people among Americans. The largest full-time group in ACTION, the Peace Corps has volunteers from every state serving more than a thousand different projects each year throughout the world. Peace Corps service begins in response to a host country's request. Over five thousand requests are received each year. The planning, programming, training, selection, and supervision of volunteers are shared by the host country government and the United States. Almost half of all Peace Corps volunteers are engaged in some kind of educational project. Many work as teachers overseas; others are involved in teacher training programs. Nearly one quarter of the volunteers are concerned with agriculture or rural development. Other projects include urban development, public works, health, business, and public management.

Volunteers in Service to America (VISTA) supports volunteers to work in locally sponsored projects in the United States designed to strengthen and supplement efforts to eliminate poverty and poverty-related human, social, and environmental problems. Volunteers work in areas of education, health, community planning, housing, economic development, and social services. Any private or public nonprofit organization engaged in anti-poverty work may sponsor a VISTA project. Sponsors provide volunteers with transportation, supervision, and in-service training. The volunteer is provided a living allowance, travel to and from the project, a vacation stipend, and medical insurance by ACTION.

The National Student Volunteer Program helps high school and college students set up volunteer activities by providing technical materials to the young volunteers as well as liaison assistance with groups in need of services. The program distributes how-to manuals, program kits, funding guides, and training resource materials.

The Retired Senior Volunteer Program provides grants and technical assistance to establish and expand projects that provide meaningful part-time volunteer activities for retired persons aged sixty or more. Through the Foster Grandparent Program, low-income volunteers aged sixty or more offer love and friendship to children in hospitals and other institutions.

The Service Corps of Retired Executives (SCORE) provides free business counseling to small businesses and community organizations. Cosponsored by ACTION and the Small Business Association, SCORE provides technical assistance to chapters composed of five or more business persons. The Active Corps of Executives is composed of executives still active in the work force who are also willing to give their time and experience to help other businesses and organizations grow.

Since 1971 six new programs have been initiated by ACTION, including the University Year for ACTION, ACTION Cooperative Volunteers, Program for Local Service, School Partnership, Senior Companion Program, and the United Nations Volunteers ACTION.

Combining community service with academic study, the University Year for ACTION (UYA) allows students to receive a year of university credit while working with local agencies in poverty areas on poverty-related human, social, and environmental problems. Encouraging academic involvement in poverty communities, UYA administers volunteer projects at the local level through the universities. The institution provides limited administrative and volunteer support costs. Grants are provided by ACTION for both project planning and operations. Students participating must be aged eighteen or more.

ACTION Cooperative Volunteers is a full-time program designed as a means of sharing ACTION's volunteer resources and programing experience with federal, state, and local government agencies and private nonprofit organizations. These agencies and institutions contribute to the direct cost of supporting the volunteers during their first year of service.

The Program for Local Service (PLS) was launched by the state of Washington and ACTION in 1973 as an experimental program. It is designed to provide full-time volunteers with opportunities for service in community projects concerning human and environmental needs, particularly those related to poverty, through a system of recruitment, placement, and management of local volunteers. The state or local government unit or delegate agency provides volunteer job descriptions, on-the-job training when necessary, and placement supervision. Each sponsor is awarded a grant by ACTION for programing and support of volunteers. PLS volunteers must be age eighteen or more and serve full time for one year.

School Partnership, a program activated by Peace Corps volunteers, brings funds raised by a sponsoring group in the United States to a community overseas. Student organizations, clubs, and church groups donate money for building materials for schools, health clinics, or other needed facilities in developing countries. The village supplies the necessary land, labor, and personnel. From 1964 to 1975 school partners built more than nineteen hundred schools.

The Senior Companion Program provides grants and technical assistance to set up and operate projects that help adults with special needs in health, education, and welfare. Senior companions must be low-income persons and aged sixty or more. Projects are administered by public or private nonprofit agencies or organizations. These agencies accept full responsibility for the development, implementation, and management of the project, including recruitment, selection, assignment, orientation, and in-service instruction for senior companion volunteers. The agencies also provide meals, transportation, and supervision.

Through the United Nations Volunteers ACTION, volunteers serve with those from other countries in United Nations programs.

All ACTION programs can be combined or used independently to meet community needs. The programs are funded separately but share the same administrative structure under the director of ACTION.

ACTION Education Programs Office of
UYA (University Year of Action)
806 Connecticut Avenue NW
Washington, D.C. 20525 USA

ACTIVISM, FACULTY
See Unrest, Campus.

ACTIVISM, STUDENT
See Unrest, Campus.

ACTIVITIES, STUDENT
See College Unions; Extracurricular Activities on Campus; Fraternities; Sport, Inter-university; Students, Student Services, and Student Organizations; Student Volunteer Programs.

ACTUARIAL SCIENCE (Field of Study)

Actuarial science is concerned with the measurement and use of probabilities of occurrence of events, usually beyond human control, which generally result in financial losses. Also, actuarial science is concerned with the measurement of the amount of future benefit payments from all kinds of private and public insurance, annuity, and welfare plans. The probabilities are used, together with the known or estimated benefit payments, to determine the premiums or cost of private and public insurance and pension plans. Generally the probabilities that are used are related to the design of social devices which spread the financial losses befalling certain members of society over the many individuals who were exposed to the risk of financial loss but who did not suffer loss. The probabilities are measured by collection and analysis of statistical data. Similarly, when the amount and/or form of benefit payment is not specifically known in advance, estimates are made by collection and analysis of prior statistical data and by analysis of possible future economic and social changes.

The divisions of the field are identified by the different types of losses, such as loss of life and loss of property through fire. Each of the areas has developed specialized techniques for handling the specific risk. The following are the major fields: (1) life insurance and pensions, in which probabilities of survival and other contingencies are used to determine the cost of benefits payable in event of premature death or upon retirement; (2) health insurance, in which frequency of occurrence and financial cost of illness or injury are used to determine premiums; (3) property and casualty insurance, which is concerned with the frequency of occurrence and extent of damage to property from natural catastrophes and accidents, such as fire, transportation loss, theft, and automobile collision, as well as loss arising from automobile and other accidents, workmen's compensation, and fidelity losses; (4) social insurance, which makes use of demographic data, birthrates, death rates, and migration to provide estimates of costs and revenues for various governmental social programs.

This branch differs from the others because it is concerned primarily with total costs and total revenues of the covered populations and does not directly relate price or cost to the magnitude of hazard.

In addition to these major areas in the field of actuarial science, there are six related fields (the first four so closely related that some actuaries have become specialists in them): (1) Statistics is a primary related field because the measurement of probability is based on the collection and interpretation of data. (2) Accounting is vitally important because the revenue and outgo of an insurance plan must be monitored to determine whether the actual occurrence of events conforms to the assumptions made in determining the premiums. Also, an important element in the costs of insurance plans is the expense of operation. The actuary must use the results of careful and thoughtful cost accounting in his premium and other value calculations. (3) Economics and investments must be understood because many insurance plans are of a long-term nature, requiring the investment of funds collected at one time for payment at a later time. In addition, the determination of the price of insurance has the same economic consideration as pricing in general. (4) Law, particularly contract law, is important to actuaries because insurance usually takes the form of a legal contract. Also, some of the concerns of actuaries are prescribed by statute. (5) Medicine is related to life and health insurance because the physical condition of the insured individual is a medical determination and a factor in the probability of survival. Actuaries do not have extensive medical training, but they do attempt to understand some of the more common aspects of medicine. Some data collection has been undertaken in cooperation with the medical profession. Rehabilitation for certain accident and illness cases can have a significant effect on insurance costs. (6) Biology—especially the biological process of aging—is important to actuaries in helping them estimate life insurance, pension, and social insurance costs.

The need for measuring probabilities of survival apparently arose in the seventeenth century, when some governments sought to finance their national debt by selling life annuities. There were also early plans to provide pensions and dependents' benefits to the clergy. As economies became more complex, the need for protection against loss became important, both for consumer goods which were subject to transportation losses and for capital goods subject to many other hazards. Awareness of the value of a human being as an economic provider for his dependents produced elementary commercial forms of life insurance in the early nineteenth century. The actuarial problems of the first insurance companies were tackled as special problems by mathematicians. By the middle of the nineteenth century, some persons with mathematical backgrounds began to specialize in actuarial problems—thereby becoming the first professional actuaries.

These early practitioners soon formed national or regional associations for discussion and research. The first such association was the Institute of Actuaries in Great Britain, formed in 1848. By the end of the nineteenth century, similar national associations had been formed in Western Europe, the United States, Canada, and Japan. After its formation, an association's next step was to develop standards for admission. These standards usually took the form of examinations based on an extensive syllabus. As the body of knowledge expanded, it became difficult for applicants to prepare for the examinations without further education; consequently, in the early twentieth century, programs and courses were established in colleges and universities in many countries. A notable exception was the United Kingdom, which had evolved the first series of professional association examinations but waited until the late 1960s to develop significant university programs.

Recent developments in actuarial science can be classified under three headings: use of computers, new risks, and state regulation. Because many basic actuarial problems require extensive calculation, actuaries were among the first to put the computer to commercial use. Among the new risks brought about by social or economic developments are the problems of developing methods of covering the enormous potential losses involved in mass transportation through jumbo jets and the unknown risks associated with atomic energy. In addition, the new concept of no-fault automobile insurance has changed the costs to insurers. Worldwide inflationary trends also have created a new hazard, the loss in value of money for the long-term coverages of life insurance and pension plans, and have led to the development of benefits indexed in some way to the cost of living. The third development, regulation of insurance by the state, exists in many forms. In the United States and Japan, private insurance is subjected to extensive, complex state regulation, and the trend internationally is toward increasing regulation. This development may relieve the actuary of some of the judgments he would normally make; at the same time, it calls for understanding of a more complex environment. Consider, for instance, the complexity of income taxation of insurance companies. In the United States the federal government, in the interest of investors in the stock of insurance companies, insists that generally accepted accounting principles be applied to the financial reporting of insurance companies; as a result, more precise actuarial judgments in reserve calculations are required. Related to the area of state regulation is the trend toward recognizing the problems of the consumer; actuaries must consider how the consumer can be helped to understand a product whose basic elements are probability and compound interest.

Approximately 55 percent of the world's actuaries are employed in the United States and Canada; 25 percent in the British Commonwealth (except Canada); 16 percent in other European countries; 3 percent in Latin America; and 1 percent in the rest of the world.

Historically, the British professional associations had an early and significant impact on the training of actuaries internationally. The Institute of Actuaries started examinations at its inception in 1848; shortly thereafter the Faculty of Actuaries also conducted examinations. Soon a system of correspondence tutoring was developed, so that candidates in all parts of the British Empire could acquire the training necessary to pass these demanding examinations. The few persons wanting to become actuaries in other parts of Asia and Africa usually participated in this program. In the 1960s a university course was developed in Australia, and since then several courses have been established in universities in the United Kingdom. Satisfactory completion of appropriate university courses gave credit for certain of the professional examinations. Thus, for the part of the world subject to British influence, the method of training was that of individuals preparing for a professional examination by correspondence courses.

The training of actuaries in the United States and Canada has developed in common for the two countries. Most United States and Canadian actuaries become qualified by first earning a baccalaureate degree, majoring in mathematics. They then study (usually without the benefit of academic programs but with informal assistance from local actuaries) to prepare for the examinations administered by two professional associations: the Society of Actuaries and the Casualty Actuarial Society. Actuarial science courses of varying lengths have been developed at about twenty colleges and universities in the two countries. Although such courses are helpful in preparing for the professional examinations, no recognition for them is given by the professional associations. However, the possibility of giving credit for a certain portion of the associations' examinations for satisfactory performance in suitable university courses is under consideration. Also, in the United States the Pension Reform Act of 1974 gives recognition to college and university courses as part of the qualifications toward becoming an "Enrolled Actuary." United States and Canadian college and university programs in the actuarial field had virtually no international aspects until the 1970s, when some candidates from Asia and Africa began taking academic courses in actuarial science in United States and Canadian colleges and universities.

Actuarial training in many countries in Western Europe has been accomplished by the establishment of a special chair or a special curriculum in actuarial science at a major university. These countries include Austria, Belgium, Denmark, France, Italy, Norway, Spain, and Sweden. Members of the relatively small European national associations established a larger international association, the International Association of Actuaries, in 1894. Actuaries from all parts of the world participate in the activities of the association, which holds a week-long meeting every fourth year for the purpose of exchanging ideas internationally. One of its early contributions was the promulgation of a notation for actuarial mathematics which has gained worldwide acceptance.

The rest of the world, for the most part, does not have a particular method of acquiring actuarial training. However, at least two Latin American countries, Argentina and Mexico, have special curricula in a major university. Special courses also are available in Israel.

The number and scope of special actuarial courses given at colleges and universities in various parts of the world are increasing. However, most persons seeking to become actuaries still must prepare for and pass some professional association examinations without benefit of academic training.

GEOFFREY CROFTS

Levels and Programs of Study

Programs in actuarial science generally require as a minimum prerequisite a secondary education. Mature students, especially those with relevant work experience,
are sometimes admitted with lower qualifications. Programs lead to the following awards: certificate or diploma, Bachelor of Science or Arts, Master of Science or Arts, the doctorate, or their equivalents. Programs deal with the principles and practices of actuarial science and consist of classroom sessions, practice, seminars, and, on advanced levels, group discussion and seminars dealing with specialties in actuarial science.

Programs that lead to an award not equivalent to a first university degree emphasize actuarial practices rather than the underlying principles of insurance or mathematics. Principal course content usually includes the mathematics of investment, the construction of life tables, principles of actuarial data collection, experience rating, and usually basic mathematics such as probability theory, calculus, analytical geometry, and algebra. Background courses usually include insurance law, investment policy, risk theory, principles of economics, and principles of accountancy.

Programs that lead to a first university degree deal with both practical and theoretical aspects of actuarial science and generally require three or four years of study. Principal course content usually includes general mathematics, differential and integral calculus, introductory analysis, differential equations, and probability theory. Specialized courses are usually selected from the mathematics of investment and credit, introductory life contingencies, finite calculus, theory of life and other contingencies, and selected topics such as preparation and analysis of raw data, application of operational research, risk theory, financing of pensions, social insurance, and demography.

Programs that lead to a postgraduate university degree emphasize original research work as substantiated by the presentation of a scholarly thesis or dissertation. Principal subject matter areas within which courses and research projects tend to fall include advanced probability theory, selected topics in actuarial science, insurance law and regulations, annuities, and investment policy for reserves.

[This section was based on UNESCO's *International Standard Classification of Education (ISCED): Three Stage Classification System, 1974* (Paris: UNESCO, 1974).]

Major International and National Organizations

INTERNATIONAL

International Actuarial Association (IAA)
Association actuarielle internationale (AAI)
9 rue des Chevaliers
1050 Brussels, Belgium
   The major international organization in its field. Founded as the Permanent Committee for International Actuarial Congresses/Comité permanent des congrès internationaux d'actuaires.

International Association of Consulting
   Actuaries (IACA)
de Lairessestraat 117
Amsterdam, Netherlands

NATIONAL

Argentina:
   Instituto actuarial argentino
   Rivadavia 954, Piso 60
   Buenos Aires

Australia:
   Actuarial Society of Australia and
      New Zealand
   % Australian Mutual Provident Society
   87 Pitt Street
   Sydney, New South Wales

Belgium:
   Association royale des actuaires belges
   14 rue des Finances
   Brussels

Brazil:
   Instituto brasileiro de atuaria
   avenida Marechal Camara 171
   Rio de Janeiro

Canada:
   Canadian Institute of Actuaries
   Suite 50b, 116 Albert Street
   Ottawa, Ontario K7P563

Federal Republic of Germany:
   Deutsche Gesellschaft für
      Versicherungsmathematik
   Von Werth Strasse 4-14
   Cologne

France:
   Institut des actuaires français
   247 rue Saint-Honoré
   Paris

India:
   Actuarial Society of India
   % Life Insurance Corporation of India
   Oriental Building, Mahatma Gandhi
      Road
   Fort, Bombay 1

Italy:
   Istituto degli attuari
   via dell'Arancio 66
   Rome

Mexico:
   Asociación mexicana de actuarios
   avenida Juarez No. 4, Desp. 705
   Mexico, D.F.

Netherlands:
   Het actuarieel genootschap
   2 Leideweg
   Utrecht

Norway:
   Den norske aktuarforening
   IBM
   P.O. Box 1379
   Oslo

South Africa:
   Actuarial Society of South Africa
   P.O. Box 4464
   Cape Town

Switzerland:
   Association des actuaires suisses
   Aeschemplatz 7
   Basel

United Kingdom:
   Institute of Actuaries
   Staple Inn Bldgs., Holborn
   London WC1, England

United States:
   Society of Actuaries
   208 South La Salle Street
   Chicago, Illinois 60604

   Casual Actuarial Society
   200 East 42nd Street
   New York, NY 10017

Principal Information Sources

GENERAL

Guides to the literature in the field are:

Pemberton, J. E. *How to Find Out in Mathematics: A Guide to Sources of Information.* (2nd ed.)

Oxford, England: Pergamon Press, 1969. Includes a section in appendix on actuarial science.

Pendleton, O. W. *How to Find Out About Insurance.* Oxford, England: Pergamon Press, 1967. Guide to the field of insurance; includes bibliographies, encyclopedias, dictionaries, periodicals, and directories.

Thomas, R. E. *Insurance: A Guide to Information Sources.* Detroit: Gale Research, 1971. Management Information Guide Series No. 21. Includes general sources of information in the field of insurance as well as a section on insurance and actuarial science education in the United States.

Some introductory works in the field include:

Cockerell, H. A. L. *Insurance.* London: English Universities Press, 1964.

Jordan, C. W. *Life Contingencies.* (2nd ed.) Chicago: Society of Actuaries, 1967.

Wolfenden, H. H. *Fundamental Principles of Mathematics Statistics.* Toronto, Ontario: Macmillan of Canada, 1942.

A historical account of the actuarial profession is provided by:

Mitchell, R. B. *From Actuarius to Actuary: The Growth of a Dynamic Profession in Canada and the United States.* Chicago: Society of Actuaries, 1974.

CURRENT BIBLIOGRAPHIES

Internationale Bibliographie der Versicherungsliteratur/International Bibliography of Insurance/ Bibliographie internationale d'assurance. Bern, Switzerland: Herbert Lang, 1964–. Text and titles are in German, English, and French.

Journals in the field of actuarial science which include current sources of information are:

Journal of the Institute of Actuaries. Oxford, England: Alden Press, 1851–.

Transactions of the Society of Actuaries. Chicago: Society of Actuaries, 1949–.

Statistical indexing and abstracting services also cover the field of actuarial science.

PERIODICALS

Some important periodicals in the field are *The Actuary* (US), *American Mathematical Monthly, Annals of Mathematics* (US), *Annals of Statistics* (US), *Computer Journal* (UK), *Journal of the American Statistical Association, Journal of the Institute of Actuaries* (UK), *Journal of Risk and Insurance* (US), *Mathematics of Computation* (US),

Operational Research Quarterly (US and UK), *Operations Research* (US), *Transactions of the Actuarial Society of Australasia, Transactions of the Society of Actuaries* (US).

For an international listing of periodicals in the field of insurance see:

Pendleton, O. W. *How to Find Out About Insurance.* Oxford, England: Pergamon Press, 1967, pp. 41–75.

ENCYCLOPEDIAS, DICTIONARIES, HANDBOOKS

Finke, E. *Handwörterbuch des Versicherungswesens.* (2 vols.) Darmstadt, Federal Republic of Germany: Verlag Hoppenstedt, 1958. Encyclopedia dealing primarily with German law and practice.

International Insurance Dictionary. Bern, Switzerland: European Conference of Insurance Supervisory Services, 1959. Multilingual dictionary in English, German, Dutch, French, Italian, Spanish, Portuguese, Danish, Swedish, Norwegian, and Finnish.

DIRECTORIES

Assekuranz-Compass. Vienna: Wischniowsky, 1965. A trilingual international insurance directory which includes information on companies, agents, and laws governing the insurance profession.

Morith, R. J. *Risk and Insurance Instruction in American Colleges and Universities.* Philadelphia: Huebner Foundation for Insurance Education, 1972. Comprehensive survey of programs and courses offered in the field in the United States.

Pendleton, O. W. *How to Find Out About Insurance.* Oxford, England: Pergamon Press, 1967, pp. 75–95. Lists general directories to insurance companies, agents, associations, and/or educational institutions in various countries throughout the world.

ADMINISTRATION, BRANCH CAMPUSES

See Branch Campuses.

ADMINISTRATION, EDUCATIONAL

See Educational Administration (field of study).

ADMINISTRATION EFFICIENCY

See Evaluation of Administrators.

ADMINISTRATION, GENERAL, ORGANIZATION FOR

See General Administration, Organization for.

ADMINISTRATION, PUBLIC

See Public Administration (field of study).

ADMINISTRATIVE POLICIES

See Business Management of Higher Education; Computers, Role of in Higher Education: Computers in Administration; Consultants, Use of; Development, College and University; Evaluation of Administrators; Financial Affairs; Financing of Higher Education; General Administration, Organization for; Governance and Control of Higher Education; Planning, Development, and Coordination; Publications, Higher Education; Research.

ADMINISTRATIVE SUPPORT ACTIVITIES TRAINING

See Business and Office Technologies (field of study).

ADMISSIONS: AN INTERNATIONAL PERSPECTIVE

The ways in which students are officially admitted to institutions of higher learning differ throughout the world. Although these differences manifest themselves primarily in specific requirements, they also grow out of circumstances such as limited availability of places and the structure of agencies empowered to grant admission.

Basic Requirements for Admission to Higher Education

Throughout the world the basic requirement for admission to higher education is the secondary school-leaving certificate, diploma, or equivalent. (Some countries offer a special form of admission for those who enroll with no intention of attaining a degree or diploma, but only degree-oriented programs will be considered here.)

In many countries this school-leaving certificate is awarded on two levels. For example, the French *baccalauréat* and the British General Certificate of Education (GCE)—advanced level affirm that a student has completed twelve or thirteen years of schooling and passed a terminal examination; the *brevet d'études du premier cycle* (BEPC) and the GCE—ordinary level indicate that he has completed only ten or eleven years and passed an examination on that level. The former certificates have traditionally been the prerequisite for admission to university-level education; the less demanding certificate has given access to nonuniversity higher education institutions. In some countries, such as the United States, where only one certificate—the high school diploma—is offered, the degree of achievement represented by that one diploma determines the level of education to which the student may aspire.

Since World War II, however, worldwide efforts have been increasing to offer alternatives to the secondary school-leaving examination and certificate and thereby broaden access to higher education. Whether the rationale is economic—greater access to higher education will increase the skilled manpower pool—or philosophical—higher education should not be the province of an elite class—the result has been the same. Both university and nonuniversity higher education institutions are granting admission to those who have not formally obtained the traditionally required secondary school-leaving certificate. Thus, the concept of equivalency—granting credit for nonformal or nontraditional education—has attained increasing importance.

The criterion of what constitutes equivalency varies and is perhaps most significant at the university level, where admission requirements have traditionally been stringent and access limited. At this level equivalency has often meant that the certificate is waived in favor of a substitute examination leading to an equivalent certificate. In the United States, for example, a student who is over eighteen and who has not completed secondary school may take a test administered by the state board of education under the General Educational Development program. Passing the test gives the student the equivalent of a secondary school-leaving certificate and allows access to most higher education institutions.

Equivalency examinations are often available to adults with work experience. In the Federal Republic of Germany, for instance, special examinations leading to university admission are provided for applicants who have work experience but have not completed secondary school. In France an examination may be given to candidates without the *baccalauréat* who are twenty years old by October 1 of the year of the examination and have two years of work experience. A similar scheme is followed in most of the former French African colonies, such as Senegal, Mali, and Togo. Norwegian universities waive entrance requirements for those over age twenty-five with five years of work experience; Swedish institutions, for those over age twenty-four with four years of work experience.

Requirement of the full secondary school-leaving certificate for university admission may also be waived in those countries that offer two-year preparatory programs within higher education institutions. Thus, in India students who do not complete the final two years of secondary schooling may take a university entrance examination to admit them into some universities for an intermediate course leading to an equivalent preuniversity certificate. In exceptional cases Yugoslavia will also waive the full secondary school-leaving certificate for those entering a two-year preparatory program within the university.

Increasingly common is horizontal transfer—the acceptance by a university of a nonuniversity higher education diploma or certificate as admission qualification to a first-degree program. In Ja-

maica, Barbados, and other participatory branches of the University of the West Indies, for example, students who hold certificates or diplomas from agricultural, teacher training, commercial, or technical institutions may apply for admission to the university. In Benin students completing the second cycle of the middle school or a comprehensive polytechnic school and employed persons who have received specialized training may be admitted to one of the specialized institutes of the university based on the decision of a council of guidance. A variation of this method occurs in Yugoslavia, where a student who has completed eight years of elementary schooling and has graduated from a school for skilled workers may, after an entrance examination, be admitted to a university faculty where the field of study corresponds to that of the school. As trained manpower becomes increasingly important in the 1970s, almost all countries are honoring some form of transfer system to universities from nonuniversity higher education institutions.

Still another form of equivalency is advanced placement, a policy whereby university students who score well on standard subject matter examinations may forgo at least some courses in those subjects as a requisite for obtaining their degrees. In the United States secondary school students who have demonstrated exceptional ability may be allowed to undertake college courses before completing their secondary education.

Admission requirements for nonuniversity higher education have generally been less stringent than those for universities. The ten-year school-leaving certificate or high school diploma, indicating a minimal mastery of academic subjects, is the usual prerequisite for admission to professional/technical/vocational and community college higher education. But this requirement in some countries may be waived, particularly in fields that the government deems of high priority because of manpower shortages.

Equivalency, then, represents a response to an increasing demand for higher education. Its privileges are often extended to those who are beyond the normal school-leaving age, and their work or life experience frequently is taken into consideration as a substitute for theoretical skills.

Open Admissions

The secondary school-leaving certificate or equivalent is often only a minimum requirement for admission to higher education in that it alone does not assure entry, particularly at the university level. When it does assure entry, the policy is known as open admissions.

Proponents of this policy contend that the preuniversity selection process is undemocratic or intellectually elitist and that all students should be given the opportunity to prove their ability in the college classroom. Such a notion is not without precedent. Proprietary colleges—privately owned institutions—have traditionally accepted some students without secondary school-leaving certificates or equivalent education. Many public nonuniversity institutions have also followed this policy, although vocational schools may impose some restrictions regarding fields of study pursued at the secondary level. At the university level open admission has generally been confined to correspondence universities, such as the University of South Africa, or to state universities with a populist tradition, such as those in the midwest and western United States.

In many instances, however, this apparent openness has been countered by fees which prohibit entry to less wealthy students. In other instances the school-leaving certificate has guaranteed automatic access provided it was earned at a particular type of secondary school. Thus, before the 1960s the German *Abitur* assured university entrance, but it could be earned only at the *Gymnasium*, a college-preparatory school where a rigid selection of students had already taken place.

Since World War II, the worldwide spread of secondary education, the opening of college preparatory schools to a wider range of students, and the initiation of equivalency have influenced the increase in the number of holders of the secondary school certificate. The concept of equal access has, thus, taken on new significance. Traditionally selective institutions—for example, the City University of New York—have sought to implement the idea. Although it has much to recommend it and certainly serves to provide as much education as possible to as many as wish it, open admissions faces obvious problems, including a lack of available facilities and staff, the divergence of staff energies toward remedial education, and the possible lowering of degree standards. The problems encountered in Italy are a case in point. There open admissions led to such a great influx of students that the government attempted to impose restrictions on university entrance, provoking strong resistance on the part of students who foresee these restrictions as a return of elitist education.

Other Modifications of Basic Requirements

Far more customary than open admissions is the retention of specific requirements for admission other than the secondary school-leaving certificate. These requirements may have their genesis in national, political, or economic considerations; historical tradition; or availability of space; in each case they serve to limit access.

Screening at the school level. The most common method of limiting access to higher education is to impose examinations at lower levels. In Kenya, for example, examinations are given at the termination of both primary and secondary levels. Only about 20 percent of primary school graduates go on to secondary schools; of that 20 percent, only 10 to 15 percent continue to higher education institutions.

Institutions may also require students to achieve a particular level of competence in a school-leaving examination before being considered for admission. This method of selectivity is most clearly illustrated in the British system, where the General Certificate of Education is granted at two levels, with universities considering only students at the advanced level. In addition, many universities prescribe the nature and number of subjects to be pursued at the advanced level. Thus, although students may have a school-leaving certificate, the additional requirements ultimately determine their access to the university.

Many of the other Commonwealth countries follow a similar selection system. Thus, a prerequisite for admission to higher education in West African nations such as Benin, the Gambia, Ghana, Nigeria, and Sierra Leone is a General Certificate of Education or a West African Examinations Council certificate. However, individual institutions may require a varying number of subjects at both the ordinary and advanced levels, with universities generally requiring more passes at the advanced level than nonuniversity institutions. In East Africa Kenya, Uganda, and Tanzania also follow the British model. The East African Examinations Council administers an ordinary-level examination which leads to the East African Certificate of Education and allows access to some professional nonuniversity higher education; a later examination leads to the East African Advanced Certificate, necessary for university admission. South African and Asian countries which have the same colonial heritage generally follow a similar system.

Many other countries also use level of success on school-leaving examinations as a restriction on admission. In countries subscribing to the pre-1960s' French system of secondary education, the subjects in which the *baccalauréat* is taken may limit access not only to higher education but also to particular fields of study. In Romania applicants with the highest marks on the *baccalauréat* examination receive priority admission to university study. In Sweden students applying to restricted fields of study, such as medicine, must have an average grade of more than 4 on a scale of 1 to 5 to be admitted.

A variation of this process occurs when institutions require, or give priority to, applicants who have focused on fields of study at the secondary level corresponding to those to be followed at the tertiary level. In the Netherlands, for instance, at least one subject at the preuniversity level must be relevant to the program studied at the university level. Admission to certain faculties is restricted, because of overcrowding, but selection is made only by a general lottery.

Entrance examinations. As a substitute for, or in addition to, secondary school-level achievement, many institutions of higher education require applicants to pass one or more entrance examinations. These examinations may be national or particular to the institution or faculty to which the student applies.

In the United States many institutions require students to achieve a particular score, determined by the institution, on nationally administered examinations of mathematical and verbal ability and of subject matter mastery prepared by the College Entrance Examination Board and the American College Testing Program. A similar system is used in the Philippines, where a National College Entrance Examination was first given in 1974. In Chile prior to 1966, university admission was contingent upon passing the *bachillerato* examination, but increasing dissatisfaction with the examination led to its replacement by a national academic achievement test, *Prueba de aptitud académica* (PAA). Admission to first-degree programs is now decided on the basis of a combination of grade point average in secondary school, scores on the PAA, and tests of specific knowledge.

More common than national examinations are institutional examinations. In Japan, only a limited number of students are allowed to continue secondary education into the tenth through the twelfth grades. Completion of grade 12 qualifies them to take a competitive entrance examination administered by the institution to which they apply. Similar competitive examinations are given in countries as diverse as Thailand, Brazil, Greece, India, Iran, Afghanistan, Spain, and Norway.

In almost all countries with some form of *numerus clausus,* or restricted admission, such as the Soviet Union, students are required to pass entrance examinations given by the faculty to which they desire admission. Often, as in Bangladesh, students who are rejected by one faculty may apply for entry to a program for which there is less demand.

Preparatory courses. Another method of limiting access to higher education is that of a preparatory program required for admission. In France, for instance, there is no limit placed on the number of students admitted to the universities; but other institutions, such as the *grandes écoles,* limit enrollment by a competitive examination open only to students who have completed a post-*baccalauréat* course of one to three years in designated preparatory schools. In Spain first-degree candidates must complete a preuniversity orientation course *(curso de orientación universitaria)* before being granted full admission.

Work requirements. Besides such academic requirements, many countries, particularly those in Eastern Europe and Asia, require that applicants complete a prescribed number of years of work. The constitution of the People's Republic of China stipulates that "cultural education and art, physical education, health work, and scientific work must all serve proletarian politics, serve workers, peasants, and soldiers, and be combined with proletarian labor," and China implements this policy by requiring that only students with several years of experience in production or the armed forces and with the recommendation of their fellow workers may be admitted to institutions of higher learning. The Soviet Union has a two-year work requirement for admission into most fields of study. In Poland students who have worked one

year in industry receive extra points on university entrance examinations. Bulgaria and Romania, among other countries with a Marxist-Leninist orientation, also have work requirements. Tanzania allows no students to enter higher education institutions before they have worked two years. The Scandinavian countries give credit for work experience in selecting students for higher education and require practical experience for admission to many fields of study, such as teacher training and engineering. Algeria, for example, while rejecting the Chinese system of mandatory work experience as too exclusive, admits only exceptionally gifted students without such experience.

Although work experience is probably the most common nonacademic admissions requirement throughout the world, others exist. There are age requirements in most countries. Applicants must be eighteen to enter an Austrian university, and few students under thirty are eligible for admission in the People's Republic of China. In general, the age requirement is based on the number of years normally needed to complete the secondary school requirement or work requirement. Students applying for admission to nonuniversity-level education may thus be younger than those applying for university-level education. In Hungary students, at age sixteen, may, in lieu of secondary or vocational schools, work part time for two years or attend a two-year continuation school for industrial or agricultural studies. Exceptions are made for particular cases, that is, advanced placement in the United States. At the other end of the scale, older students have also gained greater acceptance. For example, persons in Sweden who are over twenty-five years of age and have four years or more of work experience have access to the higher education institutions. Adult and continuing education programs, whereby a student may apply to higher education several years after receiving the secondary school certificate, have been increasing.

Language is generally a further prerequisite in that some evidence of proficiency in the language of instruction is required. Countries with a tradition of two languages present particular problems. In Pakistan, Saudi Arabia, the Sudan, and Sweden, students must prove their aptitude in English. In Algeria, Morocco, Syria, and Tunisia, the language of instruction is Arabic, but French may be required as a second language. Language proficiency may also be demanded for certain fields of study.

Discriminatory restrictions. Not infrequently, admissions are limited on a prejudicial basis. In South Africa a student must be white or have an official exemption to enter any of the white institutions, only black students are allowed into black institutions, and Asian students must attend institutions for students of Asian extraction. In Haiti a loyalty oath is a prerequisite to admission. In countries with a Muslim tradition exclusion may be based on both sex and religion. For example, in Saudi Arabia, only Muslim men can be admitted into the two Islamic universities; separate facilities exist for men and women at the secular University of Riyadh and at King Abdul Aziz University. Religious requirements also exist elsewhere. Thus, Vatican City allows non-Roman Catholics to enroll in its universities, but access may be difficult in certain fields of study.

Quotas

Since World War II, as nations have improved their secondary school systems and broadened their enrollments, there has been a worldwide increase in applications for higher education. This increase, coupled with policies to develop manpower in specific areas and lower the number of overeducated and unemployed, has led many countries and institutions to exercise greater control over admissions. The demand that applicants fulfill specific requirements is one kind of control; another is the imposition of quotas—the deliberate limiting of available spaces. Such limits may be imposed by governments, by government in conjunction with institutions, or by institutions alone.

In countries with strong central control of education, government quotas are important in the admission process. Most socialist nations have a quota system which is determined by the government with the cooperation of the higher education institutions, based on the economic needs of the country. In the Soviet Union the Ministry of Education, in consultation with specific institutions, determines how many and in which institutions spaces will be available to candidates. In Czechoslovakia the government similarly sets quotas in accordance with industry's production plans. In Bulgaria the Committee on Planning and the Committee for Science, Technical Progress, and Higher Education sets quotas, and in Hungary quotas are determined by the National Planning Office and concerned government agencies.

Although a country's economic need may be primary in determining space, it is not necessarily the only consideration. Both Sweden and Finland are concerned with balancing supply and demand in education as well as with serving all those interested in further studies and impose quotas only in certain overcrowded fields. Government-determined quotas may also exist in capitalist countries when overenrollment becomes a major problem. In Greece quotas are determined by the Ministry of Education in conjunction with specific institutions. In 1973 the Federal Republic of Germany decided that a *Zentralstelle für die Vergabe von Studienplätzen* (ZVS) should control admission to fields which were overenrolled. The committee that governs ZVS decides what fields require quotas and assigns places to students on the basis of their preferences and qualifications. If a student does not gain his choice, he may enter a related field that is not restricted or wait a semester and reapply.

Quotas may also be determined by institutions without government intervention.

In the Netherlands, where universities enjoy a high degree of autonomy, limits are determined by faculties or institutions solely in terms of capacity. Most universities and nonuniversity institutions in the United States similarly determine their own enrollment limits.

In most cases a quota system is used to exclude students; however, it may be an inclusive policy. In India, for example, a proportion of places are reserved in higher education institutions for women and students of special castes or tribes, who need meet only minimum qualifications for enrollment. Since the passage of civil rights legislation in the United States, many universities have reserved places for disadvantaged groups, particularly blacks and Hispanics.

Agencies of Admission

World differences in admissions practice also extend to application procedures. In general, three major application systems can be distinguished.

Some countries, especially those with quotas imposed by the central government, rely on a national admissions agency. Students in the Federal Republic of Germany send applications to ZVS, not to the universities, and indicate their choices of university and field of study in order of preference. ZVS verifies their academic qualifications and then assigns them to an institution and a field of study. Great Britain has a similar system. Admission to first-degree courses in such universities as Oxford, Sussex and Queens in Northern Ireland is sought through the Universities Central Council on Admissions (UCCA). UCCA, operating as a clearinghouse for student applications, matches the universities with the applicant pool. Each faculty or college then evaluates and selects students directed to it through UCCA. Where university admission requirements are government controlled and fairly standardized, applications procedures present few problems.

In other countries students apply directly to the institution to which they seek admission, even if admission is more or less controlled by government authority. In the Soviet Union final selections are made by institutional admissions committees, which include a member of the governing body of the institution and representatives of the local party, the government, trade unions, general education schools, and the student body. In the United States, although institutions may use nationally administered entrance examinations, such as those of the College Entrance Examination Board, to screen candidates, they jealously guard their right to make final admissions selections. Thus, to assure acceptance students must make multiple applications and adapt each one to the institution's specific priorities.

In still other countries, such as most francophone African and many Latin American nations, students make application to a specific faculty within an institution. In the Netherlands students apply to both a university and a specific faculty and if the specific application is refused, they may apply to another faculty. In India, however, rejection by a specific faculty constitutes university rejection, and the student must wait until the following year to reapply.

Admission to Graduate Education

In general, admission to graduate programs awarding second- and third-level degrees is contingent on acquiring the first or undergraduate degree. But just as the secondary school-leaving certificate or equivalent does not assure entry into higher education, so the first degree does not assure acceptance into advanced education.

Admission to graduate programs is usually based on performance at the first-degree level and may be limited to students who have pursued a related field during their undergraduate specialization. In addition, a graduate entrance examination may be required, such as the Graduate Record Examination in the United States, or a test of professional aptitude for programs such as law, medicine, and business.

Although admission to doctoral programs often requires not only the first but also a second degree, the latter requirement is frequently waived, and students fulfilling admission requirements for the second degree can be admitted directly into doctoral programs. During the 1960s, when a shortage of doctoral candidates was anticipated, some institutions in the United States even recruited unusually gifted applicants directly from secondary school into programs designed to grant Ph.D. degrees in six years with provision for bachelor's and master's degrees as an option within the program. Other exceptions exist as well. In the Netherlands, for instance, where undergraduate university education may last as long as eight years, graduate students seeking the doctoral degree must only find a mentor willing to supervise their research and dissertation for admission to doctoral study.

Nontraditional Higher Education Institutions

The requirements and limitations discussed so far apply to admission into traditional university or nonuniversity education. Many countries also award certificates, diplomas, or even a first degree in programs which are outside traditional higher education. In the Soviet Union a large proportion of enrollment in higher education is in part-time correspondence or evening programs, where admission requirements are the same as those of the full-time student, with an additional year of study to compensate for the difference of hours. The Open University in Great Britain, which has no formal admission requirements, is designed for students who are over age twenty-one and who do not have access to the regular universities. This degree-granting institution, geared to those who need greater flexibility in their programs of study, makes use of televised lectures, regional tutorial centers, and independent work. The Federal Republic of Germany also provides alternatives to regular university study in cooperative education programs offered through the universities and in correspondence courses. In 1975 it created an open university similar to Great Britain's in the North Rhine–Westphalia area. These examples of nontraditional institutions demonstrate the ways in which higher education is becoming increasingly available to students and society through greater flexibility and openness of access.

Bibliography

Admission Policy in Swedish Postsecondary Education. Stockholm: Organisation for Economic Co-operation and Development, 1973.

Australian Universities Commission Fifth Report. Canberra: Australian Government Publishing Service, 1972.

"Black and Other Minority Admissions to Large Universities. A Four Year National Survey of Policies and Outcomes." *Research in Higher Education,* 1974, *2,* 221–230.

Bouen, L. (Ed.) *Higher Education in Egypt— 1974.* Washington, D.C.: American Friends of the Middle East, 1975.

Brickman, W. W. *Educational Reform and Renewal in Contemporary Spain.* Washington, D.C.: U.S. Government Printing Office, 1972.

Carbone, R. F. "Too Many Students!" *Chronicle of Higher Education,* March 17, 1975, p. 24.

"Changes in Higher Education in the People's Republic of China." *Higher Education,* 1975, *4*(1), 45–60.

Clark, D. O., and Mertz, R. *The Coastal Countries of the Arabian Peninsula: Kuwait, Bahrain, Qatar, United Arab Emirates, Sultanate of Oman, People's Democratic Republic of Yemen, and Yemen Arab Republic: A Study of the Educational Systems and a Guide to the Academic Placement of Students in United States Educational Institutions.* Washington, D.C.: American Association of Collegiate Registrars and Admissions Officers, 1974.

Development of Higher Education 1950–1967. Paris: Organisation for Economic Co-operation and Development, 1970.

"Facilitating Minority Admissions: Some Legal Considerations." *College and University,* 1973, *48*(3), 171–176.

Frey, J. S. *Turkey: A Study of the Educational System of Turkey and a Guide to the Academic Placement of Students from Turkey in United States Educational Institutions.* Washington, D.C.: American Association of Collegiate Registrars and Admissions Officers, 1972.

Greek Ministry of National Education and Religion, General Directorate of General Education. *Education in Greece.* Athens: National Printing Office, 1973.

Harrell, W. A. *The Brazilian Education System: A Summary.* Washington, D.C.: U.S. Government Printing Office, 1970.

Hefling, J. *Libya: A Study of the Educational System of the Libyan Arab Republic and a Guide to the Academic Placement of Students from Libya in United States Educational Institutions.* Washington, D.C.: American Association of Collegiate Registrars and Admissions Officers, 1972.

Henderson, R. M. *Colombia.* World Education Series. Washington, D.C.: U.S. Government Printing Office, 1974.

"Higher Education in China." *Social Policy,* 1974, *5*(4), 30–37.

Jarmon, H., Ellsworth, G., and Patrick, W. S. *Republic of Vietnam.* World Education Series. Washington, D.C.: American Association of Collegiate Registrars and Admissions Officers, 1970.

Kompetenskommittén. *Om behörighet och antagning till högskolan.* Stockholm: Statens offentliga utredningar, Utbildningsdepartementet, 1974.

Korea. World Education Series. Washington, D.C.: American Association of Collegiate Registrars and Admissions Officers, 1967.

Open Tertiary Education. Draft Report of the Committee on Open University to the Australian Commission. Canberra: Australian Government Publishing Service, 1974.

"Planning for Universal Access in the Context of Uncertainty." *Higher Education,* 1975, *4*(1), 1–82.

Renner, R. R. *Education for a New Colombia.* Washington, D.C.: U.S. Government Printing Office, 1971.

"Restricted Admissions in Switzerland." *Change,* 1974, *6*(9), 14–17.

"Rethinking the University in Latin America." *Prospects,* 1974, *4*(3), 315–333.

Slocum, J. B. *Iran: A Study of the Educational System and Guide to the Admission and Academic Placement of Iranian Students in Colleges and Universities in the United States.* Washington, D.C.: American Association of Collegiate Registrars and Admissions Officers, 1970.

Wagner, E. *The United Arab Republic: A Study of the Educational System of the United Arab Republic and a Guide to the Academic Placement of Students from the United Arab Republic in United States Educational Institutions.* Washington, D.C.: American Association of Collegiate Registrars and Admissions Officers, 1970.

"Widening the Base for Higher Education: A Study of Scandinavian Institutions." *Western European Education,* 1974, *2*(6), 3–85.

JOHN A. CURRY
PHYLLIS M. SCHAEN

See also: Access of Minorities; Access to Higher Education; Articulation: Europe; Articulation: United States; Credit, Assessment of Learning for Postsecondary Education; Examinations and Tests.

ADULT EDUCATION

1. OVERVIEW—A GLOBAL PERSPECTIVE

2. ADMINISTRATION

3. GOVERNMENT PROGRAMS

4. ROLE OF LABOR AND INDUSTRY

5. ADULT EDUCATION IN DEVELOPING COUNTRIES

6. ELDERLY, PROGRAMS FOR THE

7. POSTEXPERIENCE EDUCATION

1. OVERVIEW—A GLOBAL PERSPECTIVE

Throughout history a few adults in each generation and in each culture have consciously tried to further their education by one means or another, but only since World War II has adult education emerged as an explicitly designated social institution and assumed worldwide importance. In every country adult education has tended to evolve in response to ad hoc stimuli, without reference to any agreed philosophy or national plan. As a result, it presents a variety of forms, and, as yet, there is no universally accepted definition of its nature or functions. Adult education in one country seldom corresponds to its counterpart in another country. However, when one looks closely at the ways in which adults consciously pursue their learning, one sees no lack of cross-cultural similarity. The task is to find a formula for describing adult education in a way that makes it possible to discuss trends, issues, and problems in an intelligible global context.

In recent times this task has been undertaken both by UNESCO and by professional adult educators. UNESCO has sponsored, at intervals of approximately ten years, three international conferences (Elsinore, Denmark, 1949; Montreal, Quebec, 1960; Tokyo, Japan, 1972); at each one, notable progress was made in clarifying the aims and functions of adult education. Professional adult educators, based largely in university departments, have gone far to establish adult education as a discrete field of study within the overall field of education.

For purely statistical purposes it is reasonable to use the UNESCO International Standard Classification of Education (ISCED) definition: "Adult Education . . . is synonymous with 'out-of-school' education and means education provided for the benefit, and adapted to the needs, of persons not in the regular school and university system and generally fifteen and older" *(Proposals for the Collection of Adult Education Statistics, 1974)*. However, to cover all educational experiences deliberately designed for adults, one needs a more comprehensive definition, such as that adopted by the Organisation for Economic Co-operation and Development (OECD): "Adult education refers to any activity or programme deliberately designed by a providing agent to satisfy any learning need or interest that may be experienced at any stage in his or her life by a person who is over the statutory school-leaving age and whose principal activity is no longer in education. Its ambit spans non-vocational, vocational, general, formal and non-formal studies as well as education with a collective social purpose" (OECD, 1975).

The OECD definition embodies two clarifying principles: (1) an adult is considered to be a person who is over the applicable school-leaving age in his country and who is not a full-time student, and (2) adult education is concerned, not with adventitious learning, but with sequential studies planned and monitored by an agent. An advantage of the OECD interpretation is that it embraces nonformal as well as formal education. One of the national goals of adult education is to enable adults to complete their formal academic education up to a desired level. Commonly, though not necessarily, this is done by offering courses directly parallel to those offered by the formal system. Some countries give top priority to primary or basic education, some to secondary education, and some to postsecondary education. Apart from vocational training, adult education seeks to satisfy a wide variety of nonformal learning needs outside established educational institutions. In addition, adult education can be pursued informally through the mass media or group activities.

Providing Agencies

The unplanned development of adult education has fostered a broad range of providing agencies. Three major distinctions among such agencies can be drawn. One is between governmental (or public) and nongovernmental (or private) agencies. Broadly speaking, private agencies predominated in virtually all countries until after World War II. By 1975 all countries were making at least some direct provision for the education of adults, but the extent of this provision varied greatly. In many developing countries and in those with autocratic regimes, adult education tends to be a tacit or explicit monopoly of the state; in others, nongovernmental agencies continue to flourish. At the same time, whether or not it is the chief providing agent, the state usually ensures that the overall provision is adequate and, where it is not, may itself subsidize nongovernmental agencies.

A second important distinction is between profit and nonprofit agencies. Viewing adult education as an important social service, many agencies eschew profit making and, as far as possible, try to keep down or altogether suppress charges to participants. Other agencies, however, have always existed for the purpose of financial gain, including many correspondence schools and the extension units of private universities. In addition, a large group of agencies, while scorning profits, are obliged to be self-financing.

A third distinction is the nature of the agency's commitment. Many agencies, such as the Folk High Schools in Denmark and the Workers' Educational Associations in Sweden and the United Kingdom, exist solely for the purpose of providing education to adults. Many basically noneducational organizations, such as the military services, many trade unions, some industrial and commercial enterprises, women's clubs, and a host of other voluntary associations, treat adult education as a vital secondary aim. Other agencies, such as religious bodies, political parties, and health and welfare agencies, include a specific educational purpose among their aims or use education as one means of achieving their aims. One set of agencies—notably, libraries—may generically be termed auxiliaries of adult education, since they enrich and sometimes directly service the work of other agencies. Finally, a little-known world of clubs, societies, and amenity groups that undoubtedly provide learning opportunities for their members flourishes in many communities.

As already observed, the provision of adult education has traditionally been unevenly distributed. Since about 1960 the situation has perceptibly changed because of two factors: increasing intervention of the public authorities, and steps taken by the agencies themselves to coordinate their efforts.

State intervention is most conspicuous in the developing countries. Faced with the challenge of nation building, these countries are obliged to take stock of the available physical and human resources and to ensure that they are harnessed in pursuit of developmental goals; these countries, in other words, wish to directly control the education of the adult population. Simultaneously, such countries perceive that development cannot be achieved without popular understanding of the government's aims and problems and without

increasing the efficiency of the labor force, especially in rural areas. Since bringing about the required level of understanding and improving occupational skills clearly necessitate active learning, public authorities in developing countries are giving priority to national schemes for the education of adults to a degree that has been rare even in industrially advanced countries.

If industrially advanced countries do not closely relate adult education to their economic and social policies, they nevertheless accord it higher priority than in the past because of their increasing desire to promote social justice. Many governments now accept, in principle, that all adults should have the right to reach almost any educational level to which they aspire and certainly to complete the upper-secondary or first-degree cycle. Moreover, government authorities and many employers have come to realize that, in the present age of rapid social and technological change, education has become a lifelong process. This is particularly true of vocational education. Men and women in the work force are continually obliged to learn new skills and to adapt to new conditions, either to perform their jobs more effectively or to be reabsorbed into the labor market. An efficient economy calls for a mobile and versatile working population; hence, opportunities must be provided for workers to upgrade themselves or to transfer to different types of jobs. Although occupational training is their first concern, public authorities are also showing more interest in the potentiality of adult education as an instrument for dealing with social problems.

The moment that a state begins to accord adult education higher priority, it is obliged to ensure that facilities are more equitably distributed. Since World War II many countries have witnessed serious attempts to rationalize and expand the existing provision—attempts that have been greatly facilitated by a notable improvement in the administrative competence of existing agencies and by their ability to collaborate with public authorities.

Factors that can be identified among

current measures to rationalize and expand adult education provisions include the formulation of national policies, enactment of legislation, creation of coordinating mechanisms, financial innovations, provision of accommodation, and staff development.

National planning is inevitably associated more with developing than with developed countries; most developing countries include at least a reference to the role of adult education in their long-term national development plans. In addition, some developing countries (for example, Peru and Tanzania) have devised nationwide adult education systems, centrally administered and controlled. And, while only a minority of countries has nationwide plans, the great majority has at least enunciated a policy toward adult education. Sometimes the policy is expressed in abstract terms and amounts to no more than a declaration of intent. Certain countries (for example, Yugoslavia) specify that public authorities shall provide adult education and give some indication of the resources to be made available.

Those dedicated either politically or professionally to the expansion of learning opportunities for adults argue with rising insistence, that mandatory enabling legislation is an essential prerequisite. In practice, legislation is on the increase, though still relatively weak and permissive. The one sector of adult education that has clearly benefited from legislation is vocational training; some countries give employees the right to paid educational leave. Laws have also been enacted entitling illiterates to attend literacy classes during working hours and requiring all public institutions to offer their facilities to adult education classes at times when they are not required for their primary purpose.

The need for effective coordinating mechanisms is now almost universally acknowledged, although in practice the rule of the jungle still prevails in many countries. At the national level, one of two mechanisms is used: a statutory board or a national association. Statutory boards have been established primarily in developing

countries; the Adult Education Board of Kenya is often cited as a model. Consisting of representatives of government ministries, adult agencies, employers, trade unions, and miscellaneous interest groups, the function of such boards is to draw up a national scheme for allocating and overseeing the use of resources and for ensuring maximum coordination and minimum duplication among agencies. In the United Kingdom and the United States, national associations date from the earlier part of the twentieth century. What distinguishes the recent past is the proliferation of national associations, the diversification of their functions, and the increasing sophistication of their operational behavior. These associations, which commonly receive government support, contain representatives of all the agencies directly or indirectly concerned with adult education. Their efficacy as pressure groups varies considerably according to national circumstances, but all contribute substantially to the overall growth of learning opportunities for adults.

Coordination at the local level is ultimately even more important than national coordination but is also far more neglected, probably because associations usually employ full-time officials at the national and not at the local level. Nevertheless, in many localities adult education committees play a significant coordinating role.

Economic Factors

The economics of adult education is a twilight zone that researchers are just beginning to explore. The gravest weakness of adult education is its unstable financial base. It is a frequent complaint that, when economic blizzards blow, adult education is the first sector to be left to the wolves. The reason why researchers neglect the economic factor seems to be the practical difficulty of obtaining reliable data. Such data as are available from ministries of education show unequivocally that public expenditure on adult education represents only a small fraction of the expenditure on education in general. The picture is blurred in many countries by the fact that other sectors of government—notably agriculture and labor but also sometimes health and community development—may well devote large sums to specific forms of adult education. In the last analysis, however, the evidence is overwhelming that public expenditure on all forms of adult education is slight, except in those few countries (such as Norway, Sweden, and Tanzania) with a deliberate policy to the contrary.

In certain industrially advanced countries, such as the United States, the aggregate expenditure on adult education by nongovernmental agencies is far greater than that by public authorities; however, the greater part of this expenditure is borne by industrial and commercial firms in training employees. Adult education agencies in general are constantly struggling to remain afloat financially.

In a number of industrially advanced countries, such as Austria and Sweden, and in a few developing countries, such as Nigeria, public authorities encourage the provision of adult education by nongovernmental agencies. Acknowledging that these agencies perform a service that would otherwise fall to government, public authorities generally help defray the total nongovernmental expenditure. The practice whereby government authorities finance specific nongovernmental programs judged to be social priorities—for example, those concerned with literacy or community development—is also spreading.

Staffing

Adult education cannot be expanded beyond a certain level in the absence of professionally qualified staff. Recognizing this requirement, public authorities and nongovernmental agencies alike are striving to build up cadres of full-time personnel. Traditionally, adult education services were planned and administered largely by part-time staff, many of whom worked on a purely voluntary basis. There are still far more part-time and voluntary workers than full-time ones, although the number

of full-time staff has increased spectacularly since the mid 1960s. Consequently, there has been a determined drive to define the functions of administrators and organizers more precisely and to create a profession of adult educators; this growing body of professionals is attempting to strengthen the field in all its aspects and to exert influence on policymakers and on public opinion. In a given country there is a manifest correlation between the size of the full-time staff and the overall well-being of adult education.

The expansion of full-time staff has also led to a demand for the introduction or expansion of professional training courses. Adult education departments in universities used to be rare. In 1975 it was argued that there were not enough of them, and although some countries still have no facilities, university training courses for adult educators are steadily expanding in most countries. These vary from the long and advanced courses leading to a Doctor of Philosophy in North America to the intensive one-year course typical of British practice. Courses are supplemented by numerous professional conferences, seminars, and workshops, chiefly designed for practicing adult educators.

On the whole the teaching of adults is still a part-time pursuit. The number of full-time teachers, however, appears to be growing rapidly in occupational training. In addition, a significant trend developing in some countries—for example, Kenya and the Philippines—includes the appointment of full-time teachers and the creation of institutions solely or partially designed for adults.

Research and International Cooperation

Adult education is being identified as a sector of education worthy of systematic investigation for three reasons: (1) the professionalization of adult education and the spread of training courses; (2) a new (though as yet small) official demand for more information about the education of adults as a social phenomenon; and (3) the curiosity of certain scholars. Some research into adult education is being conducted outside the universities, but for the most part it is a university preserve. As a rule, university departments of adult education are expected to perform the dual function of providing professional training courses and undertaking research. After 1960 the amount of research increased considerably, which led to progress in fixing parameters for the field and in defining its nature.

A combination of factors, including the desire of researchers to build on knowledge accumulated in other countries, has recently intensified the process of internationalizing adult education. International cooperation takes several forms: information exchange, regional and intercontinental conferences, educator visits, and bilateral and multilateral schemes. The Federal Republic of Germany, for example, has made a specialty of giving aid to selected projects in selected countries. The impact of these forms of international cooperation is illustrated by the outstanding success of the Third International Conference on Adult Education, held in Tokyo in 1972 under the sponsorship of UNESCO, and by the foundation in 1973 of the International Council for Adult Education.

Major Issues

The various trends described above indicate that adult education is currently expanding at an unprecedented rate. Nevertheless, many major issues and problems remain. The most serious issue concerns the composition of the clientele. In nearly all countries the majority of adult education agencies were established to provide assistance to adults who had not been able to benefit much, if at all, from initial schooling, and it is still widely believed that adult education should mainly serve the interests of the underprivileged. In reality, however, the evidence about participation furnished by country after country, regardless of ideological or geographical factors, shows conclusively that those who would appear to need most help participate least in the

available programs. The more initial education people receive, the more they seek further education; the less education they receive, the less they seek it. Consequently, the main contemporary challenge facing adult education is to avoid the trap of reinforcing privilege by ensuring that the interests of the needy as well as the privileged are properly served.

A second issue concerns the relationship between adult education and the regular or formal system of education. In general, adult education is either administered separately from the state educational system or occupies a peripheral position. Many adult educators are convinced that it is disastrous for their field to be administratively controlled by the formal system because it is always treated as a poor relation, starved of resources and leadership. At the same time, there is a trend to break down the rigidity of existing educational structures at all levels and to move, however tentatively, toward systems of recurrent or lifelong education. In these new circumstances it would seem politically desirable, depending on each national situation, to integrate adult education with other educational services. The necessary preconditions are that adult education be guaranteed structural security, room for growth, and effective machinery to ensure constructive interaction between it and the regular system.

A third issue concerns the scope of the learning opportunities to be offered. Demands for the introduction of recurrent education systems and for the expansion of adult education are largely inspired by governmental desire to extend formal education opportunities to adults and to increase provision for occupational training. There is a danger that other forms of adult education—above all, nonvocational liberal studies and community development, the very forms that were dominant in the past—will in the future be neglected by public authorities. Such neglect would most likely mean that the needs of many adults would be met only by nonformal programs and the judicious use of the mass media. In other words, emphasis on formal education and occupational training militates against the extension of learning opportunities to the whole spectrum of social groups.

Many other issues and problems face adult education, largely because its scope is wide; the administrative, financial, and institutional structures presently sustaining it are imperfect; and its links with other social activities are sketchy. These weaknesses, however, arise mainly from its dramatic growth. In nearly all countries adult education has suddenly come of age. The challenge before it now is how to consolidate its rapid achievements.

Bibliography

Hely, A. S. M. *New Trends in Adult Education: From Elsinore to Montreal.* Paris: UNESCO, 1962.

Huberman, A. M. *Some Models of Adult Learning and Adult Change.* Strasbourg, France: Council of Europe, 1972.

Learning Opportunities for Adults. Paris: OECD, 1975.

Lowe, J. *The Education of Adults: A World Perspective.* Paris: UNESCO, 1975.

Proposals for the Collection of Adult Education Statistics. Paris: UNESCO, 1974.

Recurrent Education: A Strategy for Lifelong Learning. Paris: OECD, 1973.

A Retrospective International Survey of Adult Education: Montreal to Tokyo. Paris: UNESCO, 1972.

Simpson, J. A. *Today and Tomorrow in European Adult Education.* Strasbourg, France: Council of Europe, 1972.

Third International Conference: Final Report. Paris: UNESCO, 1972.

JOHN LOWE

2. ADMINISTRATION

Any contributor to a discussion of adult education must necessarily preface his observations with a comment on the subject's diversity. Three or four decades ago, adult education—at least in North America, the United Kingdom, and parts of Western Europe—would have been seen as a rather elitist exercise for a self-selecting minority intent on furthering an already substantial

formal education. By the mid 1970s, however, education for adults had become much more widely based in a variety of life contexts, such as employment, health, home and family, recreation, culture, community, and retirement. With all its diversity and vast growth, the majority of informed opinion—not least that of concerned administrators—would agree that the normative position of adult education, described so graphically by Clark (1958) as "marginal," is entirely unsatisfactory for the needs of modern societies the world over. Organizations such as UNESCO, the Organisation for Economic Co-operation and Development (OECD), and the World Bank have advocated radical alternatives to the "front-end" or "apprenticeship" model of educational systems, with indicative terms, such as *lifelong, recurrent,* and *continuing.* There are discernible trends—not least those of new labor market requirements and popular demand—of a slow evolution toward the adoption of these new models. Nevertheless, the basic reality for most administrators still requires the exercise of utmost ingenuity in maneuvering around the margins of educational expenditure and in exploiting the varieties of existing resources in order to provide for the growing demand for education in later life.

For the most part this essay assumes that marginality, or at best peripherality, is the order of the day, whatever the base for administrative action—national, provincial, local, special-interest organization, university, or college. Indeed, many long-established traditional institutions solely committed to educational provision for adults—such as the Danish Folk High Schools or the Workers' Educational Associations in such countries as Australia, New Zealand, Canada, India, Egypt, Israel, Ghana, Sierra Leone, and those of Western Europe—find their resource situation threatened as their increasing dependence on the public purse places them on the fringe of educational benefits dominated by the escalating costs of formal schooling.

Providing Systems

In a world overview of administrative practice, it is necessary to consider the various broad patterns or systems adopted according to national or local circumstances. It should be understood that these are not mutually exclusive (nor exhaustive); indeed there is evidence in several instances of beneficial compatibility where two or more operate in a given area, especially in areas of particularly pressing need.

Educational subsystem. An educational subsystem exists when there is a legal acceptance—by nation, state, or province—of the need to provide education for adult people. However, the scale, scope, or range of such a subsystem is frequently not fixed; the subsystem depends upon the use of existing educational plant and personnel at times when they are not being used by the major educational system. Examples of educational subsystems include the adult education work of British extension and adult education divisions and of Canadian community colleges, as well as the legally required extension divisions of public universities and technical and agricultural institutions in many parts of the world. An exception in style (although not in essence) is exemplified by the German Adult Education Association *(Deutscher Volkshochschul-Verband:* DVV), which is officially in charge of adult education in several of the states of the Federal Republic of Germany and which represents at federal level the interests of the adult education centers *(Volkshochschulen).*

Cooperating network. The essential notion in this approach is that of cooperation between a wide diversity of special interests to promote and provide for the essential educational dimension required in each. Thus, health services, social work, agricultural extension, and technical services, as well as overtly educational organizations, are brought together in a series of planning exercises and cooperative projects. This model was strongly advocated in a report prepared by a United Kingdom commission, chaired by Lionel Russell, entitled *Adult Education: A Plan for Development.* The report proposed the establishment of national, regional, and local development councils composed of several organizations and suggested that the various levels of government be required to service and fund the councils and their work. A similar broad front policy was advocated by the International Commission for the Development of Education, chaired by Edgar Faure *(Learning to Be,* 1973).

Special project. The Health Education Project in Tanzania, the Program on Agricultural Credit and Cooperation in Afghanistan, the Training Opportunities Scheme in the United Kingdom, and the Adult Basic Education Program in the United States are all examples of special projects. Such projects promise the greatest growth rate in education for adults. All these programs reflect a national political commitment toward a relatively narrow, clearly definable, educational objective. This political commitment is a crucial prerequisite for program funding. Many such projects are highly cost-effective, since little capital expenditure is involved and existing professional personnel and volunteers are deployed. A small, mobile cadre of organizers/trainers is essential; often, centrally produced learning materials, including broadcast media programs, are used.

Critics of these rather narrow, unilateral educational interventions point out that they tend to disregard related strands of growth, learning, and development. However, if care is taken about cooperative modes of operation, and if a substantial period of training and network building is allowed, such projects can be most effective, as evaluations in both Tanzania and Brazil—with the Brazilian Literacy Movement *(Movimento brasileiro de alfabetização:* MOBRAL)—have revealed.

Polyvalent team project. Clearly, all previously discussed models have involved, to a greater or lesser extent, team concepts in the management of staff and resources.

What is implied here, however, is not merely a cooperative effort toward agreed educational objectives, but an institution, agency, or service whose total efforts are primarily geared toward economic or social ends utilizing varied instrumental educational procedures to achieve those ends. Examples are the Polyvalent Centers in Italy, the inner-urban community development projects in the United Kingdom, the Brigade Centers in Botswana, and the Village Polytechnics in Kenya and India. The major management problems in these enterprises tend to be at the local rather than the national level. For example, projects may have difficulties in gaining the acceptance of local power groups, may encounter resource problems (where they depend on regional and local finance and distribution networks), and may be in danger of becoming a prop for local dependence rather than a stimulus to local self-help. Nevertheless, most known examples have shown impressive contributions in their respective areas. The general administrative role in polyvalent projects subsumes many elements. The most obvious element is that of control: the systematic carrying out of agreed policy, checks on efficiency of the organization, and proper public accountability for financial expenditure. Another element, often not fully understood, is the political aspect: sensibility to the nuances of national, regional, or local political power bases; the ability to handle committees and special interest groups; and the ability to work with peers and colleagues. Finally, perhaps most neglected, is the crucial development element: when essentially dynamic purposes and objectives have been defined, it is necessary to continually evaluate the changing needs of individuals, communities, and societies, so that appropriate changes in the disposition of resources can be made.

Modes of Operation

Some essential administrative principles relating to the broad generic patterns of adult education must also be considered.

Cooperation. It is clear that cooperation is a basic mode of operation, much more so than in many other areas of public administration. Administrators of educational services must provide students with numerous lateral connections and networks, and frequently these will not be part of the educational hierarchy or tradition. Much of the labor force will be part time, paraprofessional, or voluntary. Many projects will require an alliance between central and local government departments and voluntary community organizations, the latter with long-developed traditions and mores and strongly defended independence. But the "cost of cooperation," cited by economists and systems analysts, can be considerable.

Identification of program needs. Another key preoccupation for managers of adult education services is the identification of needs for appropriate program planning. Over the years various procedures have been adopted for this purpose: documented social indicators, local pilot questionnaires, social network analyses, public meetings, student or consumer committees, recommendations from other social organizations in closer contact and frequent dialog with particular areas or strata or subcultures—plus inspired guesswork. Ideally, the comprehensive neighborhood service should have responsible managers involved in all segments of the community so that they are informed—directly or indirectly—of its needs and demands, growth points and deprivations. But again, such personal involvement is often heavily time-consuming, a fact that middle management must consider when devising job specifications and work schedules for field staff.

Recruitment and development. Staff recruitment and development—encompassing selection, orientation, training, pastoral care, and field appraisal—are major administrative concerns. Most adult education services depend on a small but vital cadre of full-time organizers and leaders. Thus, the management responsibility in this aspect of the enterprise is particularly critical. High motivation, flexibility, and a modicum of social skills are important considerations in the recruitment and development of staff. Unfortunately, the development of administrative staff is frequently neglected or underresourced. Clearly, if the mobilization, basic training, and subsequent deployment of the armies of part-time paraprofessionals and volunteers are to be successfully accomplished, the highest importance must attach to the full-time field professionals. Career structures and pay scales, however, frequently encourage the best field personnel to aim for administrative positions, where their talents are not as relevant or as effective.

Feedback systems. Feedback systems are increasingly important as part of quality control and improvement and as part of a more participatory management style. Student councils, wide-ranging representation on governing bodies, community consultative committees, self-programing groups—all have their place in modern adult education services. More rigorous evaluation procedures are also employed by some agencies and institutions, particularly in special projects, where the objectives can be more clearly defined.

Impact of external factors. Numerous incidental and instrumental factors impinge on the administration of adult education. These are the outcome of national or local cultural traditions, economic circumstances, and political realities. Two such factors are paid educational leave and entry requirements for particular professional qualification programs. In some fifty countries of the world, there is either legislation or a large-scale collective agreement whereby adult workers in varieties of productive employment are released for educational or training purposes without loss of normal remuneration. Where such enactments take place, the pressure on existing services grows substantially.

Similarly, the task is greatly complicated when independent professional bodies see fit to vary their qualification requirements, frequently inhibiting or at least hindering adults' involvement and progress. Occasionally, where enlightened discussion has preceded administrative diktat, reforms in program sequencing—modular structures, transferable credit accumulation, preparation or link courses—actually assist the adult education manager better to serve the needs of the people.

In this latter respect, the cooperation of the broadcast media—both radio and television—can also greatly aid the adult education manager. Too often the broadcasting authorities are either utterly indifferent to educational concerns or else so obsessed with their own educational presentations as to preclude the possibility of advertising others. A government statute or charter requiring full cooperation between educator and broadcaster can be an instrumental factor in achieving adult educational goals.

Planning and finance. No plan is worthy of the name if its cost implications—including cost-benefit and cost-effectiveness—are not included. Planning in other fields of administration is often seen as a logistical, demographical, quasi-mathematical exercise. And, for certain adult education special projects, techniques such as planned program budgeting (PPB) systems analysis and rate-of-return analyses have been employed. However, for most adult education administrators, planning and finance are essentially political exercises, involving skills such as lobbying, persuasion, social engineering, and, often, exploitation of willing subordinates and staff. Many general services for adults are financed on the margins of educational budgets, subject to annual scrutiny and revision. At best such revision can produce a steady incremental development toward planned service levels or objectives; at worst it can require savage interdepartmental in-fighting for scarce, sometimes shrinking, financial resources. In all these circumstances success depends on the adult education administrator's familiarity with the political-financial process and its executive machinery at all levels.

Much of the effort to improve the administration of adult education has been in technical areas, such as program planning, multipurpose plant usage, and staff training. More recently the "manpower requirement" approach has been more in evidence, as government and labor market bodies have perceived the paramount importance of training (and retraining) to keep pace with rapidly changing technologies. It would be foolish to ignore these efforts, as there are obvious national, even supranational, developmental needs implicit in this notion. However, most known manpower planning trials have exhibited severe conceptional limitations plus great difficulties of practical application, and some notorious mistakes have resulted.

As with "rate-of-return" approaches to educational planning, the economic models currently available have not been adequate to cope with the large number of uncontrollable variables inherent in the educational enterprise. Cohort analysis provides a more promising approach to planning, particularly if genuine recurrent or continuing systems are to be introduced. In this technique planning is based not on the proportion of population enrolled in and processed by the education system but on the major steps in the life cycle of all groups, whether graduates, dropouts, or nonjoiners. Thus, formal, nonformal, and informal programs can be viewed as equal, viable sections of a single integrated learning system, to which formal and nonformal adult education would be central.

There are known alternative systems of education, as previously mentioned, in which recurrent or continuing education is the central focus. In such systems the education of adults is accorded the highest priority by the state and other groups in society. Attempts on the part of administrators to bring about such universal support for adult learning requires an effort of imagination, political will, and professional development that is perhaps the greatest adult education program of all.

Bibliography

Bryan, A. (Ed.) *The Organisation of Adult Education: A Critical Analysis.* Leicester, England: City of Leicester Polytechnic, 1970.

Clark, B. R. "The Marginality of Adult Education." *Notes and Essays on Education for Adults,* No. 20. Boston: Center for the Study of Liberal Education for Adults, 1958.

Decrow, R. *Administrative Practices in University Evening Colleges.* Chicago: Center for the Study of Liberal Education for Adults, 1957.

Education. Sector Working Paper Series. Washington, D.C.: World Bank, 1974.

Houghton, V. P., and Richardson, K. *Recurrent Education.* London: Ward Locke, 1974.

Jessup, F. W. *Lifelong Learning.* Oxford, England: Pergamon Press, 1969.

Knowles, A. S. (Ed.) *Handbook of College and University Administration.* New York: McGraw-Hill, 1970.

Learning to Be. Paris: UNESCO, 1973.

Melby, E. O. *Administering Community Education.* Englewood Cliffs, New Jersey: Prentice-Hall, 1955.

Planning Better Programs. Washington, D.C.: Adult Education Association, 1955.

Professional Standards for Adult Education Administrators. Sacramento: California State Department of Education, 1955.

Siegle, P. E., and Whipple, J. B. *New Directions in Programming University Adult Education.* Chicago: Center for the Study of Liberal Education for Adults, 1957.

Snow, R. H. *Community Adult Education: A Guide for Program Development and Planning.* New York: Putnam's, 1955.

Stock, A. K. "Management of Adult Education: The LEA Sector." In *Proceedings of the Third Annual Conference of University Teaching and Research in the Education of Adults.* Manchester, England: Department of Adult Education, Manchester University, 1973.

Stock, A. K. "Management Problems in the Education of Adults." In *Proceedings of the Third Annual Conference of University Teaching and Research in the Education of Adults.* Manchester, England: Department of Adult Education, Manchester University, 1973.

Stock, A. K. "A Symposium on the Management of Adult Education." In *Proceedings of the Third Annual Conference of University Teaching and Research in the Education of Adults.* Manchester, England: Department of Adult Education, Manchester University, 1973.

Thatcher, J. H. (Ed.) *Public School Adult Education: A Guide to Administrators.* Washington, D.C.: National Association of Public School Adult Educators, 1963.

United Kingdom, Department of Education and Science. *Adult Education: A Plan for Development.* London: H. M. Stationery Office, 1973.

Verner, C., and White, T. (Eds.) *Administration of Adult Education.* Washington, D.C.: Adult Education Association, 1965.

ARTHUR K. STOCK

3. GOVERNMENT PROGRAMS

Because of the many heterogeneous forms of adult education activity, government support for such activity is expressed in a variety of ways. Responsibility for different types of programs is generally spread throughout different units of government, with considerable sharing of responsibility for adult education planning and activity among government sectors. Many countries that experienced difficulty in assigning responsibility for adult education to a particular ministry now recognize the necessity for broad participation. In Nigeria, for example, agencies responsible for adult education are administered by the Ministry of Education in some states and by the Ministry of Information or the Ministry of Local Government in others. These official agencies, while giving the bulk of their attention to literacy, also provide for vocational education, upgrading of educational levels, and education in areas of social interest and concern.

In Indonesia a directorate for community education is operated by the Department of Education and Culture, but it is officially recognized that adult education is also the responsibility of the Departments of Religion, Information, Agriculture, Health, Manpower, Social Affairs, Interior, and other government agencies. In Tanzania a directorate of adult education in the Ministry of National Education assumes main responsibility for adult education. Thailand's National Committee on Adult Education is chaired by the minister for education, and the director general of elementary and adult education acts as secretary. The committee formulates general policy, plans, and objectives for all adult education activities in the country.

Financial Support

Government subscription to adult education is indicated primarily by the financial support given to adult education programs. While many countries have attempted to delineate the role of central and local authorities in adult education as defined legislatively or acknowledged more generally, different approaches have been taken by free-market and planned economies.

Free-market economies. In Great Britain support is extended not only directly, through financial grants to actual adult education bodies, but also indirectly, by subvention to voluntary bodies that provide adult education as an auxiliary service. Both forms of aid are dispensed by the Department of Education and Science and by local educational authorities.

In the United States funding and organization occur at both federal and state levels. Federal and state policies relating to adult education have evolved essentially in areas connected with economic activity. Basic education has been supported to help economically disadvantaged sections and to improve work skills at all (including professional) levels. In general the same emphases are seen in other countries, both developed and developing. However, it has often been felt by government planners that budgetary allocations could reflect greater recognition of the importance of nonformal education.

In many countries financial support for adult education is governed by legislation. In Kenya and Singapore, for example, boards and associations of adult education derive their authority from legislation. In the United States many laws relate to government support of adult education in the areas of manpower development, training, and vocational and basic education for adults. In addition, more specific types of legislation relate to particular sector institutions. For example, the National Vocational Training Institute of Ghana was established under a National Vocational Training Act passed in 1970; and a law in Kenya, similar to the United Kingdom Industrial Training Act, requires firms to pay a levy into a training fund, so that companies conducting training programs can be reimbursed out of this fund. In Brazil it has been law since 1946 for commercial establishments to pay a 1 percent payroll tax to support the National Service for Commercial Apprenticeship, which provides courses for minors in their employ.

Another form of government subsidy is cost sharing. In the Ivory Coast the bulk of the cost of training transport mechanics is borne by the Ministry of Technical Education and Vocational Training, but retraining costs are borne by employers. The ministry and industry also share costs in the training of office secretaries. In Singapore joint industrial training centers have been established by the government and a number of multinational enterprises. Ongoing expenses are shared, but the government provides capital for the establishment of these centers; participating firms also provide in-plant training after in-center training has been completed.

Another mode of cost sharing is between government and participants. In India literacy programs administered by the government have been financed on the basis of a 75 percent subvention from government funds, with 25 percent raised by voluntary effort at the local level. In the Philippines teaching costs in evening vocational classes are shared between the government and participants on a 10 to 90 percent basis; training facilities and equipment belong to the daytime institution in whose premises these courses are held.

External aid organizations also participate with governments in sharing the costs of adult education projects. In Nigeria, for example, the Vocational Training and Common Facilities Centre was set up in 1969 on the basis of state sponsorship in cooperation with the International Labour Organisation (ILO); costs are shared equally between the government and the ILO. In Singapore the government and the Friedrich Ebert Foundation of the Federal Republic of Germany have jointly established the Centre for Production and Training for Adult Education Television (CEPTA TV), whose aim is the production of adult education television programs and other audiovisual material and their distribution in the East Asian and Southeast Asian regions.

Support of adult education is often in the form of subsidies and incentives. The ILO has in many cases successfully called on governments of member states to participate in measures allowing workers access to various types of paid educational leave—as distinct from holidays with pay—in order to give workers opportunity and incentive to acquire the further education and training needed to carry out their duties at work and to assume their responsibilities in the community. In some countries senior citizens or pensioners are allowed to attend adult education classes without charge. The University of Singapore offers concession rates to members of the local armed forces.

Some governments give outright grants to voluntary institutions providing adult education, training subsidies for industrial education, and scholarships for local or overseas training. Another form of support is to provide means of accreditation for courses offered by recognized bodies, such as the Council for National Academic Awards (CNAA) in the United Kingdom. Other means include support for conferences, seminars, research, and commissions of inquiry.

Incentives may also be given to adult education teachers apart from their payment or token honorarium. In many countries adult education teachers receive promotion in their full-time jobs, certificates of recognition, letters of appreciation, and even medals.

Planned economies. In countries where the economy is fully under government control, adult education becomes a totally government concern. A portion of the constitution of the Soviet Union, for example, states that the right of the citizens to education is ensured (among other ways) by the utmost development of evening and extramural education and by the organization of free vocational, technical, and agricultural training for working people in factories and on state and collective farms. In fact, attempts are often made to create favorable conditions for combining study with work, and assistance is given for acquisition of appropriate educational equipment.

In Yugoslavia a general law on education, promulgated in 1958, incorporates adult education into the educational system, giving it equal status with other branches of education and, indeed, making it obligatory for schools to contribute to the development of adult education. In Czechoslovakia, throughout the period after World War II, several Communist Party resolutions indicated the party's view of the importance of adult education and of the necessity for its ideological and political direction as a mass-based institution.

One of the principal adult education instruments in the Soviet Union (as well as in several other socialist countries) is the people's university. People's universities are actually further education, not higher education, institutions and have their bases in educational, social, cultural, administrative, and occupational enterprises. Those who take courses in people's universities may also prepare for examinations of, and be awarded qualifications by, secondary or higher educational establishments. People's universities train citizens for public service; run courses for parents and teachers; offer instruction in special disciplines; and guide clientele in their general educational, cultural, and professional development. These universities are staffed mostly by voluntary workers, who may receive incentives such as bonuses, gifts, business and holiday tours, and official decorations.

Other provisions also abound. In the Soviet Union both industrial and agricul-

tural workers are obliged to participate in periodic retraining. Even specialists have to attend advanced training courses every five or six years. In Yugoslavia workers' universities organize vocational, technical, and management training.

The place of adult education is equally defined in less developed socialist countries. In Cuba, for example, adult education is free and well integrated with the nation's social, political, and economic institutions. Literacy has been given special emphasis and encouragement through a series of official resolutions. Cuban adult education in general is the specific concern of the Vice-Ministry of Adult Education, which has established departments for worker and farmer education, on-the-job training, the youth movement, foreign-language teaching, and teacher training. A well-known polyvalent adult education center at Cienfuegos is Cuba's equivalent of the workers' and people's universities.

Although the vast majority of adult education teachers in socialist countries are voluntary workers, they receive as much careful training as the full-time professional staff. Full-time courses are provided at postsecondary institutions in Hungary, for example, as well as in-service training for professional and volunteer workers. In Czechoslovakia a standard system of training adult educators imparts ideological direction along with the necessary pedagogic skills. Young intellectuals are encouraged to take part in volunteer activities.

Adult education is integrated into the life of the People's Republic of China no less (perhaps even more) than in other socialist countries. Factories, neighborhood committees, farming communes, museums, colleges—a variety of organizations sponsor adult education. Political study to reinforce revolutionary zeal or socialist consciousness is everywhere organized and encouraged. The People's Republic of China, viewed in terms of adult education, is being transformed into a huge university, where continuing education is almost mandatory to maintain ideology, carry work skills to higher and higher levels, and ensure human development. Thousands of schools (called May 7th Schools in commemoration of a 1966 letter written by Mao Tse-tung, chairman of the Communist Party, calling for a more revolutionary attitude toward education) have been established for cadres, senior civil servants, professionals, and even ambassadors to periodically review their education. These residential educational establishments offer a combined work and study experience.

Literacy and School Equivalency Programs

In the developing countries illiteracy is a dominant problem that governments try to combat with various social, political, and personal inducements. But financial constraints are so formidable that, in Egypt and Saudi Arabia, for example, thought has been given to legislation that would compel industries to spend some portion of their profits on education and training or make them responsible for literacy among their employees. The emphasis here is on work-oriented and functional literacy, for obvious economic reasons. International bodies also try to support the efforts of governments. UNESCO itself has taken the lead in vigorously encouraging governments to give as much financial, technical, moral, and other support as possible to combat illiteracy. Two well-known international awards recognize meritorious work in this field: the Mohammed Riza Pahlevi Prize (named after the shah of Iran) and the Nadezhda K. Krupskaya Prize (named after Lenin's widow).

The People's Republic of China has taken vigorous measures, such as establishing winter schools for peasants, sparetime classes for factory workers, and study groups in communes and community locations. In Brazil the government has allocated funds for the establishment of a Brazilian literacy movement (MOBRAL: *Movimento brasileiro de alfabetização*), aimed at a 90 percent literacy rate by 1980. MOBRAL was founded under the Ministry of Education and Culture and is an autonomous

administrative body. Its resources include 30 percent of the net income from the federal football lottery plus 1 percent of the corporate income tax. It has been claimed that, in relation to general UNESCO estimates, the cost of literacy in Brazil is one of the lowest in the world.

Illiteracy is a condition that affects developed as well as developing countries. In the United Kingdom, for example, it has been estimated that there are over two million functionally illiterate adults. In Canada various adult basic education (functional, work-oriented literacy) programs have been initiated, including New Start and Basic Literacy for Adult Development (BLADE). Basic education is financed by the federal government and is implemented by the provinces.

Adult basic education programs in the United States are principally the responsibility of the individual states but receive support from the federal Office of Education; the Departments of Defense, Labor, Interior, and Justice; and the Veterans Administration. The Appalachian Region Satellite Experiment, designed especially to combat undereducation in a disadvantaged area of the United States, uses a satellite communication system to deliver in-service training to teachers, largely in adult education.

Another American program, General Educational Development (GED), leads to high school equivalency certificates. Adult learning centers and other institutions in the United States where GED programs are run are heavily financed by the government. In the United Kingdom, as part of the officially supported further education program, colleges of further education provide courses to adults preparing for school-leaving examinations as well as commercial and business education qualifications. The adult education centers *(Volkshochschulen)* in the Federal Republic of Germany and the Scandinavian folk high schools in Western Europe provide similar programs. Thailand provides school equivalency programs that take half the time of the normal school studies. And in Malaysia the Ministry of Education runs night classes for adults who wish to prepare for school-leaving certificate examinations.

Extension programs at university level prepare adults for the acquisition of university degrees. University adult education in the United States is supported by relatively small state subsidies and relies heavily on tuition fees. An up-to-date example of university part-time degree provision, using a mixed-media approach, is Britain's Open University, a highly approved government project that is being emulated in other countries.

Vocational Programs

The primary social justification for adult education has been the development of manpower resources for employment or improved employment opportunities. Technical and vocational education aimed at optimizing employment opportunities is a heavily supported area of adult education. In many countries legislation designed to encourage vocational education has been enacted. The Canadian Adult Occupational Training Act, for example, relates to programs of basic training for skill development.

In the United States various laws, like the Vocational Education Act and the Manpower Development Training Act, govern and encourage the organization of vocational and technical education. Federal funds are used to support vocational and technical education in the public schools, which also organize tuition-free training or retraining programs for adults. The federal and state governments play prominent roles in industrial training through tax exemptions. Tax incentives are also being applied in other countries to induce firms to train people in a highly competitive labor market.

In Ghana the National Vocational Training Institute conducts various forms of training. Initially the joint financial responsibility of the government of Ghana and the United Nations Development Programme through the International Labour Organisation, the institute may also receive aid from international or charitable organizations and collect fees from industry. Singapore's Industrial Training Board and Kenya's National Industrial Training Council are also concerned with a broad spectrum of trades to help sustain and develop the industrial sector.

Governments are frequently concerned not only with the specific vocational needs of workers but also with their total development, which includes academic, cultural, civic, as well as technical development, especially within the urban situation. UNESCO has provided financial and technical assistance toward the establishment of two polyvalent adult education centers, one in Cienfuegos, Cuba, and the other in Bombay, India. The Bombay center, known as the *Shramik vidyapith,* plans to seek support from industries, trade unions, and participants themselves, in addition to funds provided by the Indian government.

In countries all over the world the armed forces have supported national development, providing skill training and general educational development (sometimes up to university level) for servicemen, who would add to the country's pool of skilled manpower after their return to civilian life. Frequently basic education programs are required for those in the armed services. In the United Kingdom special preliminary education is given to a small percentage of recruits who need further training in communication skills and mathematics, while others may be given training to prepare them for school-leaving and even university examinations; general educational programs for personal enrichment and development are also offered. It has been reported that, in the People's Republic of China, 60 percent of the educational provision for the Chinese soldier has been for military training, while 25 percent has been for political education and 15 percent for basic communication and mathematical skills.

Another important educational provision within the public service is training for government employees. In the United States the Government Employees Training Act sponsors the training of civil servants. Centers for training of staff in the civil service have become quite common. In Kenya the civil service training institute is known as the Kenyan Institute of Administration; in Singapore it is known as the Staff Development Institute.

Extension and Community Development Programs

Literacy and basic education, technical training, university involvement, and the efforts of specific government agencies have been combined in improvement programs at the local level for rural change and development. Such programs have long covered a variety of activities: improvement of crop production (for example, rice in the Philippines and Cambodia and maize in Ghana and Mexico), training of officials for rural development work, training for technical employment in rural industries and businesses, health and diet improvement, and family planning cooperatives. Whether they are called cooperative extension, as in the United States, or community development, as in less developed areas, these programs are aimed at developing skills and initiative for self-help and problem solving, principally in the rural context.

Examples of variations of sponsorship of such programs abound. In Algeria the Ministry of Agriculture and Agrarian Reform administers effective vocational training for all sorts of agricultural workers. In Zambia the World Council of Churches and other church groups bear about half the costs of a farm college, with the remaining support coming from the government and profits on the sale of farm produce. In several parts of Africa, farmer training centers have been established to promote agricultural reform. In Kenya such centers are funded by the government. In Tanzania the government has helped launch an integrated development project that is supported by the German Kübel Foundation. It is quite common for developing countries to receive technical assistance for the development of rural education from more advanced countries and agencies, like UNESCO, the Food and Agriculture Organization, and the International Labour Organisation.

That rural education is a universal need is shown by the vast cooperative extension service that has developed over the last hundred years or more in the United States. This service, supported through a sharing of costs among federal, state, and county authorities, represents the joint efforts of the Department of Agriculture and land-grant universities.

Informal Programs

Adult education does not take place only in the context of systematically structured learning situations. A host of informal circumstances provide educational influences. Libraries, museums, art galleries, and cultural organizations have some organized programs of lectures, workshops, and seminars, but their greater influence is in providing continuing informal education.

In the United States public libraries and so-called learning centers provide aids to those participating in adult education programs, especially in adult basic education. Free services enable adults enrolled in basic education classes to use the resources of the library or reading center, which may include films, tapes, recordings, programed texts, and television, in addition to printed material.

Reading for the new literate and the provision of appropriate materials are heavily stressed in the literacy programs of various countries. Indonesia, for example, has made elaborate efforts to produce appropriate reading materials by combining the experience of content specialists in various subjects; research workers who identify community problems and appropriate word lists; and textbook writers, artists, and printers. The materials are distributed through village and people's libraries, set up for the general educational advancement and, more particularly, for the attainment and maintenance of literacy.

Museums also play an important adult education role. In developing countries, where nation building is an important objective, museums of various kinds may be used to focus the attention of citizens on nationalistic goals. Museums of history, anthropology, archeology, ethnology, science, industry, fine arts, war, and revolution, and other institutions that reflect the culture of a country, undertake specific educational programs and mount exhibitions for purposes of educational enrichment. Because of the close relationship between museums and national objectives, governments give museums substantial support, although a small source of income comes from entrance fees. In many countries the terms *national museum* and *national gallery* (or, in some places, *city museum* and *public gallery*) indicate public concern and public interest in the institution. However, the very high expenditure of museum maintenance usually necessitates private subvention of museum activity.

Future Development

One trend already discernible in the United States, Great Britain, and the Soviet Union and other socialist states is the development of more comprehensive policies for adult education—policies that integrate it into the whole scenario of lifelong education. In Norway, for example, a proposed law dealing with adult education would make the government as responsible for adult education as it is for school education.

In the Federal Republic of Germany the *Volkschochschulen* (adult education centers) have long striven for integration of adult education with the traditional school and higher education systems. But state intervention should be represented not only by financial support but also by a harmonious coordination of various activities. In Tasmania, Australia, for example, a commonwealth policy in adult education, with the creation of a comprehensive state service adaptable to changing demands, has been suggested.

Rising costs of education may force countries with a low gross national product to seek solutions through nonformal education. Certain West African states (Mali and Upper Volta) have organized low-cost, work-oriented, basic education schemes for rural out-of-school youth—a departure from Western-imported styles of school organization—and have returned to traditional African teaching approaches.

The search for more economical means of delivering education has focused attention on developments in educational technology that utilize programed instruction, telephone and face-to-face conferences, laboratory kits, radio, television, electronic hardware and software, and satellite communications.

The use of radio is now widespread throughout the world for all sorts of education programs. In Colombia the experience of *Acción cultural popular* (Action for Popular Culture), a movement sponsored by the Catholic church with occasional government subsidy, has influenced the continuing development of rural radio and multimedia projects all over Latin America. The use of radio for adult education has become common, as indicated by rural radio forums and radio clubs in Canada, India, and various parts of Africa.

The use of mass media will assume greater importance in the future, particularly the simultaneous utilization of a mix of media instruments—radio, newsletters, bulletins, posters, slides, films, and, wherever possible, the organized use of television. Experimental use of television has been widely conducted—for example, in India, France, Japan, Italy, and Senegal, where tele-clubs are being sponsored by UNESCO. The use of television involves high costs and low coverage, but future developments may be indicated by the Philippine experience of using less costly transmitting technology and cheaper recording and receiving equipment. Optimum use of receivers may also be contrived through organization of group viewing and discussion.

Current experiments in the use of satellites to relay television and radio broadcasts in India, Brazil, and the United States may indicate the cost effectiveness of the use of such systems, especially where large areas are involved. On the other side of the coin, traditional folk and national cultural media are also being used for nonformal education, as exemplified by the shadow plays called *wayang kulit* in Indonesia and Malaysia and *nang yai* or *nang taloong* in Thailand.

Bibliography

Adult Education and National Development. Commonwealth Foundation Occasional Paper No. 15. London: Marlborough House, 1973.

Catalogue and Index to the Computer-Stored Data and to the Microfiche Series of International Reports on Education Relating to the UNESCO Third World Conference on Adult Education (Tokyo, 1972). Paris and Geneva: UNESCO International Bureau of Educational Reference Service, 1974.

Coles, E. T. *Adult Education in Developing Countries.* Oxford, England: Pergamon Press, 1969.

Lowe, J. *Adult Education and Nation Building.* Edinburgh: Edinburgh University Press, 1970.

Lowe, J. *Adult Education in England and Wales: A Critical Survey.* London: Michael Joseph, 1970.

Perspectives of Adult Education: The United States and a Projection for the Future. Washington, D.C.: United States Department of Health, Education and Welfare, Office of Education, 1972.

Sheffield, J. R., and Diejomaoh, V. P. *Nonformal Education in African Development.* New York: African-American Institute, 1972.

Smith, R. M., Aker, G. F., and Kidd, J. R. (Eds.) *Handbook of Adult Education.* Washington, D.C.: Adult Education Association, 1970.

JOSEPH F. CONCEICAO

See also: Financing of Higher Education; Open University; Sweden, Kingdom of.

4. ROLE OF LABOR AND INDUSTRY

The educational needs of working men and women have always influenced the history of adult education. Preparation for work and life was recognized in the classical educational theories of ancient Greece and Rome, in the curricula of the earliest Arab and Indian universities, and in the preparation for leadership through competitive examinations in China more than a thousand years ago. The industrial revolution, however, led to the emergence of organizations of wage earners and employers, to educational needs unknown to medieval artisans and their guilds, and in time to new dimensions in the quality and quantity of educational provisions for working men and women—a trend of growth and innovation that has continued to this day.

This article concentrates on an essentially contemporary phenomenon: the specific roles of industry and labor in encouraging, developing, and participating in adult education programs related to or sponsored by institutions of higher education. These roles tend to differ according to the nature and structure of the society of which they are a part. A cursory international survey of this kind is inevitably subject to the caveat that, while major trends can be discerned, generalizations are often qualified by exceptions arising from particular conditions of the social, economic, political, or cultural environment.

Historical Background and Major Trends

Both industry and labor, as major groups in modern societies, recognize the importance of adult education as a means of personal advancement, as a pathway for social mobility, and as an instrument for strengthening democratic institutions. Each group tends to emphasize different interests: industry favors vocational and technical training, skill improvement at all levels, and executive development; labor leans toward educational programs for collective advancement that are designed to meet the needs of workers as producers, consumers, and members of their organizations. But the role of labor and industry in adult education cannot be considered apart from the role both have played in public higher education and in developing educational programs outside of postsecondary institutions. Labor and industry's participation in programs of adult education is, in many cases, an outgrowth of or an adjunct to their participation in other educational programs and must be considered in that context.

Industrialized countries with mixed economies. Priorities and emphases vary from country to country and with different periods of time. Industry in the United States, for example, has contributed substantially to higher education, expecting universities and colleges to produce the qualified and specialized personnel essential for the development of free enterprise in a market economy. Private endowments, public foundations, and major corporations have all participated in the extensive development of schools of business administration and management studies within American universities, which enroll promising employees for undergraduate, graduate, or special programs in executive development. This practice is supplemented by widespread collaboration between industry and academic circles in a broad range of adult education programs of in-service training, recurrent education, and professional refresher training.

Historically, American unions have placed the highest priority on efforts to develop public education and to secure public funds for education at all levels. While both labor and industry have supported and benefited from such educational innovations as land-grant colleges, American unions have generally been less than satisfied with the formal school system, particularly with its neglect of views and needs that labor considers important. Consequently, labor unions have for many years operated educational programs for their own members, leaders, and representatives. After World War II, unions and universities collaborated in developing joint programs of labor studies, with emphasis on the broad subjects needed by the American worker to understand and cope with a rapidly changing world.

In Britain, the cradle of the industrial revolution, the universities initially responded to educational challenges by their tradition of preparing the elite for leading roles through study of human problems in a well documented past society. Since liberal studies devoid of vocational emphasis often proved unreliable as preparation for industrial careers, universities began to evolve a more utilitarian approach, with emphasis on economics, statistics, and other practical courses. A bridge between higher education institutions and industry was created in the form of university extramural departments, stimulated by the collaboration of industry and labor during World War I.

In 1903 the founding of the Workers' Educational Association (WEA) in London and Oxford, England, marked another step in meeting the growing demand for education by working men and women. In bringing together groups of adult students, for whom tutors were provided by university extramural departments, the WEA determined the subject areas while universities made sure that the programs were academically sound. Day-release courses, in which workers are allowed time off from work to attend school (with the wage bill paid by the management or, in some cases, by the union), also obtained the support of both labor and industry. In Britain a combined approach to day-release courses is often made by the universities and the WEA; universities approach management, and the WEA approaches the unions within the firm.

In addition to courses offered at Ruskin College in Oxford, England—a labor-oriented institution supported largely by the trade unions—major British unions have developed trade union education programs of their own. Moreover, the Trades Union Congress has, since the late 1960s, assumed increasing coordination of workers' education activities. Finally, the entire field of adult education has been undergoing review.

In other industrialized countries the history of adult education includes many comparable initiatives. For more than a century the Folk High School (founded by the Danish theologian and poet Nikolai Grundtvig to prepare rural youth for democratic life) and similar institutions created subsequently by the Danish labor movement have prepared both rural and urban workers for social and political democratization. In all the Scandinavian countries the WEA has evolved into powerful specialized institutions—veritable educational arms of the labor movement—leaving the role of universities rather marginal in workers' education, if not in adult education. The renaissance of a strong labor movement in the Federal Republic of Germany after World War II stimulated dynamic educational programs among the unions, while the development of "codetermination" in major German industries was facilitated by special training for workers' representatives. Similarly, the introduction of workers' participation in economic enterprises in Yugoslavia was accompanied by extensive and intensive educational programs at all levels, designed to ensure the proper functioning of the system.

Countries with planned economies. In the socialist countries, the roles of industry, labor, and the educational system, including adult education, are integrated and coordinated within the framework of centralized planning. The urgent need for preparing workers and peasants for new professional and political functions was the dominant imperative in the early history of all of the socialist countries. Educational programs involving both labor and industry were required for subsequent periods of economic reform or post–World War II reconstruction in the Soviet Union and the Eastern European socialist countries. Similar exigencies led the People's Republic of China to restructure its institutions of higher education to meet social and economic developmental needs, producing in recent years such innovations as the peasant and commune colleges in rural areas and worker colleges in urban industrial complexes.

In all the socialist countries, adult education programs in institutions of higher education are closely linked with industry through cooperation and coordination between the academic structure and the world of labor and production. This relationship entails not only dovetailing educational and production plans and involving students in the production process but often the recruitment and placement of students and trainees.

Developing countries. In the Third World neither labor nor industry has, with some notable exceptions, played a major role in encouraging, developing, or participating in adult education programs associated with institutions of higher education. Public authorities take pride of place both in fixing priorities of university curricula and in sponsoring adult education programs designed for training elites or for nation building through civics, literacy, and community development.

Incipient trade unions lack resources for sustained educational work, but some national trade union centers in Africa, Asia, Latin America, and the Caribbean have succeeded in mobilizing international aid and local resources to establish labor colleges, union institutes, and other systematic educational programs of their own. Outstanding examples may be found as far apart as Argentina, Barbados, Colombia, Lebanon, Malaysia, Mexico, Nigeria, and Zaire. Heavy government support for labor institutes and related bodies is evident in such countries as Egypt, India, Iraq, Syria, Tanzania, and Zambia.

Some of the major labor education institutions in the Third World have been established by international and regional trade union organizations. The International Confederation of Free Trade Unions, for example, created the Asian Trade Union College in Calcutta in 1952 (since relocated in New Delhi) and has trained thousands of labor leaders and union officers in the region. In Latin America the labor education activities of the International Metalworkers Federation constitutes another example of successful programs of long standing, sponsored by world industrial federations of workers.

The national trade union centers of the main industrialized countries have long conducted training programs and study tours for labor leaders from the developing countries. The best-known examples are the three regional educational arms of the AFL-CIO (American Federation of Labor–Congress of Industrial Organizations)—the American Institute of Free Labor Development, the African American Labor Center, and the Asian American Free Labor Institute—all of which are headquartered in Washington, D.C., but work through a network of field representatives stationed in various countries of Africa, Asia, Latin America, and the Caribbean.

All of these labor-sponsored programs, unlike joint programs with academic institutions, utilize university staff and facilities only occasionally. In the developing countries, unions, industry, and the universities are still too preoccupied with consolidating their basic functions to be able to sustain intensive collaboration in the field of adult education, even though they recognize its crucial importance in economic and social development.

Through this kaleidoscope of national trends in countries of widely different systems of political, social, and economic organization runs a common thread of increasing participation by both labor and industry in the determination and implementation of adult education policies and programs. In 1974 international recognition and action culminated in the establishment of an international labor convention and the adoption of a recommendation on paid educational leave by the International Labor Conference—itself a prime example of tripartite collaboration between labor, management, and public authorities. These international standards emphasized that adult education must relate to rapid tech-

nological change and to workers' needs arising from economic, social, and cultural development. In addition to providing for the granting of paid leave for specific periods during working hours for vocational and other training at any level, the conference also advocated this for general, social, civic, and trade union education. These standards represent an international consensus on the respective roles of labor and industry in major fields of adult education.

Labor Studies and Industrial Relations

Universities in a number of industrialized countries have developed—with advisory support from trade unions and employers' organizations—credit programs leading to Bachelor of Arts, Master of Arts, and Doctor of Philosophy degrees in labor and industrial relations. Various universities and colleges have established similar credit or noncredit programs in labor studies. While the curricula and content of these two types of programs overlap in many ways, the essential difference lies in their approach. Labor studies concentrate on problems of work, the place of work, and the role of workers and their organizations in society. Consequently, such programs require close relations with labor organizations—either in the form of joint activities, with varying degrees of responsibility and collaboration between the academic institution and the interested unions, or in more structured, longer-term programs, with labor representatives playing an advisory role in the determination of academic policy and curricula. Labor studies typically lead to service in the labor movement; the shorter noncredit programs are usually assimilated into in-service or refresher training within labor organizations.

Industrial relations programs, on the other hand, are generally designed to prepare students for careers in management and government as well as in unions. A typical program would include an integrated, multidisciplinary curriculum in the social sciences; fields of concentration would include unions, management, and labor relations policy; organizational behavior and personnel administration; and manpower utilization and human resources development. Areas of particular interest would include collective bargaining and labor-management relations in the public and private sectors; multinational industrial relations and comparative labor problems; wage, price, and income policies; labor markets; employment practices; and manpower planning and training.

Labor studies cover many similar content areas but with relatively heavy concentration on labor history and the development of the labor movement; the structure and administration of trade unions; collective bargaining, grievance procedures, and other methods of dispute settlement; labor law and social legislation; and labor education methods and techniques. Labor studies in universities and colleges tend also to include broad courses relating to labor and the economy; work in contemporary society; politics and the government; work and alienation; organized labor and the urban crisis; the special problems of minority workers, public employees, and farm workers; and comparative labor movements and international labor affairs. In the United States labor studies are offered in thirty states and have reached thousands of trade unionists at the local and regional levels. Three dozen graduate and undergraduate university degree programs are offered in industrial relations; however, relatively few graduates have found employment in the unions.

Business Administration and Management Development

Industry in the advanced market economy countries has long played an established role in providing in-service, on-the-job training to its employees. Some leading corporations in the United States conduct and sponsor training programs with content comparable to programs of postsecondary institutions. Most of these programs are geared to meet the particular needs of the corporations, businesses, and industries offering the programs. In many instances the corporations, businesses, and industries have made arrangements with universities and colleges to give credit for the programs conducted and award degrees based on a satisfactory amount of work. Rapid technological change—particularly in such industries as electronics, computers, and business machines—not only has upgraded the sophistication and complexity of such training but also has obliged corporations to increase their cooperation with universities and to develop advanced degrees of their own. Some leading corporations in the United States—for example, International Business Machines, American Telephone and Telegraph, and General Electric—offer bachelor degrees; Arthur D. Little, a large management consultant firm in Cambridge, Massachusetts, grants a Master of Business Administration. The Management Education Institute at Arthur D. Little trains hundreds of executives from scores of foreign countries in a ten-month course. This kind of activity suggests increasing competition among industry, profit-making training institutions, traditional universities and colleges, and adult education programs in attempting to bridge the gap between academic courses and training for the world of work.

In Western Europe an early example of industry-oriented programs was that established in the *Centre d'études industrielles* (Center of Industrial Studies) in Geneva, Switzerland, to train managers for the international operations of the Aluminum Company of Canada. The influence of American programs of management development spread during the 1950s, when thousands of European managers were sent to the United States under the Marshall Plan to observe productivity, management methods, and education. By the 1960s nearly all the Western European countries had instituted management schools with comparable curricula but with national and local adaptations. Examples of such schools include the Administrative Staff College, the Tavistock Institute of

Human Relations, and the London and Manchester Business Schools in the United Kingdom; the *Centre de recherches d'études des chefs d'entreprises* (Research and Study Center for Business Managers) and the *Institut d'administration des entreprises* (Institute of Business Administration) in major universities of France; the *Universitätsseminar der Wirtschaft* (University Seminar on Economics) in Cologne, and similar centers in the Federal Republic of Germany; the *Stichting studiecentrum bed riyfsbeleid* (Study Center for Management) in Arnhem, the Netherlands; and the *Institut pour l'étude des méthodes de direction d'entreprise* (Institute for the Study of Business Management Methods) in Lausanne, Switzerland. The establishment of the European Association of Management Training Centres (EAMTC) and the European Research Group on Management (ERGOM) in Brussels marks the latest phase of consolidation and intra-European cooperation in this field.

An ultimate example of sophisticated and complex management programs is the Inter-University Program for Advancement Management, started in 1968 by a consortium of labor, Belgian firms, and the management centers of five Belgian universities. University staff provide tutoring and research guidance, beginning with a two-month preparatory course; the participating firms receive fellows for specific projects comprising a three-month diagnostic phase and a four-month action phase, punctuated by one month of observation and discussion with staff from major United States firms and universities.

The scope and content of management training programs in the Soviet Union and other socialist countries are determined by the special role of industry and labor in these countries; by the nature of the socialist economy, which involves public ownership of the means of production; and by the leading role assumed by state enterprises and governmental administrative agencies within the framework of national, regional, and local planning.

In contrast to market economies, managerial development programs in the socialist countries do not provide training and skill improvement only to enterprise directors, factory managers, and supervisors. Personnel in other agencies and sectors—industrial ministries; economic planning, financial, and administrative agencies; the cooperative sectors, trade unions, and other mass organizations—are trained as well. Industry and labor also influence the structure of adult education programs within institutions of higher education for training management specialists with work experience as well as the structure of other forms of instruction for improving management skills, including refresher courses; in-service training; special programs sponsored by administrative agencies; conferences and seminars; radio, television, and correspondence courses; popular universities; and other bodies.

Management training programs at institutions of higher education in the Soviet Union provide a foundation of managerial theory and methods, with heavy emphasis on economic education in courses on national economic planning and management; economics of industry and agriculture; scientific organization of labor; and methods and techniques of economic analysis, statistics, mathematics, and cybernetics for management. Advanced training for production managers includes industrial management, political economy, mathematical planning methods and economic calculation, statistics, computers, economic data processing, and specialized training for industrial enterprises. The Moscow Institute of National Economy provides an outstanding program for high-level managers, and various faculties offer training for middle-level managerial personnel. These programs are supplemented by a variety of shorter courses offered at skill improvement institutes and refresher courses offered in the larger enterprises and establishments. The diversified Soviet network of skill improvement programs is designed to meet the impact of new scientific and technological developments, changes in the national economy and economic policy, and innovative methods and techniques in the management sciences themselves.

Considerable development of national management centers in most of the Eastern European socialist countries occurred in the early 1960s, including the National Management Training Centers at Bucharest, Romania, and Warsaw, Poland; the Institute and Faculty of Management at Prague, Czechoslovakia; and the Academy of Social Management at Sofia, Bulgaria.

Patterns of Organization and Collaboration

The ways in which industry and labor organizations play their roles in adult education in different countries naturally vary with the structure of the society, the political and economic systems, and other individual national characteristics.

An outstanding example of highly structured patterns of organization and collaboration within a mixed economy is that of Sweden, where voluntary organizations of industry and labor directly and indirectly influence the development of adult education. Similar patterns are discernible in Denmark, Finland, and Norway, with relatively minor differences. The major central occupational organizations—*Svenska arbetsgivareföreningen* (SAF: Swedish Employers' Confederation), *Landsorganisationen* (LO: Confederation of Swedish Trade Unions), and *Tjänstemännens centralorganisation* (TCO: Central Organization of Salaried Employees)—not only coordinate and negotiate national agreements on conditions of work and employment but also represent their respective constituencies on public or joint bodies responsible for educational policy and appoint their specialists to serve on commissions of inquiry in this field. Their representatives on the National Board of Education, the National Labor Market Board, the Labor Market Vocational Council, and similar bodies present industry's and labor's views and suggestions on various programs of education and training, curricula, and alloca-

tion of responsibility for education among business, labor, and government.

More directly, the central labor and industry organizations organize or sponsor their own educational programs. The SAF, for example, operates major managerial development and specialist training programs, such as one established in the early 1950s, in collaboration with the Stockholm School of Economics Association; the Institute of Further Training, sponsored by the Association of Graduates from the Stockholm and Göteborg Schools of Economics; and the Swedish Institute of Management, associated with the Federation of Swedish Industries. A wide variety of management development courses is given at the SAF residential training center at Yxtaholm, a manor estate about sixty miles southwest of Stockholm. A comparable center in Denmark is operated by the Danish Employers' Federation at Eglund.

Correspondingly, all of the Scandinavian national trade union organizations, including major industrial federations, conduct educational programs for their officers, representatives, and membership. Moreover, they collaborate closely with the WEA (which, in the Scandinavian countries, forms a part of the labor movement, together with the unions, the cooperatives, the temperance organizations, and the Social Democratic parties). In Sweden, for example, the WEA *(Arbetarnas bildningsförbund)* is allied with the LO, and the *Tjänstemännens bildningsförening* (TBV: Salaried Employees' Educational Association) is allied with the TCO. Another instance of the role of the labor movement in adult education is the specialized publishing center, *Brevskolan,* a major provider in Sweden of books and study materials, including those used in study circles (small discussion groups meeting once or twice weekly with the leader of a study program) and mass-media educational programs.

Labor and industry, as tax-paying individuals and organizations, contribute substantially to the public funds used in many industrialized countries and some developing nations to finance adult education programs associated with institutions of higher education. In the United Kingdom and the Scandinavian countries, for example, courses sponsored by voluntary bodies, like the WEA and the Scandinavian study circles, and the relevant activities of the university extramural departments are largely supported by public funds and grants, usually calculated as a major percentage of teaching costs. It has been estimated that in England and Wales five times as much financial support has come from public funds (through the extramural departments, the WEA, and their joint committees) than has been provided by the Trades Union Congress itself.

Moreover, universities backed by state funding use a part of their budget for specialized units, such as labor institutes, labor studies departments, and labor-management institutes. The continuing growth of university services of this kind in many industrialized countries has channeled more public funds into the education of workers than would have been possible through direct support of the educational work of the unions themselves. In Third World countries the considerable development over many years of such academic institutions as the extramural department of the University of Ibadan in Nigeria, the Labor Education Center of the University of the Philippines, the Labor Relations Institute of the University of Puerto Rico, and the Trade Union Education Institute of the University of West Indies in Jamaica attests to both the availability of public funding and the viability of patterns of university-union collaboration.

The sevenfold increase of university labor institutes in France in less than twenty years is instructive. Following the pioneer leadership of the University of Strasbourg, similar institutes were created at the Universities of Paris (Sceaux), Aix-en-Provence, Grenoble, Nancy, Lyons, and Bordeaux. For example, the Paris institute, entitled *Institut de science sociale du travail* (Labor Sociology Institute), runs a large number of separate one- to two-week courses for the three major trade union confederations and their industrial federations; the unions are represented strongly on the board of the institute and play a dynamic role in the determination of curricula, scope, and content of the courses. The Advanced Education Act of 1968 made some structural changes, integrating the institutes more fully into the universities as teaching and research units; however, the act has not affected the quality of the programs or the excellent relations with the different unions involved. The act of 1959 provided substantial financing, while the Continuing Vocational Training Act of 1971 offered additional resources—from .8 percent of wages to state aid estimated at over two thousand million francs annually. In addition to funding teaching and operating expenses through the Ministry of National Education, the Ministry of Labor grants annual subsidies to the labor institutes and to the individual trade union schools.

In the United States national and state legislation, collective bargaining, and company- or union-based schemes make up a diversified mosaic of provisions for adult education, with innovative patterns of collaboration among labor, industry, and institutions of higher education. Universities and colleges compete for benefits by submitting proposals under such federal legislation as the Adult Education Act (Title I) and the Comprehensive Employment and Training Act of 1973. In addition, the Intergovernmental Personnel Act of 1970 provides federal aid for training programs in labor-management relations for public employees.

Collective bargaining between labor and industry has resulted in funding for education and training that is based on fixed contributions by management; such contributions are calculated on the basis of a percentage of the payroll, a cents-per-hour payment, or some other acceptable formula. The Joint Industry Board of the Electric Industry in New York City, for example, sponsors a ten-million-dollar educational and cultural trust fund; the yearly expenditure of two million dollars is based on 1 percent of the payroll of the employers involved. This trust fund enables hundreds of members of the Industrial Brotherhood of Electrical Workers to benefit from numerous educational activities, including credit and degree courses at the New York City Labor College (a joint undertaking of the Empire State College, Cornell University, and the New York City Labor Council). An educational fund financed by New York City agencies—the main employers of members of the American Federation of State, County, and Municipal Employees (AFSCME)—helped one AFSCME district to institute a major educational program, including courses leading to a Bachelor of Arts degree at New Rochelle College.

The National Opinion Research Center estimated in 1962 that over half of the adult education carried out in the United States was provided by organizations whose primary function is not educational; by 1970 industry expenditures on education and training accounted for about one third of all educational spending in the country. Aside from various forms of apprenticeship and in-plant training, induction schemes for new employees, and other training programs, many American companies operate tuition-refund plans both as an employee benefit and as a training tool. Major corporations such as American Airlines, American Telephone and Telegraph, E. I. duPont de Nemours, Exxon, General Electric, Kimberly-Clark, Mobil Oil, and National City Bank offer tuition-refund opportunities to employees desiring to pursue various types of courses in institutions of higher education. Since 1964 the United Auto Workers union has negotiated with the automobile companies various tuition-refund programs, providing for as much as $500 annually to an eligible worker taking approved courses in any accredited college or university.

A major problem of tuition-refund plans, particularly those provided unilaterally by corporations, has been the low rate of participation. Efforts are under way to remedy this poor response by increasing educational counseling, allowing more release time for employees to register for and pursue courses, offering incentive payments for goal completion, and enhancing company recognition of workers' educational efforts through increased income and job responsibilities.

The most complete structure of academic progression in labor studies is presented by Rutgers University in New Jersey, where two undergraduate colleges (University College for part-time working students and Livingston College for full-time day students) offer a Bachelor of Arts degree; the Graduate School of Arts and Sciences provides a Master of Arts in Labor Studies; and the Graduate School of Education offers a doctorate with emphasis on labor studies. The Federated Department of Labor Studies, which coordinates these units, and the Labor Education Center, which operates under the University Extension's Institute of Labor Management Relations, enjoy full labor support through the Trade Union Consulting Committee and labor members of the State Advisory Council of the Institute of Labor Management Relations.

Perspective for the Future

Adult educators associated with institutions of higher education are at the convergence of two increasingly powerful streams of contemporary forces—the drive for more democratization (economic and educational as well as political and social) and the concept of lifelong learning and permanent education. Both profoundly affect the role of labor and industry in adult education at a time when many universities and colleges themselves are experiencing a crisis of renewal and reform.

As democratization thrusts new and increasing responsibilities on labor and industry, it creates a corresponding need for the knowledge necessary to exercise those responsibilities. The growing clientele from the world of work will demand a larger share of those areas of adult education that best serve their interests and a greater participation in decision making and implementation of educational policies. Both labor and industry are likely to play increasingly active roles in breaking down educational compartments, removing artificial barriers between formal and informal education, linking theory and practice, and otherwise furthering the trend toward lifelong integrated education.

On a worldwide basis the dominant forms of adult education in the future will provide vocational training and recurrent education for technological change; social education for nation building; workers' education for participation in economic and social developments; management development schemes; adult education programs on social security, occupational safety, health, and labor, management, and government relations; cooperative education; and all forms of adult education for rural development.

Compared with the traditional concept of narrow areas of adult education, some of these programs already command greater resources—public and private—while others are developing innovative methods and techniques. All respond to individual as well as social needs and will shape the society of tomorrow.

Bibliography

AFL-CIO Labor Studies Center. Silver Spring, Maryland: American Federation of Labor–Congress of Industrial Organizations, 1975.

Arbetarnas bildningsförbund. *Workers' Education in Sweden*. Stockholm: Arbetarnas bildningsförbund, 1971.

Berrill, K. *Lifetime Education—The Outlook in Britain*. London: Birkbeck College, 1972.

Connery, R. H. (Ed.) *The Corporation and the Campus*. New York: Praeger, 1970.

Education in Economics for Workers and Their Representatives: Report of Regional Trade Union Seminar, Düsseldorf, November 1971. Paris: Organisation for Economic Co-operation and Development, 1971.

Finnigan, J. *Industrial Training Management*. London: Business Books, 1970.

Harbison, F. *Human Resources as the Wealth of Nations*. New York: Oxford University Press, 1973.

Indian University Association for Continuing Education and University of Madras. *Continuing Education and Universities*. New Delhi: New India Press, 1971.

Janne, H. *The University and the Needs of Contemporary Society*. Paris: International Association of Universities, 1970.

Katkhanov, K. "Economic Education for Students." *Soviet Education*, May 1973, *15*, 81–88.

Kerrison, I. L. H., and Levine, H. A. *Labor Leadership Education: A Union-University Approach*. Westport, Connecticut: Greenwood Press, 1973.

Levine, H. A. *Union-University and Inter-University Cooperation in Workers' Education in the U.S.A*. Geneva: International Labour Office, 1973.

Mailick, S. (Ed.) *The Making of the Manager: A World View*. Garden City, New York: Doubleday, 1974.

McGrath, E. H. *Training for Life and Leadership in Industry*. New Delhi: J.E.A. Publications, 1971.

Nyberg, R. (Ed.) *Educational Reform in Finland in the 1970s*. Helsinki: Ministry of Education, 1970.

Paid Educational Leave. Geneva: International Labour Office, 1973–1974.

Pan-American Union. *Report of the Mission on Labor Studies in Latin American Universities*. Washington, D.C.: Pan-American Union, 1969.

The Role of Universities in Workers' Education. Geneva: International Labour Office, 1974.

Trade Unions and Training for the Future. London: Trades Union Congress, 1972.

Training Full-Time Officers. London: Trades Union Congress, 1972.

Training in Africa Directory. Dakar, Senegal: UNESCO, 1974.

Tugbiyele, E. A. (Ed.) *Report on a National Conference on Workers' Education*. Lagos, Nigeria: Federal Ministry of Labor, 1971.

Unions, the T.U.C. and Industrial Training. London: Trades Union Congress, 1971.

Valeev, M. "Securing a High Level for the Economic Education of the Masses." *Soviet Education*, May 1973, *15*, 20–31.

Vermilye, D. W. (Ed.) *Lifelong Learners—A New Clientele for Higher Education: Current Issues in Higher Education 1974*. San Francisco: Jossey-Bass, 1974.

Viklund, B. *Trade Union Educational Work*. Stockholm: Swedish Trade Union Confederation, 1969.

PAUL B. J. CHU

See also: Aid to Other Nations: Multinational Corporations and Lateral Aid; Faculty Unionism: The United States and Great Britain; International Management Education; Sweden, Kingdom of.

5. ADULT EDUCATION IN DEVELOPING COUNTRIES

It is difficult to comprehend all the variations of adult education in the developing countries. The countries themselves are different in size and population, in historical evolution, in ideology, and in percentage of illiteracy. In some it may be said that the absence of well-developed programs of adult education constitutes a factor of underdevelopment; in others, such as Tanzania and Cuba, the role of adult education is probably greater than that in any of the developed countries. Some general trends and characteristics, however, can be discerned.

Increasingly, the term *adult education* (and its equivalents in other languages) is being utilized as the generic term to include all measures of planned learning for men and women over the statutory school-leaving age. A popular definition is this: "Adult Education is a process whereby persons who no longer attend school on a regular and full-time basis (unless specially designed for adult education) undertake sequential and organized activities with the conscious intention of bringing about changes in information, knowledge, understanding or skill, appreciations or attitudes; or for the purpose of identifying and solving personal or community problems" *(Exeter Papers,* 1969).

Other terms that are often subsumed under that of adult education, although they may apply to children as well, are *informal education* (for those educative activities that occur in the family or other primary groups); *nonformal* education (for activities carried on outside the organized school system); *literacy, functional literacy, adult basic education,* or *basic education* (all of which define a level of education that includes a mastery of fundamental learning skills and knowledge sufficient for a person to function in his own culture); and *continuing* or *recurrent education* (which denotes a stage beyond the basic acquisition). While problems of definition and difficulties of translation remain, areas of agreement have enlarged.

An international instrument on the development of adult education has been developed at UNESCO. This instrument, which defines the characteristics of the subject area in application, was approved unanimously at the General Conference of UNESCO in 1976. When countries begin to endorse it, there will be a considerable extension of agreement about the meaning and form of the entire field.

Differences Among Developing Countries

Developing countries are almost infinitely varied, and the rough contemporary classification of "developing" and "least developed" countries is not very satisfactory. There are differences in size of country (from Barbados, a tiny island, to giant Brazil); in population (Chad numbers only a fraction of the people of the People's Republic of China); in historical evolution and traditions (compare Zambia, scarcely a decade old, with India); in language (compare some Latin American states, where almost the entire population speaks Spanish, with Indonesia, where there are hundreds of language variations); in economic and financial resources (compare Kuwait with Mali). Illiteracy in some developing countries is less than 5 percent; in others, 95 percent of the women may be illiterate. There are also extraordinary differences in the general will or expectation of peoples about the values of education and in the organization of adult education. In Tanzania, for example, adult education operates with well-developed goals and a well-designed educational infrastructure; in nearby Burundi, adult education is lacking in most requirements.

Common Notions and Concepts

As previously noted, one of the problems with adult education is the lack of agreement about what it constitutes. Nevertheless, the growth of adult education and the diffusion of certain concepts have occurred with remarkable speed. At the time of the 1960 World Conference in Montreal, Canada, Ministries of Education in most of the least developed and many other countries—except those engaged in literacy campaigns—showed little concern for adult education. With respect to national organization, however, the situation has altered dramatically in many countries, since 118 member states voted unanimously for a resolution adopted by the UNESCO General Conference on November 16, 1964. The resolution states "that all countries should regard the various forms of out-of-school and adult education as an integral part of any educational system, so that all men and women, throughout their lives, may have opportunities for pursuing education conducive alike to their individual advancement and to their active participation in civic life and in the social and economic development of their country."

Another change has been the acceptance of the notion of *éducation permanente* or lifelong learning. While the terms themselves are not new, their first international expression and definition occurred in the report of the UNESCO International Committee for the Advancement of Adult Education in 1965. Since that time the notion of lifelong learning has permeated every country, and at least seventy-five nations are on record as accepting it as a basic concept in their educational plan, as was recommended by the most prestigious international body studying education—the Faure Commission—in its report *Learning to Be* (1973).

While most developing countries have accepted the achievement of functional literacy as a national goal, very few—Cuba and perhaps Burma—have reached it. There is a growing acceptance of the right of every citizen to basic education (Kidd, 1974). However, while the proportion of adult illiterates is steadily decreasing, the total number of illiterates has continued to rise, due to a heavy birthrate in most developing countries.

Many developing countries have evolved programs of vocational training for workers, and some have organized workers' education as well. Some developing countries have significant programs of educa-

tion for rural development. In general, however, despite such notable exceptions as the People's Republic of China, programs of education and training directed to rural areas have been slower to develop and have been given lesser resources than those for urban workers.

Most developing countries have made some use of the mass media in their training and educational efforts, and some employ the cinema for instruction as well. India, Indonesia, and Botswana, among others, utilize traditional art forms, such as the dance, puppet theater, and social drama, for instruction as well as for entertainment.

Most countries also accept the notion of balanced development, which implies coherent educational programs related to jobs, health and nutrition, family planning, community planning, economic and political understanding, and a well-planned educational system that comprehends all of them. However, these matters are still the concern of separate ministries in most countries, and coordination is rare.

Instruments of Influence

Most developing countries have been influenced by major industrial countries—primarily the United States, Great Britain, France, the Federal Republic of Germany, Sweden, Denmark, Canada, Israel, Yugoslavia, the Soviet Union, and the People's Republic of China—and these influences indelibly mark the organization, methods, and goals of their adult education programs. However, the view is now generally held that adult education must serve the particular needs of a country or region, must utilize indigenous cultural strengths, and must not be limited by the characteristics of educational practices designed to serve other cultures. The decade from 1965 to 1975 has been marked not only by far-reaching cultural borrowing but also by rejection of nonrelevant forms of adult education. It has also been a period when the developing countries began to exchange ideas and programs among themselves, to look for models in Cuba, or Brazil, or Tanzania rather than in more highly developed countries.

While self-determination is much more in evidence, former colonial powers, such as Great Britain and France, and other countries, such as the United States and the Soviet Union, still constitute major influences on education. For example, the American practice of universities' developing programs of graduate instruction in adult education is now being copied in many developing countries.

Intergovernmental organizations also affect policies and programs. UNESCO serves as a channel of ideas and concepts as well as an organizer of regional conferences in which experiences are exchanged and regional agreements on educational goals reached. Probably no single events have had the same impact on the growth of adult education as the three UNESCO world conferences on adult education, held in Elsinore, Denmark, in 1949; in Montreal, Canada, in 1960; and in Tokyo, Japan, in 1972. The study and advance preparation that took place in most countries and the governmental measures that followed the recommendations of these conferences have had marked effect.

The International Labour Organisation (ILO) has a well-developed department of workers' education with field services in most countries. ILO has sent many missions to plan workers' education, has assisted with the formation of labor colleges in such countries as Guyana, Barbados, and the Philippines, and has mounted programs of education concerning cooperatives and rural economic growth in countries such as India, Iran, and Benin.

The World Health Organization, the Food and Agriculture Organization, and the United Nations Environment Programme are more specialized, but each has influenced the development of educational programs for adults. The chief sources of support for programs are now the World Bank and the United Nations Development Programme. The fact that many United Nations missions to developing countries have included experts from each agency may have had some impact on achieving coherence in the educational programs of developing countries.

The World Bank has announced its intention to increase support for educational development, based on the conviction: "that every individual should receive a basic minimum education as soon as financial resources and the priorities of development permit; that skills should be developed selectively in response to specific and urgent needs; that educational policies should be formulated to respond flexibly to the need to develop educational systems (non-formal, informal and formal) so that the specific requirements of each society might be met; that opportunities should be extended throughout an educational system for those underprivileged groups who have been thwarted in their desire to enter the mainstream of their country's economic and social life. This must include more equitable access to education for the poor, the ill-fed, women, and rural dwellers" *(Education Sector Working Paper, 1975).*

Historically, adult education has advanced as much or more by voluntary effort as by state institutions, and so it has been internationally. There are exceptions of course—francophone countries do not have many examples of voluntary adult education projects.

Some churches continue to organize adult education projects in developing countries. It is a rare country that can prepare a history of adult education without scrutinizing the records of church or missionary societies. Many projects of literacy, community development, vocational training, agricultural extension, health education, and civic and political consciousness were first started by religious groups, including Islamic groups. Other nongovernmental agencies responsible for diffusing ideas of adult education include political parties, labor unions and cooperatives, and bodies fostering libraries, museums, and the arts.

The work of nongovernmental agencies goes on through the channels of a number of international organizations, notably the

World Council of Churches, the World Alliance of the YMCA (Young Men's Christian Association), the International Workers Education Association, the International Co-operative Alliance, the International Congress of University Adult Education, the International Council for Correspondence Education, and the International Federation of Library Associations. In 1973 representatives of national and regional organizations of adult education banded together to form the International Council for Adult Education, which acts as a general clearinghouse.

National Organizations

The main developments in any form of education occur because of leadership within a country. Unlike other forms of education, adult education has not had many examples of coherent and systematic national organization, at least until the early decades of the twentieth century. At that time national voluntary organizations were initiated in such countries as England, the United States, India, and Canada; in later decades, countries such as Kenya and Zambia developed boards of adult education, appointed and responsible to their respective governments. Governmental and voluntary organizations operate in some countries, although developing countries are more likely to utilize governmental instruments. In most cases the initiative comes from the Ministry of Education, but Ministries of Defense, Labor, and Agriculture may also become active.

It is not likely that any single plan or form of organization will suit the conditions of developing countries, but some functions are similar and necessary. At the world conference on National Organization for Adult Education, representatives of thirty-six countries noted that the functions of a national agency for adult education should include (*Report of National Organization for Adult Education,* 1975):

(a) *Establishing and maintaining two-way communication* with the organizations and institutions *inside* the country that offer various forms of adult education.

(b) *Fostering coordination* of the efforts of adult education agencies, government, non-governmental, and university, etc., inside the country.

(c) *Fostering co-operation and integration* of all forms of education, for all ages.

(d) *Establishing and maintaining two-way communication* with adult education interests *exterior* to the country: (1) UN agencies, such as UNESCO; (2) International NGO's (example, International Congress of University Adult Education); and (3) adult education organizations in other countries.

(e) Acting as an *advocate* on behalf of adult education, its needs and values, and developing a favourable climate for adult education, and extending it to those yet unserved.

(f) *Examining and appraising* laws, institutions and practices in the country from the perspective of their contribution to adult education.

(g) *Encouraging and fostering training* in adult education and the preparation and continuing education of practitioners of every kind.

(h) *Encouraging the development of research in adult education.*

(i) *Encouraging the experimentation, demonstration and refinement of methods and organization* in adult education.

(j) Encouraging the development of professional *standards* and *ethical practices* in adult education.

(k) *Identifying national social goals,* their implications for adult education, and fostering co-operation to achieve these goals.

(l) *Offering consultation and technical advice* about adult education.

(m) *Increasing the amount and sharing the resources* for adult education.

Representative Cases

Both the similarities and the differences in adult education in developing countries can best be perceived through analysis of some examples. In Tanzania a decision was taken by the highest authorities—President Julius Nyéreré and the ruling Tanu party—to include economic, social, political, and health developments in the education and training of all citizens. It is an integrated program that affects all aspects of life in Tanzania, where more money and personnel have been invested in education and training than in any country of comparable size.

Brazil, a giant in comparison with the population and resources of Tanzania, has put its major stress on eliminating illiteracy and on vocational and management training for industry. MOBRAL *(Movimento brasileiro de alfabetização)*, a national organization to achieve literacy, has enrolled millions of men and women, more than six million of whom had passed the minimum literacy tests by 1975. It has developed effective methods and materials, is training teachers and amateurs, and uses methods of evaluation that are as fully developed as anywhere. MOBRAL does not depend solely on the government for financial support; it receives contributions from industry, labor unions, agricultural organizations, and the national football lottery.

In the Philippines adult education is fostered by a department of the Ministry of Education through several avenues: workers' education sponsored by government agencies and unions, agricultural extension, and private activities of churches and universities. The variation in programs is remarkable, but coordination has not progressed very far. Both variety of educational service and lack of coordination are found in other Asian countries as well.

In most developing countries, usually the first step taken is to try to eliminate illiteracy among workers and then among other adults. Cuba achieved functional literacy for all adults in a single concentrated campaign in the early 1960s. Cuba's success depended on the combined efforts of the army, school and university teachers, professional men and women, college and secondary school students, military personnel, and the Ministries of Education, Agriculture, and Health. Continuing efforts seek to maintain and extend education through rural communes, workers' organizations, sports and leisure clubs, manpower and professional training, and the mass media. The work of many departments is coordinated under the Ministry of Education, headed by the vice-minister for adult education.

Costa Rica, a small country in Central America, is comparatively well advanced economically. Most of the adults have had a basic education in the common schools.

The Ministry of Education provides vocational training, and agricultural extension is offered to farmers over the entire country. The universities have no special department of adult education but do offer some preparation for those who will engage in community development of various kinds. The most notable institution of adult education is the privately funded *Instituto centroamericano de extensión de la cultura* (ICECU: Central American Institute for the Extension of Culture), a project for making education on economic, political, and cultural subjects available to people in all parts of the country through regular radio broadcasts and the widespread sale of publications in rather simple Spanish. So successful has Costa Rica's program become that it is also utilized by several other Latin American countries.

The countries where greatest progress has been made all exhibit national forms of organization that provide sustained drive; recruit and train adult education teachers, amateurs, and organizers; experiment with methods; and utilize all available media. Whether national leadership is provided under government or voluntary auspices or in some combination does not seem significant, but sustained leadership is a prime requirement.

While there are other successful examples, the complete story is far from satisfying. In at least forty countries—many of them the least developed countries—there is little understanding of what can be achieved through adult education, no national plan, and only sparse commitment of resources. There are signs that a change is coming even in these countries, but it will require intensive national efforts and international support.

Role of the University

The participation of the university in adult education in developing countries displays considerable variation. In no other sphere has the influence of Western countries so affected performance. For example, universities that have developed under

French influence give markedly different attention to adult education than those modeled after British or American or Canadian universities.

In some developing countries, universities take little part in adult education; the university is seen as responsible for training selected young people for intellectual pursuits, the professions, and basic research. In other countries, particularly in Latin America, the university student body includes adults attending part-time. In some, notably the smaller islands of the British West Indies, the provision of adult education programing, often called the Extra Mural Service, constitutes the university. In still others there are well-developed university or agricultural extension programs modeled after American universities or extramural services adapted from English universities.

Increasingly, the needs of adult education are beginning to be perceived as a responsibility of the university. In Kenya, Tanzania, and Zambia, special Institutes of Adult Education have been developed for teaching and research within the university structure. The institute in Dar es Salaam, Tanzania, has over fifty faculty members. In other universities—for example, the University of Rajasthan in India and the University of Tehran in Iran—the faculties or institutes of education are beginning to take responsibility for the professional preparation of adult educators. Since most professions—as well as managers in business and government—now recognize the need for continuing education and training, some universities are beginning to provide for such education. Universities in Canada, the United States, England, the Federal Republic of Germany, and Yugoslavia have been responsible for research and instruction in comparative adult education.

Despite the fact that the mass media play such an important role in adult education, reaching millions of people, few universities have given much attention to research or training for this purpose. Moreover,

no university has concentrated on the linguistic, sociological, anthropological, and psychological problems of literacy. Of course, few university professors have any experience or training to qualify them for working with illiterates, but the host of research, training, and managerial matters associated with mass educational programs has gone almost unnoticed by universities.

Trends and Implications

Differences and variations in adult education remain in developing countries, and some are being intensified. Nonetheless, underlying similarities and trends have begun to appear. In all developing countries there has been some acceptance of the notion of lifelong learning; where some attempt has been made to carry out this concept, it proved necessary to plan for all parts and components as one coherent system. In most developing countries it is understood that major economic and social goals cannot be achieved without measures of adult education, including education for civic and political consciousness, health and nutrition, and vocational training. In all developing countries it has become evident that it is not possible to educate everyone by simply multiplying traditional forms of elementary education. In most developing countries it is better understood that the expectations and aspirations of people deeply affect how productive they can become and that programs of the arts must be at the center of the adult curriculum. In most developing countries it is now better understood that a major target must be the education of women. In increasing numbers of developing countries, it is becoming accepted that universities have a responsibility for the preparation of adult educators, for the continuing education of managers and professional personnel, and for research about adult education.

One way of summarizing these trends is to note that universities in most developing countries have recognized, or are beginning to recognize, their responsibility toward all problems of development, and that the basic and continuing education of all citizens is one of the essential components of that task.

Bibliography

Coombs, P. H. *New Paths to Learning.* New York: International Council for Educational Development, 1973.

Coombs, P. H. (Ed.) *Education for Rural Development.* New York: Praeger, 1975.

Education Sector Working Paper. Washington, D.C.: World Bank, 1975.

Exeter Papers. Syracuse, New York: Syracuse University Press, 1969.

Hely, A. S. M. *New Trends in Adult Education.* Paris: UNESCO, 1962.

Kidd, J. R. *Whilst Time Is Burning.* Ottawa, Ontario: International Development Research Centre, 1974.

Kidd, J. R. (Ed.) *Anthology of Comparative Adult Education.* Syracuse, New York: Syracuse University Press, 1975.

Learning to Be. Paris: UNESCO, 1973.

Lowe, J. (Ed.) *Adult Education and Nation-Building.* Edinburgh: Edinburgh University Press, 1970.

Lowe, J. (Ed.) *Education and Nation Building in the Third World.* Edinburgh: Scottish Academic Press, 1971.

Lowe, J. *The Education of Adults: A World Perspective.* Paris: Organisation for Economic Co-operation and Development, 1975.

Report of National Organization for Adult Education. Toronto, Ontario: International Council for Adult Education, 1975.

The School and Continuing Education, Paris: UNESCO, 1972.

Simpson, J. A. *Today and Tomorrow in European Adult Education.* Strasbourg, France: Council of Europe, 1972.

The UNESCO Third World Conference on Adult Education. Paris: UNESCO, 1975.

J. ROBY KIDD

See also: Agriculture in Higher Education; Illiteracy of Adults; International Development, Role of Higher Education in.

6. ELDERLY, PROGRAMS FOR THE

Many countries are experiencing intensive efforts to improve the quality of life of older persons. A greater awareness of the needs and problems of the elderly is evidenced in social policy development, the implementation of innovative programs and services, and the growth of self-advocacy organizations. Beyond concern over basic survival needs, the question of what constitutes an appropriate and meaningful social role for the elderly person is being addressed more frequently. Institutions of higher education are a significant resource for involvement in revitalizing, socializing, and self-actualizing activities for elderly persons.

A variety of educational programs for the elderly exists in many countries, but relatively few institutions of higher education have thoroughly explored this area. In countries where social and educational resources are limited, it has not been possible to devote sufficient attention to the needs of the elderly. A recent search of the literature and broad international sampling of professionals revealed a paucity of programs designed specifically for older people. Most of the existing activity is taking place in European countries and in North America. Institutions of higher education in other areas have not yet directed serious attention to the question of how their unique resources could meet the needs of the elderly population for educational, social, and cultural opportunities.

Social Characteristics

Persons in their later years are referred to by a variety of terms: elderly, older persons, older adults, senior citizens, the aged, and persons of the third age. To define old age more adequately, cultural, chronological, and functional factors have to be considered, since each society views its older population from a unique perspective. There is little consensus as to precisely when old age begins. Some individuals may be considered old at forty-five, while people much older may be healthier and more active. Retirement is often used as a point of reference, but this concept does not apply to all persons or to all cultures. To understand the status of the elderly, it is useful to note that international aging statistics for 1970 showed 291,000,000 persons sixty years of age and older. This represents an increase of over 100,000,000 persons in that age category since 1950. By 1985 it is expected that the total number may reach 406,000,000, and, by the year 2000, the figure is expected to reach 585,000,000. This ratio represents 16 percent of the total population in developed countries and 7 percent in developing nations *(The Aging,* 1975).

With this substantial shift toward an older population, new social problems demanding new solutions will inevitably evolve. One important consideration relates to the improved functional status of older persons, most of whom are able to remain in their homes and to be relatively self-sufficient. In some parts of the world, people live to very old age without significant signs of mental, physical, or emotional deterioration. Significantly, older persons constitute an increasingly larger percentage of the total population of all countries. Individuality and diversity characterize their life styles, and, as such, the elderly represent an important human resource of experience, ability, and wisdom.

In considering the quality of life of the elderly and the currently available resources, one should give first priority to human survival needs, including income, health, housing, nutrition, and transportation. Other needs—for spiritual fulfillment, socialization, learning, and self-actualization—are also an important societal responsibility; such needs become more pressing in light of the trend in many societies toward increasing leisure time, earlier retirement, healthier and longer life, and higher levels of educational attainment.

The Older Learner

From an international perspective, no substantial precedent exists for the programs for the elderly that are being developed in specific institutions of higher education in a limited number of countries. Traditionally, older persons have participated on an individual, voluntary basis in special classes or seminars available through extramural or noncredit programs. A few aged individuals have been able to enroll

in degree programs as regular students. Educational programs uniquely designed for older persons, however, have been slow in developing, and special outreach efforts to involve the elderly have not taken place. Basic resources for higher education are limited in many countries, but there is evidence of significant efforts to develop relevant programs for the elderly or to make existing programs more accessible.

A pervasive myth prevails in some cultures that older persons cannot learn or adapt to change. But the gerontological literature makes it increasingly clear that learning ability and psychological development continue into the later years of life and that potential barriers to learning can be overcome by utilizing research findings to establish optimum learning conditions (Arenberg and Robertson, 1974). An understanding of physical and psychological factors can lead to teaching methods that will enhance the educational experiences of the older learner.

In many societies older learners today are actually better educated, more socially and politically aware, and more interested in an active, useful role in daily life. Educational opportunities should respond to the identified needs of these individuals. Needs assessment surveys aimed at the older population are useful in distinguishing special educational needs. The unique learning needs of the elderly have been conceptualized by McCluskey (1974) as falling within five categories: the older person's ability to cope successfully with life situations, to express himself through activities in a personally self-fulfilling manner, to continue contributing meaningful service to society, to exercise influence both personally and publicly, and to continue to improve his status and image.

Historically, numerous agencies, institutions, public and private schools, workers' associations, and other groups have provided a variety of educational offerings geared to the needs of all adults and, in some cases, specifically to older persons. Typical of these programs are the preretirement courses consisting of classes that focus on the problems and opportunities inherent in the transition from an employed to a retired status. Preparation-for-retirement courses deal not only with practical concerns but also with attitudinal and emotional stresses and adjustments. Another educational area associated with the elderly involves recreational activity and skill programs, such as dancing, games, travel, cooking, and crafts. Classes more educational in nature are frequently offered in such areas as language training, current events, academic subjects, or basic education. The media—including radio, television, newspapers, and magazines—play a very important role in providing more ready access to these various educational opportunities. Correspondence courses are also broadly utilized in some areas of the world. All of these programs can generally be categorized under the heading of adult education.

Until the early 1970s national and institutional priorities in higher education related more specifically to younger populations, and economic restrictions and social pressures still contribute to the retention of traditional educational models and policies. There is a growing feeling, however, that higher education has a responsibility to be more responsive to the learning needs of the total population. Universities and colleges in several countries have begun to accept this challenge and are providing programs to involve older persons.

Representative Programs

Several approaches are being utilized to include the elderly within the framework of current educational programs. Older adults frequently participate in extramural or extension courses for the general adult population. The same is true for radio or television programs sponsored by colleges and universities. Where educational priorities permit, the elderly enroll as either full- or part-time students in regular courses. In a few cases they participate as full residents, taking courses, using dining and residential facilities, and mingling with younger students.

Some institutions have established special programs to meet the needs of the elderly for more in-depth knowledge and information in a variety of traditional academic areas and to provide creative outlets in artistic and intellectual areas for needs that cannot be satisfied at other levels. Another significant purpose is to provide the kinds of courses and experiences that enable the older person to relate more effectively to the rapid changes in all facets of contemporary living. This future orientation may address itself to political, scientific, economic, and technological change, as well as to evolving social, philosophical, and spiritual values and customs. Finally, the intellectual environment and ambience in the higher education setting provide a unique opportunity for stimulating discussions, lectures, and social experiences.

Université du troisième âge. Initiated in 1973 at the University of Toulouse in France, the University of the Third Age has already established an international reputation and stimulated the development of similar programs throughout France and in other European countries. The basic program model, designed specifically for older persons, consists of two six-week sessions and an intersession during the summer. All elderly persons, regardless of educational background, are welcome to participate in the various activities. Special courses of a practical and an intellectual nature geared to the needs and interests of the elderly are offered. Classes are held mainly at the university outside the regular academic year; however, younger students are available for contact and exchange. A diverse program of social, cultural, and physical activities complements more traditional sessions of lecture and discussion.

University of British Columbia. After a successful 1974 summer session focused on the learning needs of the elderly, the University of British Columbia in Vancouver, Canada, decided to open its doors to senior citizens over sixty-five to take credit courses during the regular academic year. During a six-week summer session, credit and special-interest programs are offered free to the elderly. Residential facilities are available. As the program has evolved, senior citizens have been given a greater role in program planning.

University of Kentucky. The University of Kentucky in Lexington pioneered in the development of tuition-free classes for credit or noncredit. Each year the university's Council on Aging provides scholarships and enrolls a limited group of persons over sixty-five who are in reasonably good health and well-motivated. The third age scholars can enroll in any regular class on a space-available basis and typically participate in one or more classes per semester. They may also enroll in special courses designed specifically for the elderly. The concept of permitting the older adults to enroll on a space-available, tuition-free basis is now being implemented in a large number of colleges and universities throughout the United States.

Inamino Gakuen University. This free, four-year university in Kakegowa, Japan, has been designed solely for the elderly population of one geographical area. A broad standardized curriculum and specialized classes are offered to students one day per week. For those unable to attend weekly sessions, correspondence courses are available. Residential facilities also make it possible for handicapped elderly to attend classes at specified times. Active student clubs extend learning and social possibilities. The concept of a university created specifically for older persons is also being developed in the United States.

Institute of Retired Professionals. Established for many years, the program at the New School for Social Research in New York City is aimed at retired professionals, businessmen, and other well-educated older adults who seek a stimulating learning environment. The participants enact the roles of both students and teachers. Most classes use the discussion group for-mat, which provides maximum involvement and interaction. Membership fees cover participation in the institute activities plus one regular course each semester at the New School.

Community colleges. One of the fastest-growing examples of involvement with elderly persons and their needs can be seen in the two-year community colleges of the United States and Canada. Many of these institutions have already established a variety of approaches to serving older adults: special educational programs, the delivery of social services, community consultation and planning, and the opportunity to participate in regular degree or certificate programs on a credit or non-credit basis.

Trends and Implications

On the whole, the future looks promising for greater involvement of the third age population in programs offered through institutions of higher learning. Older persons are beginning to take a more active role in their own behalf, to demand greater educational opportunities at all levels, and to take more responsibility for leadership in program development.

Institutions of higher education will need to consider how to adapt to a diverse and highly motivated older student population. In subsequent years older cohorts will be increasingly better educated, and their needs for social, recreational, and educational experiences will continue to expand. Ongoing needs assessment and outreach will be essential components of a responsible, relevant educational effort. Questions of program costs, location of classes, class length, educational environment, curriculum, educational materials, transportation, counseling, and food and comfort services will require a fresh, innovative approach and continuing scrutiny. There will be a great need for research and planning to determine the most appropriate role and use of existing resources.

In developing this educational role, special attention should be given to several crucial concerns. One is the need of the elderly to cope with the rapid changes taking place in society, not only in practical areas that affect their daily lives but in areas of evolving values and life styles. Concurrently, greater opportunities for exchange and interaction must be provided for younger and older age groups. Realistic programs and goals need to be developed to enable qualified older persons to continue to pursue credit and noncredit educational programs offering degrees or certificates. These programs should relate to the specific educational needs of the elderly in particular localities for either career or life satisfaction goals. Presentations and performances of a cultural or intellectual nature, as well as social activities, will provide older persons with an added dimension of enrichment and stimulation.

Universities and colleges are in a unique position to influence societal attitudes toward improvement of the quality of life of the elderly. These institutions need to become more aware of the leading role they can play in anticipating and providing for the needs of a larger, better educated, healthier, and more animated third age population.

Bibliography

The Aging: Trends and Policies. New York: United Nations Department of Economic and Social Affairs, 1975.

Arenberg, D., and Robertson, E. "The Older Individual as Learner." In S. M. Grabowski and W. Mason (Eds.), *Learning for Aging.* Washington, D.C.: Adult Education Association and Educational Resources Information Center Clearinghouse on Adult Education, 1974.

Carlson, C. *New Education for New Students: A Senior Citizen Project.* Bakersfield, California: Bakersfield College, 1974.

Fulton, O. "Higher Education in the 80's. Part III: Recurrent Education." *Universities Quarterly,* Winter 1973, *28,* 30–37.

Grabowski, S. M., and Mason, W. (Eds.) *Learning for Aging.* Washington, D.C.: Adult Education Association and Educational Resources Information Center Clearinghouse on Adult Education, 1974.

Groombridge, B. (Ed.) *Adult Education and Television.* London: National Institute of Adult Education, 1966.

Hendrickson, A. (Ed.) *A Manual on Planning Educational Programs for Older Adults.* Tallahassee: Florida State University, 1973.

Hiemstra, R. P. "Educational Planning for Older Adults: A Survey of 'Expressive' Versus 'Instrumental' Preferences." *International Journal of Aging and Human Development,* 1973, *4*(2), 147–156.

Korim, A. S. *Older Americans and Community Colleges: A Guide for Program Implementation.* Washington, D.C.: American Association of Community and Junior Colleges, 1974.

Leisure and the Third Age. Paris: International Center of Social Gerontology, 1972.

Lowe, J. (Ed.) *Adult Education and Nation Building.* Edinburgh: Edinburgh University Press, 1970.

McCluskey, H. "Education for Aging: The Scope of the Field and Perspectives for the Future." In S. M. Grabowski and W. Mason (Eds.), *Learning for Aging.* Washington, D.C.: Adult Education Association and Educational Resources Information Center Clearinghouse on Adult Education, 1974.

Never Too Old to Learn. New York: Academy for Educational Development, 1974.

Parkyn, G. W. *Towards a Conceptual Model of Life-Long Education.* Paris: UNESCO, 1973.

"Prefectural 'University' for Elderly Reawakens Delight in Learning." *Japan Report,* May 1975, *21,* 7.

Scott, F. G. "Innovative Educational Opportunities for Older Persons." *Adult Leadership,* April 1974, *22,* 337–343.

Simpson, J. A. *Today and Tomorrow in European Adult Education.* Strasbourg, France: Council of Europe, 1972.

Stetar, J. M. "Community Colleges and the Educational Needs of Older Adults." *Journal of Higher Education,* December 1974, *45,* 717–721.

Vellas, P. "Les universités du troisième age." *Echanges internationaux et développement,* April 1975, *35,* 58–88.

E. PERCIL STANFORD

DAVID C. PRITCHARD

7. POSTEXPERIENCE EDUCATION

Postexperience higher education can be defined as education for persons who have already completed a degree program or gained its equivalent through practical work and who have had professional experience. Courses that update or refresh professional knowledge or retrain or improve specialized skills may lead to a certificate or diploma but not directly to a higher degree. Postexperience education differs from other forms of adult education or from the broad function of university extension in two ways: its aims are more clearly defined, and its content is more closely linked with practice.

The modern world is in the process of rapid scientific, technological, and socioeconomic development that leads to rapid obsolescence of previous knowledge and the emergence of new areas of knowledge and research and new branches of industry. Research in the field of higher education shows, for example, that only a relatively small proportion of the knowledge gained by engineers during their initial university studies remains useful five years after graduation. In addition, surveys in several countries have shown that many university graduates do not work in their original fields of study and that the character of many jobs changes at least once or twice during an individual's career. Such facts, and many more that might be quoted, prove that universities cannot provide their undergraduates with all the knowledge they will need during the whole of their active working lives. Thus, the need to refresh and expand knowledge and to retrain workers for new types of activity becomes more and more urgent. Lifelong postexperience higher education programs are needed to keep specialists at an adequate level of competence and to orient manpower toward new sectors of the economy.

The rapid development of higher education during 1950 to 1970, with as many as four times the previous number of students, produced large numbers of specialists now working in various branches of the economy. Simply from a quantitative point of view, the vast number of former graduates requires that postexperience opportunities be offered on a systematic basis. Already, in the majority of countries, it is considered as a major function of higher education systems.

Types of Programs

Postexperience higher education was initiated mainly in the 1960s, although in some fields, such as medicine, teacher training, and agriculture, it was organized somewhat earlier. In a few countries it existed as early as the late 1940s and early 1950s. By the mid 1970s courses were being offered at most universities, with management the field of greatest activity, followed closely by engineering, medicine, teacher training, and agriculture.

A close correlation exists between socioeconomic planning and the development of postexperience higher education. As a result, postexperience higher education is developing more successfully in countries where manpower planning is linked with planning of higher education (for example, in the Soviet Union, the German Democratic Republic, and other socialist countries). In other countries, it is carried out in a fragmented manner, uncoordinated with manpower retraining needs or government policy, and offered instead in response to industrial, economic, and social demands that reflect indirect socioeconomic planning. In these cases postexperience higher education is accomplished through government support and funding of significant industrial, community, and research activities or projects. In the less developed countries postexperience education is largely government-sponsored, to train civil servants. The developed countries are using postexperience training to refresh or retrain many professional specialists for new or different types of work.

For example, professional societies in the United States, such as the American Medical Association Council on Medical Education and the American Dental Association Council on Dental Education, provide continuing education programs on a national level for practitioners. Local programs are frequently provided by the faculty and staff of various professional schools or local sections of the particular professional organizations. This approach applies not only to allopathic medicine and dentistry but also to pharmacy, podiatry, optometry, nursing, osteopathic and veterinary medicine, and the various allied health professions (such as medical laboratory science; physical, occupational, and respiratory therapies; medical records administration; and X-ray technology).

Organization and Financing

Organizational patterns for postexperience higher education are varied, both at the national and at the local institutional or professional society levels. In the Soviet Union such courses are organized in the universities under the Ministry of Higher and Specialized Secondary Education and in specialized institutions under industrial ministries and other government bodies, with the financing, general methodological leadership, and coordination of activities assumed by the Ministry of Higher Education. In the United States postexperience higher education, though relatively well developed, is, with notable exceptions, considered as part of the extension function of universities and must therefore be at least partially self-supporting if not income producing. However, state institutions usually subsidize postexperience courses, and industry frequently provides job-related advanced training to employees at no cost. The United Kingdom stands midway between these two situations. Government-sponsored postexperience higher education exists in many fields (medicine is covered by postgraduate medical faculties and management by regional centers); university extramural departments also organize such courses. In universities, postexperience education is usually offered through existing university departments or divisions for such traditional fields as medicine and engineering or through the creation of new units specifically created for training in such fields as management and university-level teaching staff.

In the German Democratic Republic and in Latin America, postexperience higher education is directed by administrative units dealing with all types of further education, including postgraduate studies.

The full-time block-release course predominates in postexperience higher education, but evening and correspondence courses also exist. The form the course takes is crucial to the achievement of its objectives. Full-time courses offer several advantages: participants can be trained in specialized fields in a relatively short time; training can serve wide national or even international needs; administration of courses is easy; and dropout rates are usually low. However, full-time courses are more expensive than part-time courses, since they involve transportation and housing costs in addition to normal tuition and related expenses. Although part-time courses, either daytime or evening, are more difficult to administer and can only serve local demand, the unit costs are lower, and effectiveness is often higher than in full-time courses, since participants have more time for independent study and more opportunity to apply newly acquired ideas in their everyday work.

Some correlation exists between methods of financing postexperience training and its organizational pattern. Where funds come either from government sources for postexperience education in general or from contributors who do not specify the particular use to which the money should be put, universities have flexibility in designing organizational patterns to suit particular situations. Where there are direct relationships between the universities and funding organizations, the pattern is less flexible. The problem is to find the optimum correlation between these two general patterns.

In both industrialized and developing countries, where a specific government policy has been elaborated and legislation enacted for postexperience higher education, government is the most important source of direct and indirect financing. Industry is the second most important source of funding in highly developed countries, and participants themselves are the third. Contributions from regular university budgets are usually very modest, as are those from professional societies in countries where such institutions play an important role in economic life. In spite of the multiplicity of sources of finance in developed countries, where no clearly stated government policy toward postexperience higher education exists, scarcity of funds is a major problem. The less developed countries have even more restricted sources of finance; the government provides most funding.

Faculty

Postexperience students enter their courses with diverse backgrounds as well as specific and often unique learning objectives. As a result, faculty members must be managers of a complex learning process designed to accommodate these backgrounds and objectives. Faculty must encourage a learning climate that facilitates self-directed inquiry, individual and group needs assessment, structures for mutual planning, and minimum dependency and tension on the part of the students. The challenge facing faculty members is to design, provide, or suggest the proper mix of learning experiences for each member of a class. To cope with this challenge, faculty must be familiar with a variety of learning modes, media, equipment, and outside resources.

The participation of outside experts as adjunct faculty members generally depends on the policies of the sponsoring institution and the field of study. In the United States, outside experts from industry, government, and consulting and research organizations typically comprise 25 percent of postexperience higher education faculty. Notable exceptions occur at some institutions, such as Northeastern University in Boston, where 80 percent of the engineering postexperience faculty are full-time professionals or consultants. Northeastern's programs also make extensive use of guest lecturers, with continuity

provided by faculty coordinators present at all sessions. Some of these programs are conducted by two to four faculty members working in a team; such an approach enables each faculty member to make the most appropriate contribution to the program, as when university-based professors present underlying scientific principles and industry-based practitioners discuss pragmatic case studies and applications.

Methods of Instruction

One encouraging phenomenon in institutions where postexperience higher education is highly developed is that government, industry, professional societies, university staff, and participants all take some part in formulating curricula and contributing to the organization of the educational process. Nevertheless, the major burden of preparing curricula rests with university faculty and staff, who must take into consideration the requirements of other agencies.

The most important forms of instruction are conferences, lectures, group discussions, laboratory work, and, less frequently, programed instruction. These forms accent active teaching and learning, where participants have the opportunity to express their own views or react to the views expressed by teachers. Discussions following lectures are considered an important means of active feedback, even for off-campus students. Many sponsoring institutions state as a requirement for their courses that participants prepare themselves by reading a list of materials beforehand. In some fields new teaching and learning arrangements are being developed. For example, in the United States the State University of New York at Buffalo provides lectures in medicine and health-related sciences by telephone to hospitals where groups gather to hear the lectures and take part in the discussion that follows. Some medical schools operate computerized information services that enable medical practitioners to ask the computer questions of diagnosis and treatment.

Evaluation

Evaluation of postexperience higher education should provide information about the amount and quality of work done, whether the education is socially valuable, and means of improving the course. At least five aspects of evaluation can be distinguished.

1. *Evaluation of participants' performance* is normally effected on the basis of work done during the course. Sometimes oral or written examinations are used, but, generally speaking, examinations are not the rule in postexperience higher education. A form of appraisal that seems to be very suitable to this type of education is self-evaluation by participants, and a trend toward such evaluation can be seen. An important evaluation method in the field of medicine is that of three- to six-month follow-up surveys on changes in patient care as a result of training and new knowledge.

2. *Participants' own evaluation of the course,* the most highly developed form of evaluation, is generally accomplished by questionnaires, either circulated at the course or posted afterward. In other cases a group of participants is selected to evaluate the course in a discussion. In an interesting application at the Uttar Pradesh Agricultural University in India, evaluation of the course begins not when the course finishes but before it starts. As soon as they arrive, participants evaluate the curriculum and its relevance to their practical work, after which it is revised in accordance with their needs.

3. *Evaluation of courses by outside organizations* is infrequent but can be particularly useful in ensuring that courses will continue and that they will be considered valuable by consumers. For example, participants' continuing links with universities after completing postexperience courses is considered a sign of a good program. The Soviet Union and German Democratic Republic use this type of evaluation for postexperience higher education as well as for normal university courses. In some other countries, outside evaluation takes the form of accreditation by professional societies. And some employers assess the work performance of course participants over a period of years and compare it with a control group.

4. *Evaluation of the overall economic, scientific, and technical effects of postexperience higher education* is the most fundamental but most difficult type of evaluation to carry out. The University of Novi Sad, Yugoslavia, has made some attempts to measure the economic effect of its postexperience agricultural courses. Other attempts have been made to measure scientific and technological effects by comparing the number of new ideas or patents produced by former participants of postexperience courses with their output before the course.

5. *Evaluation of the impact of postexperience higher education on university performance* reveals, for example, that participants in postexperience courses generally have considerable information on real economic and technical problems, have practical knowledge of the latest achievements in their particular fields, and are aware of new areas of university research.

Outlook for the Future

The field of postexperience higher education is still in an experimental stage, and many questions about its effectiveness remain unresolved. Of major importance are developments of the following kinds: a system of indices and criteria for comparing different forms and methods of training; specific teaching and learning methods that take into account the diverse nature of participants; methods for motivating independent study among specialists not attending organized courses; models of prospective specialties and determination of permanent and changing areas of knowledge necessary to each; and methods of planning postexperience programs. The bibliography lists a number of studies conducted by international or intergovernmental agencies involved in the field of postexperience higher education. However, a great deal of research remains to be done in this relatively new and important area.

Bibliography

Broadbent, D. "Continuing Education and Retraining of Engineers and Technicians." *Journal of Engineering Education in Southeast Asia,* 1971, *1.*

Continuing Education for Physicians. Technical Report Series 534. Geneva: World Health Organization, 1973.

Fassbender. S. *Wie lehrt und lernt Man Management?* Frankfurt/Main, Federal Republic of Germany: Fritz Knapp Verlag, 1973.

French, D. D. *The Sources, Selection and Development of Faculty for Continuing Engineering Studies Programs.* Continuing Engineering Studies Series, 9. Washington, D.C.: American Society for Engineering Education, November 1, 1974.

Greenaway, H. *Training of University Teachers.* London: Society for Research into Higher Education, 1971.

Grisard, D. *L'université et la formational permanente.* Dijon, France: Institut de recherche sur l'économie de l'éducation, 1974.

Knowles, M. S. *The Modern Practice of Adult Education.* New York: Association Press, 1970.

Liapunov, A. "The Retraining of Engineers in the Soviet Union." *Bulletin of the International Association of Universities,* 1973, *21*(1), 10–12.

Onushkin, V. G. *The Role of Universities in Post-Experience Higher Education.* Paris: International Institute for Educational Planning, 1974.

Recurrent Education Policy and Development in OECD Countries. Paris: Organisation for Economic Co-operation and Development, 1973–74.

Report of the Meeting of the International Working Group on Continuing Education of Engineers. Paris: UNESCO, June 1973.

Stoikov, V. "Recurrent Education: Some Neglected Economic Issues." *International Labour Review,* July/August 1973, *108* (2–3) 187–208.

Styler, W. E. "Post-Experience and the Universities." Hull, England: University of Hull, Department of Adult Education, 1973.

                                   VICTOR G. ONUSHKIN

See also: Credit, Assessment of Learning for Postsecondary Education; Graduate and Professional Education: Postdoctoral Education.

ADULT EDUCATION ASSOCIATION OF THE U.S.A.

In May 1951 the American Association for Adult Education and the Department of Adult Education of the National Education Association were dissolved and their membership merged into a new organization, the Adult Education Association of the U.S.A. (AEA). Membership consists of individuals and institutions interested in and committed to the field of adult education. The association's affiliate is the Council of National Organizations for Adult Education.

AEA is governed by an executive committee composed of the steering committee (officers, comptroller, and executive director), twelve regional representatives, two one-year-term representatives-at-large, a graduate student in adult education, and representatives of the Council of National Organizations and the Council of Affiliate Organizations (made up of state and local adult education associations). Association activities are administered by an executive director and seven staff members and are financed through membership dues and sale of publications.

AEA serves its constituents and the cause of adult education through field services; legislative activities; special projects; an information service; and state, regional, and national conferences.

The AEA publications are *Adult Leadership,* ten issues a year; *Adult Education,* quarterly; Leadership Pamphlet Series, topical collection of published articles; *Leader's Digest,* selection of articles from past volumes of *Adult Leadership;* and adult education monographs.

810 18th Street NW
Washington, D.C. 20006 USA

ADULT EDUCATION, TEACHER TRAINING FOR (Field of Study)

Adult education (also called further education, century education, postsecondary education, recurrent education, continuing education, permanent education, lifelong education, or out-of-school education) involves a return to organized learning activity by individuals who because of age, employment, or family situations cannot conveniently be enrolled in the established school system. Nearly all adults who participate in an organized learning program do so on a part-time basis. Many programs are highly individualized: correspondence education (called "distance" education in much of Europe), radio broadcasts (particularly of literacy or other mass education programs), and television "sunrise semester" classes (usually lecture series, often offering academic credit from a sponsoring university at nonpeak viewing hours). The most common adult education programs are offered at established elementary or secondary schools, colleges and universities, libraries, museums, religious institutions, and a wide range of voluntary associations. In fact, every membership organization that has a point of view usually endeavors to share it through so-called educational activities with as large an audience as possible.

Another brand of adult education is literacy education—offered by local school authorities, churches, voluntary societies, and, in the United States, sometimes by community colleges. Other adult education programs are vocational (including agriculture) and technical education, secondary school completions, continuing professional development, and liberal education in the arts and humanities. Increasingly, in the industrialized nations as well as in the economically developing countries, learning opportunities are available to adults in such areas as nutrition and health, consumer education, and infant and child care.

Adult educators cannot agree on whether adult education is a "fourth level" of education, flowing sequentially after elementary, secondary, and higher education, or whether it is an integral part of all three. There also are differences of opinion as to whether the education of adults can be carried on successfully by agencies set up primarily for the education of young adults or whether it can best be undertaken by churches, libraries, community development departments, or other agencies established to deal exclusively with adults. In many countries the function is divided: a Ministry of Education provides for the education of children, and a Ministry of Community Development provides for the education of adults. In some countries there are workers' universities or folk high schools or employer-organized classes, which operate independently of the national Ministry of Education or local educational authorities or institutions of higher education. But in many other countries the burden of providing educational opportunities for adults falls on the public education authority, on the universities, and on other established agencies whose primary purpose is not the education of adults. There are many arguments to support such a procedure: cost effectiveness, public responsibility, access to a trained teaching staff, availability of instructional facilities in remote and rural areas, and a steadily growing and unmet need.

As a self-conscious and organized movement, adult education is a twentieth-century development. But from the school of Socrates through the classes in English for the foreign born offered by public schools in the United States during the melting-pot years of the nineteenth and early twentieth centuries, and the folk high school movement in the Scandinavian countries in the latter half of the nineteenth century, adults have been receiving systematic, organized instruction. In countries influenced by the British educational system, extramural programs for adults have long been offered to extend university training to individuals unable to attend classes at a college or university. One of the most significant innovations in adult education in the United States was the agricultural extension program, authorized by Congress in 1914, which brought the demonstration method of instruction to rural Americans through a series of program "extensions" of the agricultural colleges.

The concept of education as a lifelong process became fully developed in the United States shortly after the turn of the nineteenth century. The rapid expansion of lyceums (local assemblies which presented debates and lectures on topics of current interest), followed later by the chautauquas (annual assemblies offering programs and lectures, patterned after the original assembly held first in 1874 in Chautauqua, New York, and later held in all parts of the United States), spurred the adult education movement. In the United Kingdom the workers' education movement fulfilled a similar function. In the 1970s adult education is a significant part of education on all levels, and the facilities and resources available for the education of adults grow with each decade—although, because of the complexities of modern industrial societies, the needs always outstrip the resources.

Adult education demands a wide range of training experiences, on at least three levels: (1) highly technical and theoretical preparation programs for individuals engaged full time in policy development, teacher training, and long-range planning; (2) brief orientation programs for beginning teachers and field workers—often part-time and volunteer workers; and, in between, (3) training programs for organizers, administrators, and career teachers.

Because of the relative newness of adult education as an organized field of study and because of the universal nature of its concerns, both graduate and undergraduate programs originally relied heavily on the social sciences (including general education and agricultural education) in curriculum building. Since the 1960s, however, a body of research and theoretical knowledge specifically related to the education of adults has developed, and adult education is increasingly identified as a distinct discipline.

Diploma programs in adult education may be followed at leading universities in Eastern Europe and in Africa; usually such programs are offered in the school of education within a university. In most of the unindustrialized and developing countries, however, there are no undergraduate programs for individuals specializing in the education of adults. For example, in South America, Asia, and some countries in Africa, where there are very few degree programs in adult education, teachers and designers of many of the in-service education programs for workers engaged in the operational aspects of adult education at the village or community level have themselves had no formal or academic training in adult education. Often in such cases specialists in the media or in such disciplines as food and agriculture, engineering, or family planning are influential in the planning and development of adult education programs.

Graduate programs are most numerous in North America and Europe. In the United States the first Ph.D. program in adult education dates from 1935, and by 1971 there were sixty-eight doctoral-level programs. About two thirds of the advanced degree programs are in North America, one third in Europe. At the University of Sydney (Australia), a Master of Education degree is offered in adult education. In addition—partly because of the training of foreign nationals in the graduate adult education programs of North American and European universities, and partly through the use of specialists from other disciplines—seminars and institutes are available in the industrialized and the developing countries for present or potential managers, senior instructional staff, and organizers of adult education activities. These programs, usually limited to individuals with prior experience as teachers or field workers, often combine academic training with intern-type learning experiences.

In the Federal Republic of Germany refresher courses for full-time teachers, correspondence courses for full-time and part-time adult educators, and subject matter or media seminars are regularly offered as in-service training courses for full- and part-time teachers. The program, organized and sponsored by the *Deutscher Volkshochschul-Verband,* combines adult education theory with actual practice, and is designed for teachers who have a university degree.

In the People's Republic of China selected part-time teachers from the communes are brought into educational centers for six to eight months of training before returning to continue teaching in the classes found in nearly every factory and agricultural commune. The emphasis of the training programs is on the methodology of the literacy effort, the improvement of health practices, and the control of venereal disease. In the May 7 schools, established as a part of the Cultural Revolution's educational reforms, civil servants and party leaders work at agricultural and other manual jobs while receiving more formal types of continuing education. Similar "paid-leave" training programs are common in the Soviet Union.

In Tanzania literacy teachers and health officers were involved in a series of trainer-of-trainers seminars as the first step of an effort that eventually provided 70,000 group leaders for a mass health education campaign.

On a multinational level the fellowship program of the International Labour Organisation in Geneva and the programs of the Mount Carmel Training Center in Haifa, Israel, offer theoretical training and supervised fieldwork for leaders in workers' education and community development. Under the auspices of UNESCO, literacy and community development training centers are maintained in Egypt for service to the Arab states and in Mexico for Latin America.

Far more prevalent, because of the larger numbers to be served, are the short courses and institutes for beginning adult education workers. Such training programs—which range from a day, or even a few hours, to several weeks or for the length of a summer school term—are diverse and can be expected to emphasize immediately applicable techniques and procedures. One example of this type of program is the two-week residential workshop in Thailand for teachers in the primary and secondary schools; the purpose of this workshop is to introduce the skills required to teach combined functional literacy and family-planning programs to adults. Other examples are short courses given in Singapore for workers employed in the community centers and for teachers of adults in the classes organized to give instruction in any of the four official languages. In the United States brief orientation programs (as brief as a few hours) are provided for adult education teachers who are reaching a new clientele; for example, teachers learn to use interpreters in classes in which the deaf are enrolled. In contrast, agricultural, literacy, urban-living, and health education workers may attend summer-long residential programs. In Colombia, Honduras, and Botswana, volunteers receive training in how to organize listening groups and promote attendance among villagers receiving radio lessons in reading, farm practices, hygiene, and social progress.

Some students of the field believe that advances in adult education will be best obtained if training is more closely integrated into ongoing educational programs. This approach to adult education is found in the concept of the *animateur* (animator or "moving spirit"), where the primary teacher is given training in ways of identifying promising young adults who can become agents for cultural development and social change. Examples of this kind of training are found in France, French-speaking Africa, and parts of Canada. Similarly, Yugoslavia's standard system of training is designed to provide all students enrolled in the universities with some knowledge of informal, out-of-school methods of adult education.

In the foreseeable future all three levels of training programs are expected to attract more students. In North America and

Europe graduate and undergraduate programs probably will maintain their position
of importance, and African countries may
be the scene of the greatest growth in the
opening of new programs in higher education. Training programs at this level, if they
are to retain their influence, will need to
attract additional students with a background in health education, agriculture,
mass communication, and other specialties.
The professional preparation programs
will need to offer enriched opportunities
for internship and on-the-job study and,
in so doing, will provide greater support
and trainer-of-trainer services to the
middle-level programs for administrators
and career teachers. Finally, the continuing
extension of adult education programs into
community and village life—and, in some
countries, into factories—will require increasing numbers of volunteers and part-
time field workers and teachers. If the
workers at the contact level are to function
effectively, they will need the support
services available from the professional
and intermediate levels.

ROBERT A. LUKE

Levels and Programs of Study

Programs for teacher training in adult
education generally require as a prerequisite a secondary education, though mature
students with related work experience are
often admitted with lower educational
qualifications. For short programs—especially programs designed to improve the
qualifications of teachers or programs for
out-of-school instructors—related work
experience is usually given greater weight
than educational qualifications. Study at
the postgraduate university level usually
requires the holding of an initial teacher
qualification, demonstrated potential for
study at that level, and, in some programs,
experience in teaching or administration
at an appropriate level. Usual awards for
successful completion are certificate or
diploma, teaching certificate or diploma,
master's degree, the doctorate, or their
equivalents.

Programs that lead to awards not equivalent to a first university degree are designed
to train students as teachers or out-of-school
instructors in adult education, including
adult literacy and extension and other
types of adult education, and consist of
lectures and practice teaching. Emphasis
is placed on practice teaching and on the
practical aspects of adult education rather
than on the theory of education. Programs
for teachers, generally full time for two to
four years, are usually given in a teachers
college or special adult education training
institution; those for instructors are often
part time for one year or less.

Principal course content is geared to the
problems of the adults to be educated, but
usually includes the history, philosophy,
psychology, and sociology of education;
specific courses related to problems of the
teaching and retraining of adults; relevant
vocational or academic subjects; lesson
planning; audiovisual aids; and school
administration. In addition, time is devoted
to observing experienced teachers and to
supervised practice teaching.

For staff of extension and other types of
nonformal education, emphasis is given
to sociology related to development, adult
and adolescent psychology, learning theory
and the study of attitude change, methods
of demonstration, and the practical use of
communication methods and media.

Programs at the first university degree
level are designed to train adult education
teachers (in and out of school) qualified to
teach at the second level and the third non-
degree level of education and consist of
lectures, group discussion, and practice
teaching. The programs, full or part time
for the equivalent of one year's full-time
study or less, are usually given in a teachers
college, a university, or a special adult education training institution. They consist
primarily of courses in pedagogy (teacher
training) and related subjects such as the
theory of education. Usually included are
courses in the history, philosophy, psychology, and sociology of education; the
theory and practice of teaching in general

and of teaching and retraining adults; and special problems encountered in communicating with adults from varied backgrounds. In addition, time is devoted to observing experienced teachers and to supervised practice teaching. Principal course content for those planning to engage in extension work and other types of out-of-school education emphasizes the subject matter to be taught, sociology related to the groups concerned, learning theory, attitudes and reactions to change, and practice demonstrations.

Programs that lead to a postgraduate university degree are designed to prepare specialists in teaching and curriculum development in adult or continuing education. Programs usually last from one to three years, full time, and may consist of a certain number of prescribed courses, demonstrated facility in one or more foreign languages, and the preparation of a thesis or dissertation involving original research into a particular problem within the major subject. Through seminars, directed reading, and independent research, the student seeks to acquire a comprehensive grasp of one field within the general field of adult education—for instance, adult counseling, adult education within the community, problems relating to the education of older people, or extension or other types of nonformal education—and may prepare one or more subjects in related or other areas of education.

[This section was based on UNESCO's *International Standard Classification of Education (ISCED): Three Stage System, 1974* (Paris: UNESCO, 1974).]

Major International and National Organizations

INTERNATIONAL

African Adult Education Association
% Institute of Adult Education
University of Ghana
Legon, Accra, Ghana
    Arranges for research into problems of adult education in Africa; acts as a clearinghouse for

information; publishes a journal, newsletter, and reports.

Asian South Pacific Bureau of Adult Education
% Indian Adult Education Association
17B Indraprastha Marg
New Delhi 1, India

Council of Europe, Council for Cultural
    Co-operation
Committee for Out-of-School Education and
    Cultural Development
avenue de l'Europe
67 Strasbourg, France

Division of Adult Education
UNESCO
place de Fontenoy
75700 Paris, France

European Association for Catholic Adult
    Education
Dransdorferweg 15/IV
53 Bonn, Federal Republic of Germany

European Bureau of Adult Education
Nieueweg 4, P.O. Box 367
Amersfoort, Netherlands
    Conducts study sessions and research; provides an abstracting service.

Interamerican Federation for Adult Education
Apartado 20.016, San Martin
Caracas, Venezuela
    Coordinates and strengthens adult education associations in Latin America; publishes miscellaneous documents.

International Congress of University Adult
    Education
Department of Educational Studies
11 Buccleuch Place
Edinburgh EH8 9JT, Scotland
    Works to establish regional information and library centers and to improve educator exchanges; conducts conferences and seminars and publishes a journal.

International Council for Adult Education
P.O. Box 250, Station F
Toronto, Ontario, Canada
    Provides communication between individuals and organizations engaged in adult education throughout the world; undertakes studies, conferences, and other activities.

Literacy International
% Indian Adult Education Association
17B Indraprastha Marg
New Delhi 1, India
    Conducts seminars, workshops, and conferences for professional literacy workers; provides an information and documentation service.

Regional Council for Adult Education and
Literacy in Africa
Conseil régional pour l'éducation et
l'alphabétisation des adultes en Afrique
(CREAA)
Permanent Secretary: P.N.A.
Ministère de la santé publique et des affaires
sociales
Lomé, Togo

UNESCO Institute for Education
Feldbrunnenstrasse 70
D-2000 Hamburg 13, Federal Republic of
Germany
Current activity centers on a long-range
and comprehensive program of research and
development and information on lifelong
education.

World Confederation of Organizations of the
Teaching Profession
Adult Education Commission
5 avenue de Moulin
1110 Morges, Switzerland
Composed of national, associate, and international organizations totaling five million
teachers in eighty-five countries; publishes
material on various aspects of the teaching
profession.

NATIONAL

Australia:
Australian Association of Adult
Education
P.O. Box 1346
Canberra City, ACT 2601

Canada:
Canadian Association for Adult
Education
228 St. George St.
Toronto 5, Ontario

Denmark:
Scandinavian Adult Education
Information Office
Faervergade 27
Copenhagen

Federal Republic of Germany:
Deutscher Volkshochschule-Verband
Heerstrasse 100
53 Bonn–Bad Godesberg

Finland:
Finnish Association of Adult Education
Organizations
Museokatu 18 A2
Helsinki

France:
Institut national pour la formation des
adultes
Nancy

India:
Indian Adult Education Association
17B Indraprastha Marg
New Delhi 1

Ireland:
Irish National Adult Education
Association
62-63 Eccles Street
Dublin 7

Italy:
Unione italiana della cultura popolare
via Daverio 7
Milan

Kenya:
Board of Adult Education
Gill House, Government Road
P.O. Box 30117
Nairobi

New Zealand:
National Council of Adult Education
P.O. Box 12-114
Wellington

Nigeria:
Nigerian National Council for Adult
Education (NNCAE)
% Department of Adult Education
University of Ibadan
Ibadan

Norway:
Norwegian Adult Education Institute
University of Trondheim
7001 Trondheim

Soviet Union:
All-Union Society for the Spread of
Scientific Knowledge
Proezd Serova 4, Pod'ezd 8
Moscow

Sweden:
Adult Education Association
Drottninggatan 77
III 60 Stockholm

Switzerland:
Swiss Federation for Adult Education
Beckenhofstrasse 6, Postfach CH-8057
Zurich

Tanzania:
National Adult Education Association
of Tanzania
P.O. Box 20679
Dar es Salaam

United Kingdom:
National Institute of Adult Education
35 Queen Anne Street
London W1M 0BL, England

Scottish Institute of Adult Education
Alloa, Clackmannanshire, Scotland

United States:
Council of National Organizations for
Adult Education
810 18th Street NW
Washington, D.C. 20006
Federation of national and interna-
tional organizations with a concern for
adult education.

Adult Education Association of the USA
810 18th Street NW
Washington, D.C. 20006

Commission of Professors of Adult
Education
208 Agricultural Hall, University of
Wisconsin
Madison, Wisconsin 53706

Zambia:
Zambia Adult Education Association
P.O. Box RW 232
Ridgeway, Lusaka

For additional international and national
organizations see:

Adult Education Division, UNESCO. "Address
List of Adult Education Associations." Paris:
UNESCO, 1973. Available from UNESCO,
place de Fontenoy, 75700 Paris, France.
European Bureau of Adult Education. *Directory
of Adult Education Organizations in Europe.*
Amersfoort, Netherlands: European Bureau
of Adult Education, 1972.
Library of Continuing Education. *Directory of
Adult Education Organizations.* Syracuse,
New York: Syracuse University, 1970. Com-
prehensive and international in scope.

Principal Information Sources

GENERAL

Guides to the literature include:

*Adult Basic Education. National Teacher Training
Study.* Part I: *Review of the Literature.* Kansas
City: University of Missouri, 1972. (ERIC
Doc. ED 065 787.) Abstracts of 278 docu-
ments related to teacher training in adult
basic education and 134 items (unannotated)
related to the topic. Supplemented by ERIC
Doc. ED 095 275, produced in April 1974.
"Adult Education." In *Bibliography of Publica-
tions Issued by UNESCO or Under Its Auspices:
The First 25 Years: 1946–1971.* Paris:
UNESCO, 1973, pp. 142–146.
"Bibliographic Essay." In C. O. Houle, *The
Design of Education.* San Francisco: Jossey-

Bass, 1972, pp. 237–302. All English-
language items.
Dave, R. H. *Lifelong Education and the School:
Abstracts and Bibliography.* Hamburg, Federal
Republic of Germany: UNESCO Institute
for Education, 1973.
Educational Documentation and Information, 1972,
185, entire issue. A thematic bibliography
entitled "Lifelong Education."
Kelley, T. (Ed.) *A European Bibliography of Adult
Education: A Select List of Works in English,
French and German Published up to and In-
cluding the Year 1973.* London: National
Institute of Adult Education, 1975.
Kleis, R. J. *Bibliography on Continuing Education.*
East Lansing: Michigan State University,
Office of Studies in Continuing Education,
1972. (ERIC Doc. ED 078 242.)
*Die Mitarbeiter im Weiterbildungsbereich: Ausbil-
dung, Berufsbildung, Fortbildung; Internationale Bibliographie.* Münster, Federal Republic
of Germany: Deutsches Institut für wissenschaftliche Pädagogik, 1973. Bibliography
of books and articles, mainly in English and
German, dealing with the training of adult
educators.
Paulston, R. G. *Non-formal Education: An Annotated Bibliography.* New York: Praeger,
1972. Comprehensive guide to the literature
through 1971 on nonformal education.

Overviews and introductions to the field
include:

*Adult Education: Special Experimental Demonstra-
tion and Teacher Training Projects Fiscal Year
1974.* Washington, D.C.: Department of
Health, Education, and Welfare, Bureau of
Occupational and Adult Education, 1974.
Clegg, D. O. *Adult Teaching and Learning. Heuris-
tics of Adult Education: Courses of Study for
Professional Preparation of Educators of Adults.*
Boulder: University of Colorado; Fort Col-
lins: Department of Education, Colorado
State University, 1970. (ERIC Doc. ED
060 400.)
*Convergence: An International Journal of Adult
Education.* March 1968, *1* (1), entire issue.
Special issue devoted to the training of adult
educators.
Ericksen, S. C. *Motivation for Learning: A Guide
for Teachers of the Young Adult.* Ann Arbor:
University of Michigan Press, 1974.
Houle, C. O. "The Educators of Adults." In
R. M. Smith and others (Eds.), *Handbook of
Adult Education.* New York: Macmillan for
the Adult Education Association of the USA,
1970, pp. 109–120.
Knowles, M. *The Modern Practice of Adult Educa-
tion.* New York: Association Press, 1970.

Langerman, P. D. (Ed.) *You Can Be a Successful Teacher of Adults: NAPCAE's Authoritative Sourcebook and Information Guide.* Washington, D.C.: National Association for Public Continuing and Adult Education, 1974.

Lengrand, P. *An Introduction to Lifelong Education.* Paris: UNESCO, 1970.

Lowe, J. *The Education of Adults: A World Perspective.* Toronto, Ontario: UNESCO/Ontario Institute for Studies in Education, 1975.

The Training of Functional Literacy Personnel: A Practical Guide. Paris: UNESCO, 1973. Intended for adult educators; studies the organization of teacher training, methods of recruitment, and training of instructors.

The Training of the Part-Time Teacher of Adults. Manchester, England: Manchester University Department of Adult Education, 1972.

Workers in Adult Education: Their Status, Recruitment and Professional Training. Strasbourg, France: Council of Europe, Council for Cultural Co-operation, 1966.

Comparative education sources include:

Bennett, C., and others. (Eds.) *Comparative Studies in Adult Education: An Anthology.* Syracuse, New York: Syracuse University, Publications and Continuing Education, 1975. A project of the International Council for Adult Education.

Hawes, H. W. R. *Lifelong Education, Schools and Curricula in Developing Countries.* UIE Monograph No. 4. Hamburg, Federal Republic of Germany: UNESCO Institute for Education, 1975.

Houghton, V. P., and Richardson, K. *Recurrent Education.* London: Ward Lock, 1974.

International Conference on Adult Education, 3rd, Tokyo, 1972. Final Report. Paris: UNESCO, 1972.

Internationales Jahrbuch für Erwachsenenbildung. Heidelberg, Federal Republic of Germany: Quelle und Meyer, 1969–. Attempts to provide a central publication for the regular interchange of information and ideas about adult education on an international scale. Articles are in French, German, or English, with summaries in the other two languages.

Janne, H., and Roggemans, M. *New Trends in Adult Education: Concepts and Recent Empirical Achievements.* Paris: UNESCO, International Commission on the Development of Education, 1972.

Karanja, J. J. "Training for Adult Education." In L. O. Edstrom and others. (Eds.), *Mass Education: Studies in Adult Education and Teaching by Correspondence in Some Developing Countries.* New York: Africana Publishing, 1970, pp. 354–367.

Kidd, J. R. *A Tale of Three Cities; Elsinore, Montreal, Tokyo: The Influence of Three UNESCO World Conferences upon the Development of Adult Education.* Syracuse, New York: Syracuse University, Publications in Continuing Education, 1974.

Lifelong Education. New Delhi: Asian Institute of Educational Planning and Administration, 1970.

Mushkin, S. J. *Recurrent Education.* Washington, D.C.: National Institute of Education, 1973.

Okedara, J. T. "The Training of Adult Education Personnel: A Comparative Study." *Society and Leisure,* 1973, *2,* 119–138.

Peers, R. *Adult Education: A Comparative Study.* London: Routledge and Kegan Paul, 1972.

Permanent Education: A Compendium of Studies. Strasbourg, France: Council of Europe, 1970.

Prospects: Quarterly Review of Education (UNESCO). Autumn 1974, *4* (3). Special issue on adult education.

Prosser, R. *Adult Education in Developing Countries.* Nairobi, Kenya: East Africa Publishing House, 1970. See especially "Training of Adult Educators," pp. 145–149.

A Retrospective International Survey of Adult Education: Montreal 1960 to Tokyo 1972. Paris: UNESCO, 1972. Third International Conference on Adult Education, Tokyo, July 25–August 7, 1972. (ERIC Doc. 068 760.)

Simpson, J. A. *Today and Tomorrow in European Adult Education: A Study of the Present Situation and Future Developments.* Strasbourg, France: Council of Europe, 1972. See especially "The Profession of Adult Educator," pp. 171–180.

Stoikov, V. *The Economics of Recurrent Education and Training.* Geneva: International Labour Organisation, 1975.

Tymowski, J., and Januszkiewicz, F. *Post Secondary Education of Persons Already Gainfully Employed in European Socialist Countries.* Warsaw: Institute for Science, Policy and Higher Education, 1975.

Waniewicz, I. *Broadcasting for Adult Education: A Guidebook to Worldwide Experience.* Paris: UNESCO, 1972.

Wood, A. *Informal Education and Development in Africa.* The Hague: Mouton, 1974.

Histories of the field include:

Grattan, C. H. *In Quest of Knowledge: A Historical Perspective on Adult Education.* New York: Arno Press, 1971. Reprint of 1955 edition; history of adult education from ancient times to the present, with emphasis on the British and American experience.

Kelley, T. *A History of Adult Education in Great Britain*. Liverpool, England: University of Liverpool Press, 1962.

CURRENT BIBLIOGRAPHIES

International Bibliography, Information, Documentation. New York: Unipub, 1973–. A quarterly publication, listing publications of the United Nations system, with annotations. Lists only English-language publications or multilingual editions which include English. Subject headings for adult education, literacy, education, and teacher training.

Literary Documentation: An International Bulletin for Libraries and Information Centres. Tehran, Iran: International Institute for Adult Literacy Methods, 1972–. Published quarterly. Provides abstracts.

Studies in Adult Education. London: National Institute of Adult Education, 1969–. Published semiannually. Includes articles which mainly concern adult education in the United Kingdom, but the reviews have a strong international slant. Reviews books, journal issues, and new bibliographical guides and reports on new journals in the field.

PERIODICALS

Kulich, J. "Select Bibliography of Periodicals in International and Comparative Studies Related to Adult Education." *Convergence*, 1970, *3*, 82–90. Aimed at adult educators engaged in the comparative study of adult education.

Important journals in the field include *Adult Education* (UK), *Adult Education* (US), *Adult Education in Finland, Adult Education Information Notes* (UNESCO, France), *Adult Leadership* (US), *African Adult Education, Aften og ungdomskolen* (Denmark), *Aontas* (Ireland), *ASBAE Journal* (Asian South Pacific Bureau of Adult Education, India), *Australian Journal of Adult Education, Continuing Education* (US), *Continuing Education in New Zealand, Continuous Learning* (Canada), *Convergence* (Canada), *La cultura popolare* (Italy), *Education permanente* (Switzerland), *Erwachsenenbildung* (FRG), *Erwachsenenbildung in Österreich, Indian Journal of Adult Education, International Congress of University Adult Education Journal* (Canada), *Kenya Journal of Adult Education, Journal of Extension* (US), *Literacy Discussion* (Iran), *Notes and Studies* (European Bureau of Adult Education, Netherlands), *Society and Leisure* (Czechoslovakia), *Tidskrift för svenska folkhögskolan* (Sweden), *Volkshochschule im Westen* (FRG).

DICTIONARIES AND HANDBOOKS

Dickinson, G. *Teaching Adults: A Handbook for Instructors*. Toronto, Ontario: New Press, 1973. Deals with the nature of learning, course planning, principles of instruction, and evaluation of learning.

European Bureau of Adult Education. *List of Terms Used in Adult Education*. Amersfoort, Netherlands: European Bureau of Adult Education, 1972. A preliminary list.

Rotnes, K. *Adult Education Thesaurus*. Oslo: Norsk pedagogisk studiesamling, 1973.

Smith, R. M., and others. (Eds.) *Handbook of Adult Education*. New York: Macmillan for the Adult Education Association of the USA, 1970.

Terminology About Adult Continuing Education: A Preliminary Structure and a Suggested Developmental Process. Washington, D.C.: National Center for Educational Statistics, 1971. (ERIC Doc. ED 065 761.)

DIRECTORIES

Directory of Adult Education Centres in Africa. Dakar, Senegal: Regional Office for Education in Africa, Documentation Section, 1974. Lists adult education programs offered on all levels at institutions in countries south of the Sahara.

Grabowski, S., and Glenn, A. *Directory of Resources in Adult Education, 1974:* De Kalb, Illinois: ERIC Clearinghouse on Career Education, Northern Illinois University, 1974. Lists associations, periodicals, information systems, individuals and agencies, graduate programs, and documents considered "classics." Strong United States slant.

Knoll, J. H. (Ed.) *Research and Training in Adult Education*. Edinburgh: International Congress of University Adult Education, 1972. Attempts to identify institutions throughout the world offering training and research facilities in adult education, including levels of academic qualifications, numbers qualifying during 1969–1971, staff employed, and research undertaken.

White, A. S. *Worldwide Register of Adult Education*. Allenhurst, New Jersey: Aurea Publications, 1973. Directory of university extension departments, correspondence schools, and testing centers in forty-two countries, with emphasis on the United States, Canada, and the United Kingdom.

RESEARCH CENTERS, INSTITUTES, INFORMATION CENTERS

The following directories identify research facilities internationally:

Directory of Adult Education Centres in Africa. Dakar, Senegal: Regional Office for Education in Africa, Documentation Section, 1974.

Knoll, J. H. (Ed.) *Research and Training in Adult Education.* Edinburgh: International Congress of University Adult Education, 1972. Identifies institutions worldwide conducting research in adult education.

Kulich, J. *World Survey of Research in Comparative Adult Education: A Directory of Institutions and Personnel, 1972.* Toronto: Ontario Institute for Studies in Education; Vancouver: Centre for Continuing Education, University of British Columbia, 1972.

Libraries, information services, and documentation centers dealing with adult education are listed in the following:

Directory of Libraries and Information Centres in the Field of Literacy. Tehran, Iran: UNESCO International Institute for Adult Education, 1973.

International Directory of Documentation and Information Services in Adult Education. Paris: UNESCO, 1975.

UNESCO, Department of Curriculum, Structures and Methods of Education, Adult Education Division. *Adult Education Documentation Centres: Information Compiled About Their Activities.* Paris: UNESCO, 1973.

[Bibliography prepared by Marie Lannon.]

AERONAUTICAL AND ASTRONAUTICAL ENGINEERING
(Field of Study)

The term *aeronautics* designates those disciplines involved in flight through the atmosphere, and the term *astronautics* those disciplines involved in exoatmospheric flight. Both fields require very precise engineering expertise in a variety of areas. One such area is structural mechanics. In flight through the atmosphere and in exoatmospheric flight, the flight vehicle must overcome gravitational attraction by generating aerodynamic lift or by accelerating to very high speeds. Consequently, its inert mass or structural weight must be kept very low in order to maximize useful load. At the same time, the vehicle must operate in a hostile environment (thermal protection is often needed), and the structure must be designed so that it can safely withstand high loads. The discipline of structural mechanics, therefore, must be developed to the point where high strength/weight ratios can be achieved considerably above those required for ground-based structures.

A second area of importance to aeronautical and astronautical engineering is thermodynamics. The inert weight of the propulsion systems required to maintain flight or to accelerate to the high speeds necessary for escape from a gravitational field must be low weight; at the same time, the engine efficiency must be high, so that the fuel load will not use up an inordinate amount of useful load. Thus, a high degree of competence in thermodynamics and in methods of energy conservation is required.

A high degree of competence in dynamics and electronics is also required for aeronautical and astronautical engineers. Since a flight vehicle operates in three-dimensional space, as opposed to the more conventional two-dimensional movements of surface transportation, dynamic analyses are necessary. In addition, when the vehicle eventually either lands on a planet or performs a rendezvous with another vehicle, a high degree of precision in guidance and control is required. Furthermore, because of the difficulty in controlling the vehicle in three dimensions, particularly in the presence of atmospheric and gravitational disturbances, automatic control equipment must frequently be employed as an aid to the human pilot or as a means of operating an unmanned vehicle from a remote site.

Mechanics and physics of fluids is another important discipline to aeronautical and astronautical engineers. Aircraft fly through the atmosphere at all times, and spacecraft fly through the atmosphere during the boost and reentry phases. An understanding of the mechanics and physics of fluids over a wide spectrum of speeds (from the low-speed flight of the final touchdown and landing of the vehicle to the supersonic speeds and hypersonic reentry velocities) is therefore essential to establish the loads and performance of the vehicle.

Finally, because of the very high performance and, hence, engineering precision required in the development of aircraft and spacecraft and the complex systems needed to support them, the overall system must be optimized in order to achieve an economical device useful to society. Consequently, the area of operations analysis and systems design becomes important to the field. Also, economics and environmental concerns (for example, the minimization of environmental impact from noise or pollution) are important in aeronautical and astronautical engineering.

The major branches of aeronautical and astronautical engineering may be grouped as follows: (1) structures, materials, and aeroelasticity; (2) energy conversion and propulsion; (3) instrumentation, guidance, and control; (4) mechanics and physics of fluids; and (5) aeronautical and astronautical systems. The branch of structures, materials, and aeroelasticity covers structural design and includes, for example, finite element theory, shell theory, structural dynamics, fatigue, and advanced composites. Energy conversion and propulsion involves the design and development of gas turbine propulsion systems for aircraft and rockets for spacecraft; this branch includes liquid, solid, nuclear, and the more exotic space propulsion concepts. Instrumentation, guidance, and control is a broad field concerned with the mechanical and electronic interfaces with the vehicle; digital and analog computer aids; measurement systems involving laser, gyroscopic, and microwave devices; and the problem of the interface between the vehicle and its operator, including the psychology and physiology of human spatial orientation and response under conditions of stress. Mechanics and physics of fluids deals with ideal potential flows, turbulent shear flows, vortex systems, sonic booms, and the interaction of gases with solid surfaces. Finally, activities in the field of aeronautical and astronautical systems center primarily on space systems engineering and air transportation systems, the end goal of which is the integration of all the basic disciplines related to aeronautical and astronautical systems and their application to the design

and analysis of an optimum operating system. Concern is not only with the vehicle but with the total supporting system, including ground facilities, interaction with other systems, economics, and societal impact.

Aeronautics and astronautics are related to many disciplines. The concerns of aeronautical and astronautical engineering are found in other engineering branches, such as electrical engineering; because of the exigencies mentioned above, however, the aerospace engineer requires a somewhat specialized and in-depth training in many fields. The most closely allied discipline is electronics and computer science; the areas of potential fields, closed loop control systems, and stochastic phenomena are also important to aerospace engineering. Mechanical engineering also provides some support in aeronautical and astronautical engineering, particularly in the areas of thermodynamics. Civil engineering, too, may soon provide some support to the field in the area of structural dynamics; because of wind loads and earthquakes, civil engineers must consider structural dynamics, although earth-based structures have design requirements quite different from those of flight vehicles.

The science of flight developed almost simultaneously with its implementation at the beginning of the century and by the early 1920s was well developed. Formal education in the United States started at the Massachusetts Institute of Technology (in Cambridge, Massachusetts) in 1914. Commercial development grew rapidly during the 1930s, but the progress was interrupted by World War II, when the technology used was essentially that of the prewar years. The development of the jet transport in the early 1950s and the start of the space program shortly thereafter provided a major impetus to education in this area as aircraft took over the major portion of common carrier transportation and the great potentials of space-based operations began to be realized.

Aerospace engineering is a remarkably

international operation, and no one nation has dominated the field. Although the United States has supplied over 80 percent of all commercial jet transports in the world, the United Kingdom was the first nation to put a commercial jet into operation, and the Anglo-French *Concorde* will most likely be the first supersonic jet to carry passengers on a regular basis. Similarly, although the United States has a broader space program than the Soviet Union and was the first to land on the moon, the Soviet Union was the first in orbit in both manned and unmanned vehicles. The Soviet Union has also built and operated a much larger heavy-lift helicopter than the United States and sold it commercially abroad. In military aircraft the Germans were the first to fly a jet fighter and also developed the swept-wing concept. The United States, however, was the first to fly supersonically. Exchange between scholars and engineers of different nations has traditionally been free and highly productive. Even political differences have not been an insurmountable barrier, and it is expected that the *Apollo-Soyuz* cooperative effort between the United States and the Soviet Union will lead to future cooperation in space development and exploration.

Well-developed degree programs in aeronautical and astronautical engineering may be found in a variety of institutes and universities throughout the world. Canada, the United States, the Soviet Union, the People's Republic of China, the Republic of China, Australia, Egypt, Israel, Brazil, Japan, India, South Africa, and all Western European nations offer formal degree programs in the field. Since aircraft fly across national boundaries and carry nationals of many countries, safety requirements dictate that there be a degree of uniformity in maintenance and operational practices. Consequently, throughout the world there is relatively little difference in the emphasis placed on the various disciplines leading to the training of an aerospace engineer. Competence in the various disciplines re-

lated to aeronautical and astronautical engineering is required, and most universities have found that a student well trained at the bachelor's or master's level in one country is adequately prepared to pursue an advanced course of study in another. Only the United States and the Soviet Union are involved to any great extent in the space program, and what information exists indicates that practices in both countries are very similar.

RENE HARCOURT MILLER

Levels and Programs of Study

Programs in aerospace and aeronautical engineering generally require as a minimum prerequisite a secondary education and lead to the following awards: certificate or diploma, Bachelor of Science or Engineering, Master of Science or Engineering, the Ph.D., or their equivalents. Programs deal with the principles and practices of aerospace engineering and consist of classroom and laboratory instruction and, on advanced levels, study, seminar or group discussion, and research in specialized areas of aerospace engineering.

Programs that lead to an award not equivalent to a first university degree deal with the principles and practices of aeronautical and space engineering technology. These programs, which generally emphasize the application of mathematics and physics to problems in the aeronautical and space industries, last two or three years, full time. Principal course content usually includes some of the following: mathematics, chemistry, physics, materials science, basic electronics and electricity, thermodynamics, aerodynamics, instrumentation and controls, strength of materials, engineering economics, aeronautical and astronautical design, and machine processes.

Programs that lead to a first university degree deal with the principles and practices of aerospace and aeronautical engineering. Principal course content usually includes basic courses in structural design, materials, aeroelasticity, energy conversion, propulsion, instrumentation, flight guidance, mechanics and physics of fluids, automatic control, and aeronautical and astronautical systems, as well as background courses in such fields as physics and mathematics.

Programs that lead to a postgraduate university degree deal with advanced studies in specialized areas of aerospace and astronautical engineering. Emphasis is placed on original research work as substantiated by the presentation and defense of a scholarly thesis or dissertation. The advanced degree is usually designated as one in Aerospace or Aeronautics and Astronautics but sometimes may have a subdesignation by discipline, such as Instrumentation, Flight Transportation, Materials Engineering, or Biomedical Engineering.

[This section was based on UNESCO's *International Standard Classification of Education (ISCED): Three Stage Classification System, 1974* (Paris: UNESCO, 1974).]

Major International and National Organizations

INTERNATIONAL

Advisory Group for Aeronautical Research
 and Development
64 rue de Varenne
Paris 17e, France

Aerospace Medical Association
Washington National Airport
Washington, D.C. 20001 USA

International Academy of Astronautics
250 rue St.-Jacques
Paris 5e, France

International Academy of Aviation and
 Space Medicine
35 rue Cardinal Mercier
Brussels, Belgium

International Aeronautical Federation
Fédération aéronautique internationale
6 rue Galilae
75782 Paris, France

International Council on the Aeronautical
 Sciences
% American Institute of Aeronautics and
 Astronautics
1290 Avenue of the Americas
New York, New York 10019 USA

International Technical Institute of Flight
 Engineers
Centre gambart de lignières
Boîte Postale 241
Aéroport d'Orly
Seine, France

NATIONAL

Australia:
  Australia National Aerospace
   Organization
  19 Gregory Street
  P.O. Box 79
  Yagoona, New South Wales 219

Canada:
  Canadian Aeronautics and Space
   Institute
  Commonwealth Building
  77 Metcalfe Street
  Ottawa 4, Ontario

Japan:
  Japan Society for Aeronautical and
   Space Sciences
  Hilo kaikan 3, 1-chome
  Tamura-cho, Shiba, Minato-ku
  Tokyo

United Kingdom:
  Royal Aeronautical Society
  4 Hamilton Place
  London, England

United States:
  American Institute of Aeronautics and
   Astronautics
  1290 Avenue of the Americas
  New York, New York 10019

  National Aerospace Education Council
  806 15th Street NW
  Washington, D.C. 20005

For a complete listing of international and national organizations see:

Interavia ABC: World Directory of Aviation and Astronautics. Geneva: Interavia, 1975.
World Aviation Directory, Including World Space Directory. Washington, D.C.: Ziff-Davis, 1975. Published semi-annually.

Principal Information Sources

GENERAL

Guides to the literature of aeronautics and astronautics include:

Aeronautical Engineering Index 1947–1957 (renamed *Aerospace Engineering Index* in 1958). New York: Institute of the Aeronautical Sciences, 1948–1960. Important sources of information for early literature in the field.

Aerospace Bibliography. (6th ed.) Washington, D.C.: National Aeronautics and Space Administration, 1972. A comprehensive annotated bibliography of books, reference materials, and periodicals dealing with space science.

Fry, B. M., and Mohrhardt, F. E. *A Guide to Information Sources in Space Science and Technology.* New York: Wiley-Interscience, 1963. A significant guide to the field; includes indexing and abstracting services, specialized sources of information dealing with various aspects of space sciences, handbooks and encyclopedias, bibliographies, information centers, and other reference books.

Guide to Literature in Aerospace Engineering. Washington, D.C.: American Society for Engineering Education, 1971.

Index Aeronauticus. London: Great Britain Ministry of Supply, 1945–1968. Abstracts from international literature.

International Space Bibliography. New York: United Nations, 1966.

Ordway, F. I. *Annotated Bibliography of Space Science and Technology, with an Astronautical Supplement. A History of Astronautical Literature—1931 Through 1961.* (3rd ed.) Washington, D.C.: ARFOR Publication, Astronautics Education Division, 1962.

Sokoll, A. H. *Literatur zur Aero- und Astronautik: Ein bibliographischer Wegweiser.* Munich, Federal Republic of Germany: Alkos-Verlag, 1961.

Sources of Information on Space Technology. Hatfield, England: Technical Information Service, 1962.

Introductions to the field are provided by the following works:

Ordway, F. *Basic Astronautics: An Introduction to Space Science, Engineering and Medicine.* Englewood Cliffs, New Jersey: Prentice-Hall, 1962.

Stuhlinger, E., and Mesmet, G. (Eds.) *Space Science and Engineering.* New York: McGraw-Hill, 1965.

Vertregt, M. *Principles of Astronautics.* (2nd ed.) Amsterdam: Elsevier, 1965.

For a history of aeronautics see:

Gibbs-Smith, C. H., and others. *Aeronautics.* London: H. M. Stationery Office, 1966.

Science Museum, London. *Aviation: An Historical Survey from Its Origins to the End of World War II.* London: H. M. Stationery Office, 1970.

For a guide to the literature on the history of space exploration from its beginnings through 1967 consult:

Dickson, K. M. *History of Aeronautics and Astronautics: A Preliminary Bibliography.* Washington, D.C.: National Aeronautics and Space Administration, 1968. International in scope; includes sources in several languages.

The following works deal with educational and/or professional aspects of aerospace engineering:

Brooking, W. J. (Ed.) *Engineering Technicians.* Chicago: Ferguson, 1969. Discusses educational and professional opportunities for engineering technicians, including the aerospace engineering technician.

Space Research in United Kingdom Universities. London: Royal Society, 1963–. Published annually.

Strickler, M. K. (Ed.) *An Introduction to Aerospace Education.* Valencia, California: American Family Enterprises, 1968.

Your Career as an Aerospace Engineer. Washington, D.C.: American Institute of Aeronautics and Astronautics, 1974. Includes a list of accredited engineering schools in the United States.

For a discussion of international cooperation in space programs see:

Space Activities and Resources: A Review of United Nations, International, and National Programs. New York: United Nations, 1965.

CURRENT BIBLIOGRAPHIES

The most important comprehensive abstracting services, international in scope, are:

International Aerospace Abstracts. New York: American Institute of Aeronautics and Astronautics, 1961–. A significant abstracting service which covers literature in journals, books, and conference proceedings. Also includes translations of important articles.

Scientific and Technical Aerospace Reports: A Semi-Monthly Abstract Journal with Indexes. Washington, D.C.: National Aeronautics and Space Administration, 1963–. Covers international report literature in the field.

Current information in the field is also provided by the following abstracting and indexing services:

Bibliographies of Aerospace Science: A Continuing Bibliography. Washington, D.C.: National Aeronautics and Space Administration, 1964–.

Bulletin signalétique. Paris: Service de documentation et d'information technique de l'aéronautique, 1945–. Includes the aerospace sciences.

Referativnyĭ zhurnal: Vozdushnyi transport (Abstracts on Air Transport); Raketostroyeniye (Abstracts on Design and Construction of Spacecraft). Moscow: Akademiia nauk, SSSR, Institut nauchnoĭ informatsii, 1962–.

Progress reports are additional useful sources of current information and developments in the field:

Progress in Aeronautical Sciences. Oxford, England: Pergamon Press, 1961–.
Progress in Aerospace Sciences. Oxford, England: Pergamon Press, 1970–.

PERIODICALS

Among the most important periodicals in the field are Acta Astronautica (UK), Aeronautical Journal (UK), Aerospace (US), Aerospace Technology (US), Astronautics and Aeronautics (US), Aviation et astronautique (Belgium), Aviation, Space and Environmental Medicine (US, formerly Aerospace Medicine), Aviation Week and Space Technology (US), Flight International (UK), Flying (US), Interavia (Switzerland), Journal of the Astronautical Sciences (US), Kosmicheskiye issledovaniya (USSR), Recherche aérospatiale (France), Raumfahrtforschung/Space Flight Research (FRG), Schweizer Aero Revue, Soviet Aeronautics, Space World (US).

Guides to periodical literature include:

Fry, B. M., and Mohrhardt, F. E. A Guide to the Literature in Space Science and Technology. New York: Wiley-Interscience, 1963. See pp. 468–484 for a serial publications index.
Ulrich's International Periodicals Directory. New York: Bowker, biennial.
U.S. Library of Congress, Science and Technology Division. Aeronautical and Space Serial Publications: A World List. Washington, D.C.: U.S. Library of Congress, 1962. Lists over 4500 titles from 76 countries.

ENCYCLOPEDIAS, DICTIONARIES, HANDBOOKS

AGARD Aeronautical Multilingual Dictionary. Oxford, England: Pergamon Press, 1960. This work, produced by the North Atlantic Treaty Organization, Advisory Group for Aeronautical Research and Development, is in eight languages: English, French, German, Spanish, Italian, Dutch, Turkish, and Russian. First supplement, 1963.
Astronautical Multilingual Dictionary of the International Academy of Astronautics. Prague: Academia, 1970. In English, Russian, German, French, Spanish, Italian, and Czechoslovakian.
Dorian, A. F., and Osenton, J. (Eds.) Elsevier's Dictionary of Aeronautics in Six Languages: English/American, French, Spanish, Italian, Portuguese and German. Amsterdam: Elsevier, 1964.
Galiana, T. de. Concise Encyclopedia of Astronautics. London: Collins, 1968.
Glossary of Aeronautical and Astronautical Terms. (6th ed.) London: British Standards Institution, 1964–1970. An English dictionary.
Koelle, H. H., and Braun, W. von. Handbook of Astronautical Engineering. (18th ed.) New York: McGraw-Hill, 1961. A standard handbook.
Marks, R. W. (Ed.) The New Dictionary and Handbook of Aerospace. New York: Praeger, 1969.
McGraw-Hill Encyclopedia of Space. New York: McGraw-Hill, 1968. Covers space activities of many nations.

DIRECTORIES

Interavia ABC: World Directory of Aviation and Astronautics. (23rd ed.) Geneva: Interavia, 1975. An annual international directory of organizations, research centers, universities, companies, and services in the field.
International Directory of Facilities for Education and Training in Basic Subjects Related to the Peaceful Uses of Outer Space. New York: United Nations, 1968. Includes lists of organizations, societies, and educational facilities dealing with peaceful uses of space.
Kneifel, J. L. World Directory of Civil Aviation Institutes and Governmental Civil Aviation Departments. Berlin, Federal Republic of Germany: John L. Kneifel, 1973. Lists institutes, universities, and research centers involved with aeronautics and astronautics in Africa; North, Central, and South America; Australia; and Europe.
Peterson's Annual Guides to Graduate Study, 1976. Book 5: Engineering and Applied Sciences. Princeton, New Jersey: Peterson's Guides, 1975. See section on "Mechanics, Aerospace and Mechanical Engineering Programs." Lists university offerings in aerospace engineering in the United States.

AFARS AND ISSAS

Population: 200,000 (estimate). Student enrollment in primary school: 7700; secondary school: 1600. [Figures are for 1973.]

The Afars and Issas has been under French administration since 1885. Although there are independence movements in the territory, general elections in November 1974 reconfirmed the French presence. The Afars and Issas is located on the Gulf of Aden and bordered by Ethiopia in the east and Somalia in the west.

The educational system follows the French pattern. Four years of education are compulsory and available in twenty-one public and six private primary schools; however, since large numbers of the population are nomadic, education mainly reaches urban dwellers. There are two public secondary schools *(lycées),* one general and one technical, and nine private secondary schools. Most of the teachers are French. There is also a teacher training school, the *école normale.*

Some scholarships are awarded by the French government for study abroad.

AFFIRMATIVE ACTION

The concept of equality, the desire for an equitable distribution of opportunities and rewards, and the strong determination to build a nation of shared power and resources are at the foundation of the Declaration of Independence and the Constitution of the United States. The framers of these documents had lived through a system that would deny these basic rights as they understood them. Urged on by an inner demand to establish a system wherein one's human rights, whether legal, moral, or natural, would be guaranteed, the thirteen colonies declared themselves free, equal, and united.

There seems to be little doubt about the rights that this dangerous and drastic action was intended to perfect and protect (1) the right to be immune from private and public interference in the pursuit of an individual goal; (2) the privilege to develop one's interest and talents or to choose one's profession without being forced to surrender one's individuality; and (3) the right to have government ensure and protect privileges and immunities in relation to civil, economic, educational, political, and social rights against encroachments and unreasonable restrictions.

Historical Pursuit of Equal Opportunity

The Declaration of Independence listed the misdeeds inflicted on the colonies by an insensitive and totalitarian crown and declared, in the words of the delegates: "We hold these truths to be self-evident, that all men are created equal, that they are endowed by their Creator with certain unalienable Rights, that among these are Life, Liberty and the pursuit of Happiness." Following the Declaration of Independence, the Continental Congress drafted and published a Constitution that was adopted by the new nation—the United States. Although the Constitution was less idealistic than the Declaration of Independence, it too contained language strongly supportive of individual freedom, justice, liberty, and the right to live free of discrimination and bigotry.

The glaring exclusion of black people from this umbrella of protection and support was to be corrected, in part, about seventy years later, in a twelve-year effort beginning with the Emancipation Proclamation in 1863 and ending with the Civil Rights Act of 1875. The Emancipation Proclamation, which declared slavery abolished in those Confederate states that were in rebellion against the Union on January 1, 1863, and which was extended throughout the United States by the adoption of the Thirteenth Amendment (1865), was the first federal effort to end the legally sanctioned, systematic exclusion of a whole group of people from the enjoyment of civil, political, and economic rights and privileges. The Emancipation Proclamation and the Thirteenth Amendment did little more than remove the chains from the slaves. Consequently, the Fourteenth Amendment (1868) was introduced and adopted to confer citizenship on black people and to provide the Congress the power to assure and enforce those rights against any abridgement. Finally, the Fifteenth Amendment (1870) was adopted to expressly guarantee the right to vote. A reasonable construction of the amendments would suggest that the country had erected a formidable enough barrier to all governmental and private acts of discrimination. But when the various states enacted the "black codes," returning the black man to a point just short of slavery, Congress provided further protection by enacting Civil Rights Acts in 1866 (14 Stat. 27), 1870 (16 Stat. 140), 1871 (17 Stat. 13), and 1875 (18 Stat. 335). The purpose of these acts was "the freedom of the slave race, the security and firm establishment of that freedom" *(Slaughter-House Cases,* 83 U.S. 36 [1873]).

To ensure some measure of fair treatment to black citizens, the government announced, as the policy of the United States, steps to erase vestiges of bias in its national life. As early as 1883 the Congress declared that the civil service should appoint on the basis of merit and that notice of anyone's religion as a negative factor for federal employment was specifically forbidden (Civil Service Act of 1883, AKA the Pendleton Act, 22 Stat. 403 [1883] Ch. 12, 1958, U.S. Civil Service Commission Rule VIII [1883]). However, the Civil Rights Acts and the post–Civil War amendments on which they were founded were all but emasculated by the United States Supreme Court shortly after they were passed. The devitalization process began with the *Slaughter-House Cases* of 1873 and culminated in the rulings of the *Civil Rights Cases* (109 U.S. 3 [1883]). The *Slaughter-House Cases* represented a judicial assault that reduced the black man to the status of peasantry. In these cases the Court's opinion focused primarily on the Privileges and Immunities Clause of the Fourteenth Amendment, virtually stripping it of any meaning for black Americans.

The next judicial retreat came in *U.S. v. Reese* (92 U.S. 214 [1876]), in which the Court invalidated key portions of the Enforcement Act of 1870 (41st Congress, 2nd Session [May 31, 1870], p. 95). Reinstating the misuse of neutral principles, the Court concluded that "the Fifteenth Amendment does not confer the right of suffrage upon anyone. It prevents the State, or the United

States, however, from giving preference, in this particular, to one citizen over another, on account of race, color, or previous condition of servitude" (p. 95).

In *Hall* v. *DeCuir* (95 U.S. 485 [1878]) the Court ruled as unconstitutional a state statute prohibiting segregation on steamboats operating on the Mississippi. The Court held that the Commerce Clause did not prohibit segregation and that, in the face of the supremacy of federal law, a state (Louisiana) could not enact a nondiscrimination statute if the results placed an undue burden on commerce. The retrogressive movement of the Court, reflective of the national opinion about black people's rights, was nearly completed in 1883. In the *Civil Rights Cases,* the act of March 1, 1875 (18 Stat. 336, secs. 1, 2), was held to be unsupported by the Thirteenth and Fourteenth Amendments. Thus, the provisions that "all persons within the jurisdiction of the United States shall be entitled to the full and equal enjoyment of the accommodations of inns, public conveyances, theaters, and other places of public amusement" was invalid. Justice John Marshall Harlan (1833–1911) of Kentucky dissented, as he did later in *Plessy* v. *Ferguson* (163 U.S. 537 [1896]), establishing himself as the visionary conscience of a reactionary era.

The great depression of the 1930s did more than any other single event since the Civil War to project the true employment conditions of millions of men and women, particularly black people and women. President Franklin D. Roosevelt and the United States Congress had moved to alleviate the widespread unemployment by placing the United States government in the posture of employer of last resort. Observing the continuing racial discrimination in employment practices, the Congress again declared, in the Unemployment Relief Act of 1933, "That in employing citizens for the purpose of the Act no discrimination shall be made on account of race, color, or creed" (48 Stat. 22 [1933]).

It was not until 1940, however, that the United States government enacted rules barring racial discrimination in federal employment. By executive order (presidential action) the civil service was ordered to forbid racial as well as religious discrimination against applicants, as well as against those who were already in federal employment (Executive Order 8587, 5 Fed. Reg. 445 [1940]). In the same year, in a parallel action, Congress adopted the Ramspeck Act (54 Stat. 1211 [1940], Title I, 5 U.S.C. Sec. 631 A [1958]), broadening the coverage of the Civil Service Commission and strengthening the concept of equal employment opportunity in the federal service. The Ramspeck Act directed the civil service commissioner thus: "In carrying out the provisions of this title, and the provisions of the Classification Act of 1923, as amended, there shall be no discrimination against any person, on account of race, creed, or color."

It was during this period that the federal government, particularly the executive branch, began to scrutinize the conduct of those persons and organizations who, by means of gaining federal contracts, were offering training and employment to others (National Industrial Recovery Act [1933], Title II, 48 Stat. 200; 44 Code of Federal Regulations [C.F.R.], sec. 265–33 [1938]).

Racial discrimination persisted despite the strong and clear declarations by the executive and legislative branches of government. Federal employment officers and those who contracted for the public dollar saw the statements as mere policy—matters of public relations—but without sanctions or standards of enforcement, and doubted whether the government had the desire, or the will, to compel obedience to these provisions. The existence of these glaring contradictions of policy versus practice was not lost on black leaders of the 1930s and 1940s. In the words of Jervis Anderson (1972–1973, p. 241):

For the majority of black Americans, the new deal had turned out to be a revolution only in expectations. By late 1940 and early 1941, with Hitler's armies marching across Europe, Amer-

ican's defense industry began to boom. "We Americans," President Franklin Roosevelt assured the threatened European democracies, "are vitally concerned in your defense of freedom. We are putting forth our energies, our resources and our organizing powers to give you the strength to regain and maintain the free world. We shall send you in ever increasing numbers, ships, planes, tanks, and guns." But the Americans reaping the benefits of the industrial boom—getting the jobs to build the ships, the planes, the tanks, and the guns—were almost entirely white. Turned away at the gates of defense plants, the masses of blacks remained largely on relief—what most of them had gotten out of the New Deal—or in temporary emergency work.

Executive orders. Disappointed and incensed over the government's failure to act and ensure equal opportunity in employment, civil rights and labor leader A. Philip Randolph (born 1889) led other black leaders, such as NAACP leader Walter Francis White (1893–1955), educator Mary McLeod Bethune (1875–1955), and National Urban League leader Lester B. Granger (born 1896), in a call for more than 100,000 black people to march on Washington, D.C., to protest discrimination and to demand jobs. Of immediate concern were those agencies, institutions, and persons who held federal contracts but who failed or refused to hire black people. Realizing the seriousness of the situation and the resoluteness of the leaders, President Roosevelt issued Executive Order 8802 (6 Fed. Reg. 3109 [1941]) on June 25, 1941, launching for the first time a Fair Employment Practices Committee (FEPC). The committee was an independent agency answerable directly and only to the President. Roosevelt declared that the policy of the government was "to encourage full participation in the national defense program by all citizens of the United States, regardless of race, creed, color, or national origin, in the firm belief that the democratic way of life within the nation can be defended successfully only with the help and support of all groups within its borders."

The FEPC, as a part of the Office of

Production Management, required that all government contractors include a nondiscrimination clause in all defense contracts. The scope of the order seemed broad enough, but the committee was empowered only to accept and evaluate complaints of bias or noncompliance. The FEPC was not granted enforcement powers, nor was it authorized to impose sanctions. Its powers were advisory only, and probably its greatest contribution was made through drafting policy statements and holding public hearings in various sections of the country. Recognizing its inability to effect any meaningful change in either attitude or practice without the powers to enforce, the committee ceased its operations in 1943. Roosevelt, still under the pressure and scrutiny of black citizens, established a second FEPC (Executive Order 9346, 8 Fed. Reg. 7183 [1943]) and granted it powers to investigate beyond the defense contractors. This committee had authority to receive complaints, conduct public hearings, and recommend appropriate actions or remedies to the President. But it too lacked enforcement powers and ceased to function in 1946. Despite the ultimate failure of the FEPC, under Roosevelt the central government had taken notice of its powers to negotiate, persuade, and effect public policy through its far-reaching contracting and spending powers.

Presidents Harry S Truman and Dwight D. Eisenhower continued the use of moral suasion, public relations, public opinion, and negotiation to obtain compliance with federal policy on nondiscrimination. First, Truman issued a series of executive orders directing certain government agencies to include nondiscrimination clauses in their contracts. Then, on December 3, 1951, he issued Executive Order 10308 (16 Fed. Reg. 12303 [1951]), creating the Committee on Government Contract Compliance. It was an eleven-member group composed of representatives of industry, the public, and the five principal government contracting agencies. On August 13, 1953, President Eisenhower replaced the Truman committee with the President's Committee on Government Contracts, a fifteen-member group composed of representatives of industry, labor, government, and the public (Executive Order 10479, 18 Fed. Reg. 4899 [1953]).

It was during the brief administration of John F. Kennedy that steps were taken to move federal contract compliance beyond an act of supplication to a level of demand. Truman had been advised by his Committee on Government Contract Compliance that enforcement of the nondiscrimination provisions that appeared in all government contracts could, and would, virtually eliminate employment discrimination in the United States. Faced with continuing evidence of widespread inequality in the world of work, accompanied by an equal measure of bias and denial with regard to opportunities for education and training, Kennedy initiated a massive attack against discrimination in Executive Order 10925 (26 Fed. Reg. 1977 [1961]) issued on March 6, 1961.

The Kennedy order was the first to set forth sanctions and penalties that could be imposed against contractors who failed to adhere to its provisions. Sensing the loss of talent and the cumulative damage inflicted on the country by many years of blatant and subtle exertions of discriminatory conduct, Kennedy not only sought an end to job bias but called on each federal contractor and subcontractor to take affirmative action to eliminate the present and continuing effects of past discrimination. Perceiving another avenue of evasive action, Kennedy amended Executive Order 10925 on June 22, 1963, by issuing Executive Order 11114 (28 Fed. Reg. 6485, 3 C.F.R. [1959–63] Comp. 774). The amendment extended the nondiscrimination provisions then mandatory in federal procurement contracts to all federally assisted construction contracts.

Congressional action. Following the assassination of President Kennedy, the Congress enacted the Civil Rights Act of 1964 (42 U.S.C. 55 2000 et seq. [1964]), Title VII of which provided for the establishment of the Equal Employment Opportunity Commission (EEOC). The EEOC would have a single mission: "to investigate charges of discrimination practice and to prosecute, if necessary, violations of Title VII. The Commission also has the authority to initiate investigations and, if necessary, charges of discriminatory practices, and many dramatic and expensive settlements have resulted from the exercise of this power."

President Lyndon B. Johnson added to this arsenal of governmental legal weaponry against employment discrimination by issuing Executive Order 11246 (30 Fed. Reg. 12319 [1965]) as amended by 11375 (32 Fed. Reg. 14303 [1967]). Johnson's order established the Office of Federal Contract Compliance to monitor the enforcement and implementation of the nondiscriminatory provisions of the order. Executive Order 11246, as amended, gave the Department of Labor, or the appropriate contracting agency, the power (1) to publish the names of noncomplying contractors or unions; (2) to recommend suits by the Justice Department to compel compliance; (3) to recommend action by EEOC or the Justice Department under Title VII, as amended by the 1972 act, giving the EEOC authority to file suit in a federal district court; (4) to cancel the contract of a noncomplying employer; and (5) to prevent a noncomplying employer from participating in future government contracts until the employer has shown a willingness to comply (American Management Association, 1975).

Of equal importance to our discussion is the Equal Pay Act of 1963 (29 U.S.C. SS 206 d [1963] amending 29 U.S.C. SS SS 201 et seq., the Fair Labor Standards Act of 1938). "The Equal Pay Act prohibits an employer from discriminating between employees on the basis of sex by paying wages to employees at a rate less than the rate at which he pays wages to employees of the opposite sex for equal work on jobs the performance of which requires equal skill, effort, and responsibility, and which

are performed under similar working conditions" *(Shultz* v. *Wheaton Glass Company,* 421 F 2nd 259, cert. denied 398 U.S. 905 [1970] reversing 284 F. Suppl. 23 [1968]).

Applicability of Equal Employment Opportunity and Affirmative Action Regulations to Higher Education

Institutions of higher education, although they function as major employers and hold hundreds of millions of dollars in governmental contracts, were left to do very much as they pleased until the mid 1960s, except for the relentless pressure by black citizens against racial discrimination (in 1935, *University of Maryland* v. *Murray,* 165 Md. 478) in admissions—with its employment spinoff effect. The glaring absence of "minority-group" persons— Asian Americans, black/Afro Americans, Mexican Americans (Chicanos), Puerto Ricans and other Spanish-heritaged Americans, and native Americans (Indians)— and nonminority (Caucasian) women from the student bodies, faculties, and administrative staffs of these institutions did not seem to bother those who made decisions regarding such matters; nor did that fact seem to worry the government or the general populace. But the 1960s changed all that. The campuses found themselves confronted with their own contradictions— an avid espousal of equality on the one hand, and a self-imposed, and defended, negative behavior on the other.

Minority students were urging—demanding—that (1) greater numbers of minority students be admitted to institutions of higher education; (2) these institutions appoint persons to their faculties whose backgrounds (racially and ethnically) were similar to their students; (3) there be instituted curricular changes that would include courses and materials reflective of the experiences of all people, not just Caucasians; and (4) members of minority groups be appointed to administrative and staff positions and employed as workers on college and university projects. As the pressure intensified, some institutions began to admit small numbers of minority students. These minor manifestations of change were accelerated after the assassination of civil rights leader Martin Luther King, Jr., in 1968. Public opinion, moral suasion, and the pressure of black students and black faculty members caused educational institutions to begin a reexamination of their employment policies and public posturing.

However much the pressure and push from minority-group faculty and students might have challenged some institutions, the whole of higher education did not seem to take equal employment (certainly not affirmative action) seriously until the Women's Equity Action League (WEAL) filed a historic industry-wide complaint against educational institutions on January 31, 1970. WEAL requested the Secretary of Labor to determine the extent and degree to which institutions were discriminating on the basis of sex in the following areas: admissions, financial aid, scholarship and fellowship assistance, appointment and employment practices, working conditions and environment, classifications and promotions, and differential pay scales. WEAL's complaint, in the nature of a class action, called on the Secretary of Labor to review, for compliance performance, the personnel policies of all educational institutions holding federal contracts.

It is accurate to say that WEAL's action initiated a national campaign to eliminate sex-based discrimination in higher education (Carnegie Council on Policy Studies in Higher Education, 1975, p. 97). Educational institutions, federal agencies, labor unions, the Congress, and the White House had moved only slowly when requests came from members of minority groups. And unless and until the judiciary ordered the instruments of social control to alter their conduct, little was done. But with women, most of whom were white and middle class, the white middle-class men who sat in decisional authority were forced to pause and to reevaluate their tactics. After all, this

movement was being led by their wives, mothers, sisters, and sweethearts; and because sex discrimination has not been as pervasive as racial discrimination, many of these women had attended similar (or the same) institutions as the white male administrators and faculty members.

Schools like Radcliffe, Barnard, Sarah Lawrence, Smith, Wellesley, Vassar, Pembroke, Hunter, and other single-sex women's colleges, which were developed almost exclusively for middle- and upper-class white women, along with large private and state universities, had graduated thousands of women with impeccable credentials who could not obtain treatment equal with men with respect to employment. Consequently, the Department of Health, Education and Welfare (HEW), with power delegated by the Department of Labor, directed its Office for Civil Rights (OCR) to inspect the hiring conduct of the educational establishment. Just as the federal machinery was preparing to respond to WEAL's broadside, complaints were filed against several individual institutions by WEAL and its sister organizations, the National Organization for Women (NOW) and the Professional Women's Caucus.

Although virtually ignored up to 1970, guidelines and regulations had been issued by HEW in May 1968 that set forth the legal requirements under the President's executive order. In the face of the complaints filed by WEAL, NOW, and the Professional Women's Caucus, there was a declared need for greater detail; so the Secretary of Labor issued another set of guidelines and regulations known as Order Number 4 (CFR, Chapter 60, Title 41) in February 1970. Order Number 4 covered only underutilization of minority-group persons. To cover reported discrimination against both minority-group members and all women, the Office for Federal Contract Compliance, Department of Labor, issued Revised Order Number 4 (Fed. Reg. Vol. 36, No. 234 [1971]; amended [1973]) on December 4, 1971. Under Revised Order Number 4, the implementational regulations of Executive Order 11246 as amended, private institutions holding federal contracts of $50,000 or more and fifty or more employees were required to develop a written affirmative action program within 120 days of the receipt of such contract. Institutions under state and local governmental control—public institutions—were not affected by Revised Order Number 4. The order was amended early in 1973 and made applicable to public institutions.

Institutions of higher education, which held enviable and majestic records of teaching the concepts of equality and calling on others to engage in bias-free conduct, were not at all inspired to initiate a spirited investigation of their own records of employment and educational opportunities. Some institutions admitted that they had not done all that they could, or should, have done to ensure equal educational and employment opportunity without regard to race, color, religion, sex, or national origin; and they promised that if left alone they would take the necessary and proper steps to comply with the law and to make equal opportunity available to all qualified persons. After all, they seemed to be saying, the academic institutions knew higher education much better than anyone else; consequently, they argued, as the experts in the education industry, should not they be the ones to develop the procedures and programs for effecting this new order? Members of minority groups, women's groups, and the federal government were not enthusiastic about education's offer to clean its own house. They pressed for compliance. Some institutions resisted, and many white males in academia who objected to the new regulations began to characterize the effort as an assault against the integrity of the institutions and as a clear and present danger to the freedoms and standards enjoyed by the educational establishment. Investigations went forward. Charges and countercharges were made with respect to the effectiveness or ineffectiveness of the government's actions. From within the academy came the claim that the pressure

of the civil rights enforcement was tinkering with the delicate balance of federal versus private and federal versus state control of nonfederal property. Critics of affirmative action further contended that the heavy hand of the government, using the federal contract as a device to force social change and reform, was transgressing on private rights and abusing its constitutional powers. Moreover, they contended, the far-reaching and formidable presence of the government as a purchaser of goods and services would force institutions to adopt quotas of minorities and women. It would, they alleged, compel reverse discrimination, cause the appointment of people (minorities and women) who were unqualified for specific positions by promoting preferential treatment for members of minority groups and women. Proponents of affirmative action were equally uncertain of the justness of their cause and proclaimed their shock over the high level of resistance exhibited by educational institutions.

Guidelines for Implementation of Equal Opportunity

Faced with an unexpected push from both sides of the compliance and enforcement question, HEW's Office for Civil Rights found itself unable, with its small staff—most of whom had had little training in educational administration—to deal with academia. HEW's next move was to issue *Higher Education Guidelines: Executive Order 11246,* on October 1, 1972 (United States Department of Health, Education and Welfare, 1972).

The *Guidelines* set forth its provisions in detail in three parts. The first part, "Legal Provision," assigns to OCR the authority to enforce Executive Order 11246 as amended by Executive Order 11375, which prohibits employment discrimination on the basis of race, color, religion, sex, or national origin to anyone signing a government contract in excess of $10,000; these provisions apply to educational institutions as well as to all other contractors.

The requirements of the executive order are implemented by a Department of Labor regulation (41 Code of Federal Regulations Chapter 60, Part 60-1, "Obligations of Contractors and Subcontractors" [Tab B]) to be applied against all educational institutions, public or private.

There are two main concepts delineated in Executive Order 11246: nondiscrimination and affirmative action. The former requires the elimination of all practices, deliberate or inadvertent, operating to the detriment of any employee; the latter requires the employer to institute a program to overcome existing discriminatory practices by making additional efforts to recruit, employ, and promote qualified members of groups formerly excluded, principally women and members of minority groups (the latter defined as Asian American, black American, native American Indian, and Spanish-surnamed American).

To ensure implementation of the requirements of Executive Order 11246, employers are required to set not only goals to be attained for the employment of women and minority groups but timetables for the achievement of these goals. However, the executive order also protects the interests of the employer by expressly stating that no existing performance standard should be lowered merely to ensure compliance with the executive order.

The second part of *Guidelines,* "Personnel Policies and Practices," describes in detail the procedures that employers must follow to comply with Executive Order 11246. Recruitment policies must be as active for women and for members of minority groups as it has been in the past for the favored group of white males; recruitment practices must include utilization of employee referral and location facilities commonly employed by women and by members of minority groups as well as publication in all advertisements as being an "equal opportunity employer." Recruitment policies must include use of all possible sources of personnel, and recruitment practices must consider all posi-

tions as available to all qualified applicants.

Procedures for hiring personnel following recruitment must also follow practices explicitly designed to prevent discriminatory procedures against women and members of minority groups. Assignment of titles and academic appointments must be made on criteria applicable to all personnel equally. Moreover, compliance with the executive order must be effected only by means of vacancies created by normal growth and attrition of existing positions; to displace or dismiss currently employed personnel is expressly forbidden as a means of such compliance.

Policies for limiting simultaneous employment of two members of the same family (antinepotism policies) must either be eliminated altogether or at the least be designed so as not to operate to the detriment of any one member on account of sex.

Placement, job classification, and assignment procedures must be reviewed carefully to eliminate any possibility of discrimination against women and members of minority groups by means of separate job classifications for these employees. All job classification criteria must be equally applicable to all personnel.

To comply actively with the provisions of the executive order, training programs to provide necessary remedial training opportunities to previously disadvantaged personnel must be instituted to ensure the eligibility of these people for appropriate job classifications. Whenever there are existing job training programs, these programs must be available to all qualified personnel on an equal basis.

Promotion policies must also include remedial procedures and validation for all criteria for promotion according to outlines provided by the Department of Labor regulation (41 CFR 60-2.24).

Termination policies must affect all employees equally. However, if an incumbent is found to have been discriminated against in terms of seniority, the policies for dismissal for reason of seniority must be adjusted suitably to the benefit of the disadvantaged person insofar as necessary to assure that person fair treatment.

Conditions of work must be the same for all members of each job classification; all qualified personnel must have equal access to membership on decision-making committees, to availability of professional leaves of absence, and to the use of such institutional facilities as dining halls and faculty clubs.

Policies regarding rights and benefits and salary must adhere closely to the concept of equal pay for equal work. All criteria for determining salary by job classification should be made available to all present and potential employees. Level of pay must be determined on the basis of capability and record of performance, not on the basis of former salary, which may be low for women and for members of minority groups.

Title VII of the Civil Rights Act of 1964, the Equal Pay Act, and the National Labor Relations Act all authorize the use of back pay as a remedy for past discriminatory practices. The executive order provides access to this remedy for those employees not protected by the three preceding statutes. These payments should be included as an integral part, as needed, in an affirmative action program.

All types of paid and unpaid leaves of absence must be available to all qualified personnel.

Sex discrimination guidelines (41 CFR 60-20, Tab D) provide explicit instructions regarding employment policies relating to pregnancy and childbirth. Leaves of absence pertaining to pregnancy and childbirth must be granted on a basis equal to that for leaves of absence for other personal reasons; mandatory leaves must be required only by the recommendation of a physician; the length of leave, whether mandatory or voluntary, should be based on medical need relating to pregnancy and childbirth. Reinstatement to the employee's original position, or to one of like status and pay, without loss of seniority or accrued benefits, is specified. The revised guidelines on sex discrimination (37 Fed. Reg. 6835) also apply to university employers. Child care leaves, as well as pregnancy and childbirth leaves, are to be considered on criteria equal to those in effect for other personal leaves.

All fringe benefits—including medical, hospital, accident, life insurance, and retirement benefits; profit-sharing and bonus plans; and leaves of absence—and all other terms and conditions of employment must be equally available and applicable to all personnel, both men and women, in each job classification. Department of Labor sex discrimination guidelines specify that benefits paid to both sexes must be equal (see also Title VII of the Civil Rights Act of 1964).

To improve employment opportunities for women and members of minority groups, the Department of Labor regulation (41 CFR 60-2.24) encourages the establishment of child care programs, which are seen to benefit all employees, not just women and members of minority groups.

The provisions of Executive Order 11246 encourage the establishment of sound standards of due process for the hearing of employee grievances. These procedures may then take precedence over jurisdiction by the federal government in the management of employee affairs. These grievance procedures should be in writing and available to all present and prospective employees.

The third part of the *Guidelines,* "Development of Affirmative Action Programs," discusses under seven sections what employers must do to implement affirmative action programs. (1) Each employer should have a written policy statement, over the signature of the chief administrative officer, setting forth the legal obligation and policy for the guidance of all subsidiary personnel, employees, and the community affected by the employers. (2) All supervisory personnel must know what the law requires, what the employer's policy is, and how to interpret and implement this policy within the area of their responsibility. (3) An executive of the contractor should be appointed as director of equal employment opportunity programs; the formation of an advisory council of representatives of women and minority groups is encouraged. This director must be able to supply information relative to job discrimination to the persons involved in administering the equal employment opportunity program. (4) There must be a system of auditing and reporting the implementation of the equal employment opportunity program to ensure compliance with Executive Order 11246. (5) The Office of Civil Rights urges that contractors make public its affirmative action programs, in accordance with 41 CFR 60-2.21. (6) Affirmative action plans accepted by the Office for Civil Rights are subject to disclosure to the public under the Freedom of Information Act (5 USC 552), with certain specified exceptions. (7) To develop and implement a plan, employers are urged to involve personnel at all levels, academic and nonacademic, to ensure its acceptability and practicality.

In 1972 the case of *deFunis* v. *Odegaard and the University of Washington* (82 Wn. 2d 11, 507 p 2d 1169 [1973]; 416 U.S. 312 [1974]) raised the issue to the level of the Supreme Court. The central question was whether race could or should be used as a factor, or taken into account, when selecting from among a qualified group of persons for admission to a professional school (law in this instance); and more particularly when such action is taken in pursuit of an affirmative action policy to mitigate the inordinate underrepresentation of specific minority groups. Persons and groups in favor of affirmative recruiting, admission, and hiring argued that an answer in the negative would bring affirmative action programs to an end. Few cases or controversies have produced a level of acrimony as high as that introduced by the *deFunis* matter (Ginger, 1974).

Proponents of the *deFunis* case and opponents of affirmative action joined forces and told the world that highly qualified white students were being denied seats in schools. The major newspapers, maga-

zines, and electronic media broadcast the same message. Talk-show moderators and marginal politicians sought to make capital with their constituents by suggesting that a major cause of economic and social problems was traceable to the imposition of disparate standards as described by the backers of deFunis. Because deFunis was completing law school when the matter came up for hearing, the United States Supreme Court held the matter moot (Leonard, 1974a; "deFunis and Its Impact," 1975).

The *deFunis* controversy joined the following issues: (1) Is it enough to remove long-standing and traditional barriers that deny entry and impede the progress of minority students? (2) Can years of "affirmative exclusion" be overcome or erased by a present policy of neutrality? (3) Does the affirmative inclusion of minority-group persons call for a bending of established admissions and hiring criteria or the establishment of a broadening of the variables to be considered? (4) Should institutions of higher education have societal missions and responsibilities to admit, educate, train, and hire members of minority groups? (5) Is a state of inequality, established by illegal and unconstitutional acts and conduct, perpetuated and protected by an engagement of neutral principles?

The intensity of the debate continued: how to apply affirmative action principles and practices to higher education and whether to mandate affirmative action in higher education at all (Leonard, 1974b). By 1975 HEW had, along with many educational institutions and other agencies, been charged with mal-, mis-, and nonfeasance with respect to the enforcement of federal antidiscrimination laws involving educational institutions. The National Organization for Women had filed such a complaint in the federal courts; the comptroller general of the United States had issued a report calling for improved programs by nonconstruction federal contractors (United States General Accounting Office, 1975); the United States Commission on Civil Rights had issued a report

(1975) deploring the lack of progress made, and the resistance encountered, in higher education; and the Carnegie Council on Policy Studies in Higher Education, in its report (1975, p. xi) on affirmative action, had observed: "Affirmative Action is today one of the most important issues before the higher education community. It affects the life changes of many individuals and the degree of independence of higher education from increasing governmental controls. It involves the highest principles of academic and political life, the goals and tactics of important interest groups, and the quality of public administration in an important area of action." Then, characterizing this period of civil rights enforcement as one of "transition" in higher education, the council addressed the very hub of the matter:

Higher education long ago, in keeping with its own principles of finding merit wherever it could be found and rewarding it, should have been searching more actively for merit among women and minorities. It has failed its own principles and impoverished its own performance by the neglect of large pools of potential academic competence. It has looked for merit mostly within 40 percent of the population and largely neglected the other 60 percent. The accumulated loss of talent is staggering to contemplate. It has been a very major source of inefficiency in the academic world in the utilization of potentially available resources.

Two, [affirmative action in higher education] should take place in the 1970s and beyond. The 1960s saw a doubling of faculty members. The 1980s may even see a slight decline. The effort at redress of past errors comes 10 years too late to be easily effective. Now there are too few new appointments and too many candidates even from among the majority male group alone. The transition will take longer and will involve more individual disappointments than if it had taken place earlier. We do not expect, however, that the very ablest, including white males, will fail to find some opportunities within higher education—although, often, they will not be appointed at institutions of their first choice, their talents will not be lost to use [Carnegie Council on Policy Studies, 1975, p. 3].

Bibliography

American Management Association. *How to Eliminate Discriminatory Practices: A Guide to EEO Compliance.* New York: American Management Association, 1975.

Anderson, J. *A. Philip Randolph: A Biographical Portrait.* New York: Harcourt Brace Jovanovich, 1972–1973.

Carnegie Council on Policy Studies in Higher Education. *Making Affirmative Action Work in Higher Education: An Analysis of Institutional and Federal Policies with Recommendations.* San Francisco: Jossey-Bass, 1975.

"deFunis and Its Impact." *Black Law Journal,* 1975, *4,* 269.

Ginger, A. F. *DeFunis Versus Odegaard and the University of Washington.* (3 vols.) Dobbs Ferry, New York: Oceana, 1974.

Leonard, W. J. "DeFunis v. Odegaard: An Invitation to Look Backward." *Black Law Journal,* 1974a, *3,* 224–231.

Leonard, W. J. "Introduction to the Conference 'A Step Toward Equality: Affirmative Action and Equal Employment Opportunity.'" *Black Law Journal,* 1974b, *4,* 214.

United States Commission on Civil Rights. *The Federal Civil Rights Enforcement Effort—1974: To Ensure Educational Opportunity.* Washington, D.C.: U.S. Commission on Civil Rights, 1975.

United States Department of Health, Education and Welfare. *Higher Education Guidelines: Executive Order 11246.* Washington, D.C.: Office for Civil Rights, 1972.

United States General Accounting Office. *The Equal Employment Opportunity Program for Federal Nonconstruction Contractors Can Be Improved.* Washington, D.C.: U.S. General Accounting Office, 1975.

WALTER J. LEONARD

See also: Women and Higher Education: Equal Rights and Affirmative Action.

AFGHANISTAN, REPUBLIC OF

Population: 16,300,000. Student enrollment in primary school: 694,240; secondary school (academic, vocational, technical): 176,736; higher education: 12,970 (university: 8681; nonuniversity: 4289). Language of instruction: Dari (Persian) and Pashto; English and French in some faculties. Academic calendar: March to January, two semesters. [Figures are for 1974–75.]

The pre-Islamic period, which lasted until the Arab conquest in the seventh century and the subsequent Islamic period, were major influences in the development of Afghanistan's educational system. The aim of education during the pre-Islamic period was to provide moral enlightenment for the student. Instruction centered on the Vedas, the earliest Hindu sacred writings, and later on the teachings of Buddha. Only males attended these sessions, which were held in the royal palaces.

After the introduction of Islam, mosques became the centers of education. The Koran, the Muslim holy book, was the basis of instruction, taught by the religious leaders, the *mullas.* In addition, the curriculum included Islamic history and literature, grammar, logic, and philosophy.

In 1850 the first two secular schools were started by Amir Dost Mohammed Khan, who ruled from 1826 to 1839 and from 1842 to 1863. These schools used foreign instructors in mathematics, geography, and chemistry; however, religious training continued, and the mosque schools provided the only education available in most parts of Afghanistan until the early 1900s. In 1904 the first modern school was established in Kabul over the objections of the *mullas.* Named for its founder, Habibullah Khan, who ruled from 1901 to 1919, the Habibia school was at first patterned after the Aligarh Muslim University in India. Although the school's teaching staff were Muslim religious scholars, the curriculum included secular as well as religious subjects. Habibullah Khan also founded a teacher training college, a military academy, and a school for army officers.

During the reform rule of Habibulla Khan's son, Amir Amanullah Khan (1919–1929), the first vocational schools and a girls' school were opened, and a number of primary schools for boys were started in rural and urban areas. At this time, Habibia became an academic high school patterned after the French *lycée.* Three more high schools were established in 1923, another in 1928.

The growth of education in Afghanistan in the late 1920s was mainly the result of an increase in foreign influence and cooperation, which has continued until today. Amanullah Khan provided the first higher education when he arranged for children of leading Afghan families to study at universities in France, Germany, Italy, and Turkey. In turn, teachers from these countries were recruited to staff Afghan high schools.

The first higher education institution in Afghanistan dates back to 1932, when the Faculty of Medicine was established in Kabul. Other faculties were added—law (1938), science (1942), and letters (1944)—and in 1947 the faculties combined to form Kabul University. In 1976 the university has ten faculties and a polytechnic institute, which trains engineers for various specialties such as construction, mining, petroleum, and transportation.

By the early 1960s religious influences were lessening in Afghanistan, and secular education received more attention. The middle 1960s were also marked by student unrest, as university students sought a voice in political and university decision making. The 1960s were a period of important growth in higher education. In 1963 a medical college under the egis of Kabul University was started in Nangarhar and became the University of Nangarhar in 1972. Nangarhar now has only a faculty of medicine, but additional faculties are planned. With the assistance of UNESCO and UNICEF, a teacher training academy and a higher teacher training college were established in 1964. The same year the faculties of Kabul University moved to a new campus in Ali Abad, built with the cooperation of the United States Agency for International Development (USAID).

In the early 1970s Afghanistan expanded its teacher training program to prepare for the eventual replacement of foreign staff by Afghans in the nation's school system. New teacher training schools and colleges were built as part of an extensive program to train new Afghan teachers and to provide additional training for experienced teachers.

National Educational Policy and Legal Basis of Educational System

The government of Afghanistan regards education as an important factor in the economic and technical development of the country. The aim of the government is to provide basic education for all Afghans.

Although the First Five-Year Plan, which was adopted in 1956, placed particular stress on developing primary education, it also included plans for the expansion of Kabul University. The success of the first plan made it possible for the Second Five-Year Plan, which ended in March 1967, to give priority to the expansion of vocational and higher education.

Subsequent plans have continued to focus on means to achieve the national goals of a literate society and to provide a free, effective, and balanced system of education at all levels.

In anticipation of a new constitution, the educational system functions under Presidential Decree 205 of August 21, 1973, which states and elaborates on the government's commitment to provide education at all levels.

Types of Institutions, Programs and Degrees

Higher education in Afghanistan is provided by the two universities—Kabul University and the University of Nangarhar—and by other higher education institutions.

Kabul University has ten faculties: agriculture, economics, engineering, law and political science, letters and humanities, medicine, pharmacy, sciences, Islamic law, and veterinary science. The university also has a polytechnic institute and maintains a university hospital.

Four years of study are required for the first degree, Bachelor of Arts or Bachelor of Science, in all fields except engineering and technology, which require five years for the first degree, and medicine, which requires seven years for the degree of Doctor of Medicine (M.D.). The only advanced degree is a master's degree in Dari and Pashto.

The program of study in each faculty is highly specialized, and, in many cases, students are directed to a field of study because of limited space in a faculty or because predetermined national manpower needs have imposed quotas.

Many faculties operate with interna-

tional cooperation. For instance, the faculty of medicine, established with French and Turkish assistance, now operates in close cooperation with the University of Lyon in France. The medical program includes one year of premedical studies in mathematics, physics, chemistry, and biology; five years of classroom and laboratory work directly related to medicine; and one year of internship. The faculty also runs a five-hundred-bed men's hospital, a three-hundred-bed women's hospital, and a large polyclinic in Kabul. In 1967 a cobalt radiotherapy unit was installed in the faculty's Nadir Shah Hospital with the assistance of the International Atomic Energy Commission.

The faculty of science has close ties with the faculty of natural sciences and mathematics of *Rheinische Friedrich-Wilhelms-Universität* in Bonn (Federal Republic of Germany). Since 1962 several of the German professors have been seconded to Kabul, while Afghan staff members have studied in the Federal Republic of Germany. Equipment for the faculty's laboratories has also been provided by the German university.

The faculty of engineering was first set up as a section of the faculty of science in 1956 under a contract with USAID. In 1958, with the cooperation of the University of Wyoming in the United States, it became the faculty of agriculture and engineering. In 1963 the faculty of engineering became independent and received teachers and equipment for its laboratories from a consortium of eleven American midwestern universities. Under a separate technical cooperation agreement, the Polytechnic Institute operates in close cooperation with the Soviet Union.

Nangarhar University consists of a faculty of medicine, which offers a seven-year program leading to the Doctor of Medicine. The faculty was originally founded to supplement the number of physicians trained especially for the eastern part of the country. Students are expected to participate extensively in providing medical care in the villages in the area and among nomads.

Third-level education is available at

a number of nonuniversity institutions. Advanced commercial training is offered at the Institute of Industrial Administration. Students who successfully complete grade 12 of a vocational/commercial high school may enroll in the institute. The three-year program prepares students for management-level positions in industry, banks, and public administration.

Several teacher training schools and colleges provide programs at the middle, high school, and college levels; the programs are designed for practicing and new teachers. The regular teacher training program lasts one to three years, while the in-service program consists of intense short-term courses and part-time courses that extend over several years. The higher teachers colleges operate a two-year program for high school graduates. Students who complete the program are qualified to teach in middle schools. The Teacher Training Academy has a program designed to develop a corps of education specialists. University graduates who have a year's teaching experience are admitted to the program. These students work with education specialists from UNESCO at the academy and are then given scholarships for further training abroad.

Further technical education is offered at the Afghan Institute of Technology, which provides a four-year program, grades 9 through 13, in the fields of architecture, mechanics, electricity, construction, and motor and aircraft repair. USAID has provided the institute with teachers, advisers, and laboratory equipment.

In an effort to raise the literacy rate, the Ministry of Education has established literacy centers throughout the country. Adult education courses through the high school level are available at the ministry's night schools. Other ministries administer programs which offer practical training in their area of competency.

Relationship with Secondary Education and Admission Requirements

The government provides free and compulsory primary education. Traditionally this education was offered in primary schools (grades 1–6); village schools (grades 1–3), which provide education similar to that offered in mosque schools and permit entrance into the fourth grade); and middle schools (grades 7–9). Recent reforms have redefined compulsory education as eight years, which entail some changes in the traditional pattern.

Secondary education consists of general or vocational education offered in Afghan vocational schools or *lycées* and leads to a secondary school-leaving certificate.

Admission to higher education is based on the secondary school-leaving certificate and a university entrance examination. The university also admits a number of foreign students in accordance with cultural exchange agreements. These students are not required to pass the entrance examination but must have a secondary school-leaving certificate or its equivalent.

Administration and Control

The entire educational system is highly centralized under the Ministry of Education. Both university and nonuniversity higher education institutions are directly administered by the minister of higher education, who appoints administrative and academic staff. Kabul University is headed by a president, the University of Nangarhar by a chancellor. Both work under the guidance of the ministry and are assisted by deans, who head individual faculties. Responsibility for academic affairs is vested in a council of deans.

Financing and Student Financial Aid

Higher education institutions are financed mainly by the state. Afghanistan has been the recipient of considerable foreign aid to develop its tertiary education.

Higher education in Afghanistan is free. The government provides a number of study grants to cover room and board and expenses for students and also distributes many scholarships to needy students based on merit and academic standing. The Afghan government, foreign governments and universities, and agencies of the United

Nations have provided scholarships for study abroad. The Bureau of Cultural Relations in the Department of Education is in charge of the coordination and organization of all foreign scholarships and fellowship training. These scholarships are available to undergraduate students to pursue a field of study not offered in Afghanistan, and for postgraduate study. Upon their return from abroad, scholarship recipients are required to fulfill a government work requirement.

Student Social Background and Access to Education

Many factors have limited the access of Afghan students to higher education. Due to financial restrictions, needed school facilities have not been available in all areas; secondary schools especially have been concentrated in the larger urban centers. Education has been particularly inaccessible for the country's large nomadic population. Expansion of enrollments in higher education has been hampered by financial and space restrictions.

Opposition to education for women has come from both religious leaders and parents. Women finally achieved entry to the university in 1960, and a separate section was established for women in the faculty of theology in 1964.

Teaching Staff and Research Activities

Members of the university teaching staff are classified as professor, associate or assistant professor, lecturer, assistant lecturer, demonstrator, and teaching assistant. The minimum requirement for all members of the teaching staff is a bachelor's degree. Promotion is contingent on three years of successful service and the contribution of an original work in the teacher's specialty. All teachers are civil servants appointed by the government. Salaries are based on academic rank, and academic qualifications.

A University Research Center, created in 1967, encourages research at the university. The center provides advice to faculty members and students on the planning and conduct of research projects; evaluates proposals and research in progress; reviews papers intended for publication; and makes arrangements for collaboration with foreign research scholars or teams. The center is governed by a board composed of professors and is financed from the university's research fund.

Current Problems and Trends

The rapid expansion of the population and the demand for education on all levels have created problems in higher education. Students who attend a higher education institution often cannot find employment after graduation. Attempts are being made to counter this problem by curriculum reforms which would lay greater stress on training the technicians needed by the country. Other problems arise from the lack of trained teachers, which can result in a deterioration of standards and student wastage, especially on the lower levels. A prerequisite to improvement of education for women is the training of women teachers. Few facilities currently exist to provide this training.

To improve the facilities for teacher training, a nationwide educational broadcasting service, designed to provide information for teachers, was established through UNESCO. In 1970 a two-year program for the training of primary and middle school teachers on an in-service basis and in training colleges was initiated. The program is conducted by experienced Afghan teachers and is compulsory.

International Cooperation

Afghanistan's educational system reflects a long history of international cooperation. Foreign assistance in the forms of financing, advisers, teaching staff, and equipment has in large part been responsible for the development of higher education. Multilateral programs conducted through the United Nations; bilateral programs established with more than ten countries; and intergovernmental programs such as the Colombo Plan for Co-operative Economic Development in South and

Southeast Asia, which provides regional assistance for technical training, contribute to educational development. Many Afghan students study abroad for their undergraduate and postgraduate degrees. Higher education institutions in Afghanistan, in turn, provide undergraduate education for students from other countries. All faculties at Kabul University accept foreign students.

[Assistance received through the Afghan National Commission for UNESCO, Kabul.]

Bibliography

Duprée, L. *Afghanistan.* Princeton, New Jersey: Princeton University Press, 1973.

Education in Afghanistan During the Last Fifty Years. Vol. 1. Kabul: Ministry of Education, Planning Department, 1968.

Further Education of Teachers in Service in Asia: A Regional Survey. Bangkok, Thailand: UNESCO Regional Office for Education in Asia, 1973.

Mujaddidi, G. H. "The Development of Higher Education in Afghanistan: Kabul University." *Bulletin of the UNESCO Regional Office for Education in Asia,* September 1972, *8* (1).

Naushad, G. N. "Educational Administration in the Republic of Afghanistan." *Bulletin of the UNESCO Regional Office for Education in Asia,* June 1974, *10* (15).

Newell, R. S. *The Politics of Afghanistan.* Ithaca, New York: Cornell University Press, 1972.

Smith, H. H. *Area Handbook for Afghanistan.* Washington, D.C.: U.S. Government Printing Office, 1973.

See also: Archives: Africa and Asia, National Archives of; Religious Influences in Higher Education: Islam.

AFRICA AND ASIA, NATIONAL ARCHIVES OF

See Archives: Africa and Asia, National Archives of.

AFRICA, SOUTHERN: REGIONAL ANALYSIS

The primary focus of this regional analysis is the dual system of higher education in southern Africa, with a reference to the universities in central Africa. Some countries in southern Africa are now independent (with majority rule); others are still under colonial rule. The independent countries of the region are the two former Portuguese colonies of Angola and Mozambique; the former British High Commission Territories, which became Botswana, Lesotho, Swaziland, Malawi, and Zambia; the former French colony of Madagascar; and the former Belgian-administered trust territory Rwanda. The colonial states are Rhodesia, South Africa, and Namibia (Southwest Africa).

Higher Education in Colonial Southern Africa

Higher education in southern Africa falls into two categories, given the political realities of the area—the universities and colleges of colonial southern Africa (Rhodesia and South Africa) and the newer institutions that have been established in postcolonial southern African countries. Institutions in Rhodesia and South Africa are the oldest in the region, originally created mainly for the education of the sons and daughters of the colonial settlers. Settlers regarded, and still regard, education of the region's African population as either superfluous (in light of the lowest role assigned to the African in the socioeconomic system); or harmful, for they fear a rise in political consciousness among African university students. Student-initiated racial riots in South Africa have, of course, confirmed the fear of the colonial settlers.

For the black Africans the white settlers therefore created a separate and inferior system—Bantu education. An apologist for separate education for Africans and an opponent of African advancement such as Hendrik F. Verwoerd, who became prime minister of South Africa in 1958, argued: "Equip him [the native] to meet the demands which the economic life of South Africa will impose upon him. . . . There is no place for the native in the European society above the level of certain forms of labor" ("Bantu Education," 1954, p. 7).

This statement expanded on the stated aims of Bantu education as presented by the Eiselen Commission in 1949: "The aims of Bantu education are the development of character and intellect, and equipping of the child for his future work and surrounding" *(Report of the Commission on Native Education, 1949–1951, 1952, paragraph 607; also see "Bantu Education," 1954, and Union of South Africa, 1954).*

Such thinking resulted in the passage of the Separate Universities Education Bill in South Africa, later named the Extension of University Bill in 1959. This bill dealt the death blow to the open university approach. The Extension of University law provided for the establishment of three more black university colleges (one in Natal for the Zulus, one in Transvaal for the Sothos, and one in the Cape Province for Africans of mixed descent); a university for Indians was subsequently established in Durban. The open universities, such as the University of the Witwatersrand and the University of Cape Town, which had traditionally admitted a limited number of Africans, were now barred to them.

An analysis of higher education designed for Africans in colonial southern Africa shows that the fundamental purpose of the separate system is to guarantee African acceptance of the colonial status quo. As one *Rhodesia Herald* correspondent commented: "I do not consider it right that we should educate the native in any way that will unfit him for service. He is and always should be the hewer of wood and drawer of water for his master the European" (Parker, 1960, p. 72). The inferior system of education has also fostered a narrow and tribal chauvinism that has created barriers among different nonwhite groups. Some university-level institutions were, of course, established for Africans, such as the University of Fort Hare in South Africa. And a few Africans were admitted into multiracial institutions, such as the University of Rhodesia. These efforts, however, were exceptions to the general rule that higher education in colonial southern Africa ex-

isted essentially for the settlers. It should also be noted that the few Africans who did manage to obtain higher education were, for the most part, trained as secondary school teachers, not as scientists, engineers, researchers, and other such professionals vital to a nation's advancement.

Higher Education in Postcolonial Southern Africa

The second category of universities in the region includes those relatively new institutions established in postcolonial southern Africa. Such institutions include the Universities of Zambia; Malawi; Dar es Salaam; Madagascar; Rwanda; Angola; Mozambique; and Botswana, Lesotho and Swaziland. Apart from the prestige attached to the establishment of national universities, the underlying rationale for the founding of these institutions was the need for high-level manpower able to deal with the problems of development and administration in the new countries. Indeed, the general aim of higher education in postcolonial southern Africa is the development and strengthening of an educational system relevant to the needs of the developing countries, with particular emphasis on the natural sciences and technologies so necessary for the promotion of social and economic growth.

Curriculum

With the exception of the natural and physical sciences, the curriculum in a typical colonial-controlled southern African university exhibits two general features. First is a European, or Eurocentric, emphasis on the history, geography, government, philosophy, and literature of Western, and specifically European, civilization. The apparent assumption underlying this orientation is that it is European culture that has produced mankind's significant efforts. Such disciplines as African history and culture receive no emphasis whatsoever. Though the university community may well never acknowledge this orientation of the curriculum, an examination of scholarly literature emanating from institutions of higher learning in the region, including work in history and social anthropology, clearly reveals a Eurocentric focus.

The second feature of the higher education curriculum in colonial southern Africa is the embellishment of the political status quo, or, at least, maintenance of a discreet silence by academics regarding the political situation in southern Africa. Either out of sympathy with the existing order or out of fear of reprisals for voicing criticism, members of academic communities in the colonial countries do not ordinarily challenge the political system. Indeed, those who do speak out do so at great risk. One may be deported summarily, for example. The Rhodesian regime has, in fact, deported foreign lecturers from the University of Rhodesia every year since 1966, sometimes as many as three or four at the same time; others face imprisonment or detention without trial. Professors are harassed by police, and at times they have to submit their writing for censorship (Cefkin, 1966). Such prospects are enough to silence many voices. In colonial southern Africa, the curriculum is thus a foreign one for the African people. Except for the natural sciences, the disciplines taught tend to reinforce the status quo. The social or economic problems of the vast majority of the population are either ignored or, when subjected to academic scrutiny, not analyzed objectively.

The independent countries. It is difficult to generalize about the cultural and political features of higher education curriculum in the black-ruled states of southern Africa. It seems, though, that these states fall into two subdivisions.

One subdivision consists of neocolonial states (such as Malawi, Zambia, Botswana, Lesotho, and Swaziland) that, while enjoying independent black rule, seem dedicated to emulation in all respects of the advanced Western nations. Hence, the university is seen as a place for training a new black elite able to take over leadership in government, industry, and all other vital areas

of national concern. The curriculum in such basically traditional institutions remains modeled on European programs. Though there is nothing wrong in borrowing from Western institutions of higher learning, and, indeed, some African universities have greatly benefited from careful borrowing of ideas compatible with national development efforts, indiscriminate adoption of Western ideas and values can ignore the pressing local needs and priorities of African development. In short, the new African educational philosophy should be not British, Russian, American, or French, but African. Those elements of Western higher education relevant in the African context should be incorporated into the curriculum. Standards of excellence necessary to a fine university system do, of course, know no national or cultural boundary. But in general the emphasis in African higher education should be on the utilitarian functions of the university and the educational programs should include elements of indigenous African civilization—its languages and history, its social and national systems, its music and mythology.

Some of these concerns were expressed at the Tananarive Conference, held in Madagascar in 1962, on the relevance of higher education in African states. This conference made the following recommendation: "As students of Africa are exposed to the scientific and cultural aspects of the outside world, they need to be thoroughly grounded in a firm knowledge of their own cultural heritage. The education for the future citizens of Africa must be a modern African education" (Burns, 1965, p. 204). Such an orientation, of course, placed "great emphasis in natural sciences and technology," as Greenough suggests in a UNESCO publication (1966, p. 21).

The second subdivision of independent southern African countries consists of those states (such as Madagascar and Mozambique) that are making serious efforts to decolonize. Decolonization in this case is seen not merely as a matter of raising a new flag but as a process encompassing the decolonization of the culture as a whole. The university is eminently suited to aid in this process and to suggest new lines of genuinely independent development in these countries. The University of Dar es Salaam is perhaps the best example of this type of institution. Its students are expected to be socially committed; one of its ways of ensuring this commitment is that each student, no matter what his specialization, must take a series of interrelated development courses that analyze the Tanzanian, East Africa, and African/Third World realities and investigate the theoretical and practical possibilities for transcending those realities. In a general way, Tanzania aims at training "workers," not "bosses." Similarly, Mozambique and other African countries have, with some modifications of course, articulated Tanzania's progressive pragmatic philosophy of higher education.

Whether these efforts will succeed is still difficult to judge. What is clear is that there is a vigorous and deliberate attempt to avoid a neocolonial pattern of development both in the country as a whole and within the university in particular.

Academic Freedom

Professor Ali Mazrui of the University of Michigan has suggested that academic freedom is highly circumscribed in much of Africa (Mazrui, 1975). Arguing that such freedom in independent Africa depends largely on the nature of the regime, he identifies three kinds of political leadership in Africa: the "elder tradition," "the warrior tradition," and the "sage tradition."

The elder tradition refers to a regime headed by a father figure (Jomo Kenyatta in Kenya, for example) whose word is law and who punishes those of his "children" who step out of line, including university students and lecturers. The warrior tradition refers to military regimes. These political leaders are often extremely harsh in their treatment of dissidents, including the university population. A classic example

is the military harassment at Makerere University in Kampala, Uganda. In July 1976—on the order of President Idi Amin, whose son alleged that some students had snubbed him—Ugandan troops stormed the university, killing a number of students. The sage tradition refers to an intellectual political leadership with a more or less clearly enunciated ideology. This leadership will tolerate dissent, including academic dissent, provided it does not depart radically from official national ideology; again, Tanzania serves as a good example.

The Mazrui formulation is plausible, for it is scarcely doubted that many new African states are intolerant of opposition or manifestations of disloyalty. However, Mazrui does oversimplify insofar as he does not address himself to the crucial question of the role of the African university in social progress and development— of the university's responsibility to defend ideals threatened by political maneuverings. The university fulfills its vital role through the quality of work it produces; the research it engages in; the student it turns out; the relevance of its curriculum to the environment in which it operates; and the commitment, dedication, and zeal with which those who work within it apply themselves to these tasks. Academic freedom is really the ability to exercise one's intellect and talents responsibly, without fear of reprisal. In colonial southern Africa, that fear is the constant companion of those academics who dare speak out. In the newly independent states, academic freedom exists in greatly varying degrees, ranging from the severe and even murderous depredations of certain military regimes to the relatively tolerant and benign attitudes of other governments.

Trends and Problems

A survey of literature on the problems of higher education in southern Africa shows that while individual institutions have their unique problems, most universities in the region share common difficulties. Among them are continued dependence on foreign nations for the training of necessary manpower (as in Rwanda) and teacher training too inadequate to avoid reliance on expatriates (in Zambia, Botswana, and Lesotho); political constraints that stifle excellence (in Rhodesia and South Africa); and finances insufficient for the necessary revision of colonial curricula and expansion of existing programs in line with national development efforts.

In spite of these many difficulties and obstacles challenging colleges and universities in southern Africa, there is every reason to be optimistic and confident about their future. The typical southern African student, highly motivated because of colonial deprivation, is a tremendous asset, sure to contribute to the success of higher education in the region. Despite problems and conflicts, higher education is crucial to development in the nations of southern Africa.

Bibliography

Bantu Education, Policy for the Immediate Future. A Statement by the Honourable H. F. Verwoerd, Minister of Native Affairs of the Parliament of the Union of South Africa, 7 June 1954. Pretoria, South Africa: Information Service of the Department of Bantu Administration and Development, 1954.

Brookes, E. H. *Native Education in South Africa.* Pretoria, South Africa: Van Schaik, 1930.

Burns, D. G. *African Education: An Introductory Survey of Education in Commonwealth Countries.* London: Oxford University Press, 1965.

Cefkin, L. J. "Rhodesia: A University Crisis." *African Report,* June 1966, *11*(6), 16–19.

de Sousa Ferreira, E. *Portuguese Colonialism in Africa: The End of an Era.* Paris: UNESCO, 1974.

Duminy, P. A. (Ed.) *Trends and Challenges in the Education of the South African Bantu.* Pretoria, South Africa: Fort Hare University Press, 1967.

Greenough, G. *African Prospect.* Paris: UNESCO, 1966.

Hanf, T. D., Dias, P. V., Wolff, J. H., and Mann, W. *Education et développement au Rwanda.* Munich, Federal Republic of Germany: Weltform Verlag, 1974.

Harbison, F., and Myers, C. (Eds.) *Manpower and Education.* New York: McGraw-Hill, 1965.

Lewis, L. J. (Ed.) *The Phelps-Stokes Reports on Education in Africa.* London: Oxford University Press, 1962.

Marquard, L. *Short History of South Africa.* New York: Oxford University Press, 1968.

Mazrui, A. "The African University as a Multinational Corporation: Problems of Penetration and Dependency." *Harvard Educational Review,* 1975, *45*(2), 91–241.

Murphree, M. W. *Education, Race and Employment in Rhodesia.* Salisbury, Rhodesia: Association of Round Tables in Central Africa, 1975.

1975 Prospectus: Graduate and Diploma Studies. Salisbury: University of Rhodesia, 1975.

Parker, F. *African Development and Education in Southern Rhodesia.* International Educational Monograph No. 2. Columbus: Ohio State University Press, 1960.

Report of the Commission on Native Education, 1949–1951. U. G. No. 53/1951. Pretoria, South Africa: Government Printer, 1952.

Rose, B. (Ed.) *Education in Southern Africa.* Johannesburg, South Africa: Macmillan, 1970.

Sasnett, M., and Sepmeyer, I. *Educational Systems of Africa.* Berkeley: University of California Press, 1966.

Scanlon, D. G. *Traditions of African Education.* New York: Columbia University Press, 1963.

Stimie, C. M. *Education in the Republic of South Africa.* Pretoria, South Africa: South African Human Sciences Research Council, 1972.

Union of South Africa. *Senate Debates,* 2nd Session, 11th Parliament, 5th Senate, June 7–June 11, 1954, cols. 2595–2622.

Yesufu, T. M. (Ed.) *Creating the African University: Emerging Issues of the 1970s.* Ibadan, Nigeria: Oxford University Press, 1973.

FORBES M. MADZONGWE

See also: Botswana, Republic of; Lesotho, Kingdom of; Madagascar, Democratic Republic of; Malawi, Republic of; Mozambique, People's Republic of; Namibia; Rhodesia; Rwanda, Republic of; South Africa, Republic of; Swaziland, Kingdom of; Zambia, Republic of.

AFRICA, SUB-SAHARAN: REGIONAL ANALYSIS

The first known and perhaps the oldest university in sub-Saharan Africa—the region south of the Sahara and north of the river Limpopo—was the University of Sankore in Tombouctou, Mali, which flourished four centuries ago. Sons of the kings of the ancient kingdom of Songhai quitted the palaces of Gao, and the children of the Touraregs deserted their great tents to receive an education there. Although Sankore has ceased to exist, its ruins still attract many scholars and tourists, and a magnificent mosque now stands near the old university site in Mali. At the nonformal level, a form of indigenous higher education still exists in Africa. Secret cults serve as higher education institutions; it is through them that the secret of power (real and imaginary), profound native philosophy and science, and the theology of animism are mastered by the select or the elect.

While higher education thus is not new to Africa, the establishment of modern universities is of recent development. Except for the University of Liberia and the Fourah Bay College in Sierra Leone, which were founded in the nineteenth century, all other sub-Saharan universities were established during the latter half of the twentieth century.

There are principally two types of universities in the region, the anglophone and the francophone. The former group consists of those universities or colleges established by British colonial governments in West and East Africa; the latter is made up of institutions established by the French colonial regime principally in West and Central Africa. In each area the system of higher education was fashioned after the metropolitan country's own university system in all respects. These colonial universities were affiliated to universities in Britain and France, and their degrees were awarded or guaranteed by the "parent" institutions.

A few autonomous universities have also been founded: Haile Selassie I University (now Addis Ababa University) was opened in 1961 by the Ethiopian government; like the University of Nigeria and the University of Sierra Leone, it has a strong American orientation. In Liberia the University of Liberia and the Cuttington College and Divinity School award their own diplomas and degrees. The former was founded as Liberia College of Liberal Arts, Fine Arts, and Sciences and acquired the status of a university in 1951; it is fully financed by the Liberian government. Cuttington College—which was founded in 1889 by the Protestant Episcopal Church of America and which has been continuously open since that time with the exception of the years 1929 to 1949—is financed and controlled by the Episcopal Church in collaboration with the Methodist Board of Foreign Missions. Also independent are the Universities of Nigeria (1960), Lagos (1962), Ahmadu Bello (1962), and Ife (1961) in Nigeria (established after the country's independence in 1960) and the University of Lovanium (now National University) in former Belgian Congo (now Zaire), opened in 1954 while Zaire was still a colony of Belgium.

History and Development: The European Pattern

For the most part, however, African higher education developed under the influence of the metropolitan countries. To fully appreciate the problems and challenges of African universities in the 1970s, it is necessary to review briefly the British and French colonial policies on education in Africa prior to and since its independence.

British influence. The beginning of higher education in British Africa dates back to the abolition of slavery and the resettlement of freed slaves in Freetown, Sierra Leone, in 1787. The first African known to have received a university education was, in fact, an ex-slave: Samuel Adjai Crowther, who was educated in the United Kingdom and repatriated to Sierra Leone in 1822; he became the first African bishop in 1861. As in the case of primary and secondary education, it was the Christian missions that pioneered the establishment of institutions for higher education in West Africa. The Church Missionary Society founded the Fourah Bay College in 1827 to "train ministers of religion, teachers and lay-workers for the church"; it catered specifically to the higher education needs of the ex-slaves. In 1876 it was affiliated to Durham University, England, as a degree-granting institution. For over 120 years, Fourah Bay College served as the academic mecca of West Africa, drawing most of its student population from Nigeria, Ghana, Sierra Leone, and Gambia.

Until 1882 the British government had no written or oral statement on the subject of education for Africans on any level. However, in that year the government appointed one inspector of schools for the whole of British West Africa and passed an ordinance creating a board of education. The written policy that resulted from this action was a terse statement in which the Privy Council to the Colonial Office on Education considered how the industrial schools for the colored races might be conducted in the colonies to make the child labor available for meeting some part of their educational expenses. The document emphasized religious instruction and the value of missionary teaching, stressed character development, and called for better development of the African peasant on the land. Undoubtedly, its main purpose was to improve and increase exportable African raw materials by cultivating the African peasant as a producing agent.

Between 1920 and 1924 the Phelps-Stokes Fund of New York, a private American foundation, conducted a survey of British East, Central, and West Africa. The mission visited West Africa in 1920–21 to investigate the nature of existing education for Africans there. It was appalled by what it saw. It noted that the British government had neglected African education, and the survey exposed, among other things, the hiatus between what the few available schools were teaching and the actual needs of the people. The report (Lewis, 1962) echoed and reechoed in Africa and London. It was this exposure that led the British government to appoint an Advisory Committee on Native Education in British Tropical African Dependencies in 1923 and forced the government's hand in issuing a comprehensive "Memorandum on Education Policy in British Tropical Africa" in 1925. It was here that a com-

prehensive educational policy—which included attention to study on the higher education level—was first articulated: "A complete education system should include primary (including infant) education; secondary education of different types; technical and vocational schools and institutions some of which may hereafter reach university rank in such subjects as teacher education, medicine and agriculture, adult education; the education of the whole community should advance *pari passu*" (Fafunwa, 1971, p. 23). The British colonial government's first attempt to implement this policy on the tertiary level was the establishment of departmental training courses, particularly in technical fields, for its junior workers and young school leavers—the aim being to train the Africans for the lower echelons of the civil service. While the intent of the government was clear in this instance, no attempt was made at the time to determine what would be the future place of the educated African in the larger society, nor was the educational system developed with any such coherent purpose in mind.

Three major royal commission reports truly set the tone and the pace for the evolution of African higher education in the British dependencies: the *Report of the Commission on Higher Education in East Africa* (1937), the *Report of the Commission on Higher Education in West Africa* (1945), and the *Report of the Commission on Higher Education in the Colonies* (1945). The findings of these commissions led to the establishment of universities in Sierra Leone, Ghana, Nigeria, Uganda, Tanzania, Kenya, Malawi, Zambia, and the transnational University of Botswana, Lesotho, and Swaziland, all of which were founded as autonomous institutions or had attained degree-granting status by 1972.

French influence. While Britain was unsure of what policy to follow in African education between 1800 and 1925, the French pursued a deliberate policy based on the economic and political objectives of the metropolitan country. As far back as

1829 the French government decreed that French would be the sole language of instruction in Senegal, one of its oldest colonies in Africa. And in 1900 Pierre Foncin, one of the leading exponents of French colonial policy on education, expressed the desirability of using the educational system to foster in Africans a "psychological bond" with the metropolitan country, as an assurance that even in the case of their (probable) political independence, they would "remain . . . French in language, thought, and spirit" (Bolibaugh, 1964, p. 86). Consequently, the French policy was to educate an African elite that would be assimilated into the French culture, giving them an education identical with that offered to Frenchmen anywhere. The masses, meanwhile, were to learn French and be given vocational training. The educated Africans were regarded as "French overseas" or black Frenchmen; they were represented in the French Academy, the French parliament, and French political parties in Paris.

It is within this environment that higher education was established in francophone Africa. Unlike the situation in British Africa, there was no agitation for the founding of an autonomous university on French West African soil. In fact, the view in 1950 of at least one West African representative in the French National Assembly was that quality education in African universities depended on their maintaining a curriculum that paralleled the metropolitan system as closely as possible (Thompson and Adoff, 1958, p. 539).

The French government's first step toward the development of tertiary-level education in Africa was to introduce centers for higher education in all of its territories; this took place between 1957 and 1965. During this period the University of Dakar in Senegal was the only university in French Africa south of the Sahara. Centers for higher education were established in Togo (1962); Central African Republic, Chad, Republic of Congo, and Ivory Coast (1959); Burundi and Gabon (1960); Cameroon (1961); Dahomey and Mali (1962); Guinea and Rwanda (1963); and Upper Volta (1965). The centers uniformly offered law, science, and arts; in certain countries medicine, education, agriculture, or administration were also included in the curriculum. In all cases the centers were financed, controlled, and staffed by the French government. By the next decade many of these centers had become universities—but they maintained their very close ties with France and with French universities. In the mid 1970s, while most anglophone African universities were granting their own degrees, all of the francophone universities were extensions of universities in the French metropolis, and their degrees were underwritten by French universities; France, unlike Britain, was financing and staffing these universities and maintaining strong control over the curriculum.

Features Unique to the Region

In spite of their colonial heritage, many sub-Saharan African universities have contributed to the social and economic development of their respective countries. They continue to supply high-level manpower and have also initiated programs to Africanize the curriculum and to train intermediate-level manpower. Many of the universities have departments of adult education and extension services and are involved directly or indirectly in the administration and development of preschool, primary, secondary, and teacher education.

Contributions to development. Particularly in the anglophone countries, where there is less commitment to the metropolitan model, there have been conscious attempts to make the universities more African-oriented, whereas in francophone and other non-English-speaking countries, the institutions follow practices obtaining in the metropolitan countries. For instance, most universities in English-speaking Africa have institutes or departments of African studies, where research and teaching in such cultural areas as African music, art, history, politics, dance, and literature are vigorously pursued. A related feature in the anglophone countries is the compulsory national service scheme for undergraduates or new graduates in Ethiopia (1960s), Tanzania (1968), and Nigeria (1973). Students are required to serve for a year in rural areas as medical assistants, teachers, pupil engineers, and the like, in the hope that this firsthand involvement in the problems of their country will prepare them to become development-oriented graduate citizens.

Adult education and agricultural extension. The adult education department, sometimes called the extramural or continuing education department, is designed to meet the needs of youth and adults by providing evening classes for persons who wish to complete their secondary education, study for university entrance examinations, or obtain industrial or commercial skills in order to procure better employment. The courses offered may be either academic or practical in such subjects as history, economics, shorthand and typing, accountancy, bookkeeping, mathematics, and English. Some departments organize seminars and workshops for farmers, small businessmen, lawyers, engineers, and other specialists who wish to update their knowledge in their respective fields.

At the University of Nigeria in Nsukka, illiterate farmers were encouraged to attend a week's conference in 1963 and subsequent years on maize or yam production with a view toward acquainting them with the latest procedures in this area. Between 1962 and 1965 the University of Ibadan's extramural department, in collaboration with UNESCO, offered a functional literacy program for tobacco farmers in Oyo, a town in western Nigeria. The program was based on tobacco growing, and text materials were intimately related to the tobacco farmers' experience. At the University of Ife the department of extension education sponsors a rural development program aimed at formulating a widely applicable model for rural development based on studies of selected villages in Ife Division. The program was launched in 1971. The project site, which is located about ten miles from the university campus, also serves as a laboratory for the training of rural development and agricultural extension workers and as a research center for testing community development theories and extension methodology designed to raise the standard of living in the area. The high-yield crops, such as maize, cowpea, tomato, cassava, yam, and palm, have been introduced as a result; storage facilities have been built, and farmers have been assisted in marketing their products collectively. The extension department also provides health and nutrition programs in cooperation with the University of Ife faculty of health sciences and home economics. Recently (1973) the adult education department of the same university produced a functional literacy program in the local language, developing textbooks that emphasize the vocabulary and concerns of the local farmers. About thirty farmers and their wives from one village who participated in the program learned to read and write within three months. Similar literacy campaigns have been planned for other villages. Newsletters designed to maintain the skills of the new literates are circulated regularly.

University involvement in primary, secondary, and teacher education. Members of faculties, institutes, and departments of education participate in conferences, seminars, task forces, and committees on curriculum development, which may be organized by either the government or the ministries of education; in addition, they conduct research and surveys on primary, secondary, or teacher education problems in collaboration with ministry of education personnel. Such research projects may be funded by the universities themselves, or, occasionally, by the ministries of education or a foreign foundation. University institutes—patterned conceptually on their British counterparts—also help to organize preservice and in-service courses for teachers at all levels. Many of the in-service courses make use of university facilities during the summer holidays; some, however, are conducted during the academic year by institutes with full-time staff and full-time students. In Lesotho, Uganda, Liberia, Ghana, Ethiopia, and other anglophone countries, projects connected with the curriculum, teacher education, and primary and secondary education are being pursued in an attempt to give the African child an education with better surrender value.

The Institute of Education at the University of Ife launched in 1970 a six-year experimental project using Yoruba (a major local language) as the principal language of instruction throughout the six years of primary-level education, with English as as a second language. The project was predicated on two hypotheses: (1) that the child would benefit culturally, socially, linguistically, and cognitively by being taught in his mother tongue; (2) that the child's command of English would be improved if he learned it as a separate subject from a specially trained teacher. On a conceptual level, the project aims to develop and evaluate a primary school curriculum, including methodology and materials, that is equally relevant and functional for those children who will go on to secondary school and those who will not. It is also hoped that the use of Yoruba in the classroom will help primary students bridge the gap between home and school. About fifteen hundred children and sixty teachers in primary schools were involved in this experiment.

Issues in Sub-Saharan African Higher Education

The issues most important in sub-Saharan African higher education in the 1970s focus on redefining the university's vital functions. Often the tendency to imitate metropolitan systems has led educators to ignore the pressing needs of their own environment—mass illiteracy, low-level economic development, and shortages of technical and skilled labor. Consequently, in the wake of independence for many sub-Saharan countries, the universities were caught between the old and the emerging new social and economic systems—a situation that has created both tension and an impetus toward reform.

Need for reevaluation. There is often a greater affinity between metropolitan professors and their African counterparts than between African professors and other African professionals. In addition, there is mutual distrust between government officials and university officials. The question thus arises: How can a balance be achieved between university autonomy and academic freedom on the one hand and public or national accountability on the other hand? There is a need for involvement and cooperation between government and university, particularly in the areas of research, agriculture, technology, health sciences, and educational planning on all levels.

Between 1940 and 1960 the newly independent countries of Africa and their people relied upon higher education to improve their economic and social well-being. Education in general, and higher education in particular, received substantial allocations from government budgets—in some cases, as much as 20 to 40 percent. Facilities and resources—such as gigantic buildings, sophisticated equipment, and scholarships—were generously provided. In addition, professors, graduates, and undergraduates enjoyed enviable positions in the society. Thousands of young men and women found this educational environment to be attractive, and university enrollment figures grew phenomenally in many African countries. Higher education became a means by which students of poor parentage could climb both the social and the economic ladders. The taxpayers, the government, and the university people themselves were living under the illusion that carbon copies of Oxford, Cambridge, Harvard, and Moscow Universities in Africa would effectively serve the needs of their people, failing to realize that a university in a developing society has a different role to play. They freely borrowed staff, equipment, ideas, and practices from the metropolitan countries.

By the late 1960s and early 1970s, however, the taxpayers and the governments began to question the role of universities in their midst. They felt that their universities were failing them because they had not helped to improve the economy; in fact, university education was becoming too expensive for poor countries to finance. While the people and the government recognized the important role the universities were playing in training highly skilled manpower, they also noticed that the universities were not developing the proportion of technical manpower needed for a relatively poor region. In addition, some of the graduates who held academic qualifications had no practical skills to contribute to the development of the nation. The general population began to perceive the university community as an elitist group that, while willing to admit some new entrants, ensured that the group would remain small enough to retain its elitist character. In other words, the universities were regarded as parasites on the economy—as islands of privilege in a sea of poverty.

African academics themselves began during the same period to express dissatisfaction with colonial traditions in higher education. As a means of exploring ways to improve the higher education system, the Association of African Universities, which is composed of the vice-chancellors (presidents) of the forty-two African universities in the anglophone and francophone countries, organized a unique seminar and workshop called "Creating the African University: Emerging Issues of the 1970s." The participants, who included junior and senior academics from all African universities, identified and discussed the following issues: (1) evolving an African academic community; (2) Africanizing higher education; (3) overcoming intellec-

tual dependence and providing intellectual leadership; (4) designating the university's roles and priorities in national and regional development; (5) pursuing avenues of research beneficial to African society; and (6) organizing continuing education, extramural work, and other nontraditional programs. The conferees also formulated a redefinition of the African university's role: "[To create] a community essentially of African scholars, men and women, old and young, lettered and unlettered, dedicated to serve knowledge to its community and committed to the total development of the African society with the objective of the total liberation of the common man from all that hampers his well-being physically, materially, and intellectually" (Fafunwa, 1974).

University's Role in Development

Although African universities have been major suppliers of high-level manpower, training teachers for schools and technical and administrative officers for governments, commercial houses, and industrial concerns, there are further ways in which an Africanized higher education system can contribute to national and regional development during the final quarter of the twentieth century. For instance, university sponsorship of extramural and extension services could cease to be "extra" and become a normal function of the higher education system, and those engaged in this work could cease to be regarded as second-class citizens within the university community. Faculty members could be encouraged to write text materials for primary and secondary levels and not, as is often the case, be denied adequate recognition for their work because such exercises are not "academic" pursuits. In sub-Saharan countries, where there is a dearth of primary and secondary school materials and where high-level manpower is concentrated within the academic community, such involvement would be more valuable to the society than the production of highly scholarly papers.

The Africanization of university faculty in the region should, in fact, be a priority. The average African professor in the 1970s is not any different in attitude—only in color—from his expatriate counterpart. Both were probably trained in the same overseas institution and both have absorbed an affluent society's ideas of what a university should be. African academics, by and large, have research orientations and attitudes about teaching and curriculum that are appropriate to a developed economy; they need to be oriented, or decolonized, and sensitized to the needs of the African people. This awareness has to underlie any attempts to produce a relevant curriculum.

The next priority is to change the university structure, which in many places is inflexible if not impervious to change. The final pressing question for African educators at the end of the twentieth century is: How do we go about making our universities more responsive to the needs and aspirations of the people? The European model is proving not only inadequate but expensive and largely irrelevant. What is international or universal in a university is the common search for knowledge and truth—not particular knowledge or truth, and not the models or structures or traditions whereby they are sought in other countries. Beyond an adherence to these universal goals, the African universities need not conform to anything else. The principle of total commitment to nation building implies that a university should be ready and willing to assist the nation in whatever capacity and at whatever level it is called on. The African universities should be propelled by their own societal momentum and not by the dictates of a foreign institution, ideology, or idiosyncrasy.

Bibliography

Altbach, P. G. "Education and Neocolonialism." *Teachers College Record,* May 1971, 72, 543–558.

Ashby, E. *African Universities and Western Tradition.* Cambridge, Massachusetts: Harvard University Press, 1964.

Bolibaugh, J. B. "French Educational Strategies for sub-Saharan Africa: Their Intent, Derivation, and Development." Unpublished doctoral dissertation, Stanford University, Stanford, California, 1964.

Conidec, P. F. "La contribution des universités de nouveaux états à la formation des cadres supérieurs." *Penant,* July-September 1965, *75,* 305–317.

Fafunwa, A. B. *New Perspectives in African Education.* London: Macmillan, 1967.

Fafunwa, A. B. *A History of Nigerian Higher Education.* London: Macmillan, 1971.

Fafunwa, A. B. *Growth and Development of Nigerian Universities.* Paper Number 4. Washington, D.C.: Overseas Liaison Committee, 1974.

Hailey, L. *The Future of Colonial Peoples.* Princeton, New Jersey: Princeton University Press, 1944.

Kitchen, H. (Ed.) *The Educated African.* New York: Praeger, 1962.

Lewis, L. J. (Ed.) *Phelps-Stokes Report on Education in Tropical Africa.* London: Oxford University Press, 1962.

Report of the Commission on Higher Education in the Colonies. Cmd. 6647. London: H. M. Stationery Office, 1945.

Report of the Commission on Higher Education in East Africa. Colonial Number 142. London: H. M. Stationery Office, 1937.

Report of the Commission on Higher Education in West Africa. Cmd. 6655. London: H. M. Stationery Office, 1945.

Reports of the Inter-University Council for Higher Education in the Colonies. London: H. M. Stationery Office, 1948–1950.

Thompson, V., and Adoff, R. *French West Africa.* London: Allen & Unwin, 1958.

Trudeau, E. *Higher Education in English Speaking Africa: An Annotated Bibliography.* New York: Fordham University Press, 1964.

UNESCO. *L'avenir de l'enseignement supérieur en Afrique.* Paris: UNESCO, 1963.

Yesufu, T. M. (Ed.) *Creating the African University: Emerging Issues of the 1970s.* London: Oxford University Press, 1973.

A. BABS FAFUNWA

See also: Benin, People's Republic of; Burundi, Republic of; Botswana, Republic of; Cameroon, United Republic of; Central African Empire; Chad, Republic of; Congo, People's Republic of the; Ethiopia; Gabon Republic; Gambia, Republic of; Ghana, Republic of; Guinea, Republic of; Kenya, Republic of; Lesotho, Kingdom of; Liberia, Republic of; Malawi, Republic of; Mali, Republic of; Nigeria, Federal Republic of;

Rwanda, Republic of; Senegal, Republic of; Sierra Leone, Republic of; Swaziland, Kingdom of; Tanzania, United Republic of; Togo, Republic of; Uganda, Republic of; Upper Volta, Republic of; Zaire, Republic of: Zambia, Republic of.

AFRICAN ADULT EDUCATION ASSOCIATION

The African Adult Education Association (AAEA) was founded in January 1968 at Makerere University in Kampala, Uganda, with forty members from ten countries. The idea for such an organization dates back to a meeting of African adult educators held in 1954 in Accra, Ghana, organized jointly by the University of Ghana and the International Federation of Workers' Educational Associations. In 1964, at a conference held at Kivukoni College in Dar es Salaam, Tanzania, the possibility of an international association was discussed; and in 1965, at the Evelyn Hone College in Lusaka, Zambia, the Adult Education Association of East and Central Africa was formed. As countries outside East and Central Africa became interested, the members decided to form the present Africa-wide association.

Membership consists of persons engaged in various forms of adult education, employed by governments, universities, private enterprises, and voluntary organizations. Persons concerned with university adult education have played a leading part in administering the association and sustaining its growth.

In an effort to promote adult education in Africa, AAEA sponsors studies of adult education in contemporary Africa and acts as a clearinghouse for information on all forms of adult education relating to Africa. The association seeks to inform policymakers and the public of the importance of adult education to development and encourages high professional standards and better training for adult education workers.

AAEA is a small volunteer organization with limited resources. Every two years major policies are subjected to a vote of the membership at a general meeting. Ordinary business is managed by an executive committee consisting of twelve members from eight African countries. The association has one affiliated national adult education association, the Nigerian National Council for Adult Education, and thirty-eight institutional members, including the Kenya National Board of Adult Education and a number of major African universities. Individual members number approximately 140. AAEA is the only regional African adult education body accepted by UNESCO for nongovernmental organization status.

The AAEA's most important activities are its conferences, planned biennially. Reports have been printed of the 1968 and 1971 conference proceedings. The association also publishes occasional newsletters, issued by various African universities, and *Journal of African Adult Education.* In addition, a members' handbook and fly sheets of conference resolutions have been published in French and English for distribution to governments and the media.

Institute of Adult Studies
University of Nairobi
Nairobi, Kenya

LALAGE BOWN

AFRICAN-AMERICAN INSTITUTE, United States

Since its founding in 1953, the African-American Institute has sought to assist the development of new African nations and improve understanding between Africa and America. AAI, a private, nonprofit organization administered by a board of trustees, works closely with governments and universities in programs of education and training for African students. These programs are made possible through contracts with the United States government and grants from major foundations, corporations, and private donors.

The institute's Africa Policy Information Center (APIC) offers advisory and consultative services to businesses, educational institutions, and the media. AAI also provides specialized information services to the United States Congress. Legislators and their aides are familiarized with the scope of African issues through a series of seminars.

The AAI School Services Division generates programs in the nation's schools, assists national educational associations, evaluates existing materials, and develops new materials to bring Africa to life in the classroom.

The AAI's Educators to Africa Association (ETAA) offers low-cost charter flights to meet the growing interest in Africa. ETAA also offers university-accredited study seminars at African universities.

The African American Dialogues are a series of meetings that enable distinguished Africans and Americans to discuss major issues in African-American relations. Dialogue participants have included leading representatives from the legislative and executive branches of government, as well as from the media, business, education, religious, philanthropic, and black communities. African delegates have included heads of state, foreign ministers, other African government officials, representatives of southern African liberation movements, educators, and other private-sector representatives. The Conferences of African and American Representatives, another conference series, affords an opportunity for American senators and representatives to meet with officials of African governments.

The African Educators Program, funded by the Carnegie Corporation of New York, encourages scholars, administrators, and educational experts from Commonwealth-member African nations to broaden their professional perspectives through visits to other African countries and North America. The International Visitors Program, funded by the Bureau of Educational and Cultural Affairs of the United States Department of State, also brings African visitors to the United States.

AAI, maintaining important contacts with a wide range of African government officials, arranges meetings and programs for African delegates to the United Nations General Assembly. The Women's Africa Committee, an AAI-affiliated group, offers hospitality and educational activities as well as orientation programs for African women in the New York City area and provides support to overseas programs such as the Ethiopian Women's Welfare Association.

African countries, American universities, and the American government cooperate with AAI in a number of scholarship programs. The African Fellowship Graduate Program (AFGRAD) sponsors postgraduate studies for highly qualified academic and governmental personnel. The African Scholarship Program of American Universities (ASPAU) aids African students who wish to study at American universities.

Two AAI programs provide assistance to southern Africans. The Southern African Student Program (SASP) assists southern African students in the United States who face problems finding jobs, continuing their education, and handling visa problems due to their inability to return to their home countries. The Southern African Refugee Education Project (SAREP) offers educational assistance to African refugees from countries still under white rule and funds scholarships to African institutions at the postsecondary, vocational, and university levels. Funded by the Office of Refugee and Migration Affairs of the United States Department of State, the program manifests AAI's concern for displaced Africans from the remaining minority-ruled countries of southern Africa.

AAI provides African university administrators with training on American university campuses through its African University Student Internship Program (AUSIP). The institute responds to requests from African universities for assistance in recruiting faculty within the United States, often screening American candidates for posts at African universities.

The institute has responded to emergency needs, which have reached catastrophic proportions in Africa, by aiding several fund-raising efforts for victims of the devastating drought in the Sahel. The AAI's long-range development program, including research and conferences, focuses on African rural problems.

The AAI publications include *Africa Report*, bimonthly magazine; and *African Update*, bimonthly news report. *Non-Formal Education in African Development* is a comprehensive survey of rural development and training programs outside the formal school system in selected African countries. A second volume on nonformal education, *The Road to the Village: Case Studies in African Community Development*, is a collection of research reports that indicate how various aid programs meet the needs of African villagers. A conference report, *The Absolute Poor*, describes grass-roots efforts and external aid programs.

833 United Nations Plaza
New York, New York 10017 USA

AFRICAN AND MALAGASY COUNCIL FOR HIGHER EDUCATION
(Conseil africain et malgache pour l'enseignement supérieur)

The idea of the *Conseil africain et malgache pour l'enseignement supérieur* (CAMES: African and Malagasy Council for Higher Education) was generated in 1966 during a conference of the ministers of education of the Afro-Malagasy French-speaking countries. In 1968 African and Malagasy heads of states and governments decided to set up CAMES; its basic organization was approved by member states in 1972 and 1973.

CAMES was formed to ensure coordination between member states in the fields of higher education, research, and cultural promotion. It provides up-to-date information on the functioning of all existing institutions of higher education and research, serves as a center of analysis and synthesis of projects in the field of educational policy,

and offers a permanent framework for cultural and scientific cooperation. The council attempts to reduce the double uses and wastages of funds for higher education and research; and promotes structures and curricula adapted to the conditions, realities, and needs of the member states. CAMES initiates and encourages the exchange of students, teachers, and researchers on disciplinary or interdisciplinary levels.

Two senior officials from each member state's Ministry of Education act as delegates to the council. Chancellors and directors of higher education institutes are automatically members of the council and are entitled to a deliberative vote. The council meets once a year before the annual conference of ministers of education. The ministers' conference, the supreme authority of CAMES, directs the council's activities.

The general secretariat prepares the agendas of the council and carries out the decisions of the conference of ministers. A convention, adopted by the ministers of education and signed by the African, Malagasy, and Mauritian heads of state and government, defines the status of the administrative personnel of the general secretariat, which has its seat in Ouagadougou, Upper Volta.

The budget of CAMES is supplied by contributions of member states and financial aid of friendly organizations and countries. France, United States, Canada, and Belgium have provided or continue to provide substantial aid to CAMES.

The council developed the first African curricula for higher education. An inter-African general agreement on equivalences or validity of university diplomas in Africa and Malagasy was established in February 1972. The agreement, signed by the ministers of education, sets the conditions for preparation and award of degrees and diplomas in the area.

A conference held in Ouagadougou in December 1973 studied recommendations for an exchange of teachers and researchers to tighten the bonds between French- and English-speaking African universities. A project of inter-African competitive examinations for the recruitment of competent higher education teachers is being considered by CAMES as well as an institute of traditional African medicine and pharmacopoeia.

The council, in an effort to establish contacts among French-, English-, and Arabic-speaking countries, maintains relationships with the Association of Partially or Wholly French-Language Universities, United Nations Development Programme, United Nations Economic Commission for Africa, Cultural Committee of the Organization of African Unity, African International Institute, and Standing Conference of Rectors and Vice-Chancellors of the European Universities.

The general secretariat publishes lists of teachers and researchers working in African and Malagasy universities.

B.P. 134

Ouagadougou, Upper Volta

AFRICAN NATIONAL ARCHIVES
See Archives: Africa and Asia, National Archives of.

AFRICAN SCIENCE POLICIES
See Science Policies: Less Developed Countries: Arab World.

AFRICAN STUDIES
See Area Studies (field of study).

AGED, HIGHER EDUCATION FOR THE
See Adult Education: Elderly, Programs for the.

AGENCIES FOR ACCREDITATION
See Academic Standards and Accreditation.

AGRIBUSINESS EDUCATION
See Agriculture in Higher Education: Agribusiness and Agribusiness Education.

AGRICULTURAL ECONOMICS
(Field of Study)

Agricultural economics, a branch of applied economics, consists of the application of economic techniques and ways of thinking to agricultural and rural activities. Economics is concerned with the relation of means to ends and the obtaining of maximum benefits from scarce resources which may be used in alternative ways. Agricultural economics aims, therefore, at analyzing agricultural activities and providing guidance for maximizing returns from agricultural resources. Its distinctiveness as a subject arises from the importance and peculiarities of agriculture and rural life.

There are distinct stages in the agricultural process, from the combination of resources (land, labor, capital, and other inputs) on the individual farm, through food marketing, processing, and distribution channels, to the satisfaction of the ultimate consumer. In most countries governments deliberately intervene in production and distribution processes and provide the larger economic and political framework within which agriculture must operate. Further intervention occurs in international trade in agricultural inputs and products. Determination and operation of policies in these matters then become important considerations. The field, therefore, divides broadly into agricultural production, including farm management; supply, demand, and prices, marketing and distribution, and international trade in relation to agricultural products; and agricultural policy, including location of production, land use, agrarian reform, and rural and community development. Finance and credit are needed to assemble and organize the factors of production in commercial agriculture, and their provision and use constitute a further branch of the study.

Agricultural economics is closely allied to rural sociology, history, and geography. Agriculture is remarkable in the extent to which processes of production and ways of life are intermingled. Places of work and units of production are also the homes and environment of the people concerned. Thus, efficiency of production and the welfare of rural workers are closely linked with the rural social organization. Also, because understanding of the present situation, its problems and potentials for development, cannot be adequate without knowledge of background and traditions and the factors which have stimulated and impeded change, history is considered an allied field. Since agricultural potential is closely related to soils, terrain, and climate, an agricultural economist must be familiar with the field of geography.

The origins of agricultural economics can be traced back to the eighteenth century, when the leader of the Physiocrats, François Quesnay (1694–1774), in France, analyzed the capital needs of agricultural businesses and developed the concept of the "entrepreneur" in farming; and Arthur Young (1740–1820) in England, in the context of the "agricultural revolution," expounded his doctrine of "that proportioned farm, which is of all others the most profitable." Young's work was continued and developed by Albrecht Thaer (1752–1828) in Germany, where Johann Heinrich von Thünen (1783–1850) made further contributions, particularly to theory of price formation and location of production. Von Thünen's influence is apparent in later German studies, including the works of Friedrich Aereboe and Theodor Brinkmann in the early twentieth century. In England David Ricardo (1772–1823) formulated his famous theory of rent. Agricultural economics concerns continued to be treated within general economics until after World War I, when the field developed rapidly as a distinctive academic discipline. The works of C. S. Orwin at Oxford University and A. W. Ashby at the University of Wales exemplify the emergence of this field as a separate discipline.

During the first half of the twentieth century the study of agricultural economics also became prominent in other European countries. In Switzerland Ernst Laur suc-

cessfully developed and integrated agricultural business economics and scientific agrarian policy with special reference to peasant farming. Italian interest in economic aspects of agriculture can be traced back to the eighteenth century; but the subject emerged anew in the interwar period, largely under the influence of Arrigo Serpieri, with the development of "case-study" research methodology in the context of a fascist state. Interesting work proceeded in Russia in a contrasting political environment; particularly noteworthy is the work of A. N. Chelintzev and A. W. Chayanov on the economics of peasant farming.

Meanwhile, in the United States the collection and use of agricultural statistics for production adjustments had begun in 1840; and from 1867, at the University of Illinois, J. M. Gregory had stimulated interest in the economic aspects of agriculture. The agricultural depression of the 1890s led to intensification of study, and in the early years of the twentieth century an independent tradition of agricultural economics was taking shape, influenced particularly by R. T. Ely, T. N. Carver, E. C. Nourse, and H. C. Taylor, and later by G. F. Warren and J. D. Black. Characteristic of United States development is the integration of all aspects in elementary treatment, together with intense specialization in advanced theory and research. Agricultural production economics thus reached extreme theoretical refinement; land economics and agricultural marketing also became special subjects, although agricultural policy tended to be relatively neglected in early decades.

American and British influence spread to Canada, Australia, and later to the developing countries of Latin America, Asia, and the Pacific region. Subsequent developments have reflected local conditions and requirements. European countries other than those already mentioned tended to absorb ideas from many sources; German and Swiss influences were strongest in Scandinavia, for example.

Formal education in agricultural economics began in Germany and the United States in the latter part of the nineteenth century. Courses were listed at Cornell University and the University of Illinois in 1868. In England formal teaching in the subject began at the University of Cambridge in 1896.

Significant changes in agricultural economics have occurred as a result of the development and application of sophisticated statistical and econometric techniques, such as linear and quadratic programming and game theory, aided by computer technology. There have also been important changes in scope and emphasis in the field. With growing concentration on economic planning in almost all countries, it becomes increasingly unrealistic to consider agriculture in isolation. In the highly developed countries agricultural economics is playing a growing role in regional planning and development, where agricultural activities need to be integrated with manufacturing and service industries; in the developing countries agricultural economics is becoming more and more important in rural planning and development, where the necessity arises to promote agriculture from subsistence to commercial production and to broaden the production and employment base of the rural areas. Agricultural economics is also becoming of vital importance in world development in connection with various international organizations such as the World Bank and United Nations agencies, where there is a need to relate land use and food production to human requirements on an international scale. These developments are increasingly interdisciplinary.

The field of agricultural economics is fully international. Most countries have their own research and education establishments or are closely linked with such establishments in other countries. Since its foundation in 1929 the International Conference of Agricultural Economists (now the International Association of Agricultural Economists) has had growing influence, through its members and publications, in the communication of ideas and in the unification of the subject.

Most countries regard agricultural economics as important and offer or can obtain training to meet first-degree standards according to principles and subject definitions which are widely consistent, although emphasis varies nationally and regionally to some extent, reflecting the state of development and requirements of the countries. The special—but by no means exclusive—interests of various regions may be represented as follows: in the United States and Canada, there is interest in agricultural adjustment, the world situation, and interdisciplinary studies. In the United Kingdom and Commonwealth nations, international groupings and trade (especially the European Economic Community), regional development and rural development, and agricultural adjustment are primary areas of concern. Other European countries concentrate on international groupings and trade, agricultural structure, and cooperation. Special interests in Latin America, Asia, Africa, and the Middle East include rural development, including land reform; production and trade, especially in relevant agricultural commodities; land settlement; and community development. In Soviet and Eastern European countries, basic training is influenced considerably by Marxist economics. The requirements of centrally planned economies lead to research and teaching emphasis on data collection and analysis; determination of production norms and targets; cooperative and collective arrangements; agroindustrial complexes; comprehensive national, regional, and local planning; and determination of priorities.

J. OWEN JONES

Levels and Programs of Study

Programs in agricultural economics generally require as a minimum prerequisite a secondary education and lead to the following awards: certificate or diploma, bachelor's degree (B.Sc.), master's degree (M.Sc.), the doctorate (Ph.D.), or their equivalents. Programs deal with the principles and practices of agricultural economics and consist primarily of classroom and field instruction.

Programs that lead to an award not equivalent to a first university degree include the following courses: principles of agricultural economics, principles of marketing, farming systems, farm management, production economics, accounting and financial records, agricultural policy, and farm credit policy. Background courses usually include mathematics, principles of economics, crop husbandry, animal husbandry, and agricultural engineering.

Programs that lead to a first university degree deal with both the principles and practices of agricultural economics but stress management theory and the analysis of forces affecting agricultural organizations. Principal course content usually includes some of the following: principles of economics, principles of agricultural economics, marketing of agricultural products, production economics, farming systems, farm management and organization, cost control in agriculture, price theory, economics of natural resource use, and agriculture and government. Background courses usually include economic theory, money and banking, labor economics, statistics, principles of accounting, botany, ecology, chemistry, soil science, principles of crop husbandry, principles of animal husbandry, agronomy, and rural institutions (including cooperatives).

Programs that lead to a postgraduate university degree consist primarily of study and research dealing with advanced specialties in the field of agricultural economics. Emphasis is given to original research work as substantiated by the presentation of a scholarly thesis or dissertation. Principal subject matter areas within which courses and research projects tend to fall include farm management, farming systems, farm finance, farm policy planning and implementation, marketing of agricultural products, farm cost control, farm production economics, and trade in agricultural products. Subject areas within which background studies tend to fall include business management, accountancy, economics, law

and jurisprudence, public finance and taxation policy, agricultural cooperation and rural sociology, natural resource use, economics and planning, area development planning, and spatial equilibrium of agricultural production.

[This section was based on UNESCO's *International Standard Classification of Education (ISCED): Three Stage Classification System, 1974* (Paris: UNESCO, 1974).]

Major International and National Organizations

INTERNATIONAL

Commonwealth Bureau of Agricultural
   Economics
Bureau de l'économie agricole du
   Commonwealth
Dartington House, Little Clarendon Street
Oxford OX1 2HH, England

International Association of Agricultural
   Economists (IAAE)
Association internationale des économistes
   agronomiques
600 South Michigan Avenue
Chicago, Illinois 60605 USA
   Major international organization in the field; members are from over eighty member countries.

NATIONAL

Australia:
   Agricultural Economics Society
   Suite 302, Clunies Ross House
   191 Royal Parade
   Parkville, Victoria 3052

Belgium:
   Institut économique agricole
   18 boulevard de Berlaimont
   Brussels

Canada:
   Canadian Agricultural Economics Society
   151 Slater Street, Suite 907
   Ottawa, Ontario K1P 5H4

Chile:
   Instituto agrario de estudios económicos
   Casilla 13907, Correo 15
   San Antonio 220
   Santiago

India:
   Indian Society of Agricultural Economics
   46-48 Esplanade Mansions
   Mahatma Gandhi Road
   Bombay, Maharashtra State

Italy:
Società italiana de economia agraria
Istituto di economia e politica agraria
Piazzale Cascine 18
Florence

Japan:
Nippon nogyo keizai gakkai
Agricultural Economic Society
% University of Tokyo
Tokyo

United Kingdom:
Agricultural Economics Society
% University of Manchester
Manchester 13, England

United States:
American Agricultural Economics
Association
Department of Agricultural Economics
University of Kentucky
Lexington, Kentucky 40506

Principal Information Sources

GENERAL

Guides to the literature include:

American Agricultural Economics Association. *American Bibliography of Agricultural Economics.* Lexington: University of Kentucky, Department of Agricultural Economics, 1971–1975.

Boalch, D. H. *Current Agricultural Serials.* (2 vols.) Oxford, England: International Association of Agricultural Librarians and Documentalists, 1965.

Bush, E. A. R. *Agriculture: A Bibliographic Guide.* (2 vols.) London: Macdonald, 1974. Includes a section on agricultural economics; lists bibliographies, dictionaries, abstracts, periodicals, and general reference books.

Dillon, J. L., and McFarlane, G. C. *An Australasian Bibliography of Agricultural Economics 1788–1960.* Sydney, New South Wales: Government Press, 1967.

Fletcher, J. (Ed.) *The Use of Economics Literature.* London: Butterworth, 1971. Includes a section on agricultural economics.

Hazelwood, A. *The Economics of Development: An Annotated List of Books and Articles Published 1958–1962.* London: Oxford University Press, 1964.

Rural Institutions/Institutions rurales/Instituciones rurales Index 1945–66. Rome: Food and Agriculture Organization, Documentation Center, 1968. Provides indexes in English, French, and Spanish covering economic aspects of agriculture and rural organizations.

Selected Lists of American Agricultural Books in Print and Current Periodicals. Beltsville, Maryland: United States Department of Agriculture, National Agriculture Library, 1975. Includes sources on agricultural economics and rural sociology.

A history of agricultural economics in the United States is offered by:

Nou, J. "Studies in the Development of Agricultural Economics in Europe." *Lantbrukshogskolans annaler,* 1967, *33,* 1–611.

Taylor, H. C., and Taylor, A. D. *The Story of Agricultural Economics in the United States, 1840–1932: Men, Services, Ideas.* Ames: Iowa State College Press, 1952.

Works dealing with education and educational planning in agricultural economics include:

Agricultural Education at the University Level. Paris: Organisation for Economic Co-operation and Development (OECD), 1965. Discussion of agricultural education in nineteen OECD countries.

Axinn, G. H. "Function and Dysfunction in Education for Rural Development: An International Survey." Paper presented at annual meeting of the Rural Sociological Society, Montreal, Quebec, August 1974.

Coverdale, G. M. *Planning Education in Relation to Rural Development.* Paris: UNESCO, 1974.

Education in a Rural Environment. Paris: UNESCO, 1974.

Report of the Joint Advisory Committee on Agricultural Education. London: H. M. Stationery Office, 1974.

Overviews and introductions to the field include:

Agrawal, G. D., and Bansil, P. C. *Economic Theory as Applied to Agriculture.* Delhi: Uikas Publications, 1971.

Bishop, C., and Toussaint, W. D. *Introduction to Agricultural Economic Analysis.* New York: Wiley, 1958.

Black, J. D. *Economics for Agriculture.* Cambridge, Massachusetts: Harvard University Press, 1959.

Capstick, M. *The Economics of Agriculture.* New York: St. Martin's, 1971.

Hayami, Y., and Ruttan, V. W. *Agricultural Development: An International Perspective.* Baltimore: Johns Hopkins University Press, 1971. Includes bibliographical references.

Jones, E. L., and Woolf, S. J. *Agrarian Change and Economic Development: The Historical Problems.* London: Methuen, 1969.

Mellor, J. W. *The Economics of Agricultural Development.* Ithaca, New York: Cornell University Press, 1966.

Metcalf, D. *The Economics of Agriculture.* Baltimore: Penguin, 1969.

Ross, R. C. *An Introduction to Agricultural Economics.* New York: McGraw-Hill, 1951. Includes bibliographies.

Schultz, T. W. *Economic Growth and Agriculture.* New York: McGraw-Hill, 1968.

Tuck, R. H. *An Introduction to the Principles of Agricultural Economics.* Essex, England: Longman, 1961.

CURRENT BIBLIOGRAPHIES

Agrindex. Rome: Food and Agriculture Organization, 1975–. An international indexing service which includes sections on economic development and rural sociology and agricultural education.

Biological and Agricultural Index (formerly *Agricultural Index*). New York: Wilson, 1916–. Lists English-language sources.

Commonwealth Bureau of Agricultural Economics. *World Agricultural Economics and Rural Sociology Abstracts.* Farnham Royal, Bucks, England: Commonwealth Agricultural Bureaux, 1959–. Published monthly. The most significant and comprehensive abstracting service in its field.

United States Department of Agriculture, National Agriculture Library. *Bibliography of Agriculture.* Scottsdale, Arizona: Oryx Press, 1942–. Contains a section on agricultural economics.

PERIODICALS

Periodicals of importance to the field of agricultural economics include *Agricultural Economics Research* (US), *Agricultural Economist* (India), *American Journal of Agricultural Economics, Annuario dell'agricoltura italiana, Australian Journal of Agricultural Economics, Ekonomika sel'skogo khozyaistva* (USSR), *Indian Journal of Agricultural Economics, Land Economics: A Quarterly Journal Devoted to the Study of Economics and Social Institutions* (US), *Monthly Bulletin of Agricultural Economics and Statistics* (FAO, Italy), *OECD Agricultural Review* (US), *Oxford Agrarian Studies* (UK), *Quarterly Review of Agricultural Economics* (Australia), *Rivista di economia agraria* (Italy), *Rural Sociology* (US).

For a more complete listing of journals see:

1000 Selected Journals in Agricultural and Related Subjects. Beltsville, Maryland: United States Department of Agriculture, National Agricultural Library, 1973. An international listing.

Ulrich's International Periodicals Directory. New York: Bowker, biennial.

ENCYCLOPEDIAS, DICTIONARIES, HANDBOOKS

Haensch, G., and Haberkamp, G. *Dictionary of*

Agriculture: German, English, French, Spanish. (3rd ed.) Amsterdam: Elsevier, 1966.

Válogatott kitejezések āz agrárokonómia es a társtu dományágak köréböl. Selected Agricultural Economic and Allied Terms. Budapest: Magyar tudományos akadémia agrárgazdasági kutato intézete, 1964. Also in English, German, French, and Russian.

DIRECTORIES

Educational directories which include information on agricultural study are:

American Colleges and Universities. Washington, D.C.: American Council of Education, 1928–. Published triennially.

Commonwealth Universities Yearbook. London: Association of Commonwealth Universities, 1914–. Published annually.

International Handbook of Universities. Paris: International Association of Universities, 1959–. Published triennially.

Owen, W. F., and Glahe, F. R. *Guide to Graduate Study in Economics and Agricultural Economics: United States of America and Canada.* (3rd ed.) Homewood, Illinois: American Economic Association, 1974.

AGRICULTURAL EDUCATION, TEACHER TRAINING FOR
(Field of Study)

Teacher training programs in agriculture prepare individuals for instructional and leadership positions in educational programs for agricultural practitioners. The main purpose of these teacher training programs is to develop understandings and competencies that relate to planning, conducting, and evaluating education and training activities. Agricultural education is combined with general education and technical agriculture to fulfill the widespread need for professional preparation at the undergraduate and postgraduate levels.

Throughout the world there are numerous formal and nonformal practitioner-level education and training programs. These programs operate in a wide range of institutional settings, organizational arrangements, and sponsorships. Formal programs may be located in secondary schools, specialized agricultural schools, and postsecondary institutes. Agricultural extension and rural community development efforts are typical of nonformal programs. Training of agricultural workers and managers may be concentrated upon specific skills or may be part of a more comprehensive educational program.

Agricultural extension, which transmits knowledge from the researcher to the practitioner, is internationally recognized as the principal outreach effort of higher institutions and government agencies in agriculture. Through national sponsorship and close association with agricultural colleges and research centers, professional extension personnel serve as subject matter specialists, communications specialists, program administrators, supervisors, and operational-level extension personnel. In some countries leadership in extension is the responsibility of government agencies, while in others much of it is provided by institutions of higher education in agriculture.

The other major type of program operates principally through regular schools (under the sponsorship of education departments) and specialized agricultural schools (frequently administered by agriculture departments). The intent of some school programs is to orient students to agriculture, with relatively little attention given to vocational proficiency. Others prepare persons for farming. Still other programs train students for government service in agriculture or for employment in occupations closely related to farming.

Most prospective agriculture teachers and extension workers are trained broadly in all major agricultural subjects, so that they can undertake educational assignments requiring a general understanding of the field. Exceptions occur especially in the more technologically advanced nations, where specialization is more apparent. Some teachers and extension workers are prepared as specialists for technical-level programs or as extension specialists. These persons frequently work with others who have a more general orientation.

Additionally, farming experience, acquired beforehand or as a part of the training program, is a typical requirement for agricultural education students. Formal course work in agriculture sometimes includes specially designed courses for agricultural education majors, such as in farm mechanics.

Most agricultural education programs also emphasize the psychology of learning, principles and techniques of teaching, and the philosophy of education and extension. Agricultural education majors are also exposed to principles of education and training organizations, program planning, and evaluation of outcomes. Internships in an educational setting provide additional experience and at the same time help determine whether the student is suited to the particular role.

Agricultural education becomes more specialized at the postgraduate level and is offered in only a few countries. Most postgraduate degree holders in this field have been trained in Europe and North America. Postgraduate programs, involving course work, seminars, and research, prepare teacher trainers, administrators, supervisors, researchers, and other persons for leadership positions in practitioner education and training at the national, intermediate, and local levels. Students are frequently given part-time faculty assignments and supported with a stipend. Programs reflect the backgrounds and professional aspirations of individual students, as determined by the student and one or more faculty advisers.

Program patterns in agricultural education vary considerably within and among countries. Many programs for beginning agriculture teachers and extension agents, such as in the United States, the Philippines, and Sierra Leone, are variations of a bachelor's degree program in agriculture. In such cases, agricultural education course work forms an integral part of the degree program. The program at Ohio State University, for example, prepares both extension agents and vocational agriculture teachers. Many other countries provide agricultural education courses separate from a degree in agriculture. If the trainee is preparing to become a teacher, the pedogogical training is likely to be provided by a specialized teacher training college under the sponsorship of the education department. A trainee in agricultural extension will probably study under the sponsorship of the agriculture department.

Special institutes are sometimes created to train persons for extension worker roles. Programs at these institutions, which normally lead to a certificate or diploma, rather than a degree, typically combine training in practical agriculture with preparation in extension methods and techniques.

Agricultural education programs also vary in their balance between preservice and in-service preparation. Departments of agricultural education in the United States offer much in-service training to teachers, extension agents, and others associated with agricultural practitioner education and training programs.

Higher institutions of agriculture have traditionally been the setting for programs in agricultural education because they have generated much of the new scientific agricultural knowledge. Many of these institutions became engaged in informal outreach programs, either solicited or unsolicited, during their earlier stages. Their staff members conducted training activities and individual consultation for practitioners. As formal extension programs were started, and vocational education in agriculture was introduced into schools, graduates of agricultural colleges were employed as extension agents and teachers. Consequently, special departments of agricultural education, or agricultural extension, were established within colleges of agriculture.

Other higher education institutions also participate in agricultural education. In the United States, for example, approximately half of the departments of agricultural education are located in colleges of educa-

tion. Students receive their instruction in technical agriculture in the college of agriculture and their general education from other colleges or departments on the same campus. In some countries college of agriculture graduates are prepared for teaching in one-year degree programs at teacher training colleges or institutes, usually under the sponsorship of the education department. Training is almost entirely pedagogical, with varying degrees of emphasis on specific requirements for teaching agriculture. Extension workers in these countries are likely to receive their professional training in colleges of agriculture or in specially created extension training centers.

Several factors indicate continued expansion and change in agricultural education. One is the explosion of available new agricultural technology. Another is increased practitioner confidence in scientific findings as agriculture continues its transition from a tradition base to a science base. Still another is the fact that agricultural education is continually improving as a result of long and varied experiences, investigation, and analysis. A final contributing factor to the future importance of agricultural education is the widespread belief that the world's future depends heavily upon an ever expanding supply of food.

[For lists of organizations and information sources in the field of agricultural education, see the bibliography for "Agriculture, Forestry, and Fisheries."]

WAYNE E. SCHROEDER

AGRICULTURAL ENGINEERING
(Field of Study)

There is worldwide variation in the range of engineering activities grouped under the discipline of agricultural engineering. In some parts of the world agricultural engineering (a name first used in the late 1800s or early 1900s) is merely the application of already developed mechanisms, systems, and techniques for improving the production and storage of agricultural materials. In other regions this initial and elementary concept of agricultural engineering has become more sophisticated as the concepts of both engineering and agriculture have changed. In these regions agricultural engineering includes all engineering technology related to the production, harvesting, transport, primary on-farm to final off-farm processing, storage, and distribution of feed, fiber, food, and fuel from agricultural, forest, and marine biological materials. The field may include engineering activities which in some areas are referred to as *agricultural mechanization* and *farm, rural, forest, food, feed,* or *biological engineering* in addition to those under the more universally accepted term *agricultural engineering.*

The primary objectives of the field of agricultural engineering are considered to be all or any combination of the following: (1) to increase or protect agricultural production by providing suitable environment for growth, harvesting, processing, transport, and storage; (2) to maintain or change the natural characteristics of biological products for a particular use; and (3) to reduce the physical drudgery and provide desirable amenities for agricultural workers.

Typically the field of agricultural engineering is divided into a number of branches which are related to agricultural needs or traditional engineering fields. The more usual ones are agricultural machinery and/or power, soil and water engineering, agricultural processing, animal and plant environmental control, agricultural structures, rural electrification, and rural planning. Other areas which in some cases may be considered branches of agricultural engineering are food, forest, biological, and marine engineering.

Like any other engineering field, agricultural engineering education must have a strong physical science base, with special attention to chemistry and physics. Since materials being handled in agricultural engineering are of a biological nature, an equally strong base is desirable in the biological sciences, particularly biology and physiology. Likewise, the agricultural sciences (such as agronomy, soils, and the plant and animal sciences) are necessary for an individual to practice successfully as an agricultural engineer. And since an agricultural engineer is first of all an engineer, he must have an understanding of and an ability in the engineering sciences—at least in the areas of materials, fluid and heat flow, computations, and mechanisms.

The first attempts at applying engineering principles to agriculture were undoubtedly made by early man through combinations of imagination, motivation, and chance. However, the field did not become identifiable until the beginning of the industrial revolution in North America and the rapid settlement of that continent. The application of engineering to agriculture was an important part of the industrial revolution, as exemplified by the invention of the cotton gin, the steel plow, and the reaper. The availability of cheap energy (coal and wood) and large areas of fertile virgin lands in North America, spurred the application of mechanisms and other engineering techniques to agriculture. Early settlers wanted to command and work large areas of free land to improve their standard of living, but this was possible only through the better application of human, animal, and heat energy to the land. Following the efforts of inventors and cultivators in applying engineering to agriculture in the late 1800s and early 1900s, a few practicing engineers became interested in the possibilities of systematically applying engineering to agriculture. At this point, agricultural engineering began as a profession.

In the early 1900s interest in agricultural engineering education developed in more heavily industrialized areas of Europe and North America. Education was formalized through shop courses and later by agricultural engineering options in fields such as mechanical and civil engineering. Still later, specific curricula in agricultural engineering were instituted. The first recognized curriculum was established in the United States at Iowa State College of the Mechanic Arts, Ames, Iowa, in 1907. Options or separate curricula since then have developed all over the world.

The educational trend in agricultural engineering has been to emphasize the biological sciences and the physical sciences as foundation disciplines. There is also a trend toward a greater number of advanced degrees and greater specialization within the field. These trends are generally international in nature; however, many developing countries are following the various evolutionary steps taken earlier in North America. In many areas, particularly in the less developed countries, machines and mechanisms are still of greatest interest, but there has been a movement toward engineering systems and techniques with less emphasis on power units and machines for applying energy. With the current concern for energy conservation, agricultural engineering education must focus considerable attention on development of machines, systems, and techniques which lead toward increased productivity per unit of energy expended.

Educational programs in agricultural engineering aim at new techniques of tillage, planting, cultivation, protection of crops and animals from pests, harvesting, transport, processing, and storage. Some of the new techniques include solar heat collection in environmentally controlled buildings and the drying of crops with solar heated air. Also, lasers for surveying purposes were first used by agricultural engineers; similarly, air-pressure-supported buildings were initially used for greenhouses and environmentally controlled storage. Also, early attempts were made to conserve energy and materials in agricultural production processing and distribution; there was particular emphasis on reducing the amount of chemicals used for insect control and controlling irrigation water to avoid waste from runoff and deep percolation. In the mid 1970s atten-

tion is also being given to the production of food in the oceans—aquaculture—and the agricultural engineer can find a place in this endeavor too. Associate (two-year) programs leading toward certification as a technician in support of agricultural engineering are also being considered and tried. This technical support should encourage and allow the agricultural engineer to concentrate his energies toward becoming more professional.

The field is becoming rapidly internationalized, largely through the realization that engineering is often the vehicle to achieve the full potential of scientific breakthroughs in the plant and animal areas. The increased development of international contacts and organizations composed of agricultural engineers from various countries, the exchange of students and faculty, and the ease with which individuals can work on advanced degrees in countries other than where they obtained their first degree—all attest to the international nature of the field.

The major differences in agricultural engineering programs around the world developed during the twentieth century. In one type of program, agricultural courses are included in the more traditional fields of engineering: agricultural power and machinery development under mechanical engineering, agricultural structures and soil and water control under civil engineering, food processing and manufacturing under chemical engineering, and equipment for controlling environmental processes and agricultural electrical power applications under electrical engineering. Under such a program, students interested in engineering application to agriculture would take a conventional engineering program with electives aimed toward agricultural production, storage, processing, and/or distribution. In another type of program, students enroll in one of the existing agricultural disciplines of the plant or animal sciences, with emphasis on additional mathematics and physics and some applied engineering courses under civil, mechanical, electrical, or chemical engineering. A third program is one especially designed for the discipline of agricultural engineering. But regardless of the program in any particular country, there is a strong recognition of the need for a rigorous physical and biological sciences base to develop a well-rounded professional who can handle the engineering problems faced in agriculture. Therefore, programs which have been largely developed on traditional engineering lines are being given a biological emphasis, and those developed on biological lines are being given a physical science emphasis.

The United Kingdom and the Commonwealth are gradually changing from the concept of offering agricultural engineering only as an advanced degree to programs where agricultural engineering is a unique first degree. Many of the countries in Central and South America, Africa, the Middle East, and Asia have not yet seriously committed themselves to agricultural engineering as a unique engineering field—although one of these countries, India, has recently developed large agricultural engineering programs. Many countries in these areas reflect engineering and agricultural educational patterns established under foreign domination. Socialist countries such as the People's Republic of China, the Soviet Union, and Eastern European countries appear to be developing agricultural engineering educational programs which emphasize the specialized needs of agricultural production. These countries are making use of professionals from agricultural or the biological sciences and from traditional engineering fields in a team effort to answer or solve the engineering problems found in agriculture. Agricultural engineering in these countries is developing both from engineering programs and from biological science programs. Other countries have trained and educated individuals in engineering and the biological sciences but have not instituted specific programs for agricultural engineering. The growing worldwide em-

phasis on food and fiber in an energy-conscious environment will bring about greater emphasis on agricultural engineering as a special and unique field able to contribute to the solution of one of the primary problems of mankind—food.

BYRON L. BONDURANT

Levels and Programs of Study

Programs in agricultural engineering generally require as a minimum prerequisite a secondary education, usually with emphasis on science and mathematics, and lead to the following degrees: Bachelor of Science or Engineering, Master of Science or Engineering, the doctorate, or their equivalents. Programs deal with the principles and practices of agricultural engineering and consist of classroom and laboratory instruction, fieldwork, and, on advanced levels, study, seminar or group discussion, and research dealing with specialized areas of agricultural engineering. Agricultural engineering is concerned with the application of mechanization for the development of farmland; soil and water conservation; irrigation; crop production and protection; harvesting, handling, storage, and processing of agricultural products; the design of farm structures and machinery; and the design and construction of farm equipment.

Programs that lead to a first university degree emphasize the principles and practices of agricultural engineering. Principal course content usually includes some of the following: soil and water conservation, irrigation and drainage design, analysis of agricultural structures, and analysis of agricultural production systems. Elective courses from other engineering disciplines make up part of the program. Background courses usually include mathematics, natural sciences, and social sciences.

Programs that lead to a postgraduate university degree deal with specialized areas of agricultural engineering. Emphasis is placed on original research work as substantiated by the presentation and defense of a scholarly thesis or dissertation. Principal subject matter areas within which courses and research projects tend to fall include agricultural equipment application and methods, design of farm machinery and structures, processing equipment and methods for agricultural products, drainage of agricultural land, design and operation of irrigation systems, quality of water supplies, waste treatment in agricultural industries, pollution problems in agriculture, and application of power sources in agriculture. Subject areas within which background studies tend to fall include appropriate specialties from other engineering programs and appropriate specialties from related fields such as agriculture, natural sciences, social sciences, commercial and business administration, mathematics, statistics, and computer science.

[This section was based on UNESCO's *International Standard Classification of Education (ISCED)* (Paris: UNESCO, 1976).]

Major International and National Organizations

INTERNATIONAL

International Commission of Agricultural
  Engineers
Commission internationale de génie
  rural (CIGR)
17–21 rue de Javel
75015 Paris, France

International Confederation of Technical
  Agricultural Engineers
24 Beethovenstrasse
8002 Zurich, Switzerland

Liaison Committee of Agricultural Engineers
  for the EEC Countries
Coupure Links 533
9000 Ghent, Belgium

NATIONAL

Australia:
  Agricultural Engineering Society
  c/o National Science Center
  191 Royal Parade
  Parkville, Victoria 3052

Japan:
  Agricultural Engineering Society of Japan
  Nogyo-doboku gakkai
  c/o University of Tokyo
  Tokyo

United Kingdom:
  Institution of Agricultural Engineers
  6 Queen Square
  London WC 1, England

United States:
  American Society of Agricultural
    Engineers
  2950 Niles Road
  St. Joseph, Michigan 49085

For a more complete listing of national organizations see:

Minerva, Wissenschaftliche Gesellschaften. Berlin, Federal Republic of Germany: de Gruyter, 1972.
World Guide to Scientific Associations. Pullach/Munich, Federal Republic of Germany: Verlag Dokumentation, 1974.

Principal Information Sources

GENERAL

Guides to the literature in the field of agricultural engineering include:

Agricultural and Horticultural Engineering Abstracts. Silsoe, England: National Institute of Agriculture, 1950–1966. Consists of seventeen volumes and covers world literature in the field.
Blanchard, J. R., and Ostvold, H. *Literature of Agricultural Research.* Berkeley: University of California Press, 1958. Includes annotated entries on agricultural engineering.
Hall, C. W. *Agricultural Engineering Index, 1907–1960.* Reynoldsburg, Ohio: Agricultural Consulting Association, 1961.
Hall, G. E., and Hall, C. W. *Agricultural Engineering Index, 1961–1970.* St. Joseph, Michigan: American Society of Agricultural Engineers, 1971. Continues *Agricultural Engineering Index 1907–1960.*
Mohammad, R. *Selected Bibliography on Agricultural Engineering, 1951–1968.* Lyallpur: Faculty of Agricultural Engineering and Technology, West Pakistan Agricultural University, 1969.
Roberts, E. *Guide to Literature on Agricultural Engineering.* Washington, D.C.: American Society for Engineering Education, 1971. Comprehensive guide to literature, covering bibliographies, abstracting and indexing services, dictionaries, handbooks, and directories.
Selected Articles on Agricultural Engineering. Jerusalem: Israel Program for Scientific Translations, 1965.

Overviews of the field include:

Bowers, W., and Jones, B. A. *Engineering Appli-*

cation in Agriculture. Champaign, Illinois: Stipes, 1959.

McColly, H. F., and Martin, J. W. *Introduction to Agricultural Engineering.* New York: McGraw-Hill, 1955.

A discussion of agricultural engineering education in developing regions is offered by:

Peikert, F. W. "Engineering Education Projects for Improving Agriculture in Developing Countries." Paper presented at American Society for Engineering Education Annual Conference, June 1975, at Colorado State University, Ft. Collins, Colorado.

CURRENT BIBLIOGRAPHIES

Abstracting and indexing services for agricultural engineering include:

Applied Mechanics Reviews. New York: American Society of Mechanical Engineers, 1948–.

Biological and Agricultural Index (formerly *Agricultural Index*). New York: Wilson, 1916–. Includes a section on agricultural engineering.

Bulletin signalétique. Part 380: *Sciences agricoles;* Part 890: *Sciences de l'ingénieur.* Paris: Centre national de la recherche scientifique, 1940–. International in scope.

Engineering Index. New York: Engineering Index, Inc., 1884–. Covers world literature in all aspects of engineering.

Food Science and Technology Abstracts. Farnham Royal, Bucks, England: Commonwealth Agricultural Bureaux, 1969–. Includes literature from over fifty countries.

U.S. Department of Agriculture, National Agricultural Library. *Bibliography of Agriculture.* Scottsdale, Arizona: Oryx Press, 1942–. A monthly index to literature on agriculture and related fields; international in scope.

PERIODICALS

Some periodicals in the field are *Agricultural Engineering* (US), *Agricultural Engineering Australia, Agricultural Engineering Journal* (Philippines), *Archiv für Landtechnik* (FRG), *Canadian Agricultural Engineering, Journal and Proceedings of the Institution of Agricultural Engineers* (UK), *Journal of Agricultural Engineering* (India), *Journal of Agricultural Engineering Research* (UK), *Soil Mechanics and Foundation Engineering* (US; translation of USSR publication *Osnovaniya fundamenty i mekhanika gruntor*), *Transactions of the American Society of Agricultural Engineers, World Irrigation* (US).

For a more complete listing see:

Roberts, E. *Guide to Literature on Agricultural Engineering.* Washington, D.C.: American Society for Engineering Education, 1971, pp. 16–19.

ENCYCLOPEDIAS, DICTIONARIES, HANDBOOKS

Farrall, A. W., and Albrecht, C. F. *Agricultural Engineering; A Dictionary and Handbook.* Danville, Illinois: Interstate, 1965.

Haensch, G. *Dictionary of Agriculture: German, English, French, Spanish.* (3rd ed.) Amsterdam: Elsevier, 1966.

Hall, C. W., Farrall, A. W., and Rippen, A. L. *Encyclopedia of Food Engineering.* Westport, Connecticut: Avi, 1971.

Hine, H. J. *Dictionary of Agricultural Engineering.* Cambridge, England: Heffer, 1961.

Lueger, O. *Lexikon der Technik.* Stuttgart, Federal Republic of Germany: Deutsche Verlags-Anstalt, 1960.

Richey, C. B., and others. *Agricultural Engineer's Handbook.* New York: McGraw-Hill, 1961.

Vollmer, E. *Encyclopedia of Hydraulics, Soil and Foundation Engineering.* New York: American Elsevier, 1967.

DIRECTORIES

Agricultural Engineers' Yearbook. St. Joseph, Michigan: American Society of Agricultural Engineers, 1954–. An annual directory which includes a section on "Agricultural Engineering/Educational Programs—USA and Canada."

Directory of Engineering College Research and Graduate Study. Washington, D.C.: American Society for Engineering Education, annual. Lists research and graduate programs available at institutions in the United States, Canada, and Puerto Rico.

International Directory of Agricultural Engineering Institutions/Répertoire international des institutions de génie rural/Repertorio internacional de instituciones de ingeniería rural. Rome: Food and Agriculture Organization, 1973. The most comprehensive international directory in the field; covers government services, institutes, and departments of agriculture at universities and colleges in 115 countries. Includes information on training, research, and publications at each institution.

Peterson's Annual Guides to Graduate Study, 1976. Book 5: *Engineering and Applied Sciences.* Princeton, New Jersey: Peterson's Guides, 1975. See section on "Agricultural Engineering Programs" for a listing of United States institutions.

World Directory of Agricultural Libraries and Documentation Centres. Harpenden, England: International Association of Agricultural

Librarians and Documentalists, 1960. Includes a listing of libraries, publications of the libraries, and periodicals in the field.

AGRICULTURAL RESEARCH, EXTENSION SERVICES, AND FIELD STATIONS

See Agriculture in Higher Education: Agricultural Research, Extension Services, and Field Stations.

AGRICULTURAL RESEARCH INFORMATION SERVICE

See International Bank for Reconstruction and Development.

AGRICULTURE, FORESTRY, AND FISHERIES (Field of Study)

Work in agriculture, forestry, and fisheries occupies a large part of the population of every nation, both developed and developing. Continuous education at all levels in agriculture, forestry, and fisheries is essential because every nation's primary objective is to improve production, processing, distribution, and use of food and other agricultural products, forests and forest products, and fishery products. Since more and more trained people are needed in these fields, commercial agriculture, forestry, and fisheries could· not advance or even be maintained without continuous education.

Higher education in agriculture, forestry, and fisheries is based on biology, chemistry, physics, the social sciences, economics, mathematics, and statistics. Students usually start by taking courses in the basic sciences and then proceed with the application of these sciences to the various aspects of agriculture, forestry, and fisheries. The study of agriculture, forestry, and fisheries in colleges and universities is often subdivided into the following areas: plant sciences (crop science, horticulture, forestry), animal sciences (animal science, dairy science, poultry

science, fisheries science, wildlife), agricultural engineering, soil and water science and technology, entomology, plant pathology, food science and technology, agricultural education, and agricultural economics.

Among the plant sciences, crop science includes the crops generally grown on a field scale, the cereals or grains, legumes for seed, and forage, root, fiber, tuber, sugar, drug, oil, and rubber crops; horticulture includes fruits, vegetables, and ornamental plants; and forestry includes public and private forestlands and forest culture, processing, and use. In some countries—for instance, the United Kingdom and the Netherlands—horticulture is separated from agriculture. Similarly, forestry is sometimes separated from agriculture, in a separate school or college or as part of a school of natural resources.

The plant sciences are often subdivided according to discipline: plant physiology, plant breeding or genetics, crop production and management, crop protection, and crop utilization. Forestry schools or colleges may be divided into such disciplines or departments as forest tree physiology, forest ecology, forest hydrology, forest entomology, forest pathology, forestry economics, forest mensuration, forest administration or management and policy, tree improvement and genetics, forest soils, and wood science. Finally, in some institutions the plant sciences are grouped together as one division in a college, so that the subdivisions common to all plant sciences can be taught and administered more efficiently.

Among the animal sciences, animal science itself includes beef cattle, swine, goats, horses, and small animals such as mink, foxes, rabbits, and laboratory animals (rats, mice, and guinea pigs); dairy science includes dairy cattle and the production, processing, and distribution of milk and milk products; poultry science includes chickens, turkeys, ducks, or other domesticated fowl, and the production, processing, and distribution of poultry meat and egg products; fisheries science includes not only fish but also aquatic animals, both vertebrates and invertebrates, and their exploitation for benefit to man; the wildlife area includes not only wildlife but also habitats of economic, cultural, esthetic, historical, and scientific value.

Animal sciences in some developing countries are combined in the early stages with veterinary science; fisheries science and wildlife higher education were developed more recently, and in some cases they are combined into one department in a college of agriculture. They may be a part of a college or school of natural resources, and in a few cases they have become separate schools or colleges.

Like the plant sciences, the animal sciences sometimes are subdivided according to discipline: animal breeding or genetics; animal physiology; animal nutrition; animal production, processing, and distribution. The animal sciences in a few institutions have been grouped together as a division in a college, so that disciplinary areas common to all animal sciences can be taught and administered more efficiently.

Agricultural engineering applies engineering to the design, production, and use of equipment, machinery, systems for production, harvesting, transporting, storing, and processing of plants and animals and their products.

Soil and water science and technology, which applies the basic sciences to soils and water, concerns the management of soils and water for benefit to man in farming, forestry, road building, urbanization, and recreation. It includes particularly tillage, fertilization, drainage, and irrigation.

Entomology, a biological science of insects and other small animals, is concerned mainly with the study and control of insects that are harmful or useful to man, cultivated plants, and domestic animals.

Plant pathology is a biological science concerned primarily with the nature, epidemiology, and control of diseases of plants that are useful to man.

Food science and technology is the study of the composition, properties, processing, and storage of food and food ingredients. It is a separate department in some institutions in the developed countries, but a phase of it often is also a section of each commodity department or area; for instance, dairy technology may be a section of dairy science; and fruit and vegetable technology may be studied as part of horticulture.

Agricultural education is a separate area or department in agricultural colleges in most developed countries. It combines education and general agriculture to prepare teachers for secondary or technical schools, general extension workers and administrators, and government agricultural employees. In developing countries emphasis is given mainly to preparation for general agricultural extension.

The agricultural economics department in agricultural colleges usually applies economics and other social sciences to agriculture, forestry, and fisheries. Its specializations in the developed countries are farm management, agricultural prices, marketing and distribution, agricultural statistics, agricultural policy, agricultural credit and finance, land use, land tenure and agrarian reform, farm cooperatives, rural and community development, foreign trade, and international agricultural development. Rural sociology usually is a division in the same department, but in a few instances it is a separate department.

The cultivation of plants, particularly flowers, and the husbandry of animals was recorded in Egypt, India, and China as early as 3000 B.C. However, efforts to relate agriculture to human needs started during the Renaissance. When modern science began in the sixteenth and seventeenth centuries, essays on agriculture began to appear, and it was suggested that agriculture be taught in schools.

Agricultural societies began to be formed in the latter half of the eighteenth century in Europe and near the end of that century in the United States. Almost concurrently livestock exhibitions and fairs were developed as a means of learning about agriculture and husbandry. Academies, schools, and colleges soon grew from these societies, fair boards, commissions, and associations.

The early agricultural schools and colleges were concerned mainly with the development and application of natural sciences. A considerable body of literature on agricultural subjects was accumulated in the seventeenth and eighteenth centuries, and at least two hundred authors of agricultural writings were recognized in Great Britain by 1800. Higher agricultural education received considerable attention in Europe and the United States in the early nineteenth century. For example, a significant period in the United States started about 1845, with public discussions about the establishment of agricultural colleges in each state, and culminated in the passage of the Morrill Act of 1862, creating land-grant colleges and universities in each state. These land-grant colleges, unlike the so-called literacy colleges, were to serve the farmer and mechanic. The colleges usually included land for agricultural research and for students to obtain practical farm experience. Colleges also held open house for a few days each year, so that farmers and the public could observe and hear discussions on new findings in agriculture. Legislation in 1887 established federal support to state experiment stations, and legislation in 1914 established federal/state cooperation in agricultural extension.

Unlike higher education in agriculture in other countries, the land-grant college combines higher education, research, and extension. The land-grant college model is gradually spreading to developing countries of Asia, Africa, and Latin America—where traditionally the functions of research and extension have been administered by the Ministry of Agriculture, while higher education in agriculture has been under the Ministry of Education; as a result, the necessary coordination between higher education, research, and extension has not taken place.

The first stage of higher education in

agriculture, forestry, and fisheries is the two- or three-year programs in technical agricultural colleges, institutes, or academies. The usual minimum educational prerequisite is completion of secondary-level education. In some of the colleges in developing countries, the institution combines one or two years of secondary-level education with one to three years of higher-level education. These colleges, which may include the preparation of technicians in agribusiness as well as in production, do not offer full degree programs, and therefore they award a diploma or certificate. Some developing countries do not have higher education in agriculture, forestry, and fisheries beyond this first stage.

Many colleges and universities in the developed countries, and an increasing number in the developing countries, have programs leading to a B.S. degree or equivalent in agriculture, forestry, or fisheries. These programs emphasize basic sciences, communication skills, general education, and a general knowledge of agriculture, forestry, or fisheries.

Specialization takes place mostly in advanced programs for M.S. or Ph.D. degrees, which are awarded in each of the divisions in most of the developed countries. Advanced degree programs gradually are being organized in the developing countries. Many students from the developing countries are obtaining advanced degrees in agriculture in the developed countries, many of these financed under international technical assistance programs. As these trained professionals return to their own countries, they are helping to develop advanced degree programs in the colleges and universities.

In many countries, especially in Europe, the advanced degrees are obtained, without formal course work, through research, a thesis, and an oral examination. Some United States universities offer M.S. degrees with formal course work only; research training is required for the Ph.D. degree.

Higher education in agriculture usually

began in separate colleges of agriculture, with basic sciences included as support programs. In the United States these support programs gradually developed into separate colleges; other fields of higher education were then added, so that the original institution became a university, with agriculture as one of its colleges or schools. The other colleges in the university provide the basic sciences and related courses to the students in the agricultural college.

Higher education in agriculture in some developing countries has been added as a department or college to an existing government-supported university. However, where the existing university is traditional, difficulty arises in changing it to a land-grant type of institution with strong relationships to practical research and extension education. Higher education in agriculture has developed much more in the government-supported, research-oriented institutions than in private or nongovernment universities.

Higher education in agriculture, forestry, and fisheries is becoming more and more international in scope, particularly in the developing countries. This follows from increasing concern for the expanding world food requirements and the need for worldwide development of agriculture, fisheries, and forestry. Colleges of agriculture in the United States and some other developed countries have directors of international programs. Study-abroad programs and international study tours are increasing, and faculty are assigned to technical assistance programs abroad. International linkages of scientists, educators, and universities are developing.

In Canada and the United States higher education in agriculture, forestry, and fisheries is mostly a provincial or state function. Canadian higher education in agriculture is provided in six provincial institutions and two private universities. In the United States it is provided primarily in sixty-eight land-grant colleges and 250 other institutions. Enrollments continue to increase; individual United States universities have

more students in agriculture, forestry, and fisheries than many developing countries have in total. Admittance has been open to all students who have completed secondary education. The largest number of foreign students, mostly at the graduate degree level, are being trained in the United States. An increasing number of United States students are being trained for foreign work.

All Mediterranean-area countries offer higher education in agriculture, and some have programs in forestry and fisheries. Access is generally based on graduation from a secondary school or a general or agricultural technical school, but in some countries entrance examinations are demanded. Spain and Portugal include significant amounts of practical work in their first-degree programs. Graduate study in the Mediterranean area is generally less developed than in other regions of Europe.

Recent developments in higher education in Western Europe outside the Mediterranean area include fewer, more encompassing fields of specialization and more options within a specialty. Advanced degree programs have also been developed in many countries, and Western European universities have been attempting to train students from foreign countries and to prepare local students for foreign work.

In Latin America public universities are the primary sources of higher education in agriculture, forestry, and fisheries. The more than two hundred Latin American colleges exhibit a great variety in program, curricula, and course content. The major development of university programs occurred in the 1960s. Fisheries education has just begun. Staffing has been a problem, particularly the part-time appointments and the lifelong tenure tradition. Advanced degree programs with cooperative arrangements between universities have been developing rapidly. The early development of agriculture, forestry, and fisheries education at the university level was independent of research and extension services, but in recent years the uniting of education, research, and extension has begun to occur. Changes in higher agricultural education include the diversification of programs to move from training agronomists to more specialized persons such as animal scientists.

In Africa higher agriculture, forestry, and fisheries education varies considerably, but it is not well developed in many countries. The French-speaking countries typically have two levels of higher education. The higher level produces planners, policymakers, and top managers. The lower level produces graduates for middle-management positions. The English-speaking countries have accepted the British university pattern of bachelor's degrees (first, second, and third class). Postgraduate education is available in only a few universities in the English-speaking countries. Most former French colonies do not have university-level institutions for agriculture, probably because of the French emphasis on urban universities. Since the 1950s the United States influence has resulted in land-grant institutions in some of the new African universities.

At least 189 universities offer higher education in agriculture, forestry, and fisheries in Asia and the Far East. Over 70 percent of these institutions were government established. Administrative control of the government agricultural colleges may be in the Ministry of Education, Department of Agriculture, Governing Board, or State Department. Some countries in this region have a problem of financing all of the small agricultural colleges.

Theoretical rather than practical instruction has been a problem of most agricultural colleges. Agricultural education in Asia has consequently been criticized as as having too little practical emphasis and a surplus of professional workers.

Most universities do not have funding for research or for extension work. The University of the Philippines College of Agriculture at Los Baños and some newer land-grant agricultural universities in India operate with funds for instruction, research, and extension. The United States land-grant college influence has stimulated research and extension functions, but the limited commitment to research has been a major restraint in higher education in agriculture in most countries.

The Near East has adequate capacity in its higher agricultural, forestry, and fishery institutions despite considerable imbalance in location and variation in their quality. The location of university facilities in urban areas creates a problem in relating programs to rural societies. But considerable progress in institutions and programs has been made since 1950, when there were only four higher colleges of agriculture.

The curricula in agriculture, forestry, and fisheries for individual institutions in the Soviet Union and in Eastern Europe are normally prescribed by the state. Only in Yugoslavia do self-governing faculties determine curricula. Entrance examinations are generally required, and standards are annually adjusted to limit enrollment to institutional capacities. The widely developed system of scholarships serves a high proportion of the students. Yugoslavia is an exception, but its student loan program serves a similar purpose.

Special emphasis is given to postgraduate and teacher training development. Colleges provide postgraduate studies through refresher courses, wider studies (another field), and specialization studies. Advanced degrees are offered by most higher education institutions. Doctoral degrees in agricultural science are awarded by different units: in Romania, by the Agricultural University; in Hungary and Bulgaria, by the Academy of Agricultural Sciences; and in Yugoslavia, Czechoslovakia, and Poland, by all faculties.

The Soviet system of higher education in agriculture, forestry, and fisheries is similar to that in Eastern Europe. In 1969 ninety-eight specialized institutions of higher learning were preparing students in twenty agricultural specialties and fifteen specialties involving the service of agriculture. The Ministry of Agriculture supervises all these institutions. Full-time training and correspondence (part-time) training serve nearly equal numbers of students. All higher education graduates defend theses. The entire system has numerous economic support mechanisms for students in higher education, such as scholarships higher than state grants and student discounts. Most agricultural academies and colleges offer postgraduate courses, and over one hundred specialties are available.

Australia and New Zealand are developed countries which depend on agricultural production for export income. Their higher education in agriculture has addressed plant and animal sciences. Australia does not have a university whose primary mission is agricultural education, but degree courses are available in at least six universities. New Zealand has two agricultural universities, which offer a limited number of specialty degrees in horticulture, biochemistry, agricultural engineering, and food science. In recent years Australia has upgraded a number of agricultural "colleges" to colleges of higher education, but there were apparent problems related to transfer of work to universities, since the quality of work at colleges previously was considered only secondary level.

The South Pacific islands have seen rapid growth in agricultural education in the 1960s, with the establishment of agricultural colleges in Fiji, New Guinea, and Western Samoa. These institutions apparently have not reached higher education status.

[The author acknowledges the use of materials provided by G. W. Leske.]

MERVIN G. SMITH

Levels and Programs of Study

Programs in agriculture, forestry, and fisheries generally require as a minimum educational prerequisite a secondary education, although mature students with relevant work experience may be admitted with lower educational qualifications. Programs deal with theoretical and practical aspects of agriculture, forestry, and fishery operations and consist of classroom work,

field instruction, seminars, and research. Programs lead to the following awards: certificate or diploma, bachelor's degree (B.Sc.), master's degree (M.Sc.), the doctorate (Ph.D.), or their equivalents.

Programs that lead to an award not equivalent to a first university degree are designed to impart the theoretical and practical knowledge required for such operations as ownership and/or management of a medium- or small-scale agricultural enterprise or work as a technician. Programs at this level stress the application of technology in relevant operations rather than the theoretical and scientific principles of the subjects studied. Principal course content usually includes some of the following: animal science; crop science; horticulture; soil and water technology; agricultural economics and farm management; health of animals; food technology (for example, dairying and fruit processing); management and utilization of forest resources, including watersheds; management and conservation of wildlife and recreation areas; and management, utilization, and conservation of fishery resources. Usual background courses include areas in the natural sciences, such as biology and chemistry; the social sciences, such as economics and sociology; and mathematics and statistics.

Programs and courses may be full time or part time and usually include practical demonstration as well as student participation in relevant operations, either as an employee or in practice sessions. Refresher courses are common. These programs are sponsored and conducted by many kinds of agencies, both public and private, including institutes of technology, specialized training centers, research and development agencies, and cooperative societies.

Programs that lead to a first university degree consist of theoretical and practical aspects of agricultural, forestry, and fishery operations. These programs are intended to prepare students for careers as agricultural, forestry, or fishery scientists in such areas as research, data analysis, and management in large-scale enterprises or institutes; as advisers to governments, enterprises, or institutes concerned with protecting the health of animals; and in some countries as veterinarians. These programs typically emphasize the theoretical, general, and scientific principles of the subjects included, although practical application is not ignored. Students are sometimes encouraged to undertake original work, especially in the final phases of the programs.

Principal course content of agricultural programs usually includes aspects of animal science, crop science, poultry science, dairy science, plant pathology, entomology, horticulture, soil and water sciences, agricultural economics and management of agricultural operations, veterinary science, and food sciences and technology. Forestry programs include the cultivation, protection, and management of forest crops, the science and technology of forest ranges, and the protection and management of watersheds and recreational areas. Programs in fishery science and technology usually include fish cultivation and fishery management; and wildlife programs often include wildlife preservation, management, and ecology. Usual background courses often include biological sciences, such as zoology, entomology, botany, and microbiology; chemistry courses of various kinds; social science courses, such as economics and sociology; and courses in mathematics and statistics.

Programs followed are either full time or part time, day or evening; and, although usually sponsored by a university or technological college, they may be conducted by correspondence or through radio or television broadcasts. In the main, however, these programs are followed by full-time students in universities or similar institutions.

Programs that lead to a postgraduate university degree emphasize the theoretical and scientific principles of the subjects included. Original research work, as substantiated by the presentation and defense of a scholarly thesis, is usually an impor-

tant element. High-level specialization in particular aspects of agricultural, forestry, and fisheries science is a feature of these programs.

The programs may emphasize specialized areas of animal science, including dairy or poultry science; crop science; horticulture; plant pathology; entomology; soil and water sciences; agricultural economics and management of agricultural operations; veterinary science; food sciences and technology; forestry economics and forest management; wood science; forest cropping and protection of forest resources, including management of watersheds and recreational areas; fishery economics and fishery management; fishery science and technology, including fish culture; agricultural engineering; or wildlife management, including conservation and ecology. Usual background studies deal with advanced specialized courses in such closely related fields as biological sciences, natural sciences, social sciences, mathematics, and statistics.

Advanced-level programs are generally full time, but they are frequently carried on in combination with part-time employment as laboratory instructor or research assistant.

[This section was based on UNESCO's *International Standard Classification of Education (ISCED)* (Paris: UNESCO, 1976).]

Major International and National Organizations

INTERNATIONAL

Association for the Advancement of
 Agricultural Sciences in Africa (AAASA)
Association pour l'avancement en Afrique des
 . sciences de l'agriculture
P.O. Box 30087
Addis Ababa, Ethiopia

Committee of Agricultural Organizations in the
 European Economic Community
Comité des organisations professionnelles
 agricoles de la Communauté européenne
 économique
8 rue de Spa
1040 Brussels, Belgium

Commonwealth Agricultural Bureaux
Farnham House, Farnham Royal
Slough, Bucks, SL2 3BN, England

European Confederation of Agriculture
C.P. 87, 5200 Brugg
Aargau, Switzerland

Food and Agriculture Organization of the
    United Nations (FAO)
Organisation des Nations unies pour
    l'alimentation et l'agriculture
via delle Terme di Caracalla
00100 Rome, Italy
    Principal agricultural organization concerned
with agricultural education at the university
level. Regional offices in Africa, Latin America,
Near East, and North America.

Inter-American Institute of Agricultural
    Sciences (IAIAS)
Instituto interamericano de ciencias agrícolas
Turrialba, Costa Rica

International Association of Agricultural
    Librarians and Documentalists (IAALD)
Association internationale de bibliothécaires et
    documentalistes agricoles
IAALD Library, Tropical Products Institute
52/62 Gray's Inn Road
London WCIX 8LU, England

International Association of Agricultural
    Students (IAAS)
Association internationale des étudiants en
    agriculture (AIEA)
Bulowsvej 13
DK-1870 Copenhagen, Denmark

    Additional international organizations in the
various fields of agriculture may be found in:

Yearbook of International Organizations. Brussels: Union of International Associations,
    1948–. Published biennially.

NATIONAL

For complete listings of national organizations and learned societies in the agricultural
sciences throughout the world see:

Minerva, Wissenschaftliche Gesellschaften. Berlin,
    Federal Republic of Germany: de Gruyter,
    1972.
The World of Learning. London: Europa, 1947–.
    Published annually.

Principal Information Sources

GENERAL

Guides to the literature of agriculture include:

Blanchard, J. R., and Ostvold, H. *Literature of
    Agricultural Research.* Berkeley: University of
    California Press, 1958. Somewhat dated but
    a classic guide to reference materials; includes bibliographies, abstracting and indexing services, encyclopedias, dictionaries,
    periodicals, and directories. Covers various
    areas of agriculture: general agriculture,
    plant sciences, animal sciences, food and nutrition, physical sciences, and social sciences.
Bush, E. A. R. *Agriculture: A Bibliographic Guide.*
    (2 vols.) London: Macdonald, 1974. Covers
    all aspects of agriculture.
Frauendorfer, S. V. *Surveying of Abstracting Services and Current Bibliographical Tools in Agriculture, Forestry, Fisheries, Nutrition, Veterinary
    Medicine and Related Subjects.* Munich, Federal Republic of Germany: BLV Verlagsgesellschaft, 1969.
Fundaburk, E. L. *Reference Materials and Periodicals in Economics: An International List in
    Four Volumes.* Vol. 1: *Agriculture.* Metuchen,
    New Jersey: Scarecrow Press, 1971. An unannotated listing.
Hirst, F. C., Loosjes, T. P., and Koster, G.
    Primer for Agricultural Libraries. Wageningen,
    Netherlands: Pudoc, 1967.
Lauch, R. *Internationales Handbuch der Bibliographien des Landbaues/World Bibliography of
    Agricultural Bibliographies.* Munich, Federal
    Republic of Germany: Bayerischer Landwirtschaftsverlag, 1957. Supplemented by
    "Bibliographical News" in *Quarterly Bulletin
    of the International Association of Agricultural
    Librarians and Documentalists.* Harpenden,
    England: IAALD, 1956–.
*Selected List of American Agricultural Books in
    Print and Current Periodicals.* Beltsville, Maryland: National Agricultural Library, June
    1975. An extensive listing of books on various aspects of agriculture and related subjects published by United States publishers.
Singhvi, M. L., and Shrimaldi, D. S. *Reference
    Sources in Agriculture: An Annotated Bibliography.* Udaipur, India: Rajasthan ·College of
    Agriculture, Consumers Cooperative Society, 1962. International source; covers plant
    science, animal science, and technological
    fields of agriculture. Includes many Indian
    sources.
United States Department of Agriculture. *Dictionary Catalog of the National Agricultural
    Library, 1862–1965.* Totowa, New Jersey:
    Rowman & Littlefield, 1967. Includes holdings of the National Agriculture Library.
Velásquez, G. P., and Nadurille, T. R. *Obras
    de referencias agrícolas en español.* Mexico City:
    Instituto nacional de investigaciones agrícolas, 1967. Guide to Latin American reference materials.

Winston, H. N. M. *Man and the Environment: A Bibliography of Selected Publications of the United Nations System 1946–71.* New York: Bowker, 1972. Includes sources dealing with various aspects of the agricultural sciences.

Overviews and introductions to the field include:

Gondé, H., Carré, G., Jussiaux, P., and Gondé, R. *Cours d'agriculture moderne.* Paris: La maison rustique, 1968. An introductory text in four parts.

Robinson, D. H. (Ed.) *Fream's Elements of Agriculture: A Textbook Prepared Under the Authority of the Royal Agricultural Society of England.* (14th ed.) London: Murray, 1962. An introduction to the many aspects of agriculture, including soil science, animal and plant breeding, crop cultivation, crop diseases, poultry, and livestock.

Watson, J. A. S., and More, J. A. *Agriculture: The Science and Practice of Farming.* (11th ed. by J. A. MacMillan.) Edinburgh: Oliver & Boyd, 1962.

Histories of the field include:

Gove, H. *The Story of the F.A.O.* New York: Van Nostrand, 1955. A narrative history of the Food and Agriculture Organization of the United Nations; includes a region-by-region and country-by-country survey.

Gras, N. S. B. *History of Agriculture in Europe and America.* (2nd ed.) New York: Appleton-Century-Crofts, 1940.

Historia Agriculturae. Groningen, Netherlands: Wolters-Noordhoff, 1953–. A yearbook, issued by the Stichting Nederlands agronomisch-historisch instituut, which contains a world bibliography of works on agricultural history.

For works dealing with comparative education and research in agriculture see:

African Agricultural Research Capabilities. Washington, D.C.: Committee on African Agricultural Research Capabilities, National Academy of Science, 1974. Includes a discussion of the relationship between research and training in agriculture and the development needs of various countries.

Agan, R. "Latin American Conference on Agricultural Education." *Agricultural Education Magazine,* January 1971, *43*(7), 174–175.

Agricultural and Forestry Education in the Czechoslovak Socialist Republic. Prague: State Agricultural Publishing House, 1966.

Agricultural Education and Training: Annual Review of Selected Developments. Rome: FAO, 1967–. Discussion of agricultural education and training internationally.

Agricultural Education at the University Level. Paris: Organisation for Economic Co-operation and Development, 1965. Discussion of the curricula and state of studies of agricultural education in nineteen OECD countries.

Agricultural Education in Asia: A Regional Survey. Paris: UNESCO, 1971. A survey of educational facilities in Asia. Includes a general discussion as well as a survey of nineteen countries.

Agricultural Education, Investigation and Extension in Mexico: A Preliminary Study. Monterrey, Mexico: Instituto tecnológico y de estudios superiores, 1964.

Agricultural Education in the World. Vol. I: *Europe,* 1935; Vol. 2: *Europe,* 1936; Vol. 3: *North America,* 1938; Vol. 4: *Central and South America, Asia, Africa, and Oceania,* 1940. Rome: International Institute of Agriculture, 1935–1940. Dated but of historical interest.

Agricultural Education Magazine. Columbus, Ohio: Agricultural Education Magazine, Inc., 1929–. See especially October 1975, *48*(4). Entire issue is devoted to agricultural education; includes articles on agricultural education in various countries and regions.

Agriculture and General Education. New York: Unipub, 1972.

Ashton, J., and Lord, R. F. (Eds.) *Research, Education, and Extension in Agriculture.* Edinburgh: Oliver & Boyd, 1969. Discussion of agricultural education and research in Britain; includes bibliographies.

Blum, A. A. "Trends in Non-Vocational Agriculture—An International Review." *Agricultural Education Magazine,* October 1972, *45*(4), 86–87.

Consensus and Conflict in Agricultural Education: A Comparative Study of Four Australian Agricultural Colleges. St. Lucia, Brisbane: University of Queensland Press, 1973.

Drawbaugh, C. C., and Hull, W. L. *Agricultural Education: Approaches to Learning and Teaching.* Columbus, Ohio: Merrill, 1971. Designed to aid teachers.

Eicher, C. K. *Research on Agricultural Development in Five English-Speaking Countries in West Africa.* New York: Agricultural Development Council, 1970.

Farquhar, R. N. *Agricultural Education in Australia.* Hawthorn, Victoria: Australian Council for Educational Research, 1966. Thorough discussion of agricultural education on all levels of study.

Higher Agricultural Education in Africa: Report of a Seminar Held in Sudan at the University of Khartoum, 7–15 December 1965. Rome: FAO, 1967.

McLaughlin, P. F. M. *Research on Agricultural Development in East Africa.* New York: Agricultural Development Council, 1967.

Peterson, M. J. "The 1970 World of Agricultural Education." *Agricultural Education Magazine,* "May 1971, *43*(11), 284–286.

Richards, J. M., Jr. "Characteristics of United States, Japanese, and British Commonwealth Universities Offering Education in Agriculture." *Research in Higher Education,* 1975, *3*(2), 99–109. A comparative discussion of United States, Japan, and British Commonwealth universities that offer training in agriculture.

Stevens, G. Z. *Agriculture Education.* New York: Center for Applied Research in Education, 1967.

Sources on agricultural extension include:

Axinn, G. H., and Thorat, S. S. *Modernizing World Agriculture: A Comparative Study of Agricultural Extension Education Systems.* New York: Praeger, 1972.

Mukhopadhyay, A. *Agricultural Extension: A Field Study.* Columbia, Missouri: South Asia Books, 1971.

Rice, E. G. *Extension in the Andes.* Agency for International Development Evaluation Paper 3A. Washington, D.C.: AID, April 1971.

Saville, A. H. *Extension in Rural Communities.* London: Oxford University Press, 1966.

True, A. C. *History of Agricultural Extension Work in the United States 1785–1923.* New York: Arno, 1969. Reprint of 1928 edition.

Williams, D. B. *Agricultural Extension Service in Australia, Britain, and the United States of America.* Melbourne: Melbourne University Press, 1968.

Current Bibliographies

Current sources of information in the field include:

Abstracts from Current Scientific and Technical Literature. Leatherhead, Surrey, England: British Food Manufacturing Industries Research Association, 1948–.

Abstracts on Tropical Agriculture. Amsterdam: Koninklijk instituut voor de tropen, January 1975–.

Agrindex. Rome: FAO, 1975–. An international indexing service that includes sources on agriculture, education, extension, rural sociology, plant production and protection, forestry, animal production, fisheries, food science, and nutrition.

"Bibliographical News." In *Quarterly Bulletin of the IAALD.* Harpenden, England: International Association of Agricultural Librarians and Documentalists, 1956–. Reviews new agricultural reference works.

Biological Abstracts. Philadelphia: Biosciences Information Service of Biological Abstracts, 1927–. Includes literature on agriculture.

Biological and Agricultural Index (formerly *Agricultural Index*). New York: Wilson, 1916–. Lists English-language sources.

Bulletin signalétique. Section 380: *Agronomie, zootechnie, phytopathologie, industries alimentaires.* Paris: Centre national de la recherche scientifique, 1940–. Covers world literature in agriculture.

CC-ABES (Current Contents: Agriculture, Biology and Environmental Sciences). Philadelphia: Institute for Scientific Information, 1970–.

Landwirtschaftliches Zentralblatt. Berlin, Federal Republic of Germany: Deutsche Akademie der Landwirtschaftswissenschaften, 1955–. An abstracting service for agriculture.

National Agricultural Library. *Bibliography of Agriculture.* Scottsdale, Arizona: Oryx Press, 1946–. Monthly index to literature on agriculture and related sciences.

State of Food and Agriculture. Rome: FAO, 1947–. An annual review of world developments in food and agriculture; one of the most important publications of the FAO.

United States Department of Agriculture. *National Agricultural Library Catalogue.* Totowa, New Jersey: Rowman & Littlefield, 1966–. Covers books and materials cataloged by the NAL.

Yearbook of Agricultural Cooperation. London: Routledge and Kegan Paul, 1927–. Survey of agricultural cooperation in various countries.

PERIODICALS

Periodicals of importance to the field of agriculture include *Agricoltura* (Italy), *Agricoltura d'Italia* (Italy), *Agricultura* (Belgium), *Agricultura de las Américas* (US), *Agricultural Education* (US), *Agricultural History* (US), *Agricultural Research* (US), *Agriculture* (Canada), *Agriculture* (UK), *Agriculture and Environment* (Netherlands), *Agrochemia* (Poland), *Agronómico* (Brazil), *Agronomski glasnik* (Yugoslavia), *Agronomy Journal* (US), *Annales Agronomiques* (France), *Aomori nogyo* (Japan), *Australian Journal of Agricultural Research,* *Coopération agricole* (France), *Coopercotia* (Brazil), *East African Agricultural and Forestry Journal* (Kenya), *Grundförbättring* (Sweden), *Indian Journal of Agricultural Research, Indian Journal of Agricultural Science, Indian Journal of Extension Education, Intensive Agriculture* (India), *Italia agricola* (Italy), *Journal of Agricultural Science* (UK), *Journal of Agriculture* (Australia), *Journal of Extension* (US), *Journal of the Science of Food and*

Agriculture (UK), *Landwirtschaftliche Forschung* (FRG), *Netherlands Journal of Agricultural Science, OECD Agricultural Review* (US), *Revista de agricultura* (Brazil), *Rhodesian Journal of Agricultural Research, Tropical Agriculture* (UK), *Turrialba* (Costa Rica), *World Agriculture/Agriculture dans le monde* (France), *World Agriculture, Forestry and Fisheries/Sekai no norinsuisan* (Japan), *Zeitschrift für Acker- und Pflanzenbau/Journal of Agriculture and Plant Cultivation* (FRG), *Zeitschrift für ausländische Landwirtschaft/Quarterly Journal of International Agriculture/Journal trimestriel d'agriculture internationale* (FRG), *Zemledeliye* (USSR).

For extensive listings of periodicals see:

Boalch, D. H. (Ed.) *Current Agricultural Serials: A World List.* (2 vols.) Wageningen, Netherlands: Pudoc, 1965–1967.

List of Serials Currently Received by the Food and Agriculture Organization of the United Nations Library. Rome: FAO, 1973.

National Agricultural Library. *List of Serials Currently Received by the National Agricultural Library.* Washington, D.C.: U.S. Government Printing Office, 1974.

1000 Selected Journals in Agriculture and Related Subjects. Beltsville, Maryland: National Agricultural Library, 1973. An international listing covering all aspects of agriculture and related fields.

Ulrich's International Periodicals Directory. New York: Bowker, biennial.

ENCYCLOPEDIAS, DICTIONARIES, HANDBOOKS

Bibliography of Interlingual Scientific and Technical Dictionaries. Paris: UNESCO, 1953. Provides a list of interlingual dictionaries in agriculture.

Blanck, F. C. *Handbook for Food and Agriculture.* New York: Van Nostrand Reinhold, 1955.

Haensch, G., and Haberkamp, G. *Dictionary of Agriculture: German, French, English, Spanish.* (3rd ed.) Amsterdam: Elsevier, 1966.

Hunter, H. (Ed.) *Baillière's Encyclopedia of Scientific Agriculture.* London: Baillière Tindall, 1931.

Kratochvil, V., and Urbanova, S. *Agricultural Dictionary in Eight Languages/Nyolc-nyelvü mezögazdasagi szotar: Russian, Bulgarian, Czech, Polish, Hungarian, Romanian, German, English.* (2 vols.) New York: International Publications Service, 1970.

McGraw-Hill Encyclopedia of Science and Technology. New York: McGraw-Hill, 1971. Includes articles on agriculture.

Wilcox, E. V. *Modern Farmers' Encyclopedia of Agriculture: A Compendium of Farm Science and Practice.* New York: Judd, 1952.

Winburne, J. N. (Ed.) *A Dictionary of Agriculture and Allied Terminology.* East Lansing: Michigan State University Press, 1962.

DIRECTORIES

Directories which include information on the agricultural sciences and agricultural study are:

American Colleges and Universities. Washington, D.C.: American Council on Education, 1928–. Published quadrennially.

Catalogue of Social and Economic Development Institutes and Programs: Training. Paris: OECD, 1970.

Commonwealth Universities Yearbook. London: Association of Commonwealth Universities, 1914–. Published annually.

Hall, T. H. R. *World Crops International Directory and Handbook.* London: Leonard Hill, 1967. Includes listings of research centers and organizations, principal agricultural journals, and manufacturers of agricultural machinery and equipment.

International Handbook of Universities. Paris: International Association of Universities, 1959–. Published triennially.

McCabe, M. S., and Swanson, G. E. *International Directory of Extension Organizations and Extension Training Institutions.* Madison, Wisconsin: Midwest Universities Consortium for International Activities (MUCIA), 1975.

Stevenson, R. A. *Graduate Study in the United States: An Introduction for the Prospective A/D/C Fellow.* New York: Agricultural Development Council, 1968.

Von Klemperer, L. *International Education: A Directory of Resource Materials on Comparative Education and Study in Another Country.* Garrett Park, Maryland: Author, 1973. Includes educational directories in the agricultural sciences on the international, regional, and national levels.

The World of Learning. London: Europa, 1947–. Published annually. Lists universities, colleges, institutes, research centers, learned societies, and libraries throughout the world.

RESEARCH CENTERS, INSTITUTES, INFORMATION CENTERS

Directories to research institutes in agriculture include:

Boalch, D. H. (Ed.) *World Directory of Agricultural Libraries and Documentation Centres.* Harpenden, England: IAALD, 1960. Records nearly two thousand libraries in over one hundred countries. Out of print; a new and revised edition is being planned.

Directory of Agricultural Research Institutions and Projects in West Africa, Pilot Project. Rome: FAO, 1973.

Directory of Institutes, Universities, and Other Organizations Where Research on Agriculture, Animal Husbandry, Forestry and Fisheries Is in Progress. Karachi, Pakistan: Agricultural Research Council, 1966. A directory of agricultural research in Pakistan.

Estaciones experimentales agricolas de América latina. Washington, D.C.: Inter-American Development Bank, 1971.

Index of Agricultural Research Institutions and Stations in Africa. Rome: FAO, n.d.

Index of Agricultural Research Institutes of Europe. Rome: FAO, 1963.

Minerva, Forschungsinstitute. Berlin, Federal Republic of Germany: de Gruyter, 1972. Lists institutes throughout the world.

National Agricultural Library. *Directory of Information Resources in Agriculture and Biology.* Washington, D.C.: U.S. Government Printing Office, 1971. A United States directory to agricultural information sources, designed primarily for agricultural researchers and teachers.

Paylore, P. *Arid-Lands Research Institutes: A World Directory.* Tucson: University of Arizona Press, 1967.

Major agricultural libraries and important centers for documentation and information in the world are:

Colombia:
   Biblioteca del Centro internacional
      de agricultura tropical (CIAT)
   Cali

Costa Rica:
   Inter-American Center for Agricultural
      Documentation and Information
   Turrialba

Czechoslovakia:
   International Center of Information in
      Agriculture and Forestry
   Centre international d'information agricole
      et forestière
   Slezska 7, Prague 2

Federal Republic of Germany:
   Zentralbibliothek der Landbauwissenschaft
   Bonn

Indonesia:
   Lembaga perpustakaan, biologi dan
      pertanian
   Bibliotheca bogoriensis
   Bogor

Italy:
   David Lubin Memorial Library
   Food and Agriculture Organization
   via delle Terme di Caracalla
   Rome

International Information System for the
   Agricultural Sciences and Technology
   (AGRIS)
AGRIS Coordinating Centre of the
   United Nations
via delle Terme di Caracalla
Rome

Japan:
   Investigation and Documentation Division
   Agriculture, Forestry & Fisheries Research
      Council
   Ministry of Agriculture and Forestry
   Tokyo

Kenya:
   East African Agriculture and Forestry
      Research Organization
   East African Veterinary Research
      Organization
   Nairobi

Luxembourg:
   Commission of the European Communities
   Centre for Information and Documentation
   29 rue Aldringer
   Luxembourg

Morocco:
   Centre national de documentation
   5 Zankat Mostaghenem, B.P. 826
   Rabat

Nigeria:
   International Institute of Tropical
      Agriculture (IITA)
   Ibadan

Philippines:
   International Rice Research
      Institute (IRRI)
   Manila

Soviet Union:
   All-Union Institute of Scientific and
      Technical Information and Economic
      Research in Agriculture
   Orlikov per. 1/11
   Moscow I-139

   Tsentralnaia nauchnaia
      selskokhoziaistvennaia biblioteka
   Central Agricultural Library
   Moscow

United Kingdom:
   International Association for Agricultural
      Libraries and Documentalists (IAALD)
   Library, Tropical Products Institute
   56/62 Gray's Inn Road
   London WCIX 8LU, England

   Library of the Ministry of Agriculture,
      Fisheries and Food (MAFF)
   London, England

United States:
    National Agricultural Library (NAL)
    Beltsville, Maryland 20705

Research centers involved with agricultural extension are:

India:
    Department of Extension Education
    Indian Agricultural Research Institute
    New Delhi

Netherlands:
    Department of Extension Education
    Agricultural University
    Herenstraat 25
    Wageningen

United States:
    Division of Extension and Vocational
        Education
    University of Wisconsin
    Madison, Wisconsin 53706

    Rural Development Committee
    Cornell University
    Ithaca, New York 14850

See also: Agricultural Economics; Animal Science; Crop Science; Dairy Science; Entomology; Fisheries Science; Food Science and Technology; Forestry; Horticulture; Plant Pathology; Poultry Science; Soil and Water Science and Technology; Wildlife Ecology and Management.

AGRICULTURE IN
HIGHER EDUCATION

1. EARLY HISTORY OF AGRICULTURAL
    EDUCATION

2. AGRICULTURAL RESEARCH,
    EXTENSION SERVICES, AND
    FIELD STATIONS

3. AGRIBUSINESS AND
    AGRIBUSINESS EDUCATION

4. INTERNATIONAL COOPERATION
    IN AGRICULTURE

1. EARLY HISTORY OF
AGRICULTURAL EDUCATION

Formal instruction in agricultural education began at the turn of the eighteenth century. While these initial efforts may have lacked the scholarly luster of a university, they did form a basis for further growth and expansion of this educational discipline throughout the world.

German agriculturists must be credited with contributing most significantly to the early agricultural education concept and the direction it has taken since the turn of the century. The persistence of these early educators in maintaining a dual approach—that is, teaching both the theoretical and the practical aspects of agricultural production—resulted in a strong, educationally sound framework within which instruction in agriculture could be provided and made to flourish. The approach to agricultural education set forth by these educators is evident in present-day approaches to providing agricultural education at all levels throughout the world.

The development of agricultural education programs and curricula in institutions of higher education began in 1727 in Germany and within a hundred years had spread to all other European countries, the British Isles, and the North American continent. The pattern of development was basically the same in each country. A synopsis of the growth of agricultural education during this period is provided below.

Germany

The first agricultural school in Germany, established in 1722 by King Friedrich Wilhelm I at Königshorst in the duchy of Brandenburg, was designed to train farmers' daughters in the science of dairying. The school was maintained by the king until his death. In 1780 Friedrich II (Frederick the Great) recognized the school as merely an "ordinary academy of buttermaking." The reputation of the school declined under his leadership and ceased to exist at the turn of the century for want of students. However, the foundation was laid for including the study of agricultural sciences at German universities when Friedrich I established professorships of public administration at the Universities of Halle/Salle and Frankfurt/Oder in 1727. Agricultural science, a part of public administration, was introduced as a new subject to be taught along with economics and law enforcement.

In 1769 Johann Beckmann, in his book entitled *The Principles of German Agriculture (Die Grundsätze der deutschen Landwirtschaft)*, described technical agriculture as consisting of questions of crop and animal husbandry. Beckmann's work led to the establishment in 1771 of the first university institute with an agricultural discipline, the Veterinary Institute of Göttingen. This institute served as an example when the Veterinary College was established in Hanover in 1778 and the School of Veterinary Pharmacy in Berlin in 1790. Emphasis on the study of questions of crop husbandry did not develop until Albrecht Daniel von Thaer suggested the establishment of training centers for the study of modern farming methods. In 1807 Thaer founded a private academy of agriculture at Möglin, near Berlin in the duchy of Brandenburg, to demonstrate in practical experiments his theories of progressive farming methods. The academy consisted of a farm of a thousand acres and a college for instruction. In 1810 Thaer's efforts were recognized by appointment as professor of agriculture at the University of Berlin. Because of his conviction that agriculture could not be understood entirely nor adequately by attending lectures, Thaer resigned his professorship in 1811 and devoted his efforts to improving the program at Möglin. In 1824 the academy at Möglin was raised to the status of Royal Academy of Agriculture. This academy served as an example for the formation of other notable academies, such as Hohenheim (1818), near Stuttgart in southern Germany; Tharandt (1829); Poppelsdorf, near Bonn (1847); and Wende (1851), near Göttingen. In 1851 the Agricultural Academy at Göttingen offered, for the first time, a complete course of agricultural instruction. Other such academies were established at Schleisheim (1822), Jena (1826), Eldena (1835), Wiesbaden (1836), Regenwald (1842), and Prosdau (1826). Many of these have since been closed or transferred to university sites, and many have become institutes or royal academies. The Agricultural Academy at Hohenheim and the Royal University of Göttingen are the most notable of these institutions and have had the most influence on the development of agricultural education throughout Europe.

France

The first agricultural school in France was founded at La Rochette, near Melun, in 1763. In 1771 a second school was established at Annel, near Compiègne. Due to a growing interest in formal instruction in agriculture during this period, a plan for a national school of agriculture was submitted to the National Assembly of France in 1789. The efforts of these first schools appear to have had little effect on the National Assembly, since it did not approve the plan for such a school.

In 1822 Mathieu de Dombasle demonstrated on a farm at Roville that alternate cropping could profitably replace the three-field system of cropping that was predominant in the country. The effect of this work revolutionized farming practices throughout the country and led to the establishment of three regional agricultural schools—at Montpellier in southern France (1872), Gran Jouan (1841) in Brittany, and Grignon (1826) in the Seine-et-Oise—and the *Institut national agronomique de France* (National Agricultural Institute of France) (1848) at the Palace of Versailles. Of these institutions, the *Institut national agronomique de France* was the highest in order, being equivalent to a university. Attached to the institute were three large farms of several hundred acres and collections of numerous breeds of horses, cattle, sheep, and swine. Changes in the political climate of the country and the failure to recognize the value of a great scientific school of agriculture forced closure of the institute in 1852.

In 1876, through the efforts of Eugène Tisserand, then inspector general of agriculture, and the professors and students of the former *Institut national agronomique de France*, a law was passed by the National Assembly of France that reestablished the former institute under the title *Institut national agronomique.* The restored institute was moved from the Palace of Versailles to Paris. In lieu of any practical farm, it was given a small farm of 100 acres near Paris, at Joinville-le-Pont, for purposes of demonstration and experiment.

Of the three regional schools of agriculture, the school located at Grignon was the most distinguished. It was comparable to the agricultural academy at Hohenheim in Germany and had the same status as the Royal Agricultural College at Cirencester in England. The school at Grignon was established by Auguste Bella on a farm consisting of 1160 acres. The curriculum in each of these schools stressed both the theoretical and practical aspects of the most perfect methods of cultivation for the regions of the country in which they were located.

Belgium

Two institutions played prominent roles in the early development of higher education in agriculture in Belgium: the State Agricultural Institute at Gembloux and the Catholic School of Agriculture at Louvain. The State Agricultural Institute at Gembloux was established by a national law passed in 1860. The institute was organized similarly to the regional school of agriculture at Grignon in France and the agricultural academy at Hohenheim in Germany. As was the case with these established institutions of higher learning, stress was placed on both the theoretical and practical aspects of the latest methods of crop cultivation and animal husbandry of the agriculture prevalent in the country. The course of instruction lasted three years, and students who passed their final examinations satisfactorily received the diploma of agricultural engineer. A diploma from the institute was required for employment in controlling forests, drainage, and irrigation.

The Catholic School of Agriculture at Louvain was established in 1838 as a department of the faculty of sciences at the Catholic University of Louvain. Students were expected to complete a very exhaustive three-year course of study covering the same subjects taught at Gembloux, with the addition of religion, philosophy, and history, all of which were brought to bear on the treatment of such prominent subjects in the curriculum as the history of agriculture and comparative agriculture.

Netherlands

Agricultural education began formally in the Netherlands in 1842 with the establishment of a free school in agriculture at Hären in the province of Groningen. Instruction was given in mathematics; mechanics; the physical, biological, and social sciences; agricultural implements; and practical and colonial agriculture. Theory was taught during the winter in the town of Groningen and practical instruction given during the summer at a model farm at Hären. The school closed in 1863 because of the dissension that developed over this division of instruction. An attempt to reestablish the school in 1870 failed, and the committee that directed the school was dissolved.

In 1869 a communal school of agriculture was opened at Warffum in the province of Groningen. It was supported financially by the government, and professors of the state school (*école moyenne supérieure*), established in 1869 in the commune, were charged with some branches of instruction. One professor taught all agricultural subjects. Because of a lack of students, the school was closed in 1873. During this year a similar school was established at Wageningen, near the Rhine River, in the province of Gelderland. It was annexed to the *école moyenne supérieure* of the commune. However, after several years of operation with unsatisfactory results and a change of mind by the minister of the interior, the school became a State School of Agriculture in 1876. The school had as its purpose to provide four levels of instruction in agriculture: (1) a high school (*hoogere burger school*—equivalent to the German *Realschule*), (2) a lower agricultural school, (3) a higher agricultural school, and (4) an experimental and analytical station. The school had excellent school buildings, museums, and laboratories and possessed a farm of eighteen acres with ample farm buildings and appliances. The higher agricultural school was designed for instruction of the sons of landowners and tenant farmers who required advanced scientific and professional education and for land agents and administrators of estates in the Netherlands and the Dutch East Indies.

Denmark

The role of agriculture has been appreciated and promoted in Denmark since 1769. In that year, the Royal Agricultural Society of Denmark was established for the promotion of all phases of rural industry. It had among its purposes the holding of meetings on subjects of scientific importance or practical interest, the publication and distribution of books on rural economy, the rendering of advice on dairying and diseases of livestock, the promotion of agricultural experiments, and the placement of agricultural and dairy apprentices on farms. The efforts of this group led to the establishment of a course of lectures for young agriculturalists on the management of the domesticated animal at the Royal Veterinary School in Copenhagen in 1773.

In 1801 a professor of agriculture was appointed to the faculty of the University of Copenhagen to give lectures on agricultural subjects and report on the state of agriculture in the country. In 1849 a professor of rural economy was appointed to the Polytechnic School (Denmark Technical University), where instruction was given in agricultural chemistry. During the war of 1848 to 1850, however, these institutions were relegated to a state of near nonexistence. With the conclusion of the war, these institutions began once again to prosper. In 1856 a complete course of instruction in agriculture was added to the agriculture curriculum at the Royal

Veterinary School at Copenhagen, and the institution was renamed the Royal Agricultural and Veterinary Academy of Copenhagen.

Other European Countries

As a result of the early efforts of German agricultural educators and their interest in promoting agricultural education in their country, agricultural institutes and colleges developed throughout the European continent. Among those distinguishing themselves as outstanding agricultural institutions of higher learning were the *Università degli studi di Pisa* (State University of Pisa) in Italy, established in 1840; the *Instituto superior de agronomia* (Higher Institute of Agriculture) in Lisbon, established in 1852; and the *Instituto nacional agronómico* (National Agricultural Institute) in Madrid, established in 1855. The programs at each of these institutions were patterned after Thaer's approach to agricultural education, stressing both the theoretical and practical aspects of the agriculture prevalent in the geographic regions in which they were located.

England

Promotion of formal education in agriculture in England originated with the English Agricultural Society, established in 1838. In 1840 the society was granted a royal charter of incorporation and renamed the Royal Agricultural Society of England. Among its founding objectives was that of taking measures for the improvement of the education of those who depend on the cultivation of the soil for their support. The efforts of this society spurned the development of higher education in agriculture throughout England.

The Royal Agricultural College at Cirencester was chartered in March of 1845 with the purpose of teaching the science of agriculture and related sciences and the practical application of these sciences to the cultivation of the soil and the rearing and management of livestock. The college grew out of a resolution adopted by the

Cirencester and Fairfield Farmers' Club stressing the importance of a specific education for those engaged in agricultural pursuits.

Instruction in the theory of agriculture was provided through lectures and laboratory exercises, and practical applications were demonstrated on the college farm. Practical aspects of the program also included attendance at sales and markets, farm excursions, and experiments. The farm included five hundred acres and was managed to reflect the best of agricultural practices in the area of the country in which the college was located. In 1880 a college of agriculture in Downton, Wiltshire, near Salisbury, was opened under the name of Wilts and Hauts Agricultural College. The school was established with the purpose of training students for positions as landowners, surveyors, and farmers. The instructional program covered a two-year period and included the study of physical and biological sciences, commercial subjects, land surveying, veterinary surgery, agriculture, dairy and pastoral farming, estate management, land agency, and forestry. At the conclusion of the two-year program of study, students had sufficient background to pass the examinations of the Royal Agricultural Society of England, the Highland and Agricultural Society, and the Institution of Surveyors.

Scotland

The first university chair of agriculture in Scotland was founded in Edinburgh in 1790. It was followed in 1840 by the establishment of a lectureship in agricultural chemistry at the University of Aberdeen. In 1856 the Highland and Agricultural Society obtained a supplementary charter enabling it to conduct examinations and grant diplomas. These examinations led to the provision of teaching facilities. In 1876 the borough of South Kensington's science and art department issued a syllabus of instruction for agricultural education in the elementary school, evening classes, and advanced courses. This scheme necessitated some special training for

teachers, and beginning in 1877 the University of Aberdeen provided adequate courses for that purpose. The Universities of Edinburgh and Glasgow followed suit in 1888. At Edinburgh certain extramural lectures were combined with lectures by the professor of agriculture to provide a course in agricultural science. At Glasgow instruction in agriculture was given at the Technical College. At Ayrshire a highly successful educational program in dairying had been established in 1860. By 1889 an instructor and the necessary teaching equipment and facilities had been established at the Dairy School at Kilmarnok.

In 1896 the powers of the Scottish Education Department were extended to include agricultural education. Some teaching centers gradually developed into fully incorporated agricultural colleges associated with a definite area of the country. The West of Scotland College, associated with the dairy school at Kilmarnok, was incorporated in 1899; the East of Scotland College, associated with Edinburgh, was incorporated in 1901; and the North of Scotland College, associated with Aberdeen, was incorporated in 1904. It was the purpose of these colleges to provide a complete and efficient course of agricultural instruction, both scientific and practical; to serve as an advisory center for the agricultural community within its area; and to organize a system of agricultural instruction throughout each of the associated countries.

Canada

Attempts to improve agriculture and encourage people to use better farming methods began in Canada in the province of Ontario before the end of the eighteenth century. In 1792 an agricultural society was established at Niagara, then known as Newark. While little is known about the society's work and overall usefulness, it did lead to the establishment of similar societies throughout the province of Ontario and eventually all of Canada. These societies did much to stimulate the growing of grain, the importation of livestock, and the improvement of agricultural production methods.

The first major effort to provide higher education in agriculture came about in 1844, when a chair of agriculture was established by statute at the University of Toronto. After the establishment of this chair, however, little improvement in the agricultural program occurred for some time. As a result, considerable agitation from various agricultural groups throughout the province caused a college of agriculture to be established at Guelph in 1874 under the title Ontario Agricultural College and Experimental Farm. The institution was later renamed the Ontario Agricultural College. It was located on a 550-acre farm near Guelph in a purebred stock center of the province. The college was modeled after the Royal Agricultural College at Cirencester and developing agricultural colleges in the United States. The original program of study extended over a two-year period and consisted of formal instruction on agricultural subjects and practical work on the farm.

In 1887 the Ontario Agricultural College became affiliated with the University of Toronto and began to emphasize reaching more people through extension courses offered throughout the province. Because of its success in dealing with the agricultural needs of the province, the program of study was expanded to extend over a four-year period. The college grew to international prominence and stimulated the development of similar institutions of higher learning in agriculture in the other Canadian provinces in the early twentieth century. Among these were the Nova Scotia Agricultural College, Oka Agricultural College (Quebec Province), Manitoba Agricultural College, and the Saskatchewan College of Agriculture.

United States

The importance of agriculture was recognized in the United States before the colonies broke their political ties with England. The American Philosophical Society, founded in 1743, published numerous articles on agricultural subjects. While the society was developed to promote scientific developments in the country, it led to the organization of the Philadelphia society for the Promotion of Agriculture in 1785. The Philadelphia society had as its purpose the promotion of a greater increase of agricultural products within the American states. In addition, it encouraged the establishment of other societies throughout the country. By 1789 the society had honorary members in thirteen states, including George Washington, Robert Livingston, Noah Webster, Benjamin Franklin, and Timothy Pickering.

By example and through its honorary members, the Philadelphia society caused similar societies to emerge in other states. In 1785 the South Carolina Society for Promoting and Improving Agriculture and Other Rural Concerns, later known as the Agricultural Society of South Carolina, was organized. The Kennebec Agricultural Society was formed at Hallowell, Maine, in 1787. An organization entitled the New Jersey Society for Promoting Agriculture, Commerce and Arts was established in 1781, which led to the founding of several other similar societies within the state. The New York Society for the Promotion of Agriculture, Arts, and Manufacturers was organized in 1791. Similar societies were established in Massachusetts in 1792, Connecticut in 1794, New Hampshire in 1814, the District of Columbia in 1809, and Virginia in 1811.

Interest in agriculture, prompted by the work of the various agricultural societies, and interest in broadening the whole spectrum of public education in America led to the establishment of the Gardiner Lyceum at Gardiner, Maine, in 1821. The school was organized under the direction of Robert Hallowell Gardiner on land lying along the Kennebec River. The purpose of the school was to provide instruction in mathematics, mechanics, navigation, and those branches of natural philosophy and chemistry that were needed to develop scientific farmers and skillful mechanics.

The New York State Agricultural College was incorporated by an act of the New York State Assembly on April 15, 1853. In the act it was stated that the farm belonging to the college should be not less than three hundred acres and that the plan of instruction should include practical and scientific agriculture and the study of subjects related to agriculture. The school was opened in 1860 but with the advent of the Civil War was closed, and later efforts to reopen the school did not succeed. These efforts did eventually result in the establishment of the New York College of Agriculture at Ithaca, New York, in 1863.

At the same time that agriculturalists in the State of New York were struggling to establish an agricultural college, similar efforts to establish agricultural schools were under way in Michigan, Maryland, Iowa, Minnesota, and Pennsylvania. After considerable public debate over whether Michigan should have two state universities, Michigan Agricultural College, later to be called Michigan State University, was established in 1857 at Lansing. In 1856 the Maryland legislature passed legislation to establish an agriculture college. The college was located on a 428-acre farm within ten miles of Washington, D.C., at College Park. Funds for the college were raised by stock subscriptions. In 1916 its title was changed to Maryland State College of Agriculture; in 1920 it was combined with other schools and became the University of Maryland. The Agricultural College of Pennsylvania was chartered in May of 1862 and later (1874) renamed Pennsylvania State College. The Iowa legislature passed a bill providing for a state agricultural college and farm in 1858. The college was located on 648 acres near the town of Ames, Iowa.

Interest in agricultural education grew rapidly in the United States during this period. The need for such education was promoted extensively through the media and in the legislative halls of all the states as well as in Congress. Riding the crest of the wave of public support for this national trend, Jonathan Baldwin Turner, then professor at Illinois Jackson College at Jacksonville, Illinois, and publisher of the journal *Prairie Farmer,* proposed in 1852 that Congress grant public lands to each state for the establishment of industrial universities. In 1851 and 1852, Turner's plan for an industrial university in each state attracted wide-spread attention throughout the country. In 1853 the governor of Illinois approved resolutions passed by both houses of the state legislature asking the Congress to support and make provisions for public lands for industrial universities. After much public discussion and political maneuvering, the Morrill-Wade Act was passed by Congress in 1862. The act was referred to as the Morrill Land-Grant Bill in honor of Justin Smith Morrill of Vermont, who successfully promoted the bill through Congress. It was the purpose of the act "to donate public lands to the several states and territories which may provide colleges for the benefit of agriculture and the mechanical arts."

Iowa was the first state to accept the provisions of the act on September 11, 1862. Similar actions were taken by Vermont and Connecticut in the same year. Fourteen states accepted the act in 1863, two in 1864, one in 1865, six in 1866, four in 1867, three in 1868, one in 1869, and two in 1870.

Bibliography

The Agricultural College of Pennsylvania. Philadelphia: Williams S. Young, 1862.

Bretignière, L., and Risch, L. *Histoire de Grignon.* Châteauroux, France: Imprimerie typographique et lithographique Langlois, 1910.

General Organization and Finance of Agricultural Education and Research in Scotland. Edinburgh: H. M. Stationery Office, 1924.

Jenkins, H. M. *Report on Agricultural Education in North Germany, France, Denmark, Belgium, Holland, and the United Kingdom.* Vol. 2. London: Eyre and Spottiswoode, 1884.

Leake, A. H. *The Means and Methods of Agricultural Education.* Boston: Houghton Mifflin, 1915.

Loudeu, J. C. *Encyclopaedia of Agriculture.* London: Longman, 1835.

Madill, A. J. *History of Agricultural Education in*

Ontario. Toronto, Ontario: University of
Toronto Press, 1937.

Morton, J. A. *Cyclopedia of Agriculture*. London:
Blackie and Son, 1855.

Richardson, A. E. V. *Agricultural Education and
Agricultural Development in America*. Melbourne, Australia: N. J. Green, 1918.

Robertson, J. W. *Royal Commission on Industrial
Training and Technical Education: Report of
the Commissioners, Part IV*. Ottawa, Ontario:
C. H. Parmelee, 1913.

*Second Report of the Royal Commission of Technical
Instruction*. Vol. 1. London: Eyre and Spottiswoode, 1884.

Tornow, W. *The Trends of Agricultural Research
Development in Germany*. Münster, Federal
Republic of Germany: Landwirtschaftsver-
lag Hiltrup, 1958.

True, C. T. *A History of Agricultural Education
in the United States, 1785–1925*. Washington,
D.C.: U.S. Government Printing Office,
1929.

Welch, A. S. *Report on the Organization and
Management of Seven Agricultural Schools in
Germany, Belgium, and England*. Washington,
D.C.: U.S. Government Printing Office,
1885.

ALAN A. KAHLER

2. AGRICULTURAL RESEARCH, EXTENSION SERVICES, AND FIELD STATIONS

Agricultural extension education and the research and field stations related to them are found in every part of the world. Because of the nature of their work, programs in these systems are seldom conducted within postsecondary institutions. However, the majority are significantly influenced by institutions of higher education in their use of research and, on occasion, in administration.

The function of learning—by observation and instruction—which particular crops and livestock will grow better under which particular circumstances is as old as agriculture itself. Every rural social system has some kind of learning going on within it—encompassing those activities that have been labeled, in highly specialized and differentiated formal systems, as agricultural research or agricultural extension.

The agricultural extension education function is found in every modern nation-state in a number of organizations that vary in form and function. Some are modifications of models employed in other lands, imposed by colonial governments and shared through international technical assistance programs. Others are indigenous developments—the products of gradual evolution.

Agricultural Extension Education

Independent of its origin, each agricultural extension education organization shares a number of characteristics with extension education units in other countries. There is, first, the rural social system—the people of an area to be served. Sometimes this system is labeled the "target system." The second component is the rural development stimulation system, sometimes known as the change system. This system is an organization designed to facilitate learning within the rural social system. Finally, the personnel of rural development stimulation systems are often known as change agents, reflecting the fact that their success or failure tends to be measured in terms of change within the rural social systems.

Strategic alternatives. Agricultural extension education systems and the research units connected to them vary according to basic strategy. In some countries, the basic strategy is rural development, which is defined in terms of positive change on behalf of the inhabitants of a rural social system. Much more frequently, the strategy is one of increasing agricultural productivity.

If the goal is production oriented, the usual basic strategy is to provide technical assistance to agricultural producers—to teach them how to select the right crops, to use appropriate cultural practices, and to reap the largest possible harvest. Such strategies tend to follow the assumptions of the process of diffusion of innovations. The basic assumption of this process is that once an appropriate innovation is adopted by some agricultural producers, and is successful, it will spread to others in a predictable way (Rogers and Shoemaker, 1968).

Alternative strategies go beyond agricultural productivity and involve supplying inputs to agricultural production and marketing its outputs. Other strategies are more broadly based in their concern with community development and seek such goals as rural solidarity. Still others are concerned with rural equity and the quality of life of all those who live in the countryside.

A good example of the first strategy is that of the Ministry of Agriculture in Kenya, whose extension goal is to promote the adoption of productivity-increasing agricultural innovations. The Special Rural Development Program, established by the government of Kenya in 1970, has a somewhat broader objective: "to increase incomes, employment, and the quality of rural life" (Ascroft, Röling, Kariuki, and Chege, 1973, p. 12).

Strategies regarding agricultural productivity. Organizations that follow a strategy of supporting agricultural production tend to be primarily engaged in either research or education. The agricultural experiment stations found throughout Europe and North America were replicated in European colonies in Asia, Africa, and Latin America.

In the absence of specifically organized agricultural extension education units, these agricultural research stations have developed outreach programs. Stations have organized field days and invited farmers and other agricultural producers to see which varieties grow best, and they have given samples of seed to farmers to replicate new varieties. In places where literacy is relatively high, they have published not only scientific reports of their achievements but also farmers' bulletins and other materials directed at those who might make use of such research. In the United States, for example, agricultural experiment stations officially conducted such extension education activities from the mid 1870s until 1912, when the agricultural exten-

sion services of various states began to organize.

As extension education became formally organized in various parts of the world (most organization has occurred since 1950), some units, within ministries of agriculture and elsewhere, tried to carry out the education function without applied research. One major problem of such units, as exemplified by the extension division of the Ministry of Agriculture in Pakistan prior to the "green revolution," was that while there was an excellent organization, there was nothing "to extend." If the basic model is one of providing technical assistance to growers, then technical knowledge that is useful and practical, and that growers can adopt, is essential.

A strategic question is whether the organization will attempt only to provide education or will also supply services. In the United States, a political battle beginning in 1914 kept the Cooperative Extension Service involved in "pure" education. This unique organization (founded between 1910 and 1914), receiving financial and other support from the United States Department of Agriculture on a national basis, also received state support through the land-grant colleges and universities and county support through county governments. Since it flourished in the United States, where ample agricultural inputs (inputs include machinery, credit, seed, fertilizer, insecticides, and fungicides) were supplied through the private sector and credit was available to the major clientele, the organization did not supply inputs or market outputs. Close association and sponsorship by county and state farm bureaus and national support from the American Farm Bureau Federation are said to have kept the service tuned to the needs of larger and more commercial farmers and inept with respect to smaller and less credit-worthy farmers (McConnell, 1969). Other units in the United States, such as the Farmers' Home Administration, did supply inputs as well as credit and helped with marketing of outputs, as well as carrying on extension education. However, such organizations have been seen as natural "enemies" of the main extension education system in the United States.

In countries where the private sector does not supply such inputs as credit, feed, seed, and fertilizer on a timely basis, education services are useless unless the extension education organizations are also able to provide the supply inputs. Agricultural productivity goals are more likely to be achieved in countries where there is a system covering not only the supply of inputs and education about productivity but also the marketing of outputs and the governance and control of price and quality throughout the system (Axinn and Thorat, 1972, Chapter 1).

Extension services as nonformal education and research. In the more highly differentiated social systems, agricultural extension education is merely one of several kinds of adult and nonformal education. In Europe and North America particularly, public schools and colleges and universities carry on adult education programs, often with special activities for rural people. Community development programs in such countries often have agricultural productivity goals. The folk high schools of the Scandinavian countries (boarding schools for rural youth) are classic examples of formal education for the children of farmers designed to prepare them to assume productive roles in agriculture.

Similarly, agricultural research in more highly developed countries tends to be conducted by both the public and the private and industrial sectors. However, farmers throughout the world have made the case for their special research needs separate from those of industrial research and development. Research in agriculture is expensive. They argue that while large industries can afford to invest a certain percentage of their income in the development of new products, agriculture tends to be divided into so many small units that none of them, individually, can afford to invest in research. Based on this argument,

governments throughout the world have set up both basic and applied research units in agriculture, designed to import plant and animal materials from other parts of the world; to test and develop new varieties, strains, and breeds; and to improve cultural practices. The information and the germ plasm created in these programs are passed on to rural people.

Thus, almost every country has at least one national program of agricultural research and agricultural extension education in the public sector. These programs may be combined in one organization or split into two or more separate and sometimes competing organizations. In addition, there are usually smaller and more localized programs of research and extension education within each nation-state.

Extent and Scope of Worldwide Distribution

Agricultural extension education systems are described either as one type of rural development stimulation system or as rural development acquisition systems (Axinn, 1975). Acquisition systems tend to be controlled by the rural people for whom their service is designed; stimulation systems are generally controlled by outsiders whose goals are to bring about change within the rural social system.

Thus, agricultural extension education systems may be broadly classified as being organized from the "outside" or from the "inside." Extension organizations sponsored by farmers' associations are an example of the latter, while those sponsored by ministries of agriculture or by educational institutions are usually "outside" organizations. In addition, there are many combinations of the two.

An international directory of extension organizations in seventy-eight countries shows sixty supported entirely by the national ministry of agriculture and three by other ministries of central government (McCabe and Swanson, 1975). In that summary, only five of the agricultural extension systems are jointly supported by a ministry of agriculture and a farmers' organization. Another eight are supported by various levels of government, including local, provincial, and central. Educational institutions are involved, along with farmers' organizations and government organizations, in only two systems—one in Brazil and the other the Cooperative Extension Service of the United States.

The international directory basically lists agriculturally oriented programs. None of those listed are aimed at general community or rural development. Forty-three are concerned only with production of the various crops, while thirty-five work in addition on marketing, supply, and community relations.

Of the seventy-eight, two were organized and operating in the present agency prior to 1875. Another five developed between 1876 and 1900, and six more developed between 1901 and 1925. From 1925 to 1950, another sixteen were started, and twenty-nine developed between 1951 and 1960. Following World War II, there was extensive development of extension education organizations throughout Asia, Africa, and Latin America, usually with support from a European or North American government or from an international agency.

International, national, and regional approaches. Organizationally, the extension education function may be found in a great variety of structures. Often, but not always, extension organizations are associated with applied agricultural research.

The standard British model is based on the National Agricultural Advisory Service (NAAS) in the United Kingdom. NAAS, begun in 1946, became the Agricultural Development and Advisory Service in 1971. As NAAS, it was a part of the Ministry of Agriculture and thus integrated with government. The major function of NAAS was advisory; it specialized in extension education and had no connection with the supply, marketing, research, and educational functions of the ministry.

There have been a number of variations on this model in the former British colonies. The extension education component is typically part of a ministry of agriculture but is also often closely related to the supply function and sometimes to the marketing function. Research is usually found in quite separate units of the same ministry.

In contrast, the Thana Training and Development Center of Comilla in Bangladesh combines a great variety of components in one organization. This experimental program, which has been highly successful, combines supply, marketing, research, education, and governance functions into one organization designed to serve the production component of the rural economy. It is somewhat similar to the commune in the People's Republic of China, working through a series of brigades. In some ways the *kibbutzim* (agricultural communal societies) of Israel go even further, including the production function as well as all the other functions.

Malaysia provides an example of the evolution from the standard British colony model, first to an extension education system based in a ministry of agriculture, and then toward a broader collection of functional components designed specifically to meet the problems of the society. Seeing the success of farmers' associations in the Republic of China, the Ministry of Agriculture in Malaysia is deliberately developing such associations in its own country. It is gradually turning over the extension education function to these farmers' associations, which are deeply involved in the supply of credit and other production inputs and in the marketing of agricultural products.

Still another configuration is found in the traditional United States model, in which the research function has been nurtured in the same organization that carries on both the extension education function and the higher education function in agriculture. Land-grant colleges and universities in the United States, with their three-way tradition of research, extension, and resident instruction, are largely independent of government and avoid the supply and marketing functions. However, even within the country there is great variation. The Farmers' Home Administration, for example, did not fit the traditional United States model.

Applied research in agriculture seems to have been most effective when carried on directly by farmers concerned about their own crops. Traditionally, farmers have learned which yams or potatoes to save for seed and which to consume prior to the next growing season. This research has been formalized in educational institutions and in governments throughout the world, with educational institutions apparently more successful than governments, although the experience is varied. More recently, international networks have been developed around such crops as rice, maize, and wheat. Outstanding examples are the International Rice Research Institute of the Philippines and the International Maize and Wheat Center in Chipingo, Mexico. Such institutes in various parts of the world are providing for international exchange of knowledge, experience, and newly developed germ plasm. As an example of international cooperation, it is most promising.

Conversely, in extension education success seems to be much more limited, although there have been attempts on the part of international agencies, such as the United Nations Food and Agriculture Organization, to exchange materials among countries. Social, cultural, and religious differences have made organizational and program implementation experience more difficult to diffuse. Moreover, the content of particular programs seems to be much more dependent on location. The record of failure in international exchange is great, because those who wish to spread extension education have too often simply replicated the artifacts of their own national systems rather than developing appropriate systems for the target country. In his study of extension education in the Andes, for example, Rice (1971) illustrates the in-

eptness of a program that only transferred artifacts from another country.

Alternatives of doctrine. Agricultural extension education and research systems may be compared with each other on the basis of their doctrines—that is of their concept of what the organization stands for, what it hopes to achieve, and the styles of action it intends to use.

The doctrine of an extension education system sets the pace for its program and determines the nature of its organization, structure, and image of itself. Some systems see themselves as essentially technical assistance organizations, whose job is to provide technical information to producers, marketers, or suppliers in the system. Others see themselves more broadly as trying to help the entire rural social system to develop; such systems may call themselves "community development" organizations.

Australia, Japan, and the United Kingdom are outstanding examples of systems with a primarily technical assistance doctrine. Both India and Pakistan have gone through periods of a much broader community development concept, while Egypt and the Republic of China have combined these approaches in various ways. The People's Republic of China, Tanzania, and several small projects within other countries have completely integrated the education function with production, marketing, supply, and governance, and espouse a doctrine of equity (Axinn and Thorat, 1972).

In general, there has been increasing criticism of production-oriented doctrines in both agricultural extension and research. Particularly from the "hungry" nations of Asia, Africa, and Latin America, there is increasing pressure for both agricultural research and extension education that espouse a doctrine of general rural welfare and equity. Research of this sort takes into account employment generation as well as yield per acre, for example. Extension education that follows this doctrine might be more concerned with development of effective demand among people in the countryside than with an increase in the food supply.

Multiple versus unitary approaches. It is rare to find a nation-state with a single organization and monolithic structure carrying on either agricultural research or extension education. However, in such relatively small island nations as Barbados and Cyprus the extension service is part of the Ministry of Agriculture, and in Togo the *Société régionale d'aménagement et du développement maritime* (Regional Society for Management and for Maritime Development) receives its support through the Department of Rural Economy. More often, there is one major agricultural extension organization, usually attached to a ministry of agriculture, and a variety of smaller organizations, some of which compete. Some work in only one crop, such as sugar (often connected with a particular refinery); some may be connected with schools and relate to a ministry of education, and others, the rural development acquisition systems, may be organized and operated by the rural people they serve.

It is also possible to have multiple or unitary sources of financial support, multiple types of clientele or a single group, multiple programs or a single program, and unified leadership or diffuse control.

A comparative study of field extension workers in Nigeria employed under multi-commodity and single-commodity extension organizations found that the workers deployed under the single-commodity system reported superior performance and were rated higher by farmers than those working in general extension (Ekpere, 1973). On the other hand, organizations with multiple programing are sometimes able to build strong cadres of loyal clientele as they shift topics according to need.

Types of Organizations

Most agricultural research organizations and agricultural extension education organizations are sponsored by government ministries or departments, but some are sponsored by users, by educational institutions, or by military organizations.

Sponsorship by government. Extension and research organizations sponsored by government usually have a heavy bias toward agricultural production. For example, the Department of Extension Training of the Ministry of Agriculture in Malawi has three major program objectives. The first two emphasize self-sufficiency in food supply and encouragement of increased production of cash crops for export. The improvement of the standard of living in rural Malawi falls into third place.

Similarly, the Agricultural Extension Service of the Ministry of Agriculture in Lebanon has as its first objective the planning and execution of the extension program. Its second goal is to train farmers in improved practices in agriculture.

In the Federal Republic of Germany, where financial support comes from the Ministries of Agriculture in eleven states and from the Federal Republic, along with the six chambers of agriculture, the *Bundesministerium für Ernährung, Landwirtschaft und Forsten* (Federal Ministry for Nutrition, Agriculture, and Forestry) emphasizes education for the individual farmer over community development. The ministry gives independent individual advice to farmers to enable them to make their own decisions and attempts to convince them of the need for purposeful action to organize and develop their enterprises. A final goal is that of assistance to farmers in improving productivity "in order to increase farm income and welfare of the people working on the farm."

By contrast, in the Republic of China, where there is joint sponsorship by farmers' associations and local governments as well as by the provincial Department of Agriculture and Forestry, the first objective is "to educate rural people in order to obtain new knowledge, apply new skills, and develop new attitudes." Further goals are the development of rural people "for better farming and better business" and the improvement of their lives "socially, mentally, and physically."

A broader program is supported by the Office of Rural Development in the Republic of Korea, which gets its basic support from the Ministry of Agriculture. Its objectives include the introduction of new farming techniques, the productive use of off-farm season, the improvement of rural life, the training of rural leaders, and the strengthening of institutional cooperation.

Sponsorship by military organizations. Extension education organizations sponsored by military units are usually temporary, following a military coup or occurring during periods of revolution. While such groups usually support productivity over other considerations, some have been associated with movements designed to develop equity and have placed equity goals first.

Sources of financial support. Some financial support for extension education and applied research in agriculture has come entirely from outside the rural social system or even the nation-state. In recent years, the United Nations Development Programme, working through the United Nations Food and Agriculture Organization or UNESCO, has intervened in a variety of ways in furtherance of agricultural extension education. The World Bank and individual bilateral aid agencies have also attempted to assist in this movement.

In most cases, however, financial support for agricultural extension and its accompanying applied research comes directly from the central government. In a few instances, it is funneled through educational institutions, and in a very few countries, government funds are channeled through farmers' organizations. There are various combinations.

In Argentina, however, a special tax on agricultural exports has provided continuity and program independence to the *Instituto nacional de tecnología agropecuaria* (INTA: National Institute for Farming and Animal Husbandry Technology), which carries on agricultural research and extension activity on a national scale.

Any agricultural extension education organization that persists over time is likely to be linked with its own government and educational system. It may also have linkages to political parties, to farmers' organizations, to those who manufacture and distribute fertilizers and livestock feeds, and to banking and credit institutions.

Control of extension education organizations. There are several patterns of control around the world. The United States has been able to maintain control from the bottom up—that is, programs of cooperative extension work in agriculture and home economics have systematically and forcefully insisted on hearing the voice of rural men and women in determining program activities. Since county governments share in the cost, local people have also controlled the selection and employment of the paid staff of American extension education organizations.

However, authority usually rests with government, and particularly central government, although farmers' organizations definitely influence extension and applied research in a few countries. There are also cases of influence from political parties, from military organizations, and from labor unions. In Kerala state in India a moderately successful attempt has been made to organize small farmers and landless laborers along labor union lines.

Modes of structure. The choice of structure is critical. In some countries, the subunits within an agricultural extension education system are divided by program content or specialty. Thus, there may be a rice extension service, a livestock extension service, and a horticultural crops extension program. Others are divided by a type of farming area or by land type. In an alternative scheme, administration is by geographical units, with programs cutting across the various specialties. Extension and research efforts organized by area tend to be more responsive to the needs and interests of the people being served, while those organized by program content or special field are often more responsive to central decision making and to production goals set by the staff.

Relationships with clientele organizations are also related to structure. Some extension units act as servants of their farmer clientele. The Ujamma village of Tanzania, the Agricultural Society of Iceland, the *Dirección general de extensión agrícola* (Office of Agricultural Extension) of Mexico, and the 4-H Clubs in the United States tend to see themselves in this way. Some extension organizations are the creators and supporters of clientele organizations; others tend to dominate clientele; still others are independent of them; and a few compete with their clientele organizations.

Types of Staffing

Most agricultural research and education units are administered by professional public servants who are a part of central government. Only rarely do farmers play administrative roles. In some cases politicians are in charge of administration, and in a very few countries agriculturalists, economists, or sociologists professionally concerned with rural development administer extension education and agricultural research.

Agricultural extension education efforts are often described by a ratio of personnel to clientele. Since personnel are of many different types, simple numbers are meaningless. The variety of communication methods used also makes the ratio of personnel to clientele irrelevant. Some extension education organizations rely heavily on the use of such mass communications channels as radio, television, and the newspapers, while others work mostly through an individual advisory service, given by one staff member to one client.

Professional staff. The professional staff in extension education tends to be oriented to agriculture and reflects a variety of perceptions of the work. Some extension education systems employ a professional staff of generalists, who are able to identify local needs and seek appropriate technical information. Others employ specialists, who find opportunities for the use of specialized information among their clientele. Professional staff may also be distinguished by orientation. Some staff members are

oriented toward their clientele, some toward their professions, while others are oriented toward the bureaucracy of which agricultural extension and research organizations are a part.

In general, the greater the social distance between an agricultural extension education officer and the rural people being served, the less chance there is of effective extension education. Similarly, the greater the social distance between those managing applied research in agriculture and those managing farms, the less likely it is that the results of the research will be useful and applicable on those farms (Axinn and Thorat, 1972, p. 189).

Nonprofessional staff. Throughout the world nonprofessional staff members participate in both agricultural extension and research efforts. Although they generally have limited formal training in agriculture, nonprofessionals fill key posts as field overseers, demonstrators, and managers of research plots. Also, since agricultural extension and research organizations tend to be large and far-flung, administrative and "housekeeping" persons are needed along with the agriculturalists. In some organizations the administrators tend to dominate the organization. When this happens, program effectiveness may be seriously impaired.

Volunteers. Still another type of personnel who plays a key role in agricultural extension education and research is the volunteer. In Japan, for example, master farmers formed the backbone of organized extension education at the time that Japan was making its greatest progress in productivity. Volunteer leaders have assisted with youth programs in agricultural extension in various places in the world and have made notable contributions.

Training. There is a worldwide trend toward more formal preservice and inservice training for agricultural extension and research personnel, reflected in the rather high requirements for formal education. Of seventy countries that responded to a recent questionnaire about their training programs, all required a minimum of ten years formal education for administrative and supervisory personnel, and fifty-nine countries required fourteen or more years of training (McCabe and Swanson, 1975).

Agricultural extension officers, often referred to as professionals, are usually distinguished from village-level workers, sometimes called technicians. However, according to the same study, requirements in fifty-six countries ranged from twelve to seventeen years of preservice training for agricultural extension officers. The lowest recorded requirement was six years, and most countries required at least eight years. Of the twenty-eight countries reporting the employment of village-level workers, nineteen required twelve or more years of schooling, and only one had a requirement as low as five years.

Many of these training units were started in the mid 1960s. For example, the Netherlands started a program in 1964, followed by a similar program in 1965 in England, in 1966 in Northern Ireland, in 1967 in Finland, in 1968 in Denmark, in 1969 in Norway, and in 1971 in Sweden. All focus on the training of field staff and teachers. Most are associated with universities, and their content includes discussion of extension education methods and techniques. They receive financial support from their governments, universities, and other organizations, and conduct short courses of one to four weeks in addition to regular classes for undergraduate students. Some of the European units mentioned above were modeled after a program started in the Federal Republic of Germany in 1956.

Preparation requirements of the extent demanded in these countries may be excessive, as they tend to increase the social distance between agricultural extension personnel and the farm people they serve.

The *International Directory of Extension Organizations and Extension Training Institutions* (McCabe and Swanson, 1975) supplies breakdowns of assignment and training for 184,678 agricultural extension education personnel in seventy countries. It does not include some of the larger systems, such as those of the United States, the Soviet Union, Nigeria, Tanzania, and the United Kingdom. However, in the countries included, an average professional extension staff has 2638 members, with 212 in administrative and supervisory ranks, 158 technical specialists, 831 extension officers, and 1437 village-level workers.

Since the countries included vary greatly in size, there is also a tremendous range in the number of both clientele and professional staff members. In India there are 105,395 professional staff members, five in Syria, ten in Kuwait, ten in Montserrat, and eleven in Barbados.

Contrasts within the data are both revealing and misleading. For example, Spain and Sri Lanka report, respectively, 2013 and 2172 professional extension employees. However, Spain has over 3,000,000 agricultural holdings, whereas Sri Lanka reports only 1,169,000. All of Spain's extension staff have at least fourteen years of professional preparation, whereas 1535 of Sri Lanka's staff work at the village level and average only eleven years of preservice training.

Further, some 4500 professional extension workers in the United Kingdom and approximately 16,000 in the United States are not included in the study, nor are others in Eastern Europe and Central Asia. In the People's Republic of China, there were 38,000 people taking part in 7690 agrotechnical extension stations in 1960, and it is projected that the numbers have increased since (Stavis, 1974). The 16,000 in the United States are distributed differently in different states.

It is clear that formal credentials, such as school certificates and bachelor's and master's degrees, have been critical in the selection of personnel for extension. Formal education is accompanied by various kinds of orientation and indoctrination training and by vigorous programs of in-service training in many countries. Most extension organizations have a special unit for training of personnel, some within the major organization and others separate from it, usually in association with a university.

Types of Programs

The programs developed within extension education systems vary depending on the source of control within the program, its structure, objectives, and the numbers and orientation of its personnel.

Planning processes. Program planning varies greatly within agricultural extension education efforts. Although many declare that they develop programs on the basis of the needs and interests of rural people, most systems do their program planning from the top down or from the center out. Thus, typically, production targets are set in a ministry of agriculture within the central government. These targets are divided among the regions and districts of the country, and each extension officer at the bottom level receives his quota of production targets. These targets then become the core around which the program is planned.

By contrast, in those countries where farmers' organizations or rural people have exercised more control, programs are in fact planned from the bottom up. Rural people meet and identify their problems, decide what the nature of the extension education program should be, and pass that information up the hierarchy. Still others are a combination of these two approaches and result in a dialog between rural people with felt needs and professional agriculturalists with technical knowledge and government officials concerned with policy and price.

Objectives. The sources of the goals of program activities range from government policies to political programs. Objectives may be drawn from knowledge or subject matter, from staff preferences, from clientele preferences, from the estimates of felt needs of clientele, and from the sheer bias of extension officers. For example, an island-wide extension service was started by the Jamaica Agricultural Service in 1895. The objectives of that service, according to Henderson (1973, p. 3), were to collect and disseminate useful agricultural information among farmers, to encourage the improved cultivation of products and better breeds of livestock, and to watch over the interests of the agricultural industry generally.

The cycle of agricultural extension program development may include such aspects as an analysis of the situation, an identification of problems (opportunities), the establishment of goals (targets), and an analysis of barriers (reasons why goals have not already been achieved). Appropriate messages are then formulated, audiences designated for each message, and the best combination of channels to carry messages to audiences is selected. Treatments are designed for each message in order to achieve the greates' impact, and appropriately treated messages are sent via selected channels to designated audiences. The extent to which goals have been achieved is evaluated and the planners then repeat the process from the beginning (Axinn and Thorat, 1972, p. 190).

Operations. The methods and techniques used in agricultural extension education are as diverse as the cultures served. Throughout the world, young people who grow up on farms learn the techniques of agriculture and homemaking from their parents. In addition, agricultural fairs and competitive expositions in which the largest melons or the reddest tomatoes are placed in competition are older than recorded history. Such agricultural-centered gatherings as cattle shows, sheepherding competitions, cattle-management competitions (ancestors of the modern rodeo), and competitions among sheepherding dogs are a consistent feature of rural life. However, the result demonstration is probably the most commonly deployed and most effective technique in modern agricultural extension education. It has remained dominant since its introduction among Louisiana rice farmers by Seaman A. Knapp (Bailey, 1945).

By means of the result demonstration, cultural practices, new seeds, and other innovations developed in the agricultural experimental stations are applied in the field, either by agricultural extension personnel or by farmers themselves. Others see the results of the demonstration and try the new method or strain the next growing season. When the innovation is judged by farmers to be to their advantage, it spreads rapidly and widely. If the innovation does not prove appropriate, it soon dies away.

To speed communication in this nonformal education process, agricultural extension officers often conduct tours of the result of demonstrations and publish newsletters, booklets, posters, and other materials showing the results. Participating farmers also meet with various groups to describe their achievements. Some agricultural extension systems deliberately organize rural development acquisition systems—farmers' clubs, youth clubs, local cooperatives, and other groups—in order to have an audience for such presentations.

Studies of time use by agricultural extension workers indicate that they spend a large proportion of their time in visits to individual farms. They talk with farm operators and exchange useful bits of information, often passing on the knowledge learned by one farmer to his neighbors.

Most agricultural extension education systems employ some personnel who specialize in one crop or one type of livestock or in some special aspect of farming. Only nine of the seventy countries in the McCabe and Swanson (1975) study had no such specialized personnel. However, the average country, with a total staff of 2638, had only 158 specialists, or one to every fourteen field extension officers.

The method demonstration, in which extension officers or others demonstrate the methods employed in a particular agricultural practice, is also widely used. For example, a field extension officer will go from farm to farm to show individuals how to prune fruit trees, shear sheep, space plants, or apply fertilizer. A great variety of instructional aids is also employed by agricultural extension education workers. Some countries use radio extensively, sometimes organizing radio farm forums in which organized listener groups participate in regular meetings at the time of broadcasts directed to them. These broadcasts may be coordinated with printed material and exchange of correspondence. In some places television is used in this manner (Read, 1972). The processes used in the operation of agricultural extension services are as broad as the opportunities offered by nonformal education and the communication process (Berlo, 1960; Axinn, 1969).

Evaluation. Evaluating the effectiveness of applied research is a significant aspect of operations. Research stations measure yields per acre and quality of production in terms of nutrient levels, attractiveness to consumers, control of insects and diseases, and related matters. Increasingly, a farm management bias has been introduced, and agricultural research is evaluated in terms of the potential costs and benefits to utilizers of its products.

Measurements are also made of the inputs in extension education by broad reporting of activities carried on by extension staff and the distribution of clientele. Measuring the effect or impact of the work of the extension staff is difficult and expensive and thus infrequent (Byrn, 1959). To obtain benefit-cost ratios, it becomes necessary to do systematic evaluative research (Axinn, 1968). The high cost of such research and the fear that practitioners will be shown to be less than appropriately effective have kept this kind of evaluation to a minimum.

Control. The control of agricultural extension education activities is a serious consideration. Although most personnel see themselves as trying to do the most good for the most people, others have different views. The internal assumption is usually that the spread of technology among rural people will improve their economic status, which, in turn, will increase their social and political status. At the same time, the increase in food productivity will result in greater quantities of higher quality available at lower price to consumers throughout the country.

However, what is done is influenced by the nature of financial support, by the location of sponsorship, by the type of clientele, by the staff itself, by the kind of doctrine that the organization espouses, and by other political influences. For example, McConnell (1969) suggests that the American Farm Bureau Federation and the manufacturers of agricultural implements and other inputs in the United States helped alter the program of the Cooperative Extension Service in the United States over the years so that it served the larger commercial farmers at the expense of smaller and less economic operators. The latter were gradually driven off the farm by the pressure of the economies of scale.

Similarly, in much of Asia, accusations have been made that agricultural extension officers, with their "superior" education, represent the large landowners and moneylenders and often program, perhaps inadvertently, to the detriment of landless laborers and small holders. One of the innovations developed in the People's Republic of China is an agricultural extension education system in which control is divided equitably among utilizers of the service and overseen by a political party, thus presumably ensuring equity in the distribution of the benefits of such education (Stavis, 1974).

Major Issues and Trends

While there are several individual issues in the field of extension education, most are related to the general issue of the choice between agricultural productivity goals and rural life development goals. Until the 1960s the trend had been toward an emphasis on productivity, but it seems to be shifting gradually toward concern with the quality of rural life.

Issues of program goals. The issue of control is a major concern in agricultural ap-

plied research and in agricultural extension education. Some systems, as indicated above, tend to be controlled by the central government rather than by the rural people who till the soil and tend the livestock. When controlled by the government, research tends to be directed toward crops for export in order to earn foreign exchange, and food crop research is designed to give those in the cities the highest quantity at the lowest cost. Extension education systems organized by ministries of agriculture tend to have production orientations.

In a system in which the rural people on the land determine the program goals, there is generally less concern about productivity and more concern about their own diets, the health of their wives and children, the distribution of the education system, roads, and housing.

Another issue is the debate between the production emphasis within agriculture and a broader definition of agriculture. Some agricultural extension systems focus only on the farmer as client and devote their major energies to the techniques and skills he uses in putting into operation the results of applied agricultural research. An alternative is to carry on similar work with those who supply the inputs to agricultural production, such as feed, seed, fertilizer, machinery, and credit. A related possibility is to focus on those who market the outputs and are concerned about storage of food crops, processing of foods, packaging and distribution, as well as wholesaling and retailing of food. Some extension systems have become involved in these three aspects of the total process (production, supply, and marketing), while others are further concerned with governance and related matters.

Among extension systems, most emphasize agriculture and agricultural productivity as a main goal. Others seek community development and solidarity among rural people as more appropriate goals. As Taylor, Ensminger, Johnson, and Joyce (1967) observed, whether a system starts with a major emphasis on community development or on technical assistance, it will incorporate both if it is sufficiently long-lived.

Another goal-related issue is that of education versus other services. Some extension education systems have tried to assume only educational goals and are concerned solely with what is learned by whom. Others have decided that rural people who learn about a new type of farming and do not have the seed required will only become frustrated. Therefore, these systems become involved in the distribution of feed and seed, fertilizer, insecticides, and fungicides. Often, when marketing systems are inadequate, extension education systems purchase farmers' produce, store it, and perhaps transport it to marketing centers.

Underlying all these controversies is the doctrinal difference between emphasis on rural life versus emphasis on agricultural productivity. Most agricultural extension education programs are primarily focused on increasing productivity. A few are concerned with the quality of rural life. While the numbers of those so concerned varies (and seems to be increasing), they remain a relatively small portion of the total activity.

Issues of program means. Also among the issues confronting extension education systems are such matters as the type of staff, organization, and programs to be deployed. The extent of formal education required of staff members and the choice of a pattern of control—and thus of program emphasis—are particular issues of program means. Another issue, also mentioned above, is whether to organize by area or by special field. Here again, when responsiveness to rural people is stressed, there is a tendency to organize by area.

A continuing issue is that of the relative investment of time and energy in individual activities, such as the setting up of result demonstrations on an individual farm, in comparison with larger-scale activities, such as organizing groups and carrying out meetings, tours, and other group activities. A third alternative is heavy reliance on the

mass communications media. The choice among communication channels depends very much on the nature of the communication already going on in a particular rural social system, the types of messages being sent, and other local conditions.

Trends. Two major trends could be identified by 1975. One trend concerns equity versus productivity. Although many agricultural extension education efforts in the late 1800s were concerned with country life in general and with the welfare of rural people, there has been an increasing focus on productivity. The assumption has been that if those who till the soil produce a greater quantity of better-quality crops and livestock, other aspects of their lives will improve. However, world experience does not substantiate this claim. Economies of scale have come to be the major technical achievement of agricultural research, resulting in increased efficiency for larger and larger farm operations, increased capitalization per farm, and increased spread between the small farmers and the large farmers. Large-acreage farms have become, increasingly, commercial business operations that employ more capital than any one family could control and produce at high rates of efficiency. Other farmers left in the countryside have thus become relatively poor.

However, the attention called to this phenomenon in the last decade has affected this trend, as has increased communication with the People's Republic of China. Thus, there has been a growing shift in direction, and agricultural extension education systems are likely to put equity goals ahead of productivity goals for the next several decades.

Another major trend is a difference in the kind of attention being given to the world food problem. The assumptions of the last half century have been that supply was the central problem, that if food supplies could only be increased, there would be less hunger and famine in the world. However, there has developed an increasing awareness of the lack of effective demand on the part of millions of poor people, both in the urban centers and in the rural countryside. Thus, one can expect an increasing concern in agricultural extension education with the demand side of the equation and with activities designed to increase the effective demand among those who live in the rural world.

Bibliography

Ascroft, J., Röling, N., Kariuki, J., and Chege, F. *Extension and the Forgotten Farmer: Bulletin NR37 of the Institute for Development Studies, University of Nairobi.* Wageningen, Netherlands: Afdelingen voor sociale wetenschappen van de Landbouwhogeschool, 1973.

Axinn, G. H. "A Conceptual Framework for Analysis of Communication in Rural Social Systems." Paper presented at the annual meeting of the Rural Sociological Society, Boston, Massachusetts, August 26, 1968.

Axinn, G. H. "A Strategy of Communication in the Development Process." Paper presented at the Society for International Development Eleventh World Conference, New Delhi, India, November 14–17, 1969.

Axinn, G. H. "Changing Perspectives on Rural Development." In *Approaches to Rural Development in Asia.* Kuala Lumpur, Malaysia: Asian Centre for Development Administration, 1975.

Axinn, G. H., and Thorat, S. S. *Modernizing World Agriculture: A Comparative Study of Agricultural Extension Education Systems.* New York: Praeger, 1972.

Bailey, J. C. *Seaman A. Knapp, Schoolmaster of American Agriculture.* New York: Columbia University Press, 1945.

Berlo, D. K. *The Process of Communication.* New York: Holt, Rinehart and Winston, 1960.

Bruner, E. de S., Sanders, E. T., and Ensminger, D. *Farmers of the World—The Development of Agricultural Extension.* New York: Columbia University Press, 1945.

Byrn, D. (Ed.) *Evaluation in Extension.* Topeka, Kansas: H. M. Ives, 1959.

Ekpere, J. A. "A Comparative Study of Job Performance Under Two Approaches to Agricultural Extension Organization in the Midwestern State of Nigeria." Unpublished doctoral dissertation, University of Wisconsin, Madison, 1973.

Henderson, T. H. "The University of the West Indies in Agricultural Extension Work in the Caribbean." *Agricultural Progress,* 1973, *48.*

Leagans, J. P., and Loomis, C. P. *Behavioral*

Change in Agriculture: Concepts and Strategies for Influencing Transition.* Ithaca, New York: Cornell University Press, 1971.

McCabe, M. S., and Swanson, B. E. *International Directory of Extension Organizations and Extension Training Institutions.* Madison, Wisconsin: Midwest Universities Consortium for International Activities, 1975.

McConnell, G. *The Decline of Agrarian Democracy.* New York: Atheneum, 1969.

Ogura, T. *Agricultural Development in Modern Japan.* Tokyo: Fuji, 1963.

Read, H. *Communication: Methods for All Media.* Urbana: University of Illinois Press, 1972.

Rice, E. G. *Extension in the Andes.* Washington, D.C.: Agency for International Development, 1971.

Rogers, E. M., and Shoemaker, F. *Communication of Innovations: A Cross-Cultural Approach.* New York: Free Press, 1968.

Savile, A. H. *Extension in Rural Communities.* London: Oxford University Press, 1966.

Stavis, B. *Making Green Revolution, The Politics of Agricultural Development in China.* Rural Development Committee, Monograph No. 1. Ithaca, New York: Cornell University Press, 1974.

Taylor, C. C., Ensminger, D., Johnson, H. W., and Joyce, J. *India's Roots of Democracy: A Sociological Analysis of Rural India's Experience in Planned Development Since Independence.* New York: Praeger, 1967.

Williams, D. B. *Agricultural Extension—Farm Extension Services in Australia, Britain, and the United States of America.* Melbourne, Australia: Melbourne University Press, 1968.

GEORGE H. AXINN

See also: Public Service Role of Higher Education.

3. AGRIBUSINESS AND AGRIBUSINESS EDUCATION

Recognition of agribusiness as a field of management education and research evolved from the work begun in 1952 in the Program in Business and Agriculture at Harvard University's Graduate School of Business Administration. The original objectives of that program were to "conduct studies of agricultural and industrial relationships through analyses of technical, economic, and human factors which govern these relationships, particularly the decision-making points, and stimulate sound action in the light of these studies so that industry and agriculture may contribute most efficiently toward meeting their responsibilities in our growing economy" (Graduate School of Business Administration, Harvard University, 1952). Thus from the start the focus was on the relationships that link production agriculture to the modern industrial economy.

The term *agribusiness* was coined in 1957 and defined as "the sum total of all operations involved in the manufacture and distribution of farm supplies; production operations on the farm; and the storage, processing and distribution of farm commodities and items made from them" (Davis and Goldberg, 1957). Simultaneously, the concept of total "agribusiness commodity system" emerged as the basic tool for research and analysis in the new field. This total system was conceived as including not only all the vertical stages through which a food or fiber product passes from initial farm input to ultimate consumer but also all the coordinating mechanisms that hold the system together and the environmental framework in which the process operates.

A direct and important interface exists between the systems approach to decision making and the content and organization of agribusiness management education programs in both advanced and emerging nations. To understand these programs, it is necessary to describe the nature of agribusiness commodity systems and their application to planning and policymaking.

Scope of Agribusiness

The field of agribusiness includes all agriculture and agriculture-related activities. It is designed to link farming with both the earlier stages of input procurement and the later stages of storage, processing, distribution, and marketing. The final outputs of agribusiness include all the food and fiber products consumed by the world's population. Within this broad definition, agribusiness possibly includes as much as 60 percent of total global business activity. The ratio is significantly higher in many developing countries, where pro-

duction agriculture is still the primary source of employment and income. Viewed in this way, agribusiness is concerned with mankind's most critical problems—providing an expanding population with an adequate, nutritionally balanced, and equitably priced supply of food. By far the major portion of human effort throughout history has been devoted to this task.

As the gap between "haves" and "have-nots" widens and the world approaches the limits of its physical resources, the need to improve food production and distribution on a global basis becomes ever more apparent. This is the area in which analysis of the vertical and horizontal relationships between agriculture and related economic activities is most needed and application of this knowledge is most critical.

Unique characteristics of agribusiness. The need for analyses of vertical and horizontal interactions is particularly great in agribusiness because of its unique agronomic characteristics, which are largely beyond the direct control of participants in the system. The timing of production depends on the specific requirements for planting and harvesting each individual plant or tree crop. Similarly, animal production is a function of livestock breeding cycles. The level of total farm output in any crop year depends, in large part, on the weather. The combination of these factors leads almost inevitably to cyclical and unpredictable fluctuations in supply. Since food consumption is relatively stable by comparison, the variations in supply result in frequent and serious supply-demand imbalances.

Furthermore, the demand for food tends to be relatively inelastic with respect to both income and price. In a free market economy, therefore, small changes in production usually produce much larger fluctuations in prices, especially at the farm level. The total gross income of farmers tends to decline as their aggregate output increases. Such results have proven to be unacceptable to farmers, consumers, and society as a whole.

One important consequence of this inherent instability is that governments play a more significant role in agribusiness than they do in most industrial systems, especially in developing nations. In many countries, for example, government institutions participate as partners with private investors in joint agricultural ventures. In almost all countries, developed as well as developing, government stabilization agencies buy, sell, and store basic farm commodities. The United States is the only major trading nation in which responsibility for agricultural exports and imports is primarily in the hands of private enterprise.

Agribusiness commodity systems. Because of its broad scope, the field of agribusiness is very complex. The concept of an agribusiness commodity system was developed as a means for coping with this complexity in both theory and application. Research, analysis, and policy development are feasible if the field can be disaggregated into specific commodity systems. Primary emphasis is thus placed on the interactions within the vertical structure for producing each individual farm commodity and marketing the food and fiber products derived from it, and on the relationship between each vertical structure and its social, political, and economic environment.

The purpose of an agribusiness commodity system is to satisfy the economic demands and nutritional needs of ultimate consumers. Such a system comprises four interrelated components: direct participants, coordinating mechanisms, external environment, and government.

The direct participants, who perform all the functional tasks required for the system to serve its basic purpose, include input supplier, farm producer, transport and storage operator, processor, distributor, wholesaler, retailer, and consumer. The fundamental assumption underlying the use of the system is that participants at all levels must be aware of the total structure of which they are a part and understand the interaction of its parts in order to develop effective policies and plans.

Perhaps the most distinctive characteristic of agribusiness commodity systems is the number and variety of coordinating mechanisms that have evolved to cope with uncertainty and link the stages of commodity flow. These mechanisms include such varied practices and institutions as open market prices, futures markets, contracts, vertical integration, cooperatives, cooperative-corporate joint ventures, financial and credit institutions, trade associations, and information sources. Particular coordinating devices vary greatly over time and from commodity to commodity depending on the stage of development, the nature of demand, and the sophistication of participants.

To develop workable coordinating machinery, both private managers and public administrators understand the external environmental frame in which a specific commodity system operates. The first step in using the systems approach as an aid to decision making is to assess the ways in which economic, social, political, or technological changes are likely to impact system performance. This task is more difficult and more essential during periods of rapid change, such as those that characterized world agribusiness since 1972–73.

In agribusiness, government is best treated as a distinct system component, performing at various times the functions of all other components—direct participant, coordinator, or external factor. Its influence ranges from establishing the broad economic and social climate in which agribusiness functions to enforcing specific detailed regulations. In few other areas of human endeavor is the need for public-private coordination so vital.

Agribusiness Management Education

The degree to which an agribusiness commodity system succeeds in providing consumers with high-quality food and fiber at affordable cost is basically a function of the level of human performance within the system. Since the systems approach argues that managers will perform more effectively if they understand the coordinated operation of the total system, it follows that their preparation for a managerial role must provide an opportunity to develop such understanding. Thus, the content and form of management education and training programs should be determined by and reflect the structure and dynamics of the commodity systems they are designed to serve.

The commodity system–education interface. In general, education related to agriculture has been largely technical in nature and heavily oriented toward the farm production stage of the system. This was and still is true even of many farm management courses, where the managerial content is relatively minor. On the other hand, general management students or business administrators rarely had the opportunity to analyze the unique problems arising in agribusiness.

The emphasis on technology at the farm level has been even more pronounced in research than in education and training. The impressive contributions of agricultural research to improved farm productivity are well documented. By contrast, relatively little has been done to improve the functioning of the forward stages of storage processing and distribution even technically, let alone in terms of a totally integrated management system.

Although courses and programs emphasizing a total systems approach have proliferated rapidly since the early 1960s in response to a growing need for better-trained managers, it is only very recently that conceptual tools designed specifically to translate the characteristics of specific commodity systems into requirements for management education have been developed. One study of the usefulness of an agribusiness commodity systems approach for the agricultural education system of Central America was undertaken by the Program in Business and Agriculture at Harvard's Graduate School of Business Administration, with the support of the United States Agency for International Development (AID) and recently published in book form (Goldberg and others, 1974). The five component steps of the study were (1) identification of key needs of the economy, (2) commodity systems approach to analysis of a specific agroindustry, (3) identification of problems, (4) delineation of educational needs, and (5) determination of educational content and methodology. Steps four and five, of course, interacted with the existing educational system and defined the need for the expansion of that system. Once the educational system became established, a program could be implemented.

Thus, the approach was based on identifying the problems and needs of a particular commodity system through a comprehensive analysis of its structure, dynamics, and performance within the overall social and economic priorities of the region. These were first stated in terms of basic educational priorities and then transformed into proposals for developing specific course materials and teaching methodologies.

Although the major emphasis was on managerial and administrative needs, one feature of the approach was the use of a systems concept to relate these needs to other job levels, including technicians, foremen, and laborers. Just as the performance of the commodity system itself depends on the coordination of its parts, the performance of the educational system supporting it depends on balancing the total training needs at all levels. The unique value of the educational-need matrix is that it provides a means to pinpoint those who need training and to delineate what their training needs are on the basis of actual problems confronted in their operations (Goldberg and others, 1974).

Characteristics of a systems approach to education. For both public and private managers, the most critical problems frequently derive from their need to understand the interrelated aspects which affect overall system behavior. It is possible to identify several distinguishing characteristics of an

Agriculture in Higher Education

effective systems approach to education which have emerged from both conceptual development and applied experience to date.

It is clear that a total education and training package should offer coordinated courses or programs for all stages of an operational commodity system and for all levels of the educational system. This, in turn, requires much closer cooperation and integration of activities among individual educational institutions than has been achieved in the past. Since the discipline is an integrative one, the educational delivery system must also be integrated.

To achieve the necessary total-system perspective, agribusiness education and research must adopt a market-oriented approach similar to that required of managers. Goals should be stated in terms of user needs rather than desired technological improvement. This requires recognition of national priorities and resource limitations as well as identification of problems of a specific commodity system.

The approach is also integrative among existing academic fields of inquiry; it uses methodology from courses in marketing, production, control, finance, managerial economics, human behavior, and other functional fields in combination with material from traditional offerings in farm management, agricultural production, agronomy, food science, and agricultural economics. Of particular interest is the merging of offerings from the new agribusiness area with established programs in economic development and nutrition.

Finally, a growing number of systems approach studies of individual commodities indicate clearly that the managerial requirements for skills in planning, coordination, and control are common to a diverse range of market structures, environmental conditions, and national objectives. These studies will provide the foundation for further development of agribusiness management education systems based on new conceptual constructs and a broader applied experience.

Agribusiness Management Programs

Three agribusiness management programs have been in operation long enough to provide some perspective on their performance in catering to a diverse clientele of present and future agribusiness leaders in markedly different environmental settings. These programs are located at Harvard University; Arthur D. Little, Inc., in Cambridge, Massachusetts; and the University of the Philippines in Manila.

Graduate School of Business Administration, Harvard University. Harvard's Program in Business and Agriculture was formally inaugurated in December 1952. As noted previously, it was through the work of this program that the term *agribusiness* was coined and the concept of an agribusiness commodity system developed. From its inception, the Harvard agribusiness program has been marked by a strong emphasis on applied research, the development of educational courses and materials for use in the master's and doctoral degree programs, and executive education seminars. Over more than two decades, the scope of the research activities has evolved from early pioneering work on conceptual development to more recent studies of specific United States and international commodity systems; the business, financial, and organizational aspects of farmer cooperatives; and the agribusiness and management education needs of developing countries. The interaction and mutual reinforcement of teaching and research represent a unique strength that has contributed significantly to Harvard's leadership position in agribusiness education.

The agribusiness courses in both the master's and doctoral programs are based on the premise that the ultimate purpose of an agribusiness system is to satisfy the economic needs of consumers and other system participants in a socially beneficial manner. Major emphasis is placed on the importance of market, as opposed to production, orientation, and overall system viability. The objective is to train decision makers, policymakers, and educators to develop and use a systematized conceptual perspective that stresses the roles played by the principal actors in a commodity system, the arrangements by which they coordinate their activities, and the environmental pressures that have impacts upon the system.

The agribusiness courses are offered to second-year M.B.A. students and have included one-semester courses in domestic and international agribusiness management, management of integrated firms in the food industry, relationships between government and business entities in agribusiness, simulation models applied to agribusiness decision making, and the preparation of agribusiness management research reports. Two doctoral agribusiness reading seminars are also offered in the D.B.A. program. Agribusiness at Harvard is viewed as an integrative field that draws heavily on the traditional functional areas of finance, marketing, business policy, and international trade. It also requires an understanding of logistics, managerial economics, and simulation models.

Both the degree programs and the executive education seminars offered in the United States and abroad make extensive use of the case method of teaching. Cases are developed to emphasize the vertical stages of a commodity system and the institutions that coordinate them. The focus is on decision-making problems faced by participants, administrators, coordinators, and policymakers. A major goal of the program is to continuously develop new and up-to-date case material from all areas of world agribusiness.

Arthur D. Little Management Education Institute. The Arthur D. Little, Inc., Program in Agro-Industrial and Industrial Development began in 1964 as an experiment with the express objective of serving the specialized training needs of government administrators in emerging economies. Today the company's Management Education Institute awards a Master of Science degree to candidates successfully completing the program. As it has grown, the Institute has maintained its unique specialization in catering to the needs of managers in developing economies, and its program is open to middle- and senior-level managers or administrators in government, private industry, and multinational organizations, or to people planning careers in this field.

Because of its economic development orientation, the program strives to provide participants with an understanding of basic management disciplines within the context of national priorities, and their relationship to corporate policies, incentives, and investments. To accomplish this, the program emphasizes relevance, practicality, and application, all built upon an initial foundation of economic and administrative theory. Professionals with extensive actual experience participate in case studies and simulation exercises.

Agribusiness management is offered during the final phase of the program, which is designed to integrate and apply skills from the standpoint of management practice and national economic planning. The agribusiness course focuses on understanding the nature of food systems and their management and analyzing strategic and operational problems of public and private sector agribusiness institutions, and emphasizes the role of agribusiness in the economic development process. Stress is placed on the coordinating mechanisms that link exports of basic commodities from producer countries to world markets. A combination of lectures, cases, and actual field analyses is used. Because of the importance of agroindustry in the development process, cases and simulation exercises offered in other functional areas of the program reflect a significant agribusiness orientation.

University of the Philippines. One of the earliest comprehensive agribusiness education programs outside the United States was established at the University of the Philippines. At the undergraduate level, the university offers a program requiring two years in the College of Business Administration and three in the College of Agriculture. The curriculum is oriented toward training based on case material prepared in the division of research, and is oriented toward Philippine agribusiness conditions.

An interesting aspect of the development of agribusiness management education in the Philippines is the growth of cooperation among institutions within the Philippines and the Southeast Asian region as a whole. The four leading Philippine universities, for example, have formed an Inter-University Steering Committee for Agribusiness, the purpose of which is to interchange faculty and teaching materials, thus facilitating a more rapid expansion of agribusiness education programs. Another cooperative venture is the Southeast Asia Regional Center for Agriculture, which was organized as a joint project of the ministries of education in seven countries to develop a regional agribusiness training and research center. This center operates in conjunction with the Asian Institute of Management, which is already established as a regional graduate school.

To provide the training necessary to develop professional competence in agricultural business and management, the Graduate School of Business of the University of the Philippines offers a master's degree in agricultural business management. The two-year graduate program uses a commodity system orientation stressing those aspects of decision making unique to agribusiness. The program is designed for persons with experience or interest in private agroindustry, as well as for public officials concerned with agribusiness.

The agribusiness content of the master's program includes courses in advanced farm management, which builds on the undergraduate program; introduction to agribusiness, which identifies problems and opportunities in the major Philippine commodity systems; agribusiness management, which emphasizes integrative arrangements that relate a firm to its markets and the institutional setting of agroindustry; economics of marketing Philippine farm commodities in domestic and international markets; and public problems in agriculture, which provides a critical analysis of government programs. Various methods of instruction are employed, with heavy emphasis on the case method.

Future Developments

World food supplies and prices have been more unstable since 1972 than at any other time during the last forty years. This has caused a growing concern over basic global capacity to meet the future food demands of an expanding and more affluent population. Although chronic food shortages in any absolute sense do not appear to be a real threat in the near future, recent developments have created enormous pressures for change in world food and agribusiness systems.

Of the many issues facing private and public policymakers in food industries, five appear to be significant in their implications for the future direction of agribusiness education: (1) the accomplishment of a large-scale transition from subsistence to commercial agriculture in the developing countries; (2) the emergence of new organizational structures as the result of the continued industrialization of farming in developed economies; (3) the implications for the future behavior and control of agribusiness commodity systems resulting from economic pressures leading to further concentration of food distribution and marketing; (4) the adoption of new policies for stabilizing international commodity markets; and (5) the establishment of roles to be played by private and public institutions to adapt to these changes.

Although discussion of these fundamental issues is not within the scope of this article, it is possible to delineate some of the implications for future agribusiness management education programs. Predominant is the concept that a national or regional perspective is no longer adequate. Educators and managers alike increasingly recognize that they are part of a global agribusiness system. Recent fluctuations in world commodity and energy prices have dramatically illustrated the interdependent nature of commodity systems in exporting and importing countries. Future educational programs must reflect these interdependencies.

The increasingly global nature of agribusiness also points to the need for developing new coordinating mechanisms on an international basis. It is particularly important for planners and policymakers in the private and public sectors of both developed and developing countries to work closely together in solving the critical problems of providing adequate food consumption and nutrition for all the world's population.

Nowhere is the disparity between haves and have-nots more apparent than in their relative shares of global food supplies. While developed countries have been increasing both the level and quality of per capita food consumption, less developed countries are still faced with chronic malnutrition and the threat of mass starvation when crop failures occur. Furthermore, despite their efforts to achieve self-sufficiency, the poorer countries have become increasingly dependent on the richer ones for their food supplies. Unless progress can be made in halting or reversing these trends, confrontations between rich and poor countries could escalate dangerously. Solutions appear to depend as much on policy decisions as on a technical capacity to increase food production. A critical challenge facing agribusiness educators is the need to develop new mechanisms for the international transfer of agricultural technology on a basis that is relevant to the social, cultural, and economic realities of those areas with food deficits.

Bibliography

Davis, J. H., and Goldberg, R. A. *A Concept of Agribusiness.* Cambridge, Massachusetts: Graduate School of Business Administration, Harvard University, 1957.

Goldberg, R. A., and others. *Agribusiness Management for Developing Countries—Latin America.* Cambridge, Massachusetts: Ballinger, 1974.
Graduate School of Business Administration, Harvard University. *Advisory Committee to Program in Business and Agriculture.* Cambridge, Massachusetts: Graduate School of Business Administration, Harvard University, 1952.

LEONARD M. WILSON

4. INTERNATIONAL COOPERATION IN AGRICULTURE

A global approach to agricultural problems through international cooperation has become an accepted process. Governments throughout the world are increasingly aware of the need to share scientific agricultural knowledge if they are to contend with the constant threat of famine faced by hundreds of millions of their populations. This awareness has led to cooperative food conferences, studies of global food production and distribution, and the international involvement of educational institutions.

On December 4, 1974, the President of the United States requested the National Academy of Sciences to assume leadership in a two-year assessment of the world food and nutrition problem and to make recommendations for its solution. In an interim report made in November 1975, the study's steering committee recommended, among other things, a strengthening of existing educational programs and the establishment of new ones. Specifically, the proposal called for the expansion of post–high school training in the agricultural sciences, of doctoral research on food and nutritional problems, and of postdoctoral training in agricultural research and operational project work (Handler, 1975).

These recommendations of the National Academy of Sciences illustrate that the solutions to agricultural problems depend upon a concerted program of research, education, and international cooperation. Hopefully these recommendations will be followed to add to the effectiveness of current programs.

Development of the Exchange of Agricultural Knowledge

The exchange of agricultural information may have originated with nomadic tribes that carried with them their ideas on plant cultivation and animal husbandry. With the coming of commerce, conquest, and colonization, the frequency of such exchanges increased. The oldest pictographs found in the Middle East, featuring grains, wines, and oils, indicate an early interest in agriculture. The Greeks and Romans sent farmers into their new territories to improve local agriculture, and the Romans built irrigation systems all over their expanded dominions. Later, merchants from Baghdad, Cairo, Athens, Venice, Genoa, and Lisbon brought spices, teas, and silks to Europe and the Near East from the Orient.

As colonization spread to the Americas, the crossbreeding of animals and plants was accelerated. More than two thirds of North and South American plant life and all its domesticated animals bear imported genes. Such crossbreeding must follow on all continents as international cooperation in agriculture proceeds (Porter, 1967).

Early institutes and botanical gardens. Agricultural research institutes and botanical gardens developed in the Middle Ages, when famine was commonplace in Europe and monarchs sent forth expeditions to foreign lands to find and stabilize food supplies. At this time agricultural higher education began in the form of correspondence among men of letters who had commercial interests in the import of food and other agricultural products such as indigo, cotton, tobacco, and lumber. This correspondence was soon followed by the exchange and testing of botanical materials.

Later, Great Britain became a leader in the establishment of agricultural institutes. Its London Office of Information describes colonial efforts: "The establishment of botanic gardens in many overseas countries, where new improved strains of crop plants were grown to ascertain their suitability for local conditions, followed on the establishment [in 1841] of the Royal Botanic Gardens at Kew. This early step to assist agriculture in tropical countries has proved of great significance in the subsequent growth of agriculture in the Far East. Botanic gardens were usually placed in charge of men with *botanical training,* often from Kew, many of whom exerted a strong influence in the countries in which they worked" *(Britain and the Developing Countries,* 1966, p. 7).

Most other colonial powers had comparable exchanges with their dependent territories. The Netherlands Botanical Garden at Bogor, Indonesia, matched the British garden in Calcutta, India; the Belgians maintained a similar garden at Yangambi, Zaire. The famous State Agricultural University at Wageningen, Netherlands, with its widely patronized International Agricultural Center (which welcomed 1159 guests from ninety-two countries in 1974), is typical of what has evolved from these early efforts in exchanges.

Through most of the nineteenth century, scientists trained in the institutes and universities of Europe. To a lesser degree North America provided scientific leadership in the colonies. But a scientific approach to agriculture was slow to develop at all educational centers.

Land-grant colleges in the United States. At the time of the American Revolution in 1776, 90 percent of the population of the United States was engaged in farming. Two hundred years later less than 10 percent of its population followed agricultural pursuits. This shift from self-sufficient family farming to highly commercial and industrialized agriculture placed a growing burden on the science of farming and a consequent burden on the educational institutions which might provide that science.

By far the most important institutional development of the nineteenth century was the creation, by President Abraham Lincoln (1809–1865) in 1862, of the United

States Department of Agriculture and the land-grant college system. The schools and research stations of this land-grant system were later to become a focal point for world agricultural science. For example, during the nineteenth century scientists from Cornell University assisted in the creation of a school of agricultural science at Nanking, China, and, following an initiative of the United States Commissioner of Agriculture, the Massachusetts Agricultural College established a similar school in Hokkaido, Japan.

The nineteenth century witnessed a steady development across North America of schools that taught agricultural science. In these schools researchers received and resolved agricultural production problems as part of a cycle that moved those research results into the discipline concerned and spread the resulting knowledge to ever more farmers. The thirst of a great and growing agriculture for the science and scientists it needed was successful in creating an institutional base that soon demanded world prominence and, in many respects, preeminence.

Many land-grant institutions, such as Cornell University, imported European scientists to help develop their curricula and formalize disciplines. Well into the twentieth century most of the leading professors of the land-grant colleges were spending some time in French, German, and other European schools.

Expanded programs. The early twentieth century saw the consolidation of the United States land-grant universities and colleges into an impressive educational system of the greatest collection of agricultural resources in the world. The more complex farm production became, the greater were the demands on the land-grant institutions to provide scientific support to agriculture. As farms became larger, more prospective farmers went to college and stayed there longer to gain the added scientific knowledge required by modern farming. To further increase its effectiveness, the land-grant system added an extension service in 1914 that made both adult education and field services more accessible to farmers. The agricultural recession of the 1920s and 1930s forced scientists to develop new methods of increasing agricultural productivity and helped to establish numerous aids to education and agriculture, including extensive credit arrangements, direct aids for the improvement of farm practices, increased support for teaching and research staffs, and considerable financial assistance to students.

The fame and preeminence in agricultural science of the United States land-grant system attracted students and postdoctoral trainees from all over the world. These students, in turn, added to the scientific capacity of the system. Specialized colleges for agriculture were created by many other countries. The British set up research centers and schools of agriculture in India such as those at Delhi, Poona, Kanpur, Nagpur, Lyallpur, Coimbatore, and Sabour. In the Caribbean, tropical agricultural research centers were established in Barbados and Trinidad. These British-sponsored research centers were patterned in part after the agricultural school and soil science station that Sir John B. Lawes (1814–1900) established privately in 1843 at Rothamsted, England. Despite the prominence of agricultural science in the United States, research in tropical and subtropical agriculture still depends heavily on centers created by the European colonial powers (*Britain and the Developing Countries,* 1966).

Early international studies of the economic aspects of agriculture. During the nineteenth century many countries, because of increased global trade, began to recognize the importance of economic research and statistics. Most early economics was based on agriculture that was thought to be the only source of useful quantitative data. To meet global demands for better economic information, the International Institute of Statistics was organized in London in 1885 and thereafter met biennially.

As early as 1889 Jeremiah M. Rusk, the

United States Secretary of Agriculture, stressed the need for information on worldwide production and consumption of agricultural products. This need in part reflected the uncertain market for increasing United States agricultural exports, which were becoming an important source of foreign exchange. In addition, the war of 1898 gave the United States fruitful investment opportunities in foreign agricultural development, particularly in the Philippines and the Caribbean.

Three notable initiatives in the field of economics and statistics provided the groundwork for an explosion of worldwide activity in agricultural science. First, the International Cooperative Alliance was formed in 1902 in Manchester, England, as an outgrowth of several socialist-oriented cooperative movements sponsored largely by labor organizations in the interest of consumers. Parallel cooperative movements developed in Scandinavia, Great Britain, and parts of the United States. Second, the International Institute of Agriculture, conceived by David Lubin (1849–1919) and proposed to the International Agricultural Congress held in Budapest in 1896, was established in Rome in 1905. Third, in 1929 the International Conference of Agricultural Economists was created at Dartington Hall, Devon, England, by Leonard Knight Elmhirst (1893–1975), whose studies at Cornell had convinced him that the new discipline of agricultural economics should have an international scope.

The International Institute of Agriculture was highly active, eventually employing a staff of over one hundred men and women of some thirty different nationalities. The institute published several series of journals, monographs, yearbooks, and special reports in both French and English. In 1930 and again in 1940 it attempted a world census of agriculture, and perhaps its most effective activities were the biennial general assemblies and special meetings held at various locations across Europe. It never did achieve, however, Lubin's

prime aim of making commodity intelligence so widely available that speculation controlled by insiders could not absorb the investments of less knowledgeable men (Yates, 1955). A half century after its founding, the Institute was absorbed by the Food and Agriculture Organization (FAO) of the United Nations.

International Programs

World leadership in agriculture is shared by the United States and Canada, the European Community, and multilaterally by the Food and Agriculture Organization of the United Nations.

FAO. The FAO sponsors a broad educational program that features agricultural training and seminars. It also sponsors a fellowship program related to technical assistance projects. The FAO employs nearly four thousand professionals drawn from its 136 member nations. The training programs of the FAO are coordinated with the activities of the World Bank, the World Health Organization, the United Nations Development Programme, and the United Nations Educational, Scientific and Cultural Organization (UNESCO). These programs take place at universities, colleges, and other facilities of the member nations. In particular, extensive use has been made of North American educational institutions. The FAO concentrates on six program areas: reducing food losses both in the field and in storage, increasing the production of protein foods, extending the cultivation of high-yielding crop varieties, improving foreign exchange earnings and savings in developing countries, improving the economic and social conditions of rural people, and raising the level of planning for agricultural development. The FAO has convened world food congresses and assisted in the World Food Conference of 1974. This organization is a major technical forum for world agriculture and is jointly responsible with the United Nations for the World Food Program.

IFAP. A year after the establishment of FAO, an international organization of farmers known as the International Federation of Agricultural Producers (IFAP) was formed. In effect, IFAP has the same relationship to FAO that a national farm organization has to a national department or ministry of agriculture. It is an agricultural pressure group serving the interests of farmers around the world. Its policies deal with matters of direct economic importance to its members as well as with improvement of agriculture and farm life in developing countries. One of its key positions is that the spread of general education is fundamental to the adoption of modern agricultural techniques on a large scale.

Bilateral programs. Bilateral education and training programs play a major role in agricultural development, although historically these programs have been increasingly influenced by the policies of the United Nations and its specialized agencies. Countries active in the bilateral development process of agriculture include the United States, Canada, Denmark, France, the Federal Republic of Germany, Israel, Japan, the People's Republic of China, the Republic of China, Sweden, and the United Kingdom.

Owing in part to the significant strength of its agricultural colleges, the United States has been a leader in providing training fellowships to foreign students as well as in assisting in the creation of educational institutions around the world. One of its most striking achievements was a cooperative effort with India that, since 1952, has resulted in the creation of nine Indian universities patterned after the United States land-grant colleges. The first of these Indian universities, Uttar Pradesh Agricultural University at Pant Nagar in Uttar Pradesh, was established in 1960 through the joint efforts of the United States Agency for International Development (AID) and the University of Illinois. The University of Illinois also assisted in the establishment of the Jawaharlal Nehru Agricultural University in Madhya Pradesh in 1964. Ohio State University took part in

the establishment of the University of Udaipur in the state of Rajasthan in 1962, the Punjab Agricultural University in the state of Punjab in 1962, and the Haryana Agricultural University in the state of Haryana in 1970. Kansas State University assisted in creating Andhra Pradesh Agricultural University at Rajendranagar in the state of Andhra Pradesh in 1964. The University of Missouri took part in founding the Orissa University of Agriculture and Technology at Bhubaneswar in the state of Orissa in 1962. Pennsylvania State University was active in organizing the Marathwada Agricultural University in the state of Maharashtra in 1967, and the University of Tennessee was involved in the development of the Mysore University of Agricultural Sciences in the state of Mysore in 1963. During this process of establishing Indian universities, more than three hundred staff members of the United States land-grant colleges worked in India, and more than one thousand Indian faculty members and graduate students studied in the United States. The growth of these Indian agricultural universities has been very rapid. By 1973 their professional staffs had tripled, enrollments had more than doubled, and graduate enrollments had increased sixfold (Read, 1974, Table 10).

Both the Ford and Rockefeller Foundations cooperated in the Indian agricultural university projects. The development of agriculture and education has been a significant goal of the assistance programs for developing countries of these foundations. For example, roughly half of the Ford Foundation's assistance to India between 1950 and 1974 was for agricultural and educational purposes. The importance of the relationship between education, agriculture, and governmental action was summed up by the Ford Foundation's senior agricultural adviser: "Whether or not a national capacity in science and technology is created depends to a considerable degree on the educational and science policies adopted. Effective national policies are the direct responsibility of sovereign nations. Thus, the necessity for indigenous capacity to formulate, execute and evaluate policies and programs" (Hardin, 1974, p. 9).

The Indian projects have had their counterparts in many other parts of the world. In 1968 AID reported sixty-eight institutional building projects undertaken by United States universities in the following regions: Africa, sixteen; Far East, twelve; Latin America, twenty-four; and South Asia, sixteen.

Nearly fifty years before the American involvement in India the British Colonial Office had opened several large research centers in that country and set up "colleges to teach agricultural science with the object of providing scientifically trained indigenous staff for the State Agricultural Departments and, by linking teaching with research into regional problems, preparing students for their future duties" *(Britain and the Developing Countries, 1966, p. 11)*. This concept was very similar to the American land-grant college concept of teaching agricultural research and providing adult education to apply the results of research programs.

Although few developing countries have matched the number of specialized agricultural universities created in India, substantial and perhaps more rapid progress in this area has been achieved in countries such as Israel, the Republic of Korea, the Philippines, and the Republic of China. Generally more and more developing countries will be relying upon foreign training only for doctoral specialization and postdoctoral training. Vocational and undergraduate needs will be met by local institutions. That this shift may already be under way is indicated by the decreasing numbers of participants in United States training fellowships.

The creation of indigenous institutions has been a difficult but necessary first step in developing more effective methods of transferring technology to the smallest and weakest of the world's farmers. Language and other cultural barriers make higher education and graduate training

in foreign countries available only to the brightest and often the most fortunate citizens. Language will remain a problem in many countries where literacy is low or difficult languages and multiple dialects limit scientific exchange. Language difficulties are a critical aspect of agricultural development as illiteracy is more pervasive in rural areas.

Private programs. A number of major private institutions provide regional centers for agricultural education and research, among them the American University of Beirut; Ward College of Buenos Aires; and more recently established, the International School of Agricultural Sciences at the University of Naples. Training centers sponsored by multinational corporations are also scattered around the globe, some with a singular objective, such as the hybrid seed stations of Cargill at Pergamino, Argentina, and Asgrow at Cremona, Italy. The spread of industrialized agriculture has given added impetus to other research centers, particularly in the mechanical and petrochemical fields. Shell Oil Company has a petrochemical training station at Borgo a Mazzano, Italy, to which it brings technicians from the Middle East and Africa. The Fiat Automotive Company operates a similar training station for farm machinery technicians in Turin, Italy. Courses cover not only the theory of such practices as pest control and water conservation but also the field application of newer techniques *(Italconsult, 1967)*.

International Research in Agriculture

It has been postulated that world food production must be doubled by the year 2000 to meet the needs of an expanding population and that most of that increase in production must come from within the developing countries themselves by improving the productivity of land already under cultivation. It has been further suggested that a greater utilization of existing international agricultural research organizations would be an important approach to the achievement of these goals.

CGIAR. The Consultative Group on International Agricultural Research (CGIAR) operates in twenty-nine countries and enjoys the support of the FAO, the World Bank, the United Nations Development Programme, and major foundations. It was formed in 1971 to promote the Green Revolution—a worldwide effort to expand food production by adapting and spreading technology to the developing areas. CGIAR today sponsors a dozen major centers located in developing countries. These centers attempt to deal with the major problems that must be solved if food production in the poorest parts of the world is to be increased.

CGIAR centers develop joint research programs with national research groups in their host countries. Most centers are situated near a university where joint programs and training can best be carried on. They can also call upon leading scientists throughout the world for assistance.

Among the crops under study at the centers are rice, maize, wheat, potatoes, grain, legumes, sorghum, millet, and cassava. Tropical agriculture in both humid and semiarid areas is studied at three additional centers, and two other centers are devoted to the study of animal husbandry. CGIAR centers conduct research of the highest quality and enjoy strong associations with national and regional research institutions in other parts of the world. They also carry on sophisticated training programs and assist in the local training of research scientists and production workers. Among the successes of the centers to date are the development, improvement, and propagation of the short-stem rices and wheats and high-protein corn.

A need for coordination. The effective coordination of international agricultural research and training is an extremely complex process. Literally hundreds of institutions throughout the world are engaged in such programs, with relatively few safeguards against duplication of effort (Overseas Liaison Committee, 1973). Nor does a satisfactory method of correlating research results exist. In an effort to correct

this situation FAO has initiated two programs: AGRIS, which is an attempt to record all agricultural documentation; and CARIS, which concerns itself with the recording of current agricultural research.

International Cooperation

A prototype of international cooperation was the Marshall Plan for European reconstruction after World War II. The Marshall Plan, also known as the European Recovery Program (ERP), eventually led to the formation of the Organisation for Economic Co-operation and Development (OECD). Proposed by General George Catlett Marshall (1880–1959). United States Secretary of State, the plan was a multibillion-dollar general program of economic aid to post–World War II Europe. Its impact was unusually large and swift because of the substantial technical base and relatively high level of education in the cooperating countries. Heavy investments in agriculture resulted in some of the sharpest improvements in technology the world has ever seen. In Italy the maize crop was almost completely hybridized in five years by using adapted and locally developed seeds. Across Europe cereal production was modernized and industrialized to the point of transforming a crop deficit into a crop surplus. To accomplish these improvements, hundreds of training centers were established in the cooperating European countries, and thousands of European students went to the United States and other countries for training in new skills. Most of these centers were eventually absorbed by European educational institutions, and their work is still being carried on by universities in Louvain, Belgium; Lyon, France; Wageningen, Netherlands; Naples and Bergamo, Italy; and Oxford, Cambridge, Reading, and Newcastle, England.

Cooperation in trade and investment. Wide fluctuations in agricultural commodity prices, and consequently exchange earnings, have brought about several international meetings aimed at normalizing agricultural trade and promoting reasonable investment to ensure more adequate food supplies. In 1948 an international meeting at governmental level was held in Havana to attempt an institutional approach to these problems by creating an organization to be known as the International Trade Organization (ITO). Led by the United States, the meeting postponed a decision on ITO and created instead a General Agreement on Tariffs and Trade (GATT).

In 1964 the developing countries created a United Nations Conference on Trade and Development, and in 1975, impatient with that institution, they resolved in the United Nations to create a New International Economic Order (United Nations, 1974). This resolution stated that the fruits of world production had to be more equitably distributed, regardless of the economic concepts that must be altered.

The World Bank Group, consisting of the International Bank for Reconstruction and Development and its affiliates, is having an increasing influence on agriculture not only in the number and quality of its projects but also in the proportion of its funds invested in agriculture. In addition, the World Bank and the International Monetary Fund support agriculture through their assistance in the creation of educational and research centers (McNamara, 1975). Such involvement has been in response to the constantly increasing need for food to meet the needs of a growing population and the dependence of large parts of the developing world on agriculture for their livelihood. Thus, if the developing nations are to be helped, their agricultural programs must be supported.

Future Cooperation

International cooperation in agriculture must increase steadily in response to the demands of an exploding world population, the probability that renewable plant life will become a more important source of energy, and the increasing scientific complexity of agriculture. Effective policies of cooperation will necessarily involve the expansion of higher education, the improvement of research techniques, and an effective program to generate public awareness of the need for cooperation.

Educational and professional organizations have demonstrated an ability to cooperate on an international basis to develop genuine agricultural improvements. Attempts to develop an effective structure of economic and political cooperation have met with less success, and international cooperation in economic or political matters bearing upon agriculture requires much improvement.

Bibliography

Britain and the Developing Countries. London: Central Office of Information, 1966.

Consultative Group on Agricultural Research. *International Research in Agriculture.* New York: United Nations Development Programme, 1974.

Department of Information. *A Short History of the Agricultural University at Wageningen.* Wageningen, Netherlands: State Agricultural University, 1976.

Economic Research Service. *Foreign Agriculture Training Activities Annual Statistical Summary, 1975.* Washington, D.C.: U.S. Department of Agriculture, 1975.

Food and Agriculture Organization of the United Nations. *Report of the World Food Conference to the 29th Session of the General Assembly of the United Nations.* New York: FAO, 1974. Document E/5587.

Food and Agriculture Organization of the United Nations. *Resolutions Adopted by the World Food Conference.* Rome: FAO, 1974. Document 64/INF/12.

Handler, P. *World Food and Nutrition Study; Interim Report.* Washington, D.C.: National Academy of Sciences, 1975.

Hardin, L. S. *Ford Foundation Agricultural Programs: Observations and Issues.* Edited reprint of presentations at Ford Foundation Seminars, Ibadan, Nigeria, April 29–May 3, 1974; and Chengmai, Thailand, May 8–10, 1974.

Italconsult, 1957–1967, Società generale per progettazioni, consulenze e partecipazioni. Milan: Istituto grafico Vanzetti e Vanaletti, March 1967.

McNamara, R. S. *Address to the Board of Governors.* Washington, D.C.: International Bank for Reconstruction and Development, 1975.

Overseas Liaison Committee. *International*

Directory for Educational Liaison. Washington, D.C.: American Council on Education, 1973.

Porter, J. "Origins of Technical Assistance in Agriculture." Unpublished papers prepared for the Economic Research Service, United States Department of Agriculture, 1967.

Read, H. *Partners with India.* Champaign-Urbana: University of Illinois, College of Agriculture, 1974.

United Nations. *New International Economic Order, Declaration and Programme of Action on the Establishment of.* New York: Special Resolution 3202 of the Sixth Special Session of the General Assembly, May 16, 1974.

United States Agency for International Development. *Institution Building: A Source Book.* Washington, D.C.: U.S. Department of State, 1974.

United States Department of Agriculture, Office of Information. *Century of Service: The First 100 Years of the United States Department of Agriculture.* Washington, D.C.: U.S. Government Printing Office, 1963.

Winzer, K. *Agriculture in the Federal Republic of Germany.* Bonn–Bad Godesberg, Federal Republic of Germany: Federal Ministry for Food, Agriculture and Forestry, 1971.

Wortman, S. *Strategies for Agricultural Education in Developing Countries.* New York: Rockefeller Foundation, 1976.

Yates, P. L. *So Bold an Aim—Ten Years of International Cooperation Toward Freedom from Want.* Rome: Stabilimento tipografico Fausto Failini, 1955.

ROBERT C. TETRO

See also: Aid to Other Nations.

AID TO OTHER NATIONS

1. INTERNATIONAL COOPERATION—
OVERVIEW

2. COLONIAL POLICIES AND PRACTICES

3. BILATERAL PARTICIPATION IN
HIGHER EDUCATION

4. MULTINATIONAL CORPORATIONS
AND LATERAL AID

5. TECHNOLOGY TRANSFER

1. INTERNATIONAL COOPERATION—
OVERVIEW

International cooperation substitutes education for the gun and club as the principal power for transmuting the real world to a more nearly ideal one. Higher education contributes to international cooperation, although informal contacts outside the structures of formal education in economic, technical, political, social, and religious fields may expand human understanding as much as, if not more than, conventional colleges and universities. The impact of the growing interaction that has resulted from the technological and communications revolutions may be one of the most characteristic features of the modern era.

History and Growth of
International Cooperation

The impulse to transcend nationality in the discovery and expansion of knowledge is almost as old as formal learning itself. Migration of the master teacher was a common practice of the early cultures, East and West. Knowledge grew by natural exchange, the impulse to know what lay over the hill.

In the early formal academies of the tribal or royal courts bordering the Mediterranean and in the comparable "schools" of Asia, students were drawn from distant lands, and information exchange was a common practice. With the dispersion of religious communities in the ensuing centuries, knowledge was cradled, conserved, and ultimately created and shared beyond national boundaries, and with global intent. The manner in which the Hebraic, Christian, and Islamic traditions fostered and replicated educational institutions, traditions, and knowledge is well known. The same is true for Hindi, Buddhist, and other traditions of the East.

The missionary outreach in educational, medical, agricultural, and scientific fields has been invaluable in the training of indigenous leadership and in developing an infrastructure in communications, languages, and skills. Many of the earliest educational efforts in the emerging nations were mission supported; and leadership in many newly independent nations came from this early training.

A succession of modern wars, the post-war aftermath of urgent, unsolved human, and therefore global, problems; and the resources and promise of an international technological and communications link—all have ushered into this century, and accelerated since World War II, a new era of international cooperation in higher education. The creation of UNESCO, with its comprehensive purpose "to contribute to peace and security by promoting collaboration among the nations through education, science, and culture in order to further universal respect for justice, for the rule of law, and for the human rights and fundamental freedoms which are affirmed for the peoples of the world, without distinction of race, sex, language, or religion, by the Charter of the United Nations," gathers up a whole array of initiatives in this field (*World of Learning*, 1975, p. 13). UNESCO incorporated the International Bureau of Education (founded in 1925) in 1969 and established the International Institute for Educational Planning in 1963. It works closely with the International Council of Scientific Unions, founded in 1931 and comprised of sixteen unions, nine committees, and seven commissions (*World of Learning*, 1975, p. 17).

UNESCO collaborates as well with the International Council for Philosophy and Humanistic Studies, founded in Paris in 1949 under UNESCO auspices and comprised of thirteen philosophical and humanistic unions (*World of Learning*, 1975, p. 20). In 1950 it encouraged founding of the International Association of Universities, with 699 members in 111 countries (*World of Learning*, 1975, p. 22).

The creation of the United Nations University, headquartered in Tokyo, by the General Assembly of the United Nations in December 1972 marks the latest of these sustained and systematic efforts to link the countries of the world by a network of research and educational institutions aimed at international cooperation in addressing the critical issues of human survival. The early 1970s has seen the establishment of both global and regional organizations for international cooperation on the environment, the seas, international law, human rights, literacy, and educational planning.

Types of International Cooperation

The accelerated climate of cooperation—fed by the contact, travel, commerce, communications, and cultural flow of people and knowledge characteristic of the second half of the twentieth century—infuses virtually every type of educational impact. Cultural tours, short- and long-termed, academic and nonacademic, are popular features of travel and governmental agencies and are included in the outreach and nontraditional functions of colleges and universities throughout the world.

Faculty and student exchanges. The exchange of faculty and students, sustained in some countries by national legislation and in others by private foundations and grants, continues to accelerate. According to the Institute of International Education, the number of foreign students in the United States alone has gone from 6500 in 1921–22, to 121,363 in 1968–69, to 219,721 in 1975. Reciprocally, United States students going abroad have increased from 9877 in 1955–56 to 39,800 in 1973–74. An equal acceleration has occurred in most other countries.

Study-abroad programs, in which groups of students, with or without resident instructors from their own colleges and universities, live and study in other countries, were popular in the 1950s and 1960s in the United States and, in some measure, in Western European nations. Critics have classified these programs as academic enclaves or foreign ghettos, and immersion into the real culture of the visiting nation has often been minimal. Modified versions of the programs that disperse the group into homes and encourage more direct contact with the foreign culture have sustained their growth.

Lecturing and teaching exchange programs, conducted on a worldwide basis, have also fostered international cooperation in education. For example, the Mutual Educational and Cultural Exchange program, popularly known as the Fulbright program, has provided funds for United States lecturers to travel and teach abroad and has also offered travel grants to foreign teachers to enable them to visit colleges and universities in the United States. The British Council offers similar awards to encourage the interchange of teachers in Western and Eastern Europe.

Research. Research efforts are growing rapidly. They are fostered by a wide variety of organizations and agencies; internationally, by the United Nations and UNESCO agencies and functions; regionally, by such commissions and associations as the Council for Cultural Co-operation of the Council of Europe. International professional associations sponsor research programs, and there is much interinstitutional, interprofessional, and personal research, particularly in the fields of agriculture, energy, space, and habitat.

Exchange of research information is, for the most part, confined to national or regional interests. Though governments and private agencies and organizations engage in information services, these are often self-serving and lack the overlay of objectivity that educational research and instruction bring. The International Council for Educational Development of New York maintains a data bank and informational system on educational programs; and the University of Pittsburgh provides an International and Development Education Clearinghouse.

Business and industry. Business and industry, both national and multinational, are generating new forms of international cooperation. In the field of management education, for example, many international links have been forged. Multinational corporations have established their own schools and have joined together in cooperative efforts to educate their managers at institutes such as the *Centre d'études industrielles* (CEI: International Management Development Institute) in Geneva.

Overseas subsidiaries of American corporations contribute to education in their foreign locations. Ford Motor Company has been responsible for building schools in Latin America, and International Business Machines (IBM) has built scientific centers around the world.

Sport. One of the oldest forms of international cooperation is sport, exemplified by the Olympic Games. The games reflect the Greek ideal of education as embodied in the balanced development of body, mind and soul—the integration of the gymnasium, academe, and temple.

The international university. Even as cooperation centers around the interactions of our natural, human, symbolic, and ideal worlds, so the types of cooperation in these areas suggest their own mechanisms. The university, that instrument of self-criticism and self-renewal, is the most comprehensive and logical instrument of cooperation. New experiments in many nations—such as the Friends World College in the United States, the Patrice Lumumba People's Friendship University in the Soviet Union, Nordenfjord World University in Denmark, and the already mentioned United Nations University—attest to the vitality and imagination of new forms of international education.

Bibliography

Association of World Colleges and Universities. *Report of the Conference on Alternative Designs for World Universities (Nordenfjord World University, Denmark, August 19–25, 1973).* New York: Association of World Colleges and Universities, 1973.

Becker, J. M. *Teaching International Relations.* Boulder, Colorado: ERIC Clearinghouse for Social Studies/Social Science Education, 1972.

Boehm, E. H. *Bibliographies on International Relations and World Affairs: An Annotated Directory.* Santa Barbara, California: ABC-Clio, 1965.

Brickman, W. M. "In Retrospect, 1965–75." *International Educational and Cultural Exchange,* 1975, *11*(1), 31–36.

Cancino, F. C. "A Regional Convention on the Recognition of Diplomas." *Prospects,* 1975, *5*(2), 265–268.

Cellarius, R. A., and Platt, J. "Councils of

Urgent Studies." *Science,* 1972, *177*(4050), 670–676.

Cerych, L. *A Global Approach to Higher Education.* Occasional Paper No. 3. New York: International Council for Educational Development, 1972.

Cormack, M. L. *An Evaluation of Research on Educational Exchange.* Washington, D.C.: American Educational Research Association, 1968.

Cotner, T. E. *International Educational Exchange: A Selected Bibliography.* Washington, D.C.: U.S. Office of Education, 1961.

Crabbs, R. F., and Holmquist, F. W. *United States Higher Education and World Affairs: A Partially Annotated Bibliography.* Ch. 19. New York: Praeger, 1968.

Douglas, J. H. "Education for Development." *Science News,* March 1975, *107,* 213–214.

Education and World Affairs Organization. *Internationalizing the U.S. Professional School.* New York: Education and World Affairs Organization, 1969.

Eith, W. "The State of University Cooperation." *Western European Education,* 1974, *5*(4), 56–70.

Gardner, R. N. *The Global Partnership.* New York: Praeger, 1968.

Hannigan, J. A. *Publications of the Carnegie Endowment for International Peace, 1910–1967, Including International Conciliation, 1924–1967.* New York: Carnegie Endowment for International Peace, 1971.

Hanson, H. "The International Baccalaureate." *International Educational and Cultural Exchange,* Summer 1971, 7, 10–14.

Hinkle, R. J. "A Geo-Political Critique of Study Abroad." *International Education,* 1972, *2*(1), 74–79.

Hutchinson, E. "A Case Study in Co-operation— The European Bureau of Adult Education." *Convergence,* 1973, *6*(3, 4), 40–48.

International Association of Universities. *A Critical Approach to Inter-University Co-operation.* Paper No. 13. Paris: International Association of Universities, 1974.

Kent State University, Center for International and Comparative Programs. *Report of the Conference on Alternative Designs for World Universities (Nordenfjord World University, Denmark, August 19–25, 1973).* Kent, Ohio: Kent State University, Center for International and Comparative Programs, 1973.

Lorenz, J. G. "International Transfer of Information." In C. A. Cudo (Ed.), *Annual Review of Information Science and Technology.* Chicago: Encyclopaedia Britannica, 1969.

"Mutual Recognition of Diplomas." *Western European Education,* Fall 1974, *6,* 60–62.

National Association for Foreign Student Affairs. *Selected Speeches, 27th Annual Conference of the National Association for Foreign Student Affairs (Washington, D.C., May 7–11, 1975).* Washington, D.C.: National Association for Foreign Student Affairs, 1975.

"Research Cooperation and Integration." *Western European Education,* 1970, *2*(1), 22.

Rosen, S. M. *The Development of People's Friendship University in Moscow.* Washington, D.C.: Institute of International Studies, 1973.

Taylor, H. "A University for the World." *Phi Delta Kappa,* 1974, *116*(1), 39–40.

Tollett, K. S. "Community and Higher Education." *Daedalus,* 1975, *104*(1), 278–297.

UNESCO. *Vacation Study Abroad: Vacation Courses and Scholarships.* Paris: UNESCO, 1970.

United States Department of Health, Education and Welfare, Division of International Education, Office of Education. *Bibliography: Publications in Comparative and International Education.* Washington, D.C.: U.S. Office of Education, 1974.

United States Department of Health, Education and Welfare, Office of Education. *Research and Training Opportunities Abroad and Foreign Curriculum Consultants in the United States 1975–76.* Washington, D.C.: U.S. Office of Education, 1974.

United States Department of State, Bureau of Educational and Cultural Affairs. *Directory of Contacts for International Educational, Cultural and Scientific Exchange Programs.* Washington, D.C.: U.S. Government Printing Office, 1974.

Wane, M. "International University Projects." *Higher Education,* August 1973, *2,* 357–360.

Werdel, J. A. "International Programs/Issues: Ten Commandments for International Cooperation." *Bulletin of the American Society for Information Science,* 1975, *2*(4).

White, L. C. *International Non-Governmental Organizations.* New Brunswick, New Jersey: Rutgers University Press, 1951.

"World Leaders Express Their Views." *International Education and Cultural Exchange,* 1975, *11*(1), 17–19.

The World of Learning 1975–76. (26th ed.) London: Europa, 1975.

Yates, A. *Current Problems of Teacher Education, Report of a Meeting of International Experts.* Hamburg, Federal Republic of Germany: UNESCO, 1970.

Zweig, M. *The Idea of a World University.* Carbondale: Southern Illinois University Press, 1967.

GLENN A. OLDS

See also: International Development, Role of in Higher Education.

2. COLONIAL POLICIES AND PRACTICES

Colonialism is the recent and contemporary term for what was once called imperialism. Essentially, it refers to the rule by one people over another group in an area distant from the rulers' mother country. Commonly underlying the relationship of the two peoples is the assumption of military, political, economic, and cultural superiority of the colonizers. The subordinate people retain that status until it is broken by revolution, war, or voluntary termination.

Traditional Colonialism

Colonialism has had several connotations. In ancient times, colonies were established by a national or ethnic group at a location remote from the homeland—for example, settlements of Greeks in western Asia, North Africa, and southern Italy, and colonies of Romans in Western Europe, North Africa, and western Asia. Other colonial groups in the ancient and medieval eras were the Egyptians, Phoenicians, Jews, Persians, Indians, Chinese, Mongols, and Arabs.

From the age of discovery onward, the Spaniards, Portuguese, Dutch, English, French, and other peoples acquired territory for economic purposes. During the nineteenth century, Germany, Belgium, Italy, Russia, and the United States joined the colonial powers. At the same time, however, the Latin American countries freed themselves from Spanish and Portuguese imperialism. Then, in 1914, Turkey lost all its possessions west of the Maritsa river after the Balkan wars; the close of World War I saw the loss of the German colonies; and World War II deprived Italy and Japan of their territorial acquisitions. Since then the trend has been for the further breakup of colonial empires and for new nations to arise out of their ruins. Although there were some exceptions to this generalization—for example, the United States retains Guam, Samoa, the Virgin Islands, and Puerto Rico—by the mid 1970s it became evident that the era of traditional colonialism was now part of history.

Prominent among colonial educators were foreign missionaries, who repre-

sented independent enterprise but were frequently associated with colonialism. Buddhist, Christian, and Moslem missions have been in operation since ancient times and have involved educational activity. Hence, to the extent that missionaries trained natives as priests, they could be said to have been engaged in higher education, as in what is now the southwestern United States during the seventeenth century. As a general rule, however, missionaries carried on their work in accordance with the principle of the subordination of paganism to faith *(infideles debent subici fidelibus)*—the maxim corresponding to the early modern European law whereby a ruler could impose his religion on his subjects *(cuius regio eius religio)*.

There have been many criticisms, denunciations, and rejections of colonialism since the nineteenth century. In Volume I of *Das Kapital,* for example, Karl Marx connected colonialism with capitalism and excoriated both as evil. Lenin elaborated the Marxian critique, looking on imperialism as "the highest stage of capitalism"—that is, the final phase prior to its replacement by socialism. The political characteristics of imperialism (or colonialism), asserted Lenin repeatedly, are "reaction all along the line and increased national oppression."

There is little doubt that much of the criticism of colonialism is amply justified by the evidence of centuries. From the political point of view, it is difficult, if not impossible, to say anything positive about colonialism. Yet an impartial study of this phenomenon leads to hypotheses, inferences, and conclusions that reveal that not all colonization was injurious and iniquitous. In *The Politics of Modernization,* David Apter calls attention to the role of colonial systems "as primary instruments of modernization" of what had been regarded as backward areas (1967, p. 54). Specifically, colonial nations provided the foundations for the government of the newer nations: railroads, highways, hospitals, schools, trained civil servants, and administrative procedures. In the words of Adam

Curle (1970, p. 45): "It would be hypocritical of the colonial powers to maintain that all this was done out of love for the subject people; but it would be bigoted on the part of the latter to maintain that nothing was done without the ulterior purpose of more efficient exploitation."

Among the abundance of critiques, some of them totally negative, of the impact of colonialism on education, there can also be found positive assessments. James S. Coleman, a renowned political scientist and Africanist, acknowledges the quantitative and qualitative shortcomings of colonial education and sees "the educational stagnation in many countries in Latin America [especially Brazil]" as "the legacy of premodern colonialism." However, Coleman also makes the significant point that "countries that missed both the stimulation and the humiliation of modern colonial rule, such as Afghanistan, Ethiopia, Liberia, and Haiti, also rank very low educationally" (Coleman, 1965, p. 35). As he sees it, the establishment of a modern school system in colonies "was the single most important factor in the rise and spread of nationalist sentiment and activity," since it made possible the emergence of "an indigenous elite which demanded the transfer of political power to itself on the basis of the political values of the Western liberal tradition or the ethical imperatives of Christianity, both of which had been learned in the schools" (Coleman, 1965, p. 36). The educational aims, content, and procedures of the colonial schools carried within themselves the seeds of the destruction of colonialism. In addition, the educational system of the Western colonial powers left a deep mark on the later educational enterprise of the emerging nations. The very idea of education, not for its own or for a liberalizing sake but for an objective related to vocationalism and social mobility, did not depart with the colonial powers. With few exceptions, the new countries tended to place power in the hands of those whose substantial education conferred on them the status of an elite.

Colonial Higher Education in Historical Perspective

Higher education in an international context is frequently identified with an advanced scholastic status whereby an individual, possessed of a general education, can pursue specialized studies. There is a presupposition that higher education is built on a structure, even if somewhat loose, of primary and secondary education. However, such a structure did not always exist. Thus, in speaking of higher education historically it is necessary to define it flexibly.

A colonial power did not necessarily provide higher educational facilities *in situ.* Even in ancient times, there were instances when members of a subject people were sent to the colonizers' country for advanced study. As governor of Britain, Gnaeus Julius Agricola, the father-in-law of Tacitus, made provisions for the education of selected Britons at home, and he may also have sent some to absorb the higher learning in Rome. The higher educational institutions at ancient Athens, Alexandria, and Rome were available to both Romans and colonials, with some of the colonials (Plutarch, Quintilian) employed as professors. Evidently, those in the colonies who had the time, funds, ambition, and ability had the opportunity to seek learning wherever it was dispensed. It is noteworthy that colonial higher education in the Roman world benefited both the superior and the subordinate. Even if exaggerated, Juvenal's claim contained at least a kernel of truth: "Today the whole world enjoys Greek culture and Latin culture" (Marrou, 1964, p. 395).

Apart from some Islamic activity in India after the seventh century, there does not seem to have been much in the way of colonial higher education until early modern times. The Moslems brought Arabic and Persian learning with them to India, but it reached only small numbers of their own people and of Indians. What prevented the growth of higher education in Moslem-occupied India was the frequent disorder, except in such brief intervals as the reign of the Mogul Emperor Akbar the Great (1555–1605). Non-Indian higher learning appeared on a large scale with the advent of the British. In 1784, Governor General Warren Hastings founded the Calcutta *madrassa* (Islamic higher institute), while in 1792 Governor Jonathan Duncan of Bombay established the government-supported Sanskrit College in Varanasi (Bradby, 1939).

The centuries from the later Middle Ages through the Renaissance and into the eighteenth century were a period of exploration and conquest. Portugal initiated contact with West and East Africa, India, and the Far East during the fifteenth and sixteenth centuries, while Spain undertook the colonization of Latin America and the Philippine Islands. After 1540 the Society of Jesus (Jesuits) began to send its members as missionaries to Japan, China, India, Latin America, and other areas. The Franciscans, Augustinians, and Dominicans also established missions. As a general rule, the Portuguese trained natives as priests and, in some instances, even made it possible for some to become bishops. However, unlike the Spaniards, they did not organize institutions for higher education beyond advanced schools in Babia and Rio de Janeiro in the sixteenth century.

As early as 1538, the Spanish conquerors established the University of Santo Domingo, the first in the Western Hemisphere, followed by the University of Mexico and the University of San Marcos (Lima, Peru) in 1551. Other advanced schools were founded by the Spanish colonists in Mexico, the Philippines, Guatemala, and Argentina from the sixteenth through the nineteenth centuries, up to the very beginning of the Latin American revolutionary period. Illustrative was the opening of the University of Antioquia in Medellín, Colombia (1803), and of the University of León in Nicaragua (1812). Although these institutions were organized on the model of the University of Salamanca in Spain and were intended for the Spanish colonials, there were opportunities, especially in the

ology and pedagogy, for natives. On an obviously much smaller scale, a similar situation obtained for the Brazilian higher institutions, which drew their inspiration from the University of Coimbra in Portugal (Benjamin, 1965).

Sweden established the University of Dorpat (Tartu) in 1632 and the University of Helsinki in 1640 in colonial lands. French colonization in Canada was marked by the introduction of higher education by the Jesuits at the *Collège de Québec* in the mid seventeenth century. However, there were no higher schools by the time New France ceased to exist in 1736. Under British colonization, seventeen institutions were founded prior to the formation of the Dominion of Canada in 1867. These included the University of New Brunswick (1785), McGill University (1821), the University of Toronto (1827), the bilingual University of Ottawa (1848), and the French-speaking Laval University in Quebec City (1852).

In the thirteen colonies, the core of what is now the United States of America, nine institutions of higher studies were opened prior to independence in 1776. These establishments were created by the colonists themselves for their own children, although young persons were also sent to study in England. There was a plan for a college for Indians, in early seventeenth-century Virginia, but nothing came of it. A few young Indians were enrolled at Harvard College, while Dartmouth College made specific provisions for them. In general, it cannot be said that Indians were intrigued by the idea of higher education at the hands of the British colonists.

The Dutch sent an African student to study at the famous University of Leiden in the Netherlands during the eighteenth century. In Indonesia, they were not successful in persuading young nationals to enroll in their advanced Latin programs (Neill, 1966).

Of special interest is the career of Anthony William Amo, a native of Axim, in the Gold Coast of Africa. Under the patronage of the Princess of Brunswick, he obtained a doctor's degree in philosophy at the University of Halle-Wittenberg in 1734. He published several works in Latin and lectured on philosophy in Germany (Groves, 1948–1958).

Not usually considered in the general accounts of colonialism is the instance of the occupation of Russia by the Mongols from 1237 to the end of the fifteenth century. There should be no shock for the lack of higher education during this period, inasmuch as the Asian invaders were not practitioners of the advanced learning arts.

Colonial Higher Education From the Nineteenth to the Mid Twentieth Century

During this century and a half, the proper focus is on colonialism in Asia and Africa. However, the colonial status of New Zealand and Australia is also relevant. New Zealand had no higher institutions by the time it achieved self-governing status in 1853, but there were four by the end of the nineteenth century: Otago (1869), Canterbury (1873), Auckland (1882), and Wellington (1897). Australia, which was not a commonwealth until 1901, had a number of such schools before that date: the Universities of Sydney (1850), Melbourne (1853), Adelaide (1874), and Tasmania (1890), as well as technological and pedagogical institutes. There seems to be no evidence of attendance by Maoris in New Zealand or Aborigines in Australia.

In addition, during this period, Russia organized the University of Warsaw (1818) and the Helsinki University of Technology (1908). In Iceland the Danish authority opened the University of Iceland at Reykjavík in 1911. A newcomer to colonialism, the United States sent Cuban teachers for advanced study to the mainland and provided institutions of higher learning in Hawaii (1908), Puerto Rico (1910), and Alaska (1922). The most active colonial power in the field of education was, however, Great Britain.

British colonialism and education. When Cyprus became an independent govern-

ment within the British Commonwealth in 1960, it already possessed a Greek and a Turkish teachers' training college and a college of forestry. Another British colony, Jamaica, became self-governing in 1962, its University of the West Indies having been founded in 1948. (Interestingly, higher education in the West Indies area can be traced to Codrington College [1745], which was affiliated in 1875 with the University of Durham in England.) The modern Royal University of Malta dates from 1947, fifteen years prior to independence from Britain. Finally, when the British gave up Guyana in 1966, they had established a university three years earlier. It may be inferred, therefore, that the British colonial authority planned the modernization of its colonies by providing institutions of higher education in advance of independence. The universities in the United Kingdom, especially the University of London, were also open to colonial students for residential academic work as well as for external study and examination at home.

In Asia the most active area in colonial higher education was the Indian subcontinent. As previously mentioned, the British colonial power had opened facilities for higher education at Calcutta and Varanasi during the closing decades of the eighteenth century. The aim of these schools was to prepare individuals to become competent in the Islamic and Hindu languages and laws. The reversal of this trend began with the opening of the Hindu College in 1817 at Calcutta by Ram Mohan Roy, a modernist Hindu, and several prominent representatives of the British Raj (ruling power, from the Sanskrit word for king). The aim of this uniquely sponsored school was to furnish instruction in the English language and literature, as well as the sciences, history, and geography, so that Indian students could obtain intellectual and commercial advantages. Owing to financial and administrative difficulties, Hindu College (now Presidency College, University of Calcutta) received government aid and came under some official control

(McCully, 1940, p. 22). The pro-Western tendency was strengthened immeasurably by Thomas B. Macaulay's famous Minute of February 2, 1835 which downgraded "the whole native literature of India and Arabia" as inferior to "a single shelf of a good European library" (quoted in McCully, 1940, p. 69).

India appears to provide a most unusual case study of colonial higher education. By 1857, the year of the establishment of the Universities of Calcutta, Bombay, and Madras, British India already had twenty-seven colleges. To these were added the University of the Punjab in Lahore (1882) and the University of Allahabad in 1887. In 1946–47, the year prior to independence, India had eighteen universities and 933 colleges with a total student body of 225,000 (Altbach, 1971, p. 319).

While such growth was impressive in the context of colonial policy and practice concerning higher education in other areas, there were some flaws in the system. According to Sir Eric Ashby, a British scholar who is a leading world specialist on higher education: "From 1854 to 1919 the British rulers of India deliberately maintained powers of governmental control over universities which no British university would have tolerated" (Ashby and Anderson, 1966, p. 141). Even the mildly liberal recommendations on academic autonomy made by the commission under the chairmanship of the famous comparative educationist, Sir Michael Sadler, were not actually put into operation. Moreover, "students were required to study subjects that were culturally alien to them in a language that was not their own" (Ashby and Anderson, 1966, p. 142). On the other hand, a nationalist movement began to grow in the 1880s, a development that contributed ultimately to the achievement of independence. However critical Indians and some Britons became of the higher educational system instituted by the Raj, it would seem that India benefited at least as much as it suffered under colonial education.

Under British colonialism, Ceylon (now Sri Lanka) had a medical college in 1870, a university college in 1921, and a university in 1942. In addition, there was a technical college in Colombo (1893), while an agricultural school was opened at Peradeniya in 1916, thirty-two years before independence. Among the other British colonial educational foundations in Asia were the Universities of Hong Kong (1911); Rangoon in Burma (1920); Malaya in Kuala Lumpur, Malaysia (1949); and several institutions in Singapore: King Edward VII College of Medicine (1905), Raffles College (1929), University of Malaya in Singapore (1949; the three institutions were merged in 1962 to form the University of Singapore), and Nanyang University (1953). The Hebrew University of Jerusalem was inaugurated in 1925 in the presence of the British Mandatory authorities.

Other colonial powers. Higher institutions in Asia were also established under other colonial powers. The Universities of Saigon (1917) and Hanoi (1918) in Vietnam were established under French rule. In occupied Korea, the Japanese permitted instruction at Ewha Women's University (1886), at Jungang and Yonsei Universities (1918), at the University of Korea (1929), and at Sookmyung Women's University (1938). Between 1898 and 1946, when the Philippines was a colony of the United States, twenty-two universities were established. Among these were Silliman University (1901), the University of the Philippines (1908), the University of Manila (1913), and the Far Eastern University (Manila, 1928). In Lebanon the American University of Beirut was founded by the American Protestant mission in 1866, and the University of St. Joseph was founded by the Jesuits in 1881. The Aleppo Medical School was established in Syria in 1903 and the University of Baghdad in Iraq in 1908, while both were part of the Turkish empire. During the French Mandatory Government of Syria, the University of Damascus (1923) was created. Although the Dutch colonial authority did not provide a university in Indonesia, it did make available a college of engineering in Bandung (1920), and a law school (1924) and a medical school (1927) in Batavia (Djakarta in Indonesia, 1924). The universities of the Netherlands were available for Indonesians, but few of them actually studied there.

Colonial education in Africa. Higher education was not imported by western European countries as an innovation into Africa. Islamic higher learning came into being with the el-Zaitouna *madrassa* in Tunis (732), followed by al-Qarawiyin in Fès (Morocco, 859), and al-Azhar University in Egypt (970). During the sixteenth century, the black Islamic University of Sankore in Timbuktu became well known, and there were also such institutions in the Futa, North Nigeria, and Niger River areas, all in West Africa.

Colonization was going on in Africa all through ancient and medieval times, mainly through the expansion of Islam. The era of African discovery and exploration, beginning with the activities of Prince Henry the Navigator of Portugal in the fifteenth century, was marked by the inauguration of Christian missions in West and East Africa. The growth of English trade in the sixteenth century and that of the Dutch in the seventeenth led to colonial settlements in West and South Africa and to the development of traffic in slavery. The nineteenth century saw the arrival of the Belgians, French, Germans, and Italians as colonizers, with the Spaniards joining in the twentieth.

Western colonial educational activities did not come into being until the arrival, after the turn of the nineteenth century, of the representatives of the Church Missionary Society (CMS) in Africa and the East. The CMS had been founded in London in 1799. Before long, the American, Danish, Dutch, French, Norwegian, Swedish, and Swiss missionaries inaugurated their Protestant educational functions. Portuguese Jesuits had opened in 1697, at Sena in the Congo area, a seminary for the training of sons of native chiefs along with those of Portuguese colonists. However, there is no record of higher education until the founding by Protestant missionaries in 1827 of Fourah Bay College, Freetown, Sierra Leone. This "development of importance in education" was reinforced in 1876 by the affiliation of this school with the University of Durham in England, a procedure that permitted Africans to earn bachelor's degrees. The Reverend Edward Jones, an American Negro, became the principal in 1841 (Groves, 1948–1958).

The only other colonial institutions of higher education of significance in Africa during the nineteenth century were those established by Britain in South Africa—Cape Town (1829), Rhodes (1855), and Stellenbosch (1866)—and the schools of law, science and letters founded in 1879, which later became University of Algiers, established by the French in 1909 in Algeria. Clearly, the development of colonial higher education in nineteenth-century Africa was very limited in scope and area.

The first four decades of the twentieth century were marked by a slow and sparse development in colonial higher education, almost exclusively under British auspices. The Gordon Memorial College (1902) in Khartoum, Sudan, was followed by the University of Cairo (1908); the Technical College (1921) in Makerere, Uganda; the Prince of Wales College (1924) at Achimota, Ghana; and the Yaba Medical School (1932) and Higher College (1931) in Nigeria. In South Africa, the Universities of Pretoria (1908) and Natal (1909) were organized and the newly formed Union of South Africa incorporated the already existing Universities of the Orange Free State, the Witwatersrand, Potchefstroom, and South Africa. In addition, higher education was made available to blacks, coloreds, and Asians in the University College of Fort Hare (1916). In the French colonial region, a decree in 1918 created a medical school in Dakar, Senegal. This institution grew by virtue of the additional decrees of 1923, 1925, and 1927.

Lord Ashby called attention to "the resistance of the British government to the pressures for universities in Africa," stressing that "the colonial governments were too impoverished, and the missionaries too preoccupied with their task of combining schooling with proselytization, to devote funds or time to higher education" (Ashby, 1964, p. 15). After World War I, however, "this complacent isolationism was brought to an end" with the appointment in 1923, by the Colonial Office, of a blue-ribbon Advisory Committee on Native Education in Tropical Africa (later Advisory Committee on Education in the Colonies). Its membership included such distinguished educational experts as Sir Fredrick Lugard, Sir James Currie, and Sir Michael Sadler. While the objective of this group was to deal with education in general, ostensibly below university level, its initial memorandum contained a reference to the need for providing facilities for advanced learning in Africa. One conclusion of this forward-looking white paper stated that "As resources permit, the door of advancement through higher education in Africa must be increasingly opened for those who by character, ability and temperament show themselves fitted to profit by such education" (Ashby and Anderson, 1966, p. 191). Although this idea was developed in subsequent reports and statements during the 1920s and 1930s, no specific move was made to translate idea into reality.

Colonial Higher Education After World War II

World War II was a barrier but it did not prevent vigorous proselytizing, such as the Channon Memorandum (1940) and the Channon Report (1943). The latter document, dated May 15, 1943, was a report of the Sub-Committee on Higher Education of the Advisory Committee on Education in the Colonies. It warned that "it would show a lack of vision if we do not seize the opportunities now available to us, and profiting by past experience, plan the future universities of Africa and Malaya on sound and fruitful lines from the very

beginning" (Ashby and Anderson, 1966, p. 502). An immediate outcome was the appointment, in July, 1943, of the Asquith and the Elliot Commissions to submit recommendations for the expansion of higher education in the colonies, particularly in Africa. The publication of both reports took place in 1945, and "at long last Britain had declared a policy for higher education in the colonies" (Ashby, 1964). Furthermore, Parliament passed that year the second Colonial Development and Welfare Act with increased funds for education. The road was now clear for a postwar colonial policy to improve the status of the inhabitants of the colonies and to prepare them as citizens of democratic self-governing countries within the British Commonwealth of Nations (Evans and Evans, 1952, p. 550).

Consequences of the Asquith Report. The consequences of these actions were increasingly visible during the next decade and after. The recommendations by the Asquith Report for "the immediate setting up of university colleges" with "no undue delay in converting these colleges into universities" (quoted in Carr-Saunders, 1961, p. 35) did not have to wait for action. As expressed by the report, the aim of the planned institutions was "to give to these Colonial students an opportunity for self-development which will enable them to fit themselves for the management of their own concerns; to train themselves for their future responsibilities by gaining the expert knowledge necessary for the service of their own communities; and finally to take their place among those who are contributing to the intellectual life and scientific progress of man" (quoted in Carr-Saunders, 1961, pp. 40–41). In making its exit as a long-time colonial power, Britain was taking specific steps to facilitate the birth and growth of the emerging nations.

In line with the intent of the Asquith Commission, two institutions of higher learning made their appearance in 1948— the University College of the Gold Coast

(Ghana) at Accra and the University College of Ibadan in Nigeria. These initial "Asquith colleges" were followed by the University College of East Africa, Makerere, Uganda (1949); the University Colleges of Nairobi, Kenya, and Khartoum, Sudan (1951); the Kumasi College of Technology in Ghana (1951); and the University College of Rhodesia and Nyasaland (1955).

Other colonial powers. In the French areas, advanced education was provided in institutes of higher studies in Dakar, Senegal (1949), and Madagascar (1955); and the University of Abidjan, Ivory Coast (1958). The Belgians opened Lovanium University (1954), now part of the National University of Zaire, in Kinshasa; and the University of the Belgian Congo and Ruanda-Urundi (1956) in Lubumbashi. The National University of Somalia came into existence in Mogadisho (1954) under Italian auspices. Neither the Spanish nor the Portuguese territories possessed higher education institutions, although some Africans were sent annually to universities in Spain and Portugal. By the time the colonial era was over in Africa, most countries had established some advanced school for the native inhabitants.

Retrospect and Prospect

From the perspective of history, there can be little doubt of the lack of interest and concern on the part of colonial powers for the higher education needs of their wards. There is considerable justice in the criticisms of colonialism and of colonial education in general and higher education in particular. Yet it would not be true to the historical record to deny the continuity within the newer nations of higher education institutions and patterns originating in the colonial era. Nationalism leading to independence was very often born in colonial higher education institutions or fostered by the educational experiences of colonials in the universities of the mother countries. One outstanding example is President Habib Bourguiba of Tunisia, a former student in France. It is also note-worthy that Africanization in education has not necessarily brought about the rejection of European educational aims and content.

It is true, however, that some colonial powers did more for higher education than others. Britain seems to have made the most thoroughly planned contribution, and that of France was also substantial. Lesser achievements were recorded by the Netherlands, Belgium, Spain, and Portugal. Furthermore, in some instances the departing authority—Belgium in the Congo, for instance—did little to assure the availability of skilled personnel to carry on governmental activities. Nonetheless, colonialism cannot be totally condemned, insofar as education is concerned.

There are several very extreme critiques of colonialism in regard to higher education, among them the communist-oriented criticism of the International Union of Students of "the total inadequacy of educational facilities in the colonial and dependent countries which results in a complete denial of education to the people of these countries" (*Colonial Education,* 1950, p. 21). The sponsors of this statement give no sources for their denunciation.

On a more sophisticated level, a distinguished African writer complains of the survival of neocolonialism after the end of official imperialist domination. To Moumouni, any remaining dependence by a new nation on a European one is evidence of imperialism. Even more, the provision of technical aid by an industrial country is to be regarded as an imperialist imposition on the new nation (Moumouni, 1968, p. 101).

The motives of the colonial powers included economic exploitation, political power, and national and international prestige. The interbellum Nazi Germany demanded colonies ("Wir brauchen Kolonien"). Nevertheless, the higher educational enterprise of the European powers—in the colonies and at home—did make possible the emergence of many new nations that are able to exert an influence, far out of proportion to the length of their governmental history, on the affairs of the entire world.

Bibliography

Abernethy, D. B. *The Political Dilemma of Popular Education: An African Case.* Stanford, California: Stanford University Press, 1969.

Adams, D., and Bjork, M. *Education in Developing Areas.* New York: McKay, 1969.

Almond, G. A., and Coleman, J. A. *The Politics of Developing Areas.* Princeton, New Jersey: Princeton University Press, 1960.

Altbach, P. "Higher Education in India." In B. Burns, P. Altbach, C. Kerr, and J. Perkins (Eds.), *Higher Education in Nine Countries: A Comparative Study of Colleges and Universities Abroad.* New York: McGraw-Hill, 1971.

Altbach, P. G., and Kelly, D. H. (Eds.) *Higher Education in Developing Nations; A Selected Bibliography, 1969–1974.* New York: Praeger, 1974.

Apter, D. E. *The Politics of Modernization.* Chicago: University of Chicago Press, 1967.

Ashby, E. *African Universities and Western Tradition.* Cambridge, Massachusetts: Harvard University Press, 1964.

Ashby, E., and Anderson, M. *Universities: British, Indian, African.* Cambridge, Massachusetts: Harvard University Press, 1966.

Becker, H. T. *Das Schulwesen in Afrika.* Berlin, Federal Republic of Germany: de Gruyter, 1943.

Benjamin, H. R. W. *Higher Education in the American Republics.* New York: McGraw-Hill, 1965.

Berman, E. H. (Ed.) *African Reactions to Missionary Education.* New York: Teachers College Press, Columbia University, 1975.

Bradby, E. (Ed.) *The University Outside Europe.* London: Oxford University Press, 1939.

Brown, G. N., and Hiskett, M. (Eds.) *Conflict and Harmony in Education in Tropical Africa.* London: Allen & Unwin, 1975.

Burn, B. B., Altbach, P., Kerr, C., and Perkins, J. A. *Higher Education in Nine Countries: A Comparative Study of Colleges and Universities Abroad.* New York: McGraw-Hill, 1971.

Butts, R. F. *The Education of the West: A Formative Chapter in the History of Civilization.* New York: McGraw-Hill, 1973.

Carr-Saunders, A. M. *New Universities Overseas.* London: Allen & Unwin, 1961.

Coleman, J. S. *Nigeria: Background to Nationalism.* Berkeley: University of California Press, 1958.

Coleman, J. S. (Ed.) *Education and Political Development.* Princeton, New Jersey: Princeton University Press, 1965.

Colonial Education. Prague: International Union of Students, 1950.

Cowan, L. G., O'Connell, J., and Scanlon, D. G. (Eds.) *Education and Nation-Building in Africa.* New York: Praeger, 1965.

Curle, A. *Educational Strategies for Developing Societies.* (2nd ed.) London: Tavistock, 1970.

DeMarco, R. *The Italianization of African Natives: Government Native Education in the Italian Colonies, 1890–1937.* New York: Teachers College Press, Columbia University, 1943.

Educational Policy in British Tropical Africa: Memorandum Submitted to the Secretary of State for the Colonies by the Advisory Committee on Native Education in the British Tropical African Dependencies. Cmd. 2374. London: H. M. Stationery Office, 1925.

Emerson, R., and Fieldhouse, D. K. "Colonialism." In D. Sills (Ed.), *International Encyclopedia of the Social Sciences.* Vol. 3. New York: Macmillan, 1968.

Evans, P. C., and Evans, C. "The British Tropical Dependencies: Introduction." In *The Yearbook of Education: 1952.* London: Evans, 1952.

Ferreira, E. *Portuguese Colonialism in Africa, the End of an Era: The Effects of Portuguese Colonialism in Education, Science, Culture and Information.* Paris: UNESCO, 1974.

Furnivall, J. S. *Colonial Policy and Practice: A Comparative Study of Burma and Netherlands India.* Cambridge, England: Cambridge University Press, 1948.

Groves, C. R. *The Planting of Christianity in Africa.* (4 vols.) London: Butterworth, 1948–1958.

Hailey, Lord W. M. *An African Survey: A Study of Problems in Africa South of the Sahara.* London: Oxford University Press, 1957.

Harbison, F., and Myers, C. A. (Eds.) *Manpower and Education: Country Studies in Economic Development.* New York: McGraw-Hill, 1965.

Kitchen, H. (Ed.) *The Educated African.* New York: Praeger, 1962.

Lannoy, C. de, and Linden, H. *Histoire de l'expansion coloniale des peuples européens.* (3 vols.) Brussels: Lamertin, 1902–1921.

Lewis, L. J. *Education Policy and Practice in British Tropical Areas.* London: Nelson, 1954.

Marrou, H. I. *A History of Education in Antiquity.* New York: New American Library, 1964.

Mayhew, A. *The Education of India.* London: Faber and Gwyer, 1926.

McCully, B. T. *English Education and the Origins of Indian Nationalism.* New York: Columbia University Press, 1940.

Moumouni, A. *L'éducation en Afrique*. Paris: Maspero, 1964. (Translated by Phyllis N. Ott as *Education in Africa*. New York: Praeger, 1968.)

Mumford, W. B. *A Comparative Survey of Native Education in Various Dependencies*. London: Evans, 1937.

Mumford, W. B., and Orde-Brown, G. S. J. *Africans Learn to Be French*. London: Evans, 1937.

Neill, S. *Colonialism and Christian Missions*. New York: McGraw-Hill, 1966.

Report of the Commission on Higher Education in West Africa. (Elliot Commission.) Cmd. 6655. London: H. M. Stationery Office, 1945.

Report of the Commission on Higher Education in the Colonies. (Asquith Commission.) Cmd. 6647. London: H. M. Stationery Office, 1945.

Rysakoff, A. *The Nationality Policy of the Soviet Union*. New York: International Universities Press, 1933.

Scanlon, D. G. (Ed.) *Traditions of African Education*. New York: Teachers College Press, Columbia University, 1964.

Straus-Hupe, R., and Hazard, H. W. (Eds.) *The Idea of Colonialism*. New York: Praeger, 1958.

Walker, E. A. *Colonies*. Cambridge, England: Cambridge University Press, 1944.

Wyndham, H. A. *Native Education: Ceylon, Java, Formosa, Philippines, French Indo-China and British Malaya*. London: Royal Institute of International Affairs, 1933.

WILLIAM W. BRICKMAN

See also: Agriculture in Higher Education: Early History of Agricultural Education; History of Higher Education.

3. BILATERAL PARTICIPATION IN HIGHER EDUCATION

Assistance of a bilateral nature has been provided for the development of higher education in many countries throughout the world by private organizations, foundations, institutions of higher learning, and national governments.

During the early development of any country there is interest in providing programs and institutions that will satisfy that country's internal needs. Initially, the emphasis is on instruction for those who come to the institutions for a formal education. With growth and progress, atten-

tion can be turned to assisting others who have not yet attained the same level of achievement. That is why, at about the turn of the twentieth century, institutions of higher learning began expanding their realm of influence beyond the individual campus. Most progressive institutions now have as an integral part of their educational process an international dimension, for world affairs have caused educational institutions to become more international in scope and interest.

Donor Countries and Agencies

Several countries and organizations have been involved in providing bilateral aid to higher education in developing nations. Some of the leaders have been Canada, the Federal Republic of Germany, Great Britain, the Netherlands, Norway, Sweden, the Organization of Petroleum Exporting Countries (OPEC), the United Nations, and the United States. Although some assistance has come from these countries and regions for several decades, the main support took hold in the 1950s, became more evident in the 1960s, and has continued into the 1970s.

Canada. The Canadian International Development Agency (CIDA) was established in 1968, replacing the External Aid Office. CIDA administers Canada's official development assistance, including food aid, emergency relief, technical and educational assistance, and development loans. About 75 percent of Canadian assistance is provided bilaterally in cooperation with more than seventy developing countries in five main regions: Asia, commonwealth Africa, francophone Africa, the Caribbean, and Latin America.

During 1971–72, 1756 students and trainees were involved in courses under CIDA auspices in Canada. That same year 864 Canadian teachers were involved in service overseas, mainly in Africa. In recent years emphasis has shifted toward the support of technical institutions, teacher training programs, and regional universities and institutions, as well as arrangements for training of students from developing countries in other countries (Overseas Liaison Committee, 1973).

Federal Republic of Germany. In recent years the Federal Republic has been involved in many international activities through private foundations, national academies, and the federal government. The *Deutscher akademischer Austauschdienst* (DAAD: German Academic Exchange Service) was founded in 1925 at the initiative of the University of Heidelberg and was reestablished in 1950. DAAD, whose members are the universities represented on the West German Rectors Conference, participates in university partnerships and educational aid programs in developing countries. On the basis of mutual cooperation between corresponding institutions in the developing countries and the Federal Republic of Germany, universities and research institutes are being established and developed in Latin America, Africa, and Asia. DAAD assists with the training of local university lecturers and arranges exchanges of visiting professors between foreign and German universities.

Since 1963 DAAD has offered African and Southeast Asian students local scholarships that are tenable at universities in those regions. During 1974 there were 2349 DAAD scholarship holders from abroad studying in Germany; 505 in-country scholarship holders in Africa, Asia, and Latin America; and 1287 German DAAD scholarship holders studying or carrying out research abroad. In addition, 2863 German academic staff members were working abroad.

The main functions of DAAD are to award scholarships to German and foreign students, to send lecturers to foreign universities, to draw up exchange programs for university teachers and for student trainees, to provide an information and placement service for German scholars abroad, to arrange short study visits for groups of foreign and German scientists and students, and to issue publications on academic life in the Federal Republic of Germany and abroad (Geimer and Geimer, 1974).

Great Britain. A good example of cooperation between established universities and the development of new universities in emerging nations can be found in programs of the Inter-University Council for Higher Education Overseas (IUC). Organized in 1946 by the universities of the United Kingdom at the request of the British government, IUC was incorporated in 1971 and is supported through funding from the Overseas Development Administration (ODM). Since 1971 it has been involved in a program of "Cooperation Through Links" (Inter-University Council, 1975), in which the British universities have become associated with some thirty-five overseas universities in twenty-five countries. IUC assists in their development by providing advice on academic policy and planning, by helping with staffing, by arranging training opportunities in Britain, and by supporting cooperative link arrangements with departments in British universities. In 1974 there were approximately 120 links involving assistance and cooperation in research, training, academic planning, and university administration.

Among the aims of IUC are encouraging cooperation insofar as it is mutually desired between the universities in the United Kingdom and institutions of specified countries; and generally assisting in the development of higher education in these countries and areas by providing advisory services and administering technical assistance projects.

During 1973, 5519 British experts were serving overseas in the field of education; 1502 were working in development planning and public administration; 2211 in economic infrastructure; 1227 in agriculture and natural resources; 800 in health and social welfare; and 257 in industry, mining, and commerce.

An important spin-off from the IUC program is that British universities have derived much benefit from the cooperative association. Many British universities have academic staff with first-hand experience as university teachers in developing countries and have broadened their view and depth of understanding to the benefit of the whole academic climate within the universities of the United Kingdom (Inter-University Council, 1975).

Netherlands. The history of international education in the Netherlands goes back to the beginning of the 1950s. The first institutes were organized in 1951 as the Netherlands Universities Foundation for International Cooperation (NUFFIC) and the International Training Center (ITC). NUFFIC was established by all the Netherlands universities, with its most important tasks being to provide university education for foreigners and to facilitate scientific research by foreigners and possibly also by Netherlanders. ITC was established as a separate foundation through the cooperation of the government, the Delft University of Technology, and the state Agricultural University at Wageningen.

Although the Royal Tropical Institute was founded in 1910, it was not until 1967, when an international center was constructed on the campus, that it took on an international flavor. To achieve an efficient and coordinated approach to the problems of bilateral cooperation in the field of agriculture, the International Agricultural Center was founded in 1951. Later the Institute of Social Studies was created to train students and university staff from many countries.

The Philips Company established the Philips International Institute in 1957 to train graduate engineers or scientists from developing countries in Philips techniques, thus indicating that private enterprise also has a responsibility for realizing better conditions in the world.

Through these special institutes there has been a large transfer of both students and teachers. Special cooperative projects under the auspices of the Ghanian and Netherlands governments have been conducted in Ghana in cooperation with the University of Cape Coast. A similar relationship has been developed with the University of Indonesia. Popular courses of study have included hydraulic engineering, sanitary engineering, and hydrology. From 1957 to 1970 these courses have been attended by 933 engineers from 87 different countries. Other courses have received special consideration in that they have involved postgraduate students from many countries. In 1969 a course on land drainage was held for Peruvian engineers, and the lectures were given in Spanish. An agreement between the government of Kenya and the Royal Tropical Institute in 1964 enabled the creation of a Medical Research Center in Nairobi (Franks, 1971).

Norway. The Norwegian Agency for International Development (NORAD: *Norsk utviklingshjelp*) administers the country's bilateral aid programs. Norway is committed to the idea of providing help to developing countries and plans to increase its overall development aid to 1 percent of the gross national product of the country by 1978.

NORAD deals primarily with seven partner countries: Tanzania, Kenya, Zambia, Botswana, Uganda, India, and Pakistan; however, assistance is not limited strictly to those countries. Approximately half of the bilateral assistance goes to projects in fishing and agriculture. Higher education receives special attention; for example, funds have been provided to the University of Nairobi, in Kenya, to build up the school of journalism, to improve the faculty of veterinary sciences, and to construct a natural science complex with a residence hall for three hundred students. During 1974 an agreement was reached between Tanzania and Norway on the setting up of a department of forestry at Morogoro under the jurisdiction of the University of Dar es Salaam.

Norway also operates a scholarship program, under which scholarships are offered to applicants from any of the developing countries. The 1974 NORAD appropriation provided for 328 fellowships for study in Norway and 86 fellowships for studies in the home country or a third country. The NORAD fellows that year came from forty different developing countries, the majority from Egypt, India, Tanzania, Kenya, and Thailand.

In 1974 the board of NORAD drew up new guidelines for support to research studies. The purpose was to stimulate Norwegian institutions and enterprises to make more determined, active, and comprehensive research effort in fields that might be of significance to developing countries. Some of the first projects included work on African botany and a study of forest soils in East Africa (*Norway's Assistance to Developing Countries in 1974,* 1975).

Sweden. The Swedish International Development Authority (SIDA) is the administrative organ in charge of Sweden's overseas development assistance. Swedish aid is concentrated in specific countries and areas of interest such as Kenya, Tanzania, Ethiopia, Tunisia, India, and Pakistan. Although it has contributed to multilateral development programs since 1950, Sweden has been heavily involved in bilateral aid since 1962, and approximately half of the 1 percent of its gross national product that went to assist developing countries in 1975 was for bilateral cooperation.

SIDA programs for higher education relate to educational assistance and the recruitment and training of personnel for technical assistance activities in developing countries. One thing that is emphasized is the integration of projects with each other and with the administrative and financial framework of the country involved (Overseas Liaison Committee, 1973).

OPEC countries. Until the early 1970s much of the assistance for higher education was carried out through the relationship that existed between a developed nation and a developing nation. Then, with the formation of the Organization of Petroleum Exporting Countries (OPEC), and the increased revenue to those countries from the sale of oil, a new dimension entered the scene of higher education. Many

of these countries, especially Iran, Saudi Arabia, and Venezuela, recognized the value of developing their human resources in order that the future needs of the nation might best be served (Edgerton, 1975).

For many years Iran has been sending students abroad for advanced degree training. However, in 1973–74 the number jumped by 22 percent over the previous year, with the anticipation of additional increases in future years. The Iranian government also became very active in forming new relationships with several leading United States institutions. Cooperative agreements involved not only the training of Iranian students but an increased emphasis on further developing the Iranian system of higher education.

The government of Venezuela made a concerted effort to widen access to education for youth outside the metropolitan areas by announcing its *Programa de becas Gran Mariscal de Ayacucho* (Grand Marshal of Ayacucho Scholarship Program) in 1973. This program, designed to provide scholarships for up to 10,000 Venezuelan students each year in Venezuela, the United States, and other countries, represents a massive investment for the future development of the country.

During the 1973–74 academic year Saudi Arabia student enrollment in higher education abroad exceeded one thousand for the first time. More recently Saudi Arabia has vigorously explored the possibility of increasing that number manyfold and is also seeking cooperation with the United States and other countries for assistance in research, educational training, and institutional development.

The signing of joint commissions between the United States and individual countries from the Middle East is certain to arouse heightened interest in educational development for some time.

United Nations. Since its inception following World War II, the United Nations has been an effective and enthusiastic supporter of all kinds of international education, including bilateral educational programs. It would be futile to attempt to list the individual organizations receiving aid from the United Nations. Organizations through which the United Nations operates its educational support include the United Nations Development Programme, which administers programs carried out by the International Labour Organisation; the Food and Agriculture Organization; the United Nations Educational, Scientific and Cultural Organization; the World Health Organization; the World Bank; the International Civil Aviation Organization; the International Telecommunication Union; the World Meteorological Organization; the International Atomic Energy Agency; the Universal Postal Union; the Inter-Governmental Maritime Consultative Organization; the United Nations Conference on Trade and Development; the United Nations Industrial Development Organization; the Inter-American Development Bank; the African Development Bank; and the Asian Development Bank.

The United Nations Educational, Scientific and Cultural Organization (UNESCO) was created in 1946 as part of the United Nations system. Its major areas of emphasis have been scientific and educational advancement in the developing countries and, recently, the problems of environment in the more developed industrial countries.

The purpose of the United Nations Institute for Training and Research (UNITAR) is to enhance the effectiveness of the United Nations in achieving its major objectives, particularly with regard to the maintenance of peace and security and the promotion of economic and social development. UNITAR provides training courses in diplomacy, the functioning of United Nations structures, and United Nations developmental and environmental programs. UNITAR hopes also to establish a program for the continuing examination of major world trends and developments having implications for the future of humanity.

The United Nations Research Institute for Social Development collects information and methodologies of value in developmental planning and provides material for training in social planning.

The World Health Organization seeks to ensure the physical, mental, and social well-being of all peoples and performs a wide range of research, training, and documentation activities.

United States Involvement

The first official United States cultural exchange relationship started in 1840 with a joint resolution of Congress, which provided for the exchange of published materials between the Library of Congress and foreign libraries. In 1900 a group of approximately thirteen hundred teachers from Cuba came to the United States for a summer of study. The Rhodes fund to promote understanding between England and Germany and the United States through the exchange of students was set up in 1902. Then in the 1930s the United States joined the Convention for the Promotion of Inter-American Cultural Relations, which provided for the exchange of graduate students and professors among the countries of the Americas (Hays, 1975).

As the number of students, teachers, and scholars traveling in and out of the United States increased, the involvement of the government grew. In February 1938 President Franklin Delano Roosevelt suggested to his cabinet the necessity for a program of cultural relations with Latin America. In 1939 the Inter-Departmental Committee of Cooperation was established, coordinating the efforts of twenty-five federal agencies; it administered educational exchange programs based on bilateral agreements. In October 1939 a General Advisory Committee was created to allow private citizens an opportunity to advise the government about cultural activities. Of four conferences held in 1939 dealing with cultural affairs, the largest was on education. It was attended by six hundred university and college professors and leaders from forty-six states (Speakman, 1966).

Educational exchange. Immediately after World War II, Senator William Fulbright, once a Rhodes scholar himself, introduced the amendment to the Surplus Property Act of 1944, as Amended (the Fulbright Act), which authorized the creation of an educational program and which was signed into law on August 1, 1946, by President Harry S Truman. This act was further extended and expanded by the Mutual Educational and Cultural Exchange Act of 1961 (the Fulbright-Hays Act), approved by President John F. Kennedy on September 21, 1961. Senator Fulbright has since stated: "It was my thought then, and it is now, that if large numbers of people know and understand the people from nations other than their own, they may develop a capacity for empathy, a distaste for killing other men, and an inclination to peace" (Fulbright, 1975).

During the academic year 1973–74 funds were used to finance the studies of approximately 1160 American students abroad and of 3346 foreign students in the United States (Board of Foreign Scholarships, 1974). Fulbright grants are made to United States citizens and foreign nationals for a variety of educational activities, including university lecturing, advanced research, graduate study, and teaching. Coordinated through the Institute of International Education (IIE), Fulbright grants cover transportation, tuition, maintenance, and incidental expenses. From 1946 through 1976 the number of government grantees steadily increased and seems unlikely to slow down in the foreseeable future. The Fulbright program has been the core of the United States educational exchange program throughout the world.

United States Secretary of State Henry A. Kissinger has stated: "The Fulbright exchange was an expansive concept founded upon a global vision. It has grown to meet new realities. A program which once promoted the solidarity of the West now sustains exchanges between the United States and 122 countries around the globe. It expressed, it helps us to master, the growing interdependence of the world" (Board of Foreign Scholarships, 1974, p. 26).

Agency for International Development. The Agency for International Development (AID) was created in 1961 as the United States government organization offering bilateral assistance to developing countries, mostly in Southeast Asia and the Indian subcontinent. This agency places high priority on its educational activities, which include training local agricultural extension agents and establishing agricultural universities, assisting in the construction of new schools and teacher training, and operating several textbook distribution programs. Most AID programs operate by means of contracts with United States universities or consortia of universities and require the services of United States educational experts. Many other organizations, each offering its own bilateral assistance program, receive support from the Agency for International Development: the Agricultural Development Council (New York City); the Overseas Liaison Committee of the American Council on Education (Washington, D.C.); the American Council of Voluntary Agencies for Foreign Service, Inc. (New York City); the Bureau of Technical Assistance (AID, Washington, D.C.); the Interdisciplinary Communications Program of the Smithsonian Institution (Washington, D.C.); the Maternal and Child Health/Family Planning, Training and Research Center (Nashville, Tennessee); the Midwest Universities Consortium for International Activities, Inc. (East Lansing, Michigan); the Consortium for International Development (Logan, Utah), the Research and Training Network, Agricultural Development Council (New York City); the Technical Assistance Information Clearing House (New York City); and the TransCentury Corporation (Washington, D.C.) (Overseas Liaison Committee, 1973).

National Academy of Sciences. Although

it is not a government agency, the National Academy of Sciences (NAS) is listed in the *United States Government Manual* as a quasi-official agency. Founded in 1863, the National Academy of Sciences has among its purposes to assist the United States government whenever asked in scientific matters, for which it is reimbursed only for expenses incurred. In 1916 the academy was asked by President Woodrow Wilson to organize the National Research Council; in 1964 it founded the National Academy of Engineering as an autonomous parallel institution; and in 1971 it chartered the Institute of Medicine. The National Research Council does not maintain laboratories of its own but supports the work of individual scientists and engineers and coordinates investigations dealing with broad problems of research both nationally and internationally. NAS directly administers annually about $50,000,000 provided by contributions, grants, and contracts from federal and state agencies, private industry and foundations, scientific societies, and individuals. Its programs include committees and conferences, research projects, and fellowships *(United States Government Manual 1975/1976,* 1975).

National Science Foundation. Established in 1950, the National Science Foundation (NSF) initiates and supports fundamental and applied research in all scientific disciplines by means of grants, contracts, and cooperative agreements awarded to university, nonprofit, and other research organizations. Support is also given to problem-oriented interdisciplinary research. Improvement of science education at all levels is encouraged; fellowships are awarded on a competitive basis in the mathematical, physical, medical, biological, engineering, and social sciences, and in the history and philosophy of science. Its international activities include programs to improve information systems and services available to United States and foreign scientists, to foster interchange of information among United States and foreign

scientists, and to provide support for the translation of foreign scientific information. In addition, NSF supports the exchange of American and foreign scientific personnel as well as the development of international science education programs *(United States Government Manual 1975/1976,* 1975).

Division of International Education, Office of Education. The Division of International Education (DIE) of the Office of Education, United States Department of Health, Education and Welfare, plans and administers programs designed to expand and improve the international dimensions of American education. Of the six programs that the division operates within the United States, one program, the Foreign Curriculum Consultant program, authorized by the Fulbright-Hays Act, brings experts from other countries to the United States to assist selected American educational institutions in planning and developing their curricula in foreign language and area studies. Six additional programs, conducted primarily abroad under the auspices of the Fulbright-Hays Act, provide individuals, groups, and institutions with opportunities for research, training, and curriculum development and improvement.

The Doctoral Dissertation Research Abroad program enables advanced graduate students, prospective teachers, and scholars to engage in full-time dissertation research abroad in modern foreign languages, area studies, and world affairs.

The Faculty Research Abroad program is designed to help higher education institutions strengthen their international studies programs by assisting key faculty members to maintain expertise, update curricula, and improve teaching methods and materials in foreign languages and world affairs.

The Group Projects Abroad program provides grants to United States educational institutions or nonprofit educational organizations for training, research, curriculum development, and instructional materials preparation or acquisition in international and intercultural studies. Participants may include college and university faculty members; experienced elementary and secondary school teachers, curriculum supervisors, and administrators; and selected higher education students specializing in foreign language and area studies.

The Advanced Language Training program supports intensive advanced training at United States colleges and universities in certain major non-Western languages for which suitable instruction is available in countries outside the United States.

The Seminars Abroad program provides opportunities for teachers and social studies curriculum specialists at the elementary, secondary, and college levels to participate in short-term seminars outside the United States.

The Teacher Exchange program provides opportunities for elementary and secondary school teachers and, in some cases, college instructors and assistant professors to participate in teacher-exchange programs with other countries on a direct exchange or a one-way basis.

In addition to grant programs, DIE provides four services in the field of international education. The Comparative Education staff researches and publishes studies on the educational systems of other countries. The International Organizations staff works with international organizations, such as UNESCO or the Organisation for Economic Co-operation and Development, in the preparation of reports, surveys, and special studies on American education. It also assists in the development of position papers for international conferences, nominates American educators to serve as delegates to international meetings, recruits American educators for UNESCO field positions in other countries, maintains liaison with other United States government departments and agencies dealing with the educational programs of international organizations, and serves on related interagency committees. The Facilitative Services staff assists visiting foreign educators by itinerary planning and educational counseling. The Clearinghouse staff responds to inquiries through brochures, information pamphlets, letters, and other references about such international activities as student exchange programs, regular academic-year-abroad programs, general educational tours for teachers or students, overseas employment, or programs of financial assistance to foreign students.

Other United States government assistance. In addition to assistance disbursed by the Agency for International Development, the National Academy of Sciences, and the National Science Foundation, the United States government participates in a wide variety of programs for bilateral educational cooperation, by means of special congressional appropriations or by means of other governmental agencies. Organizations receiving this assistance include the American Association of State Colleges and Universities (Washington, D.C.); the American Council of Learned Societies (New York City); the Committee on International Exchange of Persons (Washington, D.C.—U.S. Department of State, Bureau of Educational and Cultural Affairs; principal private agency that cooperates in administering the Senior Fulbright-Hays program); the Council for Intercultural Studies and Programs (New York City); the Institute of International Education (New York City); the Institute of International Studies (Washington, D.C.—U.S. Office of Education); the Interdisciplinary Communications Program of the Smithsonian Institution (Washington, D.C.—National Institutes of Health; Office of Naval Research and Interdisciplinary Communications Associates, Inc.); the Library of Congress, Exchange and Gift Division and Overseas Programs Division (Washington, D.C.); the National Association for Foreign Student Affairs (Washington, D.C.); National Endowments for the Arts and for the Humanities (Washington, D.C.); the National Institutes of Health—Fogarty International Center for Advanced Study in the Health Sciences (Bethesda, Maryland); and the Population Council (New York City) (Overseas Liaison Committee, 1973).

Foundations

Foundations throughout the world have taken a special interest in international education as silent partners. In many instances they have been able to fill gaps left by other agencies, governments, or universities. A list of foundations may be found in the *Yearbook of International Organizations* (1974, pp. S38–S41). One such organization is the Alexander von Humboldt Foundation, in Bonn–Bad Godesberg, which was organized in 1860 under the Board of Trustees of the Prussian Academy of Science. Although the foundation became inoperative during both world wars, the Federal Republic of Germany reestablished it in 1953. It now awards 440 research fellowships annually to outstanding international candidates for advanced study in Germany. Outstanding German scholars accept prospective fellows to work under them (Lynen, 1975). Another foundation with international programs, the *Fondation universitaire,* in Brussels, was created in 1920 to support scholars, researchers, and students in the social, natural, and applied sciences. It is funded by the Belgian government and provides fellowship grants to graduate students for scientific study abroad (Overseas Liaison Committee, 1973).

Many United States foundations fill an important role in assisting with the bilateral development of higher education, especially in developing countries. Such organizations include the Edward W. Hazen Foundation (New Haven, Connecticut), established in 1925, with interests in educational projects of a pioneering nature. This foundation has engaged in the improvement of liberal higher education and of international cultural exchanges, and has given special attention to higher education in developing societies. The W. K.

Kellogg Foundation (Battle Creek, Michigan), founded in 1930, concentrates much of its effort on health, agriculture, and expanded programs, as well as on opportunities in higher education.

Carnegie Corporation. The Carnegie Corporation of New York was organized in 1911 as a philanthropic foundation concerned with the advancement and diffusion of knowledge and understanding. Carnegie grants have supported programs in teacher training, curriculum reform, and educational research at universities in Africa, the Caribbean, and the South Pacific. Since 1970 special emphasis has been placed on assisting in the development of several African universities, including the University of Botswana, Lesotho and Swaziland; the University of Nigeria in Nsukka; and Makerere University, Kampala, Uganda. Organizations conducting their own bilateral educational programs that receive support from the Carnegie Corporation include the Overseas Liaison Committee of the American Council on Education (Washington, D.C.) and the Institute of International Education (New York City) (Overseas Liaison Committee, 1973).

Ford Foundation. Established in 1936, initially to provide assistance at the local level, the Ford Foundation has now become involved in worldwide charitable, educational, and scientific activities. The foundation provides assistance in the development of promising new approaches to undergraduate and graduate instruction and supports research or training within the United States and other developed countries. The Ford Foundation maintains a large international division with overseas offices and representatives that attempt to keep appraised of the needs of institutions of higher learning in developing nations. For example, Latin American students have received grants to support graduate studies and research in recognized institutions; and in recent years the foundation has provided graduate training abroad for staff members from several

African universities. Thus, it has an interest in solving the educational needs of the growing nations of the world.

The Ford Foundation supports the bilateral educational programs of the following organizations in addition to its own programs: the Agricultural Development Council (New York City); the Overseas Liaison Committee of the American Council on Education (Washington, D.C.); the Foreign Area Fellowship Program of the American Council of Learned Societies and the Social Science Research Council (New York City); the Institute of International Education (New York City); the International Legal Center (New York City); the International Studies Association (Minneapolis, Minnesota); the Midwest Universities Consortium for International Activities, Inc. (East Lansing, Michigan); and the Population Council (New York City) (Overseas Liaison Committee, 1973).

Rockefeller Foundation. In 1913 the Rockefeller Foundation was chartered as a nonprofit organization with an interest in promoting cultural development in the United States and throughout the world. Among its present objectives are the conquest of hunger and the development of higher education. University development programs by the foundation have been concentrated in the Philippines, Indonesia, Thailand, Colombia, Brazil, Kenya, Nigeria, Zaire, Uganda, and Tanzania. The establishment of regional centers at the graduate level has been emphasized. In addition, the foundation has participated in the development of international agricultural research institutes in Mexico, the Philippines, Colombia, and Nigeria. Basic agricultural research is being conducted at the centers, which also serve as research training grounds for young agricultural scientists from many nations. In addition, the Rockefeller Foundation supports the Population Council (New York City) in its program of bilateral educational cooperation (Overseas Liaison Committee, 1973).

Other organizations. Other organizations

are concerned with problems in specific regions. The African-American Institute (New York City); the Asia Foundation (San Francisco, California), and the Organization of American States (Washington, D.C.) assist local as well as regional organizations in a wide range of research and training. Financial support is provided to needy educational institutions, and scholarships are available for graduate training in the organizations' home areas and abroad (Overseas Liaison Committee, 1973).

The Future

Cultural and educational exchange among nations appears to enjoy a bright outlook for the future. There will continue to be an emphasis on the developing countries and an interest in cooperation and sharing on the part of the more advanced nations. A high-quality liberal education in the next century will include more basic courses relevant to the development and emergence of new nations. Increasingly, students will seek the international component and include it in their curriculum, so that they can become personally involved in one or more world cultures in addition to their own.

University leaders throughout the world will explore opportunities in the realm of expanding educational cooperation, particularly as it relates to scholarship, instructional development, research, and the dissemination of ideas. Leaders from developing nations will be less interested in the traditional forms of assistance and more interested in real cooperation and collaboration on an equal basis. Areas of mutual interest will be explored so that a truly bilateral relationship will be established.

Opportunities for effective educational interchange are almost limitless. All nations must become involved: those from Africa, Latin America, the Near East, the Far East, the oil-producing countries, the communist-bloc nations, and North America.

Governments will continue to carry a

major share of the financial burden in developing and maintaining institutions of higher learning. Nevertheless, private institutes, academies, and foundations will continue to play a key role in filling the gaps and seeing that worthwhile objectives are sought. Universities will be called upon to broaden their perspectives and continue their role as seekers of truth and instigators of new methods of educational development.

It is entirely possible that the study of international education can lead to a better understanding of man. National systems of education are inadequate for the challenges of the time, and new institutions need to be created to bridge the gaps created by a strict nationalism. As Poulsen has stated: "Education must become truly universal if we are to realize the common humanity of man" (Poulsen, 1969, p. 7).

Bibliography

Altbach, P. G., and Kelly, D. H. *Higher Education in Developing Nations: A Selected Bibliography, 1969–1974.* New York: Praeger, 1975.

Beeby, C. E. *The Quality of Education in Developing Countries.* Cambridge, Massachusetts: Harvard University Press, 1966.

Board of Foreign Scholarships. *Report on Exchanges, December 1974, Twelfth Annual Report.* Washington, D.C.: U.S. Government Printing Office, 1974.

Butts, R. F. *American Education in International Development.* New York: Harper & Row, 1963.

Carnegie Corporation of New York. *Quarterly,* April 1963, *11*(2).

Carter, W. D. *Study Abroad and Educational Development.* Paris: UNESCO, 1973.

Edgerton, W. B. "Trends in Educational Exchange." *Exchange,* 1975, *11*(1).

Franks, H. G. *The Dutch System of International Education.* The Hague: Netherlands Universities Foundation for International Cooperation, 1971.

Fulbright, J. W. "The Creative Power of Exchange." *Exchange,* 1975, *11*(1).

Geimer, R., and Geimer, H. *Science in the Federal Republic of Germany—Organization and Promotion.* (3rd ed.) Bonn–Bad Godesberg, Federal Republic of Germany: Deutscher akademischer Austauschdienst, 1974.

Hays, W. L. "A View from the Hill." *Exchange,* 1975, *11*(1)

Inter-University Council. *Cooperation Through Links.* London: IUC, 1975.

Lynen, F. *Aims and Functions of the Alexander von Humboldt Foundation.* Bonn–Bad Godesberg, Federal Republic of Germany: Alexander von Humboldt Foundation, 1975.

Mutual Education Exchange Program. *Abroad Under the Fulbright-Hays Act, 1977–78.* Washington, D.C.: Council for International Exchange of Scholars, 1976.

Norway's Assistance to Developing Countries in 1974. Oslo: Norwegian Agency for International Development, 1975.

Overseas Liaison Committee. *International Directory for Educational Liaison.* Washington, D.C.: Overseas Liaison Committee, 1973.

Poulsen, F. R. *Changing Dimensions in International Education.* Tucson: University of Arizona Press, 1969.

Speakman, C. E., Jr. *International Exchange in Education.* New York: Center for Applied Research in Education, 1966.

Study Abroad: International Scholarships and Courses. Paris: UNESCO, 1974.

United States Government Manual, 1975/1976. Revised May 1, 1975. Washington, D.C.: Office of the Federal Register, National Archives and Records Service, General Services Administration, 1975.

Weidner, E. W. *The World Role of Universities.* New York: McGraw-Hill, 1962.

Yearbook of International Organizations. Brussels: Union of International Associations, 1974.

KEITH R. ALLRED

See also: International Development, Role of in Higher Education.

4. MULTINATIONAL CORPORATIONS AND LATERAL AID

The world economy has changed rapidly since 1950. National borders are no longer the strong bulwarks against the economic fluctuations of neighboring or even distant countries. The world is moving steadily toward a global economy: an economy woven together by the trade patterns of all nations.

Part of this movement has been caused by the rapid growth of multinational corporations—corporations that transcend national boundaries in their operations. Since World War II, foreign trade has increased dramatically; in the twenty-four-year period between 1950 and 1974, exports from the United States rose from $10,100,000,000 to $98,000,000,000, representing approximately an 870 percent increase. In that same period, direct foreign investments by the United States climbed from $11,800,000,000 to $118,600,000,000—a 900 percent rise. These figures indicate that world trade and investment will continue to tie the economies of the world closer together and that multinational corporations will play an important role in the process.

In 1970 multinational corporations accounted for close to 15 percent of the three-trillion-dollar total gross world product (GWP). Predictions peg the 1980 contribution of these companies at almost 50 percent of the gross world product (Teague, 1971).

Multinationalism is not merely a phenomenon of American business. Of the $450,000,000,000 pumped into the world economy by multinationals, 44 percent came from companies based in the United States that operated abroad; 22 percent came from foreign companies that operated in the United States; and 33 percent came from interproduction between nations (Teague, 1971).

The United States, with its large market of affluent consumers, is increasingly becoming a host nation for corporations of other nations. Direct investment by foreign companies in the United States grew 108 percent between 1960 and 1972, climbing from $6,900,000,000 to $14,400,000,000 (Dent, 1974), and reached $21,700,000,000 by the end of 1974.

The economic crisis of the 1970s centering around the production and distribution of oil has not only highlighted the economic interdependence of all nations but has fanned the fire of worldwide foreign investment. Nations newly rich in oil have huge surpluses of revenues, which cannot be spent completely in their own countries. The problem of recycling the skyrocketing pile of petrodollars held by these nations severely shook the structure of the international financial system in the fall of 1974. The problem is not over: the $60,000,000,000 1974 petrodollar surplus should mushroom to between $200,000,000,000 and $250,000,000,000 by 1978 ("Estimates of Petrodollar Surplus," 1975).

Future capital movements should see a continuation of the move away from traditional exporting and toward direct investment. Much of the 1974 and 1975 petrodollar surplus went to finance direct and portfolio investment in foreign countries. There can be little doubt that this trend will continue. More and more of the trade decisions of countries will be wrested out of the hands of nation-states and placed in the hands of private corporations. The world market will no longer be the exclusive preserve of the giant companies and the developed nations. Smaller enterprises and less developed countries will continue to enter the multinational arena, realizing that they too can expand profits through investments abroad. There should be a continued trend for foreign direct investment to expand out of the traditional areas of raw material extraction and manufacturing and into the service areas, such as consulting, education, advertising, and law.

Current Impact on Education

The continued internationalization of world business and growth of multinational corporations has had a substantial impact on higher education through direct donations of funds to educational institutions and through the creation of new programs to educate a new type of corporate manager.

Direct donations. Corporations have long played an important role in the educational system of the United States. Alfred P. Sloan, former chairman of the board of General Motors, once stated: "When the annals of our time are recorded, it will most likely be found that the two greatest contributions of our time have been the

U.S. university and the U.S. corporation: both mighty forces, both uniquely American. If these forces can go forward together in understanding and cooperation, there is perhaps no problem beyond their joint power of resolution. If, however, they choose to go their separate ways, there is no solution of any problem affecting either that is likely to be long lasting" (*Handbook of Aid to Higher Education by Corporations,* 1974, p. Aiii).

For the most part, American business appears to have heeded Sloan's advice. The Council on Financial Aid to Education estimates that two thirds of the total funds received annually by all colleges and universities in the United States comes from corporate endowments. In addition, almost 15 percent of all voluntary funds, or annual contributions, to education in the United States are from corporations *(Handbook of Aid to Higher Education by Corporations,* 1974).

In the academic year ending June 1974, total corporate giving to higher education in the United States reached almost $475,000,000. Of this figure, 75 percent ($356,000,000) was given directly to colleges and universities, while the remaining 25 percent was given in other forms of corporate aid to education, such as scholarships and fellowships awarded either directly to the student or through associations and foundations. The $356,000,000 spent by corporations represents 15.8 percent of the total package of voluntary support contributions that universities and colleges in the United States received from various donors in that year (*CFAE Newsletter,* 1975).

It is difficult to estimate what portion of this figure can be attributed to corporations having worldwide operations. However, many large multinationals, such as International Business Machines Corporation (IBM), International Telephone and Telegraph Corporation (ITT), and Exxon Corporation, are substantial contributors to the United States educational system. The same is true for the British Petroleum Company Limited in England, Volkswagen A.G. in Germany, and Dentsu Advertising

Limited in Japan. In addition, many of the major philanthropic foundations—such as Ford, Carnegie, and Rockefeller in the United States, Pahlevi in Iran, and Agnelli in Italy—have their roots in industry and multinationalism.

Outside the United States, where government support of private education is more prevalent, corporations have played a vital part in the growth of management education. In Europe, where business schools were a rare exception prior to World War II, corporations met the challenge of filling the gap that existed in the academic offerings of universities, which were more concerned with traditional academic disciplines than with business management. Corporations established their own schools or joined together in cooperative efforts to educate their managers at institutes such as the *Centre d'études industrielles* (CEI: International Management Development Institute) in Geneva and IMEDE Management Development Institute in Lausanne, Switzerland. These world-renowned institutes were established by Alcan Aluminum Corporation of Canada and by Nestle Alimentara S.A. of Switzerland, respectively.

In France the *Ecole des hautes études commerciales du nord,* the oldest and one of the leading French schools of business, was founded in 1881 and is supported directly by the chamber of commerce. Other schools of business, such as the *Ecole supérieure des sciences économiques et commerciales* (ESSEC), founded in 1935 to offer excellent full-time instruction in business as well as many part-time evening and institute-type programs, are heavily dependent on contributions from corporations.

The Iran Center for Management Studies in Tehran, which was founded in 1970, was made possible by major contributions for both working capital and endowment by Iranian and foreign multinational corporations and continues to receive strong industry support.

Overseas subsidiaries contribute to education in their foreign locations. Although the amount of such contributions is difficult to estimate, experts believe that industry involvement in host country charitable donations is growing steadily. Richard Barnet and Ronald Muller (1974) have pointed out that the amount of donations is undoubtedly substantial. At the University of Warwick in England, for example, there is a Barclay's Bank Chair of Management Information Systems, a Volkswagen Chair of German, and a British Leyland Motors Chair of Industrial Relations. Schools in France and the Federal Republic of Germany are highly endowed, as are Japanese, Iranian, and Canadian schools (Barnet and Muller, 1974).

In Mexico, Ralston Purina, Singer, Pullman-Kellogg, and Carnation Companies have all made contributions to Querétaro University in Querétaro, according to Barnet and Muller. At Anáhuac University in Mexico City the law school was donated by Chase Manhattan Bank, and Eastman Kodak contributed a laboratory facility (Barnet and Muller, 1974). Ford Motor Company has been responsible for building eighty-two schools in Latin America, and IBM has built scientific centers around the world.

The Asian Institute of Management (AIM) is another example of regional development by multinational corporations and local industry. Located in a suburb of Manila, this nonprofit institute offers high-quality management education to students and executives primarily from sixteen Asian nations. Without strong industry support, the institute would never have been realized. The Manila-based Ayala Corporation donated land for the institute's site, and a leading Filipino businessman, Eugenio Lopez, underwrote construction of all the facilities. Chairman of the board and one of the founders is Washington C. Sycip, head of the largest auditing and management consulting firm outside of the United States. Among the corporate donors that have enabled the institute to continue and expand are Caltex (Philippines) Incorporated, First National City Bank, IBM, Mobil Oil–Philippines, Pepsi Cola Bottling Company, Procter and Gamble PMC, and U.S. Industries Philippines Incorporated.

In addition, many national and international companies have established scholarships to provide educational opportunities for worthy scholars. For example, college scholarships to deserving students are awarded by Citibank in the Philippines, Greece, Indonesia, and the Bahamas. Citibank's Bahamas representative discussed their rationale by stating that "the government of the Bahamas has placed great stress on the education of its people in recent years and the branch felt that the university scholarship program was the best way to demonstrate its concern for the government's educational goals" (*Top Management Report*, 1975, p. 30).

In 1974 McGraw-Hill Incorporated and other major publishers from the United States made available nearly forty tons of books at a substantial discount to the Franklin Book Program, which was conducting a massive "book lift" to war-torn Bangladesh under a United States Agency for International Development (AID) relief and rehabilitation grant. The books sent to Bangladesh were to replenish six university libraries badly damaged during the 1971 war (*Top Management Report*, 1975).

Changes in management programs. The transnational nature of modern business requires that the manager of today know more than the functional areas of business, such as accounting, finance, marketing, and research, which are traditional to the business school curriculum. Political science, regional economics, cultural anthropology, and languages are all increasingly needed in the management perspective as corporations cross national borders. Growing internationalism has created the need for a new breed of manager, who can function across national boundaries and adjust to cultural differences, and whose business knowledge can cross over normal functional lines to tie him to a worldwide environment.

Fayerweather, Boddewyn, and Engberg (1966) point out in their book on international business education that it is not just the overseas manager who must be schooled in international matters. Using the United States as an example, there are actually five classes of managers affected by the growing internationalization of world business. These include (1) United States personnel; (2) United States–based foreign personnel; (3) managers in the United States with direct international responsibilities; (4) managers in the United States without direct responsibility but affected by international business; and (5) managers who are indirectly affected and need to know about international business in order to be intelligent businessmen. In addition, the politician who legislates, government officials who administer, and agency representatives who enforce the legislation must be equally aware of the scope and impact of multinational corporate activity.

The fifth category of manager—the manager who is indirectly affected by international business—is growing daily. Even though the direct growth of multinationalism skyrockets annually, it is the indirect impact of multinationalism on local economies that is making it imperative for higher education to have a more global perspective. Despite its rapid growth and economic importance, international business is still very much of an uncharted and unstructured educational discipline. As a field, international business did not actually come into existence until the 1950s. The number of courses, texts, research projects, and related materials has grown steadily since that time.

For example, the Harvard Intercollegiate Case Clearing House, an organization that categorizes, publishes, and sells business case studies to professors for classroom use, began listing international and foreign cases in 1959. At that time, they had 242 such case listings. In 1969 there were over 1800 such titles and the number is still growing (Terpstra, 1970).

Research into the field has also increased.

A study of business research by Richard W. Wright found that, prior to 1960, only about sixteen research projects in international business were being published annually (Wright, 1970). By 1972 the annual number had jumped to 111. Current research shows increasing sophistication and concern with the broader policy problems of strategy and structure of international business.

Some universities are now offering international business courses as a part of their required core curriculum, while others have developed special international business programs. A few have centers where research is carried out and international managers receive continuing education on topical matters. New York University, Columbia University, the University of Indiana, George Washington University, the University of California at Berkeley and Los Angeles, and the University of Michigan all have large international business programs. The University of Pennsylvania has a separate international business unit; Harvard University has a Multinational Studies Center; and Cleveland State University is in the process of developing a World Trade Education Center.

All schools, whatever their approach to business education, are being changed by the growth of multinational business. The old philosophy that "business is business" and can be taught universally is being challenged by a changing world and the growth of international business. International business is not adequately covered in the traditional business curriculum of most business schools and is sorely lacking in the social sciences.

The American Assembly of Collegiate Schools of Business has adopted the policy of requiring all member schools to internationalize core curricula because of the changing requirements of business. For many schools, this internationalization will take the form of a required course in the various degree programs that would offer the student an insight into the divergent nature of business operations overseas as compared to operations within his own national borders. Such a course may be either an introductory-level course or a business policy course at the end of the student's program. Other schools have decided that the best approach is to internationalize all functional areas; that is, to have a section of courses in accounting, marketing, finance, and production devoted to international operations. Other schools, while offering core courses, have developed major fields of study in international business. One of the more complete is at George Washington University, where, in addition to the introductory-level courses in international business and economics, courses are offered in such areas as international marketing management, international financial management, international production, management of international research and development, legal aspects of international business, comparative business management, international communication, and business policy for the multinational enterprise. Major fields of study are available at the bachelor's, master's, and doctoral level.

In 1969 a nationwide survey by the Academy of United States Business Schools found that 85 percent of the 111 responding colleges and universities offered international business courses and programs. These respondent schools were members of both the American Assembly of Collegiate Schools of Business and the Academy of International Business (the leading professional group in the study of multinational operations) and accounted for 44 percent of all business degrees awarded at the bachelor's level in the United States; 70 percent of all master's degrees; and 90 percent of all doctoral degrees. Of the surveyed schools, seventy-three offered courses at the master's level and twenty offered courses at the doctoral level. Most of the universities were located on either the east or west coast of the United States (Terpstra, 1970).

The study also found that, although there was a great variety of courses, the most popular were those in general international business and international marketing. These courses were followed in frequency by those dealing with international management, international finance, and international advertising (Terpstra, 1970). No ancillary data are available on specific courses in such related areas as political science and economics; however, the topic of multinationalism on the part of corporations has added a new dimension to studies in these and other closely related fields, such as sociology, psychology, and law.

There can be little doubt that the field of international business education will continue to grow and that multinational corporations will play an important role in its development. The time will come when knowledge of the international dimensions of management will be as important to the future manager as the basic core curriculum of accounting, finance, marketing, and mathematics is today. Even students who do not plan to follow an international business career will find that they will need this knowledge to be effective managers, government officials, or politicians. The importance of world trade and commerce has long been understood by the Europeans and the Japanese. As the United States, with its high standard of living and heavy consumption patterns, increasingly becomes a target of foreign investors, the "domestic" manager will suddenly find himself thrust even more into the international arena.

The growth of multinational corporations has created the need for a macro approach to business operations and education. International business is fraught with problems of both a transnational and environmental nature, which are not of concern to purely domestic firms. Transnational problems include tariff regulations, double taxation, exchange and currency fluctuations, special antitrust problems, and political requirements. Special sociocultural problems caused by conducting business in a foreign country may include language, customs, methods of doing business, and the cultural attitudes of employees and customers.

International business students and managers need to be knowledgeable in areas that include (1) technical aspects of international trade, taxation, finance, and marketing; (2) behavioral science aspects of the social, political, and cultural environment of nations; (3) comparative business studies of worldwide industries; (4) area business studies; (5) language; and (6) international business management and administration. Instruction in the last area should teach the future manager how to organize, manage, evaluate, and make decisions in the international firm based at home and in a foreign environment. The overall objectives of an international business education should be to sensitize the potential manager to the intricacies of global business operations and to develop both a knowledge of international subject matter and a cultural empathy that will allow him to function efficiently in any environment.

Changes in other disciplines. The growth of worldwide business will continue to have an impact on other educational disciplines as well. The booming industries and development of the oil-rich countries have caused a growth in educational facilities of all kinds internationally. Expansion of physical facilities will be matched by increasing enrollments in colleges and universities around the world as the need for global specialists in fields such as engineering, the environment, telecommunications, and world health grows.

In the developing nations of the world, education should flourish as economic growth increases and stabilizes. Not only literate technicians but also local managers and future multinational executives will be required. The growing nationalism experienced in the 1970s should have a profound impact on the future ability of giant corporations to transfer management skills from the home office, without drawing on the existing talent within the host nation.

Perhaps the biggest change will come in the area of linguistic education. According to a survey in Europe, approximately 60 percent of Italian businessmen and 50 percent of French and German businessmen could not understand written or spoken English (Heyman, 1973). Language as a

requirement in universities throughout the United States has dropped greatly. If the trend toward global corporations continues, the need for managers trained in more than one language will undoubtedly become imperative.

Potential Impact on Education

Multinational corporations will continue to exercise a great degree of influence on higher education, both through the growth of multinationalism itself and through continued support of programs for higher education. In a report by the special Brookings panel, *The International Dimension of Management Education* (1975, pp. 1–3), the panel concluded:

International business enterprises—and even very large ones—are nothing new, nor is their entanglement in political affairs within and between nation states. But in recent years, the MNC has become a phenomenon of new magnitude, emerging with breathtaking speed. A development not yet in ebb, it has arisen from a confluence of (1) ever-changing technology in the production, financing, and distribution of products, (2) new forms of information gathering, processing, and transmission, (3) the weakening of the postwar *Pax Americana,* and (4) the hard fact of heterogeneity in the worldwide distribution of natural resources, human skills, social and political institutions, and rates of growth of consumption and saving.

The earlier transnational corporation that produced for domestic and export markets is being replaced or surrounded by diversified corporations or conglomerates with numerous subsidiaries that buy, produce, and sell in many countries, often worldwide. Even domestic business is increasingly affected by international influences related to raw material sources, exchange rates, foreign economic policies, and domestically situated foreign competition. . . . In short, a global rationalization of economic activities is occurring on a scale and in dimensions hitherto unknown. It may not continue at the same pace, but there is no reason to expect a major turnabout soon. We must now accept and cope with a new kind of world economic and business environment. The implications for everyone are enormous.

An immediate implication is that we have entered a period of adjustments and surprises, the kinds of realignment that follow major structural changes as aftershocks follow an earthquake. Confusion and often anxiety are present to a degree greater than usual, bringing with them a sharp increase in conflict over such broad issues as jobs, incomes, and wealth, as well as markets, technology transfers, capital movements, prices, taxes, profits, and differing standards as regards such things as bribery and corruption. The conflicting parties are interested "stakeholders": employees, organized labor, competitors, suppliers, customers, taxpayers, owners, local governments, and nation-states themselves, both developed and developing. To the extent they are not embraced in these categories, they also include the managers in their fiduciary roles for other stakeholders.

The realignment, uncertainty, and acrimony will be unusually sharp in the near term, meaning five to ten years, as new laws, new institutions, new attitudes and expectations, new procedures, and new leaders emerge. Then, perhaps, the strife will decrease as the world adapts to its economic organization.

Multinational firms are now a major factor in both the world economy and world politics. They are rich and powerful and therefore are coming under increasing scrutiny by the public. Some observers see them as future world unifiers, others as another form of neocolonialism. Supporters see them as creating trade revenues for the United States, opponents view them as exporting jobs. The need for knowledgeable international businessmen who can manage these growing giants will become increasingly critical in the years to come, as will the need for astute officials capable of developing the legislative structure that will be necessary to govern these corporate giants. To higher education worldwide falls the task of providing the educated manpower necessary to accomplish these managerial objectives.

Bibliography

Barnet, R. J., and Muller, R. E. *Global Reach: The Power of the Multinational Corporations.* New York: Simon & Schuster, 1974.

CFAE Newsletter. New York: Council for Financial Aid to Education, April 1975.

Dent, F. B. "The Multinational Corporation—Toward a World Economy." *Financial Executive,* February 1974, *42,* 42–47.

"Estimates of Petrodollar Surplus Are Cut." *Wall Street Journal,* May 23, 1975, p. 4.

Fayerweather, J., Boddewyn, J., and Engberg, H. *International Business Education.* New York: New York University Press, 1966.

Handbook of Aid to Higher Education by Corporations. New York: Council for Financial Aid to Education, 1974.

Heyman, P. "Multinationalism—European Style: A New Way of Integration." *Report from Europe,* November–December 1973.

The International Dimension of Management Education. Washington, D.C.: Brookings Institution, 1975.

Teague, B. "Multinational Corporations: Profiles and Prospects." *Conference Board Record,* September 1971, *8*(9), 20–31.

Terpstra, V. "University Education for International Business." *Journal of International Business Studies,* 1970, *1,* 89–96.

Top Management Report on Government-Business Corporation in the Field of International Public Affairs. Washington, D.C.: International Management and Development Institute, 1975.

Wright, R. W. "Trends in International Business Research." *Journal of International Business Studies,* 1970, *1,* 109–123.

PHILLIP D. GRUB

See also: International Management Education; Philanthropy and Foundations.

5. TECHNOLOGY TRANSFER

Technology is the systematic use of all technical knowledge, methods, and operations in the control of nature; technology and social organization overlap insofar as technology usually incorporates administrative systems and work organization. *General technology* is information common to a sector; *system-specific technology* is information used in the manufacture of a particular product or in the provision of a specific service; and *enterprise-specific technology* is information specific to a particular enterprise or to a unit providing services but which cannot be attributed to any particular product or service. Technology never exists in isolation; it is *product-embodied* or *process-embodied* and, in varying degrees, *person-embodied,* as it always exists in someone's mind.

Technology transfer refers to the communication and adoption of technology in an enterprise, industry, economic sector, or region. Technology transfer can take place internationally as well as within a single country. It can involve both *vertical* transfer, when information is transmitted from basic to applied research, from applied research to development, and from development to production; and *horizontal* transfer, when technology used in one place, organization, or context is transferred and used in another place, organization, or context. Horizontal technology transfer includes several phases. *Material transfer* is characterized by the simple transfer of new materials, such as seeds, plants, animals, machines, and the relevant management techniques. *Design transfer* involves the transfer of information in the form of blueprints, journals, and books. During this phase new plant materials, animal breeding stock, or prototype machinery may be introduced for testing or copying; new plants and animals may be subjected to systematic tests, propagation, and selection; and machines may be tested and designs modified in accordance with local conditions and individual tasks. *Capacity transfer*, through the transfer of scientific and technical knowledge, works to institutionalize a new capacity for a continuous stream of locally adapted technology, so that a locality or country can become less dependent on prototypes developed elsewhere. It corresponds to the creation of an independent problem-solving capability. Consequently, particularly important in capacity transfer are the movement of individual scientists and engineers and the building of research and educational institutions.

Technology Transfer and Economic Growth

The role of technology in the development process is not a simple, easily isolated and identified phenomenon, but it is generally agreed that technological change is the most crucial single variable in economic growth. The specific role of technology transfer between countries has received serious attention only since World War II,

and a better understanding of the transfer process and its inherent obstacles is important in formulating policies designed for faster and easier transfer on a large scale. The removal of obstacles to technology transfer—economic, political, social, legal, and institutional—helps to stimulate economic growth, but a number of inhibiting conflicts remain in the relations between technology suppliers and recipients.

The availability of modern transferable technology has increased the interdependence of countries and shifted developmental concern from indigenous technological evolution to the transfer of technology from one country to another. The technological gap between developing and industrialized countries is of relatively recent origin, as the economic progress of the industrialized countries has been achieved only in the last century. Uneven development—which is at the core of technology transfers—has been the rule as nations move through various modes of production. India was economically superior to Britain before becoming an exploited colony. Britain, once the center of industrialization, is rapidly declining in relative importance. India is now slowly reemerging and gathering strength, albeit more slowly than another potential giant, the People's Republic of China. Many of the national superiorities of the 1970s are likely to be transitory, and technology transfer will play an important role in future transitions. However, the ability to control the technology transfer, rather than the availability of technology, is going to be the decisive factor.

Goulet (1975b, p. 14) concludes that "technology is perhaps the most vital arena where cultures and subcultures will either survive or be crushed. Their absorptive capacity will be tested in this arena." Borrowed technology contributes to the expanding vitality of the borrowing culture only insofar as it both nourishes and draws nourishment from the activities that led to borrowing in the first place. If it becomes a substitute for native forces, it is destructive rather than constructive.

Technology transfer during the last quarter of the twentieth century is likely to differ from that of earlier periods, not only because demand for it is increasing as countries and regions are drawn into much closer interaction and differences in material production among nations are increasingly obvious, but also because technology is much more intimately related to science than in the past. Thus, the developing countries must attempt not only to approach, by adaptation, a much higher level of science and technology, but they must also reach for science and technology that are continually and rapidly moving to higher levels. And practically all this advancement takes place in the industrialized countries. For example, increased activity and interest of engineers are needed to transfer and apply skills in more creative ways. Consequently, postsecondary engineering curricula in donor as well as recipient countries must be designed with this in mind. In industrialized countries engineering curricula must respond to the needs of an increasing number of foreign graduates residing in industrialized countries. In developing countries, new curricula are urgently needed in order to help engineers participate in the development, control, and redirection of technology transfer.

Transfer Mechanisms

A mechanism for transferring technology is any means for making available to a production unit those elements of technical knowledge required to set up or operate production facilities. Considering the range of technologies that may be transferred, it is hardly surprising that a wide variety of mechanisms can be used. These mechanisms include the flow of published information, such as technical journals and books; foreign travel of students, engineers, and scientists; and technical aid and cooperation programs arranged by governments. Person-embodied decisional or capacity technology is generally channeled through nonprofit institutions such as government agencies, universities, and foundations. However, most technology relevant for production is channeled by commercial units, and it is generally the commercial exchange of technology—the importation of machinery, equipment, agreements on patents, licensing, and know-how—through direct foreign investments and multinational corporations that is the focus of discussions on technology transfer mechanisms. Goulet (1975b, p. 44) also notes that "much of what is called technology transfer in aid literature is not technology transfer in the strict sense but rather technical assistance whose aim is to initiate people into scientific knowledge or some learnable skill. The primary aim of transfers, however, is system-specific or enterprise-specific technology, the only kind which directly affects the production of goods or the provision of services. At best, technical assistance serves as an infrastructural investment which may benefit future production."

Goulet (1975b) differentiates six or more modes of technology transfer, including direct investment by a large corporation into its subsidiaries, patents agreements, licensing agreements, servicing contracts, provision of training, and supply of technical manuals and instructions. However, a simple two-part distinction can be used in the analysis of transfer mechanisms. On the one hand, transfer can occur through *direct* relationships between suppliers—each responsible for some of the technical knowledge required—and the recipient. On the other hand, a single enterprise in an advanced country can be responsible for supervision of the whole transfer and play an intermediary or *indirect* role by giving subcontracts to other specialist enterprises in advanced countries. In spite of the complexity of the transfer process, mechanisms might be classified into two broad groups: (1) mechanisms that are used when recipient enterprises are in direct contact with suppliers of technical knowledge and (2) mechanisms that are used when an enterprise in an advanced country plays an intermediary role in the transfer process. The intermediary then provides a "package" of technical knowledge to the recipient."

In terms of transfer mechanisms, limited to the elements of technical knowledge that are needed to set up specific new production facilities rather than such general facilities, providing technical information in general is a different and wider problem involving a larger number of other mechanisms than technology transfer (Brooks, 1966).

Direct transfer mechanisms. Direct transfer mechanisms include contracting of individual experts and consultants, engaging engineering design and plant construction enterprises, training nationals for specific production projects, providing technical information, and transferring the process technology embodied in capital goods by importing equipment.

The direct purchase of plant and equipment from manufacturers or suppliers plays an important role in technology transfer, but process technology embodied in machinery is only one element of technical knowledge that a production enterprise may need. For example, plant and equipment for the production of petrochemicals may be purchased directly, but the technical knowledge needed to operate such plants may be available only from chemical companies in advanced countries. The conditions for direct transfer through machinery suppliers are probably most favorable where technologies are "mature," technological advance is relatively slow, and proprietary technology is not extensive.

Indirect transfer mechanisms. Indirect mechanisms of technology transfer involve an enterprise in the advanced country acting as an intermediary. A number of contractual arrangements are used in the indirect transfer of technology—wholly

owned subsidiaries, licensing agreements, turnkey-plant agreements, management contracts, service agreements, and engineering and construction agreements. The intermediaries may be a contracting group, but more often they are enterprises engaged in production activities of the same type as those transferred. Frequently, such enterprises initiate the transfer, particularly when the intermediary company establishes a wholly owned subsidiary in the developing country.

The use of an intermediary is justified for the following reasons: (1) deficiencies in the recipient's ability to use technology, (2) the use of proprietary process technology in the transfer process, and (3) the use of trademarks and brand names in the transfer process. As the company that owns the process technology is generally the intermediary and often controls other parts of the transfer as well, the recipient has little incentive to diversify its sources of technical knowledge. The supplier usually has well-established links with engineering designers and construction companies acquainted with its process technologies, and substitute technology may not be acceptable for the equipment or procedures of a project. Because returns normally depend on the economic success of the recipient, the supplier has an interest in ensuring that the plant is properly designed and constructed and that production and marketing operations are managed efficiently. Often, the most efficient way to guarantee success is to obtain an agreement for de facto control over the construction and possibly also the operation of the project. In addition, the market for products to be manufactured with transferred technology is well established and conditioned to the brand names and trademarks of specific foreign suppliers. Consequently, enterprises installing new production facilities may be concerned as much with the right to use established foreign brand names on their products as with the technologies needed to manufacture them.

The most successful agents of rapid

though not always relevant transfer of capital-embodied technology are the subsidiaries of multinational companies. The activities in such transfer are not restricted to blueprints or to advice by experts. The parent firm and its specialists usually act as one unit in the actual operation, and all the know-how and skills of the parent company are transferred to the new unit; new workers are educated through on-the-job training. The entrepreneurial capacity of the parent company is mobilized in order to integrate the various elements of the new production unit.

It is difficult to reach any general conclusion about the advantages and disadvantages of direct and indirect transfer. However, it is desirable for the recipient to diversify its sources of technology, either by using as many direct transfer mechanisms as possible or by having agreements with a number of intermediaries. The more the supplier controls the transfer process, the less the recipient will be required to use and develop its skills. Undiversified technology transfer thus perpetuates the technological dependence of the developing country and limits its enterprises to a passive role in industrial activities.

Problems in International Transfer

In international technology transfer involving two or more parties, a number of conflicting interests exist, the most outstanding of which are costs and technological relevance.

Costs. The transfer of technology is by no means without cost. Like any economic activity, it uses up resources. The costs of building a plant in another country generally include engineering consultation prior to construction, transfer of engineering information, conversion of the process or product, supervision of the detailed engineering, and research and development to adapt technology. There may be added expenses due to low labor productivity and poor product quality while workers learn to utilize the new technology. The sum of these costs represents, at least crudely, the

value of the resources used in transferring knowledge not embodied in purchased equipment and materials. One study (Mansfield, 1975) of twenty-six projects, in which a multinational company transferred technology abroad, indicated that, on the average, the transfer accounted for about 36 percent of the total cost of electrical and machinery projects and about 10 percent of the total cost of chemical and refining projects.

Geographical distribution of research expenditures. A distinctive feature of the international economy is the uneven geographical distribution of expenditure to acquire new knowledge. Most spending occurs in rich countries, very little in poor countries. The United Nations has estimated that 98 percent of all spending on research and development in nonsocialist countries takes place in the industrialized countries, and 70 percent in the United States alone. Only 2 percent of research and development expenditure is located in developing countries. In absolute terms, the industrialized countries spend forty-nine times as much as the developing countries on research, and in per capita terms they spend nearly 135 times as much (Rabinowitch and Rabinowitch, 1975, p. 190).

There are severe limitations as to what the developing countries as a group can do to correct imbalances in world trade and to participate in the new economic order. Codes of conduct for technology transfer are being worked out by various organizations, including the United Nations Conference on Trade and Development (UNCTAD). However, the heart of the problem is the value of proprietary knowledge and the price it should bring. Comparative studies are needed not only to clarify the issues but also to change attitudes. If technology transfer between the industrialized and developing countries is to continue to be important, there must be closer cooperation between social scientists in donor countries and their colleagues in recipient countries.

The location of research is of great significance to developing countries, since it affects the types of problems to be investigated, the nature of solutions, and the groups who will benefit most directly. For example, over half of the research currently conducted in the industrialized countries is of no immediate relevance to the development prospects of poor countries because it centers on defense, space, and atomic energy. Other research is directly prejudicial to the interests of at least some developing countries insofar as it leads to substitutes for products coming from these countries.

When discussing the transfer of technology one must be aware that this is a process that integrates a large number of complementary elements. If one element is missing, the other elements will be useless, or their effectiveness will be highly reduced. The elements can be divided into the following broad categories, which are all undergoing changes in response to technology transfer: (1) social systems and human attitudes, (2) knowledge and human skills, and (3) physical elements in which modern technology is embodied.

Technology has usually been transferred in the interest of industrialized countries and multinational companies, but consensus is growing that it is essential for the developing countries to build up their capacity to re-create production capability rather than import the production capacity. However, there is no relevant precedent and only a limited understanding of what critical elements constitute such a capacity and the sequence in which they should be introduced. Consequently, it is essential for most developing countries to allocate more resources for policy-oriented research on issues related to technology transfer.

The need for adaptations. As a rule, advanced technologies cannot be directly transferred to developing countries without adaptation for use in a low-productivity economy and social action to create a hospitable environment. There are great differences in the contexts of technical

operation between low- and high-productivity economies. For example, advanced technologies have developed in temperate climates, while agricultural developing societies are found for the most part in tropical and subtropical zones. Consequently, different flora and fauna flourish in each. The structure of the soil and the practices appropriate to soil conservation differ as well. Different crops present different problems of cultivation, preservation, and processing. Different diseases attack men, animals, and plants, and where diseases are the same, their vectors are likely to differ. Correspondingly, it is not possible to transfer technologies and the sciences of agriculture, horticulture, animal husbandry, medicine, and public health developed in the temperate zones to countries in the tropical and subtropical zones without considerable adaptation.

Furthermore, the effects of industrialization on employment will not be felt for several decades, as impact on employment is a function not only of the rate but also of the absolute size of industrialization. The expansion of industrial manufacturing cannot alone provide solutions to the employment problem in most developing countries. A manufacturing sector employing 20 percent of the labor force would need to increase employment by 15 percent per year just to absorb the increment in a work force growing at an annual rate of 3 percent, and manufacturing output must grow by more than 15 percent if increases in labor productivity are taken into account. The initial effects of technology transfer may in fact be negative, owing to disemployment of people from traditional industries and crafts that are either competed out or modernized.

As a consequence, the agricultural labor force in many developing countries may actually increase in absolute as well as in relative terms over the coming decades. Agricultural technology of the industrialized countries almost from the beginning aimed at the improvement of yields, while the agricultural labor force was declining, first relatively and then absolutely. Consequently, this technology is, on the whole, not acceptable to conditions in the developing countries—with some important exceptions, such as new methods of preventing plant diseases and high-yielding seeds. As mechanization generally disemploys workers and contributes little to higher yields per hectare, it must be instituted selectively; meanwhile, most yields can be increased by labor-intensive methods. However, modern technology makes it possible to establish new industries with minimal disturbance of the institutional framework and minimal diffusion of skills throughout the labor force. Different conditions should therefore rule the transfer of technology to the industrial and to the agricultural sectors in developing countries.

Thus, there is strong justification for a nation developing its own technological capability—internal and external conditions are rapidly changing; relevant knowledge is often not immediately available, and so local research must be initiated; and technical forces must be trained to build up a problem-solving capability for the future. As an example of the need for indigenous adaptability on many levels, Solo (1971, p. 483) discusses the hypothetical need to control insects on a tropical plantation. There might be equipment in use elsewhere which can be used for spraying insecticides, but it would have to be adapted on the spot to climate and terrain, to the shape of the infested plant, and to the locus of its infestation or to the skill of indigenous labor. Such on-the-spot adjustment of already designed equipment would be adaptation at the first level. It might then be necessary to compound and produce an appropriate insecticide which would require knowledge of the chemistry of pesticides and of the habits and vulnerabilities of the insect to be controlled. To design this new component of technology by reference to existing knowledge would be a second-level adaptation. And if, as is frequently the case, not enough is yet

known about the habits and vulnerabilities of the pest or the pesticidal efficacy of locally available materials or the possibilities of control through the use of the pest's own parasites, then a conceptual analytic apparatus of science must be turned to search for the new information which is required. This development-orientation of science is the third level in the adaptation of advanced technology.

The environment may be favorable to the incorporation of a new technology; the new technology may be transferable; and all the skills to adapt it for transfer may be available in a developing country—but it may still fail to be incorporated into actual operations. Such failures are not confined to developing countries; they occur everywhere and are part of almost every ultimately successful innovation. For transformation to any new technology, there must be not only the capacity to transform but also the competence to evaluate the technical feasibility and economics benefits of change, the power to effect change, and the motivation to transform an existing organization. For instance, international patent conventions are, on the whole, detrimental to the interests of developing countries. Such restrictive business practices as the protection of trademarks and abuses of patent rights in developing countris granting them similarly affect the transfer of technology.

Developing countries would like to facilitate their access to patented and non-patented proprietary technology under what they consider fair and reasonable terms. It is therefore essential to develop technology suited to the productive structures of developing countries and accelerate the growth of indigenous technology.

A number of international organizations are actively promoting increased technology transfer. Aside from financial institutions such as the International Bank for Reconstruction and Development (World Bank) and regional development banks, efforts are generally limited to technical assistance programs. International

financial institutions have often been criticized for promoting technology transfer
which is very little different from that
taking place directly between commercial
enterprises. To control and direct technology transfer to the greater benefit of the
recipients will require several important
reforms: First, recipients should create an
institutional machinery specifically to deal
with the transfer of technology. Second, a
part of research and development expenditures in the industrialized countries
should be directed to subjects of particular relevance to the developing countries.
And third, international organizations
such as the United Nations Industrial
Development Organization (UNIDO)
and the United Nations Conference on
Trade and Development (UNCTAD)
should formulate and implement policies
that are more beneficial to the recipients.
Given the global power structure and
vested interests in the industrialized countries, these changes are likely to come slowly.

Bibliography

Baranson, J. *Industrial Technologies for Devel-
oping Economies.* Praeger Special Studies in
International Economics and Development.
New York: Praeger, 1969.
Brooks, H. *National Science Policy and Technol-
ogy Transfer.* Proceedings of a Conference
on Technology Transfer and Innovation.
Washington, D.C.: National Science Foun-
dation, 1966.
Cooper, C., and Sercovich, F. *The Channels and
Mechanisms for the Transfer of Technology from
Developed to Developing Countries.* UNCTAD
TD/B/AC.11/5. Geneva: United Nations
Conference on Trade and Development,
April 27, 1971.
Goulet, D. "Exporting Technology to the Third
World—A Guide to Terms and Issues."
In *Perspectives on Development and Social
Change.* Cambridge, Massachusetts: Center
for the Study of Development and Social
Change, 1975a.
Goulet, D. "The Paradox of Technology Trans-
fer." *Bulletin of the Atomic Scientists,* June
1975b, *31,* 39–46.
Hawthorne, P. *The Transfer of Technology.* Paris:
Organisation for Economic Co-operation
and Development, 1971.

Mansfield, E. "International Technology
Transfer: Forms, Resource Requirements,
and Policies." *American Economic Review,*
May 1975, *65,* 372–376.
Myrdal, G. "The Transfer of Technology to
Underdeveloped Countries." *Scientific
American,* 1974, *231*(3), 173–182.
Nabseth, L., and Ray, G. F. (Eds.) *The Diffu-
sion of New Industrial Processes.* Cambridge,
England: Cambridge University Press, 1974.
Rabinowitch, E., and Rabinowitch, V. *Views of
Science, Technology, and Development.* Elms-
ford, New York: Pergamon Press, 1975.
Rosenberg, N. "Economic Development and
the Transfer of Technology: Some Histor-
ical Perspectives." *Technology and Culture,*
1970, *2*(1), 550–575.
Solo, R. "The Capacity to Assimilate an Ad-
vanced Technology." In N. Rosenberg (Ed.),
The Economics of Technological Change. Har-
mondsworth, Middlesex, England: Penguin,
1971.
Spencer, L., and Woroniak, A. (Eds.) *The Trans-
fer of Technology to Developing Countries.*
Praeger Special Studies in International
Economics and Development. New York:
Praeger, 1967.
Sutton, A. C. *Western Technology and Soviet
Economic Development.* (3 vols.) Stanford,
California: Hoover Institution Press, 1971.
Transfer of Technology. UNCTAD TD 106.
Geneva: United Nations Conference on
Trade and Development, November 10,
1971.
Vernon, R. (Ed.) *The Technology Factor in Inter-
national Trade.* New York: National Bureau
of Economic Research, 1970.

JON SIGURDSON

See also: Agriculture in Higher Education:
International Cooperation in Agriculture;
Science Policies.

AID TO THE UNIVERSITIES
(Higher Education Report), Switzerland

Aid to the Universities (Berne: Federal Department of the Interior, 1964), a report
of the special commission established by the
Swiss Federal Department of the Interior,
assesses the existing and future financial
requirements of Swiss higher education
institutions, with particular emphasis on
the financing of the cantonal universities.

The commission considered the organization, students, staff, facilities, and unity

of teaching and research in higher education institutions during the winter semester of 1962–63 and reviewed institutional expenses since 1950. Future expenditures for higher education, in the commission's view, will be determined by the need for more teaching and scientific staff, the necessity for institutional development, the degree of coordination between institutions, and the possible establishment of new universities. The report examines federal involvement in the financing of cantonal universities, the necessity of federal subsidies, the principles that govern the granting of such aid, and the role of Swiss national funds for scientific research.

The commission proposes an increase in higher education expenditures from 212,000,000 Swiss francs in 1962 to 1,000,000,000 in 1975 in order to meet a needed increase in staff and new construction. It concludes that in the national interest the federal government must allocate subsidies to those cantons which maintain universities. This subsidy, which should reach approximately 400,000,000 Swiss francs by 1975, would be administered by a special body representing the federal government, university cantons, universities, and national funds for scientific research.

AIMS OF HIGHER EDUCATION
See Philosophies of Higher Education, Historical and Contemporary.

ALBANIA, PEOPLE'S SOCIALIST REPUBLIC OF

Population: 2,296,000. Student enrollment in primary school: 569,000; secondary school: 102,600 (general, 32,900; vocational, 69,700); higher education: 28,600. Language of instruction: Albanian. Percentage of national budget expended on education and culture: 5.2%.[Figures are for 1973]

The structure of higher education in the People's Socialist Republic of Albania was promulgated into law on June 11, 1963, and modified in 1969. According to Article 24 of Law 3697, higher education in Albania is divided into four components: the State University of Tiranë, the Higher State Institute of Agriculture, the Pedagogical Institute, and other institutes of higher education. The basis for this system of higher education is rooted in significant historical events, which reflect the Albanian people's aspirations for cultural affirmation and a national consciousness. Commencing with the proselytizing activities of Turkish, Italian, and Greek clerics as early as the fifteenth century, and those of the Austrian, Italian, and French occupation forces during World War I, Albania's history is replete with movements for nationalistic education (Thomas, 1969, pp. 2,4).

Higher education did not emerge significantly in Albania until the advent of two major reforms, in 1934 and 1938, under the reign of King Zog I of Albania (1928–1939). The Educational Reform Law of 1938, in particular, provided for the establishment of trade schools, technical institutes, normal schools, and *lycées* (Thomas, 1969, p. 6). However, before this law and the Educational Reform Law of 1934 could be carried out completely, Albania became embroiled in World War II, commencing with the invasion of its territory by Italian forces on April 7, 1939. Consequently, a stable educational system did not emerge in Albania until the advent of its National Liberation Movement and the subsequent establishment of the Office of Education by the communist provisional government on May 24, 1944. From that point on, Albania's current educational direction was set.

Following the resolutions for education adopted by the Educational Congress of Korçë (November 25–27, 1944), the first major reform of the Albanian school system under the present government took place in 1946 (Thomas, 1969, p. 22). The educational changes stipulated in this reform were influenced greatly by the Yugoslavs and corresponded to the Soviet pattern of education. The reorganization of Albania's school system called for conformance with Marxist-Leninist theory, the needs and perspectives of socialism, the general politics of the Party of Labor, socialist pedagogy, modern world science, patriotic and democratic traditions of the culture, and experiences of the Soviet schools (Beqja, 1964, p. 90). The government's plan "to democratize the schools, to relate them to life, and to bring about a radical change in their programs, texts, subjects, and methods of instruction" (*Bashkimi*, July 17, 1946, p. 2) was codified in the Educational Law of August 17, 1946.

By 1948 political differences with Yugoslavia had increased to the point where Albania felt it necessary to sever its ties with that country and turn more directly to the Soviet Union for educational assistance. As a result, it enacted a decree-law that modified the Educational Law of 1946. Most notably, the new law provided for the compulsory education of all children between seven and fourteen years of age and for the improvement of instructional programs in the schools. In rapid order, successive modifications of the Educational Law of 1946 provided for the adoption of Soviet texts, the establishment of *teknikums* (two-year trade schools), and the school attendance of all illiterates between twelve and forty years of age.

The first steps toward higher education took place with the establishment, in 1946, of the two-year Teachers Training College in Tiranë to prepare teachers for the country's seven-year schools. Subsequently, in 1951, the Advanced Teachers' Training College, the Higher Institute of Agriculture, and the Higher Polytechnical Institute were founded. The Higher Institute of Medicine was established in 1952 and the Higher Institute of Economics in 1954. All these institutions were combined to form the nucleus of the State University of Tiranë in 1957 (*Education for All*, 1973, p. 9).

The years 1954 to 1957 were particularly noteworthy in the development of higher education in Albania. Greater attention was given to its administration, especially as it concerned the broadening and the improvement of course offerings in the institutes that had been established. Among these were the State Conservatory of Music, the Higher School of Drama, the Higher Institute of Figurative Arts (now the Higher Institute of Fine Arts), the Institute of Physical Culture and Sports, the two-year Teachers' Training College in Shkoder, some twenty-two branches of the State University of Tiranë, and other higher institutes (*Education for All*, 1973, p. 9).

Also during these years, the Russian language was gradually introduced in the country's seven-year schools; the Party of Labor continued to disseminate its ideology in all the schools; and polytechnical education was implemented in the schools of general, as well as technical, education. The higher institutes, along with Albania's trade and technical schools, focused more extensively on providing students with work experiences in industrial centers, agricultural cooperatives, tractor stations, and social and government agencies.

In 1954 the Ministry of Education's name was changed to the Ministry of Education and Culture. Its relationship to the ideology of the Albanian Party of Labor, the government, and the Soviet Union was reaffirmed under Regulation 55 of the law set forth on March 16, 1954, stating that "the Ministry of Education and Culture is the highest state organ that directs the development of education and culture in the People's Republic of Albania. In its work it is guided by the decisions and directives of the Party and government, and has as its guiding principle the Communist education of the new generation, and the dissemination of culture to the masses, supported by the school experiences of the Soviet culture" (*Gazeta Zyrtare*, April 15, 1954, pp. 191–192).

Increasing political differences between the Soviet Union and Albania, coupled with difficulties in the economy, compelled Albania to reassess its educational directions in 1960. Consequently, a major reorganization of the country's school system was set into motion under the Educational Reform of 1960 (Thomas, 1969, p. 45). Henceforth, schools were to be tied more closely to life, and teaching to productive work. The reorganization called for the establishment of eight-year schools as the basic component of general, polytechnical, and practical work education. Middle (secondary) schools were to provide three-year programs of general and polytechnical education (grades 9 to 11), and, later, four-year programs (grades 9 to 12). The network of the lower technical-professional (trade) schools was to be extended, so that greater numbers of workers could be educated. To meet this need, evening, special-shift, correspondence, and seasonal classes were to be established on a continuing education basis.

The decade of the 1960s was especially significant to the current progress of education in the People's Republic of Albania. During that decade the scientific-materialistic philosophy of Marx and Lenin was extended throughout the educational system. Schools were to be ideologically pure; communist education in the schools was to be, as always, "correct and scientific." The precedent for these changes had been established shortly after World War II, when Enver Hoxha, the first secretary of the Party of Labor, proclaimed the ideological and political nature of the developing Albanian educational systems as follows: "The schools should be the driving force for the ideas and principles of the Party's politics, its tasks, and aims for the working masses; it should educate children of all strata of the populace, on the basis of these principles, to fight against every foreign ideology and against foreign influence on children" (Ylli, 1950, p. 2). The Educational Reform of 1960 intensified this direction when it required the schools to "educate the new generation with the

spirit and devotion to the issues of socialism and communism, with unlimited love for the people, for the Motherland, for our glorious Party of Labor, the organization of all the achievements of our people, with love for our countries and camps of socialism, and for all the workers of the world" (*Bashkimi,* June 22, 1960, p. 3).

The Albanian school system in 1975, including that of higher education, reflected the total reconstruction that had taken place since the report of the Party of Labor's politburo at the eighth plenum of its central committee, June 26–28, 1969. In 1968 a central committee (*komisioni qëndror*) composed of fifty-five members and headed by Mehmet Shehu, Albania's premier, was created to assume full control of the country's educational system. The resultant reform in 1969 set forth three broad goals, which are presently implemented in Albania's schools: (1) The ideological and political education of Albania's new generation *(brezi i ri)* was to be extended, so that the country's socialist revolution could be carried out more rapidly. (2) More cadres were to be educated to meet the needs of the economy, particularly in science and technology. (3) Increasing emphasis was to be given to connecting theoretical school preparation with production in work enterprises and with physical training and military service (Afezolli, 1969, pp. 24–25).

The Party of Labor's concern for improving the education of Albania's youth, teachers, and working populace was not without foundation. In 1968 some 8 percent of the country's students had terminated their education after four years of schooling, up to 40 percent had been retained in various grades of the eight-year schools, and up to 30 percent had repeated grades in some of the middle schools. Only 60.3 percent of the teachers in the eight-year schools were reportedly qualified to teach. Additionally, it was felt that the country's laborers and villagers were being educated inadequately and that the ideological and political education of Albania's youth was deficient, especially in the eight-year and middle schools (Thomas, 1973, pp. 107–119).

Relationship with Secondary Education and Admission Requirements

As currently implemented, Albania's educational network integrates formal education in the schools, work in productive enterprises, physical education, and military service for all students. Two broad components support this integration: (1) the full-time education of the country's youth and (2) the part-time education of workers and villagers.

Full-time education for young Albanians requires that they undergo preschool education from ages three to six and that they complete the program of the eight-year school. Upon graduation from the eight-year school, they may enter the country's labor force or attend various middle schools. These consist of four-year general schools of education, four-year professional (trades, art, medical, pedagogical) schools, and one- or two-year lower technical (trade) schools (Thomas, 1969, p. 54).

Part-time education enables Albania's fully employed laborers and villagers to commence their schooling in the third grade and to complete the basic eight-year program in six years. The school program for workers and villagers is similar to that undertaken by full-time students except that the former are required to undertake one additional year of preparatory schooling before entering Albania's schools of higher education. Special shift, evening, correspondence, and seasonal classes function so that the part-time students can continue their education while fully employed. Classes are coordinated with the working shifts of the country's laborers and villagers for this purpose. Evening and correspondence classes meet three times a week. The workload of students in higher education who attend these classes is reduced from eight to six hours on these days, so that they may take advantage of the opportunity to extend their education. Part-time educa-

tion is further encouraged through paid leaves, so that laborers and villagers may take the examinations required to graduate from the country's various levels of schooling.

Graduates of Albania's general and vocational secondary schools must serve one full year in work enterprises before they are permitted to continue their education. During this one-year probationary period, the graduates are placed under the direct supervision of the workers and villagers with whom they work and are subject to their approval. Consequently, their admission to schools of higher education is based on their work results and behavior during this work period; their political image; their proficiency in learning; and the recommendations of their teachers, the school collective, the youth organization, and the work collective (*Education for All*, 1973, p. 26). Preliminary examinations for the admission of students to higher schools are not utilized, so that all are given an opportunity to pursue their education on a part-time or full-time basis.

Administration and Control

Although the state university and the higher institutes function under the direction of the Ministry of Education and Culture and under the guidance of the Party of Labor, the Union of Albanian Working Youth (*Bashkimi i rinisë të punës i Shqipërisë*) has a significant role in the governance of secondary and higher education. One of its central tasks is to assure that Albania's state university and higher institutes carry out the ideology and politics of the party and the state. In keeping with the Party of Labor's emphasis on "relating learning to life," the union's young people are also engaged in the socialist construction of Albania through work experiences dictated by the needs of the country's economy.

A rector is responsible for the administration of the university in cooperation with the university council, which is the chief governing body. The university is divided into seven faculties, each of which is headed by a dean. Directors are in charge of the institutes of the university.

The Higher State Institute of Agriculture, which also is headed by a rector, is divided into three faculties, each administered by a dean.

Programs and Degrees

Studies in the full-time higher institutes of Albania encompass programs lasting three to four years, and in some disciplines five years, and lead to professional titles in fields such as pharmacy (four years); engineering, technology, and dentistry (five years); and agriculture, forestry, and veterinary science (four to five years). Students who continue their education on a part-time basis customarily attend an additional year.

The school year comprises seven months of study (including physical education), two months of work in various enterprises, one month of military training, and two months of vacation.

Financing and Student Financial Aid

Albania's 1975 state budget consisted of 7,300,000,000 leks (5 leks = U.S. $1) in income and 7,100,000,000 leks in expenditures, with a surplus of 200,000,000 leks. Approximately 24 percent of this budget was spent on social and cultural development (*Albania Report,* January–March 1975, p. 1). With a projected enrollment of over 30,000 students in higher education, a portion of these funds was spent to provide scholarships, books, board, and clothing for students. In 1973 more than 60 percent of the students in higher education were provided scholarships (*Education for All,* 1973, p. 41).

Relationship with Industry

Students in higher education are deeply involved in the industrialization of their country. The university statutes limit class work to thirty-six hours a week for full-time students and to eighteen hours a week for part-time students, so that time is available for them to gain practical work experi-

ence in industrial, agricultural, social, and governmental enterprises. Consequently, Albania is able to maintain its work production schedules through this additional source of labor and, at the same time, provide for the continuing education of its young people in its higher institutions of learning.

JOHN I. THOMAS

Bibliography

Afezolli, S. "A New Step Towards the Mass Character of the Albanian School." *New Albania,* 1969, *23* (1).

Albania Report. (Edited by Albanian Affairs Study Group, New York.)

Bashkimi, July 17, 1946.

Bashkimi, June 22, 1960.

Beqja, H. "Rreth transformimëve demokratike dhe socialistë në arësimin tonë popullor në kuadrin e reformës arësimore të vitit 1946." *Arësimi Popullor,* March–April 1964.

Education for All. Tiranë: Naim Frashëri Publishing House, 1973.

Gazeta Zyrtare, April 15, 1954.

Thomas, J. I. *Education for Communism: School and State in the People's Republic of Albania.* Palo Alto, California: Hoover Institution Press, 1969.

Thomas, J. I. "Communist Education in Albania." *Paedagogica Historica,* 1973, *13* (1), 107–119.

Vjetari statistikor i Republikës popullore të Shqipërisë, 1971–72. Tiranë: Drejtoria e statistikës, 1973.

Ylli, K. "Për një edukatë dhe ideologji më të shëndoshë në shkollat tona." *Zëri i Popullit,* October 18, 1950.

See also: Eastern European Socialist Countries: Regional Analysis; Women and Higher Education: Equal Rights and Affirmative Action.

ALEUTS

See Access of Minorities: The North American Indian.

ALGERIA, DEMOCRATIC AND POPULAR REPUBLIC OF

Population: 15,266,000 (1975). Student enrollment in primary school: 2,499,605; secondary school (academic, vocational, technical): 419,759; higher education: 44,000. Student enrollment in higher education as percentage of age group (18–22): 2.71%. Language of instruction: Arabic and French. Academic calendar: September to July, two semesters. Percentage of gross domestic product (GDP) expended on higher education: .9%. Percentage of national budget expended in 1975 on all education: 19.2%; higher education: 3.17%. [Unless otherwise indicated, figures are for 1974–75. Source: Ministry of Higher Education and Scientific Research.]

Before 1830, the year of the invasion of Algeria by the French and the beginning of the era of colonial occupation, a number of university centers existed in Algeria, offering traditional education in such subjects as Muslim law, theology, rhetoric, Arab grammar, history, geography, mathematics, and astronomy. The principal university centers were established in Tlemcen, Mazouna, Constantine, and Bougie. According to historians who accompanied the invading forces, the literacy rate of the Algerian population was quite high. However, the period of colonial occupation began with the systematic destruction of all cultural and social institutions, among which were the university centers. French replaced Arabic as the language of administration, and Arabic was relegated to religious use. At independence in 1962, 15 percent of the adult population but only 7 percent of the female population were literate in Arabic or French, the two languages spoken in the country.

The new nation inherited an elitist educational system which had been designed by the French to train subordinate personnel and to spread French culture. At independence, after 132 years as a French colony, the country had only a few educated citizens: some one hundred lawyers, a few dozen pharmacists, physicians, and dentists; and a handful of engineers. The new Algerian government, perceiving education as an important tool of government, gave it prompt attention. The goals were to make education responsible to the needs of the new country.

In the first year of statehood the Algerian government faced two mammoth problems. It needed to educate as many as possible as soon as possible. The French had held nearly all administrative, managerial, and academic posts during the occupation. Their exodus had left a vacuum, yet in 1963 less than one Algerian in ten was enrolled in a school or training program which would equip him to assume these vacancies. Secondly, Arabic, which was the spoken language of the population, had to be promoted as the first language for the millions of illiterate adults and children.

The reform of education began with the establishment of a compulsory nine years of general education for every young Algerian. Arabic was introduced into the educational system to ensure a rebirth of Algerian culture and sense of identity, although French was given priority as a first foreign language to bridge the gap between older and younger generations and smooth the transition between two systems. The continued use of French also facilitated the transfer of technological knowledge from the outside world and provided time for the modernization of Arabic.

Although democratization and Arabization were prime targets of the new educational system, they were not unique to postindependence. During the early years of colonization, Algerian resistance had focused on a determined rejection of anything remotely related to French culture (Turin, 1971). Resistance to French advances coupled with allegiance to traditional values had kept the Algerian society somewhat united and made the French *mission civilisatrice* (civilizing mission) a little harder to execute. In the 1880s a system of compulsory education was organized in France. Perceiving Algeria as simply three more French provinces, the French authorities imposed their educational policy in Algeria. However, it was not effective until after World War I. The sustained contact with European culture during and after the war altered Algerian resistance, and discharged soldiers and returning Algerian laborers sought public education for their children. Other efforts to establish French education in Algeria were manifest in the founding of a French-language School of Medicine and Pharmacy (1859) and Higher Schools of Law, Science, and Letters (1879) as well as a School of Agriculture and a School of Public Works (1906). In 1909 these institutions were amalgamated to form the University of Algiers. However, access was almost entirely reserved for children of the occupying forces, and few Algerians had an opportunity to acquire higher education within the country. Although during this period the Algerians made concessions to French culture, they simultaneously developed anticolonial and nationalist institutions (Lacheraf, 1965).

One of the most important of these institutions in terms of scholarly accomplishments and Arabization was the Association of Reformist Ulamas (scientists), which was founded in 1931 by Sheikh Abdel Hamid Ben Badis, a learned Islamic theologian. He conceived the slogan "Islam is my religion, Arabic is my language, Algeria is my fatherland," which defined the scholarly and political program of his association. By 1936 its members had founded and were operating some 130 so-called free schools, which had a modern curriculum offering mathematics, history, geography, and natural sciences, as well as Arabic grammar, Islamic religion, and law. By 1950 some 50,000 students had attended the schools, the most distinguished graduates going on to the Universities of al-Qarawiyin in Morocco, el-Zaitouna in Tunisia, or al-Azhar in Egypt to pursue further graduate work. The schools were closed in 1956 as a result of nationalist activities. By 1959, only 1600 small Koranic schools were left to teach elementary Arabic to about 50,000 pupils, but in 1962 most of these schools were incorporated into the new educational system.

In 1971 the Higher Education Reform was initiated. Its primary objective was the democratization of the inherited elitist educational system.

The independent government of Algeria recognized that the cultural level

and technological power of a people constitute the best base for economic and social development and that real political freedom is contingent upon the development of men, the diffusion of scientific knowledge, and the development of modern technology. Thus, hundreds of millions of dollars have been invested in the construction of schools designed to provide general education for children, in the establishment of a great number of schools at the middle and secondary level, and in the establishment of university institutions for technical training and higher specialized schools. In addition, thousands of scholarships have been distributed for training students abroad.

As a result of these efforts, Algeria has become almost self-sufficient in terms of manpower in fourteen years. Training policy within the framework of the Cultural Revolution has the following objectives: to revive the Arab language as a national language; to provide scientific and technological education; to accept foreign influences and thus modernization of action and thought; to promote a modern concept of Islam as a religion of progress and social equality; to democratize education; to revive a national Arabic-Islamic culture in all its manifestations; and to spread ideas which express the socialist attitude of the country. The Cultural Revolution constitutes a response to the challenge presented by the modern world to a nation whose existence has been jeopardized by intellectual and economic pressures and even military force.

Legal Basis of Educational System

Until 1971, legislation that applied to Algerian higher education consisted largely of texts dating from the period of colonization. These texts had been incorporated into an education law of December 1962. In September 1971 a higher education reform was initiated. Five major categories of legal texts were established to regulate higher education: ordinances, decrees, judgments, circulars, and decisions. Ordinances concern matters such as the organization of the universities, the creation of new universities, the financial rules applicable to university institutions, and the system of scholarships. The ordinances are promulgated by the president of the Council of the Revolution in the name of the people of Algeria. Decrees establish new university degrees and determine the duration of study for the degrees. They also regulate access to higher education; stipulate general rules for programs leading to degrees; and determine amounts of scholarships. High functionaries of the Ministry of Higher Education and Scientific Research and the rectors of the universities are also nominated by decrees, promulgated by the head of the government. Judgments determine university degree programs, spell out the content of these programs, and determine rules of organization for examinations and the progress of studies leading to a diploma.

The heads of the units of the university (Algerian universities are subdivided into units rather than faculties or departments) and the permanent teaching staff are nominated through judgments, which are signed by the minister of higher education and scientific research. Circulars consist of commentary on legal texts or regulations and elaborate on the judgments. They are established by the minister of higher education and scientific research. Decisions are regulations that apply to minor problems, such as establishing the list of candidates for a competition or examination or authorizing the transfer of files for university students to another university. Decisions can be established either by the minister or director of central administration, the Ministry of Higher Education and Scientific Research, or the rectors.

Types of Institutions

Higher education in Algeria is offered at universities, at university centers, and at a number of specialized higher education institutions. The minister of higher educa-tion and scientific research is responsible for most of these institutions. There are six universities, four of which offer a full range of studies. These include the University of Algiers, founded in 1909; the University of Oran, founded in 1967; the University of Constantine, founded in 1969; and the University of Annába, founded in 1975. Two universities specialize in science and technology: the University of Sciences and Technology of Algiers (1974) and the University of Sciences and Technology of Oran (1975), both of which are divided into institutes specializing in a well-defined scientific or technical field of study. Only one university center actually functions, the University Center of Tlemcen, founded in 1974. It provides the first two years of study for diplomas in science and technology. There are four institutes and specialized schools: *Ecole nationale supérieure d'enseignement polytechnique,* located in Oran and founded in 1970, trains teachers for secondary schools; *Ecole normale supérieure,* founded in 1964, is located in Algiers and has branches in Oran and Constantine; *Ecole nationale vétérinaire,* founded in 1971, is also located in Algiers; *Institut national agronomique,* founded in 1966, prepares students for the *diplôme d'ingénieur agronome* and other specialties at the doctoral level. In January 1975 the *Institut des télécommunications d'Oran,* previously under the responsibility of the Ministry of Telecommunications, was added to the four other schools.

A University of Science and Technology in Blida (80 kilometers south-southwest of Algiers) and a university at Sétif (320 kilometers south-southeast of Algiers) are in the planning stage.

In addition, different ministries are responsible for institutions of higher learning which train students in fields of study corresponding to the particular concern of the ministry. The Ministry of Industry and Energy is responsible for the National Institute of Hydrocarbons, the National Institute of Light Industry, and the Petroleum Institute, which are all located at Bou Merdes, about 60 kilometers east of Algiers.

The Ministry of State for Transport maintains an Institute of Hydrometeorology at Oran. The Ministry of the Interior manages the National School of Administration. The Ministry of Defense administers the National School of Engineers and Technicians at Cap Tamenfoust (30 kilometers east of Algiers) and a National Institute of Geodetic Sciences at Arzew (400 kilometers west of Algiers). The secretary of state for hydraulics oversees an Institute of Hydrotechnology and of Land Improvement at Blida. The Institute of Planning Techniques is under the authority of the secretary of state for planning.

Relationship with Secondary Education

Responsibility for education is divided between two ministries, the Ministry of Primary and Secondary Education and the Ministry of Higher Education and Scientific Research.

Preuniversity education has been traditionally divided into three levels: primary, intermediate, and secondary. Primary education lasted six years and was open to children aged six years or less. Intermediate education, lasting four years, was open to children aged twelve or thirteen who successfully passed an examination called *examen d'accès á l'enseignement moyen* (admission examination to intermediate education).

Until 1974–75 children aged thirteen or more who passed an examination entitled *certificat d'études primaires* could continue into the second year of intermediate study after a special examination; however, in 1975–76 a compulsory system of basic schooling lasting nine years and including the years of primary and middle schooling was put into effect. At the end of the ninth year the student receives a *brevet,* entitling him to continue into secondary education.

Secondary education lasts three years. It is provided either in technical schools, which prepare students for the *diplôme de technicien* in different fields of study, or in *lycées. Lycées* offer specialization in three areas: sciences, mathematics, and humanities; all of these programs lead to the school-leaving certificate, the *baccalauréat,* with mention of specialty.

Admission Requirements

Admission to the university requires the *baccalauréat* in the appropriate specialization. Entrance examinations are given to applicants who did not receive the *baccalauréat* but completed secondary schooling and to those students who wish to enter a field different from their secondary specialization.

For the higher professional schools, admission is based on the *baccalauréat* or equivalent qualifications and requires a competitive examination *(concours).*

There is no discrimination on the basis of sex, creed, or religion. In order to encourage adult and war veteran education, there is no age limit at any institution. Algerian and foreign students can register at any university or institute provided they meet admission requirements.

Administration and Control

The minister of higher education and scientific research has responsibility for the administration, financing, and teaching in all institutions of higher education not under a specialized ministry.

The highest single authority within the university is the rector, appointed by decree of the head of government, who is assisted by a council of institutes *(conseil d'instituts)* composed of the directors of all institutes. The rector may be aided by one or several vice-rectors. Although the university has financial autonomy, it does not have academic authority. Diplomas and degrees are established by the head of government; programs of study, examination regulations, requirements for diplomas and degrees, and the awarding of diplomas are the responsibility of the

Ministry of Higher Education and Scientific Research.

Participation of the teaching staff and students in the management of the universities is limited and concerns only the application of government regulations. Students and teachers meet in the academic coordinating committees to deal with problems such as duration of employment, examination schedules, and the placement of students in laboratory groups. However, the academic committees can, on the advice of the rector, make recommendations to the Ministry of Higher Education and Scientific Research.

The specialized institutes and schools are administered by a director, who is appointed by decree of the head of government and has the same duties as the rector.

In accordance with the Charter of the Socialist Management of Enterprises, promulgated in December 1971, a fundamental modification in the structure of management of the universities, institutes, and specialized schools is anticipated. The new structure, influenced by measures already implemented in state enterprises, has as its objectives to include all members of the university community—teachers, students, and administrative and technical personnel—in all facets of management of the institution (administration, teaching, and research) and to introduce a system of elective offices. The proposed structural changes have not yet been implemented.

Programs and Degrees

Algerian universities offer a full range of academic study. The first degree, the *licence,* is offered in a number of fields after six semesters. The *licence* in technical fields and technical diplomas, however, requires eight semesters of study. The diplomas for engineers, veterinary doctors, and architects require a study period of ten semesters, and the Doctor of Medicine takes six years or twelve semesters.

Advanced degrees are also awarded. The *magister* can be achieved after a minimum of two semesters beyond the diplo-

mas of engineer, veterinary doctor, or architect and after a minimum of four semesters beyond a degree. A doctoral degree in sciences, *doctorat en sciences,* requires a minimum of six semesters beyond the *magister.* Advanced medical study is offered at two levels: the diploma of specialized medical study, *diplôme d'études médicales spéciales,* lasts a minimum of three semesters beyond the doctor of medicine; a doctoral degree in medical sciences, *doctorat en sciences médicales,* takes four semesters after the advanced medical diploma.

Diplomas below degree level are also awarded on completion of short-cycle programs. The diploma of higher technician requires two years of study; the higher technological diploma (which admits students with the certificate of intermediate education) requires four years of study.

Financing and Student Financial Aid

Higher education is entirely financed by the state, which annually determines resources and public expenditures. The recurrent budget is allocated annually for expenditures related to personnel and administration at all levels of education under the ministry.

Capital expenditure is also determined annually, but within the framework of the Fourth National Development Plan. For the academic year 1975–76 the recurrent budget of the Ministry of Higher Education and Scientific Research comprised 541,722,000 dinars, or the equivalent of US$135,430,000, while the capital budget was expanded to US$389,000,000.

Students pay an annual registration fee of 55 dinars (US$13.75); certain university institutions also require insurance against school accidents (US$5.50 per year), and students pay a social security fee and medical insurance.

Tuition in Algerian institutions of higher education is free, and the government may provide subsidies for books, supplies, registration fees, and insurance. These subsidies are delineated in the presidential ordinance of December 3, 1971, which outlines the conditions for scholarships, advanced wages *(pré-salaire),* and practical training.

The scholarship is allocated by the state to students at the universities and institutions of higher education, to cover study fees and living expenses. It is based on the financial means, the nature of the study, and study results and favors students with high examination scores. Scholarship recipients hold social service positions during summer vacations and after completion of their studies are required to work in the state civil service administration; this latter requirement extends to all students. The amount of scholarship varies from a monthly allocation of 350 dinars (US$87.50) for theoretical study to 450 dinars (US$112.50) for technological study.

Advanced wages are available for students in a field of study accorded national priority; that is, fields such as technological sciences (at the level of *licence),* agronomy (diploma of agricultural engineer), and veterinary sciences (diploma of veterinary doctor). Advanced wages are granted under the same academic conditions as scholarships; in addition, students are expected to work in the relevant ministry. Students working in the field receive a daily payment of $1.50; fees for their travel expenses are paid from the state budget.

In addition, holders of scholarships and advanced wages have automatic access to student housing. The student residences and restaurants are run in each university city by a special center; three fourths of its budget is subsidized by the state; the rest of its budget is provided by fees from students for room and board.

Student Social Background and Access to Education

No studies have yet been made on the socioeconomic backgrounds of Algerian students. However, education has been encouraged by the extension of education to rural areas and to all social classes in the cities; the systematic granting of scholarships to low-income groups at intermediate schools and secondary schools; and the fact that social mobility is almost exclusively dependent on university diplomas.

The percentage of women students has grown from .5 percent of the total enrollments in 1962–63 to 33 percent in 1975–76. Women are the majority at the institutes of social sciences and in foreign languages, numbering almost 90 percent of total enrollment. In technological fields, however, women constitute only about 5 percent of enrollments. In medicine women constitute 43 percent; in chemistry and biology, approximately 40 percent of the enrollment.

The National Union of Young Algerians is a national youth organization attracting students regardless of social background, professional activities, or academic standing. Other student organizations at higher education institutions, generally focusing on cultural activities, are supported by government funds.

Teaching Staff

There are four teaching ranks. *Assistants,* who are required to hold a master's degree, are in charge of practical and laboratory work. An assistant cannot serve more than three years and must resign if he is not promoted. A *maître-assistant* (lecturer), who must hold a doctoral degree, supervises laboratory study or gives lectures under the supervision of a *maître de conférences* (senior lecturer). Lecturers are promoted after having submitted a thesis for the *doctorat en sciences.* The *docent* or *maître de conférences* lectures, supervises research for the Ph.D. or a *doctorat en sciences* degree, or conducts research; promotion is based on scientific and academic achievements. The *professeur* (professor) lectures and undertakes or supervises research.

The status of the teaching staff—that is, the conditions of their recruitment, their duties, their remuneration, and requirements for their promotion—is set by presidential decree, in accordance with civil service regulations.

Each teaching rank is represented by a commission, which consists of representa-

tives elected from among the teaching staff
of the rank, as well as representatives delegated from the Ministry of Higher Education and Scientific Research. This commission determines the promotion of each
teacher in the rank.

Research Activities

A state agency, the National Office of
Scientific Research, directed by a director
general who is nominated by presidential
decree, is charged with the funding, management, and control of scientific research
under the egis of the Ministry of Higher
Education and Scientific Research.

This office consists of research centers,
each of which specializes in a particular
scientific or technological field. Scientific
personnel at these centers are mainly teachers, who are already employed by the
university, and permanent researchers.
Scientific research is determined by the
government, which approves a plan of
scientific research submitted by the National Council of Scientific Research, presided over by the minister of higher education and scientific research. This council
consists of representatives (elected or designated) from state agencies, universities,
and public associations. The responsibilities of the council are divided among seven
commissions, each in charge of a particular
area of science. The research is financed
through the National Office of Scientific
Research. However, the National Office
of Scientific Research may also conclude
agreements with national societies which
assure financing of the research.

In addition to research financed by the
National Office of Scientific Research,
universities can finance—within the limits
of their own budget—research of an academic character not provided for in the
National Plan of Scientific Research but
pertinent to the preparation of doctorates.

Current Problems and Trends

The Algerian university was strongly influenced by the French system of higher

education, which prevailed until 1971. The
reform of higher education, launched by
the then Minister of Higher Education
and Scientific Research, Mohamed Seddik
Benyahia, has six essential goals: (1) to
make the university into a training and a
problem-solving institution in order to
accelerate the socioeconomic development
of the nation; (2) to expand the university's
tasks beyond those of mainly training graduates; (3) to revise programs so that students will be trained to understand and
rectify the problems of the nation and also
to implement recent developments in all
fields of science and technology; (4) to
promote knowledge and use of the national
language; (5) to modernize the methods
of teaching in order to increase the output
of students; (6) to orient students toward
interdisciplinary transfer, in order to develop a sufficient number of specialists in
fields where manpower is needed and to
avoid an overproduction of professionals
in fields of lesser need.

The success of the educational reform
has been considerable. Among the measures promoting this success are a reorganization of studies, from a university year
with a single series of examinations in
June—a system which leads to a high failure rate—into two semesters with better
student performance evaluation; introduction of a modular system of study,
which allows greater flexibility in the programs; and practical training in industry
and agriculture.

Relationship with Industry

There is cooperation between the university and industry to design and improve
programs. Financial aid constitutes another
manifestation of a close relationship between industry and higher education. Algerian national industrial societies may
give subsidies for training and are responsible for the advanced wages of certain
higher technicians in their field of specialty.
Industry also has an impact on student
orientation. Through salary enticements

national industries exert a large influence over the kind of training that a student chooses. The petroleum industry, for example, attracts a large number of students because it offers high wages.

International Cooperation

Algeria has cultural agreements with sixteen countries. These agreements include exchange of teachers, students, and cultural information. In addition, students of more than sixty nationalities are enrolled in Algerian universities, and Algerian government scholarships are awarded to students from some forty-six different nations. Each year more than two hundred visiting professors from different foreign universities lecture in Algeria for varying lengths of time.

[Revised and expanded by Mourad Benachenhou, Directeur des enseignements, Ministère de l'enseignement supérieur et de la recherche scientifique, Algiers.]

MOURAD BELGUEDJ

Bibliography

Annuaire statistique 1975. Algiers: Secrétariat d'état au plan, 1975.

Benachenou, M. *L'Algérie: Histoire et société.* Algiers: Edition populaire de l'armée, n.d.

L'enseignement supérieur. Algiers: Ministère de l'information et de la culture, 1973.

Lacheraf, M. *L'Algérie: Nation et société.* Paris: Maspero, 1965.

Lacoste, Y., Nouschi, A., and Prenant, A. *L'Algérie: Passé et présent.* Paris: Editions sociales, 1960.

Merad, A. *Le réformisme musulman en Algérie de 1925 à 1940: Essai d'histoire religieuse et sociale.* The Hague: Mouton, 1967.

Réforme de l'enseignement 1947–1977. (3 vols.) Algiers: Ministère de l'enseignement primaire et secondaire, n.d.

La réforme de l'enseignement supérieur: Textes officiels. Algiers: Ministère de l'enseignement supérieur et de la recherche scientifique, 1971.

République française. *Université d'Alger, cinquantenaire, 1909–59.* Algiers: Mohammad Racim, n.d.

Turin, Y. *Affrontements culturels dans l'Algérie coloniale: Ecoles, médecines, religion—1830–1880.* Paris: Maspero, 1971.

See also: Arab World: Regional Analysis; Archives: Africa and Asia, National Archives of; Science Policies: Less Developed Countries: Arab World.

ALL-INDIA ASSOCIATION OF HIGHER EDUCATION

See Religious Influences in Higher Education: Catholicism.

ALL INDIA FEDERATION OF UNIVERSITY AND COLLEGE TEACHERS' ORGANIZATIONS

University and college teachers of India met in December 1961 in Trivandrum, Kerala to form an ad hoc committee to draft the constitution of the All India Federation of University and College Teachers' Organizations. In 1962 the constitution was adopted at Varanasi, Uttar Pradesh, and in 1963 the first conference of the federation was held in Calcutta, West Bengal. The State Federation of University and College Teachers' Associations and university and college teachers' associations in various Indian states are affiliated with the federation.

The federation studies educational problems, especially in Indian colleges and universities, and works for the advancement of teaching and research. Promoting the interests of Indian university and college teachers, the federation seeks to develop feelings of fraternity among the teachers, to encourage international understanding, to work for national solidarity, and to create healthy public opinion in favor of a well-planned university education.

The federation has successfully advocated an integrated pay scale for all university and college teachers. It maintains a close liaison with the Indian University Grants Commission.

Publications include souvenir volumes of annual conferences and a newsletter.

433c Husainabad
Jaunpur, India

HRIDAYA NARAYAN SINGH

ALL INDIA STUDENTS' FEDERATION

The All India Students' Federation (AISF) was formed in 1936 to unify Indian students into a powerful student movement during India's struggle for independence. After independence in 1947, AISF organized several seminars, symposia, and debates involving educators and students to discuss problems of national reconstruction and educational reforms. In the latter part of the 1960s, AISF played a leading role in the student struggles in northern India.

AISF aims to infuse patriotism among Indian students; educate them in the ideology of Marxism-Leninism; unite them in the defense of national independence and sovereignty; and mobilize them in struggles for radical economic reforms, meaningful land reforms, and a better social order. The student group supports the right to free education and employment for all men and women in India without any distinction of caste, creed, color, or sex; the achievement of a scientific system of education dedicated to socialism, secularism, and democracy; and the eradication of illiteracy from among the masses.

The federation offers annual festivals on provincial and district levels; on local levels it offers sports, games, excursions, and picnics.

AISF publishes ten periodicals in regional languages and two central organs, both biweekly.

4/7 Asaf Ali Road
New Delhi 1, India

ALUMNI AFFAIRS

Graduates or former students of a co-educational institution are referred to as alumni. The term is derived from the Latin word *alumnus,* meaning a pupil or foster son. Female graduates are referred to as alumnae, or alumna in the singular form. Alumni, in turn, refer to the institution that they attended as their alma mater, the cherishing or foster mother.

Alumni programs and alumni associations are basically a North American phenomenon. The large-scale cultivation of alumni is little known outside the United States and Canada, although progressive institutions in Latin America and the Philippines have been seriously considering the initiation of such activities. In the United States the cultivation of the alumni by the college as a constituency to provide continuous support, financial and otherwise, began in 1821 at Williams College, a private institution in Massachusetts. Alumni programs at public universities were first developed in the early twentieth century.

The relationship between the college and its alumni has been likened to a two-way street in which each serves the interests of the other. Alumni may serve their institution by rendering four major services: (1) the ambassadorial service of representing the college well; (2) the advisory service of providing their talents on governing boards, development councils, and professional advisory groups for curriculum development; (3) the recruiting service of directing well-qualified applicants to the college; and (4) the fund-raising service of strengthening the college's resources.

The responsibilities of a college or university to its alumni include (1) the provision of good avenues of alumni communication through a vigorous program of publications, clubs, and campus events; (2) the provision of opportunities for alumni interested in continuing education or some other form of intellectual stimulation; (3) the utilization of alumni in developing public understanding and support for the institution; (4) the maintenance of academic integrity through programs of high quality that give alumni a sense of satisfaction in serving education and their college or alma mater; and (5) the maintenance of institutional integrity in relations with alumni as evidenced by an unpatronizing attitude by the college, an absence of raw exploitation of financial potential, and an alumni fund-raising effort that has objectives worthy of alumni sacrifice and dedication.

Alumni Offices and Associations

To facilitate these mutual relationships, foster among the alumni a spirit of fraternalism and loyalty to their alma mater, and to encourage them to become active in programs designed to enhance the welfare of their institution, most American colleges operate an alumni office and support an alumni association.

Alumni offices. Most alumni offices consist of an executive secretary or director and a trained staff whose salaries are paid by the institution and who organize and coordinate alumni associations, clubs, chapters, programs, and services and strive to develop positive and productive public relations with its constituency. The staff must interpret the college and its mission to the alumni in such a way as to gain their support and cooperation. They also interpret the alumni reactions and suggestions to the college administration and faculty so that the college will better be able to continue its educational efforts and endeavors. In this role of liaison between the institution and its alumni, the office should be closely allied with the office of the president. Sometimes the alumni director reports to a vice-president or similarly ranked official in charge of university development, university relations, or university advancement. But whatever the chain of command, the alumni staff should be represented at the upper decision-making level of the administration in order to be effective in organizing alumni support.

One of the major responsibilities of an alumni office is the maintenance of alumni records, including an accurate mailing list and a roster of all graduates and former students. In many institutions alumni records also include a biographical index that contains such pertinent data as the graduate's date and place of birth; parent or guardian; years of attendance at the institution; degrees earned; major subject; membership in societies, fraternities, honoraries, and sports associations; and, if possible, his first place of employment after graduation. Ideally, this biographical file is kept up to date by the alumni office staff throughout the career of each alumnus.

Alumni associations. Membership in the alumni association may be voluntary or automatic, but most associations utilize membership dues to finance their operations. The alumni association traditionally has its own constitution and bylaws that define the responsibilities and functions of the association and its elected officers and make clear the relationship of the association to the institution.

At some American colleges and universities, the alumni association is totally independent, and some alumni associations have their own building and office facilities off campus. At other institutions, the alumni association has on-campus facilities provided by the institution. Some associations pay rent to the university for the use of such facilities, while others receive these capital services in recognition of their contributions to the college.

The officers and the governing board or council of the alumni association meet at regular intervals to advise the alumni office director and his staff in areas of alumni programing. At such meetings the alumni program is coordinated in such a manner as can best serve alumni as well as university objectives and goals. At those institutions where healthy—two-way—alumni relations are in effect, the college or university officials often meet with alumni association officers and members to discuss university problems and policies with them. In many instances, alumni are elected or appointed to the college or university board of trustees or board of directors in appreciation of their talents and services, thereby becoming effective leaders for the school at every level of the organization.

Classes, clubs, and chapters. Alumni associations can be organized into classes as well as into clubs or chapters. Alumni usually become permanently identified with a class in accordance with their year of graduation. It is customary in many colleges to elect a president or a class secretary for life. These class officers assume the responsibility of maintaining a class roster of names and addresses, keeping in touch with their classmates, and working with the alumni office on campus in arranging class reunions or special functions. A major duty of class presidents or secretaries is to organize reunions, usually at five- or ten-year intervals. At some institutions, class officers are elected or reelected at each reunion instead of serving lifelong terms.

A by-product of effective class organizations and programing is a successful class fund-raising effort. Most college classes have a class treasurer whose function it is to sequester all possible profits from dances, banquets, and sales of books or other items in the name of his class. Such proceeds, added to personal contributions from class members and the collection of dues, often provide a sizable class gift to the school. Often such a gift is presented on the occasion of a special class reunion. The class organization thus becomes a part of the university's fund-raising program.

Some university alumni associations are organized by individual professional schools. Most alumni associations are also organized on a geographical basis, with alumni residing in the same region forming a local alumni club or chapter. Alumni elect club or chapter officers and conduct programs to meet the wishes of alumni in the community. While these programs may be largely social in nature, such as picnics, banquets, outings, receptions, and cocktail parties, they are usually designed to support some program of their alma mater.

Many alumni clubs sponsor special events for their own members and for the community to raise money for scholarships, the college library, athletic programs, or other university activities. When a university or college is conducting a major fund-raising campaign, efforts are usually made to uti-lize the services of alumni clubs and chapters in the campaign.

In addition to serving as vehicles for fund-raising projects, area alumni clubs often engage in service projects involving their members or students who are about to enter their university. Many alumni clubs sponsor an annual social event to which they invite new students and their parents. The purpose of such an event is to acquaint the incoming students with the alumni, to help them get oriented to college life, and to answer questions about the institution. Usually a representative of the university attends the event and advises the new students on their college careers.

Another service provided by alumni clubs is that of helping recent graduates to locate jobs and housing in their communities. Alumni can render the ambassadorial service expected of them by helping to recruit outstanding students for their alma mater, by interviewing applicants for scholarships, and by attending high school "college nights" to provide information about their college or university. If university professors or administrators visit a city or area in which alumni are located, most alumni clubs make an effort to welcome the visitor and to arrange a reception, luncheon, or dinner in his honor.

Alumni Programs

In the United States alumni are often accused of placing too much emphasis on organized intercollegiate athletics, to the detriment of academic pursuits. This charge is not well founded. While all institutions, especially those better known for successful sports programs, have a coterie of ardent alumni sports fans, the large majority of graduates and former students have a broader view of their college relationship. Sports events receive more publicity, but alumni programs touch on many other areas of interest. It is not unusual to see college alumni deeply involved in continuing education, art exhibits, concerts, lectures, and other cultural events as part of an organized alumni program. For example, alumni programing increasingly includes an annual weekend, a week, or as much as a month, set aside for an "alumni college" or an "education vacation" during which alumni return to the campus for lectures and classes by favorite professors on subjects of special interest.

Honor awards. Honor awards are always a part of alumni programs. To encourage and reward good citizenship and responsible involvement in local, state, national, and international affairs, many college alumni associations select outstanding persons from among their ranks for distinguished service recognition. The Alumnus or Alumna of the Year is recognized on almost every college or university campus in one form or another. At the same time, many alumni programs encourage outstanding faculty teaching and research by providing recognition through monetary rewards and through the establishment of named scholarships, lectureships, professorships, or academic chairs. In these ways, alumni of American colleges and universities play an important role in educational development.

Placement and advisory services. Placement and advisory services are important in alumni programing. Many institutions bring back successful alumni in representative professions to participate in student career days, job placement, and recruitment. In addition, alumni often are asked to serve on advisory boards in academic divisions and on faculty and administrative committees concerned with such matters as curriculum development and teaching techniques.

Alumni-student relations. The most successful alumni affairs officers are those who develop a good relationship with undergraduates on campus before these students become alumni themselves. Such a relationship is best accomplished through a positive public relations program that involves student participation in alumni affairs at an early stage of the students' careers. Many universities operate special programs designed to acquaint students

with the purposes and functions of their future alumni association. In addition, universities often give complimentary copies of their alumni publications to students and invite students to contribute articles or photographs for inclusion in alumni publications.

Frequently undergraduate and graduate students are invited to alumni functions; they may even have representation on alumni boards. In some schools, students serve as hosts for alumni-sponsored events. A more organized effort often includes special dinners or outings sponsored by alumni for students and student organizations. Since scholarships are provided by alumni contributions, many institutions identify scholarship recipients as alumni scholars and make a special effort to include them in alumni programs. Alumni associations also sponsor student debate tournaments, sports events, musical performances, and other such activities. Student speakers at area alumni clubs, workshops, and seminars learn to recognize the values of an active service association. Through such activities, students become acquainted with alumni leaders and become encouraged to continue their alumni associations after graduation. The development of student-alumni associations or student foundations organized on the model of an alumni association and under its sponsorship often results from such programs.

Fund raising. American colleges encourage alumni to make voluntary contributions to supplement student fees and state allocations, at public universities or colleges, and to supplement endowment income and tuition, at private institutions. It is generally felt that institutions with successful alumni programs will have greater success in securing such gift funds.

Fund raising is a by-product of good alumni relations. The various members of an institution's public, if duly impressed with the caliber of the school and convinced of the worth of its objectives, will respond to requests for financial support. Alumni affairs, parents' organizations, and relations with other publics are integral parts of a development program. Each member of the university or college community is invited to play a role in this overall effort. The prestigious American institutions are those that have successfully developed the support of alumni, parents, and other friends. The vast talents and resources of this support are channeled into building a more effective institution, making possible many facilities and programs that could not materialize otherwise. Endowed chairs and professorships, millions in scholarship funds, research facilities, libraries, art collections, museums, laboratories, university hospitals, buildings, and all kinds of facilities on hundreds of college campuses were made possible with gifts from alumni and other friends of the institutions that cultivated their support through effective alumni and public relations programs.

International alumni programing. Thousands of students from around the world have graduated from or studied at American colleges, universities, and independent schools. By definition, they are alumni of their respective alma maters. However, very few American institutions have developed alumni programs that include their former foreign students, referred to as international alumni. Some colleges and universities maintain alumni clubs in other countries. A few have special alumni newsletters to send abroad, and a limited number involve international alumni members in college activities.

In the 1970s efforts were being made to expand participation by international alumni. Such efforts are an extension of international educational and cultural exchange, until now confined to students and teachers.

The Council for Advancement and Support of Education (CASE) has named an international alumni committee to study and develop activities in this area. Surveys of existing programs have been made. International alumni of American institutions are being identified and contacted. Mail-

ing lists for individual institutions are being prepared. In these endeavors, CASE is working closely with the National Association for Foreign Student Affairs (NAFSA), and the national conferences and assemblies of both organizations now include sessions and workshops on international alumni programing.

Alumni tours. Alumni tours are sponsored by many college and university alumni associations throughout the United States. These tours are either fund-raising ventures, social events, or part of a university's continuing education effort. As international alumni programing develops, efforts will be made to use alumni tours as a means of involving graduates living in other countries. It is possible to have international alumni take part in the alumni tour activities of their United States alma maters by acting as country hosts, club program speakers, local contacts for the alumni tour group, and participants in reunion efforts. Alumni around the world can duplicate the work of alumni in the United States, serving as recruiters, interviewers of prospective students, and alumni ambassadors of their American institutions.

Alumni Publications

Every alumni affairs program includes publication of an alumni magazine, a newsletter, newspaper, or other form of periodical designed to keep alumni informed and interested in campus affairs. These alumni periodicals range in format from the elaborate to the very simple. Many feature photographs of campus and off-campus events. They report on alumni program activities, carry feature stories on outstanding graduates of the institution, and deliver the latest news from the campus. Some concentrate on the literary efforts of faculty, students, or even alumni. They publish results of athletic events, news on faculty research and publications, and messages from presidents and deans. Some alumni magazines deal with current events in news items and feature articles about domestic, national, and international affairs. Professional journals are often included in the alumni publication effort. All but a few contain "class notes" that bring readers up to date on the whereabouts and activities of classmates around the world. Many associations extend their magazine or newspaper publication efforts with alumni directories, college histories, song books, and handbooks or guides.

The alumni publications are an essential part of the university's total effort to maintain personal contact, to keep alumni informed of campus developments, and to report on institutional progress and failure.

Professional Associations in Alumni Affairs and Public Relations

Alumni relations is public relations aimed at a very specific segment of the public. For many years, two professional associations served college and university administrators responsible for alumni affairs, university development, and public relations. In 1976 these two organizations, the American College Public Relations Association and the American Alumni Council, merged to avoid duplication of services and more efficiently service their clientele. The new organization, known as the Council for Advancement and Support of Education, provides state-of-the-art information and programs in the areas of alumni administration, university development, fund raising, governmental relations, institutional relations, informational services, publications, and executive management. Membership in CASE includes more than seven thousand individuals employed in nearly two thousand colleges, universities, two-year institutions, and independent schools.

Bibliography

Ingraham, M. H. *The Mirror of Brass*. Madison: University of Wisconsin Press, 1968.
Millett, J. D. *The Academic Community*. New York: McGraw-Hill, 1962.
Murdoch, K. "Alumni Relations." In A. S Knowles (Ed.), *Handbook of College and University Administration*. (General vol.) New York: McGraw-Hill, 1970.

The "How To" of Educational Fund Raising. Washington, D.C.: American Alumni Council, 1955.
Sailor, R. W. "A Primer of Alumni Work, American Alumni Council." Ithaca, New York: Cayuga Press, 1954.

JOHN E. DOLIBOIS

See also: Development, College and University; Promotional Methods in Higher Education; Public Relations.

ALUMNI FINANCIAL SUPPORT
See Development, College and University.

ALUMNI, INTERNATIONAL
See Exchange, International: Campus International Offices.

AMERICAN ACADEMY OF ARTS AND SCIENCES

The American Academy of Arts and Sciences, founded during the American Revolution by intellectual leaders prominent in laying the philosophical foundations of the new nation, is an honorary society devoted to the promotion of knowledge. Members, including approximately twenty-three hundred fellows and four hundred foreign honorary members, are leaders in the scholastic, scientific, business, and governmental professions. The academy serves as an institutional framework where varied intellectual resources can be brought to bear on the resolution of complex problems facing mankind.

The academy is engaged in an active program of study and publication on scholarly issues as well as on major national and international problems, especially those that require the expertise of several disciplines. The academy recognizes outstanding contributions by a series of awards, including a social science prize, the Rumford Medal in physics, the Emerson-Thoreau Medal in literature, and the Amory Prize in medicine. The activities of the academy are financed by contributions from government, private foundations, and interested individuals as well as endowment funds.

In 1965 the academy's Commission on the Year 2000 was established to indicate future consequences of public policy decisions, to anticipate future social and intellectual problems, and to begin formulating alternative solutions so that society will have more options and thus be able to make moral choices. Among the topics discussed and reported on by thirty-five outstanding scholars in plenary meetings and working sessions were structures of intellectual institutions, population and the age balance, the knowledge "explosion" and its consequences (in the curriculum of education and the meaning of training), the consequences of meritocracy, and the use of leisure. Edited working papers·of the commission, defunct since 1972, appeared in the summer 1967 edition of the academy publication *Daedalus.*

The international program of the academy has centered mainly on issues relating to arms control and scientific and technological development. The American Academy and the National Academy of Sciences cosponsor American participation in the Pugwash Conferences on Science and World Affairs. Conceived by Albert Einstein and Bertrand Russell in the 1950s as a private forum for scientists from the West and the East, these meetings bring together leading scientists from developed and developing countries to discuss problems of world security and international cooperation. In addition, individual Pugwash groups in various countries organize symposia on more specific topics. The American Pugwash Committee has sponsored symposia on such topics as "The Future of the Sea-Based Deterrent," "The Impact of New Technologies on the Arms Race," and "What Can Scientists Do for Development?"

The academy also sponsors the Committee on International Studies of Arms Control, which is primarily concerned with exchanges between United States and Soviet scientists. The committee organized a summer study on new directions in arms control.

The academy participates in the development and continuing support of the International Centre for Insect Physiology and Ecology (ICIPE), an international scientific research institute located in Nairobi, Kenya. Established through the efforts of a consortium of academies of science and scientific societies, ICIPE attacks global problems of insect pest control in the fields of public health, agriculture, and the environment.

The American Academy has joined with the National Academy of Sciences in cosponsoring American participation in the development of the International Foundation for Science (IFS), whose aim is to support the research of young scientists and technical investigators in developing countries. The foundation seeks out young scientists of outstanding merit from developing countries and provides them with material and support in their work on the condition that the research activity takes place in the territory and for the benefit of a developing country. The IFS was formally established in Stockholm in 1972.

The academy has held a seminar on United States-Japanese relations, a conference on Indian-American scientific cooperation, and a series of meetings on the People's Republic of China. The academy publishes *Bulletin,* monthly; *Daedalus,* quarterly journal; and *Records,* annual report.

165 Allendale Street
Jamaica Plain Station
Boston, Massachusetts 02130 USA
PATRICIA FLAHERTY

AMERICAN ASSOCIATION FOR HIGHER EDUCATION

Founded in 1870, the American Association for Higher Education (AAHE) was one of the four original departments of the National Education Association. It became a separate nonprofit professional organization in 1969. The purpose of the association is to clarify and help resolve critical issues in postsecondary education: teaching, learning, decision making, academic freedom, individual rights, finances, and institutional goals.

There are six types of AAHE membership: regular, for faculty, administrators, trustees, and other professionals in higher education; student, for full-time students only; retired, for persons fully retired; contributing, for members wishing to give additional support to AAHE; sustaining, for members wishing to make a substantial contribution; and life, for persons wishing regular membership throughout their lives. Membership numbers over nine thousand.

The association has both a national conference held in March and regional conferences; these conferences deal with and often forecast issues vital to postsecondary education.

Activities include liaison with government agencies; Nexus, a rapid referral service that provides information, mostly by telephone, on new or old programs in postsecondary education; and the Inter-institutional Cooperative Program, a national information center that stimulates discussion on all forms of educational cooperation from bilateral arrangements to the largest multipurpose consortia. A national seminar on cooperation is held each fall and spring.

Publications include *College and University Bulletin,* monthly newsletter; *Current Issues in Higher Education, ERIC-AAHE Research Reports;* and *Journal of Higher Education,* monthly journal cosponsored by AAHE and Ohio State University Press.

One Dupont Circle
Washington, D.C. 20036 USA

AMERICAN ASSOCIATION OF COLLEGES FOR TEACHER EDUCATION

The American Association of Colleges for Teacher Education (AACTE) is a na-tional, voluntary, professional association of more than 860 colleges and universities. The AACTE member institutions collectively prepare more than 90 percent of America's educational personnel through undergraduate and graduate programs. AACTE promotes effective preparation of quality educational personnel, including sound initial training and lifelong improvement to respond to the needs of a rapidly changing, complex society. The association serves as a clearinghouse for information on teacher education.

Association programs include an annual meeting, workshops, seminars, and a special biennial School for Executives. The national office is staffed by an executive director, five associate directors, and more than thirty supporting personnel.

The association develops accreditation standards and contributes to funding for the National Council for Accreditation of Teacher Education. Other key concerns include international education and multicultural education.

Publications of AACTE include *AACTE Bulletin, Yearbook, Directory,* and *Journal of Teacher Education.* Books, periodicals, and monographs are published regularly.

One Dupont Circle
Washington, D.C. 20036 USA

AMERICAN ASSOCIATION OF COLLEGIATE REGISTRARS AND ADMISSIONS OFFICERS

The American Association of Collegiate Registrars and Admissions Officers (AACRAO), founded in 1910, is represented at over two thousand colleges and universities. Its total membership of 5800 includes college and university registrars, and admissions, financial aid, and institutional research officials. Formerly called the American Association of Collegiate Registrars, AACRAO seeks to advance higher education and encourage professionalism in offices of admissions, financial aid, institutional research, records, and registration. An executive secretary, assisted by an elected executive committee, operates the Washington national headquarters. Activities consist of administering a placement service to aid colleges and universities in filling vacancies in the areas of records, registration, admissions, institutional research, and financial aid; encouraging, conducting, and cooperating in research projects intended to further the purpose of the association; promoting regional associations of registrars, admissions directors, and related officers; and establishing committees to give attention to current problems and concerns.

In 1964 AACRAO contracted with the United States Agency for International Development to provide credential analyst and consultant sources and to conduct studies designed to improve the selection and admission of AID participants for study in United States academic institutions. The AACRAO-AID Participant Selection and Placement Study—a study of some one thousand foreign students and their admissions, placement, and education experiences in United States institutions— was undertaken in 1967. AACRAO received a special certificate of commendation for this work. The association also conducts workshops on the evaluation of foreign student credentials. An example is the African workshop, which was cosponsored by the National Association for Foreign Student Affairs and partially financed by the Bureau of Educational Affairs of the United States Department of State.

Publications include a quarterly newsletter; *College and University,* quarterly journal; *Report of Credit Given by Educational Institutions,* annual; and World Educations Series, a special series of booklets concerning the educational systems of foreign countries and guides to the academic placement of foreign students. This series is produced with the help of a special grant from the Bureau of Cultural and Educational Affairs of the United States Department of State.

One Dupont Circle
Washington, D.C. 20036 USA

AMERICAN ASSOCIATION OF COMMUNITY AND JUNIOR COLLEGES

The American Association of Community and Junior Colleges (AACJC), a nonprofit organization established in 1920, is made up of two-year colleges, both public and private, in addition to a number of individuals from these institutions.

Membership in the association is institutional. The president of the member college is the institution's representative, unless someone else is designated by the college. Institutional associates (institutions other than community and junior colleges) and individual associates also receive association services but do not participate in its governance.

Organized to provide national leadership of community-based postsecondary education, AACJC has four objectives: to represent the interests of member institutions in Washington, D.C., at foundations, and in other decision-making centers of national significance; to include in its membership, as fully as possible, all community-based postsecondary institutions; to promote the growth, acceptance, and effective practice of the concept of community-based postsecondary education; and to alert member institutions to trends and issues in society.

The AACJC Office of Governmental Affairs maintains a liaison with leaders in major branches of the United States government and provides information about legislation affecting education to Congress and government agencies. In addition, the office conducts workshops throughout the United States on such topics as proposal writing and federal liaison.

Special projects, supported by foundations or governmental agencies, provide member institutions with information and program assistance in such areas as occupational education and community services. Such projects provide more than half of the association's annual budget.

The yearly assembly gives attention to social and educational issues and addresses recommendations to the association, member colleges, and government bodies. One hundred trustees, administrators, faculty, students, and invited participants attend the assembly. Follow-up discussions and action take place at local, state, regional, and national levels.

Because the association unites many different groups with special interests, some have banded together into councils. Each council has its own constitution, officers, program, and finances. Councils recognized by the AACJC board of directors are formally affiliated with the association. Existing councils include the National Council of State Directors, Council of Universities and Colleges, National Council on Learning, National Council on Resource Development, Council on Public Relations, National Council on Student Development, Council on Black African Affairs, *Congreso nacional de asuntos colegiales* (National Congress of Affairs of Secondary Education), National Council on Community Services, American Association of Women in Community and Junior Colleges, and Council for Occupational Education.

The association has an international office that is engaged in developing an international association of persons, agencies, and institutions concerned with community-based postsecondary education.

The AACJC publications include *Community and Junior College Journal,* monthly magazine; *Community and Junior College News,* monthly newsletter; *Directory,* annual; and *Special,* occasional newsletter on legislative affairs.

One Dupont Circle
Washington, D.C. 20036 USA

AMERICAN ASSOCIATION OF STATE COLLEGES AND UNIVERSITIES

The American Association of State Colleges and Universities (AASCU), founded in 1961, has a membership of 313 state-supported colleges and universities in the United States. Most member institutions share a common development from single-purpose schools to comprehensive institutions. Although some of the colleges and universities were established originally as junior colleges, technical schools, and seminaries, the vast majority were founded as normal schools to prepare elementary and secondary school teachers.

All member institutions are four-year colleges or universities offering the baccalaureate; some offer postgraduate work at the master's and doctoral level, but their primary commitment is to the excellence of undergraduate teaching. Their common goals are to create and maintain a learning environment which will enrich the student's life and to extend the opportunity for higher education to all those willing and eager to learn, regardless of income, family heritage, and personal circumstances. AASCU provides these institutions with a national voice in the formation of policies which affect higher education.

AASCU is supported by membership dues. Special projects, such as the Office of Health Related Program Development and the Servicemen's Opportunity College Project, are funded by government agencies. In addition, AASCU has received funds from private foundations interested in furthering the goals of the association, and thus the development of state colleges and universities. The offices of the executive director and the assistant executive director coordinate AASCU activities and special projects.

The AASCU Office of Program Development assists institutions in the exploration of new curricula and services. The office encourages a continual self-evaluation of the institution's role to ensure that its programs reflect its true objectives and the realistic needs of its constituency.

The Office of International Programs works to broaden and intensify the international-intercultural experiences of an institution through its administrators, faculty, and students. The office arranges faculty exchanges, lecture trips, and seminars for educators from the United States and abroad. Study centers in Mexico, Italy,

Canada, and India offer a living-learning experience for students.

The Office of Governmental Relations works on behalf of AASCU members in policy development at both the federal and state levels. Through its own policy and fiscal analysis, it provides information to members of the United States Congress and to state officials considering changes in policy. By providing a continual flow of information to AASCU members and by working with other educational associations and such interested groups as labor, business, and women, the office attempts to maintain a strong fiscal base for public colleges and universities.

The Office of Federal Programs assists AASCU members in obtaining funds for special campus projects. Serving as a liaison between the campus and federal and private agencies, the office seeks appropriate sponsors for research and demonstration projects.

Through a regular newsletter and a publication series, the Office of Information and Research keeps members informed of events which have an impact on state college and university goals and provides information for the development of new programs and changing roles. Additionally, the office works to keep the public informed of the role, goals, and problems of state colleges and universities.

One Dupont Circle
Washington, D.C. 20036 USA

AMERICAN ASSOCIATION OF UNIVERSITY ADMINISTRATORS

The American Association of University Administrators (AAUA) was founded in 1971 at the State University of New York, Buffalo, to encourage better administration of higher education and to assist career administrators in their professional development. Membership includes more than 1300 administrators, primarily in the United States.

The purposes of the organization are to

establish, promote, and perpetuate ethical and professional standards for administrators and institutions of higher education; to cultivate the mutuality of interests of those engaged in or concerned with the administration of higher education; and to represent the interests of AAUA members in the affairs of institutions of higher education, locally or nationally.

Governed by a board of directors composed of thirty administrators, including presidents, vice-presidents, deans, and directors of higher education institutions in the United States, the association is entirely dependent on annual membership dues for financial support.

Regional seminars are held each year throughout the United States on such topics as collective bargaining, accountability, and politics of higher education. AAUA provides a free referral service for members seeking a change in position and for institutions looking for professional administrators. A national assembly is held annually in the spring on a theme of significance to administrators.

The association has issued policy statements concerning collective bargaining, requests for assistance from administrators or institutions of higher education, use of the association's name in sponsoring activities, and rights of administrators.

Any full-time college or university employee who is engaged in the administration of higher education can become an active member. Graduate students in institutions of higher learning who are preparing for careers in higher education administration are eligible for career membership. An active member who has retired from active service becomes an emeritus member. Anyone interested in the administration of higher education, but who does not fit the other membership categories, can be considered an associate member.

A group composed of at least twenty-five active members may establish a chapter to promote AAUA activities at an institution, in a state, or within a region. Existing chapters include Alabama Alpha, a state chapter;

Rutgers, an institutional chapter in New Jersey; and Western New York, which draws its membership from that region.

AAUA publishes *Communiqué*, a quarterly newsletter that includes brief summaries of conference speeches and activities.

1 Library Circle
Crosby Hall
State University of New York, Buffalo
Buffalo, New York 14214 USA

AMERICAN ASSOCIATION OF UNIVERSITY PROFESSORS

In January 1915, at the instigation of a small group of Johns Hopkins University faculty members, over six hundred professors met in New York and organized the American Association of University Professors. The purpose of AAUP, according to the constitution adopted at this first meeting, was "to facilitate a more effective cooperation among teachers and investigators in universities and colleges and in professional schools of similar grade for the promotion of the interests of higher education and research, and in general to increase the usefulness and advance the standards and ideals of the profession." In 1959 the words *standards and ideals* were changed to *standards, ideals, and welfare.* John Dewey, professor of philosophy at Columbia University, was elected the first president of AAUP, and A. O. Lovejoy, philosophy professor at Johns Hopkins University, the first secretary.

The association's revenue comes almost entirely from the dues of its members. A council, composed of thirty elected members and officers, is the governing body. The general secretary serves as chief administrative officer. The AAUP headquarters is in Washington, D.C., with regional offices in New York and San Francisco.

Teachers, researchers, librarians, and counselors with faculty status at accredited American institutions of higher education are eligible for active membership in AAUP. A group of at least seven members at an institution can organize a local chapter, and chapters can organize state conferences. As of January 1, 1974, there was 75,069 members in 2215 institutions, 1355 chapters, and 45 state conferences.

The main work of AAUP has been the development of its defense, both procedurally and substantively, of academic freedom and tenure. Under the auspices of its Committee A on Academic Freedom and Tenure, AAUP became the recognized guardian of these principles in United States higher education. The basic document of this defense is the 1940 *Statement of Principles on Academic Freedom and Tenure,* authored jointly by AAUP and the Association of American Colleges. By 1974 over ninety professional and learned societies in the United States endorsed the statement, now regarded as a basic charter of academic common law.

Cases of faculty members claiming injury under a serious abrogation of principles contained in the 1940 statement and requesting association assistance are investigated by an ad hoc committee that submits a report to Committee A. Significant reports are authorized by Committee A for publication in the quarterly *AAUP Bulletin.* On the basis of a report, the membership at an annual meeting can place an institution on the association's list of censured administrations. Removal of censure occurs by action of an annual meeting and is recommended when questions of redress are resolved and when institutional regulations on academic freedom and tenure are consistent with policies and principles supported by the association.

The second major program is an annual survey of faculty salaries, under the auspices of Committee Z on the Economic Status of the Profession. Begun in 1958 with 282 voluntarily participating institutions, the survey grew by 1974 to include 1637 different campuses and an additional 72 medical schools. The survey report, which appears every summer in the *AAUP Bulletin,* is used by economic analysts; by governing boards, administrations, and faculties in public and private sectors of higher education; and by legislators and legislative committees at state and federal levels.

At its annual meeting in 1972, the association voted to continue supporting the principles of collective bargaining. By 1974, under the auspices of Committee N on Representation of Economic and Professional Interests, local chapters at thirty institutions had become the exclusive representatives for the faculty at collective bargaining sessions.

One Dupont Circle
Washington, D.C. 20036 USA

AMERICAN CHEMICAL SOCIETY

Founded in 1876, the American Chemical Society (ACS), with more than 100,000 members, is the world's largest scholarly society devoted to a single science. In 1937 the society was granted a national charter by the United States Congress and legally designated a scientific and educational society.

The society encourages high standards of professional ethics, education, and attainments of chemists and chemical engineers; it also encourages the diffusion of chemical knowledge. ACS is active at every educational level, including high school, college and university, and continuing education.

In the 1960s ACS was involved in the development of two new curricula, CHEM Study and the Chemical Bond Approach. These curricula have become the point of departure for most work in curricular innovation in high school chemistry throughout the world. Career literature prepared by the society is widely distributed through high school guidance counselors and also through the education committees of the society's 175 local chapters. The James Bryant Conant Awards in High School Chemistry Teaching—nine regional awards and one national award—are offered annually by the society.

In 1967 ACS established a staff office for chemical education in junior colleges. During the late 1960s the National Science Foundation supported an ACS project that developed the ChemTec curriculum for the two-year training of chemical technicians. The curriculum has served as a prototype for technician projects by other scientific societies.

At the four-year-college level, the ACS Committee on Professional Training develops minimum standards for undergraduate chemistry programs leading to the bachelor's degree. These standards, updated periodically, deal not only with curriculum but also with faculty training, laboratory and library facilities, and teaching load. The committee inspects departments, by invitation only, and publishes a list of those meeting the standards. About half of the 1050 departments giving degrees in chemistry are on the approved list. ACS bears the entire cost of this program.

Any college student majoring in chemistry, chemical engineering, or a related discipline may, by paying a nominal fee, become an affiliate of ACS. Each affiliate receives a subscription to one ACS publication and special member rates for all others. A film library provides films gratis to student affiliate chapters. Student affiliates may also use the society's employment service. There are about six thousand affiliates and six hundred chapters in this program.

The ACS National Chemistry Examination Program, a popular service of the ACS Division of Chemical Education, develops, publishes, and distributes standard examinations in chemistry at high school, college, and graduate-level placements. The division conducts the Two-Year College Chemistry Conferences (quarterly) and symposia for college chemistry teachers (biannually) on such topics as new chemistry concepts, developments in curriculum, teaching methods, instrumentation, and professional status. Biennial summer conferences deal with major issues in chemical education.

The ACS Award in Chemical Education is presented annually by the division for significant achievement in chemical education.

Another college-level service is Academic Openings, triannual listings of teaching and postdoctoral research vacancies in colleges, universities, and junior colleges in the United States and Canada. Available gratis to all who request copies, the listing serves new graduates, employed teachers who want to change jobs, and chemists interested in teaching opportunities. College Chemistry Seniors is a special placement service for chemistry majors interested in graduate work. Seniors majoring in chemistry or chemical engineering may submit their résumés to be photo-reproduced and sent to graduate departments. The service is available without cost to students, including those who are not ACS affiliates.

The ACS Petroleum Research Fund administers an annual income of approximately three and a half million dollars for college and university faculty research grants. The fund awards starter grants to young unestablished members who find it difficult to attract research support elsewhere.

In 1965 the society established the ACS Short Courses, the first in a series of continuing education programs. The ACS Short Courses consist of two- to five-day presentations by small teaching staffs of subjects selected to meet the continuing education needs of chemists. About fifty sessions are presented nationwide through the year. Total participation in the first ten years of the program was about 25,000.

The ACS Audio Courses, initiated in 1970, are study units at college and continuing education levels in chemistry, chemical engineering, and related subjects. Each course includes a tape recording of the subject matter and an accompanying reference manual. Some twenty-five audio courses are used in colleges, universities, and company training programs in the United States and, though the courses are in English, in about forty foreign countries.

The society offers film and correspondence interaction courses. With the support of the National Science Foundation, the society is developing two series of multimedia user-controlled courses, involving computer and audiovisual augmentation, for continuing education of chemists in industry.

The ACS continuing education program covers new technologies and discoveries in chemistry; college curriculum introduced in the last ten to twenty years; refresher courses in sciences peripheral to chemistry; and courses in nontechnical topics such as chemical marketing, management of research and development, business aspects of chemistry, patent practices, laboratory safety, and technical writing. The short courses are available to companies for in-house use. Many local ACS chapters have lending libraries of audio courses for use by their members. Any unemployed ACS member may attend short courses free and have free access to audio courses.

The ACS publications include two journals: *Chemistry,* for superior high school students, and *Journal of Chemical Education,* for college chemistry teachers. The society also publishes and distributes *Selected Titles in Chemistry,* annotated bibliography of inexpensive books for the general reader.

Other ACS publications include *College Chemistry Faculties,* biennial directory of all college and university teachers of chemistry and related subjects in the United States and Canada, and *Directory of Graduate Research,* listing of graduate faculties in United States and Canadian institutions offering the Ph.D. degree in chemistry, biochemistry, chemical engineering, and medicinal chemistry. The latter directory describes graduate research activities in each department and also gives bibliographical references to all recent publications of each professor.

1155 16th Street NW
Washington, D.C. 20036 USA

MOSES PASSER

AMERICAN COLLEGE
HEALTH ASSOCIATION

Founded in 1920, the American College Health Association (ACHA) promotes health in its broadest aspects for students and other members of the college community. Membership is open to nonprofit institutions of higher education and individuals interested in health service on college and university campuses.

The ACHA membership includes over 1500 physicians, administrators, dentists, nurses, educators, and ecologists representing 550 institutions of higher education in the United States. Individual members are affiliated with one of ten ACHA sections: administration, athletic medicine, clinical medicine, dental health, environmental health and safety, health education, junior community colleges, mental health, nursing, or students.

All members are assessed membership dues, based on size of enrollment for institutions and annual earned income for individuals. Other sources of funding are publication sales and service charges. Specific projects receive foundation or federal grants.

The organization offers a broad range of consultation services to institutions, including a review of their total health program. An annual meeting is held each spring to discuss education programs of general interest as well as programs designed to meet the needs of the ten ACHA sections.

The ACHA publications include *Recommended Standards and Practices for a College Health Program,* a detailed outline for the design of a program to meet the comprehensive health needs of an academic community, and *Development of Health Programs for Junior and Community Colleges.* The association also publishes *Journal of the American Health Association,* professional journal; and *Action,* newsletter containing higher education reports, legislative and medical affairs, and news of ACHA activities. A number of brochures addressed to health problems

of the college student are offered by ACHA for distribution to the college community.
2807 Central Street
Evanston, Illinois 60201 USA

AMERICAN COLLEGE
PERSONNEL ASSOCIATION

Founded in 1952, the American College Personnel Association (ACPA) is a division of the American Personnel and Guidance Association (APGA), a professional organization with over 36,000 members in the United States and more than fifty other countries.

ACPA, whose membership numbers over 7500, is open to APGA members employed in student personnel work in higher education in such areas as teaching, administration, counseling, and research. A student membership is open to graduate students interested in personnel work.

Through representation at congressional hearings and government agencies, ACPA gives national attention to the interests of its members. It also carries out special research projects and surveys.

ACPA publishes *Journal of College Student Personnel,* bimonthly.
1607 New Hampshire Avenue NW
Washington, D.C. 20009 USA

AMERICAN COLLEGE
TESTING PROGRAM

A national and nonprofit organization founded in 1959, the American College Testing Program (ACT) originated as an admissions testing service. ACT now offers a number of educational services and programs in the United States. Concerned with individuals who plan to enter or continue some sort of postsecondary education, ACT's guidance, assessment, and financial-need-analysis services are designed primarily to assist high school and college students. With increased emphasis on continuing education, however, adults are also using ACT services.

A staff of about 500 directs ACT activities from a national office in Iowa City, Iowa, and twelve regional offices throughout the United States. ACT also maintains a special office located in the National Center for Higher Education in Washington, D.C.

The national and international activities of ACT are governed by two representative bodies, the thirty-seven-member ACT corporation and sixteen-member ACT board of trustees. The corporation, which holds at least one national meeting each year to set broad policy, is made up of elected representatives from thirty-seven states and regions. The trustees, who meet four times a year to direct the management of ACT, are selected by the corporate members.

Coordinated educational services that are developed, administered, and controlled by ACT are identified as resident programs. The ACT Assessment Program, an expanded and improved version of the original ACT service, is required or recommended for use by student applicants at more than 2500 colleges and other postsecondary schools. The guidance-oriented program is used each year by approximately one million students planning for some type of postsecondary education. Related services include the ACT Educational Opportunity Service and descriptive and predictive ACT Research Services.

The ACT Student Assistance Program is made up of two coordinated services. The ACT Student Need Analysis Service, used each year by more than 400,000 student aid applicants, is designed to assist students and aid administrators in applying for and awarding financial aid for postsecondary education. The other service, ACT Profile of Financial Aid Applicants, is a management service that provides general information about a school's financial aid program.

Developmental and administrative activities are carried out by ACT on a contractual basis with educational associations and governmental agencies. Two educational services that have been developed by ACT are distributed, administered, and scored by a publishing firm: ACT Career Planning Program for Grades 8–11 and ACT Assessment of Career Development.

Extensive research aimed at developing and improving ACT services is carried out by personnel within ACT's Research and Development Division, consisting of three major departments. The Test Development Department is responsible for continued development of standardized tests. The Developmental Research Department is concerned with development of nontest portions of new services and improvements in those portions of existing services. The ACT Research Services develops and administers a variety of descriptive and predictive research services and special questionnaires provided by ACT for high schools and postsecondary institutions. General educational research is also conducted within all three areas.

In addition to dozens of informational and interpretive books and brochures related to its services, ACT publishes ACT Research Report Series, ACT Monograph Series, ACT Special Report Series, ACT Essays on Education, and *Activity,* a newsletter issued four times a year.

Box 168
Iowa City, Iowa 52240 USA

AMERICAN CONFERENCE OF ACADEMIC DEANS

The American Conference of Academic Deans (ACAD) was founded in January 1945 in Atlantic City, at a meeting of the Association of American Colleges (AAC). The association provides opportunities for academic deans of liberal arts colleges to meet together, share experiences, exchange views, and discuss common problems.

Membership, originally limited to deans of institutions that were members of AAC, was extended to liberal arts deans of all four-year colleges or universities in 1968. By 1974 membership numbered 500. ACAD is the only United States organization for deans of both public and private liberal arts institutions.

Funded through dues which are institutional rather than individual, ACAD is incorporated as a nonprofit association in the District of Columbia. Thirteen members comprise the board of directors.

The ACAD meetings are held in conjunction with the meetings of the Association of American Colleges to enable the deans of ACAD and the presidents and other administrators of AAC to attend sessions of both organizations. The meetings are planned cooperatively and have a common theme.

In 1974 ACAD, in collaboration with AAC and the Council of Colleges of Arts and Sciences, sponsored a one-week summer workshop to provide in-depth educational experience for approximately fifty novice and experienced deans in the liberal arts. Also in 1974 the deans established an office in association with the Council of Colleges of Arts and Sciences at AAC headquarters in Washington, D.C.

The conference publishes the proceedings of its annual meetings. In 1969, after the twenty-fifth annual meeting, the conference published *American Conference of Academic Deans—Developments and Abstracts, 1945–1969*.

1818 R Street NW
Washington, D.C. 20009 USA

AMERICAN COUNCIL OF LEARNED SOCIETIES

The American Council of Learned Societies (ACLS), founded in 1919, is a private nonprofit federation of forty scholarly organizations in the United States concerned with the humanities and the humanistic aspects of the social sciences. The purpose of the council is the advancement of humanistic studies in all fields of learning and the maintenance and strengthening of relations among national societies devoted to such studies.

The council and its activities are supported by income from endowment, dues of constituent societies, subscriptions of ACLS associate universities and colleges, grants from philanthropic foundations, government grants and contracts, and private gifts.

The council provides aid to individual scholars who are conducting research in the humanities. The aid program consists of fellowships, study fellowships, grants-in-aid, and travel grants for participation in international congresses and conferences abroad. In all of the programs, except the American Studies for Foreign Scholars, applicants must be citizens or permanent residents of the United States or Canada.

The ACLS fellowships provide opportunities for scholars to engage in post-doctoral research in the humanities. Recipients must be able to devote six to twelve months to full-time work on their projects. The maximum award is $12,000. There is a fifty-year age limit for applicants.

Study fellowships enable young scholars in the humanities to enlarge their range of knowledge by study inside or outside the humanities in disciplines other than their present specialization. Social and natural scientists who wish to study a humanistic discipline are also invited to apply. The maximum stipend does not exceed $12,000.

The grants-in-aid program provides funds in support of individual research. Expenses for which grants are applicable include travel and maintenance. Awards are made twice annually. Stipends do not exceed $2500.

ACLS administers two travel grant programs enabling American humanists and social scientists with a strong humanistic orientation to participate in international scholarly meetings abroad. The ACLS Travel Grant Program gives scholars an opportunity to present the results of their research or preside at the scholarly sessions of such meetings. Twenty-six of the council's constituent societies and five other professional organizations serve as recommending agencies for these grants. The ACLS-NEH Travel Grant Program, operating with funds made available by the National Endowment for the Humanities, supports humanists and social scientists from the United States who, by reason of office or voting membership in international bodies, must attend meetings abroad in policymaking capacities. The program also enables United States humanists—particularly junior scholars—to participate in international congresses and research conferences abroad.

Through the support of research and planning conferences, the council explores important problems of scholarship, gets advice in planning new programs, brings together scholars from various disciplines, and responds to varied needs of scholars and scholarly groups. Some of these conferences are initiated by ACLS; others have outside sponsorship.

A special project of ACLS is the American Studies Program, designed to encourage the initiation and development of various branches of American studies in institutions of higher education abroad. The program, begun in 1960 and supported by grants from the Ford Foundation, operates in Europe, Australia, Japan, New Zealand, and Taiwan. More than 550 scholars from 32 countries have come to the United States to undertake advanced research in the general area of American studies. The program has also made grants to institutions of higher education in these countries to help establish teaching posts and to increase library resources.

An important international activity sponsored jointly by ACLS and the Social Science Research Council is the International Research and Exchanges Board (IREX). IREX carries out exchanges of humanistic and social science scholars among the United States, the Soviet Union, and six East European countries: Bulgaria, Czechoslovakia, Hungary, Poland, Romania, and Yugoslavia.

ACLS also conducts nine area studies programs entitled Africa, Contemporary China, East Europe, Japan, Korea, Latin America, Near and Middle East, South Asia, and Soviet Russia. Each of these programs makes grants to aid United States scholars with their research and teaching and initiates activities to improve research and teaching of its area in the United States.

Since 1932 ACLS has maintained the Universities Service Centre, located in Hong Kong, which aids China scholars of any nationality by sponsoring visas to enter the colony for study or research and by providing working space, a library of basic reference works and periodicals, and other research services.

The ACLS publications include *Dictionary of American Biography, Dictionary of Scientific Biography,* and editions of the American Philosophers series. ACLS also publishes a newsletter four times a year and an annual report.

345 East 46th Street
New York, New York 10017 USA

AMERICAN COUNCIL ON EDUCATION

The American Council on Education (ACE) was founded during World War I as the Emergency Council on Education to coordinate services of educational institutions and organizations to the federal government. In July 1918, recognizing the need for cooperative educational efforts in time of peace as well as war, the members of the council changed the name to American Council on Education to mark the end of the transient and emergency character of the council and to indicate its broader scope.

The fourteen founding organizations were American Association for the Advancement of Science, American Association of University Professors, Association of American Agricultural Colleges and Experiment Stations, Association of American Colleges, Association of American Medical Colleges, Association of American Universities, Association of Urban Universities, Catholic Educational Association, National Association of State Universities, National Council of Normal School Presidents and Principals, National Education Association, National Council of Education, Department of Superintendence, and Society for the Promotion of Engineering Education.

Composed of approximately 1600 institutions of higher education and national and regional educational associations, ACE is a center for the improvement of education at all levels, with particular emphasis on postsecondary education. Its membership and activities reflect the distinctive character of the United States educational system, which comprises a large number of autonomous units working together for the establishment and improvement of educational standards, policies, and procedures.

The council operates through a permanent staff, advisory commissions, and special committees. Outstanding leaders in education, related fields, and public life serve on council commissions and committees and take active part in conferences and studies sponsored by ACE.

The work of the council is financed by membership dues and grants from foundations, learned societies, and professional groups. The council also occasionally undertakes special research projects related to higher education under government contract.

In 1968 the council accepted a grant of $2,500,000 from the W. K. Kellogg Foundation toward the financing of the National Center for Higher Education in Washington, D.C. The center provides central office, service, and meeting facilities for ACE and other independent educational associations.

The ACE Office of Governmental Relations monitors federal legislation, appropriations, and administrative policies that affect postsecondary education—not only the federal government's educational programs but also such other matters as tax, wage-price, energy, and antidiscrimination

policies. Members of the office staff give testimony at congressional hearings, present oral or written comments on proposed regulations and guidelines, and prepare a biennial statement on federal policy affecting postsecondary education.

The Office of Academic Affairs focuses on issues relating to students, faculty, and curricula. The staff analyzes selected curricular and institutional needs at various levels of postsecondary education and stimulates discussion of academic issues among professional and lay groups through conferences, monographs, seminars, studies, special reports, and other activities. The office serves as a clearinghouse for ideas and information concerning the recruitment, preparation, placement, in-service training, and effective utilization of teachers. ACE conducts inquiries into intellectual, social, and personal aspects of college and university life.

The Office of Women in Higher Education develops policy statements and special reports concerning equal opportunities for women in higher education at the student, faculty, and administrative levels. The office assists in the development of workshop materials and conference programs for the advancement of professional women in postsecondary education.

Institutes, workshops, and internships, offered by the Office of Leadership Development in Higher Education, identify and develop potential executive resources in colleges and universities. The two divisions of this office are the Institute for College and University Administrators, which provides professional development seminars on administrative decision making and academic leadership for recently appointed presidents, deans, and business officers; and the Academic Administration Internship Program, which selects forty fellows each year to serve one-year internships at policymaking and top operational levels in colleges and universities.

A data resource center, storing tapes generated by council surveys as well as data collected by the United States Office of Education, is operated by the Office of Administrative Affairs and Educational Studies. The office provides information to the higher education community and to governmental agencies concerned with postsecondary education and offers advice on management information systems designed to improve planning and use of resources in postsecondary education. The office publishes *Fact Book on Higher Education,* which contains tables and charts on enrollment, social and economic factors in higher education, students, faculty, and degrees.

From data generated by council research studies as well as research conducted by other public and private groups, the Policy Analysis Service develops information on public policy and institutional issues in postsecondary education. The service undertakes short- and long-range projects to document and analyze alternatives and rank priorities, and develops position papers on major issues. It disseminates selected summaries of its findings in *Policy Briefs,* a periodical.

The Office on Educational Credit is concerned with policies and procedures for awarding credit for nontraditional learning. Specifically, the office evaluates educational programs sponsored by business, industry, and government (including military correspondence programs); administers the General Educational Development Testing Program, which enables qualified adults to earn high school credentials; and makes recommendations to colleges and universities regarding the granting of credit from the College-Level Examination Program tests. The office publishes *Guide to the Evaluation Experiences in the Armed Services,* annually.

The Overseas Liaison Committee promotes communication between the academic community in the United States and governments, research institutions, and universities in developing countries. The committee provides consulting and advisory services to universities, public and private educational and donor agencies, and government ministries abroad and undertakes surveys and analyses of educational systems and program operations. The committee also operates a communications network in cooperation with rural development scholars and practitioners to facilitate the exchange of information and ideas across a wide range of integrated rural development activities. The committee's International Seminar Series fosters dialogue between scholars in the United States and developing countries on research priorities, access problems, and opportunities for collaborative research. The committee has published *International Directory for Educational Liaison* (1973).

The International Education Project is a source of current information on the status of international education—for ACE members, federal legislators, administrators of public and academic programs, and the policymakers from various sectors of higher education. The project has developed recommendations for federal support to international studies and has established four task forces to survey and report on areas of concern to international education: diffusion, overseas skill maintenance, language competences, and transnational research collaboration. The project publishes a monthly newsletter, *International Interaction.*

Other council publications, in addition to those already mentioned, are *Educational Record,* quarterly journal; *Higher Education and National Affairs,* newsletter; *American Universities and Colleges* and *American Junior Colleges,* standard directories of United States four-year and two-year postsecondary educational institutions. Books, monographs, and special reports are also published—many of them in cooperation with other higher education associations. A publications catalog is available upon request.

One Dupont Circle
Washington, D.C. 20036 USA

AMERICAN FEDERATION
OF TEACHERS

The American Federation of Teachers (AFT) is an autonomous national teachers union composed of approximately two thousand locals from every educational sector—nearly 250 of them on college and university campuses. AFT, affiliated with the American Federation of Labor–Congress of Industrial Organizations (AFL-CIO), has 450,000 members.

College locals have existed in the American Federation of Teachers since 1916. All faculty members are eligible for membership. Anyone in a college who has power to recommend hiring and firing may not become a member, although department heads ordinarily are not prohibited from joining. In all cases, the local itself determines eligibility through its constitution. More than 35,000 college teachers belong to AFT. The AFT locals are the collective bargaining agents on more than eighty campuses.

The AFT executive council, composed of thirty vice-presidents and the president, governs the union. The president and vice-presidents are subject to elections every two years. Vice-presidents, assigned to specific geographical areas, serve without remuneration. Their duties depend on actions of conventions or a national referendum of the AFT membership. The Colleges and Universities Department works under the direction of the president and the executive council.

The AFT's supreme governing body is the annual convention. Delegates to this convention are elected by local union members. Each affiliated local with a membership of twenty-five or less may elect one delegate to the annual convention. For each additional hundred members, or major fraction thereof, one additional delegate may be elected.

To form an AFT college local, at least ten faculty members sign an AFT charter application and forward a charter fee and membership dues to the national office. The local sets its own dues at a constitutionally stipulated annual minimum fee.

AFT is concerned with the rights of faculty regarding personnel records, academic freedom, salaries, participation in institutional policymaking, facilities, grievance procedure, professional improvement, and reimbursement for expenses pertaining to teaching and professional improvement.

The AFT publications include *American Teacher,* monthly newspaper; and *On Campus,* newsletter issued monthly by the Colleges and Universities Department.

1012 14th Street, NW
Washington, D.C. 20005 USA

AMERICAN INDIANS

See Access of Minorities: The North American Indian.

AMERICAN SAMOA

Population: 29,191. Student enrollment in primary school: 6130 (3030 females); secondary school: 2034 (926 females); higher education: 950 (500 females). Percentage of national budget expended on education: 22.3%. [Figures are for 1974–75. Source: Education Department, American Samoa.]

American Samoa, a United States territory composed of seven islands southwest of Hawaii, is under the jurisdiction of the United States Department of the Interior.

Education is compulsory for ages six to eighteen. Twenty-seven consolidated elementary schools, four senior high schools, and one community college are government supported. The government also maintains 156 village early childhood education centers.

In the 1960s the United States started an economic development program, which led to the establishment of new schools and the beginning of some televised instruction.

The American Samoa Community College is the only school of higher education. It is a coeducational, state-controlled institution founded in 1970. Two years of study lead to an Associate in Arts (A.A.) degree. Tuition is free, but the government grants 85 scholarships for additional expenses or for study abroad. In 1974 there were 185 students studying abroad; the principal country of study is the United States.

See also: Arab World: Regional Analysis; Archives: Africa and Asia, National Archives of; Science Policies: Less Developed Countries: Arab World.

AMERICAN UNIVERSITIES FIELD STAFF

The American Universities Field Staff (AUFS) was founded in 1952 as a nonprofit membership corporation to develop, finance, and direct a corps of individuals to study contemporary affairs in various areas of the world. The staff makes the result of these studies available to member institutions through reports and personal services.

The consortium base of AUFS includes twelve member institutions. Administrators from these institutions form the AUFS board of trustees. Liaison committees on each campus coordinate visits of AUFS staff members and integrate other AUFS activities within their schools.

AUFS has eighteen staff members stationed around the globe. These staff members make periodic teaching visits to member schools. A series of documentaries—filmed, produced, and distributed by AUFS—focus on modernization in traditional rural societies.

AUFS maintains the Center for Mediterranean Studies in Rome and the Center for Asian and Pacific Studies in Singapore. Conferences and undergraduate group-study programs are held at these centers.

In addition to area studies, staff members examine specific problems or sets of problems in collaboration with experts in appropriate disciplines at member universities. Topics have included world population problems, including demographic analysis of population growth trends, purpose and effectiveness of public policy,

and relationships of population growth to the environment and resource funds; and the dynamics of cultural and concomitant educational change in a number of foreign societies.

The AUFS book publication program draws on information developed at overseas conferences and also on the work of individual authors. Bibliographies on Asia, Africa, Eastern Europe, and Latin America are also published. The AUFS periodicals include *Fieldstaff Reports,* journal of reports written by the overseas staff; and *Common Ground,* quarterly journal.

3 Lebanon Street
Hanover, New Hampshire 03755 USA

ANACOSTIA NEIGHBORHOOD MUSEUM
See Smithsonian Institution.

ANDEAN COMMON MARKET COUNTRIES, SCIENCE POLICIES OF
See Science Policies: Advanced Developing Countries: Andean Common Market Countries.

ANDORRA, VALLEYS OF

Population: 26,600 (1975). Student enrollment in primary school: 3779 (1842 females); secondary school: 1626 (786 females). Language of instruction: French and Spanish. [Unless otherwise indicated, figures are for 1974–1975.]

The principality of Andorra in the Pyrenees is bounded by France and Spain. Education in Andorra may be achieved in the home; in private schools, which follow either the French or the Spanish system; or in schools outside Andorra. The graduation certificate in the French system is the *baccalauréat;* in the Spanish system, the *bachillerato.* Graduates will be accepted in French and Spanish institutions of higher education on equal terms with citizens of those countries. The governments of

France and Spain also offer scholarships to Andorran students. Graduates have full right to pursue their profession in Andorra or in the country that has provided their education.

ANGOLA

Population: 6,500,000 (1975 estimate). Student enrollment in primary school: 516,000; secondary school (academic, vocational, technical): 74,000; university: 2900. Language of instruction: Portuguese. Academic calendar: October to June. Percentage of national budget expended on all education: 10.2% [Unless otherwise noted, figures are for 1971–72.]

Angola achieved independence on November 11, 1975, marking the end of five hundred years of Portuguese colonial rule in Africa. A country of great ethnic, linguistic, social, and cultural diversity, it has two major population groups: the indigenous group, consisting of Africans; and the nonindigenous group, made up largely of Portuguese settlers. The ethnic composition of Africans is subdivided into Khosians, believed to be descended from aboriginal races now residing in southern Angola; and Bantus, who account for 90 percent of the African population.

After independence—because Portugal left Angola without any formal handover of power—the country had the unique distinction of having two different names and two rival governments: the People's Republic of Angola with a Luanda-based government, proclaimed by the Popular Movement for the Liberation of Angola (MPLA), under the presidency of Agostino Neto; and the People's Democratic Republic of Angola, in Huambo (which the Portuguese had called Nova Lisboa), proclaimed by Jonas Savambi, leader of the National Union for the Total Independence of Angola (UNITA), which formed a coalition government with Holden Roberto's National Front for the Liberation of Angola (FNLA). Angola's independence occurred amidst heavy fighting, with MPLA on one side and UNITA-FNLA on the other side, following the collapse of a pre-independence transitional government. By 1976 MPLA had secured control of the government.

Although during the years of its occupation Portugal claimed that its colonization in Angola was a civilizing mission, educational statistics and statements made by colonial government and Catholic church officials have indicated otherwise. In 1950 the census revealed that 97 percent of the 4,145,200 Africans in the country were illiterate. In 1966 it was estimated that 60 percent of the whites were literate and that less than 10 percent of Africans were literate. By the time of Angola's independence, 90 percent of the Africans were still illiterate. An official inquiry made in all rural areas in Angola in 1971 (except those areas under the control of liberation movements) showed that, in 1969–70, 48.5 percent of children of shepherds and 20 percent of farm children did not attend school because of a lack of educational facilities. The numbers of Africans who entered high schools or commercial and technical schools were negligible.

Further, a survey of official statements shows that Portuguese educational authorities favored education for servitude. In a Christmas message of 1960, the Patriarch of Lisbon, Cardinal Cerejeira, speaking on colonial education, said: "We need schools in Africa, but schools in which we show the nature, the way to dignity of man and glory of the nation that protects him. . . . We want to teach the native to read and count but not to make doctors" (quoted in de Sousa Ferreira, 1974, p. 113). Twelve years later, the then Portuguese minister of overseas territories, Joaquim da Silva Cunha, in an attempt to articulate Portugal's colonial educational policy, reiterated the above position: "Education cannot have as its objective the mere spreading of knowledge; its objectives should be the formation of citizens capable of feeling to the full the imperatives of Portuguese life, knowing how to interpret them, making them a constant reality, in order to secure the continuation of the nation" (*UNESCO Courier*, November 1973).

Thus, although Portugal attempted to legitimize its domination of the colonial territories as a civilizing mission, economic exploitation was certainly a major motive. The educational system also was structured to produce semiskilled African workers to furnish the manpower necessary for the colonial economy. The ultimate goal of education was what government officials called "Portuguezation of the natives." To ensure Portuguezation, Portuguese language was obligatory in all educational activities except in religious instruction, where African vernacular was permissible (Article 17 of the *Missionary Statute*). The government also required that all bishops and apostolic vicars and everyone connected with educating the Africans must be of Portuguese nationality. Again, this was a strategy to ensure Portuguezation. Such a strategy is manifest throughout the educational history of Angola.

In 1605 the first primary school in Angola was founded in Luanda by missionaries of the Society of Jesus. Several years later, formal education in these schools was extended to include literature and ethics, in addition to religious instruction (Avila de Azevedo, 1958, p. 119). Occupational training was also provided. Servants living near schools learned trades: tailoring, shoemaking, pottery, ceramics, and caulking.

Education was exclusively in the hands of the Jesuits until the middle of the eighteenth century, when the Marquis de Pombel expelled them from Portugal as well as its colonies. It should also be noted that in addition to their missionary and educational activity, Jesuit missionaries were engaged in slave traffic between Angola and Brazil (de Sousa Ferreira, 1974, p. 49).

The first specific government provision for education in the overseas colonies was authorized by decrees of 1845 and 1869. As a result, there slowly developed what might be called a village system of educa-tion. Government schools—staffed by parish priests, partially educated Africans, and even soldiers—were common in forts and administrative centers. Few students in these schools, however, succeeded in acquiring basic literacy (Abshire and Samuels, 1969, pp. 187–189).

The arrival of English Baptists in the north of Angola in 1878 marked the beginning of participation of Protestant missionaries (from several European countries and from North America) in the development of education in Angola. Unlike the Catholic missionaries, whose curricula included little more than the catechism, Protestant missionaries had a great concern for literacy, since reading the Bible and other religious books was an important facet of their schools.

The passage of Decree 77 of 1921, which forbade the use of African languages in schools except for religious instruction, gave an advantage to the Catholic missionaries. A major educational event in the history of Portuguese Africa was the signing of a missionary accord with the Vatican in 1940, making Catholic missions an arm of the state in Portuguezation of the Africans.

Although Portugal claimed that there was no racial discrimination in its educational system, educational opportunities for Africans in Angola were limited. Schools were located mainly in the administrative centers or cities. Rural schools were attended almost exclusively by Africans, while the enrollment in the better-equipped and better-staffed urban schools varied from a few Africans to only whites.

The First Republic (the Salazar administration, 1932–1968) marked an educational setback for Angola and for Portugal's other overseas colonies. Reduction of financial aid to Catholic missions crippled their educational programs. The establishment of the Department of Native Affairs, which separated the education of rural Africans from that of the Portuguese and *assimilados* (those with constitutional rights), dealt African education a further blow; as a result, when the education of Africans was surrendered to missionaries, they could not cope with the demands.

In an attempt to reduce mounting criticism against its colonial policy and its lack of sensitivity to African advancement, Portugal made some fundamental modifications in its educational policy in Africa in the 1960s. These reforms included expansion of education unprecedented in the colonial history of Portugal. However, the expansion was quantitative and confined almost exclusively to primary education. Although textbooks were considerably Africanized as part of the new educational policy of the 1960s, a close analysis will show that there was little change of philosophy: Portuguese values still were upheld, and a conscious identification with Portuguese identity was promoted.

Throughout its history, the education given to Africans in Angola was strictly controlled. By limiting educational opportunities and the development of an educational leadership group, by systematically banishing "cultural undesirables," and by isolating Africans from Western liberal institutions, the Portuguese had hoped to maintain their authoritarian rule—a strategy explicitly stated by Salazar: "The present administration has no intention of hastening its own eventual doom by exposing its impressionable wards to that portion of the Western world's intellectual heritage" (quoted in Harris, 1958, p. 15).

The foundation of the *Estudos gerais universitários de Angola,* in 1963, which became the University of Luanda in 1969, did little to alleviate the lack of educational preparation for the African population. In 1972 the university enrolled some 2900 students. However, due to the abolition of the *estatuto indígena* (indigenous statute) in 1961, no breakdown as to race is available; therefore, it is not possible to ascertain how many, if any, Africans are actually attending the university.

Types of Institutions

Higher education in Angola is offered at the University of Luanda. The creation

of the university was largely motivated by the need to find better and more efficient ways of exploring and exploiting the country's immense natural resources. This motivation is reflected in the technical characteristics of the university's programs of study: veterinary medicine, engineering, economics, mining and geology, agriculture and forestry, biology, and medicine. The university was expected to have great importance in the development of the country's economic, social, and political life.

Relationship with Secondary Education and Admission Requirements

In 1975 two types of primary education existed in Angola: the state-run primary education (standard primary schools), mainly in urban centers and exclusively for whites and *assimilados;* and the rudimentary primary education, commonly known as "adaptation" (*ensino de adaptação*), for Africans in rural areas.

The primary schools, consisting of four grades, duplicated the school system of metropolitan Portugal. Attendance was compulsory for whites and *assimilados* between the ages of seven and twelve. Government and private schools provided this education. Rudimentary education, whose operation was entrusted to Catholic missionaries, provided instruction in assimilation and indoctrination of Africans into the Portuguese world. These schools, which provided Africans with a second-grade education, were of poor quality and much less adequately staffed than the state-run primary schools. For example, of all students enrolled in primary schools in Angola in 1967–1970, 4.4 percent completed primary education (passed the final examination of the fourth grade). The highest percentage (9.58 percent) was in Luanda, which had standard primary schools; the lowest percentage was in Cuando-Cubango (1.96 percent), which had rudimentary or "adaptation" schools. This dual approach to primary education presented some problems to African students. It was found that transfer from rudimentary schools to first grade in regular primary schools and the requirement that all instruction be in Portuguese created an initial handicap to African students. Also, African students found it hard to raise tuition to enter regular primary schools, since they could transfer only to tuition-paying institutions, whereas whites and *assimilados* could attend tuition-free regular primary schools.

Like primary education, secondary schools were either state operated or privately run by Catholic missionaries; but unlike primary education, secondary education was separated by sex. As of 1975 there were two major branches of secondary education: lyceum (classical-academic secondary education) and technical-professional secondary education (geared to providing career skills). The lyceum program consisted of seven grades divided into three cycles. The first cycle (*primeiro ciclo*) of two years combined with the second cycle (*segundo ciclo*) of three years to provide general education and was considered a sufficient qualification to civil service and other government occupations. The certificate awarded was *carta do curso geral dos liceus* (general education certificate). The third cycle (*terceiro ciclo*) provided two years of the preuniversity preparation, an equivalent of American junior college. At the completion of this cycle, students passing a final examination were issued a Certificate of Secondary Education (*carta do curso complementar liceus*). Entry to the university was based upon this certificate and an examination. Technical-professional secondary education ranged from preparatory technical schools, crafts and trades, commercial and industrial schools, and training schools for civil service, to agricultural training schools.

Teacher training was also provided at the secondary level. The majority of teachers of normal primary education, who were almost exclusively Portuguese or of mixed ancestry, attended a two-year teacher training course after the completion of five years of secondary education. In 1970 Angola had fifteen teacher training institutions (for general primary schools) with 1402 teaching interns enrolled. Teachers

for station (post) schools were given four years of training following four years of primary education. In 1970 Angola had only eleven such training establishments with an enrollment of 225. Secondary school teachers generally were trained overseas; only a few were locally trained (for instance, twenty-seven teachers received university training at the University of Luanda in 1970). In 1975 there was a serious shortage of qualified teachers in Angola, especially in secondary education, many having left the country just prior to and immediately after independence.

Administration and Control

At the time of the creation of the University of Luanda, Portugal had granted autonomous status administratively, financially, and pedagogically to institutions of higher education in its overseas provinces. Portugal still exercised some control over the university.

The rector was the chief executive officer of the university, responsible for its operation. His major functions were academic and fiscal management. The rector was appointed by the president of the country and functioned under the Overseas Ministry of Education. The day-to-day operation of the university was coordinated by a council of directors with representation from the faculties of the university, while academic matters were handled by the senate.

Programs and Degrees

At the time of the establishment of the university, its 286 students were enrolled in the following faculties: education, engineering, medicine and surgery, agronomy, and veterinary medicine. By the academic year 1966–67 courses of study were expanded to include geology, mining, and several fields of engineering. The number of students had increased to 590 (Lisboa, 1970, p. 295).

Since the University of Luanda was established under the same legislation as that of institutions of higher education in metropolitan Portugal, the level of courses of study was identical, and this allowed reciprocal exchange of students. For example, 339 students from Angola studied in Portugal as exchange students in 1970.

The University of Luanda grants the following degrees: *bacharel,* requiring three years of study; *licenciado,* requiring two additional years; and a doctorate, requiring two or three more years. Students in good academic standing are admitted into the *licenciado* program after obtaining a *bacharel* degree. Two to three years are required to complete the *licenciado* requirements. Practicums or field experience is emphasized in all advanced degrees.

Financing

Expenditure on education during the 1960s and 1970s does not show an increase that would be commensurate with stated educational aims or with the need to improve the low level of general education. The educational expenditure in the second development plan (1959–1964) was about 7 percent of the total budget; the third development plan (1968–1973) estimated an educational expenditure of slightly over 10 percent (de Sousa Ferreira, 1974, pp. 99–100). The extent of government expenditure on education after independence is not yet known.

Student Financial Aid

The University of Luanda charges tuition. Students pay fees for academic instruction and other administrative services rendered. Students in good academic standing who come from lower-income families are subsidized by scholarships. There are three kinds of scholarship subsidies: full scholarship, waiver or exemption of fees, and reduction of fees. These scholarships are provided directly by the government through the Ministry of Education or are granted by private institutions or foundations and other sources such as trade union funds.

Scholarships are also awarded for exchange programs. A number of students used to study in metropolitan Portugal for a year or so before the end of their studies at the University of Luanda. In 1970, 339 students from Angola were reported to have participated in the student exchange program, attending institutions in Portugal. Hardly any Africans participated in the program, partly because of lack of funds and partly because of the technical selective processes working against their inclusion.

Teaching Staff

Until 1975 professors at the University of Luanda were of Portuguese origin. This, of course, was in line with the Portuguese major objective—complete Portuguezation. A great number of professors have left; as a result, the university is currently understaffed, and the few professors who have remained are heavily overworked.

Ranking of the teaching personnel at the University of Luanda is as follows: *monitores* (monitors), students (usually in the fifth year of study) who aid a professor; *assistentes* (assistants); *professores auxiliares* (assistant professors); and *professores extraordinários* and *catedráticos* (extraordinary and full professors).

Current Problems and Trends

Higher education in Angola will be greatly influenced by the final political orientation of the government, whether capitalist or communist. However, it can be safely assumed that the University of Luanda will play a crucial role in both the reconstruction program and the creation of the new society. President Neto has already suggested that schools and technological training institutions be used to transform Angola into a modern nation, "capable of reaping and distributing the fruits of its national abundance."

International Cooperation

Aside from student exchange programs, in which students from Angola attend metropolitan Portuguese institutions, student exchange programs have been confined to extracurricular activities such as visits of choral groups, sporting teams, and theater and other cultural groups. The Overseas Ministry of Education encouraged such activities, as was reflected by its readiness to subsidize the costs. Some private organizations also participated in the financing of the exchange programs. For example, the organization *Procuradoria dos estudantes ultramarinos* was instrumental in helping bring students from Angola and other Portuguese provinces to Portugal. *Procuradoria dos estudantes* also assisted exchange students by arranging for holiday trips, lodging arrangements, and grants and subsidies. The major objective of the sponsors of the exchange program was, basically, to avoid the isolation of the overseas students by integrating them into the metropolitan culture. This again was a way to ensure Portuguezation of those in the overseas provinces.

Students desiring to study in other countries besides Portugal made arrangements either directly through the foreign diplomatic mission of that country or through nationalist movements. In this way, scholarships, mainly to the United States, were granted to many Angolan students (Madzongwe, 1973).

FORBES M. MADZONGWE

Bibliography

Abshire, D. M., and Samuels, M. A. (Eds.) *Portuguese Africa, A Handbook.* New York: Praeger, 1969.
de Azevedo, A. *Politica do ensino em Africa.* Lisbon: Junta de investigações do ultramar, 1958
Chilicote, R. H. *Portuguese Africa.* Englewood Cliffs, New Jersey: Prentice-Hall, 1967.
Duffy, J. *Portuguese Africa.* Cambridge, Massachusetts: Harvard University Press, 1968.
Duffy, J. *A Question of Slavery.* Cambridge, Massachusetts: Harvard University Press, 1967.
Harris, M. *Portugal's African Wards.* New York: American Committee on Africa, 1958.
Herrick, A. B., and others. *Area Handbook for Angola.* Washington, D.C.: U.S. Government Printing Office, 1967.
Lisboa, E. "Education in Angola and Mozambique." In B. Rose (Ed.), *Education in Southern Africa.* Johannesburg, South Africa: Collier Macmillan South Africa, 1970.
Madzongwe, F. "The Southern Africa Student Program 1961–1971: An Analysis of a Program to Train Leaders for Southern Africa." Unpublished doctoral dissertation, Clark University, Worcester, Massachusetts, 1973.
dos Santos, M. S. *História do ensino em Angola.* Luanda: Edição dos serviços de educação, 1970.
de Sousa Ferreira, E. *Portuguese Colonialism from South Africa to Europe.* Fribourg, Switzerland: Universitätsverlag, 1972.
de Sousa Ferreira, E. *Portuguese Colonialism in Africa: The End of an Era.* Paris: UNESCO, 1974.

See also: Africa, Southern: Regional Analysis; Archives: Africa and Asia, National Archives of.

ANIMAL SCIENCE
(Field of Study)

Animal science is the scientific study of animals, their products, and the many businesses and industries related to animal production. Animal agriculture encompasses farms, ranches, feedlots, livestock markets, feed and fertilizer stores, animal product processing plants, retail food stores, eating establishments, and other businesses involved in animal production, marketing, distribution, and consumption. There are actually more than five hundred distinct occupations in animal agriculture, two thirds of which are in closely related enterprises off the farm.

Animal science includes studies of beef cattle, swine, sheep, goats, horses, small animals (mink, foxes, rabbits), and laboratory animals (rats, mice, and guinea pigs). The food animals are excellent sources of high-quality protein. In the United States people acquire about two thirds of their protein from food of animal origin; in most other countries animal products provide a lesser percentage of the human protein intake. The world is short of protein; and animals, especially ruminants (cattle, sheep, goats, and game animals), have an important role to play in increasing world protein production. The ruminants are actually walking protein factories, since they can utilize forages (pasture, hay, and silage) which humans do not consume and convert them into high-quality animal protein. The demand for animal protein foods and their by-products is ever increasing as new products are developed and old ones are improved. Insulin, which is used to treat millions of human diabetics and is still obtained from the pancreas of slaughtered animals is another example of an important use of animal products. Horses, which were once mainly a source of farm power, are also becoming increasingly important for sport and recreation. Finally, expanding basic research for animals and humans has increased the demand for laboratory animals such as the rat, mouse, guinea pig, and rabbit.

Animal scientists are usually specialists in breeding and genetics, physiology, nutrition, meats, or production. Advanced students working for M.S. or Ph.D. degrees usually specialize in one of these five areas. Each of these areas, however, is closely related to other disciplines; for example, the nutritionist might be oriented strongly to biochemistry, microbiology, chemistry, or physics. Students working toward a B.S. degree in animal science usually have curricular options which include production, agribusiness, science, feed or food industry, preveterinary medicine, and laboratory animal science.

At least 50 percent, and sometimes more, of the animal science curriculum usually is devoted to basic science and general education courses. Such courses as communications, chemistry, physics, mathematics, biology, botany, social science, humanities, accounting, and economics provide a background for the animal science specialty. Since animal agriculture also involves land utilization, forages and crops, fertilization, irrigation, pesticides, insecticides, farm machinery, computer use, cost accounting, record keeping, money management, and marketing, animal science students also need courses in other areas of agriculture. The remaining courses are in animal science.

The trend in the United States and the other developed nations, and to a lesser extent in the developing countries, is to give the students more freedom in selecting elective courses so that they can prepare more adequately for their specific area of interest. The rigid curriculum of the past has changed to one with fewer required courses, more options, and more elective courses.

Animal science had its beginning with the domestication of animals in the Neolithic or new Stone Age. As man has become more and more dependent upon animals and their products through the centuries, improved practices in animal husbandry and scientific research (especially in the industrially advanced nations) have resulted in livestock of improved productivity and quality. The low-producing, poor-quality animal was gradually replaced as farmers improved their animal production practices. For example, in the United States the Texas longhorns were replaced by meat-type steers; the Arkansas razorbacks gave way to quality meat-type hogs; and the native sheep were replaced by modern mutton-type and wool-type animals. The increase in productivity occurred first in Europe, then in the United States and other developed nations. The developing countries still lag behind in increasing the quality and productivity of their animals.

Animal science was first called *animal husbandry* or *animal industry,* and it is still called that in some of the developing countries. Since the 1950s, however, when programs became more science oriented, the name generally has been changed to *animal science.*

Animal production did not become very scientific until the twentieth century, but since 1900—and especially since the 1920s—great progress has been made. So far, the progress has been greatest in the industrially advanced nations; but greater productivity will occur in the future in all areas of the world as scientific methods are applied to animal production, so that more young per dam and more product per animal can be produced. Future animal production practices may include manipulating reproductive processes so that sex control, multiple births, ova transplants, and other innovations become routine. New feeds may be used that do not yet exist, and the genetic base for selection may be considerably different. Finally, animal product processing, quality control, packaging, and distribution may be changed considerably in the future.

Because students in animal science and the needs of industry keep changing throughout the world, the curricula must be flexible to permit changes. For example, because an increasing number of animal science students do not have a farm background, more laboratories on the farm and/or elective off-campus practical experience courses (or on-the-job training) on farms, ranches, or agribusiness operations may be required. Another development in animal science is that an increasing number of women are enrolling in the field. Also, though still inadequately developed, visual aids are being used more. Good visual aids can eliminate the need for certain laboratories and/or field trips to observe some practices in the animal field. Finally, more business, finance, and economics courses are being recommended for animal science students, since a good animal producer needs also to be a good businessman in order to operate efficiently and profitably.

Among the areas increasing in importance in animal science are equine production and management programs. In many of the developed areas of the world, more and more people are using horses for sports and/or companion animals for riding and recreation. In the United States, for example, more people attend horse races than football or baseball games, and similar high attendances occur in many other countries. It is quite possible that considerably more attention will be paid to horse programs in the future. Another increasingly important program is laboratory animal science, which is being given as an option for a B.S. degree in animal science in the United States and in some other countries. Graduates in this branch are working in zoos,

small-animal research laboratories, pet shows, kennels, animal training operations, and other areas involving small animals. Also, courses for students who are not majoring in animal science or agriculture are being developed. Finally, interdisciplinary programs are increasing. Effective programs are being developed where a team of scientists can be used to solve complicated and difficult problems.

Animal science training programs are usually adequate in the developed countries of the world. The curricula will vary somewhat between areas and countries depending on the kind of livestock involved and the type of production system used. Often, however, training in animal science in the developing countries is inadequate — specifically, in most of Latin America and in much of Asia and Africa. In some countries, especially in Latin America, animal science professors do not have a farm background, and animals are not available at the university to use in teaching laboratories. As a result, the students lack practical or applied training. This lack of training is one reason why the developing countries, which have 60 percent of the world's livestock and poultry, produce only 22 percent of the world's meat, milk, and eggs. Thus, one of the great needs in the developing countries is to improve animal science programs. More emphasis by the United States and other developed countries on programs designed to assist the developing countries to produce more of their own food may help eradicate world hunger by enabling the developing countries to become more self-sufficient in animal and other food production. As the population of the world grows, career opportunities in animal science will continue to increase to meet the demands for more protein and more food.

T. J. CUNHA

Levels and Programs of Study

Programs in animal science generally require as a minimum prerequisite a secondary education and lead to the following awards: diploma or certificate, bachelor's degree (B.Sc.), master's degree (M.Sc.), the doctorate (Ph.D.), or their equivalents. Programs deal with the principles and practices of animal husbandry—that is, the study and investigation of the application of scientific methods in the breeding, nutrition, and care of domestic animals— and consist of lectures, classroom, and field instruction.

Programs that lead to an award not equivalent to a first university degree stress the principles and practices of agricultural technology. Principal course content usually includes some of the following: animal anatomy and physiology, animal breeding, livestock production, animal pathology, animal nutrition, poultry breeding, and poultry products technology. Background courses usually include zoology, ·microbiology, chemistry, marketing, and farm management.

Programs leading to a first university degree deal with the practical and theoretical aspects of animal science. Principal course content usually includes animal (and poultry) breeding, ruminant and non-ruminant nutrition, principles of animal nutrition, genetic improvement of farm animals, animal anatomy and physiology, poultry science, dairy science, and farm management. Background courses often included, in addition to general agricultural courses, are those in the biological sciences, chemistry, and the social sciences.

Programs that lead to a postgraduate university degree consist primarily of study and research dealing with advanced specialties in the field of animal husbandry. Emphasis is given to original research work as substantiated by the presentation of a scholarly thesis or dissertation. Principal subject matter areas within which courses and research projects tend to fall include animal genetics, animal breeding, animal nutrition, production of animal products, and control of animal environment. Subject areas within which background studies tend to fall include specialties in biology, biochemistry, biophysics, and statistical analysis.

[This section was based on UNESCO's *International Standard Classification of Education (ISCED): Three Stage Classification System, 1974* (Paris: UNESCO, 1974).]

Major International and National Organizations

INTERNATIONAL

Commonwealth Bureau of Animal Breeding
  and Genetics
The King's Building
West Mains Road
Edinburgh, 9, Scotland

Commonwealth Bureau of Animal Nutrition
Bucksburn
Aberdeen AB2 95B, Scotland

European Association for Animal Production
via Barnaba Oriani 28
Rome, Italy

NATIONAL

Federal Republic of Germany:
  Deutsche Gesellschaft für
    Züchtungskunde e.V.
  Adenauerallee 176
  53 Bonn

Japan:
  Nippon ikushu gakkai
  Japanese Society of Breeding
  %University of Tokyo
  Tokyo

People's Republic of China:
  Chung-kuo hsu mu shou i hsueh hui
  Chinese Society of Animal Husbandry
    and Veterinary Sciences
  % Department of Animal Husbandry
    and Veterinary Sciences
  Peking Agricultural University
  Peking, Hopeh

United Kingdom:
  British Society of Animal Production
  West of Scotland Agricultural College
  Annbank 234
  Auchincruive, Ayr, Scotland

United States:
  American Society of Animal Science
  113 North Neil Street
  Champaign, Illinois 61820

Principal Information Sources

GENERAL

Guides to the literature and information sources in animal science include:

Blanchard, J. R., and Ostvold, H. *Literature of Agricultural Research.* Berkeley: University of California Press, 1958. Includes a section on animal sciences.

Bush, E. A. R. *Agriculture: A Bibliographic Guide.* (2 vols.) London: Macdonald, 1974. A comprehensive guide to the literature covering various aspects of animal sciences; includes guides to the literature, bibliographies, abstracts, periodicals, dictionaries, and general reference works.

Information Sources on the Animal Feed Industry. UNIDO Guides to Information Sources, No. 13. Vienna: United Nations Industrial Development Organization, 1975. Includes professional and research organizations, information services, directories, handbooks, dictionaries, bibliographies, and periodicals.

Selected List of American Agricultural Books in Print and Current Periodicals. Beltsville, Maryland: National Agricultural Library, United States Department of Agriculture, 1975. Includes sources on animal science, breeding and reproduction, feeding and nutrition, veterinary medicine, and cattle.

Singhri, M. L., and Shrimali, D. S. *Reference Sources in Agriculture: An Annotated Bibliography.* Jaipur, India: Rajasthan College of Agriculture, Consumers Cooperative Society, 1962. Includes sources on animal science.

Smith, R. C. *Guide to the Literature of the Zoological Sciences.* (6th ed.) Minneapolis: Burgess, 1962.

Overviews and introductions to the field include:

Acker, D. *Animal Science and Industry.* (2nd ed.) Englewood Cliffs, New Jersey: Prentice-Hall, 1971.

Anderson, A. L., and Kiser, J. J. *Introductory Animal Science.* (Rev. ed.) New York: Macmillan, 1963.

Briggs, H. N., and Briggs, D. M. *Modern Breeds of Livestock.* (3rd ed.) London: Macmillan, 1969.

Byerly, T. C. *Livestock and Livestock Products.* Englewood Cliffs, New Jersey: Prentice-Hall, 1964.

Campbell, J. R., and Lasley, J. F. *The Science of Animals That Serve Mankind.* New York: McGraw-Hill, 1969.

Cole, H. H. *Introduction to Livestock Production.* San Francisco: W. H. Freeman, 1962.

Cole, H. H., and Ronning, M. *Animal Agriculture.* San Francisco: W. H. Freeman, 1974.

Ensminger, M. C. *Animal Science.* (6th ed.) Danville, Illinois: Interstate, 1969.

Park, R. D. *Animal Husbandry.* (2nd ed.) London: Oxford University Press, 1970.

Thomas, D. G. M., and Davies, W. J. *Animal Husbandry.* London: Cassell, 1971.

Histories of the field include:

McGovern, G. S. (Ed.) *Agricultural Thought in the Twentieth Century.* Indianapolis, Indiana: Bobbs-Merrill, 1967.

Zeuner, F. E. A. *A History of Domesticated Animals.* London: Hutchinson, 1962.

For works dealing with education in animal science see:

Animal Husbandry, Agricultural Education. Proceedings from the Symposium on International Animal Agriculture. Urbana: University of Illinois College of Agriculture, 1969.

Bentley, O. G. "New Challenges for Animal Science Teaching." *Journal of Animal Science,* July 1968, *27,* 863–867.

Kaufman, R. G., and others. "Improving the Effectiveness of Teaching Animal Science." *Journal of Animal Science,* January 1971, *32,* 161–164.

Kolmer, L. "Animal Science Extension Education: The Challenge and the Opportunity." *Journal of Animal Science,* September 1967, *26,* 1011–1016.

Kottman, R. M., Postlethwait, S. N., Overcast, W. W., Ward, G. M., and Lindquist, N. S. "Symposium: Effective Teaching in Dairy Science." *Journal of Dairy Science,* March 1966, *49* (3), 319–330.

Meyer, J. H. "New Directions and Opportunities for Animal Science Research." *Journal of Animal Science,* April 1972, *34,* 677–689.

Report of FAO International Conference on Animal Husbandry Education. Report of conference held in Göttingen, Federal Republic of Germany, July 25–30, 1966. Rome: Food and Agriculture Organization, 1966.

Vohnout, K. "Education of Animal Scientists from Developing Countries Outside Their Country." *Journal of Animal Science,* January 1973, *36,* 161–166.

The *Journal of Animal Science* regularly includes articles dealing with animal science education.

CURRENT BIBLIOGRAPHIES

Agrindex. Rome: Food and Agriculture Organization, 1975–. An international indexing service which covers animal production and agricultural education.

Biological Abstracts. Philadelphia: Biosciences Information Service of Biological Abstracts, 1926–. Covers genetics, physiology, livestock, breeding, and feeding.

Biological and Agricultural Index (formerly *Agricultural Index*). New York: Wilson, 1916–.

Commonwealth Bureau of Animal Breeding and Genetics. *Animal Breeding Abstracts, Compiled from World Literature.* Edinburgh: Commonwealth Agricultural Bureaux, 1933–.

Food Science and Technology Abstracts. Farnham Royal, Bucks, England: Commonwealth Agricultural Bureaux, 1969–. Covers livestock products, processing, preservation, and analysis.

Landwirtschaftliches Zentralblatt. Vol. 3: *Tierzucht, Tierernährung, Fischerei.* Berlin, Federal Republic of Germany: Deutsche Akademie der Landwirtschaft, 1955–. Abstracts world literature on the animal industry.

Nutrition Abstracts and Reviews. Farnham Royal, Bucks, England: Commonwealth Agricultural Bureaux, 1931–. Abstracts world literature on human and animal nutrition.

Referativnyĭ zhurnal. 58: Zhivotnovodstvoi veterinariya. Moscow: Akademia nauk, SSSR, Institut nauchnoĭ informatsii, 1964–.

United States Department of Agriculture, National Agricultural Library. *Bibliography of Agriculture.* Scottsdale, Arizona: Oryx Press, 1942–. International in scope; covers animal husbandry and livestock.

PERIODICALS

Important periodicals in the field of animal science include *Agroanimalia* (South Africa), *Alimentazione animale* (Italy), *Animal Behaviour* (UK), *Animal Nutrition and Health* (US), *Animal Protection* (US), *Annales de zoologie-écologie animale* (France), *Australian Journal of Experimental Agriculture and Animal Husbandry, Canadian Journal of Animal Science, Indian Journal of Animal Sciences, Journal of Animal Sciences* (US), *Journal of Livestock and Agriculture* (US), *Keurstamboeker* (Netherlands), *Livestock Farming* (UK), *Molochnoye i myasnoye skotovodstvo* (USSR), *Produzione animale* (Italy), *Revista de zootecnía* (Argentina), *World Animal Review* (Italy), *World Review of Animal Production* (Italy), *Zeitschrift für Tierzüchtung und Züchtungsbiologie/Journal of Animal Breeding and Genetics* (FRG), *Zhivotnovodstvo* (USSR), *Züchtungskunde* (FRG).

For a complete listing of journals see:

1000 Selected Journals in Agricultural and Related Subjects. Beltsville, Maryland: United States Department of Agriculture, National Agricultural Library, 1973.

Ulrich's International Periodicals Directory. New York: Bowker, biennial. See "Poultry and Livestock."

ENCYCLOPEDIAS, DICTIONARIES, HANDBOOKS

Food and Agriculture Organization and European Organization for Animal Production.

Vocabulary of Animal Husbandry. Rome: Food and Agriculture Organization, 1959.

Knight, R. L. *Dictionary of Genetics, Including Terms Used in Cytology, Animal Breeding, and Evolution.* Waltham, Massachusetts: Chronica Botanica, 1948.

Marenac, L. N., and Aublet, H. *Encyclopédie du cheval.* (2nd ed.) Paris: Librairie Maloine, 1969.

Mason, I. L. *A World Dictionary of Livestock, Breeds, Types, and Varieties.* (Rev. ed.) Farnham Royal, Bucks, England: Commonwealth Agricultural Bureaux, 1969.

Miller, W. C. *Encyclopedia of Animal Care.* (10th ed.) Baltimore: Williams & Wilkins, 1972. Formerly *Black's Veterinary Dictionary.*

Steinmetz, H. *Livestock Feeding and Management: Multilingual Illustrated Dictionary.* (2nd ed.) Betzdorf, Federal Republic of Germany: Steinmetz, 1966.

DIRECTORIES

Index of Agricultural Research Institutions in Europe Concerned with Animal Production and Their Principal Lines of Investigation. Rome: Food and Agriculture Organization, 1953.

Webb, H. R. *Directory of Australian Grassland and Animal Production Research Centers.* St. Lucia, Brisbane: University of Queensland Press, 1970.

ANTHROPOLOGY (Field of Study)

Anthropology, from the Greek *anthropos* (man) and *logia* (study), is the comparative study of mankind. Although concerned primarily with *Homo sapiens*, anthropology also studies living and extinct animals, particularly mammals and primates. The purposes of anthropology include providing data on the history of mankind; describing the ways of life of currently viable societies; and developing generalizations, laws, and theories pertaining to social processes, cultural regularities, and human abilities.

Anthropology can be divided into four subfields. The first of these subfields, biological or physical anthropology, is concerned principally with humans as biological organisms. It can be subdivided into three main areas of study: human biological evolution, human genetics, and subhuman primates. Biological anthropologists reconstruct the major biological stages of human evolution and identify the processes and environmental conditions that account for these changes. To go from description to explanation necessitates an understanding of human genetics and primatology—the study of man's closest nonhuman relatives.

The second subfield is archeology, the study of societies that no longer exist. Archeologists reconstruct ancient systems from materials that have endured. Particularly valuable materials include remains from garbage dumps (which reveal information on dietary patterns and economy), artifacts or manufactured items (which provide information on economy, trade, and technology), and potsherds or fragments of earthenware (which indicate technological and artistic life). Techniques used for the dating of finds provide either relative dating (X is older than Y) or absolute dating (age of X is given in years, with an error margin; for example 3000 B.C. ± 300).

Sociocultural anthropology, the third subfield, may be seen as a combination of social anthropology (dealing with institutional and structural relationships within communities) and cultural anthropology (dealing with the beliefs, values, and the sentiments of a population). Sociocultural anthropology is traditionally divided into two aspects: ethnography and ethnology. Ethnography, the generalizing side of sociocultural anthropology, attempts to develop and test hypotheses and to formulate laws and theories. The ethnologist, referred to by the British as the "comparative sociologist," attempts to explain the differences and similarities in the customs of various societies. The ethnologist tries to explain such human universals as the incest taboo, the family, religion, and mental illness, as well as customs of more limited distribution.

In making a study of the life-style of a group, referred to as "doing fieldwork," the sociocultural anthropologist spends a year or more "in the field," learning the culture by living it. This method of participant-observer research leads to a descriptive study of a society, called an ethnography. The major areas of specialization for ethnographic research are Africa, the Middle East, South America, North America, the Caribbean, the Pacific, India, and China.

Sociocultural anthropology can also be discussed in terms of its topical subareas. That is, apart from attempting to become expert in some ethnographic area, such as Africa, and doing ethnographies on some tribal people within that area, the sociocultural anthropologist will generally select a topical area for special consideration. These topical subareas include economic anthropology, political anthropology, the anthropology of kinship and the family, psychological anthropology, and the anthropological study of myth and religion.

The fourth subfield of anthropology is linguistics. As a student of comparative languages, the anthropological linguist formulates theories concerning the evolution of languages, the current universal aspects of languages, and linguistic change. Descriptive or structural linguistics is the study of the characteristic sound units in a language and its grammatical system. Historical linguistics deals with changes in language over time, including the influences that languages have on each other. And the comparatively new field of cognitive anthropology concerns the ways in which speakers of a given language classify and conceptualize phenomena; language, according to cognitive anthropology, structures the manner in which phenomena are known.

Culture and evolution are the central ideas which tie together the many and complex sides of anthropology. In both biological anthropology and archeology, the focus is on the evolution of an animal (*Homo sapiens*) capable of creating, transmitting, and changing culture. Sociocultural anthropology centers directly on the many manifestations of culture, including the linguistic and the archeological.

Social anthropology is closely related to sociology, economics, political science, biology, genetics, and history; psychological anthropology is related to psychiatry, psychology, and educational theory; archeology is related to geology, ecology, and cartography; and biological anthropology is related to anatomy and other medical specialties as well as to biology.

Sociologists have tended to focus their research on Western "developed" and "complex" systems, leaving the "primitive" and the exotic to anthropology. However, an increasing number of anthropologists are concerned with contemporary Western society and are applying to that society the techniques that they have devised in dealing with other societies.

Working with larger populations, the sociologist uses questionnaires and statistical techniques. Sociologists tend to concern themselves more with the reliability of the data; anthropologists, with the validity of the data.

Economists and political scientists generally restrict their studies to very specialized areas of modern nations. Anthropologists also occasionally use the nation as a unit of study. The historian, like the anthropologist, is interested in the past, but the focus tends to be more on identifying precisely what happened and when, rather than on developing theories of human behavior.

Herodotus (484–425 B.C.), the Greek traveler and historian, can be considered the first sophisticated cultural anthropologist whose writings are preserved and widely known. But professional anthropology starts with Edward Tylor (1832–1917) in England and Lewis Henry Morgan (1818–1881) in America. Since Tylor and Morgan, concern with ancient origins of man has been replaced in social anthropology by concern with man's current and recent functioning. Leaders in this shift were Franz Boas (1858–1942), Bronisław Malinowski (1884–1942), and A. R. Radcliffe-Brown (1881–1955). Boas fought against global generalizations in favor of

creating a large information pool on living cultures. Malinowski depicted cultures as satisfying the primary (biological) and secondary (social) needs of its members. Radcliffe-Brown was concerned with identifying the ways in which societies maintain their basic structures. Students of these modern masters dominated much of sociocultural anthropology until the 1960s, when a strong new interest in evolution followed on the work of Leslie White and Julian Steward; and Claude Levi-Strauss introduced an approach, known as structuralism, that focuses on shared mental processes. In addition, numerous innovative areas have opened up. One such area is urban anthropology.

In the past, anthropological research was generally done by the lone researcher working in a small community in a non-Western, technologically "simple" society. In the 1970s, however, more and more anthropologists are engaged in team research in complex, highly industrialized societies. The problems studied include poverty, racial strife, the effects of contact between industrial and nonindustrial populations, the problems of statehood (particularly in areas that have recently attained independence from colonial powers), war, and mental illness.

Cognitive anthropology, another new area, attempts to answer two questions as carefully and as completely as possible: (1) What material phenomena are important for people practicing in a given culture? (2) How do people organize these phenomena? Taxonomies and paradigms are developed by controlling questioning and summarized by formal analysis.

Programed animal communication is an attempt to understand the upper limits of prehuman thinking by teaching chimpanzees to communicate by symbolic means. Washoe, a female chimp, was taught to communicate with people by using the gestures of the American sign language for the deaf. Her repertoire amounted to over 160 symbols. Sarah, another female, learned to manipulate 130 magnetic plastic symbols on a magnetic board and to construct simple sentences.

Through the leadership of Sol Tax, the journal *Current Anthropology* has emerged as the major international anthropological forum. By means of "CA treatment," long articles are published along with comments on them sent in by scholars from every country that has professional anthropology.

In 1972–73, 276 institutions in the United States and Canada had anthropology programs, and 295 doctorates were awarded. Advanced degrees are available in a growing number of universities outside of North America. A majority of universities in the United Kingdom, France, Germany, Scandinavia, India, Australia, and Japan provide degrees either in anthropology or in closely linked disciplines. The number of museums that offer opportunities for anthropological research and training also is constantly growing.

To survive economically as a professional anthropologist, it is advantageous to have a Ph.D. degree. Doctorates in anthropology are awarded in the United States and Canada, in almost all European countries, and in many countries in Asia and Africa. Leading departments in the United States are those at Harvard University, the University of Chicago, Columbia University, the University of California (Berkeley), Yale University, the University of Michigan, Cornell University, the University of Pennsylvania, the University of California at Los Angeles (UCLA), the University of Wisconsin, and the University of Arizona.

Required empirical research or "fieldwork" transforms a graduate student into a full-fledged professional anthropologist. United States universities generally require graduate students to complete basic courses. British departments, however, generally do not require graduate students to attend regular courses. The dissertation and its defense are the major requirements for the Ph.D.

Training for physical (biological) anthropology (called *anthropology* on the continent of Europe) is quite separate from that for cultural anthropology. And in many European universities—for example, the University of Freiburg—cultural anthropology is primarily what United States anthropologists call folklore. Ethnography is a subject by itself in Eastern Europe, and there is none of what United States anthropologists would call social anthropology. And in the United Kingdom, archeology is studied separately from social anthropology. In other words, the integrated four-field approach is still largely a United States approach. Latin American universities are more in the tradition of Europe. India has patterned its approach on the British mode: Oxford-Cambridge. Japan, to judge from Hokkaido University, has followed the European pattern of physical anthropology as separate and of ethnology in the folklore or descriptive ethnography mode. The University of Edinburgh, however, has an anthropology program similar to those in the United States.

MORRIS FREILICH

Levels and Programs of Study

Programs in anthropology require as a minimum educational prerequisite a secondary education and lead to the following degrees: bachelor's (B.A.), master's (M.A., M.Sc.), the doctorate (Ph.D.), or their equivalents. Programs consist of classroom instruction, seminar or group discussion, and research and deal with the principles and practices of primitive human societies, including social organization and art forms.

Programs that lead to a first university degree generally include some of the following courses: comparative anthropology, physical anthropology, kinship systems in primitive societies, culture and personality in primitive societies, social organization of preliterate societies, economic anthropology, religion in primitive societies, languages in preliterate cultures, comparative ethnology, and methods in cultural anthropology. Background courses often included are general archeology, principles of linguistics, comparative sociology, social psychology, experimental analysis of social behavior, geology, history, and statistical analysis.

Programs that lead to a postgraduate university degree emphasize the theoretical and historical aspects of the subjects studied. Original research work, as substantiated by the presentation and defense of a scholarly thesis or dissertation, is required. At this level, individual programs are usually highly specialized. Principal subject matter areas within which study and research projects tend to fall include comparative anthropology, physical anthropology, social organization in preliterate societies, methods of social control in primitive societies, religion in primitive societies, the family and extended family (clan) in primitive societies, and language in preliterate cultures. Many specialized programs include study in other related branches of anthropology as well as study in specialties of related subjects such as linguistics, sociology, psychology, archeology, religion, law, economics, natural sciences, and the fine arts.

[This section was based on UNESCO's *International Standard Classification of Education (ISCED)* (Paris: UNESCO, 1976).]

Major International and National Organizations

INTERNATIONAL

International African Institute
Institut international africain
210 High Holborn
London WC1V 7BW, England

International Society for Ethnology and
    Folklore
Société internationale d'ethnographie et de
    folklore
Institut de folklore
25 strada Nikos Beloiannis
Bucharest 36, Romania

International Union of Anthropological and
    Ethnological Sciences
Union internationale des sciences
    anthropologiques et ethnologiques
Institut für Ethnologie, Freie Universität
    Berlin

Thielallee 43
1 Berlin 33 (Dahlem), Federal Republic of
    Germany

NATIONAL

A small sampling of national anthropological organizations worldwide includes:

Argentina:
    Sociedad argentina de antropología
    Moreno 350
    Buenos Aires

Australia:
    Australian Association of Social
        Anthropologists
    Department of Anthropology
    University of Western Australia
    Nedlands, W. A. 6009

Canada:
    Canadian Sociological and
        Anthropological Association
    Postal Box 878
    Montreal, Quebec

Chile:
    Sociedad chilena de antropología
    Rosas 1388
    Santiago

Federal Republic of Germany:
    Berliner Gesellschaft für Anthropologie,
        Ethnologie und Urgeschichte
    Schloss Charlottenburg (Langhansbau)
    1 Berlin 19

    Deutsche Gesellschaft für Völkerkunde
    % Rautenstrauch-Joest-Museum
    Ubierring 45
    5 Cologne

France:
    Société d'anthropologie de Paris
    1 rue René Panhard
    75013 Paris

Hungary:
    Magyar néprajzi társaság
    Könyves Kálmán-krt. 40
    H-1087 Budapest

India:
    Indian Anthropological Society
    35 Ballygunge Circular Road
    Calcutta 19

Italy:
    Istituto italiano di antropologia
    Città universitaria
    Rome

Japan:
    Nippon jinruigaku kai
    Department of Anthropology, Faculty of

Science
University of Tokyo
Bunkyo-ku, Tokyo

Mexico:
Sociedad mexicana de antropología
Córdoba 45
Mexico, D. F.

Netherlands:
Koninklijk instituut voor taal-, land- en
volkenkunde
Stationsplein 10
Leiden

Peru:
Instituto de estudios etnológicos
Alfonso Ugarte 650
Lima

Poland:
Polskie towarzystwo ludoznawxze
Wrocław
Szewska 36

Portugal:
Sociedade portuguêsa de antropologia e
etnologia
Facultade de ciências, Universidade do
Pôrto
Oporto

Switzerland:
Schweizerische Gesellschaft für
Volkskunde
Société suisse des traditions populaires
Augustinergasse 19
4000 Basel

United Kingdom:
Royal Anthropological Institute of Great
Britain and Ireland
36 Craven Street
London WC2N 5NG, England

United States:
American Anthropological Association
1703 New Hampshire Avenue NW
Washington, D.C. 20009

For a more complete listing of anthropological associations see:

The Archaeologists' Year Book 1973–74: An International Directory of Archaeology and Anthropology. Park Ridge, New Jersey: Noyes Press, 1973.

"Fourth International Directory of Anthropological Institutions." *Current Anthropology,* 1967, *8,* 647–751. To be updated.

Minerva, Wissenschaftliche Gesellschaften. Berlin, Federal Republic of Germany: de Gruyter, 1972.

The World of Learning. London: Europa, 1947–. Published annually.

Principal Information Sources

GENERAL

Guides to the literature include:

Beckham, R. S. "A Basic List of Books and Periodicals for College Libraries." In D. G. Mandelbaum and others (Eds.), *Resources for the Teaching of Anthropology.* Berkeley: University of California Press, 1963. See pages 77–316.

Cone, C. A. *Guide to Cultural Anthropology.* Glenview, Illinois: Scott, Foresman, 1969.

Harvard University, Peabody Museum of Archaeology and Ethnology. *Catalogue of the Library.* (54 vols.) Boston: Hall, 1963. Supplement 1 (12 vols.), 1970; Supplement 2, 1971; Supplement 3 (7 vols.), 1975.

University of Minnesota, Department of Anthropology Library Committee. *Guide to Basic Sources in Anthropology.* Minneapolis: University of Minnesota Bookstores, 1971.

White, C. M., and others. (Eds.) *Sources of Information in the Social Sciences.* (2nd ed.) Chicago: American Library Association, 1973. Pages 307–374 provide a guide to the literature of anthropology.

A sampling of the many overviews and introductions to the field includes:

Evans-Pritchard, E. E. *Social Anthropology.* New York: Free Press, 1952.

Firth, R. W. *Elements of Social Organization.* (2nd ed.) London: Watts, 1951.

Fried, M. *The Study of Anthropology.* New York: Crowell, 1972.

Harris, M. *Culture, People, Nature: An Introduction to General Anthropology.* (2nd ed.) New York: Crowell, 1975.

Hockett, C. F. *Man's Place in Nature.* New York: McGraw-Hill, 1973.

Kroeber, A. L. *Anthropology: Culture, Patterns and Processes.* New York: Harcourt Brace Jovanovich, 1963.

LaBarre, W. *The Human Animal.* Chicago: University of Chicago Press, 1954.

Historical perspectives of the field may be found in this sampling:

De Laguna, F. (Ed.) *Selected Papers from the "American Anthropologist," 1888–1920.* New York: Harper & Row, 1960. See especially the essay by A. I. Hallowell, "The Beginnings of Anthropology in America."

De Waal Malefijt, A. *Images of Man: A History of Anthropological Thought.* New York: Knopf, 1974.

Harris, M. *The Rise of Anthropological Theory.* New York: Crowell, 1968.

Penniman, T. K. *A Hundred Years of Anthropology.* (3rd rev. ed.) London: Duckworth, 1965.

Stocking, G. W., Jr. *Race, Culture, and Evolution: Essays in the History of Anthropology.* New York: Free Press, 1968.

Sources discussing education and training in the field include:

American Association of Physical Anthropology, Study Committee. "Graduate Training in Physical Anthropology: Report of the AAPA Study Committee." *American Journal of Physical Anthropology,* 1971, *34*(2), 279–305.
Burnett, J. H., and others. *Anthropology and Education: An Annotated Bibliographic Guide.* New Haven, Connecticut: Human Relations Area Files, 1974.
Frantz, C. *The Student Anthropologist's Handbook: A Guide to Research, Training, and Career.* Cambridge, Massachusetts: Schenkman, 1972.
Freilich, M. (Ed.) *Marginal Natives: Anthropologists at Work.* New York: Harper & Row, 1970.
Mandelbaum, D. G., and others. (Eds.) *Resources for the Teaching of Anthropology.* Berkeley: University of California Press, 1963.

CURRENT BIBLIOGRAPHIES

Abstracts in Anthropology. Westport, Connecticut: Greenwood Press, 1970–.
Annual Review of Anthropology. Palo Alto, California: Annual Reviews, Inc., 1972–. Supersedes *Biennial Review of Anthropology 1959–1971.*
Bulletin signalétique. Section 521: *Sociologie—Ethnologie.* Paris: Centre national de la recherche scientifique, 1961–.
Current Anthropology. Chicago: University of Chicago Press, 1960–.
Demos. Berlin, German Democratic Republic: Akademie-Verlag, 1960–.
International Bibliography of Social and Cultural Anthropology. London: Tavistock; Chicago: Aldine, 1955–.
Quarterly Check-List of Ethnology and Sociology. Darien, Connecticut: American Bibliographic Service, 1958–.
Royal Anthropological Institute of Great Britain and Ireland, Library. *Anthropological Index to Current Periodicals in the Library.* London: Royal Anthropological Institute of Great Britain and Ireland, 1963–.

PERIODICALS

A sampling of the journals for the field includes *Africa* (UK), *América indígena* (Mexico), *American Anthropologist* (US), *American Antiquity* (US), *American Ethnologist* (US), *American Journal of Physical Anthropology* (US), *Anthropological Journal of Canada, Anthropological Linguistics* (US), *L'anthropologie* (France), *Anthropos* (Switzerland), *Antiquity* (UK), *Canadian Review of Sociology and Anthropology, Cultures* (France), *Current Anthropology* (US), *Ethnographia* (Hungary), *Ethnohistory* (US), *Ethnology* (US), *Ethos* (US), *L'homme* (France), *Human Organization* (US), *Journal of American Linguistics, Journal of Anthropological Research* (US), *Journal of Field Archaeology* (US), *Journal of Human Evolution* (Italy), *Man* (UK), *Mankind* (Australia), *Oceania* (Australia), *Reviews in Anthropology* (US), *Sovetskaia arkheologiia* (Soviet Union), *Sovetskaia etnografiia* (Soviet Union), *World Archaeology* (UK), *Zeitschrift für Ethnologie* (FRG).

For a more complete listing of anthropology journals see:

Tax, S., and others. (Eds.) *Serial Publications in Anthropology.* Chicago: University of Chicago Press, 1973.
Ulrich's International Periodicals Directory. New York: Bowker, biennial.

ENCYCLOPEDIAS, DICTIONARIES, HANDBOOKS

Biasutti, R. *Le razze e il popoli della terra.* (3rd ed., 4 vols.) Turin, Italy: UTET (Unione tipagrafico-editrice torinese), 1959.
Davies, D. N. *A Dictionary of Anthropology.* New York: Crane, Russak, 1972.
Frantz, C. *The Student Anthropologist's Handbook.* Cambridge, Massachusetts: Schenkman, 1972.
Honigmann, J. *Handbook of Social and Cultural Anthropology.* Chicago: Rand McNally, 1973.
Hunter, D. E., and Whitten, P. M. *Encyclopedia of Anthropology.* New York: Harper & Row, 1976.
International Dictionary of Regional European Ethnology and Folklore. Copenhagen: Rosenkilde and Bagger, 1960–1965. Polyglot dictionary of general ethnology and folklore.
Murdock, G. P. *Outline of World Cultures.* (4th rev. ed.) New Haven, Connecticut: Human Relations Area Files, 1972. Basic source for identification of tribes and geographical areas.
Naroll, R. S., and Cohen, R. (Eds.) *A Handbook of Method in Cultural Anthropology.* Garden City, New York: Natural History Press, 1970.
Royal Anthropological Institute. *Notes and Queries on Anthropology.* (6th ed.) London: Routledge and Kegan Paul, 1951.
Seligman, R. A. (Ed.) *Encyclopedia of the Social Sciences.* New York: Macmillan, 1948. Volume 1 provides a survey of the field of anthropology.
Sills, D. L. (Ed.) *International Encyclopedia of the Social Sciences.* New York: Macmillan, 1968.
Winick, C. *Dictionary of Anthropology.* Totowa,

New Jersey: Rowman & Littlefield, 1970.

DIRECTORIES

ALSED Directory of Specialists and Research Institutions. New York: UNESCO, 1974. Directory of specialists and institutions involved in anthropology and language science in educational development (ALSED) in forty-six countries.

The Archaeologists' Year Book 1973: An International Directory of Archaeology and Anthropology. Park Ridge, New Jersey: Noyes Press, 1973.

"Fourth International Directory of Anthropological Institutions." *Current Anthropology,* 1967, *8,* 647–751. To be updated.

Guide to Departments of Anthropology. Washington, D.C.: American Anthropological Association, 1962–. A guide to anthropological education in the United States, Canada, and Mexico.

Hudson, K., and Nicholls, A. (Eds.) *The Directory of World Museums.* New York: Columbia University Press, 1975. A comprehensive, international directory of museums; includes a bibliography of national and regional museum directories and articles.

Minerva, Forschungsinstitute. Berlin, Federal Republic of German: de Gruyter, 1972.

Museums of the World/Museen der Welt: A Directory of 17,000 Museums in 148 Countries, Including a Subject Index. Pullach/Munich, Federal Republic of Germany: Verlag Dokumentation, 1975.

Research Centers Directory. (5th ed.) Detroit: Gale Research, 1975.

The World of Learning. London: Europa, 1947– Published annually.

[Bibliography prepared by Antonio Rodriguez-Buckingham.]

See also: Archeology.

ANTIDISCRIMINATION

See Access of Minorities; Affirmative Action; Legal Aspects of Higher Education; Women and Higher Education: Equal Rights and Affirmative Action.

ANTIGUA

Population: 76,000 (1975 estimate). Student enrollment in primary school: 14,330 (6970 females); secondary school: 4003 (2211 females); postsecondary education: 235 (130 females); university (abroad): 94 (35 females). Language of instruction: English. [Figures are for 1974.]

Antigua—with its dependency, Barbuda, in the Leeward Islands in the Caribbean—is a state associated with the United Kingdom. It is one of the territories contributing to the University of the West Indies, whose main campus is located in Mona, Jamaica, with branch campuses located in Cave Hill, Barbados, and St. Augustine, Trinidad. The Department of Extra-Mural Studies of UWI has a resident tutor in Antigua, and one of its university centers is also located there. In 1974 ninety-four Antiguan students attended the University of the West Indies.

[Information supplied by the Ministry of Education, St. Johns, Antigua.]

See also: Caribbean: Regional Analysis.

APPOINTMENT OF ACADEMIC PERSONNEL

See Recruitment, Appointment, Promotion, and Termination of Academic Personnel.

ARAB LEAGUE EDUCATIONAL, CULTURAL AND SCIENTIFIC ORGANIZATION

The Arab League Educational, Cultural and Scientific Organization (ALECSO), a specialized agency of fifteen countries, was founded in 1966 by the Council of the League of Arab States and became operational after its first general conference in July 1970. It was set up to implement and broaden Arab endeavors in the fields of education, culture, and science.

The organization aims to unify the Arab world through education, science, and culture; raise the standard of culture in the Arab region; and coordinate Arab efforts in building up better policies of education. ALECSO promotes scientific research, assists in the collection of relevant information, and encourages exchange of experts and experiences. It also safeguards and develops Arab heritage and encourages cooperation between the Arab world and other foreign countries, within the framework of international cooperation.

The biennial general conference, composed of representatives of each member state, lays down the broad outlines of the organization's work; invites Arab governments and nongovernmental bodies to hold conferences in education, culture, and science; and gives advice to the Council of the League of Arab States. The conference elects the members of the executive board and appoints the director general.

The head of the general conference acts as a consultant to the executive board. The meetings of the board are also attended by the director general. The board prepares the agenda of the general conference; supervises the execution of the projects approved by the conference; renders advice to the Council of the League of Arab States between the ordinary sessions of the general conference; and passes recommendations concerning the acceptance of new member states. The board meets twice a year in ordinary sessions.

ALECSO is financed by dues of member states, determined according to their shares in the budget of the League of Arab States. Grants and donations make up the Special Fund for Cultural Development in the Arab states.

ALECSO is composed of a department of education, a department of science, a department of documentation and information, a department of social sciences, humanities, and culture, and an Institute of Arab Manuscripts. A department of finance and administration handles the financial affairs of ALECSO.

Conferences, seminars, and committees are organized by ALECSO's department of education to study educational problems facing the Arab states. Educational research is encouraged in cooperation with local, regional, and international unions,

organizations, and centers. ALECSO provides grants, scholarships, and prizes in postgraduate studies for Arab students.

ALECSO seeks to promote the development of science in the Arab states through the department of science. The department cooperates with international organizations in long-term programs; participates in seminars and conferences; and conducts research on the use of natural resources available in the Arab region.

The department of documentation and information serves other departments of ALECSO, as well as the educational, cultural, and scientific conferences, in the fields of documentation and bibliographical and statistical research.

The department of social sciences, humanities, and culture encourages cultural cooperation through the spread of the Arabic language and culture and the establishment of schools, institutes, and cultural centers abroad.

The Institute of Arab Manuscripts helps libraries with their indexing and publishes a periodical review dealing with and identifying Arab manuscripts. The institute collects indexes of Arab manuscripts from public and private libraries as well as individual owners and unifies them in a general index. Valuable Arab manuscripts are photographed and put at the disposal of scholars and research workers; enlarged copies of manuscripts are also loaned to other countries.

Other organs of ALECSO include the Arab Regional Literacy Organization, Higher Institute of Arabic Studies, Permanent Arabization Centre, and Office of the Permanent Delegation to UNESCO. The Arab Regional Literacy Organization, seeking to combat illiteracy in the Arab countries, sends experts to the Arab countries to help in planning, training, and organization; it also conducts study courses, workshops, and research in the field of literacy. The Higher Institute for Arabic Studies propagates Arab culture through teaching and lecturing; it has a library of materials dealing with the origin of Arab culture and civilization and their contribution to humanity, science, and world progress. The Permanent Arabization Centre collects and tabulates all Arab research work and cooperates with linguistic institutions, specialized scientific organizations, and Arabization branches in Arab countries. The center encourages the use of classical Arabic instead of colloquial Arabic or foreign languages used in some Arabic countries. The center publishes dictionaries in mathematics, physics, chemistry, and politics. The Office of the Permanent Delegation to UNESCO promotes cooperation with ALECSO through conferences, councils, and committees and through exchanges of documents, publications, and reports.

Publications of ALECSO include *Information Documentation Newsletter, Bulletin of Educational Statistics, Bulletin of Publications in the Arab World,* and translations and books on topics of Arab interest.

109 Tahrir Street-Dokki

Cairo, Egypt

See also: Science Policies: Less Developed Countries: Arab World.

ARAB WORLD: REGIONAL ANALYSIS

There are two basic types of Arab higher education: traditional classical Arab-Islamic, which evolved shortly after the advent of Islam in the seventh century A.D., and modern Western, which was introduced early in the nineteenth century and has had a striking development in the twentieth century. From the 1820s to the mid 1900s, these two types of education went their separate ways, with little in common between them—one under religious auspices, the other under Ministries of Education or of Higher Education. They differed in their organization, in general outlook, in curricula, and in training of teaching staffs. They produced two different kinds of cultured human beings—one religiously and linguistically oriented, the other impressed with the attitudes and outlook of modern

sciences (natural, social, and humanistic). Since World War II the two types have begun to come together and, at least in Egypt, seem to have been integrated into one system of higher education.

Early Arab-Islamic Education

Islamic education had its modest beginnings soon after the start of the Islamic movement in 610 A.D. Its spiritual father and first teacher was the Prophet Mohammed to whom the *Qur'an* (Koran) was revealed. The first verse revealed was a command: "Read in the name of Thy Lord who has created, . . ." Literally, the word *Qur'an* means the act of reading, but it has come to mean the sacred book of Islam. As the verses of the Koran were revealed, they were either written down by the few people who could read and write or memorized and passed on orally. The Prophet was there to interpret them, to answer questions, to guide the steps of the new believers. The ability to read was at a premium, so much so that a slave or prisoner could earn his freedom by teaching some believers to read and write. From the very early days of Islam, the mosque was a center of learning as well as of prayer. From these beginnings Arab-Islamic higher education developed.

Islamic education gradually crystallized into two types of schools: an ungraded lower school to teach the general public the Koran and reading, writing, and arithmetic; and an equally ungraded higher school *(madrassa)* or university mosque, offering advanced and specialized instruction. In the seventh and eighth centuries, as Islam spread rapidly in Western and Central Asia, North Africa, and Spain, it absorbed large numbers of people of different races, languages, religions, and cultures. These converts needed to learn the Koran and its language, Arabic, which was also the language of the ruling race. Great intellectual activity during the seventh, eighth, and ninth centuries led to the rise of the basic Islamic *Sunni* and *Shiite* schools of theological doctrine and jurisprudence, the codification of the Arabic language and grammar, and the collection of a vast amount of pre-Islamic and early Islamic poetry. The resulting body of knowledge was known to the Arabs as the traditional *(naqliya)* sciences. Simultaneously, the Arabs had to take a stand toward Persian, Indian, and especially Greek thought. A great movement arose for the translation of Greek works of science, medicine, mathematics, astronomy, philosophy, and logic. To these the Arabs later added Indian mathematics and astronomy and their own creations in medicine, algebra, botany, and optics, which were known as the rational *(aqliya)* sciences.

These two sets of sciences constituted the backbone of the curriculum of higher education. The traditional sciences were taught mainly in mosques and *madrassas.* Logic, arithmetic, and some astronomy were taught in these two institutions mainly as tool subjects, though there is evidence that medicine was taught in some *madrassas.* A large number of *madrassas* were founded and endowed all over the Islamic world, many of them still surviving. The rational and practical sciences were mostly cultivated outside the mosques and *madrassas* in such institutions as hospitals and libraries. This division did not prevent some *shaykhs* (Islamic scholars) from personally pursuing such studies as medicine, philosophy, mathematics, and astronomy.

Arab-Islamic higher education thus came to be increasingly identified with the interpretation and propagation of Islam. Its teaching mosques and *madrassas* were schools with a mission to be undertaken by the scholars as a service for the sake of God *(al-'ilm liwajh Illah)* and of winning His favor. Accordingly, the early *shaykhs* refrained from taking any pecuniary rewards for their services and charged no fees. It was only later, as pious endowments began to multiply, that the practice of paying *shaykhs* out of the endowment gradually developed. The revenue from the endowments also provided stipends for students

to live on. Thus, students from all over the Islamic world flocked to the main centers of learning and had no financial difficulty living and learning for many years. *Al-rihlah fi talab al-'ilm* (travel for the sake of learning) became a current practice.

Teaching was carried on in circles around a *shaykh,* who propounded his subject, usually on the basis of a book of his own or one of a great authority. Individual students sought one such teacher and studied a book with him until the *shaykh* was satisfied with their performance and gave them a licence *(ijazah)* certifying that they had satisfactorily completed the study of the book with him. Students normally read other books with either the same or other *shaykhs* until they themselves felt sufficiently confident to undertake teaching. Students had the freedom to question, discuss, and sometimes challenge the views of their teachers. It was incumbent upon the *shaykh* to tolerate the questionings of his students and to defend his point of view. This system produced most of the religious and administrative personnel of the Arab and Islamic countries in all their ranks and variety of functions. It had its creative period in the first five centuries of the *Hijra* (the period following Mohammed's migration from Mecca in 622 A.D.). As Arab society began to decline, however, learning became less creative, resorting merely to the transmission of ideas and doctrines of the earlier era. Instead of original works, writers produced mostly commentaries on existing works, notes on the commentaries, and compendia that sometimes were put in verse to facilitate memorization. The cultivation of the rational sciences also declined drastically. By the end of the eighteenth century, the system was a mere echo of its brilliant past.

Advent of Modern Higher Education

Toward the end of the sixteenth century, as Europe began to expand eastward, defeating the once powerful Ottoman empire in a number of land and naval battles, and at the end of the eighteenth century, as Bonaparte occupied Egypt, Ottoman and Egyptian rulers alike were forced to recognize the military as well as the administrative superiority of the Western countries. Mehemet Ali, who became the viceroy of Egypt in 1805 after the withdrawal of the French armies, began to send students to Europe in the second decade of the nineteenth century in an endeavor to adopt Western military techniques. He invited French military advisers to Egypt and founded modern military schools as well as schools of engineering, medicine, pharmacy, and veterinary medicine based on Western science and technology. During his regime a whole new system of education was introduced, consisting of primary and secondary schools to prepare students for higher institutions. An extensive movement of translation of Western works was initiated, with students returning from Europe serving as the translators. In effect, a new system of education was established parallel to the old. The two systems ran side by side until World War II. A similar evolution took place in the Ottoman empire, of which the Arab countries in Asia and in North Africa (except Morocco) were a part.

Throughout the nineteenth century, modern higher education in Egypt consisted of only a few professional schools of the Western type. The first modern university-type institution in the Arab World was the Syrian Protestant College, established in Beirut in 1866 by American missionaries, which with the acquisition of several higher schools became the American University of Beirut in 1920. In 1875 the French Jesuit order established the Université Saint Joseph, also in Beirut. From 1859 onward, the French government in Algeria founded schools of medicine, pharmacy, law, letters, and sciences that became the University of Algiers in 1909. The private Egyptian University, founded in 1908 in Cairo (which was in fact a faculty of arts), invited some Western and

Egyptian scholars to lecture in it, and the American Protestant mission in Egypt established the American University in Cairo in 1919.

The first public higher education institution was the Syrian University (now the University of Damascus), officially founded in 1923, although its schools of medicine and law had been in existence for some years. The second public institution was the Egyptian University, founded in 1925, which annexed the private Egyptian University as its faculty of arts. The state University of Alexandria was founded in 1942.

To these four foreign and three national modern universities must be added the three millennial Arab-Islamic university mosques of Zitouna in Tunis, founded in the eighth century A.D.; Qarawiyin in Fez, founded in 859 A.D.; and al-Azhar in Cairo, founded in 970 A.D.—bringing the total number of Arab universities before the end of World War II to ten. The three venerable Islamic universities continued to teach the traditional Islamic sciences, though with some curricular and administrative adaptations. The two types of universities existed in parallel but quite separately from 1820 to 1945. Clearly, modern higher education was not a continuation of the old Arab-Islamic system but an importation from the West to meet the needs of Arab countries in the modern world.

Post–World War II Developments

The development of higher education during the post–World War II period occurred on both the modern secular and religious educational fronts. As more Arab countries regained their independence, many of them proceeded to found their own universities. By 1975 there were forty-seven Arab universities, of which forty were modern secular and seven religious, although two of the religious institutions contained both religious and modern facilities. Egypt had the largest number of universities—eleven; Iraq and Saudi Arabia had six each; Lebanon had five; Algeria, Libya, Sudan, and Syria, three each; Morocco, two; and Jordan, Kuwait, Somalia, Tunisia, and the Yemen Arab Republic, one each. In addition, there were over one hundred colleges and institutes of higher education outside the university system, bringing the total enrollment in 1970 to 425,000 (of that, approximately 100,000 were women). Compared with only 27,000 students in 1945, this represents an increase in total enrollment of 1577 percent *(Statistical Yearbook,* 1973).

Among the motives underlying the rapid development in the founding of new universities was the desire of the new independent states to train the necessary manpower for administration and for economic, social, and cultural development. As in other parts of the developing world, the university also became a kind of status symbol. Moreover, the rapid growth of primary and secondary education tremendously increased the pressure of applicants for admission to higher institutions.

The post–World War II period also witnessed several tendencies in the development of the religious universities and higher institutions. One is the creation of new religious universities. Islamic universities were founded—in Beida, Libya; Omdurman, Sudan; and Medina and Riyadh, Saudi Arabia—and the Catholic Maronite church established the University of the Holy Ghost in Kaslik, a suburb north of Beirut.

A second tendency is the incorpoation of independent colleges of Islamic law and religion into the modern universities, sometimes with the status of faculties, as, for example, the colleges of *Shari'a* (Islamic law) in Baghdad and Damascus, which were incorporated into the universities of these two cities. Of somewhat the same nature was the transfer of the three schools of religion, Islamic law, and Arabic of the old Zitouna University in Tunis to the modern University of Tunis.

A third tendency is exemplified by al-Azhar, in what came to be called the "re-form" of that venerable institution. Starting in the 1870s, repeated calls by Egyptian thinkers and religious men brought about a series of laws, introducing curricular and organizational reforms. The most radical of these laws, passed in 1961, was aimed at removing the barriers between al-Azhar and other universities and eliminating differences between its graduates and those of other institutions by ensuring a common denominator of knowledge and experience for all students. It also standardized university degrees all over the country. While maintaining the authority of the rector of al-Azhar in all matters of religion, the law divides the institution into five bodies: (1) a policymaking supreme council presided over by the rector and made up of members drawn from the hierarchy of al-Azhar, representatives of some ministries, and specialists in university education; (2) an Academy of Islamic Research, consisting of up to fifty scholars drawn from Egypt and other Islamic countries, that is charged with all matters of research and the expression of opinions about all doctrinal and social problems related to the Islamic faith; (3) Islamic cultural missions charged with publications, translations, and Islamic relations, including sending missions abroad and receiving students on scholarships from various parts of the world; (4) the university proper; and (5) al-Azhar Institutes, which are primary and secondary schools first established in the 1930s to prepare students for study at al-Azhar, with a curriculum consisting primarily of religious and Arabic studies.

With respect to the university, the law adds to the already existing three faculties of Islamic theology, jurisprudence, and Arabic, faculties of administration, engineering and industry, agriculture, and medicine. It establishes, as well, al-Azhar's University College for Women, which started to offer courses in the several fields taught at the university in the academic year 1961–62. The law also brings the university's organization in line with that of other Egyptian universities, with a rector and a university council and with faculties, their deans, councils, and departments. Academic ranks are made almost identical with those of other universities, thus opening the way for the exchange of teaching staff between al-Azhar and other universities.

The curricula at al-Azhar secondary institutes are being modernized, combining religious and modern studies drawn up by a joint committee representing the university and the Ministry of Education. The bearers of secondary certificates from the institutes are entitled not only to enter al-Azhar but also other universities, provided they spend an additional year studying such modern subjects as were missed at the institutes. Conversely, bearers of the General Certificate of Secondary Education of the Ministry of Education can be admitted to al-Azhar University if they pass a special test ensuring the equivalence of their certificate with that of al-Azhar secondary institutes, costing them an extra year of study. Thus, there is equality of opportunity for all students. To all intents and purposes, the law of 1961 has transformed al-Azhar into a modern university, with the gulf between religious and secular higher education, which had existed in Egypt for nearly a century and a half, virtually bridged.

Contemporary University Practices

One cannot give a general description of Arab higher education without slighting the many exceptions due to the different social, political, and legal practices in the twenty Arab countries and the varied origins of their higher education institutions. In the discussions that follow, some of the more significant exceptions are pointed out and described briefly. In the main, the account deals only with public higher education, along with reference to private institutions that demonstrate some interesting atypical or promising practice.

Government and organization of public universities. Generally speaking, the laws governing universities give them an autonomous status as corporate bodies. Most of the public universities are under the authority either of a minister of education or a minister of higher education. Algeria, Egypt, Iraq, Morocco, Saudi Arabia, and Syria have ministries of higher education. Egypt, Iraq and Syria also have supreme university councils responsible for laying down general policies, approving plans of development and founding new institutions, and coordinating matters relating to admissions, examinations, academic staff, degrees, and finance. The Egyptian council is composed entirely of university representatives and five members experienced in university education. The Iraqi council, while having a number of university representatives, also includes the minister of education, presidents of scientific and atomic research bodies and the teachers association, a student selected by the National Union of Students, heads of departments at the Ministry of Higher Education and Scientific Research, and up to five distinguished Iraqi or Arab thinkers, scholars, or specialists. Its functions are not limited to higher education questions and policies but cover the supervision of scientific foundations, presenting annual reports about them and recommending action concerning them. The fact that the Iraqi council is presided over by the president of the republic gives it added weight. It is in reality the body that recommends state policies with respect to higher education and scientific research and development.

Most public universities follow the same organizational patterns, with faculties, institutes, and departments; a university council or senate; faculty councils and departmental meetings; university presidents (sometimes called rectors or vice-chancellors) who preside over the councils; deans who preside over the faculties; and directors of institutes and chairmen of departments. In some cases, the president of a university has the rank and powers of a minister over his institution. He is usually nominated by the university council and appointed by the highest authority in the state. The appointment of deans and professors also comes from higher authority. Most Arab governments reserve the right to be the final authority in the appointment of the senior officials and the professors of universities, which of course sets some limitations on university autonomy. University and faculty councils, some of which have begun to include student members, have their standing and ad hoc committees to study and recommend action in matters related to their terms of reference. University councils or senates are charged with approving university policy, granting degrees, and making recommendations in such areas as the budget, new programs, appointments, promotions, and new degrees for approval by the supreme council or higher authorities. Faculty councils coordinate departmental activities, approve curricula where necessary, and recommend appointments, promotions, and the granting of degrees. Departments initiate action on curricula, degrees, appointments, promotions of teaching staff, and departmental plans.

There are a number of significant deviations from this general pattern of university governance. The University of Jordan is governed by a board of trustees of ten members (appointed by the king) whose functions are to uphold university autonomy, raise funds, approve the budget, and manage finances. In conjunction with the university council, it recommends the establishment of new faculties, institutes, and departments and nominates candidates for the presidency of the university.

The University of Khartoum follows the British pattern. Executive authority is vested in a council of thirty members consisting of the vice-chancellor (president); honorary treasurer; eleven members of the university staff; eleven members drawn from various ministries, Parliament, and some public bodies like the Gezira Board, the Civil Service Commission, and the Sudan Chamber of Commerce; and six members-at-large drawn from the princi-

pal learned professions in the country and elected by the council. The duties of the council are to elect the chancellor, manage the university's finances and properties, and appoint the academic staff. On the recommendation of the university senate, it institutes degrees and other distinctions to be conferred by the university and, in consultation with the senate, it creates, affiliates, or discontinues colleges and institutes. The chancellor elected by the council is usually the head of state. He appoints the vice-chancellor and approves borrowing by the council when it exceeds £ 100,000 (Sudanese). Otherwise, his functions are mostly ceremonial. The vice-chancellor is the chief administrator of the university, presiding over the senate and advising the council on matters of policy, finance, and administration.

The five universities and various private or public colleges in Lebanon have perhaps the largest measure of autonomy of all higher institutions in the Arab states. Subject to their own charters, they organize their own internal affairs, determine the curricula, and conduct their work entirely as they see fit. The only powers the Lebanese Ministry of Education reserves for itself relative to the private institutions are to require the Lebanese baccalaureate or its equivalent for admission to higher institutions and to recognize the degrees that meet its conditions. While the public Lebanese University does enjoy a large measure of autonomy, it nevertheless has to secure the approval of the government for the appointment of its permanent academic staff and for the establishment of new faculties and institutes and has to follow state financial regulations. Lebanon also has a supreme advisory council, presided over by the minister of national education and composed of the presidents of the five universities. Its function is to advise on matters concerning cooperation among the universities and to be an instrument for the expression of views on higher education and the exchange of useful information. The council rarely meets, however, and each of the universities goes its own way.

Accessibility and admission to higher education. At least four factors influence accessibility to higher education in the Arab states. The first is the great effort these states have been making, particularly since the mid 1950s, in instituting free and universal primary education. In most cases, primary school enrollments quadrupled and quintupled between 1950 and 1970, which has led to an increase in higher education enrollment from 52,000 to 425,000, or eight times, during the same period. The second centers on the fact that between 90 and 95 percent of adolescents entering secondary education pursue literary and scientific rather than technical or vocational studies. Since they acquire no employable skills, most of them compete for admission to universities or other higher insitutions. The third is the world phenomenon of the awakening of the social classes, which, though less pronounced as yet in the Arab states, has nevertheless contributed markedly to the increase in university enrollment, particularly on the part of students from urban areas. Although rural students have greater opportunity to enter higher education than before, they still remain largely at a disadvantage compared to urban students. The fourth concerns the emancipation of women, especially in the northern Arab countries in Asia and in Arab countries in North Africa. Softening of the segregation of the sexes and entry of women into the professions and business establishments have given a great impetus to the education of women. The enrollment of women students was approximately 25 percent of the total enrollment in higher education in 1970, the proportion ranging from 8 to 51 percent in various Arab countries, which compares well with some of the advanced countries.

The admission process normally begins with the colleges, faculties, and universities fixing the number of students to be admitted in the following year. The decision, usually taken in consultation with, or with the approval of, the ministry, is based on the estimate of places available, the supply of specialists in certain fields, and, in a few cases, on the provisions of an economic and social development plan. Admission is based on the completion of secondary education sanctioned by government examinations leading to the granting of a certificate of secondary education or, in some countries, of the *baccalauréat*. Students holding certificates of technical, agricultural, commercial, and home economics secondary schools or sections are increasingly being allowed to join the faculties or colleges corresponding to their studies. Thus, technical school students are eligible for admission to colleges of engineering or applied engineering, agricultural secondary school students to colleges of agriculture, and so on. Selection is based primarily on a student's grades and rank in government secondary school examinations. In addition to the general requirements of the secondary certificate, faculties may impose their own requirements, such as a higher passing mark in the student's intended major. Some countries refuse to admit students with secondary certificates dating more than two years before their application for admission. Others impose an upper age limit (for example, twenty-four). Such measures are clearly intended to reduce the pressure of applications.

Having more than one public university, two or three countries have established clearinghouses for the sifting of applications, sometimes with computer help. The student states his first, second, and sometimes third preference of college, its location, and the subject of his study and specialization. If he is considered qualified for admission, an effort is made to satisfy his wishes as far as practicable. If the student is not satisfied with the final decision, he may ask for reconsideration of his case.

Academic staffing. The academic staffs of most of the public universities are divided by rank: professor, assistant professor, instructor, and demonstrator. Some universities add an assistant instructor between instructor and demonstrator. A demonstrator is usually a high-ranking graduate holding the first degree of his university who acts in such capacities as assisting in the laboratories, helping students in their studies, leading discussions in sectional meetings of the classes, and sometimes in correcting test papers. In most countries he is considered outside the academic staff. Often he is expected to prepare for his master's degree while serving as demonstrator, failing which he is removed to some teaching position outside the university, usually in secondary schools. Iraq, following the American practice in this respect, has introduced the rank of associate professor. Some have also added the rank (variously named in Arabic) that might be called distinguished professor. The Egyptian universities at one time allowed one professor per department, known as a professor with a chair *(professeur titulaire* in French), who acted as head of the department. Legislation now allows more than one professor per department in order to open more opportunities for promotion and to encourage specialization within the same discipline. The universities of the three countries of North Africa follow the French practice of ranking—for example, *professeur, maître de conférences,* and *assistant.*

In the early decades of the modern universities a significant proportion of the senior professors were foreign. This is no longer the case. Foreign professors are becoming something of a rarity, though the way is open for visiting professors. By 1975 most of the professors, associate professors, and assistant professors had their doctorates from well-known European and American universities. With the establishment of doctoral programs in Egyptian and a few other Arab universities, the number of home-trained academic staff is beginning to increase. However, the flow of Arab graduate students to European and American universities has not stopped, so that there is little danger of inbreeding.

Promotion is based mainly on the amount and quality of the research and publications

of the individual academic staff member, though seniority of course plays a role. Usually there are faculty committees that study promotion cases and make recommendations. These committees go through the faculty and university councils before being finally approved by ministerial authorities. The retirement age is sixty in some countries and sixty-five in others. Universities usually have their own staff disciplinary regulations and arrangements. Theoretically, faculty members enjoy a certain immunity, though academic staff members—sometimes even presidents— have been removed or transferred as a result of outside pressure. Salary scales are often those of the public service in general or equated with them; they may be even higher. Some countries have special laws fixing the salary scales of the academic staff of universities.

Curricula. The curriculum depends to a large extent on those university patterns that have influenced modern Arab higher education: Arab-Islamic, French, American, British, and the comparatively new Egyptian. The curricula of Islamic education, described earlier in the article, survive to this day in the six Islamic universities, though they have undergone some reorganization and modernization (for example, the introduction of some foreign languages and science courses).

The French pattern is best exemplified by the programs of the Jesuit *Université Saint Joseph* in Beirut—a private university associated for the most part with the University of Lyons in France—and by the universities of North Africa, where the French practice of separating such schools as engineering and agriculture from the universities prevails. In the faculties of arts and sciences curricula are based in most part on earning three to five certificates in order to obtain a *licence.* Teaching is very largely in French, except in certain schools of law, Arabic language and literature, and education. In some of the other public universities, French influence is exercised through Arab graduates of French universities who become professors and administrators in the Arab universities.

The American pattern is best represented by the American University of Beirut, the American University in Cairo, and some colleges in Lebanon, where the course-credit semestral system, with required and elective courses, prevails. Students choose their major in one or two related fields, so that each student has the program of his choice within certain university regulations. Some faculties of education, engineering, and business (where most of the professors are American trained) generally follow the American pattern of professional education, except for annual instead of semestral courses and fixed programs of study with little or no electives. However, some universities in Iraq, Kuwait, Saudi Arabia, and Jordan, as well as the faculty of science in the Lebanese University, have adopted the semestral course-credit system, and other universities are considering its adoption.

The British type of higher education is best exemplified by the University of Khartoum, Sudan, which had its roots in two colleges founded by the British authorities and, with the addition of other faculties, became the University of Khartoum in 1956. It is organized along the lines of British universities, with instruction still largely in English. For the most part its senior academic staff were educated in British universities. Its syllabi and examinations are patterned after those of British universities, notably the University of London, and prepare students for British-type degrees. In other Arab countries British influence lingers in some faculties, such as science, medicine, and engineering, where curricula and degree requirements have been inspired by British practice.

Finally, there is what might be called the Egyptian pattern, which has evolved since the 1930s combining certain features of the Arab-Islamic, the French, and the English patterns. Undergraduate study is usually in four-year colleges, except in some professional schools where study takes five or six years. The programs of study consist almost entirely of required courses with a specific number of lecture, discussion, or practical periods. Once the student chooses his department and his major within the department, nearly all his courses are required. On the graduate level, the student usually spends one year attending courses leading to the higher diploma examinations. He then spends about a year preparing his master's thesis, and two or more years writing his doctoral dissertation. The Egyptian pattern has spread to other Arab countries, particularly those in which Egyptian university administrators and professors had a hand in founding the universities.

Since the foundation of the Association of Arab Universities in 1964, a trend has begun for the assimilation of the various patterns. The association has been conducting studies on university education, has sponsored meetings of deans of faculties dealing with the same sectors of knowledge, and has been holding biennial conferences. The objective of these activities is the creation of a common denominator of university policies, organization, and philosophy that might eventually lead to a new Arab pattern of higher education.

In the area of curricular innovations, three developments at the American University of Beirut can be cited: (1) An interdisciplinary program has been introduced, mainly on the graduate level, in which several departments or faculties cooperate. The program consists of courses given by the relevant departments or faculties and of specially designed courses taught cooperatively by staff members of several departments. In addition to the interdisciplinary approach, the faculty of arts and sciences has drawn up a list of courses offered in other faculties that a student of any major can elect and for which he can receive credit toward graduation. (2) The faculty of arts and sciences allows a student who at the beginning of his senior (fourth) year has an average of eighty-two in his major to undertake independent study.

Such a student can choose, under the supervision of a professor of his choice, a course of directed study of three to six credits that involves independent research, original creative compositions, directed reading, and the preparation of a report or thesis on his work in the course. (3) The faculty of arts and sciences has started to distinguish between an ordinary major and a teaching major. In the former a student may study intensively certain aspects of his major, such as physical chemistry, as a preliminary to further specialization. In the latter the student who is preparing to teach in junior and senior high schools must follow an all-around program, say in chemistry, that would qualify him to teach the various aspects of his field competently. Such a student can still choose a few courses to deepen his knowledge in one aspect of chemistry. Several departments have developed such programs, and some of the Egyptian universities have also introduced interdisciplinary courses into some of their curricula.

Methods of teaching. The lecture is the most prevalent method of teaching. In some institutions students are allowed to interrupt the lecturer to ask questions or discuss a point. In others, notably those of the French tradition, such interruption is rarely allowed. Any questions or discussions take place after class, during practice periods, or in sections formed for the purpose of discussing points raised in the lecture and having difficult concepts explained by the assistant in charge.

Next to the lecture, the textbook is the students' principal source of knowledge. There is a growing practice, often insisted on by the students, whereby professors publish their lectures in book form, which encourages absenteeism and cramming at the end of the year. Assignments in reference works are frequent in the better universities. Class reports, term papers, and graduation theses are often required.

Laboratory, workshop, or field experience are required in university science courses and in scientific and technological professional schools. Medical faculties, of course, have their hospitals, outpatient clinics, and pathological, radiological, and other laboratories. The use of radio, open- and closed-circuit television, films and filmstrips, videotapes, language laboratories, and similar modern media of instruction is spreading, especially in the wealthier countries.

Graduate study and research. Nearly all the modern universities in the Arab World started as undergraduate teaching institutions and later expanded to include graduate work. The American University of Beirut, founded in 1866, granted its first master's degree in 1907. A few of its professors conducted their own research, notably in Arabic grammar and language and in botany. During most of the century of its existence, the Jesuit Université Saint Joseph has been a noted center of Oriental and Arabic literary and lexicographic research. Since the institution's founding in 1923, a number of professors of the Syrian University (now the University of Damascus) have been conducting extensive lexicographic research in finding or coining Arabic scientific terms as part of their university teaching or in connection with the Syrian Arabic Language Academy. The public Egyptian University (now the University of Cairo), founded in 1925, began in the early 1930s to introduce graduate work and encourage research. It was followed in the 1940s and 1950s by the Universities of Alexandria, Ain Shams, and Assiut. Other new Arab universities entered the graduate field in the 1960s and 1970s.

Based on data from the Association of Arab Universities (which compiles statistics only for member institutions, at least seventeen universities in the Arab region were offering graduate work in 1975. In 1972–73 graduate enrollment in ten Arab universities and the American University of Beirut was 25,692. The total output of graduate degrees and diplomas exceeded 4000 in 1970 and was probably nearer 5000 by 1975. The Egyptian universities alone conferred a total of 4104 graduate degrees and diplomas in 1972, of which 402 were doctorates, 964 master's, and 2738 higher diplomas. Some Egyptian universities publish digests of their master's and doctor's degrees.

Student research leading to graduate degrees has been expanding in an increasing number of universities. One foreign language (and sometimes two) is required before a student can undertake graduate research. Master's and doctor's theses are normally written in Arabic, but many theses in science and technology are written in English or French. Taking the universities as a whole, most of the academic fields are covered.

Professorial research may be carried out by individual professors, or by teams of professors on their own, without much help from the universities. Team research sometimes takes place in cooperation with professors of other Arab or foreign universities. Some universities have their own research funds, dispensed to professors by special committees. Professors may also apply to Arab and foreign foundations for research funds. There is an increasing demand for orienting research toward the heritage, problems, and resources of the Arab World, without neglecting basic research.

National science councils give grants to university professors or to universities in support of research projects that interest them. Some national councils have built and equipped their own laboratories, which are used by their own staff or by professors and graduate students doing research for them. In one or two cases this practice has resulted in duplication and sometimes in the neglect of university laboratories.

Student and faculty exchange. Most universities in the Arab states receive students from other Arab and Islamic countries and some students from non-Islamic countries of Europe, Asia, Africa, and the Americas. Many of them offer free tuition to a sizable portion of these students, sometimes including free board and lodging. According to data gathered from *Statistical Yearbook* (1973), individual Arab countries with the largest proportion of foreign students in the early 1970s were: Lebanon (the smallest country), 54 percent of total enrollment in 1972–73; Syria, 20 percent in 1970; Saudi Arabia, 16.7 percent in 1971–72; Algeria, 11.9 percent in 1969–70; Egypt, 7.5 percent in 1970; and Iraq, 7.4 percent in 1971–72. In 1970 the total number of foreign and Arab students in the six Arab countries (not their home countries) was 48,182, of which roughly nine tenths were Arab. In addition, there were 33,394 Arab students in forty-five non-Arab countries, bringing the total of Arab students studying away from their home countries to about 80,000. Normally, more than half of these are on full or partial scholarshps from their governments, universities, national science and research councils, private foundations, or international, regional, or bilateral agencies. In the rapidly developing Arab World, returning students, especially those from European and American universities, have little difficulty in finding employment. It is from individuals educated abroad that the main intellectual, artistic, and professional leadership has been drawn in the last half century.

The movement for the exchange of professors among Arab states is also extensive. It started in the 1930s when the Iraq Ministry of Education, in seeking to develop its professional colleges, agreed with the Egyptian Ministry of Education on a formula for deputing Egyptian university staff to teach in the colleges of Iraq. One of the first nonpolitical activities of the Arab League was the adoption of a cultural agreement calling for the exchange of students, teachers, and publications. Without the extensive exchange of professors that has taken place since the 1940s, the rapid increase in Arab universities and colleges would have been impossible. In this activity Egypt played the principal role. Its professors and university administrators helped found the Universities of Riyadh (Saudi Arabia), Kuwait, Libya, San'a (Yemen Arab

Republic), and the Higher Teachers College of Qatar. The University of Cairo opened a branch in Khartoum, and the University of Alexandria helped found the Beirut Arab University, both of which are closely tied to the mother universities in curricula and examinations, number of Egyptian academic staff, and authority to grant degrees. In fact, Egyptian higher education authorities have declared that one of the missions of the Egyptian universities is to train experts and teachers for service abroad, and that it is necessary that this be taken into account in their plans for university development.

An appreciable number of professors from Iraq, Syria, and Jordan are teaching in the universities of Kuwait and the gulf countries, Saudi Arabia, Libya, and the countries of North Africa. Many in North Africa are also participating in the Arabization movement by writing, translating, or adapting textbooks and helping in the coinage of scientific terminology. There is also a fairly large number of Arab professors and holders of higher degrees teaching in the countries of Europe and America, where some are engaged in front-line research.

Problems, Issues, and Trends

As earlier sections of this article point out, there have been many significant developments in Arab higher education in the period since World War II: extensive cultural cooperation, especially efforts by industrialized Arab countries in founding and staffing higher education institutions in less developed states and in Arabization of education in countries like Algeria and Morocco, where Western influence is still strong; the provision of grants and stipends to students in public universities; the tendency to train academic staff in Arab universities rather than abroad; the attempt to unify old Arab-Islamic and modern institutions of higher education; and the opportunity for development afforded by the sharp rise in national income from petroleum in no less than half the Arab countries. While these events have pro-

vided unprecedented opportunity and challenge to higher education, they have also created a number of problems, issues, and trends.

Rapid increase in enrollment. The growth of enrollment in Arab higher education was running at an average rate of 12.3 percent between 1960 and 1965 and 7.5 percent between 1965 and 1970, exceeding the world average in both instances. As a result, two sets of problems have arisen: (1) overproduction of university graduates in some countries and in certain fields, raising the specter of unemployment among university graduates, and (2) lowering of academic standards, mainly due to the failure of higher education facilities to keep pace with the growth of enrollment.

With respect to employment opportunities for university graduates, the total number of students graduating from higher institutions around 1970 was in excess of 56,000, of whom 32,500 were graduates of Egyptian institutions. The absorptive capacity of the job market varies from country to country according to their developmental needs and the newness of their higher education institutions. In this context the Arab countries can be grouped into three categories: recipients, donors, and both recipients and donors.

The recipient countries have so far been Algeria, Libya, and those of the Arabian peninsula—the North African countries mainly for assistance in the Arabization of government services and instruction, which has necessitated importation of teachers and specialists in Arabic from the eastern Arab countries. In the donor category have been Egypt, Syria, Jordan, and the educated Palestinians. Iraq and Lebanon are both donors and recipients. Early in the 1960s there was a comparatively large migration of university personnel out of Iraq. With recent expansion of its universities and plans to use the new high rise of oil income in development projects, Iraq has been trying—with some success— to attract this migrant talent back and to invite talented and highly qualified Arabs of other nationalities who have served in the countries of Western Europe and the Americas to accept teaching, research, and other positions in its institutions. Lebanese and foreign entrepreneurial companies, operating mainly in the countries of the Arabian peninsula, as well as governments and native companies of peninsula countries, have been recruiting a large number of Lebanese university graduates for service in the peninsula. Conversely, the American University of Beirut, the Université Saint Joseph, and the Beirut Arab University habitually invite foreign professors from the United States, England, France, Egypt, and other countries. Similarly, the numerous European and American companies and banks operating in Lebanon and the Middle East continue to import some of their own expert personnel. As their universities develop and their scholarship students return, the recipient countries may not continue to be recipients for long.

Enrollment in Humanities vs. Sciences

In nearly all the Arab states, enrollment in the humanities, the law, and the social sciences far outnumbers enrollment in the pure and applied sciences and technology. This situation is just the opposite of what the Arab World with its vast undeveloped resources needs. A number of countries adopted a policy of encouraging entry into the scientific and technological fields and of limiting entry into the humanistic and legal fields. A study of the distribution of students by fields of study in nine countries during the decade of the 1960s (Hassān, 1974) showed marked gains in enrollment in the science fields in six countries, with gains in the arts and legal fields in only three countries, which suggests that the discrepancy is gradually being eliminated. That the problem still persists, however, is shown by the fact that out of 56,000 students graduating in thirteen Arab countries around 1970, 35,000 were in arts, law, and business, and only 21,000 in science, medicine, agriculture, and the technological fields. Whatever unemployment exists is mainly in the nonscientific fields.

Five or six Arab countries have conducted manpower studies, with the Egyptian studies linked directly to education. A manpower committee working under the Egyptian National Planning Institute has produced manpower figures in fifty-two fields grouped into the following seven categories: managers, specialists, technicians and supervisors, assistant technicians, skilled labor, semiskilled labor, and unskilled labor (Hassān, 1974, pp. 137–141). Of the seven groups, the first three require some form of higher training, mainly in universities, colleges, and higher institutions. Taking 1960 as the base year, the committee projected the manpower needs in five-year periods up to 1985 and concluded that by 1985 Egypt will have to train about 150,000 managers, 500,000 specialists, and more than 1,000,000 technicians and supervisors. The expansion of the universities and independent colleges that has taken place and is being planned will probably meet the targets in the first two categories, but the present facilities for training technicians and supervisors are so much below the need as to represent a real bottleneck. The committee proposed three methods for increasing the number of trained technicians: (1) up-training present skilled manpower by special training courses, (2) providing five-year training courses for holders of the preparatory (junior high) school certificates, and (3) providing facilities for two- to three-year training for holders of the general secondary certificate.

Several other Arab countries have also concluded that lack of technicians and supervisors is one of the main factors retarding development. Accordingly, there is a trend toward establishment of more centers or institutes for the training of technicians, usually with a course lasting two years beyond the secondary school.

Lowering of academic standards. It is generally agreed by Arab higher education authorities that the increase in academic staff, classrooms, laboratories, and other facilities has not, in most universities, kept pace with the expansion of student enrollment and that, consequently, academic standards have suffered. Nowhere is this trend more apparent than in the student-teacher ratios reported by the Association of Arab Universities (1973a). The university-wide student-teacher ratios varied between 14 to 1 and 121 to 1 in the seventeen public universities for which figures were available for the academic year 1972–73. These ratios compare with 12.4 to 1 at the private American University of Beirut in 1974–75—probably the lowest ratio in the Arab area. The scientific and technological faculties fared much better than the faculties of arts, law, and business. Eight faculties of science had a range between 10 to 1 and 19 to 1. The remaining nine science faculties had a range between 21 to 1 and 87 to 1. By comparison, the faculties of arts in eight public universities had a range between 16 to 1 and 30 to 1. The remaining nine arts faculties had a range between 40 to 1 and 1059 to 1. These ratios do not take into account the demonstrators and assistant teachers, since most universities do not consider them teaching staff. Nevertheless, many universities are being obliged to use them for teaching purposes. The dearth of professors has given rise to the phenomenon of the "traveling professor," who divides his time between his own university and one or more others, concentrating his lecture hours in two or three days a week in each university and usually receiving additional compensation. This practice, of course, increases the teaching load of the professor at the expense of his research and the quality of his teaching. The implication is quite clear that the unrelenting pressure of students is seriously affecting academic standards in a number of universities. Information is not easily available for the growth rate of such university facilities as buildings, laboratories, and equipment, but in this respect the universities of the richer countries seem to be faring better.

How to reduce the pressure of students on the higher education institutions has preoccupied educational authorities for at least two decades. Various devices have been tried, such as limiting the number of students to be admitted each year or setting up age limits and other restrictive measures. Public pressure often succeeds in breaking these down. Many countries have founded two-year institutes of technological and other practical subjects in an attempt to divert part of the torrent of students to them, but this approach has not fully solved the problem.

As Akrawi (1975) has pointed out, the problem goes much deeper. It lies not only in the rapid expansion of primary and secondary education but also in the single-track and bookish quality of this education, which, by not preparing the student for life, leaves him no alternative other than seeking to enter the universities and academic colleges. Akrawi (1967, 1970, 1975) has proposed that, to be effective, reform should aim at creating a variety of educational avenues, starting with primary school, and that the educational systems, their organization, and their content should be rethought and reorganized. He has formulated a plan that would tend to reduce the pressure on the universities by providing students with many alternative choices from primary school through secondary school and middle college. Such an approach would not only help universities maintain their standards but, at the same time, enable the universities to help meet the developmental needs of the Arab countries.

Relevance of higher education to the needs of the modern Arab World. Modern Arab higher education is essentially borrowed from the West, as much in its organization as in its content and methods. The knowledge it presents to students stems mainly from Western research and experimentation, with a minimum attributable to research by Arab scholars. Consequently, the knowledge acquired by Arab students often has an abstract quality. The fact that schools and universities do transmit the Arab-Islamic culture through the study of religion, Arabic language and literature,

Islamic history of the Arab Near East, and study of the modern Arab World attenuates the alienating effects of its Western-oriented education. Nevertheless, it remains largely true that teaching of social and behavioral sciences, as well as agricultural, medical, public health, business, and industrial subjects, is based largely on knowledge drawn from Western sources.

What, then, can be done to enhance the indigenous character of higher education? Some of what is being done has already been noted; two other steps seem to be indicated. One is to develop at least a few of the present universities into centers of excellence that can educate—for academic service as well as for public and private enterprises—qualified men and women of the highest standard. Such graduates would have the advantage of being trained within the context of the culture, the problems, and the needs of their countries. The fact that some universities are now rushing to set up master's and doctoral programs without adequate preparation is bound to result in second-rate graduates and academic staff. The second is to ensure that a substantial part of the studies and of professorial and graduate student research is concerned with national situations, problems, needs, and resources. Nearly all the disciplines cultivated at the universities have regional, national, and local aspects, with all their ramifications, whether in the pure and applied sciences or in the humanistic, social, and behavioral sciences, or even in the professional medical, technological, agricultural, legal, educational, and business fields. As research in these areas increases, its accumulated findings will percolate to the undergraduate and graduate courses offered by the universities and colleges—indeed, to secondary and even elementary education. Only then can it be claimed that higher education and its institutions have been acclimatized to the Arab environment. The attainment of these two goals to a satisfactory degree will probably preoccupy the Arab university authorities throughout the remaining twenty-five years of the twentieth century.

Student movements and participation. Crises in modern Arab history are often reflected in the universities and their students, resulting in demonstrations, strikes, and similar disruptive activities. In the days of foreign occupations and mandates over the Arab World, student activities were mostly directed against foreign occupations. As the Arab countries became independent and political parties sprang up within them, student groups became one of the powerful arms of such parties. This politization had a divisive influence on the student body, often disrupting studies at the universities. Some governments extended control and direction of the student movements through the device of a national union of students, which in turn was under the guidance and coordination of an office of youth welfare—an agency of the government subject to government policy. As a result, student strikes and demonstrations were reduced to a minimum. Students have their own councils and committees to control all student activities in their institutions, which constitutes a kind of conditional student government.

The call for student participation in university policymaking and decision making started in the decade from 1965 to 1975 as a reflection of happenings in Europe and the United States and of some tendencies in Soviet education. Perhaps the best example is in Lebanon, where student groups are divided by type of university and by political party. Student groups in the universities and other higher institutions are affiliated with a national union of students, which has been preoccupied with Arab and Lebanese national and social problems, using demonstrations and strikes as a method of realizing its demands where necessary.

Some universities and some countries have experimented with student participation through a university-wide student council, branch student committees in the faculties, and student representation in faculty and departmental meetings and in curriculum, disciplinary, scholarship, and even examination committees. In one or two countries students are represented on the university council or senate. In Lebanon the student council of the Lebanese University has played a role in protecting the autonomy of the university and in applying pressure for the establishment of new professional faculties at the university in order to provide poor students with an opportunity to enter the medical, engineering, and agricultural professions without having to pay the high tuition fees charged by the private universities.

Impact of New Situations in the Arab World

The rapid growth of oil revenues, estimated at about fifty billion dollars in 1974, has created new opportunities for development in the Arab states. The idea is now widespread that oil-rich states should use their wealth to achieve the status of an advanced nation by the year 2000—before the oil dries up—and that they should work out good relationships with the developing as well as the developed countries of the world. About half of the Arab states have oil reserves and substantial oil revenues. Current thinking is that these states should not only take determined steps to develop themselves but also to assist in the development of the remaining Arab states through investments, loans, or outright gifts. In addition, they should assist the developing nations of Asia and Africa and pump back funds into the economies of the advanced countries, partly by contracting with them for big Arab development projects and partly by investments in these countries. This assistance and development needs careful planning. In the October 18–19, 1974, Beirut newspaper *al-Nahar,* President Houari Boumédiene of Algeria asserted that planning on the state level is no longer adequate, advocating comprehensive planning embracing all the Arab area.

What are the implications to Arab higher education of the sharp rise of the oil revenues and the new situation that it has created in the Arab states? One is quantitative expansion. The United Nations demographic division estimates that by the year 2000 the population of the Arab World will exceed three hundred million. If the increase in higher education enrollment were to be estimated conservatively as rising from an enrollment ratio of 0.4 percent to 1.0 percent between 1970 and the year 2000, this would mean enrollment of more than three million students. Since the enrollment in 1975 was less than half a million, it will take careful planning to avoid lowering of academic standards.

The adverse effects of the rapid expansion on academic standards have already been noted. There has been a call for their improvement by such means as preparation and selection of academic staff, higher salary scales and other incentives, and better libraries, laboratories, field facilities, and workshops. Akrawi (1967, 1970, 1975) has argued that a satisfactory standard of excellence cannot be attained without maintaining cooperative relationships with the outstanding universities of the advanced world through such means as exchange of graduate students, professors, publications, and educators to help in planning curricula and research. In return, promising Arab professors, lecturers, and instructors should be sent to cooperating universities of the advanced countries for further research and teaching experience. A regular shuttle of academic personnel should be maintained to ensure the continuous flow of new ideas, discoveries, and curricular practices. Arab higher education should eventually aim at nothing less than producing manpower of excellence at the technician, professional, and advanced research levels. Its internal academic arrangements and facilities should be such as to encourage its best professors, through maturation of scholarship and field experience, to become experts of world caliber in their fields. One major step that can be taken to ensure high-quality education is to require students entering an Arab university to have a good command of at least one of the two modern languages current in the Arab world—namely, English and French.

The new world role of the Arab countries necessitates that Arab universities foster the study of foreign languages and cultures—Western, Asiatic, or African. Some Arab universities have already started to move in this direction. The University of Khartoum has created an Institute of African Studies, and Tunisia has established the Bourguiba Institute of Languages. Conversely, some universities have established centers for the teaching of Arabic as a foreign language.

Three practices relative to languages of instruction are followed in the Arab World: (1) teaching almost entirely in a foreign language, which prevails mainly in the three foreign universities; (2) teaching the scientific, mathematical, and technological subjects largely in a foreign language and the humanistic, social, and behavioral sciences in Arabic; (3) teaching entirely in Arabic, which was pioneered by the University of Damascus in the early 1920s and now prevails in all the Syrian universities and in some newer Arab countries, such as Libya and the Yemen Arab Republic.

The legal position in nearly all the Arab states is that Arabic is the language of instruction in the universities, but that the university authorities may decide to teach some courses in a foreign language when necessary. This position has had the effect of sanctioning, if not encouraging, the continuation of the two-edged practice of teaching scientific subjects in a foreign language and humanistic subjects in Arabic. Most writers on the subject insist that the national interest requires that teaching on the university level be in Arabic, pointing out that Arabic is the language of a whole civilization and, at one time, was able to express adequately all the scientific, philosophical, legal, and social ideas. It is one of the main functions of the universities, through teaching in Arabic, to develop this

language so that it becomes an adequate vehicle for the transmission of the modern sciences. The very character of Arabic gives it a flexibility that opens opportunities to use the thousands of derivatives to express adequately the various concepts and nuances of modern thought. Moreover, neoclassical Arabic is the only language that provides a common basis of understanding and unity among Arab peoples spread out over a wide area, from the Arabian gulf to the Atlantic Ocean. Finally, Arabic culture can be expressed and disseminated to the Arab masses only through the one language they understand: Arabic.

At the same time, teaching in Arabic should not mean diminishing knowledge of modern foreign languages. Proficiency in these languages would enable students to go directly to the foreign source of knowledge during their periods of study at the universities and to continue to grow professionally after their graduation. Except for those who come to the universities from a few private schools, Arab students are rarely able to read foreign source materials. Consequently, there is a call for strengthening teaching of foreign languages in the secondary schools. The University of Damascus has established a special institute for the teaching of English, French, Russian, and German. No student in any of the faculties of the university is granted a first degree unless he produces a certificate verifying that he has successfully passed the examination of the institute. At the Second General Conference of Arab Universities and Contemporary Arab Society (Association of Arab Universities, 1973b), it was proposed that each faculty or institute of the university specify at least one subject in which a foreign language will be used in teaching, in examinations, and in reference reading.

While the above arguments are largely justified, the common practice of teaching the physical sciences in a foreign language and the humanistic and social sciences in Arabic is not a satisfactory one. It accentuates the gap between what has been called the two cultures—the scientific and the humanistic—producing two sets of Arab thinkers, one thinking scientifically in a foreign language, the other thinking humanistically and socially in Arabic. The two would not only find it difficult to understand each other, but most scientists would experience difficulty in transmitting their knowledge to their people in Arabic. A compromise approach might be found in providing instruction in all fields mainly in Arabic and partially in one foreign language. To arrive at this goal, one possible practice would be to begin teaching one or two subjects a year in a foreign language, starting with the last two years of secondary school and continuing through the university. The subjects could be varied from year to year to ensure that students have mastered their specialty before graduation in two languages. There are, of course, other methods of achieving bilingualism in Arab higher education, and bold experimentation in this area is called for.

Bibliography

Ahwani, A. F. *al-Tarbiya fil-Islam.* Cairo: Issa al-Babi al-Halabi, 1955.

Akrawi, M. "The University Tradition in the Middle East." In *The University and the Man of Tomorrow: The Centennial Lectures.* Beirut: American University of Beirut, 1967.

Akrawi, M. "The University and Government in the Middle East." In C. Nader and A. Zahlan (Eds.), *Science and Technology in Developing Countries.* Cambridge, England: Cambridge University Press, 1969.

Akrawi, M. "Dawr al-jami'at fil-hayat al-'Arabiya al-mu'asira." In *Al-Mawsim al-thaqafi li-jami'at al-Kuwait.* Khaldieh, Kuwait: Kuwait University, 1970.

Akrawi, M. "The Teaching Process in the Faculty of Arts and Sciences of the American University of Beirut, Lebanon." In V. G. Onushkin (Ed.), *Planning the Development of Universities—III.* Paris: UNESCO, 1974.

Akrawi, M. "Tathmir al-'aidat al-petroliya al-'Arabiya fil-inma' al-tarbawi wal-thaqafi al-'Arabi." In H. Sa'ab (Ed.), *Tathmir al-aidat al-petroliya fil-inma' al-'Arabi.* Beirut: Development Studies Association, 1975.

Association of Arab Universities. *Bayan ihsa'i bi-a'dad al-tullab wa a'da' hay'at al-tadris bil-jami'at al-'Arabiya.* Cairo: Association of Arab Universities, 1973a.

Association of Arab Universities. *Al-Mu'tamar al-'am al-thani lil-jami'at al-'Arabiya wal-mujtama' al-'Arabi al-mu'asir.* Cairo: Cairo University Press, 1973b.

Borg, T., and others. *The Institute of Languages and Translation, al-Azhar University: A Review of Programs with Guidelines for Future Development.* Cairo: Institute of Languages and Translation, n.d. (In English and Arabic.)

Bowles, F., and others. *Sudan: Higher Education.* Serial No. 3066/RMO.RD/EHT. Paris: UNESCO, 1974.

Budair, A. A. F. *Al-Amir Ahmad Fu'ad wa nash'at al-jami'a al-misriya.* Cairo: Fuad I University Press, 1950.

Dodge, B. *The American University of Beirut: A Brief History of the University and the Lands Which It Serves.* Beirut: Kayat's, 1950.

Dodge, B. *Muslim Education in Medieval Times.* Washington, D.C.: Middle East Institute, 1962.

Dodge, B. *Al-Azhar: A Millenium of Muslim Learning.* Memorial edition. Washington, D.C.: Middle East Institute, 1974.

Dujaili, H. *Taqaddum al-ta'lim al-'ali fil-'Iraq.* Baghdad, Iraq: Irshad Press, 1963.

Egyptian National Institute of Planning. *Takhtit al-quwa al-'amila fil-jumhuriya al-'Arabiya al-muttahida.* (2 vols.) Cairo: Egyptian Institute, 1966–1971.

al-Ghannam, M. A. *Qadiyat al-'ard wal-talab fi khirriji al-jami'at fil-Iraq.* Baghdad, Iraq: University of Baghdad, 1967.

al-Ghannam, M. A., and Omar, H. R. *Wastage in Higher Education in the Arab Republic of Egypt.* Beirut: Regional Centre for Educational Planning and Administration in the Arab Countries, n.d.

Ghusayni, R. "Student Activism at Lebanon's Universities." Unpublished Ph.D. Dissertation, Stanford University, 1974.

al-Hamdani, M. *A Comparison Between Two Arab Universities: Khartoum University and Baghdad University.* Baghdad: Educational Research Center, University of Baghdad, n.d.

Hassan, M. M. *Tatwir khutat al-ta'lim fi daw'al-ma'raka wa 'alaqatuha bil-quwa al-'amila: al-Ta'lim al-'ali wal-jami'i.* Cairo: Cairo University Press, 1974.

Iraq Minisry of Higher Education and Scientific Research. *Kitab al-mu'tamer al-awwal lil-ta'lim al-jami'i fil-Iraq.* Baghdad: Local Government Press, n.d.

Iraq Ministry of Higher Education and Scientific Research. *Ijtima'at ta'lim al-'ulum al-sirfa.* Baghdad: Iraq Ministry, 1971.

Iraq Ministry of Higher Education and Scientific Research. *Taqrir halaqat takhtit al-ta'lim al-'ali fil-Iraq.* Baghdad: Local Government Press, 1971.

Isma'il, H. M. "Formation of the Teaching Staff at Cairo University." In V. G. Onushkin (Ed.), *Planning the Development of Universities—III.* Paris: UNESCO, 1974.

Al-Kitab al-dhahabi: Jami'at al-qarawiyyin fi dhikr-aha al-mi'a ba'd al-alf. Rabat, Morocco: Ministry of National Education, n.d.

League of Arab States, Directorate of Culture. *Mushkilat al-ta'lim al-jami'i fil-bilad al-'Arabiya.* Cairo: Atlas Press, n.d.

Matthews, R. D., and Akrawi, M. *Education in Arab Countries of the Near East.* Washington, D.C.: American Council on Education, 1949.

Matveyev, A., Adamson, C., and Bose, S. K. *Arab Republic of Egypt: The Feasibility of Establishing Technical Universities in the Arab Republic of Egypt.* Paris: UNESCO, 1972.

Qubain, F. I. *Education and Science in the Arab World.* Baltimore: Johns Hopkins University Press, 1966.

République tunisienne. *IVᵉ plan de développement économique et social, 1973–1976.* (2 vols.) Tunis, Tunisia: Imprimerie Société l'action d'édition et de presse, 1973.

Rifa'i, N. "Access to the University of Damascus, Syrian Arab Republic, and the Employment of Graduates." In V. G. Onushkin (Ed.), *Planning the Development of Universities—III.* Paris: UNESCO, 1974.

Rybnikov, K. A. *Iraq: Development and Reform of Higher Education.* Paris: UNESCO, 1971.

el-Sa'id, S. M. *The Expansion of Higher Education in the United Arab Republic.* Cairo: Cairo University Press, 1960.

Shalaby, A. *History of Muslim Education,* Beirut: Dar al-Kashshaf, 1954. (Also in Arabic: *Tarikh al-tarbiya al-Islamiya.*)

Sa'udi Arabia, Ministry of Education, Statistical Section. *Progress of Education in Sa'udi Arabia/380–1932 A.H., 1960–1972 A.D.* Riyadh, Saudia Arabia: Ministry of Education, 1973. (In Arabic and English.)

al-Sayyid, A. A. *Al-Ta'lim al-'ali: Mushkilatuhu wa usus takhtītihi.* Cairo: University of Cairo Press, 1963. (Also in English and French).

al-Shamma', K. *Dirasat tandhim jami'at Baghdad.* (2 vols.) Baghdad, 'Iraq: University of Baghdad, 1967.

Statistical Yearbook, 1972. Paris: UNESCO, 1973.

Supreme Council of the Universities of the UAR. *Mudhakkira fi sha'n al-malamih al-ra'isiya lil-siyassa al-muqtaraha lil-ta'lim al-jami'i.* Cairo: Cairo University Press, 1967.

Supreme Council of the Universities of the UAR. *Mu'tamarat al-ta'lim al-jami'i wal-'ali: al-Taqrīr.* Cairo: Ain Shams University Press, 1967.

Supreme Council of the Universities of the UAR. *Al-Nadwa al-'ilmiya 'an al-idara al-jāmi'iya.* Cairo: Ain Shams and Cairo University Presses, 1970.

Syrian Arab Republic, Ministry of Higher Education. *Al-Mu'tamar al-tarbawi li-tatwir al-ta'lim al-'ali wal-jami'i.* (2 vols.) Damascus, Syria: Damascus University Press, 1971.

Totah, K. *The Contributions of the Arabs to Education.* New York: Columbia University Teachers College, 1926.

Tritton, A. S. *Materials on Muslim Education in the Middle Ages.* London: Luzac, 1957.

United Arab Republic, Ministry of Higher Education. *Al-Ta'lim al-'ali fi 12 sana.* Cairo: Ministry of Higher Education, 1964.

United Arab Republic: Reform and Development of Higher Education. Paris: UNESCO, 1969.

University of Baghdad. *Dirasat fil-takhtit al-jami'i.* Baghdad, Iraq: Government Press, 1965.

Waardenburg, J. J. *Les universités dans le monde arabe actuel.* (2 vols.) Paris and The Hague: Mouton, 1966.

MATTA AKRAWI

See also: Algeria, Democratic and Popular Republic of; Egypt, Arab Republic of; Jordan, Hashemite Kingdom of; Lebanon, Republic of; Libyan Arab Republic; Morocco, Kingdom of; Qatar, State of; Saudi Arabia, Kingdom of; Sudan, Democratic Republic of the; Syrian Arab Republic; Tunisia, Republic of; Yemen Arab Republic; Yemen, People's Democratic Republic of.

ARCHEOLOGY (Field of Study)

Archeology attempts to reconstruct the human past through the retrieval, preservation, and interpretation of man's remains. Tombs and skeletons, pots and pollen, temples, texts, and tephra are the data that the archeologist uses to re-create history. Usually, however, an archeologist emphasizes just one approach to antiquity. For example, he may study a single geographical region as it changes over a long period of time; he may study a culture common to several geographical areas; or he may specialize in technical and formal studies of the design and function of artifacts. Regional studies such as Egyptology or Near Eastern or Meso-American archeology require broad understanding of geographically discrete areas. Studies of this type demand a knowledge of the many cultures, languages, and art forms which existed together or succeeded one another. For example, a Near Eastern archeologist might be concerned with developing taxonomies and typologies for the remains of a series of sites in modern Iraq and Iran. He will determine which objects or languages or social systems or entire cultures may be termed Sumerian, Akkadian, Assyrian, Babylonian, and Elamite. Examples of the study of single cultures which spread over broad geographical areas are Byzantine archeology, Islamic archeology, and Classical archeology. Here the concern is with the historical growth, development, and change of a particular culture. Examples of formal and technical specialties devoted to understanding the design and function of artifacts are lithic and ceramic technologies (the analysis of stone working and pottery making).

Since 1925 interdependence among these three major ways of seeing the past has grown, and archeology has become more dependent on other disciplines—particularly the disciplines of science and technology. Sophisticated information systems, for example, have enabled archeologists to acquire, store, retrieve, manipulate, and model data to an extent undreamed of in the 1940s. Moreover, chemistry and physics are now used routinely to test an artifact's composition and date, and dendrochronology and palynology provide absolute dating methods that permit correlations among strata, artifacts, and real time. In addition, contemporary ecological studies provide available models for understanding settlement patterns and potential explanations for subsistence strategies. Political geography provides models for the distribution of towns and the development of trade; and anthropology, ethnography, and sociology contribute analogies that are used to explain past human behaviors when no written record exists.

Archeology was not originally an academic discipline; until the nineteenth century it was antiquarianism, practiced by "amateurs," men of means and leisure who traveled to lands of ancient high cultures and collected monuments and movable treasure. Those who could not travel abroad turned to the cairns, mounds, and other standing monuments within their own borders and wrote local histories and joined a national society for the presentation of papers and the discussion of ideas. The Society of Dillettanti, for example, founded in England about 1734, sponsored James Stuart and Nicholas Revett's survey of Athenian monuments, published in 1762 as *The Antiquities of Athens*. The oldest archeological society in the Soviet Union, the Imperial Odessa Society of History and Antiquity, was founded in 1839 to study the classical antiquity of the Black Sea region.

As they became more learned, these antiquarians contributed much to the formation of specialized museums. Private collections and those of the societies themselves, moreover, contributed to the development of museums to display and preserve antiquities. The British Museum opened in 1759; the *Nationalmuseet* (National Museum) of Copenhagen was founded in 1807; and the Kerch State Historico-Archaeological Museum in the Soviet Union was founded in 1826. The acquisitive policies of museums, growing royal patronage, and eventual government sponsorship led to the development of research institutes with professional staffs. The *Académie des inscriptions et belles-lettres*, founded in Paris in 1663 to choose inscriptions for medals and dedications for royal monuments, had become a research body by 1701. Its publication *Journal des savants* first appeared in 1665 and is still being published.

The German Archeological Society in Rome became the Joint German-Italian Institute of Archeological Correspondence in 1829. Upon its takeover by the state it became, in 1870, the *Deutsches archäologisches Institut*. From the late nineteenth century on, the *Prüssische Akademie der Wissenschaften zu Berlin* sponsored such works as the *Corpus of Inscriptions*, the *Corpus of Ancient Pottery*, and the *Catalogue of Sarcophagi*. In the 1850s an Imperial Archaeological Commission within the Ministry of the Court of St. Petersburg was created to issue excavation permits and oversee archeological remains, and in 1877 the first Archaeological Institute was established, also at St. Petersburg.

Simultaneously, archeology began to develop as an academic discipline. In 1831 Jean François Champollion, who deciphered the Rosetta stone, was elected to the first European chair of Egyptology at the *Collège de France*. In the 1880s a British professorship of Classical archeology was established at Oxford. In the United States the Smithsonian Institution was founded in 1846, followed by the Peabody Museum of Archaeology and Ethnology at Harvard University (one of the first United States institutions employing full-time archeologists) in 1866 and the Bureau of American Ethnography in 1879. In 1886 Daniel G. Brinton became the first professor of American archeology at an American university, the University of Pennsylvania. He was followed by Frederic Ward Putnam at Harvard University in 1887; Putnam was also instrumental in establishing departments of anthropology which were integrated with archeology at the University of California at Los Angeles and at New York's American Museum of Natural History. At the turn of the century, Franz Boas at Columbia University was training the first generation of graduate students in anthropology. Among them were Alfred L. Kroeber, Edward Sapir, Robert H. Lowie, and Ruth Bunzel.

Despite the growth of societies, museums, expeditions, and academic chairs, archeology before the mid nineteenth century lacked an adequate theoretical framework. The major obstacle to the development of such a theory was the generally accepted belief, in the West at least, that the earth and its people had not changed since the world was created except for some modification caused by the Biblical flood. The antiquity of the world was dated to 4004 B.C., and every object discovered was attributed to a known historical group: the Gauls, the Angles, the Goths, or the Slavs.

The impetus for change in this theocentric view arose from the work of geologists and geographers. In the late eighteenth century, the Scottish geologist James Hutton first advanced the theory of uniformitarianism, the belief that the forces creating the geographical features of the earth's surface today are the same natural forces that operated in antiquity. Integral to this theory is stratigraphy, the view that the layers of the earth's surface were laid down sequentially, the oldest at greater relative depth from the surface than the most recent. In 1830–1833 Charles Lyell published his *Principles of Geology*, which established the theory of uniformitarianism as part of archeology. Somewhat later, following the work of the Danish scientists C. J. Thomsen (1788–1865) and Jens Jacob Asmussen Worssae (1821–1885), the three-stage chronological division of ancient cultures into Stone, Bronze, and Iron Ages became widely accepted. This system, familiar to the ancient Romans, Greeks, and Chinese but lost to Christendom for almost two millennia, is still in use today.

Further proof of the antiquity of humanity occurred with the discovery of fossil bones and artifacts associated with extinct fauna: the excavation of the Brixham Cave by a committee from the Royal and Geographical Societies in 1858–59; the discoveries of Jacques Boucher de Crèvecœur de Perthes in the Somme Valley in 1837; the discovery of Neanderthal fossils in Germany in 1857; and Charles Darwin's fossil studies and experiments, culminating in the publication in 1859 of *On the Origin of Species by Means of Natural Selection*.

Three recent developments in archeology deserve special mention. First is the use of thermoluminescence, carbon 14, amino acid racemization, sonar, and radar to date and help recover objects. Of perhaps equal importance has been the influence on archeology of social anthropology's theories of cultural relativity. Consequently, the tendency to read modern Western motives and values into ancient cultures is gradually being abandoned. Finally, there continues to be a change in the training of archeologists. Fieldwork—that is, participation in actual excavation under professional guidance—is gradually becoming a major part of postbaccalaureate education.

Formal education and training in archeology is well developed in Western Europe, North America, and the Soviet Union. In Europe emphasis is placed on geology and biology; on prehistory; on exact observation of detail, measurement, and the inductive method. In the United States, however, archeology is often considered part of anthropology. In the Soviet Union it is taught as a tool of history and defined, therefore, as the science of human social development governed by a single Marxist law.

The basic pattern of education almost everywhere, however, begins at the postbaccalaureate level. Students earning advanced degrees specialize in a geographical area, a time period, or a particular technical aspect of archeology. Ancillary studies involve biology, ecology, art history, ancient languages, and religion. Advanced graduate students may assume the responsibilities for conducting excavations. The pattern of graduate training follows the classical tradition established in most disciplines in European universities and imported to the Americas, North Africa, the Near East, and the Indian subcontinent by visiting scholars, missionaries, and colonialists.

Yet with all this specialized training there is a tendency to bring archeology back into the public forum. Therefore, recent educational innovation includes emphasis on adult education courses, training of "amateurs" to do technical work, professionals serving as advisers to amateur archeological societies, and public lectures and courses sponsored by museums and archeological associations. Increasing urbanization and the consequent destruction of monuments, the growth of nationalism, and the treatment of archeological remains as nonrenewable resources and irreplaceable cultural patrimony have resulted in greater public participation in and support

for the field in all countries. The greatest need in education today is for cooperation between archeologists and the public to preserve our common heritage.

MARY KATHLEEN BROWN

Levels and Programs of Study

Programs in archeology generally require as a minimum prerequisite a secondary education and lead to the following degrees: bachelor's (B.A.), master's (M.A.), the doctorate (Ph.D.), or their equivalents. Programs deal with the study of the material remains of man's past and consist primarily of classroom sessions, group discussion, and research.

Programs that lead to a first university degree usually include some of the following courses: the general history and development of archeology, archeological terminology, archeological problems, archeological records, archeological classification, professional archeology, the techniques and principles of excavation, methods of assigning dates, typology, the study of civilizations, the development of archeological techniques, and classical and medieval sciences. Background courses usually include ancient history, the natural sciences, world literature, foreign languages, philosophy, economics, and sociology.

Programs that lead to a postgraduate university degree emphasize research work as substantiated by the presentation of a scholarly thesis or dissertation. Principal subject matter areas in which courses and research projects tend to fall include the general history and development of archeology, archeological records, archeological classification and terminology, the materials and techniques of archeology, research techniques in archeology, and civilizations (for example, early man or the New World prior to urban civilization). Emphasis is frequently placed on practical work in museums and the interpretation of artifacts. Participation in excavation and exploration may be an essential feature of the program. Subject areas within which background studies tend to fall include ancient history, the natural sciences, world literature, foreign languages, and philosophy.

[This section was based on UNESCO's *International Standard Classification of Education (ISCED)* (Paris: UNESCO, 1976).]

Major International and National Organizations

INTERNATIONAL

Association of Roman Ceramic Archaeologists
Rei Cretariae Romanae Fautores (RCRF)
Museum Kamstraat 45
Nijmegen, Netherlands

International Association for Classical
   Archaeology
49 Piazza San Marco
00186 Rome, Italy

International Centre for the Study of the
   Preservation and Restoration of Cultural
   Property
256 via Cavour
00184 Rome, Italy

International Council of Monuments and Sites
   (ICOMOS)
Conseil international des monuments et des
   sites
Hôtel Saint Aignan
75 rue de Temple
75003 Paris, France

International Council of Museums (ICOM)
Conseil international des musées
UNESCO House
7 place de Fontenoy
75015 Paris, France

International Federation of the Societies of
   Classical Studies
11 avenue René Coty
75014 Paris, France

International Institute for the Conservation of
   Historic and Artistic Works
608 Grand Buildings
Trafalgar Square
London WC2N 5HN, England

International Union of Prehistoric and
   Protohistoric Sciences
Union internationale des sciences
   préhistoriques et protohistoriques
Universiteitsstraat 16
9000 Ghent, Belgium

NATIONAL

Algeria:
   Société archéologique du département de
     Constantine
   Musée Gustave Mercier
   Constantine

Belgium:
   Société royale d'archéologie de Bruxelles
   Musée de la Porte de Hal
   Brussels

Bolivia:
   Sociedad arqueológica de Bolivia
   avenida Chacaltava 500, Casilla 1587
   La Paz

Bulgaria:
   Archäologisches Institut der bulgarischen
     Akademie der Wissenschaften
   ul. Stamboliiski 2
   Sofia

Cuba:
   Junta nacional de arqueología y etnología
   Palacio Condé Lombillo
   Plaza de la Catedral
   Havana

Egypt:
   Société d'archéologie copte
   222 avenue Ramses
   al-Abbassiah
   Cairo

Federal Republic of Germany:
   Archäologische Gesellschaft zu Berlin
   Schlossstrasse 1
   1 Berlin 19 (Charlottenburg)

Finland:
   Finnische Altertumsgesellschaft
   Nationalmuseum
   Mannerheimintie 34
   00100 Helsinki 10

France:
   Société française d'archéologie
   Palais de Chaillot
   75116 Paris

Greece:
   Archaeologiki hetairia
   135 Panepistimiou 22
   Athens

Iceland:
   Islenzka fornleifafélag, Hid
   Postfach 1439
   Reykjavík

India:
   Archaeological Survey of India
   New Delhi 11

Israel:
  Israel Association of Archaeologists
  P.O.B. 586
  Jerusalem

Italy:
  Associazione archeologica romana
  Piazza Cenci 56
  Rome

Japan:
  Nippon kokogakkai
  % Tokyo National Museum
  Ueno Park
  Tokyo

Panama:
  Comisión nacional de arqueología y
    monumentos históricos
  Panama City

Peru:
  Patronato nacional de arqueología
  11° piso del Edificio del Ministerio de
    educación pública
  Lima

Poland:
  Polskie towarzystwo archeologiczne
  ul. Jezuická 6
  Warsaw

Portugal:
  Associação dos arqueólogos
    portuguêses
  Largo do Carmo
  Lisbon

Saudi Arabia:
  Arab Archaeological Society
  Mecca

South Africa:
  South African Archaeological Association
  5 Alfred Road
  Rondebosch (Cape Province)

Switzerland:
  Schweizerische Gesellschaft für Ur- und
    Frühgeschichte
  Rheinsprung 20
  4001 Basel

Turkey:
  Türk tarih kurumu
  Kizilay Sok 1
  Ankara

United Kingdom:
  British Archaeological Association
  % History of Art Department, Birkbeck
    College
  Malet Street
  London WC1, England

United States:
  Archaeological Institute of America
  260 West Broadway
  New York, New York 10013

Uruguay:
  Sociedad de amigos de arqueología
  Buenos Aires 652, Casilla 399
  Montevideo

For a list of national organizations concerned with archeology see:

The Archaeologists' Year Book 1973–74: An International Directory of Archaeology and Anthropology. Park Ridge, New Jersey: Noyes Press, 1973.

Minerva, Wissenschaftliche Gesellschaften. Berlin, Federal Republic of Germany: de Gruyter, 1972.

Principal Information Sources

GENERAL

Guides to literature in the field include:

Cone, C. A. *Guide to Cultural Anthropology.* Glenview, Illinois: Scott, Foresman, 1969. Deutsches archäologisches Institut. *Römische Abteilung Bibliothek.* Boston: Hall, 1969. A major bibliographical source for archeology.

Harvard University, Peabody Museum of Archaeology and Ethnology. *Catalogue of the Library.* (54 vols.) Boston: Hall, 1963. Supplement 1 (12 vols.), 1970; Supplement 2, 1971; Supplement 3 (7 vols.), 1975.

White, C. M., and others. (Eds.) *Sources of Information in the Social Sciences.* (2nd ed.) Chicago: American Library Association, 1973. Pp. 307–374. Includes sources on archeology and anthropology.

Some introductions to archeology are:

Childe, V. G. *A Short Introduction to Archaeology.* London: Muller, 1956.

Clark, G. *Archaeology and Society.* Cambridge, Massachusetts: Harvard University Press, 1957.

Piggott, S. *Approach to Archaeology.* London: Black, 1959.

Wheeler, M. *Archaeology from the Earth.* Oxford, England: Clarendon Press, 1954.

Wooley, L. *Digging Up the Past.* Harmondsworth, Middlesex, England: Penguin, 1956.

Some histories of archeology are provided by:

Clark, G. *World Prehistory: A New Outline.* (2nd ed.) Cambridge, England: Cambridge University Press, 1969. Provides an outline of man's prehistory.

Daniel, G. E. *The Origins and Growth of Archaeology.* New York: Crowell, 1967.

Eydoux, H. P. *In Search of Lost Worlds: The Story of Archaeology.* New York: World, 1971.

Marek, K. *Gods, Graves, and Scholars.* New York: Knopf, 1951.

CURRENT BIBLIOGRAPHIES

The following sources and abstracts provide current coverage of the field of archeology:

Abstracts of New World Archaeology. Washington, D.C.: Society for American Archaeology, 1960–.

Annuario bibliografico di archeologia. Modena, Italy: Società tipografica modenese, 1954–.

Archäologische Bibliographie: Beilage zum Jahrbuch des Deutschen archäologischen Instituts. Berlin, Federal Republic of Germany: de Gruyter, 1914–.

Art and Archaeology Technical Abstracts. New York: New York University Press, 1966–.

Art Index. New York: Wilson, 1929–.

Bibliographie annuelle de l'âge de la pierre taillée paléolithique et mésolithique. Paris: Bureau de recherches géologiques, géophysiques et minières, 1958–.

British Archaeological Abstracts. London: Council for British Archaeology, 1968–.

Bulletin signalétique. Section 525: *Préhistoire;* Section 526: *Art et archéologie.* Paris: Centre national de la recherche scientifique, 1961–.

COWA Surveys and Bibliographies. Cambridge, Massachusetts: Council for Old World Archaeology, 1958–. A biennial publication providing a series of area reports on current archeological activity in some twenty-two areas.

I.I.C. Abstracts: Abstracts of the Technical Literature on Archaeology and the Fine Arts. London: International Institute for Conservation of Historic Artistic Works, 1955–.

Répertoire d'art et d'archéologie. Paris: Morancé, 1910–.

PERIODICALS

Some of the important journals in the field are: *Acta Archaeologica* (Hungary), *American Antiquity, American Journal of Archaeology, Antiquaries Journal* (UK), *Antiquity* (UK), *Archaeological News Letter* (UK), *Archaeology* (US), *Archäologischer Anzeiger* (FRG), *Archeologia* (Italy), *Art and Archaeology Newsletter* (US), *Buried History* (Australia), *Prehistoric Society Proceedings* (UK), *Revue archéologique* (France), *Sovetskaia arkheologiia* (USSR), *Zeitschrift für schweizerische Archäologie und Kunstgeschichte/Revue suisse d'art et d'archéologie* (Switzerland).

For additional titles see:

Bruns, G., and others. (Eds.) *Deutsches archäologisches Institut: Zeitschriftenverzeichnis.* Wiesbaden, Federal Republic of Germany: Steiner Verlag, 1964.

Catalogo dei periodici della biblioteca dell'Istituto nazionale di archeologia e storia dell'arte. Rome: Palombi, 1947.

Indici dei periodici attivi. Modena, Italy: Società tipografica modenese, 1956. Supplements *Catalogo dei periodici* listed above.

ENCYCLOPEDIAS, DICTIONARIES, HANDBOOKS

Cottrell, L. (Ed.) *The Concise Encyclopedia of Archaeology.* New York: Hawthorn, 1960.

Dictionnaire archéologique des techniques. Paris: Editions de l'Accueil, 1963. Provides articles on techniques for the field.

Ebert, M. *Reallexikon der Vorgeschichte.* Berlin, Federal Republic of Germany: de Gruyter, 1924–1932.

Filip, J. *Enzyklopädisches Handbuch zur Ur- und Frühgeschichte Europas.* Stuttgart, Federal Republic of Germany: Kohlhammer, 1966–.

Reau, L. *Dictionnaire polyglotte des termes d'art et d'archéologie.* Paris: Presses universitaires de France, 1953. A useful polyglot dictionary for the field.

Some useful handbooks and manuals for the field are:

Cotter, J. L. *Handbook for Historical Archaeology.* Philadelphia: n.p., 1968.

Déchelette, J. *Manuel d'archéologie préhistorique, celtique et gallo-romaine.* Paris: Picard, 1924–1934.

Furon, R. *Manuel de préhistoire générale, géologe et biogéographie, évolution de l'humanité, archéologie préhistorique, les métaux et la protohistoire.* (5th ed.) Paris: Payot, 1966.

Leroit-Gourhan, A., and others. *La préhistoire.* Paris: Presses universitaires de France, 1966.

Müller-Karpe, H. *Handbuch der Vorgeschichte.* Munich, Federal Republic of Germany: Beck, 1966–.

Otto, W., and Herbig, R. *Handbuch der Archäologie im Rahmen des Handbuchs der Altertumswissenschaft.* Munich, Federal Republic of Germany: Beck, 1939–1954.

Stewart, J. L. *An Archaeological Guide and Glossary:* Kendal, Westmoreland, England: T. Wilson, 1958.

Trump, D., and Bray, W. *American Heritage Guide to Archaeology.* New York: American Heritage, 1970.

DIRECTORIES

Directories to study in the field include:

ALSED Directory of Specialists and Research In-

stitutions. Paris: UNESCO, 1974. Directory of specialists and institutions involved in anthropology and language science in educational development (ALSED) in forty-six countries.

American Universities and Colleges. Washington, D.C.: American Council on Education, 1928–. Published quadrennially.

The Archaeologists' Year Book 1973–74: An International Directory of Archaeology and Anthropology. Park Ridge, New Jersey: Noyes Press, 1973.

Brown, P., and Lesniak, C. (Eds.) *Archaeology in American Colleges.* New York: Archaeological Institute of America, 1970. Provides information on archeological education in the United States.

Commonwealth Universities Yearbook. London: Association of Commonwealth Universities, 1914–. Published annually.

"Fourth International Directory of Anthropological Institutions." *Current Anthropology,* 1967, *8,* 647–751. Includes information on educational and research institutions, professional associations, museums, and agencies subsidizing research in archeology. To be updated.

World Guide to Universities. Pullach/Munich, Federal Republic of Germany: Verlag Dokumentation; New York: Bowker, 1972.

The World of Learning. London: Europa, 1947–. Published annually.

RESEARCH CENTERS, INSTITUTES,
INFORMATION CENTERS

Guides to museums, research, and information centers are:

Hudson, K., and Nicholls, A. (Eds.) *The Directory of World Museums.* New York: Columbia University Press, 1975.

Minerva, Forschungsinstitute. Berlin, Federal Republic of Germany: de Gruyter, 1972.

Museums of the World/Museen der Welt: A Directory of 17,000 Museums in 148 Countries, Including a Subject Index. Pullach/Munich, Federal Republic of Germany: Verlag Dokumentation, 1975.

Répertoire international des laboratoires de musées et des ateliers de restauration. Rome: International Centre for the Study of the Preservation and the Restoration of Cultural Property, 1960. Provides a list of museum laboratories and restoration workshops.

Research Centers Directory. (5th ed.) Detroit: Gale Research, 1975.

[Bibliography prepared by Kathy Berg.]

See also: Anthropology.

ARCHITECT, SELECTION OF

See Building and Construction Administration.

ARCHITECTURE
(Field of Study)

Architecture gives order to society's building activities. The architect's most characteristic activity is design, the predetermination of a building's form and materials. But architects also serve their clients, individuals or organizations, by coordinating a number of factors that affect the outcome of the building process, including the technical systems used in the construction of a building, their costs, and their relative impact on the operation of the building once it is in use. The architect must also consider the public interest, explicitly with respect to issues of health and safety, more ambiguously with respect to community appearance and ease of use. The architect's professional role and status has become complicated by the fact that the goals of those empowered to build are not necessarily congruent with the goals of those who actually use the buildings which are provided or with the environmental interests of the public.

Education in architecture includes study of design processes; study of the physical processes that impinge on buildings and the technologies available for construction; examination and analysis of previously constructed buildings and their use; and consideration of the social and environmental consequences of specific building activities. Traditionally architectural education has emphasized the visual appearance of buildings as evidenced in drawings and representational models. The "design studio," where a group of twelve to twenty students practice designing buildings under the tutelage of a design instructor, remains the central educational vehicle in the field. Work in the studio is generally expected to integrate the student's understanding of the various elements of building and to provide opportunities for the student to exercise judgment regarding the most suitable building forms and processes.

The architect's role has been an integrative one, synthesizing disciplines rather than separating them. Several early branches of architecture have either migrated to or been absorbed by other disciplines with more firmly established academic or methodological traditions. Thus, architectural history, although it has its own professional society, is primarily allied with art history. Similarly, the analysis of building structure, while still an integral part of architectural curricula, is primarily allied with civil engineering. Building technology shares faculty and combines programs with architecture and the related engineering disciplines; building technology curricula include construction processes, environmental controls, acoustics, and materials. Urban design occupies a similar position with respect to planning curricula; the most successful urban design programs have been staffed jointly by architects and planners and have brought the architect's concern with physical form together with the planner's skills in process management and problem identification. Typical curricula include real estate economics, public policy formation, urban sociology, and planning process.

New branches of the field have established greater methodological clarity. These subfields—concerned with design methods, programing, user-oriented research, and industrialized building systems—have drawn their stimulus respectively from developments in computers and operation research, psychology, and industrial management. They attempt to establish more explicit objectives and procedures for architecture and to develop guidelines for research and evaluation.

Planning, landscape architecture, and interior architecture are related fields that have established themselves as independent disciplines, although landscape architecture programs are sometimes located in schools of forestry rather than allied with architecture. In addition, civil engineering and mechanical engineering contribute to the building process in important ways. In the 1960s and early 1970s, however, they have paid less attention to problems associated with the building industry, and there has been a consequent gap in the development of appropriate technology for architecture. The various aspects of the visual arts should be considered as allied professions in that they also attempt to give significant form to visual experience. However, in architecture a too close reliance on visual order has sometimes obscured the many factors that must be considered in the creation of buildings.

In many instances graduates in architecture can take additional graduate work in these related fields, especially planning. Another recent pattern is for architects to take additional graduate study in business management or law. This development reflects the increasing legal and managerial complexity of the practice of architecture for institutions, government agencies, and corporate bodies—the organizations that initiate most building activity.

Formal education in architecture was initiated in the royal academies of Europe, first in France *(Académie d'architecture,* 1671) and then elsewhere. These academies emphasized theoretical considerations—in contrast to the craft apprenticeship that had characterized the education of most previous master builders. In the nineteenth century the rise of professional associations and a decline in royal patronage were accompanied by the establishment of more formal institutions, most notably the *Ecole des beaux-arts* in Paris, which was formed in 1816 and remained the most authoritative center for architectural education well into the twentieth century. In this school various categories of architectural knowledge were analyzed and separated into distinct courses of instruction, although the *atelier* (workshop) directed by a master was the primary source of design instruction. Over time the number of *ateliers* multiplied and developed distinctly different characters dominated by the personalities of the respective masters. This pattern of education, which reached its peak in the early twentieth century, left its mark indelibly on subsequent forms of architectural education. In the United States, for example, most of the first teachers of architecture were trained at the *Ecole des beaux-arts*. Even after schools were established in the United States, many American architects in the early twentieth century received part or all of their technical training at the *Ecole des beaux-arts* in Paris; this training was reinforced by the establishment of the Beaux-Arts Society of Architects in New York in 1894 and later by the Beaux-Arts Institute of Design, also in New York.

In the United Kingdom the Architectural Society, founded in 1831, was concerned primarily with providing facilities for teaching. In the United States the first autonomous course of architectural instruction was established at the Massachusetts Institute of Technology in 1866, followed by the University of Illinois (then the Illinois State Industrial University) in 1868, Cornell University in 1871, and Syracuse University in 1873. Study of classical models abroad was deemed so important that traveling fellowships were established, and in 1894 the American Academy in Rome was created as a center for study in archeology, architecture, and the fine arts. A number of such national academies were founded in Rome and Athens.

The most renowned alternative to the *Ecole des beaux-arts* system was the *Bauhaus* school, founded in Weimar in 1919 and then later directed by the German architect Walter Gropius (1883–1969). Whereas the *beaux-arts* education was based mainly on the emulation of well-established precedents that illustrated prototypical building forms and predictable patterns of organization, the *Bauhaus* related architectural form directly to emerging technologies of construction, rather than to classical or medieval precedents. Because new technologies did not need to be limited by conventional building forms, they opened new construction opportunities for expression. At the same time, the visual arts in general and painting in particular were rejecting the traditional limitations on visual form imposed by conventional subject matter and modes of representation. A revolution in thinking about visual organization was brought about by an insistence on fundamental geometric forms and relationships without reference to particularizing detail. Release from similitude to previous buildings or objects made possible new building types and an unprecedented scale of development. With the demise of the *Bauhaus* under Nazi harassment, many of its faculty emigrated to England and the United States. They brought about major changes in architectural education in the United States, where until very recently most schools of architecture taught introductory "basic design" courses inspired by the *Bauhaus* model. As an activity intended to control the disposition of building resources, architecture is inherently political. The profession's roots lie in the most powerful institutions of the past (for example, cathedral building and royal commissions). Until recently, its history was written almost exclusively in terms of the great building programs of established institutions (religious buildings, palaces, country manors, government buildings and, more recently, corporate headquarters).

Current thinking about architecture is focused much more clearly on the needs and interests of those people who actually use and experience buildings and on a reexamination of the underlying conceptions of service that have controlled the architect's craft and dominated education in the field. Briefly, the traditions and the profession are under attack from two positions. On the one hand are critics who contend that the profession has not been effective in establishing techniques for the control of building production. These critics look to more precisely defined objectives and the advancement of technology as the means for improved performance. On the other hand are those critics who find that the profession has been ineffective in providing environments which are satisfying for their inhabitants, especially those remote from the centers of power in our society. These latter critics fall into two groups: those who consider that more careful attention to the interests and activities of users will lead to the provision of improved environments, and those who consider that political and economic change is a necessary precondition for the creation of satisfactory human environments.

A recent increase in the ability of the schools to conduct research is perhaps the most important factor in the development of the field as an academic discipline. While the volume of academic research conducted is considerably smaller than in other disciplines, there has nonetheless been a marked increase accompanied by a broadening of interest among graduate students and faculty and the evolution of a cadre of young professionals trained in research techniques. Since 1965 several schools in the United States have established doctoral programs, signaling their intent to contribute to the development of knowledge in the field and reflecting a more favorable climate for research funding.

In the United States there are three basic types of education leading to an accredited degree in architecture: five-year undergraduate programs, "4 + 2" programs combining undergraduate and graduate study, and graduate programs. Students in five-year schools usually enter directly into the architecture program during their first year of college and concentrate their major attention on architecture throughout their studies. Combination ("4 + 2") programs provide a more general undergraduate education with a major preprofessional program in architecture or environmental design, followed by an intensive two-year graduate program in architecture. Students with a college degree who have not previously studied architecture can enroll in some schools for a full program of study

in architecture, generally for three or four years. A number of schools in the United States also offer a second professional degree, providing opportunities for advanced study and/or specialization. Graduates of accredited schools of architecture then undertake a two- or three-year period of professional internship before being considered for professional registration in the states and national certification by the National Council of Architectural Registration Boards.

Schools in the United States, represented by the Association of Collegiate Schools of Architecture, have zealously guarded their diversity of approach, reckoning that their ability to meet new challenges to the profession is lodged in their independence of thought and responsiveness to local conditions. Schools in the United Kingdom, on the other hand, are closely linked with the Royal Institute of British Architects and its processes of certification. The schools there are more consistently structured and generally more attentive to the technical details of construction than are their counterparts in the United States.

European schools of architecture are often based in technical universities; such schools in the Federal Republic of Germany and Switzerland are notable for the levels of technical achievement that their students' work demonstrates. Schools in Italy are large and have often recently been dominated by political controversy. Under student pressure the *Ecole des beaux-arts* in France had a major reconstruction in the late 1960s; now there are a series of *beaux-arts* schools representing differing intellectual and political positions and a variety of university-based schools of architecture, mostly outside Paris. Scandinavian schools operate with greater public acceptance of the architectural profession than is found in the United States or even in the United Kingdom. The schools are technically demanding, heavily populated, and well established, even though they sometimes exist as independent academies rather than as integral elements of a university structure. Danish students are required to have direct experience with a building craft before completing their studies.

Architectural education in Eastern Europe and the Soviet Union is linked to practice in government agencies and is followed directly by a period of government service. Schools of architecture in Asia and Africa have generally been based on the prototype of the colonial system of which they have been part and are often staffed by faculty who have studied in the United Kingdom, France, or the United States. In India there are eighteen schools of architecture, in South Korea ten, and in other Far Eastern countries one or two. In the Middle East, Turkey has nine schools; Egypt six; Iraq and Israel, only one each. In Africa five countries (Ghana, Ethiopia, Kenya, Nigeria, Sudan) have one school each. Caribbean and Latin American countries have many schools (Mexico, sixteen; Colombia, nine; Argentina, nine). Often these schools are linked with engineering, and their graduates play direct roles in the building industry. Many of these schools have highly developed standards of design and technical competence.

Schools of architecture in the various countries differ considerably in size, standards of technical competence, and projected roles for the graduates of their programs. In almost all cases the building problems of the society are rapidly changing along with massive urbanization, shifting energy resources, and the pressures for income redistribution. The challenge to the schools is to provide the opportunity for students to develop skills that can be useful in these changing local conditions and to foster continued development of the fields of knowledge on which professional activity is based.

DONLYN LYNDON

Levels and Programs of Study

Programs in architecture generally require as a minimum prerequisite a secondary education and lead to the following awards: certificate or diploma, bachelor's degree (B.Sc., B.Arch.), master's degree (M.Arch., M.Sc.), the doctorate (Ph.D.), or their equivalents. Programs deal with theory, techniques, and practice of the various fields of architecture (architecture; landscape architecture; city, town, and community planning; and urban design) and consist of classroom instruction, group discussions, projects, and where applicable, fieldwork.

Programs that lead to an award not equivalent to a first university degree deal with the principles and methods of architecture, landscape architecture, and city or regional (town or community) planning. These programs are designed to prepare students for careers as relatively high-level technicians and stress the practical and technological aspects of the subjects included, with relatively little time spent on the more general, theoretical, and historical principles. The principal kinds of programs included are those dealing with structural architecture (building technology, draftsmanship, building materials, building services, measurement, surveying and design procedures), landscape architecture (planting design, earth grading, and drainage and irrigation systems), and town or community planning (urban planning projects, urban redevelopment, and urban transit systems in relation to community planning). Programs of this type usually include background courses designed to supplement the major subject. They usually include some courses in related architectural and planning programs, and courses in fields such as mathematics, statistics, natural sciences, social sciences, and the humanities.

Some programs are of relatively short duration and include retraining, refresher, and sandwich courses. Practical demonstrations, fieldwork, and projects designed to enhance the student's appreciation of the subjects form an important part of these programs. Programs are usually conducted at institutes of technology or technical colleges, although they may be sponsored by a variety of agencies.

Programs that lead to a first university

degree deal with the theory, experimental techniques, and fieldwork methods of programs in architecture, landscape architecture, and city or regional (town or community) planning. These programs stress the theoretical and scientific principles of the subjects included as well as mastery of the techniques and methods used. Experimental techniques and methods are also stressed as a basis for research and investigation. The principal kinds of programs included are those dealing with architecture (for example, the history of architecture, architectural design, structural theory, integrated building systems, and social implications of architecture), landscape architecture (for example, landscape graphics, principles of landscape architecture, and landscape design), and city or regional planning (principles of urban planning, social and institutional determinants for physical urban planning, contemporary urban problems, and problems and methods of urban redevelopment. A program in any aspect of these subjects usually includes background courses in closely related areas, such as other disciplines in architecture and planning, as well as relevant courses in engineering, natural sciences, and social sciences. In landscape architecture, relevant agricultural specialties may also be included. Most programs also include selected courses in mathematics, the humanities, commercial or business administration, and, where relevant, computer science.

Programs may be full time or part time, day or evening. At this level, however, most programs are full time, although students may undertake them on a part-time basis. The part-time programs are mainly refresher courses. Most programs are conducted in universities, technical colleges, or institutes, but some are provided through correspondence or through broadcasts (radio or television).

Programs that lead to a postgraduate university degree are concerned with theory, experimental techniques, and research methods in architecture and city or regional (town or community) planning. At this level, emphasis is given to the theoretical principles of the subjects included; and original work, as substantiated by the presentation and defense of a scholarly thesis or dissertation, is usually important. The programs followed by individual students are usually based on one specialized area within architecture (for example, the history of architecture, environmental control in building structures, or integrated building systems); landscape architecture (landscape design, the siting of structures, landscape environmental control); city and regional planning (principles of urban land use, social and institutional determinants for physical urban planning, metropolitan area development, urban renewal or redevelopment); or urban design. Many programs in architectural and planning specialties at this level include background study in related architectural or town-planning subjects and related specialties in engineering, mathematics, natural sciences, and social sciences, designed to supplement the study of the principal subject involved. Additional background study may also include relevant specialties in such fields as commercial and business administration, law and jurisprudence, or the humanities.

In the main, these programs are full time, although advanced students often do part-time teaching or supervise less advanced students in work on projects or in fieldwork. Examples of part-time programs are refresher courses and special courses designed to introduce new methods and techniques to those already employed in their specialties.

[This section was based on UNESCO's *International Standard Classification of Education (ISCED)* (Paris: UNESCO, 1976).]

Major International and National Organizations

INTERNATIONAL

Commonwealth Association of Architects
66 Portland Place
London W1N 4AD, England

International Congresses for Modern
    Architecture

Congrès internationaux d'architecture
  moderne (CIAM)
12b Posthoornstraat
Rotterdam, Netherlands

International Council for Building Research,
  Studies and Documentation
Conseil international du bâtiment pour la
  recherche, l'étude et la documentation (CIB)
704 Weena
P.O. Box 299
Rotterdam, Netherlands

International Union of Architects (IUA)
Union internationale des architectes (UIA)
1 rue d'Ulm
Paris, France

International Union of Women Architects
Union internationale des femmes architectes
  (UIFA)
14 rue Dumont d'Urville
75016 Paris, France

Panamerican Federation of Architects'
  Associations
Federación panamericana de asociaciones de
  arquitectos (FPAA)
25 de Mayo 444, 55 piso
Montevideo, Uruguay

United Nations Center for Housing, Building
  and Planning
Department of Economic and Social Affairs
United Nations Secretariat
New York, New York 10017 USA

United Nations Economic and Social
  Commission for Asia and the Far East
Sub-Committee on Housing, Building and
  Planning
Sala Santitham
Bangkok, Thailand

United Nations Economic Commission for
  Africa (ECA)
Commission économique des nations unies
  pour l'Afrique (CEA)
Africa Hall
P.O. Box 3001
Addis Ababa, Ethiopia

United Nations Economic Commission for
  Europe (ECE)
Committee on Housing, Building and Planning
Palais des Nations
Geneva, Switzerland

United Nations Economic Commission for
  Latin America (ECLA)
Central American Sub-Committee on Housing,
  Building and Planning
Santiago, Chile

For additional international organizations
consult:

*Directory of Building Research Information and
Development Organizations.* Rotterdam: Inter-
national Council for Building Research,
Studies and Documentation, 1971. Provides
a few additional international organizations
in architecture and related fields.
Yearbook of International Organizations. Brussels:
Union of International Associations, biennial.

NATIONAL

Argentina:
  Sociedad central de arquitectos
  Montevideo 942
  Buenos Aires

Australia:
  Royal Australian Institute of Architects
  118 Alfred Street
  Milson's Point, New South Wales

Belgium:
  Fédération royale des sociétés
    d'architectes de Belgique
  21 rue Ernest Allard
  Brussels

Brazil:
  Associação brasileira de escolas de
    arquitetura (ABEO)
  Rua Maranhão 88
  São Paulo

Canada:
  Royal Architectural Institute of Canada
  157 Slater Street, Suite 1104
  Ottawa, Ontario K1PA 5H3

Egypt:
  Syndicat des ingénieurs et architectes
  30 26th July Street
  Cairo

Federal Republic of Germany:
  Bund deutscher Architekten
  Ippendorfer Allee 14b
  5300 Bonn

German Democratic Republic:
  Bund deutscher Architekten
  Breite Strasse 36
  102 Berlin

Ghana:
  Ghana Institute of Architects
  P.O. Box M272
  Accra

Hong Kong:
  Hong Kong Institute of Architects
  P.O. Box 2192
  Hong Kong

India:
  Indian Institute of Architects
  Prospect Chamber Annex
  Dodabhai Naoroji Road
  Bombay

Italy:
>   Associazione nazionale ingegneri ed
>   architetti
>   24 Piazza Sallustio
>   Rome

Japan:
>   Japan Architects Association
>   Kenchiku-kaikan 4-10
>   Jingumae 2-chome, Shibuya-ku
>   Tokyo

People's Republic of China:
>   Architectural Society of the People's
>   Republic of China
>   Pai Wang Chuang, West District
>   Peking

South Africa:
>   Institute of South African Architects
>   P.O. Box 31750
>   Braamfontein, Johannesburg

Soviet Union:
>   Union des architectes soviétiques
>   Qulitsa Chtchousseva 3
>   Moscow K-1

Sri Lanka:
>   Sri Lanka Institute of Architects
>   50 Rosmead Place
>   Colombo 7

Uganda:
>   East Africa Institute of Architects
>   P.O. Box 3216
>   Kampala

United Kingdom:
>   Royal Institute of British Architects
>   66 Portland Place
>   London W1N 4AD, England

United States:
>   American Institute of Architects
>   1735 New York Avenue NW
>   Washington, D.C. 20006
>
>   Association of Collegiate Schools of
>   Architecture
>   1735 New York Avenue NW
>   Washington, D.C. 20006

For further listings of national associations consult:

Directory of Building Research Information and Development Organizations. Rotterdam: International Council for Building Research, Studies and Documentation, 1971. A comprehensive listing of national organizations.

Directory of European Associations. Beckenham, Kent, England: CBD Research, 1971.

RIBA Directory of Members. London: Royal Institute of British Architects, annual. Lists architectural societies in countries throughout the world.

Principal Information Sources

GENERAL

Guides to the literature of the field include:

Bibliography on Housing, Building, and Planning for Use of Overseas Missions of the U.S. Agency for International Development. Washington, D.C.: U.S. Department of Housing and Urban Development Library, 1969. General information sources in the field, with an emphasis on the United States.

Phillips, M. *Guide to Architectural Information.* Lansdale, Pennsylvania: Design Data Center, 1971. Guide to architectural information for the professional; includes handbooks, indexes, and bibliographies.

Smith, D. L. *How to Find Out in Architecture and Building.* Oxford, England: Pergamon Press, 1967. Comprehensive coverage; includes bibliographies, indexing and abstracting services, periodicals, dictionaries, handbooks, and encyclopedias.

Overviews and introductions to the field include:

Doxiadis, C. A. *Architecture in Transition.* London: Hutchinson, 1963.

Giedion, S. *Space, Time and Architecture: The Growth of a New Tradition.* (5th ed.) Cambridge, Massachusetts: Harvard University Press, 1967.

Gropius, W. *Scope of Total Architecture.* New York: Harper & Row, 1955.

Norberg-Schulz, C. *Intentions in Architecture.* Cambridge, Massachusetts: MIT Press, 1966.

Rasmussen, S. E. *Experiencing Architecture.* (2nd ed.) Cambridge, Massachusetts: MIT Press, 1962.

Rasmussen, S. E. *Towns and Buildings.* Cambridge, Massachusetts: MIT Press, 1969.

Rosenau, H. *Boulée's Treatise on Architecture.* London: Alec Tiranti, 1953. A classic work.

Thompson, D. W. *On Growth and Form.* Cambidge, England: Cambridge University Press, 1952.

Viollet-le-Duc, E. *The Discourses on Architecture.* New York: Grove Press, 1959. A classic work.

Wright, F. L. *The Future of Architecture.* New York: Horizon Press, 1953.

Histories of the field include the following:

Allsopp, B. *A General History of Architecture from the Earliest Civilizations to the Present Day.* London: Pitman, 1955.

Braun, H. *Historical Architecture: The Development of Structure and Design.* London: Faber & Faber, 1953.

Fletcher, B. F. *A History of Architecture on the Comparative Method.* (18th ed.) New York: Scribner's, 1975.

Million, H. A. *Key Monuments of the History of Architecture.* New York: Abrams, 1964.

Pevsner, N. *An Outline of European Architecture.* (7th ed.) Harmondsworth, Middlesex, England: Penguin, 1963.

Works dealing with comparative education include:

Bertini, G. "Scuole di architettura: Analisi comparata dei piani di studio in vigore presso dodici facoltà dell'Europa e degli USA." *Casabella,* 1968, *328,* 26–35. A comparative survey of the plans of study at twelve universities in Europe and the United States; in Italian and English.

"The Education of the Architect." *UIA; Revue de l'Union internationale des architectes,* April 1967, *44,* 23–31.

"Education, Practise, and Organizations." *Architect's Journal,* October 1969, *150* (42), 971–981. Discusses architectural education in Africa, Asia, and Britain.

"Enseignement de l'architecture." *Architecture d'aujourd'hui,* April/May 1969, *40,* entire issue. Covers architectural education in a number of countries.

"Formation-fonction-position." *Architecture, formes et fonctions,* 1969, *15,* 9–78.

Journal of Architectural Education. Washington, D.C.: Association of Collegiate Schools of Architecture, 1972–. Published quarterly. Regularly includes articles on education in the United States; occasionally discusses education in other countries as well.

Koerte, A. "Architectural Education: The Global Village?" *Canadian Architect,* July 1970, *15* (7), 51–54.

Layton, E. *The Practical Training of Architects.* London: Royal Institute of British Architects, 1962. Useful although slightly outdated summary of practices in the United Kingdom; comparison with United States and the Federal Republic of Germany.

"UNESCO and the Training of Architects: Report on the Zurich Conference of June 1970." *Architectura* (Bucharest), 1971, *4,* 8–12.

CURRENT BIBLIOGRAPHIES

Architectural Index. Boulder, Colorado: Architectural Index, 1950.

Architectural Periodicals Index. (Formerly *Annual Review of Periodical Articles.*) London: Royal Institute of British Architects, 1973–. Index to journal articles.

Bauinformation. Berlin, German Democratic Republic: Bauakademie der Deutschen Demokratischen Republik, 1966–.

Building Abstracts Service. Prague: Vyzkummy ustar vysterby a architektway, 1959–.

Building Science Abstracts. London: H. M. Stationery Office, 1928–.

Bygglitteratur: Building Abstract Service. Stockholm: Institutet för byggdokumentation/ Swedish Institute of Building Documentation, 1951–.

CSIRO Index. East Melbourne, Victoria: Commonwealth Scientific and Industrial Research Organizations, 1952/53–.

Ekistic Index. Athens: Center for Ekistics, 1968–.

Homes and Home Building. Washington, D.C.: National Association of Home Builders, National Housing Center Library, 1967–. United States index for professional builders.

Housing and Planning References. Washington, D.C.: U.S. Government Printing Office, 1948–. Compiled by the United States Department of Housing and Urban Development Library.

PERIODICALS

Abitare (Italy), *American Institute of Architects Journal, Architect's Journal* (UK), *Architectural Culture/Kenchiku bunka* (Japan), *Architectural Design* (UK), *Architectural Record* (US), *Architectural Review* (UK), *Architecture* (Bulgaria), *Architecture Canada, Architecture d'aujourd'hui* (France), *Architektura CSR* (Czechoslovakia), *Arkhitektura SSSR* (USSR), *Arkitektur* (Sweden), *Arkkitehti/Finnish Architectural Review, Arquitectura* (Spain), *Bauen & Wohnen* (Switzerland), *Bouw* (Netherlands), *Casabella* (Italy), *Centre scientifique et technique du bâtiment cahiers* (France), *Indian Architect, Journal of Aesthetic Education* (US), *Journal of Architectural Education* (US), *Oppositions* (US), *Overseas Building Notes* (UK), *Progressive Architecture* (US), *Royal Institute of British Architects Journal, South African Builder.*

A more extensive listing of architectural and related periodicals may be found in the following:

Avery Index to Architectural Periodicals. (15 vols.) Boston: Hall, 1973. Indexes journal articles. *Supplement,* 1975.

Williams, F. E. "Trade Journals and Government Periodicals on Architectural, Construction, Engineering, and Building Materials Industries in Foreign Countries." Part 1: "Selected European Countries"; Part 2: "Selected Foreign Countries." *Construction Review,* June 1975, *25* (5), 4–31; August 1975, *25* (7), 4–25.

Ulrich's International Periodicals Directory. New York: Bowker, biennial.

ENCYCLOPEDIAS, DICTIONARIES, HANDBOOKS

Bucksch, H. *Wörterbuch für Architektur, Hochbau und Baustoffe/Dictionary of Architecture, Build-*

ing *Construction and Materials.* Wiesbaden, Federal Republic of Germany: Bauverlag GMBH, 1974.

Cagnacci Schwicker, A. *International Dictionary of Building Construction.* Milan, Italy: Hoepli, 1972. English-French-German-Italian.

Callender, J. H. *Time-Saver Standards.* (4th ed.) New York: McGraw-Hill, 1966. United States measurements for building types are given.

Mansum, C. J. van. *Elsevier's Dictionary of Building Construction.* Amsterdam: Elsevier, 1959. English-French-Dutch-German.

Neufert, E. *Architect's Data.* London: Crosby Lockwood Staples, 1970. Measurements are given in metric and nonmetric.

Ramsey, C. G., and Sleeper, H. R. *Architectural Graphic Standards.* (6th ed.) New York: Wiley, 1970. United States measurements are given.

Vocabulaire international des termes d'urbanisme et d'architecture/Internationales Wörterbuch für Städtebau und Architektur/International Vocabulary of Town Planning and Architecture. Paris: Société de diffusion des techniques du bâtiment et des travaux publics, 1970–.

Walker, T. D. *Plan Graphics; Drawing, Delineation, Lettering.* West Lafayette, Indiana: PDA Publishers, 1975.

Wasmuths Lexikon der Baukunst. Berlin, Federal Republic of Germany: Ernst Wasmuth, 1929. Dictionary of architectural history.

Zboinski, A., and Tyszynski, L. *Dictionary of Architecture and Building in Four Languages.* Oxford, England: Pergamon Press, 1963. English-German-Polish-Russian.

DIRECTORIES

Architectural Schools in North America. Washington, D.C.: Association of Collegiate Schools of Architecture, biennial.

International Handbook of Universities. Paris: International Association of Universities, triennial.

List of Recognized Schools of Architecture. London: Commonwealth Association of Architects, n.d.

RIBA Directory of Members. London: Royal Institute of British Architects, annual. Includes a list of schools of architecture in the Commonwealth.

World List—Schools of Architecture. Paris: International Union of Architects, 1975.

RESEARCH CENTERS, INSTITUTES, INFORMATION CENTERS

"Building, Housing and Allied Research Centers Throughout the World." *Overseas Building Notes,* August 1975, *163,* entire issue. Garston, England: Building Research Station.

HUD International Information Sources Series: Urban Institutions Abroad. Washington, D.C.: U.S. Department of Housing and Urban Development, Office of International Affairs, 1974. Lists research centers and government departments.

Miller, W. C. *Architectural Research Centers: An Annotated Directory.* (2 vols.) Monticello, Illinois: Council of Planning Librarians, 1971 and 1972. Lists university- and nonuniversity-based centers in the United States and foreign research centers by country.

[Bibliography prepared by Ann Longfellow]

See also: City and Regional Planning; Landscape Architecture; Urban Design.

ARCHIVES

1. ARCHIVAL RESOURCES, HISTORY AND DEVELOPMENT OF

2. AFRICA AND ASIA, NATIONAL ARCHIVES OF

3. CANADA, PUBLIC ARCHIVES OF

4. FRANCE, NATIONAL ARCHIVES OF

5. FEDERAL REPUBLIC OF GERMANY, GERMAN DEMOCRATIC REPUBLIC, AND AUSTRIA, NATIONAL ARCHIVES OF

6. MEDITERRANEAN, THE VATICAN, AND LATIN AMERICA, NATIONAL ARCHIVES OF

7. NORTHERN EUROPE, NATIONAL ARCHIVES OF

8. PUBLIC RECORD OFFICE, LONDON

9. UNITED STATES, NATIONAL ARCHIVES OF

1. ARCHIVAL RESOURCES, HISTORY AND DEVELOPMENT OF

Archives are organized records of a government, business, church, organization, institution, family, or individual that are retained for administrative or research use. As the retained records of society, archives have been kept in special rooms since the dawn of recorded history. Derived from the Greek word for government house, the term *archives* refers both to the location and to the contents of an archival repository. Archives are usually created by statutory or other written authorization.

The basic concept of archives lies in the evaluation or appraisal of documentation relating to the organization, functions, policies, decisions, procedures, operations, or other activities of the creating agency. The archivist selects records having archival value or continuing usefulness after the original purposes for which the records were created have been served. His primary concern is the evaluation of documentation to select that portion which has sufficient value to justify the costs of retention, description, and preservation. All recorded information, stated policies, and reported actions document activities that may interest some researcher, but only those records transferred to archival custody become archives.

Evaluation criteria include evidential value, informational content, cost of storage and preservation, volume, time span and recurrence of comparable data, uniqueness, comprehensibility, and collective evaluation in relation with other records. In records appraisal, the archivist applies the scholar's principles of external and internal criticism to documents to assess their future usefulness. Unlike the scholar and the librarian, however, the archivist usually engages in the evaluation and description of aggregates or collections of documentation.

Archives are arranged or organized according to the principle of provenance, or the doctrine of *respect des fonds* (respect for the sources), which requires the archivist to organize records according to source rather than subject content. This method of arrangement maintains the functional relationships and protects the evidentiary integrity of the records. Thus, the first task of the archivist is to become familiar with the administrative history of the organization or institution that he serves. Its structure will determine the organization of the archives. Unlike librarians, archivists do not have preconceived, standard systems for arranging documentation.

The second principle of archival arrangement is the doctrine of original order, which requires the archivist to maintain the existing order given to the records by their creators. If this order has been disturbed or destroyed, the archivist seeks to reestablish it. In archival usage, arrangement means the ordering of whole groups of records in relation to each other, the ordering of record series or files within groups, and the ordering of file units and individual items within series. A record series is a group of documents having a common arrangement and a common relationship to the functions of the office that created them. Unlike librarians, archivists do not rearrange records for the convenience of users.

The development of archival institutions has paralleled the rising awareness of political and institutional responsibilities to contemporaries and to posterity. The passive concept of an archives as a retrieval system, or as the recorded memory of the institution that is to be tapped for information or confirmation, has gradually given way to a wider recognition of the archives as a professional office, charged with the evaluation of large quantities of documentation and the selection and protection of records for future use. The archivist bears responsibility for deciding which aspects of society and which specific activities shall be documented and thus preserved. In meeting their obligation to transmit documentation of the past and present to the future, archivists have benefited from modern man's increased awareness of the significance of records.

Types of Archives

The principal archival establishments are the national archives of countries with long recorded histories. Second in significance are the governmental archives of states, provinces, counties, regional departments, and cities. Public archives include the archives of public universities, regional authorities, international and regional organizations, and special agencies or ministries that maintain their own archives. Nonpublic archives include repositories for the records of churches; businesses; private institutions of higher education; professional, occupational, political, and social organizations; families; and prominent individuals. In addition, there are regional or subject matter collections. These categories are not mutually exclusive; public archival establishments do not hold all municipal and notarial records, and some church and industrial records may be an integral part of a public archives.

The terms *public archives* and *private archives* indicate the governmental or nongovernmental character of the source of most of the records held and do not indicate that the archives are open or closed to the public. All distinctions as to types of archives depend on the traditions and political development of the country. An archival repository may contain official records, printed or published archives, personal papers or manuscripts, pictorial records and photographs, cartographic records, microforms, machine-readable records, and sound recordings.

Access to Archives

Finding aids. Although the archivist does not rearrange records for the convenience of users, one of his most important tasks is the preparation of the instruments of research, or finding aids, which assist users by describing and indexing the contents of archives. Since retention of materials is based in part on future research needs, finding aids must be designed for long-term use.

Finding aids represent a major investment of the archivist's time and may describe holdings at the repository, record group or major administrative unit, record series, folder, or item level. They may be published, duplicated, typewritten, or handwritten cards, or computer printouts. In preparing these aids, the archivist accounts for the origin and records the name of the record series or collection and its volume, inclusive dates, and arrangement. In describing the subject matter content, he may prepare a narrative description or list the contents by container or folder. He will prepare indexes and special guides for extensive or heavily used records to anticipate the needs of users and to facilitate searching.

While processing records, the archivist may call on such related disciplines as paleography, diplomatics, sphragistics, and sigillography. Paleography involves the analysis of ancient handwriting to determine the origin and period. When a document is compared with known samples of handwriting, the evidence may be validated. Diplomatics is the critical study of official documents, especially medieval, to decipher and determine the age, authenticity, signatures, or textual emendations of the handwriting and to obtain an exact reproduction of the original copy or edition of a text or document. The sciences of sphragistics and sigillography permit authentication of documents through the study of seals and signets to determine their history, age, distinction of types, manner of use, and legal function.

Restriction of access. The office of origin or the person transferring records to archival custody retains rights of access. While it is desirable that archives should be open as soon as possible to other users and researchers, it has been a common procedure to restrict access to records until the passage of a specific period of time or the occurrence of a specific event. However, research methodologies are the direct result of societal and institutional needs. In response to these needs, national archives have reduced many seventy-five- and fifty-year general restrictions to twenty-five and thirty years. Other restrictions may be based on the estimated lifetime of the individuals mentioned in the records or on the legal circumstances under which the record was created or obtained.

Governments that have recognized their obligation to establish ownership over public records and to place them under the care of trained professional archivists have also recognized the rights of citizens and scholars to have access to public records. The papers of officials accumulated in the course of public business are public property. However, the public's right to know has conceptual and practical limits, to protect national security, privacy, and political liberty and to ensure the creation and preservation of historical sources. In addition to restrictions on access to archives, repositories also have restrictions designed to protect the documents from damage or theft and to protect the copyright or literary property rights of authors.

Records Management and Technological Influences

A rapid increase in the amount of documentation generated by twentieth-century institutions has created new opportunities and problems for archivists. Faced with huge masses of records—and the indiscriminate desires of scholars that everything of interest to them be saved—archivists have turned their attention to the records-making and records-keeping procedures of the offices of origin. Their initial concern was to improve evaluation procedures and to begin the process of evaluation at an earlier time. They soon discovered that records-making and records-keeping procedures cost more in salaries, space, and equipment than any other governmental housekeeping activity.

Records management. As archival concerns merged with management concerns, the field of records management developed. Records management means the creation, processing, and maintenance of the fewest and best records at the lowest possible cost in salaries, space, and equipment. It may include forms management, correspondence management, filing and classi-

fication, control of reports and instructions, and mail management. Also classified under records management are microfilming and reproduction services, systems and procedures analysis, space utilization, advice on the proper equipment and machines to use in the processing of paper work, procedures for the orderly retirement of noncurrent records, and the establishment of record centers for the low-cost storage of inactive records.

In records creation and processing, the archivist and records manager are largely concerned with systems analysis and educational and training programs. But most archival activity has been in the area of records retention and disposal. Archivists have established record centers for the low-cost storage of inactive records. Common characteristics of record centers include a high ratio of cubic feet of records stored for each square foot of storage space; a low cost per cubic foot of records stored, due to low costs of site, construction, shelving, and containers; control over records through deposit or transfer lists showing box and shelf numbers and retention period; minimal reference costs due to handling by clerical staff and infrequent use. All documents sent to record centers are covered by schedules listing title, dates, description, volume, arrangement, and retention period for each record series.

A sound records management program effects substantial savings in storage costs and is an integral part of a successful archival program, for once instituted, it relieves the archivist of much routine and repetitive work. Such a program ensures that documents with archival value will not be discarded by mistake and will be transferred in orderly fashion to the archives.

Technological developments. Microphotography has been a major technological influence on archival practice. Microforms (microreproductions) are produced photographically on either transparent or opaque materials in a size too small to be read by the unaided eye. There are several kinds of microforms. Some are in the form of roll microfilm in 16-, 35-, and 105-millimeter widths. Rolls may also be enclosed in a cassette. Microfiche is a four-by-six transparent sheet that holds sixty to ninety-eight pages, including targets and spacing. Microcards are opaque cards, each holding about forty pages. Unitized aperture cards are a combination of machine sorting and microphotography. Microfilm strips and jackets are especially adaptable for automated retrieval systems. Computer output microfilm (COM) is a microphotographic image produced directly from information recorded on magnetic tape.

The administrative applications of microfilm include space saving; procedural recording of documents processed in the regular course of business; preserving of original documents; and providing of security copies for the protection of documents from wars, riots, vandalism, bombs, and natural disasters. The archival applications of microfilm include provision of a reference service, by which large quantities of documents may be copied more economically than by photocopying; collection of documents for special research interests; complementary filming to secure a documentary heritage retained in another archives; and publication of documents for sale to research institutions. Archival microfilming requires conformity to physical and documentary standards.

In institutions of higher education, trends in microfilming include the purchase of reader-printers, readers, and cassettes for student and faculty use in public areas, and the purchase of fiche readers for convenience in libraries, instructional carrels, and COM fiche reference locations. Problems in the area of microfilming in higher education institutions include the lack of systems studies before purchase and the underutilization of equipment. Additionally, records have been retained in microform when it would have been cheaper to destroy the originals after a reasonable retention period.

Audiovisual archives represent a second major development in archives. Photography, sound recordings, and their combination in motion pictures and videotapes have produced both useful new archival sources and unique problems in archival evaluation, description, and preservation. Recorded oral history interviews provide additional problems in methodology.

Magnetic data storage and retrieval systems have also affected archives, since computer technology permits the compact storage, programed manipulation, and retrieval of large amounts of data in a series of fast and accurate operations. Computer technology has led management to rely heavily on automated data-processing systems. The advantages of computers in locating and processing data are related to cost factors and the value of the information. Automated data-processing systems affect archives in three ways. First, machine-readable records are appraised, acquired, and stored by archives. Second, the archives may develop an automated system for the control of its own holdings. Third, users may use the automated methods in the analysis of archival sources. While few archival institutions have automated systems for the comprehensive control and subject retrieval of information about their holdings, most have faced the problem of evaluating machine-readable records and have encountered researchers intent on the quantification of historical data.

Institutions of Higher Education as Generators and Consumers of Archival Documentation

Most civilizations develop institutions responsible for preserving, adding to, and transmitting culture and learning to future generations. Since the late nineteenth century, institutions of higher education have grown rapidly. Charged with the responsibility for advanced education, academic institutions needed the documentation maintained by archives for administrative purposes and research. The volume of paper work associated with teaching, research, and public service activities has increased as rapidly as the quantity of records accumulated in government and business activities. The establishment of university and college archives was the logical step to secure effective control over noncurrent records of continuing value.

As curators of our documentary heritage, archivists have close ties with universities. The development of scientific history in the nineteenth century was a major stimulus for the creation of modern archival institutions in government and universities. Scholars anxious to consult actual documents so that they might write "objective" history needed access to archives. Thus, many national and local archives were founded and the need grew for professionally trained archivists.

Compared to government, business, and church archives, academic archives are more likely to be associated with large libraries and to serve more demanding patrons. They generally have smaller staffs, budgets, and holdings, and rely on students and part-time assistants. Academic archives handle records with a great variety of subject content and tend to be associated with collections of regional historical material and literary manuscripts. Many archivists and researchers have been attracted to universities because of their traditional role as centers for scientific, economic, and social research. The association of academic archives with libraries, in which both share facilities and resources, is often due to the peculiar nature of university administrative staff organization. Most university administrations have been more concerned with financial management and routine business functions than with administrative documentation and the intellectual contributions of faculty, students, and staff. Administrative responsibility for official records is most common where the increased efficiency of a records management program has been recognized.

Though they receive a small part of the money spent annually on archives, university archives in the United States are responsible for a disproportionately important part of the nation's documentary heritage. The records of higher education and of fields of learning have a special value in modern society. Societies that are distinguished for technology, political institutions, and mass education require a continuing scientific examination of their progress and a continuing preparation of a large group of citizens for civic leadership. Thus, the papers of faculty, students, and alumni are a vital part of the academic archives' resources. The archivist has a major role to play in citizenship education by instructing students in the careful examination of documentary evidence and the consideration of all viewpoints.

Archival Associations

Archivists are associated through professional organizations in all major nations of the world and, since 1948, through the International Council on Archives supported by UNESCO. From its offices at 2 place de Fontenoy, Paris VIIe, France, the International Council on Archives publishes *Archivum,* an annual international review on archives, which features directories of repositories, surveys of problems, and reports of international meetings. The council also sponsors a quadrennial international congress on archives; round-table meetings; special studies of archival subjects; and regional technical assistance programs in Africa, Asia, and Latin America. An International Archival Development Fund assists the world's developing countries in building effective modern national archival structures and services.

In the United States the national association is the Society of American Archivists (310 Library, Post Office Box 8198, University of Illinois at Chicago Circle, Chicago, Illinois 60680). Since 1938 the society has published *American Archivist,* a quarterly journal containing articles on archival theory and practice, reviews, bibliographies, news, and technical notes and abstracts. The society also publishes a bimonthly *Newsletter,* directories of archivists, and special volumes. It sponsors an annual meeting and joint sessions with historical and library associations and cosponsors regional conferences. There are twenty-two regional archival associations in the United States. Similar archival associations exist in Canada, France, Germany, the United Kingdom, and most of the nations of Europe.

International Programs and Cooperation

While higher education is vitally concerned with archival resources, international programs are largely administered by national archival establishments through contacts with UNESCO and the International Council on Archives. In congresses and staff reports, the council has emphasized the access and availability of archival sources, comparative studies of archival problems, technical assistance programs for developing countries, and directories of archival agencies.

Archival Publications

An international perspective on archival practice is essential in a consideration of professional literature. Archivists have a strong nationalistic tradition. Employed by the state to gain the confidence of administrative officials and to preserve state secrets, archivists have served the state and its interests. Never a numerous profession, few archivists have contributed to their professional literature. Much of what has been written falls into the categories of accounts of unique personal experience, manuals for internal operations, and specialized monographs on obscure topics. Given the breadth of archival concerns, it is necessary to draw on the literature of several nations.

The continuity of professional writing is maintained through the publication of archival journals by national archival establishments, often in cooperation with national archival organizations. In the United States, the Society of American Archivists,

as mentioned above, publishes a quarterly and a newsletter; the National Archives and Records Service publishes *Prologue*; and regional archival associations publish newsletters. In Great Britain the Society of Archivists publishes the *Journal of the Society of Archivists,* and the British Records Association publishes *Archives.* In France the Association of French Archivists publishes *Gazette des archives,* and the *Ecole des chartes* publishes the *Bibliothèque de l'Ecole des chartes.* The German Democratic Republic publishes *Archivmitteilungen* in Berlin; in the Federal Republic of Germany the Bavarian State Archives publishes *Archivalische Zeitschrift,* and the North Rhine–Westphalian State Archives publishes *Archivar.* In the Soviet Union *Sovetskiye arkhivy* is the principal archival journal. Other representative European archival journals include *Archívni časopis* (Czechoslovakia), *Nederlands archievenblad* (Netherlands), *Nordisk arkivynt* (Denmark), *Rassegna degli archivi di stato* (Italy), *Archeion* (Poland), and *Archivist* (Yugoslavia). In India the National Archives publishes *Indian Archives.*

The basic statement of modern archival principles and theory appears in *Manual for the Arrangement and Description of Archives* (Muller, Feith, and Fruin, 1940). The principal British statement is found in *Manual of Archive Administration* (Jenkinson, 1937); American interpretations are found in Schellenberg (1965) and Holmes (1964). Basic texts for terminology include *Elsevier's Lexicon of Archive Terminology* (Hardenberg, 1964) and "A Basic Glossary for Archivists, Manuscript Curators and Records Managers" (Evans, 1974).

Contemporary archival practice is best covered in *Manuel d'archivistique* (Direction of French Archives and the Association of French Archivists, 1970); auxiliary sciences are covered in *L'histoire et ses méthodes* (Librairie Gallimard, 1961). The Russian manual is *Archival Theory and Practice in the USSR* (Belov and Nikiforov, 1966), while German practice is covered in *Urkunden- und Aktenlehre der Neuzeit* (Meisner, 1950),

Archivkunde (Brenneke and Leesch, 1953), and *Archivverwaltungslehre* (Enders, 1968). The best modern works on British archives—including Emmison (1966) and Carter (1973)—relate to local records. While there is no single volume on American practice, the Staff Information Papers and Bulletins of the National Archives and Records Service have been the most influential publications. Tropical countries are discussed in *A Manual of Tropical Archivology* (Pérotin, 1966).

The archivist is especially concerned with the security, environment, structure, and layout of his building and the quality of the paper, boxes, and folders used for his records. He must protect documents from the dangers of heat, light, air, moisture, insects and rodents, and adjacent materials, and from the inherent characteristics of documents and people. Deacidification and lamination are among the techniques used by archivists and restorators in the restoration and preservation of documentation. Most of the literature on archival preservation and security has appeared in articles or technical news notes in general archival journals or in specialized publications such as *Mitteilungen der Arbeitsgemeinschaft der Archivrestauratoren.* The best manuals in English are *Conservation of Library Materials* (Cunha, 1967) and *Document Repair* (Wardle, 1971). The only comprehensive work on archival buildings and equipment is that of Duchein (1966).

Records management and technological influences have been favorite topics of archival writers. A major contribution of American archivists is represented by the *Records Management Handbooks,* published by the National Archives and Records Service since 1954. *Records Management* (Benedon, 1969) is a comprehensive one-volume guide. In addition, the *American Society for Information Science Journal, Records Management Quarterly,* and *Records Management Journal* contain articles on records management developments. The most useful publications on microphotography are *Microphotography for Archives* (Leisinger, 1968), the equipment guides of the National Microfilm Association, and "Summary of Current Research on Archival Microfilm" (McCamy and Pope, 1965).

The history of archival development is incomplete, but significant contributions have been made by Posner (1972), Meisner (1969), and the *Société de l'Ecole des chartes* (1921). A history of American archives can be drawn from Posner (1964), Gondos (1972), and Jones (1969).

The use of archives and archival resources are the most popular subjects for archival writers. Trained as researchers and oriented toward a scholarly clientele, archivists are especially concerned with descriptions of their holdings. Despite this emphasis, the most effective way to obtain current information on archival resources is to contact the archivist in charge of the institution.

The most recent general directory is the "International Directory of Archives" (UNESCO and International Council on Archives, 1975). With 2515 entries for 132 countries, the directory is weakest for the United States, where it lists eleven entries for the National Archives, fifty state archives, and four municipal archives; university, church, and business archives are omitted. This deficiency is remedied in the field of higher education by *College and University Archives in the United States and Canada* (Helmuth, 1972).

Archivists in institutions of higher education have produced few major contributions to archival literature. The first general publication in the United States was *University Archives* (Stevens, 1965). The Illinois program is discussed by Brichford (1970a, 1970b); in addition, *Scientific and Technological Documentation* (Brichford, 1969) contains discussions of evaluation, processing, and special types of records that are of general applicability. Most university archives are associated with libraries, and archivists are often in charge of collections of historical and literary manuscripts. The best discussion of the related field of manuscripts librarianship appears in Duckett (1975).

Archival bibliographies are regularly

published in leading journals, such as *American Archivist* and *Archivar.* The leading American bibliography is *Modern Archives and Manuscripts: A Select Bibliographic Guide* (Evans, 1975).

Notes on Selection of Archives for Discussion

There are many internationally significant archives that deserve separate treatment. For convenience of discussion, the archival world has been divided into eight geographical divisions, which are covered in the individual essays that follow.

Bibliography

Belov, G. A., and Nikiforov, L. (Eds.) *Archival Theory and Practice in the USSR.* Moscow: Vysshaia Shkola, 1966.

Benedon, W. *Records Management.* Englewood Cliffs, New Jersey: Prentice-Hall, 1969.

Brennecke, A., and Leesch, W. *Archivkunde.* Leipzig, German Democratic Republic: Koehler & Amelang, 1953.

Brichford, M. *Scientific and Technological Documentation.* Urbana, Illinois: University of Illinois, 1969.

Brichford, M. "The Illiarch: University of Illinois Archives." *Illinois Libraries,* 1970a, *52,* 182–204.

Brichford, M. "Scholarly Research and Archival Programs." *Illinois Libraries,* 1970b, *52,* 150–153.

Carter, G. A. *J. L. Hobbs' Local History and the Library.* London: André Deutsch, 1973.

Cunha, G. D. M. *Conservation of Library Materials.* Metuchen, New Jersey: Scarecrow Press, 1967.

Direction of French Archives and the Association of French Archivists. *Manuel d'archivistique.* Paris: Imprimerie nationale, 1970.

Duchein, M. *Les bâtiments et équipements d'archives.* Paris: International Council on Archives, 1966.

Duckett, K. W. *Modern Manuscripts.* Nashville, Tennessee: American Association for State and Local History, 1975.

Emmison, F. G. *Archives and Local History.* London: Methuen, 1966.

Enders, G. *Archivverwaltungslehre.* (3rd ed.) Berlin, Federal Republic of Germany: Verlag der Wissenschaften, 1968.

Evans, F. B. "A Basic Glossary for Archivists, Manuscript Curators and Records Managers." *American Archivist,* July 1974, *37,* 415–433.

Evans, F. B. *Modern Archives and Manuscripts: A Select Bibliographic Guide.* Worcester, Massachusetts: Society of American Archivists, 1975.

Gondos, V. *The Movement for a National Archives of the United States.* Ann Arbor, Michigan: University Microfilms, 1972.

Guide to the Contents of the Public Record Office. London: H. M. Stationery Office, 1963.

Hardenberg, H. (Comp.) *Elsevier's Lexicon of Archive Terminology.* New York: American Elsevier, 1964.

Helmuth, R. W. (Comp.) *College and University Archives in the United States and Canada.* Ann Arbor, Michigan: Society of American Archivists, 1972.

Historical Manuscript Commission. *Record Repositories in Great Britain.* London: H. M. Stationery Office, 1973.

Holmes, O. W. "Archival Arrangement." *American Archivist,* January 1964, *27,* 21–41.

Jenkinson, H. *Manual of Archive Administration.* London: Lund Humphries, 1937.

Jones, H. G. *The Records of a Nation.* New York: Atheneum, 1969.

Leisinger, A. H. *Microphotography for Archives.* Washington, D.C.: International Council on Archives, 1968.

Librairie Gallimard. *L'histoire et ses méthodes.* Paris: Librairie Gallimard, 1961.

Library of Congress. *The National Union Catalog of Manuscript Collections.* Washington, D.C.: Library of Congress, 1962.

McCamy, C. S., and Pope, C. I. "Summary of Current Research on Archival Microfilm." In *National Bureau of Standards Technical Note No. 261.* Washington, D.C.: National Bureau of Standards, 1965.

Meisner, H. O. *Urkunden- und Aktenlehre der Neuzeit.* Leipzig, German Democratic Republic: Koehler & Amelang, 1950.

Meisner, H. O. *Archivalienkunde vom 16. Jahrhundert bis 1918.* Göttingen, Federal Republic of Germany: Vandenhoeck & Ruprecht, 1969.

Muller, S., Feith, J. A., and Fruin, R. *Manual for the Arrangement and Description of Archives.* New York: Wilson, 1940.

Pérotin, Y. (Ed.) *A Manual of Tropical Archivology.* Paris: Mouton, 1966.

Posner, E. *American State Archives.* Chicago: University of Chicago Press, 1964.

Posner, E. *Archives in the Ancient World.* Cambridge, Massachusetts: Harvard University Press, 1972.

Schellenberg, T. R. *The Management of Archives.* New York: Columbia University Press, 1965.

Société de l'Ecole des chartes. *Ecole nationale des chartes, livre du centenaire, 1821–1921.* Paris: Picard, 1921.

Société de l'Ecole des chartes. *Liste des archivistes paléographes*. Paris: Société de l'Ecole des chartes, 1972.

Stevens, R. (Comp.) *University Archives*. Ann Arbor, Michigan: Edwards Brothers, 1965.

Suelflow, A. (Comp.) *A Preliminary Guide to Church Records Repositories*. St. Louis, Missouri: Society of American Archivists, 1969.

UNESCO and the International Council on Archives. "International Directory of Archives." *Archivum*, 1975, *22–23*, 222–260.

United States Government Printing Office. *Guide to the National Archives of the United States*. Washington, D.C.: U.S. Government Printing Office, 1974.

Verein deutscher Archivare. *Archivare an deutschen und österreichischen Archiven*. Wiesbaden, Federal Republic of Germany: Verein deutscher Archivare, 1968.

Wardle, D. B. *Document Repair*. London: Society of Archivists, 1971.

Zeigler, C. "Archival Practices Survey." *American Archivist*, April 1975, *38*, 191–203.

MAYNARD BRICHFORD

2. AFRICA AND ASIA, NATIONAL ARCHIVES OF

Africa and Asia contain some of the oldest civilizations of which we have knowledge. Millennia before Christ, there were states in Africa and Asia in which orderly, stable, and literate administrations produced and used archival materials on a considerable scale. The study of these ancient records has become a specialized branch of archeology, since these records differ so much in language and form from those of more recent times. Materials used in the making of these archives included clay, wood and wax tablets, incised stone, papyrus, parchments and leathers, and palm leaf. Quantities of these materials have been collected and are in the museums of all the major nations.

Effect of Colonialism on Archives

Most of the ancient empires of Asia and Africa suffered serious breaks in the continuity of their administration in the period between ancient and modern times; thus, almost no continuous archival record remains. Invasions, migrations, and colonization broke the continuity, without always introducing new archival traditions. The Arab invasions after the seventh century brought Islamic and Arabic traditions to most of the northern parts of Africa and along the eastern coasts, as well as into large parts of Asia. In North Africa, the Middle East, India, and Southeast Asia, literate Islamic administrations left many records. These documents, expressed in language and writing unfamiliar to most Western scholars, have also been collected in specialized museums in many countries. Other colonizations, such as those of the Indians and Chinese in Southeast Asia or the east coast of Africa, did not produce considerable documentary records.

Where there were no literate administrations, there were no written archives. In such areas evidence has been preserved largely in the form of oral tradition or histories, and in most parts of Africa and Asia evidences of popular culture or activity continue to exist in nonarchival form. Recording oral traditions or recollections is likely to remain an essential part of the collecting of source materials for all countries in Africa and Asia. Modern administrations that have been set up as a result of colonial influence, even if they are sovereign and independent, remain to a large extent alien structures employing an elite bureaucratic class with systems and languages common to international administration.

Archives are the documentary remains of orderly administrations that employ systematic methods of keeping information. In most places in Africa and Asia systematic administration developed between the seventeenth and twentieth centuries, mainly during the last decades of the nineteenth century. The degree and nature of colonial domination varied greatly from country to country. However, because archives of colonial administration were always created and retained in the metropolitan capitals and because archives created in the colonies often were brought back to the home country, considerable archival sources for the place and period are to be found in the colonizing countries. Also, missionary and commercial organizations with headquarters in the developed world accumulated archival material at their headquarters rather than in the colonies.

Today, the last half of the twentieth century, virtually all the colonized areas of Africa and Asia have achieved administrative and political, if not cultural and economic, independence and have set up archive-producing governments. For the most part Africa and Asia have also established national archives repositories where those archives may be consulted, although the age, completeness, or openness of these institutions varies greatly. These archives normally contain the records of the independent government of the country, and sometimes those of the government's immediate predecessors. Thus the archives of recent times can be expected to be reasonably complete. But for the archives of their earlier periods, Asia and Africa must rely on the records stored in the repositories of former colonial powers.

Archival Sources Outside Africa and Asia

Because early archives for Africa and Asia are outside the two regions, the International Council on Archives and UNESCO have been publishing an eleven-volume survey of archival sources for the history of African nations. By 1975, nine volumes had been published; these volumes cover archives in the Federal Republic of Germany, Spain, and France with two separate volumes on libraries, Italy (two volumes), the Vatican, Scandinavia, and Great Britain. In 1975, the volume covering the United States was in progress. The British and American volumes will cover records relating to the whole continent of Africa; the other volumes will cover only records that relate to sub-Saharan Africa (including the Democratic Republic of Madagascar and the islands).

To some extent parallel with the publication of these volumes, the Institute of Historical Research at the University of London has published a series of guides to materials for West African history. There are volumes covering Belgium and the Netherlands, Portugal, Italy, and France. Another parallel survey is P. Duinan's *Handbook of American Resources for African Studies* (1967). The Library of Congress's bibliographical services include a coverage of official publications of African governments, mainly the anglophone group of countries, which is supplemented by their publication (in progress) on microfilm (EP Microform Ltd, 1974). The International Union of Academics series *Fontes Historiae Africanae (Bulletin of Information* published from the University of Ghana, Accra, from 1975) is to include the texts of documents held both within and outside Africa.

The enormously varied character of Asian civilizations has so far deterred any comparable survey of Asia. However, several institutions outside Asia have collected source material or have established bibliographic services relating to the source data. The principal such institutions in English-speaking countries are the School of Oriental and African Studies, University of London; the Hoover Institution, Stanford University; the African Studies Library, Boston; and the Library of Congress, Washington, D.C. Many other universities, libraries, and museums in North America and Europe hold important collections of African and (more especially) Asian material. And as mentioned, former colonial powers commonly maintain archival institutions that hold records dealing with colonial areas. Of those institutions listed in the "International Directory of Archives," the following deserve particular mention: the India Office Library and Records, London, England; the Overseas Archives Department, Aix-en-Provence, France; the Archives of the Indies, Seville, Spain; and the Vatican archives. Most of these groups publish reports, texts, or inventories.

During the late 1960s a number of areas, with support from UNESCO, set up regional branches of the International Coun-

cil on Archives: the Arab Countries Branch
of the International Council on Archives
(ARBICA); East and Central Africa Branch
of the International Council on Archives
(ECARBICA); and the Southeast Asia
Branch of the International Council on
Archives (SARBICA). Each of these organizations maintains a secretariat and
publishes a journal in which questions
concerning the content, use, or administration of their archives are discussed. All
branches liaise with each other through
the secretariat of the International Council
on Archives, 60 rue des Francs-Bourgeois,
Paris, France, to which preliminary inquiries may be addressed.

African and Asian repositories are included in the "International Directory of
Archives," published in volumes 22 and
23 of *Archivum* (1975). A previous issue
of *Archivum,* volume 20 (1970), gives the
texts of archival legislation for African
and Asian countries.

National Archives in Africa

The national archives in Africa cover
four geographical areas: North Africa, the
Francophone countries, the Spanish- and
Portuguese-speaking countries, and South
and Central Africa.

North Africa. There are national archives
in Algeria, Egypt, Libya, Morocco, Sudan,
and Tunisia. Algeria publishes an archival
periodical. In Libya, the records of Italian
administration were destroyed in 1944,
but an inventory of relevant records in
Italian ministries is given by Giglio (Leiden,
1971–1972). The University of Bergen
has investigated Sultanic and family records in Darfur (1972–1973) in the Sudan,
and there are some lists of Turkish archives
in Tunisia. The principal external sources
for this subregion are in Britain (Egypt,
Sudan); France (Algeria, Morocco, Tunisia); Italy (Libya); Spain, Portugal, and
Turkey.

The francophone countries. There are
national archives in Burundi (although
not much is known of the organization or
contents of this repository), Cameroon,

Central African Republic, Chad, Congo,
Benin, Gabon, Guinea, Ivory Coast, Madagascar, Mali, Mauritania, Niger, Rwanda
(similar uncertainties as in Burundi exist
here), Senegal, Togo, Upper Volta, and
Zaire. The Ivory Coast is being developed
as a model archival service. Senegal and
Congo (Brazzaville) were repositories for
the former French administrations of West
and Equatorial Africa, respectively; consequently, there are archives in Dakar and
Brazzaville that bear upon the other countries carved out of those federations.
However, many records, especially those
from the Equatorial group, were taken to
France at the time of independence. Inventories, some extensive, have been published for records held by Guinea, Senegal,
Madagascar, and Zaire, but this kind of
published literature is still rare. The principal external sources for this area are in
Belgium (Zaire, Rwanda, Burundi) and
France, but there are some Arabic sources.
Sources in Britain, Denmark, the Netherlands, and Portugal should be consulted
for the littoral countries.

Spanish- and Portuguese-speaking countries.
National archives exist in Angola, Guinea-
Bissau, Mozambique, São Tomé, and Equa-
torial Guinea. Angola and Mozambique
have extensive publications of inventories
and texts of documents. The *Boletim do
Arquivo Historico e da Biblioteca do Museo de
Angola* publishes lists, and there are forty-
six volumes of documents in *Arquivos de
Angola* (1959).

The anglophone countries. There are national archives in Botswana, Gambia, Ghana,
Kenya, Lesotho, Malawi, Mauritius, Nigeria, Sierra Leone, Swaziland, Tanzania,
and Zambia. In Liberia and Uganda attempts are being made to establish archives
services. The situation in Ethiopia is uncertain. Many of these offices publish annual
reports; inventories, guides, or texts have
been published by Kenya, Sierra Leone,
Tanzania, Zambia, and, especially, Mauritius, which has an *Archives Bulletin* and a
publication fund. Kenya has a microfilming project with the University of Syracuse

in the United States, and Tanzania has a joint project with the archives school at Marburg, in the Federal Republic of Germany. Principal external sources are in Great Britain, France (Mauritius), Federal Republic of Germany (Tanzania, Ghana), South Africa (Botswana, Lesotho, Swaziland), Rhodesia (Malawi, Zambia), the Netherlands, and Denmark (West Africa).

South and Central Africa. South Africa and Rhodesia have long-established archives services. The South African service, based at Pretoria, has branches at the Cape, Transvaal, Orange Free State, Natal, Transkei, and Namibia. There is a *South African Archives Journal,* and some branch repositories, particularly those at the Cape and Natal, have published texts or guides, some in Afrikaans. The University of Witwatersrand has important collections and publishes a guide. Rhodesia also has an extensive publications program. Principal external sources are in Britain, the Netherlands, Portugal, and the Federal Republic of Germany.

National Archives in Asia

The national archives in Asia cover the geographical areas of the Middle East, South Asia, Southeast Asia, and East Asia.

The Middle East. There are national archives in Iraq, Iran, Israel, Lebanon, Syria, and Saudi Arabia. Turkey has two archival repositories, in Istanbul and Ankara. Some manuscript preservation is being undertaken in the Yemen. The most developed archival system in this area is in Israel, where records of international Jewry are collected; guides, texts, and lists are published. The principal external sources are in Britain, France, the Soviet Union, and India.

South Asia. Afghanistan, Bangladesh, India, Nepal, Pakistan, and Sri Lanka have national archives. The capital of India has a central archives and two federal branches; some fifteen states also maintain state archives. The journal *Indian Archives* contains descriptions of the holdings and organization of many of the archives of nations in Africa and Asia. India also has an extensive program of publishing archival texts, but there are few published guides or inventories. At least two major libraries, Madras and Calcutta, have important documentary collections, and there is an Indian Historical Records Commission. The archives of Nepal and Afghanistan are newly established. The principal external sources are in Britain, France, and Portugal (Wainwright and Matthews, 1965).

Southeast Asia. There are national archives in Indonesia, Malaysia (with branches in Sabah and Sarawak), the Philippines, Singapore, and Thailand. Most likely there was some sort of organization for archives in Cambodia, Laos, and both parts of Vietnam until the wars of the 1970s. There does not seem to have been any archival establishment in Burma. In Thailand the National Library holds important sections of the early royal archives. The Institute of Southeast Asian Studies in Singapore disseminates research materials on microfilm. The archives of the former French administration of Indochina are or were in Hanoi. The principal external sources are in Britain (Burma, Malaysia, Singapore), the Netherlands (Indonesia), Spain (the Philippines), Portugal (Malaysia, Indonesia), the United States (the Philippines, Thailand), France (Cambodia, Laos, Vietnam), India (Malaysia, Indonesia), and presumably the People's Republic of China (Wainwright and Matthews, 1965).

East Asia. Formal national archives exist in Hong Kong, the Republic of China, Japan, and Mongolia. Presumably archives also exist in the People's Republic of China, both in Peking and the main provincial cities, such as Shanghai. The situation in North and South Korea and Macao is uncertain. Taiwan has several archival collections, which include material brought from mainland China; some of this material is historical and some is concerned with irredentist Chinese political movements. The archives of Japan are recently established. There do not seem to be any formal publishing programs as yet, nor are there any organized expositions of documents or inventories available from any of these sources. Much information can be gathered, however, from Russian- and Western-language abstracts of Chinese journals. The principal external sources are in Britain, the Soviet Union, France, Portugal, Germany, and the United States.

Bibliography

Akermi, C. "L'Activite archivistique dans le monde arabe." *Archives et Bibliothèques de Belgique,* 1968, *39,* 64–77.

Alsberg, P. A. *Guide to the Archives in Israel.* Jerusalem, Israel: Israel Archives Association, 1973.

Angel, H. E. "Archives in Developing Countries: Iran as a Case Study." *The American Archivist,* 1972, *35,* 173–181.

Antonelli, G. *Mise sur Pied d'un Service national d'Archives et de Pré-archivage: Liban.* Paris: UNESCO, 1974.

Axelson, E. *Documents on the Portuguese in Mozambique and Central Africa, 1497–1840.* Lisbon, Portugal, 1962 (in progress).

Baxter, T. W. *Guide to the Public Archives of Rhodesia: Volume I, 1890–1923.* Salisbury, Rhodesia: National Archives of Rhodesia, 1969.

Baxter, T. W., and Burke, E. E. *A Guide to the Historical Manuscripts in the National Archives.* Salisbury, Rhodesia: National Archives of Rhodesia, 1970.

Botha, C. G. *The Public Archives of South Africa, 1652–1910.* New York: B. Franklin, 1969 (originally published 1928).

Centro de Estudos Historicos Ultramarinos. *Catalogo dos Manuscritos de Macau.* Lisbon, Portugal, 1963.

Charpy, J. (Ed.) *Repertoire des Archives.* Rufisque, Senegal: Gouvernement Général de l'Afrique Occidentale Française, 1954–1958.

Diamond, I. A. *Afghanistan: Establishment of a National Archives Service.* Paris: UNESCO, 1974.

Duinan, P. *Handbook of American Resources for African Studies.* Palo Alto, California: Stanford University Press, 1967.

Dumett, R. E. "Survey of Research Materials in the National Archives of Ghana." *Mitteilungen der Basler Afrika Bibliographien* II, Shwäbisch Gmünd: Afrika-Verlag der kreis, Postfach 44, D-7070, 1974.

English, P. T. "Archives of Uganda." *The American Archivist,* 1955, *18,* 225–230.

Foley, D. M. "Liberia's Archival Collection." *African Studies Bulletin,* 1968, *11,* 217–220.

Giglio, C. Gli archivi storici del . . . Ministero dell' Africa i Italiana e del Ministero degli affari esterni. Gli archivi del Ministero della Difesa. Leiden, Netherlands: Brill, 1971–1972.

Glenisson, J. "Les Archives de l'Afrique Equatoriale Française." *Gazette des Archives,* 1957, New Series *22,* 23–30.

Graham, I., and Halwindi, B. C. *Guide to the Public Archives of Zambia: Volume I, 1895–1940.* Lusaka, Zambia: National Archives of Zambia, 1970.

Gregory, R. O., Mason, R. M., and Spenser, L. P. (Comps.) *A Guide to the Kenyan National Archives, to the Microfilms of the Provincial and District Annual Reports, Record Books, and Handing-Over Reports, etc.* Syracuse, New York: Syracuse University Press, 1968.

Hedtke, C. H. "The Ch'ing Dynasty Archives." In S. J. Palmer (Ed.), *Studies in Asian Genealogy.* Provo, Utah: Brigham Young University Press, 1972.

Hobbs, C. "Southeast Asian Archival Materials." *International Library Review,* 1969, *1,* 359–368.

Holt, P. M. "The Mahdist Archives and Related Documents." *Archives,* 1961–1962, *5,* 193–200.

Johnson, G. W., Jr. "The Archival System of Former French West Africa." *African Studies Bulletin,* 1965, *8,* 48–58.

Keswani, D. G. "Archival Sources of Southeast Asian History in the National Archives of India." *Southeast Asian Archives,* 1969, *2,* 3–10.

Low, D. A., Iltis, J. C., and Wainwright, M. D. (Eds.) *Government Archives in South Asia: A Guide to National and State Archives in Ceylon, India and Pakistan.* Cambridge, England: Cambridge University Press, 1969.

Mast, H., and Li Yun-Han. "Changing Times at the Historical Archives Commission of the Kuomintang." *Journal of Asian Studies,* 1971, *30,* 413–418.

Mauritius Archives. *Brief Guide to the Mauritius Archives.* Port Louis, Mauritius: Government of Mauritius, 1970.

Nguyen Hung Cuong. "Etat des Documents d'Archives en langue Française au Viet-Nam." *Southeast Asian Archives,* 1969, *2,* 139–147.

Pearson, J. D. "Materials for a Survey of Manuscripts and Archives in or Relating to Africa." *Library Materials on Africa,* 1972, *10,* 126–178.

Pearson, J. D. "Manuscripts and Archives Relating to Africa." *African Research and Documentation,* 1973, *1,* 11–18.

Shen Ching-Hung. "Historical Documents in the Manchu Language, Taiwan." *National Palace Museum Bulletin,* 1968, *3,* 1–4, 12–13.

Sheriff, G. *Catàlogue of Archives, the Property of the Government of Sierra Leone, Deposited at Fourah Bay College.* Freetown, Sierra Leone: Government of Sierra Leone, 1962.

UNESCO and International Council on Archives. "International Directory of Archives." *Archivum,* 1975, 22–23.

Valette, J. J. "Les Archives de Madagascar." *Gazette des Archives,* 1965, New Series *38,* 127–133.

Van Grieken-Taverniers, M. "Archives." *Livre Blanc de l'Académie royale des Sciences d'Outremer, Volume I.* Bruxelles, L'Académie royale des Sciences d'Outremer, 1962.

Wainwright, M. D., and Matthews, N. (Eds.) *A Guide to Western Manuscripts and Documents in the British Isles Relating to South and Southeast Asia.* Oxford, England: Oxford University Press, 1965.

Waniko, S. S. *The Arrangement and Classification of Nigerian Archives.* Lagos, Nigeria, 1958.

Webb, C. de B. *Guide to the Official Records of the Colony of Natal.* Pietermaritzburg, South Africa; University of Natal Press, 1968.

Wright, S. "Book and Manuscript Collection in Ethiopia." *Journal of Ethiopian Studies,* 1964, *2,* 11824.

MICHAEL COOK

3. CANADA, PUBLIC ARCHIVES OF

The Public Archives, the archives of the federal government of Canada, has a dual role. As a research institution, it is responsible for acquiring from any source all significant archival material "of every kind, nature and description" relating to all aspects of Canadian life and to the development of the country, and for providing suitable research services and facilities to make this material available to the public. As an essential part of the government administration, it has broad responsibilities for the promotion of efficiency and economy in the management of its records.

History of the Federal Archives

Provision for the creation of a federal archives was first made by an order-in-council of June 20, 1872, which appointed an officer in the Department of Agriculture to assemble, index, and place at the disposal of researchers the historical documents relating to Canadian history. In 1873 a keeper of the records was appointed in the Department of the Secretary of State to preserve historical records of the federal government departments. The two offices were combined in 1903, but remained in the Department of Agriculture. After 1903 the archives looked after both government records and private papers and carried out an extensive program of copying at home and abroad. In 1912 the archives became by statute an autonomous department and was named the Public Archives of Canada. The duties of the Public Archives in the field of records management were enlarged until it reached its present level of authority and responsibility by an order-in-council in 1966.

Division of Archives

Because of the federal constitution of Canada, archives are divided between the federal government and the provinces. The records of New France (before 1760) are preserved in the National Archives of Quebec, in offices located in Quebec City, Montreal, and Trois-Rivières. These records consist mainly of ordinances of the intendants (officers possessing civil and maritime jurisdiction), records relating to land grants and roads, judicial archives, notarial documents, and civil status registers.

After 1760, records generally remained with the provinces until they joined the confederation. However, most of the records affecting the provinces of Quebec and Ontario for the period 1760 to 1867 were retained by the federal government at the time of confederation in 1867. These are primarily records of the executive council, the provincial secretaries, and the governor general's office, as well as British military records created in Canada. They also include a few records of other departments, such as agriculture, public works, and militia. All historical records retained by the federal government are now in the Public Archives of Canada. Records retained by the provinces are under the responsibility of the provincial archives in each province.

Records Deposited in the Archives Branch

The historical records and papers of the Public Archives are under the direction of the Archives Branch. These documents are preserved in eight divisions: the Public Records Division, the Manuscript Division, the Machine-Readable Archives, the National Map Collection, the Picture Division, the National Photography Collection, the National Film Archives, and the Library Division.

Public Records Division. The records of the federal government in manuscript form (handwritten, typewritten, occasionally printed) are preserved in the Public Records Division. They are divided into one hundred record groups; these groups consist of the records of one department or agency, or of an important branch of a department, and usually correspond to one filing system. Occasionally, the Public Records Division assembles in a collective record group several small agencies, organizations, or commissions, such as commissions of inquiry, interdepartmental committees, or federal-provincial conferences. The records of the Department of National Defence, the Royal Canadian Mounted Police, and the Department of External Affairs are all deposited in the Public Archives. The records of the Canadian parliament are also deposited, by agreement, but the records of the Supreme Court and of the federal courts are retained in archives of the courts. The records of crown corporations, such as Air Canada, Canadian National Railways, and the Central Mortgage and Housing Corporation, have been deposited, by agreements, while other corporations, such as Atomic Energy of Canada Limited, have kept their records. Holdings of the division occupy approximately twenty thousand linear meters on the shelves. Most records can be consulted after twenty years, but in many cases more recent records can be consulted with the permission of the originating department.

Manuscript Division. The Manuscript Division, for reasons of convenience, looks after the early records of Quebec and Ontario, from 1760 to 1867. However, the bulk of its holdings consists of two kinds of documents: private papers of individuals and of business, cultural, and other societies; and copies of documents, private and public, from all parts of Canada, and from France and England, that relate to Canada from the sixteenth century to the present.

The holdings of the division are divided into thirty-five manuscript groups. Of these, two groups contain copies of official archives of the Canadian provinces; seven groups contain copies (on microfilm or handwritten) made in France from official repositories *(Archives nationales; Archives des colonies; Archives de la marine; Archives de la guerre; Ministère des affaires étrangères; Archives départementales, municipales, maritimes, et de bibliothèque);* six groups contain copies made in England from official repositories (Colonial Office, Admiralty and War Office, Foreign Office, Audit Office and Treasury, Post Office, and Customs and Plantations Office); one group contains documents copied in other countries (United States, Chile, and Republic of China). The other groups place together private papers and records by subject, date, or type of documents. Among these are such diverse groups as Indians and fur trade, Hudson's Bay Company, prime ministers' papers, and religious archives. Holdings of the division amount to about eight thousand meters and five thousand reels of microfilm.

In addition, the division has on deposit recent papers of ministers and prime ministers, most of which will eventually be transferred formally to its holdings.

Machine-Readable Archives. The Machine-Readable Archives division was established to look after both private and government records maintained in machine-readable form. Sixty government files have been transferred to this division, including those of the Royal Commission on Bilingualism and Biculturalism, which make extensive use of computer documents.

National Map Collection. The National Map Collection brings together the cartographic records of Canada, archival and current, as well as architectural and engineering drawings of national interest, from the federal government and all other sources. In addition, the Map Division has a rich collection of atlases bearing the names of most of the great mapmakers who have flourished since the Age of Discovery, and a select collection of foreign maps, mostly topographical, covering every country of the world. The Map Division holds more than 500,000 Canadian maps and drawings, and 200,000 maps of foreign countries.

Picture Division. The Picture Division collects paintings, drawings, and prints that document the development of Canada; the acquisition and preservation of purely artistic works is the function of the National Gallery of Canada. The division has over 75,000 items; most important are the watercolors by British military topographers. In addition, the Picture Division has an important collection of war posters from many countries, an extensive collection of costume documentation, and the main body of Canadian-produced comic books and associated art work. The Heraldry Unit is responsible for arms, flags, and seals; it keeps files on official heraldic devices presently used in Canada or connected with Canadian history. Finally, the National Medal Collection contains about eight thousand items relating to Canada or produced by Canadian artists.

National Photography Collection. The National Photography Collection is the largest collection of historical photographic records in Canada. The division is the official repository for noncurrent photographs for the federal government, starting with those taken in the 1850s. It is also responsible for a representative cross section of documentary photographs concerning Canadian development, as well as for records of the work of notable Canadian photographers and of the progress of photography in Canada. The National

Photography Collection holds nearly four million negatives and prints. The largest single collection is that of the Department of National Defence, extending from 1885 to the present.

National Film Archives. The National Film Archives is responsible for newsreels, documentaries, and full-length feature movies, television productions, and historical sound recordings. The historical sound recordings section contains over fifteen thousand hours of recorded speech and interviews of national interest. This section also conducts oral history programs. The collection of Canadian film is already extensive, consisting of over forty thousand reels. Films come from both the public and private sectors and have historical, cultural, or social interest. An ambitious program for the preservation of television programs, again from both the public and private sectors, has been initiated. Conversion from nitrate to safety film is in progress. The National Film Archives is also the custodian of an important documentation library on Canadian and foreign cinema.

Library Division. The Library Division has more than eighty thousand books, pamphlets, periodicals, and government publications. Most of these relate to Canada and its development, but many deal with the specialized areas of the Public Archives, such as art, cartography, photography, medals, microfilming, restoration, records management, and archival science.

The Archives Branch of the Public Archives also maintains offices in London and Paris, where the search for Canadian source material continues, and where researchers receive advice and guidance.

Public Archives' Services to the Public

For historical documents, services to the public are extensive. As part of its records management operation, the Public Archives controls three record centers in Ottawa, Ontario, for personnel files, military forces records, and general records, and regional record centers in Vancouver,

British Columbia; Edmonton, Alberta; Winnipeg, Manitoba; Toronto, Ontario; Montreal, Quebec; and Halifax, Nova Scotia. The dormant records in these centers are usually less than thirty years old and can be consulted only with the permission of the originating department. While documents in the archives may not be taken out of the archives building, the search rooms are open twenty-four hours a day for accredited researchers. Documents that are on microfilm can be borrowed through interlibrary loan. Reproduction of material in the archives may be obtained at reasonable rates. In addition, the archives provides a reference and limited research service by telephone or correspondence for those needing information on its holdings.

Over the years, the Public Archives has published annual reports; a *Guide* (Public Archives of Canada, 1975), compiled from the reports issued between 1872 and 1972, is also available. In addition, several inventories, other finding aids, and a selection of documents have been published by the archives. It has also produced several exhibitions for which catalogs were printed, and, in collaboration with the government's National Film Board, some slides series on Canadian subjects.

As part of its diffusion program, the Public Archives has deposited, in each of the ten provincial archives, numerous microfilms of records that are either of national interest or of particular interest to a given province.

The relations of the Public Archives with the learned professions, particularly with the Canadian Historical Association, have been very close. Since its formation in 1921, the office of the treasurer of the association has been located in the Public Archives. Since 1966 the Public Archives, in cooperation with the universities of Canada, has compiled the *Register of Dissertations,* which is published by the Canadian Historical Association. In cooperation with nearly two hundred archival institutions in Canada, the Public Archives pre-

pared a *Union List of Manuscripts* in 1968, which was revised in 1975. Finally, in cooperation with some fifty Canadian map libraries, the archives is preparing a union list of maps in Canadian repositories.

Bibliography

Canadian Historical Association. *Register of Post-Graduate Dissertations in Progress in History and Related Subjects.* Ottawa, Ontario: Public Archives of Canada, annual.

Maurice, E. G. (Ed.) *Union List of Manuscripts in Canadian Repositories.* Ottawa, Ontario: Public Archives of Canada, 1975.

Public Archives of Canada. *Archives: Mirror of Canada Past.* Toronto, Ontario: University of Toronto Press, 1972.

Public Archives of Canada. *List of Publications of the Public Archives of Canada.* Ottawa, Ontario: Information Canada, 1974.

Public Archives of Canada. *Guide to the Reports of the Public Archives of Canada, 1872–1972.* Ottawa, Ontario: Information Canada, 1975.

BERNARD WEILBRENNER

4. FRANCE, NATIONAL ARCHIVES OF

According to the official French definition, archives are "any kind of documents, whatever their date or form, produced and/or received by any public or private person and/or institution, in the course of their activity, and preserved for future use" *(Manuel d'archivistique français,* 1970, p. 23).* This definition differs slightly from the English and American one, since it includes in the field of archives documents of a private nature, even personal papers. The French make no distinction between manuscripts and archives, records and archives, or even historical and modern archives. All documents "produced and/or received . . . by any . . . person and/or institution" are considered to be archives, either potentially or actually.

Since France is a country where private property is guaranteed by law, archives are termed public or private, according to whether they are public or private property. Their being "public" does not necessarily mean that they are open to public inspection. For instance, recent government and administration archives are not yet accessible to the public, whereas many "private" archives are liberally open to searchers.

All public archives in France—except the archives of the Ministry of Foreign Affairs and of the army, navy, and air force—are under the authority of the *Direction des archives de France,* an institution belonging to the Ministry of Cultural Affairs. The *Direction des archives de France* issues rules and internal regulations that are applicable to all public archives repositories. Thus, it makes sure that all the rules governing, for instance, accessibility of archives for research, classification, and description are the same throughout the country. For the same reason, all archivists (the official name is *conservateurs d'archives*) working in public archives repositories from Lille to Ajaccio, and even from Fort-de-France, Martinique, to Saint-Denis, Réunion, belong to one professional body, follow one career, and are appointed by one authority.

History of the French Public Archives

The present state of administrative centralization of French public archives goes back to the French Revolution, when, from 1789 to 1792, all the existing institutions of the old France were gradually suppressed. Until that time, archives in France, as in all other European countries, had been kept by their owners. The king had his own archives, partly at Versailles, partly at Paris; the various government offices kept theirs on their own premises; the archives of the parliament of Paris were preserved in the Palace of Justice, near the Sainte-Chapelle. Each abbey, convent, church, hospital, feudal lord, public notary, and justice court kept its archives, for better or for worse (more often for worse), without any kind of public control; the only exceptions were notaries and parish vicars, who had the legal responsibility for baptism, marriage, and death registers. These archives were maintained not for historical research but for utilitarian reasons, as proofs of rights, privileges, noble descent,

and the ownership of land and property.

When all the institutions of the *ancien régime* disappeared, one by one, in the great revolutionary upheaval of 1789 to 1792, all the archives were taken over by the state—or nation, as it was then termed—and a centralized organization was created. The organization created at that time remains, with a few changes, the French public archives.

Organization of the French Public Archives

The archives of the state—that is, of the central institutions of the nation—include those of the government, the National Assembly and Senate, the Council of State, and the Court of Finances. Since the beginning of the French Revolution, these have formed the National Archives, together with the corresponding archives of the *ancien régime* (the archives of the king, the royal government, and the parliament of Paris). As there is only one state, there is only one National Archives, whose headquarters is in Paris (60 rue des Francs-Bourgeois, F-75141 Paris Cedex 03). However, for practical reasons of decentralization, the National Archives has one outside branch, in Aix-en-Provence (for archives from the former colonies), and two other annexes, in Fontainebleau and Saint-Gilles, which are not open to the public.

The archives of the *départements* (the administrative divisions of France) form the departmental archives, together with the corresponding archives of the *ancien régime* on the territory that now constitutes the *départements.* There are as many departmental archives as there are *départements* (ninety-five in France and four overseas, each headed by a prefect appointed by the government). The archives are always located in the capital town of the *département.*

Municipalities (towns or villages) and hospitals keep their own archives, which form the municipal archives (or communal archives—the terms are synonymous) and the hospital archives, respectively.

The four categories of archives—national, departmental, municipal, and hospital—are all under the authority of the *Direction des archives de France,* which is at the same address as the National Archives. Therefore, all are subject to the same rules regarding public research.

Accessibility of French Public Archives

According to a law dating from 1794 (the second year of the Republic), the general rule is that public archives in France are open to public inspection. However, some restrictions are necessary to protect both the right of citizens to privacy and the legal interests of the state or the citizens.

The current legislation on the matter is a decree of November 10, 1970, which states that as a rule, all archives prior to July 10, 1940, are freely available to searchers (it is anticipated that the date will soon be changed to 1945 or 1946). Some categories of documents, because of their confidential or personal nature, will be available only after a longer delay. Lists of those restricted documents are published in the *Journal officiel* under government regulations. The main categories of restricted documents and the period of their restriction are as follows: personal files of civil servants, one hundred years after their birth; files of judicial proceedings, one hundred years; birth, marriage, and death registers, one hundred years; notaries' archives, one hundred years; fiscal archives, one hundred or sixty years; medical archives, one hundred years (or, when they deal with hereditary diseases, 150 years).

For archives that are not freely accessible under these rules, special authorization can be requested from the *Direction des archives de France.* Full explanation must be given in support of the request.

The documents are, as a rule, made available in their original form. Only when documents are especially precious or fragile is a microfilm communicated instead of the original.

Any bona fide searcher is admitted to the search rooms of French public archive repositories. For non-French searchers, some identification from their diplomatic or university authority is required on their first visit. Addresses and opening hours of the repositories are to be found in the "International Directory of Archives" (UNESCO and International Council on Archives, 1975).

Under special conditions, documents from one repository can be obtained in another repository. However, this is possible only within continental France; overseas *départements* and, of course, foreign countries are not included in this arrangement.

A central *Bureau des renseignements* (Information Office) at the National Archives provides all necessary data on the conditions of research in French public archives. The *Salle des inventaires* (Catalog Room), close to the *Bureau des renseignements,* contains all printed finding aids available in French archives, as well as many typed or handwritten ones. A complete list of all available finding aids *(Etat général des inventaires),* whatever their form or nature, will be published.

Historical Resources of French Archives

As suggested above, the contents of French public archive repositories are both homogeneous—since they are all organized along the same lines and ruled by the same regulations—and various—since they have received, along the centuries, archives from many different sources.

The origins of documents kept in French public archive repositories are manyfold. There are archives of the *ancien régime* period, many of which go back as far as the Middle Ages (eleventh and twelfth centuries, although some come from the seventh and eighth centuries). Mainly feudal and church archives, they become more diversified as they near the end of the *ancien régime.* Archives have also been legally transferred from public institutions since the French Revolution. (Under the law, all public institutions should transfer their records to public archives repositories "as soon as they cease to be useful to their work.") In addition, there are archives donated or deposited by private donors or depositors, persons, and institutions, such as banks, private firms, societies, or families. Finally, archives are purchased by the *Direction des archives de France.*

The National Archives

The main repository, for richness of historical content, is the National Archives. The holdings of the National Archives are arranged in two main *sections,* according to whether they date from before the French Revolution *(Section ancienne)* or after the French Revolution *(Section moderne).* Other sections have been created in recent years for documents of a special nature (microfilms, audiovisual archives) and for archives of private origin, whether donated, deposited, or purchased. Archives from former colonies form a separate unit at Aix-en-Provence. The archives of the former Ministry for the Colonies (or *Ministère de la France d'outre-mer*) form yet another section, housed in a separate building in Paris (27 rue Oudinot, 75007 Paris).

The collection of the National Archives is enormous in size: more than 350,000 linear meters of shelves, of several billion documents, contained in about two million boxes or bundles. Unfortunately, no general guide exists for their content. The only global survey is the *Etat sommaire par séries des documents conservés aux archives nationales* (1891), which is largely out of date, of course, for all the archives received since that date. A new *Etat sommaire* is scheduled for 1977. A short but accurate survey of the historical resources of the Archives is given in "France, Archives nationales" (1965).

For the *Section ancienne,* the main archives groups (known as *série* or *fonds*) include the *Trésor des chartes (série J),* consisting of what remains of the kings' personal archives from 956 to the end of the Middle Ages; the *Parlement de Paris (série X),* an impressive sequence of 26,525 registers and files originating from the Supreme Court of Justice of the Monarchy, from 1254 to 1791; the *Châtelet de Paris (série Y),* 18,800 registers and files from the Criminal Court of Paris from 1255 to 1791; the *Monuments historiques (série K)* and *Monuments ecclésiastiques (série L),* containing many archives from civil and church institutions (some of them as early as the seventh century), which were mixed in a rather unfortunate manner during the French Revolution; the *Conseil du roi (série E)* and *Contrôle général des finances (série G^7),* essential for a knowledge of the economic, financial, and political state of France in the seventeenth and eighteenth centuries; and the *Maison du roi (série O),* consisting of all the plans and building records of the royal residences, such as Versailles, Compiègne, and Fontainebleau.

For the period of the French Revolution, the main *séries* are *A, B, C, D* (archives of the *Assemblée nationale constituante, Assemblée législative, Convention,* and other assemblies of the revolution, along with those of their committees which played a prominent role from 1792 to 1794), and *W (Tribunal révolutionnaire).*

The bulk of the archives transferred by the ministries since the French Revolution form *série F,* divided into thirty-three *sous-séries,* and *série BB* (archives from the *Ministère de la justice*). Of special interest for history are *sous-séries F^1* to *F^7* (general administration), *sous-série F^{17}* (public instruction), and *sous-séries F^{30}* to *F^{34}* (financial administration).

The government of Napoleon I, which was very centralized, left a special archives group, *série AF,* called *Secrétairerie d'état impériale.* Nearly all administrative matters are represented in this group, but not, of course, military matters.

Among twentieth-century documents, the archives of the Vichy period are not yet open to public inspection, nor are the de Gaulle and Pompidou personal papers, both donated to the *Archives nationales* after the deaths of their owners.

Among the private archives donated or deposited in the National Archives, or acquired by it, special mention can be made of the archives of the Orléans dynasty, donated by the Comte de Paris in 1969. A complete inventory of the private archives in the National Archives (not including the so-called economic archives of banks and industrial and commercial firms) was published in 1973 (Tourtier-Bonazzi and Huart).

Departmental Archives

Not all departmental archives repositories contain the same holdings, and not all of them have the same historical interest. Nevertheless all of them have basically the same kinds of archives groups. In all of them the historian can find archives from medieval and *ancien régime* abbeys, convents, bishoprics, chapters, and churches *(séries G and H),* many of which go back to the tenth, ninth, and even eighth centuries. There are also archives from feudal families *(série E)* and, in former capitals of feudal states, archives from those states (for example, Nantes for Brittany, Rouen for Normandy, Dijon for Burgundy). In addition, there are archives from justice courts and public notaries, before and after the French Revolution *(séries B, E, U);* archives from the revolutionary assemblies, tribunals, and administrations *(série L);* archives from the *Préfectures,* created in 1800 *(séries M, N, O);* archives from financial administrations *(séries P and Q),* and from military *(série R),* educational *(série T),* religious *(série V),* and social *(série X)* institutions. Finally, there are donated, deposited, and purchased private archives *(série J).*

Many departmental archives repositories have printed guides of their contents (see UNESCO and International Council on Archives, 1975).

Municipal and Hospital Archives

Comparatively few French towns—about eighty—have genuine archives repositories organized in the same manner as the departmental archives. However, in all towns (except perhaps the smallest

ones) searchers can normally consult the archives, provided that they have taken the precaution to write beforehand.

The contents of municipal archives are often very interesting from the standpoint of economic and social history. The archives of some of the main towns, such as Marseilles, Lyons, Bordeaux, Toulouse, and Strasbourg, are of outstanding importance. Unfortunately, the municipal archives of Paris disappeared in 1871, when the Hôtel-de-Ville was destroyed by fire during the *Commune* riot.

Hospital archives are also interesting for the historian of economics, as well as for historians of medicine and public health. Paris and Lyons have very rich and well-organized hospital archives repositories. In some other towns, ancient hospital archives have been deposited in the departmental archives or in the municipal archives.

Other Archives

A brief mention should be made of a few other categories of public archives of historical interest. Besides the *Archives des affaires étrangères* (at 37 quai d'Orsay, F75007 Paris) and *Archives des armées* (at Château de Vincennes, F94300 Vincennes), there are archives in chambers of commerce (especially Marseilles), universities (though few universities keep archives older than fifty or sixty years; older archives are in the departmental archives), bishoprics (containing archives dating from after the French Revolution), and academies.

Information on all French archives can be obtained from the *Direction des archives de France.*

Bibliography

Association des archivistes français. *Manuel d'archivistique: Théorie et pratique des archives publiques en France.* Paris: Direction des archives de France, 1970.

Carbone, S. *Gli archivi francesi.* Quaderni della rassegna degli archivi di stato No. 3. Rome: Direzione archivi di stato, Ministero dell'interno, 1960.

Duchein, M. "Les archives de France." *Archives*

et bibliothèques de Belgique, 1970, *41,* 397–428.

Etat des inventaires des Archives nationales, départementales, communales et hospitalières au 1ᵉʳ janvier 1937. Paris: Direction des archives de France, 1938; *Supplément 1937–1954.* Paris: Direction des archives, 1955.

Etat général par fonds des archives départementales: Ancien régime et période révolutionnaire. Paris: Direction des archives de France, 1903.

Etat sommaire par séries des documents conservés aux Archives nationales. Paris: Direction des archives de France, 1891.

Favier, J. *Les archives.* Collection que sais-je, No. 805. Paris: Presses universitaires de France, 1959.

"France, Archives nationales." *Archivum,* 1965, *15,* 163–171.

Langlois, C. V., and Stein, H. *Les archives de l'histoire de France.* (3rd ed.) Paris: Picard, 1891.

Tourtier-Bonazzi, D. de, and Huart, S. d'. *Archives nationales. Archives privées. Etat des fonds de la série AP.* Vol. 1. Paris: Direction des archives de France, 1973.

UNESCO and the International Council on Archives. "International Directory of Archives." *Archivum,* 1975, *22–23,* 222–260.

MICHEL DUCHEIN

5. FEDERAL REPUBLIC OF GERMANY, GERMAN DEMOCRATIC REPUBLIC, AND AUSTRIA, NATIONAL ARCHIVES OF

German constitutional history has been characterized by two parallel developments: the central authority, represented by the emperor and king of the Holy Roman Empire, and the territorial powers of the princes and of their states. Similarly, with the exception of the nineteenth century, there have always been two types of state archives: central archives of the *Reich* or *Bund* (federation) known as the *Reichsarchive* (usually with ephemeral holdings, located at various places, such as Mainz, Regensburg, Wetzlar, and Vienna); and regional or territorial archives, the *Länderarchive,* which usually can boast of much more comprehensive materials on German history. All the German states *(Länder)* and most of the towns have their own archival offices, independent of each other and of the central archives.

When the Holy Roman Empire came to an end in 1806, the holdings of the central archives, consisting of records of the various imperial institutions and authorities, were taken over by the different state governments. The majority of these holdings were transferred to Vienna and can be found today in the *Österreichisches Staatsarchiv.* In 1866, during the Prussian-Austrian War and the decline of the German Federation *(Deutscher Bund,* 1815–1866*),* most federal records in Frankfurt am Main were also transferred to Vienna. German historians demanded the creation of national archives during the nineteenth century; these demands were repeated by historians of liberalism and of the new German *Reich (Deutsches Reich,* 1871–1945*).* Not until the end of World War I, however, was a national archives established in Germany. The new archives, the *Reichsarchiv,* founded in October 1919 in Potsdam, served chiefly as a collecting point for the departmental records of the *Reich* and its central administration. In addition, the *Reichsarchiv* began to acquire nonpublic materials, such as records of political parties and organizations, private papers of eminent personalities, and press materials. Research departments for military, economic, and political history were established, but only the department of military history survived. The *Reichsarchiv* moved into a new building in 1935.

Although the *Reichsarchiv* was more centralized than its predecessor, it represented a centralized organization rather than a single central institution. Thus, although the majority of its holdings were kept in Potsdam, records of disbanded military organizations from World War I were kept in "outposts" in Dresden and Stuttgart, and part of the records of the Holy Roman Empire and of the German Federation were kept in an outpost in Frankfurt am Main.

In 1936 the idea of a central national archives suffered a decisive defeat, since in the course of rearming the German armed forces, an independent army archives organization, *Heeresarchiv Potsdam,* was created. This organization, placed within the War Department, included the outposts of Dresden and Stuttgart, the army archives of Bavaria in Munich, and, in 1940, the army archives of Austria. However, the archives of the German navy and of the young but tradition-oriented air force were kept in Berlin and remained outside the army organization. Fifty percent of the holdings of the *Reichsarchiv* and the *Heeresarchiv* were evacuated during World War II before a British air raid destroyed a great part of the city of Potsdam and the *Reichsarchiv* itself on April 14, 1945.

Federal Republic of Germany

At the end of World War II, those files and papers of the *Reich*, the German armed forces, and the Nazi Party that were in the Western zones of occupation were seized by the allied forces and subsequently transferred to a large extent to Great Britain and to the United States. The state archives within the German *Länder* continued their archival work, but a new central archival institution was not set up for several years.

History of the Bundesarchiv. In response to demands of such eminent German archivists as Bernhard Vollmer and of German historians, the Federal Republic of Germany established the Federal Archives, the *Bundesarchiv* (D-5400 Koblenz 1, Am Wöllershof 12, P.O.B. 32D) in June 1952. The new central archives were charged with collecting, categorizing, and editing the records and audiovisual materials of the federal government, the armed forces, and the Nazi Party and other political organizations, as well as collecting the archives from the previous *Reichsarchiv* and the former Prussian state archives. The central archives system for the federal government had not yet been completed as of 1976. Although the Department of Defense decided to transfer its records as well as those of the *Bundeswehr* (the new federal armed forces) to the *Bundesarchiv* in 1954, the *Auswärtiges Amt* (Department of State) retained its own archives. The German *Bundestag* (parliament) set up an independent archival institution as well.

Organization of the Bundesarchiv. The *Bundesarchiv* has four divisions, an administrative branch, and several outposts. The first division, the Office of Departmental Affairs, primarily serves as an office of the president of the archives but also includes technical services, such as restoration and repair shops, reproduction sections, storage areas, and a computer center. The second division is the public record office for all civil departments of the former *Reich* (1871–1945) and of the federal government of the Federal Republic of Germany (established 1949). Nonpublic archives, particularly private papers, political party records, and audiovisual materials, form the third division. The fourth division, the military archives, is located in Freiburg im Breisgau.

Holdings of the Bundesarchiv. As of 1975 these holdings included 171,000 feet of records; 79,000 volumes of official manuscripts; 1,600,000 photographs, posters, and sound recordings; and 114 feet of documentary and fiction films. The holdings of the main archives in Koblenz include the *Reich* archives from 1867 to 1945, the archives of German authorities in the Allied zones from 1945 to 1949, and the records of the federal government since 1949. Important record groups for the *Reich* period are the *Reichskanzlei* (State Chancery) (reference number R43), covering the period since 1919; the *Auswärtiges Amt* (Foreign Office) (R85), with records on trade policy and international law from 1867 to 1920; the *Reichsjustizministerium* (State Ministry of Justice) (R22), covering 1877 and 1935 to 1945; the *Reichsfinanzministerium* (State Ministry of Finance) (R2), with nearly complete records from 1930 to the present and some records concerning duty and trade policy dating back to 1878; the *Reichswirtschaftsministerium* (State Ministry of National Economy) (R7), 1917–1945; the *Reichsministerium für Rüstung und Kriegsproduktion* (State Ministry of Defense and War Production) (R3), 1940–1945; the *Reichsministerium des Innern* (State Ministry of Interior) (R18), 1879–1945;

the *Reichsministerium für Wissenschaft, Erziehung und Volksbildung* (State Ministry of Science, Education and Culture) (R55), 1934–1945; *the Reichsministerium für Volksaufklärung und Propaganda* (State Ministry of Public Enlightenment and Propaganda) (R55), 1933–1945; the *Reichsarbeitsministerium* (State Ministry of Labor) (R41), 1918–1945; and the *Reichsministerium für Ernährung, Landwirtschaft und Forsten* (State Ministry of Nutrition, Agriculture and Forestry) (R14), 1916–1921. In all, section R contains 154 different record groups.

The records of the former Nazi Party constitute another set of record groups within the *Bundesarchiv,* with reference numbers NS 1 to 38. These archival holdings are supplemented by vast numbers of biographical files and other archival materials within the United States document center in West Berlin. The materials on the post–World War II period, including the records of the German authorities in the allied occupation zones from 1945 to 1949, form section Z, with forty-two separate record groups. There are already as many as 103 record groups for the Federal Republic of Germany, but these can be used only by special permission of the department concerned.

The *Bundesarchiv* holds an important collection of private papers (350 separate groups) of politicians, high-ranking civil servants, party leaders, trade unionists, military persons, and academics dating back to the nineteenth century and includes the private papers of the two first presidents of the Federal Republic of Germany, Theodor Heuss and Heinrich Lübke. The *Zeitgeschichtliche Sammlungen* (documentation for contemporary history) contains records of political parties and organizations, trade unions, associations of various professional organizations, and vast collections of press material from 1867 to the present. Another collection contains official printed materials of the *Reich* and the Prussian and federal governments (1815–1866 and 1949–   ), and the printed materials of the Nazi Party are also in the ar-

chives. The audiovisual archives have an audio branch (with important items from the Nazi period) and a photography section (with about 1,300,000 items from the nineteenth and twentieth centuries, particularly rich for the Nazi period and the two world wars). The photography section also holds a collection of political posters dating back to the first decade of the twentieth century.

The *Bundesarchiv-Filmarchiv* is housed in the headquarters at Koblenz. The storage area, technical services, and facilities for using the archives are housed in a separate building on the Festung Ehrenbreitstein. The *Filmarchiv* has collected the documentary films produced by all governmental agencies before 1945 (that is, those that were found in West Germany after World War II or that were returned by the United States) and still receives negatives and copies of all films produced by federal departments and agencies. In addition, there is an important collection of German newsreels. The *Bundesarchiv-Filmarchiv* has also rescued a large number of nitrate films (both private and commercial) from deterioration by copying the films on safety material. Since 1969 the *Filmarchiv* has launched a program for the preservation of old and new German fiction films.

Outposts of the Bundesarchiv. The *Bundesarchiv, Aussenstelle Frankfurt/Main* (D-6000 Frankfurt/Main, Seckbächer Gasse 4), one of five outposts, was set up in 1925 through the cooperation of the *Reichsarchiv* and the city of Frankfurt for the preservation of those archives of the Holy Roman Empire and of the German Federation (1815–1866) that had remained in Germany (that is, they were not transferred to Austria during the nineteenth century or distributed to the archives of the *Länder*). This outpost was incorporated by the *Bundesarchiv* in 1953. The most significant record groups are the *Reichskammergericht* (Imperial High Court of Justice), covering 1495 to 1806; the *Deutscher Bund* (German Confederation), covering 1815 to 1866 and including the *Deutsche Bundesversammlung* (Assembly of the German Diet); the *Provi-*

sorische Zentralgewalt (Provisional Central Control), covering 1848 to 1849 and including records of the *Reich* government during the Revolution of 1848; and the *Deutsche Verfassungsgebende Reichsversammlung* (German Constitutional Assembly) and the *Nationalversammlung in der Paulskirche* (National Assembly in the Church of St. Paul in Frankfurt), covering 1848 to 1849. This outpost also contains records of student corporations and organizations, such as the *Deutsche Burschenschaft* (a corporation of students at German universities) and the *Verband der Vereine deutscher Studenten* (an association of German student organizations) and collections of private papers, including family archives.

The *Bundesarchiv-Militärarchiv* (D-7800 Freiburg/Breisgau, Wiesentalstrasse 10), the fourth division of the *Bundesarchiv*, began its professional activities in 1954 in Koblenz, but was transferred to Freiburg in 1967 to improve the research facilities for the staff of the historical research center of the defense department *(Militärgeschichtliches Forschungsamt)*, which at that time was incorporated into the *Bundesarchiv-Militärarchiv*. This *Bundesarchiv* outpost holds all records that have been returned by the United States since 1960 of the former German *Wehrmacht* (armed forces) and preserves the archives of the former German navy *(Marinearchiv, 1848–1945)*. A military record center, annexed to the *Militärarchiv*, holds inactive records of the defense department, military agencies, and armed forces *(Bundeswehr)* (new federal armed forces). These holdings contain military records, maps, and other paraphernalia of the former Prussian army (1867–1918), the *Reichswehr* (German defensive land and naval forces, 1919–1921), and the *Wehrmacht* (armed forces, 1935–1945) as well as those of the *Bundeswehr*. The outpost also holds important collections of materials relating to military history, particularly official records and private papers of high-ranking military persons.

The *Bundesarchiv-Zentralnachweisstelle* (central information office) (D-5106 Kornelimünster, Alte Abtei) was set up in 1946 under the name *Zentralarchiv des Hauptversorgungsamtes Nordrhein-Westfalen;* it became part of the *Bundesarchiv* in 1954. This outpost contains the personnel files, card indexes, and staff lists of the former German *Wehrmacht* (including military personnel of Austria), the *Waffen-SS*, the *Reichsarbeitsdienst* (state labor office), and the *Organisation Todt*.

The *Bundesarchiv-Zwischenarchiv* (interim archives) (D-5205 St. Augustin near Bonn, Richthofenstrasse 52) is the federal record center for all departments of the federal government in Bonn except the Department of Defense and the Foreign Office.

By the initiative of the president of the Federal Republic of Germany, the *Bundesarchiv-Erinnerungsstätte für die Freiheitsbewegungen in der deutschen Geschichte* (memorial for the struggle for independence in German history) (D-7550 Rastatt/Baden, Schloss/Herrenstrasse) was created in 1974 in Rastatt, where the remaining troops of the German revolutionary army of 1849 were defeated by the Prussian army. This outpost exhibits archival materials concerning the history of movements for liberty and democracy in Germany, provides public lectures to visiting groups, maintains permanent exhibition of archival materials on revolutionary movements, and arranges research conferences.

Independent archives. There are several important archives that are independent of the *Bundesarchiv*. The *Auswärtiges Amt, Politisches Archiv* (Department of State, political archives) (D-5300 Bonn, Adenauerallee 99-103) is the archive of the German Foreign Office, which has kept its own records since its origin in 1867 (with the exception of records concerning trade politics and international law that are in the *Bundesarchiv* and some older materials in the *Zentrales Staatsarchiv* of the German Democratic Republic). Installed in 1921 in Berlin and transferred to Bonn in 1954, the *Politisches Archiv* holds the records of the Foreign Office returned by the Western allies from 1956 to 1959. The archives, organized as a section within the Foreign Office, include a collection of private papers of former members of the diplomatic service and of Foreign Office ministers.

The foundation of the *Geheimes Staatsarchiv* (Stiftung preussischer Kulturbesitz, D-1000 Berlin 33 [Dahlem], Archivstrasse 12–14)—the central archives of the former state of Prussia—dates back to medieval times. Reorganized in 1598, the holdings were grouped archivally for the first time in 1639. Most of the collection was evacuated during World War II to what was to become the Soviet zone of occupation, and they now form the second division of the *Zentrales Staatsarchiv* of the German Democratic Republic. Nevertheless, the archival holdings of the *Geheimes Staatsarchiv* still contain important historical documents on Prussia and are indispensable to studies of German history.

The Federal Republic of Germany is a federation of ten states *(Länder)* plus West Berlin. Each state independently administers its own state archives *(Länderarchiv Verwaltungen)*, with archival holdings of regional, local, and national significance. Most of the state archives have early origins, and neither regional nor national German history can be adequately studied without these archival source materials. The main state archives in the Federal Republic of Germany are in Baden-Württemberg: *Hauptstaatsarchiv Stuttgart* (D-7000 Stuttgart 1, Konrad-Adenauer-Strasse 4); Bavaria: *Bayerisches Hauptstaatsarchiv* (D-8000 Munich 2, Arcisstrasse 12, P.O.B. 200507); West Berlin: *Landesarchiv Berlin* (D-1000 Berlin 12, Strasse des 17. Juni 112 [Ernst-Reuter-Haus]); Bremen: *Staatsarchiv Bremen* (D-2800 Bremen 1, Präsident-Kennedy-Platz 2); Hamburg: *Staatsarchiv Hamburg* (D-2000 Hamburg 36, ABC-Strasse 19); Hesse: *Hessisches Hauptstaatsarchiv Wiesbaden* (D-6200 Wiesbaden, Mainzer Strasse 80); Lower Saxony: *Niedersächsisches Hauptstaatsarchiv in Hannover* (D-3000 Hanover, Am Archive 1); North Rhine–Westphalia: *Hauptstaats-*

archiv Düsseldorf (D-4000 Düsseldorf 30; Mauerstrasse 55); Rhineland-Palatinate: *Landeshauptarchiv Koblenz* (D-5400 Koblenz, Karmeliterstrasse 1); Saarland: *Landesarchiv Saarbrücken* (D-6600 Saarbrücken 1, Am Ludwigplatz 14); Schleswig-Holstein: *Landesarchiv Schleswig-Holstein* (D-2380 Schleswig, Schloss Gottorf).

German Democratic Republic

In the Soviet zone of occupation, the military authorities in 1946 ordered the creation of *Zentralarchiv für die sowjetische Besatzungszone* (central archives for the Soviet occupation zone) (DDR-15 Potsdam, Berliner Strasse 98-101), which succeeded the *Reichsarchiv* as well as the former Prussian state archives *(Preussisches geheimes Staatsarchiv)* and the Hohenzollern archives *(Brandenburg-Preussisches Hausarchiv)*. Because most of the holdings of the former *Reichsarchiv* and *Preussisches Geheimes Staatsarchiv* were evacuated into the present territory of the German Democratic Republic during World War II, the *Zentralarchiv* was given control of about two thirds of the records of the former *Deutsches Reich* and of Prussia, particularly after the Soviet Union had returned the records of German governmental departments during the 1950s.

The tasks of the central archives in Potsdam were to collect (1) the archival materials of the former *Reichsarchiv, Preussisches geheimes Staatsarchiv,* and Hohenzollern *Hausarchiv;* (2) the records of the *Reich* government and of the new German authorities within the Soviet zone of occupation; (3) the records of political parties, trade unions, economic organizations, trusts, private firms, and other national organizations; and (4) to launch a documentation program for contemporary German history.

After the foundation of the German Democratic Republic in 1949, the archives were renamed *Deutsches Zentralarchiv;* in 1974 the name was changed again to *Zentrales Staatsarchiv.* During the following years a centralized organization for all archival institutions within the German Democratic Republic developed and was administered at the top by the Potsdam headquarters. This centralized organization constitutes a division within the Department of Interior of the German Democratic Republic. Professional archival work in state institutions is based on progressive archives legislation, which is influenced by similar developments within the Soviet Union *(Verordnung über das staatliche Archivwesen vom 17. Juni 1965).*

The central archives system, however, is still incomplete: the Department of Defense and the armed forces of the German Democratic Republic *(Nationale Volksarmee)* transfer their inactive records to the *Deutsches Militärarchiv,* which is outside the organization of the *Zentrales Staatsarchiv,* and although the audiovisual source material contains different collections, it lacks documentary and fiction films.

Organization of the Zentrales Staatsarchiv. The archives are organized by divisions. At the headquarters in Potsdam are the historical division 1 (for the archives up to 1945) and the division for socialism (for the archives since 1945, including sections for records management and services). The archives of the former Prussian *Geheimes Staatsarchiv* and of the Prussian government departments and administrative agencies, dissolved at the end of World War II, are housed in the historical division 2; this division is an outpost of the *Zentrales Staatsarchiv* in Merseburg/Saale. The centralized record center for the administration of central government within the German Democratic Republic forms division 3 and was placed at an outpost in Coswig/Anhalt in 1965.

Holdings of the Zentrales Staatsarchiv. The holdings of the main archives at Potsdam (historical division 1) cover the period of the *Deutsches Reich* (1867–1945). The most important record groups in this division are the *Reichstag* (Parliament) (1867–1938); the *Bundesrat/Reichsrat,* (Federal Council/Council of the State) (1874–1934); the *Büro des Reichspräsidenten/Präsidialkanzlei*

(Office of the President of the *Reich*/Presidential Chancellory) (1919–1939); the *Reichskanzlei* (Chancery) (1878–1945), complete for the imperial period up to 1918; the *Auswärtiges Amt* (1867–1945), including those records that had been turned over to the *Reichsarchiv* before 1945, particularly records of German embassies; the *Reichsamt/Reichsministerium des Innern* (State Ministry of the Interior) (1867–1945); the *Reichskommissar für die Überwachung der öffentlichen Ordnung* (federal commissioner for the supervision of public order) (1920–1929), most important for the history of the right- and left-wing political movements during the Weimar period; the *Reichsfinanzministerium* (State Ministry of Finance) (1867–1945), particularly rich in materials on the imperial and Weimar periods up to 1929; the *Reichsjustizministerium* (State Ministry of Justice) (1877–1945), complete up to 1933; the *Reichswirtschaftsministerium* (State Ministry of National Economy) (1917–1945); the *Reichsarbeitsministerium* (State Ministry of Labor) (1879–1944); the *Reichspostministerium* (General Post Office) (1867–1928); the *Reichsministerium für Wissenschaft, Erziehung und Volksbildung* (State Ministry for Science, Education, and National Instruction) (1867–1945); the *Reichsministerium für Volksaufklärung und Propaganda* (1933–1945); and the *Reichsministerium für die kirchlichen Angelegenheiten* (Ministry for Clerical Affairs) (1933–1945).

The *Zentrales Staatsarchiv* has an extremely rich collection of the records of political parties (excluding those of the Social Democratic and Communist parties), political organizations and associations, professional associations and industrial groups, and industrial trusts and private firms. In addition, the *Zentrales Staatsarchiv* houses about 350 collections of private papers, including those of members of Parliament and members of the economic and academic elite before 1945. The *Zentrales Staatsarchiv* also has vast collections of manuscripts and documents concerning the war of 1870–1871, World War I, the revolution of 1918, and the history of occupied German territories after World War I. Finally, there are collections of autographs, genealogical papers, and heraldic material (covering the period from 1708 to 1932), and a cartographic collection of about 25,000 items.

Outposts of the Zentrales Staatsarchiv. The *Zentrales Staatsarchiv, Historische Abteilung II* (historical division 2) (DDR-42, Merseburg, Weisse Mauer 48), set up as a collection point for archives and documents in 1948, contains all archives and records of the former Prussian *Geheimes Staatsarchiv* and the Hohenzollern *Hausarchiv* as well as those of Prussian authorities and agencies that were evacuated during World War II to the territory of the present German Democratic Republic and that were not returned to the *Geheimes Staatsarchiv* in West Berlin after 1945. In addition, the Merseburg outpost has an important collection of private papers of eminent personalities in Prussian history, particularly of the nineteenth century.

The second outpost, the *Zentrales Staatsarchiv, Dienststelle Coswig* (DDR-4522 Coswig/Anhalt) forms division 3 of the *Zentrales Staatsarchiv* and serves as a record center for the departments of the German Democratic Republic and its central administrative bodies, and for other central institutions, including public-owned industrial and commercial organizations.

Independent archives. The *Deutsches Militärarchiv* (DDR-15 Potsdam) is one of two important independent archives. Founded in 1965, it contains the military archives of the German Democratic Republic and houses the archival remnants of the former *Heeresarchiv Potsdam* and of the *Heeresarchiv* in Dresden. The holdings of the *Deutsches Militärarchiv* include a significant collection of private papers of military persons.

A second independent institution, the *Staatliches Filmarchiv der DDR* (DDR-108 Berlin, Kronenstrasse 10), founded in 1955, is the central film archives of the German Democratic Republic. This insti-tution provides centralized archival service for the public broadcasting and television corporation of the German Democratic Republic, and its holdings cover all periods of both fiction and documentary film production in Germany.

Republic of Austria

The Austrian state archives governing board—*Österreichisches Staatsarchiv: Generaldirektion* (A-1010 Vienna I, Minoritenplatz 1)—administers the central archives of Austria in Vienna. It was created by legislation in 1945—replacing the *Reichsarchiv Vienna,* which had been formed in 1940 after the *Anschluss* (annexation of Austria by Germany)—and actually began operating in 1947. The board is chaired by the *Bundeskanzleramt* (Chancellor's Office). The divisions of the *Österreichisches Staatsarchiv* under the *Generaldirektion* are the *Haus-, Hof- und Staatsarchiv* (division 1), the *Allgemeines Verwaltungsarchiv* (division 2), the *Finanz- und Hofkammerarchiv* (division 3), the *Kriegsarchiv* (division 4), and the *Archiv für Verkehrswesen* (division 5).

The *Haus-, Hof- und Staatsarchiv* (A-1010 Vienna I, Minoritenplatz 1) is one of the greatest archival institutions in Europe. Until 1806, it was the central archive of the Holy Roman Empire. The tripartite name can be understood by its component parts: *Haus* means the family papers of the Hapsburg dynasty; *Hof,* the court and legal records of the Austrian monarchy as well as of the Hapsburg kaisers of the *Reich;* and *Staat,* the records of the administrative boards of the *Reich* as well as of the Austrian territories. The institution was created by the centralization of older archives in 1749 by Empress Maria Theresa.

The most important holdings in this archive are the *Reichshofkanzlei* (State Court Chancery) (c. 1400–1806); the *Reichshofrat* (state privy councillor) (fifteenth century to 1806); the *Mainzer Erzkanzlerarchiv* (archives of the archchancellor of Mainz) (fifteenth century to 1806); the *Staatskanzlei* (Chancery of the State) (fourteenth century to 1848); the *Ministerium des Äussern* (Ministry of Foreign Affairs) (1848–1918), including archives of embassies and consulates (seventeenth century to 1918); the *Staatenabteilungen* (division of states), containing diplomatic correspondences of the *Reichshofkanzlei*, and the *Staatskanzlei* (thirteenth century to 1860); the *Grosse Korrespondenz* (fifteenth to nineteenth century); the *Habsburgisch, lothringische und estensische Hausarchive* (thirteenth to nineteenth century); the *Hofarchive* (1495 to the twentieth century); the *Urkunden* (charters, 816–1918); the *Handschriftensammlungen* (manuscript collections, ninth to twentieth century); the *Österreichische Akten* (Austrian documents) (fifteenth to eighteenth century); the *Ungarische Akten* (Hungarian documents) (sixteenth to nineteenth century); the *Italien, Spanien, Belgien* (fifteenth to eighteenth century); and the *Staatsamt resp. Bundeskanzleramt auswärtige Angelegenheiten* (government office respective to the Chancellor of Foreign Affairs) (1918–1938), including archives of embassies and consulates. Vast collections of private papers and family archives, particularly of the *Reich* and Austrian nobility, are also included.

The *Allgemeines Verwaltungsarchiv* (General Administrative Archives) (A-1010 Vienna I, Wallnerstrasse 6 a), set up in 1945, was formed by the former *Staatsarchiv des Innern und der Justiz* (State Archives of the Interior and Justice) and by the archives of the *Ministerium für Kultus und Unterricht* (Ministry of Culture and Instruction). In time, the archives of the departments of agriculture, trade, and public works were added. Portions of these archives date back to the sixteenth century; however, the records are complete for the period of the first Austrian republic (1918–1938) and for the central administrative institutions during the period from 1938 to 1945 when Austria was part of the *Deutsches Reich*.

The *Finanz- und Hofkammerarchiv* (Finance and Court Chamber Archives) (A-1010 Vienna I, Himmelpfortgasse 8 und Johannesgasse 6) was created by the unification of the *Hofkammerarchiv* and the archives of the Department of Finance in 1945. The history of the *Hofkammerarchiv* dates back to 1527, the year the *Hofkammer* was created by Emperor Ferdinand I, and the archival holdings were categorized and listed as early as the eighteenth century. The poet Franz Grillparzer served as head of the *Hofkammerarchiv* from 1832 to 1856. The *Finanzarchiv* was created in 1893 within the *Finanzministerium* (Finance Ministry), and the archives are comprehensive for the nineteenth and twentieth centuries.

The *Kriegsarchiv* (War Archives) (A-1010 Vienna VII, Stiftsgasse 2) has a long history. The first archivist for the records of the *Hofkriegsrat* (Court Council of War) was appointed through the initiative of Prince Eugene in 1711. In 1801 a separate *Kriegsarchiv* was set up; it was united with the older *Hofkriegsarchiv* in 1846. In the late eighteenth century, the archives were charged with serving the armed forces of Austria as an information center for military sciences. These archives are extremely rich in German history as well as in the history of most countries of southern and southeastern Europe. Most significant is its vast collection of military cartography (nearly 300,000 items).

Shortly after the foundation of the *Eisenbahnministerium* (Ministry of Railroads) in 1896, the *Archiv für Verkehrswesen* (Archives for Communication) (A-1030 Vienna III, Aspangstrasse 33) was established to preserve all historical records and maps concerning Austrian railway construction and administration. In 1920 the archives acquired the records of the *Verkehrsministerium* (Ministry of Communication), including those of the postal services.

Bibliography

Absolon, R. "Das Bundesarchiv, Abteilung Zentralnachweisstelle." *Der Archivar*, 1955, 8, 179–188.

Absolon, R. *Sammlung Wehrrechtlicher Gutachten und Vorschriften.* Vol. 1. Federal Republic of Germany, Kornelimünster: Bundesarchiv, 1963.

Archivalische Quellennachweise zur Geschichte der

deutschen Arbeiterbewegung im Deutschen Zentralarchiv Potsdam. Vol. 1. Berlin, German Democratic Republic: Staatsverlag, 1962. *Der Archivar*, 1947, *1*.

Barkhausen, H. "Probleme der Filmarchivierung." *Der Archivar*, 1967, *20*, 361–368.

Boberach, H. "Das Schriftgut der staatlichen Verwaltung, der Wehrmacht und der NSDAP aus der Zeit von 1933–1945. Versuch einer Bilanz." *Der Archivar*, 1969, *22*, 137–152.

Booms, H. "Zusammenfassung des militärischen Archivgutes im Bundesarchiv." *Der Archivar*, 1968, *21*, 237–240.

Breneke, A., and Leesch, W. *Archivkunde. Ein Beitrag zur Theorie und Geschichte des europäischen Archivwesens.* Munich, Federal Republic of Germany: Verlag Dokumentation, 1970.

Demeter, K. "Das Bundesarchiv Abteilung Frankfurt/M." *Archivalische Zeitschrift*, 1954, *49*, 111–125.

Deutsches Zentralarchiv 1946–1971. Potsdam, German Democratic Republic: Deutsches Zentralarchiv, 1971.

Dräger, U., and Lehrmann, I. "Zur Geschichte und Auflösung des Brandenburg-Preussischen Hausarchivs." *Archivmitteilungen*, 1969, *6*, 230–239.

Facius, F., Booms, M., and Boberach, H. *Das Bundesarchiv und seine Bestände.* (2nd ed.) Boppard, Federal Republic of Germany: Harald Boldt Verlag, 1968.

Findbücher zu Beständen des Bundesarchivs. Vols. 1–13. Koblenz, Federal Republic of Germany: Bundesarchiv, 1970–1975.

Franz, E. G. *Einführung in die Archivkunde.* Darmstadt, Federal Republic of Germany: Wissenschaftliche Buchgesellschaft, 1974.

Gesamtinventar des Wiener Haus-, Hof- und Staatsarchivs. (5 vols.) Vienna: Verlag A. Holzhausens Nachfolger, 1936–1940.

Goldinger, W. *Geschichte des österreichischen Archivwesens.* Horn, Austria: Ferdinand Berger, 1957.

Inventar des allgemeinen Archivs des Ministeriums des Innern. Vienna: Federal Austrian Printing Office, 1909.

Inventar des Archivs des K. K. Finanzministeriums. Vienna: Federal Austrian Printing Office, 1911.

Inventar des Kriegsarchivs Wien. (2 vols.) Horn, Austria: Ferdinand Berger, 1953.

Johann, G. "Der Neubau des Bundesarchiv-Zwischenarchivs bei Bonn." *Archivalische Zeitschrift*, 1972, *68*, 93–98.

Kahlenberg, F. P. "Das Zwischenarchiv des Bundesarchivs." *Archivalische Zeitschrift*, 1968, *64*, 27–40.

Kahlenberg, F. P. *Deutsche Archive in West und Ost. Zur Entwicklung des staatlichen Archivwesens seit 1945.* Düsseldorf, Federal Republic of Germany: Droste, 1972.

Klaue, W. "Das Staatliche Filmarchiv der DDR." *Archivmitteilungen*, 1961, *5*, 146–151.

Kohte, W. *Photographische, phonographische, kinematographische Dokumente und audiovisuelle Archive.* Moscow: Eighth International Congress on Archives, 1972.

Mechtler, P. *Inventar des Verkehrsarchivs Wien.* Vienna: 1959.

Nissen, G. "Das Schicksal der ausgelagerten Bestände des Preussischen Geheimen Staatsarchivs und des Brandenburg-Preussischen Hausarchivs und ihr jetziger Zustand." *Archivalische Zeitschrift*, 1954, *49*, 139–150.

Philippi, H. "Das Politische Archiv des Auswärtigen Amtes. Rückführung und Übersicht über die Bestände." *Der Archivar*, 1960, *13*, 199–218.

Rogge, H. "Das Reichsarchiv." *Archivalische Zeitschrift*, 1925, *35*, 119–133.

Schmid, G. "Die Verluste in den Beständen des ehemaligen Reichsarchivs im 2.Weltkrieg." In *Archivar und Historiker. Zum 65. Geburtstag von Heinrich O. Meissner.* Berlin, German Democratic Republic: Rütten & Loening, 1956.

Schriften des Bundesarchivs. Vols. 1–21. Boppard, Federal Republic of Germany: Harald Boldt Verlag, 1955–1975.

Scrinium. Zeitschrift des Verbandes österreichischer Archivare, 1969, *1*.

Stahl, F. C. "Die Bestände des Bundesarchivs-Militärarchivs." *Militärgeschichtliche Mitteilungen*, 1968, *2*, 139–144.

Taschenbuch Archivwesen der DDR. Berlin, Staatsverlag der DDR, 1971.

Übersicht über die Bestände des Deutschen Zentralarchivs Potsdam. Berlin, German Democratic Republic: Rütten & Loening, 1957.

Übersicht über die Bestände des Geheimen Staatsarchivs in Berlin-Dahlem. (2 vols.) Cologne and Berlin, German Democratic Republic: Grot'sche Verlagsbuchhandlung, 1966–1967.

Übersicht über die Bestände des Geheimen Staatsarchivs zu Berlin-Dahlem. Vol. 3. Leipzig, German Democratic Republic: Verlag S. Hirzel, 1934–1935, 1939.

Verzeichnis der Archivare an Archiven der Bundesrepublik Deutschland mit Land Berlin, in der Deutschen Demokratischen Republik, der Republik Österreich und der Schweizerischen Eidgenossenschaft. (12th ed.) Wiesbaden, Federal Republic of Germany: Verein deutscher Archivare, 1975.

Vietsch, E. v., and Kohte, W. *Das Bundesarchiv, Entwicklung und Aufgaben.* Boppard, Federal

Republic of Germany: Harald Boldt Verlag, 1966.

Volkmann, H. "Der Neubau des staatlichen Filmarchivs der DDR." *Archivmitteilungen*, 1968, *1*, 27–35.

Zipfel, E. "Die Organisation des Reichsarchivs von der Gründung bis zur Bildung der Wehrmacht 1919–1937." *Archivalische Zeitschrift*, 1939, *45*, 1–6.

FRIEDRICH P. KAHLENBERG

6. MEDITERRANEAN, THE VATICAN, AND LATIN AMERICA, NATIONAL ARCHIVES OF

This essay outlines the major holdings of the archival institutions of Spain and Italy; the Vatican archives are also discussed. In addition, there are brief listings of the major archives in Latin America.

Spain

The system of Spanish archives, responding to its history and to various political and administrative divisions, includes archives of a general historical, regional, and provincial nature. Each archives collects documentation about the administrative and judicial bodies of the state. The most important of these, for reasons of antiquity, are the Archives of the Crown of Aragon (ninth century), the Archives of Simancas (1540), the Archives of the Indies (1785), and the National Historical Archives (1866). These collections house the documentation of the kingdoms of Aragon, Castile, the Indies (America), and all other territories, from their earliest days to the present. The Spanish presence in Europe and throughout the world is recorded in these resources, which are of interest not only for the study of Spain's national history but also for that of the many nations and peoples with which Spain had political, economic, religious, and cultural relations.

Archives of the Crown of Aragon. The Archives of the Crown of Aragon (in Barcelona) contains 44,559 books and 4606 bundles, which occupy 6232 linear meters. The oldest documentation dates from 889. This archives is divided into thirteen sections: *Cancillería real* (Royal Chancery,

ninth to eighteenth centuries); *Real patrimonio* (Royal Estate); *Consejo supremo de Aragón* (High Council of Aragon); *Procesos* (Legal Proceedings); *Generalidad de Cataluña* (Legislative Assembly of Catalonia); *Ordenes religiosas y militares* (Religious and Military Orders); *Gran priorato de Cataluña de la Orden de San Juan de Jerusalem* (Catalan Priory of St. John of Jerusalem); *Audiencias y justicia* (Royal Tribunal and Courts of Justice); *Guerra de independencia* (the War for Independence); *Archivos notariales* (Notarial Archives); *Diversos* (Miscellaneous); *Sigilografía* (Sigillography); *Hacienda* (Treasury).

The documents contained in the Archives of the Crown of Aragon serve as a base for all historical studies of Catalonia. Because of the importance of this kingdom to the entire Mediterranean, especially during the Middle Ages, they also contain information about the European, African, and Asian countries of the area. The chancery of Catalonia, through its relations with the Vatican, was very well organized, and its registers are of great historical importance. The archives has published *Colección de documentos inéditos* and a short guide, *Guía abreviada*, in addition to indexes and catalogs of the resources.

Archives of Simancas. The Archives of Simancas (in Simancas, province of Valladolid) was at one time the archives of the Crown of Castile, and its documentation deals primarily with the monarchs of the house of Austria. It possesses 4979 books, 68,242 bundles, and 3012 maps, plans, and stamps that occupy 9494 linear meters. It has fourteen divisions: *Patronato real* (Royal Estate, 834–1851); *Secretaría de estado* (Secretary of State, fifteenth to eighteenth centuries); *Secretarías de los consejos de Flandes, Italia y Portugal* (Councils of Flanders, Italy, and Portugal); *Visitas de Italia* (Italian Council of Ministers); *Consejo real de Castilla* (Royal Council of Castile); *Cámara de Castilla* (Royal House of Castile); *Patronato eclesiástico* (Ecclesiastical Estate, 1482–1715); *Gracia y justicia* (Ministry of Justice, sixteenth to nineteenth centuries); *Registro del sello de corte* (Royal Registry, 1475–1689); *Casa real: Obras y bosques* (Royal Residence and Lands); *Guerra y marina* (the Navy, sixteenth to eighteenth centuries); *Hacienda de la Corona de Castilla* (Treasury, fifteenth to eighteenth centuries); *Mapas, planos y dibujos* (Maps, Plans, and Drawings, sixteenth to eighteenth centuries); and *Varios* (Miscellaneous). These resources are indispensable to a thorough knowledge of European history, since much of Europe was in contact with Spain for patrimonial, political, and economic reasons. There are published indexes and catalogs to this collection, such as the research guide, *Guía del investigador* (Bores, 1962).

Archives of the Indies. The Archives of the Indies (in Seville) was created by Charles III to preserve all documentation of the overseas provinces that had previously been housed in various locations throughout Spain; it includes 43,110 bundles and 6066 maps and plans. These occupy 7957 linear meters, divided as follows: *Patronato real* (Royal Estate, 1480–1790); *Contaduría general del Consejo de Indias* (General Accounting for the Council of the Indies, 1510–1778); *Casa de la contratación de Indias* (Trade Commission of the Indies, 1492–1795); *Justicia* (Justice, 1515–1617); *Gobierno* (Government, 1492–1854); *Escribanía de cámara de justicia* (Correspondence of the Judiciary, 1525–1761); *Secretaría del juzgado de arribadas de Cádiz y comisaria interventora de hacienda pública en Cádiz* (Court for Emergency Procedures and Overseeing of the Public Treasury of Cadiz, 1700–1821); *Correos* (Postal Service, 1763–1846); *Estado* (State, 1700–1836); *Ultramar* (Overseas Possessions, 1605–1870); *Capitanía general de la isla de Cuba* (Captain Generalcy of the Island of Cuba, 1585–1867); *Consulados de Sevilla y Cádiz* (Consulates of Seville and Cadiz, 1543–1857); *Títulos de Castilla* (Castilian Titles, eighteenth to nineteenth centuries); *Papeles de España* (Spanish Papers, 1650–1841); *Tribunal de cuentas* (Accounting, 1851–1887); and *Mapas, planos, dibujos y estampas* (Maps, Plans, Drawings, and Engravings).

The Archives of the Indies houses documentation relative to the American and Philippine provinces from their discovery to the end of the Spanish Empire. It includes all administrative, military, and religious papers sent to the central authorities in Spain. The holdings represent a part of the total documentation produced in the development of these territories, some of which remains at the place of origin.

National Historical Archives. The National Historical Archives (in Madrid) was created to house the documentation of administrative bodies no longer active (for example, convents and monasteries taken over by the state). This archives, the richest in the country, contains 57,127 books and 156,167 bundles and occupies 31,220 linear meters. Its sections include *Clero secular y regular* (Secular and Regular Clergy, eighteenth to nineteenth centuries); *Ordenes militares* (Military Orders, twelfth to twentieth centuries); *Estado* (State, seventeenth to nineteenth centuries); *Juros* (Rights of Ownership, fourteenth to nineteenth centuries); *Universidades y colegios* (Universities and Schools); *Sigilografía* (Sigillography); *Inquisición* (the Inquisition); *Consejos suprimidos* (Eliminated Councils); *Códices y cartularios* (Codices and Archives); *Ultramar* (Overseas Possessions, eighteenth century to 1898); *Osuna; Diversos* (Miscellaneous); and *Fondos modernos* (Modern Resources, seventeenth to nineteenth centuries).

The archives contains documentation of the House of Bourbon as well as information concerning many now defunct institutions (councils, the Inquisition, military orders). It also provides substantial ecclesiastical documentation, much of it from the Middle Ages. These documents of Spain and its overseas possessions aid in the study of European and American history and provide information concerning Spain's relations with African and Oriental territories. There is a guide to the archive, *Guía del Archivo histórico nacional* (Belda, 1958), and indexes and catalogs for several of the sections.

In these major archives are preserved both public and ecclesiastical documentation of universal importance. The five regional and forty-five provincial archives in Spain contain information about all political and administrative bodies from the time of their creation to the present. In addition to the collections mentioned above, there are several ecclesiastical archives (diocesan, cathedral, parochial, monastic, and collegiate). For information concerning these, see Belda (1963).

Italy

In Italy, as in Spain, there are a number of regional archives that, for the quality and antiquity of their resources, are comparable with the Central State Archives in Rome. Because there are so many, this essay can mention only a selection of regional archives, chosen to suggest the importance and wealth of the resources in the country's archives.

Central State Archives. Created in 1871 and given official headquarters in Rome in 1939, the Central State Archives preserves documentation dating from the mid nineteenth century to the present. The collection deals primarily with civil administration, civil and military justice, governmental bodies and ministries, and personal papers. The most important divisions are *Archivi parlamentari* (Parliamentary Archives); *Corte suprema de cassazione* (Supreme Court of Appeals); *Corte di cassazione de Roma* (Court of Appeals of Rome); *Consiglio di stato* (Council of State); *Consiglio dei ministri, Presidenza* (Council of Ministers, Presidency); *Giurisdizioni speciali* (Special Jurisdictions); *tribunali militari, Corte dei conti* (military tribunals, Court of Finance); *Ministeri* (Ministries)—*Interno* (Interior), *Terre liberate* (Public Domain), *Africa italiana* (African Possessions), *Publica istruzione* (Public Instruction), *Cultura popolare* (Popular Culture), *Grazia e Giustizia* (Justice), *Lavoro e della previdenza sociale* (Labor and Social Welfare), *Tesoro* (Treasury), *Finanze* (Finance), *Agricoltura* (Agriculture), *Indus-*

tria e commercio (Industry and Commerce), *Economia nazionale* (National Economy), *Lavori publici* (Public Works), *Trasporti* (Transportation), *Communicazioni* (Communications), *Poste e dei telegrafi* (Postal System), *Guerra* (War), *Armi e munizioni* (Armaments), *Marina* (Navy), *Aeronautica* (Aerospace), and *Difesa* (Defense); *Commissariato per le sanzioni contro il fascismo* (Commissariat for the Control of Fascism); *Ispettorato generale della Guardia nazionale* (Inspector General of the National Guard); *Comando supremo* (High Command); *Comando generale dei carabinieri* (Commander General of the Police); *Archivi fascisti* (Archives of Fascism); *Republica sociale italiana* (Italian Social Republic); *Comitato di liberazione nazionale* (Committee for National Liberation); and *Carteggio di personalità* (Correspondence of the Authorities).

Florentine Archives. Founded in 1852, the archives of the state of Florence contains documents dating from 726 and is divided into five sections. The first includes *Archivio diplomatico* (Diplomatic Archives), *Archivi della Repubblica fiorentina* (Archives of the Florentine Republic), *Archivi dei Medici* (Archives of the Medici), *Archivio notariale* (Archives of the Notary), and *Archivi di famiglia* (Family Archives). In the second are the *Archivio dei Medici granduchi* (Archives of the Medici Grand Dukes), *Archivi delle Magistrature granducali* (Archives of the Magistrates of the Grand Duchy), *Archivi dei granduchi di Lorena* (Archives of the Grand Duke of Lorraine), and *Archivi delle segreterie del granducato di Toscana* (Archives of the Secretaries of the Grand Duchy of Tuscany). The third section contains *Archivi finanziari e giudiziari della Repubblica fiorentina fino alla caduta del granducato* (Financial and Judicial Archives of the Florentine Republic up to the Fall of the Grand Duchy), *Archivi delle confraternite religiose e dei conventi soppressi* (Archives of Abolished Religious Fraternities and Convents), and *Archivio di Urbino* (Archives of Urbino). In the fourth section are *Archivi moderni* (Modern Archives), *Prefuttura*

(Prefecture), and *Tribunali, Stato civil* (Tribunals, Civil State). The fifth contains microfilm.

Archives of Genoa. This archives was founded in 1815 with the addition, in 1881, of the resources of the Bank of San Giorgio. It includes *Archivio del governo, archivio segreto y archivio palese* (Governmental Archives, Restricted and Public, from 954 to 1937) and *Archivio del Banco di San Giorgio* (Archives of the Bank of San Giorgio, 1407–1845).

Mantuan Archives. One of the oldest of Italian archives, this collection was cited as early as 1199. In 1707 it was moved to Austria and was not reinstated as an Italian archive until 1866. Its sections are: *Archivio Gonzaga di Mantova* (Archives of Gonzaga of Mantua, 1128–1851); *Archivio Castiglioni* (Archives of Castiglioni, 1293–1763); *Camera di commercio di Mantova* (Chamber of Commerce of Mantua, 1300–1893); *Corporazioni religiose soppresse di Mantova e provincia* (Abolished Religious Organizations in Mantua and the Province, twelfth to eighteenth centuries); *Atti notarili* (Acts of the Notary, 1349–1859); *Senato di giustizia* (Judicial Senate, 1571–1786); *Imperiale regia delegazione austriaca* (Royal Austrian Delegation); and *Prefetture* (Prefectures). Inventories and indexes have been made of this collection.

Milanese Archives. This archives brings together the archives of the government (1781), the senate, and the judicial and financial bodies of the old duchy of Milan and successive administrations. It is divided as follows: *Archivio ducale* (Ducal Archives, 1395–1796); *Archivio del governo repubblicano* (Archives of the Republican Government, 1796–1805); *Archivio del regno d'Italia* (Archives of the Italian Crown, 1805–1814); *Archivio del regno Lombardo-Veneto* (Archives of the Lombardo-Venetian Kingdom, 1815–1859); *Atti di governo* (Governmental Acts, fifteenth to nineteenth centuries); *Archivio del fondo di religione* (Archives of Religious Resources, twelfth to eighteenth centuries); *Sezione storica* (His-

torical Section, fifteenth to nineteenth centuries); *Archivio catastale* (Archives of Public Records, eighteenth and nineteenth centuries); *Archivio notarile* (Archives of the Notary, 1700–1863); *Archivio del regio governo di Lombardia* (Archives of the Government of Lombardy, 1859–1860); *Archivio della circoscrizione provinciale di Milano* (Archives of the Provincial Boundaries of Milan, after 1860); and *Acquisti, depositi e doni* (Acquisitions, Resources, and Gifts).

Neopolitan Archives. Instituted in 1808 with resources of varying origin, this archives is divided into the following sections: *Diplomatico-politica* (Diplomatic-Political, eleventh to twentieth centuries); *Administrativa* (Administrative, 1400–1871); *Giudiziaria* (Judicial, 1500–1950); *Militare* (Military, seventeenth and eighteenth centuries); *Direzione dell'Archivio di stato* (Direction of the State Archives). Special sections dealing with Aragon, Córcega, Malta, and several royal families have been cataloged.

Archives of Palermo. This archives was created in 1814 and houses all information about the island from the period of Norman rule (eleventh century) to the present. It is divided as follows: *Tabulari delle pergamene, reales, monasticos, pontificios* (Tabulation of Manuscripts, Royal, Monastic, Pontifical); *Atti di stato (Consiglio, Cancelleria di Sicilia, Protonotaro, Deputazione, Segreteria, Curia)* (Acts of State [Council, Chancery of Sicily, Protonotary, Commission, Secretary, Court of Justice]); *Organi giudiziari* (Judicial Bodies); *Atti finanziari* (Finance, fourteenth to nineteenth centuries); *Atti notarili* (Acts of the Notary, fourteenth to nineteenth centuries); *Corporazioni religiose soppresse* (Abolished Religious Bodies). There are inventories and registers to facilitate use of these materials, as well as a general guide.

Roman Archives. This archives was created in 1871 and preserves documents of the central bodies of the Pontificate (ministries, congregations, and tribunals) dating from the fourteenth century. The papers of the secretary of state are kept in the

Vatican Archive and are of the greatest universal importance. The most important collection in the Roman Archives is the Parliamentary Archives, divided in three sections. The first includes *Signaturarum Sanctissimi* (1474–1860), *Diversorum Negotiorum* (1396–1816), and *Taxae Maleficiorum* (1431–1800). In the second are documents ordered by subject matter, and in the third are documents ordered by place of origin. There are also collections dealing with six hundred administrative, judicial, and religious bodies, which contain documents dating back to 833. All have been inventoried. (For more detailed information see Lodolini, 1960.)

Archives of Turin. This archives contains documents from the old reign of Sardinia, for which an archival building was constructed in 1731. Its sections are *Archivio di corte del regno di Sardegna* (Archives of the Reign of Sardinia, 934–1800); *Finanze* (Finances, 1215–1800); *Camerale* (Houses of Senate, 1048–1800); and *Guerra e marina* (Navy and Defense, 1500–1800). All sections have been cataloged.

Venetian Archives. The Venetian state archives was founded in 1797. In 1804 it incorporated the resources of the Austrian state. The divisions are as follows: *Archivi statali antichi* (Archives of the Ancient Governments, 697–1797); *Archivi statali moderni* (Archives of the Modern Governments, 1797 to the twentieth century); *Archivi notarili* (Archives of the Notary, 828–1830); *Archivi di enti religiosi e di corporazione artigiane* (Archives of Religious Bodies and Craft Guilds, 1015 to the nineteenth century); *Archivi di consolati esteri a Venezia* (Archives of Foreign Affairs, 1646–1866); *Archivi privati* (Private Archives, 1099–1870); and *Collezioni e miscelanee* (Miscellaneous, 731 to the nineteenth century). Indexes have been published as well as guide books (Da Mosto, 1937–1940).

Pisan Archives. Founded in 1860 with resources from the Pisan community, this archives is divided according to periods of Pisan history; *Comune libero* (Free State, 799–1406); *Comune soggetto a Firenze* (State

Controlled by Florence, 1406–1494); *Comune libero per la seconda volta* (Second Free State, 1494–1509); *Comune soggetto per la seconda volta* (Second State under Florentine Control, 1509–1808); *Dominazione francese* (French Domination, 1808–1814); *Governo toscano restaurato* (Tuscan Restoration Government, 1814 to the twentieth century).

In addition to those described above, Italy also has state archives in Apuania, Bologna, Bolzano, Brescia, Cagliari, Lucca, Modena, Parma, Reggio Emilia, Siena, Trento, Trieste, Fiume, and Zadar.

A guide for all the state archives, *Gli archivi di stato italiano*, has been published by the Ministry of the Interior (1944).

Italian documentation makes a valuable contribution to the study of the Mediterranean area. The artisans, merchants, banks, and businesses of Italy have preserved the papers of their transactions from very early times. The archives also preserve documents concerning religious organizations that have since been abolished and thus give a fairly complete picture of the historical development of private and spiritual life.

Archives of the Holy See

There are two main archives under the direction of the Holy See. The Vatican Secret Archives collects the papers of all offices of the Vatican, while the Archives of the Sacred Congregation for the Propagation of the Faith collects papers concerning the ecclesiastical business of non-Catholic countries.

Vatican Secret Archives. The Vatican Secret Archives *(Archivio segreto vaticano)* in Vatican City is the most important archives of the Holy See. The universal mission of the church makes this collection of great international value. It is divided according to the office where the material was produced: *Camera apostolica* (Chamber of Apostles, 1257–1898); *Cancelleria* (Chancery, 1198–1898); *Segreteria apostolica* (Secretary of Apostles, 1487–1678); *Segreteria dei brevi* (Secretary of the Breviary,

1566–1846); *Segreteria dei brevi ai principi* (Secretary of the Breviary of Princes, 1560–1920); *Segreteria delle lettere latine* (Secretary of Latin Letters, eighteenth and nineteenth centuries); *Segreteria di stato* (Secretary of State, 1523–1938); *Dataria* (Datary, 1417–1908); *Officium contradictarium Audientiae D. N. [Dominus Noster] Papae* (1523–1938); *Archivio dei protonotari apostolici* (Archives of the Apostles, 1600–1903); *Sacri palazzi apostolici* (Sacred Palaces of the Apostles, 1615–1918); *Archivio concistoriale* (Senate Archives, 1490–1866); *Congregazione del concilio* (Advisory Congregation, 1564–1911); *Congregazione delle indulgenze e reliquie* (Congregation of Indulgences and Relics); *Congregazione dei riti* (Congregation of Religious Rites); *Congregazione dei vescovi e regolari* (Congregation of Bishops and Regulars, 1573–1908); *Congregazione di Avignone* (Congregation of Avignon, 1693–1789); *S. Rota* (1464–1870); *Segnatura di giustizia* (Office of Justice, 1679–1760); *Archivi delle nunziature* (Archives of Papal Ambassadors, 1465–1936); *Archivio di Castel S. Angelo* (Archives of Castel San Angelo, ninth to nineteenth centuries); *Instrumenta miscellanea* (Miscellaneous Documents, 819–1899); *Miscellanea armadi I-XV* (sixteenth to nineteenth centuries); *Epoca napoleonica* (Napoleonic Age); *Armadio 54 (Cisma de Occidente y Lutero:* Western and Lutheran Schisms, fourteenth to sixteenth centuries); *Concilium Tridentinum* (Council of Trent, 1537–1588); *Armadio 64* (documents from European and Oriental countries, sixteenth century); *Archivio de Pio IX* (Archives of Pius IX).

The documentation in the Vatican Secret Archives begins in 819 and continues to the present. It has information relative to nearly every country in the world from very early times and contains material dealing with the relations between the states of medieval Europe. Because the Church of Rome was in contact with a great variety of local churches, religious orders, monarchs, cities, and states, the archives preserves information about all regions of the globe. This documentation is among the richest

available and is often more complete than that contained in the civil archives. Each section has inventories, indexes, and catalogs to aid research (see, for example, Fink, 1951).

Archives of the Sacred Congregation for the Propagation of the Faith. This archives, located in Rome, was created at the same time as the congregation to oversee ecclesiastical matters of countries that were not Catholic (1622). Early documents (1622–1893) are in a section called the Historical Archives, and later papers are part of an administrative section. There are three divisions in the Historical Archives. The first, entitled "Acts," includes records of general meetings (1622–1893), special meetings (1622–1864), and the *Congregatio Particularis de Rebus Sinarum et Indiarum Orientalium* (1655–1856). The second section, "Congresses," contains letters from missions (1622–1892) in the first series and documents of the congregation (1622–1892) in the second series. Also gathered in this section are records of papal audiences (1622–1892), briefs and bulls (1622–1952), instructions, decrees, and letters of the congregation. The third section, "Lesser Resources," includes congressional acts for the revision of rules and records of diocesan synods. Also included are Viennese resources and a miscellaneous section.

Many of these documents, arriving from all parts of the world, were presented and discussed at the regular and special meetings of the Congregation for the Propagation of the Faith. They contain valuable information about the countries and peoples affected by them. For the most part, the papers are ordered according to the place, country, or region of their origin. (More information is available in Kowalsky, 1961.)

Latin America

The archives of the countries of Latin America preserve the documentation of each country, dividing it into two basic historical periods: the colonial period of dependency on European authority and the republican or independent period. They generally contain documents from the first days of colonization to the present. In a few cases, this system has been altered, and the material has been classified either by subject or chronologically.

National Archives of Argentina. This archives, located in Buenos Aires, was first established in 1821 and designated as the National Archives in 1884. Its principal divisions are colonial and national, with each further subdivided into sections of government and finance. There are also two independent sections. In 1960 the National Archives of Graphics was incorporated into the National Archives. It includes both graphics and sound resources and is cataloged alphabetically by subjects in national and colonial sections. (For further details, see "L'Archivio generale," 1972.)

National Archives of Bolivia. The materials now in the Bolivian National Archives in Sucre were kept in the National Library until the archives were created in 1883. They are divided according to the institution of their origin: *Audiencia de Charcas* (High Court at Charcas); *Presidencia de la provincia de La Plata* (Presidency of the Province of La Plata); *Audiencia de Buenos Aires* (High Court at Buenos Aires); *Registros de escrituras públicas* (Registers of Public Papers); *Cajas reales de La Plata* (Royal Treasury of La Plata); *Cabildo de Potosí* (Municipality of Potosí); *Comandancia del ejército unido libertador* (Command of the Unified Army of Liberation); *Ministerio del interior y de gobierno* (Ministry of the Interior); *Ministerio de relaciones exteriores y culto* (Ministry of Foreign Affairs and Culture); *Ministerio de hacienda* (Ministry of Finance); *Ministerio de guerra y defensa nacional* (Ministry of War and National Defense); *Ministerio de industria* (Ministry of Industrialization); *Ministerio de fomento* (Ministry of Development); *Congreso nacional* (National Congress); *Corte suprema de justicia* (Supreme Court); *Corte superior de Chuquisaca* (Superior Court of Chuquisaca); *Prefectura de Chuquisaca* (Prefecture of Chuquisaca);

Junta de aplicaciones de Chuquisaca (Board of Applications of Chuquisaca); *Archivo de Mizque* (Archives of Mizque); *Tribunal de cuentas* (Department of the Treasury); *Biblioteca nacional de Bolivia* (National Library of Bolivia); *Archivo nacional de Bolivia* (National Archives of Bolivia). The archives have been cataloged and publish a bulletin, *Boletín y catálogo del Archivo nacional,* and a journal, *Revista de la Biblioteca nacional y del Archivo nacional.*

National Archives of Brazil. Located in Rio de Janeiro, this archives was founded in 1838 and contains both historical and current documentation. It is divided into two services, one for written documentation and one for phonographic, photographic, and cartographic documentation. The first of these services is further divided into legislative authority, judicial authority, presidency of the republic, ministries, decentralized administration, and historical documentation. The second is subdivided by material. There are sections for maps, photographs, films, microfilm, and sound materials. This collection also possesses special equipment for a more effective utilization of its resources. The archive publishes a magazine, *Mensario do Arquivo nacional.*

National Archives of Colombia. This archives, located in Bogotá, was founded in 1868 to bring together all historical and contemporary documentation. It is divided into two sections, colonial and republican. The first is limited by an imperfect organization by subject matter, devised in the nineteenth century. The second is subdivided into *Independencia* (Independence), *Gran Colombia* (Greater Colombia), and *Colombia.* Within each section the papers are further organized according to the ministry of their origin. There are several indexes and catalogs to this collection.

National Archives of Costa Rica. This archives in San José was established in 1881 to house all national documentation. It is divided into three sections: *Histórica* (Historical), *Jurídica* (Judicial), and *Administrativo-legislativa* (Administrative-Legislative), each ordered both chronologically and by subject. The collection has been cataloged. This archives publishes a review, *Revista de los Archivos nacionales*.

National Archives of Cuba. Founded in 1840 and reorganized in 1888, this archives, located in Havana, includes public, private, and diplomatic documentation. It is divided as follows: *Capitanía general* (Captain Generalcy); *Jurisdicción militar* (Military Jurisdiction); *Jurisdicción de hacienda* (Economic Jurisdiction); *Centros judiciales* (Judicial Centers); *Jurisdicción eclesiástica* (Ecclesiastical Jurisdiction); *Archivo histórico* (Historical Archives); and *Documentación de procedencia diversa* (Documentation of Other Origin). The archives has been cataloged and publishes a bulletin, *Boletín del Archivo nacional*.

National Archives of Chile. This collection was formed in 1927 by a merger of the Government Archives (1887) and the National Historical Archives (1925) and is located in Santiago. It is divided into two sections, *Administración pública: Ministerios, Intendencias, Gobernaciones, Municipalidades, Reparticiones* (Public Administration: Ministries, Mayoralities, Municipalities, Governments), and *Histórico-judicial: Corte suprema, Cortes de apelaciones, Notarias, Juzgados, Organismos coloniales* (Historical-Judicial: Supreme Court, Courts of Appeals, Notaries, Courts, Colonial Bodies). Each section has been separately cataloged.

National Archives of the Dominican Republic. This archives was created in 1936 and is located in Santo Domingo. It is divided historically: *Epoca colonial española* (Spanish Colonial Period); *Período colonial francés* (French Colonial Period); *Independencia efímera* (Partial Independence); *Dominación haitiana* (Haitian Domination); *Primera república* (First Republic); *Anexión a España y guerra de restauración* (Spanish Annexation and the War of Restoration); *Segunda república* (Second Republic); *Ocupación norteamericana* (North American Occupation); and *Período contemporáneo* (Contemporary Period).

National Historical Archives of Ecuador.

Created as a National Archives in 1884, this collection in Quito includes documentation from the sixteenth century. Its resources are *Corte suprema de justicia* (Supreme Court of Justice); *Corte suprema de justicia de Quito* (Supreme Court of Justice of Quito); *Escribanía del canton de Quito* (Notary of Quito County); *Donaciones e incautaciones* (Donations and Confiscations); and *Procedencias desconocidas* (Unknown Origins). There is a guidebook (Granizo, 1974) and a bulletin, *Boletín del Archivo nacional de historia*.

National Archives of El Salvador. All colonial and national documentation was kept at the National Palace until its destruction by fire in 1889. The collection is now preserved in the archives in San Salvador. It is divided into two sections: *Periodismo* (Journalism) and *Documentos judiciales* (Judicial Documentation). Most ministries still collect all documentation relative to their duties.

General Archives of Central America. Located in Guatemala, this archives was founded in 1846 with documentation of the captain generalcy of Guatemala, an administration much larger than that of the modern republic. To this has been added all documentation for the republic. The collection is organized by subject and is well classified and dated.

National Archives of Haiti. Founded in 1860 to preserve both colonial and republican documentation, this collection, located in Port-au-Prince, has many sections. The papers are organized chronologically and have been inventoried by the Civil Registry.

National Archives of Honduras. Founded in 1880, and located in Tegucigalpa, this archives has material dating from the sixteenth century, divided as follows: *Títulos de tierras* (Land-Holding Titles); *Documentos históricos: Colonial, federal e independiente* (Historical Documents: Colonial, Federal, and Independent); *Copiadores del registro civil* (Files of the Civil Registry); *Hemeroteca* (Periodical Library); and *Publicaciones nacionales y extranjeras* (National and Foreign Publications). Some sections have been cataloged, and two journals are published, *Revista del Archivo y la Bibliotecas nacionales* and *Boletín de la Biblioteca y Archivos nacionales.*

General Public Archives of Mexico. The General Archives of Colonial Spain *(Archivo general de la Nueva España),* founded in 1792, did not survive long and in 1823 was reestablished as the General Public Archives *(Archivo general y público).* This collection, located in Mexico City, contains both colonial and republican documentation and is divided accordingly. Each section is further organized by subject: institutions, territories, and printed documents. The archives has been indexed and cataloged and publishes a bulletin entitled *Boletín del Archivo general de la nación.*

National Archives of Nicaragua. Founded in 1883, this archives in Managua has suffered the effects of fire (1931) and earthquake (1973). Its resources consist largely of printed matter and are divided into *Hemeroteca* (Periodical Library); *Gacetas oficiales* (Official Newspapers); and *Gubernativa* (Governmental Documentation). These have been indexed chronologically.

National Archives of Panama. The first public archive of Panama City was founded in 1885, followed by the creation of a National Archives in 1912. Its sections are *Jurídica* (Judiciary); *Administrativa* (Administrative); and *Histórica: Colonial, de Colombia, República* (Historical: Colonial, Colombian, Republican). Other collections exist, including state archives and public *(no estatales)* and private *(personales)* archives. Some have been cataloged.

National Archives of Paraguay. This archives in Asunción preserves documentation dating from the sixteenth century to 1870. All later documentation is kept by the various ministries. The collections number approximately six thousand volumes.

National Archives of Peru. Created in 1861 and located in Lima, this archives preserves both colonial and republican material. The collection is divided as follows: *Histórica* (Historical, 12,000 bundles); *Notarial y ju-*

dicial (Notarial and Judicial, 13,000 diplomatic documents and 12,000 papers); *Archivo histórico de hacienda* (Historical Archives of the Treasury, 150 cubic meters of documents and books); *Archivo administrativo* (Administrative Archives, 220 cubic meters of documents); and *judicial* (Judicial, 30 cubic meters of documents). The archives has cataloged some sections and publishes a journal, *Revista del Archivo general de la nación.*

General Archives of Puerto Rico. Created in 1955 to preserve documents from the period of Spanish rule and all subsequent administrations, this archives in San Juan is organized as follows: *Capitanía general* (Captain Generalcy); *Gobierno civil* (Civil Government); *Real audiencia* (Royal High Court); *Diputación provincial* (Provincial Authority); *Intendencia* (Mayorality); *Justicia* (Justice); *Policía* (Police); *Salud* (Health); *Mansión ejecutiva* (Executive Residence); *Universidad* (University); *Planificación* (Planning); *Hacienda* (Treasury); *Departamento de estado* (Department of State); *Trabajo* (Labor); *Presupuesto* (Budget); *Hogares de Puerto Rico* (Housing); *Banco gubernamental* (Federal Bank); *Comisión industrial* (Industrial Commission); *Agricultura* (Agriculture); *Contralor* (Controller); *Instrucción* (Instruction); *Fomento económico* (Economic Development); *Transporte* (Transportation); *Transporte industrial* (Industrial Transportation); *Seguro del estado* (State Insurance); *Renovación urbana* (Urban Renewal); *Relaciones de trabajo* (Labor Relations); *Acueductos y alcantarillados* (Aqueducts and Sewers); *Bomberos* (Firefighters); *Renovación urbana y viviendas* (Urban Renewal and Housing); *Estabilización económica* (Economic Stability); *Guarda estatal* (Civil Guard); *Municipios* (Municipalities); and *Obras públicas* (Public Works). Most of these sections have been indexed and cataloged.

General Archives of Uruguay. The General Archives was established in 1926 and exists today in Montevideo as a combination of the Administrative Archives (1883) and the National Archives and Historical Museum

(1915). The collection includes administrative, judicial, and private documents. The archives has published three catalogs: *Catálogo de los libros del ex Archivo general administrativo* (1965); *Catálogo del ex Archivo y museo histórico nacional* (1966); and *Catálogo de libros: Historia de la administración* (1971).

National Archives of Venezuela. Created in 1910 to house documentation and located in Caracas, this archives is divided into three sections: *Colonia* (Colonial Period); *Independencia* (Independence); and *República* (Republic). Each is organized according to the origin of documentation and is ordered chronologically. The archives has been cataloged and publishes a bulletin, *Boletín del Archivo general de la nación.*

These collections of colonial and republican papers give full and complete information about the administrative life of the nations of Latin America. They contain information about the government, treasury, international relations, public works, and systems of education of each country.

In addition to the national archives, there are a number of valuable administrative, ecclesiastical, and private collections. A general description of these collections is available in Hill (1948) and Mendoza (1961).

Bibliography

"L'Archivio generale della nazione e l'organizzazione archivistica argentina." *Rassegna degli archivi di stato*, 1972, *32*(1), 78–90.

Belda, L. S. *Guía del Archivo histórico nacional.* Madrid: National Historical Archives, 1958.

Belda, L. S. *Bibliografía de archivos españoles y archivística.* Madrid: National Historical Archives, 1963.

Bores, A. de la P. *Guía del investigador.* Simancas, Spain: Archives of Simancas, 1962.

Da Mosto, A. *L'Archivio di stato di Venezia: Indice generale, storico, descrittivo ed analitico.* Rome: Venetian Archives, 1937–1940.

Fink, K. A. *Das vatikanische Archiv: Einführung in seine Bestände und ihre Erforschung.* Rome: W. Regenberg, 1951.

Granizo, J. F. *Guía del Archivo nacional de historia.* Quito, Ecuador: National Historical Archives, 1974.

Hill, R. H. *Los Archivos nacionales de la América latina.* Havana, Cuba: Collective Committee of Latin American Studies of the National Council of Social Science Research, 1948.

Kowalsky, N. *Inventario dell'Archivio storico della S. congregazione "de propaganda fide."* Rome: Congregation for the Propagation of the Faith, 1961.

Lodolini, A. *L'Archivio di stato di Roma: Epitome di una guida degli archivi dell'amministrazione centrale dello stato pontificio.* Rome: Roman Archives, 1960.

Mendoza, G. *La situación actual de los archivos latinoamericanos: Manual de información básica.* Washington, D.C.: Inter-American Convention on Archives, 1961.

Ministry of the Interior. *Gli archivi di stato italiano.* Bologna, Italy: Ministry of the Interior, 1944.

VINCENTA CORTES

See also: Vatican City, State of.

7. NORTHERN EUROPE, NATIONAL ARCHIVES OF

Many ties—economic, cultural, political and geographical—exist within and among the Scandinavian and the Benelux countries of Northern Europe. Until 1523 the northern countries were united under one prince. In that year, Sweden and Finland left the union, and in 1814 Denmark and Norway were separated. Iceland remained in affiliation with the Danish kingdom until 1944, when it became an independent republic. For some years the Scandinavian economy was dominated by the Netherlands. All these historical ties are reflected in the organization and content of the archival resources of Scandinavia, the Netherlands, and Belgium.

In each nation there is a single principal officer for both the central archives and the local state archives, and generally the same working principles are followed within all state archival institutions. Two main goals are common to the daily work in the archives: to serve the present administration and to serve historical research. Centralization, however, is more distinct in the Scandinavian countries than in the Netherlands and Belgium, where there is not only a larger number of archival institutions but also a considerable number of small archives with limited archival collections and staffs. The archives of the Benelux countries possess relatively more ancient material, since these countries were strongly exposed in the early Middle Ages to the political, economic, and cultural influences radiating from Southern and Central Europe.

Archival Institutions in Denmark

In 1665 the first royal archivist in Denmark was appointed and thus was founded an independent archival institution, which came to be called *Det kongelige geheimearkiv* (the Royal State Archives). In the year 1720 the Royal State Archives building was constructed near the central administration building in Copenhagen. This building is the oldest archive building still in use in Europe. Little by little, all records kept from the Middle Ages were gathered in the Royal State Archives, and the institution received regular deliveries from the highest state authorities as material was no longer needed in daily administration. In 1861 another central archival institution, the Kingdom's Archive, was established. Housed in the government building, it administered the newer records from the central administration. In 1882 the two institutions were gathered under one principal, and by the archive law of March 30, 1889, became one institution, the Danish National Archives. In 1910 the institution was moved to the old royal library, erected about 1665, but rebuilt into a modern archives building.

The Danish National Archives contains the largest selection of archival material kept from the Middle Ages up to the year 1559, with the oldest documents dating back to the twelfth century. There are unbroken rows of volumes of documents of the central administration of Denmark dating back to the late fifteenth century. The Danish National Archives receives deliveries from all ministries and government authorities. Furthermore, documents left by statesmen and politicians are systematically being collected. The private papers

from the royal family are also preserved in the Danish National Archives. Because of the long history of union between Sweden, Finland, Norway, Iceland, and Denmark, the Danish National Archives also hold many historical records of the other northern countries as well. Until 1864 Schlesweig, Holstein, and Lauenburg belonged to the Danish empire. As a result of these close political connections between Denmark and parts of Germany, many German archival materials also are included in the Danish National Archives. In the archives, too, are the Sound Dues accounts from 1485 to 1856. All ships passing through the Øresund (the Sound) had to pay tax, and the accounts that resulted are a unique source for European trade and shipping history.

Finally, the Danish National Archives also include archives from the colonial territory that Denmark appropriated in the eighteenth century, partly at the African Ivory Coast and partly in Tranquebar. These colonies, however, were sold about the middle of the nineteenth century. Of greater importance was the possession of the islands of St. Croix, St. Thomas, and St. John in the West Indies, which were sold to the United States in 1917. Many local archives from the Virgin Islands were brought to the Danish National Archives in 1919; the West Indian parish registers were brought to the Provincial Archives of Zealand.

Local officials kept their own archives until the passage of the archives law of March 30, 1889, at which time three local provincial archives were established in Copenhagen, Odense, and Viborg. Each provincial archives was given a geographical field of activity, and local officials were expected to deliver their files to these archives. Like the Danish National Archives, the provincial archives are service organs to the local administration and to those engaged in research on local history.

The provincial archives also supervise the record-keeping methods of local administration officials, including the ecclesiastical authorities. (Since 1536 the majority of the Danish population has belonged to the Evangelic-Lutheran church, which is the national church.) In 1933 a fourth provincial archives in Åbenrå was established for that part of the duchy of Schlesweig, which had come back to Denmark after a 1920 plebiscite. The Danish National Archives and the four provincial archives form an administrative unit under the conduct of the director of the National Archives.

Outside of this organization, there is yet another state archives institution, the Danish National Business Archives, located in Århus. Established in 1942, it was an independent institution until 1962, when it was taken over by the state. The Danish National Business Archives was established for the purpose of collecting the files of large economic organizations, as well as files from private concerns inside industry, the crafts, and trade.

Archival Institutions in Finland

From 1523 to 1809 Finland formed the eastern part of the Swedish kingdom, and the country was administered from Stockholm. In 1809 Finland was conquered by Russia; rather than being incorporated as a province in Russia, it was raised to an independent grand duchy, with the czar as grand duke. In 1890 a process of "Russification" began, which was interrupted by the outbreak of World War I in 1914. In December 1917 Finland declared itself an independent state, and after a bloody civil war the republic of Finland arose.

In the period from 1809 to 1917, while Finland was a grand duchy under Russia, Helsinki became the capital, and administration was centralized in that city. In 1869 an archival institution was established that collected the files of the central administration and the state authorities. An archives building was constructed in 1890. Since the independence of Finland in 1919, the central administration has been extended, and it has been necessary to enlarge the old archives building gradually with several extensions. Some historical material is kept in the National Archives in Helsinki, especially accounts from the period when Finland was part of Sweden, but additional records also are maintained in the National Archives in Stockholm.

In Finland, too, there are seven central local archives, called provincial archives, whose task it is to collect the files of the local officials. As in Denmark, the director of the National Archives is the principal of both the National Archives and the provincial archives. In 1918 a special war archives was established in Helsinki; this archives receives documents from the central as well as from the local military authorities. To some degree, the director of the National Archives also supervises this archives.

Archival Institutions in Iceland

Until 1904 Iceland was administered from Copenhagen; at that time, the special Icelandic ministry was moved to Reykjavik. In 1918 a personal union between Denmark and Iceland was established. There was a common king and common foreign service, but the entire internal administration of Iceland was conducted from Reykjavik. In 1944 Iceland became an independent republic.

In 1882 the collection began of Icelandic local archives in the capital, Reykjavik, and in 1899 the first archivist in Iceland was appointed. In 1908 a new building was established for the Icelandic National Library in which the archives were also housed. In this building the National Archives of Iceland still resides, functioning as both a national and a provincial archives.

By an agreement with Denmark in 1927, certain files from the Danish National Archives were handed over to the National Archives in Reykjavik so that the central administration of Iceland through the ages may be studied there. Files of the local officials, including church records, have never been outside Iceland.

Archival Institutions in Norway

Until 1814 Norway was a part of the Danish monarchy and was administered from Copenhagen. In 1815, by the command of the Great Powers, a personal union between Norway and Sweden was established that lasted until 1905. In this period Sweden and Norway had a common king and foreign policy. Since 1905 Norway has been an independent kingdom.

After 1814 a Norwegian central administration was organized with its headquarters in Christiania, later renamed Oslo. After some years it became necessary to establish a special Norwegian archives office, called since 1841 the National Archives. In the beginning, the National Archives were housed in rooms at the old fortress of Akershus. In 1861 the archives moved to the newly erected parliament building. In 1914 it was again moved to quarters in a defunct bank in central Oslo. A new, separate archives building on the outskirts of Oslo will be ready for use about 1978. This new building will be the largest archives building in Scandinavia, with a shelf capacity of about ninety-six kilometers (sixty miles). All archive stores will be established in an area of rock.

By various archival agreements with Denmark, the National Archives of Norway has secured possession of a considerable part of the files concerning the administration of Norway prior to 1814. In addition, the National Archives of Norway keeps the files from the central administration since 1814. However, lack of space has meant that several older files remain with the departments in which they originated.

Because of the long geographical distances, Norway was the first country in Scandinavia to establish a central provincial archives. In 1850 the "diocese archives," located in the northern Norwegian town of Trondheim, was founded. In 1885 a similar institution was established in the west Norwegian town of Bergen. There are six local

or "state archives" in Norway, and a local archives department in the north Norwegian town of Tromsø. The director of the National Archives in Norway, as in Denmark, is the head of both the National Archives and the six town archives.

Archival Institutions in Sweden

Sweden was the first among the Scandinavian countries to establish an independent institution of archives. In 1618 a special archive office (later to become the National Archives of Sweden) was created within the Royal Chancellery. This institution had rooms in the castle of Stockholm until 1846, when it was moved to a building outside the castle. During a fire in the castle in 1697, precious files were lost. In 1891 the National Archives was able to move into a new building that had been constructed specifically for that purpose. Here the National Archives had its headquarters until it was transferred in 1968 to a newly built edifice outside the center of Stockholm. All the archives magazines have been built into rocky ground. In 1975 the National Archives of Sweden was the largest archival institution in Scandinavia, comprising about 80,000 meters (over 45 miles) of files.

In the National Archives of Sweden are kept files from the Middle Ages to the present. The oldest documents date back to the eleventh century, with the bulk of the files coming from the organs of the central administration and the so-called state authorities. Concentrated efforts are being made to gather private archives, and the papers of several outstanding statesmen and politicians are currently kept in the National Archives. Because of the Swedish administration of Finland and of the Baltic and North German provinces, there is much material in the National Archives of Sweden to interest research workers from these countries.

In Sweden, too, there are seven central local archives, called provincial archives, which receive deliveries from the local state authorities, including ecclesiastical officials.

In addition, there are several special town archives in Sweden. The largest, situated in Stockholm and Malmö, serve as provincial archives for their respective regions, receiving archival deliveries from the municipal authorities as well as from the state authorities in those two towns. As provincial archives they are under the supervision of the director of the National Archives who, in Sweden, as in Denmark and Norway, is the head of the entire Swedish archives organization.

Outside this organization, there is a special war archives in Stockholm dating from 1805. Its task is to receive the files from the central and local military authorities within the army, navy, and air force. The war archives is the chief repository of the Swedish and foreign map collections—collections that are internationally renowned. Among Scandinavian archival administrations, the Swedish archives are the most advanced in modern archival development, both in the central and the local branches of the administration.

The Benelux Countries

From an international and historical point of view, there is no doubt that the files preserved in the three Benelux countries—the Netherlands, Belgium, and Luxembourg—will attract far greater interest than those in the more remote Scandinavian countries. To a greater extent than Scandinavia, the Netherlands, Belgium, and Luxembourg have been the scene of political incidents that have had a decisive influence on the entire history of Europe. Furthermore, the Netherlands has been an international economic great power and the mother country of an extensive colonial empire. Many foreign research workers therefore look to the archives of these countries for material relating to their studies.

Archival institutions in the Netherlands. The Dutch Central Archives (*Algemeen rijksarchief*), located in The Hague (the capital), primarily contains files from the province of the Netherlands and from the Dutch central authorities. During the war with Spain at the end of the sixteenth and the beginning of the seventeenth centuries, a solid union came into existence from what had been several relatively independent provinces. The modern state of the Netherlands has developed from this union. The files that describe this development are being kept in the Central Archives in The Hague. Here, too, one may find files from the great trade companies that dominated Indian as well as West Indian international trade for centuries.

In addition to the Central Archives, there are also ten local state archives in the Netherlands, all of which bear the common name of *rijksarchief*. They are located in the ancient provincial capitals, and their archival collections describe the historical development within their own narrow local area. The largest state archives are in cities such as Arnhem, Middelburg, and Utrecht.

There are also fifty-six town archives and other municipal archival institutions. The largest town archives is the town archives in Amsterdam, with 18,000 meters (over 10 miles) of files. Other significant town archives are found in Rotterdam and Utrecht, although the Rotterdam archives suffered severe losses from the German invasion in 1940. The town archives of Amsterdam contains valuable material for historians concerned with European economic history, especially in the seventeenth century. The research worker who needs more detailed information about the individual Dutch archival institutions and their collections is referred to the international archival magazine *Archivum* (UNESCO and International Council on Archives, 1975).

Another archives of considerable international interest—established in connection with the international military tribunal in Nuremberg, which convicted the Nazi war criminals—is also to be found in the Netherlands. These archives are located in the Peace Palace in The Hague. The Peace Palace is also the head office of the International Court of Justice, which was established in connection with the League of Nations.

Archival institutions in Belgium. According to the 1975 *Archivum* survey, Belgium has 109 archival institutions. The public institutions, with one common principal officer, consist of a central archives and fifteen provincial archives. The central archives *(Archives du royaume,* or *Algemeen rijksarchiv)* is located in Brussels and receives archival documents from the central authorities.

Because of Belgium's geographical position (several important European waterways run through Belgium), many Belgian towns—above all, Antwerp—have been of great significance for European trade. European historical researchers can find much important material in several Belgian archival institutions.

Generally, the Belgian provincial archives are larger than corresponding Dutch archives, and they are usually found in the historical provincial capitals. Among the most significant provincial archives *(archives de l'état,* or *rijksarchiv)* must be counted those of Beveren-Waas, Ghent, Liège, and Antwerp.

The influence of the Roman Catholic church has always been strong in Belgium. Thus, Belgium, like other Catholic countries, has a series of independent clerical archival institutions, including Episcopal archives, the files of Catholic educational establishments, and monastic archives. Some museums, universities, and other cultural institutions also have their own archives. Several of these special archives contain material of considerable age and relevance to the general development of the country. However, their focus is most often on the more limited history of the institution in question.

Archival institutions in Luxembourg. Because of its geographically important position, Luxembourg, the small independent grand duchy, has often played a part in the politics of the great powers. On occasion, it has also played an important role in the European economy. The most important

historical source material for the duchy is kept in the *Archives de l'état,* which is located in Luxembourg, the capital. This archival institution administers about 18,000 meters (over 10 miles) of files. There is also an independent town archives for the capital, with about 4,000 meters (over 2 miles) of files. The town archives primarily contain material of local historical interest.

Bibliography

Jørgensen, H. *Nordiske arkiver.* Copenhagen: Society of Danish Archivists, 1968.

Nicomède, J. *Répertoire des inventaires des archives conservées en Belgique.* Brussels: Association des archivistes et bibliothécaires, 1970.

Pirenne, L. P. L. (Ed.) *De rijksarchieven in Nederland.* Vols. 1 and 2. The Hague: Staatsoitgeverij, 1973.

UNESCO and the International Council on Archives. "International Directory of Archives." *Archivum,* 1975, *22–23,* 222–260.

                                        HARALD JØRGENSEN

8. PUBLIC RECORD OFFICE, LONDON

The Public Record Office, as the national repository of the archives of the central government of the United Kingdom, contains documents that span nine centuries of history, from 1086, the date of the survey of England known as Domesday Book, to the present day. These documents provide an unrivaled source of information for the history of England and modern Britain. They also make a valuable contribution to the history of many other countries, particularly those in which the pioneering and trading adventures of the British people led to the creation of a widespread colonial empire. This value is demonstrated by the fact that in 1974, for example, more than a quarter of the 340,000 documents produced in the public search rooms were used by readers from outside the United Kingdom. Further evidence of this worldwide interest in the documents which occupy some seventy-five miles of shelving in the Public Record Office is the very considerable demand from overseas universities and libraries for copies of documents.

History of the Public Record Office

When the Public Record Office was created by an Act of Parliament in 1838, the public records were kept in more than sixty separate buildings in London, many of which were wholly unsuitable for the storage of documents. Storage places included the Tower of London, which had been the main repository since the Middle Ages for the records of Chancery; the Chapter House and Chapel of the Pyx (the former royal treasury in the care of the monks of Westminster) at Westminster Abbey; Carlton Ride (the stables attached to Carlton House); the Royal Mews (the site of the present National Gallery) at Charing Cross and other buildings in and around the former palace of Whitehall; the vaults of Somerset House; and the Rolls Chapel in Chancery Lane. The Public Record Office Act, 1838, became law against the background of long-standing public disquiet about the conditions in which records were kept. It created the Public Record Office as the single authority with custody over the surviving public records of existing and defunct courts. The act did not have the immediate effect of providing for the central custody of the archives of the Secretaries of State, which had been kept in a separate State Paper Office since the sixteenth century, or of any of the government departments then in existence. In 1852, however, an order in council extended the scope of the act to cover both ancient and modern records.

In 1851 work was begun on a building to house the public records on a site in Chancery Lane, known as the Rolls Estate. On this site in 1232 King Henry III had founded a *Domus Conversorum,* a house for Jews converted to the Christian faith. After the expulsion of the Jews from England in 1290, the need for such an establishment obviously declined, and the office of the Keeper of the House of Converts was usually assigned to the clerk of Chancery, whose duty it was to keep the rolls and other records of Chancery. From 1377 the house with its adjacent chapel was held continu-ously by Keepers of the Rolls. In the course of time, the Keepers of the Rolls, as judges of the Court of Chancery, became known as Masters of the Rolls, the title borne today by the President of the Court of Appeal. Rolls House, rebuilt in 1717 by the architect Colin Campbell, continued to be the London residence of the Master of the Rolls until some ten years before the passage of the act. Until the closing years of the nineteenth century, Rolls Chapel remained in use for ecclesiastical purposes, while serving also as a store for records and a meeting place for the foreclosure of mortgages. Thus, the site of the present Public Record Office building, built block by block between 1851 and 1900, has had a direct connection with records and record keeping for over seven hundred years.

The building erected on the former Rolls Estate owes its size and style to the determination of Lord Langdale and Lord Romilly, the first two statutory keepers of the public records, and to the skill of Sir James Pennethorne and Sir John Taylor, the architects. The Public Record Office is a massive structure in Gothic style, built to provide the highest standard of secure storage and to resist fire and other hazards. This turreted building, known to so many scholars throughout the world, is entered from Chancery Lane under an archway, which bears the carved figures of Henry III and Edward III, the originator of the *Domus Conversorum* and its perpetuator as a perquisite of the Master of the Rolls, respectively. The last part of the building to be finished was the small museum on the site of the former Rolls Chapel. This museum contains such glass as could be removed from the old chapel, and is further adorned with three tombs—one of which, bearing the finely modeled recumbent figure in terra-cotta of Dr. John Yong, Master of the Rolls to Henry VII and Henry VIII, is attributed to Pietro Torrigiani, the Florentine sculptor of Henry VII's tomb in Westminster Abbey. Documents on permanent exhibition in the museum include Domesday Book, two exemplars of Magna

Carta, the Log Book of HMS *Victory,* royal autographs from the Black Prince onward, and representative specimens of Chancery rolls and other formal records. Also exhibited are documents of historical and literary interest from the time of Chaucer to World War II.

Records Deposited in the Public Record Office

The public records with which the 1838 act was primarily concerned, and which were the first to be moved into the new Public Record Office in the middle of the nineteenth century, date from the twelfth century. These are records of the King's Court and the divergent branches by which it discharged its judicial, administrative, and financial functions. These included records of the Chancery, the Exchequer, the courts of common law and equity, the prerogative courts, such as the Court of Star Chamber and the Court of Wards and Liveries, and the Courts Palatinate and other special jurisdictions. The Chancery, for example, in addition to voluminous records of its proceedings as a court of equity, has left several series of parchment rolls recording the texts of royal charters, letters patent, and various other administrative instruments issued under the Great Seal. One such series, the Patent Rolls, comprises some 5500 rolls which begin in 1201 and continue into the second quarter of the twentieth century in the same physical form of parchment rolls made up of skins sewn head to tail. The many classes or series of accounts and other records of the Exchequer similarly contain examples of this continuity in the form and makeup of records; in particular, the Great Rolls or Pipe Rolls of the Exchequer survived from 1129 until they were discontinued in 1832.

Before the fifteenth century, the great bulk of these records were in Latin. Except for a brief interruption between 1651 and 1660, when English was used, the records of the courts of common law, as distinct from those of equity proceedings in Chancery and other courts, together with the solemn grants recorded on the Chancery rolls, continued until 1773 to be in Latin. From the thirteenth century to the fifteenth century, certain documents, such as writs of privy seal and many parliamentary records, were in Anglo-Norman French, the language commonly used during this period for letters, petitions, and informal writings generally. English came into use for many purposes in the course of the fifteenth century, initially superseding Anglo-Norman as the common language of official documents, and eventually also replacing the Latin of more formal records.

The deposit of these early records in the new Public Record Office was soon followed by the arrival of more modern archives of government departments. Naval and military records from the Admiralty and War Office in Whitehall were supplemented by enormous transfers from naval and military establishments in and around London, including several cargoes of logbooks and muster books sent up the river by barge from Deptford Dockyard, and Ordnance records from the Tower of London. The earlier papers of the Secretaries of State, dating from the sixteenth century, were transferred from the State Paper Office in 1856. Further accessions came from the modern Foreign, Colonial, and Home Offices, which had been created by the end of the eighteenth century by the division of the duties of the Secretaries of State. Departments such as the Board of Trade, which had its origins in the Privy Council, and the Treasury, also began to move records, often unlisted and unarranged, into the Public Record Office. In 1877 amending legislation became necessary "to prevent the Public Record Office from being encumbered with documents of not sufficient public value to justify their preservation." However, the procedure introduced in 1877 for making "destruction schedules" to control the disposal of valueless records in government offices did not prevent the accumulation of vast quantities of records and did not always ensure the preservation of all the more valuable papers. This problem was not dealt with effectively until 1952, when a Committee on Departmental Records, under the chairmanship of Sir James Grigg, was set up. Its report *(Report of the Committee on Departmental Records,* 1954) made recommendations not only for new procedures for the selection of records for preservation but also for far-reaching changes in the constitution of the Public Record Office. These recommendations led to a new Public Records Act in 1958.

The Public Records Act of 1958

The 1958 act remains the statutory basis for the operations of the Public Record Office. It gave a general responsibility for public records, whether in the office or in the custody of government departments, to a Minister of the Crown, the Lord Chancellor, in place of the Master of the Rolls, who became ex officio chairman of an Advisory Council on Public Records. The head of the office was given the title Keeper of Public Records, with general responsibility for administration of the office and for custody of the records preserved in it. Other responsibilities of the keeper include the supervision of arrangements, made in government departments, for the selection of records that must be kept permanently. Public access to records selected for preservation and transferred to the Public Record Office was regulated by a fifty-year rule which, by an amending act of 1967, was reduced to a thirty-year rule.

Records Administration Division

The Records Administration Division is responsible for the selection of public records that are worth preserving permanently. The procedures used are substantially those recommended by the Grigg Committee and involve the use of disposal schedules to control standard documents, for which fixed retention periods can be agreed, and a two-stage review for the registered files, which form the majority of documents produced by government de-

partments. The Records Administration Division is also responsible for the management of an intermediate repository housing over a million feet of records still in the charge of originating departments and awaiting either destruction or submission to reviewing procedures.

Records Services and Publications Division

Once transferred to the Public Record Office, records are under the control of the Records Services and Publications Division, which is concerned with all matters affecting public records in the permanent custody of the Keeper of Public Records. Its responsibilities include storage and custody; repair and conservation; photocopying services; search rooms and postal reference services; editorial and publications programs; and a museum. The public search rooms, used by between three hundred and four hundred persons each day, are situated in three buildings in London and a fourth more remote repository in Hertfordshire. The search rooms are open to any person holding a reader's ticket, which is obtainable on an application supported by a suitable recommendation. There are no additional restrictions for visitors from overseas.

Means of Reference to Documents

Means of reference to documents in the Public Record Office are many and varied. Some manuscript and typescript lists and indexes are available only on the shelves of the search rooms; other means of reference, both lists and more detailed calendars and transcripts, have been published. Official publication of documentary sources before 1838 was undertaken by a Record Commission first appointed in 1800. This commission began by printing texts and indexes to follow the edition of the Domesday Book, which had been published by Order of Parliament in 1783. A State Paper Commission, to continue the work of publication of sources, was appointed in 1835. The Public Records Act of 1838 empowered the Master of the Rolls to print calendars and catalogs of the records in his custody, and for the next fifty years lists and calendars appeared regularly as appendices to the annual *Deputy Keeper's Report*. In 1853 the first general guide to the public records was published; its successor is the *Guide to the Contents of the Public Records,* of which the third and last volume was published in 1968. The guide will in future be updated and revised more frequently with the assistance of a computer. Calendars prepared by the Public Record Office first began to appear separately in 1856, continuing those published by the State Paper Commission. Similarly, the series of *Chronicles and Memorials of Great Britain and Ireland During the Middle Ages* (the Rolls Series) carried on a project of the Record Commission. In 1890 the Rolls Series, which had included only a few volumes based on public records, was abandoned; work was begun on several new series of texts and calendars, with the medieval records of the Chancery most strongly represented. The fact that the greater proportion of contemporary users of the public records requires access to records of the nineteenth and twentieth centuries has led to the deployment of more resources to provide finding aids and guides to these later records.

The Public Record Office at Kew

In 1977 the Public Record Office will begin a new era in its history when its long-standing accommodation problem will be solved by the opening of a new building. This new Public Record Office is at Kew, about nine miles from central London; it will become the administrative headquarters of the Public Record Office and will contain, in general terms, the records of modern government departments (even those with records dating back two or three centuries). The earlier records, as well as certain other documents that will be more conveniently kept in central London, will remain in Chancery Lane. At Kew, in a building in which the major consideration in design has been secure storage and rapid

and easy movement of up to seventy miles of records, two search rooms will provide seats for over five hundred readers, documents will be made available by a computer-controlled production system. In this new environment the Public Record Office will face with confidence the administrative, technical, and intellectual challenges that confront archivists in all countries of the world and will continue its long tradition of service to scholarship.

Bibliography

British National Archives. *Sectional List 24* [of Government Publications, including those of the Public Record Office]. London: H. M. Stationery Office, 1971.

Galbraith, V. H. *An Introduction to the Use of the Public Records.* London: Oxford University Press, 1934.

Guide to the Contents of the Public Record Office. (3 vols.) London: H. M. Stationery Office, 1963–1968.

Guide to the Public Records. Part I: *Introduction.* London: H. M. Stationery Office, 1940.

Public Record Office. *Annual Reports of the Deputy Keepers of Public Records,* 1840–1957. London: Public Record Office, annual.

Public Record Office. *Annual Reports of the Keepers of Public Records, 1958–.* London: Public Record Office, annual.

Report of the Committee on Departmental Records. London: H. M. Stationery Office, 1954.

Royal Commission on Public Records. *First Report of the Royal Commission on Public Records, 1912.* London: Royal Commission, 1912.

A. W. MABBS

9. UNITED STATES, NATIONAL ARCHIVES OF

The National Archives of the United States is both a place and a body of records. The place is a building in the classic style in the heart of Washington, D. C. The records are the permanently valuable records of the federal government from its beginnings in the latter part of the eighteenth century. They are available for use not only by federal agencies but also by scholars, students, and other researchers.

The National Archives Building, designed by John Russell Pope and constructed during the years 1931 to 1935, stands midway between the White House and the Capitol, with entrances on both Constitution and Pennsylvania Avenues. Here are preserved most existing federal records of value, and here also is the headquarters of the National Archives and Records Service (NARS), which administers the federal archival system. The NARS is part of the General Services Administration.

With its seventy-two Corinthian columns of Indiana limestone, its sweep of steps from Constitution Avenue to the bronze doors of the main entrance, and its decorative statuary, the National Archives Building forms an imposing architectural landmark in downtown Washington.

For nearly one hundred and fifty years, the government had no central agency to preserve the records of its past. It was not until 1934 that the Congress enacted and President Franklin D. Roosevelt signed into law the legislation which created the National Archives as an independent agency. The new staff faced the immense task of inventorying the records which had accumulated over a century and a half and which were scattered in numerous locations, including attics and basements. The move into the new building took place in November 1935.

As the National Archives staff began the painstaking work of assembling, arranging, and describing the records which document the nation's history, administrators and archivists alike were looking with apprehension at the proliferation of paperwork. The rapid increase in the amount of paperwork through the 1930s, as government struggled with the Depression, turned explosive as the United States mounted its massive effort in World War II. Many began to fear that the mere volume of paperwork might make the task of preparing a coherent record of the past impossible.

After the war, general recognition of the need for stronger direction in federal records management programs coincided with the stand taken by the Commission on the Reorganization of Government (the first Hoover Commission) in favor of establishing a central agency to provide "general services" for the federal government in the interests of efficiency and economy. The result was that the independent National Archives was incorporated in 1949 into the newly formed General Services Administration and assigned records management as well as archival responsibilities.

The NARS administers twenty-two institutions composing the federal archival system: the National Archives in Washington; the Washington National Records Center in Suitland, Maryland; the National Personnel Records Center in St. Louis, Missouri; and thirteen regional federal archives and records centers located in Atlanta, Georgia; Boston, Massachusetts; Chicago, Illinois; Dayton, Ohio; Denver, Colorado; Fort Worth, Texas; Kansas City, Missouri; San Francisco and Los Angeles, California; Philadelphia and Mechanicsburg, Pennsylvania; New York City; and Seattle, Washington. All of the regional centers except Dayton and Mechanicsburg have archives branches.

The other institutions in the archival system are presidential libraries: the Herbert Hoover Library at West Branch, Iowa; the Franklin D. Roosevelt Library at Hyde Park, New York; the Harry S Truman Library at Independence, Missouri; the Dwight D. Eisenhower Library at Abilene, Kansas; the John F. Kennedy Library in temporary quarters at Waltham, Massachusetts; and the Lyndon B. Johnson Library at Austin, Texas.

The NARS also administers a government-wide records management program and publishes the daily *Federal Register,* the *United States Statutes at Large,* the *Code of Federal Regulations,* the *Weekly Compilation of Presidential Documents,* and the *Public Papers of the Presidents.*

Organizationally, the NARS is headed by the Archivist of the United States, who is appointed by the Administrator of General Services. The archivist is assisted by a deputy and an executive director, the latter with specific responsibilities for administrative management and technical services.

The six major offices of the NARS are the National Archives, Federal Register, Presidential Libraries, Federal Records Centers, Records Management, and Educational Programs. The Office of the National Archives has nine divisions: Central Reference, Civil, Military, General, Cartographic, Audiovisual, Printed Documents, Records Declassification, and Special Projects. Each division has branch structures; for example, the Civil Archives Division is composed of Diplomatic, Legislative, Judicial, and Fiscal, Natural Resources; and Industrial and Social branches. Military branches are Modern Military and Old Military (with the year 1917 as the dividing line) and Captured Records. The Special Projects Division includes the Machine-Readable branch, the Center for Polar Archives, the Territorial Papers branch, and the Center for the Documentary Study of the American Revolution, which was established to serve as a central reference point for researchers during the bicentennial period.

Since its establishment, the National Archives has had jurisdiction over records of the executive branch of the federal government, and by special arrangement serves as a depository for the judicial and legislative branches of the government as well. Each executive agency is required by law to document its structure, procedures, and important activities, and the records are eventually preserved in the National Archives.

Should agencies desire to retain records which are more than fifty years old, the agencies must be prepared to justify continued custody. In practice, however, most records are offered much earlier for transfer to the National Archives. Once accessioned, they are preserved essentially in accordance with the structures of the originating agencies in the more than four hundred record groups in the National Archives.

Holdings of the NARS total more than thirteen million cubic feet of records, but almost twelve million feet consist of noncurrent records, in the regional records centers, which will be disposed of when they have outlived their usefulness. Only 1 to 3 percent of the annual paperwork and other records created by the federal government is selected as permanently valuable for retention. Most of the records which become part of the National Archives are preserved in the National Archives Building and the Washington National Records Center, although there are original documents of specific regional interest in the branch archives.

Although most of the records are textual, there are 1,500,000 maps and charts and 2,000,000 aerial photographs, 44,000 reels of motion pictures, 4,500,000 still pictures, and 66,500 sound recordings. Most holdings and textual records are open to research.

Researchers at the National Archives register with the Central Reference Division, which operates the Central Research Room and the Microfilm Research Room. There are numerous aids to assist researchers, including the general *Guide to the National Archives of the United States* and the *Catalog of National Archives Microfilm Publications*. A current edition of the *Select List of Publications of the National Archives and Records Service* describes various publications which may be obtained free of charge or by purchase. Among the publications that may be obtained free or by purchase are numerous inventories, guides, select lists, and pamphlets. Published quarterly is *Prologue: The Journal of the National Archives*. Printed facsimiles of many historic documents in the National Archives also may be purchased.

The archives branches have become important regional research centers. Not only do they hold valuable original records, including those of federal district and circuit courts, but they also have microfilm copies of many of the most important records in the National Archives in Washington. Their microfilm copies are available for institutional loan and may be obtained from the individual branches.

The presidential libraries began with the acceptance by Congress in 1939 of the Franklin D. Roosevelt Library in New York. In 1955 additional legislation provided for the acceptance and maintenance by the government of other presidential libraries.

Major elements of the NARS sponsor conferences, institutes, and symposia to spread knowledge of the extensive resources for research in the federal archival depositories. Since the series was inaugurated in 1967, the scholarly conference series of the Office of the National Archives has dealt with research subjects ranging from polar exploration to the meaning of the American Revolution. Institutes on modern archives administration and genealogical research are held regularly in the National Archives Building, and symposia are sponsored by the branch archives, the presidential libraries, and the Office of Records Management.

Researchers are kept apprised of accessions and openings of records at the various depositories by timely notices in the quarterly *Prologue*. Such information is made available to other scholarly journals for publication.

In addition to a variety of audiovisual records available for research, the NARS operates the National Audiovisual Center, containing motion pictures, filmstrips, slide sets, videotapes, and audiotapes made by or for government agencies.

The National Historical Publications Commission, which encourages the collecting, editing, and publishing of papers of outstanding Americans and other documentary sources important to American history, is housed in the National Archives Building and is chaired by the Archivist of the United States. The Archivist also chairs the National Archives Trust Fund Board, the Administrative Committee of the Federal Register, and the National Archives Advisory Council. The latter panel advises the Administrator of General Services on policies and practices of the federal archival system. Most of its members are drawn from historical and other professional societies with strong archival interests.

The National Archives Building attracts numerous visitors annually to view its exhibits. On permanent display since 1952 in the rotunda, the main exhibition hall, are the Declaration of Independence, the Constitution, and the Bill of Rights. Only two of the five pages of the Constitution are on view; the other pages are kept in a vault below the exhibit area. All seven parchment pages of the great charters are preserved individually in sealed cases of glass and bronze, which contain inert helium and measured amounts of water vapor to prevent deterioration. The pages on display are lowered automatically each night into the massive vault twenty feet below the floor of the exhibit hall and are raised again each morning.

Flanking the great charters in the rotunda are other original documents in a Formation of the Union exhibit. Other principal exhibit areas in which displays of historical material are changed from time to time are the South Galleries and Circular Gallery, on the Constitution Avenue side of the building, and the Pennsylvania Avenue lobby. Public ceremonies are held in the National Archives Building on such days as the Fourth of July and Constitution Day (September 17), and film festivals featuring NARS motion pictures are scheduled regularly.

There are large numbers of visitors to the museum sections of the presidential libraries, where gifts of other nations to the presidents are displayed along with other memorabilia of their administrations and documentary and photographic exhibits.

The National Archives has been a model for state and local archives in the United States and has served as a training ground for archivists and technicians from many other countries. In recent years, developing nations establishing national archives and records management programs have sent representatives to Washington for training. The NARS plays a leading role in the activities of the International Council on Archives.

Bibliography

Angel, H. E. "Federal Records Management Since the Hoover Commission Report." *American Archivist,* 1953, *16*(1), 13–26.

Brooks, P. C. "Archives in the United States During World War II, 1939–45." *Library Quarterly,* 1947, *17*(4), 263–280.

Cappon, L. J. "The National Archives and the Historical Profession." *Journal of Southern History,* 1969, *35*(4), 477–499.

Child, S. B. "What Is Past Is Prologue." *American Archivist,* 1942, *5*(4), 217–227.

Connor, R. D. W. "Our National Archives." *Minnesota History,* 1936, *17*(2), 1–19.

Evans, F. B. *The Administration of Modern Archives: A Select Bibliographic Guide.* Washington, D.C.: U.S. Government Printing Office, 1970.

Evans, F. B. "The National Archives and Records Service and Its Research Resources—A Select Bibliography." *Prologue,* 1971, *3*(3), 88–112.

Grover, W. C. "Recent Developments in Federal Archival Activities." *American Archivist,* 1951, *14*(1), 3–12.

Grover, W. C. "Toward Equal Opportunities for Scholarship." *Journal of American History,* 1966, *52*(1), 715–724.

Holmes, O. W. "The National Archives and the Protection of Records in War Areas." *American Archivist,* 1946, *9*(2), 110–127.

Holmes, O. W. "The National Archives at a Turn in the Road." *American Archivist,* 1949, *12*(4), 339–354.

Jones, H. G. *The Records of a Nation: Their Management, Preservation and Use.* New York: Atheneum, 1969.

Kahn, H. "The Presidential Library: A New Institution." *Special Libraries,* 1959, *50*(1), 106–113.

Krauskopf, R. E. "The Hoover Commissions and Federal Recordkeeping." *American Archivist,* 1958, *21*(4), 371–399.

O'Neill, J. E. "Will Success Spoil the Presidential Libraries?" *American Archivist,* 1973, *36*(3), 339–351.

Paltsits, V. H. "An Historical Résumé of the Public Archives Commission from 1899 to 1921." *Annual Report of the American Historical Association for 1922,* 1922, *1,* 152–160.

Paullin, C. O. "History of the Movement for a National Archives Building in Washington, D.C." (Senate Doc. 297, 62 Cong., 2 Sess., Serial 6175.) *Congressional Record,* 1916, *53,* Pt.14, App. 1116–1119.

Posner, E. "Some Aspects of Archival Development Since the French Revolution." *American Archivist,* 1940, *3*(3), 159–172.

Rhoads, J. B. "Programs of the National Archives." *Illinois Libraries,* 1970, *52*(1), 136–143.

Shelley, F. "The Interest of J. Franklin Jameson in the National Archives: 1808–1934." *American Archivist,* 1949, *12*(2), 99–130.

White, G. T. "Government Archives Afield: The Federal Records Centers and the Historian." *Journal of American History,* 1969, *55*(1), 833–842.

JAMES B. RHOADS

ARCHIVES OF AMERICAN ART
See Smithsonian Institution.

AREA STUDIES
(Field of Study)

The study of the societies and cultures of foreign regions of the world is a natural consequence of any educational philosophy that takes the experiences and works of mankind as its province. Yet the specific growth of programs devoted to such study occurred after World War II, when increased interaction among disparate societies resulted in practical policies and efforts for mutual understanding. Referred to as foreign area studies, language and area studies, or studies of regional cultures, this effort toward global perspectives and an understanding of other cultures signifies the end of national and cultural isolation.

Prototypical programs were found before World War II in research institutes of continental Europe and embryonic curricular programs in British and American universities. Many countries helped to develop foreign area studies, moreover, because of the military need to comprehend foreign societies. But the most noteworthy surge of development occurred when universities recognized that the systematic comprehension of alien cultures embodied academic as well as strategic values. Programs—mainly undergraduate and graduate-level ones but also research ventures—burgeoned rapidly with the encouragement of private foundations and, later, the federal government. Although coverage ranged from individual countries to vast global areas, these programs generally fell into a set of regional categories: East Asia, Southeast Asia, South Asia, the Middle East, the Soviet Union and Eastern Europe, Africa, and Latin America. In the mid 1970s West European studies and American studies—long a focal point for a small coterie of scholars—joined the regional studies fields.

In keeping with the academic precedents derived from classical studies, sinology, and other regional fields of study, the humanistic disciplines have provided the backbone of area studies. In the United States, for example, history and literature provide, apart from language courses, the bulk of course offerings in programs of foreign area study. With the new emphasis on understanding contemporary cultures and societies, however, political science, economics, sociology, and anthropology are assuming vital roles in area training. Another important result of the global attention to foreign cultures has been the growth of international communities of scholarship. North American students of India, for example, maintain a level of communication with their counterparts in India that was unknown until recently except among a tiny coterie of scholars.

The appearance of ethnic studies programs, particularly on North American campuses, introduces some confusion into the field of area studies. By virtue of their multidisciplinary composition, their emphasis on indigenous language and culture, and their objective of apprehending contemporary cultures in their entirety, ethnic studies programs resemble foreign area studies. Yet it is not unusual for a program of African studies to exist side by side with a program of Afro-American studies with virtually no duplication of courses or fac-

ulty. In this sense, ethnic or multicultural studies are characteristic of ethnically plural societies and can be distinguished from foreign area studies because their attention to external cultures is more a function of establishing their own origins than of understanding the peoples of another society. Both types of studies are academically valid because they seek understanding, but appreciation and preservation play a substantial role in ethnic studies, whereas foreign area studies are typically pursued with greater detachment and with no necessary reliance on personal empathy. Nevertheless, the potential for reciprocal benefit between these programs is substantial and, for the most part, yet to be explored.

LYMAN H. LEGTERS

Levels and Programs of Study

Programs in area studies or regional cultures generally require as a minimum prerequisite a secondary education, usually in a general program, and lead to the following degrees: bachelor's, master's (M.A. or M.Sc.), the doctorate (Ph.D.), or their equivalents. In these programs a combination of the social and behavioral sciences and related disciplines is applied to analyses of the social, cultural, and ethnic problems of a particular geographical region. The programs consist of study, group discussions or seminars, and, for advanced degrees, original research work as substantiated by the presentation of a scholarly thesis or dissertation.

Principal course content for programs that lead to a first university degree usually includes the principles of sociology, principles of economics, principles of political science, physical geography, economic geography, principles of regional planning, problems of regional development, the structure of local government, urban geography, urban sociology, rural geography, rural sociology, and studies of ethnic and minority groups. Background studies often include courses in sociology, political science, mathematics, statistical analysis, and research methodology.

In programs that lead to a postgraduate university degree, principal subject matter areas within which courses and research projects tend to fall include relevant specialties in sociology, anthropology, economics, political science, geography, psychology, geology, biology, meteorology, history, languages, literature, and linguistics. Background studies include relevant specialties in philosophy, fine arts, archeology, religion, law and jurisprudence, mathematics, computer science, and statistics.

[This section was based on UNESCO's *International Standard Classification of Education (ISCED)* (Paris: UNESCO, 1976).]

AFRICAN STUDIES
(South of the Sahara)

Major International and National Organizations

INTERNATIONAL

International Congress of Africanists
%Dr. Mudimbe, Secretary General
Université nationale du Zaïre
Boîte postale 1825
Lubumbashi, Zaire
Principal international organization whose aim is to develop international cooperation in the field of African studies.

NATIONAL

National associations in Europe and America interested in African studies include:

Belgium:
Académie royale des sciences d'outre-mer
1 rue Defacqz
1050 Brussels

Canada:
Canadian Association of African Studies (CAAS)
Association canadienne des études africaines (ACEA)
Department of Geography
Carleton University
Ottawa, Ontario K15 5B6

Federal Republic of Germany:
Deutsche Afrika Gesellschaft
Markt 10-12
Bonn

Vereinigung der Afrikanisten in Deutschland (VAD)
Steinern 7
2071 Grönwohld

France:
Société des africanistes (CSSF)
Musée de l'Homme
place du Trocadéro
75116 Paris

Italy:
Istituto italo-africano
via U. Aldrovandi 16
Rome

Spain:
Instituto de estudios africanos
Castellana 5
Madrid

Sweden:
Scandinavian Institute of African Studies
P.O. Box 2126
8-750 02 Uppsala 2

United Kingdom:
African Studies Association of the United Kingdom (ASA-UK)
%Center of West African Studies
University of Birmingham
P.O. Box 363
Birmingham 15, England

Royal African Society
18 Northumberland Avenue
London WC2N 5BJ, England

United States:
African Studies Association (ASA)
218 Schiffman Center
Brandeis University
Waltham, Massachusetts 02154

Association of African Studies Programs in the United States
%Foreign and Comparative Studies Program
Syracuse University
119 College Place
Syracuse, New York 13210

Additional organizations may be found in:

Africa South of the Sahara. London: Europa, annual. Lists international, regional, and national organizations involved in Africa.
International Directory for Educational Liaison. Washington, D.C.: American Council on Education, 1973.
International Register of Organizations Undertaking Africanist Research in the Social Sciences and Humanities. London: International African Institute, 1975.

Principal Information Sources

GENERAL

Guides to the literature include:

Duignan, P. *Guide to Research and Reference Works on Sub-Saharan Africa.* Stanford, California: Hoover Institution Press, 1972. An extensive guide to library and archival materials important in reference, research, and teaching.

Duigan, P., and others. *Africa South of the Sahara: A Bibliography for Undergraduate Libraries.* Williamsport, Pennsylvania: Bro-dart, 1971.

Panofsky, H. E. *A Bibliography of Africana.* Westport, Connecticut: Greenwood Press, 1975.

CURRENT BIBLIOGRAPHIES

Accessions List, Eastern Africa. Nairobi, Kenya: U.S. Library of Congress, Nairobi Office, 1968–. Published bimonthly.

African Abstracts. London: International African Institute, 1950–. Each issue abstracts over two hundred periodicals.

Africana Journal. New York: Africana, 1970–.

The African Book Publishing Record. Oxford, England: Hans Zell, 1975–. Published quarterly.

African Books in Print. London: Mansel, 1975.

A Current Bibliography on African Affairs. Westport, Connecticut: Greenwood Periodicals, 1962–. Published monthly.

International African Bibliography. London: International African Institute, 1971–. Annual listing of over two thousand books, periodicals, and reports in many languages.

PERIODICALS

A selection from the numerous periodicals relating to African study includes *Africa* (UK), *Africa Confidential* (UK), *Africa Currents* (UK), *African Affairs* (UK), *African Development* (UK), *African Research and Documentation* (UK), *African Studies* (South Africa), *African Studies Review* (US), *Africa Report* (US), *Africa Research Bulletin* (UK), *Africa Today* (US), *Bulletin de l'Institut fondamental d'Afrique noire* (Senegal), *Bulletin of the School of Oriental and African Studies* (UK), *Cahiers d'études africaines* (France), *Canadian Journal of African Studies*, *Current Bibliography on African Affairs* (US), *International Journal of African Historical Series* (US), *Jeune Afrique* (France), *Journal de la Société des africanistes* (France), *Journal of African History* (UK), *Journal of Modern African Studies* (Lesotho), *Journal of the New African Literature and the Arts* (US), *Présence africaine* (France), *Transition* (Ghana), *West Africa* (UK).

Directories to other periodicals include:

African Studies: World List of Specialized Periodicals. The Hague: Mouton, 1970. Descriptions of 492 periodicals covering Africa south of the Sahara.

Africa South of the Sahara. London: Europa, annual. Includes a selected list of periodicals on Africa.

U.S. Library of Congress, African Section. *Africa South of the Sahara: Index to Periodical Literature, 1900–1970.* (4 vols.) Boston: Hall, 1971. A first supplement was published in 1973.

U.S. Library of Congress, African Section. *Sub-Saharan Africa: A Guide to Serials.* Washington, D.C.: Library of Congress, 1970.

ENCYCLOPEDIAS, DICTIONARIES, HANDBOOKS

The following is a selection from the numerous works that deal with Africa:

Africa South of the Sahara. London: Europa, annual. A yearbook surveying developments in economics, history, and education and containing directories of organizations.

Area Handbooks. Washington, D.C.: American University, Foreign Area Studies Division, 1961–. The volume for each country is an excellent source of basic information.

Daggs, E. *All Africa.* New York: Hastings House, 1970.

Encyclopedia Africana. Accra, Ghana, forthcoming. Projected ten volumes.

Legum, C., and Drysdale, J. *Africa Contemporary Record: Annual Survey and Documents.* London: Africa Research, annual.

Paden, J. N., and Soja, E. W. *The African Experience.* (4 vols.) Evanston, Illinois: Northwestern University Press, 1970. Teaching materials on Africa compiled for introducing African studies at the college or university level.

Potgieter, D. J. (Ed.) *Standard Encyclopedia of Southern Africa.* Cape Town, South Africa: Nasou, 1970–.

DIRECTORIES

Area Studies on U.S. Campuses: A Directory. New York: World Studies Data Bank, 1974. Lists African studies programs and centers.

Directory of African Studies in the United States. Waltham, Massachusetts: African Studies Association, biannual.

RESEARCH CENTERS, INSTITUTES, INFORMATION CENTERS

Directories to libraries, information centers, and research institutes include:

Africa South of the Sahara. London: Europa, annual. Lists national research institutions studying Africa.

Collison, R. *The Scolma Directory of Libraries and Special Collections in Africa.* (3rd ed.) Hamden, Connecticut: Archon, 1973. A guide to African materials in the United Kingdom.

Dauphin, J. C., Rosset, A., and Rupp, B. "Inventaire des ressources documentaires africanistes à Paris." *Recherche, enseignement, documentation africanistes francophones: Bulletin d'information et liaison,* 1969, *1* (1). A directory of 129 French organizations (libraries, research institutes, and information centers).

Duignan, P. *Handbook of American Resources for African Studies.* Stanford, California: Stanford University Press, 1967. A directory to nearly one hundred American library and archival collections on Africa.

International Register of Organizations Undertaking Africanist Research in the Social Sciences and Humanities. London: International African Institute, 1975. Includes a comprehensive list of international and national research organizations and institutes.

ASIAN STUDIES
(Including Oceania)

Major International and National Organizations

INTERNATIONAL

International Congress of Human Sciences in Asia and North Africa (formerly International Congress of Orientalists)
Professor Graziella de la Lama, President
El Colegio de México
Mexico D.F., Mexico

International Union of Orientalists
Union internationale des orientalistes (UIO)
77 quai du Port-du-Fouarré
94100 Saint-Maur-des-Fossés, France

NATIONAL

The following is a selection of associations interested in Asia and Asian studies:

Australia:
    Australian Association for Asian Studies
    % Professor J. A. C. Mackie
    Monash University, Clayton, Victoria 3168

Canada:
    Canadian Society for Asian Studies
    % Professor Victor Fic
    Brock University
    St. Catharines, Ontario

Federal Republic of Germany:
    Deutsche Gesellschaft für Ostasienkunde
    Rothenbaumchaussee 32
    2 Hamburg 13

    Deutsche Orient-Gesellschaft
    Takustrasse 40
    1 Berlin 33

    Deutsche morgenländische Gesellschaft
    Postfach 642
    355 Marburg/Lahn

France:
    Société asiatique
    3 rue Mazarine
    Paris 6e

India:
    Asiatic Society
    1 Park Street
    Calcutta

Italy:
    Istituto italiano per il medio e l'estremo Oriente (ISMEO)
    Palazzo Bramcaccio
    via Merulana 248
    Rome

Japan:
    Asiatic Society of Japan
    C.P.O. Box 592
    Tokyo

    Institute of Oriental Culture
    University of Tokyo
    7-3-1 Hongo, Bunkyo-ku
    Tokyo

United Kingdom:
    Royal Asiatic Society of Great Britain and Ireland
    56 Queen Anne Street
    London W1M 9LA, England

    Royal Central Asian Society
    42 Devonshire Street
    London W1N 1LN, England

    Royal Society for India, Pakistan and Ceylon
    2 Temple Chambers, Temple Avenue
    London EC4Y OHB, England

United States:
    American Oriental Society
    329 Sterling Memorial Library
    Yale Station
    New Haven, Connecticut 06520
    Includes three regional branches: Middle West Branch (MWAOS), Southwest Branch (SWAOS), and Western Branch (WAOS).

    Association for Asian Studies (AAS)
    1 Lane Hall

University of Michigan
Ann Arbor, Michigan 48104

Includes four regional councils: Southeast Asian Regional Council (SEARC), South Asia Regional Council (SARC), China and Inner Asia Regional Council (CIARC), and Northeast Asia Regional Council (NEARC).

Additional national and international organizations interested in Asia may be found in:

Asia Society, Inc. *American Institutions and Organizations Interested in Asia: A Reference Directory.* (2nd ed.) New York: Taplinger, 1961. Lists approximately one thousand programs of American institutions and organizations.

The Far East and Australia. London: Europa, annual. Lists Asian regional organizations and institutions studying the Far East and Australasia.

International Directory for Educational Liaison. Washington, D.C.: American Council on Education, 1973.

Principal Information Sources

GENERAL

The following is a sampling from the many guides to literature in the field:

Birnbaum, E. *Books on Asia from the Near East to the Far East.* Toronto, Ontario: University of Toronto Press, 1971.

Gordon, L. H. D., and Shulman, F. J. (Eds.) *Doctoral Dissertations on China: A Bibliography of Studies in Western Languages, 1945–1970.* Seattle: University of Washington Press, 1972.

Johnson, D. C. *A Guide to Reference Materials on Southeast Asia.* New Haven, Connecticut: Yale University Press, 1970.

Nunn, R. G. *Asia: A Selected and Annotated Guide to Reference Works.* Cambridge, Massachusetts: MIT Press, 1971.

Pearson, J. D. *Oriental and Asian Bibliography: An Introduction, with Some Reference to Africa.* London: Crosby Lockwood, 1966.

SarDesi, D. S., and SarDesi, B. D. *Theses and Dissertations on Southeast Asia: An International Bibliography in Social Science, Education and Fine Arts.* New York: International Publications Service, 1970.

Shulman, F. J. *Japan and Korea: An Annotated Bibliography of Doctoral Dissertations in Western Languages 1877–1969.* Chicago: American Library Association, 1970.

Shulman, F. J. *Doctoral Dissertations on South Asia, 1966–1970.* Ann Arbor: University of

Michigan, Center for South and Southeast Asia, 1972.

There are hundreds of introductions and histories to the field, among which are included:

DeBary, W. T., and Enbree, A. T. *Approaches to Asian Civilizations.* New York: Columbia University Press, 1964.

Matthew, H. G. (Ed.) *Asia in the Modern World.* New York: New American Library, 1963.

Penkola, M. *A Correlated History of the Far East, China/Korea, Japan.* Rutland, Vermont: C. E. Tuttle, 1966.

CURRENT BIBLIOGRAPHIES

Asian Bibliography. Bangkok, Thailand: United Nations, Economic Commission for Asia and the Far East (ECAFE) Library, 1952–. Published semiannually. Selected acquisitions of the library in Bangkok; social science emphasis.

Bibliographia Asiatica. Calcutta: K. K. Roy (private), 1968–.

Bibliography of Asia Studies. Ann Arbor, Michigan: Association for Asian Studies, 1957–. Published annually. Important international bibliographical contribution to the field of Asian studies.

Index Indo-Asiaticus. Calcutta: Temple Press, 1968–. Published quarterly. An international index of current periodical literature on topics relating to the culture of India and ancient Asia.

PERIODICALS

Acta Orientalia (Denmark); *Archiv orientalni* (Czechoslovakia), *Asian Affairs* (UK); *Asian Review and Art and Letters* (UK); *Asian Studies* (Japan); *Asian Survey* (US); *Asiatische Studien/ Etudes asiatiques* (Switzerland); *Association for Asian Studies, Newsletter* (US); *Bulletin of the School of Oriental and African Studies* (UK); *Central Asiatic Journal* (FRG); *China Quarterly* (UK); *East and West* (Italy); *East Asian Cultural Studies* (Japan); *France-Asie/Asia* (France); *Institut für Orientforschung; Mitteilungen* (GDR); *Journal asiatique* (France); *Journal of Asian Studies* (US); *Journal of the American Oriental Society; Journal of Asiatic Studies* (Republic of Korea); *Journal of Japanese Studies* (US); *Journal of Oriental Studies* (Japan); *Journal of the Royal Asiatic Society of Great Britain and Ireland; Journal of South Asian Studies* (Australia); *Journal of Southeast Asian Studies* (Singapore); *Modern Asian Studies* (UK); *Oriental Culture* (Japan); *Pacific Affairs* (Canada); *Wiener Zeitschrift für die Kunde des Morgenlandes* (Austria); *Zeitschrift der deutschen morgenländischen Gesellschaft* (FRG).

A more extensive listing of journals in the field may be found in:

The Far East and Australia. London: Europa, annual.

ENCYCLOPEDIAS, DICTIONARIES, HANDBOOKS

The following is a selection from the numerous works dealing with Asia. (A more extensive listing may be found in J. D. Pearson, *Oriental and Asian Bibliography,* listed above.)

Area Handbooks. Washington, D.C.: American University, Foreign Area Studies Division, 1961–. The volume for each country is an excellent source of basic information.

Chen, J. *A Practical English-Chinese Pronouncing Dictionary.* Rutland, Vermont: C. E. Tuttle, 1970.

Far East and Australasia. London: Europa, annual.

Osborne, C. (Ed.) *Australia, New Zealand, and the South Pacific: A Handbook.* New York: Praeger, 1970.

Wint, G. *Asia: A Handbook.* New York: Praeger, 1966. A reference book of basic information dealing with Asia east of Iran.

DIRECTORIES

Area Studies on U.S. Campuses: A Directory. New York: World Studies Data Bank, 1974. Lists Asian studies (including East, South, and Southeast Asia) programs and centers.

Peterson's Annual Guides to Graduate Study, 1976. Book 2: *Humanities and Social Sciences.* Princeton, New Jersey: Peterson's Guides, 1975. Lists Asian area studies in United States colleges and universities.

World Guide to Universities. New York: Bowker; Pullach/Munich, Federal Republic of Germany: Verlag Dokumentation, 1972. Lists institutions offering programs of study in the history and culture of Asia and Oceania.

The World of Learning. London: Europa, annual. Lists Asian studies research institutes and departments of Asian studies in universities throughout the world.

RESEARCH CENTERS, INSTITUTES, INFORMATION CENTERS

Directories to libraries, information centers, and research institutes include:

The Far East and Australia. London: Europa, annual. Includes an extensive listing of research institutes by country.

Pearson, J. D. *Oriental and Asian Bibliography.* London: Crosby Lockwood, 1966. Lists the principal Orientalist libraries throughout the world.

EUROPEAN STUDIES
(General and West European)

Major International and National Organizations

INTERNATIONAL

Association of Institutes for European Studies
Centre européen de la culture
122 rue de Lausanne
Geneva, Switzerland
  Coordinates activities of thirty-two member institutions in nine countries in teaching, research, and information exchange.

International Institute for Ligurian Studies
Museo Bickneli
17 bis via Romana
Bordighera, Italy
  Research on ancient monuments and regional traditions in the north-west arc of the Mediterranean; members in France, Italy, Spain, and Switzerland.

NATIONAL

United States:
    Council for European Studies
    University of Pittsburgh
    156 Mervis Hall
    Pittsburgh, Pennsylvania 15213

Additional organizations may be found in:

The Europa Yearbook. London: Europa, 1959–. Published annually.
The World of Learning. London: Europa, 1947–. Published annually.

Principal Information Sources

GENERAL

Guides to the literature include:

European Culture Centre. *The European Bibliography.* Leiden, Netherlands: A. W. Sijthoff, 1965. Briefly annotated list of books concerned with Europe as a field of specific research, a cultural unity, or as a union to be created; annotations in English, French, and German.

Gertin, P. *Initiation à la documentation écrite de la période contemporaine (fin du XVIIIe siècle à nos jours).* Liège, Belgium: Librairie Fernand Gothier, 1970. Guidebook to bibliographies, encyclopedias, yearbooks, and other literature concerning the political, economic, and social life in European countries from the eighteenth century to the present.

CURRENT BIBLIOGRAPHIES

Britain and Europe Since 1945. Brighton, England: Harvester Press, 1973–. Microfiche collection to be updated and enlarged annually.

European Studies Newsletter. Pittsburgh: Council for European Studies, University of Pittsburgh, 1972–. Each quarterly issue contains information services of interest to scholars and students of Western European affairs.

PERIODICALS

There are hundreds of journals dealing with the European area. Among those relating specifically to European studies are *Asian Journal of European Studies* (India), *Europa* (FRG), *European Studies* (UK), *European Studies Newsletter* (US), *Europea Studies Review* (US, UK), *Journal of European Studies* (UK).

For other journals see:

Ulrich's International Periodicals Directory. New York: Bowker, biennial.

Visenyi, P. E. *European Periodical Literature in the Social Sciences and the Humanities.* Metuchen, New Jersey: Scarecrow Press, 1969.

ENCYCLOPEDIAS, DICTIONARIES, HANDBOOKS

Area Handbooks. Washington, D.C.: American University, Foreign Area Studies Division, 1961–. The volume for each country provides an excellent source of basic information.

Calmann, J. *Western Europe: A Handbook.* New York: Praeger, 1967. Contains descriptive and statistical information; information on political, economic, and social affairs and on Western European integration; and a chronology of important political events for each country.

Cook, C., and Paxton, J. *European Political Facts, 1918–1972.* New York: St. Martin's, 1973. Political, social, and economic facts for thirty-five European countries.

Cosgrove, C. A. *A Reader's Guide to Britain and the European Communities.* London: Political and Economic Planning, 1970.

The Europa Yearbook. London: Europa, 1959–. Published annually. Vol. 1: *Europe.* Provides brief information on government, constitution, judicial system, and economy for each country.

European Yearbook. (21 vols.) New York: International Publications Service, 1964–1975.

Scandinavian Political Studies. New York: Columbia University Press, 1966–. Annual handbook of the political science associations of Denmark, Norway, and Sweden; contains essays and reviews as well as bibliographical surveys of political literature.

DIRECTORIES

Area Studies on U.S. Campuses: A Directory. New York: World Studies Data Bank, 1974. Lists general European studies programs in the United States.

World Guide to Universities. New York: Bowker; Pullach/Munich, Federal Republic of Germany: Verlag Dokumentation, 1972. Lists institutions offering degrees, under "Europe," "History," and "Culture."

RESEARCH CENTERS, INSTITUTES, INFORMATION CENTERS

Centre de recherches européennes
Château de Vichy
Lausanne, Switzerland

Centro studi sulle comunità europeo
Corso Strada Nrov 65
Pavia, Italy

European University Institute
Badia Fiesolana
via dei Roccettini
50124 Florence, Italy
    Conducts comparative and interdisciplinary research in European studies.

Institut d'études européennes
39 avenue F. D. Roosevelt
Brussels 5, Belgium

Institut für europäische Geschichte
Alteuniversitätsstrasse 19
65 Mainz, Federal Republic of Germany

Institute on Western Europe
420 West 118th Street
New York, New York 10027 USA

Interuniversity Centre for European Studies
1199 rue de Bleury
Pavillon Riverin 6410, C.P. 8888
Montreal, Quebec, Canada H3C 3P8

For other European studies research institutes in the United States see:

Palmer, A. M. *Research Centers Directory.* Detroit: Gale Research, 1975.

Other directories to research institutions are:

Murphy, P. W. (Comp.) *Institutes of Atlantic Studies: A Directory of Research Institutions*

Concerned with the Western Industrialized World. Washington, D.C.: Atlantic Council of the United States, 1972.

The World of Learning. London: Europa, 1947–. Published annually.

LATIN AMERICAN STUDIES

Major International and National Organizations

INTERNATIONAL

Consejo latinoamericano de ciencias sociales (CLASCO)
Lavalle 1171, 4°
Buenos Aires, Argentina

International Congress of Americanists
Alberto Rex Gonzólez, Museo de La Plata
Universidad nacional de La Plata
La Plata, Argentina
Historical and scientific study of the Americas and their inhabitants; apparently inactive since 1973.

NATIONAL

National associations in Europe and North America interested in Latin American studies include:

Canada:
 Canadian Association of Latin American Studies
 151 Slater Street, Room 210
 Ottawa, Ontario K1P 5H3

Federal Republic of Germany:
 Arbeitsgemeinschaft deutsche Lateinamerika-Forschung
 %Institut für Iberoamerika-Kunde
 Alsterglacis 8
 2 Hamburg 36

France:
 Société des américanistes
 Musée de l'Homme
 place du Trocadéro
 75116 Paris

Italy:
 Associazione italiana di studi americanistici
 Fiera internazionale P. Kennedy
 Palazzo dei Congresi
 16 129 Genoa

Netherlands:
 Studie en dokumentatie centrum voor Latijns Amerika
 University of Amsterdam
 Mawitstrade 63
 Kamer 191, Amsterdam

United Kingdom:
 Institute of Latin American Studies
 31 Tavistock Square
 London WC1, England

United States:
 Latin American Studies Association
 Box 13362 University Station
 University of Florida
 Gainesville, Florida 32601

Directories to other organizations concerned with Latin American studies and research include:

International Directory for Educational Liaison. Washington, D.C.: American Council on Education, 1973.

Pan American Associations in the United States. Washington, D.C.: Pan American Union, 1968.

Sable, M. (Ed.) *Master Directory for Latin America.* Los Angeles: University of California Press, 1965.

Principal Information Sources

GENERAL

Guides to the literature include:

American Universities Field Staff. *A Select Bibliography.* New York: American Universities Field Staff, 1973. Cumulative supplement, 1961–1971; includes Latin American area studies.

Comitas, L. *Caribbean, 1960–1965: A Topical Bibliography.* Seattle: University of Washington Press, 1968.

Griffin, C. C., and Benedict, W. J. (Eds.) *Latin America: A Guide to the Historical Literature.* Austin: University of Texas Press for the Conference on Latin American History, 1971.

Dorn, G. M. *Latin America, Spain, and Portugal: An Annotated Bibliography of Paperback Books.* Washington, D.C.: Library of Congress, 1976.

Gropp, A. E. *Bibliography of Latin American Bibliographies.* Metuchen, New Jersey: Scarecrow Press, 1968. With *Supplement, 1965–1969,* published 1971.

Gropp, A. E. *Bibliography of Latin American Bibliographies Published in Periodicals.* Metuchen, New Jersey: Scarecrow Press, 1975.

Handbook of Latin American Studies. Gainesville: University of Florida Press, 1936–. Published annually. Of first importance as a guide to Latin American materials.

Humphreys, R. A. *Latin American History. A Guide to the Literature in English.* London: Oxford University Press, 1958. Reprint, 1966.

Rodriguez, M., and Peloso, V. C. *A Guide for the Study of Culture in Central America (Humanities and Social Sciences).* Washington, D.C.: Pan American Union, 1968.

Sable, M. *A Guide to Latin American Studies.* Los Angeles: University of California, Latin American Center, 1967. Extensive annotated compilation of reference works and other literature.

Sable, M. *Latin American Studies in the Non-Western World and Eastern Europe: A Bibliography on Latin America in the Languages of Africa, Asia, the Middle East, and Eastern Europe with Transliterations and Translations in English.* Metuchen, New Jersey: Scarecrow Press, 1970.

Weaver, J. L. *Latin American Developments: A Selected Bibliography.* Santa Barbara, California: ABC-Clio, 1969.

United States Department of State, Foreign Service Institute, Center for Area and Country Studies. *Latin America: A Selected Functional and Country Bibliography.* Washington, D.C.: U.S. Government Printing Office, 1969. Part 1 covers the Latin American area; part 2 concerns the countries of Latin America.

Zimmerman, I. *Current National Bibliographies of Latin America: A State of the Art Study.* Gainesville, Florida: Center for Latin American Studies, 1971.

A selection from the many overviews and histories available for the area includes:

Bailey, H. M., and Nasatir, A. P. *Latin America: The Development of Its Civilization.* (3rd ed.) Englewood Cliffs, New Jersey: Prentice-Hall, 1973.

Crow, J. A. *The Epic of Latin America.* (2nd ed.) Garden City, New York: Doubleday, 1971.

Davis, H. E. *History of Latin America.* New York: Ronald Press, 1968.

Esquenazi-Mayo, R. *Latin American Scholarship Since World War II: Trends in History, Political Science, Literature, Geography, and Economics.* Lincoln: University of Nebraska Press, 1971.

Herring, H. *History of Latin America.* (3rd ed.) New York: Knopf, 1968.

Hilton, R. *The Latin Americans, Their Heritage and Their Destiny.* Philadelphia: Lippincott, 1973.

Rothchild, J. (Ed.) *Latin America: Yesterday and Today.* New York: Praeger, 1974. Collection of articles on many aspects of Latin America.

CURRENT BIBLIOGRAPHIES

Bibliografía actual del Caribe. Hato Rey, Puerto Rico: Biblioteca regional del Caribe, Centro norte-sur, 1971–.

British Bulletin of Publications on Latin America, the West Indies, Portugal, and Spain. London: Hispanic Council, 1947–. Published semiannually.

Handbook of Latin American Studies. Gainesville: University of Florida Press, 1936–. Published annually; comprehensive annotated bibliography; humanities and social sciences presented in alternate years.

Indice general de publicaciones periódicas latinoamericanas: Humanidades y ciencias sociales/ Index to Latin American Periodicals: Humanities and Social Sciences. Metuchen, New Jersey: Scarecrow Press, 1961–.

Inter-American Review of Bibliography. Washington, D.C.: Pan American Union, 1961–.

Latin American Research Review. Chapel Hill, North Carolina: American Studies Association, 1965–. Contains "Current Research Inventory" and newly received bibliographies and other reference works.

Padron, M. "Historiografía y bibliografía americanista." Published as a section of the *Anuario de estudios americanos.* Seville: Universidad de Sevilla, Escuela del estudios hispano-americanos, 1955–.

PERIODICALS

América latina (Brazil, *Americas* (US), *Boletín de estudios latinoamericanos* (Netherlands), *Cahiers des Amériques latines* (France), *Caribbean Studies* (Puerto Rico), *Cuadernos americanos* (Mexico), *Foro international* (Mexico), *Hispanic American Historical Review* (US), *Ibero-americano pragensia* (Czechoslovakia), *Inter-American Economic Affairs* (US), *Journal of Inter-American Studies* (US), *Journal of Latin American Studies* (UK), *Lateinamerika* (GDR), *Latin America* (UK), *Latin American Research Review* (US), *North South: Canadian Journal of Latin American Studies*, *Nueva Sociedad* (Costa Rica), *Opinião* (Brazil), *Revista interamericana de ciencias sociales* (US), *Veja* (Brazil).

Guides to other Latin American periodicals are:

Birkos, A. S., and Tambs, L. A. *Latin American Studies: Academic Writer's Guide to Periodicals.* Kent, Ohio: Kent State University Press, 1971.

Brunnschweiler, T. *Current Periodicals: A Select Bibliography in the Area of Latin American Studies.* East Lansing: Michigan State University Press, 1968.

Latin American Economic and Social Serials. Hamden, Connecticut: Archon, 1969.

Latin America: World List of Specialized Periodicals. Atlantic Highlands, New Jersey: Humanities Press, 1974.

Levi, N. *Guía de publicaciones periódicas de universidades latinoamericanas.* Mexico City: Universidad nacional autónoma de México, 1967.

Zimmerman, I. *A Guide to Current Latin American Periodicals: Humanities and Social Sciences.* Gainesville, Florida: Kallman, 1961. Old but still useful.

ENCYCLOPEDIAS, DICTIONARIES, HANDBOOKS

The following selection is only a sample of the many works available on the area:

Area Handbooks. Washington, D.C.: American University, Foreign Area Studies Division, 1961–. The volume for each country is an excellent source of basic information.

Brazil: Field Research Guide. New York: Columbia University Press, 1966.

Delpar, H. (Ed.) *Encyclopedia of Latin America.* New York: McGraw-Hill, 1974.

Enciclopedia universal ilustrada europeaamericana Barcelona: Espasa, 1907–1930. Appendix for 1930–1933; annual supplements 1935–. Extensive coverage of Latin American topics.

Grande enciclopedia Larousse. Barcelona: Espasa, 1967.

Martin, M. R., and Lovett, G. H. (Eds.) *Encyclopedia of Latin American History.* Indianapolis, Indiana: Bobbs Merrill, 1968.

The South American Handbook. Parsonage Lane, Bath, England: Trade and Travel Publications, Mendip Press, 1924–. Annual of concise and up-to-date information on the countries of Central and South America.

Stewart, J. H. (Ed.) *Handbook of South American Indians.* (7 vols.) New York: Cooper Square, n.d. Reprint of 1957 edition.

Walne, P. (Comp.) *Guide to Manuscript Sources for the History of Latin America and the Caribbean in the British Isles.* London: Oxford University Press in collaboration with the University of London Institute of Latin American Studies, 1973.

Wauchope, R. (Ed.) *Handbook of Middle American Indians.* (13 vols.) Austin: University of Texas Press, 1964–1974.

DIRECTORIES

Area Studies on U.S. Campuses: A Directory. New York: World Studies Data Bank, 1974.

Commonwealth Universities Yearbook. London: Association of Commonwealth Universities, 1941–. Published annually.

Directory of Canadian Scholars and Universities Interested in Latin American Studies. Ottawa, Ontario: Canadian Association of Latin American Studies, 1975.

Directory of Development Research and Training Institutes in Latin America. Liaison Bulletin No. 1. Paris: Organisation for Economic Co-operation and Development, 1973.

Latin American Studies in the Universities of the United Kingdom. London: University of London, Institute of Latin American Studies, 1968/69. Updated frequently.

Peterson's Annual Guides to Graduate Study, 1976. Book 2: *Humanities and Social Sciences.* Princeton, New Jersey: Peterson's Guides, 1975. Lists Latin American area studies programs in colleges and universities in the United States.

Sable, M. H. *Master Directory for Latin America.* Los Angeles: University of California Press, 1965.

A Survey of the Portuguese Language, Luso-Brazilian and Latin American Area Studies in Institutions of Higher Learning in the United States. Washington, D.C.: Brazilian Embassy and Brazilian American Cultural Institute, 1970.

World Guide to Universities. New York: Bowker; Pullach/Munich, Federal Republic of Germany: Verlag Dokumentation, 1972. See "Latin America, history."

RESEARCH CENTERS, INSTITUTES, INFORMATION CENTERS

Directories to Latin American research centers, institutes, and information/library services are:

Directory of Development Research and Training Institutes in Latin America. Paris: Organisation for Economic Co-operation and Development, 1973.

Haro, R. P. *Latin American Research in the United States and Canada: A Guide and Directory.* Chicago: American Library Association, 1971. Includes lists of library collections and Latin American research centers.

Jackson, W. V. *Library Guide for Brazilian Studies.* Pittsburgh: University of Pittsburgh Press, 1964. Surveys library resources in the United States.

Naylor, B., and others. *Directory of Libraries and Special Collections on Latin America and the West Indies.* Atlantic Highlands, New Jersey: Humanities Press, 1975.

Sable, M. *Master Directory for Latin America.* Los Angeles: University of California Press, 1965.

MIDDLE EASTERN AND NORTH AFRICAN STUDIES

Major International and National Organizations

INTERNATIONAL

Congress of Arab and Islamic Studies
Professor F. M. Pareja
Limité 5
Cuidad universitaria
Madrid 3, Spain

Promotes exchange of information among specialists in Western Europe.

International Union of Orientalists
Union internationale des orientalistes (UIO)
77 quai du Port-au-Fouarré
94100 Saint-Maur-des-Fossés, France
Principal learned society of orientalists throughout the world; it organizes congresses, research, and publications.

NATIONAL

The principal associations in the United Kingdom and the United States interested in Middle East and North African area studies are:

United Kingdom:
British Society for Middle Eastern Studies (BRISMES)
%Derek Hopwood
Middle East Library, St. Antony's College
University of Oxford
Oxford 0X1 3BD, England

Royal Asiatic Society of Great Britain and Ireland
56 Queen Anne Street
London WIM 9LA, England

United States:
American Oriental Society
329 Sterling Memorial Library
Yale Station
New Haven, Connecticut 06520

Middle East Studies Association of North America
Hagop Kezorkian Center for Near Eastern Studies
New York University
50 Washington Square South
New York, New York 10003

For a more extensive listing of organizations interested in the Middle East and North Africa, and associations and institutes studying the region, consult:

The Middle East and North Africa. London: Europa, 1948–. Published annually.

Principal Information Sources

GENERAL

Guides to the literature include:

Atiyeh, G. N. *The Contemporary Middle East 1948–1973: A Selective and Annotated Bibliography.* Boston: Hall, 1975.
Hopwood, D., and Grimwood-Jones, D. *Middle East and Islam: A Bibliographical Introduction.* Zug, Switzerland: Inter Doc, 1972. A basic collection of books on Islam and/or Middle Eastern studies.

Howard, H. N. *Middle East and North Africa: A Bibliography for Undergraduate Libraries.* Williamsport, Pennsylvania: Bro-dart, 1971.
The Middle East and North Africa. London: Europa, 1948–. Includes selections from the many introductions and histories on the Middle East and North Africa.
Pearson, J. D. *Index Islamicus, 1906–1955.* Cambridge, England: Heffer, 1958–. References to periodical literature in Western languages in all fields in the North Africa and Middle East area. Supplements are published.
Pearson, J. D. *Oriental and Asian Bibliography.* Hamden, Connecticut: Archon, 1966. Includes a chapter on histories, particularly of Oriental, Arabic, and Islamic studies.
Sauvaget, J. *Introduction to the History of the Muslim East: A Bibliographical Guide.* (2nd ed.) Berkeley: University of California Press, 1965.
Selim, G. D. *American Doctoral Dissertations on the Arab World, 1883–1968.* Washington, D.C.: Library of Congress, 1970.
Shulman, F. J. *American and British Doctoral Dissertations on Israel and Palestine in Modern Times.* Ann Arbor: University of Michigan Microfilms, 1973.
Zuwiyya, J. *The Near East.* Metuchen, New Jersey: Scarecrow Press, 1973. Lists over 3500 titles for the student and specialist interested in the culture, history, and literature of Southwest Asia and North Africa.

CURRENT BIBLIOGRAPHIES

Abstracta Islamica. Paris: P. Geuthner, 1927–.
Bibliotheca Orientalis. Leiden, Netherlands: Nederlands instituut voor het Nabije Oosten, 1943–. A bibliographical review.
Middle East Journal. Washington, D.C.: Middle East Institute, 1947–. Each issue contains a bibliography of recent periodical articles.
Orientalische Literaturzeitung. Berlin, German Democratic Republic: Akademie-Verlag GmbH, 1898–.
Quarterly Checklist of Oriental Studies. Darien, Connecticut: American Bibliographic Service, 1959–.

PERIODICALS

A selected list of periodicals on the Middle East and North Africa includes *Abr nahrain* (Netherlands), *Acta Orientalia* (Denmark), *Acta Orientalia Academiae Scientiarum Hungaricae* (Hungary), *Annuaire de l'Afrique du nord* (France), *Archiv orientalni* (Czechoslovakia), *Asiatische Studien/Etudes asiatiques* (Switzerland), *British Society for Middle Eastern Studies Bulletin, Bulletin of the School of Oriental and African Studies* (UK), *East and West* (Italy), *Folia Orientalia* (Poland), *International Journal of Middle East Studies* (US), *Islam* (FRG), *Journal asiatique* (France), *Journal* of the American Oriental Society, *Journal of the Economic and Social History of the Orient* (Netherlands), *Journal of Near Eastern Studies* (US), *Journal of the Royal Asiatic Society of Great Britain and Ireland, Middle East Journal* (US), *Journal of Semitic Studies* (UK), *Middle Eastern Studies* (UK), *Middle East Studies Association Bulletin* (US), *Mitteilungen des Instituts für Orientforschung* (GDR), *Narody Azii i Afriki* (USSR), *Orient* (FRG), *Orientalistische Literaturzeitung* (GDR), *Oriente moderno* (Italy), *Przeglad orientalistyczny* (Poland), *Rivista degli studi orientali* (Italy), *Rocznik orientalistyczny* (Poland), *Studia et Acta Orientalia* (Romania), *Studia Orientalia* (Finland), *Studies in Islam* (India), *Zeitschrift der deutschen morgenländischen Gesellschaft* (FRG).

Directories to periodicals dealing with the Middle East and Africa include:

Ljunggren, F. *The Arab World Index: An International Guide to Periodical Literature in the Social Sciences and Humanities in the Arab World 1960–64.* Cairo: American University, 1967.

Ljunggren, F., and Hamdy, M. *Annotated Guide to Journals Dealing with the Middle East and North Africa.* Cairo: American University, 1965.

The Middle East and North Africa. London: Europa, 1948–. Published annually, includes a selected list of periodicals.

3200 revues et journaux arabes. Paris: Bibliothèque nationale, 1969. Lists only journals in Arabic.

ENCYCLOPEDIAS, DICTIONARIES, HANDBOOKS

The following is a selection from the numerous works that deal with the Middle East and North Africa:

Adams, M. *The Middle East: A Handbook.* New York: Praeger, 1968.

Area Handbooks. Washington, D.C.: American University, Foreign Area Studies Division, 1961–. The volume for each country is an excellent source of basic information.

Doniach, N. S. (Ed.) *The Oxford English-Arabic Dictionary of Current Usage.* London: Oxford University Press, 1972.

Encyclopedia Judaica. Jerusalem: Encyclopedia Judaica, 1972. Useful for research on the Middle East, particularly Jewish studies.

Lewis, B. *Encyclopedia of Islam.* Leiden, Netherlands: Brill, 1954–. Considered the most important reference work in English on Islamic studies.

The Middle East and North Africa. London: Europa, 1948–. Published annually; surveys developments in economics, history, and education.

Ronart, S., and Ronart, N. *Concise Encyclopedia*

of *Arabic Civilization.* (2 vols.) New York: Praeger, 1960–1966. Useful for brief information on people, places, institutions, and events.

Wehr, H. *A Dictionary of Modern Written Arabic.* Ithaca, New York: Cornell University Press, 1961.

DIRECTORIES

Area Studies on U.S. Campuses: A Directory. New York: World Studies Data Bank, 1974. Lists Middle Eastern and North African studies programs and centers.

Directory of Graduate and Undergraduate Programs and Courses in Middle East Studies in the United States, Canada, and Abroad. New York: Middle East Studies Association, biennial. Published as a special issue to the association's *Bulletin;* the last was published as Volume 8, 1974.

Middle East Area Study Programs at American Universities and Colleges, 1970. Washington, D.C.: Middle East Institute, 1970. Lists the major Middle East studies centers in the United States and Canada.

World Guide to Universities. New York: Bowker; Pullach/Munich, Federal Republic of Germany: Verlag Dokumentation, 1972. Lists institutions offering degrees in Near East history and culture.

The World of Learning. London: Europa, 1947–. Published annually. Lists African studies research institutes in Europe, Asia, and America, and departments of African studies in the universities of the world.

RESEARCH CENTERS, INSTITUTES, INFORMATION CENTERS

Directories to libraries, information centers, and research institutes include:

Badr, A. *Directory of Archives, Libraries, Documentation Centers and Bibliographical Institutions in Arabic Speaking Countries.* Cairo: United Arab Republic National Commission for UNESCO, 1965.

The Middle East and North Africa. London: Europa, 1948–. Published annually. Includes an international listing of research institutes studying the Middle East and North Africa.

The Middle East Studies Association Bulletin. New York: MESA, New York University, 1967–. Frequently lists research facilities in the United States.

Pearson, J. D. *Oriental and Asian Bibliography: An Introduction with Some Reference to Africa.* Hamden, Connecticut: Archon, 1966. Contains an excellent list and discussion of the principal Orientalist libraries in the United Kingdom, United States, Soviet Union, and throughout Europe and Asia.

NORTH AMERICAN STUDIES
(Including Black, Chicano, and Indian Studies)

Major International and National Organizations

INTERNATIONAL

Deutsche Gesellschaft für Amerikastudien
%Anglistisches Seminar der Universität
  Mannheim Schloss
6800 Mannheim, Federal Republic of Germany
  Swiss, German, and Austrian membership.

European Association for American Studies
  (EAAS)
Amerika instituut
University of Amsterdam
Oudezijds Achterburgwal 185
Amsterdam, Netherlands

Nordic Association for American Studies
Uppsala University
Larsgatan 2
75220 Uppsala, Sweden

NATIONAL

A selection of associations interested in North American studies includes:

Canada:
  Canadian Association for American
    Studies
  %Department of English
  York University
  Downsview, Ontario M3J 1P3

France:
  Société des américanistes
  Musée de l'Homme
  place du Trocadéro
  Paris 16

United Kingdom:
  British Association for American Studies
  30 Hartham Road, Islington
  London N7, England

United States:
  American Indian Historical Society
  1451 Masonic Avenue
  San Francisco, California 94117

  American Studies Association
  Box 1, Logan Hall
  University of Pennsylvania
  Philadelphia, Pennsylvania 19174

  Association for the Study of
    Afro-American Life and History
  1401 14th Street NW
  Washington, D.C. 20005

Additional organizations may be found in:

The World of Learning. London: Europa, 1947–. Published annually.

Principal Information Sources

GENERAL

Some guides and bibliographies to the literature in North American studies are the following:

Bell, I. F., and Gallup, J. *A Reference Guide to English, American and Canadian Literature.* Vancouver: University of British Columbia Press, 1971.

Books in Canada: A National Review of Books. Toronto, Ontario: Canadian Review of Books, 1971–. Published monthly.

Clever, G. (Ed.) *A New Index to the Journal Canadian Literature.* (62 vols.) Ottawa, Ontario: Borealis Press, 1975.

Davey, F. (Ed.) *From There to Here. A Guide to English-Canadian Literature Since 1960.* Erin, Ontario: Press Porcepic, 1974.

Fee, M., Donald, G., and Cawker, D. (Eds.) *Canadian Fiction: An Annotated Bibliography.* Toronto, Ontario: Peter Martin, 1976.

Gohdes, C. *Bibliographical Guide to the Study of Literature of the USA.* Durham, North Carolina: Duke University Press, 1959.

Gómez-Quiñones, J., and Camarillo, A. (Comps.) *Selected Bibliography for Chicano Studies.* Los Angeles: University of California, Aztlan Publications, 1974.

Hayne, D., and Tirol, M. *Bibliographie critique du roman canadien-français, 1837–1900.* Toronto, Ontario: University of Toronto Press, 1969.

Index to Literature on the American Indian. San Francisco: Indian Historian Press, 1972.

Kerr, J. N., and Layng, A. *A Bibliography of Afro-American (Black) Studies.* Monticello, Illinois: Council of Planning Librarians, 1974.

Lochhead, D. (Ed.) *A Bibliography on Canadian Bibliographies.* (2nd ed.) Toronto, Ontario: University of Toronto Press, 1972.

Miller, E. W. *The Negro in America: A Bibliography.* (2nd ed., compiled by M. L. Fisher.) Cambridge, Massachusetts: Harvard University Press, 1970.

Monkman, L., and Damon, D. *Canadian Anthology.* Toronto, Ontario: W. J. Gage, 1976–77. Useful bibliography.

The Papers of the Bibliographical Society of Canada. Toronto, Ontario: Bibliographical Society of Canada, 1962.

Ryder, D. E. (Ed.) *Canadian Reference Sources: A Selective Guide.* Ottawa, Ontario: Canadian Library Association, 1973. Supplement, 1975.

Thomas, C. (Ed.) *Our Nature, Our Voices: A Guide to English-Canadian Literature to 1960.* Toronto, Ontario: New Press, 1972.

Tremaine, M. *A Bibliography of Canadian Imprints, 1751–1800.* Toronto, Ontario: University of Toronto Press, 1952.

United States Library of Congress, General Reference and Bibliography Division. *A Guide to the Study of the United States of America: Representative Books Reflecting the Development of American Life and Thought.* Washington, D.C.: U.S. Government Printing Office, 1960. An annotated bibliography dealing with all aspects of American life and history.

Watters, R. *A Checklist of Canadian Literature and Background Material, 1628–1950.* Toronto, Ontario: University of Toronto Press, 1959.

Watters, R., and Bell, I. B. *On Canadian Literature 1806–1960: A Checklist of Articles, Books, and Theses in English-Canadian Literature, Its Authors and Language.* Toronto, Ontario: University of Toronto Press, 1966.

Weimer, D. R. (Ed.) *Bibliography of American Culture, 1493–1875.* Ann Arbor: University of Michigan Microfilms, 1957. Selected articles of Americana.

Some introductions and histories to the field include:

Beaulieu, A., and others. *Guide d'histoire du Canada.* Quebec: Presses de l'Université Laval, 1969.

Bengelsdorf, W. *Ethnic Studies in Higher Education: State of the Art and Bibliography.* Washington, D.C.: American Association of State Colleges and Universities, 1972. Identifies and summarizes recent trends in ethnic studies in the United States.

Boorstin, D. J. *The Americans: The Democratic Experience.* New York: Random House, 1973.

Browne, R. B., Landrum, L., and Bottoroff, W. (Eds.) *Challenges in American Culture.* Bowling Green, Ohio: Popular Press, 1970.

Duran, L. I., and Bernard, H. R. (Comps.) *Introduction to Chicano Studies: A Reader.* New York: Macmillan, 1973.

Klinck, G. (Ed.) *Literary History of Canada.* (3 vols.) Toronto, Ontario: University of Toronto Press, 1976.

Kwiat, J., and Turpie, M. C. *Studies in American Culture: Dominant Ideas and Images.* New York: Johnson Reprint, 1971. Reprint of 1960 edition.

Leacock, E. B., and Lurie, N. O. (Eds.) *North American Indians in Historical Perspective.* New York: Random House, 1971.

Lerner, M. *America as a Civilization: Life and Thought in the United States Today.* New York: Simon & Schuster, 1957.

Meier, M. S., and Rivera, F. *The Chicanos: A History of Mexican Americans.* New York: Hill & Wang, 1972.

Merideth, R. (Comp.) *American Studies: Essays on Theory and Method.* Columbus, Ohio: Merrill, 1968.

Monkman, L., and Damon, D. *Canadian Anthology.* Toronto, Ontario: W. J. Gage, 1976–77.

Skard, S. *The American Myth and the European Mind: American Studies in Europe, 1776–1960.* Philadelphia: University of Pennsylvania Press, 1961.

Spiller, R. E., and Larrabee, E. (Eds.) *American Perspectives: The National Self-Image in the Twentieth Century.* Cambridge, Massachusetts: Harvard University Press, 1961.

Walker, D. E., Jr. *The Emergent Native Americans: A Reader in Culture Contact.* Boston: Little, Brown, 1972.

CURRENT BIBLIOGRAPHIES

America: History and Life. Santa Barbara, California: American Bibliographic Center, 1964–1973. Abstracts articles on the history of the United States and Canada and on all aspects of current North American life. Since 1974 divided into three parts.

"Articles in American Studies." In the August issue of *American Quarterly.* Philadelphia: American Studies Association, 1949–.

Canadiana: Publications of Canadian Interest Received by the National Library. Ottawa, Ontario: Information Canada, 1950–.

Canadian Periodical Index. Ottawa, Ontario: Canadian Library Association, 1938–. Published monthly. Indexes articles in the social sciences, humanities, and business.

"Recent Publications Relating to Canada." Regular feature of each quarterly issue of *Canadian Historical Review.* Toronto, Ontario: University of Toronto Press, 1920–. List of publications relating to history, economics, geography, statistics, education, religion, ethnology, and folklore.

PERIODICALS

Acadiensis (Canada), *América indígena* (Mexico), *American Heritage* (US), *American Indian Culture Center. Journal* (US), *American Quarterly* (US), *American Studies* (US), *American Studies/ International Newsletter* (US), *American Studies in Scandinavia* (Sweden), *Amerikastudien* (FRG; continues the *Jahrbuch für Amerikastudien*), *Aztlan: Chicano Journal of the Social Sciences and the Arts* (US), *Canada, Canadian Annual Review of Politics and Public Affairs, Canadian Forum, Canadian Journal of History, Canadian Literature, Canadian Notes and Queries, Canadian Review of American Studies, Dalhousie Review* (Canada),

Essays in Canadian Writing, European Association for American Studies Newsletter (Netherlands), *El grito: A Journal of Contemporary Mexican American Thought* (US), *Indian Affairs* (US), *Indian Historian* (US), *Indian Journal of American Studies* (India), *Journal de la Société des américanistes de Paris* (France), *Journal of American Studies* (UK), *Journal of Black Studies* (US), *Journal of Canadian Fiction, Journal of Canadian Studies/Revue d'études canadiennes, Journal of Negro History* (US), *Midcontinent American Studies Journal* (US), *Mosaic* (Canada), *Open Letter* (Canada), *Prospects: An Annual Journal of American Cultural Studies* (US), *Queens Quarterly* (Canada), *Red Buffalo: A Radical Journal of American Studies* (US), *Studies in Canadian Literature, University of Toronto Quarterly.*

Additional journals in the field may be found in the following:

American Indian Periodicals in the Princeton University Library: A Preliminary List. Princeton, New Jersey: Princeton University Library, 1970.
Canadian Periodical Index. Ottawa, Ontario: Canadian Library Association, 1964–.
Schneider, J. B. *A Selected List of Periodicals Relating to Negroes, with Holdings in the Libraries of Yale University.* New Haven, Connecticut: Yale University Library, 1970.
Ulrich's International Periodicals Directory. New York: Bowker, biennial.

ENCYCLOPEDIAS, DICTIONARIES, HANDBOOKS

The following selection represents a few of the many works available:

Baskin, W., and Runes, R. N. *Dictionary of Black Culture.* New York: Philosophical Library, 1973.
Concise Dictionary of American History. New York: Scribner's, 1962.
Encyclopedia Canadiana. Ottawa, Ontario: Grolier Society of Canada, 1970.
Hart, J. D. (Ed.) *The Oxford Companion to American Literature.* New York: Oxford University Press, 1965.
Hodge, F. W. (Ed.) *Handbook of American Indians North of Mexico.* (2 vols.) Washington, D.C.: Smithsonian Institution, 1907–1910.
Johnson, T. (Ed.) *The Oxford Companion to American History.* New York: Oxford University Press, 1966.
Klein, B. T. (Ed.) *Reference Encyclopedia of the American Indian.* Vol. 1. (2nd ed.) Rye, New York: Todd, 1973.
Ploski, H. A., and Kaiser, E. (Comps. and Eds.) *The Negro Almanac.* (2nd ed.) New York: Bellwether, 1971.
Sloan, I. J. (Comp. and Ed.) *Blacks in America,* 1492–1970. *A Chronology and Fact Book.* Dobbs Ferry, New York: Oceana, 1971.
Story, N. *The Oxford Companion to Canadian History and Literature.* New York: Oxford University Press, 1967.
Toye, W. (Ed.) *Supplement to the Oxford Companion to Canadian History and Literature.* New York: Oxford University Press, 1973.
Walters, S. (Ed.) *Canadian Almanac and Directory.* New York: Pitman, annual.

DIRECTORIES

Area Studies on U.S. Campuses: A Directory. New York: World Studies Data Bank, 1974. Lists North American and Indian studies programs in the United States; black and Chicano studies are listed under separate areas.
Bengelsdorf, W. *Ethnic Studies in Higher Education: State of the Art and Bibliography.* Washington, D.C.: American Association of State Colleges and Universities, 1972. Lists institutions in the United States offering programs in ethnic studies: Asian-American, black, Chicano, Indian, Puerto Rican and other Spanish-speaking people, white ethnic, and multiethnic studies.
Klein, B.T. (Ed.) *Reference Encyclopedia of the American Indian.* Vol. 1. (2nd ed.) Rye, New York: Todd, 1973. Includes college courses in the United States and Canada on the American Indian.
World Guide to Universities. New York: Bowker; Pullach/Munich, Federal Republic of Germany: Verlag Dokumentation, 1972. Lists institutions offering degrees in American studies and North American history and culture.

RESEARCH CENTERS, INSTITUTES, INFORMATION CENTERS

Information on centers of American studies in European countries can be found in the biennial newsletter of the European Association for American Studies, available from A. N. J. den Hollander, 46 Watteaustraat, Amsterdam, Netherlands.

Lists of research centers and institutes and libraries may be found in the following directories:

Research Centers Directory. (5th ed.) Detroit: Gale Research, 1975.
Schatz, W. (Ed.) *Directory of Afro-American Resources.* New York: Bowker, 1970. Lists organizations and institutions in the United States holding materials on the history and experience of black Americans.
The World of Learning. London: Europa, 1947–. Published annually.

SLAVIC AND EAST EUROPEAN STUDIES

International and National Organizations

INTERNATIONAL

Institute of Balkan Studies
% Academy of Sciences of Bulgaria
7 Noemvri 1
Sofia, Bulgaria

International Association of Slavonic
    Languages and Literature
Professor Nils Ake Nilsson
Tegnerlunden 12
111 61 Stockholm, Sweden

International Association of South-East
    European Studies
9 rue Ion Frimu
Bucharest, Romania

International Association of Teachers of
    Russian Language and Literature
ul. Krzhizhanovskogo, d. 24/35
Moscow V259, USSR

International Committee for Soviet and East
    European Studies
% Professor Adam Bromke
Department of Political Science
McMaster University
Hamilton, Ontario L8S 4M4

International Committee of Slavists
Professor M. Szymczak
Krakowskie Przedmieście 26–28
Gmach Polonistyki UW
Warsaw 64, Poland

NATIONAL

National associations in Europe and America
interested in Slavic and East European studies
include:

Canada:
    Canadian Association of Slavists
    Association canadienne des slavistes
    % Professor B. Harasymiw
    Department of Political Science
    University of Calgary
    Calgary, Alberta T2N 1N4

Federal Republic of Germany:
    Koordinationsausschuss deutscher
        Osteuropa-Institute
    Lindenbornstrasse 22
    5 Cologne-Ehrenfeld
        A general coordinating committee
    representing twelve organizations de-
    voted to various phases of Slavic and East
    European studies.

France:
    Centre de recherches sur l'URSS et les
        pays de l'est
    Université des sciences juridiques,
        politiques et sociales de Strasbourg
    place d'Athènes
    67084 Strasbourg

United Kingdom:
    British Universities Association of
        Slavists (BUAS)
    % Prof. J. C. Dumbreck
    Department of Russian Studies
    University of Manchester
    Manchester 13, England

    National Association for Soviet and East
        European Studies (NASEES)
    % Post Graduate School of Yugoslav
        Studies
    University of Bradford
    Bradford BD7 1DP, England

United States:
    American Association for the
        Advancement of Slavic Studies
        (AAASS)
    Ohio State University
    190 West 19th Avenue
    Columbus, Ohio 43210

Additional organizations may be found in:

The World of Learning. London: Europa, 1947–.
Published annually.

Principal Information Sources

GENERAL

Bezer, C. A. *Russian and Soviet Studies: A Hand-
    book.* Columbus, Ohio: American Association
    for the Advancement of Slavic Studies, 1973.
Blejwas, S. A. *East-Central European Studies: A
    Handbook for Graduate Students.* Columbus,
    Ohio: American Association for the Ad-
    vancement of Slavic Studies, 1973.
Dorotich, D. (Ed.) *A Bibliography of Canadian
    Slavists, 1951–1971.* Saskatoon: University
    of Saskatchewan, 1972.
Horecky, P. L. (Ed.) *Russia and the Soviet Union:
    A Bibliographic Guide to Western Language
    Publications.* Chicago: University of Chicago
    Press, 1965.
Horecky, P. L. (Ed.) *East Central Europe: A Guide
    to Basic Publications.* Chicago: University of
    Chicago Press, 1969.
Horecky, P. L. (Ed.) *Southeastern Europe: A
    Guide to Basic Publications.* Chicago: Univer-
    sity of Chicago Press, 1969.
Valois, P., and Hnik, T. *Soviet, East European
    and Slavonic Studies in Britain, 1972: A Bibli-*

ography. Glasgow: Institute of Soviet and East European Studies, University of Glasgow, 1973.

CURRENT BIBLIOGRAPHIES

The American Bibliography of Slavic and East European Studies. Columbus, Ohio: American Association for the Advancement of Slavic Studies, 1957–. Published irregularly.

Cahiers du monde russe et soviétique. Paris: Mouton, 1960–. Annually publishes a listing of books and articles in French in the social sciences.

M.L.A. International Bibliography. New York: Modern Language Association of America, 1921–. Published annually as supplement to *P.M.L.A.: Publications of the Modern Language Association of America*.

Modern Humanities Research Association. *Year's Work in Modern Language Studies*. London: Oxford University Press, 1931–.

Osteuropa. Stuttgart, Federal Republic of Germany: Deutsche Verlags-Anstalt, 1951–.

Südosteuropa-Bibliographie. Munich, Federal Republic of Germany: Südost Institut, 1956–.

PERIODICALS

Balkan Studies (Greece), *Cahiers du monde russe et soviétique* (France), *Canadian-American Slavic Studies* (US), *Canadian Slavonic Studies/Revue canadienne des slavistes*, *East Europe* (US), *Etudes slaves et est-européennes* (Canada), *Jahrbücher für Geschichte Osteuropas* (FRG), *Osteuropa* (FRG), *Problems of Communism* (US), *Russian Review* (US), *Slavic and East European Journal* (US), *Slavic Review* (US), *Slavonic and East European Review* (UK), *Soviet Literature* (USSR), *Soviet Review* (US), *Soviet Studies* (UK), *Studies in East European Social History* (US), *Studies in Soviet Thought* (US), *Studies on the Soviet Union* (FRG), *Ukrainian Review* (UK), *Ukrainian Studies* (US).

For a more complete listing of periodicals consult:

Birkos, A. S., and Tambs, L. A. (Comps.) *East European and Slavic Studies: Academic Writer's Guide to Periodicals*. Kent, Ohio: Kent State University Press, 1973.

The USSR and Eastern Europe: Periodicals in Western Languages. (3rd ed.) Washington, D.C.: U.S. Library of Congress, 1967. Fourth edition in preparation.

ENCYCLOPEDIAS, DICTIONARIES, HANDBOOKS

The following selection represents a few of the many works available:

Great Soviet Encyclopedia. New York: Macmillan; London: Collier Macmillan, 1973. A translation of the third edition.

Jelavich, C. (Ed.) *Language and Area Studies, East Central and Southeastern Europe: A Survey*. Chicago: University of Chicago Press, 1969.

Schopflin, G. (Ed.) *The Soviet Union and Eastern Europe: A Handbook*. New York: Praeger, 1970.

Staar, R. F. *The Communist Regimes in Eastern Europe: An Introduction*. (2nd ed.) Stanford, California: Hoover Institution Press, 1971.

DIRECTORIES

Area Studies on U.S. Campuses: A Directory. New York: World Studies Data Bank, 1974.

Study Abroad. Paris: UNESCO Press, 1974.

World Guide to Universities. New York: Bowker; Pullach/Munich, Federal Republic of Germany: Verlag Dokumentation, 1972.

The World of Learning. London: Europa, 1947–. Published annually.

RESEARCH CENTERS, INSTITUTES, INFORMATION CENTERS

Directories to libraries, information centers, and research institutes include:

Horecky, P. L. (Ed.) *East Central and Southeastern Europe: A Handbook of Library and Archival Resources in North America*. Santa Barbara, California: ABC-Clio, 1976.

Jelavich, C. (Ed.) *Language and Area Studies, East Central and Southeastern Europe: A Survey*. Chicago: University of Chicago Press, 1969.

Language and Area Centers. Washington, D.C.: U.S. Office of Education, 1968.

Walker, G., and others. *Directory of Libraries and Special Collections on Eastern Europe and the USSR*. Hamden, Connecticut: Archon, 1971.

The World of Learning. London: Europa, 1947–. Published annually.

[Bibliographies for European Studies, Latin American Studies, and North American Studies prepared by Janet Katz.]

ARGENTINA, SCIENCE POLICIES OF

See Science Policies: Less Developed Countries: Argentina, Brazil, and Mexico.

ARGENTINE REPUBLIC

Population: 25,050,000 (1974 estimate). Student enrollment in primary school: 3,778, 434; secondary school (academic, vocational, technical): 1,197,729; higher education: 497,727. Language of instruction: Spanish. Academic calendar: March to November. Percentage of gross national product (GNP) expended on all education: 3%; higher education: 1%. [Figures are for 1975. Source: Estadísticas de la educación, 1975.]

Higher education began in Argentina in 1613 when the Spanish Crown established the Universidad de Córdoba (University of Córdoba) on the petition of the bishop of Córdoba, Friar Herrando de Trejo y Sanabria. Control of the university was entrusted to the Society of Jesus. In 1767 the Jesuits were expelled from the Spanish empire, and the university was transferred to the Franciscan order, who managed it until 1808. That year it was returned to the Spanish Crown in compliance with a royal decree of 1800. After the May Revolution of 1810, the university came under the jurisdiction of the independent government of Buenos Aires. Ten years later it became the responsibility of its own provincial government as a consequence of the dissolution of the central government.

Prior to Argentina's independence in 1816 the Universidad de Córdoba was the only higher education institution in Argentina. It was governed by laws contained in Title XXII, Book I of the Digest of Laws of the Indies 1680. At its inception the aims, curriculum, and methodology of the university were inspired by the principles and values of Catholicism; scholastic theology and philosophy and the changes introduced by the Counter-Reformation were dominant influences on the educational system. However, by the end of the eighteenth and beginning of the nineteenth centuries, the influences of Descartes and of the Enlightenment philosophers were becoming evident in the increasing secularization and humanistic orientation of the university.

In 1821, five years after the province of Buenos Aires declared its independence, the government founded a second uni-

versity, the Universidad de Buenos Aires (University of Buenos Aires).

During most of the nineteenth century, only two universities existed in Argentina: Universidad de Córdoba and Universidad de Buenos Aires. Following the ratification of the national constitution in 1853, both began to receive support from the federal government. The structure and study programs at both institutions were modified and modernized at this time in accordance with the principles of the French Napoleonic university, which stressed professional education. The French influence has been the most profound in Argentina's higher education. Professional schools—particularly those concerned with medicine, law, and later civil engineering, agronomy, and public accountancy—developed; and it was not until 1910 that philosophical, historical, and literary studies reappeared. In general the university did not promote research except in the field of medicine. By preparing liberal professionals, however, it formed the country's political and economic leaders.

In 1906 the federal government nationalized the Universidad nacional de La Plata (La Plata University), which had been founded as a university in 1897 in the city of La Plata, capital of Buenos Aires province. This university—under the direction of its first rector and organizer Joaquín V. Gonzáles—attempted to initiate a new concept of education modeled on United States universities. Thus, a campus was established, and studies in the humanities, education, astronomy, natural sciences, and physics-mathematics were promoted. A museum of natural history and an astronomical observatory were also established.

Two new national universities were created in 1919 and 1921 on the foundations of older provincial institutions. The Universidad nacional del litoral (National University of the Littoral) was established in the cities of Rosario and Santa Fe, in Santa Fe province. The Universidad nacional de Tucumán (National University of

Tucumán) was created in northern Argentina.

During this same period the University Reform Movement appeared. This movement has greatly influenced higher education in Argentina as well as the rest of Latin America. The reform began in Córdoba with a violent student strike on March 13, 1918. Riots followed; the university was closed, and federal intervention was proclaimed. On June 21 the Proreform Committee made public its famous manifesto entitled *The Argentine Youth of Córdoba to the Free People of South America*, which became the movement's manifesto (often referred to as the Córdoba Manifesto).

The reformers endeavored to replace the university professors, whom they considered anachronisms linked to the status quo. They demanded modernization of curricula and teaching methods and raised the issue of decisive participation of students and graduates in university governance. They also wanted freely appointed professors and frequent examinations. These demands, especially the one concerning student cogovernance, have since become contributing factors in university and political turmoil in Latin America.

As the reform grew, some tried to find in it an influence of the Bolshevik revolution, and undoubtedly there were activists who identified with that revolution. In the main, however, reformism was simply one expression of the social and political changes that took place in Argentina after Hipólito Irigoyen, head of the Civic Radical Union, came to power as the nation's president (1916–1922). Reelected in 1928, he was ousted by a military coup by conservatives in 1930. Irigoyen's party was politically democratic to the extent that it permitted the middle class and sons of immigrants to participate in the power structure. Because reformist leaders generally came from these socioeconomic backgrounds, they received Irigoyen's silent, if limited, sanction. Although the principles of the reformists influenced legislation

and university activists in Argentina and elsewhere in Latin America, their ideas were never wholly realized, and proponents of the reform still consider their aspirations unfulfilled.

After the founding of the first national universities in 1919 and 1921, almost twenty years passed before another higher educational institution was established. In 1939, the federal government founded the *Universad nacional de Cuyo* (National University of Cuyo) in the region that includes the northwest provinces of Mendoza, San Luis, and San Juan, at the foot of the Andes. The new university, under an extraordinarily capable rector, Fernando Cruz, focused on satisfying regional needs and deepening knowledge in the field of the humanities.

In 1953 President Juan Perón founded the *Universidad obrera nacional* (National Workers' University), in Buenos Aires. This school provided postsecondary training in several branches of engineering for members of the working class who had finished their high school training in technical institutes. Regional faculties were established in various parts of the country. In 1959 this institution changed its name to *Universidad tecnológica nacional* (National Technological University).

Two new national universities were organized in 1956. The *Universidad nacional del sur* (National University of the South), in Bahía Blanca, was built on the pillars of the *Instituto tecnológico del sur* (Technological Institute of the South), a provincial institution of the province of Buenos Aires. The *Universidad nacional del nordeste* (National University of the Northeast), in Corrientes, was designed to satisfy the need for higher education in the provinces of Corrientes, Chaco, Formosa, and Misiones.

In 1955 a debate began that was to have profound implications on the development of Argentina's higher education; its subject was legislative approval of the establishment of private universities. Up to this point, federal authorities had granted only state-operated universities—be they federal or provincial—the right to confer legal titles for professional employment. Therefore, the Argentine Catholic University, founded by the Catholic Bishopric in 1912, had been forced to close. At the end of 1955, Juan Perón had been ousted by a military coup; Decree-Law 6403 reorganized higher education. Article 28—furthered by the minister of education, Atilio Dell'Oro Maini—stated that "private initiative can establish free universities and issue legal titles as long as it submits itself to legal regulations." When the constitutional system was restored in 1958, the congress—under pressure from President Arturo Frondizi—sanctioned Law 14.577 (called the "Domingorena Law," after the representative who presented it in the house), which ratified the 1955 law with some modifications.

The benefits derived from Article 28 soon become apparent. Many private universities, some Catholic and others nondenominational, were founded. Thus, although fairly recent, the private university is solidly incorporated into Argentina's higher educational system. Some private universities have achieved a high academic standard and enjoy considerable prestige. Others, because the federal government has not granted them any subsidy, have encountered difficulties, especially in financing. In general, private institutions established in and around Buenos Aires and Córdoba have succeeded because of the large population and ample resources in these areas. Those located in less advantageous areas, however, are being absorbed by state-operated universities.

The nine national universities were in full operation until 1968. In that year the *Universidad nacional del litoral* was divided, establishing a new university, *Universidad nacional de Rosario* (National University of Rosario), from its existing faculties in Rosario. Additional national universities were established in Río Cuarto, Lomas de Zamora, Luján, Santiago del Estero, Pata-

gonia, and Catamarca. Other older universities were divided: San Juan, San Luis, Salta, and Entre Ríos. Still other provincial or private universities were nationalized: Mar del Plata, Comahue, and La Pampa.

The student population has also increased substantially. The first significant increase took place at the end of the 1940s, as a consequence of three main factors: Perón's distributionist policy, which improved the standard of living; the abolishment of a registration fee in national universities (1950); and the elimination or simplification of entrance examinations. As in the rest of the world, another student population explosion occurred in Argentina at the end of the 1960s.

Legal Basis of Educational System

The legislation governing Argentina's higher education system has undergone many changes, generally as a consequence of political events. Modifications have mainly affected university governance. The manner in which rectors and professors are appointed and the degree of participation of the different university populations in governance have been subject to change. The academic structure, the characteristics of the institutions, and the teaching methods, however, have not been greatly altered.

The national constitution of 1853, which is still substantially in force, specifies that congress shall prescribe "general and university teaching plans" (Article 67, section 16). To implement this prescription, Law 1597, better known as the "Avellaneda Law," was promulgated in 1885. Named after the senator and ex-president who proposed it, this brief law grants university autonomy but establishes that professors will be designated by the executive power on the basis of terms proposed by the *consejo superior* (superior council) of the university.

As a result of political and socioeconomic changes brought about by President Perón in 1947, Law 13.031 was substituted for the Avellaneda Law. Law 13.031 subordinated the university even more to the political power. In 1949 the constitution was amended, and a large section was devoted to stating purposes of higher education (Article 37, section 4). To adapt existing legislation to the amended national constitution, another university law, 14.297, was approved in 1954.

After Perón was ousted by the military revolution of September 16, 1955, the de facto government promulgated Decree-Law 6403/55, which gave universities large autonomous powers. The law also regulated the participation of professors, students, and graduates in the university's government.

In 1966 a military coup deposed President Arturo Illia. The new president, General Juan Carlos Onganía, sanctioned Law 17.245 in 1967. This regulation placed the university in the hands of the professors and endeavored to modernize and codify the higher education system. Other laws were promulgated: Law 17.604 concerned private universities, and Law 17.778 dealt with provincial universities. These two laws have never been revoked.

The military junta that assumed power on March 24, 1976, substantially modified Law 20.654, which had been promulgated in 1974 during Perón's third presidency and which set specific percentages for student participation in university governancy, with an emergency law (Law 21.276), which completely subordinated the university to the executive power and set a limit of 180 days for the introduction of a permanent system.

Types of Institutions

Higher education is offered at the university and nonuniversity levels. Included in the university level in 1976 were twenty-seven national universities (those that depend on the federal government), twenty-five private universities (those run by private concerns but authorized by the federal government), and one provincial university. Nonuniversity higher education is provided at institutions such as *institutos superiores del profesorado secundario* (higher institutes for secondary teachers), which train teachers for the high school level in programs lasting four years, and *escuelas normales superiores* (higher normal schools), which qualify teachers for the elementary stage in programs lasting two years. In 1976 there were 421 such institutions.

Relationship with Secondary Education and Admission Requirements

Only primary school is compulsory in Argentina. It comprises seven grades for children from six to twelve years of age. High school instruction is divided into two cycles: one of three years and another of two. All high school graduates from national schools receive the title of *bachiller*. Graduates from normal schools receive the *bachiller* with a pedagogical specialization. Commercial schools award the title of commercial appraiser, technical schools graduate technicians, and agricultural schools give the title of agronomist.

All high school graduates may enter higher education, although some universities or faculties may also require an examination or a qualifying course.

Administration and Control

The *Ministerio de cultura y educación* (Ministry of Culture and Education) supervises higher education. It directly administers the *institutos del profesorado* (teachers' institutes) and the *escuelas normales superiores* (higher normal schools). Traditionally universities have enjoyed administrative and financial autonomy. The highest single administrative authority is vested in the rector. The highest administrative body is the *consejo superior* (superior council), which consists of the professors, students, and graduates; some administrative personnel may also be included. Each faculty is headed by a *decano* (dean), each department by a *director* (director). A *consejo directivo* (directive council), composed of the dean, teachers, and nonteaching staff, oversees each department or faculty.

Teaching Staff

Members of the teaching staff at Argentina's universities are classified as ordinary or special professors. The ordinary professors have the ranks of full professor *(profesor titular)*, associate professor *(asociado)*, consulting professor *(consulto)*, adjunct professor *(adjunto)*, assistant professor *(asistente)*, and head of practical study *(jefe de trabajos prácticos)*. The category also includes various ranks of auxiliary teaching staff. The ranks of special professors are honorary *(honorario)*, emeritus *(emérito)*, and visiting *(visitante)* professor.

The basic prerequisite for a teaching appointment at a university is a university title or degree. Appointments are made by the higher council after a competitive examination based upon credentials and an oral defense of those credentials before a select board. Only those professors appointed after this competition enjoy professional security, and such tenure can be surrendered only after an academic trial.

The majority of national universities have organized the structure of the teaching career, which means that university teachers are essentially civil servants committed to a professional rank rather than a university. They may thus move from one university to another within the system. Salaries are standardized and determined by the federal government in its annual budget.

Appointments in the private universities may vary according to the regulations of the specific university.

Programs and Degrees

The *Ministerio de cultura y educación* is responsible for the academic standards of the universities and other tertiary-level institutions. National, provincial, or authorized private universities grant titles of technicians, *licenciados* (title for study in arts, social sciences, and natural sciences), engineers, lawyers, and physicians. The period of study required differs for each field and varies between two and seven years.

In 1976, 32.7 percent of all university students were enrolled in basic and technological sciences, 31.1 percent in social sciences, 12.6 percent in medical sciences, and 12.3 percent in humanities.

The nonuniversity institutions award intermediate professional qualifications. In 1976, 95 percent of the students in nonuniversity higher education were following teaching specialties at the *institutos del profesorado* and *escuelas normales superiores*.

Financing

Higher education is financed almost exclusively by the federal treasury. However, national universities are permitted to receive donations and may receive remuneration for services performed. Education in these institutions is free of charge.

Authorized private universities are financed by monthly student fees and different types of contributions. Provincial institutions are supported by the respective provincial governments.

Student Financial Aid, Social Background, and Access to Education

Student scholarships, loans, and subsidies are scarce and come mostly from the university's own budget. Outside Buenos Aires, there is a large subsidized lunchroom system, which provides students—on presentation of their university credentials—with low-priced meals.

Higher education is free and thus open to all social classes. However, only 10 percent of the students come from blue-collar families.

Female enrollment is equal to that of males in the universities, and there is no racial or religious discrimination.

Research Activities

Scientific and technological research has been greatly developed in Argentine universities. Funds for these activities have since 1969 generally come from the *Secretaría de estado de ciencia y técnica* (Scientific and Technical Secretariat of the State), now dependent on the Ministry of Culture and Education. The secretariat approves research projects outlined by the universities on the basis of a national priority plan. Moreover, the *Consejo nacional de investigaciones científicas y técnicas* (CONICET: National Council of Scientific and Technical Research) grants research scholarships and pays career researchers in state and private universities. Very few projects are undertaken by private institutions.

Current Problems and Trends

The two greatest problems confronting Argentine universities are the length of the study programs and the large amount of wastage, which varies from 30 percent to 70 percent of the registered students. These problems are a consequence of many factors: financial difficulties, a large number of full-time working students, family problems, pedagogical deficiencies in teaching methods, a scarcity of teaching equipment, a lack of supervision and of vocational or professional guidance at the different levels, and an absence of student financial assistance.

Like their European counterparts, Argentine universities have stubbornly opposed teaching and methodological innovations. Despite democratization and increased student participation, their structure is basically traditional. Most innovations have taken place in new faculties— for example, in the fields of sociology, mathematics, and sciences. Of all the national universities, the National University of Luján in Buenos Aires province has undertaken the most innovative programs. Founded in 1972 and opened in 1973, it offers distance education programs, vocational and professional orientation, pedagogical assistance for teachers, and programs for students who have not yet finished high school. Special attention is given to community needs.

EMILIO FERMÍN MIGNONE

Bibliography

Actas y trabajos. (2 vols.) Rosario: Congreso universitario argentino, 1935.

Compilación (Legislación universitaria). Tucumán: Universidad nacional de Tucumán, 1970.

Del Mazo, G. *La reforma universitaria. El movimiento argentino 1918–1941.* Vol. 1. La Plata: Ediciones del Centro de estudiantes de ingeniería, 1941.

Educación, recursos humanos y desarrollo económico-social. Situación presente y necesidades futuras. (2 vols.) Buenos Aires: Presidencia de la nación, Secretaría del Consejo nacional de desarrollo, 1968.

Education, Human Resources and Development in Argentina. Paris: Organisation for Economic Co-operation and Development, 1967.

Estadísticas de la educación. Buenos Aires: Ministerio de cultura y educación de la nación, Departamento de estadística, 1975.

González, J. V. *La universidad. Teoría y acción de la reforma.* Buenos Aires: Editorial claridad, 1945.

Gutiérrez, J. M. *Origen y desarrollo de la enseñanza pública superior en Buenos Aires.* Buenos Aires: Editorial la cultura argentina, 1915.

Leyes universitarias. Buenos Aires: Ministerio de cultura y educación, Centro nacional de documentación e información educativa, 1970.

Mignone, E. F. *Política educacional.* Buenos Aires: editorial Pallas, 1955.

Mignone, E. F. *Bases para un plan integral de educación superior y universitaria.* Buenos Aires: Secretaria del Consejo nacional de desarrollo, 1968.

Mignone, E. F. "Educación: Diagnóstico, pronóstico y prospección." In *Lineamientos de un proyecto nacional.* Buenos Aires: Secretaría del Consejo nacional de seguridad, 1970.

Mignone, E. F. *Institutos superiores de formación docente. Profesorado de nivel elemental.* Buenos Aires: Ministerio de cultura y educación, 1970.

Mignone, E. F. *La reforma educativa —Documento de base.* Buenos Aires: Ministerio de cultura y educación, 1970. (Mimeographed.)

Plan nacional de desarrollo y seguridad 1971–1975. Buenos Aires: Presidencia de la nación, Secretaría del Consejo nacional de desarrollo y del Consejo nacional de seguridad, 1971.

Rodríguez Bustamante, N. *Devate parlamentario sobre la ley Avellaneda.* Buenos Aires: Editorial universitaria de Buenos Aires, 1959.

Vocos, F. J. *El problema universitario y el movimiento reformista.* Buenos Aires: Editorial Hucmul, 1962.

See also: Archives: Mediterranean, the Vatican, and Latin America, National Archives of; Science Policies: Less Developed Countries: Argentina, Brazil, and Mexico: South America: Regional Analysis.

ART AND CURRICULA
See Arts, Fine and Applied (field of study).

ART APPRECIATION
See Art Collections, College and University.

ART COLLECTIONS, COLLEGE AND UNIVERSITY

Art collections have existed at colleges and universities in Europe for centuries; portraits, silver, and religious paintings were accumulated almost from the founding of European educational institutions. Regular collecting began at the Ashmolean Museum, Oxford, as early as 1667. In the United States collections also began to develop from earliest times. The College of William and Mary and Harvard University have portraits dating from the seventeenth century. Yale acquired works of portraiture as early as 1724, and Dartmouth College displayed portraits and mineral specimens in 1793. The oldest college holdings of works collected for the purpose of art study are at Bowdoin College. James Bowdoin III left his entire art collection to the school: 142 drawings arrived at the college in 1811; paintings arrived in 1813 and 1826. The earliest museum on a college or university campus was built at Yale in 1832 to house the Trumbull Collection, given in 1831. Since then, over four hundred college collections have been founded. Among the notable museums are Fitzwilliam, at Cambridge; the *Musée de l'Ecole nationale supérieure des beaux-arts,* in Paris; the *Accademia di belle arti e liceo artistico,* in Venice; and the university museums of Dublin, Zurich, and Heidelberg. In North America there are outstanding collections in the universities in Canada and Mexico. The

collections at Harvard, Yale, Princeton, the University of Pennsylvania, and the University of Rochester are among the largest in the United States; those at the Universities of Chicago, Arizona, Michigan, Iowa, Wisconsin, California, North Carolina, Texas, and Florida are also notable. Especially important is the Rhode Island School of Design Museum. Many small colleges—among them Smith, Wellesley, Oberlin, Bowdoin, Beloit, Mills, Vassar, Connecticut College, and Dartmouth—have fine collections.

Collections range from small groups of prints and lithographs to major holdings of world art from prehistoric times to the present. Physical housing of these collections also ranges from a small room or gallery in a campus building to a separate building designed to function solely as a museum. There is no correlation between the size of a college or university and its museum. Some universities have large collections and museums of national importance, but significant collections also exist at small colleges. Some state universities have built large museum complexes, which often contain major collections and carry on extensive loan exhibition programs. Nearly every major institution of higher learning has some type of museum, although not all are art museums.

Role of Art Collections

Art collections have been playing a steadily increasing role in college and university teaching, especially as the discipline of art history has grown and expanded. The development of art collecting in colleges and universities is analogous to the creation of scientific collections and laboratories on campuses in the nineteenth century. Just as geologists or biologists use collections of specimens for study and research, the art historian uses sculpture, painting, prints, and drawings. Many find teaching from slides very inadequate; the relationship between art object and viewer in the same physical space does not occur. Collections are also used in studio courses;

instructors can demonstrate the media and techniques of art and show examples of styles from works in the collection.

In addition to direct application to art historical study or studio practice, art collections can be an important tool for teaching in all of the humanities. An art object not only embodies esthetic ideas but is also a product of its culture. The work of art results from certain social, economic, and political conditions; it is shaped by the technology and natural resources of a culture; it represents intellectual and religious ideas held by a people. Thus, the data extracted from art objects are valuable aids to research in history, government, economics, religion, and the like. Often objects are used to illustrate historical, literary, and sociological points; or the form or content of an art object is cited to support a theory or conclusion based on verbal documentation. Today, through application of archeological techniques, objects are increasingly used as vessels of information in and of themselves.

Because art objects are products of their total culture, they can be used effectively as focal points for interdisciplinary study. The artist may study a Greek vase for its form and style; the student of literature may find a classical myth portrayed; the chemist may be interested in the composition of the glaze or the action of the firing; the sociologist may delve into the purpose or function of the vessel in everyday life.

Finally, the study of objects—sometimes called museology—has become a discipline in and of itself. Many colleges and universities are teaching courses in museum practice, connoisseurship, exhibitions, museum science, and conservation. Some educational philosophies do not embrace the more practical or preprofessional aspects of such courses, but a growing number of students and educators are recognizing museum studies and work as a separate branch of learning. Harvard and New York University have had museum programs for decades. Recently, the University of Delaware, the University of Texas, the University of California at Los Angeles, the University of Michigan, and Boston University have begun museum-oriented programs based on their collections.

One of the most important considerations of the use of collections as a teaching tool is bringing objects and students into contact. Museum exhibitions, both permanent and temporary, are one means; but bringing objects more directly into the life of the student is desirable. Some colleges place works of art in student unions, libraries, and lounges; others allow pictures to be loaned or rented to students and professors for their rooms or offices; still others set up possibilities for students to buy reproductions and posters for their own use. Unfortunately, serious security problems on campus have caused discontinuance of many of these programs.

Interinstitutional Cooperation

Some educational institutions are fortunate to have a large collection for use in teaching. They can have in-house exhibitions and prepare many shows of their own material. Others have smaller collections and must cooperate with those institutions with large collections. In joint or loan exhibitions objects of art are borrowed from one or more other collections. Institutions may also exchange materials in areas where holdings are substantial, one institution contacting another to trade on a long-term loan basis for collections in an area in which it possesses only a few objects. The former practice has been standard in the museum field for many years. Often traveling shows are offered among colleges for temporary exhibition. In some states whole exhibitions can be borrowed from state museums, and the federal government makes shows available through the Smithsonian Institution Traveling Exhibition Service (SITES). The latter method of procuring objects for display is relatively new. Bowdoin and Yale have had such an exchange; and the Whitney Museum, the Metropolitan Museum, and the Boston Museum of Fine Arts also have participated in long-term loans or exchanges.

Colleges frequently lend to each other, and special shows that pool works in three or four collections have been held. College museums are sometimes at a disadvantage in securing loans, as their staffs are usually smaller than those at a regular art museum; few have registrars, and a number do not have full-time directors. Outside lenders are reluctant to permit the loan of objects under those conditions. To compensate, many colleges seek an affiliation with a larger museum in the community. Classes are brought to the local museum; sometimes whole courses are taught there, as is the practice at Boston University with the Museum of Fine Arts and Case Western Reserve with the Cleveland Museum. Occasionally, the director of a community museum is invited to be an adjunct professor in a college or university and teaches courses for the school, using museum materials. And for many years local museums have allowed professors to make assignments relating to objects in their collections. In museology programs at a college, one or more museums usually cooperate closely with the sponsoring educational institution. The museum takes interns from these programs for a period of time, during which the students prepare exhibitions and work in educational programs or on catalogs. These programs can be jointly sponsored by museums and schools, such as Winterthur (Delaware) and the University of Delaware; Cooperstown (New York), and New York State University; the Toledo Museum (Ohio), and the University of Michigan; and the Metropolitan Museum and New York University. Or the school can arrange internships at a variety of museums or different locales on a one-time basis.

Administration

Administration of college or university art museums can be quite complex. First is the problem of how the museum is to be administered. Many collections have their own director; small museums often have a member of the art department serve as

director. Most college or university museum directors report directly to the president of the institution. This has proved to be the most successful arrangement over the years. In places where the director reports to a department or committee, factional interests invariably arise, and poor administration results.

The best museums are run separately from the institution's art department. The objectives of the art faculty and the practical aspects of museum work are not easily combined. The larger the collection, the more important that it be administered separately from the teaching departments. Art history faculty will sometimes use the museum as a source for publishing their own work; shows arranged by faculty are excellent, but publications should not be self-serving to a faculty member's interest in promotion. Similarly, studio faculty are always pressing the college or university museum for exhibitions of their work. College museums are well advised to show work by their studio faculty, but only as the quality and quantity of work allows. A good solution to the obvious need for close cooperation is to make the museum director a member of the teaching faculty; he can then keep informed by attending departmental meetings and occasionally can offer courses in the art curriculum.

Some colleges and universities govern their collections through a committee or board, to whom the director of the museum is responsible. In addition, it is good to have some recourse to a committee of the board of trustees of the institution. This committee can act to approve major loans and purchases and procure improvements in physical facilities. Another helpful committee is an acquisitions advisory committee, made up of interested parties who have collections or expertise in the museum field and who can help build collections at the school. Care must be taken that any such committee is advisory. No director can remain responsible to both a committee and his president for long.

A second problematic area of administration concerns finances, particularly fund raising. Most colleges and universities carry on extensive development programs to support the college's general activities. Because there are strictures on whom the museum may approach for money, it is often left without the opportunity to get its own special funds. The Yale University Art Gallery and the Rhode Island School of Design Museum have successfully worked out programs that have raised money for their museums without hurting overall contributions, but for the most part a good solution to this problem has not been found.

A related problem is that the museum must compete with other programs for available funds. A new language laboratory is weighed against expanded painting storage; the cost of a team sport rivals the funding for a loan exhibition program. Good treasurers help avoid such conflicts, but college museums are often low among campus priorities.

Some agencies exist only for contributing to museums. A few foundations fund specific museum programs and others may offer special programs for museum purposes. The Ford Foundation, for example, has maintained a fine program for funding museum catalogs. Some smaller foundations exist primarily for support of museum activities and give money for exhibition and purchases related to the interests of the foundation. The most important such source is the National Endowment for the Arts. Since its founding in the 1960s, the endowment has done more than almost any other single source to help museums and provide badly needed funds for exhibitions, professional travel and training, conservation, catalogs, physical improvements, consultants, and so forth. The endowment was set up for museum use and does not extend into other areas, but its grants nearly always require matching funds from the museum. Care must be taken to ensure that matching funds are available from either regular budgets or endowments.

Many auxiliary services can be provided by the college to the museum. College museums are fortunate to have access to a college or university accounting department headed by well-qualified people, as well as to buildings and grounds departments, personnel services, food services, security departments, and libraries. In many cases, the college museum has better auxiliary services than large municipal or private museums. The museum director is thus relieved of worries about day-to-day operations in accounting, personnel, or maintenance. On the other hand, the director is often put in the position of a beggar with hat in hand to get cooperation. Moreover, it is very difficult for a director to have people on his staff who also report to other department heads.

Another administrative problem is the discrepancy between museum salaries and faculty salaries. Museum positions usually pay less and require an eleven-month contract. Finally, there is the question of locating an art library within the museum. Most major university galleries have an art library (often the main art library on campus) as an integral part of their operation. This material is imperative in the museum for research and comparative study of college-owned objects with other published examples.

Bibliography

Braun. E. *Museums of the World.* New York: Bowker, 1973.

Bryant, E. "The Boom in U.S. University Museums." *Art News,* September 1967, *66*(5), 30–47, 73–75.

Coleman, L. V. *The Museum in America.* Washington, D.C.: American Association of Museums, 1939. (Vol. 1, Chap. 10; Vol. 3, pp. 511–530.)

Coleman, L. V. *College and University Museums.* Washington, D.C.: American Association of Museums, 1942.

Guther, C. E. *So You Want a Good Museum.* Washington, D.C.: American Association of Museums, 1967.

Harris, J. C. *Collegiate Collections, 1776–1876.* South Hadley, Massachusetts: Mount Holyoke College, 1976.

The Organization of Museums, Practical Advice. Paris: UNESCO, 1960.

R. PETER MOOZ

See also: Business Management of Higher Education: Insurance and Risk Management; Museum Administration, College and University; Museums in Higher Education Institutions.

ART, HISTORY OF (Field of Study)

The history of art is an autonomous discipline based on historical investigation of man-made works of architecture, sculpture, and painting. The many branches of art historical scholarship are classified as *intrinsic* (or primary) and *extrinsic* (or secondary). Most modern European and American scholars normally adopt one of these approaches as their principal method, although many distinguished art historians are capable of assimilating various intrinsic and/or extrinsic approaches in any given study.

Intrinsic approaches begin from a study of the work of art itself. One intrinsic method, a method often adopted by persons associated with museums that offer conservation and restoration programs, investigates the materials and techniques of works of art, such as bronze casting or oil painting. A second intrinsic method is connoisseurship, which reconstructs the artistic personality of an individual artist or a group or school of artists by examining the authenticity, quality, dates, and provenance of their work. A third, and more important, intrinsic method identifies and interprets conventions of style. The concept of style—or the configuration of artistic characteristics that make up a manner of expression peculiar to a single work of art, the works of a single master, works by different masters of the same historical period, or works of different historical periods—provides a structure for the history of art. Art history proceeds from the assumption that the style of a work of art is a function of its historical period. Works of the same period are assumed to share certain formal conventions, while works of different periods are assumed to —

exhibit different forms. A fourth intrinsic method is iconography, which identifies and interprets the symbolic conventions of art works, as opposed to their formal conventions. Iconographers focus on the discovery and interpretation of the textual sources on which works of art are based. Closely related is iconology, which tries to reconstruct the program that served artists in the creation of their works. This method assumes that art is a symptom of principles underlying the *oeuvre* of an artist or of his personality or civilization. An iconologist strives to understand a work of art in terms of its cultural environment. After identifying the textual sources of artistic images, the iconologist interprets the inherent meaning or content of those images. Iconography is an analytical method of interpretation; iconology is a synthetic method of interpretation.

Extrinsic approaches to the history of art focus on the innumerable factors that influenced and shaped the work of art. The most widespread of these approaches are biographical studies of an artist or a group or school of artists. Allied to the biographical approach are studies in the psychology of perception and psychoanalysis. Psychoanalytic studies attempt to uncover the various chains of causation which ultimately bring a work of art into being; thus far, such studies have found little favor with the majority of American and European scholars—mainly because a study of causes is necessarily speculative and cannot be unequivocally documented. A second extrinsic approach, the social history of art, investigates the political, economic, or general social background of works of art according to the principles of the social sciences and intellectual history—political history, sociology, economics, psychology, anthropology, and at times Marxist theory. Two related approaches include the cultural history of art, which was introduced as a scholarly discipline by the Swiss historian Jakob Burckhardt (1818–1897), and *Geistesgeschichte* (intellectual history), a German method of inquiry which was first applied to art history by the Viennese art historian Max Dvořák (1874–1921). Dvořák interpreted works of art as the expression and spiritual manifestation of a unified totality of thought underlying all aspects of cultural and other human phenomena. Another extrinsic approach is the investigation of works of art in terms of the history of ideas—for instance, the concept of organic expression in architecture or the concepts of individualism, genius, and loneliness.

Disciplines allied to the history of art include antiquarianism, art appreciation, esthetics, art theory, and art criticism. The antiquarian describes, measures, weighs, and classifies works of art and artifacts; but, unlike the art historian, he makes no attempt to interpret them. Generally approaching art in a historical vacuum, art appreciation emphasizes the recreative aspect of the process of art making and relies on value judgments. In art departments of United States universities, art appreciation is generally taught as a one-semester introductory course.

Esthetics and art history differ primarily in their emphasis. The term *aesthetic* was coined by the German philosopher Alexander Baumgarten (1714–1762) in his *Meditationes* of 1735; and in the eighteenth century esthetics was first conceived by English empiricists as a distinct philosophical discipline. Esthetics is the branch of philosophy that systematically examines, defines, and assesses the processes and abilities involved in the creation, use, enjoyment, and evaluation of art, and with the response of the beholder to qualities inherent or perceived in works of art. To a large extent, it deals with recurrent patterns and the validity of standards of evaluation. The esthetician seeks to establish categories of thought and systematic definitions to express coherent points of view about the arts. He is interested in the interrelationships of all the arts: music, literature, theater and drama, cinema, and the dance, as well as the visual arts.

The art historian, too, is interested in these interrelationships, but only insofar as they illuminate meaningful historical aspects of specific works of the visual arts. Whereas the esthetician arranges and classifies his material and hypotheses according to the theories they illuminate, the art historian always deals with his objects historically, usually marshaling them chronologically and geographically, but occasionally ideologically. One of the central problems for the esthetician is the nature of art. The art historian, however, avoids all metaphysical speculation because definitions of beauty, truth, and significance do not concern him. In much of the Western world, especially in the United States and the United Kingdom, art history is nonphilosophical. (In German-speaking countries this is somewhat less true.)

As a formal academic subject in American and British education, esthetics is taught only in colleges and universities and is almost always offered by departments of philosophy. Most courses in esthetics or the philosophy of art are generally one- or two-semester undergraduate courses. Courses in esthetics or the philosophy of art are never offered by American departments of art history, but undergraduate and graduate programs in art history often require a student to take a single course in the field, depending upon the offerings in departments of philosophy.

Another discipline allied to art history is criticism, a branch of esthetics. Like esthetics, criticism deals with all the arts. The proper domain of any one critic is the oral or written description, interpretation, and evaluation of concrete works of art. Art criticism is a many-leveled activity that comprises three basic aspects: the historical, the recreative, and the judicial. The historical critic and the art historian share the same objectives, but the other two aspects of criticism have traditionally been outside the domain of art history. Recreative art criticism determines the unique qualities of an artist's work and relates them to the values and needs of the beholder. Dispensing with history, it is literary expression of high artistic merit, with a separate and different identity from its point of departure. Thus, it transforms one work of art into another. The judicial art critic evaluates the work of art in relation to other works of art, as well as current human values and needs, by reference to the normative criteria of formal artistic excellence and significance and to such values as truth, sincerity, and honesty.

Art critics may be trained as artists, philosophers (or estheticians), or art historians. Those with backgrounds in art history employ the methods and approaches of the art historian (in particular, formal analysis, the interpretation of symbolic qualities, biography, and the sociology of art) and focus on the visual arts of the twentieth century. In general, because United States and British art historians have found it difficult to establish a coherent historical perspective for contemporary art, the investigator of the visual arts is often labeled an art critic rather than an art historian. Such hair-splitting is pointless; both examine in detail works of art and make empirically meaningful and verifiable statements about them. Nonetheless, the art critic champions and promotes contemporary artists, especially younger ones, and conveys his views through newspaper columns, art journals, books, museum and gallery exhibition catalogs, and radio and television. The art historian is not concerned with such promotion.

Art theory also is closely allied to art history, for it provides the vocabulary, the terminology, and the theoretical apparatus necessary for a scholarly investigation and elucidation of specific works of art. Some theories of art describe the genesis of a work of art; other theories describe the nature of works of art; still others describe the artist. They include art as imitation, as pleasure, as play, as empathy, as communication, as expression, and as quality of experience. Such theories are examined by art historians and estheticians alike, and in higher education their study takes place in departments of art and of philos-

ophy. But undergraduate and graduate courses specifically devoted to art theory are uncommon in United States higher education.

The first systematic investigation of the history of art was J. J. Winckelmann's *History of Ancient Art* (published in Dresden in 1764), which related the style of Greek art to Greek culture. As an academic discipline, art history began with the establishment of a full professorship in 1813 at the University of Göttingen in Germany. From then until the end of the nineteenth century, university chairs in art history multiplied rapidly in Germany, Austria, and Switzerland. In the United States lecturers in art history were appointed as early as the 1850s; and by the start of the twentieth century, with the increasing study of ancient Greek and Roman art in eastern universities and the growth of museums in New York, Boston, and Philadelphia, art history began to evolve into an autonomous discipline. After World War I, it began to challenge the supremacy of art history in German-speaking universities. In the 1920s a major independent center for graduate-level art history was founded in the Institute of Fine Arts associated with New York University and the Metropolitan Museum of Art. The emigration of eminent European teachers to the United States in the 1930s transformed art scholarship from an archeologically and philologically oriented discipline into a more empirical and broad-ranging discipline.

In European universities the history of art is taught by the faculty in philosophy, which is frequently divided into mathematics and natural science, on the one hand, and the humanities, on the other. In German-speaking universities classical archeology (*Archäologie*) and history of art (*Kunstgeschichte*), which commences with the art of the Middle Ages, are separate disciplines.

Institutes of art history are independent organs of all universities in the Netherlands and offer a three-year undergraduate program in art history (leading to the *candidatus* degree) and a formal graduate program (leading to the *doctorandus* degree). Enrollments in these programs have increased dramatically since 1970. As in German-speaking universities, the discipline treats Western art from the Middle Ages to the present. Ancient art and archeology are taught in institutes of classical archeology, which are affiliated with the universities. When they enter a university, Dutch students are required to declare a major field of study almost from the outset. In the art historical institutes, their first year includes lecture surveys of the history of Western art and a trip to Italy for the purpose of preparing a paper on a particular work of art. The second-year undergraduate is introduced to the profession of art history and is assigned to "work groups" dealing with the study of primary sources, iconography, patronage, and style. Courses in minor fields such as history, literature, and foreign languages are also second-year requirements. Special topics, the preparation of short papers, and a final oral examination are required in the third year. This three-year program is becoming less rigidly structured because of student demands. Since a *candidatus* ordinarily cannot find a position as an art historian, he proceeds to the *doctorandus* program, which is equivalent to the United States Master of Arts program. For nearly all art history students, this is a three-year terminal degree and requires additional papers, seminars, and a major research paper. Very few Dutch art historians eventually obtain the equivalent of a Ph.D., which is awarded after many contributions to the field, including a major book. Programs in art history in the Netherlands emphasize primary sources, iconography, and an interpretation of the arts within the context of literature, religion, and politics.

In Asia the Taiwan Normal University in Taipei offers programs in Oriental and Western art history; archeology is a separate discipline. Some universities in Japan and the Republic of Korea follow the Western model. In the People's Republic of China the educational system is in a state of upheaval. The university departments of archeology were closed during the Cultural Revolution, but some were reopened in 1972; art historians are trained in the museums.

Rarely, if ever, are graduate degree programs in the history of art offered on the continent of Africa, except where African art history is part of an African studies program. Traditionally art history has been offered in undergraduate and graduate programs (especially in Ghana and Nigeria) in the style of the nineteenth-century European academy or school of art; these programs are predominantly studio arts programs (for example, at Kumasi in Ghana and at Zaria and Nsukka in Nigeria). African art history is taught in institutes of African studies at the University of Ghana, the University of Ibadan in Nigeria, and the University of Ife in Nigeria. A student who enrolls in a Master of Arts program in African studies at the University of Ghana concentrates his work in three areas, one of which may be African art history. After taking a number of graduate lecture courses and seminars, the student writes a paper, which is designed like an examination. Formal programs in art history are becoming more common in Africa, largely in response to an increased awareness of national culture and heritage.

In the Soviet Union the advanced study of archeology and art history has exhibited a strong sense of continuity since its beginnings in the middle of the nineteenth century. For example, Soviet art historians have long considered the study of Byzantine art essential for a proper understanding of Russian art and archeology; interest in this period (as reflected in the published studies) has been passed from teacher to student for over a century.

In the mid 1970s a Soviet person wanting to study art history in a university must first pass an entrance examination administered by the faculty in history, to which the art history faculty belong. If admitted, he studies the field for three years. Undergraduate art history programs are offered only at Moscow State University (founded in 1755), Leningrad State University (founded in 1819), and the Institute of Arts in Leningrad (where the practicing arts are also taught). In his third year of study, the art history student prepares a final paper, which is evaluated by the department; this evaluation determines whether the student can become a graduate student *(aspirant)*. Graduate students in art history pursue their studies at Moscow State University, Leningrad State University, the Leningrad Institute of Arts, or the Institute of History of Arts in Moscow. The institute in Moscow is the largest and most prestigious center for art history graduate studies in the Soviet Union. The *aspirant* undertakes a three-year program of seminars and tutorials and in his third year writes a dissertation, which is evaluated by a faculty committee of five. If the dissertation is accepted, the *aspirant* receives a *kandidat* degree. The *kandidat* then seeks a position as art history instructor, museum curator, or writer on the arts for one of the state publishing houses. He can teach at a university, academy, or institute, but to attain the rank of professor he must be a *doktor,* which requires a substantial publication or second dissertation after he practices his vocation for some years. Membership in the Communist Party is not a prerequisite for a professorial position; but many professors, especially higher administrators, belong to it.

In Moscow and Leningrad the offerings in art history are divided roughly equally between Russian art and Western European art, and art history is approached from an archeological, factual, philological, iconographic, or cultural point of view; traditionally the esthetic or artistic (visual) aspects of works of art have not been emphasized. Soviet art historians focus either on tracing the sources of art works back to early or lost archetypes or on interpreting art works in relation to literature, religion, or social life. The selection of subject matter is considered very important by the Soviet art historian, and this selection and the approach to it are not made on the basis of political theory or socialist realism. Nearly all professors in art history at Leningrad and Moscow universities, however, have published at least one book or paper on an art historical topic viewed within a political or social framework.

In university departments of art in the United States, classical archeology is sometimes taught along with postclassical European, American, Oriental, and primitive art. The oldest United States universities, such as Harvard, Yale, and Princeton, have always excluded the studio (practicing) arts from their departments of art history, but in universities in the Middle West and on the West Coast the history of art was often introduced as a "service" to the studio arts and was sometimes taught by artists with little or no university training in history of art. Since World War II, both the studio and art history units of such art departments have grown at a tremendous rate, and since the 1960s combined art history and studio departments of art reveal a growing tendency to split into two separate departments.

Before 1930 the forty-eight doctoral dissertations accepted by Harvard, Yale, and Princeton universities were devoted to a topic in ancient, medieval, or Italian art before 1500; Western European art after 1600 and Oriental art did not receive scholarly notice until the mid 1930s, in part as a result of immigrant scholar-teachers. University teaching of the arts of the "primitive" tribes in Africa and the South Seas began after World War II and expanded rapidly in the 1960s, and this momentum continued into the 1970s. In a few American universities in the 1970s the study of the arts of tribal societies is competing with European and Far Eastern art and can lead to a Ph.D. In European and African universities it is confined to museums and anthropology. Another development in United States art history is the study of the history of photography and film: in the early 1970s an endowed chair in this field was established at Princeton University, and the department of art history at Yale University has accepted six dissertations on film topics. A third development is the team-taught course in art and the law offered at Stanford University. A similar course was introduced in the department of fine arts at Indiana University (Bloomington) in 1975. Further, the number of graduate courses in the historiography of art has been increasing since 1965. Finally, graduate programs throughout the United States have offered courses in museum training and conservation, often taught in collaboration with major museums. Some institutions offer an M.A. degree in museum training; others offer a diploma or certificate.

Since the end of World War II, the growth in the number of undergraduate majors in art history in United States colleges and universities has been dramatic. The undergraduate major is usually required to complete a two-semester survey of Western art history and a minimum of eight semester lecture courses in different fields of world art (for example, Greek art, Roman art, Chinese art, and American art). Occasionally, the art history major is required to take one or more courses in studio art, and the study of one foreign language is recommended. Such an undergraduate major is useful but not normally required to gain admission to a graduate program in art history.

The Master of Arts and the Doctor of Philosophy are the two degree programs for graduate students. The requirements for both degrees vary widely in the United States. All United States and Canadian universities with art history graduate programs (except Harvard University) offer the M.A. degree, which requires a minimum of one year and commonly two years of full-time work (typically lecture courses, seminars, language examinations, and a research paper or written examination). In 1975 forty-six United States colleges and universities offered the Ph.D. in the history

of art. Almost all doctoral programs require the M.A. degree and customarily require a minimum of one year of residency and course work beyond the M.A., a second (and infrequently a third) foreign language, a written and/or oral qualifying examination, and a written dissertation based on original research. On the average, the Ph.D. requires five to seven years beyond the B.A. degree, including a residency requirement of two or more years. Research for the dissertation requires one year abroad, except for topics in American art. A Ph.D. candidate often assumes a museum or teaching position before he submits his dissertation; and such work delays completion of the degree, usually for two years.

Until the end of World War II, art history was never regarded as a serious subject in British universities, and even in the 1970s only a few universities offer M.A. or Ph.D. degrees in art history. In 1932 a major independent center for graduate-level history of art, the Courtauld Institute of Art, was founded by Samuel Courtauld. Affiliated with the University of London, it offers not only the M.A. and Ph.D. degrees in history of art but also a three-year B.A. honors degree exclusively in history of art. The first permanent university chair in art history in the United Kingdom was established at Oxford in 1955; Oxford offers the B.Litt. and the D.Phil. degrees in history of art. In the universities at Cambridge, Reading, and East Anglia (and at Edinburgh in Scotland) students can offer doctoral theses on an art historical subject or, by special arrangement, on the philosophy of art. In England and Scotland the history of art is limited to postantique Western European topics. Ancient, Far Eastern, and African art history are studied in institutes or archeological associations.

In general, the system in England and Scotland is more rigid than in the United States. The M.A. requires one or two years of course work, written examinations in two areas of specialization, and a general paper. Since all students entering a British university are expected to know two modern foreign languages, and sometimes even ancient Greek and Latin, there are no special language requirements for the M.A. program. For the Ph.D. a dissertation but no written examination is required, and the doctoral student concentrates on one area of specialization. Obtaining approval of a dissertation topic is difficult, and the Courtauld Institute in London requires a doctoral student to wait a full three years after approval before submitting and defending the dissertation. The M.A. is normally a prerequisite for the Ph.D., but occasionally a student with a first-class B.A. honors degree in history of art can forgo the M.A. program and proceed directly to the Ph.D.

Postdoctoral programs in history of art were not available anywhere in the world in 1975, but a student with the Ph.D. could arrange to study with a scholar or at a research institute.

W. EUGENE KLEINBAUER

Levels and Programs of Study

Programs in the history of art generally require as a minimum prerequisite a secondary education and lead to the following degrees: Bachelor of Arts, Master of Arts or Fine Arts, the doctorate, or their equivalents. Programs deal with both general and specialized aspects of the history and, in some instances, the philosophy of art and consist of study, seminar, and studio work and independent research.

Programs that lead to a first university degree are usually general in nature and may include some of the following courses: survey of art history, Greek art, Roman art, Chinese art, Renaissance art, and American art. A studio course in art is also usually required.

Programs that lead to a postgraduate university degree deal comprehensively with a specialty within the broad area of the history of art, such as Greek or Hindu sculpture, Chinese painting, or art as an expression of nationalism. Programs on the advanced level usually last between one and four years, full time, in a university or college of art and may consist of a number of prescribed courses, the achievement of a professional standard in the particular art form, demonstrated facility in one or more foreign languages, and the preparation of a thesis or dissertation based on original research into a particular problem within the major subject.

[This section was based on UNESCO's *International Standard Classification of Education (ISCED): Three Stage Classification System, 1974* (Paris: UNESCO, 1974).]

Major International and National Organizations

INTERNATIONAL

European Cultural Foundation
Fondation européenne de la culture
Jan van Goyenkade 5
Amsterdam 1007, Netherlands

International Association of Art Critics
Association internationale des critiques d'art
Palais du Louvre, Pavillon de Marsan
107 rue de Rivoli
75001 Paris, France

International Association of Art—Painting, Sculpture, Graphic Art (IAA)
Association internationale des arts plastiques
UNESCO House, 1 rue Miollis
75015 Paris, France

International Committee for the History of Art
Kunsthistorisches Institut der Universität
Liebfrauenweg 1
Bonn, Federal Republic of Germany

International Council of Monuments and Sites (ICOMOS)
Conseil international des monuments et des sites
Hôtel Saint-Aignan, 75 rue de Temple
75003 Paris, France

International Council of Museums
Conseil international des musées
UNESCO House, 1 rue Miollis
75015 Paris, France

International Foundation for Art Research
654 Madison Avenue
New York, New York 10021 USA

International Institute for Conservation of Historic and Artistic Works
608 Grand Buildings, Trafalgar Square
London WC2N 5HN, England

International Society for Education
  Through Art
106 rue du Point du Jour
Boulogne-sur-Seine, 92100 France

For additional international organizations
see:

Yearbook of International Organizations. Brussels:
  Union of International Associations, 1974.

NATIONAL
Australia:
  Australia Council
  168 Walker Street, Box 302
  North Sydney, New South Wales 2060

Austria:
  Berufsvereinigung der bildenden
    Künstler Österreichs
  Schloss Schönbrunn
  1130 Vienna

Brazil:
  "Pro Arte," Sociedade de artes, letras
    e ciências
  Rua Mexico 74
  Rio de Janeiro

Czechoslovakia:
  Czechoslovak Committee of Unions of
    Creative Artists
  Gottwaldovo Kabrezi 250
  110 00 Prague 1

Federal Republic of Germany:
  Deutscher Verein für Kunstwissenschaft
    e.V.
  Jebensstrasse 2 (Kunstbibliothek)
  1000 Berlin 12 (Charlottenburg)

Finland:
  Suomen taideyhdistys
  Taidehalli
  Nervanderinkatu 3
  00100 Helsinki 10

France:
  Comité international d'histoire de l'art
  3 rue Michelet
  Institut d'art et d'archéologie
  75006 Paris

Greece:
  Greek Archaeological Society
  Panepistimiou 22
  Athens 135

India:
  Art Society of India
  Sardar Vallabhai Patel Road
  Bombay 400 004

Italy:
  Istituto di storia dell'arte
  Centro di cultura e civiltà
  Fondazione Giorgio Cini
  Isola di San Giorgio Maggiore
  30124 Venice

Japan:
  Bijutsu-shi gakkai
  % Tokyo National Research Institute
    of Cultural Properties
  Ueno Park, Tokyo

Netherlands:
  Nederlandse museumvereniging
  %Toneelmuseum
  Herengracht 168
  1000 Amsterdam

New Zealand:
  Art Galleries and Museums Association
    of New Zealand
  % Auckland City Art Gallery
  P.O. Box 6842
  Auckland

Norway:
  Norske kunst- og kulturhistoriske museer
  Tidligere norske museers landsforbund
  St. Olavsgate 1
  Oslo 1

Poland:
  Stowarzyszenie historykow sztuki
  Rynek Glowny 22, Cracow
  ul. Jaroslawa Dabrowskiego 9, Lublin

Portugal:
  Sociedade nacional de belas artes
  Rua Barata Salgueiro 36
  Lisbon

Soviet Union:
  Sojuz hudoznikov
  Gogolevskii bul. 10
  Moscow

Spain:
  Asociación española de amigos de
    la arqueología
  Instituto central de restauración de
    obras de arte
  Paseo de la Habana, 144-C
  Madrid 16

Sweden:
  Sveriges allmänna konstforening
  Stora Nygatan 5, P.O.B. 2151
  103 14 Stockholm

Switzerland:
  Gesellschaft für schweizerische
    Kunstgeschichte
  Dalmazirain 11a
  3012 Bern

Turkey:
> Türk tarih kurumu
> Kizilay Sok 1
> Ankara

United Kingdom:
> Arts Council of Great Britain
> 105 Piccadilly
> London W1V OAU, England

United States:
> College Art Association of America
> 16 East 52nd Street
> New York, New York 10022

> National Art Education Association
> 1916 Association Drive
> Reston, Virginia 22091

For additional national and international organizations see:

International Directory of Arts. (2 vols.) Berlin, Federal Republic of Germany: Art Adress Verlag Müller GMBH, 1952/53–. Published biennially.

Principal Information Sources

GENERAL

Guides to the literature include:

Allen, J. S. (Ed.) *Dumbarton Oaks Bibliographies Based on Byzantinische Zeitschrift. Series I: Literature on Byzantine Art 1892–1967.* (2 vols.) London: Mansell, 1973.
Carrick, N. *How to Find Out About the Arts: A Guide to Sources of Information.* Elmsford, New York: Pergamon Press, 1965. Includes bibliographies, encyclopedias, dictionaries, and periodicals.
Chamberlain, M. W. *Guide to Art Reference Books.* Chicago: American Library Association, 1959. Classified and annotated bibliography of 2489 books on the fine arts. A standard reference work in the field.
Ehresmann, D. L. *Fine Arts: A Bibliographic Guide.* Littleton, Colorado: Libraries Unlimited, 1975. Classified and annotated bibliography of 1127 books published between 1900 and 1974.
Lucas, E. L. *Art Books: A Basic Bibliography of the Fine Arts.* Greenwich, Connecticut: New York Graphic Society, 1968. A classified bibliography, intended as a selection guide for college libraries. Most useful feature is a bibliography of artist monographs.
Rogers, A. R. *The Humanities: A Selective Guide to Information Sources.* Littleton, Colorado: Libraries Unlimited, 1974. Includes a section on the visual arts.

General introductions to the field are:

Arnheim, R. *Art and Visual Perception.* Berkeley: University of California Press, 1954.
Collingwood, R. G. *Principles of Art.* New York: Oxford University Press, 1938.
Focillon, H. *The Life of Forms in Art.* New York: Wittenborn, 1957.
Gombrich, E. H. *Art and Illusion.* New York: Pantheon Books, 1960.
Holt, E. B. *Literary Sources of Art History.* Princeton, New Jersey: Princeton University Press, 1947.
Kubler, G. *The Shape of Time.* New Haven, Connecticut: Yale University Press, 1962.
Malraux, A. *The Voices of Silence.* Garden City, New York: Doubleday, 1953.
Panofsky, E. *Meaning in the Visual Arts.* Garden City, New York: Doubleday, 1955.
Read, H. E. *Art and Society.* London: Faber & Faber, 1950.
Rosenberg, H. *The Anxious Object: Art Today and Its Audience.* New York: Horizon Press, 1964.

Works dealing with esthetics, art criticism, and philosophy of art include:

Langer, S. K. *Reflections on Art: A Source Book of Writings by Artists, Critics, and Philosophers.* New York: Oxford University Press, 1961.
Margolis, J. *The Language of Art and Art Criticism.* Detroit: Wayne State University Press, 1965.
Osborne, H. *Aesthetics and Art Theory: An Historical Introduction.* New York: Dutton, 1968.
Stolnitz, J. *Aesthetics and Philosophy of Art Criticism.* Boston: Houghton Mifflin, 1968.
Wollheim, R. *Art and Its Objects: An Introduction to Aesthetics.* New York: Harper & Row, 1968.

Works dealing with the historiography of art include:

Ackerman, J. "Western Art History." In R. Carpenter and J. Ackerman, *Art and Archeology.* Englewood Cliffs, New Jersey: Prentice-Hall, 1963, pp. 123–231.
Eisler, C. "*Kunstgeschichte* American Style: A Study in Migration." In D. Fleming and B. Bailyn (Eds.), *The Intellectual Migration: Europe and America, 1930–1960.* Cambridge, Massachusetts: Harvard University Press, 1969, pp. 544–629.
Gombrich, E. H. J. *Art History and the Social Sciences.* Oxford, England: Clarendon Press, 1975.
Hauser, A. *The Philosophy of Art History.* Cleveland, Ohio: World, 1963.
Kleinbauer, W. E. (Ed.) *Modern Perspectives in Western Art History: An Anthology of 20th-Century Writings on the Visual Arts.* New York: Holt, Rinehart and Winston, 1971.
Panofsky, E. "Three Decades of Art History in the United States: Impressions of a Transplanted European." In *Meaning in the Visual*

Arts: Papers In and On Art History. Garden City, New York: Doubleday, 1955, pp. 321–346. Includes a comparison of the teaching of art history in the United States and Germany prior to World War II.

Roskill, M. *What Is Art History?* London: Thames and Hudson, 1975.

Histories of art are provided by:

Cossio, M. B., and Pijoan y Soteras, J. *Summa artis historia general del arte.* Bilbao, Spain: España-Calpe, 1931–.

Gardner, H. *Art Through the Ages.* (6th ed.) New York: Harcourt Brace Jovanovich, 1975.

Janson, H. W., and Janson, D. J. *History of Art: A Survey of the Major Visual Arts from the Dawn of History to the Present Day.* (Rev. and enl. ed.) New York: Abrams, 1969.

Michel, A. *Histoire de l'art depuis les premiers temps chrétiens jusqu'à nos jours.* Paris: Colin, 1905–1929.

Pevsner, N. (Ed.) *Pelican History of Art.* Baltimore: Penguin, 1953–.

Some works dealing with comparative education, research, and national education are:

Art Education: An International Survey. Paris: UNESCO, 1972. Countries included in this survey are Argentina, Australia, Czechoslovakia, France, the Federal Republic of Germany, India, Italy, Japan, Nigeria, the United Kingdom, the United States, and the Soviet Union.

Artistic Education. New York: Istituto italiano di cultura, 1969. Detailed information on study facilities on all levels in Italy.

Ascot, R. "Art Education in Canada." *Studio International,* October 1972, *184,* 139–140.

Broadd, H. A. "What Is Art All About?" *Arts and Activities,* November 1973, *74,* 34–35.

Bryce, M. *Fine Arts Education in the Soviet Union.* Washington, D.C.: Office of Education, 1963.

Henkes, R. "Teaching Contemporary Art History." *School Arts,* March 1974, *73,* 42–43.

Jones, R. L. "Aesthetic Education: Its Historical Precedents." *Art Education,* December 1974, *27,* 12–16.

Lanier, V. "Conception and Priority in Art Education Research." *Studies in Art Education,* 1974–75, *16* (1), 26–30.

Two journals which often include articles dealing with art education are *Art Education* and *Studies in Art Education* (Washington, D.C.: National Art Education Association).

CURRENT BIBLIOGRAPHIES

Art Bibliographies Current Titles. Santa Barbara, California: ABC-Clio, 1972–.

Art Bibliographies Modern. Santa Barbara, California: ABC-Clio, 1973–.

Art Index. New York: Wilson, 1933–.

Byzantinische Zeitschrift. Munich, Federal Republic of Germany: C. H. Beck'sche Verlagsbuchhandlung, 1892–.

I. I. C. Abstracts: Abstracts of the Technical Literature on Archeology and the Fine Arts. London: International Institute for Conservation of Historic and Artistic Works, 1955–.

Metropolitan Museum of Art Library, New York. *Library Catalog.* Boston: Hall, 1960. Supplement, 1962–.

Répertoire d'art et d'archéologie. Paris: Morancé, 1910–.

Zeitschrift für Kunstgeschichte. Munich, Federal Republic of Germany: Deutscher Kunstverlag, 1924–.

PERIODICALS

American Art Journal, Antike Kunst (Switzerland), *Apollo* (UK), *Art Bulletin* (US), *Art Education* (US), *Artibus Ariae* (US), *Art in America, Art International* (Switzerland), *Bollettino d'arte* (Italy), *British Journal of Aesthetics, Burlington Magazine* (UK), *Connoisseur* (UK), *Critica d'arte* (Italy), *Gazette des beaux arts* (France), *Gnomon* (FRG), *Goya* (Spain), *Journal of Aesthetics and Art Criticism* (US), *Journal of Aesthetics Education* (US), *Journal of Philosophy* (US), *Kunstchronik* (FRG), *Kunst des Orients* (FRG), *Oud Holland, Pantheon* (FRG), *Philosophical Quarterly* (UK), *Revue de l'art* (France), *Studio International* (UK), *Zeitschrift für Kunstgeschichte* (FRG).

For a more complete listing of journals see:

Art Index. New York: Wilson, 1933–.

Chicago Art Institute, Ryerson Library. *Index to Art Periodicals.* (11 vols.) Boston: Hall, 1962.

Ulrich's International Periodicals Directory. New York: Bowker, biennial.

ENCYCLOPEDIAS, DICTIONARIES, HANDBOOKS

Adeline, J. *Adeline Art Dictionary, Including Terms in Architecture, Heralding and Archeology.* New York: Ungar, 1966.

Aurenhammer, H. *Lexikon der christlichen Ikonographie.* Vienna: Brüder Hollinek, 1959–1962.

Britannica Encyclopedia of American Art. Chicago: Encyclopaedia Britannica Educational Corporation, 1973.

Enciclopedia dell'arte antica: Classica e orientale. (7 vols.) Rome: Istituto della enciclopedia italiana, 1958–1966.

Encyclopedia of World Art. (15 vols.) New York: McGraw-Hill, 1959–1968. An important international work.

Jahn, J. *Wörterbuch der Kunst.* (6th ed.) Stuttgart, Federal Republic of Germany: Kröner, 1962.

Mayer, R. *A Dictionary of Art Terms and Techniques.* New York: Crowell, 1969.

Myers, B. S. (Ed.) *McGraw-Hill Dictionary of Art.* (5 vols.) New York: McGraw-Hill, 1969.

Osborne, H. *The Oxford Companion to Art.* New York: Oxford University Press, 1970.

Otto, W. (Ed.) *Handbuch der Archaeologie, im Rahmen des Handbuchs der Altertumswissenschaft.* Munich, Federal Republic of Germany: Beck, 1939–1953. (A new series is being planned.)

Read, H. *Encyclopedia of the Arts.* New York: Meredith, 1966.

Réau, L. *Dictionnaire polyglotte des termes d'art et d'archéologie.* Paris: Presses universitaires de France, 1953.

Sourdel-Thomine, J., and Spuler, B. *Die Kunst des Islam.* Berlin: Propylaen, 1973.

Thieme, U., and Becker, F. *Allgemeines Lexikon der bildenden Künstler von der Antike bis zur Gegenwart.* (37 vols.) Leipzig, German Democratic Republic: Seemann, 1907–1950. The most comprehensive biographical dictionary/encyclopedia of artists and architects; includes bibliographies.

Vollmer, H. *Allgemeines Lexikon der bildenden Künstler des XX. Jahrhunderts.* (6 vols.) Leipzig, German Democratic Republic: Seemann, 1953–1962. Continuation of Thieme and Becker; standard work for twentieth-century artists.

DIRECTORIES

American Art Directory. New York: Bowker, 1898–. Annual listing of art museums, universities, college art departments, art schools, and schools of art in America, as well as some in Europe.

International Directory of Arts. (2 vols.) Berlin, Federal Republic of Germany: Art Adress Verlag Müller GMBH, 1952/53–. Published biennially. The standard worldwide directory of the arts. Volume 1 contains names and addresses of museums, art galleries, schools, colleges, artists, collectors, and art associations. Volume 2 contains names and addresses of art and antique dealers, galleries, art publishers, art periodicals, art booksellers, restorers, experts, and dealers.

Survey of Ph.D. Programs in Art History. New York: College Art Association of America, Committee on Graduate Education in Art History, 1975. A United States directory to graduate study.

The World of Learning. London: Europa, 1947–. Published annually.

International directories to museums of the world include:

Handbook of Museums: Germany, Austria, Switzerland. (2 vols.) New York: Bowker, 1971. A comprehensive listing of museums and collections in German-speaking countries. Includes art museums and galleries and offers information on fields and objects in collections, library and archive collections, and collections of slides and tapes.

Museums of the World: A Directory of 175,000 Museums in 150 Countries Including a Subject Index. (2nd enl. ed.) New York: Bowker, 1975.

The Official Museum Directory, 1975. Washington, D.C.: American Association of Museums; New York: National Register Publishing, 1975. Covers the United States and Canada.

[Bibliography prepared by Kathy L. Berg.]

ARTICULATION: EUROPE

Education in medieval Europe had its beginning in cathedral schools, which provided instruction in basic literacy, numbers, and familiarity with the scriptures for those preparing for the priesthood and civil service. These cathedral schools became preparatory schools for entrance to the university and continued to function as such until well into the beginning of the nineteenth century, there being no widespread institution that provided primary or elementary education. Young people wanting to enter the *gymnasium,* the grammar school, or the *lycée* were prepared in a more private and informal setting. Often these schools also provided preparatory classes that gave pupils the grounding they needed in order to be admitted to the grammar school proper, where students were expected to study Latin in the first year.

Thus, it was not until the early nineteenth century in Europe that the school preceding the university got an articulated role as "secondary" in terms of academic competence imparted. Since after the introduction of compulsory elementary schooling in Western Europe—about the middle of the century—the age level of those enrolled in upper grades of the elementary school paralleled that of those enrolled in the lower grades in the secondary school. The upper grades in secondary school, enrolling students between the ages of fifteen and sixteen to eighteen and nineteen, tended in some countries to become identified as the university-preparatory school proper. A matriculation or "maturity" examination, such as the *baccalauréat* in France, the *Abitur* in Germany, or the General Certificate of Education (GCE) examination, advanced level, in England, was required for admission to the universities or higher education in general. Well into the twentieth century such an examination still was being taken by a small social and intellectual elite, consisting of some 2 to 5 percent of the relevant age group. The qualifying examinations were in many cases external, either conducted or controlled by the universities themselves. In Sweden, for example, prior to 1868 the universities administered the matriculation examination. Students who had completed studies at a *gymnasium* and were seeking entry into a university had to appear at the university and be examined by professors in the relevant subjects. From 1868 until 1968 the *gymnasia* were entrusted to administer set examination papers and to conduct oral examinations under the supervision of "censors," usually university professors who moved from one school to another during the examination period.

The history of articulation between secondary and postsecondary education has been somewhat different in the United States, where until the emergence of modern universities at the end of the nineteenth century, higher education was dominated by small, relatively undifferentiated colleges catering to an elite that by 1900 still consisted of only 4 percent of the relevant age group. The college with its classical curriculum served an ascriptive society, where advanced education was not primarily a means of getting ahead in society but a means of confirming one's elevated place in it. Most colleges were under the control of clergymen and therefore stressed

piety and character more than intellectual sophistication.

When, in the late nineteenth century, new universities emerged with graduate departments and professional schools, most undergraduate colleges tended to preserve their upper secondary school character in certain respects. In the first place, the American college, like the European *gymnasium* or the English grammar school, acted *in loco parentis*. In contrast, the European student, having enrolled as an undergraduate for which a "maturity" examination was required, was regarded and treated as an adult whose mores were not supervised by the university. Secondly, the college curriculum tended to assume an intermediate position between the European upper secondary and college undergraduate programs in terms of its academic requirements and level of specialization. This development brought about the practice established at American universities of considering the completion of a *gymnasium* or English grammar school the equivalent in terms of academic credit to the first two years of a four-year college education. Finally, the American college has been distinguished from the West European upper secondary school by the large degree of diversification that exists among institutions in the United States. This diversification has been due in part to the existence of a large private sector of higher education, whereas in Europe most of the secondary schools and the universities are uniformly administered by a central or state government.

Changes Affecting Articulation

Certain profound and rapid changes in the structure, functions, and contents of education during the mid twentieth century radically affected articulation between upper secondary and higher education. While secondary education became almost universal, its preparatory function for university entry gradually became less important. As enrollment in institutions of higher education soared, it increasingly became more appropriate to speak of "postsecondary" or "tertiary" rather than "higher" education. The entire concept of institutionalized education at the postsecondary level widened in response to changes that could be subsumed under the following headings: (1) the "enrollment explosion," coupled with increased specialization and vocationalization of postsecondary basic degree programs; (2) the "knowledge explosion"; and (3) admission of adult students to postsecondary institutions within a planned strategy of lifelong or recurrent education.

Enrollment explosion. Whereas in Europe as late as the 1950s an elitist secondary school still dominated, high schools in the United States as early as the 1930s enrolled a majority of the young people of relevant age. With the raising of mandatory school-leaving age in several European countries, lower secondary education became universal up to the age of fifteen or sixteen. The 1944 Education Act in England, the 1959 decree in France, and the 1962 Education Act on Comprehensive Education in Sweden are cases in point. The next step concerned the broadening and diversifying of upper secondary education in countries that still primarily catered to an elite of academic students seeking entrance to the university. By the beginning of the 1970s in some European countries, enrollments in upper secondary schools had almost reached the enrollment level at the junior and senior years of high school in the United States. Nevertheless, in spite of the increased enrollment in higher education in these European countries after 1960, a smaller percentage of upper secondary school students tended to proceed to the university.

Higher education has in several countries on both sides of the Atlantic become a "mass higher education" according to the criterion set by Martin Trow; namely, that some 15 to 20 percent of the relevant age group is the lower limit of mass higher education. (Below that limit, one would have "elite higher education.") There are several indications that before the year 2000 the majority of young people of university age will be part of the formal educational system as full- or part-time students. Then, according to Trow's taxonomy (where 50 percent is the lower limit), the state of "universal higher education" will have been reached (Trow, 1973).

Knowledge explosion. The so-called "knowledge explosion" and the specialization that accompanied it during the mid decades of the twentieth century had profound repercussions both on "knowledge production" (research) and on "knowledge distribution" (teaching). In many fields, the number of scientific publications has doubled every five to ten years since 1945, creating formidable problems just in terms of the amount of subject matter to be mastered. In addition, the specific competencies required in the society of tomorrow cannot be predicted in the way that was self-evident in a more static and ascriptive society. The consequence has been a shift from specific items in the syllabus, which might rapidly become obsolete, to more general information that can be applied to a wide—and to a large extent unforeseen—variety of tasks and situations. Top priority has to be given to the teaching of skills that are conducive to independent study inasmuch as the production of new knowledge by increasingly specialized research, as well as the application of new technology, necessitates an ability to adapt both knowledge and skills to an ever changing plethora of problems.

Admission of adults to postsecondary education. The concept of lifelong or recurrent education (the latter term being launched by the Organisation for Economic Co-operation and Development in Paris), a new planning strategy in education, has radically changed educators' concepts about the relationship between education and work, as well as the place of formal education in the total life cycle. Within the concept of recurrent education, formal schooling is not confined to the first eighteen to twenty years of life.

During the 1960s and the 1970s institutions of higher education have increasingly tended to become continuation schools for adults with some years of vocational experience. As such, many institutions act as "service stations" for in-service training programs made necessary by technological change and the ensuing restructuring of the work force. This tendency has been reinforced by the increasing demand for equality of opportunity. Whereas higher education was once a privilege enjoyed by young people who entered college directly from secondary school, the provision of recurrent education is perceived as a chance to reenter the system by many adults who "missed out" earlier in life.

Access to and Entrance Requirements in Postsecondary Education

In order to increase access to postsecondary education, both for students who proceed straight from secondary school and for adults with work experience, academic entrance requirements have been modified to enable credit to be given for work experience and to permit those who can meet minimum basic academic requirements to pursue further studies. As early as the 1950s, Brooklyn College in the United States tried to evaluate work experience in terms of an academic level of competence. In the 1970s the several member colleges of the University Without Walls and Empire State University in the United States, as well as the Open University in England, began tailoring programs to adults with work experience.

The traditional school-leaving examination in Europe—be it the *Abitur,* the *baccalauréat,* or the GCE—cannot serve as a uniform entrance requirement in a multipurpose, pluralistic, diversified system of postsecondary education. For this reason, the matriculation examination in Sweden, for example, was dropped in the 1960s. Recruitment to and programs in the Swedish *gymnasium,* traditionally the university-preparatory school, were considerably broadened in the 1960s. A royal commission appointed to study the problem recom-

mended that a distinction be made between general and special competence for university entry. The former consisted of competencies and skills that are prerequisites for higher studies in general—language skills, study skills, and an appropriate level of motivation. It was recommended that certain minimum standards be required in the mother tongue and in English as a foreign language. The latter competencies referred to the skills appropriate to the special program in which the applicant wanted to enroll.

A second commission considered the consequences of the report of the first commission in light of the recommendations of the U68 Commission (1973)—the latter having designed a blueprint for the entire system of higher education in Sweden. As a result of these studies, quotas were set for admission of secondary school graduates and of adults returning to school after some years in working life. A pilot program was launched, by which adults who were at least twenty-five years of age and had five years of work experience could be admitted ad hoc to university courses.

In 1975, the Swedish parliament, in passing a Higher Education Act based on the U68 Commission recommendations, established selection procedures for both categories of university entrants. Admission of secondary school graduates was to be based on marks from the *gymnasium* and scores on aptitude tests. Adults who met the general criteria of competence were to be admitted on the basis of age, number of years of work experience, and aptitude test scores. It was decided, however, that all applicants could, if they so wished, be considered solely on the basis of their test scores, but such scores could not be used to their disadvantage.

Entrance requirements to postsecondary education therefore are being reassessed in terms of the following conditions: an educators' movement toward universal access; a mounting political commitment to increased access in several countries; and a trend toward the development of tailor-made "course packages" designed to provide specific marketable competencies.

The historical concept of the educated man, schooled in the liberal arts, which epitomized the objectives of secondary education as a preparation for the university, is no longer valid. If a student is to be educated for a rapidly changing technological society in which scientific research has an increasing impact on everyday life, he must become familiar with the processes of research, not only in the natural and social sciences but in the humanities as well. Traditionally, laboratory experiments have been a part of instruction in the natural sciences. More able and interested secondary students can be taught, however, how the analytical tools of research are used and may eventually become motivated in pursuing studies of their own.

The subject areas and topics to be included in the curriculum are determined by the explicit objectives established for the upper secondary school in a particular national system. Overall objectives often are set by political decisions that in turn are influenced by the social, economic, and historical conditions prevailing in a particular society.

An overarching problem in an era of rapid expansion of postsecondary enrollment with concomitant vocationalization of programs is whether such a mass system can be accommodated within the shell of the traditional university. Scholarly functions, such as basic research and graduate education, are pursuits for which by definition few are selected. Nobody has seriously argued that there should be an "open" or universal admission to graduate departments that some writers have labeled the "academic core system" (Parsons and Platt, 1973). Scholarly functions that are germane to a university can easily come into conflict with the cafeteria-type system of undergraduate vocationally oriented courses. Several students of the "multiversity" have raised the question whether the two main functions, undergraduate courses on the one hand and research and graduate training on the other, should be separated. One argument in favor of keeping them together is the recruitment of prospective researchers and scholars who must be found among undergraduates, many of whom may not have planned to proceed to more advanced studies.

The net effect of the massification of higher education is that the borderline between secondary education and post-secondary education has become less distinct. It is more a matter of transferring from one age level to another in a more integrated system. The elements of research have in the process tended to move up to the graduate level of instruction concomitantly with the assignment of senior academic staff to teaching and supervision of study at the graduate level. This development has been more pronounced in some European countries than in the United States, where the undergraduate college has taken an intermediate position between the European secondary school and the university.

Bibliography

Altbach, P. G. (Ed.) *The University's Response to Societal Demands: An International Perspective.* New York: International Council for Educational Development, 1975.

Ashby, E. *Any Person, Any Study: An Essay on Higher Education in the United States.* New York: McGraw-Hill, 1971.

Ben-David, J. *American Higher Education: Directions Old and New.* New York: McGraw-Hill, 1972.

Bowman, M. J., and Anderson, C. A. *Mass Higher Education: Some Perspectives from Experiences in the United States.* Paris: Organisation for Economic Co-operation and Development, 1974.

Husén, T. "Lifelong Learning in the Educative Society." *International Review of Applied Psychology,* 1968, *17,* 87–99.

Husén, T. *The Learning Society.* New York: Barnes & Noble, 1974.

Husén, T. *Universiteten och forskningen* (University Research). Stockholm: Natur och kultur, 1975a.

Husén, T. "Re-shaping the Upper Secondary Curriculum." *Education and Culture,* Spring 1975b, *27,* 10–15.

Machlup, F. "The Illusion of Universal Higher

Education." In S. Hooks and others (Eds.), *The Idea of a Modern University.* Buffalo, New York: Prometheus Books, 1974.

Mood, A. M. *The Future of Higher Education: Some Speculations and Suggestions.* New York: McGraw-Hill, 1973.

Parsons, T., and Platt, G. *The American University.* Cambridge, Massachusetts: Harvard University Press, 1973.

Perkins, J. A., and others. *Higher Education: Crisis and Support.* New York: International Council for Educational Development, 1974.

Trow, M. *Problems in the Transition from Elite to Mass Higher Education.* Paris: Organisation for Economic Co-operation and Development, Directorate for Scientific Affairs, 1973.

U68 Commission. *Högskolan: Betänkande av 1968 års utbildningsutredning.* Stockholm: Statens offentliga utredningar, SOU 1973:2 (Government Printing Office), 1973.

Wolff, R. P. *The Ideal of the University.* Boston: Beacon Press, 1969.

TORSTEN HUSÉN

ARTICULATION: UNITED STATES

Articulation in American education can be characterized as a process, an attitude, and a goal. As a process, it is the coordination of policies and practices among sectors of the educational system to produce a smooth flow of students from one sector to another. As an attitude, it is exemplified by the willingness of educators in all sectors to work together to transcend the individual and institutional self-interest that impedes the maximum development of the student. As a goal, it is the creation of an educational system without artificial divisions, so that the whole educational period becomes one unbroken flow, which varies in speed for each individual.

Educational programs, institutions, and systems are said to be well articulated when their major components are coordinated to facilitate the efficient and maximum development of the student. The term *articulation* was initially applied to refer to the desirable relationship among subject areas at the same grade level and among grade levels in public elementary and secondary schools. More recently, the term has been widely adopted in higher education to describe the desirable relationships that should exist among all sectors of the educational system, including proprietary institutions and quasi-educational organizations such as the military, business and industry, and community agencies.

The need for articulation is most acute from grades 12 to 16, when millions of students are faced with the transition from high school to college or other institutions, from community college to senior college, and from senior college to graduate or professional school. The articulation, or coordination, of these educational sectors is never completely realized; rather, it ranges on a continuum extending from total fragmentation to total organizational integration. Currently, most American educators concerned with articulation in postsecondary education are more critical of existing fragmentation than of overcoordination. A number of changes are advocated, not to abolish the existing sectors, but to move further along the continuum toward cooperation and systematic interdependence in order to respond more effectively to the needs of learners.

A Fragmented Education System

As in most countries, education in the United States tends to occur in hierarchical layers, such as elementary school, secondary school, community college, senior college, and graduate school. This system, by moving students in certain age groups from one sector to another, is arbitrary and deals with collective, not individual, needs.

The educational sectors have different origins: the kindergarten, elementary school, and graduate school follow a German model; the four-year college is based on English practice, whereas the high school and community college are largely indigenous. These sectors also differ in philosophy and approach. Some are concerned with the general development of the child and the process of socialization;

some stress the development of democratic ideas and preparation for life; and others stress academic specialization and learning for its own sake. Some sectors deal with students in homogeneous groups and stress cooperative activities and close student-teacher relations; others emphasize individual competitiveness and impersonal student-teacher relations.

Cooperation among the various sectors is complicated in the United States by an aversion to government planning or control. As a result, there is no national curriculum or imposed coordination. Federal involvement is limited primarily to the appropriation of money for various educational purposes, and federal funds, although important, have not been directed toward coordination of the curriculum or stimulation of cooperative activities. The Tenth Amendment to the Constitution gives legal authority for education to the individual states rather than to the federal government. The states, in turn, have delegated much of their authority to local school boards and separate college and university governing boards and have retained only limited powers in central educational agencies. Some state agencies have established standards of minimum quality, but until recently few have sought to coordinate educational sectors. In fact, many states reflect the fragmented nature of postsecondary education by having separate state boards or agencies to oversee the various sectors. Private colleges and universities traditionally have had almost complete sovereignty in determining policy, procedures, and curriculum, and public institutions have been accorded great freedom to govern themselves.

This separation of sectors has been supported by the hierarchical attitudes of inferiority and superiority that exist among educators at the so-called elementary, secondary, and higher levels. This hierarchical approach contrasts with the egalitarian attitudes of an educational community in which sectors may differ in function but are of equal and interdependent value.

An enormous gap exists between educators in different sectors because faculty at each level tend to have different qualifications, belong to different professional associations, order their texts from different publishers, participate in different promotion and reward systems, and hold different conceptions of their professional roles. These differences encourage a lack of mutual respect and understanding among educators, particularly since little contact exists between sectors. For example, it is unusual for a university professor, even one who teaches introductory courses in a given discipline, to interact professionally with a high school or community college teacher who offers courses in that same discipline.

There is, of course, some formal interaction among sectors. Students move from the schools to the colleges, and colleges prepare teachers and administrators for the schools. High school counselors and university admissions officers communicate and interact with each other. But combined with the historical differences in the origins and purposes of educational sectors, the lack of governmental or voluntary coordination, and the hierarchical attitudes about status, the general lack of interaction among educators results in discontinuities. As a consequence, students are often deprived of the assistance they need to achieve basic educational competencies; they are handicapped in the attainment of educational excellence; and wasteful expenditures of time and money are incurred. A review of relations between schools and colleges, community colleges and senior colleges, and colleges or universities and other postsecondary agencies illustrates these existing discontinuities and current efforts to overcome them by improved articulation.

High School–College Relations

American high schools originated in the nineteenth century, and by the end of the century, they not only provided an additional four years of education beyond the primary school, which had expanded to seven or eight years, but they also permitted colleges to upgrade their enrollment and curricula expectations by providing a larger pool of well-prepared youth. Colleges had always had at least minimal entrance requirements, but under the influence of the German model of academic specialization, meritocracy, and excellence, they began to screen graduates of the high schools by the unilateral administration of college-constructed admissions examinations; colleges also sought to prescribe the high school curriculum of prospective students. The high schools resisted becoming preparatory schools controlled by the colleges, and as a result, before the turn of the century a series of national committees sought to resolve growing controversy over the control and function of the secondary school. In 1892, for instance, the Committee of Ten, dominated by college presidents, advocated a standard college preparatory curriculum for secondary education (Menacker, 1975, p. 15); in 1910, the Committee of Nine, more representative of secondary school leaders, called for less rigid college admission requirements and contended that the high school had broader responsibilities than college preparation. At the same time, regional accrediting associations of schools and colleges were formed, and these associations gave the high schools some voice in accreditation and in the development of external entrance examinations in basic academic subjects.

In the 1930s, the Eight Year Study demonstrated that students who graduated from less prescriptive high school programs performed as well in college as those from conventional prescribed programs (Menacker, 1975, p. 17); as a result, many colleges began to abandon rigid subject requirements and examinations in favor of greater reliance on the Scholastic Aptitude Test and similar test scores and on high school grades from a curriculum broader than the college preparatory program. Colleges liberalized their admissions

practices further to accommodate veterans returning from World War II, and as part of the cold war competition in the 1950s they participated in experimental programs to stimulate the development of talented high school students. The Advanced Placement Program created a number of college-level courses taught by secondary school faculty to talented students in the school, and it introduced the use of external examinations for these courses. Scores of the students' performance on these exams were reported to colleges at which the students applied and could result in the waiver of certain otherwise prescribed college courses or even the awarding of college credit on the basis of the examination. During the same decade, a group of colleges admitted experimental groups of talented students who had not yet completed high school and found them to be successful in all respects, although few of the colleges subsequently revised their admissions requirements or crediting practices to accommodate more than a handful of similar students.

The struggle of the high schools to maintain their freedom to determine their own curriculum proved largely successful, but it has left fears and hostility that continue to handicap close cooperation between schools and colleges. Even though articulation problems no longer focus primarily on selective college admissions and prescribed high school curricula, problems still remain in curriculum overlap, aiding the educationally disadvantaged, and providing stimulating educational opportunities for able students who are not challenged by the senior year in high school.

In terms of curriculum overlap, a number of studies over the past fifty years have indicated extensive duplication in the work of elementary schools, secondary schools, and colleges. Thus, a 1971 study indicated an overlap of between 21 and 39 percent in the content of courses offered in the last two years of high school and the first two years of college (Blanchard, 1971). Although some repetition may be desirable, unplanned duplication works a hardship on many students and needs to be corrected.

The problems faced by students who experience learning difficulties and who need some form of remediation or special assistance are now recognized by colleges because of the movement to universal access or some form of open admissions. Opening admissions for the educationally disadvantaged provides another incentive for improved articulation between secondary schools and colleges. Even colleges that continue to be highly selective in their admissions frequently have special quotas or programs for educationally disadvantaged students and share the secondary school's concern for aiding them. This is an area that poses basic questions about the complex process of learning and human development, and it calls for cooperative efforts of educators at both the school and college levels.

A third problem that calls for cooperation across sectors is the growth in many strong secondary schools of "senioritis"— an attitude held by many able seniors and even juniors that is characterized by restlessness, boredom, and lack of challenge or motivation. Among the causes of this condition are the proportions of high school students who have completed all or almost all graduation requirements by the end of their junior year and are waiting for entrance into college; the repetitive nature of traditional high school schedules and procedures; and the lack of appropriate courses for students with special talents (*What Should We Do with Our Senior Year?*, 1975).

Fortunately, it is not necessary to merely speculate about solutions for these and other articulation problems. A number of schools and colleges are engaged in efforts to address these issues and to provide a more effective learning continuum (*Linking Schools and Colleges*, 1975). The problem of curricular overlap is being approached not by prescription and regulation but by curriculum workshops and seminars that bring together school and college teachers of a specific subject, by faculty exchanges, and by cooperative in-service programs sponsored by professional organizations. In the area of improving the basic skills of disadvantaged students, cooperative centers to improve mathematics, writing, and reading have been formed by some schools and colleges, particularly in urban centers such as Boston and New York. To overcome senioritis, many colleges are providing more early admissions opportunities: they are crediting non-high school graduates by proficiency examinations; establishing dual enrollment programs that permit high school students to take work in college toward a high school diploma as well as toward a college degree; and offering college credit courses in the high school, courses which, in most cases, are taught by an approved member of the school faculty.

More unusual undertakings to improve articulation include cooperative career planning seminars for high school students; the formation of educational consortia that include all elementary schools, secondary schools, and colleges in a geographic area; and the creation of new structural units called *middle colleges*, which combine the last two grades of high school with the first two years of college and provide greater continuity to these critical years of education. Although most of these activities are of a voluntary nature, many state agencies are encouraging and supporting activities by conducting studies, seeking to eliminate legal or technical obstacles to cooperation, and sponsoring statewide conferences (Regents of the University of the State of New York, 1974).

Community College–Senior College Relations

Two-year community colleges, originally called junior colleges, began to develop in the early twentieth century and faced the difficulty of occupying the middle ground between high school and four-year college. Although many of the community colleges were created as extensions of the secondary schools, they soon began to take on the coloration of senior colleges and universities and to neglect their links with the secondary school. Some became even less willing than senior colleges to accept college-level work that students completed in high school. Nonetheless, most senior colleges took a negative view toward accepting community college work for transfer credit unless the student had taken identical courses and some form of affiliation existed between the institutions. In other words, the senior colleges' initial position toward community colleges was reminiscent of the rigid attitudes they had taken toward high schools.

The 1930s saw some evidence of a shift to senior college acceptance of equivalent rather than identical courses for transfer, but discontinuities have continued despite efforts to overcome them. In 1957–58, the Association of American Colleges, the American Association of Community and Junior Colleges, and the American Association of Collegiate Registrars and Admissions Officers formed a joint committee on junior and senior colleges to facilitate transfer. It commissioned a survey of the characteristics and transfer problems of over 7000 graduates of two-year colleges in ten states, which resulted in the book *From Junior to Senior College* (Knoell and Medsker, 1965). The joint committee also recommended that states develop master plans to define institutional roles and coordinate curricula between two- and four-year institutions and that orientation and counseling services be improved. This report and a series of regional conferences sponsored by the National Project for Improvement of Articulation Between Two-Year and Four-Year Colleges led to the publication of *Guidelines for Improving Articulation Between Junior and Senior College* (1966), but a follow-up study in 1972 indicated only limited implementation of its suggestions at the institutions that participated in the original survey (Willingham, 1972).

In 1970, another study of transfer problems, credit and course relationships, and state policies indicated that some progress was being made through articulation agreements and statewide systems of higher education (Kintzer, 1973). But many of the same problems still exist. Some senior colleges apply more rigorous standards to community college applicants than to students who enroll as freshmen or who apply from other four-year institutions. For example, some senior colleges prohibit community college students from transferring D grades, although they permit D grades earned at their institution to count toward a degree; some require a higher grade point average for the admission of community college students than of others; they may limit their access to financial aid or scholarships; and some insist on reviewing the details of community college courses before granting credit for them. Other senior colleges arbitrarily change graduation requirements and penalize community college students who have taken courses consistent with their former requirements; they often deny credit for courses that are considered occupational or vocational; and they sometimes redefine courses from lower- to upper-division level and refuse to grant credit for these courses from a community college. Such practices contribute to the common problem of community college students losing as much as one semester's credit when transferring to a senior college. Furthermore, two-year colleges may contribute to these difficulties by failing to provide their students with transfer guidelines and counseling, by not offering prerequisite courses or not developing them in consultation with four-year institutions, and by not establishing formal communication with senior institutions.

Current literature indicates ambivalence among educators about the proper role of state government in promoting improved articulation at this level. Many educators hope that improved relations will stem from private voluntary action, such as the creation by institutions of offices of articulation (Schafer, 1974); the holding of curricula meetings between instructional staff of the two sectors; the sharing of expensive resources such as computers; the negotiation of transfer agreements between individual institutions; and the formation of groups, such as the California Articulation Conference, that bring together representatives of schools, colleges, and universities in annual meetings to address problems of coordination. Other educators, although not opposed to these voluntary agreements, point out the difficulty of enforcing them and of financing articulation activities. They believe that these and other difficulties can best be resolved through coordination by state education agencies.

The literature certainly indicates a trend toward a more active role for the states through a variety of aproaches. Some states are sponsoring ad hoc research, meetings, and statewide master plans that address the issue. In other states, agencies responsible for community colleges are developing guidelines, regulations, and legal agreements with other sectors. In some states, governing boards that regulate both two- and four-year institutions are prescribing articulation. Among the states, Florida is a leader in establishing conditions governing student transfer and creating a joint committee to recommend further articulation, such as a common course numbering system between two-year and senior institutions.

College Relations with Other Postsecondary Institutions

Although much needs to be done in school–college and community college–senior college cooperation, a new and important area for articulation is the relationship between these well-established educational sectors and the less recognized educational activities of proprietary schools, community organizations, businesses, industries, and the armed forces. More accrediting agencies are beginning to recognize the legitimacy of proprietary schools, and these agencies are thus assisting the transfer and job placement of proprietary school graduates. Some states,

such as New York, are also authorizing proprietary institutions to confer academic degrees. A few colleges are attempting to make individual assessments of business and industrial programs and coordinate this form of learning with their own programs. The American Council on Education, following up its earlier work on military programs, has begun a national project to provide colleges with credit recommendations for many business and industrial courses, but the articulation of the activities of these postsecondary institutions with the more traditional sectors is still in a rudimentary stage and presents a major challenge for the next decade.

Although serious problems stem from the fragmented nature of the educational system in the United States, there is an increased awareness of the adverse effect these discontinuities have upon individual students, and there is a wide variety of activities under-way to reduce them. Much can be and is being accomplished by local and voluntary actions of educators, institutions, and professional associations, and these actions are particularly effective in changing attitudes. Educational agencies of most states are also playing a more active role in the coordination and regulation of education since they have a responsibility for developing and maintaining an effective and efficient educational system. Perhaps the current fiscal limitations facing all education, the leveling off and decline in the number of traditional college-age students, the impact of social problems on education, the interest in individualized education, and the attention devoted to competence and achievement rather than status will provide an atmosphere more conducive to improved articulation than did the conditions of expansion and affluence that characterized American higher education from the late 1940s to the early 1970s.

Bibliography

Blanchard, B. E. "Curriculum Articulation Between the College of Liberal Arts and the Secondary School, A National Survey, 1971." Educational Document 051-045.

Arlington, Virginia: ERIC Document Reproduction Service, 1971.

Carnegie Commission on Higher Education. *Continuity and Discontinuity*. New York: McGraw-Hill, 1973.

Guidelines for Improving Articulation Between Junior and Senior Colleges. Washington, D.C.: American Council on Education, 1966.

Kintzer, F. C. *Emerging Patterns of Statewide Articulation/Transfer Agreements*. Santa Monica, California: Pine Publications, 1976.

Kintzer, F. C. *Middleman in Higher Education*. San Francisco: Jossey-Bass, 1973.

Knoell, D. M., and Medsker, L. L. *From Junior to Senior College: A National Survey of the Transfer Student*. Washington, D.C.: American Council on Education, 1965.

Linking Schools and Colleges: An Inventory of Articulation Practices in New York State. Albany, New York: State Education Department, 1975.

Menacker, J. *From School to College: Articulation and Transfer*. Washington, D.C.: American Council on Education, 1975.

Regents of the University of the State of New York. *The Articulation of Secondary and Postsecondary Education*. Position Paper No. 21. Albany, New York: State Education Department, 1974.

Schafer, S. *A New Position in Higher Education: Liaison Officer for Articulation*. Gainesville, Florida: University of Florida Institute of Higher Education, 1974.

What Should We Do with Our Senior Year? Albany, New York: State Education Department, 1975.

Willingham, W. *The No. 2 Access Problem: Transfer to the Upper Division*. Washington, D.C.: ERIC Clearinghouse for Higher Education, 1972.

CHARLES W. MEINERT

ARTS, FINE AND APPLIED
(Field of Study)

The subject field for those who create and study works of art includes fine and applied arts (design), crafts, and art history. The fine are painting, drawing, sculpture, photography, film making, and printmaking. Printmaking embraces lithography, intaglio, serigraphy, woodcut, and related techniques. The design fields are graphic design, interior design, and industrial design. The term *crafts* has come to include ceramics, metalsmithing and jewelry, weaving and textile printing, woodworking, and glass making. The history, philosophy, and criticism of art is a field of study closely related to the creation of works of art, but it deals primarily with the interpretation and assessment of art from a scholarly-historical point of view. Therefore, while the artist's activity is studio production, the historian's role is to collect, preserve, and evaluate works of art.

Artists have formed a symbiotic link with poets, composers, dancers, and representatives of the other arts, who have in common the search for creative expression. To this extent, the boundaries of the arts, their stylistic changes, and their rates of progress are entirely international. The language of visual art is a universal language. This has become more evident as artists have traveled widely, and communication-technology has shortened distance and time. Technical advances in electronics (video, lasers, and computers), as well as the development of metals-plastics materials and sophisticated new machinery, have broadened the vocabulary of art forms. To some extent the distinctions among the various fields have become increasingly blurred as artists use new materials and processes.

Technology has also given rise to new outlooks and styles. Conceptual art, performance pieces, and video-computer work have come into existence only in the 1960s. They represent the confluence of more conventional attitudes and methods with science, music, and theater.

Historically, the education of young artists took place under the master-apprentice system. During the Renaissance this relationship often took the form of an atelier, in which an artist would take in several assistants to aid in the completion of commissions. In return for their help, the apprentices would receive instruction from the master. Later, private art academies were formed—sometimes by an individual artist with a substantial following or, more often, by a museum or other public institution which regarded instruction as one of its responsibilities along with collecting and conserving works of art. Higher education in the visual arts in the 1970s is centered in institutions of higher learning. The private institutions are generally more intensively specialized and somewhat smaller in size. The public institutions—the colleges and universities—tend to offer more diversified subject matter and hence a wider variety of study opportunities within and around the arts. In the United States there are large numbers of private and public institutions which offer higher education in fine and applied arts. These range in size and equipment from small junior colleges and museum-related schools to large university art departments. Comprehensive professional art schools (there are about sixty in the United States) may be affiliated with private or public universities or with major museums; or they may be independent, private schools.

Opportunities for study in the United Kingdom and Europe are somewhat restricted by the number and size of the institutions. In England, for example, there are relatively few large schools such as the Royal College of Art and the Leeds Polytechnic College of Art. Most higher education in the visual arts is carried on in the polytechnics, spaced widely across the land, and at the small, usually privately supported, academies in urban centers. On the continent the tradition of study in private academies and city-sponsored institutes is continued. It is typified by the academies in Berlin and Munich and the academies of fine arts in Florence and Rome. Universities on the European continent almost invariably have degree offerings in the history of art, but virtually none make available study in the studio fields. In Africa and Latin America most students work with individual artists at the outset and then seek advanced study in Europe or the United States. There are some exceptions—for example, the University of Mexico, which carries on a strong tradition in the crafts and mural painting. In the Soviet Union there are institutes of art in major cities. Strong emphasis is placed on cinematography, but not on experimental modes. Little is known about formal in-

struction in Eastern Europe or the People's Republic of China except that opportunities for study in visual art are very rare and subject to marked state control. Japan's center for formal study is the University of Tokyo, but Japan also has many small private academies where students can work (primarily in ceramics and other craft fields) with recognized masters. Work in casting and calligraphy, for example, is rather informal and often dependent on the initiative of students for its inception. Osaka University of the Arts is a relatively new private university devoted to higher education in the arts.

Those who seek degrees in fine and applied arts usually proceed from the Bachelor of Fine Arts degree (generally four years) to the Master of Fine Arts degree (two years of study), generally the terminal degree in United States studio fields. In the United Kingdom the first degree, earned at the end of approximately four years, is the Bachelor of Arts (replacing the former Diploma in Art and Design). Study beyond the B.A. can be undertaken, but advanced degrees vary widely in the United Kingdom, depending on the institution and the specialty field. Some schools confer master's degrees, others award certificates or diplomas, and others confer an associate degree. Advanced study in the visual arts beyond secondary levels in Europe is much more informal, culminating in a diploma or certificate of completion rather than a formal degree.

Policies relating to degrees in the United States (involving exhibition, thesis requirements, oral defenses, and other requirements) are established by the two principal national organizations in the art field, the National Association of Schools of Art and the College Art Association of America. Although some international societies attempt to transcend national boundaries within specific fields (often the design areas), there were no formal accreditation organizations outside the United States in 1975. On the other hand, formal degree requirements for advanced study in history of art are remarkably uniform. Students are expected to take the Bachelor of Arts, or "first" degree, in approximately four years of relatively generalized study. Emphasis is on the course work in history of art and on languages and other supplemental disciplines. The master's degree (M.A.) normally is earned after one to three years of more specialized course work in art history and a master's thesis. The terminal degree is the Doctor of Philosophy, conferred upon completion of course work; language and other academic requirements; and a lengthy work of original scholarly research in art history, the doctoral dissertation.

Both general and specialized study for advanced degrees is available internationally. The private professional art schools tend to offer the more specialized approach, with detailed, intensive course work often directed toward portfolio development and vocational possibilities in design areas. The larger public institutions are more generalized, providing a blend of art study with general education. Admission to programs in studio areas is frequently quite competitive—particularly in the United Kingdom, where there is great demand for admission and relatively few openings. Selections are based on the student's academic record and a portfolio of art work; and some schools, particularly in Europe, require successful completion of an entrance examination. Many institutions with strong programs in design fields have close working relationships with firms and businesses, in which their graduates subsequently find employment. Artists and designers in professional practice in urban centers frequently serve as adjunct faculty members at nearby art schools. As a result, the major institutions are found in larger cities around the world, where critical and professional expertise as well as libraries and other technical resources abound. Summer study activities are frequently arranged in other areas with particular scenic or practical advantages for relatively short-term work.

The study of the history of art dictates substantial travel for students, who must

view original works of art and their natural surroundings. Requirements for advanced degrees invariably include, therefore, ability in one or more foreign languages. These factors create the international character of the history and criticism fields. Degree requirements are noticeably similar, professional journals are employed in common, and there is extensive exchange of scholars and students among institutions.

GEORGE V. BAYLISS

Levels and Programs of Study

Programs in fine and applied arts generally require as a minimum prerequisite a secondary education. In some instances, applicants with experience or talent but with lower educational qualifications may be admitted to a program after demonstrating satisfactory performance in the subject concerned. The field includes a variety of programs that deal with principles, techniques, history, performance, and production in the fine and applied arts. Programs consist of lectures, group discussions, demonstrations, studio practice sessions, and, on advanced levels, research and seminars. Programs lead to the following awards: certificate or diploma, bachelor's degree (B.A., B.F.A.), master's degree (M.A., M.F.A.), the doctorate (Ph.D., D.F.A.), or their equivalents.

Programs that lead to an award not equivalent to a first university degree place more emphasis on techniques, performance methods, and related practical aspects of the subjects than on underlying theory or general principles. Programs are offered in drawing, painting, sculpture, printmaking, crafts, photography, cinematography, and applied or commercial art and design. Programs in any of these areas usually include courses in related fine or applied arts as well as courses in related subjects such as the humanities, social and behavioral sciences, and natural sciences. Programs may be full time or part time, day or evening. Many are of relatively short duration (in some cases, less than one year), and they include retraining, refresher, and sandwich courses. In many cases, periods of study alternate with periods of practice or work in the relevant field. Programs are usually conducted in special institutions such as colleges or institutes of art. In some cases, programs are provided in institutes of technology, technical colleges, or community colleges.

Programs that lead to a first university degree emphasize the underlying theoretical and general principles of the subjects included as well as their practical techniques and methods. The programs offered—in such areas as drawing and painting, printmaking (including lithography, serigraphy, intaglio, etching, and related techniques), sculpture, crafts, photography, cinematography, graphic design, fashion design, industrial design, and interior design—usually contain some background courses in related fine or applied arts, intended to supplement and to assist the student in mastering the theory and techniques of the major subject. Background courses from such related fields as the humanities, social and behavioral sciences, and natural sciences also are usually included. Programs may be full time or part time, day or evening. At this level, however, most programs are full time, although students may undertake them on a part-time basis. In many cases, study of the subject is supplemented by practice or performance in the relevant field. Programs are usually conducted in universities or colleges or art institutes.

Programs that lead to a postgraduate university degree consist of study, seminars, research, and performance in aspects of the fine and applied arts. At this level, emphasis is given to the theoretical, philosophical, and historical bases of the subjects included in a program, and original research or composition is often an important element. In many programs, original research work, as substantiated by the presentation and defense of a scholarly thesis, is a requirement. The programs followed by individual students at this level are usually confined to one specialized area within one of the fine or applied arts. Important

kinds of programs included are highly specialized studies within such groups as the history and philosophy of art, drawing and painting, printmaking, sculpturing, or interior design. A program in any of the above specialties usually entails some study of related aspects of the same subjects as well as special aspects of other related fine and applied arts, as a means of supplementing and assisting in the mastery of the major subject. In some cases, background studies are also included in special aspects of related subjects in the humanities, social and behavioral sciences, religion, or natural sciences. These programs are mostly full time, although advanced students may be active in their professions and therefore may undertake a program on a part-time basis. The relatively few part-time programs are refresher courses and special courses. Periods of practice or performance form an indispensable part of some programs. Programs are usually given in universities, but some are provided by special colleges of fine arts.

[This section was based on UNESCO's *International Standard Classification of Education (ISCED)* (Paris: UNESCO, 1976).]

Major International and National Organizations

INTERNATIONAL

European Cultural Foundation
Fondation européenne de la culture
Jan van Goyenkade 5
Amsterdam 1007, Netherlands

International Association of Art—Painting,
    Sculpture, Graphic Art (IAA)
Association internationale des arts plastiques
UNESCO House
1 rue Miollis
75015 Paris, France

International Association of Art Critics
Association internationale des critiques d'art
Palais du Louvre, Pavillon de Marsan
107 rue de Rivoli
75001 Paris, France

International Center for the Study and
    Preservation of Cultural Property
256 via Cavour
Rome, Italy

International Committee for the History of Art
Kunsthistorisches Institut der Universitat
Rheinische Friedrich-Wilhelms-Universität
Liebfrauenweg 1
Bonn, Federal Republic of Germany

International Council of Monuments and
    Sites (ICOMOS)
Conseil international des monuments et
    des sites
Hôtel Saint-Aignan
75 rue de Temple
75003 Paris, France

International Council of Museums
Conseil international des musées
UNESCO House
1 rue Miollis
75001 Paris, France

International Federation for Art Education
1m Rossweidli 70
Zurich 8055, Switzerland

International Foundation for Art Research
654 Madison Avenue
New York, New York 10021 USA

International Institute for Conservation of
    Historic and Artistic Works
608 Grand Buildings
Trafalgar Square
London WC2N 5HN, England

International Society for Education
    Through Art (INSEA)
106 rue du Point du Jour
92100 Boulogne-sur-Seine, France

NATIONAL

Argentina:
    Fondo nacional de las artes
    Alsina 673
    Buenos Aires

Australia:
    Australia Council
    168 Walker Street
    Box 302
    North Sydney, New South Wales 2060

Austria:
    Kunsthistorische Gesellschaft
    Universitätsstrasse
    Vienna 1

    Künstlerhaus
    Karlsplatz 5
    Vienna 1

Belgium:
    Association des artistes professionnels
        de Belgique
    461 avenue Louise
    Brussels

    Société royale des beaux-arts
    25 avenue Lambeaux
    Brussels

Canada:
    Canadian Conference of the Arts
    49 Wellington Street East
    Toronto

    Canadian Council
    151 Sparks Street
    P.O. Box 1047
    Ottawa, Ontario

France:
    Société nationale des beaux-arts
    11 rue Berryer
    Paris 8e

Italy:
    Consiglio superiore delle antichità e
        belle arti
    Ministero della pubblica istruzione
    Piazza del Popolo 18
    Rome

Mexico:
    Instituto nacional de bellas artes
    Palacio de Bellas Artes
    Mexico 1, D.F.

Netherlands:
    Netherlands Art Foundation
    Oostelyke handelskade 29
    Postbus 1258
    Amsterdam

Norway:
    Art association
    Wergelandsveien 17
    Oslo 1

South Africa:
    South African Association of Arts
    506 Commercial Union Buildings
    Greenmarket Square
    Cape Town

Sweden:
    Swedish General Art Association
    Stora Nygatan 5
    P.O.B. 2151
    10314 Stockholm 2

Switzerland:
    Société des arts
    Athenée
    Geneva

United Kingdom:
    Arts Council of Great Britain
    105 Piccadilly
    London W1, England

United States:
>   American Federation of Arts
>   41 East 65th Street
>   New York, New York 10021
>
>   Associated Councils of the Arts
>   1564 Broadway
>   New York, New York 10036
>
>   College Art Association of America
>   16 East 52nd Street
>   New York, New York 10022
>
>   National Art Education Association
>   1916 Association Drive
>   Reston, Virginia 22091
>
>   National Association of Schools of Art
>   11250 Roger Bacon Drive
>   Reston, Virginia 22090
>
>   National Endowment for the Arts
>   2401 E Street NW
>   Washington, D.C. 20506
>
>   National Endowment for the Humanities
>   806 15th Street NW
>   Washington, D.C. 20506

For further listings see:

International Directory of Arts. (2 vols.) Berlin, Federal Republic of Germany: Art Adress Verlag Müller GMBH, 1952/53–. Published biennially.

The World of Learning. London: Europa, 1947–. Published annually.

Principal Information Sources

GENERAL

Guides to the literature include:

Besterman, T. *Art and Architecture: A Bibliography of Bibliographies.* Totowa, New Jersey: Rowan and Littlefield, 1971. Classified bibliography of bibliographies.

Carrick, N. *How to Find Out About the Arts: A Guide to Sources of Information.* Elmsford, New York: Pergamon Press, 1965.

Chamberlin, M. W. *Guide to Art Reference Books.* Chicago: American Library Association, 1959. A standard work in the field of fine arts. Classified and annotated; covers reference tools, basic histories, handbooks, and periodicals. Somewhat out of date.

Dove, J. *Fine Arts.* London: Clive Bingley, 1966. Classified and annotated bibliography of a selected group of books.

Ehresman, D. L. *Fine Arts: A Bibliographic Guide to Basic Reference Works, Histories and Handbooks.* Littleton, Colorado: Libraries Unlimited, 1975. Classified, annotated bibliography.

Goldman, B. *Reading and Writing in the Arts: A Handbook.* Detroit: Wayne State University Press, 1972. Intended as a tool to provide access to reference materials. Includes bibliographies, dictionaries, library catalogs, biographies, histories, and periodicals.

Lucas, E. L. *The Harvard List of Books on Art.* Cambridge, Massachusetts: Harvard University Press, 1952. Classified, not annotated.

Lucas, E. L. *Art Books: A Basic Bibliography on the Fine Arts.* Greenwich, Connecticut: New York Graphic Society, 1968.

Podszus, C. O. *Art: A Selected Annotated Art Bibliography.* New York: n. p., 1960. General bibliography of approximately one thousand items covering all aspects of visual arts, with particular emphasis on studio practice.

Rogers, A. R. *The Humanities: A Selective Guide to Reference Sources.* Littleton, Colorado: Libraries Unlimited, 1974.

Walford, A. J. (Ed.) *Guide to Reference Materials.* London: Library Association, 1959. Supplement, 1963. Intended for general library use in all areas, but contains a good, highly selected section on the arts.

Important introductory works and historical perspectives of the field include:

Bazin, G. *Histoire de l'art de la préhistoire à nos jours.* Paris: Garamond, 1953. One-volume French survey of Eastern and Western art.

Fleming, W. *Arts and Ideas: New Brief Edition.* New York: Holt, Rinehart and Winston, 1974. General survey of all the arts.

Gardner, H. *Art Through the Ages.* (6th ed.) New York: Harcourt Brace Jovanovich, 1975. Standard world history of art.

Gombrich, E. H. *The Story of Art.* (12th ed.) New York: Phaidon Art Books, 1974. General survey of art history.

Hauser, A. *The Social History of Art.* (4 vols.) New York: Random House, 1965. Encyclopedic and factual survey stressing social forces of art history.

Janson, H. W. *History of Art.* New York: Abrams, 1969.

Robb, D. M., and Garrison, J. J. *Art in the Western World.* (3rd ed.) New York: Harper & Row, 1953.

Upjohn, E. H., Wingert, P. S., and Mahler, J. G. *History of World Art.* (2nd rev. ed.) New York: Oxford University Press, 1958.

Books and journal articles dealing with art education and careers in various countries include:

Art Education: An International Survey. Paris: UNESCO, 1972. Countries included are Argentina, Australia, Czechoslovakia, France, Federal Republic of Germany, India, Italy,

Japan, Nigeria, United Kingdom, United States, and Soviet Union.

Art/1975: The Journal of the Professional Artist. Paris: International Association of Art, 1975. Entire issue No. 70 is devoted to "UNESCO Project: The Education of Artists. A Report on Experimental and Advanced Programmes for the Education of Painters-Sculptors, Craftsmen, Graphic Designers, Industrial Designers."

Ascot, R. "Art Education in Canada." *Studio International,* October 1972, *184*(948), 139–140.

Conant, H. *Art Education.* New York: Center for Applied Research in Education, 1964.

Dennis, L. J., and Jacob, R. M. *The Arts in Higher Education.* San Francisco: Jossey-Bass, 1968.

Fausett, S. "Visits to Fourteen Colleges of Art." *Studio International,* November 1969, *178*, 148–49.

Forge, A. "L'enseignement de l'art en Grande Bretagne." *Chroniques de l'art vivant,* April 1972, *29*, 18–19.

Guitar, M. *Art Professions in the United States.* New York: Cooper Union School of Art and Architecture, 1960. A source of information for students and guidance counselors pertaining to education, preparation, and training for professional careers in art.

Holden, D. *Art Career Guide: A Guidance Handbook for Art Students, Teachers, Vocational Counselors, Parents and Job Hunters.* (3rd rev. ed.) New York: Watson-Guptill, 1973.

"International Education Year: Summary Report of the Second International Conference on the Professional Training of the Artist, Belgrade, Yugoslavia, 18–24 May, 1970." *Art: The Journal of the Professional Artist,* 1971/72, *64/65*, 10–13.

"The Professional Training of the Artist, International Conference, London, 18–14 June, 1965." *Information Bulletin: International Association of Art,* April 1966, *57/58*, 3–24.

Rothenstein, M. "Contrasts: English and American Art Students." *Studio International,* December 1972, *184*(950), 248–249.

Slade, R. "Art Education in America." *Studio International,* October 1972, *184*(948), 138–139.

Wagnar, C. E. "Art Education in Trinidad." *Leonardo,* Spring 1973, *6*(2), 131–136.

Journals that often include articles on art education are *Art Education: Journal of the National Art Education Association* (US), *Art Journal* (US), and *Studies in Art Education* (US).

CURRENT BIBLIOGRAPHIES

Art Bibliographies: Current Titles. Santa Barbara, California: ABC-Clio, 1972–. Monthly index to articles in 250 current fine arts periodicals.

Art Bibliographies: Modern. Santa Barbara, California: ABC-Clio, 1973–. Annual bibliography of books and periodical articles on twentieth-century art. Formerly *LOMA: Literature on Modern Art;* published 1969–1972.

Art Index. Wilson, 1933–. New York: Quarterly classified bibliography; basic reference tool, especially in English language.

Art/Kunst: International Bibliography of Art Books. 1972–. Basel, Switzerland: Helbing and Lichtenhahn, 1973–. Classified list of current art books.

Education Index. New York: Wilson, 1929–.

Répertoire d'art et d'archéologie. Paris: Morancé, 1910–.

The Worldwide Art Book Syllabus: A Select List of In-Print Books on the History of Art and Archeology. New York: Worldwide Books, 1966–.

PERIODICALS

Some of the important periodical literature devoted to the fine arts include *African Arts* (US), *American Art Journal, Antike Kunst* (Switzerland), *Apollo* (UK), *Ars Orientalis* (US), *Art: The Journal of the Professional Artist* (France), *Art Bulletin* (US), *Art Education* (US), *Artforum* (US), *Art in America, Artibus Asiae* (US), *Art International* (Switzerland), *Art Journal (College Art Journal)* (US), *Art News* (US), *Art Quarterly* (US), *Arts* (US), *Arts Canada, Bollettino d'arte* (Italy), *Burlington Magazine* (UK), *Canadian Art, La critica d'arte* (Italy), *Gazette des beaux-arts* (France), *Graphis* (Switzerland), *Journal of Aesthetics and Art Criticism* (US), *Journal of the Warburg and Courtauld Institutes* (UK), *National Sculpture Review* (US), *Oud-Holland* (Netherlands), *Pantheon* (FRG), *Print* (US), *Studies in Art Education* (US), *Studio International* (UK).

For additional titles see:

Chicago Art Institute, Ryerson Library. *Index to Art Periodicals.* (11 vols.) Boston: Hall, 1962.

Ulrich's International Periodicals Directory. New York: Bowker, biennial.

ENCYCLOPEDIAS, DICTIONARIES, HANDBOOKS

Adeline, J. *Adeline Art Dictionary, Including Terms in Architecture, Heraldry and Archeology.* New York: Ungar, 1966. With supplement by H. Beigel. Includes terms used in art and architecture as well as information on heraldry, iconography, symbols, and the saints and gods. First published in 1891.

Conant, H. (Ed.) *Lincoln Library of the Arts.* (2 vols.) Columbus, Ohio: Frontier Press, 1973.

Encyclopedia of World Art. (15 vols.) New York: McGraw-Hill, 1959–1968. Comprehensive encyclopedia of art and architecture; a standard reference work in the fine arts; good bibliographies with articles.

Glossarium Artis, Deutsch-Französisches Wörterbuch zur Kunst. Tübingen, Federal Republic of Germany; Strasbourg, France: Niemeyer, 1972–. German/French dictionary; each term is illustrated. The most scholarly and comprehensive dictionary of art terms; when complete, it will be the standard work in the field.

Jahn, J. *Wörterbuch der Kunst.* (6th rev. ed.) Stuttgart, Federal Republic of Germany: Kröner, 1962. General fine arts dictionary; includes terms, artists, styles, periods, and civilizations; illustrated, with bibliographies for longer articles.

Mayer, R. *A Dictionary of Art Terms and Techniques.* New York: Crowell, 1969. Coverage of frequently encountered terms and descriptions of techniques; illustrated, with bibliographies.

Murray, P., and Murray, L. *Dictionary of Art and Artists.* New York: Praeger, 1965. A quick reference for artists and movements; best for definitions and explanation of processes, techniques, and materials; illustrated.

Myers, B. S. (Ed.) *McGraw-Hill Dictionary of Art.* (5 vols.) New York: McGraw-Hill, 1969. Comprehensive illustrated dictionary of the visual arts; covers artists, styles, periods, terms, monuments, museums, places, and countries.

Osbourne, H. (Ed.) *Oxford Companion to Art.* New York: Oxford University Press, 1970. Comprehensive short entries; illustrated.

Parow, R. and Pappenheim, H. E. *Kunststile Lexikon der Stilbegriffe.* (2nd ed.) Munich, Federal Republic of Germany: Kunst und Technik, 1958. Part 1 contains a lexicon of styles, schools, movements, and art forms; Part 2 contains alphabetical listing of terms used in art. In German with French and English equivalents.

Praeger Encyclopedia of Art. New York: Praeger, 1971. Comprehensive.

Reau, L. *Dictionnaire polyglotte de termes d'art et d'archéologie.* Paris: Presses universitaires de France, 1953. Reprinted in 1975 by Ohms, Osnabrück, Federal Republic of Germany. Alphabetical listing in French; equivalents in Greek, Latin, Italian, Spanish, Portuguese, Romanian, English, German, Dutch, Swedish, Czech, Polish, and Russian.

Handbooks on techniques include:

Doerner, M. *Materials of the Artist and Their Use in Painting, with Notes on the Techniques of the Old Masters.* (Ref. ed., E. Newhaus, trans.) New York: Harcourt Brace Jovanovich, 1949.

Herbert, K. *The Complete Book of Artists Techniques.* New York: Praeger, 1958.

Mayer, R. *The Artist's Handbook of Materials and Techniques.* (3rd rev. ed.) New York: Viking, 1970.

Vasari, G. *Vasari on Technique.* (L. S. Maclehose, trans.) New York: Dover, 1960.

The following are biographical dictionaries:

Benezit, E. *Dictionnaire critique et documentaire des peintres, sculpteurs, dessinateurs et graveurs.* (8 vols.) Paris: Grund, 1948–1955. Reprinted in 1968.

Darmstädtler, R. *Künstlerlexikon: Maler, Bildhauer, Architekten.* Bern, Switzerland; Munich, Federal Republic of Germany: Francke, 1961.

Thieme, V., and Becker, F. *Allgemeines Lexikon der bildenden Künstler von der Antike bis zur Gegenwart.* (37 vols.) Leipzig, German Democratic Republic: Seemann, 1907–1950. Standard biography for fine arts.

Vollmer, H. *Allgemeines Lexikon der bildenden Künstler des XX Jahrhundert.* (6 vols.) Leipzig, German Democratic Republic: Seemann, 1953–1962. Continuation of Thieme and Becker. Standard reference for twentieth-century artists.

DIRECTORIES

American Art Directory. New York: Bowker, 1898–. Published annually. Annual listing of art museums, universities, college art departments, and art schools in the United States as well as several in Europe.

Directory of National Arts.Organizations: Membership Associations Serving the Arts. New York: Associated Council of the Arts, 1976. Lists membership organizations that are national, nongovernmental, nonprofit associations serving nonprofit, noncommercial art. Information includes address, membership, purpose, activities, publications, and annual budgets. United States associations only.

International Directory of Arts. (2 vols.) Berlin, Federal Republic of Germany: Art Adress Verlag Müller GMBH, 1952/53–. Published biennially. A worldwide listing of people and institutions affiliated with the arts. Volume 1 contains names and addresses of museums, art galleries, schools, colleges, artists, collectors, and art associations. Volume 2 contains names and addresses of art and antique dealers, galleries, art publishers, art periodicals, art booksellers, restorers, experts, and dealers. The standard directory of the arts.

Kay, E. *International Who's Who in Art and Antiques.* Cambridge, England: Melrose Press, 1972. Complete international listing of art associations and art schools.

Von Klemperer, L. *International Education: A Directory of Resource Materials on Comparative Education and Study in Another Country.* Garrett Park, Maryland: n. p., 1973. Includes some art sources.

Museum directories include:

Hudson, K., and Nicholls, A. (Eds.) *The Directory of World Museums.* New York: Columbia University Press, 1975. A comprehensive, international directory which also includes a bibliography of national and regional museum directories and articles.

Kloster, G. B. *Handbook of Museums/Handbuch der Museen.* (2 vols.) Vol. 1: *Federal Republic of Germany;* Vol. 2: *German Democratic Republic, Austria, Switzerland.* New York: Bowker; Pullach/Munich, Federal Republic of Germany: Verlag Dokumentation, 1971.

Museums of the World/Museen der Welt: A Directory of 17,000 Museums in 150 Countries, Including a Subject Index. (2nd enl. ed.) New York: Bowker, 1975.

The Official Museum Directory. 1975, United States and Canada. Washington, D.C.: American Association of Museums; New York: National Register Pub. Co., 1975. Index.

The World of Learning. London: Europa, 1947–. Published annually. Lists universities, institutes, learned associations, research centers, and museums throughout the world.

[Bibliography prepared by Nancy Cottrill.]

See also: Art, History of; Crafts; Dance; Drawing and Painting; Fashion Design; Industrial Design; Interior Design; Music; Photography and Cinematography; Printmaking; Sculpture; Theater Arts.

ASIAN COUNTRIES OF THAILAND, SRI LANKA, AND MALAYSIA, SCIENCE POLICIES OF

See Science Policies: Less Developed Countries: Asian Countries of Thailand, Sri Lanka, and Malaysia.

ASIAN COUNTRIES OF THE PHILIPPINES, INDONESIA, AND THE REPUBLIC OF KOREA, SCIENCE POLICIES OF

See Science Policies: Advanced Developing Countries: Asian Countries of the Philippines, Indonesia, and the Republic of Korea.

ASIAN NATIONAL ARCHIVES

See Archives: Africa and Asia, National Archives of.

ASIAN STUDIES

See Area Studies (field of study).

ASSESSMENT OF LEARNING FOR POSTSECONDARY EDUCATION CREDIT

See Credit, Assessment of Learning for Postsecondary Education.

ASSOCIATED UNIVERSITIES FOR INTERNATIONAL EDUCATION, United States

Associated Universities for International Education (AUIE) was organized in 1968 and incorporated as a nonprofit organization in the state of Illinois for the promotion, encouragement, and conduct of educational, scientific, and research activities in international education on behalf of member institutions.

The president of each member institution designates a representative to the AUIE board of directors. Three member institutions may sponsor an AUIE program subject to board approval. Member institutions are not required to participate in AUIE programs.

Preference for full membership is given to those institutions with substantial graduate or professional programs in international studies. Associate membership is reserved for those institutions with programs primarily at the undergraduate level. Associate member institutions are represented by nonvoting participation at board meetings and pay 50 percent of full membership dues.

The association conducts residential study programs led by the AUIE faculty and organizes field research projects. AUIE cooperates with other countries in the development of new colleges, universities, schools, and related educational systems, providing consultants, advisers, faculty instructors, and educational administrative support. Under the Foreign Lecturers Program, foreign scholars are invited to lecture at member universities and, in some instances, to spend a term in residence at an institution.

Special conferences are sponsored to explore international educational needs and to develop new programs. Through its committees and conferences, AUIE serves as a forum for exchange of information and experience among the international program directors of its member institutions.

Northern Illinois University
Lowden 101
De Kalb, Illinois 60115 USA

ASSOCIATION FOR CONTINUING HIGHER EDUCATION, United States

The Association for Continuing Higher Education (ACHE) began in 1939 as the Association of University Evening Colleges with thirty-three charter members. Although the initial emphasis was on evening college administration, the association later directed greater attention toward course planning, noncredit course development, and community needs. In the late 1940s community services and liberal education were the focal points. In the 1960s interassociational cooperation, community and junior college programs, and continuing education programs were major concerns. In 1973 the name was changed to the Association for Continuing Higher Education, to reflect the broader concerns of the membership.

An organization of institutions of higher education and their administrators of continuing education in the United States and Canada, ACHE encourages collegiate programs of education for adults as a basic function and responsibility of higher education. The association promotes high standards of professional excellence; sponsors research concerning continuing collegiate education; and provides for the interchange of information and ideas in the area of continuing education.

Membership is open to institutions of higher education that have a continuing education division; to individuals involved in continuing education; and to organizations and individuals interested in supporting the association's aims and activities. The activities of the association are funded by membership dues.

ACHE publishes *Continuing Higher Education,* quarterly newsletter; and *Proceedings,* summary of addresses, papers, and discussions presented at the association's annual meeting. Essays in continuing higher education, a series of reports and research developed by ACHE committees, are published periodically.

Office of the Executive Vice-President
1700 Asp Avenue
Norman, Oklahoma 73069 USA

ASSOCIATION FOR INSTITUTIONAL RESEARCH
See Institutional Research.

ASSOCIATION FOR TEACHER EDUCATION IN AFRICA

The Association for Teacher Education in Africa (ATEA), founded as the Afro-Anglo-American Program in Teacher Education in 1960, adopted its present title in 1969 and simultaneously came under exclusive African control. In 1971 two regional bodies that had been semi-independently formed by member institutions of ATEA—the Regional Council for Education (serving Eastern Africa) and the West African Council for Teacher Education—became the eastern regional council and the western regional council of ATEA. In November 1974 the University of Lagos Faculty of Education, Lagos, Nigeria, was chosen as the ATEA headquarters.

The association and the councils are

funded by member institutions, the French government, and the following organizations: Carnegie Corporation of New York, United States Agency for International Development, British Inter-University Council for Higher Education Overseas, Dulverton Trust, and Ford Foundation.

ATEA is made up of university departments and institutes of education in English-speaking Africa (not including Rhodesia and South Africa). Teachers College of Columbia University, University of London Institute of Education, and University of Bristol School of Education are also members. Member institutions, thirty-three in number, are distributed among fifteen countries.

The main purpose of ATEA is to strengthen teacher education in Africa through conferences, special studies, staff exchanges, and fellowships for advanced study relating to teacher education in Africa. Special studies, sponsored or co-sponsored by ATEA, include surveys of in-service teacher education and the demand for and supply of secondary school teachers, in both cases in English-speaking Africa.

Annual ATEA conferences, usually of a week's duration, have been held since 1961. Following the 1975 conference in Nairobi, it was agreed that ATEA conferences would be held biennially and regional council conferences in the intervening years. International professional and donor agencies that are interested in teacher education send observers to ATEA conferences.

Under the Afro-Anglo-American Program, staff exchanges have taken place between Teachers College, Columbia University, on the one hand and African universities and the University of London on the other. Similar exchanges between African universities are arranged through ATEA. ATEA sponsors the African Fellowship Program at Teachers College, Columbia University, financed by the Carnegie Corporation of New York. Fellows, selected from among nominees of

member universities, pursue advanced study relating to teacher education in Africa. The ATEA also sponsors African graduates with master's degrees who wish to continue their studies in United States universities.

ATEA publishes a biannual newsletter. Conference reports on ATEA and regional councils are available at the ATEA headquarters.

University of Lagos
Faculty of Education
Lagos, Nigeria

ASSOCIATION FOR WORLD EDUCATION, United States

The Association for World Education, a nonprofit educational organization, was organized in November 1970 at Racine, Wisconsin, by twenty-five delegates as the Association for World Colleges and Universities. The name was changed in 1974 to focus on all postsecondary education committed to world education. The association helps its members to communicate, share resources, and set standards for accreditation.

Over four hundred individuals and forty institutions make up the membership. Regional conferences are held each year and a worldwide conference biennially. Regional offices are in the planning stages.

The association promotes problem-oriented, creative work toward world education by institutes, workshops, research centers, and professional organizations. Joint ventures with accredited higher educational institutions are also encouraged. Each institution is urged to develop its own way of involving faculty and students in world education functions such as study abroad, overseas facilities, multinational staff, and cross-cultural relations.

The association publishes *Journal of World Education,* quarterly. With a circulation of approximately five thousand, each issue of the journal focuses on a specific theme, such as peace education, study tours, United Nations University, religion, and global education.

3 Harbor Hill Drive
Huntington, New York 11743 USA

ASSOCIATION OF AFRICAN UNIVERSITIES
(Association des universités africaines)

The Association of African Universities (AAU) was founded in November 1967 in Rabat, Morocco. The idea for such an association was conceived in September 1962, during a UNESCO conference on the future of higher education in Africa. Heads of African institutions of higher learning met in September 1963 at the University of Khartoum, Sudan, to appoint a committee charged with drafting the association's constitution and organizing the founding conference. Thirty-three African universities from twenty-six countries were among the founding members.

The association was formed to promote interchange and cooperation among university institutions in Africa. AAU collects, classifies, and disseminates information on African higher education and research; promotes cooperation among African institutions in curriculum development and degree equivalences; and encourages increased contact between members and the international academic world. The association identifies the educational and related needs of African universities and coordinates efforts to meet those needs. AAU encourages the development and wider use of African languages and organizes and supports seminars and conferences between African university teachers, administrators, and others dealing with problems of higher education in Africa. Membership in AAU numbers fifty-one universities from thirty countries.

AAU sponsors the Inter-African University Scholarship Programme (INTERAF) to provide opportunities for students to study at universities outside their own countries in fields of study not readily available at home. The program encourages the exchange of students between African countries; helps universities extend their international dimensions and make the most efficient use of facilities for human resource development in Africa; and contributes to the growing pool of university-trained manpower in fields that are important for the development of African countries.

The INTERAF scholarships are primarily for undergraduates, but the association also provides postgraduate scholarships for staff development programs. Approximately 270 scholarships are available to African students each year. INTERAF started in 1967 with eighteen students from three countries studying at six African universities. In 1975 the program supported about six hundred and fifty students from thirty-two countries studying in thirty-three universities and institutions of higher learning. The association also plans a similar program for staff exchanges.

The association offers three-month language courses in French, English, and Arabic at selected member universities for university teachers, administrators, and students. The AAU has a documentation center to provide materials on all matters of African higher education. The center offers abstracting and bibliographical services and, through affiliations with other research libraries and institutes throughout the world, collaborates with universities to support research and promote African development.

The AAU is funded by membership subscriptions and interest from an endowment fund to which a number of African governments have contributed. The Organization of African Unity also provides an annual subvention. The United States Agency for International Development is the largest single donor for INTERAF. Other donors for the scholarship program are the British Inter-University Council, the Canadian International Development Agency, and the Federal Republic of Germany's *Deutscher akademischer Austauschdienst*

(German Academic Exchange Service). The French Ministry of Cooperation, the Danish government, and the Ford Foundation provide the necessary financial support for the documentation center.

The AAU publishes a bulletin containing information on university affairs and AAU activities. The *Directory of African Universities* includes the history, location, entrance requirements, degrees awarded, student services, and publications of universities in Africa.

P.O. Box 5744
Accra-North, Ghana

ASSOCIATION OF AMERICAN COLLEGES

The Association of American Colleges (AAC) is a United States organization of colleges of liberal arts and sciences. Founded in 1915 by a group of church-related colleges, its membership now includes over seven hundred accredited institutions, privately controlled or publicly supported, that offer a liberal education at the undergraduate level. In 1974 membership was expanded beyond colleges and universities granting a baccalaureate degree to include other institutions (such as two-year colleges) that have demonstrated an effective commitment to the liberal education of undergraduate students.

Under its constitution, the association is charged with promoting higher education in general. It has consistently sought to advance the common interests of undergraduate education, regardless of institutional setting, while sustaining the principle of institutional diversity in the public interest. Since, however, seven eighths of its members are privately controlled institutions, AAC has long been regarded as the leading spokesman for the independent sector of higher education in the United States.

The professional staff, housed in the association's headquarters in Washington, D.C., consists of a president, vice-president, executive associates, and supporting staff. The staff members who regularly visit member colleges provide information or guidance on subjects germane to liberal education and the liberal arts college. Prospective candidates and search committees for executive positions, particularly for presidencies and academic deanships, often use the resource facilities of the staff.

The work of the association is supported primarily through membership dues. As a tax-exempt organization, however, it has received assistance over the years from a variety of philanthropic and corporate donors, both in support of its regular operating budget and particularly for its many special projects and services.

The association is supported by an affiliate organization, the National Council of Independent Colleges and Universities, composed of more than one thousand privately controlled institutions concerned with strengthening their relations with state and federal governments. NCICU coordinates the work of thirty-eight state associations of independent institutions. It is staffed by AAC but governed by its own board of directors. Early in 1975 AAC published *A National Policy for Private Higher Education,* a report prepared by an NCICU task force.

Through its National Policies Communication Service and Legislative Relations Service, AAC seeks to provide information and counsel to its own members and to government officials and elected representatives in all matters relating to undergraduate education.

The Federal Relations Advisory Service provides assistance on request to member colleges interested in taking advantage of various governmental programs which are keyed to the needs and resources of undergraduate schools and colleges in the arts and sciences.

AAC and the American Conference of Academic Deans (ACAD) collaborate in matters of common interest and hold joint annual meetings. In cooperation with ACAD and the Council of Colleges of Arts and Sciences (in publicly supported universities), AAC organizes workshops for academic deans. Seminars are conducted for college presidents on critical aspects of the president's functions, such as academic leadership, fund raising, and the admission and retention of students.

Although AAC has no power of mandatory prescription, it has periodically adopted formal policy statements on major personnel issues, usually in concert with other national organizations, to offer guidance to its members.

The association is administered by a board of thirteen directors, twelve elected to rotating terms by the membership, plus the president ex officio. The board is advised in some of its major areas of responsibility by three standing commissions of fifteen members each: the Commission on Institutional Affairs, concerned with institutional organization, internal management, and personnel matters; Commission on Liberal Learning, concerned with academic programs and the reform of liberal education through development of alternative curricular models; and Commission on Religion, concerned with the teaching of religion as an academic subject, campus ministry, and special problems of church-related colleges.

The official journal of the association is the quarterly *Liberal Education*. AAC also publishes reports of studies on issues of current concern to member colleges.

1818 R Street NW
Washington, D.C. 20009 USA

ASSOCIATION OF
AMERICAN UNIVERSITIES

Founded in 1900, the Association of American Universities (AAU) comprises forty-eight major public and private universities in the United States and two in Canada that are preeminent in graduate and professional education and research. AAU maintains a close working relationship with its affiliate, the Association of Graduate Schools (AGS), composed of graduate deans from member institutions. AGS meets annually, just prior to the fall meeting of AAU, to discuss problems of graduate education and make recommendations to AAU.

New AAU members are admitted by a three-fourths vote of the membership. Closed association meetings, attended by the head of each member institution, are held in the spring and fall. An AAU member is the host for the spring meeting; the fall meeting is held in Washington, D.C. AAU is funded by dues, supplemented by special assessment and by foundation or federal support for special activities.

The purposes of the association are to consider and express opinions on matters of common interest relating to university policy, particularly those relating to graduate study and research; to inform individuals and institutions of the purposes, responsibilities, and needs of universities; and to cooperate with universities in other countries. The association tries to facilitate an informal exchange of ideas and experience among the member presidents on matters of mutual interest related to university policy and to state a public position on matters of high urgency, such as the federal financing of higher education.

In 1969 the organization broadened its objectives with the establishment of the Council on Federal Relations, whose function is to consider all federal government activities that affect universities and to make recommendations to the presidents of AAU universities. To facilitate the work of the council, standing and ad hoc committees were established in a number of areas, including institutional accountability, graduate education, legislation, nondiscrimination, and student financial assistance. These activities are closely coordinated with the American Council on Education, National Association of State Universities and Land-Grant Colleges, and other higher education associations.

Since the AAU membership is comparatively small in number, the staff prepares no regular newsletter or other publications. Communication with the members tends to be informal and is timed to coincide with evolving pertinent issues.

One Dupont Circle
Washington, D.C. 20036 USA

ASSOCIATION OF ARAB UNIVERSITIES

Representatives of Arab universities meeting in Benghazi, Libya, in May 1961 for a seminar on the problems of higher education suggested the formation of an association for Arab universities. In 1964 the representatives of Arab universities met in Beirut, Lebanon, to draft the constitution of the Association of Arab Universities (AARU). A temporary secretariat was set up in 1965. A council was held, and standing committees were elected to study curricula, higher studies and academic research, affairs of the teaching staff, student affairs, libraries, laboratories, and the policy of university education. In September 1969 the first general congress was held in Alexandria, Egypt, and a permanent secretariat was founded. The second general congress was held in Cairo in February 1973.

The association has twenty-eight member universities from Algeria, Iraq, Jordan, Kuwait, Lebanon, Libya, Egypt, Syria, Sudan, Tunisia, Morocco, Qatar, and Yemen Arab Republic.

The association is governed by the general congress held every three years. The executive organ of the association is the council, composed of the rectors of member universities. The council meets twice annually. The association also has a general secretariat and a supporting staff.

The association encourages high standards of university education. It emphasizes applied research dealing with environmental problems and encourages attempts to relate research topics to plans for social and economic development in the Arab countries. The main aims of the association are to spread the Arab cultural heritage, encourage the establishment of new universities in Arab countries, promote co-

operation between Arab universities and other universities in the world, and coordinate the work of Arab universities in international organizations and conferences.

The association has offered seminars for librarians and directors of Arab university libraries and for deans in the faculties of engineering, science, veterinary medicine, agriculture, commerce, law, pharmacy, and art in Arab universities. With the cooperation of UNESCO, a regional symposium on the economic and manpower efficiency of existing research and science teaching institutions was held in Cairo in December 1971.

The association publishes a *Directory of Arab Universities* and a *Directory of Teaching Staff of Arab Universities*. Other publications are seminar reports, congress proceedings, and the *Bulletin of the Association of Arab Universities*.

Scientific Computation Center
Tharwat Street, Orman Post Office
Giza, Cairo, Egypt

ASSOCIATION OF ATLANTIC UNIVERSITIES, Canada

The Association of Atlantic Universities (AAU) was founded in 1964 to assist in the coordination of higher education, ensure high academic standards in a period of rising costs, and avoid unnecessary duplication of faculties and courses of studies. The association has sixteen members in the four Atlantic provinces of Canada (New Brunswick, Newfoundland and Labrador, Nova Scotia, and Prince Edward Island), all but one with degree-granting powers. The University of the West Indies is an associate member.

A voluntary association, AAU has no statutory authority over individual members but functions by consensus, mainly through its executive council. The council, composed of the presidents of each member institution, meets four times a year.

The most important of more than a dozen committees linked formally or informally to AAU is the Academic Vice-

Presidents' Committee. Formed in 1971, the committee is a key element in the review of new programs proposed by individual institutions, especially since the formation of the Maritime Provinces Higher Education Commission (MPHEC) in 1974. MPHEC, a grants committee for the three Maritime Provinces (New Brunswick, Nova Scotia, and Prince Edward Island), normally refers all new programs to the AAU council for comment, and the council normally passes them to the academic vice-presidents for advice. The idea of the MPHEC, put forward by AAU in its report for the Maritime Union Study, was adopted by the premiers of the three provinces as their first joint project.

The AAU committee of business officers has worked with Statistics Canada since 1970 on a national pilot project for standard reporting of university financial information. Other AAU committees group registrars, nurses, student services officers, and those responsible for continuing education. Members of the Atlantic Provinces Inter-University Committee on the Sciences include scientists from government laboratories.

One major study begun on AAU initiative in 1974, brings together the MPHEC, the Province of Newfoundland and Labrador, and the Federal Department of Communications with AAU. The study examines the best use of computer facilities in the Atlantic universities.

AAU maintains a small secretariat in Halifax. Funding is entirely from member institutions.

Suite 500
Duke Tower, Scotia Square
Halifax, Nova Scotia B3J 2L4

bers, about 550 in number, include university teachers and other scientific workers having tenure in universities or scientific institutions with a public character, such as museums, archives, and libraries. The association is not a trade union and has no single political or philosophical faith. It considers academic problems from the scholar's point of view, to raise the level of teaching and promote research; encourages friendship among teachers and research workers in all Belgian universities and research institutions; and supports freedom of teaching and research.

The association organizes an annual general assembly and also holds symposia on academic matters such as university examinations, the role of scientific staff in universities, refresher courses, transfer of scientific information, teaching methods in the university, integration of higher education, university admissions, and the future of the university.

Funded by an annual subvention from the Belgian Ministries of Education and members' contributions, the association is directed by a bureau of ten members assisted by a national council. The national council, composed of representatives of all universities and research institutions, operates under the control of a general assembly. An honorary secretary general directs the association's day-by-day activities.

The association publishes *Communication/Mededelin,* proceedings of meetings; and *Feuille d'avis/Informatieblad,* information bulletin. Both periodicals are in French and Dutch.

rue des Champs Elysées 43
1050 Brussels, Belgium

ASSOCIATION OF BELGIAN UNIVERSITY TEACHERS
(Universitas belgica)

The Association of Belgian University Teachers was founded in 1945 as a national section of the International Association of University Professors and Lecturers. Mem-

ASSOCIATION OF CARIBBEAN UNIVERSITIES AND RESEARCH INSTITUTES
(Asociación de universidades e institutos de investigación del Caribe)

The *Asociación de universidades e institutos de investigación del Caribe* (UNICA: Association of Caribbean Universities and Research

Institutes) was founded in November 1968 at a conference attended by representatives from sixteen Caribbean universities and research institutes at the University of Puerto Rico. Reports were presented at the conference by working parties set up by a group of presidents of Caribbean universities in 1966. These reports indicated that universities and research institutes in the Caribbean area could and should work together in such basic areas as agriculture, education, medicine, science and technology, and the social sciences and that university libraries in the Caribbean should develop means of cooperating with each other.

It was decided that the association should foster contact and collaboration between member institutions through conferences, meetings, newsletters, bulletins, surveys, studies, teaching materials, and joint planning of teaching and research programs.

The affairs of the forty-six-member nonprofit association—registered in accordance with Jamaican, Puerto Rican, and Colombian laws—are managed by an executive committee consisting of seven elected members and the secretary general. Members are elected at general meetings of the association for a minimum of two years. The staff consists of the secretary general as the chief executive officer, project directors, and an executive assistant.

UNICA programs are planned by groups of specialists from member institutions and include projects in education technology, teacher education, plant protection and pest control, horticultural development, urbanism, management studies, and social development.

Voting membership is open to all accredited university-level institutions, postgraduate institutions, or research centers and institutes in the Caribbean region. Associate membership is for university-level institutions beyond the Caribbean that have academic commitments in the region. Affiliate membership is open to associations with similar purposes to those of UNICA, such as the Association of Caribbean University Librarians.

The association is funded by dues from member institutions and by grants from foundations and international agencies, including the Ford Foundation, International Development Research Centre, Canadian International Development Agency, and Inter-American Foundation.

Publications include the *Caribbean Educational Bulletin,* quarterly; *UNICA Newsletter,* three times yearly; and conference proceedings. UNICA also publishes surveys of studies in the Caribbean on urbanism, social development, horticultural workers, teacher training institutions, economic integration with Latin America, and management studies in the Commonwealth countries of the Caribbean.

27 Tobago Avenue
New Kingston
Kingston 10, Jamaica, West Indies

See also: Organization of American States.

ASSOCIATION OF CHRISTIAN SCHOOLS AND COLLEGES, The Philippines

Founded in June 1964, the Association of Christian Schools and Colleges (ACSC) is incorporated under the laws of the Republic of the Philippines as a nonstock, nonprofit, educational corporation. These church-related schools are under the auspices of the following denominations: Methodist, United Church of Christ in the Philippines, American Baptist, Southern Baptist, Seventh-Day Adventist, Philippine Episcopal, Christian Missionary Alliance, and United Evangelical.

The objectives of ACSC are to elevate the standards and advance the interests of Christian schools; to promote a high sense of unity, understanding, and fellowship among the member schools and cooperating mission boards, agencies, and other bodies, in the Philippines and abroad, interested in Christian schools and education in general in the Philippines; to serve as an accrediting body for member schools; to provide special services requested by member schools; and to serve as a liaison for member schools with government and related agencies.

Of the fifty-eight member schools of ACSC, two are universities, eighteen are colleges, and thirty-eight are secondary schools. By geographical location, eighteen are in Mindanao, ten in the Visayan Islands, and thirty in Luzon. ACSC is a regular member of the Board of National Education, Coordinating Council of Private Educational Associations, and UNESCO Philippine Commission, and an associate member of the National Council of Churches in the Philippines.

ACSC has conducted, with grants from the Fund for Assistance to Private Education (a foundation funded from World War II damage funds authorized by the Congress of the United States), science and mathematics regional seminars among its member schools, with emphasis on upgrading teacher competencies and curricular innovations.

ACSC is engaged in an accreditation program for member schools. In addition, data gathered from an ACSC survey conducted in member secondary schools have served as the basis for planning project proposals designed to develop community outreach and for helping out-of-school youth learn creative and productive skills. The collated data have enabled ACSC to draw up a national project proposal which will emphasize the training and development of middle-level skills. Any qualified member schools will serve as sites for middle-level manpower training centers.

1664 Taft Avenue
Manila, Philippines

MODESTO G. RICO

ASSOCIATION OF COLLEGE HONOR SOCIETIES, United States

The Association of College Honor Societies (ACHS) was organized in 1925 by a group of college and university teachers, administrators, and representatives of six well-established honor societies. The initial honor societies were Phi Beta Kappa, liberal arts; Sigma Xi, scientific research; Tau Beta Pi, engineering; Phi Kappa Phi, all university fields; Alpha Omega Alpha, medicine; and Order of the Coif, law. The organizers met to consider the problems of character, function, membership standards, multiplicity, and duplication of honor societies. They sought to recommend appropriate classification, standards, membership cost, consolidation, or elimination of these societies.

The Association of College Honor Societies consists of national and international honor societies that meet the defined standards of the association. In general, the membership requirements are superior scholarship and/or leadership achievement either in broad fields of education or in departmental fields, at undergraduate or graduate levels. Societies are classified as general honor societies and specialized honor societies. Recognition societies (societies that confer membership in recognition of a student's interest and participation in some collegiate study or activity and have more liberal membership requirements than those prescribed for general and specialized honor societies) are not eligible for membership in the association.

The present objectives of ACHS are to encourage all general and specialized honor societies; to establish and maintain desirable standards and useful functions in higher education; and to achieve recognition for member societies. ACHS invites qualified societies to seek affiliation.

ACHS is governed by a council consisting of an official representative of each member society. The council, meeting annually, investigates and determines membership qualifications. Membership includes active voting members (societies that meet all requirements for membership in the association) and associate nonvoting members (societies that meet all the requirements except those concerning age or size). Dues from each constituent organization are set by the council.

The society publishes *Booklet of Information,* biennially.

2812 Livingston Street
Allentown, Pennsylvania 18104 USA

ASSOCIATION OF COLLEGE UNIONS–INTERNATIONAL

The Association of College Unions–International (ACU-I) was founded as the National Association of Student Unions at Ohio State University, Columbus, Ohio, in 1914, when students representing seven universities in the central United States gathered with three faculty observers to discuss problems common to campus centers. Two Canadian unions were among the twelve charter members who reorganized the association in 1922. The first president was the warden of Hart House, the union at the University of Toronto. Membership now numbers over 900 institutions in the United States, Canada, Australia, England, Hong Kong, Guatemala, Japan, and New Zealand.

One of the oldest international associations in higher education, ACU-I provides opportunities for staff members and student officers involved in student union activities to join in studying and improving their programs and services. The association assists in the development of new college unions and encourages and publishes research. It is a member of the American Council on Education.

Membership is open to any college or university that has a general cultural-recreational program and operates, or is planning, building quarters or premises (whether known as a union, center, hall, or house). Voting membership is by institutions, but nonvoting membership is also open to individual staff members on a professional basis and to students active in the union field. In 1975 there were more than 800 individual members.

The association's annual conference, primarily for union staff members, is attended by approximately 1000 representatives of some 450 institutions. Besides a wide variety of discussion sessions on union program goals, building management problems, and general issues in higher education, there are intensive preconference seminars and exhibits of products and services useful in building operations and program development.

Fifteen regional meetings are held in North America each autumn for both staff members and student officers. More than 4000 from nearly 650 institutions participate, with student attendance predominating. Fifteen regional representatives from the various geographical areas assist in the general development of the association and work with students and staff in developing regional programs, newsletters, directories, program workshops, and seminars.

The association conducts an annual workshop, where two students from each of the fifteen regions, the regional representatives, and the association's executive committee meet for a week-long discussion of union objectives and future plans. A student representative of this assembly is elected each year to sit as a voting member on the executive committee.

The standing committees of the association foster studies and programs concerned with international relations, management, outdoor recreation, the performing and visual arts, program development, and intercollegiate games. The association actively encourages research in the union field, making numerous surveys of union practices and policies and lending assistance wherever possible to authors, researchers, and graduate students doing thesis studies. In addition, to encourage the continued professional development of union staff members, ACU-I sponsors short courses, seminars, and training programs at several universities.

The association's central office, staffed by a full-time executive secretary and several assistants since 1968, operates a computerized professional registry service to match qualified candidates to job openings.

The association publishes *Proceedings,* annual conference report; *Bulletin,* illustrated journal, five times a year; *Union Wire,* bimonthly newsletter; and *Directory of Unions and Staff Members,* annual. Also published are books on union history and philosophy, monographs, and research studies dealing with building planning and operation and program guidelines. A complete list of available publications can be obtained from the ACU-I central office. All association publications since 1914 have been microfilmed and placed on microfiche cards, which may be purchased from the central office. The association exchanges current publications with more than a hundred other professional organizations and publications concerned with higher education.

Box 7286
Stanford, California 94305 USA

CHESTER A. BERRY
PORTER BUTTS

ASSOCIATION OF COLLEGES AND UNIVERSITIES FOR INTERNATIONAL-INTERCULTURAL STUDIES, United States

The Association of Colleges and Universities for International-Intercultural Studies (ACUIIS), is a consortium of colleges and universities in the United States sharing a concern for international education. The association supports programs on-campus and abroad that encourage international and intercultural studies.

ACUIIS grew out of experimental student study-travel programs of the United Methodist Division of Higher Education, Nashville, Tennessee, beginning in 1960. In 1967 the original twelve colleges participating in the early projects incorporated to form ACUIIS, with membership open to non-Methodist-affiliated institutions.

Sources of funds include member college dues, student fees, and grants from the United States Department of Health, Education and Welfare; the Department of State; the United Methodist Board of Higher Education and Ministry; and interested individuals.

The consortium includes thirty-six accredited institutions of higher education in the United States. The majority are four-year liberal arts colleges. Changes made in the bylaws at the association's annual meeting in Nashville in October 1973 provide for an associate membership for cooperating foreign institutions.

The association sponsors visits by international scholars, artists, and journalists to its member institutions as well as international programs in music, literature, economics, diplomacy, and politics. Other activities include faculty workshops on the internationalization of the curriculum; United Nations and intercultural seminars; and travel-study opportunities for both faculty and students. Foreign study programs have included trips to Africa, India, Bangladesh, Yugoslavia, Poland, and the Galapagos Islands. The association also cosponsors (with the University of Evansville, in Indiana) an ongoing year-abroad program at Harlaxton, England.

In 1969 the Graz Center, based at the University of Graz, Austria, was opened. Operating approximately two months each summer, the center offers courses in international studies, with emphasis on Eastern and Central European affairs. Participants include 80–150 American students, 10–25 European students, and an international faculty of about 15. Approximately a dozen faculty members from the United States pursue individual study and research at the center.

The association publishes *Special International Resources,* quarterly newsletter; and *International Communique,* periodic bulletin concerning the work of ACUIIS.

P.O. Box 871
Nashville, Tennessee 32303 USA

ASSOCIATION OF COMMONWEALTH UNIVERSITIES

The Association of Commonwealth Universities (ACU), founded in 1913 as the Universities Bureau of the British Empire, is the oldest international interuniversity organization. The organization was renamed the Association of Universities of the British Commonwealth in 1948 and in 1963 received a Royal Charter under its present name. A voluntary body, ACU is governed by the general meeting of vice-chancellors, presidents, rectors, and principals of member universities and a council elected by the annual general meeting. Its main activities are financed by annual contributions from its two hundred member universities. Special services of the association are paid for by the institutions concerned.

The association promotes the exchange of information, ideas, and experience among members and between members and governments, through conferences, congresses, publications, and an information service. ACU facilitates the interchange of students and teachers among the universities of the Commonwealth.

Congresses, held every five years alternately in the United Kingdom and other Commonwealth countries, bring together four delegates from each member institution and invited guests. The Conference of Executive Heads, held twice every five years, is limited to principals, vice-chancellors, presidents, and rectors of member institutions. The annual meetings of the council provide opportunities for informal discussion between council members and their colleagues in the host country. Through its free information service, ACU answers more than three thousand inquiries a year.

ACU encourages the movement of staff and students within the Commonwealth through its Appointments Service. The association provides the secretariats of the Commonwealth Scholarship Commission in the United Kingdom and Marshall Aid Commemoration Commission. With the assistance of outside funds, ACU supports academic exchanges between the developing countries of the Commonwealth and provides traveling fellowships to enable career administrators to enlarge their experience through visits to universities in other Commonwealth countries.

The *Commonwealth Universities Yearbook* is published annually by ACU. Other publications include information guides about fellowships, scholarships, and other awards available to staff and students; and handbooks of information of interest to prospective students or their parents. The *ACU Bulletin of Current Documentation* provides factual information on some of the more important recent books, reports, and other documents about university affairs that are of more than local interest.

36 Gordon Square
London WC1H 0PF, England

HUGH W. SPRINGER

ASSOCIATION OF ENGINEERS AND ARCHITECTS IN ISRAEL

The Association of Engineers and Architects in Israel (AEAI), founded in 1921, is an academic, professional organization divided into professional sections of architecture and planning; and civil, mechanical, electrical, hydraulic, agricultural, environmental, industrial, municipal, and chemical engineering. The association is an autonomous body, administered by an executive and a central committee elected from delegates at triennial conventions. The delegates are elected in direct, personal, and secret balloting, held on a regional and professional basis. The professional sections hold separate concurrent elections for their officers.

Graduates of recognized institutes of higher learning in engineering, architecture, and technology can be admitted as active members. Engineering and architecture students in their final year of studies are admitted on a special student status, leading to full membership upon graduation. Membership includes nine thousand Israeli engineers and architects and two thousand nonresident members from five continents.

AEAI handles wage and employment problems of self-employed engineers and architects, periodically drafting and publishing codes of practice and scales of fees for professional services. AEAI also holds symposia, lectures, and seminars to keep members informed of developments in their specific fields of interest. It shares the administration of postgraduate and refresher courses throughout the country in cooperation with the Technion—Israel Institute of Technology.

The association founded the Engineering Council to study public policy toward technological projects and developments, and the Building and Industry Research Institute to carry out research in the fields of building and industry.

AEAI's Central Competitions Committee appoints juries for public competitions of architectural design projects in Israel. Branches of AEAI in Tel Aviv, Haifa, Jerusalem, and Beersheba host the Engineering Club, where cabinet ministers and heads of the economic, science, and industrial communities discuss programs and problems of interest to the profession.

AEAI is affiliated with the *Union internationale des architectes* (International Union of Architects) and the World Federation of Engineering Organizations. It maintains close associations with sister organizations abroad and other academic institutions, sending representatives to congresses, conferences, and seminars organized by these and similar bodies. AEAI sponsors the triennial World Congress of Engineers and Architects in Israel. At the first congress in 1967, the International Technical Cooperation Centre (ITCC) was founded. A nonprofit organization administered by a multinational 43-member executive committee and a 171-member executive coun-

cil, ITCC seeks to promote the transfer of technology from the developed to the developing countries, with Israel acting as the chief liaison. ITCC also sponsors conferences and seminars on problems affecting the developing countries.

AEAI publishes a monthly bulletin in Hebrew and a monthly newsletter in English for overseas members. Other publications include periodicals on planning, civil engineering, and technology; and technical books for engineers, technicians, and vocational school students, issued in cooperation with government agencies and the General Federation of Labor.

The Engineer's Institute
200 Dizengoff Road
Tel Aviv, Israel 63462

ELHANAN PELLES

ASSOCIATION OF GOVERNING BOARDS OF UNIVERSITIES AND COLLEGES, United States

In 1921, approximately ninety boards of regents of public institutions in the United States formed the Association of Governing Boards of State Universities and Allied Institutions. The group opened membership to private institutions in 1963, and the name was changed to the Association of Governing Boards of Universities and Colleges (AGB). In 1964 a national office was established in Washington, D.C., with a full-time director.

A nonprofit, tax-exempt corporation, AGB seeks to aid higher education in the United States by strengthening its system of lay leadership. The organization is concerned with the problems and responsibilities of trusteeship in all sectors of higher education in the United States and with the relationship of trustees and regents with the president, faculty, and student body.

Membership includes more than 600 governing, coordinating, and advisory boards representing 960 United States campuses and numbering over 13,000 individual regents and trustees. The AGB's board of directors consists of fifteen trustees of member institutions.

Membership fees are scaled according to institutional enrollment rather than size of the governing board. Additional support funds are obtained from individual, corporation, and foundation grants.

Twice a year AGB holds a national conference to discuss higher education issues. Governing boards, both members and nonmembers, and college presidents are invited to participate.

Two periodicals are distributed to members: *AGB Reports,* journal containing articles of special interest to regents and trustees; and *AGB Notes,* newsletter designed to keep members informed about current events in higher education. AGB also has special publications on such topics as the role of governing boards, effective use of resources, and two-year-college trustees.

One Dupont Circle
Washington, D.C. 20036 USA

ASSOCIATION OF GRADUATE SCHOOLS

See Association of American Universities.

ASSOCIATION OF GRADUATES FROM INSTITUTIONS FOR HIGHER EDUCATION (Akademikernes centralorganisation), Denmark

In Denmark the *Akademikernes centralorganisation* (AC: Association of Graduates from Institutions for Higher Education) binds twenty-three organizations of graduates from universities and other institutions of higher education into one central body. These organizations include civil servants, teachers, and graduates in the professions.

There is no special organization for university teachers, but AC has a council for those who are employed in research and higher education. University teachers are civil servants with wage and employment conditions stipulated by agreements be-

tween AC and the state (the Ministry of Finance). The council concerns itself with employment conditions for university teachers and gives advice to AC management.

Gothersgade 131
1123 Copenhagen K, Denmark
KNUD BENT HEY

ASSOCIATION OF HIGHER EDUCATION (Hochschulverband), Federal Republic of Germany

Founded in 1950, the *Hochschulverband* (Association of Higher Education) is a voluntary professional association of university professors and lecturers in the Federal Republic of Germany. The association promotes the interests of university professors in their various fields of study and represents its members' interests with government agencies and the public.

The membership of 8200 is organized into unions in the eleven states and into groups at the individual universities. Seven professors, elected for two-year terms, provide the leadership for the association. A secretary and office staff maintain headquarters in Bonn–Bad Godesberg.

The association publishes *Mitteilungen des Hochschulverbandes,* six times a year, and edits a number of books on higher education.

Rheinallee 18
D-5300 Bonn–Bad Godesberg 1
Federal Republic of Germany

ASSOCIATION OF INDEPENDENT COLLEGES AND SCHOOLS, United States

In 1962 the National Association and Council of Business Schools and the American Association of Business Schools merged to form the United Business Schools Association. In 1972 the association's name was changed to the Association of Independent Colleges and Schools (AICS). Membership in AICS includes five hundred colleges and schools that have a curriculum designed to prepare people for careers in business. The majority are proprietary schools (private schools conducted for profit to serve the educational needs of business, industry, professional training, and other social and cultural areas). About 10 percent of the institutions are tax exempt; some are church related. The member institutions represent 130,000 students. The student population is 70 percent female.

In 1956 the United States Office of Education of the Department of Health, Education and Welfare recognized the Accrediting Commission for Business Schools (now called the Accrediting Commission of AICS) as a national accrediting agency for business schools. Some AICS member schools are also accredited by regional accrediting associations.

The schools offer programs of education in business and business-related subjects, both at the degree level and at the postsecondary level. High school graduation, or the equivalent, is a prerequisite to enrollment. Many students who enroll in proprietary schools have had one or more years of college in other institutions of higher education. The length of study at the proprietary school can vary from a few months to four years, ending with a certificate, a diploma, or an academic degree. The one- to two-year core curriculum provides an education program for secretaries, junior accountants, and data-processing personnel. Some schools train executive secretaries, medical secretaries, and court reporters. Most of the program offerings are closely related to job opportunities and provide particularized service to students and to the business community where the school is located.

AICS publishes the monthly *Compass,* with a circulation of five thousand. Other AICS publications are *Your Career as a Secretary, Your Career as a Legal Secretary, Accounting for Your Future,* and other guidance materials. A bibliography on proprietary schools is available from AICS.

Through the Accrediting Commission, the association publishes the *Directory of Accredited Institutions* and *Supplement to the Criteria.*

1730 M Street NW
Washington, D.C. 20036 USA

MARY B. WINE

ASSOCIATION OF INDIAN UNIVERSITIES, India

The Association of Indian Universities, formerly known as Inter-University Board of India, was established in 1925 to serve as an authorized channel of communication among universities and facilitate coordination of higher education activities. Acting as a liaison between the universities, the government of India, and other official and nonofficial organizations, the association is the chief agency for determining equivalences of degrees of both Indian and foreign origin. Membership includes ninety-three universities and institutes. Nineteen vice-chancellors act as the association's executive body. The association is supported by annual contributions from the universities and by grants from the government of India.

The association promotes games and sports among the universities and institutes through the Sports Board, composed of 103 universities and institutes. The Sports Board conducts about thirty-three tournaments in various sports and games for both men and women every year, sponsors university athletes in national tournaments, and awards about one hundred scholarships annually to outstanding athletes.

The association publishes the *University News,* monthly; *Universities Handbook;* a bibliography of doctoral theses; and a bibliography of projects conducted at Indian universities and institutes. The association also publishes the proceedings of university meetings and conferences held under its auspices.

Rouse Avenue
New Delhi 110001, India

ASSOCIATION OF INTERNATIONAL COLLEGES AND UNIVERSITIES

The Association of International Colleges and Universities (AICU), a voluntary association of American independent colleges and universities in Europe, was founded in April 1972 and incorporated as a nonprofit corporation by the Commonwealth of Massachusetts. Each member is basically a liberal arts institution, although professional and technical education are accommodated in various ways in most of the members' programs. Members of AICU include the following institutions: American University in Cairo, American College in Paris, American College in Switzerland (Leysin, Switzerland), Beirut University College, John Cabot International College in Rome, Deree-Pierce Colleges (Athens), Haigazian College (Beirut), Institute for American Universities (Aix-en-Provence, France), New England College (Arundel, England), Richmond College (Richmond, England), and Center for International Education of the Massachusetts State College System (Buzzards Bay, Massachusetts). The association is funded by its members and has an American board of trustees.

AICU aims to promote internationalism and cooperation among educational institutions of higher education in Europe; exchange information and resources; and serve as an additional source of publicity about such institutions among colleges and universities in the United States. The association conducts studies on the standards of such institutions and acts as a regional accrediting organization dedicated to the development, maintenance, and improvement of sound educational standards. It also administers monies and property donated to serve the purposes of the association.

The association strives to maintain undergraduate programs that transcend national borders yet at the same time utilize knowledge gained from the distinctive cultures. All member institutions use the modular course-credit system adapted from the American university and employ professors of many different national backgrounds.

The association publishes and distributes newsletters and reports periodically.

Deree-Pierce Colleges
P.O. Box 472
Athens, Greece

ASSOCIATION OF OVERSEAS EDUCATORS, United States

The Association of Overseas Educators (AOE), was organized at the National Education Association's Chicago convention in July 1955. The association adopted its constitution in July 1956 and was incorporated in Michigan in August 1959.

AOE serves as a central organization for individuals, universities, organizations, and agencies interested in sharing and exchanging educational information gleaned from overseas educational experiences. Active voting members have served overseas in an educational capacity. Any United States citizen may become an associate nonvoting member. Honorary nonvoting members are educators from other countries visiting the United States. Dues are paid annually to national and local groups.

The organization conducts an advisory program to prepare those who are leaving the United States for a foreign assignment; formulates and carries out an action program to influence legislation in the field of foreign policy that members deem to be in the national interest; conducts local and regional informal discussions and conferences on matters related to international affairs; and concerns itself with public and private programs for the exchange of administrators, teachers, and students. Through local and state organizations, AOE acts as host or adviser to educators who come from abroad to work in the educational system of the United States; collects information about educational exchange programs and distributes this information to local AOE units; and acts as a rallying point for all those interested in the promotion of world peace through educational and cultural interchange.

The stateside program consists of an annual business meeting, held in conjunction with the National Education Association convention. The organization also promotes educational flights to Europe and Africa; provides hospitality to foreign educators; and reports overseas educational experiences to colleagues, students, and the public. Members receive *AOE Newsletter* three times a year.

Central Michigan University
Mt. Pleasant, Michigan 48859 USA

ASSOCIATION OF PARTIALLY OR WHOLLY FRENCH-LANGUAGE UNIVERSITIES (Association des universités partiellement ou entièrement de langue française)

The *Association des universités partiellement ou entièrement de langue française* (AUPELF: Association of Partially or Wholly French-Language Universities) was founded September 1961 in Montreal, Canada, and registered in accordance with the law of the state of Quebec. The association aims to develop international cooperation in teaching and research among the partially or wholly French-language universities; to provide information or technical services for these universities; and to encourage a permanent cultural exchange among Africa, the East, and the West.

Regular membership consists of about one hundred universities in twenty-eight countries where French is the principal or one of the principal languages of teaching. Associate membership includes 15 schools and other establishments of higher education that teach in French at the university level and 125 departments or centers of French studies at non-French-speaking universities. AUPELF has consultative status with UNESCO and is a member of the International Association of Universities.

The general assembly that convenes every three years elects the secretary general. The council of administration, composed of eleven members, meets once a year. Four permanent commissions are concerned with documentation, cooperation, the French language, and university economic relations. The general secretariat is maintained at Montreal and undersecretariats in Paris and Dakar, Senegal.

AUPELF studies the evolution of the university and its place in society, circulates scientific information, arranges cultural encounters, supports new universities in developing countries, and provides information services. The association helps French departments of non-French-speaking universities and encourages relations between these departments and the university members of AUPELF in the publication of scientific books and periodicals in French. AUPELF has initiated a service charged with studying pedagogical innovations in particular fields of study and institutions. The service is equally concerned with taking stock of university activities in adult education.

Since 1968 the AUPELF Fund for International University Cooperation has supported new universities and assured the financing of original cooperative ventures conducted by the association itself. Training for young university librarians and administrators is also being financed, and plans are under way to fund professors from universities of the Maghrib, Africa, and the Orient. In 1971 and 1972 AUPELF organized seminars for French-speaking universities and publishing houses to discuss ways of improving the market for scientific and technical books.

At a 1970 AUPELF meeting in Abidjan, Ivory Coast, the role of the university as a propelling element of continuing education was discussed. At a 1971 conference in Tananarive, Malagasy Republic, AUPELF members examined the role of the university in promoting African development and emphasized the importance of interuniversity cooperation. During the international meeting in Quebec in 1972, AUPELF established an information and liaison service for more than one thousand French departments and study centers at non-French-speaking universities throughout the world.

A permanent information service on equivalence was established in 1971. At that time AUPELF published *Répertoire des études supérieures et des équivalences de titres, de diplômes et de périodes entre les universités de langue française* (Report of Higher Studies and Equivalences of Titles, Diplomas, and Length of Study Among the French-Language Universities).

AUPELF publishes *Répertoire des thèses de doctorat soutenues devant les universités de langue française* (Report of Doctoral Theses at French-Language Universities), biannually. The association also offers a microfiche service for French-language universities as well as a microedition service.

University of Montreal
B.P. 6128
Montreal 101, Quebec, Canada

ASSOCIATION OF POLYTECHNIC TEACHERS, United Kingdom

The Association of Polytechnic Teachers (APT) was founded in May 1973 to represent the interests of teaching and related staff in the thirty-one polytechnics in England, Wales, and Northern Ireland (Scotland has a separate system). APT seeks parity between polytechnics and universities over such issues as staff salaries and working conditions, to broaden understanding of polytechnic education, and to promote the concept of a polytechnic community.

APT membership at the end of 1975 was approximately three thousand. Each member also belongs to a local association in the polytechnic where he is employed. The majority of members are on the teaching staff. Funding is entirely from members' subscriptions, with a part retained by the local association.

The head office of APT is at Southsea, England, where the full-time staff consists of a chief executive, an executive officer, and a field officer based in the Midlands. Other members of the national executive are honorary, elected annually by the APT council, on which all local associations are represented in proportion to their membership. Specialist panels provide additional services to members and formulate policy in such areas as health and safety, legal assistance, education, overseas students, pensions and salaries.

Activities of APT have included proposals for a radical overhaul of the teachers' pension scheme; conferences on modular courses and teacher education in polytechnics; and action on behalf of overseas students in Britain. Submissions to committees of inquiry include the Houghton Committee on Teachers' Pay, the Parliamentary Inquiries into Department of Education and Science Priorities in Decision-Making and into University Research, and the Layfield Committee on Local Government Finance.

The main channel of communication between the executive and the membership is a monthly bulletin supplemented by information sheets. In addition, a discussion paper has been published on student services in the polytechnics.

11 Queens Keep
Clarence Parade
Southsea, England

VIVIAN S. GAY

ASSOCIATION OF PRIVATE JUNIOR COLLEGES IN JAPAN
(Nihon shiritsu tanki-daigaku kyokai), Japan

The *Nihon shiritsu tanki-daigaku kyokai* (Association of Private Junior Colleges in Japan) groups 424 private junior colleges throughout Japan. The association seeks to enrich junior college education and increase governmental financial aid to these colleges. Funded primarily through membership dues, the association also receives support from the Japanese government for group study and training.

Twelve officers operate the Tokyo head-quarters. The association has twelve research committees focusing on problems of student placement, personnel services, libraries, accounting, administration, school affairs, junior college system, and courses in home economics, kindergarten teacher training, physical education, and English and Japanese literature.

The association publishes *Junior College Education,* annually, and *Junior College Information,* monthly. *Introductory Pamphlet to the Industrial World* and *Junior College in Japan* are issued biennially. The latter is available in English.

4-2-25 Kudan-Kita
Chiyoda-ku
Tokyo, Japan

MINORU NAKAHARA

ASSOCIATION OF
PUBLIC UNIVERSITIES
(Koritsu daigaku kyokai), Japan

The *Koritsu daigaku kyokai* (Association of Public Universities) groups thirty-three public (prefectural and municipal) universities in Japan. Encouraging cooperation among the universities, the association deals with administration and management of public universities, scientific research in the universities, and educational planning.

Osaka City University
459 Sugimoto-cho, Sumiyoshi-ku
Osaka, Japan

ASSOCIATION OF SOUTHEAST
ASIAN INSTITUTIONS
OF HIGHER LEARNING

A nongovernmental organization, the Association of Southeast Asian Institutions of Higher Learning (ASAIHL) was founded in 1956 at a meeting in Bangkok of the heads of eight state universities in Southeast Asia. ASAIHL consists of forty-six members, representing institutions of higher learning in seven countries of South-

east Asia and two associate members from Japan and the United States.

The purpose of the ASAIHL is to assist member institutions to strengthen themselves through mutual self-help and achieve international distinction in teaching, research, and public service. ASAIHL fosters the development of the institutions themselves, and the cultivation of a sense of regional identity and interdependence with other regional and international organizations concerned with research and teaching. Serving as a clearinghouse of information, the association provides advisory services and promotes discussions of academic and general university development. ASAIHL assists member institutions in the recruitment and placement of faculty and staff, exchanges of professors and students, and development of cooperative arrangements on specific projects. Funding of ASAIHL comes from membership fees and foundation grants.

ASAIHL promotes academic interchange through scholar exchanges and fellowships. ASAIHL has also aided in the formation of regional learned societies, such as the Southeast Asian Social Science Association and the Southeast Asian Mathematical Society.

Seminars are held at least twice a year on specific academic topics or general university topics such as university administration. ASAIHL sponsors a lectureship at member institutions once a year to give recognition to outstanding scholars in the region.

ASAIHL publishes seminar reports, a newsletter, and *Handbook of Southeast Asian Institutions of Higher Learning.*

Ratasastra Building
Chulalongkorn University
Bangkok, Thailand

ASSOCIATION OF
SOUTHEAST ASIAN NATIONS

The Association of Southeast Asian Nations (ASEAN) was established in August 1967 to step up and stabilize economic progress in the South East Asian region. Member states are Indonesia, Malaysia, Philippines, Singapore, and Thailand. The association aims to accelerate economic growth, social progress, and cultural development in the region; to promote regional peace and stability through justice and law; to encourage collaboration on matters of common interest in the economic, social, cultural, technical, scientific, and administrative fields; to share training and research facilities; and to work for the improvement of trade, transportation, communication facilities, and living standards. Other objectives include promoting Southeast Asian studies and establishing and maintaining relationships with regional and international organizations that have similar aims.

Structurally, the association is composed of a ministerial conference, a standing committee, permanent committees, and special committees. The ministerial conference, comprised of foreign ministers of the states, meets annually; the standing committee meets once a month for consultation in Bangkok. There are permanent committees on food and agriculture at Kuala Lumpur, Malaysia; shipping at Djakarta, Indonesia; communications and air traffic services at Manila, Philippines; civil air transport at Bangkok, Thailand; commerce and industry, Singapore; transport and communications, Manila; science and technology, Djakarta; mass media, Manila; finance, Manila; tourism, Kuala Lumpur; sociocultural activities, Manila.

Special committees include the Coordinating Committee of ASEAN Nations, Bangkok; ASEAN Brussels Committee, Brussels, Belgium; ASEAN Coordinating Committee for Reconstruction and Rehabilitation of Indochina States, Kuala Lumpur; Special Committee of the ASEAN Central Banks and Monetary Authorities, Bangkok; and the ASEAN Geneva Committee, Geneva, Switzerland.

Specific efforts have been made to increase trade in the ASEAN region and the rest of the world. Established in March 1973, the ASEAN Geneva Committee deals with multilateral trade negotiations under the General Agreement on Tariffs and Trades, a multilateral treaty.

In the area of joint research and technology, technical experts and training facilities have been shared, and comprehensive programs have been drawn up to investigate such problems as food technology, corrosion of metals, and water resources. Exchanges include those for teachers, students, and social workers. Other cultural exchanges include tours by theater and dance groups, art exhibits, and sharing of films, visual aids, radio, and television programs.

Concerted efforts have been made to pool airline services, develop an Asian shipping line (June 1968 agreement between ASEAN countries), and build up the telecommunications network in the ASEAN region. In order to promote tourism, ASEAN nationals are able to visit member countries for a seven-day visa-free period. ASEAN is actively involved in tourist promotion.

Ministry of Foreign Affairs
Bangkok, Thailand

ASSOCIATION OF TEACHERS IN TECHNICAL INSTITUTES, New Zealand

The Association of Teachers in Technical Institutes (ATTI) was established to safeguard the interests of its members, to further the advancement of technical and general education, and to establish closer relations with teachers and students of technical and vocational education, both nationally and overseas.

Its membership consists of full-time tutors in the technical institutes, community colleges, and farm training institutes, as well as community education officers who are paid on technical institute salary scales. Membership in ATTI is voluntary, but more than 95 percent of those eligible are members. The present membership totals 1370.

The annual conference, consisting of representatives from each branch, is the chief policymaking body of ATTI. A national executive council—consisting of a president and two vice-presidents, elected by the annual conference, and a representative from each branch—has responsibility for the implementation and direction of association policies. The general secretary is a full-time, permanent, salaried officer of the association. The only income for ATTI is derived from membership subscriptions.

The association is recognized by the government as a service organization, with sole negotiating rights for the salaries and conditions of service for the tutors in the technical institutes and community colleges. These negotiations are conducted with the department of education. ATTI also maintains a legal aid fund, which may be used for the advice and support of members involved in disciplinary or dismissal proceedings.

ATTI is also actively engaged in consultations and negotiations with the Department of Education on certain aspects of vocational and continuing education, such as curriculum development, in-service training of tutors, establishment of tertiary teachers' certificates, and establishment of new courses. Furthermore, it is closely involved in liaison and negotiation with statutory bodies—such as the Vocational Training Council and its industry training boards, the Technician Certification Authority, and the Trades Certification Board—whose responsibilities lie in the fields of continuing education.

The publications of ATTI include the *ATTI Journal,* quarterly, and the *ATTI Newsletter,* which is published every two weeks and circulated to members.

Peters Building
80A Queens Drive
Lower Hutt, New Zealand

R. W. S. FARGHER

ASSOCIATION OF TEACHERS OF THE ROYAL UNIVERSITY OF MALTA

The Association of Teachers of the Royal University of Malta (ATRUM) was formed in 1947, with the following objectives: to develop academic fraternity among Royal University teachers and promote their general welfare; to protect the independence and freedom of teaching and research; to examine problems that may be referred to the association; to promote cooperation between the members of the different faculties; and to collaborate with other bodies, local or foreign, whose interests may be similar—in particular with national associations of university teachers, international bodies of professors and research workers. Furthermore, ATRUM aims to defend and promote the interests of the Royal University and its teachers, to secure representation on any executive or advisory body on matters affecting the Royal University and its teachers, and to deal with any other matter considered by the association to be in its interests.

Membership is open to all teachers of the university during their tenure of office and to emeritus professors of the university. Fully paid-up membership varies between seventy and eighty from year to year; funds are obtained solely through members' annual subscriptions.

ATRUM is governed by a council, consisting of the president, vice-president, secretary, treasurer, and three other members. All seats on the council are by election during the annual general meeting, held in January/February. ATRUM is affiliated with the International Association of University Professors and Lecturers.

No publications as such are issued by ATRUM. Members publish their own papers and books in their various specialties, either in ad hoc journals or as separates at the Royal University of Malta Press.

Royal University of Malta
Msida, Malta

ASSOCIATION OF UNIVERSITIES
AND COLLEGES OF CANADA
(Association des universités et collèges du Canada)

The Association of Universities and Colleges of Canada (AUCC) is a national, voluntary organization grouping sixty-three universities and colleges, including all Canadian degree-granting institutions. Founded in 1911, the association received its present name and structure in 1965 by act of the Canadian Parliament. The objective of the association is to promote the interest of higher education in Canada. It provides a forum for discussions of national and international concerns of higher education, offers a focal point for voluntary coordination of action among member institutions, and provides information on Canadian higher education to all interested individuals and groups.

Membership in AUCC is institutional. Associate membership is open to national, interuniversity groups with academic or administrative concerns. Honorary associates include the Canada Council and the National Research Council.

The association is supported by fees of member institutions. Additional support is derived from publication sales. Substantial financial assistance is received from granting bodies for major research projects.

The governing body of the association is a twenty-five-member board of directors. The president, vice-president, and members of the board are elected at the annual general meeting. The board is representative of the academic community and includes faculty, students, and administrators. The affairs of the association are administered by the executive director, who is responsible to the board of directors. He is an ex officio member of the board and secretary to the association's Committee of Presidents. The secretariat is composed of five directorates, which provide bilingual service related to the association's activities: the National Programs Directorate, the International Programs Directorate, the Office of Administration, the Finance Office, and the Information Directorate.

The National Programs Directorate is concerned with liaison with association members, other Canadian educational bodies, departments and agencies of the federal government, provincial ministries responsible for higher education, provincial grants commissions, and provincial and regional private and public bodies concerned with Canadian higher education. The directorate prepares materials and performs small research projects related to university problems. Major research projects, contracted out to commissioners, are funded from outside sources, including foundations and federal granting bodies. Projects include a Commission on Canadian Studies and a study of teaching in the health sciences. The directorate also is responsible for relations with the business community and, as part of this responsibility, administers a program of corporate scholarships and participates in an annual industry-university conference. Projects completed by the National Programs Directorate include *Planning for Planning,* a report on planning in universities and between these universities and government; *Quest for the Optimum,* a report on the rationalization of university research; *Health Manpower Output of Canadian Educational Institutions;* and *Athletic Programs in Canadian Universities.*

The International Programs Directorate is concerned with the association's relationships with other national and international educational bodies, departments and agencies of the federal government that handle Canada's external affairs, and other individuals and bodies concerned with international education. The directorate evaluates Canadian degree and diploma equivalencies for AUCC members and foreign credentials for AUCC members and government employers; administers 120 foreign government scholarships; and, under agreement with the Canadian government, is responsible for the Commonwealth Scholarship and Fellowship Plan.

The Office of Administration is responsible for the sales and distribution of all AUCC publications and provides many of the administrative services of the secretariat, including internal and external mail, files, supplies, duplicating, proofreading, translation, conference planning, and other support services. The Finance Office is responsible for all financial matters pertaining to the association. In addition, the office administers a data-processing center and an in-house printing operation.

The Information Directorate is responsible for the association's publications and reports. The association publishes *Universities and Colleges of Canada,* annual directory; *University Affairs/Affaires universitaires,* monthly news and opinion magazine which includes notices of academic and administrative positions available; and *Canadian Directory to Foundations.* The directorate provides information to Canadian and foreign students who plan to study at a Canadian university and assists individuals and groups in the Canadian and foreign academic communities by collecting and maintaining information on Canadian higher education.

The AUCC library, including approximately 12,000 books, 360 journal subscriptions, 100,000 newspaper clippings, 8000 pamphlets, and 1500 government documents, forms part of the Information Directorate. Together the two offices offer a complete information service.

151 Slater Street
Ottawa, Ontario, Canada K1P 5N1

ASSOCIATION OF UNIVERSITIES OF BANGLADESH

The Association of Universities of Bangladesh was formed in February 1972 to advise the universities and administration on matters of higher education, such as the maintenance of appropriate academic standards and coordination of university programs on teaching, research, and administration. The association consists of three members from each university, including the vice-chancellor and two other nominees of the academic council. The vice-chancellors are ex officio members while the other members serve one-year terms.

The Standing Committee of the Vice-Chancellors, consisting of all vice-chancellors, is the executive body of the association. The office of the chairperson, of the association and the standing committee, rotates annually among the vice-chancellors in sequence according to the universities' founding dates.

In 1972 the association formed an Inter-University Sports Board to promote and develop games and athletic activities among university students in Bangladesh. The board is composed of all members of the Standing Committee of Vice-Chancellors and the universities' directors of physical education. The chairperson and the secretary of the Association of Universities of Bangladesh are the ex officio chairperson and the treasurer of the board, respectively. The director of physical education of the university whose vice-chancellor is the chairperson of the association is the secretary of the sports board. The association is financed by membership fees and government grants.

An annual handbook of universities is published by the association.

25 Shyamolee Bagh
Dacca-15, Bangladesh

ASSOCIATION OF UNIVERSITY PROFESSORS, PAKISTAN

The Association of University Professors, Pakistan was formed in December 1971 following an organizational meeting of university professors in the office of the vice-chancellor of Punjab University, Lahore. University professors from Punjab

University, Lahore; the University of Engineering and Technology, Lahore; and the Agricultural University, Lyallpur, participated in forming the new organization.

The association promotes professionalism among its members; fosters cooperation in the academic community; and helps to uphold standards of education and research. Providing a forum for discussions on national and international developments in the fields of education, culture, science, and technology, the association holds conferences and seminars on matters affecting the academic life of Pakistan. The association also holds informative meetings on the foreign policy of Pakistan, educational policy, administrative reform, and certain aspects of medicine. In addition, it assists the national government in establishing policies in education, research, and culture and fosters academic freedom in educational institutions.

The structure of the association consists of a general council and a syndicate. The syndicate, acting as the executive body of the general council, is made up of two representatives from each university, a secretary general, three joint secretaries, and a treasurer. The chairperson, elected on a rotating basis, acts as the chief executive of the association and presides at the meetings of the general council.

8 Zafar Ali Road
Lahore, Pakistan

ASSOCIATION OF UNIVERSITY TEACHERS (SCOTLAND)

The Association of University Teachers (Scotland) traces its origin back to 1921, when local associations of university teachers were started in four Scottish universities. Representatives of these bodies met in council for the first time in Edinburgh on May 6, 1922, and formed the Association of University Teachers of Scotland. In 1949 the association merged with the Association of University Teachers (AUT) but retained its separate identity as AUT (Scotland).

The objectives of the association are to advance university education, scholarship, and research in Scotland; to promote better communication among university teachers; to further and safeguard their interests; and to confer with the Association of University Teachers in England, Wales, and Ireland and with other educational associations on matters pertaining to education.

Membership to AUT(S) is open to all levels of full-time university teachers, research workers, academic library staff, and senior administrative staff. Its membership as of 1974 was in excess of 22,000. It alternates the holding of its annual general meeting at each of its member universities.

The association is essentially a trade union, with branches in every university and college in Scotland. In addition, there are some attached members in certain recognized institutions and corresponding members in overseas university institutions. Local associations send representatives to a meeting of the central council twice a year. The central council, together with an executive committee, initiates and coordinates general policy and seeks the opinion of members on matters of general and academic concern. Reports are then prepared on these issues; after consideration by the local associations and final approval by the council, the reports are made available to the general public.

AUT(S) has worked for mutual understanding and exchange of views with university staffs of other countries. It has arranged social and cultural events as well as meetings between school administrators and students to discuss matters of mutual interest. AUT(S) has recommended increasing the proportion of nonprofessional staff on faculties and senates and has worked for the betterment of salaries and fringe benefits.

The *Bulletin* is published by the association six times a year and is distributed to members only.

Department of Botany
University of Glasgow W2
Glasgow, Scotland

ASSOCIATION OF UNIVERSITY TEACHERS, United Kingdom

The Association of University Teachers (AUT), founded in June 1919, aims to advance university education and research, to regulate relations between university teachers and their employers, to promote united action by university teachers, and to safeguard the interests of its members. Membership is open to all full-time university teachers, research workers, academic library staff, and senior administrative staff in the United Kingdom. AUT is essentially a trade union, with branches in every university and university college in England, Wales, Scotland, and Northern Ireland; in addition, there are some attached members in certain recognized institutions and corresponding members in overseas university institutions. The association has a present membership of over 28,000.

The local associations send representatives to a central council, which meets twice a year; its business and that of its executive committee is to determine and coordinate general policy and to secure the opinion of members on matters which, after consideration by the local associations and final approval by council, are made available to the general public and presented as the views of the association.

AUT has representative negotiating rights for salaries and salary-related matters through the national negotiating machinery.

The AUT *Bulletin* is published six times a year and is distributed to members only.

United House
1 Pembridge Road
London W 11 3HJ, England

                              LAURIE SAPPER

ASSOCIATION OF UNIVERSITY TEACHERS OF NEW ZEALAND

Founded in 1923, the Association of University Teachers of New Zealand (AUT) is a professional organization that aims to advance university education and research and to further the interests of its members. AUT is composed of 2400 members, representing 85 percent of the university teachers of New Zealand, as well as a few senior library and administrative staff members. For many years AUT was a federation of branch associations, coordinated by a national standing committee. In 1967 it became an incorporated society with a national office (at Victoria University of Wellington) staffed by a part-time executive secretary, a part-time research secretary, and two clerical assistants. The major policymaking bodies of the association are the council, which meets annually, and the executive committee, which meets three times a year. AUT is funded solely from members' subscriptions.

On topics of professional interest, AUT conducts national seminars and presents submissions to the government or other appropriate bodies. AUT has been involved in negotiations for national academic salary scales and informal arbitration on matters of concern to its members.

The official publication of the association is the *A.U.T. Bulletin*. The *Bulletin* is published approximately five times a year.

P.O. Box 28-017
Wellington, New Zealand

ASSOCIATION OF URBAN UNIVERSITIES, United States

The Association of Urban Universities, founded in 1914, is comprised of colleges and universities, both public and private, that are located in metropolitan areas throughout the United States. The association promotes the study of adult education, community service, university extension, and other problems of interest to urban universities.

An annual meeting is held for heads and chief officers of member institutions.

Jacksonville University
Jacksonville, Florida 32211 USA

ASTRONOMY (Field of Study)

Astronomy deals with the totality of the universe, over every epoch, including all constituent parts, such as galaxies, stars, interstellar matter, planets, and moons. The electronics and space eras have opened the entire electromagnetic spectrum to observation and have facilitated *in situ* studies of the greater terrestrial environment. The phenomena investigated range from the birth of the cosmos to the death of stars, including recently discovered bizarre objects that emit many billions of times more energy than our sun and others that are so massive yet densely compacted that they literally crush themselves from the universe. Responsible astronomers and august scientific organizations are even asserting that interstellar communication with extraterrestrial beings appears achievable, possibly in our lifetimes.

Within the 1965–1975 decade observational astronomy has revealed a universe previously unknown and unimagined by man; concomitantly, theoretical astrophysics has challenged the fundamental tenets of contemporary science. In a sense, modern astronomy has lost some of its traditional romantic appeal as it has become increasingly esoteric and technical; yet, in a more profound sense, it has become increasingly vital and philosophically enriching, for one of mankind's most ennobling achievements is its ability to comprehend a system far vaster than itself. Humans are now peering back to the beginning of the universe and reconstructing the entire saga of cosmic evolution— of nuclei, galaxies, stars, planets, and life. Without astronomy this epoch could not be understood.

Astronomy as a discipline may be divided into three basic groups: observational astronomy, theoretical astrophysics, and laboratory astrophysics. The first division, observational astronomy, may be further subdivided into visual astronomy, radio astronomy, and space astronomy. Visual astronomy deals with observations of celestial objects, usually photographically, in the restricted part of the electromagnetic spectrum that can be seen by the human eye. This research is traditionally done from the earth's surface with conventional telescopes, but a modern extension into the infrared is carried out from high-flying airplanes. Radio astronomy refers to observations of celestial objects in the radio portion of the electromagnetic spectrum. The antennae, which often resemble large radar dishes, can detect natural emanations from such diverse objects as Jupiter, dying stars, and exploding galaxies. Space astronomy refers to observations by detectors above the earth's surface, such as balloons, rockets, earth satellites, or deep space probes. The observations frequently are taken in both visible and nonvisible parts of the spectrum, and some space experiments analyze particles as well as light. The second division of astronomy, theoretical astrophysics, concerns the mathematical and physical examination of celestial objects and phenomena; the determination of the sun's internal temperature and composition on the basis of its external features is one example of the kind of research done in theoretical astrophysics. Laboratory astrophysics, a relatively small discipline, refers to laboratory simulations of some astronomical conditions.

Using the methods employed in these various branches of astronomy, astronomers usually specialize in basic topics, such as instruments and techniques, solar systems, the sun, stellar structure, interstellar matter, stellar motions, ultrahigh-energy stars, extragalactic objects, and cosmology.

Astronomy increasingly offers to all sciences the ultimate laboratory—the universe. Because the field unites the sciences in a multidisciplinary endeavor, it simultaneously offers a vehicle for interdisciplinary instruction. Its closest cognate areas are physics and mathematics; indeed, some authorities consider astronomy to be a subdiscipline of physics, although others perceive it as a field in its own right. Because astronomy permits examination of the physical world under the widest possible conditions, it simultaneously challenges both experimental and theoretical physics. Modern astronomy is also highly mathematical; serious research in the field requires several years of university-level mathematics preparation. As physics is the language of astronomy, so is mathematics the language of physics.

Recently chemistry and even biology have been recognized as fields related to astronomy. The origin and evolution of the chemical elements were basically astronomical phenomena, and numerous new discoveries suggest that the genesis of life may be commonplace in the universe. Such developments have even produced the new multidisciplinary field of exobiology.

Other related fields are electronics and radio engineering, allied to radio astronomy. Although radio astronomers generally are quite knowledgeable about these sister subjects, few other astronomers take formal training in them. Computer technology, however, is vital to almost all astronomers.

Astronomy, one of the oldest academic disciplines, was studied in antiquity for both practical and spiritual reasons: practical, because the heavens seemed to influence men's lives; spiritual, because the heavens were thought to be the abode of the gods. This age-old yearning to understand the system and man's place in it ultimately led to the Copernican revolution, which helped usher in an entire intellectual renaissance. From those days until approximately the middle of the nineteenth century, astronomy was taught as part of natural philosophy. Aside from its obvious utility with calendars, tides, and eclipses, from the days of Isaac Newton onward astronomy offered incomparable tests of terrestrial physical theories and also provided new, unexpected discoveries.

In the United States astronomy has been taught since the founding of the first institution of higher education, Harvard University, in the 1630s. In the United States and Western Europe from the early seventeenth century until the mid nineteenth century, astronomy became increasingly a part of the curriculum, often combined with trigonometry, navigation, and surveying. By the mid nineteenth century, however, observational astronomy matured into a discipline in its own right, and the precursors of modern astrophysics began to develop. By 1900 both theoretical and observational astronomy were taught at a number of universities in the United States, Western Europe, the Soviet Union, and a few other countries. Most of the instruction then, however, was descriptive and nonanalytical. As modern physics progressed, astronomical research and instruction became increasingly analytical. From the 1920s until the 1950s the number of professionals in the field increased only modestly, but since the late 1950s the average annual growth rate in the number of astronomers in many Western nations has been greater than that in almost any other scientific discipline. Similarly, in the United States enrollments by university nonscience students in general education courses have also risen dramatically.

Since the early 1960s the physical aspects of astronomy have become increasingly dominant. The discipline a few generations ago stressed sky surveys, positional determinations, and white-light photography; the field today places primacy on theoretical astrophysics, high-energy physics, space probes, and observations in the nonvisible spectrum. Modern astronomy, therefore, requires a solid background in advanced physics and mathematics and expertise in computers and electronics.

These trends in the discipline have been mirrored in its preparatory education. In the United States over half of all professional astronomers obtain their bachelor's degrees in physics, and the majority also obtain their doctorates in physics. Similar situations occur almost worldwide. In

Western nations preparation in astronomy is almost identical to that in physics except that a few elective courses in physics are replaced by astronomy courses.

Probably no other science is more international than astronomy. Perhaps because the universe surrounds us all and belongs to no one, astronomy has been cosmopolitan for centuries. Modern observational astronomers can obtain research time on instruments throughout the world; non-American experiments have even been placed aboard United States space vehicles. Moreover, radio astronomers link their instruments electronically, thereby crossing borders and even spanning continents. And theoreticians readily share their information anywhere. In 1975 the United States and the Soviet Union joined in the first multinational manned-space venture.

In the United States and Canada astronomy is taught only cursorily at the elementary and secondary levels, usually as part of a physics or general science course. Idiosyncratically, however, some school systems have elaborate programs and facilities. There are, for example, several hundred school planetariums. At the postsecondary level, several dozen universities offer undergraduate and graduate programs in the field; almost all of these programs stress physics.

Astronomy education in the United Kingdom generally resembles that in the United States. In Australia, however, there are few undergraduate courses specifically in astronomy. Moreover, although excellent Ph.D. programs exist in the field, they generally are less structured than in the United States and the United Kingdom; instead, with small numbers of students, they rely strongly upon colloquia and individually directed projects. In India two distinct types of astronomical studies exist: traditional and modern. The traditional, taught in Sanskrit, is semimystical. The modern studies, generally taught in English, are patterned after the British system. Some universities teach astronomy

in their mathematical courses. At least two universities give undergraduate degrees in the field, with a basically descriptive coverage; one university has a separate department of astronomy, which offers systematic courses in the field through the graduate level.

In several countries in Western Europe, astronomy is taught as a separate compulsory subject at the elementary or secondary level, but the coverage rarely goes beyond one semester. Only a few undergraduate programs are offered, although astronomy courses frequently are available for undergraduate majors in other fields. The graduate programs vary substantially, but overall they resemble their counterparts in the United States and the United Kingdom.

In Eastern Europe and the Soviet Union, astronomy often is included in the secondary school curriculum. At the undergraduate level astronomy-oriented students usually study physics and mathematics during the first few years, specializing in astronomy only in the latter years.

In Latin America some astronomy is introduced at the elementary and secondary level, but few formal programs exist at the university level. Argentina has a small but vigorous university program and Venezuela offers some courses at four universities. In most Latin countries astronomy is not available as a separate major.

Some astronomy courses are also available in Asia and Africa. In Japan astronomy is included in the general science curriculum at both the junior and senior high school levels, and undergraduate and graduate degree programs in the field are available. Indonesia has some astronomy offerings at the university level and is now expanding its curriculum. In Africa formal university-level astronomy programs are offered only in Egypt and South Africa.

RICHARD BERENDZEN

Levels and Programs of Study

Programs in astronomy generally require as a minimum prerequisite a secondary education, usually in a science program, and lead to the following degrees: Bachelor of Science, Master of Science, the Ph.D., or their equivalents. Programs that lead to a first university degree consist primarily of classroom and laboratory instruction dealing with the fundamental principles of astronomy. At this level the theoretical and general principles of the subjects studied are emphasized, although practical aspects are not ignored. Principal course content usually includes some of the following: basic astronomy, cosmology, fundamentals of celestial mechanics, solar physics, space astronomy, introductory astrophysics, stellar atmospheres, stellar interiors, stellar evolution, pulsating stars, novae and supernovae, interstellar medium and gaseous nebulae, astrometry, stellar classification, observational theory, radioastronomy, and galactic structure. Background courses often included are physics, mathematics, photometry, spectroscopy, interferometric methods, geology, statistics, humanities, social sciences, and languages.

Programs that lead to a postgraduate university degree consist of seminars, study, and laboratory work dealing with advanced topics in the field of astronomy. Emphasis is placed on original research work as substantiated by the presentation of a scholarly thesis or dissertation. Principal subject matter areas within which courses and research projects tend to fall include advanced subjects related to the field of astronomy—subjects such as astrophysical plasma kinetic theory, Riemannian geometry, general relativity theory, cosmological models, radiometers and antennae, solar physics, solar radiation, solar terrestrial effects, lunar astronomical studies, double stars, theory of stellar atmosphere, information theory of noise signals, theory of convolutions, spherical astronomy, nonequilibrium radiative transfer theory, galactic structure, and advanced astrophysics. Subject areas within which background studies tend to fall include fundamentals of celestial mechanics, solar physics, and ap-

propriate specialties in physics and mathematics.

[This section was based on UNESCO's *International Standard Classification of Education (ISCED)* (Paris: UNESCO, 1976).]

Major International and National Organizations

INTERNATIONAL

Central Bureau for Astronomical
    Telegrams (CBAT)
Smithsonian Astrophysical Observatory
60 Garden Street
Cambridge, Massachusetts 02138 USA

Committee on Space Research (COSPAR)
International Council of Scientific
    Unions (ICSU)
7 via Cornelio Celso
00161 Rome, Italy

Federation of Astronomical and Geophysical
    Services (FAGS)
URSI (Union radio-scientifique internationale)
    Secretariat
place Emile Danco 7
1180 Brussels, Belgium

International Astronomical Union (IAU)
Space Research Laboratory of the Astronomical
    Institute
21 Beneluxlaan
Utrecht, Netherlands
    This is the major association; it publishes the important *Transactions of General Assembly* and *Reports on Symposia,* and sponsors the CBAT.

NATIONAL

Australia:
    Astronomical Society of Australia
    % Commonwealth Scientific and
        Industrial Research Organisation
    Division of Radiophysics
    P.O. Box 76
    Epping, New South Wales

Canada:
    Royal Astronomical Society of Canada
    252 College Street
    Toronto 130, Ontario

Federal Republic of Germany:
    Deutsche Forschungsgemeinschaft
    German Research Society
    40 Kennedyallee
    Bad Godesberg

Japan:
    Astronomical Society of Japan
    Tokyo Astronomical Observatory
    Osawa, Mitaka, Tokyo

Soviet Union:
Academy of Sciences of the USSR
Lenin prospekt 14
Moscow

United Kingdom:
Royal Astronomical Society
Burlington House, Piccadilly
London W1, England

United States:
American Astronomical Society (AAS)
211 Fitz-Randolph Road
Princeton, New Jersey 08540

For a world directory of international organizations and national societies in the field consult:

International Physics and Astronomy Directory 1969–70. Reading, Massachusetts: W. A. Benjamin, 1970.

For additional names of international organizations see:

COSPAR Information Bulletin, August 1975, *73,* 79–82.

Principal Information Sources

GENERAL

Guides to the literature include:

Berendzen, R., and DeVorkin, D. "Resource Letter EMAA–1: Educational Materials in Astronomy and Astrophysics." *American Journal of Physics,* 1973, *41*(6), 783–807.
Bibliography of Non-Commercial Publications of Observatories and Astronomical Societies. Utrecht, Netherlands: Sonnenborgh Observatory, 1971. With supplements.
Kemp, D. A. *Astronomy and Astrophysics: A Bibliographical Guide.* London: Macdonald; Hamden, Connecticut: Archon, 1970.
Müller, E. *International Bibliography of Educational Materials in Astronomy.* Geneva: Astronomical Observatory, University of Geneva (for the IAU), 1970. Updated triennially.

Overviews and introductions to the field include:

Abell, G. *Exploration of the Universe.* (2nd ed.) New York: Holt, Rinehart and Winston, 1969.
Baker, R. H., and Frederick, L. W. *Astronomy.* New York: Van Nostrand, 1971.
Hodge, P. *Concepts of Contemporary Astronomy.* New York: McGraw-Hill, 1974.
Jastrow, R., and Thompson, M. H. *Astronomy: Fundamentals and Frontiers.* (2nd ed.) New York: Wiley, 1974.

Histories of the field include:

Abetti, G. *The History of Astronomy.* Translated from the Italian *Storia dell'astronomia* by B. B. Abetti. London: Sidgwick & Jackson, 1954.
Dreyer, J. L. E. *A History of Astronomy from Thales to Kepler.* (2nd ed.) New York: Dover, 1953.
Hoyle, F. *Astronomy.* Garden City, New York: Doubleday, 1962.
Journal for the History of Astronomy. New York: Academic Press, 1970–. A quarterly publication.
Pannekoek, A. *A History of Astronomy.* New York: Wiley-Interscience, 1961.
Shapley, H. *Source Book on Astronomy, 1900–1950.* Cambridge, Massachusetts: Harvard University Press, 1960.
Struve, O., and Zebergs, V. *Astronomy of the 20th Century.* New York: Macmillan, 1962.

Literature discussing education in the field includes:

Berendzen, R. *On the Career Development and Education of Astronomers in the U.S.* Cambridge, Massachusetts: Harvard University Archives, 1968.
Berendzen, R. *International Conference on Education in and History of Modern Astronomy.* New York: New York Academy of Science, 1972.
Journal of College Teaching, December 1973, *3*(2). This issue is on astronomy; its guest editor is R. Berendzen.
Miller, F. D. *How to Become an Astronomer.* Cambridge, Massachusetts: Sky Publishing, 1974.
Müller, E. *International Bibliography of Educational Materials in Astronomy.* Geneva: Astronomical Observatory, University of Geneva (for the IAU), 1970. Updated triennially.

CURRENT BIBLIOGRAPHIES

Astronomy and Astrophysics Abstracts. Berlin, Federal Republic of Germany: Springer-Verlag, 1969–.
Bulletin signalétique. Part 120: *Astronomie et astrophysique; Physique du globe.* Paris: Centre national de la recherche scientifique, 1961–.
International Aerospace Abstracts. New York: AIAA (American Institute of Aeronautics and Astronautics) Technical Information Service, 1961–.
Physics Abstracts. London: Institution of Electrical Engineers, 1898–.
Quarterly Check-List of Physics, Including Astronomy and Astrophysics. Darien, Connecticut: American Bibliographic Service, 1960–
Referativnyĭ zhurnal. 51: *Astronomiya.* Moscow: Akademia nauk, SSSR, Institut nauchnoĭ informatsii, 1953–. Published monthly.

PERIODICALS

Some of the important periodicals in the field are *Acta Astronomica* (Poland), *American Astronomical Society Bulletin, Astronomical Institutes of Czechoslovakia Bulletin/Astronomiceskich institutov Cechoslovakii Bulletin, Astronomical Journal* (US), *Astronomical Society of Japan. Publications, Astronomical Society of the Pacific. Publications* (US), *Astronomicheski zhurnal/Soviet Astronomy, Astronomie* (France), *Astronomische Nachrichten* (GDR) *Astronomy* (UK) *Astronomy and Astrophysics* (FRG), *Astrophysical Journal* (US), *Astrophysical Letters* (UK), *Astrophysics* (US), *Astrophysics and Space Science* (Netherlands), *British Astronomical Association Journal, COSPAR Information Bulletin* (Italy), *Icarus* (US), *International Astronomical Union Information Bulletin* (Netherlands), *Irish Astronomical Journal* (N. Ireland), *Journal for the History of Astronomy* (UK), *Journal of the British Astronomical Society, Moon* (Netherlands), *Nature* (UK), *Planetary and Space Science* (US, UK), *Royal Astronomical Society Monthly Notices* (UK), *Royal Astronomical Society of Canada Journal, Royal Astronomical Society Quarterly Journal* (UK), *Sky and Telescope* (US), *Società astronomica italiana memorie, Solar Physics* (Netherlands), *Southern Stars* (New Zealand), *Space Science Reviews* (Netherlands), *Stubll si cercetari de astronomie* (Romania).

For a list of astronomical periodicals see:

Astronomy and Astrophysics Abstracts. Berlin, Federal Republic of Germany: Springer-Verlag, 1969–.

International Aerospace Abstracts. New York: AIAA Technical Information Service, 1961–.

Kemp, D. A. *Astronomy and Astrophysics: A Bibliographical Guide.* London: Macdonald; Hamden, Connecticut: Archon, 1970. See pages xi–xxiii.

ENCYCLOPEDIAS, DICTIONARIES, HANDBOOKS

Allen, C. W. *Astrophysical Quantities.* (3rd ed.) London: Athlone Press, 1973.

Klezcek, J. *Astronomical Dictionary in Six Languages.* New York: Academic Press, 1961. Languages included are English, Russian, German, French, Italian, and Czechoslovakian.

Kuiper, G. R., and Middlehurst, B. (Eds.) *Stars and Stellar Systems Series.* Chicago: University of Chicago Press, 1960–.

Pecker, J. C. (Ed.) *Astronomer's Handbook.* London: Academic Press, International Astronomical Union, 1966.

Russian-English-Chinese Dictionary of Astronomy. (3rd ed.) London: Scientific Information Consultants, 1966.

Satterthwaite, G. B. *Encyclopedia of Astronomy.* London: Hamlyn, 1970.

Thewlis, J. (Ed.) *Encyclopaedic Dictionary of Physics.* Oxford, England: Pergamon Press, 1961–1963. Includes terms used in astronomy and astrophysics. Volume 9 is a glossary in English, French, German, Spanish, Russian, and Japanese.

Voigt, H. H. (Ed.) *Landolt-Börnstein Numerical Data and Functional Relationships in Science and Technology.* Group VI, Vol. I: *Astronomy and Astrophysics.* Berlin, Federal Republic of Germany: Springer-Verlag, 1965.

Weigert, A., and Zimmermann, H. *A Concise Encyclopedia of Astronomy.* New York: American Elsevier, 1968. A translation from German by J. H. Dickson.

DIRECTORIES

Directory of Physics and Astronomy Faculties in North American Colleges and Universities 1974/75. New York: American Institute of Physics, annual. Lists institutions and faculty in the United States, Canada, Mexico, and Central America which offer degrees in astronomy and physics.

International Physics and Astronomy Directory 1969–70. Reading, Massachusetts: W. A. Benjamin, 1970. Includes a worldwide list of academic departments and faculties of physics and astronomy.

Rigaux, F. *Les observatoires astronomiques et les astronomes.* Brussels: Observatoire royal de Belgique, 1959. Supplement, 1961.

U.S. Nautical Almanac Office. *American Ephemeris and Nautical Almanac.* Washington, D.C.: U.S. Government Printing Office, 1852–. Published annually; lists observatories worldwide by coordinates.

RESEARCH CENTERS, INSTITUTES, INFORMATION CENTERS

Center for Astrophysics (Joint Offices of the Harvard College Observatory and the Smithsonian Astrophysical Observatory)
60 Garden Street
Cambridge, Massachusetts 02138 USA

European Southern Observatory
Bergedorferstrasse 131
205 Hamburg 80, Federal Republic of Germany

European Space Research Organization
Organisation européenne de recherches spatiales
114 avenue de Neuilly
92 Neuilly-sur-Seine, France

Hale Observatories
813 Santa Barbara Street
Pasadena, California 91106 USA

International Latitude Observatory of
   Mizusawa
Mizusawa
Iwate-ken, Japan

Kitt Peak National Observatory
Tucson, Arizona 85717 USA

Lick Observatory
University of California
Santa Cruz, California 95060 USA

NASA Headquarters
Washington, D.C. 20546 USA
   The home office for dozens of centers and
institutes.

Royal Greenwich Observatory
Herstmonceuz Castle
Hailsham, Sussex, England

   See the following:

*International Physics and Astronomy Directory,
   1969–70.* Reading, Massachusetts: W. A.
   Benjamin, 1970. Includes a list of government and industrial physics and astronomy
   research facilities in the United States.
The World of Learning. London: Europa, 1947–.
   Published annually. Lists the principal research institutes and observatories in countries throughout the world.

ATHLETICS IN HIGHER EDUCATION
See Sport, Interuniversity.

ATHLETICS, INTERCOLLEGIATE
See Sport, Interuniversity.

ATOMIC ENGINEERING
See Nuclear Engineering (field of study).

ATTORNEY, UNIVERSITY

   The focus of this essay is on the role of
university counsel in the United States
(the term *university* is used in its generic
sense to include all institutions of higher
education). The employment of counsel
in the American university system is a rapidly developing trend of great interest to
educators in other countries where such
developments are beginning to take place.

   Within the tenure of some and the memory of many, there was a time when the
role of the attorney in higher education was
barely evident. Litigation was infrequent
and the perceived need for legal consultation was rare. Bequests (anticipated and actual) and property transactions accounted
for most legal work. No informed observer
of the contemporary (mid 1970s) university could draw the same conclusion. The
obvious need of institutions of higher education, as discoverers and analyzers of ideas
and preceptors of knowledge, to be legitimate in the conduct of their own affairs
has focused attention on the university
counsel as a valuable resource. The exposure of the university to litigation-prone
operations and of its governors and officers
to criticism and possible liability for failure
to observe an increasing quantity of legal
strictures has made the retention of counsel indispensable.

   This article examines the role of the
university attorney in discharging the two
classic roles of the legal profession: advice
and representation. The nature of these
roles lends itself easily to a further function—that of policy adviser. Since fulfillment of the role of policy adviser by counsel
is more the result of other factors (personalities and the ability to assess problems
and make policy judgments), it will not
be discussed here, except to note the responsibility of counsel to make sure that
the recipient of advice (the client) is fully
aware when the advice being given relates
to policy rather than law.

Higher Education and the Law

   In its broadest sense, a law is a rule, adherence to which is enforced by governmental action of some kind. Most persons
are familiar with the obvious sources of
law: national and state or provincial constitutions (or other organic enactments);
and national, state or provincial, and municipal statutes and ordinances. These laws

are usually adopted by enactment through a representative assembly or by vote of the people in an initiative or referendum. Most people also recognize as laws ministerial decrees and rules and administrative regulations and orders, validly adopted by an executive authority within the scope of its delegated responsibility. In public universities, these laws may include general orders of the governing board and of the chief executive officers of the institution. By delegation, actions of campus deans and faculty bodies may also have some effect as laws—depending on the authority of the officer or body. Often, such actions acquire a sort of common-law status, in that their force and effect are rooted in years of practice and general acceptance, with correlative expectations that actions taken within such traditional authority will be honored unless clearly overruled at a higher level.

Perhaps least understood as law are private engagements entered into in such a way as to entitle the parties to invoke the assistance of governmental processes to enforce either compliance or a remedy for violations. Contracts are the most obvious example, but there are others: trusts, simple gifts, and property transfers, to name a few. While technically only the rules that authorize resort to governmental processes are laws, the substantive effect is that the transactions themselves become laws with respect to their parties.

The matter does not end here. The internal rules of private institutions, including universities, take on many of the aspects of legislation. Governments not only make laws but enter into contracts with other governmental units and with private parties. When they do, they are usually bound to keep their engagements, much as any private entity. (A traditional exception is that the government cannot be held to a contract in excess of the power of the officer or entity that made it. But substantial inroads have been made on this rule, chiefly through application of the legal principle of estoppel; that is, it would be unfair for

the government to escape its commitments because of a limitation on its agent's authority, if the parties with whom it contracted—and possibly others—reasonably relied on the governmental agent having the power it purported to have, and if no public policy violation would result from the government's performance.)

The principle that even the sovereign may be held to its contractual promises has an especially honored place in the United States—and in the legal affairs of higher education. The leading case is *Trustees of Dartmouth College* v. *Woodward* (4 Wheat. 518, 1819). However, the principle is a sword as well as a shield. If the government (like other contractors) can decide whether or not it chooses to enter into a contract, it can also decide whom it will contract with, what promises it will make, and what it will expect from the other contracting parties. Accordingly, it may insist on adherence to governmental policies as a condition to contracts—even if these policies have little or nothing to do with the principal subject of the contract. This theory is the foundation of the American federal government's affirmative action programs as reflected in Executive Order 11246 of 1965 (as amended in 1967) and a long series of subsequent presidential and departmental rules—and it has been judicially upheld (*Contractors Association of Eastern Pennsylvania* v. *Secretary of Labor*, 442 F. 2d 159, 7th Cir., 1971; *cert. den.* 404 U.S. 854, 92 S. Ct. 98, 1971).

The enormous scope of federal financial assistance to higher education—through contracts, subventions, and grants—gives this approach a pervasive significance. Thus, a series of statutes (for example, Titles VI, VII, and IX of the Civil Rights Act of 1964, as amended in 1972, as well as Executive Order 11246 and other executive rules) conditions receipt of federal benefits on nondiscrimination and affirmative action to end the effects of past discrimination. (Virtually all forms of pernicious discrimination are covered by one or more of these enactments: race, religion, ethnicity, national origin, sex, and age.) In the event of nonadherence, federal funds may be cut off (following certain administrative procedures). The result could be serious curtailment of, or even an end to, university operations.

Because university contracts with its own personnel are often "contracts of adhesion" made under circumstances in which the employee has little or no bargaining power over the terms of the agreement, the traditional reluctance of courts to interfere in campus affairs has been tempered with a disinclination to allow the institution to excuse its own omissions on the basis of "fine-print" or "escape-hatch" provisions purporting to authorize it to make ad hoc changes in rules on any subject at any time. (The principle is illustrated in *Greene* v. *Howard University*, 412 F. 2d 1128, D.C. Cir., 1969.)

The work of university counsel is as broad as the exposure of the university to legal problems, and that (as the foregoing discussion suggests) is broad indeed. The modern university, large or small, involves a complex of legal relationships and exposures, both with respect to its internal family of students, faculty, staff, and administrators and with respect to its dealings with others. Few indices are available to measure the discerned need for university legal services. A very rough reflection may be seen in the amount of space devoted to colleges and universities in the West Publishing Company's *Decennial Digests* of reported American cases. The *Digest* for the period 1658 to 1906 devotes thirty-six pages to the topic; *Digests* covering successive ten-year periods thereafter remain at a steady level of about twelve pages each through the 1946–1956 issue; in the 1956–1966 issue, the number increases to twenty pages, and for the first nine years of the current *Digest* period (1966–1975), it runs to over eighty-four. A somewhat closer measure is seen in the growth of the National Association of College and University Attorneys. Founded in 1961, the association has grown over the ensuing fifteen years from a handful of institutions and attorneys to over seven hundred institutions and fifteen hundred attorneys.

A great many factors are responsible for the growth in the number, scope, and seriousness of legal problems affecting higher education. A major factor is an increase in the sophistication of legal analysis. Thus, as late as the 1950s, text writers still analyzed the relation of the university to its students in terms of "privilege versus right"—a useless distinction since each term was defined simply as the antonym of the other. The real issues involve concepts of much greater difficulty. The analysis by the United States Supreme Court of the university-professor relationship in terms of the complex issues of liberty and property is illustrative (*Board of Regents of Wisconsin State Colleges* v. *Roth*, 408 U.S. 564, 92 S.Ct. 2071, 1972; *Perry* v. *Sindermann*, 408 U.S. 593, 92 S.Ct. 2694, 1972).

Other reasons for the growth of legal problems can be found in the enactment of social legislation of special application to the campus and in the elimination of campus exemptions from other social legislation. Examples of the latter are the Fair Labor Standards Act; Title VII of the Civil Rights Act of 1964, as amended in 1972; the Occupational Safety and Health Act; and the Employee Retirement Income Security Act.

More broadly, campuses have felt the effects of unrelated social, economic, and international events (for example, a general rise in the level of social consciousness of students and faculty, the Vietnam war, and birthrate fluctuations); the increased availability of lawyers; and alternate means of delivery of legal services (especially through class actions and group practice). These trends, or others like them, may be expected in the future. There is, in addition, a kind of rhythm in the rise and subsidence of new areas of legal emphasis. In coming years one may expect an increasing body of new rules requiring interpretation and compliance in such areas as energy, environmental protection, and financing, as well as changes in a number of traditional relationships (for example, faculty and student) and an erosion of graduate-undergraduate and public-private distinctions. All will require careful legal analysis and, where appropriate, skilled advocacy on behalf of the university.

Nature of the Legal Relationship

At the heart of the legal profession is the attorney-client relationship. Perhaps more than any of its analogs in other special relationships recognized by the law, the principal focus of this relationship is on the protection of the party served—the client. The attorney is generally held to the highest standards of ethical conduct in dealing with the client. He is a fiduciary and has obligations of full service, disclosure, confidence, and the absence of conflicting relationships and self-dealing. All of these are obligations to the client and may be released only by the client, never by the attorney alone.

There is no reason why these standards should be any less in the case of the university counsel, whether retained or employed. But questions often arise within the complicated university community as to just who is the client. There is an inherent tension between faculty and trustee or executive bodies, often ripening into legal disputes and sometimes into litigation. In a multicampus institution similar disputes may occur among two or more of its units. But these issues are not fundamentally different from similar problems that arise in other complex bodies, governmental and private. Providing separate legal counsel to each disputing unit seems far too great a deference to the special nature of their roles and would probably lead to an increase in the number of disputes and a polarization of the parties. The institution itself should be seen as the client, rather than one or another of its faculties, boards, units, and committees. Of course, university counsel must report at a particular level or to a particular officer or body of the institution, and it is from this source

or under its authority that counsel would receive policy direction. Thus, the placement of counsel in a table of organization (or its practical equivalent) has a significance far beyond questions of budgeting or symmetry on an organization chart; it influences the attorney's discharge of responsibilities within the professional canons governing the attorney-client relationship.

Legal counsel serves the university in a variety of ways. It represents the entity and its officers and staff in administrative and court litigation, in negotiations, and in any number of other relationships. But the most significant role of counsel occurs before policy decisions are taken and, if possible, before issues with outsiders are joined.

There are two cardinal components of legal advice. The first is an assessment of the kinds of legal risk involved. The inquiry here goes to areas of legal exposure, including the laws that are (or may be) applicable to the particular proposal. The second is assessment of the degree of risk. Some actions simply cannot be taken without compliance (for example, the necessity for various permits); in some cases application of a law may be open to question, with various levels of legal consequence flowing from resolution of the question; sometimes legal risk simply cannot be eliminated, only reduced. Having advised with respect to the degree and quality of legal risk, the university counsel should attempt to work constructively and imaginatively with policy and program personnel in an effort to find a way to accomplish as many as possible of the objectives sought, with a minimum of legal risk.

Suppose, for example, a university wished to establish a "tax-sheltered" annuity program through which employees could elect to take a pay reduction, with an amount equivalent to the reduction invested in an annuity on their behalf. If done properly, no income tax is payable on the investment when it is made (Rev. Rul. 63-20, C.B. 1963-1, p 24, 1963). The basic program and objectives are, of course, policy issues.

Once they have been tentatively determined, the proposal should be given to counsel for legal analysis. The attorney may discover that no entity may establish or contract for such a program without approval of the insurance commissioner. This kind of provision is mandatory, and failure to comply would unquestionably halt the program. The attorney may find that "private-ruling" letters from the Internal Revenue Service and the state income tax authority, while not mandatory, are highly desirable for the protection of employees participating in the program; the major drawbacks to obtaining such rulings are the precision needed in formulating the request and the time consumed in processing it. Counsel may also discover that the available annuity contracts do not treat men and women equally (because of actuarial data showing greater longevity for women). Would the arrangement therefore expose the university to loss of federal funds because of noncompliance with federal affirmative action and nondiscrimination requirements? Even if it would not, what if the federal rules (or their interpretation) should change in the future—would the university then be bound to a contract, the honoring of which would place it out of compliance with federal contracts? And what of the exposure to private suits based on Title VII of the Civil Rights Act?

Further complicating features to this relatively simple example are not difficult to imagine. Other more complex problems readily come to mind, such as layoff of personnel as a result of steady-state enrollment or other financial exigency (see, for example, *Johnson* v. *Board of Regents of the University of Wisconsin System*, 377 F. Supp. 227, W.D.Wis. 1974, aff. without opinion 519 F. 2d 975, 7th Cir., 1975). Some of the legal issues leave no choice but to act in a particular way if the program is to be mounted; others suggest possible program decisions; still others can be addressed by contract solutions (for example, in the annuity case, by clauses in the master annuity contract protecting the university and its participating employees)—but only at program or financial cost. What remains is an irreducible level of risk. When the best program has been devised, consonant with policy and legal consideration, the person or board in authority can decide if the advantages sufficiently outweigh the problems.

This sort of analysis occurs, at least subliminally, in almost all decision making. What is relatively new in higher education is the explicit recognition of the necessity of competent legal advice before the policy decision is taken. It is, in essence, the practice of preventive law.

Sources of Legal Service

The three basic sources of legal counsel are staff, outside general counsel, and outside special counsel. There is a limitless number of combinations and permutations of these alternatives.

Staff counsel is, of course, counsel employed on the staff of the institution, on a full- or part-time basis. Such counsel may be found in a single university office (typically termed university or general counsel) or scattered among various offices. The attorneys may be part-time faculty or administrators (or both) or full-time counsel. Sometimes attorney members of the governing board act as counsel—a practice fraught with a number of legal drawbacks, principally based on potential conflicts of interest.

Outside counsel is a law firm or sole practitioner independent of the university, usually serving many other clients. Such counsel is generally retained on a continuing basis and thus has a continuity of service with the university. Included in this category is the arrangement in which some or all legal services to a state university are provided by a statewide governmental office that also serves all other state institutions. Occasionally this arrangement is varied by the permanent on-campus assignment of a deputy to the university.

As the name connotes, special counsel is an attorney or firm retained for a one-time or occasional matter (for example, a specific lawsuit) or to handle a particular but limited kind of problem (for example, patents or collective bargaining) on a continuing basis.

Each of these arrangements has its particular advantages and limitations. Staff attorneys develop an especially intimate knowledge of the institution, its policies, and its personnel. But because their entire energies are devoted to the institution, they may lack exposure to other kinds of legal problems and litigation. Outside counsel is the mirror image of staff counsel; its typical strengths lie in areas of the other's typical weaknesses, and vice versa. Generalizations must be limited, but there is much to be said for having both staff and outside counsel. Staff counsel is available, on a daily basis, to handle virtually all of the legal problems of the campus. Outside counsel may be retained to handle most trial litigation, so as not to entirely tie up staff counsel.

Specialization within staff counsel presents a related problem. A staff of lawyers could divide its work topically, or each attorney could develop the capacity for handling problems over a broad range. There are, again, arguments on both sides. An attorney can become more experienced and knowledgeable in an area if that field (or that and few others) is all he does. But such counsel is then unlikely to have the advantage of being able to call on other areas of the law by analogy or of looking to them for the application or distinction of precedent and legal techniques. Moreover, the temporary absence of the specialized attorney from the office may delay vital legal advice if no one else is in a position to supply it.

There has been an increasing trend among American institutions of higher education to utilize full-time staff counsel. Outside counsel, when used on a continuing basis, usually handle only litigation or special kinds of litigation or, in the case of special counsel, provide advice or representation on a special case or issue. In a 1974 national survey of seventy-three universities (public and private, mostly larger institutions), 70 percent had full-time counsel; but of these, 59 percent had not had such counsel prior to 1960 (Bealle, 1974).

There are several advantages to assigning staff counsel to one central office. Administratively, it assures continuity and consistency of advice, provides a single point of responsibility for rendering the advice, and allows for flexibility in staffing and economy in the use of expensive facilities, such as a law library. It provides important professional advantages as well. Attorneys, especially younger attorneys, work best when they deal on a daily basis with other attorneys engaged in the same enterprise. This arrangement permits an informal but constant flow and pooling of information and techniques and an opportunity to subject legal analysis to the challenge of others. Advice forged in that kind of crucible is often better reasoned than legal conclusions developed in isolation.

The office of staff counsel (however styled) usually reports to the governing board or operating head of the university. Access is the key to effective preventive law. Since counsel's time is valuable and limited, it would be useful to develop some criteria with respect to who has regular access to the attorneys. However, a sufficient degree of flexibility should be provided to accommodate those with a real need for legal advice and to allow counsel to obtain necessary information and assistance from within the university.

Use of Legal Counsel

Several suggestions for the use of university counsel are in order. The first is simply that the university employ counsel and keep that counsel sufficiently involved in the work, policies, and programs of the institution to effectively pursue the practice of preventive law. Second, the attorney should be paid. The kinds of legal problems facing the modern university are far too complex and varied and their consequences to the institution too severe to rely on volunteer services. Third, the university itself should be a member of the National Association of College and University Attorneys. This would enormously expand the resources available to its counsel through access to a national library of attorney-developed materials concerning institutions of higher education, specialized legal publications, workshops and lectures, and other attorneys serving university clients. Fourth, counsel should be encouraged to provide constructive advice and imaginative suggestions. Both the university client and the attorney must have the stamina to receive and provide forthright legal advice. University administrators should not be afraid to seek legal advice for fear of a discouraging answer. When advice is sought, counsel should be given a fair picture of everything bearing on the issue. It is usually better to provide counsel with the actual facts of a situation than with a hypothetical question. The law is characterized by differences of opinion. Counsel cannot be expected to guarantee a particular result but to provide a considered analysis of the relative legal risks presented by alternative courses of action. Fifth, legal advice should be sought at an early stage, and counsel should not delay in providing it. The courses of action available are often a function of time—the longer the delay, the fewer the options.

Above all, however, the use of legal counsel should be predicated on an open, constructive relationship between the appropriate university governors, officers, and staff, on the one hand, and their counsel, on the other.

Bibliography

Alexander, K., and Solomon, E. *College and University Law.* Charlottesville, Virginia: Michie, 1972.

Bealle, R. "Delivery of Legal Service to Institutions of Higher Education." *Journal of College and University Law,* 1974, 2(1), 5.

Blackwell, T. *College Law: A Guide for Administrators.* Washington, D.C.: American Council on Education, 1961.

Blackwell, T. *The College Law Digest, 1935–1970.*
Washington, D.C.: National Association of College and University Attorneys, 1974.

Brown, L. *Preventive Law.* Englewood Cliffs, New Jersey: Prentice-Hall, 1950.

Brubacher, J. S. *The Law and Higher Education: A Casebook.* (2 vols.) Rutherford, New Jersey: Fairleigh Dickinson University Press. 1971.

Brubacher, J. S. *The Courts and Higher Education.* San Francisco: Jossey-Bass, 1971.

Chambers, M. M. *The Colleges and the Courts, 1936–1940.* New York: Carnegie Foundation for the Advancement of Teaching, 1941.

Chambers, M. M. *The Colleges and the Courts, 1946–1950.* New York: Columbia University Press, 1952.

Chambers, M. M. *The Colleges and the Courts Since 1950.* Danville, Illinois: Interstate, 1964.

Chambers, M. M. *The Colleges and the Courts: Faculty and Staff Before the Bench.* Danville, Illinois: Interstate, 1973.

Epstein, N. "The Use and Misuse of College and University Counsel." *Journal of Higher Education,* 1974, 45(8), 635.

Sensenbrenner, R. "University Counsellor: Lore, Logic and Logistics." *Journal of College and University Law,* 1974, 2(1), 13.

Wheeler, J. "The Role of the University Counsel in Dealing with Equal Employment Opportunity Compliance Problems." *The College Counsel,* 1972, 7(1), 249.

Williams, R. *Legal Bases of Boards of Higher Education in Fifty States.* Chicago: Council of State Governments, 1971.

Young, D., and Gehrin, D. *The College Student and the Courts.* Asheville, North Carolina: College Administration Publications, 1973.

Young, D., and Gehrin, D. *College and University Business Administration.* (3d ed.) Washington, D. C.: National Association of College and University Business Officers, 1974.

NORMAN L. EPSTEIN

See also: Affirmative Action; Courts and Higher Education; Legal Aspects of Higher Education.

ATTRITION: WASTAGE IN HIGHER EDUCATION

Wastage is not an attractive word when applied to human beings, but such substitutes as attrition, student mortality, and dropping out have the drawback of implying that all shortcomings reside in the student. Yet brief reflection suggests that, while students are primarily responsible for their own failures, both the institution itself and government policies may contribute to wastage too.

The very definition of wastage rests on individual, institutional, and national conceptions of the roles, purposes, short-term objectives, and long-term aims of higher education. For example, if the role of higher education is entirely to prepare people for the professions, it can be argued that wastage is occurring if students are being recruited and educated for professions in which there is already a surplus of qualified manpower. On the other hand, if the role of higher education is primarily to impart higher learning as an end in itself or to ensure that society will continue to conserve its own and other countries' culture, then we can argue that it is right to continue to educate people in whatever field they choose, not merely in preparation for jobs that may or may not continue to exist. Both purposes of higher education are valid; the latter is perhaps more valid.

Once the broader cultural purposes of higher education are accepted, the operational definition of wastage as a percentage of those who start and do not finish courses is seen to be a rough-and-ready (though still useful) device. The student who enters higher education for even a brief period before dropping out will benefit from the experience, if only by discovering that it has no value for him. That in itself can be a positive experience, less wasteful than persisting in an education that serves none of his needs.

Wastage is therefore a concept that has to be seen within the context of an individual's motivation and personal needs as well as the needs of society. Consideration of the aims and purposes of higher education is fundamental to choice in policies, planning, and provision of higher education, be it national or institutional planning or an individual's own personal plans to invest his resources in a period of higher education.

In India the University Grant Commission (*Report for the Year* 1974) reports that

country's problem of wastage in educating people for jobs that do not exist in quantity sufficient to justify the number of people graduating. The same question is being raised in other countries where not all graduates are able to find jobs that utilize their qualifications. While this is clearly one aspect of wastage, it ignores the question of the right of the individual to pursue higher education in the subject of his choice. The question of whether higher education should be geared to the job market is a perennial one, and any argument that it should be so directed must rest squarely on the accuracy of manpower studies in determining how many graduates in each field the job market can absorb. Manpower studies, however, are never accurate; if they provided the only basis on which to determine the numbers entering higher education, the human wastage involved in young people desiring to be educated and not being admitted might be vast. In addition, strict adherence to manpower projections could lead to a serious shortfall in education for the professions. In the United States the problem is avoided largely by the provision of mass higher education; universities thus provide more than adequate numbers for most professions.

In the People's Republic of China wastage is avoided by not giving degrees or diplomas to any student. This is not to say there is no assessment. On the contrary, while examinations are not set in the way of Western countries, the very low student/staff ratio makes it possible for students to criticize each other, for teachers to criticize students, and for students to criticize teachers, so that a great deal of close assessment occurs daily. The People's Republic is clearly attempting to make higher education relevant to the needs of society (as conservative and radical people alike continually propose in Western societies). In a developing country like the People's Republic of China, this appears a sensible policy, since the greater emphasis is on primary and secondary education to build foundations rather than superstructures, a decision that has not been made in India. Advanced technological societies are, perhaps, able to afford higher education for the masses because they already have an adequate basis of primary and secondary education.

What of wastage in higher education in India and the People's Republic of China? Where can it be said that the worse wastage occurs? In India there are too many graduates, especially in law, for the job market to absorb; in the People's Republic a highly selective system may preclude capable people from higher education. It can be argued equally that no wastage occurs in Chinese higher education because of the concentration on education in lower schools, minimal to optimal recruitment to higher education, continuous assessment, absence of degrees and diplomas and jobs for all who have completed their higher education—the level of employment depending on the students' contributions to society during their period in higher education and before, and on their scholastic achievements.

How can the reasons for wastage be determined? Kerr (1971) rejects "possible universal tests" of effectiveness in systems of higher education—which include such criteria as net contribution of higher education to gross national product, the enhancement and preservation of the cultural heritage, and moral character—because such tests cannot be assessed operationally. Kerr suggests wastage rates can be explained by the quality of preparation in secondary schools and by the admissions policies of postsecondary institutions, but these are only some limited explanations. The Indian University Grants Commission, on the other hand, attributes wastage to the fact that "post-graduate departments in the universities and colleges do not always have the facilities to ensure excellence of teaching, with the result that students who become teachers perpetuate the ineffective teaching which they had themselves received as students [and] this vicious circle has to be broken

somewhere" *(Report for the Year* 1974*).* This is often true, and now many new centers for improving teaching in colleges and universities and for studies in higher education are being established in many countries.

To formulate the concept of wastage as objectively as possible, it is very helpful to consider the terms *gross wastage* and *net wastage.* Gross wastage refers to incompletion of the degrees, diplomas, or certificates for which students enroll, regardless of whether students drop out, fail, or enroll in other courses or institutions. The term *net wastage* suggests that students who have failed or dropped out might well have derived benefit from their courses and takes into account the possibility that such students might transfer to other courses, taking credits with them in the form of units passed. Since dropping out and failure might imply temporary status, net wastage is the more useful definition.

Student Variables

Selection implies that one can predict a student's performance from his record in secondary school; the difference in demands on a student in secondary school and in a university or college is not always recognized. In some countries the admissions interview is regarded as an important adjunct to selection and prediction. This is particularly so in British universities and in faculties such as medicine in many countries. Other adjuncts are examinations, such as the American Scholastic Aptitude Test, which is more objective and scientifically validated than school results.

It has been found consistently—in the United States (Sanford, 1962; Lavin, 1965), in Australia (Anderson, 1964; Sanders, 1948), in New Zealand (Parkyn, 1959), and in Britain (Choppin, 1975)—that the best single predictor is school results. But this predictor is of limited value since correlations between school and university or college performance are seldom higher than .2 or .3. On its own, therefore, school performance rarely accounts for any more than 10 percent of variance in higher education performance, and usually accounts for only 4 percent or less (Astin, 1964). Marginal correlations have been found in other studies. Furthermore, when adjuncts such as entrance interviews and examinations are added to school performance, almost no enhancement of prediction is achieved, and the practice is then to rely entirely on school results again.

Faced with the abortive efforts to improve selection, educators have attempted to predict performance by focusing on such factors as motivation; study habits and attitudes; social, psychological, and financial problems; anxiety; age; nationality; religion; the division of time between study and extracurricular activities; childhood happiness; parental discord; social class; family size; lack of self-confidence; loneliness; and lack of relevance of courses to student goals. Most of these indicators of a student's performance have little to do with prediction in statistical terms; yet there can be little doubt that, for some students, one or more of these might be of critical importance in how well they perform in higher education. Statistically, the most important variables appear to be intellectual ability (however defined), social class, and financial problems. Early deprivation and dominating parents or teachers may also stifle initiative and cognitive style. Motivation is obviously of fundamental importance but difficult to define. Persistence, an outcome of motivation, is more easily studied; yet persistence in school relates only tenuously to persistence in higher education.

Differences in ability in the upper 30 percent of the student population are not of overwhelming importance in wastage. Clearly a modicum of ability must be present for the student to succeed, but Watson (1963) reported that 33 percent of the students who are dropping out of classes were in the upper half and 20 percent were in the top 10 percent of their class in ability. Vernon (1963) reported the overall correlation between measured intelligence

and university attainment to be as low as .2, accounting for only 4 percent variance in achievement. Schonell, Roe, and Meddleton (1962) reported that, while some highly gifted students fail, many average students gain their degrees. However, Eysenck (1947) selected thirty-four well-designed studies from several hundred and found an average correlation of .58 between ability test results and various academic criteria. While this value indicates a correlation of an order rarely found in the social sciences, it still accounts for only 33 percent of the variance, leaving two thirds to be accounted for by other variables.

The factors of deprivation and of dominance on the part of parents (and perhaps teachers) may, in the case of school children, relate strongly to academic achievement, and bear only a slight relationship to social class. While it is not feasible to extrapolate with certainty from primary to higher education, it is possible that children who start life with these handicaps do not achieve as highly as they might in university or college.

Another variable is the desire for education, expressed in terms of a student's intention to stay at school and learn as much as possible. This is clearly of importance and positively related to social class, though the correlation is small. A heavy commitment to learning might be regarded as an index of motivation as opposed to participation in extracurricular activity; yet Malleson (1958, pp. 288–319) poses the more important question—how well do students who engage heavily in other activities organize their time and their work programs? Malleson reports that the great majority of students who fail to graduate do not appear to work fewer hours than those who pass.

What is perplexing about student variables is that almost every one appears to have some relationship to wastage, but the relationship in every case is weak. Multiple correlations yield little more understanding. There is no choice but to revert to selection by school performance almost as an act of faith. While there is some justification for this practice, Parkyn (1959), Anderson (1964), and Schonell, Roe, and Meddleton (1962) find that when this criterion is applied stringently, more students who would have succeeded are excluded from entering higher education than those who would have failed.

By now it is clear that other variables not directly attributable to students are at work, and it is necessary to scrutinize the institutional characteristics, policies, and practices that might affect wastage.

Institutional Variables

An extensive study of the literature shows that institutional variables have been of some interest to researchers but have been studied with far less frequency than student variables. Fishman (1962) asserts that a moratorium should be declared on investigations to improve selection and prediction of student performance, since four decades of such studies have proved inconclusive. If further studies are attempted, they should be augmented with exhaustive analyses of the following: age and sex composition of the student population, number of years spent in secondary school, quality of teaching in the schools from which students originate, time spent between school and college in a job or some other nonacademic experience, percentage of the age group entering higher education, college teaching, staff/student relations, staff/student ratios, availability of counseling, health and psychiatric services, student residence, student financing, course structures, methods of assessment, established pass/fail ratios, and the possibility of transfer of credits between courses and institutions.

There is good reason to believe that any student who is well motivated, persistent, thorough, well organized, and well adjusted will overcome every obstacle that is placed in his way. Yet it is not realistic to expect such perfection in all students. Each institution has to seek a degree of compromise and decide how far it can go in adjusting its policies to suit the needs of students. Such a compromise does not require a diminution of standards but an assessment of reality that takes into account the imperfections of the institution's own resources of money, time, and equipment; the ability and motivation of its students; and the attainments of its graduates.

Once isolated, the institutional factors involved in wastage can be assessed individually; decisions of policy and practice can then take into account how each factor, individually and in interaction with others, affects success rates. The possibilities of institutional failure appear to be obvious, yet for nearly half a century they have been ignored; explanations for wastage have been sought on the basis of student data alone.

Large differences in wastage will generally occur between departments in any single institution. Comparisons of the practices and expectations of departments provide some basis for policies and practice. For instance, are the teaching practices of each department comparable (after allowing for variations in approaches among different subject areas)? In Britain and Australia a movement toward the training of university and polytechnic teachers has been developing in response to the belief that wastage can be reduced by moving away from a purely student orientation. In addition to a new emphasis on the practical aspects of teaching—delivery, organization, small classes and one-to-one tutorials, and the use of media—one should give much attention to the formulation of the objectives of the course and the individual lecture. Unless objectives are clarified, teaching effort and time will be wasted in irrelevant busywork and overteaching. This kind of institutional wastage may be far more costly than student failures and dropouts.

Another source of wastage is caused by limiting admissions to students from secondary school, though this practice is changing as recurrent postexperience higher education becomes accepted. Students coming directly from school may have too little time to reflect on the most appropriate course of study and are not always ready to make mature choices from the available options. In contrast, the student who has tested the reality of the world outside has a mature academic, vocational, or professional goal toward which to work. In general, the responsibility for providing opportunity of choice rests with the institution not the student.

The kind of teaching a student experiences in secondary school is another possible source of wastage if, for example, it has been too didactic to be an adequate preparation for the independent study normally expected in higher education. Schonell, Roe, and Meddleton (1962) have demonstrated that it is possible for students with excellent school results but little experience of independent study to falter in higher education, while apparently less well-prepared students with greater experience of independent study do well.

In evaluating institutional wastage one must take account of the percentage of the age group entering in order to estimate the general ability of the group; the larger the percentage, the greater the spread of ability downwards.

Staff/student ratios should also be taken into account, although there is some evidence that they are of little importance in certain situations. It has been found, for example, that learning can take place better in a large lecture theater with a good lecturer than in a small group with a poor leader (Maclaine, 1965; Costin, 1972). Learning depends more on the quality of the teacher than on the size of the class. Yet it cannot be confidently asserted that a campus with a staff/student ratio of one to twenty will produce as much good learning as a campus with a ratio of one to six.

The availability of counseling, health, psychiatric, and other support services is bound to affect wastage of individual students, but clinical evidence is not usually precise enough for exact evaluation. The Minnesota Studies (Campbell, 1965) suggest, however, that students who are counseled fail less often and achieve more postgraduate degrees than those who, although they seek counseling, are denied it due to the limited availability of services.

Course structures are another consideration in wastage. Where it is possible for the students to select course units instead of a whole course, failure may be limited to only one or two units. In contrast, if a student who is nearing the end of his program and who has been successful up to that point fails his final comprehensive examination, three years of successful achievement may be wasted if a repeat or transfer elsewhere is not possible. On the other hand, greater wastage can occur under a course units system. Since more opportunities for failure exist, failure may be compounded—a possibility that requires consideration when a student plans to change from one system to another. However, where units are examined separately, there is greater opportunity for student mobility from one course or college to another with minimal wastage of successful credits.

The most unnecessary wastage of all may occur in institutions that perpetuate a constant pass/fail ratio. Studies in Britain *(Higher Education,* 1963*)* and Australia (Hohne, 1951), for example, show that an improvement in the quality of enrollment does not necessarily lead to improvement in the pass rate.

Other variables that can affect wastage are housing (provision of residences for first-year students would preclude their need to compete on the open market for accommodations, thus eliminating one distraction from studies); financial assistance (a supportive financial aid system would make continuation possible for students who would otherwise be forced to leave); a balanced sex ratio; and grading (as, for example, in the British system, where first and second honors degrees are granted to the best students with lower seconds and pass degrees for the majority, leaving few to fail). The honors system may in part account for the low overall wastage rate in Great Britain.

A comparison of the policies and practices of almost any two institutions—one with high and one with low wastage rates—will reveal differences in policies and practice that might point up modifications that could affect wastage in each.

Wastage in higher education is a reflection of the natural imperfections of humans and man-made institutions. Seeking remedies for reducing wastage does not necessarily imply a lowering of standards in students. On the contrary, awareness of the numerous possibilities for positive change is conducive to the raising of standards in practice.

Bibliography

Anderson, D. S. *Problems and Performance of University Students*. Melbourne: University of Melbourne, 1964.

Astin, A. W. "Personal and Environmental Factors Associated with College Drop-Outs Among High Aptitude Students." *Journal of Educational Psychology*, 1964, *55*, 219–266.

Campbell, D. P. *Results of Counseling Twenty-Five Years Later*. Philadelphia: Saunders, 1965.

Choppin, B. *The Prediction of Academic Success*. London: National Foundation for Educational Research, 1975.

Costin, F. "Lecturing Versus Other Methods of Teaching: A Review of Research." *British Journal of Educational Technology*, 1972, *3*(1), 4–31.

Eysenck, H. J. "Student Selection by Means of Psychological Tests—A Critical Survey." *British Journal of Educational Psychology*, 1947, *17*, 20–39.

Fishman, J. A. "Some Social Psychological Theory for Selecting and Guiding College Students." In N. Sanford (Ed.), *The American College*. New York: Wiley, 1962.

Higher Education. Report of the Committee on Higher Education Appointed by the Prime Minister. Cmnd. 2154. London: H. M. Stationery Office, 1963.

Hohne, H. H. *The Prediction of Academic Success (Faculty of Arts)*. Hawthorn, Victoria: Australian Council for Educational Research, 1951.

Husén, T. "Comparative Research on Higher Education." In *Higher Education: Crisis and Support*. Paris: Organisation for Economic Co-operation and Development, 1974.

Kerr, C. "Introduction: The Evaluation of National Systems of Higher Education." In B. B. Burn. *Higher Education in Nine Countries*. New York: McGraw-Hill, 1971.

Lavin, D. *The Prediction of Academic Performance*. New York: Wiley, 1965.

Maclaine, A. G. "A Programme for Improving Learning and Teaching at Australian Universities." *The Australian University*, 1965, *3*(3), 235–266.

Malleson, N. "Student Performance at University College London." *Universities Quarterly*, 1958, *12*(2), 288–319.

Miller, G. W. *Success, Failure and Wastage in Higher Education*. London: Harrap, 1970.

Miller, G. W. *Higher Education Research in Australia and New Zealand*. London: Society for Research into Higher Education, 1971.

Miller, G. W. "Student Drop-Out and Wastage: A Comparison Between Australian and British Universities—I." *The Australian University*, 1973, *11*(3), 239–250.

Miller, G. W. "Student Drop-Out and Wastage: A Comparison Between Australian and British Universities—II." *The Australian University*, 1974, *12*(1), 3–25.

Parkyn, G. W. *Success and Failure at the University*. Vol. 1: *Academic Success and Entrance Standards*. Wellington: New Zealand Council for Educational Research, 1959.

Parkyn, G. W. *Success and Failure at the University*. Vol. 2: *The Problem of Failure*. Wellington: New Zealand Council for Educational Research, 1967.

Reports for the Year 1972–73. New Delhi: University Grants Commision, 1974.

Sanders, C. *Student Selection and Academic Success in Australian Universities*. Sydney: Government Printer, 1948.

Sanders, C. *Psychological and Educational Bases of Academic Performance*. Melbourne: Australian Council for Educational Research, 1961.

Sanford, N. (Ed.). *The American College*. New York: Wiley, 1962.

Schonell, F. J., Roe, E., and Meddleton, I. G. *Promise and Performance: A Study of Student Progress at University Level*. London: University of London Press, 1962.

Vernon, P. E. "The Pool of Ability." In P. Halmos (Ed.), *The Sociological Review*. Monograph No. 7. Keele, England: University of Keele, 1963.

Watson, G. *Happy College Years*. New York: City University, 1963.

GORDON W. MILLER

AUDIO-VISUAL AIDS

See Educational Resources: Learning Resource Centers.

AUSTRALIA, COMMONWEALTH OF

Population: 13,131,597. Student enrollment in primary school: 1,811,124; secondary school (academic, vocational, technical): 1,062,885; higher education—university: 142,307 (1974 estimate); higher education—nonuniversity: 116,837. Student enrollment in higher education as percentage of age group (18–22): 19.8%. Language of instruction: English. Academic calendar: February/March to mid December. Percentage of gross national product (GNP) expended on education: 4.5%. [Except where otherwise noted, figures are for 1973.]

The Commonwealth of Australia is a federation composed of six states (New South Wales, Victoria, Queensland, South Australia, Western Australia, and Tasmania) and two territories (the Australian Capital Territory and the Northern Territory). Under the constitution, education is the responsibility of the states; the federal government is not empowered to make laws with regard to education except within the territories.

Higher education planning in Australia, especially between 1960 and 1975, has focused on a means to provide an extensive variety of educational opportunities that will meet the needs and demands of the nation. There has been considerable activity on the national level, through investigations by several special committees whose tasks were to review policies and procedures on various aspects of tertiary-level education and to recommend changes that would facilitate the expansion of the number and variety of available programs. The contributions of these special committees have enabled the commonwealth government to play a stimulating role in the development of postsecondary education.

Included among these special committees were the Committee on the Future of Tertiary Education in Australia (the Martin Committee), the Advisory Committee on Advanced Education (the Wark Committee), and the Committee on Open University. The Martin Committee report, *Tertiary Education in Australia* (1964), provided the major thrust for development of the current structure of postsecondary education, particularly with regard to (1) the creation of colleges of advanced education, which were subsequently developed by the Wark Committee (originally established in 1965 and superseded in 1971 by the Australian Commission on Advanced Education); and (2) the 1975 proposal to establish a single national body to make recommendations on all areas of higher education, with the exception of some subprofessional courses covered by the Australian Committee on Technical and Further Education.

The work of the Committee on Open University is one of the continuing efforts to exploit all possible alternatives and innovations that may offer worthwhile educational opportunities. In its report entitled *Open Tertiary Education* (1974), it recommended development of off-campus courses, but not necessarily by all institutions.

National Educational Policy and Legal Basis of Educational System

National policies concerning postsecondary education are aimed at cultivating an educational system which (1) will serve the diverse needs of the populace by providing a multiplicity of programs at a variety of institutions and (2) will provide an opportunity for everyone to receive a higher education.

Currently operating acts of parliament with regard to education include (1) for New South Wales: the Higher Education Act 1969 (as amended); (2) for Victoria: the Victoria Institute of Colleges Act 1965 (as amended) and the State College of Victoria Act 1972; (3) for Queensland: the Queensland Board of Education Act 1970; (4) for South Australia: the South Australian Board of Advanced Education Act; (5) for Western Australia: the Western Australian Tertiary Education Commission

Act 1970; (6) for Tasmania: the Advanced Education Act.

The Australian (federal) government is deeply involved in tertiary education throughout the commonwealth. Virtually all finance for tertiary education is in the form of grants to the states from federal funds for specified purposes and under specified conditions. Apart from the States Grants Acts, federal acts relating to tertiary education include the Universities Commission Act 1959 (as amended) and the Australian Commission on Advanced Education Act 1971.

Types of Institutions

Higher education in Australia is offered primarily by three types of institutions: universities, colleges of advanced education, and teachers colleges. The total number of universities has grown from six in 1946 to eighteen in 1975, with three new universities in the planning stages. They would be located at Campbelltown in New South Wales, at Albury-Wodonga in New South Wales, and at Geelong in Victoria.

The six oldest universities, founded in the eighteenth and early nineteenth centuries, include the University of Sydney (1850), the University of Melbourne (1853), the University of Adelaide (1874), the University of Tasmania (1890), the University of Queensland (1909), and the University of Western Australia (1911).

Colleges of advanced education vary considerably among themselves and can be distinguished from universities by their emphasis on the vocational aspects of the programs they offer; by their orientation to teaching rather than research; and by their emphasis on programs, primarily in vocational fields of study, which lead to an undergraduate diploma or degree and postgraduate diplomas by course work rather than to a postgraduate degree dependent on research. Originally established in 1966 in response to recommendations of the Martin Committee, the colleges are categorized into the following groups: (1) large multidiscipline metropolitan in-

stitutes; (2) small, generally single-discipline, metropolitan colleges; (3) multidiscipline nonmetropolitan colleges; and (4) small single-discipline country colleges (Australian Commission on Advanced Education, 1972). As of July 1973 there were seventy-seven colleges of advanced education.

The only federal university is the Australian National University, located in Canberra, in the Australian Capital Territory. The Institute of Advanced Studies at the Australian National University is totally devoted to research activities. It engages in no undergraduate teaching but trains graduate candidates for the degree of master or doctor. The other part of the Australian National University is called the School of General Studies. It offers courses leading to bachelor's and master's degrees and supervises some candidates for the research degrees of master and doctor.

Teachers colleges were once administered primarily by state educational agencies and were designated as colleges of advanced education by the commonwealth (federal) parliament in December 1973. Those teachers colleges remaining as such are for the most part private institutions run by religious organizations.

Total enrollments in the universities in 1974 were estimated at 142,307 students, an increase of 7.4 percent over the enrollment of the previous year. Of the 1974 enrollment 64.99 percent of students (92,488) were undertaking full-time programs, while 35.01 percent (49,819) were undertaking part-time programs. Colleges of advanced education (including teachers colleges) had approximately the same proportions of full-time and part-time student enrollments; when teachers colleges are excluded, however, over 50 percent of the students in colleges of advanced education were enrolled part time.

Relationship with Secondary Education and Admission Requirements

Education in Australia lies within the jurisdiction of the states. Mandatory education generally lasts eleven or twelve years;

the first six years are primary, and the remaining five or six are secondary. Completion of secondary school is usually marked by a public examination, the scores on which constitute the most widely used measure for determining admission to universities and colleges of advanced education; colleges generally have more flexible entry standards and policies than universities.

Use of the examination scores as the most important criterion for entry has been criticized for several reasons. Some of the critics contend that a single examination may not be an adequate or fair representation of a student's ability; others have criticized the restrictions placed on the secondary school programs because of the time that must be devoted to preparing students for the examination. As a result of the criticisms, states and institutions have been experimenting with other measures of student ability or with other criteria that will enhance equal access to tertiary-level institutions. The use of the examination scores has been abolished in the state of Queensland; instead, students entering institutions in 1974 were assessed primarily on secondary school evaluations of their ability. The Australian National University in the Australian Capital Territory and the University of New England in New South Wales engaged in similar programs in 1972; each admitted 20 percent and 25 percent, respectively, of the incoming class on the basis of reports of the secondary school principals. Some institutions, particularly the colleges, are experimenting with criteria such as motivation and interest. In Victoria, in a slightly different approach to providing opportunities for tertiary education, a number of institutions developed plans to admit some students for the 1974 (and subsequent) academic years on the basis of prior educational disadvantage.

Administration and Control

Universities and colleges of advanced education are public institutions established by or under an act of parliament of a state or, in the case of the territories, by an act of the federal parliament. The federal government does, however, exercise almost total de facto control over higher education throughout the commonwealth. Control is exercised through the financial power of the federal government, which has the constitutional power to "grant financial assistance to any State on such terms and conditions as the Parliament thinks fit." This power, together with the priority of federal direct taxation over revenues, has meant that the federal government has effective control over the expenditure of most public funds and thus has overall control of higher education.

The federal government's advisory bodies, the Universities Commission and the Commission on Advanced Education, make recommendations to the commonwealth (federal) government on grants to the states for tertiary education. Through these recommendations (that is, through their designation of courses qualifying for receipt of funds from the commonwealth government), both commissions exercise a critical role in determining the programs offered by these institutions. In 1974 the commonwealth government assumed complete responsibility for financing universities, colleges, and other tertiary-level institutions approved by the commonwealth minister of education; as a result, the government assumed even greater responsibility for coordinating the overall growth and development of tertiary education in Australia.

The states' responsibilities for coordination of higher education within their boundaries are variously administered by a single authority, by the state Department of Education, and/or a separate agency that is concerned only with the colleges of advanced education. The Higher Education Authority in New South Wales and the Tertiary Education Commission in Western Australia, for example, are both authorized to coordinate state responsibilities for both universities and colleges.

At the institutional level, universities and colleges of advanced education are autonomous institutions, legally responsible for administering their own affairs. Decision-making authority over institutional policies and procedures lies with the university or college council, which is created by the act of establishing the institution. Council members are generally representative of the academic, professional, and industrial communities and usually include teaching staff and student members; members of the college councils tend, in addition, to be members of the local geographical community. The chief executive is chosen by the council and is responsible to it for the administration of the institution. In universities the position of chancellor is generally an honorary position, with the vice-chancellor exercising the role of chief executive. In colleges of advanced education the equivalent position title is usually director principal. The vice-chancellor of universities is typically assisted by assistant or pro-vice-chancellors, who are appointed by the councils. The academic structure of the universities is made up of faculties headed by a dean, who is either appointed by the council (tenured position) or elected by the professors for a term of two or three years. Within each faculty the disciplines are delineated by departments headed by a professor (or head of department) who is normally appointed by council to a tenured position. The teaching staff at universities may play a formal or advisory role in institutional governance and decision making, generally through the structure of an academic senate.

The director or principal of a college is generally assisted by one or more assistant directors or deputy principals appointed by the college council. The academic structure within a college usually consists of a number of schools or faculties, each headed by a dean or head of school appointed by the council. As in the universities, the faculties or schools are umbrella organizational units consisting of departments, and each department has its own tenured or elected head.

The senior members of the adminis-trative staff are the registrar and the bursar or comptroller. The registrar is usually responsible for all matters relating to the academic administration or functioning of the college or university—such matters as admission and enrollment, record keeping, internal information systems, publications, statistics, committee secretariats, and staffing procedures. The bursar or comptroller is usually responsible for functions such as budgeting, financial administration, construction of buildings, maintenance of buildings, and other business undertakings. Registrars and comptrollers do not usually have any responsibility for determining academic policy; these areas are dealt with by the senior academic administrative staff. Senior administrative staff have some teaching responsibilities.

Programs and Degrees

The general areas of study available at Australian universities, with the percentage of university undergraduate students enrolled in each in 1971, are agriculture (1.6 percent), architecture (2 percent), arts (34.3 percent), dental science (1.2 percent), economics/commerce (14.5 percent), education (4.8 percent), engineering (10.3 percent), law (5.8 percent), medicine (6.9 percent), science (17.6 percent), and veterinary science (1.2 percent). For the colleges of advanced education, the major areas of study, with corresponding percentages for 1970–71, are agriculture (2.2 percent); applied science (11.9 percent); art and design (8 percent); building, surveying, and architecture (6.6 percent); commercial and business studies (31 percent); engineering and technology (24.8 percent); liberal studies (4.1 percent); music (1.1 percent); paramedical (7.9 percent); and teacher education (1.1 percent). Total percentages do not add up to 100 percent because of rounding and because 166 students enrolled midyear at Canberra College of Advanced Education were not included in field of study totals (Australian Commission on Advanced Education, 1972).

Programs of study at universities lead

to a bachelor's degree (usually requiring a total of three years of full-time study or the equivalent), a bachelor's degree with honors (usually requiring at least four years of full-time study or the equivalent), a master's degree (usually requiring a total of at least five to six years of full-time study or the equivalent), and a doctor's degree (which usually requires a total of at least seven to ten years of full-time study or the equivalent). The universities also offer some programs that lead to undergraduate diplomas, but these are being phased out. Most universities offer postgraduate diploma courses, most commonly in education, which usually require one year of full-time study (or its equivalent).

The total number of bachelor's degrees awarded annually by the universities increased almost five times between 1956 and 1971, from a total of 3089 in 1956 to a total of 14,994 in 1971 (17.6 percent, or 2639, were honors degrees). The annual rate of growth is expected to decline as a result of the decrease in the overall rate of growth in undergraduate enrollments, while the annual total of master's and doctor's degrees awarded has been increasing considerably, especially during the decade of the 1960s (universities conferred 8436 master's degrees and 4735 doctor's degrees in 1972). There are some indications that only very small increases or absolute declines may occur during the 1980s. There was, for example, a significant decrease in the annual rate of increase of master's and doctor's degrees issued between 1970 and 1972: from 9.6 percent in 1970, to 7.9 percent in 1971, to 5.7 percent in 1972.

Colleges of advanced education offer programs leading to undergraduate diplomas or bachelor's degrees and, to a lesser extent, to master's degrees. The colleges often offer two levels of undergraduate diplomas: an associate diploma, normally requiring two years of full-time study or the equivalent; and a diploma, usually requiring three years of full-time study or the equivalent. Bachelor's degrees offered by the colleges usually require three or four

years of full-time study or the equivalent.

In order to encourage consistency and some form of equivalence among programs offered at different colleges, the Australian Council on Awards in Advanced Education (ACAAE) was established in 1971 by joint agreement of the commonwealth and state ministers of education. The ACAAE recommended that the following categories of diplomas and degrees be offered by colleges of advanced education: (1) an associate diploma, requiring at least two years of work in an in-depth study of a restricted area or in a program of studies which emphasizes skills rather than theory; (2) a diploma, requiring a minimum of three years of full-time study, leading to professional recognition; (3) a bachelor's degree, requiring a minimum of three years of full-time study in an integrated program of major and supplementary subject areas; (4) a graduate diploma, requiring (a) a minimum of one year of full-time study after receipt of a bachelor's degree or, if permitted, a diploma award and (b) pursuit of a program of study which may or may not be of graduate level; and (5) a master's degree, requiring about two years of full-time study. Colleges of advanced education also offer substantial part-time correspondence programs.

The commonwealth government has placed considerable emphasis on the development of postsecondary education outside the universities. In accordance with the recommendations of the Australian Committee on Technical and Further Education (also known as the Kangan Committee, established in 1973), the commonwealth government approved in 1974 the creation of a special commission to study and recommend ways to enhance the quality and availability of opportunities in technical and further education (TAFE). TAFE usually refers to postsecondary education programs offered by institutions other than the universities and colleges of advanced education and supported and/or administered by a government educational agency. The Kangan Committee was particularly concerned about the fact that less than half of the persons in TAFE programs were enrolled in technological studies, a portent of future shortages of skilled technicians. The commonwealth government allocated approximately one hundred and ten million Australian dollars for use in 1975 and 1976 for the development of TAFE programs throughout the country.

Financing

Beginning with the 1974 academic year, all universities and colleges of advanced education were financed by the commonwealth government. The Commission on Advanced Education (CAE) was authorized to examine the possibility of financing other tertiary-level institutions as well. Financing is generally determined on a three-year basis, upon recommendations of the Universities Commission and the CAE, and is provided through legislation known as the States Grants Acts of the commonwealth government. The major purpose of federal assumption of total costs was the promotion of equal educational opportunity for all potential students.

Student Financial Aid

For the purpose of advancing the equality of educational opportunities, the commonwealth government abolished tuition charges and certain compulsory fees for full-time and part-time students and for students in external study programs. Students are responsible for paying only student council, student union, and sports fees. In conjunction with the abolition of tuition fees, the commonwealth government extended the program of means-tested scholarship assistance to help support full-time students. Students receiving financial aid also receive allowances to cover remaining student fees. Special allowances for dependents (spouse, children) are awarded to those qualifying for aid, as are special travel allowances, enabling students to return home three times per year. Eligibility for support is based on the adjusted income of the student's paren-

tal family; for persons already living independently of parents, the means test is applied to the student's income (or the spouse's where applicable). Part-time students are not eligible for aid.

Teaching Staff

The four main teaching and research staff positions at universities, in descending order of rank, are professor, associate professor/reader, senior lecturer, and lecturer. Available positions at each level are usually advertised, and applications are reviewed and recommendations made by a specially designated selection committee. The composition of and the procedures for appointing selection committees vary among the universities. They also may vary within an institution in accordance with the rank of the appointment under consideration. Actual appointing power generally lies with the university council but is often delegated to senior staff for appointments below the level of full professor. Selection committees for appointment to the rank of professor are frequently chaired by the vice-chancellor and include members of the administrative and academic staff of the university and, in many instances, members of the university council. Similar or identical selection committees review applications for the position of associate professor/reader and, in some cases, for senior lecturer and lecturer, although for the last two ranks the respective department head and academic staff may constitute the selection committee.

Except at the University of Western Australia, where full professors are given an initial untenured seven-year appointment, professorial appointments are tenured appointments, which are effective until the age of sixty-five; initial appointments below that level may be made for one, three, or five years prior to receiving tenure.

In 1974 the commonwealth government authorized establishment of an Academic Salaries Tribunal to set the salary rates for universities and colleges in the territories and to make recommendations for academic staff salaries at institutions within the states. The creation of the tribunal was the result of concerted attempts on the part of academic staff in universities and colleges to receive salaries equal to those given other workers throughout the economy.

There has been an increased emphasis on the importance of the research responsibilities of the teaching staff, especially since the 1960s, to the extent that the research records have become the critical measure of performance and ability when candidates are considered for appointment and promotion. In addition to the university staff whose duties include both research and teaching, there are university staff who do not teach but are, instead, engaged wholly in research activities.

At colleges of advanced education, teaching positions are generally classified as head of department, principal lecturer, senior lecturer, and lecturer. Teaching staff at the colleges are not generally required to engage in research, although there is an increasing involvement in applied (rather than theoretical) research in the colleges. Academic staff positions at the colleges are usually tenured under similar conditions to those applying at universities. While there is no formal legal protection for academic freedom, the tradition is so strong as to have the effect of legislated protection.

Research Activities

Research activities are an essential part of the contribution which universities are committed to make to the field of learning. Teaching staff are expected to devote a substantial portion of their time to research. At colleges, however, the emphasis is on the teaching of students; hence, formally sponsored research is limited, and the research that does take place is generally applied rather than basic.

There are four major sources of funds supporting research: (1) general recurrent funds, (2) special grants, (3) other grants from agencies of the commonwealth gov-

ernment, and (4) privately supported grants and contracts. In 1970, approximately 22.2 percent of the total funds spent on research conducted at universities came from general recurrent funds. Special research grants, constituting about 11.6 percent of that total, provided general support to unfinanced but potentially significant research projects engaged in by the university staff. The commonwealth government was the source of 44.9 percent of the 1970 total; included in this category are funds provided by the Australian Research Grants Committee (ARGC), which makes recommendations to the commonwealth minister for education for special research grants and which sponsors only the most "outstanding and promising" research. The general fields of study where most of the expenditures were made were science (35.5 percent); medicine (18 percent); engineering (14.4 percent); arts, economics, education, and law (13.3 percent); and agriculture (12.9 percent).

Relationship with Industry

Industry and higher education enjoy a mutually beneficial relationship. Industrial representatives participate on the governing bodies of the institutions of higher education, and industry supports institutional research activities. Another significant relationship is developing through efforts to establish programs of cooperative education, or sandwich programs, which integrate a period of study and a period of work. Although cooperative education programs are still limited at the universities, they are being extensively developed by some colleges of advanced education—in particular at the Swinburne College of Technology in Hawthorn and the New South Wales Institute of Technology in Sydney.

International Cooperation

The Australian commonwealth government fosters considerable participation in international educational activities and cooperation through (1) programs, conferences, and projects sponsored by international organizations; (2) financial assistance programs for Australian teachers and students (usually at the graduate level) to study in foreign countries and for foreign students and teachers to study in Australia; and (3) supervision of foreign students studying independently in Australia.

Australian educators have participated in numerous conferences and projects sponsored by UNESCO; in a program known as Commonwealth Cooperation in Education, supported by member nations of the British Commonwealth of Nations; and in programs sponsored by the Organisation for Economic Co-operation and Development (OECD).

The commonwealth Department of Education administers several programs which support teacher and/or student exchanges, study abroad, and study in Australia. Two opportunities provided through the Commonwealth Cooperation in Education program are the Commonwealth Scholarship and Fellowship Plan, which assists primarily postgraduate-level exchanges among Commonwealth countries; and an Australian assistance program, which is aimed at assisting national development in Commonwealth countries in Africa and the Pacific and Caribbean areas through training programs in Australia for educational personnel and through special assignment abroad for Australian educators. Some exchange or study-abroad scholarship programs administered by the commonwealth department of education include Travel Grants for Australians, a program that supports study, teaching, or research at institutions in the United States and is sponsored by the Australian-American Educational Program; the Anzac Fellowship Scheme, a three-month exchange of eminent scholars between Australia and New Zealand; the Australia-China Students Exchange Scheme; the Australian European Awards Program; and numerous grants and programs sponsored by foreign governments.

Foreign students may receive financial assistance for study in Australia through programs such as the Colombo Plan for Cooperative Economic Development in South and Southeast Asia, Commonwealth Cooperation in Education programs, the Special Commonwealth African Assistance Plan, the South Pacific Aid Program, the Australian International Awards Scheme, and programs sponsored by foreign governments.

[Special information supplied by Robert S. Davie, Assistant Director, Swinburne College of Technology; Walter Stern, Department Head, New South Wales Institute of Technology; Russell T. Dawe, Assistant Registrar, Swinburne College of Technology; and the Australian Department of Education, Melbourne.]

Educational Associations

Federation of Australian University
  Staff Associations
499 St. Kilda Road
Melbourne, Victoria 3004, Australia

Federation of Staff Associations of Australian
  Colleges of Advanced Education
172 Cheywynd Street
North Melbourne, Victoria 3051, Australia

Australian Union of Students (AUS)
97 Drummond Street
Carlton, Melbourne, Victoria 3053, Australia

Bibliography

Australian Commission on Advanced Education. *Third Report 1973–75.* Canberra: Australian Government Publishing Service, 1972.

Fifth Report of the Australian Universities Commission. Canberra: Australian Government Publishing Service, 1972.

Krane, H. H. *The Third Culture: An Integration of Technology with Art.* Melbourne: Gold Star, 1972.

McCaig, R. (Ed.) *Policy and Planning in Higher Education.* St. Lucia, Brisbane: University of Queensland, 1973.

Open Tertiary Education. Draft Report of the Committee on Open University to the Australian Universities Commission. Canberra: Australian Government Publishing Service, 1974.

Report on the Commonwealth's Role in Teacher Education. Senate Standing Committee on Education, Science and Arts. Canberra: Parliament of the Commonwealth of Australia, 1972.

Statement No. 1: Nomenclature and Guidelines for Awards in Advanced Education. Canberra:

Australian Council on Awards in Advanced Education, 1972.

Tertiary Education in Australia. Vols. 2 and 3. Report of the Committee on the Future of Tertiary Education in Australia [the Martin Committee]. Canberra: Australian Universities Commission, 1964, 1965.

Wheelwright, E. L. (Ed.) *Higher Education in Australia*. Melbourne: Federation of Australian University Staff Associations, 1965.

See also: Academic Standards and Accreditation: International; Cooperative Education and Off-Campus Experience: Sandwich Plan in Commonwealth Nations; Courts and Higher Education; Financing of Higher Education: University Grants Committees; Health Services, Worldwide University; Library Administration Outside the United States; Oceania: Regional Analysis; Science Policies: Highly Industrialized Nations: Free Market Economies: Australia and New Zealand.

AUSTRALIA, SCIENCE POLICIES OF

See Science Policies: Highly Industrialized . Nations: Australia and New Zealand.

AUSTRALIAN ASSOCIATION OF ADULT EDUCATION

The Australian Association of Adult Education was formed in 1960 to encourage interest in and support for the further development of adult education. Serving as a national information clearinghouse on adult education, the association advises governments and governmental agencies and acts as a national abstracting service. The association encourages and stimulates research, experiment, and inquiry and organizes international and national conferences. Membership consists of full-time professional adult educators and administrators and institutions, government departments, and statutory bodies, as well as any of their interested personnel.

The association's national office, staffed by a national secretary with clerical support, is located on the campus of the Australian National University in Canberra. The association is directed by an elected executive board, including a chairperson and twelve member representatives. Elections are held annually, and all members in good standing are entitled to vote. The executive board meets approximately six times annually. An annual general meeting is also held. The association receives an annual grant-in-aid from the Australian government as well as income from membership dues and publication sales.

National seminars and conferences, open to nonmembers and members, have treated such topics as the conditions, needs, and resources of adult education in Australia and the role of the Australian government in the education of adults.

The association possesses printing facilities and publishes educational material and *AVCC Education* Newsletter.

P.O. Box 1346
Canberra City, A.C.T. 2601, Australia

AUSTRALIAN VICE-CHANCELLORS' COMMITTEE

The Australian Vice-Chancellors' Committee (AVCC) developed from informal meetings of vice-chancellors beginning in 1920. Established as a formal committee in 1935 and incorporated in 1973, AVCC provides opportunities for executive heads of Australian universities to discuss matters of mutual concern. The committee studies problems and needs of Australian universities, notably their relations with other educational institutions, the Australian government, and community; consults with the universities and government; and collects and disseminates information about the universities.

The full committee meets five times a year to discuss policy matters of mutual interest to Australian universities. AVCC has no power to act on behalf of the universities. Authority resides in each university's governing body. AVCC can only make recommendations or offer advice to individual governing bodies and rely on them for implementation. The meetings of the committee are held in different universities on a rotating basis, with one meeting a year normally held in Sydney, Canberra, and Melbourne.

The AVCC executive also meets five times a year, between meetings of the full committee, and has delegated powers to make urgent decisions and handle routine business, subject to formal confirmation by the full committee. The executive, consisting of five members, is elected by the full committee. Membership includes the chairperson, deputy chairperson, and three members elected for varying terms up to three years.

Each year AVCC appoints subcommittees among its own members to oversee activities concerned with finance and statistics, research, development, teaching and students, staff and medical matters, Australian-Asian Universities Co-operation Scheme (AAUCS), and educational research and development. These subcommittees, which have power to coopt, meet as required to discuss particular problems.

The Australian-Asian Universities Co-operation Scheme (AAUCS) operates as an interuniversity undertaking. The AVCC standing committee responsible for the scheme receives a grant through the Australian Development Assistance Agency (ADAA). AAUCS offers educational aid in plant and animal sciences, food technology, forestry, agricultural economics, English-language training, and demography in Indonesia, Malaysia, and Singapore. The main focus is in East Indonesia at the Universities of Hasanuddin, Udayana, and Brawijaja. The program, which is highly integrated, includes intensive staff training courses in plant and animal sciences conducted at associated universities; follow-up research programs as a sequel to the training courses; a limited number of teaching assignments for Australian staff at associated universities; support projects in technical training, libraries, publications, and the teaching of English as a foreign language; participation in courses, seminars, and workshops organized by the associated

universities; fellowships for degree, diploma, and refresher study in Australia; and study visits by senior educational administrators to Australia.

The standing committee of AAUCS, chaired by a vice-chancellor and including about ten members drawn from Australian universities, meets twice each year. Routine business is handled by an executive committee which meets as required. Observers from ADAA connected with the plan attend meetings of both the standing committee and the executive committee. The academic aspects of the plan are handled by a part-time academic director and day-to-day operations by a full-time executive officer who is a member of the AVCC secretariat.

The AVCC Subcommittee on Educational Research and Development provides research and development backup for AVCC by collecting information, conducting applied research, and supporting development projects. The subcommittee conducts action research to study the effects of changes in policies and practices on the function of universities; monitors the current status of university education in Australia; and promotes items of information through newsletters, registers of research, and reports.

The subcommittee, chaired by a vice-chancellor, consists of six other members drawn from different universities. The day-to-day work of the subcommittee is undertaken by a full-time research information officer who is a member of the AVCC secretariat. The subcommittee meets several times a year as required.

The AVCC also appoints working parties to examine specific matters and make recommendations. Working parties have been appointed in the areas of postgraduate medical training, academic salaries, superannuation, long service leave transferability, conditions of appointment of sublecturing staff, honors degrees, open university, and F.M. broadcasting.

The AVCC has issued guidelines for interuniversity meetings to help reduce the expenses involved and to avoid duplication of effort. The committee sponsors an annual meeting of registrars and bursars (Administrative Staff Conference) and also periodic meetings of specialist administrative groups such as information officers.

AVCC conducts an annual administrative staff training course for the middle administrative group: graduate assistants, senior graduate assistants, and assistant registrars. The courses, which are residential, extend over two weeks and are organized by a planning committee appointed by the Administrative Staff Conference.

The vice-chancellor of the University of Papua New Guinea was a member of AVCC from the foundation of that university in 1966 until Papua New Guinea became self-governing in 1973. The Papua New Guinea University of Technology was created in August 1973 out of the former Papua and New Guinea Institute of Technology. Both universities are invited to participate in most AVCC activities. The AVCC has agreed to help the Papua New Guinea universities obtain staff and has prepared guidelines for the secondment of staff from Australian universities.

AVCC was directly involved in the development of a course in Australian studies at Nanyang University, Singapore, and appointed a working group to advise on the selection of a lecturer. AVCC was also invited to assist a World Bank project in reviewing agricultural education in Thailand. AVCC has a close interest in the University of the South Pacific in Fiji, and representatives of that university are invited to participate in some AVCC activities. In addition, an Australian representative, who is nominated by the committee, serves on the council of the university.

AVCC is used by government departments and agencies as a point of reference for information and advice on university matters. Members of AVCC and the Universities Commission meet informally once a year, and AVCC representatives meet regularly with the chairperson and deputy chairperson of the Universities Commis-

sion to discuss current issues. An annual meeting between the AVCC and the Department of Education is held to discuss student assistance and other matters. AVCC also works with the Department of Science on Project SCORE, the Organisation for Economic Co-operation and Development in reviewing the science policy in Australia, the Australian Research Grants Committee, and the Commonwealth Scientific and Industrial Research Organisation.

AVCC is represented on the Undergraduates Working Visits to Australia Committee, which arranges for undergraduates from the United Kingdom and Europe to visit Australia during the summer. The committee also makes representations to the Department of Immigration on matters relating to the admission of overseas students and the recruitment of overseas staff for the Australian universities.

The committee's officers maintain close liaison with officials of the Australian Union of Students and the Federation of Australian University Staff Associations. The committee also has contacts with the Australian Academy of Science, the Australian Academy of the Humanities, and the Academy of the Social Sciences in Australia.

AVCC appoints two Australian representatives to the Association of Commonwealth Universities (ACU). AVCC cooperates with the British Council on the Commonwealth University Interchange Scheme and contributes to the cost of Category 'B' visitors (those visitors for whom the British Council acts as paymaster, although they are sponsored and usually paid for by another country) each year. Formal but irregular contacts are maintained between AVCC and other interuniversity bodies throughout the world. Meetings of the executive officers of the interuniversity bodies within the Commonwealth are held at ACU congresses and conferences of executive heads.

AVCC either assists with or is responsible for the administration and selection of candidates for several awards that are competed for on an Australia-wide basis: Frank Knox Fellowship to Harvard, Gowrie Postgraduate Research Travelling Scholarship, Senior Hulme Scholarship to Oxford, Canadian Pacific Airlines Award, Nuffield Dominions Trust Appointments at Oxford Medical School, GMH Postgraduate Research Fellowship, ACU Travelling Fellowships for University Administrators, and Australian American Educational Foundation (AAEF) Travel Grants for University Administrators.

AVCC also prepares rosters to enable each university in turn to make nominations for Commonwealth University Interchange Scheme Category 'B' visitors, Commonwealth Scholarship and Fellowship Plan (CSFP) Visiting Professors and Fellows, Drapers' Company Visiting Lecturers, and Australian-European Awards. The committee provides the secretariat for the Charles Strong Memorial Trust (established in 1957 to foster study of comparative religion in Australia) and makes arrangements for visiting lecturers brought to Australia by the trust.

AVCC is funded by contributions from all Australian universities, proportionate to their recurrent income for each year. The staff includes the secretary, assistant secretary, research information officer, executive officer of AAUCS, part-time accountant, and six typist-clerks.

AVCC acts as a clearinghouse for information on matters of mutual interest to all Australian universities. An average of about thirty information summaries are published each year on Australian university activities such as term dates, conditions of service, university structure, and student participation. Lists of vacant positions at Australian and overseas universities are compiled biweekly and distributed to over a thousand individuals and institutions.

AVCC also publishes *Australian Newsletter,* a quarterly journal on university affairs; and *Education Newsletter,* a quarterly on teaching and education research. Reports resulting from investigations and conferences organized by AVCC arc issued periodically. Relevant extracts from the Hansard of the Australian Parliament are sent to vice-chancellors on a regular basis. In cooperation with the Graduate Careers Council, AVCC sponsors publications on opportunities for postgraduate study and research in Australia and overseas.

P.O. Box 1142
Canberra City, A.C.T. 2601, Australia

F. S. HAMBLY

AUSTRIA, REPUBLIC OF

Population: 7,639,000 (1976 estimate). Student enrollment in primary school: 985,286; secondary school (general, compulsory, vocational): 334,905; teacher training: 14,778; higher education: 82,372. Language of instruction: German. Academic calendar: October to June, two semesters. [Enrollment statistics are for 1974–75.]

Austria, a landlocked republic in Central Europe, once formed the core of an empire created during the reign of the Hapsburgs (1278–1918), an empire that at its zenith encompassed much of Central and Southern Europe. Following the collapse of the Hapsburg monarchy in 1918 and the dissolution of the empire, Austria was proclaimed an independent republic. The new state experienced more than two decades of economic and social upheaval followed by annexation by Nazi Germany in 1938. After World War II Austria was divided into four zones occupied by forces of France, the Soviet Union, the United Kingdom, and the United States. In 1955 the four powers recognized Austria's independence as a democratic republic and withdrew the troops which had occupied the country for a decade. The same year, the Austrian parliament passed an act that proclaimed Austria a permanently neutral state.

As in other Central European countries, education in Austria was originally provided by medieval monastery schools, which were established and operated by the church, The program of study consisted of Latin, the Scriptures, and church doctrine and led to ecclesiastical occupations. The monastery schools gradually expanded their curriculum to include secular studies (*Austria: Organization of Education*, 1973, p. 5). During the Charlemagne period (about A.D. 800), the municipal governments began to establish schools in the larger merchant towns. The curricula of these municipal schools continued to resemble those of the church-operated monastery schools until the thirteenth century; students received a basic knowledge of Latin, religion, and mathematics (Keefe and others, 1976, p. 118). The church subsequently began to establish schools, known as Latin schools, in some towns. The Latin schools were originally staffed by clerics; however, secular teaching staff were later added.

University education in Austria was first provided by the University of Vienna, established in 1365 by Rudolf IV (1358–1365). The University of Vienna was the first university in a German-speaking country and remained the only university in Austria for more than two centuries.

During the Counter-Reformation, which extended from the early sixteenth to the mid seventeenth century, the Catholic church was instrumental in expanding educational facilities at all levels. In 1552 the Society of Jesus founded the Grammar School in Vienna, a secondary-level institution, and later established grammar schools in Graz and Innsbruck. The University of Graz was established in 1585–86 as the country's second university and came under Jesuit authority in the following year. In 1622 a third university, the University of Salzburg, was established by the Benedictine order. The country's fourth university, the University of Innsbruck, was founded in 1669 with a faculty of Catholic theology as its base. Austria's prestigious Academy of Fine Arts (*Akademie der bildenden Künste*) was established in Vienna in 1692 during the height of Austrian baroque culture.

A period of educational reform was ini-

tiated during the reign of Maria Theresa (1740–1779). The Society of Jesus was dissolved in 1773, and education was increasingly placed under state control. A secular elementary system, which included three types of schools, was established in 1774. Under Maria Theresa control of secondary and higher education was assumed by the state, but reform at both levels was limited. Several new chairs in the natural sciences and law were created at the University of Vienna; however, non-Catholic students at the university were not permitted to graduate. Several special advanced schools were created during Maria Theresa's rule—among them the School of Veterinary Medicine (*Tierärztliche Hochschule*) in Vienna, established in 1767, now the University of Veterinary Medicine.

Maria Theresa's successor, Joseph II (1780–1790), forced his utilitarian objectives on the schools and adapted the university curricula to the training of civil servants. University status was withdrawn from the University of Graz in 1782 and not restored until 1829. Under Joseph, however, the universities were opened to non-Catholics. His successor, Leopold II (1790–1792), restored the Universities of Vienna, Salzburg, and Innsbruck to their former prestigious position.

During the nineteenth century, non-university higher education in Austria experienced a great period of growth in response to the development of the Austrian economy and of technology. During this same period, however, the University of Salzburg was dissolved (1810), not to be reopened until 1962. (Austria had surrendered Salzburg to Bavaria in 1809 during the Napoleonic Wars. The city was regained in 1814, but the university was not subsequently reopened.)

In 1811 the Graz School of Technology (*Technische Hochschule in Graz*) was established, followed by the Vienna School of Technology (*Technische Hochschule in Wien*) in 1815. Both schools achieved university status in the early 1870s. The School of Mining and Metallurgy (*Montanistische*

Hochschule) was established in 1840 at Leoben, and in 1867 the School of Applied Art *(Hochschule für angewandte Kunst)* was founded in Vienna. The School of Agriculture *(Hochschule für Bodenkultur)* and the School of Economics *(Hochschule für Welthandel)* were founded in Vienna in 1872 and 1898, respectively. Three schools of music and dramatic arts were also established during this period in Graz (1803), Vienna (1817), and Salzburg (1841).

The development of Austrian higher education since 1900 has largely taken the form of reorganization and expansion of existing institutions; however, three new schools have been established since 1962. In 1901 the Graz and Vienna Schools of Technology were authorized to award doctorates, and both schools were reorganized in 1955. The School of Mining and Metallurgy was raised to *Hochschule* status in 1904, while the School of Veterinary Medicine achieved this status in 1908 and was accorded the same rights and privileges as other Austrian universities in 1920. The School of Economics acquired university status in 1919 and was accorded the right to award doctorates in 1930. In 1962, while the primary and secondary levels of education were undergoing a reorganization, the University of Salzburg was reopened, and the School of Social and Economic Sciences *(Hochschule für Sozial- und Wirtschaftswissenschaften)* was founded in Linz. The latter institution began operating in 1966 and was later renamed the University of Linz.

Many changes have occurred in the Austrian higher education system since 1966, and most programs of study at the university-level institutions have been reorganized. The schools of music and dramatic art and the School of Applied Art in Linz, which had all been reorganized several times since their inception, were accorded university status in 1970 with the title of *Hochschule.* The same year the School of Educational Sciences *(Hochschule für Bildungswissenschaften)* (now the University of Educational Sciences) was founded

in Klagenfurt. The School of Artistic and Industrial Design *(Hochschule für künstlerische und industrielle Gestaltung)* was opened in Linz in 1973. From October 1, 1975, the Austrian parliament has enforced a new law on university organization which will reform all university-level institutions in the country.

National Educational Policy

Austria possesses one of the oldest educational systems in the world, a system that has maintained high standards through continual innovation and reform. Education is free at all levels for every citizen in recognition of the fact that the development of the country depends on the development of the individual.

Austrian higher education institutions are concerned with academic research and teaching. The objectives of higher education, as determined by law, are the advancement of the humanities and sciences and the training of future scholars and scientists. In addition, higher education institutions provide academic preparation for professional work and postgraduate studies on the latest developments in the arts and sciences *(Study in Austria,* 1973, pp. 8–9).

Legal Basis of Educational System

The Federal Constitutional Act of July 18, 1962, determined the respective educational responsibilities of the federal government and the provincial governments and served as the basis for the federal education acts that were subsequently enacted. The School Organization Act of July 25, 1962, and its 1965, 1966, 1971, and 1972 amendments set forth the structure and purpose of the schools, their organization, number of classes and teaching staff, length of studies, final examination schedules, and criteria for admission. The implementation of this act was intended to provide both general and vocational education for the entire school-age population, to extend the period of compulsory school attendance, and to provide additional trained technicians for the agricultural and industrial sectors.

Other acts relating to the general system of education include the School Attendance Act (1962), which introduced nine-year compulsory school attendance; the Religious Instruction Act (1949, with amendments in 1957 and 1962), which placed responsibility for all religious instruction with the legally recognized churches and religious communities; and the Private Schools Act (1962), regarding the legal and public status of private schools and state subsidies to private schools.

Prior to the enactment of the University Organization Act on April 11, 1975, university-level institutions in Austria were organized under the authority of the Higher Organization Act of July 13, 1955, and its amendments. A May 10, 1972, amendment to the act accorded advisory status and the right to submit proposals at meetings of the academic senate to representatives of the nonprofessorial research and teaching staff and students at the universities. The amendment also stipulated that representatives of the two groups may have seats and votes in the study commissions *(Studienkommissionen)*.

The University Organization Act establishes a new university structure with three cooperative levels: the institutes, the faculty, and the academic senate and rector. The act sets forth the following principles and aims: freedom of academic research and teaching, democratization of the universities, cooperation between teachers and students, freedom of study, and a structure that ensures openness in the field of policy and decision making *(Austria: Organization of Education*, 1973, p. 13). The act envisions a socially responsible university which will serve as a vehicle for social development.

Other significant recent legislation pertinent to higher education includes the General Higher Education Act of July 15, 1966, which set forth the regulations governing studies, students, examinations, and academic degrees. A number of special education acts regarding the organization and regulation of studies in certain university faculties were implemented in the late 1960s and early 1970s. Studies in the *technische Hochschulen* were reorganized by the Federal Act of July 10, 1969. The art schools were raised to university status by the Art School Organization Act of 1970; and their programs of study are regulated by the Art School Regulations Act of 1971.

Types of Institutions

University-level education in Austria is provided by eighteen higher education institutions. These can be divided into twelve degree-granting universities, five *Kunsthochschulen* (art schools), and one art academy. The universities include the four general universities in Graz, Innsbruck, Salzburg, and Vienna; the technical universities in Graz and Vienna; and six specialized universities, which were formerly *Hochschulen:* the University of Linz (formerly the School of Social and Economic Sciences in Linz), with its constituent schools of social sciences, economics, law, and technology and natural sciences; the University of Mining and Metallurgy at Leoben; the University of Agriculture, the University of Veterinary Medicine, and the University of Economics, all located in Vienna; and the University of Educational Sciences in Klagenfurt. The six art schools are the *Akademie der bildenden Künste* (Academy of Fine Arts) in Vienna, the *Hochschule für angewandte Kunst* (School of Applied Art) in Vienna, the *Hochschule für Musik und darstellende Kunst* (School of Music and Dramatic Art) in Vienna, the *Hochschule für Musik und darstellende Kunst* in Graz, the *Hochschule für Musik und darstellende Kunst "Mozarteum"* in Salzburg, and the *Hochschule für künstlerische und industrielle Gestaltung* (School of Artistic and Industrial Design) in Linz.

Nonuniversity higher education is provided by technical and vocational schools, schools for tourism, teacher training academies (for general teachers, vocational teachers, and teachers of religion), academies of social work, federal institutions for educators, and schools for higher medical/technical training.

The formal Austrian educational system is supplemented by an extensive network of adult education centers operated by the government and by private organizations. University extension services are also available at several of the higher education institutions.

Postgraduate studies are offered by university and other public institutes and by private organizations. Among these institutions are the *Diplomatische Akademie in Wien* (Diplomatic Academy of Vienna), the *Wiener medizinische Akademie für ärztliche Fortbildung* (Vienna Academy of Medicine for Postgraduate Training), and the *Österreichisches Lateinamerika-Institut* (Austrian Latin-America Institute).

Relationship with Secondary Education

Education in Austria is compulsory for children between six and fourteen years of age. The first four years of compulsory schooling, known as *Grundschule* (basic school), is provided in the *Volksschule* (primary school). At age ten, students in some rural areas continue in the four-year senior division of the primary school *(Volksschuloberstufe)*. An increasing number of students, however, are instead entering either the *Hauptschule* (upper primary school) or the lower division of the general secondary schools for a further four years of study.

The majority of students who complete eight years of compulsory education enter programs which lead to occupations. Vocational training programs that extend one to five years are offered in fields such as business, arts and crafts, and domestic science. In 1975, 60 percent of the seventeen-year-old cohort in the country were enrolled in school. Of these an estimated 35 percent were enrolled in apprentice training programs. These programs usually involve one day of classroom attendance per week (or an equivalent amount of work in night school) during the first three years of employment (Keefe and others, 1976, pp. 123–125).

A ninth year of compulsory education, the polytechnic course *(polytechnischer Lehrgang)*, is required for those students who do not intend to continue into a vocational school or a secondary school. Students who complete this ninth year of study have the option of continuing their studies in a general secondary school or a vocational school.

Upon completion of the eighth year of compulsory education, students intending to seek university admission generally enroll in one of the five-year upper secondary programs offered by the general secondary schools—the *Gymnasium* (academic secondary school), the *Realgymnasium* (science secondary school), or the *wirtschaftskundliches Realgymnasium für Mädchen* (domestic science school for girls)—or follow one of four special secondary school programs.

The upper division of the *Gymnasium* is divided into three areas of study: classical *(humanistisches Gymnasium)*, modern languages *(neusprachliches Gymnasium)*, and modern studies *(realistisches Gymnasium)*. The upper division of the *Realgymnasium* consists of two sections: natural sciences *(naturwissenschaftliches Realgymnasium)* and mathematics *(mathematisches Realgymnasium)*. The domestic science school for girls is on the same academic level as the *Gymnasium* and the *Realgymnasium*.

The programs leading to university admission are completed by the *Reifeprüfung*, the secondary school-leaving examination. Students who pass this examination receive the *Reifezeugnis* (secondary school-leaving certificate). The general secondary schools and the special secondary schools provide direct access, in most cases, to the universities and other higher education institutions. Three other types of secondary schools—the *höhere technische und gewerbliche Lehranstalten* (secondary technical and trade schools), the *Handelsakademien* (business academies), and the *höhere Lehranstalten für wirtschaftliche Frauenberufe* (higher institutions for women's occupations)—offer five-year programs that also provide access to higher education.

Adult education serves as a significant supplement to the formal educational system. Austria has 350 extramural schools for adult education and about 1900 regional centers of education. Private institutions, which provide the major portion of adult education, receive subsidies from the federal government, the provinces, and the municipalities *(Austria: Organization of Education,* 1973, p. 15). The federal government operates institutes which enroll about 250,000 students annually for the advancement of trade and commerce. Labor unions operate night schools for their members, and businesses and industry provide further training courses for their employees. Lower Austria, Carinthia, Tirol, and Styria operate compulsory continuation schools for farmers (Keefe and others, 1976, p. 124).

Admission Requirements

There are two levels of admission to university-level institutions: (1) general admission through matriculation and (2) admission to a specified field of study after matriculation. Candidates for admission are divided into three groups: regular students *(ordentliche Hörer),* special students *(ausserordentliche Hörer),* and guest students *(Gasthörer).*

For admission as a regular student to the university community, a candidate must hold the *Reifezeugnis* (secondary school-leaving certificate) of an Austrian secondary school or must have a recognized foreign equivalent. Admission to a specific field of study may involve supplementary examinations or special requirements *(Universitäten Hochschulen,* 1976, p. 11).

Special-student status may be granted to persons, nineteen years of age and older, who wish to enroll in courses for a specified period of time and who possess sufficient qualifications. Guest students are graduates of Austrian or foreign higher education institutions who wish to attend courses for a specified period of time but do not intend to enroll in a degree program. The

School of Applied Art in Vienna also has *Meisterschüler* (master students) who have passed the *Diplomprüfung* (diploma examination) and wish to pursue advanced studies of art. The art schools generally require an entrance examination and samples of work or proof of qualification for study, but do not necessarily require the *Reifezeugnis.*

Administration and Control

Higher education institutions in Austria are federal and are administered directly by the Federal Ministry of Science and Research. The art schools are under the jurisdiction of the Federal Ministry of Education and Arts. The higher education institutions are autonomous in matters of research and teaching.

The four general universities and the University of Linz have a similar administrative structure. The *akademischer Senat* (academic senate) is the highest authority of the university. It consists of the rector, the pro-rector (the rector of the previous academic year), the deans, representatives of the faculties, representatives of the *akademischer Mittelbau* (nonprofessorial research and teaching staff), and student representatives. As the chief executive officer of the university, the rector acts as its representative and is responsible for maintaining order. The rector is appointed for one year. The universities are divided into faculties, which are, in turn, divided into numerous institutes. Each faculty is headed by a dean. Other academic authorities include the *Professorenkollegium* (board of professors) and the *Studienkommissionen* (study commissions). The study commissions issue study regulations and are composed of representatives from among the professors, the nonprofessorial research and teaching staff, and students.

At the technical universities the academic authorities include the rector, the *Gesamtkollegium* (board of professors), the academic senate, the deans, the faculty boards, and the study commissions *(Study in Austria,* 1973, pp. 5–7).

The University Organization Act calls for a reorganization of the administrative structure of the universities to include three levels. The lowest level comprises the institutes, which are responsible for carrying out all research and teaching in a specific field. All institutes of a particular field or of a group of subjects form a faculty, which handles administrative tasks at the intermediate level. The main governing authorities, the academic senate and the rector, are charged with the planning, coordination, and supervision of academic research and teaching of the faculties and with the overall management of the university. According to the law, the rector's term of office will be extended to two years. The rector will serve in an assistant administrative position for one year prior to his appointment and one year after his term of office to ensure a greater continuity of leadership *(Austria: Organization of Education,* 1973, p. 14*).* The new law also provides for the creation of committees (comprised of the professors, the graduate assistants, and students), which will oversee, among other matters, university budgets, appointments, and promotions. Under the new law, the university director, who is in charge of the day-to-day administration, will report to the Ministry for Science and Research and not to the rector.

The Art School Organization Act of 1970 sets forth the administrative structure of the art schools. The rector, the chief executive officer, is responsible for the coordination of study programs and for maintaining order on campus. He is assisted by the pro-rector. The highest authority on campus is the *Gesamtkollegium* (board of professors of the entire school). The art schools are divided into departments, which are administered by *Abteilungsleiter* (department heads) and *Abteilungskollegien* (department boards) *(Study in Austria,* 1973, pp. 20–21).

Programs and Degrees

A general university education is provided by the Universities of Vienna, Graz, Innsbruck, and Salzburg. The programs of study offered vary among the universities and include architecture, civil engineering, economics, education, law, liberal arts, mathematics, medicine, natural sciences, pharmacy, philosophy, social sciences, and theology. The technical universities provide courses in civil engineering and architecture, mechanical and electrical engineering, and the natural sciences. The remaining university-level institutions generally offer one major area of study. For example, training in mining and metallurgy is provided by the University of Mining and Metallurgy in Leoben, while veterinary medicine studies are offered by the University of Veterinary Medicine in Vienna. The other institutions offer training in one of the following areas of study: agriculture, economics, social sciences and economics, educational sciences, fine arts, music and dramatic arts, or applied arts.

Degree programs offered by Austrian higher education institutions are defined by law. Courses are offered on a semester basis, with two semesters per academic year. The minimum length of time required to complete a first-degree program varies between six and ten semesters; however, most students require additional time to finish their studies. Students may select their courses and teachers. A period of practical training is a requirement for graduation in many first-degree programs.

Regular students may undertake *Diplomstudien* (diploma studies), "which provide an academic preparation for professional work and lead to a diploma degree," or *Doktoratsstudien* (doctoral studies), "which allow for the further development of the student's ability to do independent scientific or scholarly work and which lead to the degree of doctor" *(Study in Austria,* 1973, p. 8). The doctoral degree is generally awarded afer several semesters of further study beyond a diploma degree; however, in some fields the doctoral degree is the first and only degree awarded. Studies for the two main diploma degrees, the *Diplom* (diploma) and the *Magister* (master's), generally involve two or three examinations and a *Diplomarbeit* (diploma thesis). The doctoral degree program, in general, requires one to three *Rigorosen* (rigorous doctoral examinations) and a doctoral dissertation. Academic degrees are awarded on the basis of a student's success in the examinations.

The first-degree program in the social sciences generally requires a minimum of eight semesters, two diploma examinations, and a diploma thesis and leads to the Master of Social and Economic Science. Two additional semesters of study, a dissertation, and one *Rigorosum* are required for the Doctor of Social and Economic Sciences. In the liberal arts and natural sciences, a minimum of eight to ten semesters, depending upon the field of study, two diploma examinations and a diploma thesis are generally required for the first degree of *Magister* in a designated field. Two additional semesters, including a dissertation and one *Rigorosum,* are required for the doctorate in philosophy or sciences. The program in the medical sciences, which extends a minimum of ten semesters, is divided into three parts. Each part ends with a *Rigorosum.* The degree of Doctor of Medicine is awarded upon completion of the program. Studies in Catholic theology extend a minimum of eight to ten semesters, depending on the specialty, and lead to the *Magister.* An additional two semesters of study, a dissertation, and a *Rigorosum* are required for the doctorate. The program in law and political science involves a minimum of eight semesters. Study is divided into three parts, and each part is completed by a *Staatsprüfung* (state examination). To receive the degree of Doctor of Law, students must pass three *Rigorosen.*

At the technical universities the programs in the natural sciences, mechanical and electrical engineering, and civil engineering and architecture involve a minimum of eight to ten semesters, depending on the field, and two diploma examinations and a diploma thesis for the first degree

or title of *Diplomingenieur* (diploma engineer). Students who enroll in the doctoral program must first pass the second diploma examination in a technical field of study and must present a dissertation before attempting the *Rigorosum.* Successful candidates receive the degree of Doctor of Technology. The University of Technology in Vienna offers two certificate programs in the natural sciences in actuarial mathematics and in computation methods. The program in actuarial mathematics requires a minimum of six semesters and leads to the title "certified actuary," while the program in computation methods requires four semesters and leads to the title "certified computer engineer."

The program in agriculture extends a minimum of nine or ten semesters, depending on the specialty, and involves two diploma examinations and a diploma thesis for the first degree or title of *Diplomingenieur.* The degree of Doctor of Agriculture requires the completion of a dissertation and one *Rigorosum.* The first degree in veterinary medicine, the Diploma of Veterinary Surgeon, requires nine semesters of work and three state examinations. The degree of Doctor of Veterinary Medicine may be awarded upon completion of a dissertation and a *Rigorosum.* The duration of study in mining and metallurgy for the first degree, the *Magister* in mining geology and the *Diplomingenieur* in all other specialties, is ten semesters. Two diploma examinations are required. The Doctor of Mining and Metallurgy requires the completion of a dissertation and one *Rigorosum.*

The schools of music and dramatic art provide artistic training, professional training, and training for teachers and research scholars in the arts. Most of the programs in the art schools extend a minimum of six to twelve semesters and are completed by a diploma examination.

Teachers for the nation's secondary schools are trained at the higher education institutions. The general and technical universities and the University of Linz prepare teachers for the general secondary schools. The University of Economics in Vienna and the University of Linz train teachers for commercial secondary schools. The program of study in education extends a minimum of nine semesters and leads to the *Magister* degree after two diploma examinations and one diploma thesis. Students also take the final examination for teachers of secondary schools *(Lehramtsprüfung für höhere Schulen)*. The doctoral degree may be earned after two further examinations *(Rigorosen)* and a dissertation.

Art teachers are prepared at the Academy of Fine Arts in Vienna and dance teachers at the School of Music and Dramatic Art in Vienna. Music teachers receive their training at the Schools of Music and Dramatic Art in Vienna, Salzburg, and Graz. The minimum duration of study in the art, dance, and music teacher education programs varies from six to ten semesters, depending on the specialty. In addition to the secondary school teachers qualifying examination, students are required to take a diploma examination.

Primary school teachers and teachers for general compulsory school receive their training in the *pädagogische Akademien* (general teacher training academies), which offer a four-semester program on the postsecondary level. Practical training is provided in schools attached to each academy. The program of study leads to a qualifying examination.

Teachers for the vocational schools are prepared by the *berufspädagogische Akademien* (academies for vocational teachers), which offer four-semester programs in domestic science and the clothing trade. In addition, the academies provide two-semester courses for in-service teachers at vocational schools, for workshop teachers, and for teachers of shorthand and typing. The postsecondary programs offered by the academies for social work extend a minimum of four semesters and lead to a final proficiency examination.

Postgraduate studies are offered by specialized institutes of higher learning and other academic schools and private institutions. Programs provide graduates with continued scientific, academic, and practical training in special fields. The Diplomatic Academy in Vienna provides a three-semester program which requires a final examination and the presentation of a diploma thesis. The curriculum includes historical, legal, and economic subjects. Other postgraduate courses extend eight months to two years and involve intensive scientific research. Such courses include the Postgraduate Training Course on Groundwater Tracing Techniques, offered by the Technical University in Graz; the Postgraduate Course for Prospecting and Mining in Developing Countries, offered by the University of Mining and Metallurgy in Leoben; and the Postgraduate Course for Animal Production and Reproductive Biology, available at the University of Veterinary Medicine in Vienna.

Extension courses are offered by a few of the university-level institutions. Extension courses, which usually extend two to four semesters, are generally held in the evenings and require prior partial or complete university training. The university extension course for theology graduates is required for candidates training for the priesthood. Specialized training is provided in pastoral theology, religious education, and other subjects of Catholic theology. The University of Educational Sciences in Klagenfurt provides extension courses in educational technology, university didactics, adult education, group dynamics, and theory of science. Extension courses in glass-painting techniques and artistic textile techniques are available at the School of Applied Arts in Vienna. The University of Economics in Vienna provides a variety of extension courses in advertising and sales management, the tourist trades, the training of export merchants, and electronic data processing.

Financing and Student Financial Aid

Higher education in Austria is financed by the federal government. The University

Fees Act of 1972 abolished all fees for Austrian students at the universities and at other higher education institutions. Foreign students, however, are required to pay a university fee at the beginning of each semester. The fee covers the use of all facilities and libraries, course attendance, examinations, and the granting of degrees. Exemptions are granted to students from developing countries and students whose own country grants such an exemption to Austrian citizens. Tuition and examination fees are charged to all students for university extension courses *(Study in Austria,* 1973, p. 15).

The Austrian government provides scholarships that cover living expenses for needy students and that serve as an incentive to students to pursue higher studies. A 1971 amendment to the Study Encouragement Act of 1969 raised the state scholarship and income limits *(Austria: Organization of Education,* 1973, p. 14). A number of scholarships are offered by public and private organizations to outstanding foreign students in financial need.

Student Social Background and Access to Education

Education in Austria is free and theoretically open to all. Aptitude and scholastic achievement are the only requirements for advancement.

At age fourteen, students have the option of transferring to any of the various types of secondary school programs that give access to higher education. The social status of the parents and the availability of facilities often determine which educational channel is selected. Students from middle- or upper-class families and students from the larger cities are more likely to pursue higher education than are students from lower-class families and students from rural areas, where preuniversity educational facilities are often limited.

Enrollments in higher education, however, are expanding. The number and quality of the general secondary school programs are increasing, and the federal government's higher education subsidy is growing. Approximately 63,000 students were enrolled in university-level education in 1973. Of these, about 27.5 percent were women, an increase of 2.5 percent over 1970. The enrollments in higher education, however, are strictly controlled; and entrance requirements and academic standards are kept high, so that only the best-qualified students are able to gain admission (Keefe and others, 1976, pp. 84, 117, 127).

Teaching Staff

The academic staff at Austrian higher education institutions are classified as *ordentliche Hochschulprofessoren* (ordinary or full professors), *ausserordentliche Hochschulprofessoren* (extraordinary or associate professors), *emeritierte Hochschulprofessoren* (emeritus professors), *Honorarprofessoren* (honorary professors), and *Hochschuldozenten* (assistant professors). All are required to have a *venia legendi* for an academic subject at a particular school. A *venia legendi* is granted after examination to scientists who have carried out high-level scientific work. Professors are appointed by the president of the country, on the recommendation of the federal minister of science and research and with the approval of the Austrian government, from three candidates selected by the board of professors of a faculty *(Classification of Educational Systems,* 1973, p. 33; *Study in Austria,* 1973, p. 7).

Other members of the faculty include the *Hochschullektoren* (lecturers), who teach a practical subject for a specified period of time; *Gastprofessoren* (visiting professors); *Gastdozenten* (visiting assistant professors); and *Gastvortragende* (guest lecturers). The visiting teachers, who are from other national universities or from foreign universities, are entitled to teach an academic subject. In addition, there are *Lehrbeauftragte* (special lecturers) and *Instruktoren* (instructors), who are responsible for certain courses. These faculty members do not necessarily have a *venia legendi*.

In the universities, the titles *Universitätsprofessor, Universitätsdozent,* and *Universitätslektor* are used in place of *Hochschulprofessor, Hochschuldozent,* and *Hochschullektor*.

Institutions of higher learning also employ the following academic staff: *Assistenzärzte* (assistant physicians), *Hochschulassistenten* (graduate assistants), *wissenschaftliche Hilfskräfte* (junior assistants), and *Demonstratoren* (demonstrators).

Research Activities

Higher education institutions in Austria are teaching and research organs. Research is carried out at all higher education institutions and is subsidized by the federal government through the budget of the Federal Ministry for Science and Research. The expenditure for research and development within the budget of the ministry doubled between 1970 and 1973. The expenditure for research in the total federal budget rose from approximately 1 percent in 1970 to 1.5 percent in 1973 *(Austria: Organization of Education,* 1973, p. 17)*.

Current Problems and Trends

Education at all levels in Austria is under constant review in an effort to adapt educational programs to the needs of the country. In 1969 a Parliamentary School Reform Commission was established to discuss a reform of the entire educational system: its aims, content, structure, and methods. Experiments were begun in 1971–72 to develop an external school reform that would bring about a reorientation of education. Since 1972 experiments have been carried out to develop a viable internal school structure on the basis of the proposed Federal School Instruction Act. The proposed act defines the rights and duties of the teachers, the students, and the students' parents. Curriculum reform—with an emphasis on improving curricular content, tests, and the instructional media—is also being considered. Special projects in the areas of teacher training and fur-

ther training are also under way.

Since the middle 1960s significant changes have occurred in higher education, and most degree programs have been reorganized. The effects of these reforms are now being assessed. The full effect of the new Universities Reform Act, which was adopted in October 1975, will not be known for some time. However, the provisions of the law have led to widespread resistance by administrators and professors. In March of 1975, several months prior to the enforcement of the law, a number of rectors resigned and professors withdrew their services for a period of time.

The Austrian government is strengthening its support for adult education in the 1970s to make permanent education possible for all citizens. A proposed act concerning the promotion of adult education defines adult education as activity which aims at "instilling knowledge and skills, at fostering responsible judgment and action and at developing the personality" *(Austria: Organization of Education,* 1973, p. 15). Among the types of adult education mentioned in the act are political and socioeconomic education and further vocational training. As part of the new emphasis on adult education, an institute for political education and an institute for the planning and implementation of educational programs in television and radio are planned. Correspondence courses are also being developed.

Relationship with Industry

Institutions of higher learning in Austria have a close relationship with industry. During their degree study, students are required to acquire practical work experience in a number of fields of study. For example, nine months of practical work is required in engineering and in mining and metallurgy.

Postgraduate training, consisting of practical work or internships, is required in certain fields of study prior to a state professional examination. For example, most engineering specialties require three years of practical work prior to the civil engineering examination and five years of experience for a professional license. Attorneys-at-law must undergo one year of law court internship and either six years of practical experience with a practicing lawyer or a bar examination. Auditors and public accountants are required to complete six years of practical work before sitting for a final examination (*Education in Austria*, 1973, pp. 22–33).

International Cooperation

Austria follows an active policy of international cooperation in the area of higher education. In 1973 about 17 percent of the total university-level student enrollment were foreign students. Foreign student enrollment remained at about 10,500 in the early 1970s. The majority of the foreign students are from the Federal Republic of Germany (Keefe and others, 1976, p. 126).

Tuition payments at Austrian higher education institutions are waived for most students from developing countries. Higher education is also free for students from countries that have bilateral reciprocal agreements with Austria. A number of public or private organizations award scholarships to foreign students for study in Austria. The Federal Ministry of Science and Research operates several scholarship programs. Its Development Aid Scholarship Program is open to candidates from developing countries who hold a bachelor's degree and submit an official recommendation from their government. The ministry also awards scholarships under the program "Applications from All Over the World"; these scholarships are available mainly to persons who have completed their first-degree program and wish to pursue a year of specialized study or research in Austria. The ministry also operates an exchange program and a scholarship program for art students (*Study in Austria*, 1973, pp. 172–176).

Numerous German-language courses for foreign students are available in Austria, and courses on various topics are provided for foreign students during university vacation periods.

Several postgraduate study programs in Austria operate with financial assistance from international organizations. For instance, the Postgraduate Course for Prospecting and Mining in Developing Countries is sponsored by the Austrian government, UNESCO, and the Organization of American States (OAS). The Postgraduate Training Course in Groundwater Tracing Techniques operates under the sponsorship of the Federal Ministry of Science and Research and UNESCO (*Study in Austria*, 1973, p. 157).

Educational Associations

Österreichische Hochschülerschaft
Führichgasse 10
1010 Vienna, Austria

Österreichische Landesgruppe der IAUPL
Franz Kleingasse 1-48
Vienna, Austria

Bibliography

Austria: Organization of Education in 1971/73. Vienna: Ministry of Education and Arts, 1973.

Classification of Educational Systems in OECD Member Countries. Austria, Ireland, Italy. Paris: Organisation for Economic Co-operation and Development, Directorate for Scientific Affairs, 1973.

Country Education Profiles: Austria. Geneva: International Bureau of Education, 1972.

Keefe, E., and others. *Area Handbook for Austria.* Washington, D.C.: U.S. Government Printing Office, 1976.

Study in Austria. Vienna: Austrian Foreign Student Service, 1973.

Universitäten Hochschulen '76. Hochschulstudien in Österreich. Vienna: Bundesministerium für Wissenschaft und Forschung, 1976.

See also: Academic Dress and Insignia; Archives: Germany, Federal Republic of, German Democratic Republic, and Austria, National Archives of; Cooperative Education and Off-Campus Experience: Cooperative Education Worldwide; Health Services, Worldwide University; Library Administration Outside the United States; Science Policies: Highly Industrialized Nations: Western Europe.

AUSTRIAN NATIONAL UNION
OF STUDENTS
(Österreichische Hochschülerschaft)

Founded in 1950, the *Österreichische Hochschülerschaft* (OH: Austrian National Union of Students) is the official representative of all students enrolled at Austrian universities. In addition to the central organization, there are eighteen local student unions that form independent corporations under public law. Each student automatically becomes a member of the union and pays a membership fee, which constitutes the main income of OH. The Austrian Ministry of Science and Research subsidizes special projects of the union.

OH comments on legal proposals related to the interests of members, represents students in international student organizations, cooperates in the development of bills related to curricular changes, and organizes cultural and social activities. Although the union's activities originally pertained only to cultural and social issues of students, the organization also takes political stands on national and international questions not directly related to student problems. The OH policy is independent of governments and political parties, although student parties represented in the *Zentralausschuss* (student parliament) may have close relations with major political organizations.

Liechtensteinstrasse 13
A-1090 Vienna, Austria

AUTOMOTIVE ENGINEERING
See Automotive Technologies (field of study).

AUTOMOTIVE TECHNOLOGIES
(Field of Study)

The field of automotive technologies includes the technical skills and knowledge required to support the design, development, manufacture, and servicing of a complete automobile. As the automobile has become more advanced, the technical knowledge to understand the systems and subsystems has greatly increased.

There are basically three main divisions in the field of automotive technologies: design and development (designing, building prototype models, testing, evaluating, and finalizing a future vehicle), production and manufacturing (ordering tools, fixtures, components, and other materials for the vehicle), and servicing (preparing the vehicle for delivery and providing maintenance service throughout the life of the vehicle).

Many fields are related to these three main divisions. For example, the division of design and development includes the following fields: (1) styling, drafting, and detailing, which involve the transfer of body dimensions to engineering drawings or tapes; (2) materials testing, the testing of materials, connectors, and components to ensure that specifications are met; and (3) component and vehicle testing, the means by which the various components and prototype vehicles are evaluated. In the production and manufacturing division the following activities are performed: heat treating, welding, painting, sheet metal fabrication, casting, machining, processing, and assembly. To ensure the quality, specifications, and efficiency of the vehicle, a knowledge of the following is necessary: tool and die design (the means of fabricating parts and assembling a vehicle), quality control, metrology, and methods and work measurement analysis. Finally, to keep the vehicle in repair, specialists in engine, transmission, chassis, and body repair are required. Franchised dealerships as well as independent garages and service stations provide such service.

Automotive technology dates to the middle 1700s, when a carriage propelled by a large clock motor was demonstrated in Paris. From this beginning, vehicles powered by steam and electricity were developed. These were followed by the internal-combustion gasoline engine, first used to propel a four-wheeled vehicle in 1883. Since the beginning of the twentieth century, automobile manufacturing with mass production assembly line techniques has grown from buggies with engines to highly sophisticated automobiles with built-in safety, convenience, and emission control devices.

Because of the rapid growth and increased sophistication of automobile manufacturing and service, educational programs, which began about 1919, have expanded to cover all phases of the industry. The earliest educational programs were concerned with training mechanics to service the automobiles. Later, programs for training designers, draftsmen, tool and die makers, and industrial supervisors were developed. Many of these were evening programs and were part of an apprentice training program. From 1950 through 1965 one- and two-year technology programs were developed to prepare students for vocational opportunities. The period from 1965 to 1975 witnessed a large growth in community college one-year certificate and two-year associate degree programs. Privately funded institutions have also developed technology programs. Automotive manufacturers have established training centers throughout the United States and Canada to train and update mechanics, sales and service people, and insurance adjusters.

Included among the new developments in automotive technologies education is the expansion of one-year certificate programs. Such programs prepare individuals for job entry positions requiring basic knowledge and skills. In the middle 1970s the two-, three-, and four-year automotive technology programs were also greatly expanded. Graduates of the two- and three-year programs usually find employment as technicians working as support personnel to engineers, or in the service area. The four-year programs prepare

graduates for positions in design, development, testing, manufacturing, or service engineering. Other developments in educational programs for automotive technologies include the use of audiotapes for self-paced instruction, commercially available training aids, and take-apart models. These are increasingly being employed to improve instructional efficiency.

There are automotive technologies programs in the major manufacturing countries as well as the developing countries. The differences in the various programs can be illustrated by a few of the countries in the British Commonwealth. In the United Kingdom the post–high school educational system in technology offers either vocational craft programs or technician programs. The craft program is usually a release-time program of one day per week, thirty-six weeks per year, and may extend to six years. The technician program has three sections of up to two years each. The examinations for each section are nationwide. Individuals may withdraw from the program at the conclusion of individual sections and seek employment at that level of education. Most automotive technicians receive their education in this way. In Australia individual state technical colleges offer one-year certificate programs, two-year diploma programs, and three-year degree programs in technology. Finally, in South Africa most technological programs attract graduates of technical high schools. Three years of high school may apply to apprentice requirements. Two additional years are required to qualify as a journeyman. The Department of National Education operates technical colleges in most large towns as well as six advanced technical colleges which have full-time students, release-time students, or evening programs. The advanced technical colleges operate on a four-year cooperative program which has a six-month cycle of alternating work and study.

The programs offered at the three branches of the Polytechnic Institute located in Nairobi, Kenya, were developed in the United Kingdom and begin with mechanic training. In late 1974 a new educational model—using a cooperative program and including a one-year mechanics program, a two-year technicians program, and a three-year program in automotive engineering technology—was developed. Most students of these programs will be employed in local dealerships. There is a need for highly qualified service people, since virtually no technical service is available beyond the dealership.

Educational programs in technology may be supported by either the private or the public sector or by both sectors. In the Federal Republic of Germany, the United States, and Canada, automotive technology programs are operated by both sectors. In Germany the educational programs are closely tied to apprenticeship requirements. Usually these programs require six semesters of evening school. Geographically, programs are developed to support the local automotive industry. The United States and Canada offer one-year certificate, two- and three-year associate degree, and four-year baccalaureate programs. These programs cover everything from mechanic and body repair skills to the skills for the semiprofessional technologist who supports engineers and computer scientists. In Japan, on the other hand, there are no publicly supported technology programs; instead, post–high school programs (including automotive technology programs) are operated by specific industries, firms, or associations.

In the Soviet Union and Eastern European countries the educational system seems to be technically oriented. Reports indicate that training of technicians for all of industry is ongoing. With the expansion of automotive manufacturing, the educational programs are certain to provide the necessary talent at all levels of technology. Finally, in Brazil there are technological programs throughout the country, and the automotive programs are centered in São Paulo. Students in these programs are

normally graduates from technical high schools. They then attend the College of Industrial Engineering for three years and graduate as operational engineers.

JAMES BAY
HAROLD P. RODES

Levels and Programs of Study

Programs in automotive technologies generally require as a minimum prerequisite a secondary education. In some instances, mature students with relevant work experience may be admitted with lower qualifications, especially into programs designed to upgrade the performance of those already employed. Programs may lead to the following awards: certificate or diploma, associate degree, Bachelor of Science degree, or their equivalents. Programs deal with the principles and practices of automotive technology and consist of lectures, workshop study, and practice.

One-year certificate programs (programs not equivalent to a first university degree) are typically given in technological institutes. For short courses, often sponsored by employers or employers' associations, a certificate of satisfactory completion is usually awarded. Principal course content for below-university work usually includes principles of operation, diagnosing, and servicing of engines, transmissions, chassis, and body. At the below-university level, emphasis is given to the achievement of practical competence and skills. Programs often consist of alternating periods of study and work in industrial and other enterprises.

Two- and three-year programs lead to an associate degree and usually include the courses required for the certificate program, plus additional specific subjects such as air conditioning, carburetion, electronic diagnosis, technical mathematics, technical physics, blueprint reading, machine tools, and drafting.

Programs that lead to a first university degree emphasize automotive design, development, testing, and manufacturing, or service engineering. Typical courses include chemistry, calculus, technical communications, computers, fundamentals of circuits and electronics, engineering drafting, physics, metallurgy, thermodynamics, strength of materials, dynamics, fluid mechanics, and principles of automotive systems. There is generally much laboratory work required.

[Information in this section was provided by James B. Bay.]

Major International and National Organizations

INTERNATIONAL

International Automobile Federation
Fédération internationale de l'automobile
8 place de la Concorde
75008 Paris, France

International Federation of Automobile
  Engineers' and Technicians' Associations
Fédération internationale des sociétés
  d'ingénieurs des techniques de
  l'automobile (FISTA)
% Society of Automotive Engineers of
  Japan, Inc.
16-15 Takanawa 1-chome
Minato-ku
Tokyo 108, Japan

International Federation of Automobile
  Experts
Fédération internationale des experts en
  automobile (FIEA)
12 rue Victor-Masse
75009 Paris, France

Society of Automotive Engineers
400 Commonwealth Drive
Warrendale, Pennsylvania 15096 USA

World Touring and Automobile Organization
32 Chatham Place
London, England

NATIONAL

Argentina:
  Asociación de ingenieros y técnicos
    de automotores
  Marcelo T de Alvear
  636-5° Piso
  Buenos Aires

Australia:
  Society of Automotive Engineers—
    Australasia
  National Science Centre
  191 Royal Parade
  Parkville, Victoria 3052

Austria:
  Österreichischer Ingenieur und
    Architekten Verein
  Fachgruppe Kraftfahrzeugtechnik
    Ingenieurhaus
  Eschenbachgasse
  9 A-1010 Vienna

Belgium:
  Société belge des ingénieurs de
    l'automobile
  Prins Albertlei 13 B-2600
  Berchem

Czechoslovakia:
  Société scientifique et technique pour
    la construction mécanique
  Siroka, 5 Prague 1

Federal Republic of Germany:
  Verein deutscher Ingenieure
  Fachgruppe Fahrzeugtechnik A.T.G.
  Postfach 1139
  Graf. Reckestrasse 84-4
  Düsseldorf 1

France:
  Société des ingénieurs de l'automobile
  3 avenue du Président Wilson
  75116 Paris

Hungary:
  Association scientifique des ingénieurs
    et mécaniciens
  Maison de la Technique
  P.O.B. 451
  H-1372 Budapest

Italy:
  Associazione tecnica dell'automobile
  via Carlo Alberto
  61-10123 Turin

Japan:
  Society of Automotive Engineers of
    Japan, Inc.
  16-15 Takanawa 1-chome
  Minato-ku, Tokyo 108

Netherlands:
  Koninklijk instituut van ingenieurs
  Afdeeling voor verkeerskunde en
    verkeerstechniek
  Sectie voor automobieltechniek
  Prinsessegracht 23, The Hague

Poland:
  Société polonaise des ingénieurs et
    techniciens mécaniciens
  ul. Swietokrzyska 14a
  0050 Warsaw

Spain:
  Sociedad de técnicos de automoción
  avenida Generalísimo Franco
  999 Barcelona 14

Sweden:
   Svenska mekanisters riksförening—
      Division mekanik
   Box 40207
   10344 Stockholm 40

Switzerland:
   Schweizerische Automobil technische
      Gesellschaft
   Wallisellerstrasse 3
   8302 Kloten/Zurich

United Kingdom:
   Institution of ⸱Mechanical Engineers—
      Automobile Division
   1 Birdcage Walk
   Westminster, London SW1H 9JJ,
      England

Yugoslavia:
   Jugoslovensko drustvo za motore i vozila
   27 Marta 80 1100
   Belgrade

Principal Information Sources

GENERAL

Reference sources in the field of automotive technologies include the following works:

Automobile nastoiashchego i budushchego. Moscow: Publichnaia Biblioteka, 1962.

Fundaburk, E. L. *Reference Materials and Periodicals in Economics: An International List in Six Volumes.* Vol. 4: *Four Major Manufacturing Industries—Automotive, Chemical, Iron and Steel, Petroleum and Gas.* Metuchen, New Jersey: Scarecrow Press, 1972. Contains a large bibliographical section on the automotive industry. Included are bibliographies, abstracts, dictionaries, handbooks, and periodicals.

Library Catalogue. London: Institute of the Motor Industry, 1948. Includes approximately 2000 automotive-related works.

Veasey, W. I. "Sources of Information in Automobile Engineering." *Aslib Proceedings,* 1961, *13,* 167–177. A brief but concise listing of the literature, including bibliographies, abstracts, and periodicals.

Among the many general works dealing with automotive technologies (covering various aspects of the field, such as design, servicing, and production), the following are noteworthy:

Campbell, C. *The Sports Car: Its Design and Performance.* (3rd ed.) Cambridge, Massachusetts: Robert Bentley, 1969.

Crouse, H. W. *Automotive Mechanics.* (7th ed.) New York: McGraw-Hill, 1970.

Heldt, P. M. *Automobile Chassis.* Philadelphia: Chilton, 1952.

Nash, F. C. *Automotive Fundamentals.* (3rd ed.) New York: McGraw-Hill, 1969.

The following provide historical introductions to the field:

Barber, H. L. *Story of the Automobile: Its History and Development from 1760 to 1917, with an Analysis of the Standing and Prospects of the Automobile Industry.* Chicago: A. J. Munson, 1917.

Caswell, R. L. T. *Motoring History.* London: Studio Vista, 1964.

Epstein, R. C. *The Automobile Industry: Its Economics and Commercial Development.* New York: Amp Press, 1972.

For works dealing with educational and career opportunities see:

Career Development Standards for Vocational Automotive Service Instruction. Detroit: Motor Vehicle Manufacturing Association, 1973.

Career Opportunities in Automotive Service. Detroit: Motor Vehicle Manufacturing Association, 1972.

Crouse, W. H. *How to Get Ahead in the Automobile Business.* New York: McGraw-Hill, 1956.

Educational Training for the Metal Worker of 1980: Regional Trade Union. Final Report. Paris: Organisation for Economic Co-operation and Development (OECD), 1971.

Ellinger, H. E. "Automotive Technology Curriculum." *Industrial Arts and Vocational Education/Technical Education,* November 1969, *58,* 18–19.

CURRENT BIBLIOGRAPHIES

The following provide abstracts in the field of automotive technologies:

Automobile Abstracts: A Monthly Survey of World Literature. Lindley, England: Motor Industry Research Association, 1968–.

Bulletin mensuel de documentation. Paris: L'union technique de l'automobile, du motocycle et du cycle, 1947–. Published monthly.

For a progress report see:

Advances in Automotive Engineering. Oxford, England: Pergamon Press, 1963.

PERIODICALS

For a full listing of periodicals in the field see:

Fundaburk, E. L. *Reference Materials and Periodicals in Economics.* Vol. 4. Metuchen, New Jersey: Scarecrow Press, 1972, pp. 117–130.

Some of the many journals include *American Auto News, Automobile* (France), *Automobile*

(Italy), *Automobile Engineer* (UK), *Automobile International/Automóvil internacional* (US), *Automobilismo e automobilismo industriale* (Italy), *Automotive Design Engineering* (UK), *Automotive Industries* (US), *Automotive News* (US), *Avtomobil'nыı transport* (USSR), *Ingénieurs de l'automobile* (France).

The following journals include information on technical education: *American Vocational Journal* (US), *Industrial Education* (US), *School Shop* (US), *Technical Education News* (US), *Technical Education Newsletter* (US).

ENCYCLOPEDIAS, DICTIONARIES, HANDBOOKS

Carnelutti, D. *A Technical Dictionary of the Automobile, Illustrated and Systematically Arranged.* In Italian, French, English, German, and Spanish. Lausanne, Switzerland: Spes, 1964.

Georgano, G. N. (Ed.) *The Complete Encyclopedia of Motorcars 1885–1968.* New York: Dutton, 1968.

Handbuch der internationalen Automobil-Industrie/ Handbook of the International Automotive Industry/Manuel de l'industrie internationale de l'automobile. Berlin, Federal Republic of Germany: Finanz-Verlag, 1926.

Jennings, R. E. *The Automotive Dictionary.* New York: William Dogan Annual Publications Associates, 1969.

Muller, W. *Technical Dictionary of Automotive Engineering, Containing 10,000 Technical Terms.* Oxford, England: Pergamon Press, 1964. In English, with German, Russian, and French equivalents.

SAE Handbook. Warrendale, Pennsylvania: Society of Automotive Engineers, 1926–. A standard handbook, published annually.

Stekhoven, G. S. *Elsevier's Automobile Dictionary in 8 Languages: English/American, French, Italian, Spanish, Portuguese, German, Russian, Japanese.* Amsterdam: Elsevier, 1960.

Thomas, H. K. *Automotive Engineering: A Practical and Authoritative Work for Automobile Engineers, Designers, and Students.* (7 vols.) London: Pitman, 1932–1933.

Viitasalo, E. *Automotive Technical Terms.* Helsinki: Kirja-Mono Oy, 1969. Finnish terms with their Swedish, German, and English equivalents.

DIRECTORIES

Dent, H. C. *Yearbook of Technical Education and Careers in Industry.* London: Black, 1957–. A directory to technical careers and vocational study in the United Kingdom.

Directory of the Motor Industry. (2nd ed.) London: Society of Motor Manufacturers and Traders. 1963–. Published annually.

Doyle, G. R. *The World's Automobiles, 1880–1995: A Record of 75 Years of Car Building.* (2nd ed.) London: Temple Press, 1957.

Gleazer, E. J. *American Junior Colleges.* (8th ed.) Washington, D.C.: American Council on Education, 1971.

Russell, M. M. *The College Blue Book: Occupational Education.* New York: Macmillan, 1973. A United States directory.

Technical Education Yearbook. Ann Arbor, Michigan: Prakken, 1963–. Includes a directory to technical institutes in the United States, a list of professional organizations concerned with technical education, and articles on issues and problems of technical education.

AUTONOMY

From the earliest beginnings of the university in the Middle Ages down to the present century, autonomy, or self-government, has been a key ingredient in the ideology of institutions of higher education. In the medieval period, groups of scholars—whether masters or students—came together as autonomous units to form the first universities. Independence was critical, for these scholars saw their mission as the pursuit and dissemination of knowledge; to undertake this task, they had to be free of the dominance of state or municipal authority and the control of the church. At the same time, they recognized that they were operating within societies whose twin pillars were public and religious authority. Throughout the early centuries of their existence, universities had to continuously maintain a delicate balance between their rights to self-governance and the powers of the larger society in which they functioned. Though they did not always succeed, the ideal of autonomy did not wane.

As universities evolved, they took on different features in different countries, and autonomy itself appeared at different levels in the organization of higher learning. In most continental countries, for example, autonomy has traditionally been a characteristic of the most powerful position in the university—that of the senior professor, whose authority is buttressed not only by the tradition of professional freedom but also by civil service status. In England and the United States, on the other hand, autonomy has traditionally accrued not so much to the individual professor as to the individual institution. Yet, at whatever level autonomy has obtained, it has most often been viewed as necessary to the maintenance of the university's unique position in society.

In the mid 1970s, autonomy is subject to new forces that are changing the shape and direction of higher education around the world. By examining the conditions under which the modern university must function, one can begin to determine how, to what extent, and at what level autonomy may best be preserved and defended.

Seeds of Change

Three current realities are affecting autonomy in fundamental ways. The first of these realities has to do with the relation between institutions of higher education and society, the second with the increasing professionalization of society, and the third with increasing specialization within the field of higher education itself.

Interdependence of universities and society. Throughout the twentieth century, and especially since World War II, institutions of higher education and society have become ever more dependent on each other. In most countries higher education is seen as an essential component of industrial and economic progress. Sophisticated economies cannot survive without constant production of new knowledge and highly trained men and women to use that knowledge. Developing economies, too, need the knowledge and trained personnel to move their economies—indeed, their countries—toward intertwined goals of economic and social progress. Thus, governments and industries turn to the universities and other institutions of higher education for help in shaping and implementing their policies. In turn, higher education looks to these sectors for the funds and other support

required to implement these broadened purposes.

Financial aid is thus one element in the interdependence of universities and society. Because institutions of higher education everywhere are increasingly dependent on public funds, they are experiencing greater public intrusions into matters of budget and finance. Autonomy seems increasingly vulnerable. Even in countries where universities have long been supported by public funds and where autonomy has traditionally rested not with the institution but with the professors, changes in higher education are beginning to affect the shape of that autonomy. Governments in these countries are more likely to rule on such matters as allocation of staff per institution and amounts to be expended on research—decisions that were formerly made by professors or particular faculties, either individually or as part of councils of academics. In countries with a strong tradition of privately supported universities, institutional autonomy in financial matters was once taken for granted; now, however, survival calls for an ever greater turning to the public for support, with the concomitant accountability to the public that such dependence implies.

Another dimension of the interconnection between higher education and society is an informal, but no less dynamic, relationship created by the mobility of university people. University teachers, researchers, and administrators move into private industry or government and back into the academic world. An economist, for example, may retain his position at a leading university and also become a consultant to private industry or to a government agency. No longer are the offices of major corporations peopled only by employees, nor are the halls of government restricted to those with backgrounds in politics. Academics have increasingly infiltrated these sectors, reinforcing the connections between institutions of higher education and the societies of which they are a part. The ivory tower professor is increasingly being replaced by the peripatetic and versatile scholar, who is at home in many worlds.

This mobility of the academic, because it binds the university and society closer together, threatens the autonomy of institutions of higher education. Although universities need and benefit immeasurably from the presence of scholars who understand the actual workings of society, just as governments and the rest of society need the trained expertise that academics can provide, such a dynamic situation can compromise the independent workings of the university, since the university can serve society effectively only if it can maintain itself as a countervailing force in that society. It can never be the arm of government and still provide the necessary objectivity or distance that is the source of its benefits to society. Thus, as the university moves toward greater interdependence with society, it must simultaneously be alert to the possibility that the more intimate is its connection, the more vulnerable is its freedom to push back the boundaries of knowledge.

Professionalization of society. As societies grow older, their requirements change. In earlier centuries generalists were needed—people who could bring a wide range of knowledge to bear on problems of society and statecraft. Today the need is for people with specific skills at high levels of performance. Thus, in the twentieth century, the professional group has emerged as a key element in the organization of society. And the professional group, whether in medicine, law, the sciences, engineering, or education, transcends the various and more traditional sectors of society—government, industry, the university. Scholars are linked to others in their discipline through professional societies that operate at regional, national, or even international levels—well beyond the range of an individual university. The community of scholars—the medieval heritage of the university and one of the bases of autonomy—has virtually disappeared. The tie of a scholar to a particular university has been loosened, while the tie to a professional group has been reinforced.

In recent years this professionalization of faculty commitments has been paralleled by similar movements within the student body and other groups in the university. Students, seeing themselves as a group with collective interests, have become increasingly organized, with loyalties to student groups that transcend their allegiance to the individual campus. Similarly, though for different reasons, administrative and nonteaching personnel in universities—a group that has expanded greatly in numbers since the early 1960s—are turning to unions or other organizations in order to express their interests as a collectivity within the university.

Professionalization and the proliferation of special-interest groups have eroded the very concept of the university as a community, leaving the institution with a vacuum at its core. With no group that can assume responsibility for matters of university-wide concern, the university becomes vulnerable to the intervention of the state or, more generally, of public power. Moreover, fragmentation leaves the university powerless to refine and mediate the various interests expressed there, and integrity as well as autonomy suffers.

Specialization of universities. The drive for coordination, a result of increasing specialization among universities themselves, also affects autonomy. As disciplines have become ever more specialized, so too have the institutions that embrace them. With scholars in short supply for certain fields, universities have had to concentrate their energies and resources on particular areas; rising costs and scarcity of funds have enhanced the trend toward greater specialization within universities. The high cost of special library collections or laboratory equipment makes proliferation and duplication impossible to justify in financial terms.

Institutional specialization has had an inevitable accompaniment in the search for new means of coordinating the activities of individual units. No longer can any one university function as the repository of all knowledge. Institutions must turn to one another for cooperative arrangements. In the United States consortia for sharing certain kinds of facilities or students have sprung up among universities, and various kinds of systems have been created to orchestrate the specialized offerings of colleges and universities at the regional and state levels. In countries such as France and Italy, where universities have long been part of the public sector, coordination has taken place at the government level. In England coordination takes place in the University Grants Committee, which plans and allocates funds for higher education as a whole. The Federal Republic of Germany is evolving another type of coordination, that between *Länder*—the state ministries responsible for higher education—and the federal government. The phenomenon of coordination—a response to the emergence of educational systems—is virtually universal.

Though the impulse toward coordination of universities is often perceived as inevitably destructive of autonomy, its effects are more complex than that. Certainly, in a coordinated system of universities, the ability of individual units to make decisions affecting their own activities may be lessened. Yet the coordinated system as a whole may achieve considerably more autonomy than any one of its components could achieve alone. What coordination does present, therefore, is the necessity for rethinking the concept of autonomy and for determining how best to maintain it for the parts and the whole of a system of institutions.

Outlook for the Future

In the changing landscape of educational systems, autonomy will rest on three requirements.

First, any integrated educational system will have to maintain a balance between the need to be responsive to public purposes—

that is, to the society of which it is a part—and the need to defend freedom for the scholar and teacher within its borders. This task will not be easy. Institutions must demonstrate an awareness of issues of public concern. And the public must understand the connection between society's goals, on the one hand, and the independence of the scholar and the integrity of the institutions of higher education, on the other. Yet institutions themselves have done little to clarify their roles and the requisites for their contribution to society. They do not work at telling the public what they are doing, why they are doing it, and why it is that they can function effectively only if they are somewhat shielded from societal pressures. Institutions must undertake this critical task; without public understanding and appreciation of their functions, they are doomed to founder. The value of the educational enterprise is no longer self-evident. Administrators and educators must undertake a program of continuous public education that will clarify what those benefits are and why independence is necessary to achieve them. Autonomy cannot survive without this forging of public support for an institution that must maintain its independence as well as its interdependent relation with society.

Second, institutions must be flexible. Educational institutions or educational systems that become rigid and unresponsive leave themselves open to public complaint and, eventually, to public action. Again, achieving flexibility is no simple order. Universities are essentially conservative institutions, preserving and sometimes embalming their traditions and customs, curricula, and procedures. In societies experiencing rapid change at an ever-accelerating pace, educational institutions cannot afford to sit back in Buddha-like contemplation of the status quo. If they are to maintain their autonomy, institutions of higher education must demonstrate a vitality that will enable them to respond to new needs; otherwise, they will invite the intervention of outside agencies pressing for change.

Third, universities must have strong administration, which can serve to protect institutions and their scholars against outside intrusions and provide the leadership necessary to forge greater conhesiveness within an institution or an educational system. The role of administration in protecting institutional autonomy becomes apparent when one looks at those systems that lack strong administrative apparatus. In countries where the universities are directly subject to a ministry of education, they are also subject to various forms of political pressures and interests; there is no intermediate agency—no buffer—between a rector and a ministry. On the other hand, in countries where there are boards of trustees or regents serving as intermediaries between the public and the institution (including the administration), direct political pressures can be deflected.

Strong administration can also serve to protect the faculty itself, although the faculty may not always acknowledge or appreciate this function of administration. However, when public feelings run high against some act of an individual professor, it is the administration that must deal with the issue and protect the scholar from pressures for censure or removal.

Another administrative attribute central to the maintenance of autonomy is the ability to promote internal cohesiveness by welding the diverse interests of the various constituencies of the university—faculty, students, and staff. Specialization and professionalization have fragmented the internal community that the university represents; administration can fill this void and provide the leadership that will help establish a sense of a common cause and purpose among its disparate groups. Thus, the integrity of an institution depends in large part on strong and effective administrative leadership. For administrators to provide this leadership, however, several requisites are in order.

Administrators must begin to see the institution as part of a system of educational institutions and not solely as an individual entity. They must accept the need for collaboration and for the changes that collaboration implies—that an institution is but one component in a larger educational landscape and that the interests of the larger collectivity must be served as well as those of its individual members.

Administrators must also realize that the jobs of educating the public and of maintaining a proper relationship to society are continuous. There will always be tension between the institution and the public. It is the job of administration to work at creating and re-creating that critical balance between the needs of the scholar and student—the institution's internal constituency—and the needs of the society of which the university is a part.

Finally, administrators must recognize that planning will take place increasingly at levels that involve the system of institutions and not the individual institution. Because of the inevitability of this trend, the key question for institutions becomes: who shall plan? Will it be the institutions themselves, working in concert with one another, or will it be public agencies? If there is a vacuum in the planning capacities of institutions collectively, public officials will surely step in.

Doubtless, universities are not well-equipped to plan the future of higher education. Their fear that collaboration and cooperation among institutions will lead to loss of autonomy and independence has hamstrung efforts to create the kinds of working relationships that could preserve independence. The conclusion concerning the future of university autonomy thus seems paradoxical. To maintain independence, universities and other institutions must cede some of their autonomy as individual units. If they attempt to operate as individual entities, their autonomy will be subsumed by larger structures. If they can work out truly cooperative arrangements with other institutions comprising the system of higher education, they can maintain their independence and reinstate the link between autonomy and integrity.

Bibliography

Adiseshiah, M. "Objectives of an Autonomous College." *New Frontiers in Education,* April–June 1974, *4,* 58–64.

Ashby, E. "Self-Government in Modern Universities." *Science and Freedom,* December 1956, 3–10.

Ashby, E., and Anderson, M. *Universities: British, Indian, African.* Cambridge, Massachusetts: Harvard University Press, 1966.

Berdahl, R. O. *British Universities and the State.* Berkeley: University of California Press, 1959.

Berdahl, R. O. *Statewide Coordination of Higher Education.* Washington, D.C.: American Council on Education, 1971.

Bremauntz, A. *Autonomía universitaria y planeación educativa en México.* Mexico City: Ediciones jurídicas sociales, 1969.

Browne, A. "The Institution and the System: Autonomy and Coordination." In O. Knorr (Ed.), *Long-Range Planning in Higher Education.* Boulder, Colorado: Western Interstate Commission for Higher Education, 1965.

Dingerkerry, S. R. *University Autonomy in India.* Bombay: Lalvani, 1967.

Einaudi, L. "University Autonomy and Academic Freedom in Latin America." *Law and Contemporary Problems,* Summer 1963, *28,* 636–646.

Fletcher, B. *The Freedom and Autonomy of Universities.* London: SCM Press, 1968.

Glenny, L. A. *Autonomy of Public Colleges: The Challenge of Coordination.* New York: McGraw-Hill, 1959.

Glenny, L. A. "Institutional Autonomy for Whom?" In G. K. Smith (Ed.), *The Troubled Campus: Current Issues in Higher Education 1970.* San Francisco: Jossey-Bass, 1970.

Herzfeld, A., Waggoner, B., and Waggoner, G. *Autonomía, planificacíon, coordinacion, innovaciones: Perspectivas Latinoamericanas.* Lawrence: School of Arts and Sciences, University of Kansas, 1972.

Hetherington, H. "On University Autonomy." In *University Autonomy: Its Meaning Today.* Paris: International Association of Universities, 1965.

Higher Education and the Current Crises: An International Perspective. New York: International Council for Educational Development, 1976.

Higher Education: Crisis and Support: An International Perspective. New York: International Council for Educational Development, 1974.

John, V. V. "Freedom to Teach: The Idea of the Autonomous College." *New Frontiers in Education,* April–June 1974, *4,* 42–57.

Kamat, R. V. "The Case for Autonomy." *Journal of Higher Education,* 1975, *1,* 91–97.

Perkins, J. A. *The University in Transition.* Princeton, New Jersey: Princeton University Press, 1966.

Perkins, J. A. (Ed.) *The University as an Organization.* New York: McGraw-Hill, 1973.

Perkins, J. A., and Israel, B. B. (Eds.) *Higher Education: From Autonomy to Systems.* New York: International Council for Educational Development, 1972.

Puccetti, R. "Authoritarian Government and Academic Subservience: The University of Singapore." *Minerva,* April 1972, *10,* 223–241.

Robbins, L. C. "Of Academic Freedom." *Universities Quarterly,* September 1966, *20,* 420–435.

Rodriques Zorrilla, A., and Sosa, A. L. "The Principle of Autonomy and the Coordination of Education." *Democratic Education,* 1970 (3), 15–23.

Shils, E. "The Enemies of Academic Freedom." *Minerva,* October 1974, *12,* 405–415.

Singh, A. "Autonomous Colleges: The Problem of Governance." *New Frontiers in Education,* April–June 1974, *4,* 65–71.

Tünnerman, C. B. "Planificación y autonomía." *Universidades,* April–June 1972, *12,* 18–46.

The University's Response to Societal Demands: An International Perspective. New York: International Council for Educational Development, 1975.

JAMES A. PERKINS

See also: Accountability; Governance and Control of Higher Education: Governance and Administration; Participatory Democracy.

AUXILIARY ENTERPRISES

See Business Management of Higher Education; Financial Affairs: Accounting and Financial Reporting.